Social &
Personality Development

About the Author

David R. Shaffer is a professor of psychology, chair of the Social Psychology program, and past chair of the Life-Span Developmental Psychology program at the University of Georgia, where he has taught courses in human development to graduate and undergraduate students for the past 20 years. He has published extensively on such topics as altruism, attitudes and persuasion, moral development, sex roles and social behavior, self-disclosure processes, and social psychology and the law. He has also served as associate editor for the *Journal of Personality and Social Psychology, Personality and Social Psychology Bulletin*, and *Journal of Personality*. A winner of numerous distinctions for teaching effectiveness, Dr. Shaffer received the 1990 Josiah Meigs Award for Excellence in Instruction, the University of Georgia's highest instructional honor.

3RD
EDITION

Social &

Personality Development

David R. Shaffer
UNIVERSITY OF GEORGIA

£24.50

Brooks/Cole Publishing Company
PACIFIC GROVE, CALIFORNIA

I(T)P ™ The trademark ITP is used under license.

Brooks/Cole Publishing Company
A Division of Wadsworth, Inc.

Printed in the United States of America
10   9   8   7   6   5   4

Library of Congress Cataloging-in-Publication Data

Shaffer, David R. (David Reed), [date]
    Social and personality development / David R. Shaffer. — 3rd ed.
        p.   cm.
    ISBN 0-534-20760-X
    1. Personality development.   2. Socialization.   I. Title.
BF723.P4S48   1994
155.4′ 18—dc20

Sponsoring Editor: *Vicki Knight*
Editorial Associates: *Lauri Banks-Wothe and Cathleen S. Collins*
Production Coordinator: *Fiorella Ljunggren*
Production: *Cecile Joyner, The Cooper Company*
Manuscript Editor: *Micky Lawler*
Permissions Editor: *Karen Wootten*
Interior and Cover Design: *Vernon T. Boes*
Cover Photo: *Super Stock, Inc.*
Art Coordinator: *Cecile Joyner*
Interior Illustration: *Judith L. Macdonald and Lori Heckelman*
Photo Coordinator: *Larry Molmud*
Photo Researcher: *Sue C. Howard*
Typesetting: *TypeLink*
Cover Printing: *Phoenix Color Corporation*
Printing and Binding: *Arcata Graphics/Fairfield*

Photo Credits

CHAPTER 1. **7**, Cornelius de Vos, *Portrait of Antonie Renniers, His Wife, Marie Leviter.* Philadelphia Museum of Art, The W. P. Wilstach Collection; **8**, The Bettmann Archive, Inc.; **21**, Anna Kaufman Moon/Stock, Boston; **29**, (left) Brown Brothers; (right) Bob Daemmrich/The Image Works; **33**, Owen Franken/Stock, Boston.

CHAPTER 2. **40**, The Bettmann Archive, Inc.; **47**, Jon Erikson; **52**, Kira Godbe; **58**, Mary Ellen Mark/Library; **61**, Jean-Claude Lejeune/Stock, Boston.

CHAPTER 3. **79**, Archives of the History of American Psychology; **81**, Harvard University News Office; **83 and 85**, Albert Bandura; **89**, Cathy Watterson/Meese Photo Research; **97**, Elizabeth Crews/The Image Works.

CHAPTER 4. **107**, Archives of the History of American Psychology; **111**, From A. N. Meltzoff and M. K. Moore, *Science*, 1977, *198*, 75–78. © 1977 by The AAAS; **121**, Harvard University Law Office; **130**, Martha Stewart; **134**, Tom Cheek/Stock, Boston.

CHAPTER 5. **143**, C. E. Izard, R. R. Huebner, D. Risser, G. McGinnes, & L. Dougherty, ''The Young Infant's Ability to Produce Discrete Emotion Expressions.'' *Developmental Psychology*, 1980, *16*(2), 132–140; **151**, Ken Gaghen/Jeroboam, Inc.; **158**, Harlow Primate Laboratory/University of Wisconsin; **162**, Chester Higgins/Photo Researchers; **165**, Suzanne Arms/Jeroboam, Inc.; **168**, Popperfoto/Globe Photos.

CHAPTER 6. **185**, Elizabeth Crews/Stock, Boston; **191**, Jim Whitmer/Stock, Boston; **195 and 197**, Harlow Primate Laboratory/University of Wisconsin; **198**, Suzanne Arms/Jeroboam, Inc.

CHAPTER 7. **213**, Inga Morath/Magnum Photos; **216**, Kira Godbe; **221**, Skjold Photos.

CHAPTER 8. **241 and 265**, Robert Pleban; **248**, Kira Godbe.

CHAPTER 9. **280**, Frederik D. Bodin/Stock, Boston; **282**, Kira Godbe; **285 and 310**, Robert Pleban; **300**, Courtesy of David R. Shaffer; **312**, Gail Meese/Meese Photo Research; **316**, Spencer Grant/Photo Researchers.

CHAPTER 10. **333 and 349**, Frank Keillor; **340 and 341**, Robert Pleban; **343**, Dennis Bud Gray/Stock, Boston.

CHAPTER 11. **370**, Kira Godbe; **373**, Robert Pleban; **385**, Michael Weisbrot/Stock, Boston; **393**, Bob Daemmrich/Stock, Boston.

CHAPTER 12. **403**, Courtesy of David R. Shaffer; **408**, Cathy Watterson; **419**, Jim Bradshaw; **427**, Paul Fusco/Magnum Photos.

CHAPTER 13. **443**, David Austen/Stock, Boston; **451**, Elizabeth Crews/Stock, Boston; **454**, Erika Stone/Peter Arnold, Inc.; **461**, Michael Weisbrot/Stock, Boston; **465**, Elizabeth Crews; **470**, Randy Matusow/Monkmeyer Press Photo Service; **480**, San Francisco Child Abuse Council.

CHAPTER 14. **498**, Arthur Tress/Magnum Photos; **504**, Big Bird © 1991 Jim Henson Productions, Inc. CTV; **507**, David M. Grossman; **514**, Kira Godbe; **520**, Jeff M. Dunn/Stock, Boston; **524**, Paul Conklin.

CHAPTER 15. **536**, Frank Keillor; **538**, Harlow Primate Laboratory, University of Wisconsin; **540 and 567**, Gail Meese/Meese Photo Research; **541**, Courtesy of David R. Shaffer; **559**, Marquita Flemming; **560**, Elizabeth Crews.

Brief Contents

Contents

Preface

In the preface to the first edition, I expressed an opinion that the study of social and personality development had come of age and the hope that my book reflected that fact. Clearly, the former premise turned out to be correct—so correct, in fact, that the information explosion that has occurred over the past fifteen years has rendered earlier editions of this volume hopelessly obsolete.

My purpose in revising *Social and Personality Development* has been to produce a current and comprehensive overview of the discipline that reflects the best theories, research, and practical wisdom that social developmentalists have to offer. Throughout my many years of teaching, I have tried to select rigorous, research-based textbooks that are also interesting, accurate, up to date, and written in concise, precise language that my students can easily understand. I believe that a good text should talk to, rather than at, its readers, anticipating their interests, questions, and concerns and treating them as active participants in the learning process. A good "developmental" text should also stress the processes that underlie developmental change, so that students come away from the course with a firm understanding of the causes and complexities of whatever aspect(s) of development the text strives to present. Last but not least, a good text is a relevant text—one that shows how the theory and research that students are asked to digest can be applied to a number of real-life settings. The present volume represents my attempt to accomplish all of these objectives.

Philosophy

Certain philosophical views are inherent in any systematic treatment of a discipline as broad as social and personality development. My philosophy can be summarized as follows:

- *I emphasize theory and believe in theoretical eclecticism.* And my reasons for doing so are straightforward: The study of social and personality development is now a well-established scientific discipline—one that has advanced because of the efforts of a large number of researchers who have taught us so much about developing children by formulating theory and systematically evaluating their theoretical hypotheses. This area of study has a very rich theoretical tradition, and all the theories we will review have contributed in important ways to our understanding of social and personality development. Consequently, this book will not attempt to convince its readers that any one theoretical viewpoint is "best." The psychoanalytic, behavioristic, cognitive-developmental, social information-processing, ethological, ecological, and behavior genetic viewpoints (as well as several less encompassing theories that address selected aspects of development) are all treated with respect.

• *The best information about human development comes from systematic research.* To teach this course effectively, I believe that one must convince students of the value of theory and systematic research. Although there are many ways to achieve these objectives, I have chosen to contrast modern developmental psychology with its "prescientific" origins and, then, to discuss and illustrate the many methodological approaches that developmentalists use to test their theories and answer important questions about developing children and adolescents. I've taken care to explain why there is no "best method" for studying social and personality development, and I've repeatedly stressed that our most reliable knowledge is based on outcomes that can be replicated using a variety of methods.

• *I favor a strong process orientation.* A major complaint with many developmental texts is that they describe human development without explaining why it occurs. My own "process orientation" is based on the belief that students are more likely to remember what develops and when if they know and understand the reasons why these developments take place.

• *Human development is a holistic process.* Although individual researchers may concentrate on particular topics such as physical development, cognitive development, emotional development, or the development of moral reasoning, development is not piecemeal but *holistic:* Human beings are at once physical, cognitive, social, and emotional creatures, and each of these components of "self" depends, in part, on changes that are taking place in other areas of development. Clearly, this is a "specialty" book that focuses primarily on the social and emotional aspects of development. However, I have striven to paint a holistic portrait of the developing person by stressing the fundamental interplay between biological, cognitive, social, and ecological influences in my coverage of each and every facet of social and personality development that we will discuss.

• *A developmental text should be a resource book for students—one that reflects current knowledge.* I have chosen to cite more than 600 very recent studies and reviews (published since the second edition) to ensure that my coverage, as well as any outside readings that students may undertake, will represent our current understanding of a topic or topics. However, I have tried to avoid the tendency, common in textbooks, to ignore older research simply because it is older. In fact, many of the "classics" of social and personality development are prominently displayed throughout the text to illustrate important breakthroughs and to show how our knowledge about developing persons gradually builds on earlier findings and insights.

Content

Though not formally divided into parts, the book can be viewed in that way. The first four chapters (which could be construed as Part One) present an orientation to the discipline and the tools of the trade, including a thorough discussion and illustration of research methodologies (Chapter 1), and substantive reviews of psychoanalytic, ethological, sociobiological, and behavior genetic theories (Chapter 2), the behavioristic and ecological viewpoints (Chapter 3), and cognitive/ social-cognitive perspectives (Chapter 4). An important feature of this coverage is its analyses of the contributions and limitations of each research method and each of the major theoretical traditions.

Chapters 5–12 (which could be labeled Part Two) focus on the "products," or outcomes, of social and personality development, including early social and emotional development (Chapter 5) and its implications for later development (Chapter 6); development of the self (Chapter 7); achievement (Chapter 8); sex typing and sex-role development (Chapter 9); aggression and antisocial conduct (Chapter 10); altruism and prosocial development (Chapter 11); and moral development (Chapter 12).

The final section (or Part Three) of the text explores the settings and contexts in which people develop and could be labeled the "ecology" of development. Here the focus is on the family as an agent of socialization (Chapter 13) and on three important extrafamilial influences: television and schools (Chapter 14) and children's peer groups (Chapter 15).

New to This Edition

The third edition contains several important changes in the treatment of theoretical as well as topical issues. These changes include expanded coverage of both contextual and biological influences on development and a heavier emphasis on adolescent development. The empirical literature has been extensively updated, with the result that nearly half of the references date from 1987 (when the second edition appeared) through early 1993 (when this book went into production).

All chapters have been thoroughly revised to incorporate new topics and to better reflect recent developments in our discipline. The major alterations and additions from the second edition include the following:

- In Chapter 1, the coverage of the discipline's historical underpinnings has been expanded and the discussion of research methods has been reorganized to make this important material easier for the student to learn, remember, and appreciate.
- A discussion of the sociobiological perspective has been added to Chapter 2, which now also includes a stronger critique of inferences and conclusions drawn from behavior genetics research.
- Bronfenbrenner's ecological systems theory is presented in Chapter 3 to illustrate a modern contextualist perspective on social and personality development. Coverage of Vygotsky's "collaborative learning" as a central mechanism in the socialization process is also part of the revision.

- Chapter 4 has been rewritten to compare Piaget's cognitive-developmental theory with attribution theory and other modern social-cognitive perspectives.
- Chapters 5 and 6 have been extensively updated to reflect recent knowledge about the development and regulation of emotions, the personal and contextual factors that contribute to insecure emotional attachments (including the newly identified disorganized/disoriented attachment pattern), the long-term correlates of secure and insecure attachments, and the variables that most influence children's long-term adjustment to maternal employment and day care.
- Chapter 7 includes a major new section on the development of self-regulation and self-control. Also presented are a "new look" at the character of preschool children's self-concepts and extensive coverage of parental and peer contributions to children's self-esteem and adolescents' identity statuses (including recent research on problems minority youths may face in forging a personal identity).
- Recent research on the development of mastery/achievement motivation in preschool children is highlighted in Chapter 8, which also devotes much more attention to cultural and subcultural influences on achievement.
- The latest research on the modification of gender stereotypes and its implications for sex typing is an important addition to Chapter 9.
- Chapter 10 now focuses more intently on the implications of childhood aggression for the development of delinquency and antisocial conduct. Exciting new research on the *victims* of child aggression is also discussed.
- Recent research on the links between empathy, role-taking, felt responsibility, and altruism is an important addition to Chapter 11.
- A comparison of the processes by which parents and peers influence children's moral reasoning is featured in Chapter 12.
- Expanded coverage of the adolescent's quest for autonomy and the parental practices that foster or inhibit this process is included in Chapter 13. This chapter on familial influences also contains new sections on prescriptions for a healthy adjustment to divorce and on long-range developmental implications of family violence and child abuse.
- New cross-national data on schooling and academic achievement are now featured in Chapter 14.
- Chapter 15 is new and represents a broadly expanded coverage of the many ways that peers and peer groups influence social and personality development.

Writing Style

My goal has been to write a book that talks directly to its readers and treats them as active participants in an ongoing discussion. I have tried to be relatively informal and down to earth in my writing style and to rely heavily on questions, thought problems, and a number of other exercises to stimulate student interest and involvement. Many of the chapters were pretested on my own students, who provided many useful ideas for clarification and suggested several of the analogies and occasional anecdotes that I've used when introducing and explaining complex ideas. So, with the valuable assistance of my student-critics, I have attempted to prepare a volume that is substantive and challenging but that reads more like a story than an encyclopedia.

Special Features

Among the features I've included to make the book more interesting and the material easier to learn are the following:

- *Boxes*. Each chapter contains boxes that call attention to important issues, ideas, or applications. The aim of the boxes is to permit a closer and more personal examination of selected topics, while stimulating the reader to think about the questions, controversies, and practices under scrutiny. All the boxes were carefully selected to reinforce central themes in the text.
- *Outlines and chapter summaries*. Outlines at the beginning of each chapter provide the reader with a preview of what will be covered. Each chapter concludes with a succinct summary that allows the student to quickly review the chapter's major themes.
- *Glossary*. A glossary of more than 400 key terms and concepts is provided at the end of the book. It includes all items appearing in boldface type throughout the text. References for the pages in which the glossary items appear for the first time can be found in the index.
- *Subtitles*. Subtitles are employed very frequently to keep the material tightly organized and to divide the coverage into manageable bites.
- *Italics*. Italics are used liberally throughout the text to emphasize important findings and conclusions.
- *Illustrations*. Photographs, figures, and tables appear frequently throughout the text. Although these features are designed, in part, to provide visual relief and to maintain student interest, they are not merely decorations. All visual aids, including the occasional cartoons, were selected to illustrate important principles and outcomes and thereby further the educational goals of the text.
- *Testing file* (for the instructor). An extensive testing file is available to all instructors who adopt *Social and Personality Development*. The text file for each chapter consists of 60 to 110 multiple-choice items, five to ten discussion questions, and page references for the answer to each question.

Acknowledgments

As is always the case with projects as large as this one, there are many individuals whose assistance was invaluable in the planning and production of this volume. I'll begin by expressing my gratitude to the following expert reviewers for their many, many constructive and insightful comments and suggestions: James Carson of the University of California–Riverside, Beverly Fagot of the University of Oregon, Lois Hoffman of the University of Michigan–Ann Arbor, Michelle L. Kelley of Old Dominion University, Roberta Kestenbaum of the University of

Michigan–Ann Arbor, Brett Laursen of Florida Atlantic University, and Richard Reardon of the University of Oklahoma–Norman.

Special thanks go to Geraldine Moon, who coordinated the project's clerical staff, to Renea Martin, Pat Harbin, Tracy Hobus, and Sylvia Stogden, who typed drafts of individual chapters, and to Robin Moore, who typed the bulk of the text and the accompanying instructor's manual. It is difficult for me to express in words just how much their contributions have meant to me.

Last, but not least, the staff at Brooks/Cole has once again applied its professionalism and skills to the production of *Social and Personality Development* (3rd Edition). I am grateful to Fiorella Ljunggren, Production Services Manager, for her dedication to my books over the course of many years; to Micky Lawler, the manuscript editor, for her meticulous editing; to Cecile Joyner of The Cooper Company for carrying out the production of the book with skill and efficiency; to Vernon T. Boes for contributing his artistic talent and creativity to the design of the book; to Karen Wootten for securing the necessary permissions; and to Larry Molmud and Sue C. Howard for handling the photo program. Finally, sponsoring editor Vicki Knight was there from the inception of the project, providing her knowledge and wisdom and interjecting just enough humor into our discussions to keep me on track. Vicki is truly a consummate professional and is responsible for many of the improvements in this book's latest edition. I am very fortunate to have had her assistance and counsel.

David R. Shaffer

1

Introduction

To this day I can recall how I made the decision to become a psychologist. I was a first-quarter junior who had dabbled in premed, chemistry, zoology, and oceanography without firmly committing myself to any of these areas of investigation. Perhaps the single most important event that prompted me to walk over to the psychology table on that fateful fall registration day had actually occurred 18 months earlier. I am referring to the birth of my niece.

This little girl fascinated me. I found it quite remarkable that, by the tender age of 18 months, she was already quite proficient at communicating with others. I was also puzzled by the fact that, although she and I had been pals when she was 5 months old, she seemed to fear me a few months later when I returned home for the summer. This toddler knew the names of a number of objects, animals, and people (mostly TV personalities), and she had already become very fond of certain individuals, particularly her mother and her grandmother. To my way of thinking she was well on her way to "becoming human," and the process intrigued me.

After studying developing children for more than 20 years, I am more convinced than ever that the process of "becoming human," as I had called it, is remarkable in several respects. Consider the starting point. The newborn, or **neonate**, is often perceived as cute, cuddly, and lovable by its parents, but it is essentially an unknowing, dependent, demanding, and occasionally unreasonable little creature. Newborns have no prejudices or preconceptions; they speak no language; they obey no human-made laws; and they sometimes behave as if they were living for their next feeding. It is not hard to understand why John Locke (1690/1913) described the neonate as a *tabula rasa* (blank slate) receptive to any and all kinds of learning.

Irvin Child (1954, p. 655) has noted that, despite the enormous number of available behavioral options, the child is "led to develop actual behavior which is confined within a much narrower range — the range of what is customary and acceptable according to the standards of his group." Indeed, English children will learn to speak English while French children learn French. Jewish children will often develop an aversion to pork, Hindus will not eat the flesh of the sacred cow, and Christians learn that it is perfectly acceptable to consume either of these foodstuffs. American children are taught they will someday play an active role in electing their leaders, whereas Jordanian and Saudi Arabian children learn that their rulers assume that role as a birthright. Children who grow up in certain areas of the United States are likely to prefer square dancing and country music; those who live in other areas may prefer break dancing and rap music. Some children are permitted to "sass" their parents, but others are taught to obey the commands of their elders without comment. In short, the child develops in a manner and direction prescribed by his or her society, community, and family.

What I had originally described as "becoming human" is more commonly labeled **socialization**. Socialization is the process through which the child acquires the beliefs, behaviors, and values deemed significant and appropriate by other members of society. The socialization of each succeeding generation serves society in at least three ways: (1) It is a means of regulating behavior. I suspect that the penalties for rape, robbery, and murder are not the most important inhibitors of these heinous acts. Any one of us could probably walk outside, snatch someone's purse, and stand a reasonably good chance of making a few dollars without getting caught. So why don't we mug little old ladies or engage in several other low-risk but socially inappropriate behaviors? Probably because the control of antisocial acts is largely a personal matter that stems from the standards of morality — right and wrong — that we have acquired from our interactions with parents, teachers, peers, and many other agents of socialization. (2) The socialization process helps to promote the personal growth of the individual. As children interact with and become like other members of their culture, they acquire the knowledge, skills, motives, and aspirations that will enable them to function effectively within their communities. (3) Socialization perpetuates the social order. Socialized children become socialized adults who will impart what they have learned to their own children.

The study of socialization is truly an interdisciplinary science, for anthropologists, biologists, political scientists, psychologists, and sociologists have all contributed to our understanding of social and personality development. The sociologist concentrates on the *similarities* among children in their adjustment to society and its institutions. Sociologist Frederick Elkin (1960) notes:

> Although it is true that no two individuals are alike and that each person has a singular heredity, distinctive experiences, and a unique personality development, socialization focuses not on such individualizing patterns and processes but on similarities, on those aspects of development which concern the learning of, and adaptation to, the culture and society [p. 5].

Anthropologists share this interest in the products, or "common outcomes," of socialization but have proceeded a step further by studying the differences in socialization practices *across cultures* and the effects of these cultural variations on social and personality development.

Psychologists have emphasized the *processes* of socialization, or the means by which the child acquires socially approved beliefs, behaviors, and values. An important assumption of the psychological approach is that all children assimilate their social experiences in roughly the same fashion, even though the content of this experience varies from family to family, community to community, and culture to culture.

One important difference between the psychological and the sociological perspectives concerns the emphasis placed on the similarities among children. Sociologists stress the common outcomes of socialization and pay less attention to individual differences. Psychologists also expect similarities among the children of any social group, but only to the extent that members of that group hold common beliefs about how their children should be raised. You can probably recall several occasions when you envied a friend who was allowed to do something or go somewhere that you couldn't. The point of this example is that each and every one of us faces a unique set of experiences while growing up, and therefore we should not be expected to emerge as carbon copies of our parents, our peers, or the child next door. In sum, psychological theorists believe that individual personalities are an inevitable consequence of the socialization process.

The Universal Parenting Machine —A Thought Experiment

Jones, Hendrick, and Epstein (1979) have described an interesting thought experiment that touches on the major issues that we will discuss throughout this book. They title their hypothetical experiment the "Universal Parenting Machine" and describe the project as follows:

> Suppose that six infants are placed immediately after birth into a "universal parenting machine" (the UPM). To enliven the scenario, we may suppose that three infants are male and three female. The UPM is conceived as an enclosed building with advanced machinery and technology capable of taking care of all the infants' physical needs from immediately after birth to maturity. The most critical feature of the UPM is that it is constructed so that the infants will have no human contact other than with each other during their first 18 years of life. In fact, they will not even know that other human beings exist [p. 52].

Now imagine that the creation of a UPM is within the range of our technical capabilities. Let's also assume that the UPM can be set up in such a way as to create a modern-day "Garden of Eden," complete with trees, flowers, the sounds of birds chirping, and a transparent domed room so that our experimental children are exposed to the sights and sounds of the weather and the movements of the sun, the moon, and the stars. In other words, try to imagine that we have simulated a very pleasant acre of the real world that lacks at least one potentially important feature: we have omitted all other people and, indeed, the concept of a culture. Were we to expose six infants to this environment, there are many questions we might wish to ask about their development. Here are but a few:

- Perhaps the most basic question: would these children interact with one another and become social creatures? If they did, several other questions could be asked.
- Would the children love one another, depend on one another, or develop stable friendships?

- Would the children ever develop a spoken language or some other efficient method of communicating complex ideas?
- Would this environment provide the kinds of stimulation that children need to develop intellectually so that they might have complex ideas to express?
- Would these children develop sex roles and/or become sexual beings at maturity?
- Would the children develop a sense of pride in their accomplishments (assuming, of course, that they were able to accomplish anything meaningful on their own)?
- Would the children's interactions be benevolent (guided by a spirit of togetherness, cooperation, and altruism) or belligerent (destructive and aggressive)?
- Would these children ever develop standards of good and evil or right and wrong to govern their day-to-day interactions?

How would the experiment turn out? That's hard to say, for this kind of project has not been attempted (and, if current ethical guidelines prevail, probably never will). But this is a thought experiment, and there is nothing to prevent us from speculating about possible outcomes, with the help of what is known about social and personality development.

Recall that the product of socialization is a person who has acquired the beliefs, attitudes, and behaviors that are thought to be appropriate for members of his or her culture. How does the child become socialized? One point of view is that children are shaped by their culture. Were we to adopt this viewpoint quite literally, we might predict that our six experimental children would surely become little vegetables or semihumans in the absence of a prevailing social structure. The opposite side of the coin is that culture is shaped by people. Thus it is conceivable that our six children would show enough initiative to interact, to develop strong affectional ties, and to create their own little culture complete with a set of rules or customs to govern their interactions. Although this suggestion may seem quite improbable, there is at least one case in which a small group of Jewish war orphans did indeed form their own "society" in the absence of adult supervision while in a German prison camp during World War II (Freud & Dann, 1951). This group will be discussed in detail in Chapters 6 and 15.

Of course, we can't be absolutely certain that infants raised by the UPM would create the same kind of social order the young war orphans did. Furthermore, because the orphans had been integrated into adult society at a very early age, they provide few clues about the kinds of people that our experimental children might eventually become. So where do we turn to develop some predictions about the outcome of our experiment? One possibility is to examine the existing theories of social and personality development to see what hints they provide.

There are several theories of socialization, each of which makes assumptions about children and the ways they develop. In the following sections of this chapter we will compare and contrast a number of these theories on the basis of the assumptions they make. Our theoretical overview will carry over into Chapters 2, 3, and 4, where we will take a closer look at several major perspectives on social and personality development.

Once we have had an opportunity to examine the major theories, our focus will shift to a most important aspect of social development: the child's earliest interpersonal relationships. You may have observed that young infants become attached to "mama" and often voice their displeasure if separated from this intimate companion. How does this attachment originate? How does it affect the infant's reactions to strangers? Why and under what circumstances will an infant become distressed when separated from its mother or from another close companion? These issues are explored in some detail in Chapter 5. Chapter 6 addresses another important question: what happens to children who do not become attached to an adult or do not develop a sense of social responsiveness during the first two to three years of life? The answers to all these questions—particularly the last—would almost certainly provide some basis for speculation about the development of children raised by a universal parenting machine.

People clearly differ in their willingness to engage others in social interaction and to seek their attention or approval. Some individuals can be described as loners, whereas others are outgoing and gregarious. These two types differ in what is called *sociability*, or the value they place on the presence, attention, and approval of other people. Achievement is another way in which people clearly differ. Some people take great pride in their accomplishments and seem highly motivated to achieve. Others do not appear to be terribly concerned about what they have accomplished or what they are likely to accomplish in the future. Would our six experimental children come to value the presence, attention, or approval of one another? Would they develop a motive to achieve? Perhaps a review of the factors that influence children's sociability, achievement motivation, and achievement behavior will help us to decide. These topics are discussed in Chapters 7 and 8.

Recall that the children selected for our experiment were balanced with respect to biological sex (three males and three females). Would they eventually differentiate among themselves on the basis of gender? Would they develop a sense of masculinity and femininity and pursue different activities? Would they become sexual beings at maturity? There are reasons for predicting that the answers to all these questions would be yes, for gender is, after all, a biological attribute. But we should keep in mind that sex roles and standards of sexual conduct are almost certainly affected by social values and customs. Thus the sex typing and the sexual behavior of our six experimental children might well depend on the kind of social order they created, as well as on their biological heritage. The determinants of sex typing and sex-role behaviors are explored in detail in Chapter 9.

Earlier, we asked whether interactions among our six experimental children would turn out to be benevolent or belligerent. Children raised in a typical home setting display both kinds of behavior, but we should keep in mind that the socializing experiences provided by a UPM could hardly be described as typical. Nevertheless, it might be possible to make some educated guesses about the positive or negative character of these children's interactions if we had some information about the development of aggression and altruism in normally reared children. The factors that affect children's aggression and antisocial conduct are discussed in Chapter 10. The development of altruism and prosocial behavior (generosity, helpfulness, and cooperation) is the focus of Chapter 11.

One of the reasons why human beings are able to live together in ordered societies is that they have devised laws and moral norms that distinguish right from wrong and that govern their day-to-day interactions. How do children acquire a knowledge of these moral principles? What role do parents, teachers, peers, and other agents of socialization play in the moral development of the child? The answers to these questions may well provide some hints about the likelihood that children raised by a universal parenting machine would develop their own moral norms. Moral development is the topic of discussion in Chapter 12.

Since our experimental children are to be raised by a machine, they will not be exposed to a nuclear family as we know it (consisting of a mother, a father, and any number of brothers and sisters). How would the lack of family ties and familial influence affect their development? Perhaps we can gain some insight on this issue after focusing on the family as an agent of socialization in Chapter 13.

Although families may have an enormous impact on their young throughout childhood and adolescence, it is only a matter of time before other societal agents begin to exert their influence. For example, infants and toddlers are frequently exposed to alternative caregivers and a host of new playmates when their working parents place them in some kind of day care. Even those toddlers who remain at home will soon begin to learn more about the outside world once they develop an interest in television. And by age 6 to 7, virtually all youngsters in Western societies are venturing outside the home to school, a setting that requires them to adjust to the demands of a new authority figure — the classroom teacher — and to interact effectively with other little people who are similar to themselves. Does exposure to television or to formal schooling contribute in any meaningful way to the shaping of one's character? Do playmates and the peer group have a significant effect on a child's social and personality development? The answers to these questions are of obvious importance to the development of our six experimental children, who are to be raised with no exposure to the electronic media and no companions other than peers. Thus our overview of social and personality development will conclude with in-depth discussions of the major "extrafamilial" agents of socialization: television and schools (Chapter 14) and children's peer groups (Chapter 15).

In sum, we cannot specify *exactly* how children raised by a universal parenting machine would turn out. After all, we have no empirical precedents from which to work. Although we will not dwell further on our hypothetical children in this text, you may want to keep them in mind and to make some educated guesses about their future as we examine the major theories of social and personality development and review a portion of the data on children's socialization that have been collected over the past 60 to 70 years. We will begin our discussion by briefly considering how scientists became interested in the socialization process and why they have settled upon theoretically inspired empirical research as the preferred method of acquiring knowledge about developing children and adolescents.

Why Study Socialization? A Historical Perspective

Childhood in Premodern Times

Childhood and adolescence were not always regarded as the special and sensitive periods we know them to be today. In the early days of recorded history, children had few if any rights, and their lives were not always valued by the elders. For example, archeological research has shown that, as far back as 7000 B.C., children were killed as religious sacrifices and sometimes embedded in the walls of buildings to "strengthen" these structures (Bjorklund & Bjorklund, 1992). Until the fourth century A.D., Roman parents were legally entitled to kill their deformed, illegitimate, or otherwise unwanted infants; even after this active infanticide was outlawed, unwanted babies were often left to die in the wilderness or sold as servants upon reaching childhood (deMause, 1974).

Historian Philippe Aries (1962) has analyzed documents and paintings from medieval Europe and concluded that European societies before 1600 had little or no concept of childhood as we know it. Medieval children were closely cared for until they could feed, dress, and bathe themselves, but they were not often coddled by their elders (Aries, 1962;

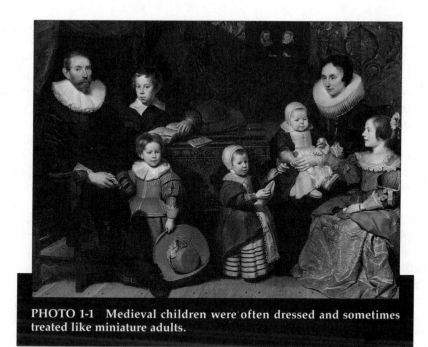

PHOTO 1-1   Medieval children were often dressed and sometimes treated like miniature adults.

deMause, 1974). At about age 6, children were dressed in downsized versions of adult clothing and were depicted in artwork as working alongside adults (usually close relations) in shops or fields or as drinking and carousing with adults at parties and orgies. And, except for exempting infants from criminal culpability, medieval law generally made no distinctions between childhood and adult offenses (Borstelmann, 1983; Kean, 1937).

During the 17th and 18th centuries, attitudes about children and child rearing began to change. Religious leaders of that era stressed that children were fragile creatures of God who should be shielded from the wild and wanton behavior of adults and, at the same time, diverted from their own stubborn and devilish ways. One method of accomplishing these objectives was to send young people to school. Although the primary purpose of schooling was to civilize children — to provide them with a proper moral and religious education — it was recognized that important subsidiary skills such as reading and writing should be taught in order to transform the innocents into "servants and workers" who would provide society "with a good labor force" (Aries, 1962, p. 10). Children were still

considered family possessions, but parents were now discouraged from abusing their sons and daughters and were urged to treat them with more warmth and affection (Aries, 1962; Despert, 1965).

Children as Subjects: The Baby Biographies

The first glimmering of a systematic study of children can be traced to the late 19th century. This was a period in which investigators from a variety of academic backgrounds began to observe and record the development of their own children and to publish these data in works known as **baby biographies**.

Perhaps the most influential of the baby biographers was Charles Darwin, who made daily records of the early development of his son (Darwin, 1877). Darwin's curiosity about child development stemmed from his earlier theory of evolution, which had appeared in his book *The Origin of Species*. Most of us are familiar with Darwin's ideas that human beings gradually evolved from lower species. But how did this theory lead him to study children? On this point Darwin was clear. He believed that young, untrained infants shared many characteristics with their subhuman ancestors. For example, he described both babies and beasts as amoral creatures who must be disciplined before they would acquire any desirable habits. Such similarities between children and animals were intriguing to Darwin because he was a firm believer in the (now-discredited) *law of recapitulation* — the notion that an individual who develops from a single cell at conception into a marvelously complex, thinking human being as a young adult will retrace the entire evolutionary history of the species, thereby illustrating the "descent of man." In sum, Darwin argued that the way to approach thorny philosophical questions about human nature was to study the origins of humanity — both in natural evolution and in developing children (Kessen, 1965). Consequently, he and many of his contemporaries turned to the baby biography, less out of an interest in development than as a means of answering questions about our evolutionary past.

Unfortunately, baby biographies left much to be desired as works of science. Observations for many of the biographies were made at irregular intervals, and different biographers emphasized very different aspects of their children's behavior. As a result, the data provided by various biographers were often not comparable. In addition, the persons making observations in these biographical studies were generally proud parents who were likely to selectively record pleasant or positive incidents while downplaying unpleasant or negative episodes. Finally, almost every baby biography was based on observations of a single child, and it is difficult to know whether conclusions based on a single case would hold for other children.

Despite these shortcomings, baby biographies were a step in the right direction. Indeed, the fact that eminent scientists such as Charles Darwin were now writing about developing children implied that human development was a topic worthy of scientific scrutiny.

Emergence of a Psychology of Childhood

Introductory textbooks in virtually all academic areas typically credit someone as the "founder" of the discipline. In developmental psychology there

PHOTO 1-2   American psychologist G. Stanley Hall (1844–1924) is recognized as one of the founders of developmental psychology.

are at least two viable candidates for this honor: G. Stanley Hall and Sigmund Freud.

Well aware of the shortcomings of baby biographies based on single subjects, the American psychologist G. Stanley Hall set out to collect more objective data on larger samples. Specifically, he was interested in the character of children's thinking, and he developed a familiar research tool — the **questionnaire** — to "discover the contents of children's minds" (Hall, 1891). What he found was that children's understanding of worldly events increases rapidly over the course of childhood. He also discovered that the reasoning of young children is rather curious at times, deviating radically from that dictated by formal logic. Hall later wrote an influential book titled *Adolescence* (1904), which was the first work to call attention to adolescence as a unique phase of the life span. Here, then, were the first large-scale scientific investigations of developing youth, and it is on this basis that Hall merits consideration as the founder of developmental psychology (White, 1992).

At about the time Hall was using questionnaires to study children's thinking, a young European neurologist was trying a different method of probing the mind and revealing its contents. The neurologist's approach was very fruitful, providing information that led him to propose a theory that revolutionized thinking about children and childhood. The neurologist was Sigmund Freud. His ideas came to be known as *psychoanalytic theory*.

In many areas of science, new theories are often revisions or modifications of old theories. But in Freud's day there were few "old" theories of human behavior to modify. Freud was truly a pioneer, formulating his psychoanalytic theory from the thousands of notes and observations he made while treating patients for various kinds of emotional disturbances.

Ever the astute observer, Freud noticed that patients would often describe very similar experiences or events that had been noteworthy to them while they were growing up. He inferred that there must be important milestones in human development that all people share. As he continued to observe his patients and listen to their accounts of their lives, Freud concluded that each milestone in the life history of a patient was meaningfully related to earlier events. He then recognized that he had the data—the pieces of the puzzle—from which to construct a comprehensive theory of human development.

The genius of Freud soon attracted many followers. Shortly after the publication of Freud's earliest theoretical monographs, the *International Journal of Psychoanalysis* was founded, and other researchers began to report their tests of Freud's thinking. By the mid-1930s much of Freud's work had been translated into other languages, and the impact of psychoanalytic theory was felt around the world. Over the years, Freud's theory proved to be quite *heuristic*—meaning that it continued to generate new research and to prompt other researchers to extend Freud's thinking. Clearly, the field of child development was alive and well by the time Freud died, in 1939.

The Role of Theory in the Scientific Enterprise

Freud's work—and other scientists' reactions to it—aptly illustrates the role theories play in the modern, scientific study of human development. Although the word *theory* is an imposing term, it so happens that theories are something everyone has. If I were to ask you why males and females appear so different as adults when they seem so similar as infants, you would undoubtedly have something to say on the issue. In answering, you would be stating or at least reflecting your own underlying theory of sex differences. So a **theory** is really nothing more than a set of concepts and propositions that allow the theorist to describe and explain some aspect of experience. In the field of psychology, theories help us to describe various patterns of behavior and to explain why those behaviors occur.

A scientific theory is a public pronouncement that indicates what a scientist believes to be true about his or her specific area of investigation (Green, 1987). And the beauty of scientific theories is that they allow us to organize our thinking about a broad range of observations and events. Imagine what life might be like for a researcher who plods away at collecting data and recording fact after fact without organizing this information around a set of concepts and propositions. Chances are that this person would eventually be swamped by a large number of seemingly unconnected facts, thus qualifying as a trivia expert who lacks a "big picture." So theories are of critical importance to the developmental sciences (or any other scientific discipline), for each of them provides us with a "lens" through which we might interpret any number of specific observations about developing individuals.

What are the characteristics of a good theory? Ideally, it should be concise, or **parsimonious**, and yet be able to explain a broad range of phenomena. A theory with few principles that accounts for a large number of empirical observations is much more useful than another theory that requires many more concepts and propositions to explain the same number (or a lesser number) of observations. In addition, good theories are **falsifiable**—that is, capable of making explicit predictions about future events so that the theory can be supported or disconfirmed. And, as implied by the falsifiability criterion, good theories are **heuristic**: they build on existing knowledge by continuing to generate testable **hypotheses** that, if confirmed by future research,

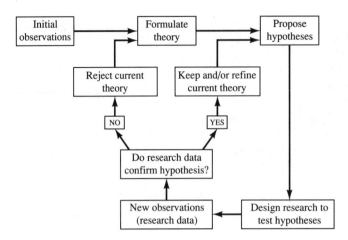

FIGURE 1-1   The role of theory in scientific investigation.

will lead to a much richer understanding of the phenomena under investigation (see Figure 1-1).

Today there are several "good" theories that have contributed to our understanding of social and personality development, and in Chapters 2–4 we will critically examine some of the more influential of these viewpoints. As we will see in the pages that follow, different theories emphasize different aspects of human behavior. In addition, each theory makes somewhat different assumptions about human nature as well as about the course and causes of development. So before we review the content of the major theories of social and personality development, it may be helpful to consider some of the more basic issues on which they differ.

Questions and Controversies about Human Development

Developmental theorists have different points of view on at least four basic issues:

1. Are children inherently good or inherently bad?
2. Is nature (biological forces) or nurture (environmental forces) the primary influence on human development?
3. Are children actively involved in the developmental process, or, rather, are they passive recipients of social and biological influences?
4. Is development continuous or discontinuous?

Early Philosophical Perspectives on Human Nature

What kind of animal are we? After debating this issue for centuries, social philosophers have produced viewpoints ranging from Thomas Hobbes's (1651/1904) doctrine of **original sin**, which held that children are inherently selfish egoists who must be controlled by society, to Jean Jacques Rousseau's doctrine of **innate purity**—the notion that children are born with an intuitive sense of right and wrong that is often misdirected by society. These two viewpoints clearly differ in their implications for child rearing. Proponents of original sin argued that parents must actively restrain their egoistic offspring, whereas the innate purists viewed children as "noble savages" who should be given the freedom to follow their inherently positive inclinations.

Another view on children and child rearing was suggested by John Locke, who believed that the mind of an infant is a *tabula rasa*, or "blank slate," that is written upon by experience. In other words, children are neither inherently good nor inherently bad, and how they turn out depends entirely on how they are raised. Like Hobbes, Locke argued in favor of disciplined child rearing to ensure that children develop good habits and acquire few if any unacceptable impulses.

As it turns out, each of these three philosophical perspectives on human nature remains with us today in one or more contemporary theories of social and personality development. Although one may search in vain for explicit statements about human nature, the theorist will typically emphasize the positive or the negative aspects of children's character or perhaps will note that positivity or negativity of character depends on the child's experiences. These assumptions about human nature are important, for they influence the content of each developmental theory — particularly what the theory has to say about child rearing.

Nature versus Nurture

One of the oldest issues among developmental theorists is the **nature/nurture** controversy: are human beings a product of their heredity and other biological predispositions, or are they shaped by the environment in which they are raised? Here are two opposing viewpoints:

> Heredity and not environment is the chief maker of man. . . . Nearly all of the misery and nearly all of the happiness in the world are due not to environment. . . . The differences among men are due to

ORIGINAL SIN

INNATE PURITY

differences in the germ cells with which they were born [Wiggam, 1923, p. 42].

> Give me a dozen healthy infants, well formed, and my own specified world to bring them up in and I'll guarantee to take any one at random and train him to become any type of specialist I might select — doctor, lawyer, artist, merchant, chief, and yes, even beggarman and thief, regardless of his talents, penchants, tendencies, abilities, vocations, and race of his ancestors. There is no such thing as an inheritance of capacity, talent, temperament, mental constitution, and behavioral characteristics [Watson, 1925, p. 82].

Clearly these are extreme positions that few contemporary researchers would be willing to endorse. Today many developmentalists believe that the relative contributions of nature and nurture depend on the aspect of development in question: social forces predominate in some areas (for example, moral development), whereas biological factors take precedence in others (for example, physical growth and development). However, they stress that most complex human attributes, such as temperament, personality, and mental health, are probably best viewed as the end products of a long and involved interplay between biological predispositions and environmental forces. Their advice to us, then, is to think less about nature *versus* nurture and more about how these two sets of influences combine or *interact* to produce developmental change.

TABULA RASA

Activity versus Passivity

Another topic of theoretical debate is the **activity/passivity issue**. Are children curious, active creatures who largely determine how agents of society treat them? Or are they passive souls on whom society fixes its stamp? Consider the implications of these opposing viewpoints. If it could be shown that children are extremely malleable—literally at the mercy of those who raise them—then perhaps individuals who turned out to be less than productive would be justified in suing their overseers for malfeasance. Indeed, one young man in the United States recently used this logic to bring a malfeasance suit against his parents. Perhaps you can anticipate the defense that the parents' lawyer would offer. Counsel would surely argue that the parents tried many strategies in an attempt to raise their child right but that he responded favorably to none of them. The implication is that this young man played an active role in determining how his parents treated him and therefore bears a large share of the responsibility for creating the climate in which he was raised.

As we will see in the next three chapters, there is an intermediate stance on this activity/passivity issue, one that leans more in the direction of an active child than a passive one. This "middle ground" is the view that human development is best described as a continuous *reciprocal interaction* between children and their environments (**reciprocal determinism**): the environment clearly affects the child, but the child's mannerisms and behaviors will also affect the environment. Thus, children are *actively involved* in creating the very environments that will influence their growth and development.

Continuity versus Discontinuity

Now think for a moment about the concept of developmental change. Do you think that the changes we experience occur very gradually? Or would you say that these changes are rather abrupt?

On one side of the **continuity/discontinuity issue** are continuity theorists, who view human development as an additive process that occurs in small steps, without sudden changes. They might represent the course of developmental change with a smooth growth curve like the one in Figure 1-2A. By contrast, discontinuity theorists describe the road to maturity as a series of abrupt changes, each of which elevates the child to a new and presumably more advanced level of functioning. These levels, or "stages," are represented by the plateaus of the discontinuous growth curve in Figure 1-2B.

A second aspect of the continuity/discontinuity issue centers on whether developmental changes are quantitative or qualitative in nature. Quantitative changes are changes in *degree*. For example, children grow taller; they run a little faster with each passing year; they acquire more and more knowledge about the world around them. By contrast, qualitative changes are changes in *kind*—changes that make the individual fundamentally different in some way than he or she was before. The transformation of a tadpole into a frog is a qualitative change. Similarly, we might regard the infant who lacks language as qualitatively different from a preschooler who speaks well, or the adolescent who is sexually mature as fundamentally different from a

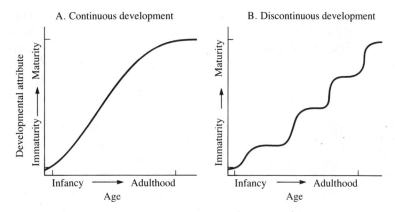

FIGURE 1-2 The course of development as described by continuity and discontinuity (stage) theorists. (Adapted from D. R. Shaffer, "Social Psychology from a Social-Developmental Perspective." In C. Hendrick (Ed.), *Perspectives on Social Psychology*. Copyright © 1977 by Lawrence Erlbaum Associates. Used by permission.)

classmate who is yet to reach puberty. Continuity theorists generally believe that developmental changes are both gradual and quantitative in nature, whereas discontinuity theorists tend to view such changes as more abrupt and qualitative. Indeed, discontinuity theorists are the ones who argue that we progress through **developmental stages**. Presumably, each of these stages represents a distinct phase within a larger sequence of development—a period of the life cycle characterized by a particular set of abilities, motives, behaviors, or emotions that occur together and form a coherent pattern.

Finally, there is a third aspect of the continuity/discontinuity debate: are there close connections between early developments and later ones, or, rather, do changes that occur early in life have little bearing on future outcomes? Continuity in this sense implies a sense of *connectedness* between earlier and later developments. Those who argue against the concept of developmental stages might see such connectedness in the *stability* of attributes over time, as might be indicated, for example, if aggressive toddlers routinely become aggressive adolescents or if particularly curious toddlers are the ones who are recognized, as adults, for creative accomplishments. Even a theorist who proposes that we pass through qualitatively distinct stages

might still see some connectedness (or continuity) to development if the abilities that characterize each successive stage are thought to evolve from those of the previous stage.

Yet there are theorists who believe that many later developments are discontinuous with, or unconnected to, earlier developments (see Kagan, 1980). The idea here is that a new behavior pattern may simply replace an old one without having evolved from it, as when an infant who once smiled at strangers comes to fear them or when a teenage girl who has previously avoided boys becomes "boy crazy." In this sense, then, the discontinuity position is that attributes apparent early in life are *plastic*—that is, subject to change in any number of ways so that they often do not carry over into adulthood.

In sum, the debate about developmental continuities and discontinuities is very complex. There is the issue of whether developmental change is gradual or abrupt, the issue of whether it is quantitative or qualitative, and the issue of whether it is or is not reliably connected to earlier developments. Why have theorists studying the same subjects (developing children and adolescents) adopted such radically different stances on these issues?

One reason for the continuity/discontinuity debate is that discontinuity theorists tend to focus on the visible products of development—the obvious changes in the child with age—whereas continuity theorists are looking at the processes that give rise to these changes. Research in developmental psychology shows that different types of developments are important at different periods of the life cycle. For example, the development of intimate emotional ties to close companions is particularly noteworthy during infancy and adolescence; one's gender identity and sex-role preferences are rapidly developing during the preschool period; moral reasoning undergoes dramatic changes during middle childhood and adolescence; and a strong concern about one's present and future roles in life becomes a preoccupation for many people during late adolescence and young adulthood. If we concentrate on *what is developing* (for example, emotional bonds, gender identity, moral reasoning, personal identities), social and personality development may often appear to be rather discontinuous, or "stagelike." But if we focus on the *processes* that underlie these developments (for example, biological maturation and learning), then development may seem much more gradual, or continuous. As we review the leading theories of social and personality development, we will see that continuity theorists do tend to concentrate on the processes that underlie developmental change, whereas stage theorists are concerned mainly with the nature or content of these changes.

Matching Assumptions with Theories

Now that we have examined the kinds of philosophical and conceptual issues on which theorists differ, let's briefly consider the patterns of assumptions made by the major social-developmental theories—the theories that we will examine in Chapters 2–4 and encounter repeatedly throughout the text.

Psychoanalytic theory.   Sigmund Freud adopted the doctrine of original sin when he formulated his psychoanalytic theory of social and personality development. His impression was that human beings were "seething cauldrons" who must constantly seek to gratify a number of innate sexual and aggressive instincts. Like Hobbes, Freud believed that the

purpose of socialization was to divert the child's socially undesirable impulses away from their natural outlets and into socially acceptable patterns of behavior. His view was that children are "molded" by the more powerful elements of society, and he depicted the young child as a relatively *passive* entity in this "socialization" process—one whose developmental outcomes (that is, personality or character) would depend largely on the emotional climate created by parents in their attempts at child rearing.

Freud viewed social and personality development as progressing through a sequence of qualitatively distinct stages, thus qualifying him as a discontinuity theorist. However, he did believe that early developments were connected to later ones and that childhood attributes could well carry over into adulthood.

In recent years, proponents of psychoanalytic theory (Erikson, 1963, 1972; Hartmann, 1958) have reassessed Freud's views and concluded that children are not nearly so sinister or so passive as Freud had assumed. Erik Erikson argues that the child is an active, curious explorer whose lifelong attempts to master the environment are not easily explained as a displacement of primitive sexual or aggressive urges. Erikson clearly stressed the positive, adaptive aspects of our character, and in this sense his viewpoint resembles that of the innate purists.

The biological viewpoint.   Like Freud, biological theorists contend that children inherit a number of attributes and behavioral predispositions that have a profound effect on their development. But, in marked contrast to Freud's passive child, the biological view is that even newborn babes are *active*, adaptive souls who are capable of influencing the character of their environments from the moment of birth. Ethologists, for example, have argued that human infants inherit several patterned behaviors (such as smiling, crying, and clinging) that serve to attract attention and/or promote contact with their caregivers—precisely the kind of experience that a baby needs to form secure emotional ties to other members of the species. Thus the biological viewpoint is that children are neither inherently good nor inherently bad but, rather, inherently active and adaptive.

Proponents of the biological perspective tend to concentrate very heavily on the hereditary bases of behavior — the nature side of the nature/nurture issue. Nevertheless, they are well aware that human beings are largely products of their environments and that little if anything of lasting developmental significance occurs automatically. To pursue our example, infants may well be biologically predisposed to beam signals (such as smiles and cries) to their caregivers, but these innate responses will eventually wane if they fail to produce favorable reactions from unresponsive companions. (In this case, the environment might be said to have overridden a biological predisposition.) Of the four major approaches to social and personality development, the biological viewpoint is really more a "point of view" than a well-articulated theory. We will see that biological studies are often useful for pinpointing some of the causes and correlates of social *behavior*; however, they are rarely sufficient, in themselves, to account for all the complexities of social and personality *development*. We will focus on biological theories of development, along with the psychoanalytic approach, in Chapter 2.

Social-learning theory. The doctrine of *tabula rasa* provides the philosophical basis for several models of socialization known collectively as social-learning theory. The most influential of the early social-learning theorists was the American psychologist John B. Watson. Watson believed that children enter the world with very little in the way of ability, knowledge, or behavioral predispositions. In other words, he viewed the neonate as a blank slate who would develop very passively and continuously in accord with the kinds of learning experiences provided by the environment.

Watson's strong belief in "environmental determinism" was generally accepted by other social-learning theorists until the 1960s. During that decade, Albert Bandura and his associates (Bandura, 1965; Bandura & Walters, 1963) criticized their colleagues for failing to recognize that children are active, thinking organisms who are quite capable of self-instruction, self-reinforcement, and, thus, some degree of self-determination. Bandura concedes that the newborn infant is a naive, unknowing creature who is quite receptive to environmental influence. Moreover, he believes (as do all social-learning theorists) that the vast majority of human social attributes are products of experience (i.e., learned) rather than innate or genetically programmed qualities. Yet, as we will see in Chapter 3, Bandura views children and their environments as being in a constant state of *reciprocal interaction*: the active, creative child affects the environment, and the resulting environment then affects the child. Thus the Bandurans are set apart from earlier social-learning theorists by their contention that children are active agents who have a hand in determining the character of their own socializing environment.

The cognitive viewpoint. Cognitive theorists Jean Piaget and Lawrence Kohlberg have adopted a perspective that resembles the doctrine of innate purity. Although these theorists do not make the assumption that humans are inherently moral, they do stress the positive aspects of human development while rejecting the notion that children are passive recipients of environmental influence. Indeed, Piaget asserts that the child is an *active* explorer who is born with a need to adapt to his or her environment.

What does Piaget mean by "adaptation"? In the biological sciences, *adaptation* refers to the organism's ability to cope with its surroundings, and the function of this adaptation is survival. Piaget's adaptation serves a similar purpose: the child must understand the environment in order to function effectively within it. Piaget contends that children become increasingly adaptive as they develop intellectually and that the environment provides the impetus for intellectual development. But he also stresses that the reorganization and extension of the child's cognitive abilities — through a qualitatively distinct sequence of stages — are undertaken *by the child when he or she is prepared for this undertaking* and are *not* "shaped" by parents, teachers, or any other external agent. In sum, active, exploring children do not simply mirror experience; they create it. And in the process they change themselves (Langer, 1969).

Lawrence Kohlberg (1966, 1969) and other social-cognitive theorists (for example, Selman, 1980) go one step further by suggesting that social and personality development depends on cognitive development and thus proceeds in a discontinuous, stagelike fashion. Their major assumption is that a person's level, or stage, of cognitive development largely determines how he or she views the world and, thus, what the person is likely to learn from his or her interactions with a demanding parent, a distressed playmate, or a deviant peer model. Cognitive perspectives on socialization and personality development are the subject of Chapter 4.

If you are like many people, you may find it difficult not to select a "favorite" theory of social and personality development after scanning several of these approaches for the first time. The reason we tend to "play favorites" is quite simple: we all make assumptions about children and the ways they develop, and perhaps we tend to favor theories whose assumptions are similar to our own. See whether you find this true of yourself. Take the short quiz in Box 1-1, and compare the overall pattern of your five responses against the several patterns that appear in the key. Then, after completing your study of Chapters 2–4, see whether the theory you prefer is the one that most closely matches the pattern of responses you favored when completing this exercise. (Let's note, however, that the best way to evaluate these theories is on the demonstrated ability of each to predict and explain significant aspects of human social and personality development, not on the basis of our first impressions or preferences.)

In the next section we will focus on the "tools of the trade"—that is, the research methods that developmentalists use to test their theories and gain a better understanding of the child's world.

Research Methods

When detectives are assigned cases to solve, they will first gather the facts, formulate hunches, and then sift through the clues or collect additional information until one of their hunches proves correct. Unraveling the mysteries of social and personality development is in many ways a similar endeavor. Investigators must carefully observe their

subjects, study the information they have collected, and then use it to draw conclusions about the ways people develop.

Our focus in this section is on the methods that researchers use to gather information about developing children and adolescents. Our first task is to understand why developmentalists consider it absolutely essential to gather all these facts. We will then discuss the advantages and disadvantages of several basic fact-finding strategies and see how these techniques might be used to detect developmental change.

The Scientific Method

The study of social and personality development is appropriately labeled a scientific enterprise because modern developmentalists have adopted a value system called the **scientific method** that guides their attempts at understanding. The scientific method is really more of an attitude or a value than a method; the attitude dictates that, above all, investigators must be *objective* and must allow their observations (or data) to decide the merits of their thinking.

In earlier eras, when social philosophers such as Hobbes, Locke, and Rousseau were presenting their views on children and child rearing, most people were likely to interpret these pronouncements as fact. It was as if the public assumed that great minds always had great insights; however, so-called great

B
O
X

1-1 | *Match Wits with the Theorists*

All of us have made certain assumptions about children and child rearing. Developmental theorists make assumptions too, and their assumptions largely determine what they may propose in the way of a theory. You may find it interesting to match wits with these influential scholars to see with whom you most agree (initially, at least). Answer the five questions that follow. Then compare the patterning of your five responses against the patterns that appear in the "key" at the end of this exercise. The pattern that comes closest to your own will tell you with which group of theorists you are most philosophically consistent.

1. Biological factors (for example, heredity, maturation) and environmental forces (for example, culture, methods of parenting) are thought to contribute to human development. All things considered,
   a. biological factors contribute more than environmental forces.
   b. biological factors and environmental forces are equally important.
   c. environmental forces contribute more than biological factors.
2. Children are:
   a. "seething cauldrons"—creatures whose basically negative impulses must be controlled.
   b. neither inherently good nor inherently bad.
   c. "noble savages"—creatures who are born with many positive and few negative inclinations.

3. Development proceeds:
   a. in stages—that is, through a series of fairly abrupt changes.
   b. continuously—in small increments without abrupt changes.
4. Children are basically:
   a. active creatures who play a major role in determining their own character.
   b. passive creatures whose character is molded by parents, teachers, and other agents of society.
5. Character attributes such as aggressiveness or dependency:
   a. first appear in childhood and remain relatively stable over time.
   b. first appear in childhood but may change rapidly at some later time.

Now transcribe your answers in the space marked "Your Pattern." Then invert the page and compare your pattern with those that appear in the key. On the basis of the five assumptions you have made, are you a budding psychoanalyst, learning theorist, cognitive developmentalist, or biological theorist?

	Question				
Your pattern:	1	2	3	4	5
	___	___	___	___	___

Key

Question:	1	2	3	4	5	*Theory and/or Theorist*
	a	a	a	b	a	Sigmund Freud's psychoanalytic theory
	c	c	a	a	a	Erik Erikson's psychosocial theory (a revision and extension of Freud's thinking)
	a or b[1]	b	a or b[2]	a	a	Biological perspectives
	c	b	b	b	b	Watson's early social-learning theory
	c	b	b	a	b	Bandura's modern social-learning theory
	b	c	a	a	b	Piaget's/Kohlberg's/Selman's cognitive viewpoints

[1]Biological theorists differ on the exact weights given to biological and social forces.

[2]Some biological theorists (the ethologists) posit critical periods, or stages, of development; others (behavior geneticists) view development as a continuous interaction between one's genetic predisposition and the environment. Distinctions between these two viewpoints will be drawn in Chapter 2.

minds may produce miserable ideas on occasion.[1] If such poorly conceived notions have implications for the ways human beings are to be treated, it behooves us to discover these erroneous assumptions before they harm anyone. The scientific method, then, is a value that helps to protect the scientific community and society at large against flawed reasoning. The protection comes from the practice of evaluating the merits of various theoretical pronouncements against the objective record, rather than simply relying on the academic, political, or social credibility of the theorist. Of course, this means that the theorist whose ideas are being evaluated must be equally objective and, thus, willing to discard pet notions when there is evidence that they have outlived their usefulness.

Gathering Data: Basic Fact-Finding Strategies

No matter what aspect of social development we hope to study—be it the emotional reactions of newborn infants, the growth of friendships among children, or the origins of drug use among adolescents—we must find ways to measure what interests us. Today researchers are fortunate to have many tried-and-true procedures that they can use to measure behavior and to test their hypotheses about human development. But, regardless of the technique one employs, scientifically useful measures must always display two important qualities: **reliability** and **validity**.

A measure is *reliable* if it yields consistent information over time and across observers. Suppose you go into a classroom and record the number of times each child behaves in an aggressive manner toward others, but your research assistant, using the same scheme to observe the same children, does not agree with your measurements. Or you measure each child's aggressiveness one week but come up with very different aggressiveness scores while applying the same measure to the same children a week later. Clearly, your observational measure of aggression is unreliable because it yields highly in-

consistent information. To be reliable and thus useful for scientific purposes, your measure would have to produce comparable estimates of children's aggression from independent observers (*interrater reliability*) and would have to yield similar scores for individual children from one testing to another shortly thereafter (*temporal stability*).

A measure is *valid* if it measures what it is supposed to measure. Perhaps you can see that an instrument must be reliable and measure consistently before it can possibly be valid. Yet reliability, by itself, does not guarantee validity. For example, a demonstrably reliable observational scheme that is intended as a measure of children's aggression may provide grossly overinflated estimates of aggressive behavior if the investigator simply classifies all acts of physical force as examples of aggression. What the researcher has failed to recognize is that many high-intensity antics may simply represent enjoyable forms of rough-and-tumble play with no harmful or aggressive intent. Clearly, researchers must demonstrate that they are measuring the attribute they say they are measuring before we can have much faith in the data they collect or the conclusions they reach.

With the importance of establishing the reliability and validity of measures in mind, let us consider some of the different ways in which aspects of human development might be measured.

SELF-REPORT METHODOLOGIES

Four common procedures that developmentalists use to gather information and test hypotheses are interviews, questionnaires, the clinical method, and case studies. Although these approaches are similar in that each asks subjects to answer questions posed by the investigator, they differ in the extent to which the investigator treats individual participants alike.

Interviews and questionnaires.   Researchers who opt for the interview or the questionnaire technique will ask the child (or the child's parents) a series of questions pertaining to one or more aspects of development. Collecting data via a questionnaire simply involves putting questions on paper and asking participants to respond to them in writing, whereas

---

[1]The intent here is not to criticize the early social philosophers. In fact, today's developmentalists (and children) are indebted to these men for helping to modify the ways in which society thought about, treated, and often exploited its young.

interviews require participants to respond orally to the investigator's queries. If the procedure is a **structured interview or questionnaire**, all who participate in the study are asked the same questions in the same order. The purpose of this standardized or structured format is to treat each person alike so that the responses of different participants can be compared.

One interesting application of the interview technique was a project in which kindergarten, second-grade, and fourth-grade children responded to 24 questions designed to assess their knowledge of social stereotypes about males and females (Williams, Bennett, & Best, 1975). Each question came in response to a different short story in which the central character was described by either stereotypically masculine adjectives (for example, *aggressive*, *forceful*, *tough*) or stereotypically feminine adjectives (for example, *emotional*, *excitable*). The child's task was to indicate whether the character in each story was male or female. Williams and his associates found that even kindergartners could usually tell whether the stories referred to boys or girls. In other words, these 5-year-olds were quite knowledgeable about gender stereotypes, although children's thinking became much more stereotyped between kindergarten and the second grade. One implication of these results is that stereotyping of the sexes must begin very early if kindergartners are already thinking along stereotyped lines.

Interviews and questionnaires have some very real shortcomings. First, neither approach can be used with very young children who cannot read or comprehend speech very well. Second, investigators must hope that the answers they receive are honest and accurate and are not merely attempts by respondents to present themselves in a favorable manner. Many children, for example, might be reluctant to admit that they have snitched money from Mother's purse or played "doctor" with the child next door. Clearly, inaccurate or untruthful responses will lead to erroneous conclusions. Finally, investigators must be careful to ensure that participants of different ages interpret questions in the same way; otherwise, the age trends observed in one's study may reflect differences in children's ability to comprehend and communicate rather than

real underlying changes in children's feelings, thoughts, or behaviors.

Despite these potential shortcomings, structured interviews and questionnaires can be excellent research tools. Both approaches are particularly useful when the interviewer *challenges* participants to display what they know about an issue, for the socially desirable response to such a challenge is likely to be a truthful or accurate answer. In the gender-stereotyping study, for example, the young participants probably considered each question a personal challenge or a puzzle to be solved and were thus motivated to answer accurately and to display exactly what they knew about males and females. Under the circumstances, then, the structured interview was an excellent method of assessing children's perceptions of the sexes.

The case study.   Yet another strategy for researching social and personality development is the **case study**. An investigator who uses this method prepares detailed descriptions of one or more individuals and then attempts to draw conclusions by analyzing these "cases." In preparing an individualized record, or case, the researcher will typically include many items of information about the individual, such as his or her family background, socioeconomic status, education and work history, health record, self-descriptions of significant life events, and performance on psychological tests. Much of the information included in any case history comes from interviews with the individual, although the questions asked are typically not standardized and may vary considerably from case to case.

Sigmund Freud was a strong proponent of the case study. He formulated a comprehensive theory of social and personality development—psychoanalytic theory—from his analyses of the life histories of his patients. Nevertheless, there are three major shortcomings of case studies that can seriously compromise their usefulness. First, the validity of the investigator's conclusions will obviously depend on the accuracy of information received from the "cases." Unfortunately, the potential for inaccuracy is great in a method in which older subjects try to recall the causes and consequences of important events that occurred years ago in childhood. Second, the data on any two (or more) individuals may not be directly comparable if the investigator has asked each participant different questions rather than posing a standard set of questions to all. Finally, the case study may lack *generalizability*; that is, conclusions drawn from the experiences of the particular individuals who were studied may not apply to most people. In fact, one recurring criticism of Freud's psychoanalytic theory is that it was formulated from the experiences and recollections of emotionally disturbed patients who were hardly typical of the general population. In sum, the case study can serve as a rich source of ideas about social and personality development. However, its limitations are many, and any conclusions drawn from case studies should be verified through the use of other research techniques.

The clinical method.   The **clinical method** is a very close relative of the interview technique. The investigator is usually interested in testing a hypothesis by presenting the research participant with a task or problem of some sort and then inviting a response. When the participant has responded, the investigator will typically ask a second question or introduce a new problem in the hope of clarifying the participant's original answer. This questioning then continues until the investigator has the information needed to evaluate the hypothesis. Although participants are often asked the same questions in the initial stages of the research, their answers to each question determine what the investigator asks next. And since participants' answers often differ, it is possible that no two participants will ever receive exactly the same line of questioning. Thus the clinical method considers each subject to be unique.

Jean Piaget, a famous Swiss psychologist, relied extensively on the clinical method to study children's moral reasoning and general intellectual development. The data from Piaget's research are largely protocol records of his interactions with individual children. Here is a small sample from Piaget's (1932/1965, p. 140) work on the development of moral reasoning—a sample showing that this young child thinks about lying in a very different way than adults do.

Piaget: Do you know what a lie is?
Clai: It's when you say what isn't true.
Piaget: Is 2 + 2 = 5 a lie?
Clai: Yes, it's a lie.
Piaget: Why?
Clai: Because it isn't right.
Piaget: Did the boy who said 2 + 2 = 5 know it wasn't right or did he make a mistake?
Clai: He made a mistake.
Piaget: Then if he made a mistake, did he tell a lie or not?
Clai: Yes, he told a lie.

We need only examine the richness of Piaget's thinking (as we will do in Chapter 4 and throughout the text) to see that the clinical method can provide a wealth of information about developing children. However, this approach is a highly controversial technique that presents some thorny interpretive problems. We have already noted the difficulties in comparing cases or protocols generated by a procedure that treats each participant differently. Furthermore, the nonstandardized probing of each participant raises the possibility that the examiner's preexisting theoretical biases may affect the questions asked and the interpretations provided. Since conclusions drawn from the clinical method depend, in part, on the investigator's *subjective* interpretations, it is always desirable to verify these insights using other research techniques.

OBSERVATIONAL METHODOLOGIES

Often researchers prefer to observe people's behavior directly rather than to ask them questions about it. One such method that many developmentalists favor is **naturalistic observation** — observing people in their common, everyday (that is, natural) surroundings. To observe children, this would usually mean going into homes, schools, or public parks and playgrounds and carefully recording what happens. Rarely will the investigator try to record every event that occurs; he or she will usually be testing a specific hypothesis about one type of behavior, such as cooperation or aggression, and will focus exclusively on acts of this kind. One strength of naturalistic observation is that it can be applied to infants and toddlers, who often cannot be studied through methods that demand verbal skills. But perhaps the greatest advantage of the observational technique is that it is the only method that can tell us how people actually behave in everyday life (Willems & Alexander, 1982).

Researchers using naturalistic observation must be extremely careful to ensure the reliability of their observational measures and to guard against **observer bias** — the tendency to confirm one's hypotheses by reading too much (or too little) into naturally occurring events. One way to achieve these ends is to specify in advance precisely the kinds of activity that qualify as examples of the behavior you hope to study. An *objective* behavioral record of this kind calls for a minimum of subjective interpretation and will help to ensure that independent observers will agree on what they have seen.

Unfortunately, the mere presence of an unfamiliar observer can cause subjects to behave rather atypically. Consider the experiences of one graduate student who perceived something other than spontaneous play while photographing children on a playground. A girl who had been playing alone with a doll jumped up when the student approached and asked him to photograph her "new

PHOTO 1-3 Children's tendency to perform for an observer is one of the problems researchers must overcome when using the method of naturalistic observation.

trick" on the monkey bars. Another child, who had been playing kickball, said "Get this" as he broke away from the game and laid a blindside tackle on an unsuspecting onlooker. Clearly, observers must try to minimize the influence they might have on the behavior of their subjects. One way to do so is to videotape the behavioral record for later viewing by members of the research team. Videotaping is particularly effective at minimizing observer influence if it is done from a concealed location or if the equipment is in place for a long period so that the children become used to this unusual machinery. If videotaping is not feasible, observers can minimize their influence by mingling with the children in their natural habitats before the actual conduct of the study. In this way, children become accustomed to the observers' presence and therefore are less likely to "perform" for them or alter their behavior in any significant way.

Rosalind Charlesworth and Willard Hartup (1967) used naturalistic observation to determine whether nursery-school children become more pleasant to one another as they grow older. Charlesworth and Hartup first defined examples of positive social reinforcers that children might dispense to one another (for example, showing affection, cooperating, sharing, giving tangible objects such as toys). Then, over a five-week period, they carefully observed a sample of 3- and 4-year-old nursery-school children, noting instances in which a child dispensed a positive social reinforcer to a classmate. The results were interesting. Not only were 4-year-olds more likely to reinforce their peers than 3-year-olds were, but they also distributed their reinforcers to a larger number of classmates. In addition, the children who gave the most social reinforcers to peers were the ones who received the most in return. So these preschoolers appeared to be partaking in a *reciprocal exchange* of positive reinforcers—a finding that suggests we could learn a great deal about the origins of social equity by observing the mutual give-and-take among young children at play in their peer groups.

One major limitation of observational research is its inability to differentiate among several possible causes for the observations made. Let's reconsider a major result of Charlesworth and Hartup's study: Do 4-year-olds reinforce peers more than 3-year-olds *because* the older children have learned that peers will return their acts of kindness? Or, rather, are 4-year-olds simply more inclined to favor *group* play activities, which just happen to provide more opportunities to give and receive social reinforcers? Either possibility can account for Charlesworth and Hartup's findings, and, unfortunately, the observational record fails to tell us which explanation is correct. In sum, there are many variables in the natural setting that may affect children's behavior, and it is often difficult to specify which of these variables or what combination of them is responsible for an observation or pattern of observations.

Finally, some behaviors occur so infrequently (for example, heroic rescues) or are so socially undesirable (for example, overt sex play, thievery) that they are unlikely to be witnessed by a strange observer in the natural environment. To study these kinds of behaviors, investigators are likely to make **structured observations** in a laboratory. The procedure would involve presenting the child with a stimulus thought to prompt the behavior in question and then surreptitiously observing the child (via hidden camera or through a one-way mirror) to see if he or she performs that behavior. For example, Leon Kuczynski (1983) got children to promise to help him with a boring task and then left them alone to work at it in a room where attractive toys were present. This procedure enabled Kuczynski to determine whether youngsters were likely to break their promise to work (a socially undesirable act) when they thought there was no one present to observe their transgression.

Besides being a feasible way of studying behaviors that occur infrequently or are unlikely to be displayed openly in the natural environment, structured observations also ensure that every participant in the sample is exposed to the *same* eliciting stimuli and has an *equal opportunity* to perform the target behavior—circumstances that are not always true in the natural setting. Of course, the major disadvantage of structured observations is that participants may not always respond to a contrived laboratory setting as they would in everyday life.

Table 1-1 provides a brief review of the data-gathering schemes that we have examined thus far. In the sections that follow, we will consider the issue of how investigators might design their research to test hypotheses and detect developmental changes.

Detecting Relationships: Correlational and Experimental Designs

Once researchers have decided what they want to study, they must then formulate a research plan, or design, that permits them to identify associations among events and behaviors and to specify the causes of these relationships. Here we consider two general research designs that investigators might employ: correlational and experimental.

THE CORRELATIONAL DESIGN

In a **correlational design** the investigator gathers information to determine whether two or more variables of interest are meaningfully related. If the researcher is testing a specific hypothesis (rather than

TABLE 1-1 *Strengths and limitations of some general methods of collecting scientific data*

Method	Strengths	Limitations
Interviews and questionnaires	Relatively quick way to gather much information; standardized format allows the investigator to make direct comparisons among data provided by different participants.	Data collected may be inaccurate, may be less than completely honest, or may reflect variations in respondents' verbal skills and ability to understand the questions.
Case studies	Very broad method that considers many sources of data when drawing inferences and conclusions about individual participants.	Kind of data collected often differs from case to case and may be inaccurate or less than honest; conclusions drawn from individual cases are subjective and may not apply to other people.
Clinical method	Flexible methodology that treats subjects as unique individuals; freedom to probe can be an aid in ensuring that the participant understands the meaning of the questions one asks.	Conclusions drawn may be unreliable in that participants are not all treated alike; flexible probes depend, in part, on the investigator's subjective interpretations of the participant's responses; can be used only with highly verbal participants.
Naturalistic observation	Allows study of behavior as it actually occurs in the real world.	Possibly subject to observer bias; observed behaviors may be influenced by observer's presence; unusual or undesirable behaviors are unlikely to be observed during the periods when observations are made.
Structured observation	Offers a standardized environment that provides every child an opportunity to perform the target behavior; excellent way to observe infrequent or socially undesirable acts.	Observations may not always represent the ways children behave in the natural environment.

conducting preliminary exploratory research), he or she will be checking to see whether these variables are related as the hypothesis specifies they should be. No attempts are made to structure or manipulate the participants' environment in any way. Instead, correlational researchers take people as they find them—already "manipulated" by natural life experiences—and try to determine whether variations in people's life experiences are associated with differences in their behaviors or patterns of development.

To illustrate the correlational approach to hypothesis testing, we will work with a simple theory specifying that youngsters learn a lot from watching television and are likely to imitate the actions of the characters they observe. One hypothesis we might derive from this theory is that, the more often children observe TV characters who display violent and aggressive acts, the more inclined they will be to behave aggressively toward their own playmates. Af-

ter selecting a sample of children to study, our next step in testing our hypothesis is to measure the two variables that we think are related. To assess children's exposure to aggressive themes on television, we might use the interview or naturalistic observational methods to determine what each child watches, and then count the number of violent and aggressive responses that occur in this programming. To measure the frequency of the children's own aggressive behavior toward peers, we could observe our sample on a playground and record how often each child behaves in a hostile, aggressive manner toward playmates. Having now gathered the data, it is time to evaluate our hypothesis.

The presence (or absence) of a relationship between variables can be determined by subjecting the data to a statistical procedure that yields a **correlation coefficient**. A correlation coefficient (symbolized by an r) provides a numerical estimate of the strength and the direction of the association between two variables. It can range in value from +1.00 to −1.00. The absolute value of *r* (disregarding its sign) tells us the *strength* of the relationship. An *r* of .00 indicates that the two variables are unrelated, whereas an *r* with an absolute value larger than .50 indicates a moderate-to-strong relationship. The sign of the correlation coefficient indicates the *direction* of the relationship. If the sign is positive, this means that, as one variable increases, the other variable also increases. For example, height and weight are positively correlated: as people grow taller, they (usually) get heavier. Negative correlations, however, indicate inverse relationships; as one variable increases, the other *decreases*. Among middle-aged men, exercise and heart disease are negatively correlated: men who exercise more often are less likely to develop heart disease.

Now let's return to our hypothesized positive relationship between televised violence and children's aggressive behavior. A number of investigators have conducted correlational studies similar to the one we have designed, and the results (reviewed in Liebert & Sprafkin, 1988) suggest a moderate positive correlation (between +.40 and +.60) between the two variables of interest: children who watch a lot of violent television programming are more likely to approve of violence and to behave more aggressively toward playmates than are other youngsters who watch little violent programming (see Figure 1-3 for a visual display).

Do these correlational studies establish that exposure to violent TV programming *causes* children to become more aggressively inclined? *No, they do not!* Although we have detected a relationship between exposure to televised violence and children's aggressive behavior, the causal direction of the relationship is not at all clear. An equally plausible alternative explanation is that relatively aggressive children are the more inclined to prefer violent programming. Another possibility is that the association between TV viewing and aggressive behavior is actually caused by a third variable we have not measured. For example, perhaps parents who endorse forceful means of conflict resolution (an unmeasured variable) cause their children to become more aggressively inclined *and* to favor violent TV

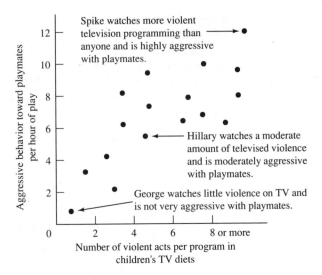

FIGURE 1-3 Plot of a hypothetical positive correlation between the amount of violence children see on television and the number of aggressive responses they display. Each dot represents a specific child who views a particular level of televised violence (shown on the horizontal axis) and commits a particular number of aggressive acts (shown on the vertical axis). Although the correlation is less than perfect, we see that, the more acts of violence a child watches on TV, the more inclined he or she is to behave aggressively toward peers.

programs. If this were true, the latter two variables could be correlated even though their relationship to each other is not one of cause and effect.

In sum, the correlational design is a versatile approach that can detect systematic relationships between any two or more variables that we might be interested in and are capable of measuring. However, its major limitation is that *it cannot unambiguously indicate that one thing causes another.* How, then, might a researcher establish the underlying causes of various behaviors or other aspects of human development? By conducting experiments.

THE EXPERIMENTAL DESIGN

In contrast to correlational studies, **experimental designs** permit a precise assessment of the cause-and-effect relationship that may exist between two variables. Let's return to the issue of whether viewing violent television programming *causes* children to become more aggressively inclined. In conducting a laboratory experiment to test this (or any) hypothesis, we would bring participants to the lab, expose them to different treatments, and record as data their responses to these treatments. The different treatments to which we expose our participants represent the **independent variable** of our experiment. To test the hypothesis that we have proposed, our independent variable (or treatments) would be the type of television program that we show to our participants. Half the children might view a program in which one or more characters behave in a violent or otherwise aggressive manner toward others, whereas the other half would watch a program in which little if any violence was portrayed. Children's reactions to the television shows would become the data, or **dependent variable**, in our experiment. Since our hypothesis centers on children's aggression, we would want to measure (as our dependent variable) how aggressively children behave after watching each type of television show. A dependent variable is called "dependent" because its value presumably "depends" on the independent variable. In the present case, we are hypothesizing that future aggression (our dependent variable) will be greater for those children who watch programs displaying violence and aggression (one level of the independent variable) than for children who watch programs portraying few if any aggressive acts (the second level of the independent variable). If we are careful experimenters and exercise precise control over *all* other factors that may affect children's aggression, then the pattern of results that we have anticipated would allow us to draw a strong conclusion: watching violent television programs *causes* children to behave more aggressively.

Several years ago an experiment similar to the one we have proposed was actually conducted (Liebert & Baron, 1972). Half of the 5- to 9-year-olds in this study watched a violent 3½-minute clip from *The Untouchables*—one that contained two fistfights, two shootings, and a stabbing. The remaining children watched 3½ minutes of a nonviolent but exciting track meet. Thus the independent variable was the type of program watched. Then each child was taken into another room and seated before a box

that had wires leading into the adjoining room. On the box was a green button labeled HELP, a red button labeled HURT, and a white light between the buttons. The experimenter announced that a child in the adjoining room would soon be playing a handle-turning game that would illuminate the white light. The subject was told that, by pushing the buttons when the light was lit, he or she could either *help* the other child by making the handle easy to turn or *hurt* the child by making the handle become very hot. When it was clear that the subject understood the instructions, the experimenter left the room, and the light came on 20 times over the next several minutes. Thus each subject had 20 opportunities to help or hurt another child. The total amount of time each subject spent pushing the HURT button served as a measure of his or her aggression—the dependent variable in this study.

The results were clear: despite the availability of an alternative, helping response, *both boys and girls were much more likely to press the HURT button (that is, behave aggressively) if they had watched the violent television program.* However, children in the two experimental conditions did not differ in their willingness to push the HELP button. So it appears that a mere 3½-minute exposure to televised violence can cause children to behave more aggressively toward a peer, even though the aggressive acts they witnessed on television bore no resemblance to those they committed themselves.

When students discuss this experiment in class, someone invariably challenges this interpretation of the results. For example, one student recently proposed the alternative interpretation "Maybe kids who saw the violent film were naturally more sadistic than those who saw the track meet." In other words, he was suggesting that children's *preexisting* levels of sadism had determined their willingness to hurt a peer and that the independent variable (type of television programming) had had no effect at all! Could he have been correct? How do we know that children in the two experimental conditions didn't differ in some important way (such as their preexisting sadistic inclinations) that may have affected their willingness to hurt a peer?

This question brings us to the crucial issue of **experimental control**. In order to conclude that the independent variable is causally related to the dependent variable, the experimenter must ensure that all other factors that could affect the dependent variable are *controlled* — that is, equivalent in each experimental condition. One way to equalize these extraneous factors is to do what Liebert and Baron (1972) did: randomly assign children to their experimental treatments. The concept of *randomization*, or **random assignment**, means that each research participant has an equal probability of being exposed to each experimental treatment or condition. Assignment of individual participants to a particular treatment is accomplished by an unbiased procedure such as the flip of a coin. If the assignment is truly random, there is only a very slim chance that participants in the two (or more) experimental conditions will differ on *any* characteristic that might affect their performance on the dependent variable; all these "extraneous" characteristics will have been randomly distributed within each condition and equalized across the different conditions. Since Liebert and Baron randomly assigned children to experimental conditions, they could be reasonably certain that the children who watched the violent TV program were not naturally more sadistic than those who watched the nonviolent program. So it was reasonable for them to conclude that the former group of children were more aggressive *because* they had watched a program in which violence and aggression were central.

A possible limitation of laboratory experiments. Critics of laboratory experimentation have argued that the tightly controlled laboratory environment is often very contrived and artificial and that children are likely to behave very differently in these surroundings than they would in a natural setting. Urie Bronfenbrenner (1977) has charged that a heavy reliance on laboratory experiments has made developmental psychology "the science of the strange behavior of children in strange situations with strange adults" (p. 19). Similarly, Robert McCall (1977) notes that experiments tell us what *can* cause a developmental change but do not necessarily pinpoint the factors that *actually do* cause such changes in natural settings. Consequently, it is quite possible that con-

clusions drawn from laboratory experiments will not always apply to the real world. In Box 1-2 we consider a step that experimentalists can take to counter this criticism or to assess the **ecological validity** of their laboratory results.

THE NATURAL (OR QUASI) EXPERIMENT

There are many issues to which the experimental method cannot or should not (for ethical reasons) be applied. Suppose, for example, that we wish to study the effects of social deprivation on infants' social and emotional development. Obviously we cannot ask one group of parents to lock their infants in an attic for two years so that we can collect the data we need. It is simply unethical to submit children to any experimental treatment that may adversely affect their physical or psychological well-being.

However, we might be able to accomplish our research objectives through a **natural (or quasi) experiment** — a study in which we observe the consequences of a natural event to which subjects have been exposed. So, if we were able to locate a group of children who were raised in impoverished institutions with very little contact with caregivers over the first two years, we could compare their social and emotional development with that of children raised at home in traditional family settings. This comparison would provide some information about the effects of early social deprivation on children's social and emotional development. (Indeed, precisely this kind of natural experiment is described in detail in Chapter 6.) The "independent variable" in a natural experiment is the "event" that subjects experience (in our example, the social deprivation experienced by institutionalized infants). The "dependent variable" is whatever outcome measure one chooses to study (in our example, social and emotional development).

Note, however, that researchers conducting natural experiments do not control the independent variable, nor do they randomly assign participants to experimental conditions; they merely observe and record the apparent outcomes of a natural happening or event. So, in the absence of tight experimental control, it is often hard to determine precisely what factor is responsible for any group differences that are found. But, even though the quasi experiment is unable to make *strong* statements about cause and effect, it is nevertheless useful: it can tell us whether a natural event could possibly have influenced those who experienced it and, thus, can provide some meaningful clues about cause and effect.

Designs to Measure Developmental Change

Social developmentalists are not interested merely in examining children's behavior at one particular point in time; instead, they hope to determine how children's feelings, thoughts, abilities, and behav-

iors *develop* or *change* over time. How might we design research to chart these developmental trends? Let's briefly consider three approaches: the cross-sectional design, the longitudinal design, and the sequential design.

THE CROSS-SECTIONAL DESIGN

In a **cross-sectional design**, groups of children who *differ in age* are studied at *the same point in time*. For example, a researcher interested in determining whether children become more generous as they mature might place 6-, 8-, and 10-year-olds in a situation in which they are afforded an opportunity to share a valuable commodity (say, candy or money)

<table><tr><td>B O X</td><td>**1-2**</td><td>*Assessing Causal Relationships in the Real World — The Field Experiment*</td></tr></table>

How can we be sure that a conclusion drawn from a laboratory experiment applies in the real world? One way is to seek converging evidence for that conclusion by conducting a similar experiment *in a natural setting* — that is, a **field experiment**. This approach combines all the advantages of naturalistic observation with the more rigorous control that experimentation allows. In addition, children typically are not apprehensive about participating in a "strange" experiment, because all the activities they undertake are everyday activities; indeed, they may not even be aware that they are being observed.

Let's consider an example of a field experiment that provides some converging evidence for the hypothesis that heavy exposure to televised violence can cause children to become more aggressively inclined. Lynette Friedrich and Aletha Stein (1973) went into a nursery school and spent three weeks becoming acquainted with the children and observing how often each of them behaved aggressively toward classmates. This initial assessment of the children's aggressive behavior provided a *baseline* against which future increases in aggression could be measured. The children were then randomly assigned to three groups. For the next

month, children in each group watched one of three types of television shows during the first half-hour of the school day. Some children always viewed violent programming (*Batman* or *Superman*), whereas others always watched either prosocial programming (*Mister Rogers' Neighborhood*) or neutral programming (featuring nature themes). At the end of this month-long treatment phase, each child was observed daily for two additional weeks to determine whether the television programming had had any effects on the amount of aggression he or she displayed toward classmates.

Friedrich and Stein reported that exposure to violent television did result in higher levels of aggressive behavior, *but only for those children who had been average or above in aggression on the earlier baseline measure.* So the results of this field experiment are consistent with Liebert and Baron's laboratory study in suggesting that exposure to violent television programming can indeed *cause* increases in aggression. Yet it also qualifies the laboratory work by implying that the instigating effects of viewing TV violence *in the natural environment* are greatest for those children who are already somewhat aggressively inclined.

with needy youngsters who are less fortunate than themselves. By comparing the responses of children in the different age groups, investigators can often identify age-related changes in generosity (see Chapter 11 for a review of this topic) or in whatever aspect of development they have chosen to study.

An important advantage of the cross-sectional method is that the investigator can collect data from subjects of different ages over a short time. For example, an investigator would not have to wait four years for her 6-year-olds to become 10-year-olds in order to determine whether children's generosity increases over this age range. She can merely sample children of different ages and test all samples at approximately the same time.

Notice, however, that, in cross-sectional research, participants at each age level are *different* people who come from different cohorts. A *cohort* is a group of people of the same age who are exposed to similar cultural environments or historical events as they are growing up. The fact that different cohorts are always involved in cross-sectional comparisons means that any age-related effects that are found in the study may not always be due to age or development but, rather, to some other feature that distinguishes individuals in different cohorts.

An example may clarify the issue. For years, cross-sectional research had consistently indicated that young adults score higher on intelligence tests than middle-aged adults, who, in turn, score higher than the elderly. But does intelligence decline with age, as these findings would seem to indicate? Not necessarily! More recent research (Schaie, 1965, 1986) reveals that individuals' intelligence test scores remain reasonably stable over the years and that the earlier studies were really measuring something quite different: cohort differences in education. The older adults in earlier cross-sectional studies had had less schooling, which could explain why they scored lower on intelligence tests than the middle-aged or young-adult samples. Their test scores had not declined but, rather, had always been lower than those of the younger adults with whom they were compared. So the earlier cross-sectional research had discovered a **cohort effect**, not true developmental change.

This example points directly to a second problem with the cross-sectional method: it tells us nothing about the development of *individuals*, because each person is observed *at only one point in time*. So cross-sectional comparisons cannot provide answers to questions such as "When will *my* child become more generous?" or "Will aggressive 2-year-olds become aggressive 5-year-olds?" To address issues like these, an investigator will often rely on a second kind of developmental comparison, the longitudinal design.

THE LONGITUDINAL DESIGN

In a **longitudinal design**, the same participants are observed repeatedly over time. For example, a researcher interested in determining whether generosity increases over middle childhood might provide 6-year-olds an opportunity to behave in a charitable fashion toward needy youngsters and then follow up with similar assessments of the generosity of *these same children* at ages 8 and 10.

The period spanned by a longitudinal study may be very long or reasonably short. The investigators may be looking at one particular aspect of development, such as generosity, or at many. By repeatedly testing the same subjects, investigators can assess the *stability* of various attributes and the patterns of developmental *change* for each person in the sample. In addition, they can identify *general* developmental trends by looking for commonalities in development that most or all individuals share. Finally, the tracking of several children over time will help investigators to understand the bases for *individual differences* in development, particularly if it can be established that different kinds of earlier experiences lead to very different outcomes.

Although we have focused on the important advantages of the longitudinal comparison, this procedure does have several drawbacks. For example, longitudinal research can be very costly and time consuming, particularly if the project spans a period of several years. Moreover, the focus of theory and research in social and personality development is constantly changing, so that longitudinal questions that seem very exciting at the beginning of a long-

PHOTOS 1-4   Leisure activities of the 1930s (left) and the 1990s (right). As these photos illustrate, the kinds of experiences that children growing up in the 1930s had were very different from those of today's youth. Many believe that cross-generational changes in the environment may limit the results of a longitudinal study to the youngsters who were growing up while the research was in progress.

term project may seem rather trivial by the time the study ends. *Subject loss* may also become a problem: children may move away, get sick, become bored with repeated testing, or have parents who, for one reason or another, will not allow them to continue in the study. The result is a smaller and potentially **nonrepresentative sample** that not only provides less information about the developmental issues in question but also may limit the conclusions of the study to those healthy children who do not move away and who remain cooperative over the long run.

Between the 1920s and the 1950s, several major longitudinal projects were undertaken to follow groups of children from infancy through adolescence, charting the course of their physical, social, emotional, and intellectual development. Clearly, studies of this kind can provide us with a wealth of information about social and personality development. (Indeed, we will be examining data from several of these projects throughout the text.) Nevertheless, these very-long-term longitudinal studies have another shortcoming, which students often

see right away: the **cross-generational problem**. Children in a longitudinal research project are typically drawn from one cohort: as a result, they will experience somewhat different cultural, family, and school environments than children in other cohorts. Consider, for example, that children raised in the 1940s lived in larger and typically less affluent families. What's more, they traveled less than modern children do and had no access to television or electronic computers. Clearly, these youngsters lived in a different world, and inferences drawn from longitudinal studies of such children may not apply to today's youth. Stated another way, cross-generational changes in the environment may limit the conclusions of a longitudinal project to those children who were growing up while the study was in progress.

We have seen that the cross-sectional and the longitudinal designs each have distinct advantages and disadvantages. Might it be possible to combine the best features of both approaches? A third kind of developmental comparison — the sequential design — tries to do just that.

THE SEQUENTIAL DESIGN

Suppose we hoped to optimize one aspect of development by creating a training program to reduce racial prejudice among 6- to 10-year-olds. Before administering our program on a large scale, we would surely want to try it out on a smaller number of children to see whether it really works. However, there are a number of questions that others may have about our program, such as "When can children first understand it?"; "At what age will children respond most favorably to the training?"; and "Do any immediate reductions in prejudice produced by our program persist over time?" To address all these issues in our research, we will need a design that measures *both* the short-term and the long-term effects of our program on children of *different ages*.

Clearly, the cross-sectional comparison, which tests participants at only one point in time, cannot tell us anything about the long-term effects of our program. The longitudinal method can tell us about long-term effects; but, since all the participants would be exposed to the program at the same age (say, age 6), a longitudinal study would not tell us whether this training would be any more (or less) effective if it were first administered when children were older.

The only approach that allows us to answer all our questions is a **sequential design** (Schaie, 1965, 1986). Sequential designs combine the best features of the cross-sectional and the longitudinal approaches by selecting participants of different ages and then studying each of these cohorts over time. For purposes of our proposed research, we might begin by administering our training program to groups of 6-, 8-, and 10-year-olds. Of course, we would want to randomly assign other 6-, 8-, and 10-year-olds to control groups that are not exposed to the training program. The children who were "trained" would then be observed and compared with their agemates in the control group to determine (1) whether the program was immediately effective at reducing racial prejudice and (2) if so, the age at which the program had its greatest *immediate* impact. This is the information we would obtain had we conducted a standard cross-sectional experiment (see the comparison labeled CS1 in Figure 1-4).

However, our choice of the sequential design allows us to measure the *enduring* effects of our program by simply retesting our samples of 6-, 8-, and 10-year-olds two years later (see comparisons labeled L1, L2, and L3 in Figure 1-4). This approach has several advantages over the standard longitudinal design. The first is a *time saving*: in only two years we have learned about the long-term effects of the program on those children who are still between the target ages of 6 and 10. A standard longitudinal comparison would require four years to provide similar information. Second, the sequential design actually yields *more information* about long-term effects than the longitudinal approach does. If we had chosen the longitudinal design, we would have data on the long-term effects of a program administered *only* to 6-year-olds. However, the sequential approach allows us to perform a second cross-sectional comparison to determine whether the program has *comparable* long-term effects when administered to 6-, 8-, and 10-year-olds (see comparison CS2 in Figure 1-4). Clearly, this combination of the cross-sectional and longitudinal designs is a rather versatile alternative to either of those approaches.

We have now discussed a variety of research designs, each of which has definite strengths and weaknesses. To help you review and compare these designs, Table 1-2 provides a brief description of each, along with its major advantages and disadvantages.

Cross-Cultural Comparisons

Developmentalists are often hesitant to publish a new finding or conclusion until they have studied enough people to determine that their "discovery" is reliable. However, their conclusions are frequently based on subjects living at one point in time within one particular society or subculture, and it is difficult to know whether these conclusions will apply to future generations or even to children currently growing up in other societies or subcultures (Lerner, 1991). Today the generalizability of findings across samples and settings has become an impor-

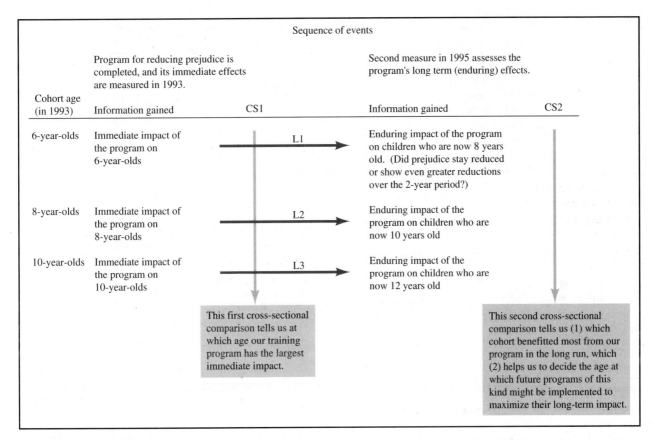

FIGURE 1-4   Illustration of a simple sequential design and a summary of the information gained from such a procedure.

tant issue, for many theorists have implied that there are "universals" in human development—events and outcomes that all children share as they progress from infancy to adulthood.

Cross-cultural studies are those in which participants from different cultural or subcultural backgrounds are observed, tested, and compared on one or more aspects of development. Studies of this kind serve many purposes. For example, they allow the investigator to determine whether conclusions drawn about the development of children from one social context (such as middle-class, white youngsters in the United States) also characterize children growing up in other societies or even those from different ethnic or socioeconomic backgrounds within the same society (for example, American children of

Hispanic ancestry or those from economically disadvantaged homes). So the **cross-cultural comparison** guards against the overgeneralization of research findings and, indeed, is the only way to determine whether there truly are "universals" in human development.

However, many investigators who favor the cross-cultural approach are looking for *differences* rather than similarities. They recognize that human beings develop in societies that have very different ideas about issues such as the proper times and procedures for disciplining children, the activities that are most appropriate for boys and for girls, the time at which childhood ends and adulthood begins, the treatment of the aged, and countless other aspects of life. They have also learned that people from

TABLE 1-2 *An overview of commonly used research designs*

Design	Procedure	Strengths	Limitations
General designs			
Correlational	Gathers information about two or more variables without researcher intervention.	Estimates the strength and direction of relationships among variables in the natural environment.	Does not permit determination of cause-and-effect relationships among variables.
Laboratory experiment	Manipulates some aspect of subjects' environment (independent variable) and measures its impact on subjects' behavior (dependent variable).	Permits determination of cause-and-effect relationships among variables.	Data obtained in artificial laboratory environment may lack generalizability to the real world.
Field experiment	Manipulates independent variable and measures its impact on the dependent variable in a natural setting.	Permits determination of cause-and-effect relationships and generalizability of findings to the real world.	Experimental treatments may be less potent and harder to control when presented in the natural environment.
Natural (quasi) experiment	Gathers information about the behavior of people who experience a real-world (natural) manipulation of their environment.	Permits a study of the impact of natural events that would be difficult or impossible to simulate in an experiment; provides strong clues about cause-and-effect relationships.	Lack of precise control over natural events or the participants exposed to them prevents the investigator from establishing definitive cause-and-effect relationships.
Developmental designs			
Cross-sectional	Observes people of different ages (or cohorts) at one point in time.	Demonstrates age differences; hints at developmental trends; relatively inexpensive; takes little time to conduct.	Age trends may reflect extraneous differences between cohorts rather than true developmental change; provides no data on the development of individuals, because each participant is observed at only one point in time.
Longitudinal	Observes people of one cohort repeatedly over time.	Provides data on the development of individuals; can reveal links between early experiences and later outcomes; indicates how individuals are alike and how they are different in the ways they change over time.	Relatively time consuming and expensive; subject loss may yield nonrepresentative sample that limits the generalizability of one's conclusions; cross-generational changes may limit one's conclusions to the cohort that was studied.
Sequential	Combines the cross-sectional and the longitudinal approaches by observing different cohorts repeatedly over time.	Discriminates true developmental trends from cohort effects; indicates whether developmental changes experienced by one cohort are similar to those experienced by other cohorts; often less costly and time consuming than the longitudinal approach.	More costly and time consuming than cross-sectional research; despite being the strongest design, may still leave questions about whether a developmental change is generalizable beyond the cohorts that were studied.

various cultures differ in the ways they perceive the world, express their emotions, think, and solve problems. So, apart from its focus on universals in development, the cross-cultural approach also illustrates that human development is heavily influenced by the cultural context in which it occurs (see Box 1-3 for a dramatic illustration of cultural influences on gender roles).

Isn't it remarkable how many methods and designs developmentalists have at their disposal? This diversity of available procedures is a definite strength, because findings gained through one procedure can

---

1-3 | *A Cross-Cultural Comparison of Gender Roles*

One of the greatest values of cross-cultural comparisons is that they can tell us whether a developmental phenomenon is or is not universal. Consider the roles that males and females play in our society. In our culture, the masculine role has traditionally required traits such as independence, assertiveness, and dominance. By contrast, females are expected to be more nurturant and sensitive to other people. Are these masculine and feminine roles universal? Could biological differences between the sexes lead to inevitable sex differences in behavior?

Some years ago, anthropologist Margaret Mead (1935) compared the gender roles adopted by people in three tribal societies on the island of New Guinea, and her observations are certainly thought provoking. In the Arapesh tribe, both men and women were taught to play what we would regard as a feminine role: they were cooperative, nonaggressive, and sensitive to the needs of others. By contrast, both men and women of the Mundugumor tribe were brought up to be hostile, aggressive, and emotionally unresponsive to other people—a masculine pattern of behavior by Western standards. Finally, the Tchambuli displayed a pattern of gender-role development that was the direct opposite of the Western pattern: males were passive, emotionally dependent, and socially sensitive, whereas females were dominant, independent, and aggressive!

Mead's cross-cultural comparison suggests that cultural dictates may have far more to do with the characteristic behavior patterns of men and women than biological differences do. So we very much need cross-cultural comparisons such as Mead's. Without them, we might easily make the mistake of assuming that whatever holds true in our society holds true every-

where; with their help, we can begin to understand the contributions of biology and environment to human development.

The roles assumed by men and women may vary dramatically from culture to culture.

then be checked and perhaps confirmed through other procedures. Indeed, such *converging evidence* demonstrates that the discovery one has made is truly a "discovery" and not merely an artifact of the method or the design used to collect the original data. So there is no "best method" for studying children and adolescents; each of the approaches we have considered has contributed substantially to our understanding of social and personality development.

Postscript: On Becoming a Wise Consumer of Scientific Information

Students often wonder why they must learn so much about the methods developmentalists use to conduct research. This is a reasonable question given that the vast majority who take this course will pursue other careers and will never conduct a scientific study of developing children or adolescents. So why not simply present the research findings and skip the methodological details?

My answer is straightforward: although survey courses such as this one are designed to provide a solid overview of theory and research in the discipline to which they pertain, they should also strive (in my opinion, at least) to help you evaluate the relevant information you may encounter in the years ahead. And you will encounter such information; even if you don't read academic journals in your role as a teacher, school administrator, nurse, probation officer, social worker, or other professional who works with developing persons, then certainly you will be exposed to such information through the popular media—television, newspapers, magazines, and the like. How can you know whether that seemingly dramatic and important new finding you've just read or heard about should be taken seriously?

This is an important issue, for new information about social and personality development is often chronicled in the popular media several months or even years before the data on which the media re-

ports are based finally make their appearance in professional journals (if they ever do). Professional journals are slow. Scientists' oral convention presentations, which are often the sources of popular media reports, must first be written, submitted for publication, and examined by other expert reviewers (who often suggest necessary revisions that are made, rereviewed, and often revised again) before a decision is made to publish the research in an academic journal. This professional publication process may take anywhere from 1½–4 years! Moreover, less than 30% of the papers developmentalists submit are judged sufficiently worthy of publication by the most rigorous and reputable journals in our discipline. So many media reports of "dramatic" new findings are based on research that other scientists don't view as very dramatic (or even worthy of publication) after all.

Even if a media report is based on a published article, coverage of the research and its conclusions is often misleading. For example, one recent network story reported on a published article saying that there was clear evidence that "alcoholism is inherited." As we will see in Chapter 2, this is a far more dramatic conclusion than the authors actually drew. Another metropolitan newspaper report summarized a recent article from the prestigious journal *Developmental Psychology* with the headline "Day care harmful for children." What was never made clear in the newspaper article was the researcher's (Howes, 1990) conclusion that *very-low-quality* day care may be harmful to the social and intellectual development of *some* preschool children but that most youngsters receiving good day care suffer no adverse effects. (The issue of day care and its effects on developing children is explored in depth in Chapter 6.) One major cause of such inaccuracies and overstatements is the fact that many reporters writing about the developmental sciences are not trained science writers and simply lack the background to properly summarize the findings of developmental research.

I don't mean to imply that you can never trust what you read; rather, I'd caution you to be skeptical and to evaluate media (and journal) reports, using the methodological information presented in this chapter. You might start by asking: How were the data gathered, and how was the study designed? Were appropriate conclusions drawn given the limitations of the method of data collection and the design (correlational vs. experimental; cross-sectional vs. longitudinal) that the investigators used? Were there proper control groups? Have the results of the study been reviewed by other experts in the field and published in a reputable academic journal? And please don't assume that published articles are unassailable. Many theses and dissertations in the developmental sciences are based on problems and shortcomings that students have identified in previously published research, and professors in courses such as this one will occasionally assign readings to give students opportunities to critique published research. So take the time to read and evaluate published reports that seem especially relevant to your profession or to your role as a parent. Not only will you have a better understanding of the research and its conclusions, but any lingering questions and doubts you may have can often be addressed through a letter (or a phone call) to the author of the article.

In sum, one must become a knowledgeable consumer in order to get the most out of what the field of social and personality development has to offer. Our discussion of research methodology was undertaken with these objectives in mind, and a solid understanding of these methodological lessons should help you to properly evaluate the research you will encounter, not only throughout this text but in many, many other sources in the years to come.

Summary

Socialization is the process through which children and adolescents acquire the beliefs, values, and behaviors deemed significant and appropriate by other members of society. The study of socialization is an interdisciplinary science. Anthropologists and sociologists concentrate on the "content," or *common outcomes*, of socialization — that is, the similarities that children and adolescents display in their adjustment to society and its institutions. Psychologists focus more intently on the means by which children become socialized and on the attributes and experiences that contribute most heavily to our *individual* personalities.

Children who lived in medieval times (and earlier) were often treated rather harshly by their elders and were afforded few of the rights, privileges, and protections of today's youth. The viewpoints of religious leaders and social philosophers of the 17th and 18th centuries contributed to a more humane outlook on children and child rearing, and shortly thereafter some individuals began to observe the behavior of their own sons and daughters and to report their findings in baby biographies. The scientific study of children did not emerge until nearly 1900 as G. Stanley Hall, in the United States, and Sigmund Freud, in Europe, began to collect data and to formulate theories about human growth and development. Soon other investigators were conducting research to evaluate and extend these theories, and the study of developmental psychology began to thrive.

The study of social and personality development is truly a theoretical discipline, with four major theoretical traditions: psychoanalytic theory, the biological viewpoint, social-learning theory, and the cognitive viewpoint. The evolution of different theories is attributable, in part, to the tendency of theorists to make different assumptions about human nature and the character of human development. Sigmund Freud, the father of psychoanalytic theory, portrayed children as "seething cauldrons" who are constantly striving to gratify *inborn* sexual and aggressive instincts. According to Freud, the development of personality proceeds through a series of stages as parents successfully divert the child's undesirable impulses away from their natural outlets and into socially acceptable patterns of behavior. Like Freud, proponents of the biological viewpoint contend that children inherit a number of attributes that will influence their social and personality development. But, rather than characterizing children as inherently negative, self-serving creatures who are passively molded by their parents, biological theorists argue that humans are active and adaptive beings whose natural inclinations are neither inherently good nor inherently bad.

Social-learning theorists view children as blank slates who come into the world with very little in the way of ability, knowledge, or behavioral predispositions. The social-learning perspective is that socialization occurs continuously and may take either a positive or a negative path, depending on the kinds of learning experiences provided by one's environment. However, the most recent versions of social-learning theory stress that children are not merely passive pawns of environmental influence but, rather, active agents who have a hand in determining the character of their own socializing environments.

Cognitive theorists emphasize the positive side of human nature by portraying children as active, adaptive explorers who are constantly trying to cope with the social, emotional, and intellectual demands of the environment. An important assumption made by cognitive theorists is that a child's level of cognitive development will determine her interpretations of and reactions to the social experiences and socializing environment that she encounters.

The best way to evaluate these theories is not on the basis of the assumptions they make but, rather, through use of the *scientific method*, collecting objective data to determine their ability to predict and explain significant aspects of social and personality development. Developmentalists are fortunate to have available a variety of useful techniques for studying developing children and adolescents and testing theoretical hypotheses. The most common methods of data gathering include self-report measures, such as interviews, questionnaires, case studies, and clinical procedures, and direct behavioral observations that are made either in the natural environment or in structured laboratory settings.

Two general research designs—*correlational* and *experimental*—permit researchers to identify relationships among variables that interest them. Although correlational studies estimate the strength and the direction of associations among variables, they cannot specify whether variables are causally related. The experimental design, however, does point to cause-and-effect relationships; the experimenter manipulates one or more independent vari-

ables, controls all other extraneous variables that might affect participants' performance, and then observes the *effect(s)* of the manipulation(s) on one or more dependent variables. Experiments may be performed in the laboratory or, alternatively, in the natural environment, thereby increasing the generalizability of the results. The impact of real-world events that researchers cannot manipulate or control can be studied in natural (quasi) experiments. However, lack of control over natural events prevents the quasi-experimenter from drawing definitive conclusions about cause and effect.

Cross-sectional, longitudinal, and sequential designs are employed to detect developmental change. The cross-sectional design assesses developmental trends by studying participants of different ages at the same point in time. It is an expedient method but limited in that it observes each participant only once and cannot tell us how individuals develop. The longitudinal design detects developmental change by repeatedly examining the same participants as they grow older. Although it provides information on the development of individuals, the longitudinal design is costly, time consuming, and subject to such problems as cross-generational changes in environments and participant loss (resulting in biased samples). The sequential design, a combination of the cross-sectional and longitudinal approaches, offers the investigator the best features of both strategies.

Cross-cultural studies, in which participants from different cultures and subcultures are compared on one or more aspects of development, are becoming increasingly important. Only by comparing people from many cultures can we identify "universal" patterns of development and, at the same time, demonstrate that other aspects of development are heavily influenced by the social context in which they occur.

 ## References

ARIES, P. (1962). *Centuries of childhood*. New York: Knopf.

BANDURA, A. (1965). Influence of models' reinforcement contingencies on the acquisition of imitative responses. *Journal of Personality and Social Psychology, 1,* 589–595.

BANDURA, A., & WALTERS, R. H. (1963). *Social learning and personality development*. New York: Holt, Rinehart & Winston.

BJORKLUND, D. F., & BJORKLUND, B. R. (1992). *Looking at children*. Pacific Grove, CA: Brooks/Cole.

BORSTELMANN, L. J. (1983). Children before psychology: Ideas about children from antiquity to the late 1800s. In P. H. Mussen (Ed.), *Handbook of child psychology* (Vol. 1). New York: Wiley.

BRONFENBRENNER, U. (1977). Toward an experimental ecology of human development. *American Psychologist, 32,* 513–531.

CHARLESWORTH, R., & HARTUP, W. W. (1967). Positive social reinforcement in the nursery school peer group. *Child Development, 38,* 993–1002.

CHILD, I. L. (1954). Socialization. In G. Lindzey (Ed.), *Handbook of social psychology*. Reading, MA: Addison-Wesley.

DARWIN, C. A. (1877). A biographical sketch of an infant. *Mind, 2,* 285–294.

deMAUSE, L. (1974). The evolution of childhood. In L. deMause (Ed.), *The history of childhood*. New York: Harper & Row.

DESPERT, J. L. (1965). *The emotionally disturbed child: Then and now*. New York: Brunner/Mazel.

ELKIN, F. (1960). *The child and society*. New York: Random House.

ERIKSON, E. H. (1963). *Childhood and society* (2nd ed.). New York: Norton.

ERIKSON, E. H. (1972). Eight ages of man. In C. S. Lavatelli & F. Stendler (Eds.), *Readings in child behavior and child development*. San Diego: Harcourt Brace Jovanovich.

FREUD, A., & DANN, S. (1951). An experiment in group upbringing. In R. Eisler, A. Freud, H. Hartmann, & E. Kris (Eds.), *The psychoanalytic study of the child* (Vol. 6). New York: International Universities Press.

FRIEDRICH, L. K., & STEIN, A. H. (1973). Aggressive and prosocial television programs and the natural behavior of preschool children. *Monographs of the Society for Research in Child Development, 38*(4, Serial No. 51).

GREEN, M. (1987). *Theories of human development: A comparative approach*. Englewood Cliffs, NJ: Prentice-Hall.

HALL, G. S. (1891). The contents of children's minds on entering school. *Pedagogical Seminary, 1,* 139–173.

HALL, G. S. (1904). *Adolescence*. New York: Appleton-Century-Crofts.

HARTMANN, H. (1958). *Ego psychology and the problem of adaptation*. New York: International Universities Press.

HOBBES, T. (1904). *Leviathan*. Cambridge, England: Cambridge University Press. (Original work published 1651.)

HOWES, C. (1990). Can age of entry into child care and the quality of child care predict adjustment in kindergarten? *Developmental Psychology, 26,* 292–303.

JONES, R. A., HENDRICK, C., & EPSTEIN, Y. (1979). *Introduction to social psychology*. Sunderland, MA: Sinauer.

KAGAN, J. (1980). Perspectives on continuity. In O. G. Brim, Jr., & J. Kagan (Eds.), *Constancy and change in human development*. Cambridge, MA: Harvard University Press.

KEAN, A. W. G. (1937). The history of the criminal liability of children. *Law Quarterly Review, 3,* 364–370.

KESSEN, W. (1965). *The child*. New York: Wiley.

KOHLBERG, L. (1966). A cognitive-developmental analysis of children's sex-role concepts and attitudes. In E. E. Maccoby (Ed.), *The development of sex differences*. Stanford, CA: Stanford University Press.

KOHLBERG, L. (1969). Stage and sequence: The cognitive-developmental approach to socialization. In D. A. Goslin (Ed.), *Handbook of socialization theory and research*. Skokie, IL: Rand McNally.

KUCZYNSKI, L. (1983). Reasoning, prohibitions, and motivations for compliance. *Developmental Psychology, 19,* 126–134.

LANGER, J. (1969). *Theories of development*. New York: Holt, Rinehart & Winston.

LERNER, R. M. (1991). Changing organism-context relations as the basic process of development: A developmental contextual perspective. *Developmental Psychology, 27,* 27–32.

LIEBERT, R. M., & BARON, R. A. (1972). Some immediate effects of televised violence on children's behavior. *Developmental Psychology, 6,* 469–475.

LIEBERT, R. M., & SPRAFKIN, J. (1988). *The early window: Effects of television on children and youth* (3rd ed.). New York: Pergamon Press.

LOCKE, J. (1913). *Some thoughts concerning education*. Sections 38 and 40. London: Cambridge University Press. (Original work published 1690.)

McCALL, R. B. (1977). Challenges to a science of developmental psychology. *Child Development, 48,* 333–344.

MEAD, M. (1935). *Sex and temperament in three primitive societies*. New York: William Morrow.

PIAGET, J. (1965). *The moral judgment of the child*. New York: Free Press. (Original work published 1932.)

SCHAIE, K. W. (1965). A general model for the study of developmental problems. *Psychological Bulletin, 64,* 91–107.

SCHAIE, K. W. (1986). Beyond calendar definitions of age, time, and cohort: The general developmental model revisited. *Developmental Review, 6,* 252–277.

SELMAN, R. L. (1980). *The growth of interpersonal understanding*. Orlando, FL: Academic Press.

WATSON, J. B. (1925). *Behaviorism*. New York: Norton.

WHITE, S. H. (1992). G. Stanley Hall: From philosophy to developmental psychology. *Developmental Psychology, 28,* 25–34.

WIGGAM, A. E. (1923). *The new decalogue of science*. Indianapolis: Bobbs-Merrill.

WILLEMS, E. P., & ALEXANDER, J. L. (1982). The naturalistic perspective in research. In B. B. Wolman (Ed.), *Handbook of developmental psychology*. Englewood Cliffs, NJ: Prentice-Hall.

WILLIAMS, J. E., BENNETT, S. M., & BEST, D. L. (1975). Awareness and expression of sex-stereotypes in young children. *Developmental Psychology, 11,* 635–642.

2 | *Psychoanalytic Theory and Modern Biological Perspectives*

Our focus in this chapter is on some of the earliest and some of the newest ideas about human social and personality development. The earlier ideas stem from Sigmund Freud's psychoanalytic theory—an approach that portrays human beings as servants to inborn biological needs that largely determine who we are and what we are likely to become. After reviewing Freud's view of human development and a contemporary psychoanalytic perspective, we will consider what modern biological theorists have to say about innate, or inborn, determinants of personality and social behavior.

The Psychoanalytic Perspective

With the possible exception of Charles Darwin's theory of evolution, no scientific theory has had a greater impact on Western thought than Sigmund Freud's psychoanalytic theory. One of my former professors once claimed that Freud's name was recognized by a larger percentage of the American people than that of any other scientific personality. And he may have been correct. Many laypersons have been exposed to at least some of Freud's ideas, and you shouldn't be surprised if friends and relatives ask your opinion of Freud (and his theory) when they learn that you are taking a psychology course.

Almost no one is neutral about Sigmund Freud. His followers thought him a genius, even though they didn't agree with all of his ideas. Yet many of his contemporaries in the medical profession ridiculed Freud, calling him a quack, a crackpot, and other, less complimentary, names. What was it about this man and his theory that made him so controversial? For one thing, he emphasized the importance of sexual urges as determinants of behavior, for children as well as for adults. In this section of the chapter, we will first consider Freud's interesting perspective on human development and then compare Freud's theory with that of his best-known follower, Erik Erikson.

PHOTO 2-1   The psychoanalytic theory of Sigmund Freud (1856–1939) changed our thinking about developing children.

Freud's Psychoanalytic Theory

Psychoanalytic theory is not a deductive approach that began with well-defined concepts and propositions from which hypotheses were derived and tested. Freud did not conduct laboratory experiments; he did not use objective instruments to collect his data; nor did he ever submit his findings to statistical analysis or describe them with tables and graphs. Freud was a practicing physician (a neurologist) who formulated his psychoanalytic theory from the observations and notes he made about the life histories of his mentally disturbed patients.

Freud observed that people are often reluctant to discuss very personal problems with a stranger, even if the stranger is a therapist. For this reason, he favored nontraditional methods of interviewing patients—methods such as hypnosis, *free association* (in which the patient discusses anything that comes to mind), and *dream analysis*. While reclining on the couch, the patient would relax and talk about anything and everything that popped into his or her head. Dreams were thought to be a particularly rich source of information, for they gave some indication of a patient's **unconscious motivations**. Freud assumed that we all dream about what we really want—for example, sex and power—unhindered by social prohibitions that tend to suppress these desires when we are awake.

During the course of therapy, Freud's patients would typically begin by discussing their current problems and then work backward, describing many of the important events of their lives. Often these retrospective accounts would end with the patient's expressing extreme discomfort over one or more events that had occurred early in childhood. As Freud listened to the associations of his patients, he was struck by the fact that each event in a person's life history seemed to be related in some meaningful way to earlier events. He then realized that these "case histories" were precisely the kind of longitudinal data from which one might formulate a comprehensive theory of personality.

From his analyses of patients' dreams, slips of the tongue, unexpected free associations, and childhood memories, Freud was able to infer that all of us experience intense conflicts that influence our behavior. As biological creatures, we have goals or motives that must be satisfied. Yet society decrees that many of these basic urges are undesirable and must be suppressed or controlled. According to Freud, these conflicts emerge at several points during childhood and play a major role in determining the course and character of one's social and personality development.

INSTINCTS, GOALS, AND MOTIVES

Freud believed that all human behavior is energized by psychodynamic forces. Presumably, each individual has a fixed amount of *psychic* (mental) energy that he or she uses to think, to learn, and to perform other mental functions.

According to Freud, a child needs psychic energy in order to satisfy basic urges. And what kinds of urges are children born with? Bad ones! Freud viewed the newborn as a "seething cauldron"—that is, an inherently negative creature who is relentlessly "driven" by two kinds of biological instincts (inborn motives), which he called **Eros** and **Thanatos**. Eros, or the life instincts, helps the child (and the species) to survive; it directs life-sustaining activities such as respiration, eating, sex, and the fulfillment of all other bodily needs. By contrast, Thanatos—the death instincts—was viewed as a set of destructive forces present in all human beings. Freud believed that Eros is stronger than Thanatos, thus enabling us to survive rather than self-destruct. But he argued that, if the psychic energy of Thanatos reaches a critical point, the death instincts will be expressed in some way. For example, Freud thought that destructive phenomena such as arson, fistfights, murder, war, and even masochism (the desire to be hurt) were expressions of the death instincts.

THREE COMPONENTS OF PERSONALITY: ID, EGO, AND SUPEREGO

According to Freud (1933), the psychic energy that serves the instincts is eventually divided among three components of personality: the id, ego, and superego.

The id: Legislator of the personality. At birth the personality is all **id**. The major function of the id is to serve the instincts by seeking objects that will satisfy them.

Have you ever heard a hungry baby cry until someone comes to feed him? A Freudian would say that the baby's cries and agitated limb movements are energized by the hunger instinct. Presumably, the id directs these actions as a means of attracting the mother or another adult and thereby producing the object (food—or, literally, the mother's breast) that reduces hunger.

According to Freud, the id obeys the **pleasure principle** by seeking immediate gratification for instinctual needs. This impulsive thinking (also called "primary-process thinking") is quite unrealistic, however, for the id will invest psychic energy in any object that seems capable of gratifying the instincts, whether or not the object can actually do so. If we had never progressed beyond this earliest type of thinking, we might gleefully ingest wax fruit to satisfy hunger, reach for an empty pop bottle when thirsty, or direct our sexual energies at racy magazines and inflatable love dolls. Perhaps you can see the problem: we would have a difficult time satisfying our needs by relying on our irrational id. Freud believed that these very difficulties lead to the development of the second major component of personality, the ego.

The ego: Executive of the personality.   According to Freud (1933), the **ego** emerges when psychic energy is diverted from the id to energize important cognitive processes such as perception, learning, and logical reasoning. The goal of the rational ego is to serve the **reality principle** — that is, to find realistic ways of gratifying the instincts. At the same time, the ego must invest some of its available psychic energy to block the id's irrational thinking.

Freud stressed that the ego is both servant and master to the id. The ego's mastery is reflected by its ability to delay gratification until reality is served. But the ego continues to serve the id as an executive serves subordinates, pondering several alternative courses of action and selecting a plan that will best satisfy the id's basic needs.

The superego: Judicial branch of the personality.   The third component of the Freudian personality is the **superego** — the person's internalized moral standards. The superego develops from the ego and strives for *perfection* rather than for pleasure or for reality (Freud, 1933). It gradually takes shape as 3- to 6-year-olds *internalize* (take on as their own) the moral standards and values of their parents. Once the superego emerges, children do not need an adult to tell them they have been good or bad; they are now aware of their own transgressions and will feel guilty or ashamed of their unethical conduct. So the superego is truly an internal censor. It insists that the ego find socially acceptable outlets for the id's undesirable impulses.

Dynamics of the personality.   Obviously, these three components of personality do not see eye to eye, and conflict is inevitable. In the mature, healthy personality a dynamic balance operates: the id communicates basic needs, the ego restrains the impulsive id long enough to find realistic methods of satisfying these needs, and the superego decides whether the ego's problem-solving strategies are morally acceptable. The ego is clearly "in the middle"; it must serve two harsh masters by striking a balance between the opposing demands of the id and the superego, all the while accommodating to the realities of the external world.

According to Freud (1940/1964), psychological problems often arise when the fixed amount of psychic energy a person has is unevenly distributed among the id, ego, and superego. For example, the sociopath who routinely lies and cheats to achieve his aims may have a very strong id, a normal ego, and a very weak superego, having never learned to respect the rights of others. By contrast, a woman who is paralyzed by anxiety at the thought of having sex with her steady may be dominated by an overly strong superego. By using clinical methods to analyze the balances (and imbalances) among the three components of personality, Freud believed that he could explain many individual differences in development as well as the origins of many psychological disorders.

FREUD'S STAGES OF PSYCHOSEXUAL DEVELOPMENT

Freud viewed the sex instinct as the most important of the life instincts because he discovered that the mental disturbances of his patients usually revolved around earlier sexual conflicts that they had **repressed**—that is, forced out of conscious awareness. Sex in childhood! Certainly the notion of childhood sexuality was among the more controversial of Freud's ideas. Yet his use of the term *sex* refers to much more than the need to copulate. Many simple bodily functions that most of us would consider rather asexual were viewed by Freud as "erotic" activities, motivated by this general life force that he called the sex instinct.

Although the sex instinct is presumably inborn, Freud (1940/1964) felt that its character changes over time, as dictated by biological **maturation**. As the sex instinct matures, its energy, or **libido**, gradually shifts from one part of the body to another, and the child enters a new stage of *psychosexual* development. Freud called these stages "psychosexual" to underscore his view that the maturation of the sex instinct leaves distinct imprints on the developing psyche (that is, the mind, or personality).

The oral stage (birth to 1 year). Freud was struck by the fact that infants spend much of the first year spitting, chewing, sucking, and biting on objects, and he concluded that the sex instinct seeks pleasure through the mouth during this **oral stage**. Feeding was thought to be a particularly rich source of oral gratification, and Freud argued that a child's later psychological development can be very much affected by the mother's feeding practices. For example, a baby girl who was weaned too early or fed on a rigid schedule would be deprived of "oral gratification" and might later become a woman who craves close contact and is overdependent on her husband. Note the implication here: Freud is saying that *early experiences can have a long-term effect on personality development*. In Box 2-1 we will see why

Freud believed that early traumas and conflicts are likely to surface in the adult personality.

The anal stage (1–3 years). As the sphincter muscles mature in the second year of life, infants acquire the ability to withhold or expel fecal material at will. Not only does voluntary defecation become the primary method of gratifying the sex instinct during this **anal stage**, but infants must endure the demands of toilet training. For the first time, outside agents are regularly interfering with instinctual impulses by insisting that the child inhibit urges to defecate (or urinate) until he reaches a designated locale. Freud believed that the emotional climate parents create during toilet training could leave lasting imprints on the personality. For example, he claimed that children who are harshly punished for their "accidents" are likely to become anxious, inhibited adults who may be messy or wasteful.

The phallic stage (3–6 years). We now come to the aspect of Freudian theory that many people find so controversial. Freud's view was that 3- to 4-year-old children have matured to the point that their genitals have become an interesting and sensitive area of the body. Libido presumably flows to this area as children derive pleasure from stroking and fondling their genitals. What is so controversial? According to Freud, all children at this age develop a strong incestuous desire for the parent of the other sex. He calls this period the **phallic stage** because he believed that the phallus (penis) assumes a critically important role in the psychosexual development of both boys and girls.

Let's examine this stage for boys. According to Freud, 4-year-old boys develop an intense sexual longing for their mothers. At the same time, they become jealous; if they could have their way, they would destroy their chief rivals for maternal affection, their fathers. Freud called this stage of affairs the **Oedipus complex** after the legendary Oedipus, King of Thebes, who unwittingly killed his father and married his mother.

Now, 3–6-year-old boys are not as powerful as King Oedipus, and they face certain defeat in their quest to win the sexual favors of their mothers. In fact, Freud suggests that a jealous young son will have many conflicts with his paternal rival and will eventually fear that his father might castrate him for his rivaling conduct. When this **castration anxiety** becomes sufficiently intense, the boy (if development is normal) will then resolve his Oedipus complex by repressing his incestuous desire for the mother and identifying with the father. This *identification with the aggressor* lessens the chances of cas-

tration, for the boy is no longer a rival. He will try to emulate the father, incorporating all the father's attitudes, attributes, and behaviors. In so doing, the son is likely to adopt a distinct preference for the masculine sex role and to become a "male" psychologically. Identification with the aggressor should also place the crowning touch on the boy's superego, for he will repress two of the most taboo of motives—incest and murder—and internalize the moral standards of his feared and respected rival. In

---

B O X **2-1** | *Early Experience, Defense Mechanisms, and the Adult Personality*

At each psychosexual stage, the id's impulses and social demands inevitably come into conflict. Even a young infant's seemingly harmless tendency to explore objects with his mouth is likely to put him at odds with his mother, thereby making him anxious, if his exploration frequently centers on objects that Mother considers inappropriate, such as her lipstick, cigarette butts, or insects that he has cornered. How do children cope with the conflicts and anxieties they experience?

Freud (1940/1964) described several mechanisms that children may use to defend themselves (literally, their egos) against the anxieties or uncertainties of growing up. One such defense mechanism—**sublimation**—occurs when the child finds socially acceptable outlets for unacceptable motives. Freud believed that frequent use of sublimation could have long-term effects on the personality. For example, a teenage girl who habitually sublimates her sexual desires by taking cold showers may become a "cleanliness nut" as an adult.

Another important ego-defense mechanism is **fixation**, or arrested development. According to Freud, the child who experiences severe conflicts at any particular stage of development may be reluctant to move or incapable of moving to the next stage, where the uncertainties are even greater. The child may then fixate at the earlier stage, and further development will be arrested or at least impaired. Freud believed that some people

become fixated at the level of primary-process thinking and consequently remain "dreamers" or "unrealistic optimists" throughout their lives. Others fixate on particular behaviors. An example is the chronic thumbsucker whose oral fixation may be expressed later in life in such substitute activities as chain smoking, incessant talking, or oral sex.

A person who experiences too much anxiety or too many conflicts at any stage of development may retreat to an earlier, less traumatic stage. Such developmental reversals are examples of an ego-defense mechanism that Freud called **regression**. For example, a 4-year-old who is made insecure by the arrival of a new baby in the house may revert to infantile acts, such as throwing temper tantrums or requesting juice from a baby bottle, to attract her share of parental attention. Even well-adjusted adults may regress from time to time in order to forget problems or to reduce anxiety. For example, masturbation is one earlier mode of sexual functioning that a person may undertake to reduce sexual conflicts or frustrations. Dreaming is a regressive activity that enables a person to resolve conflicts or obtain pleasure through the magic of wishful thinking.

In sum, Freud insists that the past lives on. He claims that early childhood experiences and conflicts may haunt us in later life and influence our adult interests, behaviors, and personalities.

short, the boy has become a well-behaved youngster—Daddy's "little man."

And what about girls? Freud contends that, before age 4, girls prefer their mothers to their fathers. But once the girl discovers that she lacks a penis, she is thought to blame her closest companion, the mother, for this "castrated" condition. This traumatic discovery results in a transfer of affection from the mother to the father. Freud believed that a girl of this age envies her father for possessing a penis and chooses him as a sex object in the hope of exerting some control over a person who has the valued organ that she lacks. (Freud assumed that the girl's *real* underlying desire was to bear her father's child, an event that would compensate for her lack of a penis, especially if the child was male.)

The female Oedipus complex (known as the **Electra complex**) bears some obvious similarities to that of the male. Children of each sex value the male phallus; girls hope to gain one, and boys hope to keep theirs. Furthermore, both boys and girls perceive the parent of the same sex as their major rival for the affection of the other parent. However, Freud was uncertain just how (or why) girls ever resolved their Electra complex. Boys fear castration, and this intense fear forces them to renounce their Oedipus complex by identifying with their fathers. But what do girls fear? After all, they supposedly believe that they have already been castrated, and they attribute this act of brutality to their mothers. To Freud's way of thinking, they no longer have any reason to fear the mother.

Why, then, does the Electra complex subside? Freud (1924/1961) assumed that it may simply fade away as the girl faces reality and recognizes the impossibility of possessing her father. However, he suggested that girls will develop weaker superegos than boys because their resolution of the Electra complex is not based on a fear of retaliation (castration anxiety) that would force them to internalize the ethical standards of their mothers (or their fathers).

The latency period (6–12 years).   Between ages 6 and 12 the child's sex instincts are relatively quiet. The sexual traumas of the phallic stage are forgot-

ten, and all available libido is channeled into socially acceptable activities (such as schoolwork or vigorous play) that consume most of the child's physical and psychic energy. The **latency period** continues until puberty, when the child suddenly experiences a number of biological changes that mark the beginning of Freud's final psychosexual stage.

The genital stage (age 12 onward).   With the onset of puberty come maturation of the reproductive system, production of sex hormones, and, according to Freud, a reactivation of the genital zone as an area of sensual pleasure. The underlying goal of the sex instinct now becomes biological reproduction through sexual intercourse. However, adolescents face conflicts in learning how to manage these new sexual urges in socially acceptable ways. Throughout adolescence and young adulthood, libido is invested in such activities as forming friendships, preparing for a career, courting, and getting married— activities that prepare the individual to eventually satisfy the mature sex instinct by having children. Here, in the **genital stage**, is where Freud believed that people remain for the rest of their lives.

CONTRIBUTIONS AND CRITICISMS OF FREUD'S THEORY

Few theories have generated as much interest or as much criticism as Freud's psychoanalytic model. Many critics contend that Freud's favorite interview techniques, free association and dream analysis, are unstandardized, hopelessly subjective, and thus poor as sources of scientific information. Let's also recall who Freud's subjects were: a relatively small number of *clinical* patients. Were the reports of these individuals accurate? Do the life histories of neurotic patients really tell us anything about the personality development of normal people? Pollsters cannot make accurate statements about public opinion by sampling a nonrepresentative population such as dock workers or old people. Why, then, should we believe that Freud's theory can be generalized beyond the abnormal population on which it is based? In sum, the theories of Freud and his closest disciples stem from unstandardized, nonobjective assessments of a population that is hardly representative of human beings in general.

Methodological criticisms notwithstanding, how plausible do you think Freud's ideas are? Are we all relentlessly driven by sexual and aggressive instincts? Could we really have experienced Oedipus or Electra complexes and simply repressed these traumatic events? Or did Freud get carried away with sex? Could the sexual conflicts that he thought so important have merely been reflections of the sexually repressive culture in which his patients lived?

Few contemporary psychologists accept all of Freud's theory. For example, there is not much evidence that the oral and anal activities of childhood predict one's later personality. Nor is there reason to believe that all children experience Oedipus or Electra complexes. To experience these conflicts, 3- to 6-year-old children would have to recognize the anatomical differences between the sexes, and there is little evidence that they do. In fact, Alan Katcher (1955) found that the majority of 4- to 5-year-olds are inept at assembling a doll so that its genitals match other parts of its body. Even 6-year-olds often make mistakes such as attaching a lower torso containing a penis to an upper body with breasts. Clearly, these "oedipal-aged" children were confused or ignorant about sex differences in genital anatomy (see also Bem, 1989), and it seems highly unlikely that they could be experiencing any castration anxiety or penis envy.

But we cannot reject all of Freud's ideas simply because some of them may seem a bit outlandish. Indeed, contemporary scholars (see, for example, Emde, 1992) have carefully reexamined Freud's work and concluded that there are several reasons why Sigmund Freud will always remain an important figure in the history of the behavioral sciences. Perhaps Freud's greatest contribution was his concept of unconscious motivation. When psychology came into being, in the middle of the 19th century, investigators were concerned with understanding isolated aspects of *conscious* experience, such as sensory processes and perceptual illusions. It was Freud who first noted that these scientists were

studying the tip of the iceberg when he proclaimed that the vast majority of psychic experience lay below the level of conscious awareness. Freud also deserves considerable credit for focusing attention on the implications of early experience for later development. Debates continue about exactly how critical early experiences are, but few developmentalists today doubt that some early experiences *can* have lasting effects. Finally, we might thank Freud for studying the *emotional* side of human development—the loves, fears, anxieties, and other powerful feelings that play important roles in our lives, as well as the defense mechanisms that we use to cope with emotional conflicts. Unfortunately, these aspects of life have often been overlooked by developmentalists who concentrate on observable behaviors or on rational thought processes.

In sum, Freud was truly a great pioneer who dared to navigate murky, uncharted waters that his predecessors had not even thought to explore. In the process, he changed our views of humankind.

Erikson's Theory of Psychosocial Development

As Freud became widely read, he attracted many followers. However, Freud's pupils did not always agree with the master, and eventually they began to modify some of his ideas and become important theorists in their own right. Among the best known of these *neo-Freudian* scholars is Erik Erikson.

COMPARING ERIKSON WITH FREUD

Erikson accepts many of Freud's ideas. He agrees that people are born with a number of basic instincts and that the personality consists of an id, ego, and superego. Erikson also assumes that development occurs in stages and that the child must successfully resolve some crisis or conflict at each stage in order to be prepared for the crises that will emerge later in life.

However, Erikson is truly a revisionist, for his theory differs from Freud's in several important respects. First, Erikson (1963, 1982) stresses that children are *active, adaptive* explorers who seek to control their environment rather than passive creatures

PHOTO 2-2 Erik Erikson (1902–) has emphasized the sociocultural determinants of personality in his theory of psychosocial development.

studied college students, combat soldiers, civil rights workers in the South, and Native American cultures. With this kind of cross-cultural background, it is hardly surprising that Erikson would emphasize social and cultural aspects of development in his own theory. In sum, Erikson's approach is truly a new theory of *psychosocial* development, rather than a restatement of Freud's psychosexual viewpoint.

EIGHT LIFE CRISES

Erikson believes that human beings face eight major crises, or conflicts, during the course of their lives. Each conflict has its own time for emerging, as dictated by both biological maturation and the social demands that we experience at particular points in life. Table 2-1 briefly describes each of Erikson's eight crises (or psychosocial stages) and lists the Freudian psychosexual stage to which it corresponds. Note that Erikson's developmental stages do not end at adolescence or young adulthood as Freud's do. Erikson sees the problems of adolescents and young adults as very different from those of middle-aged or elderly people. Most contemporary developmentalists would definitely agree.

An analysis of the first psychosocial stage—**basic trust versus mistrust**—should help to illustrate Erikson's thinking. Recall that Freud emphasized the infant's oral activities during the first year of life, and he believed that a mother's feeding practices could have a lasting impact on her child's personality. Erikson agrees. However, he goes on to argue that what is most important to an infant's later development is not merely the caregiver's feeding practices but, rather, her *overall responsiveness* to the infant and his needs. To develop a basic sense of *trust*, infants must be able to count on their primary caregivers to provide food, to relieve discomfort, to come when beckoned, to smile when smiled upon, and to display warmth and affection. Should close companions often neglect, reject, or respond inconsistently to an infant, that child will learn a very simple lesson: other people are not to be trusted.

The development of trust provides the basis for healthy coping with the second major life crisis, the

who are molded by their parents. He has also been labeled an *ego* psychologist because he believes that an individual must first understand the *realities* of the social world (an ego function) in order to adapt successfully and show a normal pattern of personal growth. So, unlike Freud, who felt that the most interesting aspects of behavior stemmed from conflicts between the id and the superego, Erikson assumes that human beings are basically rational creatures whose thoughts, feelings, and actions are largely controlled by the ego.

Yet another crucial difference between Erikson and Freud is that Erikson places much less emphasis on sexual urges and much more emphasis on social influences than Freud did. Clearly, Erikson's thinking was shaped by his own varied experiences. He was born in Denmark, was raised in Germany, and spent much of his adolescence wandering throughout Europe. After receiving his professional training, Erikson came to the United States, where he

TABLE 2-1   *Erikson's and Freud's stages of development*

Approximate Age	Erikson's Stage or "Psychosocial Crisis"	Erikson's Viewpoint: Significant Events and Social Influences	Corresponding Freudian Stage
Birth to 1 year	Basic trust versus mistrust	Infants must learn to trust others to care for their basic needs. If caregivers are rejecting or inconsistent in their care, the infant may view the world as a dangerous place filled with untrustworthy or unreliable people. The mother or primary caregiver is the key social agent.	Oral
1 to 3 years	Autonomy versus shame and doubt	Children must learn to be autonomous—to feed and dress themselves, to look after their own hygiene, and so on. Failure to achieve this independence may force the child to doubt his or her own abilities and feel shameful. Parents are the key social agents.	Anal
3 to 6 years	Initiative versus guilt	Children attempt to act grown up and will try to accept responsibilities that are beyond their capacity to handle. They sometimes undertake goals or activities that conflict with those of parents and other family members, and these conflicts may make them feel guilty. Successful resolution of this crisis requires a balance: the child must retain a sense of initiative and yet learn not to impinge on the rights, privileges, or goals of others. The family is the key social agent.	Phallic
6 to 12 years	Industry versus inferiority	Children must master important social and academic skills. This is a period when the child compares the self with peers. If sufficiently industrious, children will acquire the social and academic skills to feel self-assured. Failure to acquire these important attributes leads to feelings of inferiority. Significant social agents are teachers and peers.	Latency

SOURCE: Adapted from D. R. Shaffer, "Social Psychology from a Social-Developmental Perspective." In C. Hendrick (Ed.), *Perspectives on Social Psychology*, p. 160. Copyright © 1977 by Lawrence Erlbaum Associates. Used by permission.

conflict of **autonomy versus shame and doubt**. Infants who have learned to trust other people are likely to feel sufficiently confident to communicate their wishes and assert their wills. During the "terrible twos" phase, for example, toddlers may loudly proclaim their desire for autonomy by resisting toilet training and by favoring three words over all others: "no," "me," and "mine." However, a toddler who *mistrusts* others may lack the self-confidence to be assertive as a 2-year-old. As a result, she may fail to become autonomous and could experience shame and doubt. A year or two later this shameful, self-doubting youngster may have difficulty concocting and pursuing "bold plans" during the preschool crisis of **initiative versus guilt** and may instead be

too inhibited to want to care for a pet or to give roller skating a try. So Erikson proposes that a successful resolution of each life crisis prepares the individual for the next psychosocial conflict. By contrast, the person who fails to resolve one or more of life's social conflicts is almost certain to encounter problems in the future.

Although Erikson believes that the crises of childhood and adolescence set the stage for our adult lives, he views human beings as rational, adaptive creatures who will struggle to the very end in their attempts to cope successfully with their social environment. Charles Dickens's Scrooge, a fictional character from *A Christmas Carol*, aptly illustrates the self-centered, "stagnated" adult—one who is

TABLE 2-1   *continued*

Approximate Age	Erikson's Stage or "Psychosocial Crisis"	Erikson's Viewpoint: Significant Events and Social Influences	Corresponding Freudian Stage
12 to 20 years	Identity versus role confusion	This is the crossroad between childhood and maturity. The adolescent grapples with the question "Who am I?" Adolescents must establish basic social and occupational identities, or they will remain confused about the roles they should play as adults. The key social agent is the society of peers.	Early genital (adolescence)
20 to 40 years (young adulthood)	Intimacy versus isolation	The primary task at this stage is to form strong friendships and to achieve a sense of love and companionship (or a shared identity) with another person. Feelings of loneliness or isolation are likely to result from an inability to form friendships or an intimate relationship. Key social agents are lovers, spouses, and close friends (of both sexes).	Genital
40 to 65 years (middle adulthood)	Generativity versus stagnation	At this stage, adults face the tasks of becoming productive in their work and raising their families or otherwise looking after the needs of young people. These standards of "generativity" are defined by one's culture. Those who are unable or unwilling to assume these responsibilities will become stagnant and/or self-centered. Significant social agents are the spouse, children, and cultural norms.	Genital
Old age	Ego integrity versus despair	The older adult will look back at life, viewing it as either a meaningful, productive, and happy experience or as a major disappointment full of unfulfilled promises and unrealized goals. One's life experiences, particularly social experiences, will determine the outcome of this final life crisis.	Genital

failing at Erikson's seventh life crisis (and who has been unsuccessful at establishing a sense of intimacy as well). You may remember that old Scrooge was so absorbed in his own interests (making money) that he completely ignored the needs and wishes of his young clerk, Bob Cratchit. Scrooge's tale had a happy ending, however. By the end of the story, he had acquired a sense of intimacy and generativity that had eluded him earlier, and he was now ready to face life's final crisis in a positive frame of mind. An unlikely reversal? Not necessarily! Erikson is quite the optimist; he maintains that "there is little that cannot be remedied later, there is much [in the way of harm] that can be prevented from happening at all" (1950, p. 104).

CONTRIBUTIONS AND CRITICISMS OF ERIKSON'S THEORY

Many people prefer Erikson's theory to Freud's because they simply refuse to believe that human beings are dominated by sexual instincts. An analyst like Erikson, who stresses our rational, adaptive nature, is so much easier to accept. In addition, Erikson emphasizes many of the social conflicts and personal dilemmas that people may remember, are currently experiencing, can easily anticipate, or can see affecting people they know.

Erikson does seem to have described many of the central issues in life in his eight psychosocial stages. Indeed, we will see just how stimulating his ideas have been as we discuss such topics as the emotional development of infants (Chapter 5), the growth of self-concept in childhood and the identity crisis facing adolescents (Chapter 7), and the influence of friends and playmates on social and personality development (Chapter 15) (see also Sigelman & Shaffer, 1991, for a discussion of Erikson's contributions to the field of adult development).

On the other hand, Erikson's theory can be criticized for being vague about the *causes* of psychosocial development. What kinds of experiences must someone have to develop autonomy as a toddler, initiative as a preschooler, or a stable identity as an adolescent? Why, exactly, is a sense of trust so important for the development of autonomy, initiative, or industry? Unfortunately, Erikson is not very explicit about these important issues, owing perhaps to the *unstandardized* interviews and observations he made, which aptly illustrate psychosocial conflicts but are ill suited for revealing their underlying causes. In sum, Erikson's theory is really a *descriptive* overview of human social and emotional development that does not adequately *explain* how or why this development takes place.

Psychoanalytic Theory Today

Freud and Erikson are only two of many psychoanalysts who have had (or are having) a strong influence on the field of social and personality development. For example, psychoanalyst Karen Horney (1967) has challenged Freud's ideas about sex differences in development and is now widely credited as a founder of the discipline we know today as the Psychology of Women. Alfred Adler (1929/1964), a contemporary of Freud's, was among the first to suggest that *siblings* (and sibling rivalries) are critically important determinants of social and personality development—a proposition that we will explore in detail in Chapter 13. And American psychoanalyst Harry Stack Sullivan (1953) wrote extensively about how *chumships* (close friendships) during preadolescence set the stage for the development of intimate love relationships later in life (see Chapter 15 for a more complete discussion of this and other contributions that friends may have on social and personality development). Although

their theories clearly differ in focus, all these neo-Freudians were more inclined than was Freud to emphasize *social* contributions to personality development and to deemphasize the role of the sex instincts.

Despite the many important contributions that psychoanalytic theorists have made, only a small minority of contemporary developmentalists adhere strongly to this perspective. One reason why many researchers have abandoned the psychoanalytic approach (particularly Freud's theory) is that its propositions are difficult to verify or disconfirm. Suppose, for example, that we wanted to test the basic Freudian proposition that the healthy personality is one in which psychic energy is evenly distributed among the id, ego, and superego. How could we do it? There are objective tests that we could use to select "mentally healthy" subjects, but we have no instrument that measures psychic energy or the relative strengths of the id, ego, and superego. The point is that many psychoanalytic assertions are untestable by any method other than the interview or a clinical approach, and, unfortunately, these techniques are time consuming, expensive, and among the least objective of all methods used to study developing children.

Of course, the main reason why so many developmentalists have abandoned the psychoanalytic perspective is that other theories seem more compelling to them. One collection of theories that is currently attracting a good deal of attention is the modern biological viewpoint, to which we will now turn.

Modern Biological Perspectives

Freud's psychoanalytic theory obviously has strong biological overtones. Not only are inborn instincts the motivational components of his theory, but the maturation of the sex instinct was said to determine the course (or at least the stages) of social and personality development.

In this section we will become acquainted with two additional perspectives that emphasize biological contributions to human social and personality development. One of these streams of thought is illustrated by two modern theories—*ethology* and *sociobiology*—that have strong evolutionary overtones. These "evolutionary" approaches focus heavily on inherited attributes that characterize all members of a species and conspire to make us *alike* (that is, contribute to common developmental outcomes). By contrast, the second approach, *behavior genetics*, is concerned mainly with determining how the unique combination of genes that each of us inherits might be implicated in making individuals *different* from one another.

Evolutionary Viewpoints

The notion that biological influences play a significant role in shaping human development is alive and well in **ethology**—the scientific study of the evolutionary bases of behavior and development (Cairns, 1979). Although the origins of this theory can be traced to Charles Darwin, ethology arose from the work of Konrad Lorenz and Niko Tinbergen, two European zoologists whose animal research pointed to some important links between evolutionary processes and adaptive behaviors.[1] Other biologists (for example, E. O. Wilson, 1975) have proposed a related model, called **sociobiology**, that seeks to determine the evolutionary bases for human *social* behaviors. In the pages that follow, we will briefly examine each of these perspectives and focus on their implications for social and personality development.

ASSUMPTIONS AND
MECHANISMS OF CLASSICAL ETHOLOGY

According to Lorenz (1937, 1981) and Tinbergen (1973), members of all animal species are born with a number of "biologically programmed" attributes and behaviors that (1) are products of evolution and (2) are adaptive in that they contribute to survival.

Many species of birds, for example, seem to come biologically prepared to engage in such instinctual behaviors as following their mothers (a response called **imprinting**, which helps to protect the young from predators and to ensure that they find food), building nests, and singing songs. These biologically programmed characteristics are thought to have evolved as a result of the Darwinian process of **natural selection**; that is, over the course of evolution, birds with genes responsible for these "adaptive" behaviors were more likely to survive and to pass on their genes to future generations than were birds lacking these adaptive characteristics. Thus, over many, many generations, the genes underlying the most adaptive behaviors would become more widespread in the species, characterizing nearly all individuals.

So ethologists focus on inborn or instinctual responses (1) that members of a species share and (2) that seem to steer individuals along similar developmental paths. Where might one search for these adaptive behaviors to investigate their developmental implications? Ethologists have always preferred to study their subjects in the natural environment. Why? Simply because they believe that the inborn attributes that shape human (or animal) development are most easily identified and understood if observed in the natural settings where they evolved and have proven to be adaptive (Hinde, 1989). Ethologists do conduct laboratory studies, however, to confirm or clarify observations made in the natural environment. Indeed, we will review many such studies in Chapters 5 and 6, where we will take an in-depth look at the ethological perspective on early emotional growth and its implications for the developing personality.

ETHOLOGY AND HUMAN DEVELOPMENT

Instinctual responses that seem to promote survival are relatively easy to spot in animals. But do humans really display such behaviors? And, if they do, how might these preprogrammed responses influence their development?

Human ethologists such as John Bowlby (1969, 1973) believe that children display a wide variety of preprogrammed behaviors, each of which promotes

---

[1]Indeed, Lorenz and Tinbergen were jointly awarded a Nobel Prize in 1973 for their pioneering research in ethology.

PHOTO 2-3   The cry is a distress signal that attracts the attention of caregivers.

a particular kind of experience that will help the individual to survive and develop normally. For example, not only are infants said to be biologically programmed to convey their distress with loud, lusty cries, but ethologists also believe that caregivers are biologically predisposed to respond to such signals. So the adaptive significance of an infant's crying is to ensure that (1) the child's basic needs (for example, hunger, thirst, safety) will be met and (2) the infant will have sufficient contact with other human beings to form primary social and emotional attachments (Bowlby, 1973).

Although ethologists are especially critical of learning theorists for largely ignoring the biological bases of human development, they are well aware that development could not progress very far without learning. For example, the cry of an infant may be an innate signal that promotes the human contact from which emotional attachments emerge; however, these emotional attachments do not simply "happen" automatically. The infant must first *learn*

to discriminate familiar faces from those of strangers before he will show any evidence of emotional attachment to a regular companion. Presumably, the adaptive significance of this discriminatory learning goes back to that period in evolutionary history when humans traveled in nomadic tribes and lived outdoors. In those days it was crucial that an infant become attached to familiar companions and fearful of strangers, for failure to cry in response to a strange face might make the infant "easy pickings" for a predatory animal.

Now consider the opposite side of the coin. Some caregivers who suffer from various life stresses of their own (for example, prolonged illnesses, depression, an unhappy marriage, or even a habitually cranky baby) may be routinely inattentive or neglectful, so that the infant's cries rarely promote any contact with them. Such an infant is not likely to form strong emotional attachments to her caregivers and could remain rather shy and emotionally unresponsive to other people for years to come (Ainsworth, 1979, 1989). What this infant has *learned* from her early experiences is that her closest companions are unreliable and not to be trusted. Consequently she is likely to be ambivalent or wary around her caregivers and may later assume that other regular associates, such as teachers and peers, are equally untrustworthy individuals who should be avoided whenever possible.

How important are an individual's early learning experiences? Like Freud, the ethologists believe that they are *very* important. In fact, they have argued that there may be "critical periods" for the development of many attributes and behaviors. A **critical period** is a part of the life cycle during which the developing organism is particularly sensitive or responsive to specific environmental influences; outside this period, the same events or influences are thought to have little if any lasting effects. To illustrate: Some ethologists believe that the first three years of life is a critical period for the development of social and emotional responsiveness in human beings. Presumably, we are most uniquely susceptible to forming close emotional ties during the first three years, and, should we have little or no opportunity to do so during this period, we would find it difficult to make close friends or to enter into intimate emotional relationships with other people later in life. Clearly, this is a most interesting and provocative claim about the emotional lives of human beings—one that we will examine carefully when we consider the long-term effects of early social and emotional development in Chapter 6.

In sum, ethologists clearly acknowledge that we are largely a product of our experiences. Yet they are quick to remind us that we are inherently biological creatures whose inborn characteristics affect the kinds of learning experiences we are likely to have.

THE SOCIOBIOLOGICAL PERSPECTIVE

Ethologists are not the only ones who have concerned themselves with the evolutionary bases of behavior. Sociobiologist E. O. Wilson (1975) and his followers have attempted to explain how evolutionary processes might contribute to the development of *social* motives and behaviors. Although sociobiology is a rather provocative new field with a meager empirical base, it is worth considering briefly here because it illustrates just how interested scientists have become in the evolutionary bases of behavior and development.

Sociobiologists make different assumptions about the workings of evolution than ethologists do. Recall the ethological notion that adaptive behaviors are those that ensure survival of the *individual*. Wilson and the sociobiologists disagree with this premise, arguing instead that adaptive behaviors are those that ensure the survival of the individual's *genes*. This may seem like a subtle distinction, but it has a very important implication: according to sociobiologists, a behavior can be adaptive (and, hence, become more common over generations through natural selection) if it ensures that our genes survive. It is not necessary that the behavior ensure that *we* (as individuals) survive.

Sociobiologists cite **altruism**—a genuine concern for the welfare of others and a willingness to act on that concern—as a prime example of a social motive (or behavioral predisposition) that illustrates their viewpoint. Consider a father who risks his life reentering his burning house in an attempt to save his

twins trapped in an upstairs bedroom. This selfless behavior on the father's part is hard for an ethologist to explain—taking such a risk does not promote the *father's* survival. Sociobiologists, however, would explain the father's behavior by noting that the twins he saves (1) *carry his genes* and (2) have many more reproductive years ahead of them than he does. Thus the father's altruism is *adaptive* from a sociobiological point of view. By rescuing his children, the father has ensured the survival of *his genes* (or, more literally, those who carry his genes), even if he should perish in the process.

Although sociobiologists view genes as self-serving entities that seek to ensure their own survival, Wilson notes that human beings share many genes with one another; thus the gene-preservation process often occurs at the cultural or societal level. For example, cultural prescriptions against incest, robbery, and murder may be products of an evolutionary process that favored individuals whose social behaviors were advantageous to all members of the group, thus promoting the survival of everyone's genes. Indeed, Box 2-2 illustrates how altruism may have evolved at the group, or societal, level and cites empirical data suggesting that there may be a biological basis for certain aspects of altruism.

Contributions and Criticisms of Evolutionary Theories

If this chapter had been written in 1974, it would not have included a section on evolutionary theories. Although ethology came into being more than 30 years ago, the early ethologists studied animal behavior; only within the past 15 to 20 years have proponents of ethology made a serious attempt to specify the biological bases of human development. Moreover, sociobiology was not even recognized as a scientific discipline until 1975, the year that Wilson published his now-classic volume *Sociobiology: The New Synthesis*. So evolutionary theories of human development are themselves recent developments, and they have not yet succeeded in providing us with detailed explanations (or even with satisfactory overviews) of *all* aspects of social and personality development. Nevertheless, they have already contributed in an important way to the discipline by reminding us that every child is a biological creature who comes equipped with a number of adaptive, genetically programmed characteristics—attributes that will influence other people's reactions to the child and, thus, the course that development is likely to take. In addition, the ethologists have made a major methodological contribution by showing us the value of (1) studying human development in normal, everyday settings and (2) comparing human development to that of other species.

By way of criticism, evolutionary approaches are like psychoanalytic theory in being very hard to test. How does one demonstrate that various motives, mannerisms, and behaviors are inborn, are adap-

---

B O X   **2-2** | *Is Altruism a Part of Human Nature?*

Darwin's notion of "survival of the fittest" seems to argue against altruism as an inborn motive. Many have interpreted Darwin's idea to mean that powerful, self-serving individuals who place their own needs ahead of others' are the ones who are most likely to survive. If this were so, evolution would favor the development of selfish, egoistic motives—not altruism—as basic components of human nature.

Martin Hoffman (1981) has recently challenged this point of view, listing several reasons why the concept of "survival of the fittest" actually implies altruism. His arguments hinge on the assumption that human beings are more likely to receive protection from natural enemies and to satisfy all their basic needs if they have genes that predispose them to be socially outgoing and to live together in cooperative social groups. If this assumption is correct, then cooperative, altruistic individuals would be the ones who are most likely to survive long enough to pass on their "altruistic genes" to their offspring; individualists who "go it alone" would probably succumb to famine, predators, or some other natural disaster that they could not cope with by themselves. So, over thousands of generations, natural selection would favor the development of innate social motives such as altruism. Presumably, the tremendous survival value of being "social" makes altruism, cooperation, and other social motives much more plausible as components of human nature than competition, selfishness, and the like.

It is obviously absurd to argue that infants routinely help other people. However, Hoffman believes that even newborn babies are capable of recognizing and experiencing the emotions of others. This ability, known as **empathy**, is thought to be an important contributor to altruism, for a person must recognize that others are distressed in some way before he or she is likely to help. So Hoffman is suggesting that at least one aspect of altruism—empathy—is present at birth.

Hoffman's claim is based on an experiment (Sagi & Hoffman, 1976) in which infants less than 36 hours old listened to (1) another infant's cries; (2) an equally loud computer simulation of a crying infant, or (3) no sounds at all (silence). The infants who heard a real infant crying soon began to cry themselves, to display physical signs of agitation (such as kicking), and to grimace. Infants exposed to the simulated cry or to silence cried much less and seemed not to be very discomforted. (A more recent study by Martin & Clark, 1982, has confirmed these observations.)

Hoffman argues that there is something quite distinctive about the human cry. His contention is that infants listen to and experience the distress of (that is, empathize with) another crying infant and become distressed themselves. Of course, this finding does not conclusively demonstrate that humans are altruistic by nature. But it does imply that the capacity for empathy may be present at birth and thus may serve as a biological basis for the eventual development of altruistic behavior.

tive, or are products of evolutionary history? Harvard paleontologist Steven Jay Gould (1978) has criticized the sociobiologists in particular for constructing "just-so stories" to illustrate how various forms of social behavior have been naturally selected because of their adaptive value. A just-so story is an explanation that sounds plausible and, in fact, may be true but is not supported by any conclusive evidence. (Indeed, the explanation given in Box 2-2 for the evolution of altruism in group contexts could be considered a just-so story.) This is a strong critique, for theories that easily lend themselves to just-so stories lack one important characteristic of a *useful* scientific model: they are nearly impossible to falsify. In addition, evolutionary theories have also been criticized as being *retrospective* or "post hoc" explanations of development. One can easily apply evolutionary concepts to explain what has already happened, but can the theories *predict* what is likely to happen in the future? Many developmentalists believe that they cannot.

Finally, proponents of other viewpoints (most notably, social-learning theory) have argued that, even if the bases for certain motives or behaviors are biologically programmed, these innate responses will soon become so modified by learning that it may not be helpful to spend much time wondering about their prior evolutionary significance. Even strong, genetically influenced attributes can easily be modified by experience. Consider, for example, that young mallard ducklings clearly prefer their mothers' vocal calls to those of other birds (for example, chickens)—a behavior that ethologists say is innate and adaptive as a product of mallard evolution. Yet Gilbert Gottlieb (1991) has shown that duckling embryos that were prevented from vocalizing and exposed to chicken calls before hatching come to prefer the call of a chicken to that of a mallard mother! In this case, the ducklings' *prenatal* experiences overrode a genetic predisposition. Of course, human beings have a much greater capacity for learning than ducklings do, thus leading many critics to argue that cultural learning experiences quickly overshadow innate evolutionary mechanisms in shaping human conduct and character. Albert Bandura (1973), for example, makes the following observation when comparing aggressive behavior in humans and animals:

> [Unlike animals], man does not rely heavily on auditory, postural, or olfactory signals for conveying aggressive intent or appeasement. He has [developed] a much more intricate system of communication—namely language—for controlling aggression. National leaders can . . . better safeguard against catastrophic violence by verbal communiques than by snapping their teeth or erecting their hair, especially in view of the prevalence of baldness among the higher echelons [p. 16].

Despite these criticisms, evolutionary theories remain a valuable addition to the field of social and personality development. They have provided a healthy balance to the heavy environmental emphasis apparent in learning theories, have convinced more and more researchers to study development in the natural settings where it actually occurs, and have led to several important discoveries that were neither anticipated nor easily explained by other theoretical approaches.

Now let's turn to a second modern biological perspective that is becoming increasingly influential—the *behavior genetics* approach.

The Behavior Genetics Approach

In recent years, investigators from the fields of genetics, embryology, population biology, and psychology have asked the question "Are there specific abilities, traits, and patterns of behavior that depend very heavily on the particular combination of genes that an individual inherits, and, if so, are these attributes likely to be modified by one's experiences?" Those who focus on these issues in their research are known as *behavior geneticists*.

Before we take a closer look at the field of **behavior genetics**, it is necessary to dispel a common myth. Although behavior geneticists view development as the process through which one's **genotype** (the set of genes one inherits) comes to be expressed as a **phenotype** (one's observable characteristics and behaviors), they are *not* strict hereditarians. Instead, they believe that most behavioral attributes are end products of a long and involved interplay between hereditary predispositions and environmental influences. Consider the following example: A child who inherits genes for tall stature will almost certainly grow taller than one who inherits genes for short stature if these children are raised in the same environment. But, if the first child receives poor nutrition early in life and the second is well nourished, they may well be about the same height as adults. Thus the behavior geneticist is well aware that even attributes (such as physical stature) that seem to have a very strong hereditary component are often modified in important ways by environmental influences. This is a point to keep in mind as we discuss the implications of behavior genetics research.

How, then, do behavior geneticists differ from evolutionary theorists, who are also interested in the biological bases of development? The answer is relatively simple. As we noted earlier, evolutionary theorists study inherited attributes that characterize *all* members of a species and thus conspire to make them *alike* (that is, attributes that contribute to *common* developmental outcomes). By contrast, behavior geneticists focus on the biological bases for *variation* among members of a species. They are concerned with determining how the unique combination of genes that each of us inherits might be implicated in making us *different* from one another. Let's now consider the methods they use to approach this task.

METHODS OF ESTIMATING HEREDITARY INFLUENCES

There are two major strategies that behavior geneticists use to assess hereditary contributions to behavior: *selective breeding* and *family studies*. Each of these approaches attempts to specify the **heritability** of various attributes — that is, the amount of variation in a trait or a class of behavior that is attributable to hereditary factors.

Selective breeding. Members of any species, particularly human beings, differ considerably in their basic abilities, peculiarities, and patterns of behavior. Could these individual differences be hereditary? Do they simply reflect the fact that no two individuals (except identical twins) inherit the same pattern of genes?

Many investigators have tried to answer this question by attempting to selectively breed particular attributes in animals. A famous example of a selective-breeding experiment is R. C. Tryon's (1940) attempt to show that maze-learning ability is a heritable attribute in rats. Tryon started by testing a large number of rats for ability to run a complex maze. Rats that made few errors were labeled "maze-bright"; those that made many errors were termed "maze-dull." Then, across several successive generations, Tryon mated the brightest of the maze-bright rats while also inbreeding the dullest of the maze-dull group. This was a well-controlled experiment in that Tryon occasionally took offspring from each group and had them raised by mothers from the other group. This *cross-fostering* procedure helps to ensure that any difference in maze-learning ability between the offspring of the two strains is due to selective breeding (heredity), rather than to the type of early stimulation that the young animals received from their mother figure (environment).

Figure 2-1 shows the results of Tryon's selective-breeding experiment. Note that across generations the differences in maze-running performance between the maze-bright and the maze-dull groups became increasingly apparent. By the 18th generation, the worst performer among the maze-bright group was better at running mazes than the best performer from the maze-dull group. Clearly, Tryon had shown that maze-learning ability in rats is influenced by hereditary factors. Other investigators have used the selective-breeding technique to demonstrate clear genetic contributions to such attributes as activity level, emotionality, aggressiveness, and sex drive in rats, mice, and chickens (Plomin, DeFries, & McClearn, 1989).

Family studies. Since it is obviously unethical to conduct selective-breeding studies with humans, the field of human behavior genetics relies on an alternative methodology known as the family study. In a typical family study, persons who live in the same household are compared to see how similar they are on one or more attributes. If the attribute in

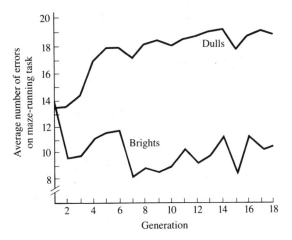

FIGURE 2-1 Maze-running performance by inbred maze-bright and maze-dull rats over 18 generations. (From *Introduction to Behavioral Genetics*, by G. E. McClearn & J. G. De-Fries, p. 214. Copyright © 1973 by W. H. Freeman. Reprinted by permission.)

question is heritable, then the similarity between any two pairs of individuals who live in the same environment should increase as a function of their **kinship** — that is, the extent to which they have the same genes.

Two kinds of family (or kinship) studies are common today. The first is the **twin design**, or **twin study**, which asks the question "Are pairs of identical twins reared together more similar to each other on various attributes than pairs of fraternal twins reared together?" If genes affect the attribute(s) in question, then identical twins should be more similar, for they have 100% of their genes in common (kinship = 1.00), whereas fraternal twins share only 50% (kinship = .50). Extending this logic, we could also predict that fraternal twins should be more similar on a heritable attribute than either half-siblings (kinship = .25) or pairs of genetically unrelated children who live in the same household (kinship = .00).

The second common family study, the **adoption design**, focuses on adoptees who are genetically unrelated to other members of their adoptive families. A researcher looking for hereditary influences would ask "Are adopted children more similar to their biological parents, whose *genes* they share

(kinship = .50), or to their adoptive parents, whose *environment* they share?" If adoptees resemble their biological parents in temperament or personality, even though these parents did not raise them, then genes must be influential in determining such attributes.

Family studies can also help us to estimate the extent to which various abilities and behaviors are influenced by the environment. To illustrate, consider a case in which two genetically unrelated adopted children are raised in the same home. Their degree of kinship with each other and with their adoptive parents is .00. Consequently, there is no reason to suspect that these children will resemble each other or their adoptive parents unless their common environment plays some part in determining their standing on the attribute in question. Another way the effects of environment can be inferred is to compare identical twins raised in the same environment with identical twins raised in different environments. The kinship of all pairs of identical twins, reared together or apart, is 1.00. So, if identical twins reared together are more alike on an attribute than identical twins reared apart, we can infer that the environment plays a role in determining that attribute.

We are now almost ready to examine the results of several family studies in order to gauge the impact of heredity and environment on complex attributes such as temperament, personality, and mental illness. To evaluate this research, however, we need to recall what a correlation is and to learn how correlation coefficients can help us to determine whether an attribute is influenced by hereditary factors.

Calculating heritabilities. In Chapter 1 we learned that correlated variables are systematically related — that is, they "go together," or covary, in some meaningful way. We also noted that *correlation coefficients* are statistics (ranging from −1.00 to +1.00) that allow us to estimate the strength and direction of the relationship (correlation) between two variables. Behavior geneticists rely on correlational techniques in their research. In a family study, they are seeking to answer the following questions: (1) Are people alike

PHOTO 2-4   Because identical twins have identical genotypes, they are a rich source of information about possible hereditary contributions to personality and social behavior.

in various attributes—are their scores correlated? (2) If so, does this resemblance increase as their genetic similarity (kinship) increases?

Let's consider a hypothetical example. Suppose we had conducted a study of 50 families, 25 that have a pair of identical twins and 25 that have a pair of fraternal twins. While conducting the study, we measured some aspect of personality in each twin and found that the correlation between identical twins on this trait was +.50 while the correlation between fraternal twins was +.30. Since members of each twin pair live in the same household, we might assume that they have had highly similar environments. Thus the fact that identical twins are more alike on this personality dimension than fraternal twins suggests that the trait in question is affected by heredity. But just how strong is the hereditary contribution?

In recent years, behavior geneticists have proposed a statistical technique to estimate the amount of variation in a characteristic that is attributable to hereditary factors. This index, called a **heritability coefficient**, is calculated as follows:

$$H = (r \text{ identical twins} - r \text{ fraternal twins}) \times 2$$

In words, the equation reads: heritability of an attribute equals the correlation between identical twins minus the correlation between fraternal twins, all multiplied by a factor of 2 (Plomin, 1990).

Now we can estimate the contribution that heredity makes to variations in the aspect of personality that we measured in our hypothetical study. Recall that the correlation between identical twins on the attribute was +.50 and the correlation between fraternal twins was +.30. Plugging these values into the formula yields the following heritability coefficient (H):

$$H = (.50 - .30) \times 2 = .20 \times 2 = .40$$

The heritability coefficient is .40, which, on a scale ranging from 0 (not at all heritable) to 1.00 (totally heritable), is moderate at best. We might conclude that, within the population from which our subjects were selected, this aspect of personality is influenced to some extent by hereditary factors. However, it appears that much of the variability among people on this trait is attributable to nonhereditary factors—that is, to environmental influences and to errors we may have made in measuring the trait (no measure is perfect).

What do heritability estimates tell us?   People have often assumed that heritability coefficients tell us whether we might have inherited various traits or characteristics. *This idea is simply incorrect.* When we talk about the heritability of an attribute, we are referring to the extent to which *differences* among individuals on that attribute are related to differences in the genes they have inherited (Erdle, 1990; Plomin, 1990). To illustrate that *heritable* means something other than "inherited," consider that everyone inherits two eyes. Agreed? Yet the heritability of eyes is .00, simply because everybody has two and there are no individual variations in "eyeness" (except for those attributable to environmental events such as accidents).

In interpreting heritability coefficients, it is important to recognize that these estimates apply only to populations and *never to individuals*. So, if you studied the heights of many pairs of 5-year-old twins and estimated the heritability of height to be

.70, you could infer that a major reason why 5-year-olds *differ* in height is that they have inherited different genes. But, since heritability estimates say nothing about individuals, it is clearly inappropriate to conclude from an *H* of .70 that 70% of Freddie Jones's height is inherited, whereas the remaining 30% reflects the contribution of environment.

Finally, heritability estimates refer only to the particular trait in question as displayed by members of a *particular population* under *particular environmental circumstances*. These are important points to keep in mind, for heritability coefficients may differ in different populations or in different environments. Suppose, for example, we located a large number of twin infants, each of whom was raised in an impoverished institution in which his or her crib was lined with sheets that prevented much physical, visual, or social contact with other infants or with adult caregivers. Previous research (which we will examine in Chapter 6) suggests that, if we measured how sociable these infants are, we would find that they vary somewhat in sociability but that virtually all of them would be much less sociable than babies raised at home — a finding we could reasonably attribute to their socially depriving early experiences. Yet, because their early rearing environment was so uniform, the only reason these twins might show any *variation* in sociability is due to difference in their genetic predispositions. The heritability coefficient for sociability would thus approach 1.0 in this sample — a far cry from the *H*'s of .25 to .40 found in studies of other populations (twins and adopted children) raised in different environments (at home with parents) (Plomin, 1990).

In sum, the term *heritable* is not a synonym for *inherited*, and heritability estimates, which may vary across populations and environments, can tell us absolutely nothing about the development of any particular individual. Nevertheless, heritability coefficients are very useful statistics — the bread and butter of behavior genetics research — because they can help us determine whether there is any hereditary basis for the *differences* that people display on any attribute we might care to study. Let's now consider what behavior geneticists have learned about the heritability of some specific aspects of development.

HEREDITARY CONTRIBUTIONS TO TEMPERAMENT, PERSONALITY, AND MENTAL HEALTH

When psychologists speak of "personality," they are referring to a broad collection of attributes — including temperament, attitudes, values, and distinctive behavioral patterns (or habits) — that seem to characterize an individual. Unfortunately, the personality consists of so many characteristics that it is virtually impossible to measure them all with any single test. However, it is possible to focus on specific aspects of personality to see whether there is any hereditary basis for the ways we behave.

Heritability of temperament. **Temperament** is a term developmentalists use to describe our tendencies to respond in predictable ways to environmental events — tendencies that some believe to be the building blocks of personality (Goldsmith et al., 1987). Although different researchers do not always define or measure temperament in precisely the same way, many would agree that such attributes as *activity level* (the typical pace or vigor of our behavior), *irritability* or *emotionality* (the degree to which we become upset over novel events), *soothability* or *self-regulation* (the ease with which we can be calmed after being upset), *fearfulness*, and *sociability* (our receptiveness to social stimulation) are important components of temperament (Buss & Plomin, 1984; Goldsmith et al., 1987; Rothbart, 1981).

To many, the very term *temperament* implies a biological foundation for individual differences in behavior — a foundation that is heritable and stable over time (Bates, 1987; Buss & Plomin, 1984). Selective-breeding studies conducted with various animal species indicate that temperamental characteristics such as activity, fearfulness, and sociability do have a strong hereditary component (see Plomin et al., 1989). Can the same be true of human beings?

Behavior geneticists have tried to answer this question by comparing the temperamental similarities of pairs of identical and fraternal twins. Several such studies are remarkably consistent in revealing that, from early infancy onward, identical twins are more alike on such temperamental dimensions as activity level, demands for attention, irritability, and sociability than fraternal twins are

(Braungart et al., 1992; Plomin, DeFries, & Fulker, 1988; Wilson & Matheny, 1986). Though the heritability estimates for these attributes are moderate at best (averaging about .40), we can conclude that at least some components of temperament are influenced by the genes we have inherited. In addition, babies from different backgrounds show distinct temperamental characteristics as early as the first few days of life. In one study, Daniel Freedman (1979) compared the temperaments of newborn Caucasian and Chinese-American infants. The ethnic differences were clear: Caucasian babies were more irritable and harder to comfort than Chinese-American babies. Since the Caucasian and the Chinese-American mothers had received the same prenatal care, it appears that the temperamental differences between their infants may well have been hereditary.

Is early temperament stable over time? Is the "fearful" 8-month-old who is highly upset by a strange face likely to remain wary of strangers at 24 months and to shun new playmates as a 4-year-old? Longitudinal research indicates that several components of temperament—namely activity level, negative emotionality (fearfulness, irritability), and attention to novelty—are moderately stable throughout infancy, childhood, and even into the early adult years (Campos, Campos, & Barrett, 1989; Caspi, Elder, & Bem, 1987, 1988; McDevitt, 1986; Ruff et al., 1990; Worobey & Blajda, 1989). Behavior geneticists point to such stability as evidence that many temperamental traits are heavily influenced by the genes we inherit. By contrast, environmentalists argue that these same temperamental stabilities may well be attributable to the child's remaining in a relatively stable, or unchanging, home environment (Wachs, 1988). However, not all individuals are so temperamentally stable.

Consider what Jerome Kagan and his associates found while conducting longitudinal studies of a temperamental attribute they call **behavioral inhibition**—the tendency to withdraw from unfamiliar people or situations (Kagan, 1989; Kagan, Reznick, & Snidman, 1988; Reznick et al., 1986). Children identified as inhibited or uninhibited when first tested at age 21 months often remained relatively

inhibited or uninhibited when retested at 4, 5½, and 7½ years of age. Not only were the inhibited children shy around peers and wary of strange adults, but they were also more cautious than uninhibited children about playing with objects that involved an element of risk (for example, a balance beam), and they often displayed intense physiological arousal (for example, increased heart rates) in response to novel situations that barely fazed the uninhibited children. The physiological data, in particular, suggested to Kagan that behavioral inhibition is a reasonably stable temperamental trait that has deep biological roots, and a recent twin study clearly implies that inhibition is a heritable attribute (see Robinson et al., 1992). Nevertheless, it was only children at the *extremes* of the continuum—the most highly inhibited and the most highly uninhibited youngsters—who displayed this long-term stability; the other children's levels of inhibition fluctuated considerably over time (Kagan, Reznick, & Gibbons, 1989). These latter findings imply that even heritable aspects of temperament are often modified by environmental forces.

A similar conclusion emerges from Alexander Thomas and Stella Chess's classic *New York Longitudinal Study* of child temperament (Thomas, Chess, & Birch, 1970; Thomas & Chess, 1977, 1986). In their earliest reports, Thomas and Chess noted that certain components of infant temperament tend to cluster together, forming broader temperamental profiles. For example, highly active infants are often very irritable and irregular in their feeding, sleeping, and bowel habits, whereas passive babies tend to be good natured and regular in their habits. Thomas and Chess found that most infants in their sample could be placed into one of three categories according to the overall patterning of their temperamental qualities:

1. **Easy temperament**. Easygoing children are even tempered, are typically in a positive mood, and are quite open and adaptable to new experiences. Their habits are regular and predictable.
2. **Difficult temperament**. Difficult children are active, irritable, and irregular in their habits. They often react very vigorously to changes in rou-

tine and are slow to adapt to new persons or situations.

3. **Slow-to-warm-up temperament**. These children are quite inactive and moody. They, too, are slow to adapt to new persons and situations, but, unlike difficult children, they typically respond to novelty or to changes in routine with mild forms of passive resistance. For example, they may resist cuddling by directing their attention elsewhere rather than by crying or kicking.

Apparently, these broader temperamental patterns may also persist over time and influence the child's adjustment to a variety of settings and situations later in life. For example, children with difficult temperaments are more likely than other children to have problems adjusting to school activities, and they are often irritable and aggressive in their interactions with siblings and peers (Brody, Stoneman, & Burke, 1987; Thomas, Chess, & Korn, 1982). By contrast, children who are slow-to-warm-up often show a different kind of adjustment problem: their hesitancy to embrace new activities and challenges may cause them to be ignored or neglected by peers (Chess & Thomas, 1984). Do these observations imply that early temperamental *profiles* are immutable and will largely determine the outcomes of our social and personality development?

No, they do not! Thomas and Chess (1986; Chess & Thomas, 1984) find that early temperamental characteristics *sometimes do* and *sometimes do not* carry over into later life. In other words, temperament can change, and one factor that often determines whether it does change is the **"goodness of fit"** between the child's temperamental style and the parents' patterns of child rearing. Let's first consider a "good fit" between temperament and child rearing. Difficult infants who fuss a lot and have trouble adapting to new routines often become less cranky and more adaptable over the long run if parents remain calm, exercise restraint, and allow these children to respond to novelty at a more leisurely pace. Indeed, Chess and Thomas (1984) report that many difficult infants who experience such patient and sensitive caregiving are no longer classifiable as

PHOTO 2-5 Difficult infants are likely to retain their difficult temperaments if parents are impatient and forceful with them.

temperamentally difficult later in childhood or adolescence. Yet it is not always easy for parents to be patient and sensitive with a highly active, moody child who resists their bids for attention; in fact, many parents become irritable, impatient, demanding, and punitive with such children. Unfortunately, these attitudes and behaviors constitute a "poor fit" with a difficult child, who is likely to become all the more fussy and resistant in response to the parents' forceful and punitive tactics. And, true to form, difficult infants are especially likely to remain difficult and to display behavior problems later in life if their parents had been impatient, demanding, and forceful with them (Chess & Thomas, 1984).

In sum, many of the temperamental characteristics that we display and that may affect our social behavior and emotional adjustment later in life are clearly influenced by the genes we have inherited. However, early temperamental patterns can be altered, and the changes in temperament commonly observed over the course of childhood suggest that this aspect of personality is highly susceptible to environmental influence.

Hereditary contributions to the adult personality.
Psychologists have often assumed that the relatively
stable traits and habits that make up our adult personalities are heavily influenced by the environment. Presumably, our feelings, attitudes, values,
and characteristic patterns of behavior have been
shaped by the familial and cultural contexts in
which we live. Behavior geneticists would not necessarily disagree with this conclusion. However,
they do believe that psychologists overestimate the
impact of the environment on the developing personality while underestimating the importance of
hereditary factors (Goldsmith, 1983).

Family studies of personality suggest that many
attributes have a hereditary component. One example of a heritable trait is **introversion/extraversion**.
Introverts are people who are generally quiet, anxious, and uncomfortable around others. As a result, they often shun social contact. Extraverts are
highly sociable people who enjoy being with others.
Identical twins are moderately similar on this attribute, and their resemblance is greater than that of
fraternal twins, ordinary siblings, or pairs of genetically unrelated children raised in the same household (Martin & Jardine, 1986; Nichols, 1978; Scarr et
al., 1981).

Another interesting attribute that may be influenced by heredity is **empathic concern**. A person
high in empathy is a compassionate soul who recognizes the needs of others and is concerned about
their welfare. In Box 2-2 we saw that newborn infants will react to the distress of another infant by
becoming distressed themselves—implying that
the capacity for empathy may be innate. But are
there any biological bases for *individual differences* in
empathic concern?

To find out, Karen Matthews and her associates
(1981) administered a test of empathic concern to 114
pairs of identical twins and 116 pairs of fraternal
twins who ranged in age from 42 to 57 years. Even
though the vast majority of these male twins had
lived apart for many years, the identical twins were
still more alike in empathic concern ($r = .41$) than
the fraternal twins ($r = .05$), suggesting that empathy is a reasonably heritable attribute. The implications of these results are interesting. In the words of

the authors, "If empathic concern . . . leads to altruistic motivation, the present study provides evidence for a genetic basis for individual differences in
altruistic behavior" (p. 246).

Just how heritable is the adult personality?   To
what extent are our personalities influenced by the
genes we have inherited? We get some idea by looking at personality resemblances among family members, as shown in Table 2-2. Note that identical twins
are more similar to each other on this composite
measure of personality than are fraternal twins.
Were we to use the twin data to estimate genetic
contributions to personality, we might conclude
that many personality traits are moderately heritable. Of course, one implication of a moderate heritability coefficient is that personality is strongly influenced by environmental factors.

What features of the environment contribute
most heavily to the development of our personalities? Developmentalists have traditionally assumed that the home environment is especially important in this regard. Yet Table 2-2 reveals that
genetically unrelated individuals *who live in the same
home* barely resemble one another on the composite
personality measure ($r = .07$). Therefore, aspects of
the home environment that all family members *share*
must not contribute much to the development of
personality. How, then, does environment affect
personality?

Behavior geneticists David Rowe and Robert
Plomin (1981) argue that the environmental influences that contribute most heavily to personality are
those that make individuals *different* from one another—that is, events, situations, and experiences
that children within any family do *not* share. An example of a **nonshared environmental influence**
within the home is a tendency of one or both parents to respond differently to sons and daughters,
to first-born and later-born children, and so on. To
the extent that two siblings are treated differently by
parents, they will experience different environments, which will increase the likelihood that their
personalities will differ in important ways. Interactions among siblings provide another source of nonshared environmental influence on the developing

TABLE 2-2   *Personality resemblances among family members at three levels of kinship*

	Kinship			
	1.00 (identical twins)	.50 (fraternal twins)	.50 (nontwin siblings)	.00 (unrelated children raised in the same household)
Personality attributes (average correlations across several personality traits)	.50	.30	.20	.07

SOURCES: J. C. Loehlin, "Fitting Heredity-Environment Models Jointly to Twin and Adoption Data from the California Psychological Inventory." *Behavior Genetics*, 1985, 15, 199–221. Also J. C. Loehlin & R. C. Nichols, *Heredity, Environment, and Personality*. Copyright © 1976 by the University of Texas Press.

personality. For example, an older sibling who habitually dominates a younger one may become generally assertive and dominant as a result of these home experiences. But for the younger child this home environment is a dominating environment that may foster the development of such personality traits as passivity, tolerance, and cooperation.

How could we ever measure the impact of something as broad as nonshared environments? One strategy used by Denise Daniels and her associates (Daniels, 1986; Daniels & Plomin, 1985) is simply to ask pairs of adolescent siblings whether they have been treated differently by their parents and/or have experienced other important differences in their lives (for example, differences in their popularity with peers). She finds that siblings do report such differences and, more important, that these nonshared environmental influences reliably predict just how different siblings are in their personalities!

The next question, then, is "Do siblings have different experiences because they have inherited different genes?" Stated another way, it is possible that a child's heritable attributes might influence how other people respond to her. For example, a difficult youngster is likely to be treated very differently by parents and peers than a sibling with an easy temperament. Although genotypes do contribute to some extent to the different experiences reported by siblings (Baker & Daniels, 1990; Daniels, 1986), there is ample reason to believe that our highly individualized, unique environments are not solely attributable to our having inherited different genes (see

Hoffman, 1991, for a lucid discussion of this point). How do we know this?

One important clue comes from studies of identical twins. Since identical twins are perfectly matched from a genetic standpoint, any *differences* between them must necessarily reflect the contribution of environmental influences that they do *not* share. Clearly, these nonshared environmental effects cannot be attributed to the twins' different genes, because identical twins have identical genotypes! So, with this fact in mind, we can estimate the effects of nonshared environmental influences (NSE) on any attribute:

$$NSE = 1 - r \text{ (correlation for identical twins on that attribute)}$$

The logic behind this formula is straightforward: because identical twins have identical genes, only environmental influences can keep pair members from resembling each other. "One minus the correlation for identical twins is therefore an estimate of all environmental causes that make identical twins *different*" (Rowe & Plomin, 1981, p. 521).

Table 2-2 shows that the average correlation for identical twins across several personality attributes is only +.50 (which implies that these twins are alike in many respects and different in many others). So it seems that nonshared environmental influences (that is, 1 − .50 = .50) are indeed important contributors to the adult personality.

Now a thought question: is it really plausible that all personality resemblances that you and your siblings display are attributable to the *genes* that you share? Are we to believe that the home environment serves mainly to make siblings *different* from one another and contributes little to their similarities? As we see in Box 2-3, there are some very good reasons why some developmentalists are reluctant to accept these conclusions.

Hereditary contributions to behavior disorders and mental illness.   Is there a hereditary basis for mental illness? Might some among us be predisposed to commit deviant or antisocial acts? Although these ideas seemed absurd 25 years ago when I was a col-

lege student, it now appears that the answer to both questions is a qualified yes.

The evidence for hereditary contributions to abnormal behavior comes from family studies in which investigators calculate **concordance rates** for various disorders. In a twin study, for example, the concordance rate for a disorder is a measure of the likelihood that the second twin will exhibit the problem, given that the first one does. If concordance rates are higher for identical twins than for fraternal twins, one can conclude that the disorder is influenced by heredity.

B O X **2-3** | *Another Perspective on Shared Environment and Personality Development*

Virtually all developmentalists would agree that non-shared environmental influences help to explain why individuals raised in the same home will have different personalities. However, those who study parenting and other family influences are quite critical of the behavior geneticists' presumption that, just because siblings differ, their shared environments must contribute very little to their developing personalities. In her recent essay on sibling similarities and differences, Lois Hoffman (1991) makes several interesting points about **shared environmental influences** — points that behavior geneticists seem to overlook. Here are three such arguments.

1. *Shared environmental experiences can create differences as well as similarities among siblings.* To illustrate this point, let's consider how younger and older siblings might react to their parents' divorce. Cognitively immature preschool children, who are likely to feel somehow responsible for the family dissolution, may experience a great deal of guilt or shame and feel quite depressed. Indeed, these emotional reactions often trigger such *regressive* behaviors as tantrums and conduct disorders, which can undermine the child's personal relationships, both within and outside the family (Hetherington, 1989). By contrast, older children react differently. Although they may be just as emotionally distressed by the divorce as their younger sibs are, older grade-school children are not as likely to feel that

they caused this event, and they will probably have social supports from outside the family (for example, friends) to help them respond more *constructively* to the turmoil at home. Finally, older preadolescent and adolescent siblings (particularly daughters) often must assume caregiver roles and other family responsibilities that promote new *competencies* and may enhance their self-esteem. Here, then, is an example of a shared environmental experience — family dissolution — that can have very different effects on siblings, depending on their age and their interpretations of the event. So shared experiences need not always be portrayed as making siblings alike (as behavior geneticists have presumed); they can contribute to personality *differences* as well.

2. *Behavior genetics research overestimates sibling personality differences and the heritability of personality.* Research such as that summarized in Table 2-2 is based on paper-and-pencil, self-report measures of personality. According to Hoffman (1991), siblings in family studies may look very *different* on self-report measures because they are each prompted to think about their own uniqueness, especially if they know that their brothers and sisters are also being tested. Identical twins, on the other hand, may look so *similar* on self-report measures because they, by virtue of their obvious physical resemblance and the similar responses they evoke from others, are prompted to focus on similarities rather

Schizophrenia is a serious form of mental illness characterized by disturbances in thinking, emotional expression, and behavior. Schizophrenics are often so deficient at forming simple concepts and making logical connections between everyday events that they are unable to distinguish fantasy from reality. As a consequence, they may experience delusions or vivid hallucinations, which contribute to their irrational and inappropriate behavior. A survey of several twin studies of schizophrenia suggests an average concordance rate of .46 for identical twins but only .14 for frater-

nal twins (Gottesman & Shields, 1982). This is a strong indication that schizophrenia is a heritable disorder. In addition, studies of adults who grew up in adoptive homes reveal that the incidence of schizophrenia (and other disorders) among these adoptees is more closely related to the incidence of schizophrenia among their biological relatives (with whom they share genes) than among members of their adoptive families (Plomin, 1990).

In recent years it has become increasingly apparent that heredity also contributes to abnormal behaviors and conditions such as alcoholism, criminality and

---

BOX 2-3 | *continued*

than differences. If those self-reporting biases occur, their effects would be to inflate the personality resemblances of identical twins and to understate the resemblance of fraternal twins and other nontwin siblings. These distortions, in turn, would cause researchers to overestimate the heritability of the trait(s) in question and to underestimate the effects of shared environmental influences.

An example should illustrate the point. When *aggression* is measured by self-report inventories, family members show little resemblance that is not attributable to their genetic similarities (Loehlin, Willerman, & Horn, 1988). In other words, aggression looks like a highly heritable attribute. By contrast, objective *behavioral* measures of aggression suggest much less genetic influence and a marked effect of the shared environment; that is, individuals who share a home environment show some obvious similarities in their aggressive inclinations—similarities that are *not* attributable to the genes they share (Plomin, 1990). So shared environment contributes to aggression in ways that are masked by reporting biases that seem to characterize the personality inventories on which behavior geneticists rely.

3. *Shared environmental influences are strongest for dimensions on which siblings are treated alike.* There are several aspects of socialization for which parents try to be consistent by treating all their children alike. For exam-

ple, they try to use roughly the same strategies and disciplinary tactics with all their children to promote moral growth and foster social and intellectual competencies. They express similar religious and political values rather than tailoring their prescriptions to the individual child. And they model similar interests and activities for all their children. Do siblings resemble one another on such aspects of personality as social competence, moral internalization, political and religious attitudes, interests and activity preferences, and orientations to cognitive challenges (that is, creativity; tolerance for ambiguity)? Yes, indeed, and the similarities they display on these attributes are often as heavily influenced (or even more so) by their shared environments as by the genes they share (Hoffman, 1991; Plomin, 1990).

In sum, Hoffman's (1991) essay makes it clear that the small resemblance siblings display on *self-report* personality inventories is *not* an adequate justification for dismissing the contributions of shared environment to personality development. Indeed, the environments siblings share not only may foster such personality *differences* (should two or more siblings react differently to the same objective event), but they are also as important as genetic influences at creating resemblances among siblings on many noteworthy aspects of personality.

delinquency, depression, hyperactivity, **manic-depression**, and a number of *neurotic disorders* (Baker et al., 1989; Mednick, Gabrielli, & Hutchings, 1984; Plomin, 1990; Rowe, Rodgers, & Meseck-Bushey, 1992). Now, perhaps you have or have had close relatives who were diagnosed as alcoholic, neurotic, manic-depressive, or schizophrenic. Rest assured that this does *not* mean that you or your children will develop these problems. Only 10–14% of children who have one schizophrenic parent ever develop any symptoms that might be labeled "schizophrenic" (Kessler, 1975). Even if you are an identical twin whose co-twin has a serious psychiatric disorder, the odds are only between 1 in 2 and 1 in 10 (depending on the disorder) that you would ever experience anything that even approaches the problem affecting your twin.

Since identical twins are often *discordant* (that is, not alike) with respect to illnesses such as schizophrenia, it is obvious that environment must be a very important contributor to behavioral abnor-·malities and mental illnesses. In other words, people do not inherit particular disorders—they inherit genetic predispositions to develop certain illnesses or deviant patterns of behavior. And, even when a child's family history suggests that such a genetic predisposition may exist, it usually takes one or more very stressful experiences (for example, rejecting parents, a failure or series of failures at school, or dissolution of the family due to divorce) to trigger the illness in question (see Plomin & Rende, 1991; Rutter, 1979). Clearly, these latter findings provide some basis for optimism, for it may be possible someday to prevent the onset of most heritable disorders. To do so, we must (1) learn more about the adverse events that precipitate these disturbances and (2) strive to develop interventions or therapeutic techniques that will help "high-risk" individuals to maintain their emotional stability in the face of environmental stress.

THE CHARACTER OF
GENOTYPE/ENVIRONMENT INTERACTIONS

After reviewing a portion of the literature and seeing how behavior geneticists estimate the contribution of heredity to various attributes, it should be clear that both heredity and environment contribute in important ways to our temperaments, personalities, and mental health. But how do they do so? Today most behavior geneticists have rejected the notion that heredity contributes a set percentage to each attribute and environment contributes the rest. Even the once-popular "rubber band" and "reaction range" hypotheses, which implied that heredity sets a range of developmental potentials for each attribute, with environment determining where within that range the individual will fall, are probably far too simple. So how do environments combine with our genotypes to influence development? In at least three ways.

Passive genotype/environment interactions.   Parents contribute to a child's development in two important respects: (1) they have provided genes—the child's biological blueprint for development—and (2) they structure a social, emotional, and intellectual environment in which the child will grow. Sandra Scarr and Kathleen McCartney (1983) propose that the environments parents provide for their children depend, in part, on the parents' own genotypes. And, because children share genes with their parents, the rearing environments to which they are exposed are correlated (and, therefore, likely to be compatible) with their *own* genotypes.

The following example illustrates some developmental implications of these **passive genotype/environment interactions**. Parents who exercise regularly and who encourage this kind of animation tend to raise children who enjoy vigorous physical activities (Shaffer, 1985). Surely it could be argued that the parents' own displays of physical activity and their inducements to exercise are potent environmental influences that contribute to their children's activity preferences. However, parents such as these may have a genetic predisposition to enjoy physical exercise, which (1) may be passed along to their children and (2) may affect the activities that they, as parents, will try to promote. Thus, not only are their children exposed to a rearing environment that encourages vigorous physical exercise, but they may also have inherited genes that predispose them to be responsive to that environment. In other words, these youngsters may come to enjoy physical exercise for both hereditary and environmental reasons—and the influences of heredity and environment are inextricably intertwined.

Evocative genotype/environment interactions. Earlier we noted that the environmental influences that may contribute most heavily to personality are "nonshared" experiences that make individuals *different* from one another. Might the differences in environments that children experience be partly due to the fact that they have inherited different genes and thus may elicit different reactions from their companions?

Scarr and McCartney (1983) think so. Their notion of **evocative genotype/environment interactions** assumes that a child's heritable attributes will affect the behavior of others toward him or her. For example, smily, active babies may receive more attention and social stimulation than moody and passive ones. Teachers may respond more favorably to physically attractive students than to their less attractive classmates. Clearly, these *reactions* of other people to the child (and the child's heritable attributes) are environmental influences that will play an important role in shaping that child's personality. So once again we see an intermingling of hereditary and environmental influences: heredity affects the character of the social environment in which the personality develops.

Active gene influences (niche picking). Finally, Scarr and McCartney (1983) propose that the environments children prefer and seek out will be those that are most compatible with their genetic predispositions. For example, a child with genes for sociability is likely to invite friends to the house, to be an avid party-goer, and to generally prefer activities that are socially stimulating. By contrast, the child with genes for shyness may actively avoid large social gatherings and choose instead to pursue activities (such as coin collecting) that can be done alone. So one implication of these **active genotype/ environment interactions** is that people with different genotypes will *select* different "environmental niches" for themselves—niches that may then have a powerful effect on their future social, emotional, and intellectual development.

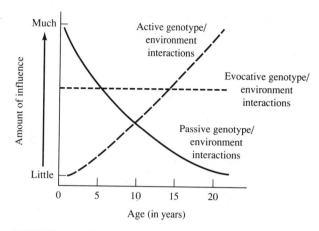

FIGURE 2-2 Relative influence of passive, evocative, and active (niche-picking) genotype/environment interactions as a function of age.

Developmental implications. According to Scarr and McCartney (1983), the relative importance of active, passive, and evocative gene influences will change over the course of development. During the first few years, infants and toddlers are not free to roam the neighborhood, choosing friends and building environmental niches. Most of their time is spent at home in an environment that parents structure for them, so that passive genotype/environment interactions are particularly important early in life. But, once children reach school age and venture away from home on a daily basis, they suddenly become much freer to pick their own interests, activities, friends, and hangouts. Thus, active, niche-building interactions should exert more and more influence on development as the child matures (see Figure 2-2). Finally, evocative genotype/ environment interactions are always important; that is, a person's heritable attributes and patterns of behavior may influence the ways other people react to him or her throughout life.

If Scarr and McCartney's theory has any merit, then virtually all siblings other than identical twins should become much less similar over time as they emerge from the relatively similar rearing environments parents impose during the early years and begin to actively select different environmental niches for themselves. Indeed, there is clear support for this assertion. Pairs of genetically unrelated adoptees who live in the same home do show some definite similarities in conduct and in intellectual performance during early and middle childhood (Scarr & Weinberg, 1978). Since these adoptees share no genes with each other or with their adoptive parents, their resemblances must be attributable to their common rearing environments. Yet, by late adolescence, genetically unrelated siblings no longer resemble each other in intelligence or personality, presumably because they have selected very different environmental niches, which, in turn, have steered them along differing developmental paths (Scarr & McCartney, 1983; Scarr et al., 1981). Even fraternal twins, who have 50% of their genes in common, are much less alike as adolescents and adults than they were as children (McCartney, Harris, & Bernieri, 1990). Apparently the genes that fraternal twins do *not* share cause these individuals to select somewhat different environmental niches, which, in turn, will contribute to their declining resemblance over time.

By contrast, pairs of identical twins continue to display some very noteworthy similarities throughout life. Why should this be? Scarr and McCartney (1983) suggest two reasons: (1) not only do identical twins elicit similar reactions from other people, but (2) their identical genotypes predispose them to prefer and to select very *similar* environments (that is, friends, interests, and activities), which will then exert comparable influences on these twin pairs and virtually guarantee that they will continue to resemble each other over time.[2]

A final comment.   After reading about Scarr and McCartney's theory, one can easily come away with the impression that our genotypes *determine* our environments and, therefore, exert the primary influence on human development. This is *not* what the theory implies. What Scarr and McCartney are saying is that people with different genotypes are *likely* to evoke different responses from others and to select different environmental niches for themselves. But it is also true that the responses they will evoke from others and the aspects of the environment that they select when building their "niches" will depend to no small extent on the particular individuals, settings, and circumstances that are available to them. To illustrate: Consider a pair of identical twins who are genetically predisposed to be outgoing and sociable. If one of them grows up with her mother in New York City and the other with a reclusive father in the Alaskan bush, the former twin will have had ample opportunity to act on her biological predispositions by mixing with other people and becoming highly extraverted, whereas her sister, lacking these opportunities, might actually become rather shy and reserved in social contexts.

This is not an unrealistic example. Studies of identical twins who were separated in infancy and reared in different environments reveal that each pair of separated co-twins showed some remarkable similarities and some striking dissimilarities (Bouchard et al., 1990; Farber, 1981). And, interestingly, the noteworthy differences these twins displayed usually centered on attributes for which their rearing environments were so dissimilar as to prevent them from ever establishing comparable niches.

Thus, although our genes may influence the kinds of life experiences we are likely to have, they do not *determine* our environments. Indeed, the events and experiences we actually encounter will depend largely on what is available to us in the particular culture or subculture in which we are raised. And, should some of the life experiences available to one person be radically discrepant from those of another, these two individuals will inevitably differ in important ways, regardless of the similarity of their genes or genetic predispositions.

Contributions and Criticisms of the Behavior Genetics Approach

Human behavior genetics is a relatively new discipline that is beginning to have a strong influence on the ways behavioral scientists look at social and per-

[2]This is not to say that identical twins do not differ in important ways from their co-twins. In fact, these twin pairs are less alike as adults than they were as children or adolescents (McCartney et al., 1990), owing perhaps to their desire to distinguish themselves from a co-twin and establish a "unique" identity. Nevertheless, adult identical twins resemble each other to a much greater degree than do adult fraternal twins or other pairs of adult siblings.

sonality development. Only 30 years ago it was generally assumed that our personalities were shaped by the familial and cultural contexts in which we lived. Presumably, everyone had a different personality because no two persons were exposed to precisely the same set of experiences as they were growing up. Today we have a plausible alternative explanation for individual differences in social and personal behavior: with the exception of identical twins, no two persons inherit precisely the same set of genes. Of course, the implication of this point of view is that our temperaments, personalities, and characteristic patterns of social conduct depend in part on the heredity blueprints that our parents passed along to us when we were conceived.

Yet the finding that many components of personality appear to be heritable (that is, influenced by genetic factors) in no way implies that genotype determines behavior or that environmental influences are unimportant. In fact, two of the major contributions of the behavior genetics approach are the notions that (1) our genotypes influence the kinds of environments that we are likely to experience, and (2) virtually all behavioral attributes of lasting developmental significance represent a long and involved interplay between nature and nurture. Perhaps Donald Hebb (1980) was not too far off in stating that behavior is determined 100% by heredity and 100% by environment, for it appears that these two sets of influences are inextricably intertwined.

Interesting as these ideas may be, there are those who argue that the behavior genetics approach is merely a general descriptive overview of how development might proceed rather than a well-articulated theory. One reason for this sentiment is that we know so little about how genes exert their effects. Genes are coded to manufacture amino acids, not to produce such attributes as sociability or creativity. Although we now suspect that genes affect behavior indirectly by influencing the *environments* that we experience and create for ourselves, we are still a long way from understanding how or why genes might impel us to prefer particular kinds of stimulation or to find certain activities especially satisfying. Moreover, behavior geneticists apply the term *environment* in a very global way, making few if any attempts to measure environmental influences

directly or to specify how the environment acts on the individual to influence behavior. Perhaps you can see the problem: the critics contend one has not *explained* development by merely postulating that unspecified environmental forces that are influenced in unknown ways by our genes will somehow shape our conduct and character.

How do environments impinge on children and adolescents to influence their development? What environmental influences, provided when, are particularly noteworthy in this regard? As we will see in our next chapter, *social-learning* theorists and proponents of *ecological theory* have explored these very issues in some detail.

Summary

This chapter focuses on some of the oldest and some of the newest ideas about human social and personality development. The older ideas stem from Sigmund Freud's *psychoanalytic theory*. Freud was a practicing neurologist who developed his theory from his observations of neurotic patients — observations that led him to conclude that human beings are born with two kinds of urges, or instincts: *Eros*, the life instincts, and *Thanatos*, the death, or destructive, instincts. Freud believed that these instincts were the source of all *psychic* (or mental) energy — the energy one uses to think, to learn, and to perform other mental functions that are necessary to gratify one's inborn goals or motives.

According to Freud, a newborn infant has a primitive, undifferentiated personality consisting of the instincts (Eros and Thanatos) and a few basic reflexes. This is the *id*, which represents all of one's basic needs, wishes, and motives. The *ego* is formed as psychic energy is diverted from the id to activate important cognitive processes, such as perception, learning, and logical reasoning, which help the child to find realistic methods of gratifying the instincts. The *superego* is the ethical component of the personality. It develops from the ego, and its function is to determine whether the ego's methods of satisfying the instincts are moral or immoral.

Freud believed that social and personality development progresses through a series of five *psychosexual stages*—oral, anal, phallic, latency, and genital—that parallel the maturation of the sex instinct. Freud assumed that the activities and conflicts that emerge at each psychosexual stage would have lasting effects on the developing personality.

Erik Erikson has extended Freud's theory by concentrating less on the sex instinct and more on important sociocultural determinants of human development. According to Erikson, people progress through a series of eight *psychosocial stages*. Each stage is characterized by a particular social conflict or "crisis" that the individual must successfully resolve in order to develop in a healthy direction. Erikson's first five stages occur at the same ages as Freud's psychosexual stages, but they differ from Freud's stages in several respects. Erikson's last three stages, which occur during young adulthood, middle age, and old age, are important extensions of Freud's developmental scheme.

Although psychoanalytic theory has strong biological overtones, there are two recent perspectives that focus even more intently on biological contributions to social and personality development. One of these perspectives—the evolutionary approach—is illustrated by two modern theories, *ethology* and *sociobiology*.

The ethologists concentrate on inherited attributes that conspire to make human beings similar to one another (that is, contribute to common developmental outcomes). Ethologists believe that children are born with a number of adaptive responses that have evolved over the course of human history and serve to channel development along particular paths. Although ethologists recognize that we are largely products of our experiences, they remind us that we are biological creatures whose innate characteristics affect the kinds of learning experiences we are likely to have.

Sociobiology is a recent attempt to explain *social* behaviors and motives in terms of an evolutionary model specifying that the survival of an individual's genes (rather than survival of the individual organism) transcends all other goals. Like ethology, sociobiology has been criticized for emphasizing evolutionary products (and processes) that are difficult to verify or falsify and that may often be overridden by environmental influences. Nevertheless, the demonstrated successes of the evolutionary models have made developmentalists more inclined to (1) view individuals as products of a long evolutionary history and (2) seek to understand how the innate behaviors that humans display might influence their social and personality development.

Proponents of a second modern biological perspective—the *behavior genetics* approach—concentrate on biological bases for *variation* among members of a species. Their major research strategy is to look for behavioral similarities and differences in family members who vary in *kinship* in order to estimate the *heritability* of various attributes—that is, the amount of variation in a trait or a class of behavior that is attributable to hereditary factors.

Results of family studies reveal that our unique genotypes do play important roles in the development of some aspects of temperament, many dimensions of personality, and several mental illnesses and abnormal patterns of behavior. Yet these findings do not imply that our genes determine social conduct or the course of social and personality development. Indeed, two of the major contributions of the behavior genetics approach have been the discoveries that (1) our genotypes influence the kinds of environments we are likely to experience or to create for ourselves, and (2) the "nature versus nurture" controversy is a moot point, because all behavioral attributes of lasting developmental significance are products of a long and involved interplay between the forces of nature and nurture.

References

ADLER, A. (1964). *Problems of neurosis*. New York: Harper & Row. (Original work published 1929.)

AINSWORTH, M. D. S. (1979). Attachment as related to mother-infant interaction. In J. S. Rosenblatt, R. A. Hinde, C. Beer, & M. Busnel (Eds.), *Advances in the study of behavior* (Vol. 9). Orlando, FL: Academic Press.

AINSWORTH, M. D. S. (1989). Attachments beyond infancy. *American Psychologist, 44,* 709–716.

BAKER, L. A., & DANIELS, D. (1990). Nonshared environmental influences and personality differences in adult twins. *Journal of Personality and Social Psychology, 58*, 103–110.

BAKER, L. A., MACK, W., MOFFITT, T. E., & MEDNICK, S. (1989). Sex differences in property crime in a Danish adoption cohort. *Behavior Genetics, 19*, 355–370.

BANDURA, A. (1973). *Aggression: A social learning analysis.* Englewood Cliffs, NJ: Prentice-Hall.

BATES, J. E. (1987). Temperament in infancy. In J. D. Osofsky (Ed.), *Handbook of infant development* (2nd ed.). New York: Wiley.

BEM, S. L. (1989). Genital knowledge and gender constancy in preschool children. *Child Development, 60*, 649–662.

BOUCHARD, T. J., JR., LYKKEN, D. T., McGUE, M., SEGAL, N. L., & TELLEGEN, A. (1990). Sources of human psychological differences: The Minnesota study of twins reared apart. *Science, 250*, 223–228.

BOWLBY, J. (1969). *Attachment and loss. Vol. 1: Attachment.* New York: Basic Books.

BOWLBY, J. (1973). *Attachment and loss. Vol. 2: Separation, anxiety, and anger.* New York: Basic Books.

BRAUNGART, J. M., PLOMIN, R., DeFRIES, J. C., & FULKER, D. W. (1992). Genetic influence on tester-rated infant temperament as assessed by Bayley's Infant Behavior Record: Nonadoptive and adoptive siblings and twins. *Developmental Psychology, 28*, 40–47.

BRODY, G. H., STONEMAN, Z., & BURKE, M. (1987). Child temperaments, maternal differential behavior, and sibling relationships. *Developmental Psychology, 23*, 354–362.

BUSS, A. H., & PLOMIN, R. (1984). *Temperament: Early developing personality traits.* Hillsdale, NJ: Erlbaum.

CAIRNS, R. B. (1979). *Social development: The origins and plasticity of interchanges.* New York: W. H. Freeman.

CAMPOS, J. J., CAMPOS, R. G., & BARRETT, K. C. (1989). Emergent themes in the study of emotional development and emotional regulation. *Developmental Psychology, 25*, 394–402.

CASPI, A., ELDER, G. H., JR., & BEM, D. J. (1987). Moving against the world: Life-course patterns of explosive children. *Developmental Psychology, 23*, 308–313.

CASPI, A., ELDER, G. H., JR., & BEM, D. J. (1988). Moving away from the world: Life-course patterns of shy children. *Developmental Psychology, 24*, 824–831.

CHESS, S., & THOMAS, A. (1984). *Origins and evolution of behavior disorders.* New York: Brunner/Mazel.

DANIELS, D. (1986). Differential experiences of siblings in the same family as predictors of adolescent sibling personality differences. *Journal of Personality and Social Psychology, 51*, 339–346.

DANIELS, D., & PLOMIN, R. (1985). Differential experience of siblings in the same family. *Developmental Psychology, 21*, 747–760.

EMDE, R. N. (1992). Individual meaning and increasing complexity: Contributions of Sigmund Freud and René Spitz to developmental psychology. *Developmental Psychology, 28*, 347–359.

ERDLE, S. (1990). Limitations of the heritability coefficient as an index of genetic and environmental influences on human behavior. *American Psychologist, 45*, 553–554.

ERIKSON, E. H. (1950). In M. J. E. Senn (Ed.), *Symposium on the healthy personality.* New York: Josiah Macy, Jr., Foundation.

ERIKSON, E. H. (1963). *Childhood and society* (2nd ed.). New York: Norton.

ERIKSON, E. H. (1982). *The life cycle completed: A review.* New York: Norton.

FARBER, S. L. (1981). *Identical twins reared apart: A reanalysis.* New York: Basic Books.

FREEDMAN, D. G. (1979). Ethnic differences in babies. *Human Nature, 2*, 36–43.

FREUD, S. (1933). *New introductory lectures in psychoanalysis.* New York: Norton.

FREUD, S. (1961). The dissolution of the Oedipus complex. In J. Strachey (Ed. & Trans.), *The standard edition of the complete psychological works of Sigmund Freud* (Vol. 19). London: Hogarth Press. (Original work published 1924.)

FREUD, S. (1964). An outline of psychoanalysis. In J. Strachey (Ed. & Trans.), *The standard edition of the complete psychological works of Sigmund Freud* (Vol. 23). London: Hogarth Press. (Original work published 1940.)

FREUD, S. (1974). *The ego and the id.* London: Hogarth Press. (Original work published 1923.)

GOLDSMITH, H. H. (1983). Genetic influences on personality from infancy to adulthood. *Child Development, 54*, 331–335.

GOLDSMITH, H. H., BUSS, A. H., PLOMIN, R., ROTHBART, M. K., THOMAS, A., CHESS, S., HINDE, R. A., & McCALL, R. B. (1987). Roundtable: What is Temperament? Four approaches. *Child Development, 58*, 505–529.

GOTTESMAN, I. I., & SHIELDS, J. (1982). *Schizophrenia: The epigenetic puzzle.* Cambridge, England: Cambridge University Press.

GOTTLIEB, G. (1991). Experiential canalization of behavioral development: Theory and commentary. *Developmental Psychology, 27*, 4–13.

GOULD, S. J. (1978). Sociobiology: The art of story telling. *New Scientist, 80*, 530–533.

HEBB, D. O. (1980). *Essay on mind.* Hillsdale, NJ: Erlbaum.

HETHERINGTON, E. M. (1989). Coping with family transitions: Winners, losers, and survivors. *Child Development, 60*, 1–14.

HINDE, R. A. (1989). Ethological and relationships approaches. In R. Vasta (Ed.), *Annals of child development. Vol. 6: Theories of child development: Revised formulations and current issues.* New York: Appleton-Century-Crofts.

HOFFMAN, L. W. (1991). The influence of the family environment on personality: Accounting for sibling differences. *Psychological Bulletin, 108*, 187–203.

HOFFMAN, M. L. (1981). Is altruism part of human nature? *Journal of Personality and Social Psychology, 40*, 121–127.

HORNEY, K. (1967). *Feminine psychology.* New York: Norton. (Original work published 1923–1937.)

KAGAN, J. (1989). The concept of behavioral inhibition to the unfamiliar. In J. S. Reznick (Ed.), *Perspectives on behavioral inhibition.* Chicago: University of Chicago Press.

KAGAN, J., REZNICK, J. S., & GIBBONS, J. (1989). Inhibited and uninhibited types of children. *Child Development, 60*, 838–845.

KAGAN, J., REZNICK, J. S., & SNIDMAN, N. (1988). Biological bases of childhood shyness. *Science, 240*, 167–171.

KATCHER, A. (1955). The discrimination of sex differences by young children. *Journal of Genetic Psychology, 87*, 131–143.

KESSLER, S. (1975). Psychiatric genetics. In D. A. Hamburg & K. Brodie (Eds.), *American handbook of psychiatry*. Vol. 6: *New psychiatric frontiers*. New York: Basic Books.

LOEHLIN, J. C. (1985). Fitting heredity-environment models jointly to twin and adoption data from the California Psychological Inventory. *Behavior Genetics, 15*, 199–221.

LOEHLIN, J. C., & NICHOLS, R. C. (1976). *Heredity, environment, and personality*. Austin: University of Texas Press.

LOEHLIN, L. C., WILLERMAN, L., & HORN, J. M. (1988). Human behavior genetics. *Annual Review of Psychology, 39*, 101–133.

LORENZ, K. Z. (1937). The companion in the bird's world. *Auk, 54*, 245–273.

LORENZ, K. Z. (1981). *The foundations of ethology*. New York: Springer–Verlag.

MARTIN, G. B., & CLARK, R. D. III (1982). Distress crying in neonates: Species and peer specificity. *Developmental Psychology, 18*, 3–9.

MARTIN, N. G., & JARDINE, R. (1986). Eysenck's contributions to behavior genetics. In S. Modgil & C. Modgil (Eds.), *Hans Eysenck: Consensus and controversy*. Philadelphia: Falmer.

MATTHEWS, K. A., BATSON, C. D., HORN, J., & ROSENMAN, R. H. (1981). "Principles in his nature which interest him in the fortune of others": The heritability of empathic concern for others. *Journal of Personality, 49*, 237–247.

McCARTNEY, K., HARRIS, M. J., & BERNIERI, F. (1990). Growing up and growing apart: A developmental meta-analysis of twin studies. *Psychological Bulletin, 107*, 226–237.

McDEVITT, S. C. (1986). Continuity and discontinuity of temperament in infancy and early childhood: A psychometric perspective. In R. Plomin & J. Dunn (Eds.), *The study of temperament: Changes, continuities, and challenges*. Hillsdale, NJ: Erlbaum.

MEDNICK, S. A., GABRIELLI, W. F., JR., & HUTCHINGS, B. (1984). Genetic influences in criminal convictions: Evidence from an adoption cohort. *Science, 224*, 891–894.

NICHOLS, R. C. (1978). Heredity and environment: Major findings from twin studies of ability, personality, and interests. *Homo, 29*, 158–173.

PLOMIN, R. (1990). *Nature and nurture: An introduction to behavior genetics*. Pacific Grove, CA: Brooks/Cole.

PLOMIN, R., DeFRIES, J. C., & FULKER, D. W. (1988). *Nature and nurture during infancy and early childhood*. New York: Cambridge University Press.

PLOMIN, R., DeFRIES, J. C., & McCLEARN, G. E. (1989). *Behavioral genetics: A primer* (2nd ed.). New York: W. H. Freeman.

PLOMIN, R., & RENDE, R. (1991). Human behavioral genetics. *Annual Review of Psychology, 42*, 161–190.

REZNICK, J. S., KAGAN, J., SNIDMAN, N., GERSTEN, M., BAAK, K., & ROSENBERG, A. (1986). Inhibited and uninhibited children: A follow-up study. *Child Development, 57*, 660–680.

ROBINSON, J. L., KAGAN, J., REZNICK, J. S., & CORLEY, R. (1992). The heritability of inhibited and uninhibited behavior: A twin study. *Developmental Psychology, 28*, 1030–1037.

ROTHBART, M. K. (1981). Measurement of temperament in infancy. *Child Development, 52*, 569–578.

ROWE, D. C., & PLOMIN, R. (1981). The importance of nonshared (E_1) environmental influences in behavioral development. *Developmental Psychology, 17*, 517–531.

ROWE, D. C., RODGERS, J. L., & MESECK-BUSHEY, S. (1992). Sibling delinquency and the family environment: Shared and unshared influences. *Child Development, 63*, 59–67.

RUFF, H. A., LAWSON, K. R., PARRINELLO, R., & WEISSBERG, R. (1990). Long–term stability of individual differences in sustained attention in the early years. *Child Development, 61*, 60–75.

RUTTER, M. (1979). Protective factors in children's responses to stress and disadvantage. In M. W. Kent & J. E. Rolf (Eds.), *Primary prevention of psychopathology*. Vol. 3: *Social competence in children*. Hanover, NH: University Press of New England.

SAGI, A., & HOFFMAN, M. L. (1976). Empathic distress in newborns. *Developmental Psychology, 12*, 175–176.

SCARR, S., & McCARTNEY, K. (1983). How people make their own environments: A theory of genotype-environment effects. *Child Development, 54*, 424–435.

SCARR, S., WEBBER, P. L., WEINBERG, R. A., & WITTIG, M. A. (1981). Personality resemblance among adolescents and their parents in biologically related and adoptive families. *Journal of Personality and Social Psychology, 40*, 885–898.

SCARR, S., & WEINBERG, R. A. (1978). The influence of family background on intellectual attainment. *American Sociological Review, 43*, 674–692.

SHAFFER, D. R. (1985). Unpublished data, Department of Psychology, University of Georgia.

SIGELMAN, C. K., & SHAFFER, D. R. (1991). *Life-span human development*. Pacific Grove, CA: Brooks/Cole.

SULLIVAN, H. S. (1953). *The interpersonal theory of psychiatry*. New York: Norton.

THOMAS, A., & CHESS, S. (1977). *Temperament and development*. New York: Brunner/Mazel.

THOMAS, A., & CHESS, S. (1986). The New York longitudinal study: From infancy to early adult life. In R. Plomin & J. Dunn (Eds.), *The study of temperament: Changes, continuities, and challenges*. Hillsdale, NJ: Erlbaum.

THOMAS, A., CHESS, S., & BIRCH, H. G. (1970). The origin of personality. *Scientific American, 223*, 102–109.

THOMAS, A., CHESS, S., & KORN, S. (1982). The reality of difficult temperament. *Merrill-Palmer Quarterly, 28*, 1–20.

TINBERGEN, N. (1973). *The animal in its world: Explorations of an ethologist, 1932–1972* (Vols. 1 & 2). Cambridge, MA: Harvard University Press.

TRYON, R. C. (1940). Genetic differences in maze learning in rats. *Yearbook of the National Society for Studies in Education, 39,* 111–119.

WACHS, T. D. (1988). Relevance of physical environment influences for toddler temperament. *Infant Behavior and Development, 11,* 431–445.

WILSON, E. O. (1975). *Sociobiology: The new synthesis.* Cambridge, MA: Harvard University Press.

WILSON, R. S., & MATHENY, A. P., JR. (1986). Behavior genetics research in infant temperament: The Louisville twin study. In R. Plomin & J. Dunn (Eds.), *The study of temperament: Changes, continuities, and challenges.* Hillsdale, NJ: Erlbaum.

WOROBEY, J., & BLAJDA, V. M. (1989). Temperament ratings at 2 weeks, 2 months, and 1 year: Differential stability of activity and emotionality. *Developmental Psychology, 25,* 257–263.

3

Environmentalist Perspectives: Social-Learning Theory and the Ecological Approach

Let's suppose that we have been transported back to the year 1910. We have just registered for a new semester, and here we are awaiting the first lecture of the first psychology course that our college has ever offered. At precisely one minute before the hour, the professor enters the hall through a side door, takes his place at the lectern, and announces to the hushed gathering: "Students, we have been given the opportunity this term to survey a new science called psychology, or the study of the mind." We listen eagerly as the professor informs us that the first half of the term will deal with the theories of a Viennese neurologist by the name of Sigmund Freud. He then begins to describe the work of several experimental psychologists who may be somewhat less familiar to us, including William James, Hermann Ebbinghaus, and Edward Titchener, who share an interest in phenomena such as emotions, volition, consciousness, and the *subjective* experience of everyday sensory events—color, sound, motion, and pain. We can already anticipate an interesting semester in the new course, which should help us solve many mysteries of the mind.

Had we taken this course three years later, we would surely have learned of another psychologist, John B. Watson, who vehemently objected to the discipline's mentalistic overtones. In 1913 Watson proclaimed:

> The time seems to have come when psychology must disregard all references to consciousness, when it need no longer delude itself into thinking that it is making mental states the object of observation. We have become so enmeshed in speculative questions concerning the elements of the mind, the nature of conscious content . . . that I, as an experimental student, feel that something is wrong with our premises and the types of problems which develop from them. . . .
>
> Psychology, as the behaviorist views it, is a purely objective, experimental branch of natural science. Its theoretical goal is the prediction and control of *behavior*. Introspection [thinking about one's own internal states] forms no essential part of its methods, nor is the scientific value of its data dependent upon the readiness with which they lend themselves to interpretation in terms of consciousness. The behaviorist . . . recognizes no dividing line between man and brute. The behavior of man, for all its refinement and complexity, forms only a

part of the behaviorist's total scheme of investigation [pp. 158–163; italics added].

Although Watson was first and foremost a learning theorist, he had some very pointed things to say about developmental processes. For example, a basic premise of his doctrine of **behaviorism** was that the "mind" of an infant is a *tabula rasa* and that *learned* associations between stimuli and responses are the building blocks of human development. According to Watson, development does not proceed through a series of stages; it is a continuous process marked by the gradual acquisition of new and more sophisticated *behavioral* patterns, or habits. Watson believed that only the simplest of human reflexes (for example, sucking, grasping) are inborn and that all of the significant aspects of one's personality are learned.

Before we take a closer look at Watson's early contributions to the field of social and personality development and consider several theories that arose from the behavioral perspective he founded, it is necessary to understand what behaviorists mean by the term *learning* and to familiarize ourselves with the ways in which learning can occur.

What Is Learning?

Learning is one of those deceptively simple terms that are actually quite complex and difficult to define. Most psychologists think of learning as a change in behavior (or behavioral potential) that satisfies the following three criteria (Domjan, 1993):

1. The individual now thinks, perceives, or reacts to the environment in a new way.
2. This change is clearly the result of one's *experiences* — that is, attributable to repetition, study, practice, or the observations one has made, rather than to heredity or the maturational process or to physiological damage resulting from injury.
3. The change is *relatively permanent*. Facts, thoughts, and behaviors that are acquired and immediately forgotten have not really been

learned; also, temporary changes attributable to fatigue, illness, or drugs do not qualify as learned responses.

How Does Learning Occur?

Learned responses or habits may be acquired in at least five ways: by *repetition* (or mere exposure), by *classical conditioning*, by *operant conditioning*, by *observation*, and by *collaboration* with a more skillful partner. Let's briefly consider each of these processes.

MERE EXPOSURE

Odds are that you can recall an occasion when you gradually became more positive toward a song, a new food, or an acquaintance the more often you encountered that stimulus. It turns out that these "mere exposure" effects are quite real: over the past several years, social psychologists have discovered that we tend to develop favorable attitudes toward objects, activities, and persons that we encounter on a regular basis—even though we may never touch the objects, partake in the activities, or interact with the persons (Baron & Byrne, 1991). Although people may say they know what they like, it seems that they often *learn* to like what they know (Domjan, 1993).

CLASSICAL CONDITIONING

A second way that one may learn is through classical conditioning. In **classical conditioning**, a neutral stimulus that initially has no effect on the subject comes to elicit a response of some sort by virtue of its association with a second, nonneutral stimulus that always evokes the response.

As an illustration, consider that young children are unlikely to lick their lips (or to do much else other than listen) the first two or three times they hear the jingling of an approaching ice-cream truck. In other words, this jingling is an initially neutral stimulus in that it does *not* elicit lip licking. Ice cream, however, will normally elicit lip licking. In the language of classical conditioning, ice cream is an **unconditioned stimulus (UCS)**, and lip licking is an unlearned or **unconditioned response (UCR)** to ice cream. If a child hears the jingling of an ice-

cream truck *and* then receives an ice [cream on] several days in succession, she should [asso]ciate this jingling with the presentation [of ice cream,] and may begin to lick her lips at the sou[nd of an] approaching vehicle. Clearly, the child's b[ehavior] has changed as a result of her experiences. I[n the] terminology of classical conditioning, she is n[ow] emitting a **conditioned response (CR)**—lip lick-ing—to an initially neutral or **conditioned stimulus (CS)**—the jingling of the ice-cream truck (see Fig-ure 3-1).

Although the lip-licking response described in this example may seem rather mundane, it is quite conceivable that every one of us has learned many things through classical conditioning—things that continue to affect us today. In fact, we will soon see why Watson believed that many fears, phobias, and other conditioned emotional responses may be ac-quired through a form of classical conditioning.

OPERANT (OR INSTRUMENTAL) CONDITIONING

In classical conditioning, learned responses are elic-ited by a conditioned stimulus. **Operant (or instru-mental) conditioning** is quite different: it requires the learner to first emit a response of some sort (that is, to actively operate on the environment) and then to associate this action with the particular outcomes, or consequences, it produces.

Two kinds of consequences are important in op-erant conditioning: reinforcers and punishments. **Reinforcers** are consequences that promote operant learning by increasing the likelihood that the re-sponse will occur in the future. For example, a mother who praises her son for displaying sympa-thy and compassion toward a distressed playmate who has fallen and skinned his knee is using praise as a reinforcer. If the boy values his mother's praise and recognizes that his compassion is what pro-duced this pleasant outcome, he is likely to respond compassionately again toward his friend (and per-haps toward other distressed companions as well) when opportunities to do so present themselves. By contrast, **punishments** are consequences that *sup-press* a response and may decrease the likelihood that it will occur again. For example, an infant whose hands are slapped every time she reaches for her mother's eyeglasses may soon refrain from

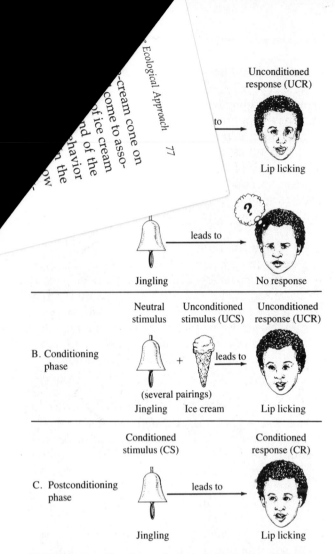

FIGURE 3-1 The three phases of classical conditioning. In the preconditioning phase, the unconditioned stimulus (UCS) always elicits an unconditioned response (UCR), whereas the conditioned stimulus (CS) never does. During the conditioning phase, the CS and UCS are paired repeatedly and eventually associated. At this point the learner passes into the postconditioning phase, in which the CS alone will elicit the original response (now called a conditioned response, or CR).

doing so. An adolescent who is grounded for sassing his father will probably think twice before repeating this "mistake." In sum, operant conditioning is a very common form of learning in which freely emitted responses become either more or less probable, depending on the consequences (reinforcers and punishments) they produce.

OBSERVATIONAL LEARNING

Observational learning is a fourth process by which we acquire new feelings, attitudes, and behaviors. If a child watches someone do something or listens attentively to that person's reasoning, he may learn to do, think, or feel as that other person did. Even toddlers can learn by observation. A 2-year-old boy may discover how to approach and pet the family dog simply by noting how his older sister does it. A 6-year-old girl may acquire a negative attitude toward members of a minority group after hearing her parents talk about these people in a disparaging way. In the language of observational learning, the individual who is observed and imitated is called a *social model*. Over the years, children are exposed to hundreds of social models and will have the opportunity to learn literally thousands of responses (some good, some bad) simply by observing others displaying them.

COLLABORATIVE LEARNING

Recently, developmentalists have come to appreciate that many culturally meaningful skills and attributes that children acquire are mastered through cooperative or collaborative dialogues between children and their socializing agents. The idea here is that parents and other more skillful associates will often assist the young child to acquire new competencies by (1) introducing challenges that she cannot master on her own; (2) providing hints, suggestions, and instructions that are carefully tailored to her current abilities; and then (3) encouraging her to enact those behaviors she is competent to perform. Gradually, as the child becomes more knowledgeable and more familiar with the task at hand, she will assume more of the planning or strategizing role from the tutor, eventually gaining the competencies to master similar challenges by herself. Notice that competencies acquired through this kind of **collaborative (or guided) learning** are not gained through mere exposure, through mere observation, or through classical or operant conditioning. Instead, a child who lacks the attribute or skill and who cannot acquire it on his own is encouraged to make gradual headway toward the goal by a more competent associate — one who provides the **scaf-**

folding and encouragement that permit this learning to unfold.

The notion that collaborative learning is an important contributor to children's socialization can be traced to Lev Vygotsky (1934/1962, 1978), a Russian developmentalist who was concerned primarily with social and cultural influences on children's *cognitive* development. Although Vygotsky is more accurately classified as a cognitive scholar than as a social-learning theorist, we will see later in this chapter that his perspective on social/cultural learning represents an important addition to (or extension of) the social-learning viewpoint.

Watson's Legacies

John B. Watson, the father of behaviorism, surely qualifies as the first *social*-learning theorist. His view that children are passive creatures who are molded by their environments carried a stern message for parents — that it was they who were largely (if not wholly) responsible for what their children would become. Watson (1928) cautioned parents to begin training their children at birth and to cut back on the coddling and babying if they hoped to instill good habits. Treat them, he said,

> as though they were young adults. . . . Let your behavior always be objective and kindly firm. Never hug and kiss them, never let them sit on your lap . . . shake hands with them in the morning. Give them a pat on the head if they have made an extraordinarily good job of a difficult task. . . . In a week's time, you will find how easy it is to be perfectly objective with your child and at the same time kindly. You will be utterly ashamed at the mawkish, sentimental way you have been handling [your child] [1928, pp. 81–82].

Clearly, Watson's doctrine of **environmental determinism** and his prescriptions for child rearing were considered rather extreme, even in his own era (Horowitz, 1992). Indeed, Watson may have taken the radical environmental stand that he did partly because other prominent theorists of the day — most notably Arnold Gesell (1880–1961) — took the equally extreme but opposing position that human development is largely a matter of biological maturation. Gesell's (1933) view was that children, like

PHOTO 3-1   John B. Watson (1878–1958) was the father of behaviorism and the first social-learning theorist.

plants, simply "bloomed," following a pattern and timetable laid out in their genes. His message for parents was more reassuring than Watson's: if you provide humane care that is tailored to the child's unique (and presumably inborn) potentials, you can sit back, relax, and watch nature take its course (Thelen & Adolph, 1992).

Why was Watson so convinced that young children are remarkably malleable organisms, subject to any and all kinds of environmental influence? It seems that this view stemmed in large part from his own earlier research, which suggested that infantile fears and other emotional reactions are easily acquired through classical conditioning. In 1920, for example, Watson and Rosalie Raynor presented a gentle white rat to a 9-month-old named Albert. Albert's initial reactions were positive ones: he crawled toward the rat and played with it as he had previously with a dog and a rabbit. Two months later came the conditioning phase. Every time little Albert reached for the white rat, Watson would slip behind him and bang a steel rod loudly with a hammer. Little Albert would then cry and shy away from the rat. In this case the loud noise is the unconditioned stimulus (UCS) because it elicits fearful behavior (the UCR) without any learning having taken place. Did little Albert eventually associate the white rat with the loud noise and come to fear his furry playmate? Indeed he did, and he also learned to shy away from other furry things, such as a rabbit and a Santa Claus mask. This extension (or **stimulus generalization**) of fear to objects other than the rat illustrates that emotional responses acquired through classical conditioning can be very powerful indeed. And, since Watson's day, other researchers have repeatedly demonstrated that many of our attitudes and prejudices may also be acquired through a classical-conditioning process (see Staats, 1975).

But perhaps the most important contribution of Watson's early research was the message it conveyed to other behaviorists, virtually all of whom worked with animals. That message was clear: apparently, human behavior obeyed many of the most basic laws of learning theory. This was an immensely important demonstration, for it helped to convince a number of influential learning theorists that human social and personality development was a topic worthy of their scientific scrutiny.

Since Watson's time, several theories have been proposed to explain social learning and the process of personality development. The earliest of these approaches appeared in the 1930s, when a group of anthropologists, psychologists, and sociologists from Yale University attempted to interpret psychoanalytic phenomena within the framework of a learning theory outlined earlier by Clark Hull, a famous experimental psychologist who worked with animals. These **"neo-Hullian" theorists** rejected Freud's idea that we harbor inborn instincts. Yet they believed that most human behaviors were performed to satisfy unlearned motives such as hunger or sex (which were relabeled **primary drives**) or learned motives such as the needs for affiliation, approval, power, and achievement (which were called **secondary drives**; Dollard & Miller, 1950; Miller & Dollard, 1941). The neo-Hullians scoffed at the Freudian notion of oral and anal fixations that might resurface in the adult personality; yet they viewed the personality as a collection of relatively stable,

learned responses, or **habits**, that can persist for a lifetime because they have proved to be *successful methods of reducing drives*. Whenever a response reduced a drive, it was said to be *reinforced* and was likely to be learned (thus becoming a habit).

An important corollary of the neo-Hullian model was that there can be no learning without reinforcement — and reinforcement required drive reduction. Clearly, this neo-Hullian view of reinforcement was similar to Freud's pleasure principle, which stated that the id will prefer strategies or responses that provide immediate gratification of instinctual needs. So, even though the neo-Hullians used different terminology than Freud did and made a major contribution to the discipline of human development by stressing that many of the motives that guide our behavior might be *learned* rather than innate, their theory was closely tied to Freud's psychoanalytic theory — a viewpoint that contemporary social-learning theorists find difficult to accept. And we will begin to see the basis for this dissatisfaction as we examine the operant-learning theory of B.F. Skinner and the cognitive social-learning theory of Albert Bandura.

Skinner's Operant-Learning Theory

While the neo-Hullians were formulating their theory of social and personality development, Harvard psychologist B.F. Skinner, a disciple of Watson's radical behaviorism, was conducting research with animals and discovering important principles that would lead to yet another social-learning theory — one that served as an important link between the neo-Hullian approach and the viewpoint that many behaviorists favor today. Perhaps Skinner's most radical departure from the earlier neo-Hullian theory was his claim that internal drives play little or no role in human social learning. Instead, he argued that most of the social responses that we acquire are freely emitted *operants* that become either more or less probable as a function of their consequences. Stated another way, Skinner (1953) proposed that the vast majority of behavior (both animal and hu-

PHOTO 3-2   B. F. Skinner (1904–1990) proposed a social-learning theory that emphasized the role of external stimuli in controlling human behavior.

man) is motivated by *external* stimuli—reinforcers and punitive events—rather than internal forces, or drives.

How are these operants acquired? As noted earlier, operant learning occurs when a person emits a response and is reinforced for that action. In Skinner's theoretical framework, a reinforcer is not something that reduces a drive but, rather, any event that increases the probability that a response will be repeated. Thus, if a 3-year-old girl were to comfort her doll while playing, receive a hug from her proud mother, and then resume her comforting with renewed vigor, a Skinnerian would say that the mother's hug had reinforced the girl's nurturant behavior.

Reinforcers may be either *positive* or *negative*. The girl in the preceding example received **positive reinforcement**, because a pleasant or positive stimulus (a hug) was added to the situation after the behavior (comforting) had occurred, and the response was subsequently repeated. Thus, positive reinforcers can be thought of as rewards that are consequences

of a particular behavior. Negative reinforcement, in contrast, is any unpleasant stimulus that is removed from the situation once a particular response has occurred. To illustrate: we've all been in cars in which an obnoxious buzzer sounds until we buckle our seatbelts. "Buckling up" becomes a stronger habit through **negative reinforcement**—that is, we learn to fasten the belt because this act ends the irritating noise. Indeed, the desire to terminate, escape, or avoid unpleasant situations is the basis for many of our habits. If a child finds that he can prevent an aversive scolding by keeping his clothes off his bedroom floor, this kind of "tidying up" should become more probable. If you find that you can avoid an incredibly boring instructor by transferring to another instructor's 8:00 A.M. section of the course, you may well become an early riser. In each of these examples, a behavior is strengthened through negative reinforcement—through the removal or elimination of something unpleasant. However, Skinner believed that most parents, failing to fully appreciate the power of negative reinforcement, rarely use it to influence their children's behavior.

You may be thinking "Wait a minute—virtually all parents use aversive stimuli to control their children's behavior!" And indeed they do. But Skinnerians are careful to distinguish between negative reinforcement and punishment. Recall that a negative reinforcer is an aversive stimulus that is *withdrawn* when the child performs a desirable act (that is, one that the reinforcing agent hopes to instill). By contrast, the most familiar form of punishment involves the *presentation* of an aversive stimulus when the child emits an undesirable response. In other words, the purpose of punishment is roughly opposite to that of reinforcement—to *suppress* unacceptable acts rather than to strengthen acceptable ones.

So it is true that parents often use *punishment* as a means of controlling their children's behavior. And there is a case to be made for its use, particularly when the punished behavior is something dangerous like playing with matches or probing electrical sockets with metallic objects. Yet operant-learning theorists contend that punishment is generally less effective than reinforcement at producing desirable changes in behavior, because punishment merely suppresses ongoing or established responses without teaching anything new. For example, a toddler who is punished for grabbing food with his hands is likely to stop eating altogether rather than to learn to use his spoon. A much simpler way to promote this desirable alternative response is to reinforce it (Skinner, 1953). Operant theorists also note that punishment may have some undesirable side effects, such as making the child angry or resentful toward the punitive agent. There is even some evidence that punishment can backfire and produce effects opposite to those intended, for parents who use harsh forms of punishment in an attempt to suppress their children's aggressive acts often end up raising extremely aggressive children. (We will explore the reason for this paradoxical effect when we take up the topic of aggression in Chapter 10.)

Skinner has taught animals to perform a wide variety of behaviors (including such incredible feats as inducing pigeons to play table tennis) by carefully reinforcing the component responses of these complex behavioral systems. Can children learn socially desirable operants if their parents, teachers, and other agents of socialization carefully shape these responses through the administration of reinforcement? Indeed they can. Even infants are susceptible to operant conditioning, as we see in the following example.

Paul Weisberg (1963) exposed 3-month-old infants to four experimental treatments to see whether he could increase the frequency with which they babbled. The infants in one experimental group received social stimulation in the form of smiles and gentle pats on the tummy whenever they happened to babble (*contingent* social stimulation). A second group was given the same kinds of social stimulation, but these gestures were *noncontingent*; that is, they were presented at random and did not depend on the infants' babbling behavior. Two other groups received nonsocial stimulation (the sound of chimes) that was either contingent or noncontingent on their babbling responses. Weisberg found that neither noncontingent social stimulation nor the sound of chimes was sufficient to reinforce babbling behavior. Babbling (a social operant) became more frequent only when it was accompanied by *contingent* social stimulation.

In analyzing these results, Skinner would argue that it makes little sense to attribute the babbling of these infants to a "babbling instinct," a learned need

to babble, or any other internal motive. Instead, the infants have learned to babble because this response produced *external* stimuli (smiles and pats) that stimulated its repetition.

Weisberg's study is only one of many showing that freely emitted social operants can be conditioned. In fact, it has been argued that a very large percentage of the truly significant human social behaviors are "conditioned" responses established through principles of operant learning (Bijou & Baer, 1978; Gewirtz, 1969; Skinner, 1953).

But are we really on firm ground trying to explain human social learning on the basis of a theory derived from research with animals? Albert Bandura (1977, 1986, 1989) doesn't think so. Bandura (1977) has argued that, even though human social behaviors are subject to the laws of operant conditioning, this does not mean that such behaviors are actually acquired in that way. Furthermore, he has criticized the Skinnerians for their radical behaviorist assumption that *external* stimuli—the reinforcers that accompany responses and the cues that direct these actions—control most human behavior. Instead, Bandura stresses that humans are *cognitive* beings—active information processors—who, unlike animals, are likely to think about the relationships between their behavior and its consequences and who are often more affected by what they *believe* will happen than by the events they actually experience. As an illustration, you need only consider your own plight as a student. Your education is costly and time consuming and may impose many demands that you find less than satisfying. Yet you tolerate the costs and unpleasantries because you can probably *anticipate* greater rewards once you obtain your degree. Your behavior is not shaped by its immediate consequences; if it were, few students would ever make it through the trials and turmoils of college. Instead, you persist as a student because you have *thought about* the long-term benefits of obtaining an education and have decided that they outweigh the short-term costs you must endure.

Perhaps from this critique you can anticipate Bandura's belief that reinforcement plays a very different role in human social learning than that suggested by either the neo-Hullians or the Skinnerians. Let's see what he has to say.

Bandura's Cognitive Social-Learning Theory

When contemporary developmentalists use the term *social-learning theory*, they are undoubtedly referring to the theory of Albert Bandura and his associates (Bandura, 1977, 1986, 1989; Mischel, 1979, 1986). This "Banduran" approach shares some important features with its neo-Hullian and Skinnerian predecessors. For example, all three theories contend that one's personality is largely a product of his or her social-learning experiences. Moreover, the three approaches use roughly the same terminology and consider such concepts as "cue," "response," "reinforcement," "punishment," "acquisition" (learning), and "stimulus generalization" to be important theoretical constructs. But, despite these basic commonalities, Bandura's theory of social learning is very different from the neo-Hullian and Skinnerian approaches.

How Does Bandura Differ from Other Social-Learning Theorists?

Notice that "drive" is not included in the list of important theoretical elements presented above. The Skinnerians were the first to criticize the neo-Hullian view that human behavior is motivated by primary and secondary drives, and Bandura echoes their criticism. He views the term *drive* as a circular motivational label that does little more than *describe* the behavior to which it refers. For example, a drive theorist who observes a person trying to amass a fortune ascribes that behavior to an "acquired drive" for money that can be inferred from the person's "money-seeking" behavior. Bandura (1977) notes:

> It is not the existence of motivated behavior that is being questioned, but whether such behavior is at all explained by ascribing it to the action of [drives]. The limitations of this type of analysis can be illustrated by considering a common activity, such as reading. . . . People spend large sums . . . purchasing reading material; . . . they engage in reading for hours on end; and they can become emotionally upset when deprived of reading material [such as a missed newspaper]. . . .

PHOTO 3-3 Albert Bandura (1925–   ) has emphasized the cognitive aspects of learning in his social-learning theory.

> One could ascribe [reading behavior] to the force of a "reading drive." . . . However, if one wanted to *predict* what people read, when, how long, and the order in which they choose to read different material, one would look not for drives, but for preceding inducements and expected benefits derived from reading [p. 3; italics added].

In other words, Bandura maintains that the social-learning theorist must identify the antecedent stimuli (cues) that trigger a response and the consequences (rewards or punishments) that maintain, alter, or suppress that response before he or she can *explain* why the response occurred. So why do people read? For any number of reasons. One person may be reading because she finds the activity pleasurable; another reader may be studying for an exam; a third may be trying to understand his income-tax form; a fourth may be planning a vacation. To attribute the behavior of these four persons to a "reading drive" is, in Bandura's opinion, a grossly oversimplified analysis of their activities.

To this point, the Skinnerians and the Bandurans are in perfect agreement. But, as we have previously noted, Skinnerian theorists assume that external stimuli—environmental cues and extrinsic reinforcers—are the primary determinants of human behavior. Bandura rejects this assertion because it ignores the individual's cognitive capabilities. Indeed, we will soon see that a response to any particular stimulus or situation depends not so much on the reinforcers or punishments that are actually forthcoming as on the person's impressions, or *cognitive representations*, of the consequences that his actions are likely to have.

Finally, recall that both the neo-Hullians and the Skinnerians assume that a child must first perform a response and then be reinforced for the action before the response will be learned. Bandura disagrees. In 1965 he made what was then considered a radical statement: children can learn by merely observing the behavior of a social model, *even though they have never attempted the responses they have witnessed or received any reinforcement for performing them.* Note the implications here: Bandura is proposing a type of "no trial" learning in which the learned response is not motivated by a drive state, elicited by a conditioned stimulus, or strengthened by a reinforcer. Impossible, said many learning theorists, for Bandura's proposition seems to ignore important principles of both classical and operant conditioning.

AN EXAMPLE OF "NO TRIAL" LEARNING WITHOUT REINFORCEMENT

But Bandura was right, although he first had to conduct what is now considered a classic experiment to prove his point (Bandura, 1965). At the beginning of this experiment, nursery-school children were taken one at a time to a semidarkened room to watch a short film. As they watched, they saw an adult model direct an unusual sequence of aggressive responses toward an inflatable Bobo doll, hitting the doll with a mallet while shouting "Sockeroo!," throwing rubber balls at the doll while shouting "Bang, bang, bang!," and so on (see Photos 3-4). There were three experimental conditions. Children in the *model rewarded* condition saw the film end as a second adult appeared and gave the aggressive model some candy and a soft drink for her "championship performance." Children as-

signed to the *model punished* condition saw an ending in which a second adult scolded and spanked the model for beating up on Bobo. Finally, children in the *no consequences* condition simply watched the model beat up on Bobo without receiving any reward or punishment.

When the film ended, each child was left alone in a playroom that contained a Bobo doll and many of the props that the model had used to work Bobo over. Hidden observers then watched the child, recording all instances in which he or she imitated one or more of the model's aggressive acts. These observations revealed how willing the children were to *perform* the responses they had seen the model display. The results of this "performance" test appear in the left-hand side of Figure 3-2. Here we see that children in the model-rewarded and the no-consequences conditions imitated more of the model's aggressive acts than children who had seen the model punished for aggressive behavior. At the very least, these results indicate that subjects in the first two conditions had learned some rather novel aggressive responses without being reinforced

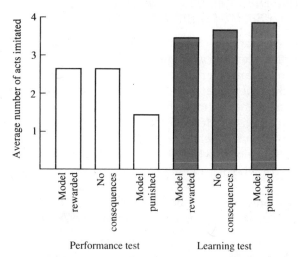

FIGURE 3-2 Average number of aggressive responses imitated during the performance test and the learning test for children who had seen a model rewarded, punished, or receiving no consequences for her actions. (Adapted from "Influence of Models' Reinforcement Contingencies on the Acquisition of Imitative Responses," by A. Bandura. *Journal of Personality and Social Psychology*, 1965, *1*, 589–595. Copyright 1965 by the American Psychological Association. Adapted by permission.)

PHOTOS 3-4 In Bandura's classic experiment, children who had watched an adult model show aggression toward a Bobo doll in several distinctive ways (top row) performed similar acts themselves (middle and bottom rows), even though they hadn't been reinforced for committing such acts.

themselves and without having had a previous opportunity to perform them. This looks very much like the kind of "no trial" observational learning that Bandura had proposed.

THE LEARNING/PERFORMANCE DISTINCTION

But one question remained: had the children in the model-rewarded and the no-consequences conditions actually *learned more* from observing the model than the children who had seen the model punished? To find out, Bandura devised a second test in which he persuaded children to show just how much they had learned. Each child was offered some juice and trinkets for reproducing all of the model's behaviors that he or she could remember. The results of this "learning" test, which appear in the right-hand portion of Figure 3-2, clearly show that children in each of the three conditions learned about the same amount by observing the model. Apparently, children in the model-punished condition had imitated fewer of the model's responses on the initial "performance" test because they felt that they too might be punished for striking Bobo. But, offered a reward, they showed that they had learned much more than their initial performances might have implied.

In sum, it is important to distinguish what children *learn* by observation and their willingness to *perform* these responses. Bandura's (1965) experiment shows that reinforcement is not necessary for observational learning. What reinforcement does is to increase the likelihood that the child will perform that which he or she has already learned by observing the model's behavior.

OBSERVATIONAL LEARNING AS THE PRIMARY DEVELOPMENTAL PROCESS

Bandura (1977) believes that the vast majority of the habits we form during our lifetimes are acquired by observing and imitating other people. According to Bandura, there are several reasons why observational learning plays such a prominent role in social and personality development. First, learning by observation is much more efficient than the trial-and-error method. When observers can learn by watching a model perform flawlessly, they are spared the needless errors that might result from attempts to perfect the same skills and abilities on their own. For this reason, parents soon discover that it is much easier to instill socially acceptable behaviors by displaying or describing these responses for the child than by differentially reinforcing the child's unguided actions. Second, many complex behaviors probably could never be learned unless children were exposed to people who modeled them. Take language, for example. It seems rather implausible that parents could ever shape babbling into words, not to mention grammatical speech, merely by rewarding and punishing these random vocalizations. Yet children who lack some bit of grammatical knowledge will often alter their sentence constructions soon after hearing this rule of grammar reflected in the speech of close companions (Bandura, 1986; Farrar, 1992). Finally, observational learning permits the young child to acquire many new responses in settings where her "models" are simply pursuing their own interests and are not trying to teach her anything in particular. Of course, some of the behaviors that young children observe and may try to imitate are actions that adults display but would like to discourage — practices such as swearing, eating between meals, and smoking. Bandura's point is that children are continually learning both desirable and undesirable responses by "keeping their eyes (and ears) open," and he is not at all surprised that social and personality development proceeds so very rapidly along so many different paths.

How Do We Learn by Observation?

It would be highly inappropriate to conclude that Bandura and his associates are the only social-learning theorists who recognize the importance of observational learning. Both the neo-Hullians (Miller & Dollard, 1941) and Skinner (1953) claimed that many behaviors are acquired through the influence of example; but their theories of imitative learning required that a modeled response be *performed* by the observer and then *reinforced* before it could be learned.

Perhaps you can see the problem with these theories. They certainly cannot explain the results of Bandura's (1965) experiment or any example of **deferred imitation**, whereby (1) the observer does not imitate the modeled response in the setting where it occurred, (2) reinforcement is not forthcoming to either the model or the observer, and (3) the observer does not display the acquired response until days, weeks, or even months later. Instances of deferred imitation are common among children. Almost every young boy watches his father shave and then tries to shave himself at a later date when Daddy is no longer present to serve as "shaving" model. In this case the model was not reinforced for shaving and is not likely to reinforce his son for undertaking what is clearly a dangerous activity for little boys.

How, then, does the child acquire the component responses involved in the act of shaving? Bandura suggests that this and all other successful instances of imitative learning occur *while the observer attends to the model and before the observer's imitative responses have been performed or reinforced*. What the observer acquires is **symbolic representations** of the model's behavior, which are stored in memory and retrieved at a later date to guide his own attempts to imitate. Bandura contends that the acquisition of modeled behavior is governed by four interrelated processes: *attention, retention, motoric reproduction*, and *motivation*.

Attentional process.   Virtually all children are exposed to a large number of social models, including parents, teachers, siblings, peers, scout leaders, and media heroes. However, Bandura (1977) notes that (1) a child must first attend carefully to any model to learn by observation, and (2) some models are more worthy of attention than others.

Whom are young children likely to select as social models? According to Bandura (1977), the most likely candidates are people who are warm and nurturant (socially responsive) and/or appear competent and powerful. Indeed, Joan Grusec and Rona Abramovitch (1982) found that nursery-school children will often attend to and imitate their teachers (powerful, competent models) and those classmates who are typically warm and responsive to them. Moreover, 5–10-year-olds prefer to imitate agemates or older models rather than a younger child, undoubtedly because they believe that younger children are less competent than they are (Brody, Graziano, & Musser, 1983; French, 1984).

Attainment of certain development milestones will also affect the child's choice of models. For example, once children are fully aware of their gender and know that it will never change (a milestone usually reached between 5 and 7 years of age), they will pay much more attention to models of their own sex (Slaby & Frey, 1975). As people mature, they develop certain interests, attitudes, and values and will normally prefer models who are in some way similar to themselves—friends or people in the same occupation, ethnic group, political party, and so on. But, even though our choice of models may become somewhat more restricted over time, we continue to learn by observing others throughout life.

Retention processes. An observer must also commit the model's behavior to memory if he or she is to reproduce these responses later, when the model is no longer present to serve as a guide. According to Bandura (1977), observers use two methods to retain the important elements of a modeled sequence. The first is the **imaginal representational system**; observers simply form retrievable sensory images of what they have seen. For example, a boy may attend to the acrobatics of a basketball star such as Michael Jordan, form images of what he has seen, and then use these images to guide his own play on the basketball court. Observers may also make use of the **verbal representational system** by translating what they have observed into summary verbal labels. Verbal representation is particularly important, for it enables the observer to retain information that would be difficult or impossible to remember by any other method. Imagine how hard it would be to open a combination safe if you simply formed images of the model turning the dial and did not trans-

late these actions into a verbal label such as "L49, R37, L18"!

Apparently, symbolic coding activities do facilitate observational learning. For example, children who are told to describe a model's actions as they observe them are later able to reproduce *more* of these responses than children who do not describe the model's behavior (Coates & Hartup, 1969). By contrast, children who are prevented from verbally encoding a model's behavior (by counting to themselves as they watch the model) are *less* capable of reproducing the model's actions than those who did not perform distracting mental activities (Bandura, Grusec, & Menlove, 1966).

Motoric reproduction processes. Symbolic representations of a modeled sequence must be translated into action before the observer can be said to have imitated the model's behavior. The rate at which this motoric reproduction unfolds depends, in part, on the observer's ability to execute all the component responses. Learners who possess the requisite skills may be able to achieve errorless imitation with little or no practice, but, if one or more constituent responses are lacking, the observer will fail to emulate the model. That is, we often learn things from models that we cannot reproduce ourselves. For example, a 4'2" boy may have acquired and retained symbolic representations of Michael Jordan's moves to the basket, but, lacking the height and agility of this amazing basketball star, he won't be able to execute a whirlybird dunk.

The adage "Practice makes perfect" certainly applies to much of our observational learning. As a novice golfer, I studied many books and "pro shop" films in an attempt to learn all facets of the Jack Nicklaus swing. I knew all the "rules"—left arm straight, head down, eyes on the ball—but I had real problems reproducing Jack's swing (or at least its results). One of my problems was that I was unable to observe my own swing to determine whether it matched my symbolic representation of the Nicklaus swing. By consulting with other golfers and by making self-corrective adjustments based on the results I was achieving, I finally developed a golf swing that satisfied me (although it would hardly have satisfied Jack Nicklaus). Bandura would describe my experiences as fairly typical, for he argues that "in most everyday learning, people usually achieve only rough approximations of new patterns of behavior by modeling and [then] refine them through self-corrective adjustments on the basis of informative feedback from performance" (1971, p. 8).

Motivational processes (reinforcement). Bandura distinguishes acquisition (learning) from performance, because people do not enact everything they learn. Recall that children in the model-punished condition of Bandura's (1965) experiment were initially quite reluctant to imitate the model's aggressive responses. They had seen the model spanked for her actions and might well have assumed that they would be punished for imitating her behavior. But, when the children were offered incentives to imitate, learned responses that had previously been inhibited were promptly translated into action. These data led Bandura to conclude that the main function of both direct and vicarious reinforcement is to regulate the *performance* of learned behavior.[1]

However, Bandura (1969) concedes that reinforcement may play a small part in the acquisition of modeled responses. If an observer knows *in advance* that he will be reinforced for correctly imitating a model, this promise of reward should motivate him to attend carefully to the model's actions and to expend some effort in retaining what he has witnessed. Thus, incentives that are anticipated before observing the model's behavior may indeed promote observational *learning*.

Clearly, what is new about Bandura's theory is the proposition that observational learning is primarily a *cognitive* activity that requires neither the enactment nor the reinforcement of the responses we acquire. Yet it can also be argued that our willingness to *perform* learned responses is also under cognitive control. In the Bandura (1965) experiment, for example, children who had seen the model rewarded for aggressive behavior were initially much more willing to imitate the model's actions than were those who had seen the model punished. While observing the consequences of the model's behavior, these youngsters had formed very different impressions (that is, cognitions) about the likely outcomes of their own imitative responses—impressions that then affected their willingness to display what they had learned by observation. According to Bandura, what determines whether we will enact the responses we have learned is not the actual consequences we receive for performing such acts but, rather, the consequences we expect to receive. And Bandura's (1965) experiment proves his point: when children in the model-punished condition were later led to expect positive outcomes for imitating the model, they became every bit as willing to do so as their counterparts in the model-rewarded condition.

Developmental Trends in Imitation and Observational Learning

Bandura's theory of observational learning assumes that an observer can construct images or other symbolic representations of a model's behavior and then use these mediators to reproduce what he or she has witnessed. When do these capabilities first appear? When do children begin to take advantage of their emerging powers of observation to acquire important new skills? And how does the character of observational learning change over time? Although Bandura had little to say about these important issues, other researchers have addressed them and have provided some answers.

Origins of imitation and observational learning. Although neonates are able to imitate a limited number of motor responses, such as sticking out their tongue (Kaitz et al., 1988), moving their head as an adult model does (Meltzoff & Moore, 1989), and possibly even mimicking facial expressions of happiness and sadness (Field et al., 1982), these early imitative capabilities soon disappear and may be nothing more than involuntary reflexes (Abravanel & Sigafoos, 1984; Vinter, 1986).[2] Volun-

---

[1]Vicarious consequences are the reinforcers and punishments experienced by social models. Bandura's (1965) experiment showed that the consequences of the model's behavior affected the willingness of observers to display what they had learned through observation. Thus, vicarious rewards and punishments are thought to regulate the performance of learned responses in much the same way as rewards and punishments that are administered directly to the learner.

[2]Nevertheless, as we will see in Chapter 5, this early reflexlike imitation and other neonatal reflexes may play an important role in promoting emotional attachments between caregivers and their infants.

tary imitation of novel responses first appears and becomes more reliable between 8 and 12 months of age (Piaget, 1951). Initially the model must be present and must continue to perform a response before the child is able to imitate. But by age 9 months some infants can imitate very simple acts with a toy up to 24 hours after they first witness them (Meltzoff, 1988c). This *deferred imitation*—the ability to reproduce the actions of a model at some point in the future—develops rapidly during the second year. By age 14 months nearly half the infants in one study imitated the simple actions of a *televised* model after a 24-hour delay (Meltzoff, 1988a), and nearly all the 14-month-olds in a second experiment were able to imitate at least three (of six) novel behaviors displayed by a live model *after a delay of one week* (Meltzoff, 1988b).

Clearly, deferred imitation is an important developmental milestone. It indicates that children are now capable of constructing symbolic representations of their experiences and then retrieving this information from memory to guide their reproduction of past events. So 14- to 24-month-old infants should now be prepared to *learn* a great deal by observing the behavior of their companions. But do they take advantage of their newly acquired imitative capabilities?

Perhaps not right away they don't. Leon Kuczynski and his associates (1987) asked mothers to record the immediate and the delayed reactions of their 12–20-month-old infants and their 25–33-month-old toddlers to the behavior of parental and peer models. The results were quite interesting. All the children imitated their models a fair percentage of the time, but there were clear age differences in the content of these imitations. The 12–20-month-olds tended to imitate affective displays, such as laughing and cheering, and other high-intensity antics like jumping, shaking the hand to and fro, and pounding on the table. In other words, their imitations were largely playful in character. By contrast, the 25–33-month-olds more often imitated *instrumental* behaviors, such as household tasks and self-care routines, and their imitations had more of a self-instructional quality to them, as if the older toddlers were now making an active attempt to (1) acquire skills their models had displayed or (2) understand the events they had witnessed. When

PHOTO 3-5   By age 2, toddlers are already acquiring important personal and social skills by imitating the adaptive acts of older social models.

imitating disciplinary encounters, for example, the 12–20-month-olds simply repeated verbal prohibitions and physical actions such as hand slapping, usually directing these responses to themselves. However, the older toddlers tended to reenact the entire scenario, including the social-influence strategies the disciplinarian had used, and they usually directed these responses to another person, an animal, or a doll. So it seems that, between the ages of 2 and 3, observational *learning* is becoming an important means by which children acquire basic personal and social competencies and gain a richer understanding of the rules and regulations they are expected to follow.

A later development in observational learning: Use of verbal mediators.   Although preschool children are rapidly acquiring language and becoming more accomplished as conversationalists, they are less likely than older children to rely on verbal labels to help them retain modeled sequences. In the study by Coates and Hartup (1969) mentioned earlier, 4–5-year-olds and 7–8-year-olds watched a short film in which an adult model displayed a number of unusual responses, such as shooting at a tower of blocks with a pop gun and throwing a beanbag between his legs. Some of the children from each age group were told to describe the model's actions as they observed them (*induced-verbalization condition*); others simply watched the model without having received any instructions (*passive-observation condition*). As shown in Figure 3-3, 4–5-year-olds who described what they were observing were later able to reproduce much more of the model's behavior than their agemates in the passive-observation condition. By contrast, 7–8-year-olds reproduced the same number of model's responses, whether or not they had been told to describe what the model was doing. This latter finding suggests that 7–8-year-olds will use verbal labels to describe what they have seen, even if they are not told to. One important implication of this study is that preschool children may generally learn *less* from social models

because they, unlike older children, do not spontaneously produce the verbal mediators that would help them retain what they have observed.

Beyond Observational Learning: Self-Regulation through Self-Produced Consequences

An adequate theory of social and personality development must explain not only how habits and behavioral tendencies are acquired but also how they are regulated and maintained. Bandura (1977, 1986) concedes that many of our habits and mannerisms are profoundly affected by the approving or disapproving responses they elicit from other people. But he also notes that people often misinterpret the idea that "human behavior is controlled by its consequences" to mean that our actions are "at the mercy of" environmental influences. Bandura's counterargument is that much of human behavior is **self-regulated** by *self-produced consequences* (self-reinforcement).

An artist who sculpts a bust from clay does not require someone at her side to differentially reinforce her every move until an acceptable product emerges. Rather, the artist has her own idea of what constitutes acceptable work and will perform self-corrective adjustments until her project meets these standards. The result of this self-scrutinizing may often be a product that far exceeds the standards of acceptable art for the layperson or, indeed, for other artists. I once knew an artist who, in his own words, had never created a "finished" product, because he was never satisfied with any of his paintings. Although this person made a substantial sum of money from the sale of his work, his failure to match his own standards of artistic merit was the major impetus for his eventual selection of another occupation.

This example of self-monitoring is not at all unusual. Bandura contends that people set **performance standards** for themselves in many areas and respond to their accomplishments either positively or negatively in accordance with these self-imposed demands.

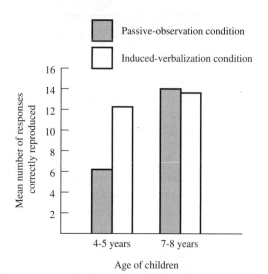

Passive-observation condition

Induced-verbalization condition

Age of children

FIGURE 3-3 Children's ability to reproduce the behavior of a social model as a function of age and verbalization instructions. (Adapted from "Age and Verbalization in Observational Learning," by B. Coates and W. W. Hartup. *Developmental Psychology*, 1969, *1*, 556–562. Copyright © 1969 by the American Psychological Association. Adapted by permission of the authors.)

Origins of performance standards. According to Bandura (1977), children acquire their performance

standards through *direct tuition* and *observational learning*. Parents often try to teach or instill certain performance standards by offering their child incentives for behavior that meets or exceeds these criteria. For example, a mother may praise her son or provide him with some material reinforcer (such as money or toys) for every grade of "B" or above on his report card. As a result of this reinforcement, the child may come to consider the grade "B" an indication of a job well done and respond to his subsequent academic accomplishments in a self-approving or self-critical fashion depending on their departure from this acquired performance standard.

Several experiments (reviewed in Bandura, 1971) show that children also learn standards of self-reinforcement displayed by social models and use these performance criteria to evaluate their own social behavior. Of course, some models are more effective in this regard than others. Generally speaking, children attempt to compare themselves with models who are similar to themselves in competence or ability. For example, a 4-year-old who is learning to swim will most likely compare her accomplishments with those of other novice swimmers.

According to Bandura (1971, 1986), the performance standards we adopt for ourselves will play a major role in shaping our self-concepts. Bandura defines *self-esteem* in terms of the discrepancies between a person's behavior and the accomplishments that he or she has selected as indications of personal merit. A man who consistently fails to satisfy his self-imposed behavioral demands will evaluate himself negatively and be low in self-esteem. But, if his accomplishments frequently match or exceed his performance standards, he will think well of himself and enjoy high self-esteem. Thus a person's feelings about the self depend on more than his or her absolute accomplishments and the reactions of others to these accomplishments; rather, the self-concept depends on the "goodness of fit" between one's behavior and one's *own* performance expectancies. Bandura notes that many very competent people who clearly "have it made" in the eyes of others may hold negative opinions of themselves for failing to reach their own lofty aspirations. He concludes that:

a harsh system of self-reinforcement gives rise to depressive reactions, chronic discouragement, feelings of worthlessness, and a lack of purposefulness. Excessive self-disparagement, in fact, is one of the defining characteristics of psychotic depression. [Researchers] have shown [that] depressed adults evaluate their performances as significantly poorer than do nondepressed subjects, even though their actual achievements are the same [1971, p. 31].

Why do we adhere to exacting performance standards?   Much of our self-regulated conduct centers on behaviors that we must inhibit (for example, snitching cookies between meals) or on other activities that originally were of little intrinsic interest to us. To illustrate: Few children enter grammar school with a strong desire to excel at particular subjects such as language or arithmetic. Yet, once they set performance standards to aim for (such as doing all their homework every day), many students will forgo interesting TV programs and other enticements until they have achieved their objectives. They may even feel so good about their perseverance that they actively reward themselves for their accomplishments (for example, by treating themselves to an ice-cream cone or a movie). And, should someone fail to meet an exacting standard, her self-imposed punishment can take many forms, not the least of which may be feeling very bad about herself.

Bandura is not at all impressed by the fact that people monitor their performances and often reward themselves. From his perspective, the challenging questions that must be answered are "Why do people *deny* themselves available rewards over which they have full control, why do they adhere to exacting standards that require difficult performances, and why do they *punish* themselves?" (1971, p. 33; italics added).

Bandura concedes that external incentives such as praise, social recognition, and awards surely contribute to the maintenance of high performance standards, whereas few accolades are bestowed on people who reward themselves for mediocre accomplishments. Modeling influences may also contribute to the maintenance of high standards; a person who often sees others refuse to reward themselves for substandard performances is less likely to reinforce

BOX 3-1 | *Delaying Gratification: Early Evidence of Self-Regulation and Self-Control*

Self-regulation is a crucial aspect of human development—one that allows us to generate our own consequences and control our own behavior, thus freeing ourselves from having to behave like weather vanes, constantly shifting in different directions in response to the momentary pushes and pulls of our immediate environments (Bandura, 1986). Social-learning theorists such as Walter Mischel and Ignatius Toner have looked for early signs of self-regulation by studying children's attempts to delay gratification. In a **"delay of gratification"** study the child is usually given a choice between two alternatives: a small reward that is available immediately or a larger reward that can only be obtained later. Of course, this choice mirrors the kinds of decisions that both children and adults must often make—choices such as deciding whether to spend this week's allowance on an inexpensive toy today or to save for several weeks for a better one, or contemplating whether to invest in an ultrasafe Treasury bond that pays small but regular dividends or to back a new but risky "growth" stock that provides no current return but could pay megadividends in the years to come. Walter Mischel (1986) argues that the ability to defer immediate gratification is absolutely essential for the attainment of all meaningful long-term goals and that an inability to resist immediate temptations spells trouble. For example:

> Inadequate delay patterns often are partial causes of antisocial and criminal conduct . . . and may victimize the individual by guaranteeing an endless chain of failure experiences. Consider, for example, the "high school dropout" who leaves school because he cannot tolerate postponing pleasures and working for more distant goals. His school failure may sentence him to future vocational hardships and prevent him from achieving durable satisfaction [p. 415].

When do children begin to delay gratification, and how do they manage to do so? Interestingly, some 2½-year-olds already show at least some limited capacity to resist immediate temptations (Vaughn, Kopp, & Krakow, 1984), although preschool children normally find it very difficult to maintain their resolve when the enticements they must resist are in plain sight (Mischel & Ebbesen, 1970; Toner & Smith, 1977). Preschoolers who are the most successful at overcoming visible temptations are those who use such *distractive* techniques as inventing games to play while waiting for the delayed reward or covering their eyes to shield themselves from the enticing alternative (Mischel & Ebbesen, 1970). Notice, then, that children's early ability to defer immediate gratification comes from *within* and is under *cognitive* control; that is, by distracting themselves, these high-delay children were able to regulate their conduct by *cognitively* transforming a potentially frustrating situation into a tolerable one.

Further evidence that the capacity for delay comes from within and is cognitively mediated stems from a study of delay patterns among kindergartners through second-graders (Toner, Moore, & Emmons, 1980). One goal of this experiment was to influence children's self-concepts by labeling some of them as "patient" individuals. Before beginning the delay-of-gratification task, the experimenter casually mentioned to half of the children "I hear that you are patient because you can wait for nice things when you can't get them right away." The remaining children heard the task-irrelevant attribution "I hear that you have some very nice friends at school." The results were clear: even when no one was present to monitor their behavior, children who had been labeled as patient were able to delay gratification far longer than those who had been labeled as having nice friends. So it seems that having an image of themselves as patient, self-disciplined individuals (a cognitive judgment about the self) helps children to maintain their resolve in the face of temptation.

We have only touched on the topic of self-regulation here, to illustrate Bandura's claim that the basis for many truly significant attributes lies within the individual and *not* in the external environment. In Chapter 7 we will take a closer look at the growth of internal regulatory mechanisms and will see that a firm sense of self-control eventually becomes (for those who achieve it) a valued aspect of the self-concept—one that predicts success and happiness in the years ahead.

his own trivial accomplishments. But in recent years Bandura (1982, 1986, 1989) has argued that the primary basis for self-denial and for adherence to exacting performance standards comes not from the external environment but from *within* the individual (see Box 3-1 for an illustration of this point in regard to young children's emerging abilities to delay immediate gratification). Once we set goals for which to strive, *self*-satisfaction becomes conditional upon making reasonable progress to achieve these objectives. Accordingly, we feel extremely proud, competent, or "efficacious" when we succeed, and we may feel anxious, guilty, shameful, or downright incompetent should our performances fall short of our self-imposed demands. So *cognitively based* perceptions of competence or **self-efficacy** stemming from successes contribute in a major way to the maintenance of high performance standards.

Self-efficacy as a contributor to personal development. Just how important are these feelings of self-efficacy for social and personality development? Bandura suggests that they may be crucial. His own research (Bandura, 1982, 1986, 1989) has shown that children are most likely to undertake, persist at, and ultimately succeed at novel or ambiguous tasks that they think they are capable of mastering, whereas they tend to avoid or give up on activities at which they feel less capable or efficacious. Research with adults paints a similar picture. For example, subjects who feel efficacious at such behaviors as stopping smoking or losing weight are much *less* inclined than those with low perceived self-efficacy to continue their smoking habits (Baer, Holt, & Lichtenstein, 1986) or to drop out of Weight Watchers programs (Mitchell & Stuart, 1984).

So our perceived self-efficacies may be more important than our actual accomplishments at determining our interests, objectives, and other personal attributes. Consider one developmental implication of this observation. If parents were to repeatedly tell their daughter that math is something "boys do better at," these statements might persuade the girl to devote less time to math than to her other classes, resulting, perhaps, in lower math grades, in "math anxiety," or in the perception that she is not very good at this subject. Not feeling particularly effi-

cacious at math, the girl may subsequently choose to avoid taking electives in math, statistics, or computer science, thereby barring the doors to many occupations that depend heavily on well-developed quantitative skills. Bandura (1982, 1986) suggests that each of us is constantly processing, evaluating, and reevaluating information about our strengths and weaknesses, thereby forming a unique pattern of self-perceived competencies. These perceptions of self-efficacy then affect the activities we choose to pursue (or to avoid), thus largely determining who we are and what we are likely to become.

Social Learning as Reciprocal Determinism

Early versions of social-learning theory were largely tributes to John Watson's *doctrine of environmental determinism*: young, unknowing children were viewed as passive recipients of environmental influence who would become whatever parents, teachers, and other agents of society groomed them to be. In fact, B. F. Skinner, the famous "radical behaviorist" of recent times, has taken a position that many students find hard to accept: not only are we products of our experiences, but we have little to say in determining the character of those experiences. In other words, Skinner (1971) is arguing that "free will," or the concept of conscious choice, is merely an illusion.

Now contrast Skinner's position with that of Bandura (1977), who has repeatedly emphasized that children are active, thinking beings who contribute in many ways to their own development. Observational learning, for example, requires the observer to actively attend to, encode, and retain the behaviors displayed by social models. Moreover, children are often free to choose the models to whom they will attend; hence they have some say about what they will learn from others.

Recently, Bandura (1986) has proposed the concept of **reciprocal determinism** to describe his view that human development reflects an interaction among the person (*P*), the person's behavior (*B*), and the environment (*E*) (see Figure 3-4). Unlike the early behaviorists, who maintained that the environment (*E*) shaped the child and his (her) behavior,

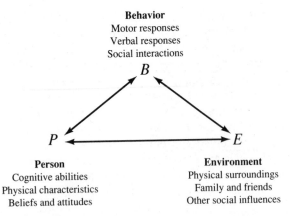

Behavior
Motor responses
Verbal responses
Social interactions

B

P   *E*

Person
Cognitive abilities
Physical characteristics
Beliefs and attitudes

Environment
Physical surroundings
Family and friends
Other social influences

FIGURE 3-4 Bandura's model of reciprocal determinism. (Adapted from A. Bandura, "The Self System in Reciprocal Determinism." *American Psychologist*, 1978, 33, 344–358. Copyright © 1978 by the American Psychological Association.)

Bandura and others (most notably Richard Bell, 1979) propose that the links among persons, behaviors, and environments are bidirectional, so that children may influence their environments by virtue of their own conduct. Consider an example.

Suppose a 4-year-old discovers that he can gain control of desirable toys by assaulting his playmates. In this case, control of a desired toy is a satisfying outcome that reinforces the child's aggressive behavior. But note that the reinforcer here is produced by the child himself—through his aggressive actions. Not only has bullying behavior been reinforced (by obtaining the toy), but *the character of the play environment has changed*. Our bully becomes more inclined to victimize his playmates in the future, and those playmates who are victimized may become even more inclined to "give in" to the bully (see Figure 3-5).

In sum, cognitive-learning theorists such as Bandura (1986) and Richard Bell (1979) characterize social and personality development as a continuous *reciprocal interaction* between children and their environments. The situation or "environment" that a child experiences will surely affect her, but her behavior is thought to affect the environment as well. The implication is that children are actively involved in shaping the very environments that will influence their growth and development.

Evaluation of Social-Learning Theory

"The more things change, the more they remain the same." It might be argued that this epigram describes the evolution of social-learning theory. Recall that John Watson, the first social-learning theorist, objected to the study of subjective, mentalistic phenomena. He argued that overt behavior was the appropriate subject matter for psychologists and that virtually all such behavior was determined by forces external to the organism. The neo-Hullians largely agreed with Watson, except for their assertion that certain organismic characteristics, such as primary and secondary drives, are important determinants of behavior. Next came the Skinnerians, who took Watson quite literally. Skinner and his disciples argued that drives and cognitive activities are unnecessary to explain behavior. From their perspective, human behavior is controlled by external stimuli that evoke various responses and by reinforcing (or punishing) stimuli that maintain, alter, or suppress these responses. But the circle has definitely closed. Bandura and his associates emphasize that children do have "minds," which they use to affect the course and outcome of their development. Thus it is fair to say that most contemporary social-learning theorists are once again interested in the "mentalistic" determinants of behavior.

Contributions of Social-Learning Theory

Developmentalists have benefited from the social-learning viewpoint in many ways. One very positive feature of this approach (indeed, Watson's most enduring legacy; see Horowitz, 1992) is that social-learning theorists stress *objectivity* in all phases of their work. Their units of analysis are typically objective behavioral responses rather than subjective phenomena that are hard to observe or measure. They carefully define their concepts, make clear-cut predictions, and conduct tightly controlled experiments to provide objective evidence for the suspected causes of developmental change. The dem-

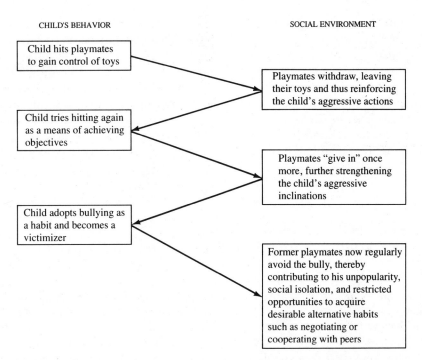

CHILD'S BEHAVIOR   SOCIAL ENVIRONMENT

FIGURE 3-5   Reciprocal determinism: A hypothetical example showing how a child both influences and is influenced by the social environment.

onstrated success of their approach has encouraged researchers from all theoretical backgrounds to become more objective when studying developing children.

The learning theorist's emphasis on overt behavior and its immediate causes has also produced a number of important clinical insights and practical applications. For example, many problem behaviors can now be treated rapidly by various behavior-modification techniques in which the therapist (1) identifies the reinforcers that sustain undesirable habits and eliminates them while (2) reinforcing alternative behaviors that are more socially desirable. Thus, childhood phobias such as a fear of school can often be eliminated in a matter of days or weeks, rather than the months (or years) that a psychoanalyst might take to probe the child's unconscious, trying to find the underlying conflict that is producing the phobic reaction.

But surely the major contribution of the social-learning approach is the wealth of information it has provided about developing children. After studying how children interpret, react to, and even shape their immediate environments, social-learning theorists have helped us to understand how and why children form emotional attachments to others, adopt sex roles, become interested in doing well at school, learn to abide by moral rules, attain (or lose) status with their peers, make friends, and so on. Throughout this text we will see that much of what we know about social and personality development stems from the research of social-learning theorists.

Criticisms of the Social-Learning Viewpoint

Despite its strengths, many view the social-learning approach as an oversimplified account of social and personality development. Consider its explanation of individual differences: presumably, individuals follow different developmental paths because no two persons grow up in exactly the same environment.

Yet critics are quick to note that each person comes into the world with something else that constitutes an equally plausible explanation for his or her "individuality" — a unique genetic inheritance. Children also mature at different rates, a factor that affects how other people will respond to them (for an interesting example, see the material in Chapter 15 on rate of maturation and popularity) and how they will react to the behavior of other people. The point is that our genetic characteristics and maturational timetables may have direct effects on development, or they may have indirect effects by determining what we are capable of learning (or would find reinforcing) at any given point in life. And when we recall the "behavior genetics" argument that our genotypes may affect the kinds of environments that we prefer and seek out, it does appear that social-learning theorists may have oversimplified the issue

---

BOX 3-2

Collaborative (Guided) Learning: The "Social" Learning That Social-Learning Theorists Overlooked

Social-learning theorists contend that adults teach children literally thousands of important lessons in either of two ways: (1) through *direct tuition* (that is, shaping the child's conduct with reinforcers and punishments) and (2) by serving as models for *observational learning*. Russian developmentalist Lev Vygotsky (1934/1962, 1978) has described a third kind of social instruction that he believes to be the most common and effective means by which parents and other more competent associates transmit significant aspects of culture to developing children. Vygotsky's brand of social learning occurs within the context of cooperative or collaborative *dialogues* between a skillful tutor, who transmits verbal instructions, and a novice pupil, who first assimilates (or internalizes) this information and then uses it to regulate his or her own activities.

Vygotsky claims that collaborative (or guided) learning occurs within the child's **zone of proximal development** — a term he uses to describe tasks that are too difficult for the child to master on his own but that can be accomplished with the assistance and encouragement of a more skillful associate. To illustrate collaborative learning as Vygotsky sees it, let's imagine that a 4-year-old boy is eager to learn to hit a wiffle ball with his plastic bat; try as he might, however, he cannot make contact when Dad pitches to him. His father, noticing that the boy always takes his eye off the ball and holds his arms too close to his body, quickly concludes that his son is not about to become a junior Babe Ruth without assistance. How might this father then proceed to help his son become a better hitter?

According to Vygotsky, the role of the more skillful collaborator is (1) to organize the learning activity so as to capitalize on the child's current abilities, (2) to then provide guidance or instruction that is within the child's capacity to understand, and, finally, (3) to encourage the child to give the activity a try. So our father, thinking that his son can't hit what he doesn't track, might first build a tee so that the wiffle ball can remain *stationary*. He then places the boy beside the tee and gives relevant verbal instructions ("bring your arms out," "keep your head up," and "WATCH THE BALL") before encouraging his son to knock the ball into the next county.

Vygotsky assumes that the child's role in collaborative learning is to take the language of the verbal instructions and use it to guide his own activities. Thus our 4-year-old might blurt "arms out" or "watch the ball" as he takes his first several dozen swings at it. As the boy learns these initial lessons, the father will provide new and more complex instructions (such as "turn your hips as you swing") to increase his son's skills, whereas the boy will verbalize these new directives (out loud or to himself) as he continues to refine his techniques. After several such dialogues (or exchanges of information), the boy should have internalized a pretty fair verbal representation of the component skills involved in batting and may now be ready to put this "private speech" to good use in guiding his attempts to hit a moving ball.

In sum, collaborative learning does not depend on the direct tuition (shaping) of new responses; nor does

of individual difference in development by downplaying the contribution of important biological factors.

Each of the social-learning theories we have reviewed is incomplete in other ways as well. For example, each chronicles one particular kind of learning as the central developmental process; for Watson it was classical conditioning, whereas Skinner championed operant learning and Bandura emphasizes observational learning. Yet, even if we become integrative theorists and concede that all these forms of learning contribute importantly to human development, apparently none of our social-learning theorists recognized the significance of *collaborative (or guided) learning*—a strategy by which human beings (and only human beings) transmit much of their culture to each successive generation (Vygotsky, 1934/1962, 1978). In Box 3-2 we take

---

BOX 3-2 | *continued*

it rest solely on lessons learned by observation (although the tutor's demonstrations of the new skill or activity may often help to clarify his or her verbal instructions). Instead, guided learning is really more of an "apprenticeship" in thinking and doing—one in which novice children learn any number of culturally relevant skills and activities through their day-to-day, "hands-on" participation in such activities, with the guidance of their parents, teachers, older siblings, or more skillful and accomplished peers (Rogoff, 1990).

Although Vygotsky developed his theory in the early part of this century, many of his works have only recently been translated from Russian. However, his ideas have already captured the attention of developmentalists, who are busily conducting research to determine how parents instruct their children and what children gain from collaborative learning experiences. To date, the research supports Vygotsky's claim that, given appropriate adult support and encouragement, children can often learn new activities and perform complex tasks that they were unable to carry out on their own (Diaz, Neal, & Vachio, 1991; Freund, 1990; Rogoff, 1990). Similar advances in problem-solving skills have been reported when children collaborate with peers as opposed to working alone (Gauvain & Rogoff, 1989), and the youngsters who gain the most from these collaborations are those who were initially much less competent than their partners (Azmitia, 1988; Radziszewska & Rogoff, 1991). So collaborative (or guided) learning, which can occur only through *social* transactions between tutor and tutee, appears to be

a very meaningful socialization process—and one that social-learning theorists seem to have overlooked.

According to Vygotsky, new skills are often easier to acquire if children receive guidance and encouragement from a more competent associate.

a closer look at this important kind of "social" learning.

Is the social-learning approach truly a developmental theory? Many critics claim that it is not, and they do so with some degree of justification. Nowhere in any social-learning theory do we find references to ages and stages of development or to qualitatively different levels of functioning. Social-learning theorists have been much more concerned with outlining a general set of principles to explain how people of *all* ages learn from their experiences, forming new habits and discarding old ones. So the social-learning approach is a "process" approach that has little to say about age-related changes in either the character of social learning itself or the kinds of behaviors it permits developing persons to acquire.

Despite the popularity of recent cognitively oriented learning theories that stress the child's active role in the developmental process, there are those who say that *no* social-learning theorist pays enough attention to the *cognitive* determinants of development. Proponents of this "cognitive-developmental" viewpoint believe that a child's cognitive abilities undergo a series of qualitative changes (or stages) that social-learning theorists completely ignore. Further, they argue that a child's impressions of and reactions to the social environment depend on his or her level of **cognitive development**. Over the past 20 years this "cognitive" perspective on social and personality development has attracted many followers, for reasons that should become quite apparent in our next chapter as we review the basic premises and implications of this interesting approach.

Finally, there is another group of critics who heartily agree with social-learning theorists that one's social and personality development depends very heavily on one's transactions with the environment. However, these critics argue that the "environment" that so powerfully influences development is really a series of social systems that interact with one another (and with the individual) in complex ways that are impossible to simulate in a laboratory. In the final section of this chapter we will briefly examine this *ecological (or contextual) perspective* and see why its proponents insist that only by studying people in their natural settings are we likely to understand how environments truly influence development.

The Ecological (or Contextual) Perspective

Although social-learning theorists are often cited as the strongest advocates of an "environmentalist" perspective on human development, there is another group of developmentalists who have offered a much richer conceptualization of environment and environmental influences than any other currently available. The **ecological perspective** to which these developmentalists adhere is not really a new theoretical model; strong proponents of any of the theories we have reviewed (or will review) can be found among the ranks of ecological psychologists. Instead, it is more accurately characterized as a different way of thinking about human development and a different approach to studying the factors that influence it (Vasta, Haith, & Miller, 1992).

To compare the ecological viewpoint with social-learning theory, let's imagine a discussion in which leading "environmentalists" are brought together and asked to respond to a very straightforward question: "What is this entity you people call environment?" In Chapter 2 we criticized the behavior geneticists for being vague on this issue, and, interestingly enough, social-learning theorists aren't much better. Traditional views offered by Watson and Skinner depict "environment" as any and all external forces that shape the individual's development. Although modern learning theorists (for example, Bandura, 1986) have backed away from this extremely mechanistic view by citing the principle of *reciprocal determinism* and acknowledging that environments both influence and *are influenced by* individuals, they continue to provide only vague descriptions of the environmental contexts in which development takes place.

What is the ecological viewpoint on environment? Perhaps the most detailed analysis of environment and environmental influences that has appeared to date is Urie Bronfenbrenner's (1979, 1989) **ecological systems model** of human development. Bronfenbrenner begins with one of the same assumptions that ethologists make: that *natural* environments are the major source of influence on developing children and adolescents—a source that is often overlooked (or simply ignored) by researchers

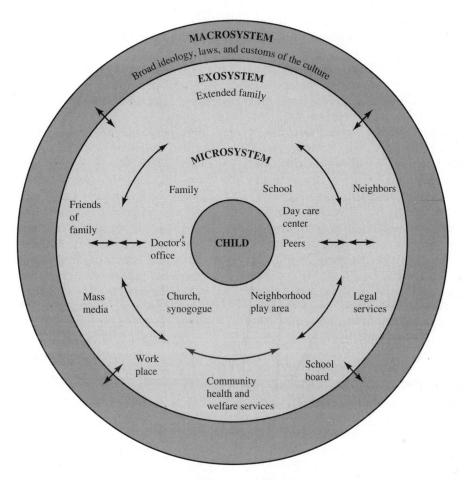

FIGURE 3-6   Bronfenbrenner's ecological model of the environment as a series of nested structures. The microsystem refers to relations between the child and the immediate environment, the mesosystem to connections among the child's immediate settings, the exosystem to social settings that affect but do not contain the child, and the macrosystem to the overarching ideology of the culture. (Adapted from *The Child: Development in a Social Context*, edited by C. B. Kopp and J. B. Krakow. © 1982, Addison-Wesley Publishing Co., Reading, Massachusetts. P. 648. Reprinted with permission.)

who choose to study development in the highly artificial context of the laboratory. Bronfenbrenner (1979) goes on to depict "environment" (or the natural ecology) as "a set of nested structures, each inside the next, like a set of Russian dolls" (p. 22). In other words, the developing individual is said to be embedded in not one but several environmental systems, ranging from immediate settings such as the family to remote contexts such as the broader culture (see Figure 3-6). Each of these systems is thought to interact, either directly or indirectly, with

the others and with the individual to influence development in complex ways. Let's take a closer look.

Bronfenbrenner's innermost environmental layer, or **microsystem**, consists of the immediate contexts that individuals actually experience. For most young infants the microsystem may be limited to the family. Yet this structure eventually becomes much more complex as children mature and are exposed to day care, preschool classes, youth groups, and neighborhood play areas. Not only are children likely to be influenced by the people present in their microsystems, but they influence those people as well. For example, an extremely irritable or difficult infant can alienate her parents or even create friction between them that may be sufficient to damage their marital relationship. Microsystems are truly dynamic systems in which each person influences and is influenced by the other persons present.

The next environmental layer, or **mesosystem**, refers to the links or interconnections among microsystems. Bronfenbrenner believes that children's development is likely to be optimized by strong, supportive links among microsystems. For example, a toddler who has established secure emotional ties to her parents may be well prepared to approach and to cooperate with other children upon entering day care (whereas one who is insecure at home may be hesitant or even hostile with peers). A child's ability to master arithmetic in elementary school may depend not only on the instruction his teacher provides but also on the extent to which such scholastic activities are valued and encouraged at home. Microsystems do interact to influence developmental outcomes—a theme that will be repeated over and over throughout the text.

Bronfenbrenner's third environmental layer, or **exosystem**, consists of settings that children never experience directly but that may still affect their development. For example, children's emotional relationships at home can be influenced considerably by whether or not their parents enjoy their work. Similarly, children's experiences in school may also be affected by their exosystem—by a social integration plan adopted by the school board, or by a plant closing in their community that results in a decline in the school's revenue.

Finally, Bronfenbrenner stresses that development always takes place in a **macrosystem**—that is, a cultural or subcultural context in which microsystems, mesosystems, and exosystems are embedded. The macrosystem is really a broad, overarching ideology that dictates (among other things) how children should be treated, what they should be taught, and which goals they should strive for. Of course, these values differ from culture to culture (and across subcultures) and can greatly influence the kinds of experiences children have in their homes, neighborhoods, schools, and all other contexts that affect them, directly or indirectly. To cite one example, the incidence of child abuse in families (a microsystem experience) is much higher in those cultures (or macrosystems) that sanction the use of physical punishment (for example, spankings) and adopt a permissive attitude toward violence (Belsky, 1980).

Although we have barely touched on the ecological perspective here, we will explore its propositions throughout the text. Perhaps you can already see, however, that it provides a much richer description of environment (and environmental influences) than anything offered by learning theorists. Each of us functions in particular microsystems that are linked by a mesosystem and embedded in the larger contexts of an exosystem and a macrosystem. To an ecological theorist it makes little sense to try to study environmental influence in contrived laboratory contexts; only by observing transactions between developing persons and their ever-changing *natural* settings will we ever understand how individuals influence and are influenced by their environments.

Summary

The father of behaviorism and social-learning theory was John B. Watson, a psychologist who claimed that newborn infants are *tabulae rasae* who are gradually conditioned by their environments to feel, think, and act in certain characteristic ways. Watson believed that learned associations between stimuli and responses (habits) are the building blocks of human development. Presumably, social and personality development is a continuous process marked by the gradual acquisition of new and more sophisticated habits. These habits may be acquired through repeated exposure to a stimulus (or *mere exposure*), *classical conditioning*, *operant conditioning*, *observational learning*, or *collaborative (or guided) learning* experiences with a more competent associate.

Since Watson's day, researchers have offered several explanations of social and personality development based on the principles of various learning theories. *Neo-Hullian theorists* assume that one's personality consists of a set of habits, each of which represents a learned association between a stimulus and a response. According to the neo-Hullians, human behavior is motivated by *primary* and *secondary* drives. Responses that prove to be reliable sources of drive reduction are learned and become habits.

By contrast, *Skinnerian* (or *operant-learning) theorists* believe that drives play little or no role in human social learning. Instead, most of our actions are freely emitted operants that become either more or less probable as a function of their consequences. In other words, human behavior is said to be controlled by *external* stimuli—reinforcers and punitive events—rather than by internal forces, or drives.

According to Bandura's *cognitive social-learning theory*, many habits and personality attributes are responses acquired by observing the behavior of social models. Bandura makes an important distinction between learning and performance. He has shown that a response need not be reinforced or even performed in order to be learned. Learning is viewed as a *cognitive* activity that occurs as the observer attends to, codes, and mentally rehearses the model's behavior—before that behavior is reinforced. From Bandura's perspective, reinforcers and punitive events are performance variables that motivate the learner to display—or suppress—what he or she has already learned.

Bandurans suggest that children play an active role in their own socialization. The process of observational learning requires the observer to actively attend to, code, rehearse, and enact the behavior displayed by social models. Furthermore, children are said to regulate their own behavior by rewarding acts that are consistent with learned standards of acceptable conduct and punishing acts that are inconsistent with those standards. Thus the bases for self-denial and for adherence to exacting performance standards come not from the external environment but from *within the individual*. Finally, Bandura emphasizes that human development is best described as the product of a continuous reciprocal interaction among personal, behavioral, and environmental factors: the environment may affect the child, but the child's behavior also affects the environment. The implication of Bandura's *reciprocal determinism* model is that children are actively involved in shaping the very environments that influence their development.

Among the strengths of the social-learning approach are its objectivity, its practical applications, and the wealth of information it has helped to generate about developing children and adolescents. Nevertheless, the learning approach is often criticized as a nondevelopmental model that (1) discounts or ignores important biological and cognitive contributions to social and personality development and (2) has overlooked the important role of collaborative (guided) learning in children's socialization.

The *ecological perspective* is a new way of looking at environment and at environmental influences on human development. The natural environment is portrayed as a set of nested environmental systems that are constantly interacting with one another and with the growing person to influence development in complex ways. Proponents of the ecological viewpoint criticize developmentalists who rely heavily on laboratory experimentation, arguing that only by observing transactions between developing persons and their ever-changing *natural* ecologies will we ever understand how individuals influence and are influenced by their environments.

References

ABRAVANEL, E., & SIGAFOOS, A. D. (1984). Exploring the presence of imitation during early infancy. *Child Development, 55*, 381–392.

AZMITIA, M. (1988). Peer interaction and problem-solving: When are two heads better than one? *Child Development, 59*, 87–96.

BAER, J. S., HOLT, C. S., & LICHTENSTEIN, E. (1986). Self-efficacy and smoking reexamined: Construct validity and clinical utility. *Journal of Consulting and Clinical Psychology, 54*, 846–852.

BANDURA, A. (1965). Influence of models' reinforcement contingencies on the acquisition of imitative responses. *Journal of Personality and Social Psychology, 1*, 589–595.

BANDURA, A. (1969). *Principles of behavior modification.* New York: Holt, Rinehart & Winston.

BANDURA, A. (1971). *Social learning theory*. Morristown, NJ: General Learning Press.

BANDURA, A. (1977). *Social learning theory*. Englewood Cliffs, NJ: Prentice-Hall.

BANDURA, A. (1982). Self-efficacy mechanism in human agency. *American Psychologist, 37*, 122–147.

BANDURA, A. (1986). *Social foundations of thought and action: A social cognitive theory*. Englewood Cliffs, NJ: Prentice-Hall.

BANDURA, A. (1989). Social cognitive theory. In R. Vasta (Ed.), *Annals of child development*. Vol. 6: *Theories of child development: Revised formulations and current issues*. Greenwich, CT: JAI Press.

BANDURA, A., GRUSEC, J. E., & MENLOVE, F. L. (1966). Observational learning as a function of symbolization and incentive set. *Child Development, 37*, 499–506.

BARON, R. A., & BYRNE, D. (1991). *Social psychology: Understanding human interaction* (6th ed.). Newton, MA: Allyn & Bacon.

BELL, R. Q. (1979). Parents, child, and reciprocal influences. *American Psychologist, 34*, 821–826.

BELSKY, J. (1980). Child maltreatment: An ecological integration. *American Psychologist, 35*, 320–335.

BIJOU, S. W., & BAER, D. M. (1978). *Behavior analysis of child development*. Englewood Cliffs, NJ: Prentice-Hall.

BRODY, G. H., GRAZIANO, W. G., & MUSSER, L. M. (1983). Familiarity and children's behavior in same-age and mixed-age peer groups. *Developmental Psychology, 19*, 568–576.

BRONFENBRENNER, U. (1979). *The ecology of human development*. Cambridge, MA: Harvard University Press.

BRONFENBRENNER, U. (1989). Ecological systems theory. In R. Vasta (Ed.), *Annals of child development*. Vol. 6: *Theories of child development: Revised formulations and current issues*. Greenwich, CT: JAI Press.

COATES, B., & HARTUP, W. W. (1969). Age and verbalization in observational learning. *Developmental Psychology, 1*, 556–562.

DIAZ, R. M., NEAL, C. J., & VACHIO, A. (1991). Maternal teaching in the zone of proximal development: A comparison of low- and high-risk dyads. *Merrill-Palmer Quarterly, 37*, 83–108.

DOLLARD, J., & MILLER, N. E. (1950). *Personality and psychotherapy: An analysis in terms of learning, thinking, and culture*. New York: McGraw-Hill.

DOMJAN, M. (1993). *The principles of learning and behavior* (3rd ed.). Pacific Grove, CA: Brooks/Cole.

FARRAR, M. J. (1992). Negative evidence and grammatical morpheme acquisition. *Developmental Psychology, 28*, 90–98.

FIELD, T. M., WOODSON, R., GREENBERG, R., & COHEN, D. (1982). Discrimination and imitation of facial expressions by neonates. *Science, 218*, 179–181.

FRENCH, D. C. (1984). Children's knowledge of the social functions of younger, older, and same-age peers. *Developmental Psychology, 55*, 1429–1433.

FREUND, L. S. (1990). Maternal regulation of children's problem-solving behavior and its impact on children's performance. *Child Development, 61*, 113–126.

GAUVAIN, M., & ROGOFF, B. (1989). Collaborative problem solving and children's planning skills. *Developmental Psychology, 25*, 139–151.

GESELL, A. (1933). Maturation and the patterning of behavior. In C. Murchison (Ed.), *A handbook of child psychology*. Worcester, MA: Clark University Press.

GEWIRTZ, J. L. (1969). Mechanisms of social learning: Some roles of stimulation and behavior in early human development. In D. A. Goslin (Ed.), *Handbook of socialization theory and research*. Skokie, IL: Rand McNally.

GRUSEC, J. E., & ABRAMOVITCH, R. (1982). Imitation of peers and adults in a natural setting: A functional analysis. *Child Development, 53*, 636–646.

HOROWITZ, F. D. (1992). John B. Watson's legacy: Learning and environment. *Developmental Psychology, 28*, 360–367.

KAITZ, M., MESCHULACH-SAFATY, O., AUERBACH, J., & EIDELMAN, A. (1988). A reexamination of newborns' ability to imitate facial expressions. *Developmental Psychology, 24*, 3–7.

KUCZYNSKI, L., ZAHN-WAXLER, C., & RADKE-YARROW, M. (1987). Development and content of imitation in the second and third years of life: A socialization perspective. *Developmental Psychology, 23*, 276–282.

MELTZOFF, A. N. (1988a). Imitation of televised models by infants. *Child Development, 59*, 1221–1229.

MELTZOFF, A. N. (1988b). Infant imitation after a 1-week delay: Long-term memory for novel acts and multiple stimuli. *Developmental Psychology, 24*, 470–476.

MELTZOFF, A. N. (1988c). Infant imitation and memory: Nine-month-olds in immediate and deferred tests. *Child Development, 59*, 217–225.

MELTZOFF, A. N., & MOORE, M. K. (1989). Imitation in newborn infants: Exploring the range of gestures imitated and the underlying mechanisms. *Developmental Psychology, 25*, 954–962.

MILLER, N. E., & DOLLARD, J. (1941). *Social learning and imitation*. New Haven, CT: Yale University Press.

MISCHEL, W. (1979). On the interface of cognition and personality: Beyond the person-situation debate. *American Psychologist, 34*, 740–754.

MISCHEL, W. (1986). *An introduction to personality* (4th ed.). Holt, Rinehart & Winston.

MISCHEL, W., & EBBESEN, E. B. (1970). Attention and delay of gratification. *Journal of Personality and Social Psychology, 16*, 329–337.

MITCHELL, C., & STUART, R. B. (1984). Effect of self-efficacy on dropout from obesity treatment. *Journal of Consulting and Clinical Psychology, 52*, 1100–1101.

PIAGET, J. (1951). *Play, dreams, and imitation in childhood*. New York: Norton.

RADZISZEWSKA, B., & ROGOFF, B. (1991). Children's guided participation in planning imaginary errands with skilled adult or peer partners. *Developmental Psychology, 27*, 381–389.

ROGOFF, B. (1990). *Apprenticeship in thinking: Cognitive development in social context*. New York: Oxford University Press.

SKINNER, B. F. (1953). *Science and human behavior*. New York: Macmillan.

SKINNER, B. F. (1971). *Beyond freedom and dignity*. New York: Knopf.

SLABY, R. G., & FREY, K. S. (1975). Development of gender constancy and selective attention to same-sex models. *Child Development, 46*, 849–856.

STAATS, A. W. (1975). *Social behaviorism*. Homewood, IL: Dorsey Press.

THELEN, E., & ADOLPH, K. E. (1992). Arnold L. Gesell: The paradox of nature and nurture. *Developmental Psychology, 28*, 368–380.

TONER, I. J., MOORE, L. P., & EMMONS, B. A. (1980). The effect of being labeled on subsequent self-control in children. *Child Development, 51*, 618–621.

TONER, I. J., & SMITH, R. A. (1977). Age and overt verbalization in delay maintenance behavior in children. *Journal of Experimental Child Psychology, 24*, 123–128.

VASTA, R., HAITH, M. M., & MILLER, S. A. (1992). *Child psychology: The modern science*. New York: Wiley.

VAUGHN, B. E., KOPP, C. B., & KRAKOW, J. B. (1984). The emergence and consolidation of self-control from eighteen to thirty months of age: Normative trends and individual differences. *Child Development, 55*, 990–1004.

VINTER, A. (1986). The role of movement in eliciting early imitations. *Child Development, 57*, 66–71.

VYGOTSKY, L. S. (1962). *Thought and language*. Cambridge, MA: MIT Press. (Original work published 1934.)

VYGOTSKY, L. S. (1978). *Mind in society: The development of higher psychological processes*. Cambridge, MA: Harvard University Press.

WATSON, J. B. (1913). Psychology as the behaviorist views it. *Psychological Review, 20*, 158–177.

WATSON, J. B. (1928). *Psychological care of the infant and child*. New York: Norton.

WATSON, J. B., & RAYNOR, R. (1920). Conditioned emotional reactions. *Journal of Experimental Psychology, 3*, 1–14.

WEISBERG, P. (1963). Social and nonsocial conditioning of infant vocalization. *Child Development, 34*, 377–388.

4 | *Cognitive Viewpoints on Social and Personality Development*

If I had written this book 30 years ago, it would not have included a chapter on cognitive contributions to social and personality development. Although the study of children's cognitive growth has a long and storied history in developmental psychology, the widespread application of cognitive-developmental theories to social-developmental issues and problems is relatively recent. Modern-day cognitive perspectives on socialization stem from the work of developmentalists (Baldwin, 1906; Kohlberg, 1966; Werner, 1957), social psychologists (for example, Heider, 1958; Kelley, 1973), and sociologists (for example, Cooley, 1902; Mead, 1934). But the person who deserves more credit than any other for directing our attention to the interconnections between children's cognitive growth and their social/personality development is Jean Piaget (1896–1980), a Swiss scholar who studied the process and products of intellectual development for more than 60 years.

We begin this chapter by examining Piaget's theory of intellectual growth and its implications for social and personality development.[1] We will see that Piaget viewed children as curious, active explorers who pass through four major stages of cognitive growth between birth and early adulthood. Each successive stage was thought to represent a new and more complex level of intellectual functioning that largely determines (1) how children encode, interpret, and respond to environmental events and thus (2) what effects these events are likely to have on their social and personality development.

Piaget's early notion that social development depends very heavily on cognitive development (as well as his demonstrations of the influence of cognition on moral development—a contribution we will discuss at length in Chapter 12) has spurned a whole new area of developmental research: the study of **social cognition**. Students of social cognition seek to determine (1) how children come to understand the thoughts, intentions, emotions, and behaviors of themselves and other people; (2) how they conceptualize their social relationships with parents, peers, friends, and authority figures (for

example, teachers); and (3) how this knowledge influences their social behavior and personality development. Although social cognition is a relatively new area of study, it is a critically important one. Throughout this text we will see that the ways in which children and adolescents think about their social experiences affect their self-concepts (Chapter 7), their propensities for achievement (Chapter 8), their gender identities and sex-role development (Chapter 9), their aggressive inclinations (Chapter 10) and altruistic behavior (Chapter 11), their moral development (Chapter 12), and their relationships with family members (Chapter 13), teachers (Chapter 14), and friends and peers (Chapter 15).

In this chapter we concentrate on one particular aspect of social cognition: how children reason about other people's attributes and how they use such information to form impressions of their companions. This research illustrates Piaget's influence on the study of social cognition. It also highlights the contributions made by *attribution* (or social information-processing) *theorists* and shows how other cognitive scholars have extended Piaget's ideas to paint a much richer portrait of the fundamental interplay between cognitive growth and social/personality development.

Piaget's Cognitive-Developmental Theory

Jean Piaget was truly a remarkable individual. At age 10 he published his first scientific article, about the behavior of a rare albino sparrow. This early interest in how animals adapt to their environments eventually led him to pursue a Ph.D. in zoology, which he completed in 1918. Piaget's secondary interest was *epistemology* (the branch of philosophy concerned with the origins of knowledge), and he hoped to be able to integrate his two interests. Thinking that psychology was the answer, Piaget journeyed to Paris, where he accepted a position at the Alfred Binet laboratories, working on the first standardized intelligence test. His experiences in this position had a profound influence on his career.

[1]Much more detailed overviews and assessments of Piaget's contributions to the study of cognitive development can be found in Bjorklund (1989) or Shaffer (1993).

In the testing approach to the study of mental ability, an estimate is made of the person's intelligence based on the number and kinds of questions that he or she answers correctly. However, Piaget soon found that he was more interested in children's *incorrect* answers than in their correct ones. He first noticed that children of about the same age were producing the same kinds of wrong answers. But why? As he proceeded to question children about their misconceptions, using the clinical method he had learned earlier while working in a psychiatric clinic, he began to realize that young children are not simply less intelligent than older children; their thought processes are completely different. Piaget then set up his own laboratory and spent 60 years charting the course of intellectual growth and attempting to determine how children progress from one mode (or stage) of thinking to another.

Piaget's View of Intelligence and Intellectual Growth

Influenced by his background in biology, Piaget (1950) defined intelligence as a basic life process that helps an organism to adapt to its environment. By "adapting," Piaget means that the organism is able to cope with the demands of its immediate situation. For example, the hungry infant who grasps a bottle and brings it to her mouth is behaving adaptively, as is the adolescent who successfully interprets a road map while traveling or changes a tire should the need arise. As children mature, they acquire ever more complex "cognitive structures" that aid them in adapting to their environments.

COGNITIVE (INTELLECTUAL) SCHEMES

A cognitive structure—or what Piaget called a **scheme**—is an organized pattern of thought or action that is used to cope with or explain some aspect of experience. For example, a 3-year-old will probably insist that the sun is alive because it comes up in the morning and goes down at night. This child is operating on the basis of a simple cognitive scheme: things that move are alive. The earliest *schemes*, formed in infancy, are simple motor habits such as

PHOTO 4-1 The cognitive-developmental theory of Swiss scholar Jean Piaget (1896–1980) has several important implications for our understanding of social and personality development.

reaching, grasping, and lifting, which prove to be highly adaptive. For example, a curious infant who combines the responses of extending an arm (reaching) and grasping with the hand is suddenly capable of satisfying his curiosity by exploring almost any interesting object that is no more than an arm's length away. Simple as these **behavioral schemes** may be, they permit infants to operate toys, to turn dials, to open cabinets, and to otherwise master their environments. Late in infancy, children are able to represent experiences mentally, forming such **symbolic schemes** as images and verbal codes. And, shortly after they enter grade school, children's schemes become **operational**, taking the form of internal mental activities or "actions of the head" (for example, mental addition or subtraction) that allow them to manipulate information and think logically about the issues and problems they encounter in everyday life. At any age, children rely on their current cognitive structures to understand the world around them. As a result, younger and older children, who construct very different kinds of schemes, will often interpret and respond to the same objects and events in very different ways.

CONSTRUCTING SCHEMES: PIAGET'S INTELLECTUAL FUNCTIONS

How do children develop more complex schemes and increase their understanding of the world? Piaget claimed that infants have no inborn knowledge or ideas about reality, as some philosophers have claimed. Nor are children simply handed information or taught how to think by adults. Instead, Piaget viewed children as **constructivists**, who actively create new understandings of the world based on their own experiences. How? By being the curious and active explorers that they are. Children watch what goes on around them; they experiment with objects they encounter; they make connections or associations between events; and they are puzzled when their current understanding or schemes fail to explain what they have experienced.

According to Piaget, children can construct new schemes because they have inherited two *intellectual functions*, which he calls *organization* and *adaptation*. **Organization** is the process by which children combine existing schemes into new and more complex intellectual structures. For example, a toddler may initially believe that anything that flies is a "birdie." As he gradually discovers that many things that are not birds can also fly, he may organize this knowledge into a new and more complex hierarchical structure, such as this one:

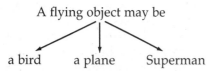

A flying object may be

a bird   a plane   Superman

Piaget believed that organization is inborn and automatic: children are constantly organizing their available schemes into higher-order systems or structures.

The goal of organization is to further the process of adaptation. As its name implies, **adaptation** is the process of adjusting to the demands of the environment. According to Piaget, adaptation occurs through two complementary activities: assimilation and accommodation.

To illustrate the adaptive function, let's return to the 3-year-old who believes that the sun is alive. Surely this idea is not something the child learned from an adult; it was apparently constructed by the child on the basis of her own worldly experiences. After all, many things that move *are* alive. As long as the child clings to this understanding, she may regard any new moving object as alive; that is, new experiences will be interpreted in terms of her current cognitive structures, a process Piaget called **assimilation**. Eventually, however, this child will encounter moving objects that almost certainly couldn't be alive, such as a paper airplane that was nothing more than a sheet of newsprint before Dad built it or a wind-up toy that invariably stops moving unless she winds it again. Now here are contradictions (or what Piaget termed **disequilibriums**) between the child's understanding and the facts to be understood. It becomes clear to the child that her "objects-that-move-are-alive" scheme needs to be revised. So she will be prompted by these disconfirming experiences to **accommodate**—that is to alter her existing schemes so that they provide a better explanation of the events she has witnessed (only things that move under their own power are alive).

So it goes through life. Piaget believes that we are continually relying on the complementary processes of assimilation and accommodation to adapt to our environments. Initially we attempt to understand new experiences or to solve problems using our current cognitive structures (assimilation). But we often find our existing schemes are inadequate for these tasks, which then prompts us to revise them (through accommodation) and to integrate them with other relevant schemes (organization) to provide a better "fit" with reality (Piaget, 1952). Biological maturation also plays an important role: as the brain and nervous system mature, children become capable of increasingly complex cognitive activities that help them to construct better understandings of what they have experienced (Piaget, 1970). Eventually, curious, active children, who are always forming new schemes and reorganizing this knowledge, will have progressed far enough to be thinking about old issues in entirely new ways; that is, they pass from one stage of cognitive development to the next higher stage.

Four Stages of Cognitive Development

Piaget proposed four major periods (or stages) of cognitive development: the *sensorimotor* stage (birth to age 2), the *preoperational* stage (age 2 to 7), the *concrete-operational* stage (age 7 to 11 or 12), and the *formal-operational* stage (age 11–12 and beyond). These stages form what Piaget called an **invariant developmental sequence**—that is, all children progress through the stages in exactly the order in which they are listed. There is no skipping of stages, because each successive stage builds on the previous stage and represents a more complex way of thinking.

THE SENSORIMOTOR STAGE
(BIRTH TO APPROXIMATELY 2 YEARS)

The **sensorimotor stage** spans the first two years, or the period that psychologists refer to as infancy. The dominant cognitive structures are behavioral schemes, which evolve as infants begin to coordinate their *sensory* input and *motor* responses in order to "act on" and get to "know" the environment. ·

During the first two years of life, infants evolve from reflexive creatures with very limited knowledge into planful problem solvers who have already learned a great deal about themselves, their close companions, and the objects and events in their everyday worlds. So dramatic are the infant's cognitive advances that Piaget divides the sensorimotor period into six substages (see Table 4-1, p. 113), which describe the child's gradual transition from a reflexive to a reflective organism. Our review will concentrate on those aspects of sensorimotor development that have influenced subsequent thinking about children's social and personality development.

Growth of intentional or goal-directed behavior. Over the first eight months, infants begin to act on objects and to discover that they can make interest-

AN INFANT
ACCOMMODATING HIS
MOUTH TO THE SHAPE
OF AN OBJECT

ing things happen. However, these discoveries emerge very gradually. Piaget believed that neonates are born with only a few basic reflexes (for example, sucking, grasping) that assist them in satisfying biological needs such as hunger. During the first month their activities are pretty much confined to exercising their innate reflexes, assimilating new objects into these reflexive schemes (for example, sucking on objects other than nipples), and accommodating their reflexes to these novel objects. The first coordinated habits emerge at 1–4 months of age as infants discover by chance that various responses that they can produce (for example, sucking their thumbs, making sounds by cooing) are satisfying and, thus, worthy of repetition. These responses, called **primary circular reactions**, are centered on the infant's own body. They are called "primary" because they are the first habits to appear and "circular" because the pleasure they bring stimulates their repetition.

Between 4 and 8 months of age, infants discover (again by chance) that they can make interesting things happen to *external* objects (such as making a rubber duck quack by squeezing it). These responses, called **secondary circular reactions**, also tend to be repeated for the pleasure they bring. Of what possible significance are these simple habits for social and personality development? According to Piaget, infants are discovering the limits and capabilities of their own bodies during the first four months and then recognizing that external objects are separate from their "physical selves" by the middle of the first year. Thus, making the distinction between "self" and "nonself" is viewed as the first step in the development of a personal identity, or self-concept.

Between 8 and 12 months of age, infants are suddenly able to coordinate two or more actions to achieve simple objectives. For example, if you place a toy that the child wants under a cushion, the child may lift the cushion with one hand while using the other to grab the toy. In this case the act of lifting the cushion is not a pleasurable response in itself; nor is it emitted by chance. Rather, it represents part of a larger *intentional* scheme in which two initially unrelated responses—lifting and grasping—are coordinated as means to an end. Piaget believed that these simple means/ends activities represent the earliest form of true problem solving.

At 12 to 18 months of age, infants begin to experiment with objects and will try to invent totally new methods of solving problems or reproducing interesting results. For example, a child who originally squeezed a rubber duck to make it quack may now decide to drop it, step on it, or crush it with a pillow to see whether these actions will have the same or different effects on the toy. These trial-and-error exploratory schemes, called **tertiary circular reactions**, signal the emergence of true curiosity.

A dramatic development takes place between 18 and 24 months of age: children begin to internalize their behavioral schemes to construct mental symbols, or images. Suddenly, 18–24-month-olds are capable of solving problems mentally, without resorting to trial-and-error experimentation. This ability, called **inner experimentation**, is illustrated in Piaget's interaction with his son, Laurent:

> Laurent is seated before a table and I place a bread crust in front of him, out of reach. Also, to the right of the child I place a stick, about 25 cm. long. At

---

BOX 4-1

Neonatal Imitation: A Closer Look at the Phenomenon and Its Possible Adaptive Significance

Several years ago, Andrew Meltzoff and Keith Moore (1977) reported a startling set of results. Apparently, 12- to 21-day-old infants were able to imitate an adult model's simple facial expressions—actions such as opening the mouth, sticking out the tongue, and puckering the lips. However, these initial findings were greeted with much skepticism. After all, these particular imitative schemes involve matching a facial gesture that babies can see with their own expressions, which they cannot see—a sophisticated skill that Piaget claimed was not available until 8 to 12 months of age. Some critics dismissed the infant's responses as pseudo-imitation: perhaps very young infants will pucker, open their mouths, or stick out their tongues because face-to-face interaction with the adult has excited them (see Olson & Sherman, 1983). Others wondered whether the adult model might not be subconsciously mimicking the facial expressions of the infants.

Although both these possibilities could conceivably account for Meltzoff and Moore's original results, they are less plausible explanations for recent demonstrations that calm infants only 36–72 hours old can reproduce the facial gestures and head movements of adult models under conditions in which *the model gestured first* and the infant's imitative *reactions* were recorded on videotape (Field et al., 1982; Meltzoff & Moore, 1989; Reissland, 1988). Because the babies in these latter studies were so very young, we might seriously entertain the possibility that neonates are biologically prepared to imitate the facial gestures of their companions (although this conclusion remains quite controversial).

Are such early imitative capabilities in any way adaptive? One might be tempted to say no, for babies apparently lose whatever capacity they have to imitate facial gestures and other gross motor responses over the first several weeks of life (see, for example, Abravanel & Sigafoos, 1984). However, the ethologists

first, Laurent tries to grasp the bread . . . and then he gives up. . . . Laurent again looks at the bread, and without moving, looks very briefly at the stick, then suddenly grasps it and directs it to the bread . . . [he then] draws the bread to him [Piaget, 1952, p. 335].

Clearly, Laurent had an important insight: the stick could be used as an extension of his arm to obtain a distant object. Trial-and-error experimentation is not apparent in this case, for Laurent's "problem solving" occurred at an internal, symbolic level.

Development of imitation. Imitation intrigued Piaget because he viewed it as a highly adaptive activity—a means by which infants might actively participate in social exchanges and add many new skills to their behavioral repertoires. However, his own observations suggested that infants are incapable of imitating *novel* responses displayed by a model until 8 to 12 months of age (the same age at

which they show clear evidence of intentionality in their own behavior). Moreover, the imitative schemes of an 8-month-old are rather imprecise. Were you to bend and straighten your finger, the infant might mimic you by opening and closing her entire hand (Piaget, 1951). Voluntary imitation becomes much more precise between 12 and 18 months, and (as we noted in Chapter 3) the major accomplishment of the second year is the emergence of *deferred imitation*—the ability to reproduce actions modeled earlier in time. Of course, this capacity for deferred imitation implies that infants are capable of generating the kinds of *symbolic* representations that promote observational learning.

What are we to make of recent claims (mentioned earlier, in Chapter 3) that *neonates* are capable of imitating simple facial gestures and motor responses? In Box 4-1 we explore this phenomenon that Piaget overlooked and discuss its possible adaptive significance.

B O X **4-1** | *continued*

might argue that this early "imitation" is a meaningful inborn ability—one that enables a baby to respond contingently to her caregivers, thereby sustaining their attention and eliciting displays of affection. Indeed, we will see in Chapter 5 that very young infants have a number of other inborn characteristics that help them

to elicit the kinds of affectionate social contact from caregivers that are necessary for normal social and emotional development. So it is quite conceivable that any rudimentary imitative capabilities that neonates display serve this same important function and are quite adaptive indeed.

Sample photographs from videotaped recordings of 2- and 3-week-old infants imitating tongue protrusion, mouth opening, and lip protrusion.

Development of object permanence.   One of the more notable achievements of the sensorimotor period is the development of **object permanence** — the idea that objects continue to exist when they are no longer visible or detectable through the other senses. If you were to remove your watch and cover it with a coffee mug, you would be well aware that the watch continues to exist. Objects have a permanence for us; out of sight is not necessarily out of mind.

According to Piaget, babies are not initially aware of this basic fact of life. Throughout the first four months, infants will not search for attractive objects that vanish; if they were interested in a watch that was then covered by a mug, they would soon lose interest, almost as if they believed that the watch had lost its identity by being transformed into a mug (Bower, 1982). At age 4 to 8 months, infants will retrieve attractive objects that are partly concealed or hidden under a transparent cover; but their continuing failure to search for objects that are completely concealed suggests that, from their perspective, disappearing objects may no longer exist.[2]

The first signs of an emerging object concept appear, according to Piaget, at 8 to 12 months of age. However, object permanence is far from complete, as we see in Piaget's demonstration with 10-month-old Jacqueline:

> Jacqueline is seated on a mattress without anything to disturb or distract her. . . . I take her [toy] parrot from her hands and hide it twice in succession under the mattress, on her left [point A]. Both times Jacqueline looks for the object immediately and grabs it. Then I take it from her hands and move it very slowly before her eyes to the corresponding place on her right, under the mattress [point B]. Jacqueline watches this movement . . . but at the moment when the parrot disappears [at point B] she turns to her left and looks where it was before [at point A] [1954, p. 51].

Jacqueline's response is typical of children at this age. When searching for a disappearing object, the 8- to 12-month-old will often look in the place where it was previously *found* rather than in the place where it was last seen. In other words, the child acts as if her *behavior* determined where the object was to appear, and consequently she does not treat the object as if it exists independent of her own activity.

Between 12 and 18 months of age, the object concept improves. Infants will now track the visible movements of objects and search for them where they were last seen. Yet the object concept is not complete, for the child cannot make the mental inferences necessary to represent and understand *invisible* displacements. Thus, if you conceal an attractive toy in your hand, place your hand behind a barrier, deposit the toy there, remove and open your empty hand, and ask the child to find the toy, 12- to 18-month-olds will search where the toy was last seen — in your hand — rather than look behind the barrier.

By 18 to 24 months of age, children are capable of mentally representing invisible displacements and using these mental inferences to guide their search for objects that disappear. The object concept is now complete.

Of what social significance is the object concept? In Chapter 5 we will see that it may play a very important role in the development of an infant's first true emotional attachments. Cognitive theorists (for example, Schaffer, 1977, 1990) have proposed that infants cannot form close emotional ties to regular companions unless these individuals have a "permanence" about them. After all, it would seem rather difficult to establish a meaningful and lasting relationship with a person who "ceases to exist" whenever he or she passes from view.

In sum, the child's intellectual achievements during the sensorimotor period are truly remarkable. In two short years, infants have evolved from reflexive and largely immobile creatures into planful thinkers who can move about on their own, solve some problems in their heads, form simple concepts, and even communicate many of their thoughts to their companions. Table 4-1 presents a brief summary of the

[2]However, Piaget's conclusion has been hotly debated. Some investigators contend that even very young infants *know* that hidden objects continue to exist; they simply *forget* where the objects are if they stay hidden more than a second or two (see Bjorklund, 1989, or Shaffer, 1993, for brief summaries of recent research on the growth of object permanence).

TABLE 4-1 *Summary of the substages and intellectual accomplishments of the sensorimotor period*

Piagetian Substage	Methods of Solving Problems or Producing Interesting Outcomes	Imitation Skills	Object Concept
1. Reflex activity (0–1 month)	Exercising and accommodating inborn reflexes	Some imitation of facial expressions and gross motor responses[1]	Tracks moving object but ignores its disappearance
2. Primary circular reactions (1–4 months)	Repeating interesting acts that are centered on one's own body	Repetition of own behavior that is mimicked by a companion	Looks intently at the spot where an object disappeared[2]
3. Secondary circular reactions (4–8 months)	Repeating interesting acts that are directed toward external objects	Same as in substage 2	Searches for partly concealed object
4. Coordination of secondary schemes (8–12 months)	Combining actions to solve simple problems (first evidence of intentionality)	Ability to eventually imitate novel responses after gradually accommodating a crude first attempt at imitation	First glimmering of object permanence; searches for and finds concealed object that has not been visibly displaced
5. Tertiary circular reactions (12–18 months)	Experimenting to find new ways to solve problems or reproduce interesting outcomes	Systematic imitation of novel responses; deferred imitation of simple motor acts	Searches for and finds object that has been visibly displaced
6. Invention of new means through mental combinations (18–24 months)	First evidence of using insight as the child solves problems at an internal, symbolic level	Deferred imitation of complex behavioral sequences	Object concept is complete; searches for and finds objects that have been hidden through invisible displacements

[1] Imitation of facial expressions is apparently an inborn ability that may bear little relation to the voluntary imitation that appears later in the first year.

[2] Many researchers now believe that the object concept may be present very early and that Piaget's research badly underestimates what young infants may know about objects (see Bjorklund, 1989; Shaffer, 1993).

SOURCES: Adapted from T. M. Field, R. Woodson, R. Greenberg, & D. Cohen, "Discrimination and Imitation of Facial Expressions by Neonates." *Science*, 1982, *218*, 179–181; also A. N. Meltzoff & M. K. Moore, "Imitation of Facial and Manual Gestures by Human Neonates." *Science*, 1977, *198*, 75–78.

major intellectual accomplishments of the first two years.

THE PREOPERATIONAL STAGE (APPROXIMATELY 2 TO 7 YEARS)

During the **preoperational stage**, children become increasingly proficient at constructing and using mental symbols (words and images) to think about the objects, situations, and events they encounter. But, despite these advances in symbolic reasoning, Piaget's descriptions of preoperational intelligence focus mainly on the limitations or deficiencies in children's thinking. Indeed, he calls this period "preoperational" because he believes that preschool children have not yet acquired the **cognitive operations** — such internal mental activities as cognitive addition or subtraction — that would enable them to think logically. As we review this intellectual stage, we will once again focus on characteristics of preoperational thought that have implications for social and personality development.

Symbolism and pretend play. The early preoperational period (ages 2–3) is marked by a dramatic increase in children's use of the **symbolic function**:

the ability to make one thing — a word or an object — stand for, or represent, something else. Consider, for example, that, because 2–3-year-olds can use words and images to represent their experiences, they are now quite capable of thinking about or even comparing objects that are no longer present. (Indeed, this increased proficiency with the use of mental symbols may help to explain why, as we saw in Chapter 3, 2–3-year-olds are suddenly using their capacity for deferred imitation to *learn* new competencies by carefully observing their parents and other social models.)

A second hallmark of the early preoperational period — one made possible by the growth of symbolism — is a dramatic increase in both the frequency and the complexity of *pretend play*: toddlers often pretend to be people they are not (mommies, superheros), and they may assume these roles with props (such as a shoe box or a stick) that symbolize role-relevant objects (a baby's crib or a ray gun). Although parents occasionally become concerned when their preschoolers immerse themselves in a world of make-believe, Piaget viewed pretend play as serious business — an activity that promotes the child's social, emotional, and intellectual development. And there is ample support for Piaget's argument. For example, preschool children who "pretend" a lot are judged to be more creative, more socially mature, and (if their play frequently includes peers) more popular than agemates who pretend less often (Connolly & Doyle, 1984; Connolly, Doyle, & Reznick, 1988; Dansky, 1980). Play also serves as a means of coping with emotional crises and reducing emotional conflicts:

> If there is a (disciplinary) scene at lunch (for example), one can be sure that an hour or two afterward it will be recreated with dolls and brought to a happier solution. Either the child disciplines her doll . . . or in play she accepts what had not been accepted at lunch (such as finishing a bowl of soup she does not like, especially if it is the doll who finishes it symbolically). . . . Generally speaking, symbolic play helps in the resolution of conflicts and also in the compensation of unsatisfied needs (and) the *inversion of roles* such as obedience and authority [Piaget & Inhelder, 1969, p. 60; italics added].

The italicized portion of Piaget and Inhelder's statement hints at another major function of symbolic play: *role taking*. During the preschool period, children become cowboys, firefighters, doctors, lawyers, nurses, or space travelers simply by donning the appropriate attire and pretending to be these things. They can become powerful authority figures (such as parents) by enacting that role with dolls or with younger brothers and sisters. In other words, pretend play enables preschool children to try out roles that other people play while encouraging them to think about the feelings of the individuals who actually live these roles. In the process, they will learn from their enactments and further their understanding of the social world in which they live (Kuczynski, Zahn-Waxler, & Radke-Yarrow, 1987; Rubin, Fein, & Vandenberg, 1983). Play is serious business indeed!

Deficiencies in preoperational reasoning. Despite the adaptive characteristics of children's symbolism and pretend play, much of what Piaget had to say about preoperational thought dwelled on its limitations. The most striking deficiency that he saw in preoperational reasoning was the child's **egocentrism** — a tendency to view the world from one's own perspective and to have difficulty recognizing another person's divergent point of view. Piaget demonstrated this tendency by first familiarizing children with an asymmetrical mountain scene (one that looked very different from different vantage points) and then asking them what an observer would see as he gazed at the scene from a vantage point other than their own. Often 3–4-year-olds said that the other person would see exactly what they saw, which Piaget interpreted as the child's failure to consider the other's divergent perspective.

If young children often have trouble with *perceptual perspective taking* (inferring what others can see and hear), imagine the difficulties they must face with *conceptual perspective taking* — that is, correctly inferring what another person may be feeling, thinking, or intending. Indeed, we will see later in this chapter that preschoolers do tend to rely on their own perspectives and thus fail to make accurate judgments about other people's motives, intentions, and desires; also, they do often assume that, if they know something, others will too (Ruffman & Olson, 1989; Sodian et al., 1991). Finally, the egocentrism that younger children display may help to explain why they sometimes appear rather cruel, selfish, inconsiderate, or unwilling to help one another. If these "insensitive" youngsters do not realize how their own actions make others feel, they may not readily experience the remorse and sympathy that might inhibit antisocial behavior or elicit acts of kindness. This hypothesized link between children's cognitive abilities (namely, their empathic capabilities and role-taking skills) and their social conduct will be discussed later in the chapter and explored in detail when we consider the topics of aggression, altruism, and moral development in Chapters 10, 11, and 12.

Between the ages of 4 and 7, egocentrism declines somewhat and children become much more proficient at classifying objects on the basis of shared perceptual features such as size, shape, and color. In fact, Piaget characterized the thinking of 4- to 6-year-olds as "**intuitive**" because their understanding of objects and events tends to "center" on their single, most salient *perceptual* feature — the way things appear to be — rather than on logical or rational thought processes.

The deficiencies of intuitive reasoning are quite obvious if we examine the results of Piaget's famous *conservation* studies (Flavell, 1963). One of these experiments begins with the child adjusting the volumes of liquid in two identical containers until each is said to have "the same amount to drink." Next the child sees the experimenter pour the liquid from one of these tall, thin containers into a short, broad container. He is then asked whether the remaining tall, thin container and the shorter, broader container have the same amount of liquid (see Figure 4-1 for an illustration of the procedure). Children younger than 6 or 7 will usually say that the tall, thin receptacle contains more liquid than the short, broad one. The child's thinking about liquids is apparently **centered** on one perceptual feature: the relative heights of the columns (tall column = more liquid). In Piaget's terminology, preoperational children are incapable of **conservation**: they do not yet realize that

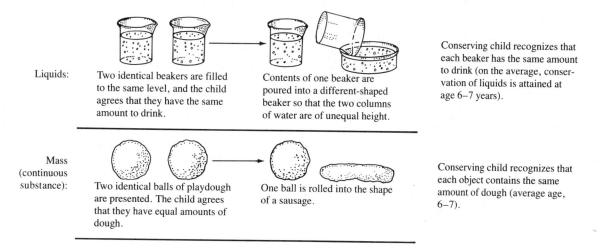

Liquids:	Two identical beakers are filled to the same level, and the child agrees that they have the same amount to drink.	Contents of one beaker are poured into a different-shaped beaker so that the two columns of water are of unequal height.	Conserving child recognizes that each beaker has the same amount to drink (on the average, conservation of liquids is attained at age 6–7 years).
Mass (continuous substance):	Two identical balls of playdough are presented. The child agrees that they have equal amounts of dough.	One ball is rolled into the shape of a sausage.	Conserving child recognizes that each object contains the same amount of dough (average age, 6–7).

FIGURE 4-1 Two of Piaget's famous conservation problems.

certain properties of a substance (such as its volume or mass) remain unchanged when its appearance is altered in some superficial way.

Why do preoperational children fail to conserve? Simply because their thinking is not yet *operational*. According to Piaget, either of two cognitive operations is necessary for conservation. The first is **reversibility**—the ability to mentally undo, or reverse, an action. At the intuitive level the child is incapable of mentally reversing the flow of action and therefore does not realize that the liquid in the short, broad container would attain its former height if it were poured back into the tall, thin container. Second, the child must be able to overcome his or her "centered" thinking in order to recognize that immediate appearances can be deceiving. Piaget suggests that children begin to "decenter" as they acquire a cognitive operation called **compensation**—the ability to focus on several aspects of a problem at the same time. Children at the intuitive stage are unable to attend simultaneously to both height and width when trying to solve the liquid conservation problem. Consequently, they fail to recognize that increases in the width of the column of liquid compensate for decreases in its height to preserve its absolute amount.

Let's consider one implication of the young child's intuitive reasoning for social and personality development. Three- to 5-year-olds clearly understand that they are boys or girls and that everyone can be classified according to gender. But the thinking of these young children about gender and its implications is quite egocentric and is dominated by appearances or "perceptual realities." Thus a 4-year-old boy might well say he could become a mommy if he wanted to, or he might conclude that a woman who cuts her hair short, wears men's clothing, and goes to work as a construction worker is now a man (McConaghy, 1979; Slaby & Frey, 1975). Impressions such as these suggest that preschool children have not yet conserved the concept of gender. In Chapter 9 we will see that the conservation of gender is an important contributor to sex-role development that is not attained until age 5 to 7—precisely the age at which children begin to conserve "nonsocial" attributes such as liquids and mass.

THE CONCRETE-OPERATIONAL STAGE (APPROXIMATELY 7 TO 11 YEARS)

According to Piaget, children at the **concrete-operational stage** are rapidly acquiring cognitive operations and applying these important new skills when thinking about objects and events that they've seen, heard, or otherwise experienced. Recall from our earlier discussion that a cognitive operation is an internal mental activity that enables the child to modify and reorganize her images and symbols to reach a logical conclusion (Flavell, 1985). For example, we've seen how the operation of *reversibility* allows the child to mentally reverse a flow of action (as with the columns of liquid in a conservation study). The operations of cognitive *addition* and *subtraction* permit the child to discover the logical relation between whole classes and subclasses by mentally adding the parts to form a superordinate whole and then reversing this action (subtracting) to once again think of the whole class as a collection of subclasses. Thus the ability to operate on one's objects of thought takes the 7- to 11-year-old far beyond the static and centered thinking of the preoperational stage.

The growth of relational logic. One of the hallmarks of concrete-operational thinking—an ability that permits us to (among other things) sharpen our self-concepts by comparing our skills and attributes with those of other people—is a better understanding of relations and relational logic. Can you remember an occasion when your gym teacher said "Line up by height from tallest to shortest"? Carrying out such a request is really quite easy for concrete operators who are now capable of **seriation**—the ability to mentally arrange items along a quantifiable dimension such as height and weight. By contrast, preoperational youngsters perform miserably on seriation tasks and would struggle to comply with the gym teacher's request.

Closely related to seriation is the concept of **transitivity**: the ability to accurately infer the relations among elements in a serial order. If, for example, Jane is taller than Susan, who is taller than Jo, then Jane has to be taller than Jo. Elementary as this inference may seem to us, Piaget claimed that children show little awareness of the transitivity principle before the stage of concrete operations.

Interestingly, however, the transitive inferences of concrete operators are generally limited to *real objects* that are *physically present*; 7- to 11-year-olds cannot yet apply this relational logic to abstract signifiers such as the *x*'s, *y*'s, and *z*'s that we use in algebra. Indeed, Piaget named this period *concrete* operations because his research implied that 7- to 11-year-olds are not yet able to apply their operational schemes to think *logically* about abstract ideas or about any hypothetical proposition that violates their conceptions of reality. Read on and you'll see why he came to this conclusion.

THE FORMAL-OPERATIONAL STAGE (AGE 11–12 AND BEYOND)

By age 11 or 12, many children are entering the last of Piaget's intellectual stages: **formal operations**. Recall that concrete operations are mental actions performed on material aspects of experience and that concrete operators can think quite logically about tangible objects and events. By contrast, formal operations are mental actions performed on *ideas* and *propositions*. No longer is thinking tied to the factual or observable, for formal operators can reason quite logically about hypothetical processes and events that may have no basis in reality.

Reactions to hypothetical propositions.   One way to determine whether a preadolescent has crossed over into the stage of formal operations is to present a thought problem that violates her views about the real world. The concrete operator, whose thinking is tied to objective reality, will often balk at hypothetical propositions. In fact, she may even reply that it is impossible to think logically about objects that don't exist or events that could never happen. By contrast, formal operators enjoy thinking about hypotheticals and are likely to generate some very unusual and creative responses. In Box 4-2 we can see the differences between concrete-operational and formal-operational thinking as children consider a hypothetical proposition that was presented in the form of an art assignment.

Hypothetical-deductive reasoning: The systematic search for answers and solutions.   The formal operator's approach to problem solving becomes increasingly systematic and abstract—much like the **hypothetical-deductive reasoning** of a scientist. We can easily compare the reasoning of formal operators with that of their younger counterparts by examining their responses to Piaget's famous *pendulum problem* (Inhelder & Piaget, 1958). Given strings of different lengths, objects of different weights to attach to one end of the strings, and a hook on which to hang the other end, the subject's task is to discover which factor influences how fast the pendulum oscillates (that is, swings back and forth during a given time period). Is it the length of the string? The heaviness of the weight? The force with which the weight is pushed? The height from which the weight is released? Or might two or more of these variables be important?

The key to solving this problem is to first identify the four factors that might control the pendulum's oscillation and then to systematically test all of these "hypotheses," varying one factor at a time while holding all the other factors constant. Formal operators, who rely on this systematic approach to hypothesis generation and testing, eventually discover that the oscillation of the pendulum depends on only one factor: the length of the string. By contrast, 9–10-year-old concrete operators are not able to generate and systematically test the full range of possibilities that would permit them to draw a logical conclusion. They often test one variable (say string length) without holding another (weight) constant; should they find that a short string with a heavy weight oscillates faster than a longer one with a lighter weight, they are likely to erroneously conclude that both string length and weight control the pendulum's oscillation.

In sum, formational-operational reasoning is rational, systematic, and abstract; the formal operator can think logically about *ideas* and *possibilities*, as well as tangible objects and events.

Personal and social consequences of formal thought.   Formal-operational thinking is a powerful tool that may change the adolescent in many ways—some good and some not so good. First the good news: as we will see later in this chapter, formal operations may pave the way for a much richer understanding of other people's psychological perspectives and the underlying causes of their behavior. It may also permit the adolescent to think logically about what is possible in life, thus paving the way for the formation of a stable identity (Chapter 7), and the formal operator becomes better equipped to make difficult personal decisions that involve weighing alternative courses of action and their probable consequences for oneself and other people (see Chapter 12, for example, on the devel-

opment of moral reasoning). So, as Piaget anticipated, advances in cognitive growth do help to lay the groundwork for changes in other aspects of social and personality development.

Now the bad news: formal operations may also be related to some of the more painful aspects of the adolescent experience. Unlike younger children, who tend to accept the world as it is and to heed the dictates of authority figures, formal operators, who can imagine hypothetical alternatives to present realities, may begin to question everything—from their parents' authority to restrict their choice of friends to the need for spending billions on imple-

---

BOX 4-2 | *Children's Responses to a Hypothetical Proposition*

Piaget (1970) has argued that the thinking of concrete operators is reality bound. Presumably most 9-year-olds would have a difficult time thinking about objects that don't exist or events that could never happen. By contrast, children entering the stage of formal operations were said to be quite capable of considering hypothetical propositions and carrying them to a logical conclusion. Indeed, Piaget suspected that many formal operators would even enjoy this type of cognitive challenge.

Several years ago a group of concrete operators (9-year-old fourth-graders) and a group of children who were at or rapidly approaching formal operations (11- to 12-year-old sixth-graders) completed the following assignment:

Suppose that you were given a third eye and that you could choose to place this eye anywhere on your body. Draw me a picture to show where you would place your "extra" eye, and then tell me why you would put it there.

All the 9-year-olds placed the third eye *on the forehead between their two natural eyes.* It seems as if these children called on their concrete experiences to complete their assignment: eyes are found somewhere around the middle of the face in all people. One 9-year-old boy remarked that the third eye should go between

the other two because "that's where a cyclops has his eye." The rationales for this eye placement were rather unimaginative. Consider the following examples:

Jim (age 9½): I would like an eye beside my two other eyes so that if one eye went out, I could still see with two.
Vickie (age 9): I want an extra eye so I can see you three times.
Tanya (age 9½): I want a third eye so I could see better.

In contrast, the older, formal-operational children gave a wide variety of responses that were not at all dependent on what they had seen previously. Furthermore, these children thought out the advantages of this hypothetical situation and provided rather imaginative rationales for placing the "extra" eye in unique locations. Here are some sample responses:

Ken (age 11½): (*Draws the extra eye on top of a tuft of hair.*) I could revolve the eye to look in all directions.
John (age 11½): (*Draws his extra eye in the palm of his left hand.*) I could see around corners and see what kind of cookie I'll get out of the cookie jar.
Tony (age 11): (*Draws a close-up of a third eye in his mouth.*) I want a third eye in my mouth because I want to see what I am eating.

When asked their opinions of the "three eye" assignment, many of the younger children considered it

ments of warfare when so many people are hungry and homeless. Indeed, the more logical inconsistencies adolescents detect in the real world, the more inclined they are to become frustrated with or even rebelliously angry toward the agents (for example, parents, the government) thought to be responsible for these imperfect states of affairs. Piaget (1970) viewed this idealistic fascination with the way things "ought to be" as a perfectly normal outgrowth of the adolescent's newly acquired abstract reasoning abilities, and he thus proclaimed formal operations as the primary cause of the "generation gap."

According to Piaget, adolescents can be so focused on themselves and their thinking that they actually become more egocentric than they were during the grade-school years. David Elkind (1967, 1981) has identified two kinds of egocentrism that adolescents often display. The **"imaginary audience"** phenomenon refers to the adolescent's feeling that she is constantly "on stage" and that everyone around her is just as concerned with and as critical of her actions or appearance as she is. Thus the teenage girl who has spent hours making up her face to hide a few pimples may be convinced that her date is repulsed by them whenever he looks

---

B O X | **4-2** | *continued*

rather silly and uninteresting. One 9-year-old remarked "This is stupid. Nobody has three eyes." However, the 11–12-year-olds enjoyed the task and continued to pester their teacher for "fun" art assignments "like the eye problem" for the remainder of the school year (Shaffer, 1973).

So the results of this demonstration are generally consistent with Piaget's theory. Older children who are at or rapidly approaching the stage of formal operations are more likely than younger, concrete operators to generate logical and creative responses to a hypothetical proposition and to enjoy this type of reasoning.

Tanya's, Ken's, and John's responses to the "third eye" assignment.

away—when, in truth, the equally self-conscious boy may be turning away because he's convinced that her looks of concern imply that his mouthwash has failed him. The second form of adolescent egocentrism is what Elkind calls the **personal fable**—a belief in the *uniqueness* of oneself and one's thinking. For example, an adolescent who receives his first "Dear John" letter may think that nobody else has ever experienced anything quite like *his* depth of despair. The personal fable may also help to explain many of the risks that adolescents take. After all, *they* are unique and would never be harmed by snorting cocaine or having unsafe sex—these negative consequences only happen to "the other guy" (or gal).

Elkind believed that both forms of adolescent egocentrism would increase as youngsters first acquire formal operations and gradually decline over time as idealism wanes. However, the data are not always consistent with his point of view. Although the imaginary-audience phenomenon is stronger among 13- to 15-year-olds than among older adolescents, it is often the 13- to 15-year-olds still functioning at the *concrete-operational* level who show the greatest self-consciousness—the reverse of what Elkind would predict (Gray & Hudson, 1984; Riley, Adams, & Nielsen, 1984). Moreover, some developmentalists have even challenged the notion that the imaginary audience and personal fable are forms of egocentrism. Instead, they believe the self-preoccupation that teenagers display may actually reflect the emergence of new social-perspective-taking skills (to be discussed later in the chapter) that make adolescents more aware of how other people *might* perceive them or react to their conduct (Lapsley et al., 1986).

Evaluation of Piaget's Theory

If you have taken a course in cognitive development (or even a rigorous one in introductory developmental psychology), you are undoubtedly aware that many of Piaget's ideas and procedures have been criticized over the years. For example, we now know that Piaget's heavy reliance on clinical interviews often underestimated children's mental competencies, either because children were incapable of articulating what they actually knew or because

they were unmotivated to do their best on the problems presented to them (Bjorklund, 1989). Moreover, children's reasoning is not always as consistent across problems as Piaget's "stagelike" depiction of it implies. For example, it may be months (or even more than a year) before a 6½-year-old concrete operator who can seriate is able to solve other concrete-operational problems, such as conservation of mass (see Figure 4-1). These observations have led many developmentalists (particularly information-processing theorists) to conclude that cognitive growth is much less stagelike than Piaget had assumed (Fischer, 1980; Flavell, 1985).

Even the many contemporary developmentalists who insist that cognitive growth is stagelike are bothered by Piaget's account of how children move from one stage of intellect to the next. Recall what Piaget says: biological maturation, in conjunction with the constant interplay among the intellectual functions of assimilation, accommodation, and organization, permits children to construct increasingly complex schemes. Eventually they will view their experiences in completely new ways as they move to the next higher intellectual stage. Clearly, this rather vague explanation of cognitive growth raises more questions than it answers. What maturational changes are necessary before children can progress from sensorimotor to preoperational functioning or from concrete operations to formal operations? What kinds of experiences must a child have before he will construct mental symbols, understand cognitive operations, or begin to operate on ideas and think about hypotheticals? Piaget is simply not very explicit about these or any other mechanisms that might enable a child to move to a higher stage of intellect. As a result, a growing number of researchers now look on his theory as an elaborate *description* of cognitive development that has limited explanatory power (Case, 1985; Gelman & Baillargeon, 1983).

Although Piaget's theory of intellectual development has some very real shortcomings and leaves many questions unanswered, it is easy when critiquing it to lose sight of the fact that researchers have been testing and confirming many of Piaget's ideas for more than 60 years (Beilin, 1992). Moreover, Piaget's notion that social development depends on cognitive development, as well as his early research on the growth of moral reasoning (which we will examine in Chapter 12), was very influential in creating the area of research we know today as *social cognition*. One social-cognitive theorist who was profoundly influenced by Piaget was Lawrence Kohlberg, a Harvard professor who formulated his own cognitive-developmental theory of social and personality development.

Kohlberg's Extension of Piaget's Theory

Kohlberg (1966, 1969) has relied heavily on Piaget's theory as a basis for understanding the growth of such social phenomena as emotional attachments, sociability, gender identity, sex typing, altruism, and moral reasoning. The basic assumptions that underlie Kohlberg's cognitive-developmental approach to socialization are as follows:

1. Cognitive development proceeds through the invariant sequence of stages that Piaget has described.

2. Emotional development parallels cognitive development. For example, true emotional attachments cannot occur until the infant develops a certain level of object permanence; sympathetic reactions that promote altruism require a lessening of egocentrism and the development of perspective-taking (role-taking) skills.

3. Social development can be described in terms of changes that occur in the self-concept as the child compares herself with other people and acquires more and more information about her niche in the social environment.

4. The child's social cognition (or understanding of the thoughts, needs, motives, and emotions of other people) will depend on her **role-taking** abilities. The more advanced the child's role taking, the better able she will be to understand the needs of others and the reasons why they behave as they do.

5. The direction of social and personality development is toward a state of equilibrium, or *reciprocity*, between the child's actions and the actions

PHOTO 4-2 Lawrence Kohlberg (1927–1987) has formulated a cognitive-developmental theory of socialization that has influenced research on altruism, sociability, sex typing, and moral development.

of others toward him. To achieve a state of social equilibrium, the child must establish a stable, workable identity so that others will respond to him in a predictable fashion. For example, children eventually develop a gender identity ("I'm a girl" or "I'm a boy") that remains constant across all situations and role relationships. The establishment of a stable gender identity is a social analogue of conservation, and it depends on the same logical operations as physical conservations.

In sum, Kohlberg's view is that social and personality development proceeds through an invariant sequence of qualitatively distinct stages. The behaviors that characterize each social stage are said to depend on the interplay between two important factors: (1) the child's level of cognitive development and (2) the kinds of social experiences the child encounters. Kohlberg does not deny the importance of social learning. Quite the contrary, he argues that socialization could not progress very far if the child failed to assimilate social experiences and accommodate to these experiences. But he is quick to remind us that the child's existing cognitive structures determine *how* he or she interprets social experiences and, hence, *what* is likely to be learned by interacting with others.

Kohlberg's stages of social and personality development vary considerably depending on which aspect of socialization he is considering. For example, the stage sequence involved in sex-role development is normally completed by the time the child enters concrete operations (age 7), whereas moral development may continue well into young adulthood. Clearly, Kohlberg and the many other social-cognitive theorists whom he (and Piaget) has influenced have had some rather interesting and provocative ideas about the course and underlying causes of social development — ideas that we will examine in some detail as we discuss the aspects of social and personality development to which their theories apply. We begin in the next section, where we will chart the changes that occur in children's knowledge and impressions of other people and see how cognitive-developmental theory and other more recent social-cognitive models can help us to explain these developments.

Social Cognition: Knowing about Others

Being appropriately "social" requires us to interact with other people, and these interactions are more likely to be harmonious if we know what our social partners are thinking or feeling and can predict how they are likely to behave. The development of children's knowledge about other people — their descriptions of others' characteristics and the inferences they make about their thoughts and behaviors — constitutes perhaps the largest area of social-cognitive research. And there are so many questions to be answered. For example, what kinds of information do children use to form impressions of others? How do these impressions change over time? And what skills are children acquiring that might explain such changes in person perception? These are the issues that we will now address.

Age Trends in Impression Formation

From early infancy, children are gathering information that they can use to classify or characterize other people. For example, even 3-month-old infants will look longer at photographs of their mothers than at those of other women (Barrera & Maurer, 1981), thus illustrating that they know who this intimate companion is and can discriminate her from strangers. By age 2½, toddlers who have acquired gender labels such as *boy* and *girl* can easily classify people in photographs as male or female (Brooks-Gunn & Lewis, 1982). Shortly thereafter, children begin to form distinct impressions of individual family members and playmates — impressions we can measure by asking them to describe their associates.

What this research indicates is that children younger than 7 or 8 seem to form very concrete, physicalistic impressions of others — impressions that are nearly devoid of any psychological characterizations (Livesley & Bromley, 1973; Peevers & Secord, 1973). Five-year-old Jenny, for example, said: "My daddy is big. He has hairy legs and eats mustard. Yuck! My daddy likes dogs — do you?" Not much of a personality profile there! When young children do use a psychological term to describe a companion, it is typically a very general attribute (such as "He's *nice*" or "She's *mean*") that they may use more as a label for the other person's recent behavior than as a description of the person's enduring characteristics (Rholes, Jones, & Wade, 1988; Rholes & Ruble, 1984).

It is not that preschoolers have *no* appreciation for the psychological qualities that people display. Indeed, we will see that 3- to 5-year-olds typically assume that others' actions reflect definite *motives* or *intentions* (Miller & Aloise, 1989), and they are well aware of how their closest peer companions typically behave in a variety of situations (Eder, 1989). In fact, 5-year-olds who are given ample information about an unknown peer, or who are encouraged to learn all they can about him (by being led to believe they will interact with this person), will not only make psychological inferences about the child but will also rely on these inferences to predict his future behavior (Feldman & Ruble, 1988; Gnepp & Chilamkurti, 1988). Nevertheless, traitlike descriptions appear to be less meaningful for younger than for older children. Five- to 7-year-olds are not especially interested in playing with a child merely because he is "nice"; but, describe the same child as owning an attractive toy, and his popularity skyrockets. By contrast, 9-year-olds are much more inclined to want to play with a child described as "nice" than with one whose most salient quality is owning an attractive toy (Boggiano, Klinger, & Main, 1986).

Between ages 7 and 16, children come to rely less on concrete attributes (possessions and physical attributes) and more on psychological descriptors to characterize their friends and acquaintances. Carl Barenboim (1981) has proposed a three-step developmental sequence to describe the changes in children's impressions during the grade-school years:

1. **Behavioral comparisons phase**. If asked to talk about people they know, 6- to 8-year-olds will compare and contrast their acquaintances in concrete *behavioral* terms, such as "José *runs* faster than Jason" or "She *draws* best in our whole class." Before this phase, children usually describe the behavior of their companions in absolute terms (for example, "José's fast"), without making explicit comparisons.
2. **Psychological constructs phase**. As they continue to observe definite regularities in a companion's behavior, 8- to 10-year-olds should begin to base their impressions on the stable *psychological* constructs, or traits, that the person is now presumed to have. For example, an 8- to 10-year-old might describe friends with statements such as "He's a stubborn idiot" or "She's generous." However, children at this phase are not yet comparing their associates on these psychological dimensions.
3. **Psychological comparisons phase**. By preadolescence (age 11 or 12), children should begin to *compare* and *contrast* others on important psychological dimensions. The statement "Bill is much more shy than Ted" is an example of a psychological comparison.

Barenboim evaluated his proposed developmental sequence by asking 6-, 8-, and 10-year-olds to describe three persons whom they knew well. Each descriptive statement was classified as a behavioral

comparison, a psychological construct (or traitlike statement), or a psychological comparison. The children were then retested one year later, so that data were available for subjects of all ages between 6 and 11.

Several interesting findings emerged. As we see in Figure 4-2, the impressions of younger children were usually stated in behavioral terms. Use of behavioral comparisons increased between the ages of 6 and 8 and began to decline at age 9. However, 9- to 11-year-olds were relying much more heavily on psychological constructs during the same period when the use of behavioral comparisons was becoming less common. The longitudinal data were also consistent with Barenboim's proposed developmental sequence: over the year between the original test and the retest, virtually all the subjects had either stayed at the same phase of impression formation or moved forward (for example, from behavioral comparisons to the psychological constructs phase). Note, however, that even the 11-year-olds rarely used psychological comparisons when stating their impressions of other people.

When do children begin to compare others on important psychological dimensions? To find out,

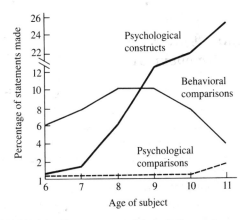

FIGURE 4-2 Percentages of descriptive statements classified as behavioral comparisons, psychological (traitlike) constructs, and psychological comparisons for children between the ages of 6 and 11. (From C. Barenboim, "The Development of Person Perception in Childhood and Adolescence: From Behavioral Comparisons to Psychological Constructs to Psychological Comparisons." *Child Development*, 1981, 52, 129–144. Copyright © 1981 by the Society for Research in Child Development. Reprinted by permission.)

Barenboim repeated his study with 10-, 12-, 14-, and 16-year-olds and found that the vast majority of 12–16-year-olds had progressed to this third level of impression formation. By contrast, fewer than 15% of the 10-year-olds *ever* used a psychological comparison when talking about their companions.

By age 14 to 16, adolescents are not only aware of the dispositional similarities and dissimilarities that characterize their acquaintances, but they are also beginning to recognize that *external*, or situational, factors (for example, illness or family strife) can cause a person to act "out of character" (Damon & Hart, 1988). So, by mid-adolescence, young people are becoming sophisticated "personality theorists" who are able to look both inside and outside a companion to explain her conduct and form coherent impressions of her character.

Why do children progress from behavioral comparisons to psychological constructs to psychological comparisons? Why do their impressions of others become increasingly integrated and abstract over time? To address these issues, we will first examine three contrasting but not altogether inconsistent "cognitive" points of view and then consider how social forces might contribute, both directly and indirectly, to the growth of social cognition.

Theories of Social-Cognitive Development

The three cognitive theories that are most often used to explain developmental trends in person perception are Piaget's cognitive approach, attribution theory, and Robert Selman's role-taking analysis.

COGNITIVE-DEVELOPMENTAL THEORY

According to cognitive-developmental theorists, the ways in which a child conceptualizes other people will depend largely on his or her own level of cognitive development. Recall that the thinking of 3- to 6-year-old "preoperational" children tends to be static and to center on the most salient perceptual aspects of stimuli and events. So it would hardly surprise a Piagetian to find that 4- to 6-year-olds describe their associates in very concrete, observable terms, mentioning their appearances and possessions, their likes and dislikes, and the actions that they can perform.

The thinking of 7–10-year-olds will change in many ways as these youngsters enter Piaget's concrete-operational stage. For example, egocentrism is becoming less pronounced, so that children may begin to appreciate that other people have points of view that differ from their own. Concrete operators are also *decentering* from perceptual illusions, becoming more proficient at *classifying* objects and events, and beginning to recognize that certain properties of an object remain invariant despite changes in its appearance (conservation). These emerging abilities to look beyond overt appearances and to infer underlying invariances might help to explain why grade-school children are suddenly noting definite regularities in their own and others' behavior and using psychological constructs, or traits, to describe these patterns.

By age 12 to 15, children are entering formal operations and are now able to think more logically and systematically about abstractions. Although the concept of a psychological trait is itself an abstraction, it is one based on regularities in concrete, observable behaviors (perhaps explaining why *concrete* operators can think in these terms). However, a trait *dimension* is even more of a mental inference or abstraction and has few if any concrete referents. Thus the ability to think in dimensional terms and to reliably order individuals along these continua (as is necessary in making psychological comparisons) implies that a person is able to operate on abstract concepts—a formal-operational ability (O'Mahoney, 1989).

Barenboim (1981) favored a cognitive-developmental interpretation when seeking to explain why children progress from behavioral comparisons to psychological constructs to psychological comparisons. And his conclusions seem quite reasonable when we recall that the shift from behavioral comparisons to psychological constructs occurs at age 8–9, soon after children have entered Piaget's concrete-operational stage and are becoming increasingly proficient at detecting regularities or invariances and classifying such events. Moreover, the shift from psychological constructs to psychological comparisons occurs at about age 12, precisely the time when many children are entering formal operations and acquiring the ability to operate on abstractions. So the points at which we see major transitions in children's impressions of others are generally consistent with the Piagetian interpretation of these events.

According to proponents of **attribution (or social information-processing) theory**, human beings are active information processors who are constantly seeking explanations, or **causal attributions**, for both their own and other people's behavior. The premise is that children's impressions of others will change, becoming much deeper and more abstract, as the children become more proficient at inferring the reasons why people behave as they do.

Theorizing about attributional processes can be traced to Fritz Heider (1958), a social psychologist who believed that all human beings are characterized by two strong motives: (1) the need to form a coherent understanding of the world and (2) the need to exert some control over the environment, thus becoming "captain of one's own ship." To satisfy these motives, we must be able to predict how people are likely to behave in a variety of situations and understand why they behave in these ways. Without such knowledge the world might seem a random, incoherent place that we would find impossible to adapt to or control.

According to Heider, a person who is seeking to explain some noteworthy behavior will tend to attribute it either to *internal* causes (for example, some characteristic or disposition of the actor) or to *external* causes (for example, something about the situation that elicited the actor's behavior or is otherwise responsible for it). This is an important distinction, for the kinds of causal attributions we make about our own or other people's behavior can influence our reactions to that behavior. Consider the following example.

Suppose a 10-year-old boy is walking across the playground when he is suddenly whacked in the back of the head by a Frisbee. He turns around and sees no one but a single classmate, who is laughing at this turn of events. What kind of "theory" does the child formulate to explain his classmate's conduct? It is likely that the boy will interpret his classmate's laughter as a sign that the classmate *intended* to hit him, and he will probably attribute the classmate's behavior to some internal (or dispositional) cause, such as the classmate's aggressiveness. Consequently, the boy is likely to be angry and may respond with some form of counteraggression. But, had the classmate expressed concern about having hit the boy with the Frisbee, and had there been another classmate present to whom the Frisbee was apparently being thrown, it is likely that the boy would view the act of hitting him as *unintentional* and would perhaps attribute it to some external (or situational) cause, such as the wind deflecting the Frisbee's path. Thus the child is not as likely to be angry, and his behavior might be very different than if he had held the classmate personally responsible for the hurt that he had experienced.

Heider and other early attribution theorists (for example, Kelley, 1973) were social psychologists who mainly studied the causal attributions of adult subjects and were not especially interested in developmental issues. Yet, once the principles underlying adult social cognition had been established, an obvious next step was to study children's interpretations of social behavior, seeking to determine how their causal attributions differ from those of adults and why they change over time. Early thinking about these issues (Secord & Peevers, 1974) was that there are at least three major milestones in the growth of children's understanding of their own and other people's behavior. First, children must recognize that individuals can be the *cause* of various actions. They must then realize that such actions are often guided by *intentions*. Finally, they must understand that individuals may behave in consistent and predictable ways (that is, have *stable* traits and dispositions). Let's briefly consider when each of these milestones might be reached.

People as causal agents. When do children first understand that people can "cause" various events? Probably very early in life. In one recent experiment (Lewis, Alessandri, & Sullivan, 1990), infants only 4 months old expressed delight upon learning that they could "cause" a baby's smiling face to appear (via slide projector) as they tripped an electrical switch with their arm motions—and they also became angry during an extinction phase, when their actions no longer produced these pleasant outcomes.

By age 2, toddlers are frequently displaying their awareness of causality in their own language (for example, "I left it [TV] on *because* I want to watch it"), and they are much more likely to recall causal event sequences than noncausal ones two weeks after observing them (Bauer & Mandler, 1989; Miller & Aloise, 1989).

Why, then, have Piaget and many others assumed that preschool children often fail to appreciate or understand causal relationships? Possibly because the problems investigators have used to test young children's causal reasoning were often extremely complex (for example, "What causes the wind?"); their clinical procedures required the preschooler to verbally justify ideas that she may have understood but could not articulate (Gelman & Kremer, 1991). Indeed, studies that rely on *nonverbal* measures reveal that even 3-year-olds know that (1) people must ordinarily be present before they might be considered the cause of an event and (2) an actor's behavior must *precede* the event to be its cause. To illustrate the latter (*temporal priority*) principle, Kun (1978) showed 3-year-olds sets of pictures depicting the following situations:

A. Scott pulled the dog's tail.
B. The dog bit Scott.
C. Scott cried.

Kun then asked the children whether A or C had caused B. The children reliably chose picture A, evidently recognizing that something Scott had done previously had caused the dog to bite him. So, for simple situations in which there appear to be only a few possible causes for an event, preschool children are quite aware that people can be (and often are) the causal agents.

Inferring intentionality. A child's knowing that a person has caused an event does not necessarily imply that he or she understands the actor's intentions. If a 4-year-old saw a playmate break his favorite toy, he would know that the playmate *caused* the damage. But, in order to interpret this event as an adult might, the child must now decide whether the playmate's actions were deliberate (intentional) or accidental (unintentional).

When do children first understand that another person may perform an act fully intending to produce a given effect? Again, the answer seems to be fairly early in life (see Miller & Aloise, 1989, for a review of the literature). For example, even 3-year-olds recognize that actors intend to produce their "successes" when striving to achieve a goal and that failures or other mistakes are unintentional (Shultz & Wells, 1985). Indeed, the attributional error shown by many preschool children is to assume that *most social behaviors are intentional*; consequently, they often fail to distinguish deliberate acts from accidents before 5–7 years of age (Miller & Aloise, 1989; Shantz, 1983). To decide whether an act and its consequences were intended, young children rely heavily on a **matching rule**: actions producing desirable outcomes for the actor (that is, those that match her motive) are more likely to be viewed as intentional than those producing unwanted or aversive outcomes (Shultz & Wells, 1985). Moreover, young children also rely on a **foreseeability heuristic**: if the actor's behavior was voluntary and its effects could have been predicted, then the behavior is viewed as intentional (Nelson-LeGall, 1985).

All children are exposed to people who engage in such deceptive practices as expressing one intent ("I forgot to invite you to the party") while serving another ("I intended to exclude you"). How and when do children become more proficient at inferring the sincerity of others' stated intentions? At least one recent study suggests that this ability improves dramatically between ages 5 and 9, as children rely more and more on a **verbal/nonverbal consistency rule** to discriminate honest messages from deceptive ones (Rotenberg, Simourd, & Moore, 1989). For example, older children know quite well that (1) telling someone you like him or her while displaying a neutral or unhappy facial expression implies that you are lying, whereas (2) if your stated intent is sincere, your nonverbal behaviors will normally be consistent with your verbal communications.

In sum, preschool children who assume that most acts are intended will become much better over the next several years at (1) distinguishing deliberate acts from accidental ones and (2) assessing the veracity of the verbal motives and intentions that other people express. Of course, this is precisely the kind of information that should help them to form clearer and more stable impressions of their companions.

Understanding dispositional characteristics. The knowledge that an actor has caused a foreseeable and intended event is not, in itself, an indication of a stable trait or disposition. Attribution theorists argue that, to view someone as exhibiting a trait, the perceiver must first (1) judge the actor's behavior to be internally caused, rather than attributable to situational constraints, and then (2) infer that this "personal" cause is reasonably stable over time and across situations.

An example may help to illustrate some of the challenges children face when deciding whether to make internal or external attributions. Suppose Johnny stays in from recess to help the birthday boy, Jimmy, with his schoolwork. Jimmy is eager to finish his schoolwork because he wants to ride his shiny new birthday bicycle. Can Jimmy assume that Johnny really wants to help him (a personal or dispositional cause), or, rather, should he simply conclude "Johnny is helping me so that I will let him ride my new bike" (an external cause)? According to causal attribution theory (Kelley, 1973), there are several schemata that Jimmy might use to infer the meaning of Johnny's behavior:

1. *The* **consistency schema**. Is Johnny often helpful, or does he rarely behave this way? If he consistently assists other people, then his willingness to help Jimmy is likely to be viewed as internally caused.

2. *The* **distinctiveness schema**. Does Johnny often help me and not other kids (high distinctiveness), or, rather, does he tend to help whoever seems to need assistance (low distinctiveness)? If Johnny is helpful to lots of other kids (that is, his behavior is low in distinctiveness), then Jimmy is more likely to assume that the helpgiving was internally caused.

3. *The* **consensus schema**. Do other kids often help me (high consensus), or is Johnny one of the few who do (low consensus)? Presumably, Jimmy is more likely to attribute Johnny's behavior to internal causes if Johnny is one of the few who will

help. Acts that everyone will perform are high in consensus and likely to be perceived as externally (that is, situationally) caused.

4. *Multiple sufficient causes and the discounting schema*. Of course, there may often be several plausible causes for an actor's behavior. In our example, Johnny may be helping Jimmy because he wants to (internal cause), because Jimmy has a new bike that Johnny might get to ride (a situational cause), or for both reasons. According to the **discounting principle** (Kelley, 1973), the role of a given cause in producing an effect will be discounted to some extent if other plausible causes are also present. Thus, Jimmy is somewhat less likely to conclude that Johnny's helpfulness is internally motivated if Jimmy has just received a new bike for his birthday (alternative "external" cause) than if he has no attractive possessions that Johnny might be hoping to use (no apparent external motivation).

By the time children enter grade school, they are using information about the consistency, the distinctiveness, and (occasionally) the consensus of an actor's behavior to determine whether personal qualities of the actor or situational constraints are responsible for an action (Sedlak & Kurtz, 1981; Shantz, 1983). There is some disagreement, though, about when children first use the discounting principle. Many investigators find no evidence for its use among 5–7-year-olds (see Shantz, 1983), whereas others report that even 3- to 5-year-olds will discount internal causes for an actor's behavior when a plausible external cause is made equally salient to them (Miller & Aloise, 1989). These age trends in the use of causal schemata suggest a very interesting question: if 5- and 6-year-olds often make dispositional attributions, deciding that an actor's behavior reflects his or her personal motives and characteristics, then why do they not use psychological constructs (traits) when describing the self and others? A study by William Rholes and Diane Ruble (1984) suggests one answer.

In Rholes and Ruble's study, children aged 5 to 10 first heard stories in which an actor's behavior varied in either consistency or distinctiveness — information that they might have used to make personal or situational attributions. The following is an example of a "high consistency" story that would be expected to yield a dispositional attribution about the actor's high ability:

> Yesterday Sam threw the basketball through the hoop almost every time he tried. In the past, Sam has almost always thrown the ball through the hoop when he tried to.

After hearing the stories, children were asked to make either dispositional or situational attributions for the actor's most recent behavior and to answer a series of questions to determine whether they viewed an actor's dispositions as *stable* causes of his

or her conduct. In the basketball story, for example, children might be asked "How many times do you think Sam could throw the ball through the hoop in the future?" (stability over time) or "How many other kinds of throwing games would Sam do well at?" (stability over situations).

As expected, Rholes and Ruble found that even 5- and 6-year-olds made dispositional attributions about the actor's current behavior if that action was either high in consistency or low in distinctiveness. But, when it came to the *prediction* questions, children younger than 9 did not seem to recognize that dispositions are stable across situations. Thus, 5–8-year-olds who viewed Sam as having high abil-

---

BOX 4-3   *Another Look at Young Children's Ability to Predict Future Behaviors*

Are 5- to 8-year-olds who make dispositional attributions about a peer's current behavior really unable to predict that child's *future* behavior? Mary Dozier (1991) doubts it. She argues that the *dichotomous* "prediction" questions Rholes and Ruble (1984) used (that is, asking the subject to indicate whether or not the target child would perform a particular act in the future) require children to speculate about which of two possible alternatives is the more probable. If young children then confuse possibilities with probabilities and reason that either course of action is *possible*, they may simply guess at what the actor would or would not do, thus appearing as if they cannot reliably predict future behavior. Dozier believes that predictive measures that are *quantitative* in nature—such as "*How much* of X will the target peer do in the future given that she's done this much X in the past?"—do not confuse possibilities with probabilities and may allow even 5-year-olds with knowledge of a child's previous behavior to make accurate predictions about that child's future conduct.

To test her hypothesis, Dozier (1991) exposed 5-, 7-, and 10-year-olds to four stories, each of which described a peer who had performed two acts. One peer had performed two "nice" acts (that is, had shared lots of toys and helped others a lot). Another peer had performed two "not nice" acts (that is, had shared little

and helped little). Finally, the two remaining peers had each performed one "nice" act and one "not nice" act, but in opposite order. After hearing each story, the subject first learned that the target peer had 12 pennies and then was asked to make a quantitative prediction: "How many of the pennies would this child share with you?"

If young children truly view others' past behaviors as having implications for future conduct, then they ought to predict that a peer who had previously performed *two* "nice" acts would share more pennies with them than one who had performed one "nice" and one "not nice" act. Moreover, this second child might be expected to share more pennies than another peer who previously performed two "not nice" acts. As shown in Figure A, this is precisely the pattern of predictions the children made—even the 5-year-olds! By contrast, 5-year-olds who made "dichotomous" predictions in a second study did not consistently indicate that a "nice" peer would perform a nicer future action than a "not nice" peer. So, apparently, younger children cannot accurately assess from a person's past behavior *whether or not* that person will perform a particular act in the future (a dichotomous prediction); but they can use the same information about prior conduct to predict *how much* of that behavior the associate is likely to display (quantitative prediction).

ity in basketball did not realize that Sam probably has the perceptual-motor skills to do well at other, similar games.

So it appears that children younger than 8 or 9 may fail to describe the self and others in "trait-like" terms, not because they fail to make internal attributions (as attribution theorists had originally thought) but because they are uncertain about the *stability* of internal causes and personal characteristics. Stated another way, traitlike terms are not very meaningful for younger children. Should a 6-year-old use a trait such as "kind" to describe someone, she is likely to be describing an apparent internal cause for that person's recent "kindly" behavior

rather than referring to a stable attribute that has definite implications for the person's future conduct. By contrast, traitlike terms are much more salient to a 9-year-old, who can use a label like "kind" as a brief and convenient way of expressing his knowledge that a person who shows kindness in one situation is likely to display the same inclination in a variety of other situations. (But see Box 4-3 for another viewpoint.)

Why might 5- to 8-year-olds often fail to recognize or appreciate the stability of personal attributes? Most social information-processing theorists believe that these younger children simply have not had enough *experience* applying causal schemata

---

4-3 | *continued*

If 5- to 8-year-olds are capable of recognizing consistencies in other people's behavior and even making predictions about their future conduct, then why do

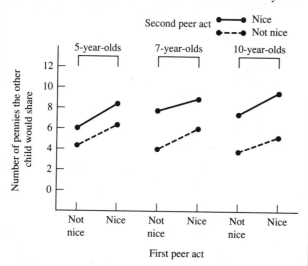

FIGURE A Predictions about the number of pennies a peer would share based on the peer's prior "nice" or "not nice" behaviors. Notice that even the 5-year-olds predicted that a peer who had earlier performed two nice acts would share more than would peers who had performed only one "nice" act or two "not nice" ones.

they not describe their acquaintances in traitlike terms? One reason may be that children may not ordinarily be motivated to seek out consistencies in others' conduct and to label them with a trait word. If we supply them the motivation, however, by describing a peer's prior conduct and leading them to believe that they will soon interact with that child, 5- to 6-year-olds suddenly begin to make traitlike inferences (for example, he's "nice," "smart," "mean," etc.) about him or her (Feldman & Ruble, 1988).

Don't misunderstand. Younger children *are* less capable than older ones at painting rich psychological portraits of other people, and for reasons that will become quite apparent in our next section. However, we can say from the research reviewed here that (1) 5- to 8-year-olds can infer at least some of the traits that their companions possess, and (2) they are more inclined to tell us what they know about the meaning and implications of these attributes if we question them in ways that permit them to display their knowledge (Dozier, 1991).

SOURCE: Text and figure adapted from M. Dozier, "Functional Measurement Assessment of Young Children's Ability to Predict Future Behavior." *Child Development*, 1991, *62*, 1091–1099. Copyright © 1991 by the Society for Research in Child Development. Reprinted by permission.

and comparing actors' behaviors (over time and across situations) to have developed the concept of stable and abiding personality characteristics (Rholes & Ruble, 1984). However, cognitive-developmental theorists attribute the younger child's shortcomings to a *cognitive* deficit: specifically, younger children's static and centered thinking, which focuses on the here-and-now (that is, the way things are at present), prevents them from recognizing the regularities or invariances in conduct that would lead to the inference of stable traits and dispositions. Robert Selman (1980) tends to side with the cognitive theorists on this issue, but he proceeds one step further, arguing that a mature understanding of the self and others depends to a large extent on one particular aspect of cognitive growth: the development of **role-taking** skills. Let's take a closer look.

SELMAN'S ROLE-TAKING ANALYSIS
OF INTERPERSONAL UNDERSTANDING

According to Selman (1980; Yeates & Selman, 1989), children will become much more proficient at understanding themselves and other people as they acquire the ability to discriminate their own perspectives from those of their companions and to see the relations between these potentially discrepant points of view. The underlying assumption of Selman's theory is straightforward: in order to "know" a person, one must be able to assume his perspective and understand his thoughts, feelings, motives, and intentions—in short, the *internal* factors that account for his behavior. If a child has not yet acquired these important role-taking skills, she may have little choice but to describe her acquaintances in terms of their external attributes—that is, their appearance, their activities, and the things they possess.

Selman has studied the development of role-taking skills by asking children to comment on a number of interpersonal dilemmas. Here is one example:

Holly is an 8-year-old girl who likes to climb trees. She is the best tree climber in the neighborhood. One day while climbing down from a tall tree, she falls . . . but does not hurt herself. Her father sees

PHOTO 4-3   Robert Selman (1942–   ) has emphasized the relationship between the development of role-taking skills and the growth of interpersonal understanding.

her fall. He is upset and asks her to promise not to climb trees any more. Holly promises. Later that day, Holly and her friends meet Shawn. Shawn's kitten is caught in a tree and can't get down. Something has to be done right away or the kitten may fall. Holly is the only one who climbs trees well enough to reach the kitten and get it down but she remembers her promise to her father [1976, p. 302].

To assess how well a child understands the perspectives of Holly, her father, and Shawn, Selman asks: "Does Holly know how Shawn feels about the kitten? How will Holly's father feel if he finds out Holly climbed the tree? What does Holly think her father will do if he finds out she climbed the tree? What would you do?" Children's responses to these probes led Selman to conclude that role-taking skills develop in a stagelike manner, as shown in Table 4-2.

Notice in examining the table that children progress from largely egocentric beings, who may be

TABLE 4-2   *Selman's stages of social perspective taking (role taking)*

Stage	*Typical Responses to the "Holly" Dilemma*
0. *Egocentric or undifferentiated perspective* (roughly 3 to 6 years) Children are unaware of any perspective other than their own. They assume that whatever they feel is right for Holly to do will be agreed on by others.	Children often assume that Holly will save the kitten. When asked how Holly's father will react to her transgression, these children think he will be "happy because he likes kittens." In other words, these children like kittens themselves, and they assume that Holly and her father also like kittens. They do not recognize that another person's viewpoint may differ from their own.
1. *Social-informational role taking* (roughly 6 to 8 years) Children now recognize that people can have perspectives that differ from their own but believe that this happens *only* because these individuals have received different information. The child is still unable to think about the thinking of others and know in advance how others will react to an event.	When asked whether Holly's father will be angry because she climbed the tree, the child may say "If he didn't know why she climbed the tree, he would be angry. But if he knew why she did it, he would realize that she had a good reason." Thus the child is saying that, if both parties have exactly the same information, they will reach the same conclusion.
2. *Self-reflective role taking* (roughly 8 to 10 years) Children now know that their own and others' points of view may conflict, even if they have received the same information. They are now able to consider the other person's viewpoint. They also recognize that the other person can put himself in their shoes, so that they are now able to anticipate the person's reactions to their behavior. However, the child cannot consider his own perspective and that of another person at the same time.	If asked whether Holly will climb the tree, the child might say "Yes. She knows that her father will understand why she did it." In so doing, the child is focusing on the father's consideration of Holly's perspective. But, if asked whether the father would want Holly to climb the tree, the child usually says no, thereby indicating that he is now assuming the father's perspective and considering the father's concern for Holly's safety.
3. *Mutual role taking* (roughly 10 to 12 years) The child can now simultaneously consider her own and another person's points of view and recognize that the other person can do the same. At this point, each party can put the self in the other's place and view the self from that vantage point before deciding how to react. The child can also assume the perspective of a disinterested third party and anticipate how each participant (self and other) will react to the viewpoint of his or her partner.	At this stage a child might describe the outcome of the "Holly" dilemma by taking the perspective of a disinterested third party and indicating that she knows that both Holly and her father are thinking about what each other is thinking. For example, one child remarked: "Holly wanted to get the kitten because she likes kittens, but she knew that she wasn't supposed to climb trees. Holly's father knew that Holly had been told not to climb trees, but he couldn't have known about [the kitten]. He'd probably punish her anyway just to enforce his rule."
4. *Social and conventional system role taking* (roughly 12 to 15 and older) The young adolescent now attempts to understand another person's perspective by comparing it with that of the social system in which he operates (that is, the view of the "generalized other"). In other words, the adolescent expects others to consider and typically assume perspectives on events that most people in their social group would take.	A stage-4 adolescent might think that Holly's father would become angry and punish her for climbing the tree because fathers generally punish children who disobey. However, adolescents sometimes recognize that other people are nontraditional or may have a personal viewpoint quite discrepant from that of the "generalized other." If so, the subject might say the reaction of Holly's father will depend on the extent to which he is unlike other fathers and does not value absolute obedience.

SOURCE: Adapted from R. L. Selman, "Social-Cognitive Understanding: A Guide to Educational and Clinical Practice." In T. Lickona (Ed.), *Moral Development and Behavior: Theory, Research and Social Issues.* New York: Holt, Rinehart & Winston. Copyright © 1976 by Holt, Rinehart & Winston.

TABLE 4-3 *Percentages of children and adolescents at each of Selman's role-taking stages as a function of their level of cognitive development*

	Role-Taking Stage				
	0 *Egocentric*	*1* *Social-* *Informational*	*2* *Self-* *Reflective*	*3* *Mutual*	*4* *Social Systems*
Piaget's Stage					
Preoperational	80	20	0	0	0
Concrete operations	0	14	32	50	4
Transitional (late concrete)	1	3	42	43	10
Early formal operations	0	6	6	65	24
Consolidated formal operations	0	12[a]	0	38	50

[a] Since only 8 consolidated formal operators were found in the sample, this figure of 12% represents only one subject.
SOURCE: Based on R. L. Selman & D. Byrne, "A Structural Developmental Analysis of Role-Taking in Middle Childhood." *Child Development*, 1974, *45*, 803–806. Copyright © 1974 by the Society for Research in Child Development; also D. Keating & L. V. Clark, "Development of Physical and Social Reasoning in Adolescence." *Developmental Psychology*, 1980, *16*, 23–30. Copyright © 1980 by the American Psychological Association.

unaware of any perspective other than their own (stage 0), to sophisticated social-cognitive theorists, who can keep several perspectives in mind and compare each with the viewpoint that "most people" would adopt (stage 4). Apparently these role-taking stages represent a true developmental sequence, for 40 of 41 boys who were repeatedly tested over a five-year period showed steady forward progression from stage to stage with no skipping of stages (Gurucharri & Selman, 1982). And one reason why role-taking skills may unfold in one particular order is that they are closely related to Piaget's invariant sequence of cognitive stages (Keating & Clark, 1980). As we see in Table 4-3, preoperational children are at Selman's first or second level of role taking (stage 0 or 1), whereas most concrete operators are at the third or fourth level (stage 2 or 3) and many formal operators have reached the fifth and final level of role taking (stage 4).

Role taking and social cognition. Not only do children's impressions of other people become increasingly abstract as they acquire important role-taking skills, but so too do their understandings of the relationships among people. Consider what children of different ages say about the meaning of friendship.

Preschoolers at Selman's egocentric (level 0) stage think that virtually any pleasant interactions between themselves and available playmates will qualify those playmates as "friends." Thus, 5-year-old Chang might describe Terry as a close friend simply because "He lives next door and plays games with me" (Damon, 1977).

Once they recognize that other children may have motives and intentions that differ from their own (Selman's stage 1), 6- to 8-year-olds begin to conceptualize a "friend" as someone who *chooses* to "do nice things for me" or who "plays the way I like to"—in a word, someone who fulfills the child's *self*-interests. However, friendships are *one-way* at this stage, for the child feels no strong pressure to reciprocate these considerations. And, should a friend fail to serve the child's interests (for example, by spurning an invitation to camp out in the back yard), she may quickly become a nonfriend.

Later, at Selman's stage 2, 8- to 10-year-olds show increasing concern for the needs of a friend and think that true friendships are *reciprocal* relationships in which each party displays affection and kindness toward the other (Furman & Bierman, 1983; Selman, 1980). Yet these stage-2 alliances can be described as "fair-weather" friendships, because they are likely to persist only as long as each person continues to please the other.

Ten- to 15-year-olds at Selman's stage 3 also think of friends as people who share, support, and do nice things for each other. But they have now expanded their notion of personal reciprocity to emphasize the exchange of *intimate* thoughts and feelings rather than superficial courtesies and such tangible commodities as toys and snacks (Berndt, 1982, 1988; Reid et al., 1989; Selman, 1980). Moreover, stage-3 youngsters no longer demand immediate reciprocity from a friend. Nor do they necessarily feel rejected when a friend spurns a suggested activity or chooses to associate with another peer; they are now better at reading each other's thoughts and feelings and can appreciate that a friend may have immediate needs that they simply cannot meet.

Finally, older adolescents (at Selman's stage 4) continue to think of close friends as faithful and trusted companions who are willing to share their innermost thoughts and feelings (Berndt & Perry, 1990). Yet these sophisticated role takers also recognize that a close friend must also be a flexible companion who cares enough to adapt to the new demands and new life circumstances that his or her partner may introduce into their relationship.

So, with the growth of role-taking skills, children's conceptions of friendship gradually change from the one-sided, self-centered view of friends as "people who benefit me" to a harmonious, reciprocal perspective in which each party truly understands the other, enjoys providing him or her with emotional support and other niceties, can more readily forgive occasional gaffes, snubs, and peculiarities, and expects these same considerations in return. Perhaps because they rest on a firmer basis of intimacy and interpersonal understanding, the close friendships of older children and adolescents tend to be rated much higher in quality and are more long lasting than those of younger children (Berndt, 1988; Berndt & Hoyle, 1985; Buhrmester, 1990).

Role taking and social status. A child's role-taking skills may also affect his or her general status in the peer group. For example, Lawrence Kurdek and Donna Krile (1982) found that the most popular children among groups of third- to eighth-graders are those who have well-developed role-taking skills. Moreover, highly sociable children and those who have established intimate friendships score higher on tests of role-taking abilities than their classmates without close friends (LeMare & Rubin, 1987; McGuire & Weisz, 1982).

Why are mature role takers likely to enjoy such a favorable status in the peer group? A study by Lynne Hudson and her associates (Hudson, Forman, & Brion-Meisels, 1982) provides one clue. Second-graders who had tested either high or low in role-taking ability were asked to teach two kindergarten children how to make caterpillars out of construction paper. As each tutor worked with the kindergartners, his or her behavior was videotaped for later analysis. Hudson et al. found that *all* the tutors were willing to assist their younger pupils if the kindergartners *explicitly asked for help*. However, good role takers were much more likely than poor role takers to respond to a kindergartner's subtle or *indirect* requests for help. For example, exaggerated straining with scissors and frequent glances at the tutor usually elicited a helpful response from a good role taker but nothing more than a smile from a poor role taker. Apparently, good role takers are better able to infer the needs of their companions so that they can respond accordingly—an ability that may help to explain why they are so popular with their peers and so successful at establishing close friendships.

THE SOCIAL-EXPERIMENTAL VIEWPOINT

Recently, developmentalists have wondered whether the growth of children's interpersonal understanding is as closely tied to cognitive development as social-cognitive theorists have assumed. Consider, for example, that, even though children's role-taking abilities are related to their performances on Piagetian measures and IQ tests (Pellegrini, 1985), it is quite possible for a child to become less egocentric and to mature intellectually *without becoming an especially skillful role taker* (Shantz, 1983). Thus there must be other, *noncognitive* factors that contribute to the growth of role-taking skills and that may even exert their own *independent* effects on children's social-cognitive development. Might social experiences play such a role? No less an authority than Jean Piaget thought so.

Social experience as a contributor to role taking. Several years ago, Piaget (1932/1965) argued that

PHOTO 4-4   Equal-status contacts with peers are an important contributor to the development of role-taking skills and interpersonal understanding.

playful interactions among grade-school children promote the development of role-taking skills and mature social judgments. Piaget's view was that, by assuming different roles while playing together, young children become more aware of discrepancies between their own perspectives and those of their playmates. When conflicts arise in play, children learn to integrate their points of view with those of their companions (that is, compromise) in order for play to continue. So Piaget assumed that equal-status contacts among peers are an important contributor to social perspective taking and the growth of interpersonal understanding.

Not only has research consistently supported Piaget's viewpoint (see, for example, Bridgeman, 1981), but it appears that some forms of peer contact may be better than others at fostering the growth of interpersonal understanding. Specifically, Janice Nelson and Francis Aboud (1985) propose that disagreements among friends are particularly important, because children tend to be more open and honest with their friends than with mere acquaintances. As a result, disagreeing friends should be more likely than disagreeing acquaintances to provide each other with the information needed to recognize and appreciate their conflicting points of view.

Nelson and Aboud tested their hypothesis by first administering a test of social awareness to two groups of 8–10-year-olds — pairs of friends and pairs of acquaintances. Items on this test were designed to measure the children's levels of reasoning about interpersonal issues such as "What is the thing to do if you lose a ball that belongs to one of your friends?" After taking the test, each pair of friends or acquaintances was asked to discuss one of the interpersonal issues on which they initially disagreed. Their levels of social understanding were then reassessed after the discussions were over.

As predicted, friends responded differently to their conflicts than acquaintances did. Friends were much more critical of their partners than acquaintances were, but they were also more likely to fully explain the rationales for their own points of view — precisely the kind of information that might be expected to promote an understanding (and perhaps an appreciation) of each other's perspectives. Prior to the discussions, pairs of friends and pairs of acquaintances made comparable scores on the social-awareness test. But, after the discussions, friends' final answers to the issue they had discussed were at a higher level of social understanding than their original answers, whereas the answers of acquaintances hadn't changed appreciably from pretest to posttest. Thus the results of this study clearly suggest that equal-status contacts among friends may be particularly important to the development of role-taking skills and interpersonal understanding.

Social experience as a direct contributor to person perception. Social contacts with peers not only contribute indirectly to social cognition by fostering the development of role-taking skills, but they are also a form of *direct experience* by which children can learn what others are like. In other words, the more experience a child has with peers, the more *motivated* she should be to try to understand them and the more *practiced* she should become at appraising the causes of their behavior (Higgins & Parsons, 1983).

Popularity is a convenient measure of social experience; that is, popular children interact more often with a wider variety of peers than do their less popular agemates (LeMare & Rubin, 1987). So, if the amount of direct experience a child has with peers exerts its own unique influence on his or her social-cognitive judgments, then popular children should outperform less popular agemates on tests of social understanding, *even when their cognitive abilities are comparable*. This is precisely what Jackie Gnepp (1989) found when she tested the ability of popular and less popular 8-year-olds to make personalized (psychological) inferences about an unfamiliar child from a small sample of the child's previous behaviors. So it seems that both social experience (as indexed by popularity) and cognitive competence (role-taking skills) contribute in their own way to the development of children's understanding of other people.

Postscript: On the Character of Social/Personality Development and Theories of Social/Personality Development

We have now completed our survey of the "grand theories" of social and personality development and are about ready to consider the aspects of development to which these theories pertain. Before we do, there are a couple of very critical (and related) points that we should keep in mind.

1. *Social/personality development is a holistic enterprise*. Although we have classified the major theories as "biological," "environmental," and "cognitive" viewpoints, each of these models acknowledges the contribution of forces other than those it emphasizes. For example, behavior geneticists focus on genetic influences but are quick to acknowledge that genes and environments interact to produce behavioral phenotypes. Modern versions of social-learning theory stress that children are *cognitive* beings—active information processors—who help to create the environments that influence their development. And proponents of the various cognitive viewpoints at least acknowledge the important role that biological forces play in cognitive development while stressing that cognitive growth, social cognition, and social behavior are reciprocally related and complexly intertwined. In other words, all modern-day theorists are well aware that changes in one aspect of development will have important im-

plications for other aspects. Consider the following example.

What determines a person's popularity with peers?[3] If you were to say that social skills are important, you would be right. Social skills such as warmth, friendliness, and a willingness to cooperate—all of which are heavily influenced by the rearing environment—are characteristics that popular children typically display. And yet we now know that such genetically influenced attributes as facial attractiveness and the age at which a child reaches puberty can have a very real effect on social life. For example, boys who reach puberty early enjoy better relations with their peers than boys who reach puberty later. Let's also note that bright children who do well in school tend to be more popular with their peers than children of average intelligence or below who perform somewhat less admirably in the classroom.

We see, then, that one's "popularity" depends not only on social skills but also on cognitive prowess and physical characteristics. As this example illustrates, development is not piecemeal but *holistic*: human beings are biological, cognitive, and social creatures, and each of these components of "self" depends, in part, on changes that are taking place in other areas of development. This **holistic perspective** is perhaps the dominant theme of human development today—and the theme around which the remainder of this book is organized.

2. *Most contemporary developmentalists are theoretically eclectic*. In reviewing our "grand" theories, we've seen that each has definite strengths and that each is subject to criticism. This basic fact, combined with the realization that human development is a holistic enterprise, has led many developmentalists to become theoretical *eclectics*—people who recognize that none of the grand theories can explain all aspects of social and personality development but that each has contributed to what we know about developing children and adolescents. The plan for the remainder of this book is to take an **eclectic approach**, borrowing from many theories to integrate their contributions into a unified, holistic portrait of the developing person. Indeed, the benefits of the

[3]The development of peer status and popularity is discussed at length in Chapter 15.

approach will become apparent in our next chapter, where we will see that psychoanalysts, ethologists, social-learning theorists, and cognitive developmentalists have all helped us to understand how and why infants establish (or, in some cases, fail to establish) secure emotional ties to their closest companions.

Summary

Jean Piaget formulated a theory of intellectual development that has many important implications for social and personality development. According to Piaget, intellectual activity is a basic life function that helps the child to adapt to the environment. He described children as active, inventive explorers who are constantly constructing *schemes* to represent what they know and modifying these cognitive structures through the processes of *organization* and *adaptation*. Organization is the process by which children rearrange their existing knowledge into higher-order structures, or schemes. Adaptation is the process of adjusting successfully to the environment, and it occurs through two complementary activities: *assimilation* and *accommodation*. Assimilation is the process by which the child tries to interpret new experiences in terms of her existing schemes. Accommodation is the process of modifying one's existing schemes in order to interpret (or otherwise cope with) new experiences. Presumably, cognitive growth results from the interplay of these intellectual functions: assimilations stimulate accommodations, which induce the reorganization of schemes, which allows further assimilations, and so on.

Piaget believed that intellectual growth proceeds through an invariant sequence of stages that can be summarized as follows:

Sensorimotor period (0–2 years). Over the first two years, infants come to "know" and understand objects and events by acting on them. The behavioral (or sensorimotor) schemes that a child creates to adapt to his surroundings are eventually internalized to form mental symbols that enable him to understand the permanence of objects (including people), to imitate the behavior of absent models, and to solve simple problems on a mental level without resorting to trial and error.

Preoperational period (roughly 2–7 years). Symbolic reasoning becomes increasingly apparent during the preoperational period as children begin to use words and images in inventive ways in their play activities. Although 2- to 7-year-olds are becoming more and more knowledgeable about the world in which they live, their thinking is quite deficient by adult standards. Piaget described preschool children as highly *egocentric*: they view events from their own perspective and have difficulty assuming another person's point of view. And their thinking is characterized by *centration*: when they encounter something new, they tend to focus only on one aspect of it — its most obvious, or perceptually salient, feature. Consequently, they often fail to solve problems that require them to evaluate several pieces of information simultaneously.

Concrete operations (roughly 7–11 years). During the period of concrete operations, children can think logically and systematically about concrete objects, events, and experiences. They can now perform arithmetical operations in their heads and mentally reverse the effects of physical actions and behavioral sequences. The acquisition of these and other *cognitive operations* permits the child to conserve, seriate, and make transitive inferences. However, they still cannot think logically about hypothetical propositions that violate their conceptions of reality.

Formal operations (age 11 or 12 and beyond). Formal-operational thinking is rational, abstract, and much like the hypothetical-deductive reasoning of a scientist. At this stage, adolescents can "think about thinking" and operate on ideas as well as on tangible objects and events. These newly emerging cognitive powers may help to explain why adolescents often seem so preoccupied with themselves and their thinking as well as so idealistic.

Although Piaget accurately described the normal *sequences* of intellectual development, he often underestimated and occasionally overestimated the child's cognitive capabilities. Some investigators have challenged Piaget's assumption that development occurs in stages, and others have criticized his theory for failing to specify how children progress from one stage of intellect to the next. But, despite its shortcomings, Piaget's theory has contributed enormously to our understanding of cognitive development and has helped to spawn a new area of study: *social cognition*. Students of social cognition seek to determine how children interpret the thoughts, motives, emotions, and behaviors of themselves and other people and how this knowledge affects their social behavior and personality development.

Lawrence Kohlberg has used Piaget's theory as a framework for understanding many social-developmental phenomena. Kohlberg's most basic assumption is that social and personality development parallels cognitive development and therefore occurs in stages. Kohlberg's stages of social and personality development vary considerably for different social attributes. We will review these stages in some detail when we discuss the aspects of development to which they apply.

The development of children's knowledge of other people is perhaps the largest area of social-cognitive research. Children younger than 7 or 8 are likely to describe friends and acquaintances in concrete terms that are nearly devoid of psychological content. But, as they compare themselves and others on noteworthy behavioral dimensions, they become more attuned to regularities in others' conduct and begin to rely on stable psychological constructs, or traits, to describe these patterns. As they approach adolescence, their impressions of others become more abstract as they begin to compare and contrast their friends and acquaintances or a number of psychological dimensions. By age 14 to 16, adolescents are becoming sophisticated "personality theorists" who know that any number of situational influences can cause a person to act "out of character."

The growth of children's social-cognitive abilities is related to cognitive development in general, to the development of attributional (or social information-processing) schemes, and to the growth of role-taking skills (to truly "know" a person, one must be able to assume her perspective and understand her thoughts, feelings, motives, and intentions). However, proponents of the *social-experimental* viewpoint are quick to note that social experiences also contribute to social-cognitive development, both indirectly (by fostering the growth of role-taking skills) and directly (by providing opportunities for children to *learn* what other people are like).

Having reviewed the "grand theories," it is clear that social and personality development is a *holistic* process that no single theory can adequately explain. Today most developmentalists are *eclectic*, meaning that they borrow from many theories, attempting to integrate these contributions into a holistic portrait of developing children and adolescents.

References

ABRAVANEL, E., & SIGAFOOS, A. D. (1984). Exploring the presence of imitation during early infancy. *Child Development*, 55, 381–392.

BALDWIN, J. M. (1906). *Social and ethical interpretations in mental development*. New York: Macmillan.

BARENBOIM, C. (1981). The development of person perception in childhood and adolescence: From behavioral comparisons to psychological constructs to psychological comparisons. *Child Development*, 52, 129–144.

BARRERA, M. E., & MAURER, D. (1981). Recognition of mother's photographed face by the three-month-old infant. *Child Development*, 52, 714–716.

BAUER, P. J., & MANDLER, J. M. (1989). One thing follows another: Effects of temporal structure on 1- to 2-year-olds' recall of events. *Developmental Psychology*, 25, 197–206.

BEILIN, H. (1992). Piaget's enduring contribution to developmental psychology. *Developmental Psychology*, 28, 191–204.

BERNDT, T. J. (1982). The features and effects of friendship in early adolescence. *Child Development*, 53, 1447–1460.

BERNDT, T. J. (1988). The nature and significance of children's friendships. In R. Vasta (Ed.), *Annals of child development* (Vol. 5). London: JAI Press.

BERNDT, T. J., & HOYLE, S. J. (1985). Stability and change in childhood and adolescent friendships. *Developmental Psychology*, 21, 1007–1015.

BERNDT, T. J., & PERRY, T. B. (1990). Distinctive features and effects of adolescent friendships. In R. Montemayor, G. R. Adams, & T. P. Gullotta (Eds.), *From childhood to adolescence: A transitional period?* London: Sage.

BJORKLUND, D. F. (1989). *Children's thinking: Developmental function and individual differences*. Pacific Grove, CA: Brooks/Cole.

BOGGIANO, A. K., KLINGER, C. A., & MAIN, D. S. (1986). Enhancing interest in peer interaction: A developmental analysis. *Child Development*, 57, 852–861.

BOWER, T. G. R. (1982). *Development in infancy.* New York: W. H. Freeman.

BRIDGEMAN, D. L. (1981). Enhanced role-taking through cooperative interdependence: A field study. *Child Development, 52,* 1231–1238.

BROOKS-GUNN, J., & LEWIS, M. (1982). The development of self-knowledge. In C. B. Kopp & J. B. Krakow (Eds.), *The child: Development in a social context.* Reading, MA: Addison-Wesley.

BUHRMESTER, D. (1990). Intimacy of friendship, interpersonal competence, and adjustment during preadolescence and adolescence. *Child Development, 61,* 1101–1111.

CASE, R. (1985). *Intellectual development: Birth to adulthood.* Orlando, FL: Academic Press.

CONNOLLY, J. A., & DOYLE, A. (1984). Relation of social fantasy play to social competence in preschoolers. *Developmental Psychology, 20,* 797–806.

CONNOLLY, J. A., DOYLE, A. B., & REZNICK, E. (1988). Social pretend play and social interaction in preschoolers. *Journal of Applied Developmental Psychology, 9,* 301–313.

COOLEY, C. H. (1902). *Human nature and the social order.* New York: Scribner's.

DAMON, W. (1977). *The social world of the child.* San Francisco: Jossey-Bass.

DAMON, W., & HART, D. (1988). *Self-understanding in childhood and adolescence.* New York: Cambridge University Press.

DANSKY, J. (1980). Make-believe: A mediator of the relationship between play and associative fluency. *Child Development, 51,* 576–579.

DOZIER, M. (1991). Functional measurement assessment of young children's ability to predict future behavior. *Child Development, 62,* 1091–1099.

EDER, R. A. (1989). The emergent personologist: The structure and content of 3½-, 5½-, and 7½-year-olds' concept of themselves and other persons. *Child Development, 60,* 1218–1228.

ELKIND, D. (1967). Egocentrism in adolescence. *Child Development, 38,* 1025–1033.

ELKIND, D. (1981). *Children and adolescents: Interpretive essays on Jean Piaget* (3rd ed.). New York: Oxford University Press.

FELDMAN, N. S., & RUBLE, D. N. (1988). The effect of personal relevance on psychological inference: A developmental analysis. *Child Development, 59,* 1339–1352.

FIELD, T. M., WOODSON, R., GREENBERG, R., & COHEN, D. (1982). Discrimination and imitation of facial expressions by neonates. *Science, 218,* 179–181.

FISCHER, K. W. (1980). A theory of cognitive development: The control and construction of hierarchies of skills. *Psychological Review, 87,* 477–531.

FLAVELL, J. H. (1963). *The developmental psychology of Jean Piaget.* New York: Van Nostrand Reinhold.

FLAVELL, J. H. (1985). *Cognitive development.* Englewood Cliffs, NJ: Prentice-Hall.

FURMAN, W., & BIERMAN, K. L. (1983). Developmental changes in young children's conceptions of friendship. *Child Development, 54,* 549–556.

GELMAN, R., & BAILLARGEON, R. (1983). A review of Piagetian concepts. In J. H. Flavell & E. M. Markman (Eds.), *Handbook of child psychology.* Vol. 3: *Cognitive development.* New York: Wiley.

GELMAN, S. S., & KREMER, K. E. (1991). Understanding natural cause: children's explanations of how objects and their properties originate. *Child Development, 62,* 396–414.

GNEPP, J. (1989). Personalized inferences of emotions and appraisals: Component processes and correlates. *Developmental Psychology, 25,* 277–288.

GNEPP, J., & CHILAMKURTI, C. (1988). Children's use of personality attributions to predict other people's emotional and behavioral reactions. *Child Development, 59,* 743–754.

GRAY, W. M., & HUDSON, L. M. (1984). Formal operations and the imaginary audience. *Developmental Psychology, 20,* 619–627.

GURUCHARRI, C., SELMAN, R. L. (1982). The development of interpersonal understanding during childhood, preadolescence, and adolescence: A longitudinal follow-up study. *Child Development, 53,* 924–927.

HEIDER, F. (1958). *The psychology of interpersonal relations.* New York: Wiley.

HIGGINS, E. T., & PARSONS, J. E. (1983). Stages as subcultures: Social-cognitive development and the social life of the child. In E. T. Higgins, W. W. Hartup, & D. N. Ruble (Eds.), *Social cognition and social development: A sociocultural perspective.* New York: Cambridge University Press.

HUDSON, L. M., FORMAN, E. R., & BRION-MEISELS, S. (1982). Role-taking as a predictor of prosocial behavior in cross-age tutors. *Child Development, 53,* 1320–1329.

INHELDER, B., & PIAGET, J. (1958). *The growth of logical thinking from childhood to adolescence.* New York: Basic Books.

KEATING, D., & CLARK, L. V. (1980). Development of physical and social reasoning in adolescence. *Developmental Psychology, 16,* 23–30.

KELLEY, H. H. (1973). The process of causal attribution. *American Psychologist, 28,* 107–128.

KOHLBERG, L. (1966). A cognitive-developmental analysis of children's sex-role concepts and attitudes. In E. E. Maccoby (Ed.), *The development of sex differences.* Stanford, CA: Stanford University Press.

KOHLBERG, L. (1969). Stage and sequence: The cognitive-developmental approach to socialization. In D. A. Goslin (Ed.), *Handbook of socialization theory and research.* Skokie, IL: Rand McNally.

KUCZYNSKI, L., ZAHN-WAXLER, C., & RADKE-YARROW, M. (1987). Development and content of imitation in the second and third years of life: A socialization perspective. *Developmental Psychology, 23,* 276–282.

KUN, A. (1978). Evidence for preschoolers' understanding of causal direction in extended causal sequences. *Child Development, 49,* 218–222.

KURDEK, L. A., & KRILE, D. (1982). A developmental analysis of the relation between peer acceptance and both interpersonal understanding and perceived social self-competence. *Child Development, 53,* 1485–1491.

LAPSLEY, D. K., MILSTEAD, M., QUINTANA, S.M., FLAN-NERY, D., & BUSS, R. R. (1986). Adolescent egocentrism and formal operations: Tests of a theoretical assumption. *Developmental Psychology, 22,* 800–807.

LeMARE, L. J., & RUBIN, K. H. (1987). Perspective taking and peer interaction: Structural and developmental analyses. *Child Development, 58,* 306–315.

LEWIS, M., ALESSANDRI, S. M., & SULLIVAN, M. W. (1990). Violation of expectancy, loss of control, and anger expressions in young infants. *Developmental Psychology, 26,* 745–751.

LIVESLEY, W. J., & BROMLEY, D. B. (1973). *Person perception in childhood and adolescence.* London: Wiley.

McCONAGHY, M. (1979). Gender permanence and the genital basis of gender: Stages in the development of constancy and gender identity. *Child Development, 50,* 1223–1226.

McGUIRE, K. D., & WEISZ, J. R. (1982). Social cognition and behavioral correlates of preadolescent chumship. *Child Development, 53,* 1478–1484.

MEAD, G. H. (1934). *Mind, self, and society.* Chicago: University of Chicago Press.

MELTZOFF, A. N., & MOORE, M. K. (1977). Imitation of facial and manual gestures by human neonates. *Science, 198,* 75–78.

MELTZOFF, A. N., & MOORE, M. K. (1989). Imitation in newborn infants: Exploring the range of gestures imitated and the underlying mechanisms. *Developmental Psychology, 25,* 954–962.

MILLER, P. H., & ALOISE, P. A. (1989). Young children's understanding of the psychological causes of behavior: A review. *Child Development, 60,* 257–285.

NELSON, J., & ABOUD, F. E. (1985). The resolution of social conflict among friends. *Child Development, 56,* 1009–1017.

NELSON-LeGALL, S. A. (1985). Motive-outcome matching and outcome foreseeability: Effects on attribution of intentionality and moral judgments. *Developmental Psychology, 21,* 332–337.

OLSON, G. M., & SHERMAN, T. (1983). A conceptual framework for the study of infant mental processes. In L. P. Lippitt (Ed.), *Advances in infancy research* (Vol. 3). Norwood, NJ: Ablex.

O'MAHONEY, J. F. (1989). Development of thinking about things and people: Social and nonsocial cognition during adolescence. *Journal of Genetic Psychology, 150,* 217–224.

PEEVERS, B. H., & SECORD, P. F. (1973). Developmental changes in attributions of descriptive concepts to persons. *Journal of Personality and Social Psychology, 27,* 120–128.

PELLEGRINI, D. S. (1985). Social cognition and competence in middle childhood. *Child Development, 56,* 253–264.

PIAGET, J. (1950). *The psychology of intelligence.* San Diego: Harcourt Brace Jovanovich.

PIAGET, J. (1951). *Play, dreams, and imitation in childhood.* New York: Norton.

PIAGET, J. (1952). *The origins of intelligence in children.* New York: International Universities Press.

PIAGET, J. (1954). *The construction of reality in the child.* New York: Basic Books.

PIAGET, J. (1965). *The moral judgment of the child.* New York: Free Press. (Original work published 1932.)

PIAGET, J. (1970). Piaget's theory. In P.H. Mussen (Ed.), *Carmichael's manual of child psychology* (Vol. 1). New York: Wiley.

PIAGET, J., & INHELDER, B. (1969). *The psychology of the child.* New York: Basic Books.

REID, M., LANDESMAN, S., TREDER, R., & JACCARD, J. (1989). "My family and friends": Six- to twelve-year-old children's perceptions of social support. *Child Development, 60,* 896–910.

REISSLAND, N. (1988). Neonatal imitation in the first hour of life: Observations in rural Nepal. *Developmental Psychology, 24,* 464–469.

RHOLES, W. S., JONES, M., & WADE, C. (1988). Children's understanding of personal disposition and its relationship to behavior. *Journal of Experimental Child Psychology, 45,* 1–17.

RHOLES, W. S., & RUBLE, D. N. (1984). Children's understanding of dispositional characteristics of others. *Child Development, 55,* 550–560.

RILEY, T., ADAMS, G. R., & NIELSEN, E. (1984). Adolescent egocentrism: The association among imaginary audience behavior, cognitive development, and parental support and rejection. *Journal of Youth and Adolescence, 13,* 401–417.

ROTENBERG, K. J., SIMOURD, L., & MOORE, D. (1989). Children's use of a verbal-nonverbal consistency principle to infer truth and lying. *Child Development, 60,* 309–322.

RUBIN, K. H., FEIN, G., & VANDENBERG, B. (1983). Play. In E. M. Hetherington (Ed.), *Handbook of child psychology.* Vol. 4: *Socialization, personality, and social development.* New York: Wiley.

RUFFMAN, T. K., & OLSON, D. R. (1989). Children's ascriptions of knowledge to others. *Developmental Psychology, 25,* 601–606.

SCHAFFER, H. R. (1977). *Mothering.* Cambridge, MA: Harvard University Press.

SCHAFFER, H. R. (1990). *Making decisions about children: Psychological questions and answers.* Cambridge, MA: Basil Blackwell.

SECORD, P. F., & PEEVERS, B. H. (1974). The development and attribution of person concepts. In T. Mischel (Ed.), *Understanding other persons.* Totowa, NJ: Rowman & Littlefield.

SEDLAK, A. J., & KURTZ, S. T. (1981). A review of children's use of causal inference principles. *Child Development, 52,* 759–784.

SELMAN, R. L. (1976). Social-cognitive understanding: A guide to educational and clinical practice. In T. Lickona (Ed.), *Moral development and behavior: Theory, research and social issues.* New York: Holt, Rinehart & Winston.

SELMAN, R. L. (1980). *The growth of interpersonal understanding.* Orlando, FL: Academic Press.

SELMAN, R. L., & BYRNE, D. (1974). A structural developmental analysis of role-taking in middle childhood. *Child Development, 45,* 803–806.

SHAFFER, D. R. (1973). *Children's responses to a hypothetical proposition*. Unpublished manuscript, Kent State University.

SHAFFER, D. R. (1993). *Developmental psychology: Childhood and adolescence* (3rd ed.). Pacific Grove, CA: Brooks/Cole.

SHANTZ, C. U. (1983). Social cognition. In P. H. Mussen (Ed.), *Handbook of child psychology*. Vol. 3: *Cognitive development*. New York: Wiley.

SHULTZ, T. R., & WELLS, D. (1985). Judging the intentionality of action-outcomes. *Developmental Psychology, 21*, 83–89.

SLABY, R. G., & FREY, K. S. (1975). Development of gender constancy and selective attention to same-sex models. *Child Development, 46*, 849–856.

SODIAN, B., TAYLOR, C., HARRIS, P. L., & PERNER, J. (1991). Early deception and the child's theory of mind: False trails and genuine markers. *Child Development, 62*, 468–483.

WERNER, H. (1957). The concept of development from a comparative and organismic point of view. In D. B. Harris (Ed.), *The concept of development*. Minneapolis: University of Minnesota Press.

YEATES, K. O., & SELMAN, R. L. (1989). Social competence in the schools: Toward an integrative developmental model for intervention. *Developmental Review, 9*, 64–100.

5 Early Social and Emotional Development I: Emotional Growth and Establishment of Affectional Ties

In 1891 G. Stanley Hall stated that adolescence is the most crucial period of the life span for the development of personality. Hall characterized the teenage years as a time when interests are solidified, long-lasting friendships emerge, and important decisions are made about one's education, career, and (in those days) choice of a mate. In other words, he viewed adolescence as the period when individuals assume personal and interpersonal identities that will carry them through their adult lives.

This viewpoint was soon challenged by Sigmund Freud (1905/1930), who believed that many of the decisions that an adolescent makes about the future are predetermined by his or her reactions to earlier life experiences. In fact, Freud proclaimed that the foundations of the adult personality are laid during the first five to six years of life and that personality development begins the moment a baby is first handed to his or her parents.

Today we know that Freud was right in at least one respect: social and emotional development does begin very early in life. Although few contemporary theorists believe that our personalities are "set in stone" during the first few years, we know that the kinds of emotional relationships infants develop with their close companions can affect the ways they relate to other people later in life. Early social experiences are important experiences — and infancy is truly a sensitive period for personality development.

Our primary focus over the next two chapters is on a major social and emotional milestone of infancy: the development of affectional ties between children and their closest companions. We will begin by briefly reviewing what is known about infants' abilities to display and regulate their own emotions and to interpret the emotions of others. Indeed, this brief overview should aptly illustrate why modern developmentalists view infants' emotional transactions with their caregivers as a critically important aspect of early social development. We will then take up the topic of emotional *attachments*, first defining the term as developmentalists do and then exploring the processes by which infants and their close companions establish these intimate affectional ties. Next we will consider two

common fears that attached infants often display and will see why these wary reactions often emerge during the latter half of the first year. And in Chapter 6 we will continue our discussion of early social and emotional development by reviewing a rapidly expanding base of evidence suggesting that the kind of emotional attachments that infants are able to establish (or the lack thereof) can have important implications for their later social, emotional, and intellectual development.

Are Babies Emotional Creatures?

Do babies have feelings? Do they experience and display specific emotions, such as happiness, sadness, fear, and anger, the way older children and adults do? Most parents think they do. In one study, more than half the mothers of 1-month-old infants said that their babies displayed at least five distinct emotional expressions: interest, surprise, joy, anger, and fear (Johnson et al., 1982). Although one might argue that this is simply a case of proud mothers reading much too much into the behavior of their babies, there is now reliable evidence that even very young infants are indeed emotional creatures.

Displaying (and Controlling) Emotions

Carroll Izard and his colleagues at the University of Delaware have studied infants' emotional expressions by videotaping babies' responses to such events as grasping an ice cube, having a toy taken away, or seeing their mothers return after a separation (Izard, 1982). Izard's procedure is straightforward: he asks raters, who are unaware of the events that an infant has experienced, to tell him what emotion the child is experiencing from the facial expression the child displays. These studies reveal that different adult raters observing the same expressions reliably see the same emotion in a baby's

Interest: brows raised; mouth may be rounded; lips may be pursed.

Fear: mouth retracted; brows level and drawn up and in; eyelids lifted.

Disgust: tongue protruding; upper lip raised; nose wrinkled.

Joy: bright eyes; cheeks lifted; mouth forms a smile.

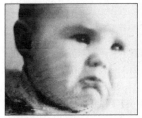

Sadness: corners of mouth turned down; inner portion of brows raised.

Anger: mouth squared at corners; brows drawn together and pointing down; eyes fixed straight ahead.

PHOTOS 5-1 Young infants display a variety of emotional expressions.

face (see Photos 5-1). Infants also respond in predictable ways to particular kinds of experiences. For example, soft sounds and novel visual displays are likely to elicit smiles and looks of interest, whereas inoculations and other painful stimuli will elicit distress from a younger infant and anger from an older one (Izard, Hembree, & Huebner, 1987).

Babies can also express emotions vocally. For example, 1-month-olds often **coo** when contented and may also display "blurts" of excitation when they are happy or interested in something—signals that

parents interpret as positive emotions and will attempt to prolong by talking to or playing with their babies (Keller & Scholmerich, 1987). Moreover, healthy neonates are capable of producing at least three distinct cries that may indicate different kinds of distress: a rhythmic "hunger" cry that starts with a whimper and becomes louder and more sustained, a "mad" cry that is also rhythmic but more intense, and a "pain" cry that begins with a high-pitched shriek, followed by a brief silence and then more vigorous crying. Peter Wolff (1969) devised an interesting experiment to see whether young, relatively inexperienced mothers could distinguish these three cries. While supposedly observing the neonates in their own rooms, Wolff played a tape recording of the infant crying and waited for the mothers to respond. And respond they did: At the sound of a high-pitched "pain" cry, mothers immediately came running to see what was wrong. However, the mothers responded much more slowly (if at all) to either "hungry" or "mad" cries. Although caregivers do become better with experience at deciphering the "meaning" of their infants' cries (Gustafson & Harris, 1990), even inexperienced adults know that, the higher the pitch of an infant's crying, the more serious and urgent his problem is (Zeskind & Marshall, 1988).

Critics of such demonstrations argue that the "emotional" expressions of infancy are really nothing more than global displays of positive and negative affect. However, these critics have not adequately explained how adults are able to show such remarkable agreement about the specific feeling an infant is experiencing (for example, distress versus disgust) when they have nothing more to go on than a tape recording of the infant's facial or vocal expression. Moreover, we've noted that babies react in very predictable ways to particular kinds of experiences; there is even some consistency to these affective displays, for the infants who react more vigorously to a distressing event at age 2 months are likely to remain the most vigorous responders when retested at ages 13–19 months (Izard et al., 1987). So early patterns of affective expression are tied to specific kinds of eliciting events and are relatively stable over time. Regardless of whether one calls them "emotions" (and most contemporary researchers do), it is obvious that infants are able to communicate a variety of feelings to their companions.

SEQUENCING OF DISCRETE EMOTIONS

Various emotions appear at different times over the first two years. At birth or shortly thereafter, babies display interest (by staring attentively at objects), distress, disgust (to bitter tastes and foul odors), and expressions of contentment (Izard, 1982; Izard & Malatesta, 1987). Other **primary emotions** that emerge between 2½ and 6 months of age are anger, sadness, surprise, and fear. It has been argued (see Izard, 1982; Malatesta et al., 1989) that the primary emotions are biologically programmed, since they appear in all normal infants at roughly the same time and are interpreted similarly in all cultures. Yet some learning is probably necessary before babies will experience and display any emotion not present at birth. Indeed, one of the strongest elicitors of surprise and joy among 2- to 8-month-olds is their discovery that they can control objects and events in their environments. Yet, disconfirmation of these *learned* expectancies (as when someone or something prevents their exerting control) is likely to sadden and *anger* 4–5-month-olds (Lewis, Alessandri, & Sullivan, 1990).

Complex (or secondary) **emotions** such as embarrassment, shame, guilt, and pride appear in the second or third year and seem closely tied to cognitive development. Michael Lewis and his associates (Lewis et al., 1989) believe that *self-conscious* emotions (such as embarrassment) will not emerge until the child can recognize herself in a mirror or a photograph (a self-referential milestone that we will discuss in detail in Chapter 7), whereas *self-evaluative* emotions (such as shame, guilt, and pride) may require *both* self-recognition and a firm understanding of rules of conduct that will allow the child to evaluate her behavior as acceptable or unacceptable.

Preliminary findings are quite consistent with Lewis's theory. For example, he has shown that the only toddlers who become noticeably embarrassed by lavish praise or by a request to "show off" for strangers are those who display self-recognition (Lewis et al., 1989). And by age 3 — or about the time children first *evaluate* their own performances in terms of "successes" and "failures" — they begin to show clear signs of *pride* (smiling, applauding, exclaiming "I did it!") when they succeed at a difficult task and *shame* (that is, a downward gaze with a slumped posture, often accompanied by statements such as "I'm no good at this") should they fail at an easy one (Lewis, Alessandri, & Sullivan, 1992; see also Stipek, Recchia, & McClintic, 1992). Let's note, however, that toddlers and young preschool children are most likely to experience these self-evaluative emotions when someone else is present to observe their behavior. Indeed, it may be well into the elementary-school period before children feel especially prideful or shameful about their conduct in the absence of external surveillance (Bussey, 1992; Harter & Whitesell, 1989).

In addition to the above findings, there are other clear indications that 18–24-month-old infants live rich emotional lives. For example, this is the age when they begin to talk about various feelings that they or their companions have experienced and will often discuss the causes of these emotions as they enact them during pretend play (Bretherton et al., 1986; Dunn, Bretherton, & Munn, 1987). In fact, many older infants and toddlers have already learned to fake certain affective expressions (for example, crying or acting peeved) in order to manipulate a companion's emotions or otherwise get their own way (Bretherton et al., 1986). They are accomplished "emoters" indeed!

SOCIALIZATION OF EMOTIONS AND EMOTIONAL SELF-REGULATION

Each society has a set of **emotional display rules** that specify the circumstances under which various emotions should or should not be expressed. For example, 12-year-olds in Western society know that they are supposed to express happiness or gratitude when they receive a gift from Grandma and, by all means, to suppress any disappointment they may feel should the gift turn out to be underwear. Indeed, these emotional "codes of conduct" are rules that children must acquire and use if they hope to get along with other people and maintain their approval. When does this learning begin?

Earlier than you might imagine! Consider that, when mothers play with 2–7-month-old infants, they restrict themselves mainly to displays of joy, interest, and surprise, thus serving as models of positive emotions for their babies (Malatesta & Haviland, 1982; Malatesta et al., 1986). Mothers also respond selectively to their infants' emotions; over the first several months they become increasingly attentive to babies' expressions of interest or surprise and less responsive to the infants' negative emotions (Malatesta et al., 1986, 1989). Through basic learning processes, then, babies are trained to display more pleasant faces and fewer unpleasant ones—and they do just that over time. Infants are quickly learning which emotional displays parents find acceptable and are even developing expressive styles that match those of their parents (Denham, 1989; Malatesta et al., 1989).

To comply with these emotional lessons, however, babies must devise strategies for regulating and controlling their emotional states. This is a difficult feat indeed for very young infants, who do manage to reduce at least some of the negative arousal by turning away from unpleasantries or by sucking vigorously on objects. Nevertheless, they must often depend on caregivers to soothe them when they are experiencing strong emotional distress (Kopp, 1989). By the end of the first year, infants have developed new means of moderating aversive arousal as they rock themselves to and fro, chew on their fingers and thumbs, and reach for and explore toys as a form of distraction (Kopp, 1989). During the second year, infants begin to knit their brows and to bite or compress their lips as they actively attempt to suppress their sadness and their anger (Malatesta et al., 1989).

By age 3, children are becoming much better at concealing at least some of their feelings. Consider what Michael Lewis (Lewis, Stanger, & Sullivan, 1989) found when he left the room, tempting many 3-year-olds to peek at a hidden toy when they weren't supposed to. When asked if they had peeked, children who did and then lied about it showed some subtle emotional leakage (detectable on film) that might have signaled their guilt or shame; that is, they emitted nervous smiles and body touches that were not displayed by truth

tellers. Yet these youngsters were already so good at covering their emotional tracks that naive adult observers could neither detect these subtle cues nor discriminate the liars from the truth tellers.

Of course, suppressing signs of guilt or shame is hardly a practice that parents would hope to encourage—but they may nevertheless do so by reacting so very negatively to whatever lies from their child they do happen to detect. Carolyn Saarni (1984, 1990) argues that children learn to comply with socially sanctioned display rules for precisely the same reasons they hide their guilt: to avoid punishment and maintain others' approval. She also believes that mastering these rules is a gradual process—one in which the child must first see the rule applied consistently and then eventually decide that it is a generally accepted practice. Indeed, even simple display rules may take a long time to master. As we see in Figure 5-1, many 7–9-year-olds are still unable to act thrilled and to mask their disappointment

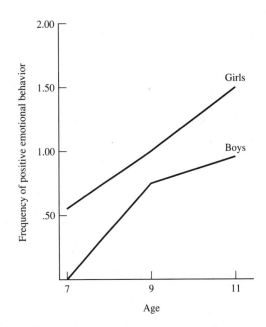

FIGURE 5-1 With age, children are more able to display positive emotional reactions after receiving a disappointing gift. (Based on C. Saarni, "An Observational Study of Children's Attempts to Monitor Their Expressive Behavior." *Child Development*, 1984, *55*, 1504–1513. Copyright © 1984 by the Society for Research in Child Development.)

upon receiving a lousy gift. And even 12–13-year-olds may fail to suppress all their anger when a respected adult exercises authority and thwarts their objectives (Underwood, Coie, & Herbsman, 1992).

Recognizing and Interpreting Emotions

When do infants first notice and respond to the emotional expressions of other people? Surprising as it may seem, they react to certain vocal signals at birth or shortly thereafter. In Box 2-2, for example, we learned that neonates who hear another infant cry will soon begin to cry themselves, thus showing their responsiveness to the distress of another baby.[1] Over the first year, parents the world over speak to infants in high-pitched tones that are acoustic concomitants of positive emotions such as happiness (Fernald & Mazzie, 1991; Grieser & Kuhl, 1988), and even 2-day-old infants pay more attention to this highly intonated speech than to the "flatter" speech that adults use when communicating with one another (Cooper & Aslin, 1990). By the end of the neonatal period (age 4–6 weeks), the infant can discriminate his mother's voice from those of female strangers when the mother speaks in her high-pitched "happy" tone but not when she speaks in a monotone (Mehler et al., 1978). Of course, this does not mean that infants recognize that their mothers are "happy," but it does imply that they are closely attending to the parameters of speech by which we convey emotions.

Currently there is some debate about when babies begin to recognize and interpret the facial expressions of emotion that others display. Although 3-month-olds prefer to look at photos of happy faces rather than at photos of neutral, sad, or angry ones (Kuchuk, Vibbert, & Bornstein, 1986; La Barbera et al., 1976), their looking preferences may simply reflect their powers of visual discrimination and do not necessarily imply that infants this young *interpret* various expressions as "happy," "angry," or "sad" (Ludemann, 1991; Nelson, 1987). Yet evidence is rapidly accumulating to suggest that young in-

fants do attend carefully and react appropriately to more natural displays of emotion. For example, 3-month-olds will not only discriminate their mother's happy, sad, or angry expressions when these facial configurations are accompanied by a happy, sad, or angry tone of voice, but they also become rather gleeful in response to a happy expression and distressed by the mother's anger or sadness (Haviland & Lelwica, 1987; Tronick, 1989).

The ability of infants to *interpret* emotional expressions is rather obvious by age 8–10 months—the point at which they begin to monitor their parents' emotional reactions to uncertain situations and to use this information to regulate their own feelings and behavior (Feinman, 1992; Klinnert et al., 1986). Indeed, this **social referencing** becomes more common with age (Walden & Baxter, 1989) and may soon extend to strangers as well: by age 12 months, infants will typically approach and play with unfamiliar toys if a nearby stranger is smiling but avoid these objects if the stranger displays a fearful expression (Klinnert et al., 1986). During the second year, infants will often look to their companions *after* they have appraised a new object or situation, which suggests that they are now using others' emotional reactions to assess the accuracy of their *own* judgments (Hornik & Gunnar, 1988).

Once toddlers begin to talk about emotions, family conversations that center on emotional experiences can help them to achieve a much richer understanding of their own and others' feelings. In fact, Judy Dunn and her associates (1991) found that, the more often 3-year-olds had discussed emotional experiences with other family members, the better they were at interpreting others' emotions three years later in grade school. Of course, the ability to identify how others are feeling and to understand why they feel that way is a central aspect of social cognition—and one that may have important social consequences in that kindergarten and first-grade children who score high on tests of emotional understanding tend to enjoy especially good relations with their peers (Cassidy et al., 1992).

Although our major focus in this chapter is on early emotional development, it should come as no surprise that children's ability to recognize and interpret others' emotional displays improves steadily

---

[1]Although ethologists have suggested that such crying may be a precursor of empathy, another interpretation is that infants find the sound of crying to be aversive and will chime in to convey their own distress.

over the preschool period (Fabes et al., 1988, 1991). Nevertheless, there are many interpretive lessons that young grade-school children have yet to learn. Not until age 8, for example, do children recognize that many situations (for instance, the approach of a big dog) are emotionally equivocal and will elicit different emotional responses from different individuals (Gnepp & Klayman, 1992). Moreover, 8-year-olds are also beginning to understand that a person can experience more than one emotional reaction to the same event (Harter, 1986; Wintre, Polivy, & Murray, 1990) and are displaying some ability to integrate contrasting facial, behavioral, and situational cues to infer what those reactions might be (Hoffner & Badzinski, 1989). Notice that these latter advances in emotional understanding occur at about the same time that children begin to describe their acquaintances in traitlike terms (see Chapter 4). Indeed, they may even depend on the same underlying cognitive developments (that is, decentration and the acquisition of reciprocal role-taking skills), although it is likely that such relevant social experiences as observing, feeling, and having opportunities to talk about "mixed" emotional reactions are important as well (Harter & Buddin, 1987).

Emotions and Early Social Development

What role do emotions play in early social development? Clearly, a baby's feelings serve a *communicative* function that is likely to affect the behavior of caregivers. For example, cries of distress summon close companions. Early suggestions of a smile or expressions of interest may convince caregivers that their baby is willing and even eager to strike up a social relationship with them. Later expressions of fear or sadness may indicate that the infant is insecure or feeling blue and needs some attention or comforting. Anger may imply that the infant wants her companions to stop whatever they are doing that is upsetting her, whereas joy serves as a prompt for caregivers to prolong an ongoing interaction or perhaps signals the baby's willingness to accept new challenges. So infant emotions are adaptive in that they promote social contact and help caregivers to adjust their behavior to the infant's needs and goals. Stated another way, the emotional expressions of infancy help infants and their close companions to "get to know each other" (Tronick, 1989).

At the same time, the infant's emerging ability to recognize and interpret others' emotions is an important achievement that enables him to infer how he should be feeling or behaving in a variety of situations. The beauty of this "social referencing" is that children can quickly acquire *knowledge* in this way. For example, a sibling's joyful reaction to the family pooch should indicate that this "ball of fur" is a friend rather than an unspeakable monster. A mother's pained expression and accompanying vocal concern might immediately suggest that the knife in one's hand is an implement to be avoided. And, given the frequency with which expressive caregivers direct an infant's attention to important aspects of the environment or display their feelings about an infant's appraisal of objects and events, it is likely that the information inherent in their emotional displays will contribute in a major way to the child's understanding of the world in which he lives (Rosen, Adamson, & Bakeman, 1992).

What Are Emotional Attachments?

Social developmentalists have discovered that the young of most higher species form close emotional ties to their mothers or to a "mother figure" during infancy. To the layperson this "attachment" appears to be a bond of love that is often attributed to maternal tendencies such as "mother instinct" or "mother love." Developmentalists are willing to concede that mothers and other close companions are likely to become attached to an infant long before the infant is attached to them. However, it now appears that mother love must be nurtured and that most infants are capable of promoting such a caregiver-to-infant bond from the moment of birth. What is an emotional **attachment**? John Bowlby (1958, 1969) uses the term to describe the strong affectional ties that bind a person to an intimate companion. According to Bowlby, people who are attached will interact often and will try to maintain proximity to each other. Thus a 12-month-old boy who is attached to his mother may show his attachment by doing whatever it takes—crying, clinging, approaching, or following—to establish or to maintain contact with her. Leslie Cohen (1974) adds that attachments are *selective* in character: the company of some people (**attachment objects**) is more pleasant or reassuring than that of others. For example, a 2-year-old girl who is attached to her mother should prefer the mother's company to that of a mere acquaintance whenever she is upset, discomforted, or afraid.

Although our focus in this chapter is on the attachments that develop between infants and their close companions, there are many other kinds of attachments that individuals may form. Older children, adolescents, and adults may not "cling" to their intimate companions in the same way that infants do, but we can certainly see some similarities between an infant's strong ties to his mother, a child's or adolescent's involvement with a particularly close friend, and an adult's emotional commitment to a spouse or a lover (Hazan & Shaver, 1987; Simpson, Rholes, & Nelligan, 1992). Indeed, people even develop intense attachments to cuddly kittens, puppies, and other house pets that respond to them and seem to enjoy their company. All these ties are similar in that the attachment object is someone (or something) special with whom we are motivated to maintain contact (Ainsworth, 1989).

How do infants and caregivers become attached to each other? Let's address this important issue by looking first at caregivers' reactions to infants.

The Caregiver's Attachment to the Infant

People sometimes find it hard to understand how a parent might become attached to a neonate. After all, newborn infants can be demanding little creatures who drool, spit up, fuss, cry, dirty their diapers on a regular basis, and often require a lot of attention at all hours of the day and night. Since babies are associated with so many distasteful consequences, why don't their parents learn to dislike them?

Early Emotional Bonding

One reason why parents may overlook or discount the negative aspects of child care is that they began to form emotional attachments to their infant *before* they experienced many of the unpleasantries of parenthood. Marshall Klaus and John Kennell (1976) believe that caregivers can become **emotionally bonded** to an infant during the first few hours after birth—provided that they are given an opportunity to get to know their baby. Specifically, Klaus and Kennell argued that early skin-to-skin contact between mothers and their babies would make mothers especially responsive to their infants and promote the development of strong mother-to-infant emotional bonds.

To test this hypothesis, Klaus and Kennell (1976) studied 28 young mothers who had just delivered full-term, healthy infants. During their three-day stay in the hospital, half the mothers followed the traditional routine: they saw their babies briefly after delivery, visited with them 6–12 hours later, and then had half-hour feeding sessions with their infants every four hours thereafter. Mothers assigned to a second, or "extended contact," group were permitted five "extra" hours a day to cuddle their babies, including an hour of skin-to-skin contact that took place within three hours of birth.

When observed one month later, the mothers who had had extended contact with their newborns stood nearer and soothed their infants more during a routine physical examination, and they held their babies closer during feeding than did mothers who had followed the normal hospital routine. A year later, extended-contact mothers were still more soothing, cuddling, and nurturing than mothers in the "normal routine" condition. As for the year-old infants, those who had had extended early contact with their mothers outperformed those who had not on tests of physical and mental development.

From this study and others reporting similar results (see Klaus & Kennell, 1982), Klaus and Kennell concluded that the sheer amount of early contact a mother has with her infant is less important than the *timing* of that contact. Indeed, their interpretation of the data is that the first 6–12 hours is a **sensitive period** for emotional bonding: presumably, mothers develop the strongest possible affection for their babies if they have had some skin-to-skin contact with them during this particular time.

WHY MIGHT EARLY CONTACT MATTER?

Why do mothers build these emotional bridges to their infants just after giving birth? Kennell, Voos, and Klaus (1979) suggested that hormones present at the time of delivery may help to focus the mother's attention on her baby and make her more susceptible to forming a strong emotional bond. If these hormones should dissipate before a mother has any extended contact with her infant, she will presumably become less responsive to her baby, much as animals do if separated from their offspring in the first few hours after giving birth.

Although the "hormonal mediation" hypothesis may sound quite plausible, there are observations that it can't easily explain. Consider, for example, that fathers who are present at birth (or soon thereafter) often become just as fascinated with a neonate as mothers do, wishing to touch, hold, or caress the baby (Greenberg & Morris, 1974). Clearly, a father's early **engrossment** with his infant is an emotional reaction very similar to that experienced by mothers and is obviously *not* due to the action of pregnancy hormones.

If the hormonal mediation hypothesis does not explain the early affection that parents display toward their newborn infants, then what does? One idea offered by ethologists is that caregivers are biologically predisposed to react favorably and with affection to a neonate's pleasing social overtures (Bowlby, 1969). Another possibility stems from social-psychological research on the interpretation of emotions. Perhaps the intense emotional arousal (fear or apprehension) that parents experience during childbirth is *reinterpreted* in a positive light when they are handed an infant who gazes attentively at them, grasps their fingers, and seems to snuggle in response to their caresses. If parents should then attribute these positive feelings to *the baby and its behavior*, it is easy to see how they might feel rather affectionate toward their neonate and become emotionally involved with him or her. However, parents who have little or no early contact with their neonates are unable to attribute their existing emotional arousal to a beautiful, responsive baby. In fact, they often end up labeling their emotions as exhaustion or a sense of relief that the ordeal of pregnancy and childbirth is finally over (Grossman et al., 1980). Perhaps you can see that these latter attributions are unlikely to make parents feel especially affectionate toward a newborn child.

IS EARLY CONTACT NECESSARY FOR OPTIMAL DEVELOPMENT?

Klaus and Kennell's **sensitive-period hypothesis** implies that new parents show a basic "readiness" to become emotionally involved with their infant during the first few hours after birth. As we have seen, there is ample evidence to support this proposition. However, Klaus and Kennell also implied that parents who have had little or no contact with their neonates during the sensitive period may never become as attached to these infants as they might had they had skin-to-skin contact with them during the first few hours. This second theoretical proposition is much more controversial.

Susan Goldberg (1983) has carefully reviewed the emotional-bonding literature and concluded that, contrary to Klaus and Kennell's claim, "early contact" effects are neither large nor long lasting. In one well-controlled study in which mothers and neonates were carefully observed for a nine-day period, the advantages of early contact steadily declined over time. By the ninth day after birth, early-contact mothers were no more affectionate or responsive toward their infants than were mothers who had had no skin-to-skin contact with their babies for several hours after delivery. Indeed, the delayed-contact mothers showed a dramatic increase in responsiveness over the nine-day observation period—suggesting that the hours immediately after birth are not nearly so critical as Klaus and Kennell assumed

(Goldberg, 1983; see also Myers, 1987). Michael Rutter (1981) adds that most adoptive parents are quite satisfied with and will develop close emotional ties to their adoptees, even though they have rarely had *any* contact with them during the neonatal period (see also Levy-Shiff, Goldshmidt, & Har-Even, 1991). Indeed, the likelihood that a mother and her infant will become securely attached is just as high in adoptive families as in nonadoptive ones (Singer et al., 1985).

In sum, research on early emotional bonding suggests that parents can become highly involved with their infants during the first few hours if they are permitted to touch, hold, cuddle, and play with their babies. As a result, many hospitals have altered their routines to allow and encourage these kinds of experiences. However, it appears that this early contact is neither crucial nor sufficient for the development of strong parent-to-infant or infant-to-parent attachments. Stable attachments between infants and caregivers are not formed in a matter of minutes, hours, or days—they build rather slowly from social interactions that take place over *many weeks and months*. So there is absolutely no reason for parents who have not had early skin-to-skin contact with their infant to assume that they will have problems establishing a warm and loving relationship with the child.

How Infants Promote Attachments

Since newborn infants spend more than 20 hours a day sleeping, crying, or being in a drowsy, semiconscious state (Berg & Berg, 1987), it is tempting to think of them as inherently asocial creatures. However, ethologists John Bowlby (1969) and Konrad Lorenz (1943) have challenged this point of view, arguing that babies are highly *sociable* companions who are born with a number of endearing qualities that should make them easy to love. Let's explore this idea further.

OH, BABY FACE: THE KEWPIE-DOLL SYNDROME

Konrad Lorenz (1943) suggested that a baby's **"kewpie doll"** appearance (that is, large forehead, big eyes, chubby cheeks, and soft, rounded features;

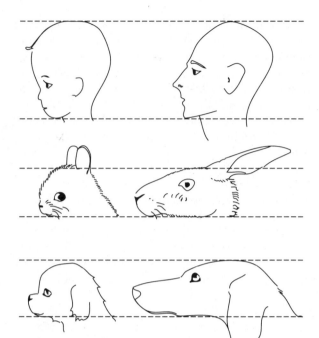

FIGURE 5-2 Infants of many species display the "kewpie-doll syndrome" that makes them appear lovable and elicits caregivers' attention. (Adapted from K. Z. Lorenz, "Die angeboren Formen moglicher Erfahrung" [The innate forms of possible existence]. *Zeitschrift fur Tierpsychologie*, 1943, 5, 233–409.)

see Figure 5-2) makes the infant appear cute or lovable to caregivers. Thomas Alley (1981) agrees. Alley found that adults judged line drawings of infant faces (and profiles) to be "adorable"—much cuter than those of 4-year-old children. Younger boys and girls also react positively to babyish facial features, although girls begin to show an even stronger interest in infants after reaching menarche (Goldberg, Blumberg, & Kriger, 1982).

Do adults respond more frequently and more favorably to attractive babies than to unattractive ones? Indeed they do (Hildebrandt & Fitzgerald, 1981; Stephan & Langlois, 1984)—even when the babies in question are their own (Barden et al., 1989; Field & Vega-Lahr, 1984). One recent study found that mothers of "unattractive" 3-month-olds reported *more* satisfaction with parenting than did mothers of "attractive" agemates; yet, filmed observations revealed that these same mothers were *less* likely than were mothers of attractive infants to cuddle or play with their babies or to respond to their bids for attention (Barden et al., 1989). Furthermore, mothers expect unattractive infants to be capable of *more* behaviors than attractive ones, probably because an unattractive infant looks "older" than an attractive agemate (Ritter, Casey, & Langlois, 1991). Although these latter studies are "early returns" that will need to be replicated before we can draw firm conclusions, they do imply that (1) attractive facial features may indeed help infants to elicit the kinds of attention that will promote social attachments, and (2) unattractive features may inhibit such contact and contribute to the development of unrealistically high expectations for an infant, without the parent even being aware of these effects.

INNATE RESPONSES AS SOCIABLE GESTURES

Not only do infants have "cute" faces, but many of their early reflexive behaviors may have an endearing quality about them (Bowlby, 1969). For example, the rooting,[2] sucking, and grasping reflexes may lead parents to believe that their infant enjoys being close to them. Smiling, which is initially a reflexive response to almost any pleasing stimulus, seems to be a particularly potent signal to caregivers, as are cooing, excitable blurting, and spontaneous babbling (Keller & Scholmerich, 1987). In fact, an adult's typical response to a baby's smiles and positive vocalizations is to smile at (or vocalize to) the infant (Gewirtz & Petrovich, 1982; Keller & Scholmerich, 1987), and parents often interpret their baby's grins, laughs, and babbles as an indication that the child is contented and that they are effective caregivers. So a smiling or babbling infant can reinforce caregiving activities and thereby increase the likelihood that parents or other nearby companions will want to attend to this happy little person in the future.

Even the reflexive cry, which is often described as aversive, can promote caregiver-to-infant attachments. Bowlby views the cry as a "distress signal" that elicits the approach of those who are responsible for the infant's care and safety. Presumably, re-

PHOTO 5-2   Few signals will attract as much attention as a baby's social smile.

sponsive caregivers who are successful at quieting their babies will then become the beneficiaries of positive responses, such as smiling and babbling, that should reinforce their caregiving behavior and make them feel even closer to their contented infants.

INTERACTIONAL SYNCHRONY

One thing that many parents find so fascinating about infants is that their babies often seem so responsive to them. Not only will full-term, healthy, neonates often stop crying, become alert, and begin to vocalize themselves when they are spoken to, but some researchers (for example, Peery, 1980) have claimed that 1-day-old infants are already capable of synchronizing their head and limb movements with those of an adult admirer. Although others are skeptical of these claims, arguing that any apparent "synchrony" in these earliest interactions reflects the adult adjusting her behavior to that of the baby (Cohn & Tronick, 1987), the fact remains that most

[2]The rooting reflex is an innate response: when an object brushes the cheek, an infant will turn its head in the direction of the touch, searching for something to suck.

normal, healthy infants are highly receptive to social contact—a characteristic that is likely to endear them to their companions.

Over the first few months, caregivers and infants will ordinarily have many opportunities to interact face to face as the caregiver feeds, bathes, diapers, or plays with the baby. One interesting feature of these early interactions is that babies cycle between periods of attention or interest, in which they may smile and make eye contact with the caregiver, and periods of inattention or avoidance, in which they quickly become overaroused and are likely to evade social overtures. Many infant-watchers now believe that these cycles of alert attention and inattention are important in establishing patterns of communication between caregivers and infants (Tronick, 1989). Should a caregiver attend carefully to a baby's cycles and limit her social stimulation to those periods when the baby is alert and receptive, she and her infant will soon develop **synchronized routines** that both parties will probably enjoy. Psychologists who have observed these interactions have likened them to "dances" in which the partners take turns responding to each other's leads. Edward Tronick (1989, p. 112) has described one such "dance" as a mother played peek-a-boo with her infant:

> The infant abruptly turns away from his mother as the game reaches its "peak" of intensity and begins to suck on his thumb and stare into space with a dull facial expression. The mother stops playing and sits back watching. . . . After a few seconds the infant turns back to her with an inviting expression. The mother moves closer, smiles, and says in a high-pitched, exaggerated voice, "Oh, now you're back!" He smiles in response and vocalizes. As they finish crowing together, the infant reinserts his thumb and looks away. The mother again waits. [Soon] the infant turns . . . to her and they greet each other with big smiles.

This is indeed an exquisite (synchronous) exchange in which each participant sends messages to which the other responds appropriately. By turning away and sucking, the excited infant is saying "Hey, I need to slow down and regulate my emotional state." His mother tells him she understands by patiently awaiting his return. As he returns, Mom tells him she's glad he's back, and he acknowledges that

signal with a smile and an excitable blurt. And, when the baby becomes overexcited a minute or two later, his mother waits for him to calm once again, and he communicates his thanks by smiling wide for her when he turns back the second time. Clearly, this is a dyad that not only interacts smoothly but quickly repairs any interactive errors.

How important are synchronous exchanges to the establishment of affectional ties? We can get some idea by contrasting synchronous interactions with conflictual, nonsynchronous ones. Suppose the mother in our example had been less patient when her infant turned away, choosing instead to click her tongue to attract his attention and to follow up by sticking her face in the baby's line of vision. According to Tronick (1989), what might well happen is that the baby would grimace, turn further away, and perhaps even push at his mother's face. The mother's intrusive actions have communicated something like "Cut the coy stuff and come play with me," whereas the infant's negative response implies "No, you cool it and give me some space." Here, then, is an exchange in which messages go unheeded and interactive errors persist—one that is undoubtedly much less pleasant for both the mother and her baby than the highly affectionate, synchronous interplay described above.

In sum, infants play a major role in persuading other people to love them. Babies are physically appealing; they come equipped with a number of reflexes and response capabilities that capture the attention and warm the hearts of their companions; and, last but not least, they are responsive to social overtures and may soon be capable of synchronizing their behavior with that of a caregiver. Daniel Stern (1977) believes that synchronized interactions between infants and their companions may occur several times a day and are particularly important contributors to social attachments. As an infant continues to interact with a particular caregiver, he will learn what this person is like and how he can regulate her attention. Of course, the caregiver should become better at interpreting the baby's signals and learning how to adjust her behavior to successfully capture and maintain his attention. As the caregiver and the infant practice their routines and become better "dance partners," their relationship becomes more satisfying for both parties and will often blossom into a strong reciprocal attachment (Isabella & Belsky, 1991).

Problems in Establishing Caregiver-to-Infant Attachments

Although we have been talking as if caregivers invariably become closely attached to their infants, this does not always happen. As we will see, some babies are hard to love, some caregivers are hard to reach, and some environments are not very conducive to the establishment of secure emotional relationships.

SOME BABIES MAY ENGENDER LITTLE AFFECTION

Even though many neonates are remarkably proficient at attracting attention and sustaining social interactions, some babies display characteristics that could annoy and even alienate their companions. For example, premature infants are alert less often than full-term infants, are more quickly over-aroused by social stimulation, and will often avoid a caregiver's bids for attention (Field, 1987; Lester, Hoffman, & Brazelton, 1985). Premature babies also tend to be physically unattractive, and their high-pitched nonrhythmic cries are perceived as much more ''sickly'' and aversive than those of healthy, full-term infants (Zeskind, 1980).

Babies born addicted to a variety of narcotic agents also display abnormal patterns of behavior that could disrupt the establishment of synchronous routines between themselves and their caregivers (Kelley-Buchanan, 1988; Lester et al., 1991). Cocaine babies, in particular, are extremely susceptible to overstimulation and will often calm down and become alert *only* if they are left alone (Adler, 1989). Of course, the problems that drug-addicted babies face in endearing themselves to their companions may stem, in part, from the less-than-adequate care they often receive from their drug-using parents (Lester et al., 1991).

Finally, some full-term and otherwise-healthy infants have very difficult temperaments: they are at risk of alienating close companions because they are extremely active and irritable, are irregular in their habits, and are likely to resist caregivers' social overtures (Crockenberg, 1981).

During the first few months, parents do find it challenging to establish stable and synchronous routines with a very irritable or unresponsive infant who is likely to squirm, fuss, and clamor (Greene, Fox, & Lewis, 1983; Malatesta et al., 1986; Van Den Boom, 1988). Mothers of fretful infants are usually quite willing to provide comfort and attend to the infants' basic needs, but they spend less time in playful and affectionate activities than mothers whose babies cry less and are more responsive to social play (Greene et al., 1983; Malatesta et al., 1986).

Fortunately, most parents eventually establish satisfying routines and secure relationships with their difficult or unresponsive infants (Easterbrooks, 1989), particularly when they feel competent, or efficacious, about their parenting behavior (Teti & Gelfand, 1991) and when they have the support and encouragement of a spouse, a grandparent, or another close associate (Crockenberg & McCluskey, 1986; Jacobson & Frye, 1991). One way to help the process along is to identify *neonates* who may be difficult to love and then to teach their caregivers how to elicit favorable responses from these sluggish or irritable companions. Box 5-1 discusses one such training program that appears to be quite effective at achieving these aims.

SOME CAREGIVERS ARE HARD TO REACH

Caregivers sometimes have personal quirks or characteristics that seriously hinder them in establishing close emotional ties to their infants. For example, insecure attachments are the *rule* rather than the exception when a child's primary caregiver has been diagnosed as clinically depressed (Radke-Yarrow et al., 1985). The problem is that depressed parents are often not sufficiently responsive to a baby's social signals to establish a satisfying and synchronous relationship. And, unfortunately, young infants of depressed mothers soon begin to match the mothers' depressive symptoms (Field et al., 1990) and will often maintain this unresponsive, depressive demeanor, even when interacting with other *non-depressed* adults (Field et al., 1988)! Clearly, depressed parents are likely to require more than Brazelton training if they are to become more involved with their infants and establish secure emotional relationships with them. One intervention that has achieved excellent success is a program in which depressed mothers are visited regularly over a 9–18-month period by a trained paraprofessional who (1) establishes a friendly, *supportive* relationship with the mother, (2) teaches her how to elicit more favorable responses from her baby, and (3) encourages her to participate in weekly parenting groups—a second important source of parenting information and social support (Lyons-Ruth et al., 1990). Indeed, even nondepressed mothers who otherwise have little social support are likely to establish more secure ties with their infants when they receive periodic assistance and encouragement from a paraprofessional (Jacobson & Frye, 1991).

Other parents who could benefit from focused interventions are those who themselves felt unloved,

neglected, or abused as children. Formerly mistreated caregivers often start out with the best intentions, vowing never to do to their children what was done to them. But they often expect their infants to be "perfect" and to love them right away. So when their babies are irritable, fussy, or inattentive (as all infants will be at times), these emotionally insecure adults may feel as if they are being rejected once again (Steele & Pollack, 1974). They may then back off or withdraw their own affection (see Biringen, 1990; Crowell & Feldman, 1988, 1991), sometimes to the point of neglecting or abusing their babies.

Finally, some caregivers may be disinclined to love their babies because their pregnancies were unplanned and their infants unwanted. In one study conducted in Czechoslovakia (Matejcek, Dytrych, & Schuller, 1979), mothers who had been denied permission to abort an unwanted pregnancy were judged to be less closely attached to their children than a group of same-aged mothers of similar mari-

---

B O X

5-1 | *Brazelton (NBAS) Training: Effects on Parents and Infants*

Irritable, unresponsive, and apathetic infants who are at risk of alienating their close companions often can be identified very soon after birth by virtue of their low scores on the **Brazelton Neonatal Behavioral Assessment Scale (NBAS)**. This simple test, which is usually administered on the third day of life and repeated several days later, is a measure of the infant's neurological health and responsiveness to stimulation. It assesses the strength of 20 infant reflexes as well as the infant's reactions to 26 situations, many of which are "social" in character (for example, responses to cuddling, the infant's orientation to the examiner's face and voice, general alertness, and irritability). High-risk infants who may fail to establish synchronized routines with caregivers are fairly easy to spot: their performance on the test is characterized by mild irritability, inalertness, lack of attention to social stimuli, and poor motor control (Brazelton, 1979; Waters, Vaughn, & Egeland, 1980). Dr. T. Barry Brazelton (1979) believes that many

of the emotional difficulties forecasted by low scores on the Brazelton test can be prevented if parents of these unresponsive babies learn how to properly stimulate and comfort their infants.

One method of teaching parents how to interact with their babies is to have them either watch or take part as the NBAS is administered to their child. The Brazelton test is well suited as a teaching device because it is designed to elicit many of the infant's most pleasing characteristics, such as smiling, cooing, and gazing. As the test proceeds, parents will see that their neonate can respond positively to other people, and they will also learn how to elicit these pleasant interactions.

"Brazelton training" has proved to be an effective strategy indeed. Mothers of high-risk children who have had the NBAS procedure demonstrated to them become more responsive in their face-to-face interactions with their babies. In addition, these infants score higher on the NBAS one month later than high-risk

tal and socioeconomic status who had not requested an abortion. Although both the ''wanted'' and the ''unwanted'' children were physically healthy at birth, over the next nine years the unwanted children were hospitalized more frequently, made lower grades in school, had less stable family lives and poorer relations with peers, and were generally more irritable than the children whose parents had wanted them. Here, then, are data suggesting that failure of a caregiver to become emotionally attached to an infant could have long-term effects on the child's physical, social, emotional, and intellectual well-being.

SOME ECOLOGICAL CONSTRAINTS ON ATTACHMENT

To this point we have noted that the character of an adult's attachment to an infant is influenced by the adult's characteristics as well as those of the infant. However, we should also recognize that interactions between infants and caregivers take place within a broader social and emotional context that may affect how a particular caregiver and infant will react to each other. For example, mothers who must care for several small children with little or no assistance may find themselves unwilling or unable to devote much attention to their newest baby, particularly if the infant is at all irritable or unresponsive (Belsky, 1981; Crockenberg, 1981). Indeed, researchers have consistently reported that, the more children a woman has had, the more negative her attitudes toward children become and the more difficult she thinks her children are to raise (Garbarino & Sherman, 1980; Hurley & Hohn, 1971).

The quality of a caregiver's relationship with his or her spouse can also have a dramatic effect on parent/infant interactions and attachments. Consider that parents who were unhappily married *prior* to the birth of their child (1) are less sensitive caregivers after the baby is born, (2) express less

---

B O X **5-1** | *continued*

infants whose mothers were not trained (Widmayer & Field, 1980).

Other research (Myers, 1982; Worobey, 1985) indicates that NBAS training also has positive effects on the parents of healthy, responsive infants. In Barbara Myers's (1982) study, either mothers or fathers in a treatment group were taught to give the NBAS to their neonates; parents in a control group received no such training. When tested four weeks later, parents who had received the Brazelton training were more knowledgeable about infant behavior, more confident in their caretaking abilities, and more satisfied with their infants than were control parents. In addition, fathers who had been trained reported that they were much more involved in caring for their infants at home than fathers who had received no training.

Although many hospitals provide brief instruction on how to diaper and bathe a baby, parents are seldom told anything about the neonate's basic abilities, such as whether newborns can see, hear, or carry on meaningful social dialogues with other people. NBAS training clearly illustrates what a new baby is capable of doing, and it appears to have a number of positive effects on both parents and their infants. This brief intervention does not always accomplish wonders (see Belsky, 1985), and even Dr. Brazelton acknowledges that more powerful and longer-term interventions may be necessary for mothers of premature infants or for families experiencing a lot of stress (Worobey & Brazelton, 1986; see also Lyons-Ruth et al., 1990). Nevertheless, NBAS training appears to be a good way to help parents and babies start out on the right foot. As Barbara Myers (1982) notes, ''The treatment is relatively inexpensive, it only takes about an hour, and the parents reported enjoying it. This type of intervention needs to be tested [further] on other populations . . . for possible consideration as a routine portion of a hospital's postpartum care'' (p. 470).

favorable attitudes about their infants and the parenting role, and (3) establish less secure ties with their infants and toddlers, compared to other parents from similar socioeconomic backgrounds whose marriages have been close and confiding (Cox et al., 1989; Howes & Markman, 1989). Why poor marriages disrupt parenting is not completely clear. One suggestion is that unhappily married parents are looking to their babies for the love and affection they lack from a spouse and may simply back off and become less affectionate when their infants fail to satisfy all their emotional needs (Pedersen, 1982). Of course, the child can contribute to the adult's withdrawal and dissatisfaction with parenting if he should pick up on the parent's unhappiness and begin to act sullen or depressed himself (Field et al., 1990; Tronick, 1989). Indeed, this may often happen, for unhappily married parents are much more likely than happily married ones to describe their babies as temperamentally difficult (Easterbrooks & Emde, 1988).

Happily married couples, on the other hand, are likely to receive active encouragement from their mates as they undertake the responsibilities of parenthood, and this positive social support may be particularly important if the baby has already shown a tendency to be irritable and unresponsive. In fact, Jay Belsky (1981) finds that neonates who are "at risk" for later emotional difficulties (as indicated by their poor performance on the Brazelton NBAS) are likely to have nonsynchronous interactions with their parents *only when the parents are unhappily married*. So it seems that a stormy marriage is a major environmental hazard that can hinder or even prevent the establishment of close emotional ties between parents and their infants.

The Infant's Attachment to Caregivers

Although adults may feel emotionally drawn to an infant very soon after the baby is born, the infant will require a little more time to form a genu-

ine attachment to caregivers. Many theories have been proposed to explain how and why infants become emotionally involved with the people around them. But, before we consider these theories, we should briefly discuss the stages that babies go through in becoming attached to a close companion.

Development of Primary Social Attachments

Many years ago, Rudolph Schaffer and Peggy Emerson (1964) studied the development of social attachments by following a group of Scottish infants from early infancy to 18 months of age. Once a month, mothers were interviewed to determine (1) how the infant responded when separated from close companions in seven situations (for example, being left in a crib; being left in the presence of strangers) and (2) to whom the infant's separation responses were directed. A child was judged to be attached to someone if separation from that person reliably elicited a protest.

Schaffer and Emerson found that infants pass through the following steps, or stages, as they develop close ties with their caregivers:

1. The **asocial stage** (0–6 weeks). The very young infant is somewhat "asocial" in that many kinds of social and nonsocial stimuli will produce a favorable reaction, and few produce any kind of protest. By the end of this period, infants are beginning to show a distinct preference for social stimuli.

2. The **stage of indiscriminate attachments** (6 weeks to 6–7 months). Now infants clearly enjoy human company but tend to be somewhat indiscriminate: they are likely to protest whenever *any* adult puts them down or leaves them alone. Although 3–6-month-olds are more likely to smile at their mothers than at strangers (Watson et al., 1979) and are often more quickly soothed by a regular caregiver, they clearly enjoy the attention they receive from just about anyone (including strangers).

3. The **stage of specific attachments** (about 7–9 months). At about 7–9 months of age, infants begin to protest only when separated from one par-

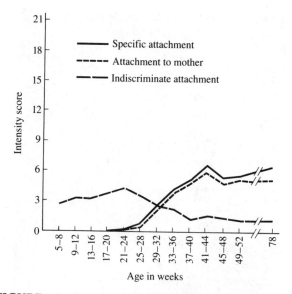

FIGURE 5-3 The developmental course of attachment during infancy. (From H. R. Schaffer & P. E. Emerson, "The Development of Social Attachments in Infancy." *Monographs of the Society for Research in Child Development*, 1964, 29(3, Serial No. 94). Copyright © 1964 by the Society for Research in Child Development. Reprinted by permission.)

ticular individual, usually the mother (see Figure 5-3). In addition, many infants begin to fear strangers at about this time. Schaffer and Emerson interpret these data as an indication that infants have formed their first true attachments.

4. The **stage of multiple attachments**. Within weeks after forming their initial attachments, about half the infants in Schaffer and Emerson's study were becoming attached to other people (fathers, siblings, grandparents, or perhaps even a regular babysitter). By 18 months of age, very few infants were attached to only one person, and some were attached to five or more.

Schaffer and Emerson originally believed that infants who are multiply attached have a "hierarchy" of attachment objects and that the individual at the top of the list is their most preferred companion. However, later research indicates that each of the infant's attachment objects may serve different functions, so that the person whom an infant prefers most may depend on the situation. For example, most infants prefer the mother's company if they are upset or frightened (Lamb & Stevenson, 1978). However, fathers seem to be preferred as playmates, possibly because much of the time they spend with their infants is "playtime" (Bretherton, 1985; Lamb, 1981).[3] Schaffer (1977) is now convinced that "being attached to several people does not necessarily imply a shallower feeling toward each one, for an infant's capacity for attachment is not like a cake that has to be [divided]. Love, even in babies, has no limits" (p. 100).

Theories of Attachment

If you have ever had a kitten or a puppy, you may have noticed that pets often seem especially responsive and affectionate to the person who feeds them. Might the same be true of human infants? Developmentalists have long debated this very point, as we will see in examining the four most influential theories of infant attachment: psychoanalytic theory, learning theory, cognitive-developmental theory, and ethological theory.

PSYCHOANALYTIC THEORY: *I LOVE YOU BECAUSE YOU FEED ME*

According to Freud, young infants are "oral" creatures who derive satisfaction from sucking and mouthing objects and should be attracted to any person who provides oral pleasure. Since it is usually mothers who "pleasure" oral infants by feeding them, it seemed logical to Freud that the mother would become the baby's primary object of security and affection, particularly if she was relaxed and generous in her feeding practices.

Erik Erikson also believes that a mother's feeding practices will influence the strength or security of her infant's attachments. However, he suggests that a mother's *overall responsiveness* to her child's needs is more important than feeding itself. According to Erikson, a caregiver who consistently responds to an infant's needs will foster a sense of *trust* in other

[3]Fathers' contributions to their infants' social and emotional development will be discussed at length in Chapter 6.

people, whereas unresponsive or inconsistent care-giving breeds mistrust. He adds that an untrusting child may well become overdependent—one who will "lean on" others, not necessarily out of love or a desire to be near but solely to ensure that his needs are met. Presumably, children who have not learned to trust others during infancy will avoid close mutual-trust relationships throughout life.

Before we examine the research on feeding practices and their contribution to social attachments, we need to consider another viewpoint that assumes that feeding is important—learning theory.

LEARNING THEORY: REWARDINGNESS LEADS TO LOVE

For quite different reasons, some learning theorists have also assumed that infants will become attached to persons who feed them and gratify their needs. Feeding was thought to be particularly important for two reasons (Sears, 1963). First, it should elicit positive responses (smiles, coos) that are likely to increase a caregiver's affection for the baby. Second (and more important to our discussion here), mothers are often able to relax with their infants while feeding and to provide them with *many comforts*—food, warmth, tender touches, soft and reassuring vocalizations, changes in scenery, and even a dry diaper (if necessary)—*all in one sitting*. What will a baby make of all this? According to learning theorists, an infant will eventually associate the mother with pleasant feelings and pleasurable sensations, so that the mother herself becomes a source of reinforcement. Once the mother (or any other caregiver) has attained this status as a **conditioned reinforcer**, the infant is attached—he or she will now do whatever is necessary (smile, cry, coo, babble, or follow) to attract the caregiver's attention or to remain near this valuable and rewarding individual.

Just how important is feeding? In 1959 Harry Harlow and Robert Zimmerman reported the results of a study designed to compare the importance of feeding and tactile stimulation for the development of social attachments in infant monkeys. The monkeys were separated from their mothers in the first day of life and reared for the next 165 days by two

PHOTO 5-3   The wire and cloth surrogate mothers used in Harlow's research. Infant monkeys remain with the cloth mother even though they must stretch to the wire mother to feed. This was one observation that led Harlow to conclude that feeding is not the most important contributor to primary social attachments.

surrogate mothers. As you can see in Photo 5-3, each surrogate mother had a face and a well-proportioned body constructed of wire. However, the body of one surrogate (the "cloth mother") was wrapped in foam rubber and covered with terrycloth. Half the infants were always fed by this warm, comfortable cloth mother, the remaining half by the rather uncomfortable "wire mother."

The research question was simple: would these infants become attached to the "mother" who fed them, or would they instead prefer the soft, cuddly terrycloth mother? It was no contest! Infants clearly preferred the cloth mother, *regardless of which mother had fed them*. Indeed, monkeys fed by the wire mother spent more than 15 hours a day clutching the *cloth* mother, compared to only an hour or so (mostly at mealtimes) with the wire mother (see Fig-

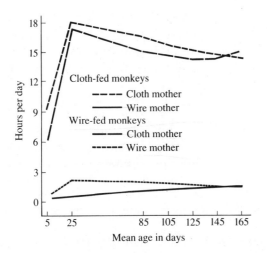

FIGURE 5-4 Average amount of time infant monkeys spent in contact with their cloth and wire mother surrogates. The monkeys spent much more of their time clinging to the cloth mother, regardless of which mother had fed them. (From H. F. Harlow & R. R. Zimmerman, "Affectional Responses in the Infant Monkey." *Science,* 1959, *130,* 421–432. Copyright © 1959 by the AAAS. Reprinted by permission.)

ure 5-4). Moreover, all infants ran directly to the cloth mother when they were frightened by novel stimuli (marching toy bears, wooden spiders) that were placed in their cages. Apparently the cloth mothers provided the reassurance the infants were seeking, for Harlow and Zimmerman noted that:

> in spite of their abject terror, the infant monkeys, after reaching the cloth mother and rubbing their bodies about hers, rapidly come to lose their fear of the frightening stimuli. Indeed, within a minute or two most of the babies were visually exploring the thing which so shortly before had seemed an object of evil. The bravest of the babies would actually leave the mother and approach the fearful monsters, under, of course, the protective gaze of their mothers [p. 423].

Clearly, Harlow and Zimmerman's classic study tells us that feeding is *not* the most important determinant of an infant's attachment to caregivers.

Although Harlow's subjects were monkeys, research with human infants paints a similar picture. In their study of Scottish infants, Schaffer and Emerson (1964) asked each mother the age at which her

child had been weaned, the amount of time it had taken to wean the child, and the feeding schedule (regular interval or demand feeding) that she had used with her baby. None of these feeding practices predicted the character of an infant's attachment to his or her mother. In fact, Schaffer and Emerson found that, in 39% of the cases, the person who usually fed, bathed, and changed the child (typically the mother) was not even the child's primary attachment object! These findings are clearly damaging to any theory claiming that feeding and feeding practices are the primary determinants of the child's first attachment.

Current viewpoints. How, then, do attachments develop? Although contemporary learning theorists no longer stress the importance of feeding per se, they continue to argue that reinforcement is the primary mechanism responsible for social attachments (Gewirtz & Petrovich, 1982). They have, in fact, ended up adopting a viewpoint similar to that of Erik Erikson: infants should be attracted to those individuals who are quick to respond to (and thereby reinforce) their social signals and who provide them with a variety of pleasant or rewarding experiences. Indeed, Schaffer and Emerson (1964) found that the two aspects of a mother's behavior that predicted the character of her infant's attachment to her were (1) her *responsiveness* to the infant's behavior and (2) the *total amount of stimulation* that she provided. Mothers who responded reliably and appropriately to their infants' bids for attention and who often played with their babies had infants who were closely attached to them.

COGNITIVE-DEVELOPMENTAL
THEORY: TO LOVE YOU, I MUST KNOW YOU

Cognitive-developmental theory has little to say about which adults are most likely to appeal to infants, but it does remind us of the holistic character of development by suggesting that the ability to form attachments depends, in part, on the infant's level of intellectual development. Before an attachment can occur, the infant must be able to discriminate familiar persons (that is, potential attachment objects) from strangers. She must also recognize that familiar companions have a "permanence" about them (object permanence), for it would be difficult indeed to form a stable relationship with a person who ceases to exist whenever she passes from view (Schaffer, 1971). So perhaps it is no accident that attachments first emerge at age 7–9 months — precisely the time when infants begin to show *clear* evidence of acquiring an object concept. Rudolph Schaffer (1971) went as far as to propose that attachments cannot occur until the *fourth sensorimotor substage* — the point at which infants first begin to search for and find objects hidden behind a screen.

Barry Lester and his associates (1974) evaluated Schaffer's hypothesis by giving 9-month-old and 12-month-old infants a test of object permanence before exposing them to brief separations from their mothers, their fathers, and a stranger. They found that 9-month-olds who scored high (stage 4 or above) in object permanence showed stronger protests when separated from their mothers than infants who scored lower (stage 3 or below). Among the 12-month-old infants, those who scored high (stage 4 or above) in object permanence showed more separation protest at the departure of *either the mother or the father* than infants whose object permanence was less well developed. Neither age group protested separations from a stranger. Using separation protest as evidence of attachments, it would appear that the cognitively advanced 9-month-olds were attached to their mothers, whereas the cognitively advanced yearlings were attached to *both* parents. Thus, Lester's findings not only are consistent with the developmental stages of attachment reported by Schaffer and Emerson (1964) but also indicate that the timing of the primary attachment is related to the child's level of object permanence.

ETHOLOGICAL THEORY: PERHAPS I WAS BORN TO LOVE

Ethologists have proposed a most interesting and influential explanation for social attachments — and one that has distinct evolutionary overtones. A major assumption of the ethological approach is that all species, including human beings, are born with a number of innate behavioral tendencies that have in some way contributed to the survival of the species over the course of evolution. Indeed, John Bowlby (1969, 1980) proposes that many of these built-in behaviors are specifically designed to promote attachments between infants and their caregivers. Even the attachment relationship itself is said to have adaptive significance, serving to protect the young from predators and other natural calamities and to ensure that their needs are met. Of course, ethologists would argue that the long-range purpose of the primary social attachment is to permit members of each successive generation to live long enough to reproduce, thereby enabling the species to survive.

Origins of the ethological viewpoint. How did ethologists ever come up with their evolutionary theory of attachment? Interestingly enough, their insights were prompted by observations of young fowl. In 1873, Spaulding first noted that chicks would follow almost any moving object — another chicken, a duck, or a human being — as soon as they were able to walk. Konrad Lorenz (1937) observed this same "following response" in young goslings, a behavior he labeled **imprinting** (or stamping in). Lorenz also noted that (1) imprinting is automatic — young fowl do not have to be taught to follow; (2) imprinting occurs only within a narrowly delimited **critical period** after the bird has hatched; and (3) imprinting is irreversible — once the bird begins to follow a particular object, it will remain attached to it.

Lorenz then concluded that imprinting was an adaptive response. Young birds should generally survive if they stay close to their mothers so that they are led to food and afforded protection. Those that wander away may starve or be eaten by predators and thus fail to pass on their genes to future generations. So, over the course of many, many generations, the imprinting response eventually became an inborn, **preadapted characteristic** that attaches a young fowl to its mother, thereby increasing its chances of survival.

Attachment in humans. Although human infants do not imprint on their mothers in the same way that young fowl do, Bowlby (1969) claims that they have inherited a number of behaviors that help them to maintain contact with others and to elicit caregiving. What preadapted behaviors do they display? In addition to crying, the signal that often brings caregivers running, infants also suck, grasp, smile, coo, and babble—the very responses that were described earlier as having an endearing quality about them. In fact, Bowlby believes that adults are just as biologically predisposed to respond to a baby's signals as the baby is to emit them. It is difficult indeed for parents to ignore an urgent cry or to fail to warm up to a baby's big grin. In sum, human infants and their caregivers are said to have evolved in ways that predispose them to respond favorably to each other and to form close attachments, thus enabling infants (and, ultimately, the species) to survive.

A common misunderstanding. Does this mean that attachments occur automatically? No indeed! Bowlby claims that secure attachments develop gradually as parents become more proficient at reading and reacting appropriately to the baby's signals and as the baby is *learning* what his parents are like and how he might regulate their attention. Yet the process can easily go awry, as illustrated by the finding that an infant's preprogrammed signals will eventually wane if they fail to produce favorable reactions from an unresponsive companion, such as a depressed mother or an unhappily married father (Ainsworth et al., 1978). So, although Bowlby believes that human beings are biologically *prepared* to form close attachments, he also stresses that secure emotional bonds will not develop unless each participant has *learned* how to respond appropriately to the behavior of the other.

Perhaps the most basic of all ethological hypotheses is that, the more close physical contact a mother has with her baby early in infancy, the more responsive she should become to the baby and the more secure the infant should feel with her. This hypothesis was recently tested in an interesting experiment by Elizabeth Anisfeld and her colleagues (1990). On the second day after delivering their babies, mothers were randomly assigned to two conditions. Half received soft, pouchlike baby carriers for trans-

porting their infants and were encouraged to use these products (close-contact group), whereas the remaining mothers were instructed in the use of the more common plastic infant seats—implements that permit less close contact than soft carriers do (control group). Follow-up sessions conducted to see how mothers and their infants were doing provided striking support for the "close contact" hypothesis. After 3½ months, mothers in the close-contact group were significantly more responsive to their infants' bids for attention than were mothers in the control group. When the babies were 13 months old, those who had had ample close contact early in infancy were more likely to be securely attached to their mothers than were babies in the control group. Of course, ethologists would explain these results by noting that the heightened "togetherness" of the close-contact pairs had provided them more opportunity to learn how to adjust to each other and to develop the interactional synchrony from which secure relationships build.

COMPARING THE FOUR THEORETICAL APPROACHES

Although the four theories we have reviewed differ in many respects, each has something to offer. Even though feeding practices are not as important as psychoanalysts had originally thought, it was Sigmund Freud who stressed that we will need to know more about mother/infant interactions if we hope to understand how babies form attachments. Erik Erikson and the learning theorists pursued Freud's early leads and concluded that caregivers do play an important role in the infant's emotional development. Presumably, infants will view a responsive companion who provides many comforts as a trustworthy and rewarding individual who is worthy of affection. Ethologists can agree with this point of view, but they add that infants are *active participants* in the attachment process, emitting preprogrammed responses that enable them to promote the very interactions from which attachments are likely to develop. Finally, cognitive theorists have contributed by showing that the timing of social attachments is related to the child's level of intellectual development. So it makes little sense to tag one of these theories as "correct" and to ignore the others; each theory has helped us to understand how infants become attached to their most intimate companions.

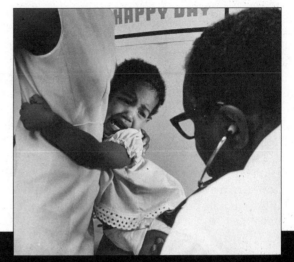

PHOTO 5-4   Although infants become more tolerant of strangers during the second year, unavoidable contact with an intrusive stranger may continue to upset many 2-, 3-, and even 4-year-olds.

Two Common Fears of Infancy

At about the same time that infants are establishing close affectional ties to a caregiver, they often begin to display negative emotional outbursts that may puzzle or even annoy close companions. In this section we will look at two of the common fears of infancy—*stranger anxiety* and *separation anxiety*—and try to determine why these negative reactions are likely to emerge during the second half of the first year.

Stranger Anxiety

Nine-month-old Billy is sitting on the floor in the den when his mother leads a strange person into the room. The stranger suddenly walks toward the child, bends over, and says "Hi, Billy! How are you?" If Billy is like many 9-month-olds, he may stare at the stranger for a moment and then turn away, whimper, and crawl toward his mother.

This wary reaction to a stranger, or **stranger anxiety**, stands in marked contrast to the smiling, babbling, and other positive greetings that infants often emit when approached by a familiar companion. Schaffer and Emerson (1964) noted that most of the infants in their sample reacted positively to strangers up until the time they had formed an attachment (usually at around 7 months of age) but then became fearful of strangers shortly thereafter. Studies of North American children tend to confirm this finding: wary reactions to strangers often emerge at 6–7 months of age, peak at 8–10 months, and gradually decline in intensity over the second year (Sroufe, 1977). However, stranger anxiety may never completely subside, for 2-, 3-, and even 4-year-olds are likely to show at least some signs of

wariness when approached by a stranger in an unfamiliar setting (Greenberg & Marvin, 1982).

Stranger anxiety was once thought to be a true developmental milestone—an inevitable response to unfamiliar company that supposedly characterized all infants who had become attached to a caregiver. However, later research revealed that infants are not always afraid of strangers and, in fact, may sometimes react rather positively to them (Levitt, 1980). In Box 5-2 we will consider the circumstances under which stranger anxiety is most likely to occur and see how medical personnel and child-care professionals might use this knowledge to head off outbreaks of fear and trembling in their offices.

Separation Anxiety

Not only do infants become wary of strangers, but they also begin to display obvious signs of discomfort when separated from their mothers or other familiar companions. For example, 10-month-old María, restrained in her playpen, is likely to cry if she sees her mother put on a coat and pick up a purse as she prepares to go shopping. If unrestrained and exposed to the same scene, 15-month-old Jenni might run and cling to her mother or at least follow her to the door. As her mother leaves and closes the door behind her, Jenni will probably cry. These reactions reflect the infants' **separation anxiety**. Separation anxiety normally appears during the latter half of the first year (at about the time infants are forming primary social attachments), peaks at 14–20 months, and gradually becomes less frequent and less intense throughout infancy and the preschool period (Kagan, 1983; Weinraub & Lewis, 1977).

Children raised in some cultural settings protest separations from their mothers at an earlier age than North American or European infants. For example, Mary Ainsworth (1967) found that Ugandan infants begin to fear such separations as early as 5–6 months of age. Why? One reason may be that Ugandan babies have much more close contact with their mothers than is typical in Western cultures; these infants sleep with their mothers, nurse for at least two years, and go wherever their mothers go, riding on the mother's hips or across her back in a cotton sling. So Ugandan infants may be quick to protest separations from their mothers because these separations are very unusual events.

Why Do Infants Fear Separation and Strangers?

We have seen that both stranger anxiety and separation anxiety emerge at about the same time as the primary social attachment and follow a predictable developmental course. Why do children who are just beginning to appreciate the pleasures of love now suddenly experience the gripping agony of fear? Let's consider three very different points of view.

The "conditioned anxiety" (or fear of separation) hypothesis. Psychoanalysts and some social-learning theorists have proposed that infants may learn to fear separations from their caregivers if prior discomforts (for example, hunger, wet diapers, and pain) have been especially frequent or intense dur-

ing periods when caregivers were not present to relieve them. In other words, infants may associate discomfort with the caregiver's absence and then express their "conditioned anxiety" by protesting whenever the caregiver is about to depart. Stranger anxiety is presumably a simple extension of separation anxiety: the child protests the approach of intrusive strangers because she fears becoming separated from or losing the person(s) to whom she is attached.

Although this **"conditioned anxiety" hypothesis** is appealing for its simplicity, there are problems with it. For example, it cannot easily explain why infants are *less* likely to protest separations from a loved one at home (where they have previously suffered many discomforts) than in a laboratory where they have never been before (Rinkoff & Corter, 1980). Nor does it adequately explain the *early* separation protests seen among Ugandan infants who have rarely been separated from their mothers and therefore have had little or no opportunity to associate pain and discomfort with the mother's absence. Let's now consider a second point of view that does explain these findings.

The ethological viewpoint. The ethological explanation for both stranger anxiety and separation anxiety is remarkably straightforward. John Bowlby (1973) suggests that there are a number of events that qualify as natural clues to danger. In other words, some situations have been so frequently associated with danger throughout a species' evolutionary history that a fear or avoidance response has become innate, or "biologically programmed." Among the events that infants may be programmed to fear are strange people, strange settings, and the "strange circumstance" of being separated from familiar companions.

Critics had a field day with this explanation when it was first proposed. After all, if Bowlby's notion of programmed fears was correct, couldn't one reasonably argue that many stimuli, including the child's eventual attachment objects, should be sufficiently unfamiliar to elicit a protest almost from birth? Yet it is important to understand that Bowlby is *not* suggesting that a fear of the unfamiliar is present *at birth*. Quite the contrary; he argues that a neonate's cognitive and perceptual capabilities are very immature and that it will take some time for the child to learn what is "familiar" and to discriminate these persons, objects, and events from those that are unfamiliar. But, once such discriminations are possible, the infant's preprogrammed "fear of the unfamiliar" should be readily apparent.

Indeed, there is some evidence for a biological mediation of children's wary responses to unfamiliar stimuli. Specifically, identical twins are much more similar than fraternal twins in the age at which they begin to fear strangers (Freedman, 1965; Plomin & DeFries, 1985), and physiologically reactive, temperamentally *inhibited* children (whom we discussed in Chapter 2) are much more wary of

---

BOX 5-2 *Combating Stranger Anxiety: Some Helpful Hints for Doctors and Child-Care Professionals*

It is not at all unusual for toddlers visiting the doctor's office to break into tears and to cling tenaciously to their parents. Some youngsters who remember previous visits may be suffering from "shot anxiety" rather than stranger anxiety, but many are simply reacting fearfully to the approach of an intrusive physician who may poke, prod, and handle them in ways that are atypical and upsetting. Fortunately, there are steps that caregivers and medical personnel (or any other stranger) can take to make such visits less terrifying for an infant or toddler. What can we suggest?

1. *Keep familiar companions available.* Infants react much more negatively to strangers when they are separated from their mothers or other close companions. Indeed, most 6–12-month-olds are not particularly wary of an approaching stranger if they are sitting on their mothers' laps; however, they will frequently whimper and cry at the stranger's approach if seated only a few feet from their mothers (Morgan & Ricciuti, 1969). Clearly, doctors and nurses can expect a more constructive response from their youngest patients if they can avoid separating them from their caregivers.

Stranger anxiety is also less likely if the caregiver issues a warm greeting to the stranger or uses a positive tone of voice when talking to the infant about the stranger (Feinman, 1992). These actions permit the child to engage in *social referencing* and to conclude that maybe the stranger really isn't all that scary if Mom and Dad seem to like him. It might not hurt, then, for medical personnel to strike up a pleasant conversation with the caregiver before directing their attention to the child.

2. *Make the setting more "familiar."* Stranger anxiety occurs less frequently in familiar settings than in unfamiliar ones. For example, few 10-month-olds are especially wary of strangers at home, but most react negatively to strange companions when tested in an unfamiliar laboratory (Sroufe, Waters, & Matas, 1974). Although it may be unrealistic to advise modern physicians to make home visits, they could make at least one of their examination rooms more homelike for young children, perhaps by placing an attractive mobile in one corner and posters of cartoon characters on the wall or by having a stuffed toy or two available for the child to play with. The infant's familiarity with a strange setting also makes a difference; whereas the vast majority (90%) of 10-month-olds become upset if a stranger approaches them within a minute after being placed in an unfamiliar room, only about half will react negatively to the stranger when they have had ten minutes to grow accustomed to this setting (Sroufe et al., 1974). Perhaps trips to the doctor would become more tolerable for an infant or a toddler if medical personnel gave the child a few minutes to familiarize herself with the examination room before making their entrance.

3. *Be a less intrusive stranger.* An infant's response to a stranger often depends on the stranger's behavior. Mary Levitt (1980) finds that strange adults can easily become "friends" if they allow the infant to take the initiative and control their earliest interactions. By contrast, intrusive strangers who approach rapidly and force themselves on the child (for example, by pinning him to an examination table or trying to pick him up) are likely to elicit feelings of terror (Sroufe, 1977). Of

strange persons and situations than their relatively nonreactive, uninhibited agemates (Kagan, Reznick, & Gibbons, 1989). (Of course, these latter findings also suggest a biological basis for *individual differences* in stranger and separation anxieties—a topic that Bowlby did not address in his theory.)

The ethological viewpoint easily explains many observations that the conditioned-anxiety hypothesis cannot. For example, Bowlby would expect infants to show stronger separation protests in an unfamiliar laboratory than at home, because the "strangeness" of the laboratory setting magnifies the apprehension they will ordinarily experience when separated from a caregiver. Moreover, ethologists would argue that Ugandan infants are quick to protest separations from their mothers

---

<table>
<tr><td>B
O
X</td><td>**5-2**</td><td>*continued*</td></tr>
</table>

course, busy physicians may not have the 20 minutes it can take for an apprehensive child to warm up to them on her own. But they don't need that much time anyway. Inge Bretherton and her associates (Bretherton, Stolberg, & Kreye, 1981) report that most 1–2-year-olds will respond favorably to a friendly stranger who (1) is not overly intrusive and (2) offers a toy (or suggests an activity) with which the infant is familiar. In fact, friendly strangers are likely to be more successful at establishing rapport with an infant if they cautiously take the initiative and allow the infant to regulate the pace of their activities rather than sitting back and waiting for the child to initiate an interaction with them (Bretherton et al., 1981).

4. *Try looking a little less strange to the child.* Stranger anxiety depends, in part, on the stranger's physical appearance. Jerome Kagan (1972) has argued that infants form mental representations, or *schemes,* for the faces that they encounter in daily life and are most likely to be afraid of people whose appearance is not easily assimilated into these existing schemes. So a doctor in a sterile white lab coat with a strange stethoscope around her neck (or a nurse with a pointed hat that may give her a "witchlike" look) can make infants and toddlers rather wary indeed! Pediatric professionals may not be able to alter physical features (for example, a huge nose or a facial scar) that might make children wary; but they can and often have shed their strange instruments and white uniforms in favor of more "normal" attire that will help their youngest patients to recognize them as members of the human race. Babysitters who favor the "punk" look might also do well to

heed this advice if establishing rapport with their young companions is a priority.

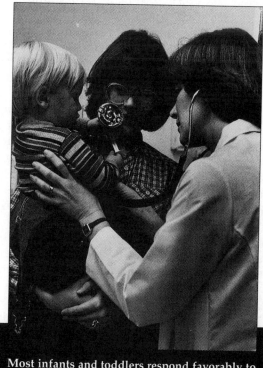

Most infants and toddlers respond favorably to a friendly stranger—even a doctor—who offers a toy.

because these separations occur so very infrequently that they qualify as highly unusual (that is, fear-provoking) events (Ainsworth, 1967).

Why, then, do stranger anxiety and separation anxiety become less intense during the second year—declining to the point that the infant will actually *initiate* separations and tolerate strangers, even after her mother has left the room? Mary Ainsworth (1979) believes that infants become less wary of strangers and separations as they begin to use their attachment objects as **secure bases** who encourage a second preprogrammed behavior—*exploring* the environment. As the infant ventures away from his secure base to explore, he should eventually discover that many novel stimuli (including friendly strangers) can be interesting and enjoyable in their own right.

Are infants less likely to fear separations that they initiate themselves? Apparently so. Harriet Rheingold and Carol Eckerman (1970) found that 10-month-olds were perfectly willing to leave their mothers and venture alone to play in a strange room. However, a second group of 10-month-olds typically cried when they were placed in the same strange room and then were left alone as their mothers departed. It appears that the first group of infants were not discomforted in the strange setting because *they* had initiated their separations, using their mothers as a secure base from which to explore.

In sum, ethologists view the anxieties of infancy as preprogrammed and adaptive concerns that help to protect the young of a species from harm by ensuring that they will remain near their caregivers. Yet the caregivers who serve this protective function are also instrumental in alleviating these programmed fears. By serving as a secure base for exploratory activities, a caregiver encourages her infant to venture into the unknown and become increasingly familiar with the environment. As a result, the child should eventually become more tolerant of separations and much less wary of stimuli (strangers and unfamiliar settings) that have previously been a source of concern.

The cognitive-developmental viewpoint. Cognitive theorists view both stranger anxiety and separation anxiety as natural outgrowths of the infant's

perceptual and cognitive development. Jerome Kagan (1972) suggests that, because 6–8-month-olds have finally developed stable schemes for the faces of familiar companions, a strange face now represents a discrepant and potentially fear-provoking stimulus. He notes that babies of this age will typically stare at a stranger before protesting, as if they are *hypothesizing*, trying to explain who this is or what has become of familiar faces that match their schemes for caregivers. Failing to answer these questions, the child becomes apprehensive and may cry in an attempt to summon familiar company.

Kagan's (1972, 1976) explanation of separation anxiety is equally interesting. He suggests that infants develop schemes not only for familiar faces (caregivers) but also for a familiar person's probable whereabouts. Moreover, he claims that violations of these "familiar faces in familiar places" schemes are the primary cause of separation distress. Consider the implications of this viewpoint. If a mother should proceed to the kitchen, leaving her 10-month-old son on the living-room floor, the infant may watch her depart but should then resume his previous activity *without protesting her departure*. He knows where his mother has gone because he has previously developed a scheme for mother-in-the-kitchen. But, should she pick up her coat and purse and walk out the front door, the child should find it difficult to account for her whereabouts and will probably cry. In sum, cognitive theorists believe that infants are most likely to protest separations when they cannot understand where their absent companions may have gone.

Indeed, infants observed at home are more likely to protest when mothers depart through an unfamiliar doorway (such as the entry to the cellar) than through a familiar one (Littenberg, Tulkin, & Kagan, 1971). Even more revealing are the results of an interesting laboratory study (Corter, Zucker, & Galligan, 1980) in which 9-month-old infants first accompanied their mothers to a strange room (Room A) and shortly thereafter watched their mothers exit into a second room (Room B). Although few infants protested immediately, they soon crawled into the adjoining room in search of their mothers. In cognitive terms, it is reasonable to assume that the infants had formed a scheme for the mother's whereabouts once they had found her in Room B. At this point the infants and their mothers reentered Room A and spent a short time together before the mother departed once again. But on this second trial she went into another room (Room C), thus violating the infant's scheme for her probable whereabouts. This time the majority of the infants fussed or cried! And where did these distressed youngsters go to search for their mothers? Generally they crawled to the doorway that matched their schemes (Room B) rather than to the portal through which they had most recently watched the mother depart (Room C). Here, then, is clear support for Kagan's theory: infants are most likely to protest separations from a caregiver when they are uncertain of her whereabouts.

Notice that Corter's 9-month-olds were looking for "Mama" *where they had previously found her*, rather than where she was last seen. This is precisely the type of error made by Piaget's 8–12-month-old infants as they first began to search for disappearing objects. Must infants have reached this "searching" phase (that is, the fourth sensorimotor substage, which Piaget believed to be the beginning of true object permanence) before they will begin forming hypotheses about the probable location of an absent caregiver? Apparently so. If an infant doesn't recognize that a departing caregiver continues to exist somewhere out of view, he or she should not try to determine her location and may not even protest her absence. As it turns out, we have already discussed a study that supports this line of reasoning. Recall that Barry Lester and his associates (1974) found that infants who had not yet begun to search for disappearing objects generally failed to protest when separated from their mothers and fathers.

Summing up.   Clearly, stranger anxiety and separation anxiety are complex emotional responses that may stem, in part, from (1) a child's general *apprehension of the unfamiliar*; (2) her inability to *explain* who a stranger may be, what he may want, or what has become of familiar companions; and (3) perhaps even a *fear of losing a companion* who provides so much warmth and security. So there is no one correct explanation for these interesting fears of infancy. Each of the theories has received some sup-

port and has helped us to understand why infants may be wary of strangers and upset when separated from loved ones.

On Easing the Pain of Separation

At some point, virtually all parents will find it necessary to leave their infants and toddlers in an unfamiliar setting (such as a nursery or a day-care center) or in the company of a stranger (for example, a babysitter) for hours at a time. Are there ways to make these separations easier or more tolerable for a young child?

Indeed there are. Marsha Weinraub and Michael Lewis (1977) found that toddlers who were separated from their mothers in an unfamiliar setting cried less and played more constructively if the mother took the time to explain that she was leaving and would soon return. Apparently, brief explanations informing the child that he or she should "play until Mommy returns" are more effective at reducing separation distress than lengthy explanations (Adams & Passman, 1981). The problem with a lengthy discourse is that it is probably quite discrepant with the caregiver's usual practices. In other words, if the child has no scheme for lengthy explanations, he or she may perceive the upcoming separation as something "out of the ordinary" and become very concerned.

Some parents try to prepare their toddlers for an upcoming separation by explaining the situation to the child anywhere from a few hours to a few days in advance. This approach may work with preschool children who have the language skills and cognitive abilities to ask pertinent questions and to rehearse the situation in their own minds, but it may backfire with younger children who lack these problem-solving capabilities. Indeed, Roderick Adams and Richard Passman (1980) found that 2-year-olds who had been prepared at home for an upcoming separation later played less constructively and were more likely to try to follow their departing mothers than were toddlers who had not been told of the separation in advance.

Separations are also less painful for older infants and toddlers if they have some reminder of the home setting with them, such as a favorite stuffed animal or a security blanket (Passman & Weisberg, 1975).[4] In fact, Richard Passman and Kathleen Longeway (1982) found that toddlers who were given sharply focused photographs of their mothers were reasonably tolerant of separations: they played more and stayed longer in an unfamiliar playroom than toddlers who were given unrecognizable (blurred) photographs of their mothers. Apparently a clear physical representation of the mother reduces separation distress, and it may help a child to remember whatever explanation a mother has given for her departure (although this latter assumption remains to be tested). Although all the children in Passman and Longeway's study were at least 20 months of age, we know that infants are capable of recognizing photographs of their mothers early in the first year (Barrera & Maurer, 1981) and that they have already begun to carefully examine and to smile at photographs of their parents by age 9–12 months (Brooks-Gunn & Lewis, 1981). So it is possible that even a 12-month-old infant, who is unlikely to understand a verbal explanation, can be made less discomforted during necessary separations if a substitute caregiver is able to produce a photograph of the infant's absent companion(s).

Finally, Megan Gunnar and her associates (1992) found that infants' reactions to brief separations are closely linked to the quality of alternative care they receive. Most of the 8–10-month-olds in Gunnar's experiment were visibly upset when their mothers left them in the company of an unfamiliar sitter. If the sitter assumed a "caretaker" role by first settling the infant in and then pursuing her own interests, infants continued to display signs of distress. But, if the sitter acted as a "playmate" by providing toys and playing with the baby, a clear majority of infants quickly stopped protesting and became no more distressed than they were when their mothers remained with them in this novel environment. What these findings seem to imply is that parents should choose sitters carefully, selecting one who

PHOTO 5-5 Necessary separations are easier to bear when toddlers have their favorite toys with them and their sitters act more like playmates than like caretakers.

enjoys interactions with infants over one who sees her function as attending to the baby's basic needs as a prelude to heading to the telephone or the refrigerator.

Reactions to the Loss of an Attachment Object

To this point the research we have reviewed has focused on children's rather immediate responses to *short-term* separations from attachment objects. How do young children react to permanent or prolonged separations from their loved ones? Do they eventually stop protesting or perhaps even forget these special companions?

Seeking to answer these questions, John Bowlby (1960) studied the behavior of children aged 15 to 30 months who were hospitalized for chronic illnesses and thus separated from their mothers for a long period. According to Bowlby, most of these children

---

[4]Lest you wonder, most children who are strongly attached to inanimate objects are well-adjusted youngsters who have satisfactory ties to their parents (Passman, 1987). Thus, object attachments are *not* a sign of emotional disturbances, even though some disturbed children become strongly attached to objects (Bowlby, 1960).

progressed through three behavioral phases during their separations. In the initial, *protest* phase, the child tried to regain his or her mother by crying, demanding her return, and resisting the attention of caretakers. This phase lasted from a few hours to more than a week. Next came the phase of *despair*. It seemed to Bowlby as if the child had given up hope of ever being reunited with his or her mother. The child became apathetic and unresponsive to toys or to other people and appeared to be in "a deep state of mourning." Next came what Bowlby called the stage of *detachment*. At this point the child appeared to have recovered, for he or she showed a renewed interest in play activities, caretakers, and other features of the environment. But the child's relationship with the mother had changed. When the mother visited, the child was cool and largely indifferent, showing hardly any protest when she left once again. It was almost as if the children were in the process of undoing their attachments to their mothers. Bowlby's observations have been replicated by Heinicke and Westheimer (1965), who studied the behavior of 2- to 3-year-old children left by their parents in a residential nursery for periods ranging from two weeks to three months.

Bowlby notes that a fourth separation phase, *permanent withdrawal from human relationships*, may occur if the child's separation from the mother is extremely prolonged or if the child loses a series of temporary attachment objects, such as nurses or babysitters, while separated from the mother. In either case, the child often becomes uninterested in making contact with others. He or she is still able to communicate with other people at their initiative but becomes more egocentric as attention shifts from human beings to fuzzy toys or other inanimate objects.

Michael Rutter (1981) has carefully reviewed these and other pertinent data and concluded that children's reactions to long-term separations are nowhere near as uniform as Bowlby suggests (see also Schaffer, 1990). According to Rutter, most children who are securely attached to their caregivers may protest and show some "despair" over a long-term separation, but they are unlikely to "detach" themselves either from their close companions (that is, parents) or from human beings in general. However, Rutter claims that infants and toddlers who have shaky, insecure relationships with companions at home may well put some psychological distance between themselves and these persons—almost as if they were becoming detached. And, should the child's attachments be sufficiently insecure, he or she may indeed choose to withdraw from human contact, sinking into a state of "affectionless psychopathology" in which it becomes exceedingly difficult to be emotionally involved with anyone.

Clearly, Rutter is proposing that there are several kinds of attachments that children may form with caregivers and that different kinds of attachments may have different implications for the child's future social and emotional well-being. In Chapter 6 we will see that he is right on both counts. Would you care to hazard a guess about whether an insecure attachment with a close companion is better than no attachment at all? This is another issue we will consider in the next chapter as we review what is known about the social, emotional, and intellectual development of children who are denied opportunities to form social attachments during their early years.

Summary

Human infants are clearly emotional beings. At birth, babies reliably display interest, distress, disgust, and contentment (as indicated by their facial expressions), with the remaining *primary emotions* (that is, anger, sadness, surprise, and fear) normally appearing by the middle of the first year. Such *complex emotions* as embarrassment, pride, guilt, and shame emerge in the second (or third) year, after children reach such cognitive milestones as self-recognition and have acquired standards for evaluating their conduct.

The socialization of emotions and emotional self-regulation begin very early, as parents model positive emotions for their infants, attend carefully to and try to prolong their infants' pleasant feelings, and become less responsive to infants' negative emotional displays. By the end of the first year, infants develop simple strategies for regulating aversive arousal; soon thereafter they will be making active attempts to suppress their sadness or anger. However, the ability to regulate and control emotions develops very slowly, and it may be well into the grade-school years before children become proficient at complying with culturally defined *emotional display rules*.

The infant's ability to recognize and interpret others' emotions improves dramatically over the first year of life. During the first six months, infants begin to discriminate and respond appropriately to their mother's naturalistic displays of emotion, and by age 8–12 months they are actively seeking emotional information from their companions. The ability to identify and interpret others' emotions continues to improve throughout the preschool and early grade-school years, aided by family conversations that center on the child's emotional experiences and those of her companions.

Emotions play at least two important roles in an infant's social development. The child's own emotional expressions are adaptive in that they promote social contact with others and assist caregivers in adjusting their behavior to the infant's needs and goals. At the same time, the infant's ability to recognize and interpret the emotions of other people serves an important *social-referencing* function by helping the child to infer how he or she should be feeling, thinking, or behaving in a wide variety of situations.

Infants begin to form affectional ties to their close companions during the first year of life. These "bonds of love," or *attachments*, serve many purposes and are important contributors to social and emotional development. Attachments are usually reciprocal relationships, for parents and other intimate companions will typically become attached to the infant.

Parents may begin to feel emotionally involved with a neonate during the first few hours if they have close contact with their baby during this period. This initial *bonding* may then be strengthened as the infant begins to emit social signals (smiles, vocalizations) that attract the attention of caregivers

and make them feel that the baby enjoys their company. If the caregiver adjusts his or her behavior to the infant's cycles of attention and inattention, eventually he (or she) and the baby will establish highly synchronized interactive routines that are satisfying to both parties and are likely to blossom into a reciprocal attachment. However, some parents may have a difficult time becoming attached to their baby if the child is irritable, unresponsive, or unwanted; if they are clinically depressed or unhappily married; or if they have other problems that prevent them from being sensitive and responsive to the infant.

Most infants have formed a primary social attachment to a close companion by 6–8 months of age, and within weeks they are establishing these affectional ties with other regular companions. Many theories have been proposed to explain how and why infants form attachments. Among the most influential theories of attachment are the psychoanalytic, the learning-theory, the cognitive-developmental, and the ethological viewpoints. Although these theories make different assumptions about the roles that infants and caregivers play in the formation of attachments, each viewpoint has contributed to our understanding of early social and emotional development.

At about the time infants are becoming attached to a close companion, they often begin to display two kinds of fear. *Stranger anxiety* refers to the child's wariness of unfamiliar people. It is by no means a universal reaction and is most likely to occur in response to an intrusive stranger who appears in an unfamiliar setting where loved ones are unavailable. *Separation anxiety* is the discomfort infants may feel when separated from the person or persons to whom they are attached. As infants develop intellectually and begin to move away from attachment objects to explore the environment, they will become increasingly familiar with strangers and better able to account for the absences of familiar companions. As a result, both stranger anxiety and separation anxiety will decline in intensity during the second year.

Brief separations from caregivers can be made more bearable for toddlers if they have some reminder of home (for example, a security blanket) with them or if the parent has provided a brief (rather than elaborate) rationale for the separation immediately before her departure. Prolonged or permanent separations from a loved one are much more stressful, and the child's ability to cope will depend on the quality of his or her emotional relationship with the departed person. Children who have stable ties with caregivers often protest and may show some short-term depression, or despair, over the loss of an attachment object. However, those who are insecure in their emotional relationships may become "detached" from close companions and, in extreme cases, may withdraw from human contact and experience difficulties in becoming involved with anyone.

References

ADAMS, R. E., & PASSMAN, R. H. (1980, March). *The effects of advance preparation upon children's behavior during brief separation from their mother.* Paper presented at annual meeting of the Southeastern Psychological Association, Washington, DC.

ADAMS, R. E., & PASSMAN, R. H. (1981). The effects of preparing two-year-olds for brief separations from their mothers. *Child Development, 52,* 1068–1071.

ADLER, T. (1989). Cocaine babies face deficits. *APA Monitor, 20,* 14.

AINSWORTH, M. D. S. (1967). *Infancy in Uganda: Infant care and the growth of love.* Baltimore: Johns Hopkins University Press.

AINSWORTH, M. D. S. (1979). Attachment as related to mother-infant interaction. In J. G. Rosenblatt, R. A. Hinde, C. Beer, & M. Busnel (Eds.), *Advances in the study of behavior* (Vol. 9). Orlando, FL: Academic Press.

AINSWORTH, M. D. S. (1989). Attachments beyond infancy. *American Psychologist, 44,* 709–716.

AINSWORTH, M. D. S., BLEHAR, M. C., WATERS, E., & WALL, S. (1978). *Patterns of attachment: A psychological study of the strange situation.* Hillsdale, NJ: Erlbaum.

ALLEY, T. R. (1981). Head shape and the perception of cuteness. *Developmental Psychology, 17,* 650–654.

ANISFELD, E., CASPER, V., NOZYCE, M., & CUNNINGHAM, N. (1990). Does infant carrying promote attachment? An experimental study of the effects of increased physical contact on the development of attachment. *Child Development, 61,* 1617–1627.

BARDEN, R. C., FORD, M. E., JENSEN, A. G., ROGERS-SALYER, M., & SALYER, K. E. (1989). Effects of craniofacial deformity in infancy on the quality of mother-infant interactions. *Child Development, 60,* 819–824.

BARRERA, M. E., & MAURER, D. (1981). Recognition of mother's photographed face by the three-month-old infant. *Child Development, 52,* 714–716.

BELSKY, J. (1981). Early human experience: A family perspective. *Developmental Psychology, 17,* 3–23.

BELSKY, J. (1985). Experimenting with the family in the newborn period. *Child Development, 56,* 407–414.

BERG, W. K., & BERG, K. M. (1987). Psychophysiological development in infancy: State, startle, and attention. In J. Osofsky (Ed.), *Handbook of infant development* (2nd ed.). New York: Wiley.

BIRINGEN, Z. (1990). Direct observation of maternal sensitivity and dyadic interactions in the home: Relations to maternal thinking. *Developmental Psychology, 26,* 278–284.

BOWER, T. G. R. (1982). *Development in infancy.* New York: W. H. Freeman.

BOWLBY, J. (1958). The nature of the child's tie to his mother. *International Journal of Psychoanalysis, 39,* 350–373.

BOWLBY, J. (1960). Separation anxiety. *International Journal of Psychoanalysis, 41,* 89–113.

BOWLBY, J. (1969). *Attachment and loss.* Vol. 1: *Attachment.* London: Hogarth Press.

BOWLBY, J. (1973). *Attachment and loss.* Vol. 2: *Separation.* London: Hogarth Press.

BOWLBY, J. (1980). *Attachment and loss.* Vol. 3: *Loss, sadness, and depression.* New York: Basic Books.

BRAZELTON, T. B. (1979). Behavioral competence of the newborn infant. *Seminars in Perinatology, 3,* 35–44.

BRETHERTON, I. (1985). Attachment theory: Retrospect and prospect. In I. Bretherton & E. Waters (Eds.), Growing points of attachment theory and research. *Monographs of the Society for Research in Child Development, 50*(Serial No. 209).

BRETHERTON, I., FRITZ, J., ZAHN-WAXLER, C., & RIDGEWAY, D. (1986). Learning to talk about emotions: A functionalist perspective. *Child Development, 57,* 529–548.

BRETHERTON, I., STOLBERG, U., & KREYE, M. (1981). Engaging strangers in proximal interaction: Infants' social initiative. *Developmental Psychology, 17,* 746–755.

BROOKS-GUNN, J., & LEWIS, M. (1981). Infant social perception: Responses to pictures of parents and strangers. *Developmental Psychology, 17,* 647–649.

BUSSEY, K. (1992). Lying and truthfulness: Children's definitions, standards, and evaluative reactions. *Child Development, 63,* 129–137.

CASSIDY, J., PARKE, R. D., BUTKOVSKY, L., & BRAUNGART, J. M. (1992). Family-peer connections: The roles of emotional expressiveness within the family and children's understanding of emotions. *Child Development, 63,* 603–618.

COHEN, L. J. (1974). The operational definition of human attachment. *Psychological Bulletin, 4,* 207–217.

COHN, J. F., & TRONICK, E. Z. (1987). Mother-infant face-to-face interaction: The sequence of dyadic states at 3, 6, and 9 months. *Developmental Psychology, 23,* 66–77.

COOPER, R. P., & ASLIN, R. N. (1990). Preference for infant-directed speech in the first month after birth. *Child Development, 61,* 1585–1595.

CORTER, C. M., ZUCKER, K. J., & GALLIGAN, R. F. (1980). Patterns in the infant's search for mother during brief episodes. *Developmental Psychology, 16,* 62–69.

COX, M. J., OWEN, M. T., LEWIS, J. M., & HENDERSON, V. K. (1989). Marriage, adult adjustment, and early parenting. *Child Development, 60,* 1015–1024.

CROCKENBERG, S. B. (1981). Infant irritability, mother responsiveness, and social support influences on the security of infant-mother attachment. *Child Development, 52,* 857–865.

CROCKENBERG, S. B., & McCLUSKEY, K. (1986). Change in maternal behavior during the baby's first year of life. *Child Development, 57,* 746–753.

CROWELL, J. A., & FELDMAN, S. S. (1988). Mothers' internal models of relationships and children's behavioral and developmental status: A study of mother-child interaction. *Child Development, 59,* 1273–1285.

CROWELL, J. A., & FELDMAN, S. S. (1991). Mothers' working models of attachment relationships and mother and child behavior during separation and reunion. *Developmental Psychology, 27,* 597–605.

DENHAM, S. A. (1989). Maternal affect and toddlers' social-emotional competence. *American Journal of Orthopsychiatry, 59,* 368–376.

DUNN, J., BRETHERTON, I., & MUNN, P. (1987). Conversations about feeling states between mothers and their young children. *Developmental Psychology, 23,* 132–139.

DUNN, J., BROWN, J., & BEARDSALL, L. (1991). Family talk about feeling states and children's later understanding of children's emotions. *Developmental Psychology, 27,* 448–455.

EASTERBROOKS, A., & EMDE, R. (1988). Marital and parent-child relationships: The role of affect in the family system. In R. Hinde & J. Stevenson-Hinde (Eds.), *Relationships within families: Mutual influences.* Oxford: Oxford University Press.

EASTERBROOKS, M. A. (1989). Quality of attachment to mother and to father: Effects of perinatal risk status. *Child Development, 60,* 825–830.

FABES, R. A., EISENBERG, N., McCORMICK, S. E., & WILSON, M. S. (1988). Preschoolers' attributions of situational determinants of others' naturally occurring emotions. *Developmental Psychology, 24,* 376–385.

FABES, R. A., EISENBERG, N., NYMAN, M., & MICHEA-LIEU, Q. (1991). Young children's appraisals of others' spontaneous emotional reactions. *Developmental Psychology, 27,* 858–866.

FEINMAN, S. (1992). *Social referencing and the social construction of reality in infancy.* New York: Plenum.

FERNALD, A., & MAZZIE, C. (1991). Prosody and focus in speech to infants and adults. *Developmental Psychology, 27,* 209–221.

FIELD, T. M. (1987). Affective and interactive disturbances in infants. In J. D. Osofsky (Ed.), *Handbook of infant development* (2nd ed.). New York: Wiley.

FIELD, T. M., HEALY, B., GOLDSTEIN, S., & GUTHERTZ, M. (1990). Behavior-state matching and synchrony in mother-infant interactions of nondepressed versus depressed dyads. *Developmental Psychology, 26,* 7–14.

FIELD, T. M., HEALY, B., GOLDSTEIN, S., PERRY, S., BENDELL, D., SCHANBERG, S., ZIMMERMAN, E. A., & KUHN, C. (1988). Infants of depressed mothers show "depressed" behavior even with nondepressed adults. *Child Development, 59,* 1569–1579.

FIELD, T. M., & VEGA-LAHR, N. (1984). Early interactions between infants with cranio-facial anomalies and their mothers. *Infant Behavior and Development, 7,* 527–530.

FREEDMAN, D. G. (1965). Hereditary control of early social behaviors. In B. M. Foss (Ed.), *Determinants of infant behavior* (Vol. 3). London: Methuen.

FREUD, S. (1930). *Three contributions to the theory of sex.* New York: Nervous and Mental Disease Publishing Co. (Original work published 1905.)

GARBARINO, J., & SHERMAN, D. (1980). High-risk neighborhoods and high-risk families: The human ecology of child maltreatment. *Child Development, 51,* 188–198.

GEWIRTZ, J. L., & PETROVICH, S. B. (1982). Early social and attachment learning in the frame of organic and cultural evolution. In T. M. Field, A. Huston, H. C. Quay, L. Troll, & G. E. Finley (Eds.), *Review of human development.* New York: Wiley.

GNEPP, J., & KLAYMAN, J. (1992). Recognition of uncertainty in emotional inferences: Reasoning about emotionally equivocal situations. *Developmental Psychology, 28,* 145–158.

GOLDBERG, S. (1983). Parent-infant bonding: Another look. *Child Development, 54,* 1355–1382.

GOLDBERG, S., BLUMBERG, S. L., & KRIGER, A. (1982). Menarche and interest in infants: Biological and social influences. *Child Development, 53,* 1544–1550.

GREENBERG, M. T., & MARVIN, R. S. (1982). Reactions of preschool children to an adult stranger: A behavioral systems approach. *Child Development, 53,* 481–490.

GREENBERG, M. T., & MORRIS, N. (1974). Engrossment: The newborn's impact upon the father. *American Journal of Orthopsychiatry, 44,* 520–531.

GREENE, J. G., FOX, N. A., & LEWIS, M. (1983). The relationship between neonatal characteristics and three-month mother-infant interaction in high-risk infants. *Child Development, 54,* 1286–1296.

GRIESER, D. L., & KUHL, P. K. (1988). Maternal speech to infants in a tonal language: Support for the universal prosodic features in motherese. *Child Development, 59,* 14–20.

GROSSMAN, F. K., EICHLER, L. S., WINICKOFF, S. A., & ASSOCIATES (1980). *Pregnancy, birth, and parenthood: Adaptations of mothers, fathers, and infants.* San Francisco: Jossey-Bass.

GUNNAR, M. R., LARSON, M. C., HERTSGAARD, L., HARRIS, M. L., & BRODERSEN, L. (1992). The stressfulness of separation among 9-month-old infants: Effects of social context variables and infant temperament. *Child Development, 63,* 290–303.

GUSTAFSON, G. E., & HARRIS, K. L. (1990). Women's responses to young infants' cries. *Developmental Psychology, 26,* 144–152.

HALL, G. S. (1891). The contents of children's minds on entering school. *Pedagogical Seminary, 1,* 139–173.

HARLOW, H. F., & ZIMMERMAN, R. R. (1959). Affectional responses in the infant monkey. *Science, 130,* 421–432.

HARTER, S. (1986). Cognitive-developmental processes in the integration of concepts about emotions and the self. *Social Cognition, 4,* 119–151.

HARTER, S., & BUDDIN, B. J. (1987). Children's understanding of the simultaneity of two emotions: A five-stage developmental acquisition sequence. *Developmental Psychology, 23,* 388–399.

HARTER, S., & WHITESELL, N. (1989). Developmental changes in children's understanding of simple, multiple, and blended emotion concepts. In C. Saarni & P. Harris (Eds.), *Children's understanding of emotion.* Cambridge, England: Cambridge University Press.

HAVILAND, J. M., & LELWICA, M. (1987). The induced affect response: 10-week-old infants' responses to three emotion expressions. *Developmental Psychology, 23,* 97–104.

HAZAN, C., & SHAVER, P. (1987). Romantic love conceptualized as an attachment process. *Journal of Personality and Social Psychology, 52,* 511–524.

HEINICKE, C. M., & WESTHEIMER, I. (1965). *Brief separations.* New York: International Universities Press.

HILDEBRANDT, K. A., & FITZGERALD, H. E. (1981). Mothers' responses to infant physical appearance. *Infant Mental Health Journal, 2,* 56–61.

HOFFNER, C., & BADZINSKI, D. M. (1989). Children's integration of facial and situational cues to emotion. *Child Development, 60,* 411–422.

HORNIK, R., & GUNNAR, M. R. (1988). A descriptive analysis of social referencing. *Child Development, 59,* 626–634.

HOWES, P., & MARKMAN, H. J. (1989). Marital quality and child functioning: A longitudinal investigation. *Child Development, 60,* 1044–1051.

HURLEY, J. R., & HOHN, R. L. (1971). Shifts in child-rearing attitudes linked with parenthood and occupation. *Developmental Psychology, 4,* 324–328.

ISABELLA, R. A., & BELSKY, J. (1991). Interactional synchrony and the origins of infant-mother attachment. *Child Development, 62,* 373–384.

IZARD, C. E. (1982). *Measuring emotions in infants and children.* New York: Cambridge University Press.

IZARD, C. E., HEMBREE, E. A., & HUEBNER, R. R. (1987). Infants' emotion expressions to acute pain: Developmental change and stability of individual differences. *Developmental Psychology, 23,* 105–113.

IZARD, C. E., & MALATESTA, C. Z. (1987). Perspectives on emotional development: I. Differential emotions theory of early emotional development. In J. D. Osofsky (Ed.), *Handbook of infant development* (2nd ed.). New York: Wiley.

JACOBSON, S. W., & FRYE, K. F. (1991). Effect of maternal support on attachment: Experimental evidence. *Child Development, 62,* 572–582.

JOHNSON, W., EMDE, R. N., PANNABECKER, B., STENBERG, C., & DAVIS, M. (1982). Maternal perception of infant emotion from birth through 18 months. *Infant Behavior and Development, 5,* 313–322.

KAGAN, J. (1972). Do infants think? *Scientific American, 226,* 74–82.

KAGAN, J. (1976). Emergent themes in human development. *American Scientist, 64,* 186–196.

KAGAN, J. (1983). Stress and coping in early development. In N. Garmezy & M. Rutter (Eds.), *Stress, coping and development in children.* New York: McGraw-Hill.

KAGAN, J., REZNICK, J. S., & GIBBONS, J. (1989). Inhibited and uninhibited types of children. *Child Development, 60,* 838–845.

KELLER, H., & SCHOLMERICH, A. (1987). Infant vocalizations and parental reactions during the first four months of life. *Developmental Psychology, 23,* 62–67.

KELLEY-BUCHANAN, C. (1988). *Peace of mind during pregnancy: An A–Z guide to the substances that could affect your unborn baby.* New York: Facts on File.

KENNELL, J. H., VOOS, D. K., & KLAUS, M. H. (1979). Parent-infant bonding. In J. D. Osofsky (Ed.), *Handbook of infant development.* New York: Wiley.

KLAUS, M. H., & KENNELL, J. H. (1976). *Maternal-infant bonding.* St. Louis: Mosby.

KLAUS, M. H., & KENNELL, J. H. (1982). *Parent-infant bonding.* St. Louis: Mosby.

KLINNERT, M. D., EMDE, R. N., BUTTERFIELD, P., & CAMPOS, J. J. (1986). Social referencing: The infant's use of emotional signals from a friendly adult with mother present. *Developmental Psychology, 22,* 427–432.

KOPP, C. B. (1989). Regulation of distress and negative emotions: A developmental view. *Developmental Psychology, 25,* 343–354.

KUCHUK, A., VIBBERT, M., & BORNSTEIN, M. H. (1986). The perception of smiling and its experiential correlates in three-month-old infants. *Child Development, 57,* 1054–1061.

La BARBERA, J. D., IZARD, C. E., VIETZE, P., & PARISI, S. A. (1976). Four- and six-month-old infants' visual responses to joy, anger, and neutral expressions. *Child Development, 47,* 535–538.

LAMB, M. E. (1981). The development of father-infant relationships. In M. E. Lamb (Ed.), *The role of the father in child development.* New York: Wiley.

LAMB, M. E., & STEVENSON, M. (1978). Father-infant relationships: Their nature and importance. *Youth and Society, 9,* 277–298.

LESTER, B. M., CORWIN, M. J., SEPKOSKI, C., SEIFER, R., PEUCKER, M., McLAUGHLIN, S., & GOLUB, H. L. (1991). Neurobehavioral syndrome in cocaine-exposed newborn infants. *Child Development, 62,* 694–705.

LESTER, B. M., HOFFMAN, J., & BRAZELTON, T. B. (1985). The rhythmic structure of mother-infant interactions in term and preterm infants. *Child Development, 56,* 15–27.

LESTER, B. M., KOTELCHUCK, M., SPELKE, E., SELLERS, M. J., & KLEIN, R. E. (1974). Separation protest in Guatemalan infants: Cross-cultural and cognitive findings. *Developmental Psychology, 10,* 79–85.

LEVITT, M. J. (1980). Contingent feedback, familiarization, and infant affect: How a stranger becomes a friend. *Developmental Psychology, 16,* 425–432.

LEVY-SHIFF, R., GOLDSHMIDT, I., & HAR-EVEN, D. (1991). Transition to parenthood in adoptive families. *Developmental Psychology, 27,* 131–140.

LEWIS, M., ALESSANDRI, S. M., & SULLIVAN, M. W. (1990). Violation of expectancy, loss of control and anger expressions in young infants. *Developmental Psychology, 26,* 745–751.

LEWIS, M., ALESSANDRI, S. M., & SULLIVAN, M. W. (1992). Differences in shame and pride as a function of children's gender and task difficulty. *Child Development, 63,* 630–638.

LEWIS, M., STANGER, C., & SULLIVAN, M. W. (1989). Deception in 3-year-olds. *Developmental Psychology, 24,* 434–440.

LEWIS, M., SULLIVAN, M. W., STANGER, C., & WEISS, M. (1989). Self-development and self-conscious emotions. *Child Development, 60,* 146–156.

LITTENBERG, R., TULKIN, S., & KAGAN, J. (1971). Cognitive components of separation anxiety. *Developmental Psychology, 4,* 387–388.

LORENZ, K. Z. (1937). The companion in the bird's world. *Auk, 54,* 254–273.

LORENZ, K. Z. (1943). Die angeboren Formen moglicher Erfahrung [The innate forms of possible experience]. *Zeitschrift fur Tierpsychologie, 5,* 233–409.

LUDEMANN, P. M. (1991). Generalized discrimination of positive facial expressions by seven- and ten-month-old infants. *Child Development, 62,* 55–67.

LYONS-RUTH, K., CONNELL, D. B., GRUNEBAUM, H. U., & BOTEIN, S. (1990). Infants at social risk: Maternal depression and family support services as mediators of infant development and security of attachment. *Child Development, 61,* 85–98.

MALATESTA, C. Z., CULVER, C., TESMAN, J. R., & SHEPARD, B. (1989). The development of emotion expression during the first two years of life. *Monographs of the Society for Research in Child Development, 54*(1–2, Serial No. 219).

MALATESTA, C. Z., GRIGORYEV, P., LAMB, C., ALBIN, M., & CULVER, C. (1986). Emotional socialization and expressive development in preterm and full-term infants. *Child Development, 57,* 316–330.

MALATESTA, C. Z., & HAVILAND, J. M. (1982). Learning display rules: The socialization of emotion expression in infancy. *Child Development, 53,* 991–1003.

MATEJCEK, Z., DYTRYCH, Z., & SCHULLER, V. (1979). The Prague study of children born from unwanted pregnancies. *International Journal of Mental Health, 7,* 63–74.

MEHLER, J., BERTONCINI, J., BARRIERE, M., & JASSIK-GERSCHENFELD, D. (1978). Infant recognition of mother's voice. *Perception, 7,* 491–497.

MORGAN, G. A., & RICCIUTI, H. N. (1969). Infants' responses to strangers during the first year. In B. M. Foss (Ed.), *Determinants of infant behavior* (Vol. 4). London: Methuen.

MYERS, B. J. (1982). Early intervention using Brazelton training with middle-class mothers and fathers of newborns. *Child Development, 53,* 462–471.

MYERS, B. J. (1987). Mother-infant bonding as a critical period. In M. H. Bornstein (Ed.), *Sensitive periods in development: Interdisciplinary perspectives.* Hillsdale, NJ: Erlbaum.

NELSON, C. A. (1987). The recognition of facial expressions in the first two years of life: Mechanisms of development. *Child Development, 58,* 889–909.

PASSMAN, R. H. (1987). Attachments to inanimate objects: Are children who have security blankets insecure? *Journal of Consulting and Clinical Psychology, 55,* 825–830.

PASSMAN, R. H., & LONGEWAY, K. P. (1982). The role of vision in maternal attachment: Giving 2-year-olds a photograph of their mother during separation. *Developmental Psychology, 18,* 530–533.

PASSMAN, R. H., & WEISBERG, P. (1975). Mothers and blankets as agents for promoting play and exploration by young children in a novel environment: The effects of social and nonsocial attachment objects. *Developmental Psychology, 11,* 170–177.

PEDERSEN, F. A. (1982). Mother, father, and infant as an interactive system. In J. Belsky (Ed.), *In the beginning.* New York: Columbia University Press.

PEERY, J. C. (1980). Neonate and adult head movement: No and yes revisited. *Developmental Psychology, 16,* 245–250.

PLOMIN, R., & DeFRIES, J. C. (1985). *Origins of individual differences in infancy.* Orlando, FL: Academic Press.

RADKE-YARROW, M., CUMMINGS, E. M., KUCZYNSKI, L., & CHAPMAN, M. (1985). Patterns of attachment in two- and three-year-olds in normal families and families with parental depression. *Child Development, 56,* 884–893.

RHEINGOLD, H. L., & ECKERMAN, C. O. (1970). The infant separates himself from his mother. *Science, 168,* 78–83.

RINKOFF, R. F., & CORTER, C. M. (1980). Effects of setting and maternal accessibility on the infant's response to brief separation. *Child Development, 51,* 603–606.

RITTER, J. M., CASEY, R. J., & LANGLOIS, J. H. (1991). Adults' responses to infants varying in appearance of age and attractiveness. *Child Development, 62,* 68–82.

ROSEN, W. D., ADAMSON, L. B., & BAKEMAN, R. (1992). An experimental investigation of infant social referencing: Mothers' messages and gender differences. *Developmental Psychology, 28,* 1172–1178.

RUTTER, M. (1981). *Maternal deprivation revisited* (2nd ed.). New York: Penguin Books.

SAARNI, C. (1984). An observational study of children's attempts to monitor their expressive behavior. *Child Development, 55,* 1504–1513.

SAARNI, C. (1990). Emotional competence: How emotions and relationships become integrated. In R. A. Thompson (Ed.), *Socioemotional development. Nebraska Symposium on Motivation* (Vol. 36). Lincoln: University of Nebraska Press.

SCHAFFER, H. R. (1971). *The growth of sociability.* Baltimore: Penguin Books.

SCHAFFER, H. R. (1977). *Mothering*. Cambridge, MA: Harvard University Press.

SCHAFFER, H. R. (1990). *Making decisions about children: Psychological questions and answers*. Cambridge, MA: Basil Blackwell.

SCHAFFER, H. R., & EMERSON, P. E. (1964). The development of social attachments in infancy. *Monographs of the Society for Research in Child Development*, 29(3, Serial No. 94).

SEARS, R. R. (1963). Dependency motivation. In M. Jones (Ed.), *Nebraska Symposium on Motivation* (Vol. 11). Lincoln: University of Nebraska Press.

SIMPSON, J. R., RHOLES, W. S., & NELLIGAN, J. S. (1992). Support seeking and support giving within couples in an anxiety-provoking situation: The role of attachment styles. *Journal of Personality and Social Psychology*, 62, 434–446.

SINGER, L. M., BRODZINSKY, D. M., RAMSAY, D., STEIR, M., & WATERS, E. (1985). Mother-infant attachments in adoptive families. *Child Development*, 56, 1543–1551.

SPAULDING, D. A. (1873). Instinct with original observation in young animals. *MacMillans Magazine*, 27, 282–283.

SROUFE, L. A. (1977). Wariness of strangers and the study of infant development. *Child Development*, 48, 1184–1199.

SROUFE, L. A., WATERS, E., & MATAS, L. (1974). Contextual determinants of infant affectional response. In M. Lewis & L. A. Rosenblum (Eds.), *The origins of fear*. New York: Wiley.

STEELE, B. F., & POLLACK, C. B. (1974). A psychiatric study of parents who abuse infants and small children. In R. E. Heller & C. H. Kempe (Eds.), *The battered child*. Chicago: University of Chicago Press.

STEPHAN, C. W., & LANGLOIS, J. H. (1984). Baby beautiful: Adult attributions of infant competence as a function of infant attractiveness. *Child Development*, 55, 576–585.

STERN, D. (1977). *The first relationship: Infant and mother*. Cambridge, MA: Harvard University Press.

STIPEK, D., RECCHIA, S., & McCLINTIC, S. (1992). Self-evaluation in young children. *Monographs of the Society for Research in Child Development*, 57(1, Serial No. 226).

TETI, D. M., & GELFAND, D. M. (1991). Behavioral competence among mothers of infants in the first year: The mediational role of maternal self-efficacy. *Child Development*, 62, 918–929.

TRONICK, E. Z. (1989). Emotions and emotional communications in infants. *American Psychologist*, 44, 112–119.

UNDERWOOD, M. K., COIE, J. D., & HERBSMAN, C. R. (1992). Display rules for anger and aggression in school-age children. *Child Development*, 63, 366–380.

VAN DEN BOOM, D. (1988). *Neonatal irritability and the development of attachment: Observation and intervention*. Leiden, The Netherlands: Author.

WALDEN, T. A., & BAXTER, A. (1989). The effect of context and age on social referencing. *Child Development*, 60, 1511–1518.

WATERS, E., VAUGHN, B. E., & EGELAND, B. R. (1980). Individual differences in mother-infant attachment relationships at age one: Antecedents in neonatal behavior in an urban, economically disadvantaged sample. *Child Development*, 51, 208–216.

WATSON, J. S., HAYES, L. A., VIETZE, P., & BECKER, J. (1979). Discriminative infant smiling to orientations of talking faces of mother and stranger. *Journal of Experimental Child Psychology*, 28, 92–99.

WEINRAUB, M., & LEWIS, M. (1977). The determinants of children's responses to separation. *Monographs of the Society for Research in Child Development*, 42(4, Serial No. 172).

WIDMAYER, S., & FIELD, T. (1980). Effects of Brazelton demonstrations on early interactions of preterm infants and their teen-age mothers. *Infant Behavior and Development*, 3, 79–89.

WINTRE, M. G., POLIVY, J., & MURRAY, M. A. (1990). Self-predictions of emotional response patterns: Age, sex, and situational determinants. *Child Development*, 61, 1124–1133.

WOLFF, P. H. (1969). The natural history of crying and other vocalizations in early infancy. In B. M. Foss (Ed.), *Determinants of infant behavior* (Vol. 4). London: Methuen.

WOROBEY, J. (1985). A review of Brazelton-based interventions to enhance parent-infant interaction. *Journal of Reproductive and Infant Psychology*, 3, 64–73.

WOROBEY, J., & BRAZELTON, T. B. (1986). Experimenting with the family in the newborn period: A commentary. *Child Development*, 57, 1298–1300.

ZESKIND, P. S. (1980). Adult responses to the cries of low and high risk infants. *Infant Behavior and Development*, 3, 167–177.

ZESKIND, P. S., & MARSHALL, T. R. (1988). The relation between variation in pitch and maternal perceptions of infant crying. *Child Development*, 59, 193–196.

6

Early Social and Emotional Development II: Individual Differences and Their Implications for Future Development

My sister once asked whether it was normal for a 10-month-old to be a "mama's boy." She then proceeded to tell me that her son Jacob often cried when she left him alone and would try to crawl to wherever she had gone. Actually, she was overstating the case. Jacob did cry when his mother disappeared from view at Grandma's house or left him alone for more than five to ten minutes at home. But in most cases Jacob reacted rather normally to a separation from his mother: he watched intently as she left and then continued whatever he was doing. My sister and I talked for a while about the nature of relationships between mothers and infants, and we eventually decided that Jacob's attachment to her was one indication that he was well on his way to becoming a socially responsive little boy.

Had he been there, Sigmund Freud would surely have endorsed our conclusion. Freud (1905/1930) repeatedly argued that the emotional events and experiences of infancy can have any number of long-term effects on developing children. In fact, he stressed that the formation of a stable mother/infant emotional bond is *absolutely necessary* for normal social and personality development, a sentiment shared by ethologist John Bowlby and the best-known psychoanalytic theorist of recent times, Erik Erikson. Erikson's view is that secure emotional attachments to caregivers provide the infant with a basic sense of *trust* that will permit him or her to form close affectional ties to other people later in life. Learning theorists such as Harry Harlow (who studied monkeys) and Robert Sears (who studied humans) believe that close contact with a mother figure allows the infant to acquire a repertoire of social skills that will enable him or her to interact effectively and appropriately with other members of the species. In sum, almost everyone agrees that the emotional events of infancy are very influential in shaping one's future development.

There are at least two ways to evaluate this **early-experience hypothesis**. First, we could try to determine whether infants who do not become securely attached to their parents turn out any different from those who do. Second, we could look at what happens to infants who have had little or no contact with a mother figure during the first two years and do not become attached to anyone. In the pages that

follow, we will consider the findings and implications of both these lines of inquiry.

Individual Differences in the Quality of Attachments

Mary Ainsworth and her associates (1978) have found that infants differ in the type (or quality) of attachments that they have with their caregivers. Ainsworth measures the quality of an infant's attachment by exposing the child to a **"strange-situations" test** consisting of eight short episodes (summarized in Table 6-1) that attempt to simulate (1) naturalistic caregiver/infant interactions in the presence of toys (to see if the infant uses the caregiver as a *secure base* from which to explore); (2) brief separations from the caregiver and encounters with strangers (which will often stress the infant); and (3) reunion episodes (to determine whether a stressed infant derives any comfort and reassurance from the caregiver and can once again become involved with toys). By recording and analyzing an infant's responses to these episodes—that is, exploratory activities, reactions to strangers and to separations, and, in particular, behaviors when reunited with the close companion—Ainsworth and her associates found that they could usually characterize his or her attachment to the caregiver in one of three ways:

1. **Secure attachment**. About 65% of 1-year-old infants fall into this category. The securely attached infant actively explores while alone with the mother and is visibly upset by separation. The infant *greets the mother warmly when she returns and will welcome physical contact with her*. The child is outgoing with strangers while the mother is present.

2. **Resistant attachment**. About 10% of 1-year-olds show this type of "insecure" attachment. These infants try to stay close to the mother but explore very little while she is present. They become very distressed as the mother departs. But, when she returns, the infants are ambivalent: they

TABLE 6-1 *The eight episodes that make up the strange-situations test*

Episode Number	Persons Present	Duration	Brief Description of Action
1	Mother, baby, and observer	30 seconds	Observer introduces mother and baby to experimental room, then leaves. (Room contains many appealing toys scattered about.)
2	Mother and baby	3 minutes	Mother is nonparticipant while baby explores; if necessary, play is stimulated after 2 minutes.
3	Stranger, mother, and baby	3 minutes	Stranger enters. First minute: stranger silent. Second minute: stranger converses with mother. Third minute: stranger approaches baby. After 3 minutes mother leaves unobtrusively.
4	Stranger and baby	3 minutes or less	First separation episode. Stranger's behavior is geared to that of baby.
5	Mother and baby	3 minutes or more	First reunion episode. Mother greets and/or comforts baby, then tries to settle him again in play. Mother then leaves, saying "bye-bye."
6	Baby alone	3 minutes or less	Second separation episode.
7	Stranger and baby	3 minutes or less	Continuation of second separation. Stranger enters and gears her behavior to that of baby.
8	Mother and baby	3 minutes	Second reunion episode. Mother enters, greets baby, then picks him up. Meanwhile stranger leaves unobtrusively.

Note: Although Ainsworth et al. designed the strange-situations test to assess the quality of infants' attachments to their mothers, the procedure can also be used to measure the kind of attachments that infants have established with other close companions (for example, fathers, regular sitters, etc.).
SOURCE: M. D. S. Ainsworth, M. C. Blehar, E. Waters, & S. Wall, *Patterns of Attachment: A Psychological Study of the Strange Situation.* Copyright © 1978 by Lawrence Erlbaum Associates, Inc. Reprinted by permission.

will *try to remain near her*, although they seem to resent her for having left them, and they are likely to *resist physical contact initiated by the mother*. Anxious/resistant infants are quite wary of strangers, even when their mothers are present.

3. **Avoidant attachment**. These infants (about 20% of 1-year-olds) also display an "insecure" attachment. They often show little distress when separated from the mother and will generally *turn away so as to ignore or avoid contact with her when she returns*. Anxious/avoidant infants are not particularly wary of strangers but may sometimes avoid or ignore them in much the same way that they avoid or ignore their mothers.

From these descriptions, it would appear that securely attached infants are reasonably happy individuals who have established an affectionate relationship with their primary caregivers. By contrast, infants in the *resistant* category are drawn to their mothers but seem not to trust them, and *avoidant* infants appear to derive little if any comfort from their mothers—almost as if they were somewhat "detached" from them.

The percentages of infants who are classified as secure, resistant, and avoidant differ somewhat from culture to culture and seem to reflect cultural variations in child rearing. For example, German parents deliberately encourage their infants to be independent and tend to discourage clingy close contact, which perhaps explains why avoidant attachments are more common in Germany than in the United States (Grossmann et al., 1985). Moreover, resistant attachments (in which infants show intense distress over separations and strangers) are much more common in cultures such as Japan, where caregivers do not encourage early separations, and Israel, where communally reared kibbutz infants are rarely exposed to adults from outside the commune (Sagi, van IJzendoorn, & Koren-Karie, 1991; van IJzendoorn & Kroonenberg, 1988). But, despite these cultural variations, the fact remains that Ainsworth's three types of attachment have been observed in many cultures and that more babies around the world fall into the secure attachment category than into either of the insecure categories (Sagi et al., 1991; van IJzendoorn & Kroonenberg, 1988).

Now a methodological note: although Ainsworth's strange-situations test is the most commonly used method of assessing attachment security, it has its critics, and new attachment measures are beginning to appear. In Box 6-1 we will briefly consider some alternatives to the strange situations, including self-report measures that are suitable for adolescents and adults.

How Do Infants Become Securely or Insecurely Attached?

Ainsworth's Caregiving Hypothesis

Mary Ainsworth (1979) believes that the quality of an infant's attachment to her mother (or any other close companion) depends largely on the kind of attention she has received. According to this **caregiving hypothesis**, mothers of *securely attached* infants are thought to be responsive caregivers from the very beginning. And evidently they are, for Ainsworth (1979) and many other researchers (for example, Isabella & Belsky, 1991; Malatesta et al.,

---

BOX 6-1 | *Alternative Methods of Assessing Attachment Quality*

Ainsworth's strange-situations test has been criticized as a relatively cumbersome procedure that creates a great deal of unnecessary stress for infants—stress that occurs in a very strange and atypical laboratory environment, where infants' behavior toward caregivers may be different from their normal interactions at home. Moreover, the "strange situations" is not very useful for characterizing the attachments of children much older than 2, who are becoming quite accustomed to (and much less stressed by) brief separations and encounters with strangers. Finally, the "strange situations" is a costly procedure in that investigators who are trying to classify the kinds of attachments their subjects have established must first receive extensive training to do so at satisfactory levels of reliability.

One alternative procedure that is becoming increasingly popular is the **Attachment Q-Set** (Waters & Deane, 1985)—a measure that both complements and extends the strange-situations test by gathering information about the attachment behaviors that infants,

toddlers, and *preschool children* display *within the familiar confines of their homes.* The most recent version of this instrument consists of 90 items, each of which is a written declarative statement about the child's behavior that a caregiver (or researcher who observes the infant and caregiver) will sort into one of three categories: "most characteristic of this child," "neither characteristic nor uncharacteristic," and "most *uncharacteristic* of this child." Some sample items from the Attachment Q-Set are "Looks to mother for reassurance when wary," "Explores objects thoroughly," "Easily comforted by mother," "Cries to prevent separation," and "Does *not* expect mother to be responsive." By examining the number and patterning of items sorted into each of the three categories, one can derive a score that indicates how *secure* the child is with his or her caregiver. Preliminary studies with this new instrument have found that children's Q-Set security scores correspond closely to their strange-situations attachment classifications (Bosso, Corter, & Abramovitch, 1990;

1989; Teti et al., 1991) find that these mothers enjoy close contact with their babies, are highly sensitive to their infants' social signals, are emotionally expressive, and are quick to encourage their infants to explore. Ainsworth's view is that infants' impressions of other people are shaped by their early experiences with primary caregivers. When a caregiver is sensitive to the infant's needs and is easily accessible, the infant should derive comfort and pleasure from their interactions and become securely attached.

Mothers of *resistant* infants seem interested in their babies and willing to provide close physical contact. However, they frequently misinterpret their infants' signals and have generally failed to establish synchronized routines with them. In some cases, part of the problem may be a "difficult" infant, for Everett Waters and his associates found

that infants classified as resistant at 1 year of age had often been rather irritable and unresponsive as neonates (Waters, Vaughn, & Egeland, 1980). Yet the infant's behavior cannot be the only contributor to a resistant attachment, since the majority of difficult babies will eventually become securely attached to their caregivers (Easterbrooks, 1989; van IJzendoorn et al., 1992). Ainsworth (1979) finds that mothers of resistant infants tend to be inconsistent in their caregiving; at times they react very enthusiastically to their babies, but their responses to the infant may depend more on their own moods than on the infant's emotional state. As a result, the infant becomes both saddened and resentful when he learns that he cannot necessarily count on the mother for emotional support and comfort *when he needs it* (see also Belsky, Rovine, & Taylor, 1984; Isabella & Belsky, 1991).

B O X   **6-1** | *continued*

Vaughn & Waters, 1990), and more and more investigators (for example, Teti et al., 1991; Vaughn et al., 1992) are now using the Attachment Q-Set as the primary (and sometimes only) measure of early attachment security in their own research.

Other new methods of assessing attachment quality include (1) Main and Cassidy's (1988) analogue of the strange situations, which focuses on the ways in which preschool and young grade-school children respond when reunited with a caregiver after a lengthy separation in a strange environment, and (2) the *Adult Attachment Interview* (George, Kaplan, & Main, 1985), in which adults are questioned extensively about their recollections of and feelings about early childhood relationships; on the basis of their responses, they are classified as having secure or insecure working models of intimate emotional ties (see Kobak & Sceery, 1988). Finally, social psychologists (for example, Bartholomew & Horowitz, 1991; Hazan & Shaver, 1987) have constructed paper-and-pencil, self-report measures, with

items modeled after Bowlby's and Ainsworth's verbal descriptions of secure, resistant, and avoidant attachments, to try to assess the quality of affectional ties that adolescents and young adults form with their boyfriends, girlfriends, and spouses.

In sum, there are now several alternatives to Ainsworth's strange-situations test—measures that permit researchers to assess the kinds of attachments that infants, children, adolescents, and adults have established with loved ones. Of course, these new measures permit us to seek answers for some intriguing questions: Are an infant's primary attachments stable over time? Do they forecast the kinds of attachments that he will establish with other people (including his own children) later in life? Later in this chapter we will address these very issues and discuss several other ways in which a child's development might be influenced by an early history of secure or insecure attachments.

There may be at least two patterns of caregiving that place infants at risk of developing *avoidant* attachments. Ainsworth and others (for example, Egeland & Farber, 1984) find that mothers of avoidant infants are often impatient with their babies and unresponsive to their signals, are likely to express negative feelings about their infants, and seem to derive little pleasure from close contact with them. Ainsworth (1979) believes that these mothers are rigid, self-centered people who are likely to *reject* their babies.

Yet, caregivers need not be extremely unresponsive or rejecting in order to promote an avoidant relationship. Russell Isabella and his associates (Isabella & Belsky, 1991; Isabella, Belsky, & von Eye, 1989) find that some infants classified as anxious and avoidant have overzealous mothers who constantly bombard them with high levels of stimulation, even during periods when the child doesn't care to be stimulated. Perhaps these infants have learned to cope with this intrusive mothering by simply turning away from or avoiding their rather insensitive caregivers so as not to become overaroused.

Finally, there is a new development. Many infants who do not clearly fall into one of Ainsworth's three attachment categories show a curious mixture of the resistant and the avoidant patterns. In reunion episodes, for example, these toddlers may act dazed and confused; or they may first seek proximity but then abruptly move away as the mother draws near; or they may display *both* patterns in different reunions. Their behavior clearly suggests an insecure attachment—one that Mary Main calls **disorganized/disoriented** (Main & Solomon, 1986, 1990).

Main suggests that infants who develop these disorganized/disoriented attachments are drawn to their caregivers but may also *fear* them because of past episodes in which they were neglected or physically abused. Indeed, the infant's approach/avoidance (or totally dazed demeanor) at reunion is quite understandable if she has experienced cycles of acceptance and abuse and doesn't know whether to approach the caregiver for comfort or to retreat for safety. Preliminary research supports Main's theorizing: although disorganized/disoriented attachments are occasionally observed in any research sample, they seem to be the *rule* rather than the exception among groups of abused infants (Carlson et al., 1989). And this same curious mixture of approach and avoidance, coupled with sadness upon reunion, also characterizes many infants whose severely depressed mothers are prone to reject them or to ignore their social signals (Radke-Yarrow et al., 1985).

Caregivers or Infants as Architects of Attachment Quality: The Temperament Hypothesis

To this point we have been talking as if caregivers were primarily responsible for the kinds of attachments their infants form. Not everyone agrees. Jerome Kagan (1984), for example, believes that the strange-situations test may really measure individual differences in infants' temperaments rather than the quality of their attachments. Recall from Chapter 2 that a majority of young infants display one of three temperamental profiles: **easy**, **difficult**, and **slow-to-warm-up** (Thomas & Chess, 1977). And, as we see in Table 6-2, the percentages of 1-year-olds who have established secure, resistant, and avoidant attachments correspond closely to the percentages of classifiable infants who fall into the easy, difficult, or slow-to-warm-up categories. Is this merely a coincidence?

Kagan doesn't think so. He suggests that a temperamentally "difficult" infant who resists changes in routine and is upset by novelty may become so distressed by the strange-situations procedure that he is unable to respond constructively to his mother's comforting and is thus classified as "anxious and *resistant*." By contrast, a friendly, easygoing child is likely to be classified as *"securely attached,"* whereas one who is shy or "slow to warm up" may appear distant or detached in the strange situations and will probably be classified as "anxious and *avoidant*." So Kagan's **temperament hypothesis** implies that infants, not caregivers, are the primary architects of their attachment classifications. Presumably, the attachment behaviors that a child displays reflect his or her own temperament.

Although such components of temperament as irritability and negative emotionality are indeed re-

TABLE 6-2   *Comparison of the percentages of young infants who can be classified as temperamentally "easy," "difficult," and "slow-to-warm-up" with the percentages of 1-year-olds who have established secure, resistant, and avoidant attachments with their mothers*

Temperamental Profile	Percentage of "Classifiable" Infants*	Attachment Classification	Percentage of 1-Year-Olds
Easy	60	Secure	65
Difficult	15	Resistant	10
Slow-to-warm-up	23	Avoidant	20

* These percentages are based only on the 65% of young infants who clearly exhibited one of the three temperamental profiles; hence they exclude the 35% of Thomas and Chess's sample who could not be classified.

SOURCES: M. D. S. Ainsworth, M. C. Blehar, E. Waters, & S. Wall, *Patterns of Attachment: A Psychological Study of the Strange Situation.* Copyright © 1978 by Lawrence Erlbaum Associates, Inc. Reprinted by permission; also A. Thomas & S. Chess, *Temperament and Development.* Copyright © 1977 by Brunner/Mazel.

lated to certain attachment behaviors (for example, separation protest) and do account for at least some of the variability in children's attachment classifications (cf. Goldsmith & Alansky, 1987; Izard et al., 1991; Vaughn et al., 1989, 1992), most experts reject Kagan's temperament hypothesis as far too simple and extreme. Consider, for example, that infants can be securely attached to one close companion and insecurely attached to another—a pattern that we would not expect if attachment classifications were merely reflections of the child's relatively stable temperamental characteristics (Sroufe, 1985). Moreover, the quality of a child's attachments to a particular caregiver can change relatively quickly if the caregiver experiences life changes (for example, divorce, a return to work) that significantly alter the way he or she interacts with the child (Thompson & Lamb, 1984). Relatively stable aspects of temperament should not be so readily modifiable. Finally, several recent longitudinal studies have measured infant temperament, infant social behavior, and maternal caregiving over the first year to see which of these factors best predicts the quality of infant attachments at age 12 months. We will concentrate on one of these studies in particular (Goldberg et al., 1986) because all the infants were premature and, thus, likely to display the inattentiveness and irritability that might place them at risk of developing insecure attachments.

At three-month intervals over the first year, ratings were made of (1) the infants' social behaviors, (2) the mothers' caregiving styles (for example, responsiveness to social signals; accessibility), and (3) the infants' temperamental characteristics. At the end of the year the infants were tested in the strange situations to determine the type of attachment they had to their mothers. The results were clear: the best predictor of infants' later attachment classifications was *the style of caregiving their mothers had used*; neither infant social behaviors nor infant temperamental characteristics reliably forecasted the quality of these attachments (see also Belsky, Rovine, & Taylor, 1984; Crockenberg & McCluskey, 1986; and Vaughn et al., 1989, for similar results). And it is important to add that the majority of Goldberg's temperamentally sluggish, "at risk" infants ended up establishing *secure* attachments with their mothers rather than the anxious, insecure relationships that might have been predicted by Kagan's temperament hypothesis (see also van IJzendoorn et al., 1992).

Although these results seem to suggest that caregivers, not infants, determine the kinds of attachments infants will establish, such a conclusion is, in itself, too extreme (Mangelsdorf et al., 1990; Vaughn et al., 1992). Irritable infants are somewhat more likely than easygoing ones to develop insecure attachments, owing perhaps to the impact of their unpleasant dispositions on caregiver/infant interactions (Goldsmith & Alansky, 1987). Indeed, it is hard to be consistently sensitive and responsive to a squirming, fussy baby, particularly for caregivers who lack social support (Crockenberg, 1981), who are not very confident about their parenting skills (Teti et al., 1991), or who are experiencing other problems (for example, depression, marital strife, economic hardships) of their own (Cox et al., 1989; McLoyd, 1990). Yet it is worth emphasizing once again, as Sarah Mangelsdorf and her colleagues (1990) recently have, that even a very irritable, temperamentally difficult infant is likely to establish a *secure* relationship with a caregiver who displays patience and who adjusts her caregiving to the baby's temperamental attributes.

Perhaps the findings we have examined are best summarized in terms of Thomas and Chess's (1977) **"goodness of fit" model**: secure attachments evolve from relationships in which there is a "good fit" between the caregiving a baby receives and his or her own temperament, whereas insecure attachments are more likely to develop when highly stressed or otherwise inflexible caregivers fail to accommodate to their infants' temperamental qualities. Indeed, one reason why "caregiver sensitivity" so consistently predicts attachment security is that the very notion of *sensitive* care implies an ability to tailor one's routines to whatever temperamental characteristics a baby might display (Sroufe, 1985).

To this point we have focused primarily on the quality of the infant's attachment to his or her mother. Do you think that the kind of attachment an infant has to the mother will have any effect on the infant's relationship with the father? We will explore this issue in the next section as we look at some of the ways fathers contribute to their infants' social and emotional development.

Beyond the Primary Attachment: Fathers as Attachment Objects

In 1975, Michael Lamb described fathers as the "forgotten contributors to child development." And he was right. Until the mid-1970s, fathers were largely ignored or treated as "biological necessities" who played only a minor role in the social and emotional development of their infants and toddlers. In fact, the literature on fatherhood at that time focused mainly on the effects of father *absence* (due to death or divorce), and even then it was felt that the absence of the father would have little if any impact on the child until the preschool period (that is, ages 2–5) and beyond.

One reason why researchers overlooked or discounted the father's early contributions is that fathers simply spend less time with babies than mothers do (Belsky, Gilstrap, & Rovine, 1984; Parke, 1981). However, fathers appear to be just as "engrossed" with neonates as mothers are (Parke, 1981), and they become increasingly involved with their infants over the first year of life (Belsky, Gilstrap, & Rovine, 1984), spending an average of nearly an hour a day interacting with their 9-month-olds (Ninio & Rinott, 1988). Fathers are most highly involved with their infants and hold more favorable attitudes about them when they are happily married (Cox et al., 1989; Levy-Shiff & Israelashvili, 1988) and when their wives encourage them to become an important part of their babies' lives (Palkowitz, 1984). How do infants react to Dad's increasing involvement?

Many infants form secure attachments to their fathers during the latter half of the first year (Lamb, 1981), particularly if the father has a positive attitude about parenting and spends a lot of time with them (Cox et al., 1992). And how do fathers compare to mothers as companions? In his classic early work on fathering, Lamb (1981) found that mothers and fathers tend to play somewhat different roles in a baby's life. Mothers are more likely than fathers to hold their infants, to soothe them, to play traditional games, and to care for their needs; fathers are more likely than mothers to provide playful physical stimulation and to initiate unusual or unpredictable games that infants often enjoy (Lamb, 1981). Although most infants prefer their mothers' company when upset or afraid (Lamb & Oppenheim, 1989), fathers are often preferred as playmates.

However, the playmate role is only one of many that fathers assume. Most fathers are quite skillful at soothing and comforting their distressed infants, and they may also serve as a "secure base" from which their babies will venture to explore the environment (Hwang, 1986; Lamb, 1981). In other words, fathers are rather versatile companions who

PHOTO 6-1   The "playmate" role is only one of many that fathers assume.

can assume any and all of the functions normally served by the other parent (of course, the same is true of mothers).

Although research on fatherhood is still a new endeavor, we have already learned that the father is a very important contributor to his infant's social, emotional, and intellectual development. Let's take a closer look at these findings.

Fathers' influence on early intellectual development.   In one of the earliest studies of fathering, Alison Clarke-Stewart (1978, 1980) found that infants whose fathers were highly involved with them scored higher on infant intelligence tests than those whose fathers were less involved. Easterbrooks and Goldberg (1984) have essentially corroborated these findings with a sample of young toddlers. Children whose fathers were highly involved with them and sensitive to their needs expressed more positive affect while working at a cognitive challenge (a jigsaw puzzle) and persisted longer at the task than

those whose fathers were less sensitive and involved. Moreover, Easterbrooks and Goldberg report that the fathers' *sensitivity* to their toddlers' needs was a better predictor of the children's cognitive performance than was fathers' overall involvement in caregiving activities. So, even with fathers, the type or *quality* of interaction may be as important (or more important) to a child's developmental outcomes as the sheer amount of contact fathers provide (see also Cox et al., 1992).

Fathers as contributors to early social and emotional development.   Although many infants form the same kind of attachment with their fathers as they have previously established with their mothers (Fox, Kimmerly, & Schafer, 1991), it is not at all unusual for a child to be secure with one parent and insecure with the other (Cox et al., 1992; Main & Weston, 1981). For example, when Mary Main and Donna Weston (1981) used the strange-situations test to measure the quality of 44 infants' attachments to their mothers and fathers, they found that 12 infants were securely attached to both parents, 11 were secure with the mother but insecure with the father, 10 were insecure with the mother but secure with the father, and 11 were insecurely attached to both parents.

What might a father add to a child's social and emotional development? One way to find out is to compare the social behavior of infants who are securely attached to their fathers and infants who are insecurely attached to their fathers. Main and Weston adopted this strategy by exposing their four groups of infants to a friendly stranger in a clown outfit who spent several minutes trying to play with the child and then turned around and cried when a person at the door told the clown he would have to leave. As the clown went through his routine, the infants were each observed and rated for (1) the extent to which they were willing to establish a positive relationship with the clown (low ratings indicated that the infant was wary or distressed) and (2) signs of emotional conflict (that is, such indications of psychological disturbance as curling up in the fetal position on the floor or vocalizing in a "social" manner to a wall).

TABLE 6-3 *Average levels of social responsiveness and emotional conflict shown by infants who were either securely or insecurely attached to their mothers and fathers*

Measure	Pattern of Attachment			
	Securely Attached to Both Parents	Secure with Mother, Insecure with Father	Insecure with Mother, Secure with Father	Insecurely Attached to Both Parents
Social responsiveness	6.94	4.87	3.30	2.45
Emotional conflict	1.17	1.00	1.80	2.50

Note: Social responsiveness ratings could vary from 1 (wary, distressed) to 9 (happy, responsive). Conflict ratings could vary from 1 (no conflict) to 5 (very conflicted).
SOURCE: M. Main & D. R. Weston, "The Quality of the Toddler's Relationship to Mother and to Father: Related to Conflict and the Readiness to Establish New Relationships." *Child Development*, 1981, 52, 932–940. Copyright © 1981 by the Society for Research in Child Development.

Table 6-3 shows the results of this stranger test. Note that infants who were securely attached to both parents were the most socially responsive. Equally important is the finding that infants who were securely attached to *at least one parent* were more friendly toward the clown and less emotionally conflicted than infants who had insecure relationships with both parents. In sum, this study illustrates the important role that fathers can play in their infants' social and emotional development. Not only are infants more socially responsive when they are securely attached to *both* the mother and the father, but it also appears that a secure attachment to the father may help to prevent harmful consequences (emotional disturbances; an exaggerated fear of other people) that could otherwise result when infants are insecurely attached to their mothers.

Implications of Attachment Quality for Later Development

Both psychoanalytic theorists (Erikson, 1963; Freud, 1905/1930) and ethologists (Bowlby, 1969) have argued that the feelings of warmth, trust, and security that infants derive from healthy attachments will set the stage for adaptive psychological functioning later in life. Of course, one implication of this viewpoint is that insecure attachments are likely to forecast less-than-optimal patterns of behavior in the years ahead.

Early correlates of secure and insecure attachments. Does the quality of an infant's early attachment relationships predict his or her behavior during toddlerhood and the preschool period? It seems to. Even though the existing data are somewhat limited in that they focus almost exclusively on infants' attachments to their mothers, the early correlates of secure and insecure attachments are very interesting indeed. For example, Susan Londerville and Mary Main (1981) found that infants who were securely attached at 12 months of age are more likely than those who were insecurely attached to obey their mothers and to cooperate with female strangers at 21 months of age. Other short-term longitudinal research reveals that infants who were securely attached at age 12–18 months are better problem solvers as 2-year-olds (Frankel & Bates, 1990; Matas, Arend, & Sroufe, 1978) and are more complex and creative in their symbolic play (Pipp, Easterbrooks, & Harmon, 1992; Slade, 1987) than children with a history of insecure attachments. And it is interesting to note that, from a peer's point of view, securely attached 2–3-year-olds are already much more attractive as playmates than are children who are insecurely attached. In fact, peers often respond in an overtly negative or aggressive way to playmates classified as "anxious and *resistant*" (Jacobson & Wille, 1986).

The relationship of early attachments to social and intellectual behavior during the *preschool* period is nicely illustrated in a longitudinal study by Everett Waters and his associates. Waters, Wippman, and Sroufe (1979) first measured the quality of children's attachments at 15 months of age and then observed these children in a nursery-school setting at age 3½. Children who had been securely attached to their mothers at age 15 months were now social leaders in the nursery school: they often initiated play activities, were generally sensitive to the needs and feelings of other children, and were very popular with their peers. Observers described these children as curious, self-directed, and eager to learn. By contrast, children who had been insecurely attached at age 15 months were socially and emotionally withdrawn, were hesitant to engage other children in play activities, and were described by observers as less curious, less interested in learning, and much less forceful in pursuing their goals (see Sroufe, Fox, & Pancake, 1983, for similar results with 4–5-year-olds).

Finally, insecurely attached preschoolers may also make poor "best friends." Kathryn Park and Everett Waters (1989) recently observed the play of 4-year-olds as each spent an hour in a playroom paired with his or her best friend. Half of the pairs consisted of children who were both securely attached to their mothers (secure/secure pairs); the other half were pairings in which one child was securely attached and the other was insecure (secure/insecure pairs). Conflict was common in both kinds of friendship pairings. However, the secure/secure pairings were usually able to resolve their differences by taking their partner's protests seriously and negotiating fair settlements, whereas members of secure/insecure pairs were much more inclined to challenge each other, to rely on forceful strategies to get their way, and to end up being angry with their partners. So friendships involving an insecurely attached child are a whole lot more coercive and less harmonious than those between youngsters who are both securely attached.

Why might attachment quality forecast later behavior?   Clearly, the preschool correlates of secure and insecure attachments are consistent with Erik Erikson's ideas about the importance of developing an early sense of "trust" in other people. Perhaps securely attached infants who have learned to trust an easily accessible and responsive caregiver become curious problem solvers later in life because they feel comfortable at venturing away from an attentive parent to explore and, as a result, they learn how to answer questions and solve problems on their own. Moreover, securely attached infants may become quite sociable and rather popular with their peers because they have already established pleasant relationships with responsive caregivers and have learned from these experiences that human beings are likely to react positively to their social overtures. By contrast, an anxious, insecure infant who has not learned to trust her caregivers may be reluctant to either (1) explore the environment and gain the initiative that would help her to answer questions or (2) completely trust other people with whom she may have dealings, including those who will become her "best friends."

Ethologists can agree in principle with Erikson's analyses but have chosen to explain any enduring effects of early attachment histories in a different way. John Bowlby (1969, 1988) and Inge Bretherton (1985, 1990) have proposed that, as infants continue to interact with primary caregivers, they will develop **internal working models**—that is, cognitive representations of *themselves* and *other people*—that are used to interpret events and to form expectations about the character of human relationships. Sensitive, responsive caregiving, for example, may lead the child to conclude that people are dependable (positive working model of others), whereas insensitive, neglectful, or abusive caregiving may lead to insecurity and a lack of trust (negative working model of others). Although this sounds very similar to Erikson's theory, the ethologists further propose that an infant will also develop a working model of the *self*—either a positive or a negative one, based largely on *his ability* to elicit (or fail to elicit) attention and comfort when he needs it. Presumably, these two working models will combine to influence the quality of the child's primary attachments and the expectations she has about future relationships. And what kinds of expectations might she form?

A recent variation of this "working models" theory appears in Figure 6-1. As shown, infants who construct positive working models of themselves and their caregivers are the ones who should (1) form *secure* primary attachments, (2) have the ego strength to approach and to master new challenges, and (3) be predisposed to establish close, mutual-trust relationships with friends and spouses later in life. By contrast, a positive model of self coupled with a negative model of others (as might result when infants can successfully attract the attention of an insensitive, overintrusive caregiver) is thought to predispose the infant to form *avoidant* attachments and to "dismiss" the importance of close emotional bonds. A negative model of self and a positive model of others should be associated with *resistant* attachments and a "preoccupation" with establishing secure emotional ties. Finally, a negative working model of both the self and others is thought to underlie *disorganized/disoriented* attachments and an emerging "fear" of being hurt (either physically or emotionally) in intimate relationships (Bartholomew & Horowitz, 1991).

Of course, caregivers also have working models of themselves and others—models that are based on their own earlier life experiences and that may affect the working models their babies construct. Indeed, Judith Crowell and Shirley Feldman (1988) found that mothers' working models of attachments, as assessed by the *Adult Attachment Interview* (see Box 6-1), accurately predicted the sensitivity of their interactions with their 2- to 4½-year-old children in a laboratory play session (with secure mothers being much more sensitive than insecure mothers). Moreover, Peter Fonagy and his associates (Fonagy, Steele, & Steele, 1991) report that mothers' working models of attachment assessed *before their babies were born* accurately predicted about 75% of the time whether their infants would establish secure or insecure attachments to them. So it seems that cognitive representations of close relationships can be transmitted from generation to generation. Indeed, Bowlby (1988) proposed that, once formed, a working model of relationships may

	MODEL OF SELF	
	Positive	Negative
MODEL OF OTHERS Positive	SECURE (Secure primary attachments)	PREOCCUPIED (Resistant primary attachments)
Negative	DISMISSING (Avoidant primary attachments)	FEARFUL (Disorganized/disoriented primary attachments)

FIGURE 6-1   Four models of close emotional relationships that evolve from the positive or negative "working models" of self and others that people construct from their experiences with intimate companions. (Adapted from K. Bartholomew & L. M. Horowitz, "Attachment Styles among Young Adults: A Test of a Four-Category Model." *Journal of Personality and Social Psychology*, 1991, *61*, 226–244. Copyright © 1991 by the American Psychological Association.)

stabilize (becoming an aspect of personality) and thereby continue to influence the character of a person's close emotional ties throughout life.

Beyond the preschool period: Correlates of attachment histories later in life.   Are there any data to imply that the quality of a child's earliest attachments can influence his or her adjustment during the grade-school years, adolescence, or young adulthood? Indeed there are. Consider that early attachments are often stable over time; most children experience the same kind of attachment relationships with their parents during the early grade-school years than they did in infancy (Main & Cassidy, 1988). Moreover, the grade-school behavioral correlates of secure and insecure attachments are similar to those characterizing secure and insecure preschoolers. Six-year-old boys who are still insecurely attached to their mothers, for example, are rated less popular and more aggressive by peers, and less intellectually competent by their first-grade teachers, than male classmates whose current ties to their mothers are secure (Cohn, 1990). Parallel findings have even been reported for young adults. For example, college students who recall their own early attachment relationships as stable and secure are rated less anxious and less hostile by peers, and report lower levels of loneliness and personal distress, than classmates who describe their early attachment histories as insecure (Kobak & Sceery, 1988). Moreover, young adults who characterize their early attachments as secure, resistant, or avoidant tend to establish the same kind of attachment relationships with their current romantic partners (Feeney & Noller, 1990; Hazan & Shaver, 1987).

Is attachment history destiny?   Although it seems that early working models of relationships may be long lasting and that there are some clear advantages to having formed secure emotional attachments early in life, the future is not always so bleak for infants who are insecurely attached. As suggested earlier, a secure relationship with another person, such as the father or perhaps a grandparent or a day-care provider, can help to offset whatever undesirable consequences might otherwise result from an insecure attachment to the mother (Clarke-Stewart, 1989). Moreover, the character of our social relationships later in childhood and adolescence will also influence our ultimate social adjustment. In fact, one recent longitudinal study found that adult social outcomes were actually predicted as well or better by peer relations during adolescence as by early attachment histories (Skolnick, 1986).

Let's also note that secure primary attachments can quickly become insecure should a mother return to work, place her infant in day care, or experience life stresses (such as marital problems, a major illness, or financial woes) that drastically alter how she and her infant respond to each other (Thompson, Lamb, & Estes, 1982). Indeed, one reason why Bowlby (and later Bretherton) used the term *working* models was to underscore that a child's cognitive representations of self, others, and close emotional relationships are dynamic and can change (for better or for worse) if later experiences with caregivers, close friends, romantic partners, or spouses imply that a revision is necessary. Finally, such major life disruptions as the divorce of one's parents or the death of a sibling can quickly undermine a child's psychological well-being, regardless of the quality of his early emotional ties.

So secure attachment histories are no guarantee of positive adjustment later in life; nor are insecure early attachments a certain indicator of poor life outcomes (Fagot & Kavanagh, 1990). Yet we should not underestimate the adaptive significance of secure early attachments, for children who have functioned adequately as infants but very poorly during the preschool period are more likely to recover and to display good social skills and self-confidence during the grade-school years if their early attachment histories were secure rather than insecure (Sroufe, Egeland, & Kreutzer, 1990).

Now let's turn to a controversial topic that has been widely debated in both the popular and the scholarly presses. The question is simple, but the answers are not: do maternal employment and alternative caregiving arrangements hinder children's emotional development?

Working Mothers, Alternative Care, and Children's Emotional Development

Working mothers are no longer exceptions to the rule. Because of changes in economic conditions over the past 20 years, both parents in many families must now work in order to maintain a standard of living similar to that achieved by their own parents with only one family breadwinner. Moreover, a growing number of single parents have little choice but to work; even the majority of those who are receiving public assistance would rather be working and report that they would do so if adequate child-care services were available to them at a reasonable cost (Stipek & McCroskey, 1989).[1] In the United States, more than 50% of mothers with infants and toddlers are now employed outside the home (Hoffman, 1989), and the comparable figure for Swedish mothers is even higher, at 85% (Andersson, 1989). Not only does work take a mother away from her

---

[1]Indeed, alternative care is expensive. The average American family spends about $3500 per year per child (25–30% of what a single mother on public assistance might hope to earn before taxes) for what is often less-than-optimal day care (Berk, 1991).

child for several hours a day, but her infants or preschool children will also have to adjust to alternative caregiving — either in-home or out-of-home care by a babysitter or relative or care provided by a day-care home or a group day-care center. Do these daily separations and contacts with alternative caregivers have adverse effects on a child's emotional development, as some theorists (for example, Fraiberg, 1977) have feared? Let's explore this issue by looking first at what we know about maternal employment.

Maternal Employment and Early Emotional Development

In her recent review of the literature, Lois Hoffman (1989) concludes that maternal employment, in itself, is unlikely either to prevent infants from establishing secure ties to their mothers or to undermine an attachment that is already secure. One reason that these daily separations may not impede the emotional development of most children is that working mothers often compensate for their absences by being especially sensitive and responsive caregivers when they are at home (Crockenberg & Litman, 1991; Hoffman, 1989). Moreover, it seems that families spend just as many hours together in "family" activities in households in which mothers are employed as in those in which only the father is employed (Easterbrooks & Goldberg, 1985). So, intensive family interactions may provide all the experience an infant needs to become (or remain) securely attached to a working mother.

Yet, not all children make such positive adjustments to work-related separations or alternative caregiving. Consider that most of the studies that show no differences in the emotional development of children of employed and nonemployed mothers have focused on *two-parent middle-class* families. Thus the working mothers in these studies may be somewhat "advantaged" in that they have a spouse to assume some responsibility for child care and to encourage them as they try to establish and maintain warm, loving relationships with their infants and toddlers. Can we assume that the results of these studies would also apply to economically disadvantaged families, particularly those in which

working mothers are single parents and have no spousal support?

Probably not. In one study of economically disadvantaged families (Vaughn, Gove, & Egeland, 1980), infants whose mothers had returned to work before the infants' first birthday were more likely to develop avoidant attachments than infants from similar backgrounds whose mothers cared for them at home. Moreover, the likelihood that these infants' attachments would become (or remain) avoidant over time was greater when the working mother was a single parent. So an early return to work by mothers who must raise children without support from a spouse can contribute to the development of anxious/avoidant emotional attachments. Even children from *middle-class* families face a slightly greater risk of developing insecure attachments if their mothers return to work during *the latter half of the first year* — the period when infants are normally establishing their primary social attachments (Barglow, Vaughn, & Molitor, 1987; Belsky & Rovine, 1988; Benn, 1986). Male infants appear to be particularly vulnerable to their mothers' early return to work and to alternative caregiving, for they are more likely than female infants to be insecure with their fathers as well (Belsky & Rovine, 1988; Chase-Lansdale & Owen, 1987).

Don't misunderstand. Researchers are *not* claiming that infants and toddlers are destined to a life of emotional insecurity if they are economically disadvantaged or if their mothers should resume employment in the first year. In fact, *most* such infants are not adversely affected, and some will even become more emotionally *secure* after their mothers return to work (Thompson et al., 1982; Vaughn et al., 1980). How can we explain these dramatic individual differences? Might the quality of alternative care that children receive make a difference? Let's see what researchers have learned.

Infants' Reactions to Alternative Care

According to experts on alternative care, a high-quality day-care facility is one that has (1) a reasonable child-to-caregiver ratio (1–3 infants, 1–4 toddlers, or 1–8 preschoolers per adult); (2) caregivers

PHOTO 6-2 High-quality day care can have beneficial effects on children's social, emotional, and intellectual development.

who are warm, emotionally expressive, and responsive to children's bids for attention; (3) little staff turnover, so that children can become familiar and feel comfortable with their new adult companions; (4) a curriculum made up of games and activities that are age appropriate; and (5) an administration that is willing (or, better yet, eager) to confer with parents about the child's progress (Howes, 1990; Howes, Phillips, & Whitebook, 1992). Given adequate training and resources, and some effort on the substitute caregiver's part, all these criteria can be achieved by a relative or regular sitter providing in-home care, by a nonrelative operating a day-care home, or by a group day-care center (Howes, 1988).

Regardless of the setting in which care is given, the quality of alternative care that children receive clearly matters. For example, high-quality day care promotes both the social responsiveness and the intellectual development of children from emotionally disadvantaged backgrounds—so much so, in fact,

that, by the time they reach kindergarten, disadvantaged day-care children score substantially higher on IQ tests than other children from similar backgrounds who were cared for at home by their mothers (Burchinal, Lee, & Ramey, 1989). Apparently, there is little risk of emotional insecurity (or any other adverse outcome) when children receive excellent alternative care—*even when that care begins very early.* Jerome Kagan and his associates (1978), for example, found that infants who entered a high-quality, university-sponsored day-care program at age 3½ to 5½ months not only developed secure attachments to their mothers but were just as socially, emotionally, and intellectually mature over the first two years of life as children from similar backgrounds who had been cared for at home. Studies conducted in Sweden (where day care is government subsidized, closely monitored, and typically of high quality) report similar positive outcomes (Lamb et al., 1988); moreover, the earlier Swedish infants enter high quality day care, the better their cognitive, social, and emotional development 6 to 12 years later in elementary and junior high school (Andersson, 1989, 1992; see also Field, 1991). Finally, Carollee Howes's (1990) recent longitudinal study of middle-class families in California indicates that early entry into day care is associated with poor social, emotional, and intellectual outcomes later in childhood *only* when the care children received was of low quality (see also Vandell, Henderson, & Wilson, 1988).

Unfortunately, infants who receive the poorest and most unstable day care are often those whose parents are living complex, stressful lives that may prevent them from becoming highly involved with or closely attached to their children (Howes, 1990). So a child's poor progress in day care may often stem as much from a disordered home life, in which parents are not all that enthused about parenting, as from the less-than-optimal alternative care that he or she receives. Let's explore this idea further.

Parents' Attitudes about Work and Parenting

According to Hoffman (1989), a mother's attitudes about working and child care may be as important to her child's social and emotional well-being as her actual employment status. Mothers tend to be much happier and much more sensitive as caregivers when their employment status matches their attitudes about working (Crockenberg & Litman, 1991; Hock & DeMeis, 1990; Stuckey, McGhee, & Bell, 1982). So, if a woman wants to work, it may make little sense to pressure her into staying home to care for her child when she might be depressed, hostile, or otherwise unresponsive in that role.

Even when children receive less-than-optimal alternative care, their outcomes will depend greatly on their parents' attitudes and behaviors. Outcomes are likely to be better if a working mother has positive attitudes *both* about working and about being a mother (Belsky & Rovine, 1988; Greenberger &

| B O X | 6-2 | *Alternative Care in Context:*
Early Emotional Development in the Kibbutz |

Our examination of day care has focused on arrangements common in Western societies; thus it may be inappropriate to generalize our findings to children in other cultures, who often receive very different kinds of alternative care. One society that employs a very different form of alternative care from those we've discussed is the modern state of Israel.

Early in the 20th century, when Zionist pioneers founded their first collective settlements, or kibbutzim, a system of communal child care was employed to enable a greater number of adults to perform economically productive work. Over the years this system of child rearing has become something of an institution. In the modern kibbutz, women are granted brief maternity leaves to deliver and care for their neonates but will generally return to work within 6 to 12 weeks after the child is born. During the hours that mothers are working, their children are cared for by specially designated caregivers (called *metaplot;* singular, *metapelet*), each of whom looks after three to four children of the same age. Children typically stay with the same metapelet for 12 to 15 months, after which they are reassigned to another metapelet. All children remain with peers and the metapelet throughout the day, except for the period between 4:00 and 7:00 P.M., when they are with their parents. At night, children of the kibbutz are assigned to *biet tinokot* and *biet yeladim* ("children's homes"), where they are looked after by "watchwomen" who periodically walk from residence to residence. Because many women in the kibbutz take turns as watchwomen, these caregivers are often quite unfamiliar to the children.

Abraham Sagi and his colleagues (Sagi et al., 1985) point out that child-rearing practices in the kibbutz differ substantially from those considered optimal by attachment theorists. For example, kibbutz babies have much less contact with parents than home-reared infants do and are monitored at night by unfamiliar watchwomen, who have many children to look after and may be slow to respond to a child's distress or other bids for attention. Moreover, women serving as primary caregivers, or metaplot, are *assigned* to this work; they may or may not be enthusiastic about serving in that capacity. For all these reasons, Sagi et al. presumed that the incidence of insecure attachments would be greater among kibbutz-reared infants than among children from the United States or Israeli children raised in home settings.

To test this hypothesis, Sagi et al. administered the strange-situations test to 86 kibbutz-reared infants aged 11–14 months. Each child was tested three times to assess the quality of his or her attachment to the mother, the father, and the metapelet. The resulting data were then compared with the patterns of attachment observed among U.S. children and among a second sample of 36 home-reared Israeli infants.

As we see in the table, Sagi et al. found that insecure attachments were more common among kibbutz-reared infants than among their U.S. counterparts or Israeli children raised at home. The latter comparison is particularly interesting in that the home-reared Israeli infants were recruited from day-care centers and thus were themselves receiving alternative care.

Goldberg, 1989). And it also helps immensely if her spouse approves of her working and supports her in her parenting role (Spitze, 1988). Ultimately, parents' attitudes about being parents, as well as the quality of care they provide at home, may have much more to do with an infant's development than the kind of alternative care he receives (Lamb et al., 1988).

In sum, we cannot draw pat conclusions about the effects of maternal employment and alternative care on infants' emotional development, for these "effects" are sometimes beneficial and sometimes harmful. We can say that most children in two-parent families are unlikely to suffer any adverse long-term effects as a result of their day-to-day separations from working parents. And, not

---

B O X

6-2 | *continued*

Attachment patterns
observed among three groups of infants

| | Type of Attachment | |
Sample	Insecure	Secure
U.S. sample		
with mother	33%	66%
Kibbutz sample		
with mother	49	48
with father	44	54
with metapelet	52	45
Home-reared Israeli sample		
with mother	25	75

Note: Percentages in some rows do not add to 100% because some infants were judged to be unattached or their attachments were not easily classifiable.
SOURCE: Adapted from A. Sagi, M. E. Lamb, K. S. Lewkowicz, R. Shoham, R. Dvir, & D. Estes, "Security of Infant-Mother-Father-and-Metapelet Attachments among Kibbutz-Reared Israeli Children." In I. Bretherton & W. Waters (Eds.), "Growing Points of Attachment Theory and Research." *Monographs of the Society for Research in Child Development*, 1985, *50*(Nos. 1–2, Serial No. 209).

Apparently the quality of caregiving that infants received from the metaplot largely determined the kinds of attachments they established, and (1) most infants under the care of a particular metapelet established exactly the same kind of attachment to her, and (2) the infants' attachment to the metapelet predicted the quality of their attachment to their fathers. Thus, some metaplot have caregiving styles that promote secure attachments, whereas others (perhaps because they are

less than enthusiastic about their assigned role) seem to promote insecure attachments.

Do the attachments that kibbutzniks establish with metaplot predict their later social and emotional behavior? One might expect that they would *not*: kibbutzniks are routinely assigned to new metaplot in the second year, and their emotional ties to their mothers and fathers might further dilute the influence of this primary attachment experience. However, Oppenheim, Sagi, and Lamb (1988) discovered otherwise when they followed up on Sagi's sample at 5 years of age. Kibbutzniks who had been secure with their metaplot at age 11–14 months were more empathic, dominant, independent, and achievement oriented as kindergartners than their counterparts who had been insecurely attached to their metaplot. Moreover, the quality of children's early attachment to their metaplot was a better predictor of their kindergarten behaviors than was the quality of their attachments to either their mothers or their fathers.

Clearly, metaplot assume an important role in the lives of kibbutzniks — a more central role than day-care providers in Western societies normally play. And research from the kibbutz also speaks to the importance of interactions with a *primary* caregiver (and the working models derived from this experience), for it was the security of the kibbutzniks' attachments to metaplot, rather than the quality of their ties to their parents, that best predicted children's social and emotional behavior four years later in kindergarten.

TABLE 6-4   *Sample parental-leave policies in modern industrialized nations*

Denmark:	Mothers receive 14 weeks' paid maternity leave after childbirth; at their option, either the mother or father may take an additional 10 weeks without pay.
Finland:	Leave for a mother or a father consists of 70 working days at full pay and an additional 188 working days at 70% pay. Unpaid leave may be extended for 3 years without jeopardizing the parent's employment.
France:	Working mothers receive 16 weeks of leave at 84% pay.
Israel:	Working mothers receive 12 weeks' paid leave and up to 40 weeks' unpaid leave.
Japan:	Working mothers receive 14 weeks' paid leave.
Poland:	Working mothers can take up to 6 months' leave with full pay and up to 2½ additional years with partial pay.
Sweden:	Working mothers receive 6 months' leave at 90% pay and an additional 6 months' unpaid leave. Mothers and fathers may share leave benefits if they wish.
United States:	Parents may take 12 weeks of unpaid leave in firms of 50 or more employees.

SOURCE: Adapted from *Looking at Children*, by D. F. Bjorklund & B. R. Bjorklund, pp. 354–355. Copyright © 1992 by Brooks/Cole Publishing Co.

surprisingly, infants from any background are likely to fare rather well if they receive sensitive, responsive care both at home and from their substitute caregivers.

What can we do to help working parents establish more secure emotional ties with their infants and to promote these infants' early social and personality development? A national policy governing parental leave for child care is one step in the right direction. In early 1993 the United States finally adopted a parental-leave policy — one guaranteeing workers in firms with 50 or more employees the right to take 12 weeks of unpaid leave to spend time with their infant, without jeopardizing their jobs. Yet this guarantee (1) does not apply to the *majority* of American workers (who are employed by firms with fewer than 50 employees) and (2) seems almost miserly compared to the often-generous parental-leave policies that many other industrialized societies have enacted (see Table 6-4).

A national policy on day care may be even more important. At present, American parents must often struggle to find and keep competent sitters or other high-quality day-care placements — due, in part, to the continuing reluctance of the U.S. government to subsidize and carefully monitor day care (as several European countries have done). Sandra Scarr (1984) finds this puzzling, since the U.S. government is quite willing to invest in children once

they are old enough to attend public school. Increasingly, employers are realizing that it is in their best interest to help workers obtain quality day care, and a few have even established day-care centers at the work site (Hymes, 1990). But, until more options are available, working parents will continue to face the challenges of finding good alternative care at a cost they can afford.

The Unattached Infant: Effects of Restricted Social Contacts during Infancy

Some infants have very limited contacts with adults during the first year or two of life and do not appear to become attached to anyone. Occasionally these socially deprived youngsters have been reared at home by very abusive or neglectful caregivers, but most of them are found in understaffed institutions where they may see a caregiver only when it is time to be fed, changed, or bathed. Will these "unattached" infants suffer as a result of their early experiences? Must infants form attachments to develop normally, as Freud and some ethologists (for example, Bowlby, 1973) have argued?

We will begin by looking at the immediate and long-range effects of social deprivation on puppies and infant monkeys — species that ordinarily form attachments and, in the case of rhesus monkeys, develop complex social networks. As we will see, this tightly controlled experimental research has helped us to understand why socially deprived children are likely to differ from those raised at home with their parents.

Effects of Social Isolation in Dogs

Thompson and Melzack (1956) describe an interesting series of experiments designed to measure the effects of social isolation on the development of Scottish-terrier puppies. Each puppy assigned to the experimental group was separated from its mother immediately after weaning and housed in a cage with opaque sides. These pups were then isolated from other puppies and from humans for several months. By contrast, puppies assigned to the control group were reared either (1) with other dogs in the laboratory or (2) in a home setting with human caretakers.

After seven to ten months both groups were tested for their fear of strange stimuli, their relative dominance, and their social responsiveness. Thompson and Melzack found that the isolated puppies were much more agitated when exposed to novel stimuli, such as an umbrella opening, than the control puppies. They were also less dominant than control puppies when placed in a situation in which they had to compete with the control puppies for a bone. The results of the social-responsiveness test were particularly interesting. Social responsiveness was measured by releasing the puppy into a large pen that contained two other dogs confined to opposite corners by chicken-wire partitions. The isolates paid very little attention to the other dogs, spending most of their time sniffing around and exploring the pen itself. Control pups, by contrast, spent a considerable amount of time barking at, wagging their tails at, and examining the other dogs. Follow-up observations revealed that the isolates' relative lack of social responsiveness persisted for several years.

Subsequent research has identified the period between 3 and 12 weeks of age as a **sensitive period** for the development of social responsiveness in dogs: puppies that are socially isolated during this period

PHOTO 6-3   Isolate monkeys often display unusual postures.

typically remain quite unreceptive to the social overtures of other dogs or human beings (see Scott, 1962, 1968) and will often display such unusual behaviors as wedging their bodies into the corner of a novel testing room, as if they were trying to retreat from this strange new environment. They are rather atypical and asocial creatures indeed.

Harlow's Studies of Socially Deprived Monkeys

Harry Harlow and his associates studied the effects of early social deprivation on rhesus monkeys by isolating newborn infants in individualized stainless steel cubicles and then carefully monitoring their progress. What they found was remarkable. Even three months of social deprivation left infants in a state of emotional shock. When removed from isolation, these pitiful creatures gave the appearance of being terrified by clutching at themselves, crouching, or burying their heads in their arms as if trying to shut out this strange new world (see Photo 6-3). They also displayed such abnormal behaviors as self-biting, rocking, and pulling out tufts of their hair. However, the three-month isolates eventually recovered. Daily 30-minute play periods with a normal agemate soon led to the development of effective social relationships that persisted into adolescence and adulthood.

The prognosis was not nearly so optimistic for infants isolated six months or longer. The six-month isolates clearly avoided normal agemates during free-play sessions, preferring instead to play by themselves with toys. What little social responsiveness they did show was directed toward other isolates, leading Harlow to conclude that *misery prefers miserable company*. Normally reared infant monkeys usually go through a phase of aggressive play in the latter half of the first year. Yet, when the isolates were attacked by other infants, they accepted the abuse without offering much defense.

As bad as this behavioral pattern may sound, the effects of 12 months of social isolation were even worse. The 12-month isolates were extremely withdrawn and apathetic, and they often had to be separated from their normal agemates, who were likely to injure or even kill these passive creatures during periods of aggressive play (Harlow & Harlow, 1977).

Follow-up studies of monkeys isolated six months or longer have found that the isolates develop bizarre patterns of social and sexual behavior during adolescence and adulthood. Harlow describes the adult sexual behavior of these monkeys as follows:

> When the females were smaller than the [normally reared] males, the girls would back away and sit down facing the males [an inadequate attempt at sexual posturing], looking appealingly at their would-be consorts. Their hearts were in the right place but nothing else was. . . . [Isolate] males were equally unsatisfactory. They approached the females with a blind . . . misdirected enthusiasm. Frequently, they would grasp the females by the side of the body and thrust laterally, leaving them working at cross purposes with reality [1962, p. 5].

Isolates as mothers.   What kind of mothers do isolate females make?[2] Harlow and his associates (Har-

[2]You may be wondering how the motherless mothers ever became pregnant if their sexual behavior was truly inadequate. In some cases, breeding males overpowered them or helped the more cooperative ones to attain a satisfactory coital posture. In other cases, isolate females were placed in a specially constructed "breeding rack" that restrained, positioned, and supported the female during copulation.

low et al., 1966) found that these **"motherless mothers"** frequently pushed their infants away, refusing to let them nurse (see Photo 6-4), and sometimes even subjected them to severe physical abuse. Yet two remarkable findings emerged from this study of "motherless mothers." First, the surviving offspring of these brutal or indifferent caregivers showed a relatively normal pattern of social development. Thus, unloving mothers are better than no mothers at all—a finding that undoubtedly surprised many social-developmental theorists. Second, the "motherless mothers" who gave birth to second and even third babies suddenly became adequate mothers. Harlow et al. (1966) proposed that the first-borns may have served a socializing function by partially compensating for the previous social deprivation of the isolates, thereby allowing these "motherless mothers" to develop enough social responsiveness to accept subsequent babies. But, despite the vast improvement in their maternal behaviors, the "motherless mothers" continued to display incompetent social and sexual responsiveness toward other adult monkeys.

Can isolate monkeys recover?   Harlow and his associates initially believed that the first six months of life was a **critical period** for the social development of rhesus monkeys: presumably, infants who were denied social stimulation and who remained unattached to another monkey for six months or longer would become forever incapable of establishing normal social and emotional relationships with other adult monkeys. However, a later experiment by Steven Suomi and Harry Harlow (1972) challenged this point of view by showing that the isolation syndrome can be reversed.

The "therapy" that proved so successful involved exposing long-term isolates to daily play sessions with *younger*, 3-month-old monkeys. Why younger companions? Mainly because a 3-month-old infant has not yet become active and aggressive in its play; the initial response of these younger associates is to approach and cling tenaciously to their isolate partners rather than to harass or attack them (as normally reared agemates do). Suomi and Harlow believed that an emotionally disturbed isolate would not only tolerate a passive, nonaggressive infant but

PHOTO 6-4   Typical abusive behavior of "mother-less" mother monkeys toward their infants.

PHOTO 6-5   Younger "therapist" monkey clinging to the back of her older isolate playmate.

might eventually be "drawn out of his shell" if he ever began to respond to the younger monkey's playful antics. Progress did prove to be painfully slow, but, by the end of 26 weeks of this **younger-peer therapy**, the isolates had recovered. Their social behaviors were normal and age appropriate, and they bore no resemblance to the pitiful, socially inept creatures described in earlier reports. Even profoundly disturbed 12-month isolates will eventually recover to become socially and sexually competent as adults if they are eased into a rehabilitative program with a younger therapist monkey (Novak, 1979).

Clearly, these dramatic reversals contradict the critical-period hypothesis, which implies that the devastating social and emotional consequences of prolonged isolation are permanent and irreversible. Perhaps it is more accurate to call the first six months of life a "sensitive" period when normally reared monkeys are rapidly developing important social skills and becoming attached to their mothers. Although social deprivation interferes with these

activities and produces a rather disturbed young monkey, recovery is possible if the patient is given the proper therapy.

Social Deprivation in Humans

Fortunately, there are both legal and ethical constraints to prevent researchers from isolating human infants for scientific purposes. Yet, in the recent past, physicians and psychologists began to discover that infants in some orphanages and foundling homes were being raised under conditions that resembled those experienced by Harlow's socially deprived monkeys. For example, it was not uncommon for an impoverished institution to have only one caregiver for every 10–20 infants. Moreover, the adults in these understaffed institutions rarely interacted with the infants except to bathe and change them or to prop a bottle against their pillow at feeding time. Infants were often housed in separate cribs with sheets hung over the railings so that, in effect, they were isolated from the world around them. To make matters worse, babies in the more impoverished of these institutions had no crib toys to manipulate and few if any opportunities to get out of their cribs and practice motor skills. Compared with infants raised in a typical home setting, these institutionalized children received very little in the way of social or sensory stimulation.

Babies raised under these conditions appear quite normal for the first three to six months of life: they cry for attention, smile and babble at caregivers, and make the proper postural adjustments when they are about to be picked up. But in the second half of the first year their behavior changes. Now they seldom cry, coo, or babble; they become rigid and fail to accommodate to the handling of caregivers; their language skills are grossly retarded; and they often appear rather depressed and uninterested in social contact (Goldfarb, 1943; Provence & Lipton, 1962; Ribble, 1943; Spitz, 1945). Here is a description of one such infant:

> Outstanding were his soberness, his forlorn appearance, and lack of animation. . . . He did not turn to adults to relieve his distress. . . . He made no demands. . . . As one made active and persistent efforts at a social exchange he became somewhat more responsive, animated and . . . active, but lapsed into his depressed . . . appearance when the adult became less active. . . . If you crank his motor you can get him to go a little; but he can't start on his own [Provence & Lipton, 1962, pp. 134–135].

What are these institutionalized infants like as schoolchildren and adolescents? The answer depends, in part, on how long they remain in the institution. William Goldfarb (1943, 1947) compared children who left an understaffed orphanage during the first year with similar children who spent their first three years at the orphanage before departing for foster homes. After interviewing, observing, and testing these children at ages 3½, 6½, 8½, and 12, Goldfarb found that the youngsters who had spent three years in the institution lagged behind the early adoptees in virtually all aspects of development. They scored poorly on IQ tests, were socially immature, were remarkably dependent on adults, had poor language skills, and were prone to behavior

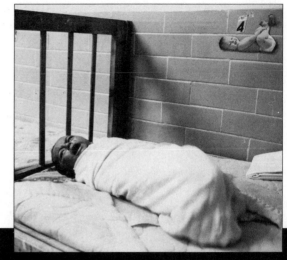

PHOTO 6-6 Children raised in barren, understaffed institutions show many signs of developmental impairment.

problems such as aggression and hyperactivity. By early adolescence they were often loners who had a difficult time relating to peers or family members.

Barbara Tizard (1977; Hodges & Tizard, 1989) has recently compared similar groups of institutionalized and early-adopted children and found that many of the developmental impairments described by Goldfarb also characterized her sample of late adoptees. The institutions in which Tizard's children lived were adequately staffed. But, because staff turnover was so high, children were cared for by as many as 80 different caregivers; thus they rarely became attached to any one adult over the first few years of life. By age 8, Tizard's late adoptees were intellectually normal and socially outgoing, and many had even formed close emotional ties to a housemother or an adoptive parent. But, despite these encouraging signs, children who had spent at least four years in the institution were more restless, more disobedient, and more unpopular in elementary school and were much more emotionally troubled and antisocial at age 16 than children adopted early in life. So it seems that prolonged institutionalization can have adverse effects that are difficult to overcome.

Finally, as Box 6-3 reveals, institutionalized infants are not the only ones to suffer developmental impairments when seriously deprived of attention and affection.

Why Is Early Deprivation Harmful?

Studies of institutionalized children (and, indeed, of those who fail to thrive; see Box 6-3) are "experiments of nature" that were not designed in a laboratory and are subject to a variety of methodological criticisms (see Longstreth, 1981; Pinneau, 1955). However, many of the results we have reviewed are so consistent across studies that most researchers have stopped arguing about whether deprivation effects are real. Today the issue is "Why do they occur?"

THE MATERNAL DEPRIVATION HYPOTHESIS

Many psychologists (for example, Bowlby, 1973; Spitz, 1965) believe that infants will not develop normally unless they receive the warm, loving attention of a stable mother figure to whom they can become attached. Presumably, children raised in understaffed institutions and animals reared in isolation will show developmental impairments because they have not had an opportunity to become emotionally involved with that special someone — typically their mother — who is constantly looking after them and attending to their needs.

Popular as this **maternal deprivation hypothesis** once was, there is no evidence that infants need to be "mothered" by a single caregiver in order to develop normally. Studies of adequately staffed institutions in the Soviet Union, the People's Republic of China, and Israel reveal that infants who are cared for by many responsive caregivers appear quite normal and are about as well adjusted later in childhood as infants who are reared at home (Bronfenbrenner, 1970; Kessen, 1975; Levy-Shiff, 1983; Oppenheim, Sagi, & Lamb, 1988). Moreover, we have seen that Harlow's infant monkeys who were isolated for three months eventually recovered from their early developmental abnormalities without ever being exposed to a mother figure. All they

needed was stimulation provided through daily contacts with other monkeys of the same age. In a similar vein, Freud and Dann (1951) reported that a group of six war orphans raised together from early infancy in a German concentration camp were neither mentally retarded nor socially unresponsive at 3 years of age, despite their very limited contact with their parents (who had been executed in Hitler's gas chambers) or other adult prisoners.[3] Apparently the stimulation that these orphans provided one another was sufficient to prevent serious developmental impairments. So infants need not become attached to a single mother figure in order to develop normally.

THE SOCIAL STIMULATION HYPOTHESIS

Are understaffed institutions breeding grounds for developmental abnormalities because they provide the infant with a monotonous *sensory* environment — one where there is little stimulation *of any kind* to encourage responsiveness? Or, rather, is it a lack of *social* stimulation that accounts for the unusual behavior and abnormal development of institutionalized children (and isolate monkeys)?

Most contemporary developmentalists favor the latter explanation, or **social stimulation hypothesis**, arguing that isolate monkeys and institutionalized humans develop abnormally because they have very little exposure to anyone who responds to their social signals. Indeed, giving isolate monkeys enriched *sensory* stimulation (in the form of slide shows) has no therapeutic effect, whereas allowing them *social* contacts with responsive peers will enable them to develop normally as they interact with these companions, become more responsive themselves, and slowly overcome their bizarre patterns of behavior (Pratt, 1967, 1969).

Sally Provence and Rose Lipton (1962) studied a sample of institutionalized infants who had toys to

[3]These children, who were orphaned in the first few months of life, received about the same amount of attention from adults that is normally received by children in severely understaffed institutional settings. We will take a closer look at these remarkable orphans in Chapter 15 when we consider the important roles that the peer group plays in a child's social and personality development.

play with, some visual and auditory exposure to other infants, but limited contact with adult caregivers. In other words, these infants were "socially deprived" although certainly not "stimulus deprived." In spite of the variety of sensory stimulation that the infants received, they showed roughly the same patterns of social, emotional, and intellectual impairment that characterized the institutionalized children from earlier studies. If we contrast this finding with the normal development of Chinese, Russian, and Israeli infants who are raised by a multitude of caregivers in communal settings, we can draw an interesting conclusion: *infants apparently need sustained interactions with responsive companions in order to develop normally*. Recall that we came to the same conclusion when we looked at the origins of the primary social attachment: infants who have regular interactions with sensitive, *responsive* caregivers are the ones who are likely to become securely attached.

Why are interactions with responsive people so important? Probably because the social stimulation an infant receives is related to his or her own behavior: people often attend to the infant *when* she cries, smiles, babbles, or gazes at them. This kind of association between one's own behavior and the behav-

---

BOX 6-3 | Emotional Deprivation and the Failure to Thrive

Otherwise-healthy children who experience too much stress and too little affection often appear rather apathetic or depressed and are likely to lag far behind their agemates in physical growth and motor development. This **"failure to thrive" syndrome** may characterize as many as 8% of preschool children in the United States and up to 5% of all patients admitted to pediatric hospitals (Lozoff, 1989).

Perhaps the most intriguing research on the failure-to-thrive syndrome was reported by Lytt Gardner (1972). Gardner studied the development of physically healthy, nonabused infants and toddlers who had received adequate physical care but very little affection from emotionally unresponsive parents. These home-reared but emotionally deprived youngsters showed many of the same abnormalities as children raised in understaffed institutions: apathy and apparent depression, a forlorn appearance, rigid body postures, retarded physical and motor development, depressed vocalization, and so on. One case involved twins—a boy and a girl—who developed quite normally for the first four months. Soon thereafter their father lost his job, their mother became pregnant with an unwanted baby, and the parents blamed each other for the hardships they were experiencing. The father then moved out of the house, and the mother focused her resentment on her infant son, becoming increasingly detached and unresponsive to his bids for attention (she did, however, provide him with adequate nutrition and physical care). Although his sister remained socially responsive and continued to grow normally, the boy at 13 months of age often failed to react to social stimulation and was *only about the size of an average 7-month-old infant*. In other words, his growth was severely retarded, a condition Gardner called **deprivation dwarfism**.

It is important to emphasize that the "deprivation dwarfs" Gardner studied were free of organic abnormalities and had received adequate nutrition and physical care. But all these children came from disordered family environments where they had been rejected by one parent (and often by both). Gardner believes that deprivation dwarfism is directly related to the infant's early social/emotional deprivation, and his conclusions are based on the behavior of many deprivation dwarfs hospitalized for observation and treatment. Here is a typical case:

> The 15-month-old child quickly responded to the attention she received from the hospital staff. She gained weight and made up for lost growth; her emotional state improved strikingly. Moreover, these changes were demonstratedly unrelated to any change in food intake. During her stay in the hospital she received the same standard nutrient dosage she

ior of caregivers may lead infants to believe that they have some *control* over their social environment. Thus the infant may become more outgoing as he learns that he can use his social signals to attract the attention and affection of his companions.

Now consider the plight of institutionalized infants: they may emit many signals but rarely receive a response from their overburdened or inattentive caregivers. What are these children likely to learn from their early experiences? Probably that attempts to attract the attention of others are useless, for nothing they do seems to matter to anyone. Consequently, they may develop a sense of **"learned help-**

lessness" and simply stop trying to exercise any control over the environment (Finkelstein & Ramey, 1977). Here, then, is a very plausible explanation for the finding that socially deprived infants are often rather passive, withdrawn, and apathetic.

Can Children Recover from Early Deprivation Effects?

Earlier we noted that severely disturbed young monkeys can overcome the effects of prolonged social isolation if they receive the proper kinds of therapy. Is the same true of human beings? Can children

---

B O X **6-3** | *continued*

had received at home. It appears to have been the enrichment of her social environment, not of her diet, that was responsible for the normalization of her growth [Gardner, 1972, p. 78].

It is relatively easy to explain the depressed social responsiveness observed among Gardner's deprivation dwarfs: these youngsters haven't had enough face-to-face contact with playful, responsive caregivers to acquire many socially responsive behaviors or even to learn that other human beings can be interesting. But why do you suppose emotional deprivation might inhibit a child's *physical* growth and development?

Undernourishment may play a role in some cases, especially if children actively resist or avoid feedings offered by their otherwise-neglectful caregivers (Lozoff, 1989). But in many other cases growth failure is apparently not diet related. (Recall that, when Gardner's deprivation dwarfs received ample doses of responsive social stimulation in the hospital, they soon began to grow rapidly on the same diet on which they had "failed to thrive" at home.) Current thinking is that lack of social and emotional stimulation may inhibit secretion of the pituitary **growth hormone**, a substance known to be essential for the normal growth and development of body cells (Tanner, 1990). Indeed, Gardner (1972) noted that deprivation dwarfs have abnormally low levels of growth hormone in their blood-

streams during periods of subnormal growth. When these youngsters entered the hospital and began to receive responsive caregiving, the secretion of growth hormone resumed, apparently enabling them to grow rapidly and make up lost ground. Yet it is important to note that, should a child's emotional deprivation continue for several years, he or she may remain smaller than normal and display long-term social and intellectual deficits as well (Brinich, Drotar, & Brinich, 1989; Lozoff, 1989).

Deprivation dwarfism and the failure-to-thrive syndrome provide yet another indication that children require love and responsive caregiving if they are to develop normally. Fortunately, we are making some headway at identifying those parents whose children may be affected. Even before giving birth, women whose children will fail to thrive are more likely than other mothers to feel unloved by their parents, to reject their own mothers as models, and to say that their own childhoods were unhappy; moreover, within days of giving birth, they are already having problems feeding and nurturing their babies (Altemeier et al., as cited in Lozoff, 1989). Like depressed mothers and those with premature infants, these women need help and would almost certainly benefit (as would their infants) from structured interventions that teach them to be sensitive, responsive companions.

who start out in an understaffed institutional setting recover from their initial handicaps, and, if so, what will they require in the way of corrective therapy?

There is now a wealth of evidence that socially deprived infants can recover from many of their handicaps if they are placed in homes where they receive ample doses of individualized attention from affectionate and responsive caregivers (Clarke & Clarke, 1976; Rutter, 1981). Recovery seems to be especially good if deprived children are placed with *highly educated, relatively affluent* parents. Audrey Clark and Jeannette Hanisee (1982), for example, studied a group of Asian orphans who had lived in institutions, foster homes, or hospitals before coming to the United States. Many were war orphans who had early histories of malnutrition or serious illness. But, despite the severe environmental insults they had endured, these children made remarkable progress. After two to three years in their highly stimulating, middle-class adoptive homes, the Asian adoptees scored significantly *above* average on both a standardized intelligence test and an assessment of social maturity.

The prognosis for recovery also depends on the *amount of time* a child has spent in a depriving early environment. Children whose deprivation lasts for the first three years or longer are likely to have lingering social, emotional, and intellectual difficulties, even after spending the next several years in stable adoptive homes (Dennis, 1973; Goldfarb, 1947) and despite showing some ability to form attachments to an adoptive parent later in childhood (Hodges & Tizard, 1989). Are late adoptees incapable of making complete recoveries? Do their lingering deficiencies imply that the first three years of life is a *critical period* for human social and emotional development, as Bowlby (1973) and others have argued?

Other researchers say no, suggesting that, even though infancy may be a *sensitive period* for emotional development, recovery may still be possible (Rutter, 1981). It stands to reason that children who develop severe problems when deprived for long periods will take longer to overcome their handicaps than children whose early deprivation was relatively brief. Moreover, we have to wonder how

Goldfarb's or Tizard's late adoptees would have fared had they been adopted into enriched home environments such as those of the Asian adoptees in Clark and Hanisee's (1982) study. Clearly, the fact that late adoptees continue to show some deficiencies as adolescents in no way establishes that they were incapable of recovery, as proponents of the critical-period hypothesis might have us believe.

Only a short time ago it was thought that six months of isolation would have irreversible effects on the social and emotional development of rhesus monkeys. Yet Harry Harlow and his associates were able to perfect a therapy to treat the harmful consequences of early social deprivation, thus rendering even their most profoundly disturbed 12-month isolates more socially and sexually competent as adults. This younger-peer therapy has now been used by Wyndol Furman, Don Rahe, and Willard Hartup (1979) to modify the behavior of socially withdrawn preschool children. Children who had been identified as social isolates in a day-care setting were exposed to a series of play sessions with a partner who was either their age or 18 months younger. The findings were indeed interesting: withdrawn children who had played with a partner became much more socially outgoing in their day-care classrooms than social isolates who had not taken part in any play sessions. In addition, the improvements in sociability were greatest for those withdrawn children who had played with a *younger* partner (see Figure 6-2). So Furman et al. (1979) obtained results with humans that are similar to those reported earlier for emotionally disturbed monkeys. Although Furman's withdrawn children could hardly be classified as emotionally ill, the results of this study are sufficiently encouraging to suggest the younger-peer treatment as one possible therapy for children who are more severely disturbed.

In sum, infants who have experienced social and emotional deprivation over the first two years show a strong capacity for recovery when they are placed in a stimulating home environment and receive individualized attention from responsive caregivers. Even severely disturbed children who are adopted after spending several years in understaffed institutions will show dramatic improvements, compared

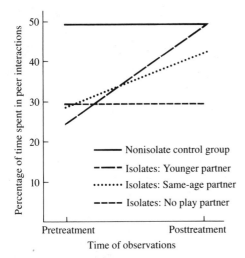

FIGURE 6-2 Percentages of time that children spent interacting with peers before and after engaging in play sessions with a younger or a same-age partner. (From W. Furman, D. F. Rahe, & W. W. Hartup, "Rehabilitation of Socially Withdrawn Preschool Children through Mixed-Age and Same-Age Socialization." *Child Development*, 1979, *50*, 915–922. Copyright © 1979 by the Society for Research in Child Development. Reprinted by permission.)

with their counterparts who have remained in a barren institutional setting (Dennis, 1973; Rutter, 1981). And, rather than being discouraged by the handicaps that continue to plague many late adoptees, we could just as easily treat their partial recoveries as an encouraging sign — one that may lead to the discovery of environmental interventions and therapeutic techniques that will enable these victims of prolonged social deprivation to put their lingering deficiencies behind them.

Summary

Psychologists from many theoretical backgrounds believe that the social and emotional events of infancy are very influential in shaping one's future development. Two ways of evaluating this *early-experience* hypothesis are (1) to look for varia-tions in the development of children who form different kinds of attachments to close companions and (2) to see what happens to socially deprived infants who have had few if any opportunities to become emotionally involved with anyone.

Research with Ainsworth's *strange-situations test* (which assesses a baby's responses to strangers, brief separations, and reunions with a caregiver) reveals that infants typically establish one of four kinds of attachment to their mothers. One kind of attachment is labeled *secure*, whereas the other three (that is, *avoidant*, *resistant*, and *disorganized/disoriented*) are thought to be emotionally insecure. Sensitive, responsive caregiving is consistently associated with the development of secure attachments, whereas inconsistent, neglectful, overintrusive, and abusive styles of caregiving predict insecure attachments. However, infant temperament may also influence the quality of early attachments by affecting the character of caregiver/infant interactions. Although most babies form primary attachments to their mothers, fathers play an important role in many infants' lives. Children's early cognitive performances are better when their fathers are highly involved with them, and infants appear to be most socially responsive when securely attached to both parents.

Research consistently indicates that people with an early history of secure attachments are more socially skilled and intellectually competent later in life than their counterparts with insecure attachment histories. However, children's *working models* of attachment relationships can change over time. Thus a secure attachment history is *no* guarantee of positive adjustment later in life; nor are initially insecure attachments a certain indicator of poor life outcomes.

It was once feared that regular separations from working parents might prevent infants from establishing secure attachments or undermine relationships that were already secure. However, there is little evidence that either a mother's employment outside the home or alternative caregiving will have such effects, provided that the day care is of good quality and that parents are sensitive and responsive caregivers when they are at home.

Some infants have had very limited contacts with caregivers during the first year or two of life; as a result, they do not become attached to anyone. Both monkeys and children who are socially deprived during infancy are likely to be withdrawn, apathetic, and (in humans) intellectually deficient. The longer infants experience such social/emotional deprivation, the more disturbed they become. However, both monkeys and humans have a strong capacity for recovery and may overcome many of their initial handicaps if placed in settings where they will receive ample amounts of individualized attention from sensitive and responsive companions.

References

AINSWORTH, M. D. S. (1979). Attachment as related to mother-infant interaction. In J. S. Rosenblatt, R. A. Hinde, C. Beer, & M. Busnel (Eds.), *Advances in the study of behavior* (Vol. 9). Orlando, FL: Academic Press.

AINSWORTH, M. D. S., BLEHAR, M. C., WATERS, E., & WALL, S. (1978). *Patterns of attachment: A psychological study of the strange situation*. Hillsdale, NJ: Erlbaum.

ANDERSSON, B. (1989). Effects of public day-care: A longitudinal study. *Child Development, 60,* 857–866.

ANDERSSON, B. (1992). Effects of day-care on cognitive and socioemotional competence of thirteen-year-old Swedish schoolchildren. *Child Development, 63,* 20–36.

BARGLOW, P., VAUGHN, B. E. & MOLITOR, N. (1987). Effects of maternal absence due to employment on the quality of infant-mother attachment in a low-risk sample. *Child Development, 58,* 945–954.

BARTHOLOMEW, K., & HOROWITZ, L. M. (1991). Attachment styles among young adults: A test of a four-category model. *Journal of Personality and Social Psychology, 61,* 226–244.

BELSKY, J., GILSTRAP, B., & ROVINE, M. (1984). The Pennsylvania Infant and Family Development Project I: Stability and change in mother-infant and father-infant interaction in a family setting. *Child Development, 55,* 692–705.

BELSKY, J., & ROVINE, M. (1988). Nonmaternal care in the first year of life and the security of infant-parent attachment. *Child Development, 59,* 157–167.

BELSKY, J., ROVINE, M., & TAYLOR, D. G. (1984). The Pennsylvania Infant and Family Development Project III: The origins of individual differences in infant-mother attachment — Maternal and infant contributions. *Child Development, 55,* 718–728.

BENN, R. K. (1986). Factors promoting secure attachment relationships between employed mothers and their sons. *Child Development, 57,* 1224–1231.

BERK, L. (1991). *Child development* (2nd ed.). Boston: Allyn & Bacon.

BOSSO, O. R., CORTER, C. M., & ABRAMOVITCH, R. (1990). *Q-sort attachment measures of 18 to 32 month old first borns: Relation to strange situation classification and to behavior toward a younger sibling.* Unpublished manuscript, University of Toronto.

BOWLBY, J. (1969). *Attachment and loss.* Vol. 1: *Attachment.* London: Hogarth Press.

BOWLBY, J. (1973). *Attachment and loss.* Vol. 2: *Separation: Anxiety and anger.* London: Hogarth Press.

BOWLBY, J. (1988). *A secure base: Clinical applications of attachment theory.* London: Routledge.

BRETHERTON, I. (1985). Attachment theory: Retrospect and prospect. In I. Bretherton & E. Waters (Eds.), Growing points of attachment theory and research. *Monographs of the Society for Research in Child Development, 50*(Nos. 1–2, Serial No. 209).

BRETHERTON, I. (1990). Open communication and internal working models: Their role in the development of attachment relationships. In R. A. Thompson (Ed.), Socioemotional development. *Nebraska Symposium on Motivation* (Vol. 36). Lincoln: University of Nebraska Press.

BRINICH, E., DROTAR, D., & BRINICH, P. (1989). Security of attachment and outcome of preschoolers with histories of nonorganic failure to thrive. *Journal of Clinical Child Psychology, 18,* 142–152.

BRONFENBRENNER, U. (1970). *Two worlds of childhood: U.S. and U.S.S.R.* New York: Russell Sage Foundation.

BURCHINAL, M., LEE, M., & RAMEY, C. (1989). Type of day-care and preschool intellectual development in disadvantaged children. *Child Development, 60,* 128–137.

CARLSON, V., CICCHETTI, D., BARNETT, D., & BRAUNWALD, K. (1989). Disorganized/disoriented attachment relationships in maltreated infants. *Developmental Psychology, 25,* 525–531.

CHASE-LANSDALE, P. L., & OWEN, M. T. (1987). Maternal employment in a family context: Effects on infant-mother and infant-father attachments. *Child Development, 58,* 1505–1512.

CLARK, E. A., & HANISEE, J. (1982). Intellectual and adaptive performance of Asian children in adoptive American settings. *Developmental Psychology, 18,* 595–599.

CLARKE, A. M., & CLARKE, A. D. B. (1976). *Early experience: Myth and evidence.* New York: Free Press.

CLARKE-STEWART, K. A. (1978). And daddy makes three: The father's impact on the mother and young child. *Child Development, 49,* 466–478.

CLARKE-STEWART, K. A. (1980). The father's contribution to children's cognitive and social development in early childhood. In F. A. Pedersen (Ed.), *The father-infant relationship: Observational studies in the family setting.* New York: Praeger.

CLARKE-STEWART, K. A. (1989). Infant day care: Maligned or malignant? *American Psychologist, 44,* 266–273.

COHN, D. A. (1990). Child-mother attachment of 6-year-olds and social competence at school. *Child Development, 61,* 152–162.

COX, M. J., OWEN, M. T., HENDERSON, V. K., & MAR-GAND, N. A. (1992). Prediction of infant-father and infant-mother attachment. *Developmental Psychology, 28,* 474–483.

COX, M. J., OWEN, M. T., LEWIS, J. M., & HENDERSON, V. K. (1989). Marriage, adult adjustment, and early parenting. *Child Development, 60,* 1015–1024.

CROCKENBERG, S. (1981). Infant irritability, maternal responsiveness, and social support influences on the security of mother-infant attachment. *Child Development, 52,* 857–865.

CROCKENBERG, S., & LITMAN, C. (1991). Effects of maternal employment on maternal and two-year-old child behavior. *Child Development, 61,* 930–953.

CROCKENBERG, S., & McCLUSKEY, K. (1986). Change in maternal behavior during the baby's first year of life. *Child Development, 57,* 746–753.

CROWELL, J. A., & FELDMAN, S. S. (1988). Mothers' internal models of relationships and children's behavioral and developmental status: A study of mother-child interaction. *Child Development, 59,* 1273–1285.

DENNIS, W. (1973). *Children of the creche.* New York: Appleton-Century-Crofts.

EASTERBROOKS, M. A. (1989). Quality of attachment to mother and to father: Effects of perinatal risk status. *Child Development, 60,* 825–830.

EASTERBROOKS, M. A., & GOLDBERG, W. A. (1984). Toddler development in the family: Impact of father involvement and parenting characteristics. *Child Development, 55,* 740–752.

EASTERBROOKS, M. A., & GOLDBERG, W. A. (1985). Effects of early maternal employment on toddlers, mothers, and fathers. *Developmental Psychology, 21,* 774–783.

EGELAND, B., & FARBER, E. A. (1984). Mother-infant attachment: Factors related to its development and changes over time. *Child Development, 55,* 753–771.

ERIKSON, E. H. (1963). *Childhood and society* (2nd ed.). New York: Norton.

FAGOT, B. I., & KAVANAGH, K. (1990). The prediction of antisocial behavior from avoidant attachment classifications. *Child Development, 61,* 864–873.

FEENEY, J. A., & NOLLER, P. (1990). Attachment style as a predictor of adult romantic relationships. *Journal of Personality and Social Psychology, 58,* 281–291.

FIELD, T. M. (1991). Quality infant day-care and grade school behavior and performance. *Child Development, 62,* 863–870.

FINKELSTEIN, N. W., & RAMEY, C. T. (1977). Learning to control the environment in infancy. *Child Development, 48,* 806–819.

FONAGY, P., STEELE, H., & STEELE, M. (1991). Maternal representations of attachment during pregnancy predict the organization of infant-mother attachment at one year of age. *Child Development, 62,* 891–905.

FOX, N. A., KIMMERLY, N. L., & SCHAFER, W. D. (1991). Attachment to mother/attachment to father: A meta-analysis. *Child Development, 62,* 210–225.

FRAIBERG, S. (1977). *Every child's birthright: In defense of mothering.* New York: Basic Books.

FRANKEL, K. A., & BATES, J. E. (1990). Mother-toddler problem-solving: Antecedents in attachment, home behavior, and temperament. *Child Development, 61,* 810–819.

FREUD, A., & DANN, S. (1951). An experiment in group upbringing. In R. S. Eisler, A. Freud, H. Hartmann, & E. Kris (Eds.), *The psychoanalytic study of the child* (Vol. 6). New York: International Universities Press.

FREUD, S. (1930). *Three contributions to the theory of sex.* New York: Nervous and Mental Disease Publishing Co. (Original work published 1905.)

FURMAN, W., RAHE, D. F., & HARTUP, W. W. (1979). Rehabilitation of socially withdrawn preschool children through mixed-age and same-age socialization. *Child Development, 50,* 915–922.

GARDNER, L. J. (1972). Deprivation dwarfism. *Scientific American, 277,* 76–82.

GEORGE, C., KAPLAN, N., & MAIN, M. (1985). *Attachment interview for adults.* Unpublished manuscript, University of California, Berkeley.

GOLDBERG, S., PERROTTA, M., MINDE, K., & CORTER, C. (1986). Maternal behavior and attachment in low-birth-weight twins and singletons. *Child Development, 57,* 34–46.

GOLDFARB, W. (1943). The effects of early institutional care on adolescent personality. *Journal of Experimental Education, 12,* 107–129.

GOLDFARB, W. (1947). Variations in adolescent adjustment in institutionally reared children. *Journal of Orthopsychiatry, 17,* 449–457.

GOLDSMITH, H. H., & ALANSKY, J. A. (1987). Maternal and infant temperamental predictors of attachment: A meta-analytic review. *Journal of Consulting and Clinical Psychology, 55,* 805–816.

GREENBERGER, E., & GOLDBERG, W. A. (1989). Work, parenting, and the socialization of children. *Developmental Psychology, 25,* 22–35.

GROSSMANN, K., GROSSMANN, K. E., SPANGLER, S., SUESS, G., & UNZNER, L. (1985). Maternal sensitivity and newborn responses as related to quality of attachment in Northern Germany. In I. Bretherton & E. Waters, Growing points of attachment theory. *Monographs of the Society for Research in Child Development, 50*(1–2, Serial No. 209).

HARLOW, H. F. (1962). The heterosexual affectional system in monkeys. *American Psychologist, 17,* 1–9.

HARLOW, H. F., & HARLOW, M. K. (1977). The young monkeys. In *Readings in developmental psychology today* (2nd ed.). Del Mar, CA: CRM Books.

HARLOW, H. F., HARLOW, M. K., DODSWORTH, R. O., & ARLING, G. L. (1966). Maternal behavior of rhesus monkeys deprived of mothering and peer associations as infants. *Proceedings of the American Philosophical Society, 110,* 88–98.

HAZAN, C., & SHAVER, P. R. (1987). Romantic love conceptualized as an attachment process. *Journal of Personality and Social Psychology, 52,* 511–524.

HOCK, E., & DeMEIS, D. K. (1990). Depression in mothers of infants: The role of maternal employment. *Developmental Psychology, 26,* 285–291.

HODGES, J., & TIZARD, B. (1989). IQ and behavioral adjustment of ex-institutional adolescents. *Journal of Child Psychology and Psychiatry, 30,* 53–75.

HOFFMAN, L. W. (1989). Effects of maternal employment in the two-parent family. *American Psychologist, 44,* 283–292.

HOWES, C. (1988). Relations between early child care and schooling. *Developmental Psychology, 24,* 53–57.

HOWES, C. (1990). Can the age of entry into child care and the quality of child care predict adjustment in kindergarten? *Developmental Psychology, 26,* 292–303.

HOWES, C., PHILLIPS, D. A., & WHITEBOOK, M. (1992). Thresholds of quality: Implications for the social development of children in center-based child care. *Child Development, 63,* 449–460.

HWANG, C. P. (1986). Behavior of Swedish primary and secondary caretaking fathers in relation to mother's presence. *Developmental Psychology, 22,* 749–751.

HYMES, J. L. (1990). *The year in review: A look at 1989.* Washington DC: National Association for the Education of Young Children.

ISABELLA, R. A., & BELSKY, J. (1991). Interactional synchrony and the origins of infant-mother attachment. *Child Development, 62,* 373–384.

ISABELLA, R. A., BELSKY, J., & von EYE, A. (1989). Origins of infant-mother attachment: An examination of interactional synchrony during the infant's first year. *Developmental Psychology, 25,* 12–21.

IZARD, C. E., HAYNES, D. M., CHISHOLM, G., & BAAK, K. (1991). Emotional determinants of infant-mother attachment. *Child Development, 62,* 906–917.

JACOBSON, J. L., & WILLE, D. E. (1986). The influence of attachment pattern on developmental changes in peer interaction from the toddler to the preschool period. *Child Development, 57,* 338–347.

KAGAN, J. (1984). *The nature of the child.* New York: Basic Books.

KAGAN, J., KEARSLEY, R. B., & ZELAZO, P. R. (1978). *Infancy: Its place in human development.* Cambridge, MA: Harvard University Press.

KESSEN, W. (1975). *Childhood in China.* New Haven, CT: Yale University Press.

KOBAK, R. R., & SCEERY, A. (1988). Attachment in late adolescence: Working models, affect regulation, and representations of self and others. *Child Development, 59,* 135–146.

LAMB, M. E. (1975). Fathers: Forgotten contributors to child development. *Human Development, 18,* 245–266.

LAMB, M. E. (1981). The development of father-infant relationships. In M. E. Lamb (Ed.), *The role of the father in child development.* New York: Wiley.

LAMB, M. E., HWANG, C., BOOKSTEIN, F. L., BROBERG, A., HULT, G., & FRODI, M. (1988). Determinants of social competence in Swedish preschoolers. *Developmental Psychology, 24,* 58–70.

LAMB, M. E., & OPPENHEIM, D. (1989). Fatherhood and father-child relations: Five years of research. In S. H. Cath, A. Gurwitt, & L. Gunsberg (Eds.), *Fathers and their families.* Hillsdale, NJ: Erlbaum.

LEVY-SHIFF, R. (1983). Adaptation and competence in early childhood: Communally-raised kibbutz children versus family raised children in the city. *Child Development, 54,* 1606–1614.

LEVY-SHIFF, R., & ISRAELASHVILI, R. (1988). Antecedents of fathering: Some further exploration. *Developmental Psychology, 24,* 434–440.

LONDERVILLE, S., & MAIN, M. (1981). Security of attachment, compliance, and maternal training methods in the second year of life. *Developmental Psychology, 17,* 289–299.

LONGSTRETH, L. E. (1981). Revisiting Skeels' final study: A critique. *Developmental Psychology, 17,* 620–625.

LOZOFF, B. (1989). Nutrition and behavior. *American Psychologist, 44,* 231–236.

MAIN, M., & CASSIDY, J. (1988). Categories of response to reunion with the parent at age 6: Predictable from infant attachment classifications and stable over a 1-month period. *Developmental Psychology, 24,* 415–426.

MAIN, M., & SOLOMON, J. (1986). Discovery of a disorganized/disoriented attachment pattern. In T. B. Brazelton & M. W. Yogman (Eds.), *Affective development in infancy.* Norwood, NJ: Ablex.

MAIN, M., & SOLOMON, J. (1990). Procedures for identifying infants as disorganized/disoriented during the Ainsworth Strange Situation. In M. T. Greenberg, D. Cicchetti, & E. M. Cummings (Eds.), *Attachment in the preschool years: Theory, research, and intervention.* Chicago: University of Chicago Press.

MAIN, M., & WESTON, D. R. (1981). The quality of the toddler's relationship to mother and to father: Related to conflict and the readiness to establish new relationships. *Child Development, 52,* 932–940.

MALATESTA, C. Z., CULVER, C., TESMAN, J. R., & SHEPARD, B. (1989). The development of emotion expression during the first two years of life. *Monographs of the Society for Research in Child Development, 54*(1–2, Serial No. 219).

MANGELSDORF, S., GUNNAR, M., KESTENBAUM, R., LANG, S., & ANDREAS, D. (1990). Infant proneness-to-distress temperament, maternal personality, and mother-infant attachment: Associations and goodness of fit. *Child Development, 61,* 820–831.

MATAS, L., AREND, R. A., & SROUFE, L. A. (1978). Continuity of adaptation in the second year: The relationship between quality of attachment and later competence. *Child Development, 49,* 547–556.

McLOYD, V. C. (1990). The impact of economic hardship on Black families and children: Psychological distress, parenting, and socioemotional development. *Child Development, 61,* 311–346.

NINIO, A., & RINOTT, N. (1988). Fathers' involvement in the care of their infants and their attributions of cognitive competence to infants. *Child Development, 59,* 652–663.

NOVAK, M. A. (1979). Social recovery of monkeys isolated for the first year of life: II. Long-term assessment. *Developmental Psychology, 15,* 50–61.

OPPENHEIM, D., SAGI, A., & LAMB, M. E. (1988). Infant-adult attachments on the kibbutz and their relation to socioemotional development 4 years later. *Developmental Psychology, 24,* 427–433.

PALKOWITZ, R. (1984). Parental attitudes and fathers' interactions with their 5-month-old infants. *Developmental Psychology, 20,* 1054–1060.

PARK, K. A., & WATERS, E. (1989). Security of attachment and preschool friendships. *Child Development, 60,* 1076–1081.

PARKE, R. D. (1981). *Fathers.* Cambridge, MA: Harvard University Press.

PINNEAU, S. R. (1955). The infantile disorders of hospitalism and anaclitic depression. *Psychological Bulletin, 52,* 429–452.

PIPP, S., EASTERBROOKS, M. A., & HARMON, R. J. (1992). The relation between attachment and knowledge of self and mother in one- to three-year-old infants. *Child Development, 63,* 738–750.

PRATT, C. L. (1967). *Social behavior of rhesus monkeys reared with varying degrees of peer experience.* Unpublished master's thesis, University of Wisconsin.

PRATT, C. L. (1969). *Effect of different degrees of early stimulation on social development.* Unpublished doctoral dissertation, University of Wisconsin.

PROVENCE, S., & LIPTON, R. C. (1962). *Infants in institutions.* New York: International Universities Press.

RADKE-YARROW, M., CUMMINGS, E. M., KUCZYNSKI, L., & CHAPMAN, M. (1985). Patterns of attachment in two- and three-year-olds in normal families and families with parental depression. *Child Development, 56,* 884–893.

RIBBLE, M. (1943). *The rights of infants.* New York: Columbia University Press.

RUTTER, M. (1981). *Maternal deprivation revisited* (2nd ed.). New York: Penguin Books.

SAGI, A., LAMB, M. E., LEWKOWICZ, K. S., SHOHAM, R., DVIR, R., & ESTES, D. (1985). Security of infant-mother, -father, and -metapelet attachments among kibbutz-reared Israeli children. In I. Bretherton & E. Waters (Eds.), *Growing points of attachment theory and research. Monographs of the Society for Research in Child Development, 50*(1–2, Serial No. 209).

SAGI, A., van IJZENDOORN, M. H., & KOREN-KARIE, N. (1991). Primary appraisal of the Strange Situation: A cross-cultural analysis of preseparation episodes. *Developmental Psychology, 27,* 587–596.

SCARR, S. (1984). *Mother care/Other care.* New York: Basic Books.

SCOTT, J. P. (1962). Critical periods in behavior development. *Science, 138,* 949–957.

SCOTT, J. P. (1968). *Early experience and the organization of behavior.* Pacific Grove, CA: Brooks/Cole.

SKOLNICK, A. (1986). Early attachment and personal relationships across the life course. In P. B. Baltes, D. L. Featherman, & R. M. Lerner (Eds.), *Life-span development and behavior* (Vol. 7). Hillsdale, NJ: Erlbaum.

SLADE, A. (1987). Quality of attachment and early symbolic play. *Developmental Psychology, 23,* 78–85.

SPITZ, R. A. (1945). Hospitalism: An inquiry into the genesis of psychiatric conditions in early childhood. In A. Freud (Ed.), *The psychoanalytic study of the child* (Vol. 1). New York: International Universities Press.

SPITZ, R. A. (1965). *The first year of life: A psychoanalytic study of normal and deviant object relations.* New York: International Universities Press.

SPITZE, G. (1988). Women's employment and family relations: A review. *Journal of Marriage and the Family, 50,* 595–618.

SROUFE, L. A. (1985). Attachment classification from the perspective of infant-caregiver relationships and infant temperament. *Child Development, 56,* 1–14.

SROUFE, L. A., EGELAND, B., & KREUTZER, T. (1990). The fate of early experience following developmental change: Longitudinal approaches to individual adaptation in childhood. *Child Development, 61,* 1363–1373.

SROUFE, L. A., FOX, N. E., & PANCAKE, V. R. (1983). Attachment and dependency in developmental perspective. *Child Development, 54,* 1615–1627.

STIPEK, D., & McCROSKEY, J. (1989). Investing in children: Government and workplace policies for parents. *American Psychologist, 44,* 416–423.

STUCKEY, M. R., McGHEE, P. E., & BELL, N. J. (1982). Parent-child interaction: The influence of maternal employment. *Developmental Psychology, 18,* 635–644.

SUOMI, S. J., & HARLOW, H. F. (1972). Social rehabilitation of isolate reared monkeys. *Developmental Psychology, 6,* 487–496.

TANNER, J. M. (1990). *Fetus into man: Physical growth from conception to maturity* (2nd ed.). Cambridge, MA: Harvard University Press.

TETI, D. M., NAKAGAWA, M., DAS, R., & WIRTH, O. (1991). Security of attachment between preschoolers and their mothers: Relations among social interaction, parenting stress, and mothers' sorts of the Attachment Q-Set. *Developmental Psychology, 27,* 440–447.

THOMAS, A., & CHESS, S. (1977). *Temperament and development.* New York: Brunner/Mazel.

THOMPSON, R. A., & LAMB, M. (1984). Continuity and change in socioemotional development during the second year. In R. N. Emde & R. J. Harmon (Eds.), *Continuities and discontinuities in development.* New York: Plenum.

THOMPSON, R. A., LAMB, M. E., & ESTES, D. (1982). Stability of infant-mother attachment and its relationship to changing life circumstances in an unselected middle-class sample. *Child Development, 53,* 144–148.

THOMPSON, W. R., & MELZACK, R. (1956). Early environment. *Scientific American, 114,* 38–42.

TIZARD, B. (1977). *Adoption: A second chance.* London: Open Books.

VANDELL, D. L., HENDERSON, V. K., & WILSON, K. S. (1988). A longitudinal study of children with day-care experiences of varying quality. *Child Development, 59,* 1286–1292.

van IJZENDOORN, M. H., GOLDBERG, S., KROONENBERG, P. M., & FRENKEL, O. J. (1992). The relative effects of maternal and child problems on quality of attachment: A meta-analysis of attachment in clinical samples. *Child Development, 63,* 840–858.

van IJZENDOORN, M. H., & KROONENBERG, P. M. (1988). Cross-cultural patterns of attachment: A meta-analysis of the Strange Situation. *Child Development, 59,* 147–156.

VAUGHN, B. E., GOVE, F. L., & EGELAND, B. R. (1980). The relationship between out-of-home care and the quality of infant-mother attachment in an economically disadvantaged population. *Child Development, 51,* 1203–1214.

VAUGHN, B. E., LEFEVER, G. B., SEIFER, R., & BARGLOW, P. (1989). Attachment behavior, attachment security, and temperament during infancy. *Child Development, 60,* 728–737.

VAUGHN, B. E., STEVENSON-HINDE, J., WATERS, E., KOTSAFTIS, A., LEFEVER, G. B., SHOULDICE, A., TRUDEL, M., & BELSKY, J. (1992). Attachment security and temperament in infancy and early childhood: Some conceptual clarifications. *Developmental Psychology, 28,* 463–473.

VAUGHN, B. E., & WATERS, E. (1990). Attachment behavior at home and in the laboratory: Q-Sort observations and strange situation classifications of one-year-olds. *Child Development, 61,* 1965–1973.

WATERS, E., & DEANE, K. E. (1985). Defining and assessing individual differences in attachment relationships: Q-methodology and the organization of behavior in infancy and early childhood. In I. Bretherton & E. Waters (Eds.), Growing points of attachment theory and research. *Monographs of the Society for Research in Child Development, 50*(1–2, Serial No. 209).

WATERS, E., VAUGHN, B. E., & EGELAND, B. R. (1980). Individual differences in mother-infant attachment relationships at age one: Antecedents in neonatal behavior in an urban, economically disadvantaged sample. *Child Development, 51,* 208–216.

WATERS, E., WIPPMAN, J., & SROUFE, L. A. (1979). Attachment, positive affect, and competence in the peer group: Two studies in construct validation. *Child Development, 50,* 821–829.

7 Becoming an Individual: Development of the Self

Who am I?

I'm a person who says what I think . . . not [one] who's going to say one thing and do the other. I'm really lucky. I've never [drunk or] done drugs, but I'm always high. I love life. I'm about five years ahead of my age. I've got a lot of different business interests . . . a construction company, oil wells, land . . . I'm trying everything. I travel a lot . . . it's difficult to be traveling and in school at the same time. [People] perceive me as being unusual . . . very mysterious, and I hope they see me as being a competitor, because I do all my talking on the field.
— *Herschel Walker*, former college student and Olympic bobsledder, and currently running-back of the Philadelphia Eagles (as quoted in Blount, 1986)

How would you answer the "Who am I" question? If you are like most adults, you would probably respond by mentioning attributes such as your gender, personal characteristics that you consider particularly noteworthy (for example, honesty, sincerity, friendliness, kindness), perhaps your political leanings, religious preferences (if any), and occupational aspirations or attainments, and your strongest interests and values. In so doing, you would be describing that elusive concept that psychologists call the **self**.

Although no one knows you as well as you do, it is a safe bet that much of what you know about yourself stems from your contacts and experiences with other people. When a college sophomore tells us that he is a friendly, likable guy who is active in his fraternity, the Black Student Union, and the Campus Crusade for Christ, he is saying that his past experiences with others and the groups to which he belongs are important determinants of his personal identity. Several decades ago, sociologists Charles Cooley (1902) and George Herbert Mead (1934) proposed that the self-concept evolves from social interactions and will undergo many changes over the course of a lifetime. Indeed, Cooley used the term **looking-glass self** to emphasize that a person's understanding of his identity is a reflection of how other people react to him: the self-concept is the image cast by a social mirror.

Cooley and Mead believed that the self and social development are completely intertwined — that they emerge together and that neither can progress very far without the other. Presumably, neonates experience people and events as "streams of impressions" and will have absolutely no concept of "self" until they realize that they exist independent of the objects and individuals that they encounter regularly. Once infants make this important distinction between self and nonself, they will establish interactive routines with their close companions (that is, develop socially) and will learn that their behavior elicits predictable reactions from others. In other words, they are acquiring information about the "social self" based on the ways people respond to their overtures. As they acquire some language and begin to interact with a larger number of other people, children's self-concepts will change. Soon toddlers are describing themselves in categorical terms relating to age ("I this many"), size and gender ("I big boy, not a baby"), and activities ("I run—zoom!")—descriptions that reflect how others respond to or label them. Mead (1934) concluded:

. . . the self has a character that is different than that of the physiological organism proper. The self is something which . . . is not initially there at birth but arises in the process of social development. That is, it develops in a given individual as a result of his relations to that process as a whole and to other individuals within the process.

Do babies really have no sense of self at birth? This issue is explored in the first section of the chapter, where we will trace the growth of the **self-concept** from infancy to young adulthood. We will then consider how children and adolescents make judgments about their self-worth and construct a sense of *self-esteem*. Our focus will then shift to a major developmental task of adolescence: the need to establish a firm, future-oriented self-portrait, or *identity*, with which to approach the responsibilities of young adulthood. Finally, the chapter concludes by examining the growth of two other components of self — *self-regulation* and *self-control* — that will figure prominently in determining what we are able to accomplish in life as well as how we get along with other people.

Of course, there are several other aspects of self (or personality) development that warrant extended coverage and will become the subject of our later chapters. In Chapter 8, for example, we will see how active and curious infants begin to take pride in their ability to make things happen — a pride that may (or may not) blossom into a strong motive to achieve and a favorable academic self-concept. In Chapter 9 we will examine the *sex-typing* process and see that a child's emerging conception of self as a male or a female can (and often does) exert a powerful influence on his or her aspirations and patterns of social conduct. Chapters 10 and 11 will focus on the development of aggressive tendencies and altruistic inclinations and, thus, provide a look at the antisocial and prosocial aspects of self. And our concern in Chapter 12 will center more directly on moral and ethical issues as we follow the child's transformation from an egocentric and seemingly self-indulgent creature who appears to respect no rules to a moral philosopher of sorts — one who may have strongly internalized a number of ethical principles to guide her own conduct and to evaluate the behavior of others.

Now let's return to the starting point and see how children come to know and understand this entity we call the "self."

Development of the Self-Concept

One Self or Two?

The 19th-century psychologist William James (1890) was among the first to propose that there is not one self but two: the **I (or private self)** and the **Me (or public self)**. In other words, he viewed the self as both a *subject*, who has experiences, thinks, and constructs knowledge, and an *object*, who can be reflected on or thought about. James put it this way:

> Whatever I may be thinking of, I am always at the same time more or less aware of *myself*, of my *personal* existence. At the same time, it is I who am aware . . . [as if] the total self . . . were duplex, partly known and knower, partly object and partly subject . . . which for shortness we may call one the *Me* and the other the *I* [p. 53].

James believed that the "I" was the central aspect of self, which, from one's own point of view, doesn't change very much over time. What changes, according to James, is the "Me," the objective manifestation of self that the "I" (and, indeed, other people) perceives and reacts to. Thus, in the quote at the beginning of this chapter, football star Herschel Walker recognizes that, despite his newfound wealth and fame (changes in "Me"), he is still only Herschel, an entity ("I") that has always been the same and is inherently no better or worse than anybody else. When asked about the adulation he receives from his fellow students, Walker replied: "It's something I've tried to discourage. I'm honored by it, but sort of ashamed of it. The way I make the best of it is to show people I'm still Herschel Walker from Wrightsville, GA. I'm just like an average person" (Blount, 1986, p. 20c).

Contemporary social psychologists make a similar distinction between the self as an active, thinking organism (subjective self) and the self as an object of thought (objective self) that influences and is influenced by others (see Duvall & Wicklund, 1972). Moreover, it appears that adults and even grade-school children reliably differ in the extent to which they are aware of and will consciously monitor their inner, or private, self, which other people can't see, and the outer, or public, components of self, which are normally available for public scrutiny (see, for example, Musser & Browne, 1991; Scheier & Carver, 1981).

Which of these aspects of self develops first? Most developmentalists believe that the "I," or private self-as-knower, must surely be the first to appear; presumably an infant must first know *that she is* (or that she exists independent of other entities) before she can understand *who* or *what* she is (Harter, 1983).

So when do infants first differentiate themselves from other people, objects, and environmental events? At what point do they sense their uniqueness and form self-images? What kinds of information do young children use to define the self, and how do their self-images change over time? These are some of the issues we will explore as we trace the development of the self-concept from birth through adolescence.

The Emerging Self:
Differentiation and Self-Recognition

Like Cooley and Mead, many developmentalists believe that infants are born without a sense of self. Psychoanalytic theorist Margaret Mahler (Mahler, Pine, & Bergman, 1975) likens the newborn to a "chick in an egg" who has no reason to differentiate the self from the surrounding environment. After all, every need the child has is soon satisfied by ever-present companions, who are simply "there" and have no identities of their own. So when do infants first gain a sense of themselves as beings who are separate from the world around them?

This is not an easy question to answer, but it may be helpful to recall Piaget's (and others') descriptions of cognitive development early in infancy. During the period of **primary circular reactions** (1–4 months), infants are repeating pleasurable acts that are centered on their own bodies (for example, sucking their thumbs and waving their arms). At 4–8 months (or the period of **secondary circular reactions**), infants have begun to repeat actions centered on some aspect of the *external* environment (for example, shaking a rattle or squeezing a noise-making toy). Thus, children may learn the limits of their own bodies during the first four months and may recognize that they can operate on objects external to this physical self by the middle of the first year. If 8-month-old infants could talk, they might answer the question "Who am I?" by saying "I am a looker, a chewer, a reacher, and a grabber who acts on objects and makes things happen."

But not everyone agrees that it takes infants 4–6 months to become self-aware. Indeed, the "I" component of self, as reflected by an infant's **personal agency**, or understanding that she can make things happen, may be present very early. At age 3 weeks, for example, infants are often emitting "fake cries" (crying sounds of low pitch and intensity that differ substantially from distress cries) that are either designed to attract the attention of caregivers or repeated because the child has discovered that she can make interesting noises and continues to do so for the sheer pleasure of experimenting with sounds (Wolff, 1969). By age 8 weeks, infants delight in the discovery that they can make an overhead mobile move or can produce interesting sights and sounds by merely kicking their legs or pulling their arms (which are attached via strings to the mobiles or to audiovisual machinery; see Lewis, Alessandri, & Sullivan, 1990; Rovee-Collier, 1987). And, when 8–12-week-old infants find (during extinction trials) that they can no longer produce such effects, they are likely to pull or to kick all the harder and to become *angry* over their loss of control (Lewis et al., 1990). Observations such as these have convinced some developmentalists that babies have both the powers of discrimination and the sense of agency to recognize that they exist, independent of other people and objects, during the first month or two of life, and possibly even sooner (Samuels, 1986; Stern, 1985).

At this point, no one can be absolutely certain about the age at which infants become self-aware. We now know that neonates are hardly the "autistic" creatures that Mahler has described, and, given the remarkable perceptual and discriminative feats of which they are capable, we might well entertain the possibility that infants are never totally unable to distinguish themselves from the environment. Yet Piaget, Mahler, and others are undoubtedly correct in one sense, for any primitive self-awareness that may be present very early will surely become much more refined (and much more apparent to scientists who study it) over the first 4–8 months of the child's life.

Once children acquire language, they begin to tell us what they know about the distinction between themselves and others. By the end of the second year, for example, many infants are already using the personal pronouns *I*, *me*, *my*, and *mine* when referring to the self and *you* when addressing a companion (Lewis & Brooks-Gunn, 1979; Stipek, Gralinski, & Kopp, 1990). This linguistic distinction between *I* (or *me*) and *you* suggests that 2-year-olds now have a firm concept of "self" and "others" (who are also recognized as selves) and have inferred from their conversations that *I* means the person (or self) who is speaking whereas *you* refers to the person who is spoken to. By contrast, autistic children (whose conceptions of self are often very disordered) frequently misuse these personal pronouns and may fail to use them at all (Fraiberg & Adelson, 1976; Spiker & Ricks, 1984).

Self-recognition.   Interestingly, an infant's appropriate use of "me" and "you" in his speech does not necessarily imply that he recognizes who "me" is — that is, an "object" with attributes unlike those of any other person or object. When do infants perceive themselves as having unique physical characteristics? When do they construct firm self-images that enable them to recognize themselves?

One way to answer these questions might be to place infants in front of a mirror and see how they respond to their reflections. Researchers who have adopted this strategy find that 5–8-month-olds enjoy looking in a mirror and will often reach out and touch their reflected images (Bertenthal & Fischer, 1978; Lewis & Brooks-Gunn, 1979). By 9–12 months of age, infants recognize the correspondence, or contingency, between their own actions and those of a mirror image, and they often delight in making the image do whatever they do. Does this gleeful reaction to the reflected image mean that the infant recognizes *himself* in the mirror? Not necessarily, for it might be argued that he enjoys looking at and playing with his mirror image because this interesting "companion" is the most responsive playmate he has ever seen (Damon & Hart, 1982).

Michael Lewis and Jeanne Brooks-Gunn (1979) have studied the development of **self-recognition** by asking mothers to surreptitiously apply a spot of rouge to their infants' faces (under the pretext of wiping the infant's nose) and then place the infants before a mirror. If infants have a scheme for their own face and recognize their mirror images as themselves, they should soon notice the new red spot and reach for or wipe their *own* face. When infants 9 to 24 months old were given this **rouge test**, the younger ones showed no self-recognition: they seemed to treat the image in the mirror as if it were "some other kid." Signs of self-recognition were observed among a few of the 15–17-month-olds, but only among the 18–24-month-olds did a majority of infants touch their own nose, apparently recognizing that they had a strange mark on *their* face (see also Bullock & Lutkenhaus, 1990).

Interestingly, infants from nomadic tribes, who have no experience with mirrors, begin to show self-recognition on the rouge test at the same age as city-reared infants (Priel & deSchonen, 1986). And many

PHOTO 7-1   Recognizing one's mirror image as "me" is a crucial milestone in the development of "self."

18–24-month-olds can even recognize themselves in photographs and will often use a personal pronoun (me) or their own name to label their photographic image (Lewis & Brooks-Gunn, 1979). Recall that 18–24 months is precisely the time when the object concept is maturing and children are internalizing their sensorimotor schemes to form mental images. So the ability to recognize the self seems closely related to the child's level of cognitive development. Even children with Down's syndrome and a variety of other mental deficiencies can recognize themselves in a mirror if they have attained a mental age of at least 18–20 months (Hill & Tomlin, 1981).

Although a certain level of cognitive development seems necessary for self-recognition, social experiences are probably of equal importance. Gordon Gallup (1979) finds that adolescent chimpanzees can easily recognize themselves in a mirror (as shown by the rouge test) — unless they have been reared in complete social isolation. In contrast to normal chimps, social isolates react to their mirror images as if they were looking at another animal! So the term *looking-glass self* applies to chimpanzees as well as to humans: reflections cast by a "social mirror" enable normal chimps to develop a knowledge of self, whereas a chimpanzee that is denied these experiences will fail to acquire a discernible self-image.

What kinds of social influences might contribute to self-recognition and to the growth of the self-concept? Attachment theorists (for example, Bowlby, 1988; Sroufe, 1990) suggest one answer. Specifically, they argue that an infant's "working models" of the self and others evolve from interactions with primary caregivers. Sensitive, responsive caregiving is thought to promote (1) a strong sense of agency, (2) a positive working model of the self and the caregiver (as the infant learns that *he* can influence the behavior of his trustworthy companion), and (3) a secure attachment. By contrast, insensitive, neglectful, or abusive caregiving may lead to (1) a weaker sense of agency, (2) a less positive working model of the self and the caregiver, and (3) an insecure attachment. These propositions, coupled with the finding (reviewed in Chapter 6) that secure attachments promote exploratory activities, might lead us to predict that securely attached infants will show earlier evidence of self-recognition than their insecurely attached agemates. One early study found precisely this association between attachment security and self-recognition (Schneider-Rosen & Cicchetti, 1984), whereas a second study found exactly the opposite pattern, with insecurely attached infants passing the rouge test earlier than their securely attached agemates (Lewis, Brooks-Gunn, & Jaskir, 1985). However, when Sandra Pipp, Ann Easterbrooks, and Robert Harmon (1992) administered a complex test of self-knowledge—one that assessed the child's awareness of her name and gender as well as self-recognition—they found that (1) securely attached 2-year-olds were already outperforming their insecurely attached agemates on the test, and (2) differences in self-knowledge between securely and insecurely attached children were even greater among a sample of 3-year-olds. Securely attached infants and toddlers also displayed more knowledge *about their mothers* than did their insecurely attached agemates. So it seems that secure attachments may not only promote the growth of self-awareness after all but may also be an important contributor to other aspects of social cognition (for example, knowing about others).

Categorical self. Shortly after infants and toddlers can recognize themselves in a mirror or photograph, they begin to notice some of the ways that people differ and to categorize themselves on these dimensions (Stipek et al., 1990)—a classification called the **categorical self**. Age is one of the first social categories that toddlers incorporate into their self-concepts—viewing themselves as "big boys" (or girls) rather than babies or adults (Edwards & Lewis, 1979). Use of age as a social category becomes much more refined during the preschool period (Edwards, 1984). For example, 3- to 5-year-olds who examine photographs of people aged 1 to 70 can easily classify them as "little boys and girls" (photographs of 2- to 6-year-olds), "big boys and girls" (7- to 13-year-olds), "mothers and fathers" (14- to 49-year-olds), and "grandmothers and grandfathers" (age 50 and older).

Gender is another social category that children recognize and react to very early in life. Brooks-Gunn and Lewis (1981) found that 9- to 12-month-old infants can easily discriminate photographs of strange women from those of strange men, and they are more likely to smile at the women. By age 18 months, infants can readily distinguish photos of themselves from those of *opposite-sex* agemates, and 2½-year-olds who have acquired the gender labels *boy* and *girl* usually know which label applies to them and can easily identify people in photographs as males or females (Brooks-Gunn & Lewis, 1981; Thompson, 1975). Their understanding of gender is far from complete, however, for even 4-year-olds are likely to say that they could change sex if they really wanted to (Kohlberg, 1969). But, by the time they enter grade school, children know that they will always be males or females and have already learned many cultural stereotypes about men and women (Williams, Bennett, & Best, 1975). Clearly, one's gender identity is an extremely important aspect of "categorical self"—one that we will discuss at length in Chapter 9.

Finally, 3–5-year-olds are becoming increasingly aware of racial and ethnic differences, although these youngsters (particularly minority children) often fail to correctly identify the category to which they belong. Native American preschoolers, for example, can easily discriminate Indians and Anglos in photographs but are less accurate in correctly specifying the category that they most resemble (Spencer & Markstrom-Adams, 1990). A similar "misidentification" phenomenon has been observed among African-American preschoolers, who display a clear pro-white bias and associate fewer positive attributes with the color black or with African-American people (Cross, 1985; Spencer, 1988). Do these pro-majority opinions imply that minority preschoolers are critical of themselves and have negative self-concepts? Probably not. Consider that African-American children typically display a strong pro-white bias *and* a highly favorable *self-concept* (Powell, 1985), and young Native Americans show a stronger preference for their own race when tested in their native language (Annis & Corenblum, 1987). So, rather than implying self-criticism or a "negative" identity, the pro-majority opinions that minority preschoolers often express may simply reflect their growing awareness of negative social stereotypes about minority groups and an egocentric tendency to view themselves as valuable by expressing a preference for socially desirable attributes (Spencer & Markstrom-Adams, 1990). By age 10 to 12, however, most minority children are displaying a clear preference toward and identification with their own racial group (Beuf, 1977; Spencer, 1982).[1]

Who Am I? Responses of Preschool Children

When asked to describe themselves, preschoolers dwell on their physical characteristics, their possessions and interpersonal relationships, and the actions they can perform (Damon & Hart, 1982). In one study (Keller, Ford, & Meachum, 1978), 3- to 5-year-olds were asked to say ten things about themselves and to complete the sentences "I am a _____" and "I am a boy/girl who _____." Approximately 50% of the children's responses to these probes and questions were *action* statements such as "I play baseball" or "I walk to school." By contrast, psychological descriptions such as "I'm happy" or "I like people" were rare among these 3- to 5-year-olds. So it seems that preschool children have a somewhat "physicalistic" conception of self that is based largely on their ability to perform various acts and make things happen.

These findings would hardly surprise Erik Erikson. In his theory of psychosocial development, Erikson (1963) proposes that 2- to 3-year-olds are struggling to become independent or autonomous, whereas 4- to 5-year-olds who have achieved a sense of **autonomy** are now acquiring new skills, achieving important objectives, and taking great pride in their accomplishments. According to Erikson, it is a healthy sign when preschool children define themselves in terms of their activities, for an activity-based self-concept reflects the sense of initiative they will need in order to cope with the difficult lessons they must learn at school.

Do preschoolers display "psychological" self-awareness? Not everyone agrees that preschoolers' self-concepts are so devoid of "psychological" awareness. Rebecca Eder (1989, 1990), for example, finds that 3½- to 5-year-olds know how they usually behave in various contexts (saying, for example, "I like to play by myself at nursery school"), and she believes that these "habit" statements are an early *psychological* characterization of self that provides the basis for later traitlike conceptions that older children will express (for example, "I'm not very sociable"). Indeed, 3- to 5-year-olds will quickly characterize themselves on psychological dimensions such as achievement if asked the appropriate contrasting questions (for example, choosing between "mostly doing things that are hard" versus "mostly doing things that are easy"). Moreover, they characterize themselves differently on different dimensions, and these self-characterizations are stable over a one-month period (Eder, 1990). Although preschool children may not be consciously aware of what it means to be "sociable" or to be an "achiever," Eder's research implies that they have rudimentary psychological conceptions of self long before they can express this knowledge in traitlike terminology (see also Miller & Aloise, 1989).

---

[1]By contrast, Anglo majority children show a clear preference for identifying with their own group at ages 5–7, and this early in-group identification is due in part to the greater esteem in which their majority group is held (Aboud, 1988).

PHOTO 7-2   Preschool children are already aware of their behavioral patterns and preferences and are using this information to form an early "psychological" portrait of the self.

Origins of the private self.   When adults think about the self, they know that they have a *public self* (or selves) that people can see (a "me") and a *private*, thinking self (or "I") that is not available for public scrutiny. Do young children make this distinction between public and private selves?

One way to find out is to ask young children "how" or "where" they think and whether other people can observe them thinking. John Flavell (as cited in Maccoby, 1980) tried this approach and found that children older than 3½ generally know that their own thinking goes on inside their heads and that others cannot observe their thought processes. Moreover, 3-year-olds must also know that other people cannot always infer what is on their minds, for (as we saw in Chapter 5) children this young are quite capable of creating false beliefs by (1) lying and hiding their guilt (Lewis, Stanger, & Sullivan, 1989) or (2) "faking" emotions (such as anger and distress) in order to "manipulate" their companions (Bretherton et al., 1986; see also Box 7-1). By age 4 to 5, children know that private mental activities are controlled by their brains (Johnson & Wellman, 1982), and they are also beginning to make a clear distinction between *private*, or problem-solving, *speech*, which is now abbreviated and often nearly inaudible, and *public* (communicative) *speech*, which is boldly articulated and consists of complete sentences (Vygotsky, 1934/1962).

So it seems that 3- to 5-year-olds have indeed begun to discriminate the private self-as-knower from the public self-as-known. But, as we will see in the next section, their understanding of the relationship between these two aspects of self is rather primitive, even compared with that of an 8-year-old.

Conceptions of Self in Middle Childhood and Adolescence

In Chapter 4 we learned that children's thinking about objects and events (that is, their general cognition) and their impressions of others (that is, social cognition) gradually become less concrete and more abstract throughout middle childhood and adolescence. The same is true of thinking about the self: children's self-descriptions gradually evolve from listings of their physical, behavioral, and other "external" attributes to sketches of their enduring inner qualities—that is, their traits, values, beliefs, and ideologies (Damon & Hart, 1982; Harter, 1990b; Livesley & Bromley, 1973). This developmental shift toward a more abstract or "psychological" portrayal of the self can be seen in the following three responses to the "Who am I?" question (Montemayor & Eisen, 1977):

9-year-old: My name is Bruce C. I have brown eyes. I have brown hair. I love! sports. I have seven people in my family. I have great! eye site. I have lots! of friends. I live at. . . . I have an uncle who is almost 7 feet tall. My teacher is Mrs. V. I play hockey! I'm almost the smartest boy in the class. I love! food. . . . I love! school.

11½-year-old: My name is A. I'm a human being . . . a girl . . . a truthful person. I'm not pretty. I do so-so in my studies. I'm a very good cellist. I'm a little tall for my age. I like several boys. . . . I'm old fashioned. I am a very good swimmer. . . . I try to be helpful. . . . Mostly I'm good, but I lose my temper. I'm not well liked by some girls and boys. I don't know if boys like me. . . .

17-year-old: I am a human being . . . a girl . . . an individual. . . . I am a Pisces. I am a moody person . . . an indecisive person . . . an ambitious person. I am a big curious person. . . . I am lonely. I am an American (God help me). I am a Democrat. I am a liberal person. I am a radical. I am a conservative. I am a pseudoliberal. I am an Atheist. I am not a classifiable person (i.e., I don't want to be) [pp. 317–318].

Although grade-school children and young adolescents are coming to rely more and more on psychological labels to describe the self, they tend to apply them in an absolute way, viewing these attributes as stable and unchanging. For example, 8- to 14-year-olds who say that they are "kind" tend to believe that kindness is an enduring aspect of their personalities that will always characterize their interactions with others (Harter, 1986; Mohr, 1978). By contrast, older adolescents who describe themselves with a trait such as "kindness" are aware that any number of extenuating circumstances can cause them to act in ways that seem inconsistent with their self-descriptions. Thus a "kindly" 20-year-old might say "I help my brother with his homework, but I don't help my sister with hers because my

BOX 7-1 | *Deception as an Indicator of Young Children's Distinctions between Public and Private Self*

Recently, Michael Chandler and his associates (Chandler, Fritz, & Hala, 1989; Hala, Chandler, & Fritz, 1991) reported a series of studies implying that children as young as 2½ make clear distinctions between what the "private self" knows and what the "public self" portrays to others. In Chandler's initial study, 2½- to 5-year-olds were introduced to a puppet named Tony, who was about to hide a "treasure" under one of four containers. After being told that Tony left white footprints wherever he went, the child played the "finder" in this treasure hunt, successfully following Tony's telltale footprints to the treasure's hiding place on three separate occasions. (They also watched the experimenter erase the footprints with a sponge after each of their "finds.") Then the child was told that it was his turn to help Tony hide the treasure and was encouraged to hide it so that a second player seated outside the room would not be able to find it.

Could these young children spontaneously generate deceptive strategies in the hope of creating a *false belief*—a belief that they knew would not correspond to what their "private selves" knew about the treasure's

true location? Indeed they could. Even the 2½-year-olds delighted at misleading the second player by (1) destroying Tony's tracks after the treasure was hidden, (2) laying down false trails (footprints) to other locations, and/or (3) blatantly lying by directing the second player to containers known to be empty. Apparently these young, preschool con artists were quite aware that the second player's beliefs about the treasure's location (1) would be influenced by the activities of their public selves (that is, their own deceptive ploys) and (2) would differ from their *own* "private" knowledge (see also Hala et al., 1991). Although other investigators have wondered just how well 2- and 3-year-olds truly understand the impact of their deceptive ploys (see Sodian et al., 1991), research is rapidly accumulating to suggest that 3-year-olds do appreciate that another person might hold a belief that they know to be false (Lewis & Osborne, 1990; Robinson & Mitchell, 1992), thus implying that awareness of an inner, private self (and that different inner selves may hold different beliefs) is present at an early age.

brother really needs help, while my sister is lazy. I mean it's fair to help him and not her'' (Damon & Hart, 1982, p. 858). What the adolescent has done is to integrate a stable attribute (kindness) with a belief (help only those who really need help) to produce a more coherent self-portrait that provides a logical explanation for two actions that appear to be inconsistent.

Reexamining the adolescent's self-concept. How do adolescents become such sophisticated self-theorists? Are they ever bothered by the inconsistencies they display in different social contexts (for example, being cheerful toward friends and surly toward parents)? Susan Harter and Ann Monsour (1992) recently addressed these issues by asking 13-, 15-, and 17-year-olds to (1) describe themselves as they are with parents, with friends, in romantic relationships, and in the classroom; (2) sort through these self-descriptions to identify any attributes they viewed as "opposites" (for example, cheerful vs. surly); and (3) report how confused they were about these inconsistencies. Based on Kurt Fischer's (1980) cognitive-developmental theory—which implies that there are three substages of formal-operational reasoning—Harter and Monsour made the following predictions:

1. The 13-year-olds will be at Fischer's first, or *single abstractions*, level of formal operations. They should generate many traitlike descriptions, but they lack the cognitive ability to compare these abstractions. Hence they should identify few opposing traits and experience little confusion over their self-descriptions.
2. The 15-year-olds should have progressed to an *abstract mappings* level of formal operations in which they actively begin to compare and contrast abstract concepts. These mid-adolescents were expected to identify many opposing attributes in their self-portraits and to interpret these contradictions as conflictual and distressing.
3. The 17-year-olds may have progressed to Fischer's *abstract systems* level of formal operations—a level in which they are able to integrate sets of abstractions into a compatible, higher-order abstraction (for example, saying

that a cheerful demeanor with friends coupled with an occasionally surly one toward acquaintances or parents implies that "I am moody"). Presumably, these older adolescents would also identify many oppositional attributes but would not be terribly confused by them.

As we see in Figure 7-1, Harter and Monsour's findings were consistent with their predictions. Thirteen-year-olds did identify fewer oppositional attributes than either the 15-year-olds or the 17-year-olds (see Figure 7-1A). And more 15-year-olds reported feeling confused or "mixed up" by inconsistencies in their self-portraits than did 13-year-olds or 17-year-olds (see Figure 7-1B).

In sum, Harter and Monsour's study indicates that, by mid-adolescence, teenagers are likely to be confused and possibly even distressed by the inconsistencies they display—almost as if they feel that they are different selves with different people and are concerned about determining which of these entities is the "real me." Although we will see in the pages that follow that some aspects of self may never be completely understood, the ability of older adolescents to create higher-order *abstract systems* may well be a major contributor to their lack of distress over oppositional attributes and to the integrated, holistic self-portraits that they display.

Further distinctions between public and private self. Mid-adolescents' concern over their inconsistencies—or their multiple "me's"—implies that they are not yet completely aware of the relationship between public and private self (or how "me" relates to "I"). Robert Selman (1980) has studied children's growing awareness of their public and private selves by asking them to consider the following dilemma:

Eight-year-old Tom is trying to decide what to buy his friend Mike for a birthday present. By chance, he meets Mike on the street and learns that Mike is extremely upset because his dog Pepper has been lost for two weeks. In fact, Mike is so upset that he tells Tom "I miss Pepper so much that I never want to look at another dog. . . ." Tom goes off only to pass by a store with a sale on puppies. Only two are left and these will soon be gone.

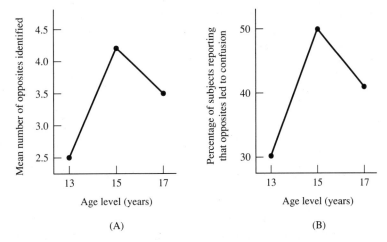

FIGURE 7-1   Average number of oppositional attributes reported by 13-, 15-, and 17-year-olds (panel A) and the percentages of 13-, 15-, and 17-year-olds who said they were confused or "mixed up" by these inconsistencies in their self-portraits (panel B). (Adapted from S. Harter & A. Monsour, "Developmental Analysis of Conflict Caused by Opposing Attributes in the Adolescent Self-Portrait." *Developmental Psychology*, 1992, *28*, 251–260. Copyright © 1992 by the American Psychological Association.)

Children were first asked whether Tom should buy Mike one of the puppies. To probe their understanding of the distinction between the private self and one's public image, they were then asked such questions as "Can you ever fool yourself into thinking that you feel one way when you really feel another?" and "Is there an inside and an outside to a person?"

Selman found that children younger than 6 did not distinguish between private feelings and public behavior, responding to the questions with statements such as "If I say that I don't want to see a puppy again, then I really won't ever want to." By contrast, most 8-year-olds recognize the difference between inner states and outward appearances, and they are likely to say that Mike would really be happy to have another puppy. Apparently, 8-year-olds show these keen insights because they are more aware than 6-year-olds that people (themselves included) can experience more than one emotional reaction to the same event (Harter, 1986; Wintre, Polivy, & Murray, 1990) and are better able to integrate potentially contrasting facial, behavioral, and situational cues to infer what those reactions might be (Hoffner & Badzinski, 1989). So, some-

where between the ages of 6 and 8, children become much more attuned to inconsistencies between a person's "public" and "private" selves and will think of the private self as the *true* self.

Thinking about the private self changes once again as young, self-reflective adolescents come to believe that they can consciously *control* their inner feelings. Thus a 14-year-old might react to the loss of a pet by saying "I could fool myself into not wanting another puppy if I kept saying to myself 'I don't want a puppy; I don't ever want to see another puppy.'" However, older adolescents eventually realize that they cannot control all their subjective experiences, because their feelings and behaviors may be influenced by factors of which they are *not consciously aware*. Consider the reply of one older adolescent when asked "Why did Mike say he didn't want . . . another puppy?"

[Mike] might not want to admit that another dog could take Pepper's place. He might feel at one level that it would be unloyal to Pepper to just go out and replace the dog. He may feel guilty about it. He doesn't want to face these feelings, so he says no dog. (Experimenter: Is he aware of this?) Probably not [Selman, 1980, p. 106].

Type of item							
	Really true for me	Sort of true for me				Sort of true for me	Really true for me
Scholastic competence	☐ 1	☐ 2	Some kids have *trouble* figuring out the answers in school	BUT	Other kids almost *always* can figure out the answers	☐ 3	☐ 4
	Really true for me	Sort of true for me				Sort of true for me	Really true for me
Behavioral conduct	☐ 1	☐ 2	Some kids usually get in *trouble* because of things they do	BUT	Other kids usually *don't* do things that get them in trouble	☐ 3	☐ 4

FIGURE 7-2 Sample items from Harter's *Self-Perception Profile for Children*. (From S. Harter, "Developmental Processes in the Construction of the Self." In T. D. Yawkey & J. E. Johnson (Eds.), *Integrative Processes and Socialization: Early to Middle Childhood*, p. 63. Hillsdale, NJ: Erlbaum. Copyright © 1988 by Erlbaum. Reprinted by permission.)

In sum, children's understanding of their private and public selves becomes increasingly abstract from middle childhood through adolescence. The concrete 6-year-old who feels that her public image is an accurate portrayal of self will gradually become a reflective adolescent who is not only aware of discrepancies between her public and private selves but also recognizes that the private "self as knower" may not always understand why the public self behaves as it does.

Self-Esteem: The Evaluative Component of Self

As children develop, they not only come to understand more and more about themselves and to construct more intricate self-portraits, but they also begin to *evaluate* the qualities that they perceive themselves as having. This aspect of self is called **self-esteem**. Children with high self-esteem are fundamentally satisfied with the type of person they are; they recognize their strong points, can acknowledge their weaknesses (often hoping to overcome them), and generally feel quite positive about the characteristics and competencies they display. By contrast, children with low self-esteem view the self in a less favorable light, often choosing to dwell on perceived inadequacies rather than on any strengths they may happen to display (Dweck & Elliott, 1983; Zupan, Hammen, & Jaenicke, 1987).

Measuring Self-Esteem

Many early studies of self-esteem attempted to characterize one's self-worth with a single score. However, subsequent research (see Harter, 1982, 1988, 1990a) indicates that children first evaluate their competencies in many different domains and only later integrate these impressions into an overall self-evaluation. Susan Harter (1986, 1990a) has developed a 36-item scale, called the *Self-Perception Profile for Children*, that assesses subjects' opinions of their overall self-worth as well as their evaluations of their competencies in five separate domains: scholastic competence, athletic competence, behavioral conduct, social acceptance, and physical appearance. Each of the six subscales contains six items, and each item requires the child to (1) select one of two statements that best describes the self and (2) indicate whether that statement is "sort of true for me" or "really true for me." Figure 7-2 illustrates sample items from the scholastic competence and the behavioral conduct subscales. As shown in the figure, each item is scored from 1 to 4, with higher scores indicating higher perceived competence on that item. Responses to the six items on each subscale are then summed to determine how positively the child evaluates his or her competencies in each of the six areas.

When Harter (1982) administered an early version of her scale to third- through ninth-graders, she found that even the third graders (8-year-olds) perceive themselves in favorable or unfavorable terms in different competency domains—indicating that children's knowledge and feelings about the self (or self-esteem) are well established by middle childhood.[2] Children also make important distinctions about their competencies in different areas, so that their "self-esteem" depends on the situation in which they find themselves. For example, a star student who considers himself bad at sports and other physical activities may enjoy high self-esteem in the classroom while feeling inadequate on the playground. Finally, children's self-ratings seem to be accurate reflections of how others perceive them. For instance, children with high scholastic self-esteem were rated quite high in intellectual competence by their teachers. Children's ratings of social self-esteem were confirmed by peers who had been asked to rate their classmates' social competencies. And children with high athletic self-esteem were more frequently chosen for team sports and were rated higher in physical competence by gym teachers than were classmates who felt physically inadequate.

Taken together, these findings suggest that both self-knowledge and self-esteem may depend to a large extent on the way others perceive and react to our behavior. This is precisely the point that Charles Cooley (1902) was making when he coined the term *looking-glass self* to explain how we construct a self-image.

PHOTO 7-3 Children who do well at school and who have lots of friends are likely to enjoy high self-esteem.

Harter (1986) also finds that children differ in the *importance* they assign to the five competency domains assessed by her scale. Moreover, youngsters who rate themselves as very competent in the areas that *they* see as most important tend to be highest in overall self-worth. So it seems that older children and adolescents' feelings of self-esteem depend both on how they think others evaluate them (that is, the social looking glass) and on how they choose to evaluate themselves (Harter, 1990a).

Which competencies are most important? Although the answer will differ somewhat from child to child, it seems that fourth- through seventh-graders often base their overall self-worth on their *academic* and *social* competencies. Thus, children who enjoy the highest self-esteem tend to be those who do well in school and who have lots of friends (Cauce, 1987; Cole, 1991; Coopersmith, 1967). These findings would not surprise Erikson (1963), who believes that the major psychosocial conflict that grade-school children face is **industry versus inferiority**. To gain a sense of "industry," children must master the important cognitive and social skills—

[2]Harter and Pike (1984) have developed a perceived competence scale for preschool and early grade-school children (4–7-year-olds) and found that youngsters in this age range do tend to perceive themselves in relatively favorable or unfavorable terms on a couple of dimensions: general competence and social acceptance. However, the authors were hesitant to interpret these self-perceptions as a firm sense of self-esteem, because 4–7-year-olds' impressions of their general competencies and social acceptance are not terribly accurate and, hence, may partly reflect a *desire* to be liked or to be "good at" a variety of activities rather than a firm set of beliefs about their actual competencies.

reading, writing, arithmetic knowledge, cooperative teamwork, and a sense of fair play—that are necessary to win the approval of both adults and peers. According to Erikson, children who acquire these skills should feel quite competent and should be adequately prepared for the next psychosocial hurdle—the identity crisis of adolescence—whereas those who fail to acquire important academic and social skills should feel inferior and may have a difficult time establishing a stable identity later in life.

Origins of Self-Esteem

Why do some children develop higher self-esteem than others? As you might guess, parents can play a crucial role. Stanley Coopersmith (1967) found that boys with high self-esteem have mothers who are highly loving and accepting, who set clear behavioral standards for them to live up to, and who allow their children to express their opinions and participate in decision making (see also Lamborn et al., 1991, for similar findings with boys *and* girls). We cannot be sure that this loving and democratic parenting style *causes* high self-esteem, but it is easy to imagine such a causal process at work. Certainly the message "You're a good kid whom I trust to follow rules and make good decisions" is likely to promote higher self-esteem than a more aloof or more controlling style in which parents may be saying, in effect, "Your inadequacies turn me off" (Isberg et al., 1989).

Of course, another reason why children differ in self-esteem is that they really do differ in the competencies on which self-esteem is based. Starting at about age 6, children begin to seek **social comparison** information that will tell them whether they are more or less competent than their peers; they glance at each other's papers and say "How many did you miss?" or make such statements as "I'm faster than you" after winning a foot race (Frey & Ruble, 1985). This kind of social comparison (1) increases with age (Stipek & Mac Iver, 1989), (2) is stronger when teachers create a highly competitive atmosphere in the classroom or on the playground (see Butler, 1989, 1990), and (3) apparently plays a very important role in shaping children's self-esteem. Yet, competency appraisals are not the only kind of comparisons that

can influence a child's perceived self-worth. For example, such correlates of socioeconomic status as the quality of one's clothes and possessions are salient dimensions for comparison, and it is perhaps not surprising that grade-school children from families on public assistance tend to express very low levels of self-esteem (Kaufman & Cicchetti, 1989).

Does Self-Esteem Change at Adolescence?

How stable are one's feelings of self-worth? Is a child who enjoys high self-esteem as an 8-year-old likely to feel especially good about himself as an adolescent? Or is it more reasonable to assume that the stresses and strains of adolescence will cause most teenagers to doubt themselves and their competencies, thereby undermining their self-esteem?

Erikson (1963) favored the latter point of view, arguing that young adolescents are likely to experience at least some erosion of self-esteem as they begin to seek a stable identity. He proposed that the many physical, cognitive, and social changes that occur at puberty force the young adolescent to conclude "I ain't what I ought to be, I ain't what I'm gonna be, but I ain't what I was" (1950, p. 139). In other words, 12- to 15-year-olds face an **"identity crisis"** in that they are no longer sure who they are and yet must also grapple with the question "Who will I become?" A failure to answer these questions leaves them confused and uncertain about their self-worth. However, Erikson believed that adolescents would eventually view themselves in more positive terms if they achieved a stable identity with which to approach the tasks of young adulthood.

Apparently some young adolescents do experience a decline in self-esteem if they are noticeably overweight (Mendelson & White, 1985) or if they are leaving elementary school as the oldest and most revered pupils and entering junior high, where they are the youngest and least competent (Simmons et al., 1979; Wigfield et al., 1991). But, before we conclude that adolescence is hazardous to our sense of self-worth, let's note that young (12–15-year-old) adolescents show no greater fluctuations in mood than the typical grade-school child (Larson & Lampman-Petraitis, 1989) and that *most* 11- to 14-

year-olds show no appreciable decline in self-esteem (Nottelmann, 1987; Petersen, 1988). In fact, it seems that, if self-images change at all during adolescence, the direction of these changes is more likely to be positive than negative (Marsh, 1989; O'Malley & Bachman, 1983; Savin-Williams & Demo, 1984). So the portrayal of adolescence as a period of personal stress and eroding self-esteem seems to characterize only a small minority of young people—primarily those who experience *many life changes* (for example, a change in schools, changing body images, onset of dating, a disruption of family life) *all at once* (see Simmons et al., 1987).

What, then, happened to Erikson's identity crisis? For the minority of adolescents who suffer a serious erosion in self-esteem, the task of coping with present realities and future possibilities may, indeed, represent a crisis—one that could even trigger suicidal thoughts (see Box 7-2). But, as we will see, most adolescents seem to treat the process of identity formation not as an aversive, disruptive crisis, but as a normal and necessary part of life.

Who Am I to Be?
Forming an Identity

According to Erikson (1963), the major developmental hurdle that adolescents face is establishing an **identity**—a unified, holistic self-portrait that integrates the private self (or "I") with all the various role-oriented public selves (or "me's") that we present to other people. An identity also implies a sense of *consistency*—a relatively stable and future-oriented impression of self that will serve as the psychological foundation for commitments to a career, to intimate relations, and to establishment of a "world view" (for example, choice of political or religious ideologies). All this is, of course, a lot for teenagers to have on their minds, and Erikson used the term "identity crisis" to capture the sense of confusion, and even anxiety, that adolescents may feel as they think about who they are today and try to decide "What kind of self can (or should) I be?"

Can you recall a time during the teenage years when you were confused about who you were, what you should be, and what you were likely to become? Is it possible that you have not yet resolved these identity issues and are still seeking answers? If so, does that make you abnormal or maladjusted?

James Marcia (1966, 1980) has developed a structured interview that enables researchers to classify adolescents into one of four *identity statuses* based on whether or not they have explored various alternatives and made firm commitments to an occupation, a religious ideology, and a set of political values. These identity statuses are as follows:

1. **Identity diffusion**. Adolescents classified as "diffuse" have not yet thought about identity issues or, having thought about them, have failed to make any firm future-oriented commitments.
2. **Foreclosure**. Persons classified as "foreclosed" have made future commitments without ever experiencing the "crisis" of deciding what really suits them best. This can easily occur if parents suggest an identity to the adolescent ("You'll go to med school, Johnny"), who then adopts this viewpoint without carefully evaluating its implications.
3. **Moratorium**. This status describes the person who is experiencing what Erikson referred to as an identity crisis. He or she has made no definite commitments but is actively exploring a number of values, interests, ideologies, and careers in search of a stable identity.
4. **Identity achievement**. The identity achiever has resolved his or her identity crisis by making relatively strong *personal* commitments to an occupation or an ideology (or both).

Age trends in identity formation.   Although Erikson assumed that the identity crisis occurred in early adolescence and was typically resolved by age 15–18, it appears that his age norms were overly optimistic. When Philip Meilman (1979) assessed the identity statuses of college-bound (or college-educated) males between the ages of 12 and 24, he did find evidence of a clear developmental progression. But, as shown in Figure 7-3, the vast majority of 12- to 18-year-olds were identity diffused or foreclosed; not until age 21 or older had the majority of participants reached the moratorium status or achieved stable identities. Similar age trends in identity formation have now been reported for both males and females from a broader sample of adolescents, many of whom were not college bound (Archer, 1982). So it seems that most American youths do not experience a strong identity crisis until late adolescence and that many people of college age are still seeking a firm, future-oriented identity (Waterman, 1988).

We might also note that the process of forging an identity is much more "uneven" than Erikson had thought (Kroger, 1988). For example, Sally Archer (1982) has assessed the identity statuses of 6th- through 12th-graders in four areas: occupational choices, gender roles, religious values, and political ideologies. She found that only 5% of her adolescents were in the same identity status in all four areas, and more than 90% were in two or three statuses across the four areas. Apparently, adolescents can achieve a strong sense of identity in one area and still be searching in others.

How painful is identity formation?   Perhaps it is unfortunate that Erikson used the term *crisis* to describe the adolescent's active search for an identity (or identities), because adolescents in the moratorium status do not appear to be all that "stressed

---

**B
O
X**

7-2   *Adolescent Suicide: The Tragic Destruction of Self*

Surprising as it may seem to anyone who has never contemplated taking his own life, suicidal thoughts are shockingly common among adolescents and young adults (Dubow et al., 1989). In one recent survey of high school students, nearly 63% reported at least one instance of suicidal thinking, and 10.5% had actually attempted suicide (Smith & Crawford, 1986). Moreover, the suicide rate among 15- to 24-year-olds has increased dramatically over the past 30 years (American Academy of Pediatrics, 1988) — so much so that suicide is now the third leading cause of death for this age group, ranking far ahead of accidents and just behind homicides (National Center for Health Statistics, 1988). Overall, females attempt suicide about three times as often as males do, but males are more often successful in their attempts. Males succeed more often simply because they tend to shun slower-acting pills in favor of more abruptly lethal means, such as ropes and guns (American Academy of Pediatrics, 1988).

Unfortunately, there is no sure way to identify young people who will try to kill themselves. Suicidal adolescents come from all races, ethnic groups, and social classes, and even popular adolescents of superior intelligence may take their own lives. Yet there are some telltale warning signs. Suicidal adolescents are often severely depressed for weeks or even months before their suicide attempts, and many have expressed the wish to die. They have often experienced deteriorating relationships with parents, peers, or romantic partners, have suffered academic failures, and have lost all interest in hobbies or other enjoyable activities as they sink into a state of hopelessness and despair and feel incapable of coping with their problems (Berman & Jobes, 1991; Rubenstein et al., 1989). Because adolescents are far less successful than adults at killing themselves when they try (see figure), many theorists believe that their suicide attempts are often a desperate "cry for help." Unlike suicidal adults, who are often determined to end it all, many suicidal adolescents are hoping to *improve* their lives; they may see their suicide attempts as a way of forcing others to take their problems seriously. But, by miscalculation or by sudden impulse, they often die before they can be helped (Berman & Jobes, 1991; Rubenstein et al., 1989).

What can be done to prevent adolescent suicides? Friends and associates can play an important role in

out." In fact, James Marcia (1980) finds that these active identity seekers feel much better about themselves and their futures than do agemates in the diffusion and foreclosure statuses. Yet, Erikson was right in characterizing identity achievement as a very healthy and adaptive development, for identity achievers do enjoy higher self-esteem and are less preoccupied with personal concerns than their counterparts in the other three identity statuses (Adams, Abraham, & Markstrom, 1987).

What may be most painful or "crisis-like" about identity seeking is a long-term failure to establish one. Erikson believed that such individuals would eventually become depressed and lacking in self-confidence as they drift aimlessly, trapped in the "diffusion" status. Or, alternatively, they might heartily embrace what Erikson called a *negative identity,* becoming a "black sheep," a "delinquent," or a "loser." Why? Because, for these foundering souls, it is better to become everything that one is not supposed to be than to have no identity at all (Erikson, 1963). Indeed, many adolescents who enter high school with low self-esteem do become delinquent and often view this deviant self-image as providing them with a boost in self-worth (Bynner, O'Malley, & Bachman, 1981; Wells, 1989).

Social influences on identity formation.   What social factors might promote or retard the adolescent's progress toward identity achievement? Evidently, parenting styles are very important. After reviewing the literature, Alan Waterman (1982) concluded that

---

BOX 7-2 | *continued*

recognizing the warning signs of suicidal thinking and urging their depressed young companions to talk about their problems. Should the adolescent divulge suicidal thoughts, companions might try to convince him or her that there are ways other than suicide to cope with distress. But perhaps the most important thing friends and associates can do is to tell what they have learned to other people who are in a better position to help—people such as the adolescent's parents, a teacher, or a school counselor. Clearly, it is better to break a confidence than to let the person die.

As for parents, perhaps the best advice is to take *all* suicidal thinking seriously, for as many as 1 in 6 teenagers who have such thoughts will actually attempt to kill themselves (Smith & Crawford, 1986). And professional assistance is definitely called for after an unsuccessful suicide attempt, because adolescents who try once are at risk of succeeding in the future if they receive little help and continue to feel incapable of coping with their problems (Berman & Jobes, 1991).

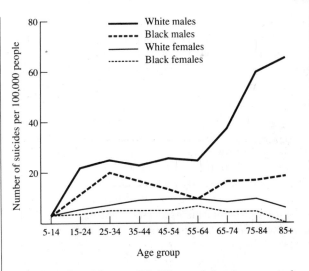

Number of suicides per 100,000 people by age, sex, and race in the United States in 1986. (Data from *Vital Statistics of the United States, 1986: Vol. 2, Mortality, Part A* (DHSS Publication No. PHS 88-1122) by the National Center for Health Statistics. Washington, DC: U.S. Government Printing Office.)

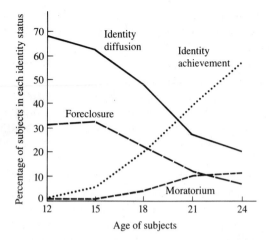

FIGURE 7-3 Percentages of subjects in each of Marcia's four identity statuses as a function of age. Note that resolution of the identity crisis occurs much later than Erikson assumed: only 4% of the 15-year-olds and 20% of the 18-year-olds had achieved a stable identity. (Adapted from P. W. Meilman, "Cross-Sectional Age Changes in Ego Identity Status during Adolescence." *Developmental Psychology*, 1979, 15, 230–231. Copyright © 1979 by the American Psychological Association. Reprinted by permission.)

close relationships with domineering parents are likely to result in identity foreclosures, whereas distant relationships with aloof or uninvolved parents provide the adolescent with little reason to think about future commitments, thereby promoting identity diffusions. By contrast, students who are classified in either the moratorium or identity achievement status appear to have a solid base of affection at home combined with the freedom to be individuals in their own right (Grotevant & Cooper, 1986). So the same loving and democratic style of parenting that seems to help children gain a strong sense of self-esteem is associated with healthy and adaptive identity outcomes in adolescence.

Does attending college help one to forge an identity? The answer is yes—and no. College attendance does seem to push people toward making career goals and stable occupational commitments (Waterman, 1982), but college students are often far behind their working peers in terms of establishing mature political and religious identities (Munro & Adams, 1977). In fact, some collegians will regress from identity achievement to the moratorium or even the

diffusion status in certain areas, most notably religion. But let's not be too critical of the college environment, for, like college students, many adults will later reopen the question of who they are if exposed to people or situations that challenge old viewpoints and offer new alternatives (Waterman, 1988).

Cultural influences on identity formation.   In a recent review of the literature, Margaret Spencer and Carol Markstrom-Adams (1990) concluded that achieving an identity may be an especially problematic and complex task for many minority youths. Indeed, existing research suggests that Native-American, Mexican-American, and (to a lesser extent) African-American adolescents are more likely to be at the foreclosure identity status than are their Anglo agemates (Abraham, 1986; Marcia, 1966; Markstrom, 1987). Why is this?

Spencer and Markstrom-Adams discuss several possibilities. First, the preponderance of negative stereotypes about minorities is hardly conducive to acquiring a solid sense of self or to feeling especially optimistic about the future. Consider, for example, that minority adolescents' growing awareness of social prejudice and the limitations it places on educational and vocational opportunities may be a major hindrance to their establishment of occupational identities (Ogbu, 1988). Moreover, minority youths frequently encounter conflicts between the values of their subculture and those of the majority culture, and members of their subcultural communities often discourage identity explorations that clash with the social and ideological traditions of their own group. In fact, it seems as if virtually all North American minorities have a term for community members who are "too white" in orientation, be it the "apple Indian syndrome" (red on the outside, white on the inside) for Native Americans, the "coconut syndrome" for Hispanics, the "banana syndrome" for Asians, or the "Oreo syndrome" for African Americans. So, in view of these conflicts, a minority adolescent's "foreclosed" identity (that is, simply adopting the viewpoints and ideologies of one's subculture) may actually be adaptive, fostering a stronger sense of personal and social well-being, at least in the short run (DeVos & Romanucci-Ross, 1982). Finally, minority parents are often reluctant to discuss racial and ethnic issues with their children, which may erect yet another barrier to identity achievement. As Spencer and Markstrom-Adams (1990) point out, parental failure to confront racial issues leaves their children ill prepared to deal constructively with either the prejudice they will encounter or the value conflicts that will emerge between their own subculture and the cultural mainstream.

What can be done to make the search for an identity a little easier for minority youths? Spencer and Markstrom-Adams believe that, first and foremost, we must strive to keep minority students in school and academically oriented, for a lack of education automatically closes many doors and virtually guarantees a life of socioeconomic disadvantage. Beyond this academic emphasis, special efforts might be made to enhance ethnic pride at home, at school, and in the community. Of course, this would require mechanisms for (1) assisting parents to become prideful transmitters of their minority subculture and (2) sensitizing teachers to the customs, traditions, communication patterns, and language of their minority pupils. Finally, the quest for racial equity and equal opportunity must continue so that the possibility of exploring a broad range of options will seem more plausible to minority adolescents who are grappling with identity issues. However, waiting until adolescence to implement new programs would be to wait too long. Spencer and Markstrom-Adams stress:

> Minority youth generally (and male minority youth specifically) should, from the early toddler and preschool years, believe that they can have a positive impact on the world. Environments could be restructured to support children's acquisition of a sense of personal efficacy and thus the [evolution] of a more constructive identity and the perception and experience of a competent self [p. 306].

Identity as preparation for intimacy.   According to Erikson (1963), the first psychosocial crisis that young adults face is **intimacy versus isolation**. And Erikson believed (see also Dyk & Adams, 1988) that one must successfully resolve an identity crisis before he or she can establish a truly intimate relationship with another person. To Erikson, true intimacy

implies a reciprocal commitment in which each partner gives of himself or herself to achieve a *shared* identity. True intimacy need not imply sexuality, but it does imply mutual trust and a genuine sensitivity to the needs, wishes, and aspirations of one's partner. So intimacy rests on one's keen awareness of oneself vis-à-vis one's partner—an achievement that may be difficult indeed for identity diffused or foreclosed individuals who have not yet thought that deeply about who or what they are.

The available research is generally consistent with Erikson's views on identity as a prerequisite for intimacy. Fitch and Adams (1983), for example, report that the majority of college students showing mature identity statuses (that is, moratorium or identity achievement) as freshmen or sophomores had established intimate relationships one year later, whereas those with diffuse identities rarely achieved intimacy with anyone over the next 12 months. Moreover, identity achievement is a much better predictor of intimate relationships for college *alumni*, who have had several years to live within and consolidate their identities, than for college students, whose identity crises may be less firmly resolved (Whitbourne & Tesch, 1985). So it seems that the establishment of a stable personal identity is a significant developmental milestone indeed—one that helps pave the way for the growth of deep and trusting emotional commitments that could conceivably last a lifetime.

Development of Self-Regulation and Self-Control

Having examined how developing children and adolescents gain information about themselves, evaluate this information, and use it to achieve an identity, we now turn to yet another critical aspect of self: *self-regulation* and the development of *self-control*.

Self-regulation refers to the *processes* by which an individual, in the absence of external instruction or surveillance, actively maintains a course of action for purposes of achieving a goal (Harter, 1983). Of course, self-regulation is necessary for **self-control** — the ability to inhibit actions (for example, rule violations) that one might otherwise be inclined to perform. As we saw in Chapter 4 when discussing Bandura's cognitive social-learning theory, self-regulation is a critical aspect of human development. It allows us to monitor our thinking and our conduct to successfully pursue important objectives, many of which we have set for ourselves. Indeed, Bandura (1986) has argued that our capacity for self-regulation is what ultimately frees us from having to react in a reflex-like way to the momentary pushes and pulls of our immediate environments.

Self-control is equally important. If people did not learn to inhibit immediate impulses and control their behavior, they would constantly be at odds with other people for violating others' rights, breaking rules, and failing to display the patience and self-sacrifice that would permit them to achieve important *long-range* objectives (for example, earning a diploma). Although many theorists have commented on the development of self-control (for example, Bandura, 1986; Freud, 1935/1960; Kopp, 1987; Mischel, 1986), all of them make two assumptions: (1) young children's behavior is almost completely controlled by external agents (for example, parents); (2) over time, some of this control is *internalized* as children adopt standards, or norms, that stress the value of self-control and acquire self-regulatory skills that permit them to adhere to these prescriptions.

Emergence of Self-Control in Infancy and Toddlerhood

When do children first display any evidence of self-regulation and self-control? Most theorists assume that these milestones occur at some point during the second year, after infants realize that they are separate, autonomous beings and that their actions have consequences that *they* have produced. Indeed, we have already discussed one such example of early *self-regulation* — lip compressing and brow knitting by 1–2-year-olds who are attempting to *control* their sadness or anger (Malatesta et al., 1989). But, on the whole, the 1–2-year-old's ability to monitor her behaviors and adjust them as necessary is very limited indeed (Bullock & Lutkenhaus, 1988).

By age 2, children are showing clear evidence of **compliance**. They are now aware of a caregiver's wishes and expectations and can voluntarily follow her requests and commands (Crockenberg & Litman, 1990; Schneider-Rosen & Wenz-Gross, 1990). Although compliant acts performed in the context of *pleasurable* interactions may themselves be pleasurable for many 2-year-olds (Kaler & Kopp, 1990), their behavior is still largely *externally* controlled by the approval they anticipate for compliance and the disapproval they associate with noncompliance (Kuczynski & Kochanska, 1990).

However, anyone who has ever spent much time with 2–3-year-olds knows that they can become extremely uncooperative and noncompliant upon entering a phase that parents sometimes call the "terrible twos." Indeed, 2–3-year-olds will often appear *defiant* by ignoring or actively spurning others' commands and instructions and insisting that they can accomplish tasks on their own (Bullock & Lutkenhaus, 1990; Erikson, 1963). According to Erikson, these toddlers are struggling with the psychosocial conflict of **autonomy versus shame and doubt**: they are resolved to display their independence and self-determination by doing things their own way, even if that means being noncompliant and risking others' disapproval.

Recently, Susan Crockenberg and Cindy Litman (1990) made an important distinction between **self-assertion** (simply refusing a request or command) and **defiance** (saying "No" and becoming angry and/or intensifying one's ongoing behavior). They view the former as the more competent form of autonomy seeking — one that is likely to promote *self-control*. They also find that the external control strategies that mothers use predict the responses of their 2-year-olds to requests and commands. Specifically, mothers who reacted to a child's "No!" (self-assertion) by intervening physically or by threatening and criticizing were likely to elicit *defiance*, whereas mothers who took an initial "No!" as an opportunity to remain firm in their demands while offering a rationale (or an incentive) for complying were likely to elicit *compliance*.

So self-assertion in the interest of achieving autonomy is a normal and even healthy developmental sign. And it seems as if the strategies that parents use in resolving these autonomy conflicts with their children may play a major role in determining whether an assertive toddler becomes negative and defiant toward authority figures or, alternatively, adopts a more cooperative and compliant posture that is conducive to the development of self-control (see also Kochanska, 1992).

Young children's emerging ability to control their impulses becomes much more apparent by the middle of the third year. In one *delay of gratification* study, Brian Vaughn and his associates (Vaughn, Kopp, & Krakow, 1984) presented 18- to 30-month-old toddlers with three challenges: (1) to refrain from touching a nearby toy telephone, (2) to not eat raisins hidden under a cup until told that they could, and (3) to not open a gift until the experimenter had finished her work. The child was then observed to see how long he or she could wait before succumbing to these powerful temptations. As shown in Figure 7-4, delay of gratification increased dramatically between 18 and 30 months of age. Moreover, there were clear individual differences in the ability of 30-month-olds to defer gratification; the single best predictor of this capacity for self-control was their level of language development: linguistically advanced children delayed longer.

What role might language play in the child's transition from an externally controlled organism to a disciplined agent of self-control? Let's see what developmentalists have learned.

The Role of Language in the Development of Self-Control

Vygotsky's viewpoint. Soviet psychologist Lev Vygotsky (1934/1962) was fascinated by his observation that preschoolers would often talk to themselves while playing or working on tasks. Unlike Piaget, who felt that these preschool monologues merely reflected children's egocentrism and were of little developmental significance, Vygotsky claimed that nonsocial speech is communicative and important. Specifically, he called it a "speech for self," or **private speech**, that helps young children to plan strategies and to monitor their behavior so that they are more likely to accomplish their goals. Vygotsky also claimed that private speech becomes more abbreviated with age, progressing from the whole

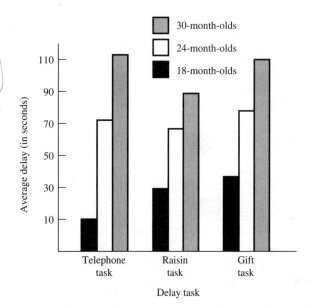

FIGURE 7-4 Average delay of gratification (in seconds) of 18-, 24-, and 30-month-olds exposed to three strong temptations. (Adapted from B. E. Vaughn, C. B. Kopp, & J. B. Krakow, "The Emergence and Consolidation of Self-Control from Eighteen to Thirty Months of Age: Normative Trends and Individual Differences." *Child Development*, 1984, *55*, 990–1004. Copyright © 1984 by the Society for Research in Child Development.)

phrases that 4-year-olds produce to the single words or even simple lip movements that are more common among grade-school children. His view is that private speech never completely disappears; instead, it simply goes underground, becoming silent or *inner speech* — the covert verbal thought that we use to organize and *regulate* our everyday activities.

Recent research is quite consistent with Vygotsky's theory. In problem-solving studies, for example, children rely more on private speech when facing *difficult* rather than easy tasks and when deciding how to proceed after making errors (Berk & Garvin, 1984; Kohlberg, Yaeger, & Hjertholm, 1968); moreover, their performance typically improves after they turn to self-instruction (Behrend, Rosengren, & Perlmutter, 1989; Bivens & Berk, 1990). And it is the *brightest* children who rely most heavily on private speech — a finding that links this language to *cognitive competence* rather than to cognitive immaturity (egocentrism) that Piaget claimed it represents (Berk, 1986; Kohlberg et al.,

1968). Finally, private speech does eventually go underground, progressing from words and phrases, to whispers and mutterings, to inner speech (Frauenglass & Diaz, 1985), and this internalization process occurs earliest among the brighter members of an elementary-school class (Berk, 1986; Kohlberg et al., 1968). So it seems that private speech is an important *self-regulating* mechanism that assists us to monitor and control our thinking and our conduct.

Luria's research.   Alexander Luria (1961) was a follower of Vygotsky who was interested in the age at which children could first use language to both initiate and *inhibit* behaviors when they tell themselves to. Of course, the ability to voluntarily inhibit behaviors is an important accomplishment—one that allows children to resist temptations to violate moral norms and to forgo immediate gratifications in the service of long-term goals. In Luria's research on early self-control, 1½- to 5-year-olds were given a rubber bulb that they were to squeeze whenever the experimenter said "press" or instructed them to say "press." When the experimenter said "don't press," or instructed them to say "don't press," they were to quit squeezing the bulb. What Luria discovered is that children younger than 3 could not respond appropriately to their own self-instructions. In fact, if they were squeezing the bulb and heard "don't press" (either from themselves or from the experimenter), they often squeezed even faster! It is not that the young child intends to disobey but, rather, that the inhibitory command "don't press" has a positive instructional component (the verb *press*) that seems to energize the ongoing response (Luria, 1961). Indeed, Eli Saltz and his associates (Saltz, Campbell, & Skotko, 1983) found that, the louder an adult's instruction to inhibit a response, the greater the likelihood that 3- and even 4-year-olds will continue to perform it, at least for short periods (see Figure 7-5). By contrast, 5–6-year-olds are more likely to respond appropriately to an adult's inhibitory commands, particularly if the command is loud or forceful.

When do children begin to follow their *own* instructions to inhibit a response? Luria (1961) found that only his 5-year-olds could respond about as well to their own speech as to that of an adult, and he concluded that this is the age at which verbal self-

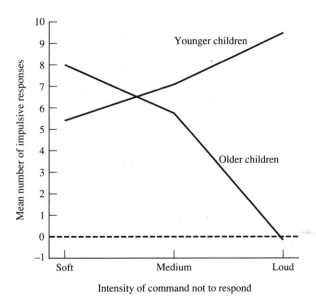

FIGURE 7-5   Average number of impulsive responses by younger (3–4-year-old) and older (5–6-year-old) children as a function of the intensity of the verbal command not to respond. (From E. Saltz, S. Campbell, & D. Skotko, "Verbal Control of Behavior: The Effects of Shouting." *Developmental Psychology*, 1983, *19*, 461–464. Copyright © 1983 by the American Psychological Association. Reprinted by permission.)

regulation becomes a powerful instrument of *self-control*.

However, we should not infer from Luria's work that children younger than 5 never use language to regulate their conduct. Indeed, preschool children often instruct themselves when playing or trying to accomplish tasks (Kohlberg et al., 1968). And recall from our earlier discussion that the 2½-year-olds who are most proficient at delaying immediate gratification are those who have progressed furthest in their language development (Vaughn et al., 1984). Nevertheless, we will see in our next section that Luria was right in one important respect: older children are much more proficient than younger ones at tailoring their self-instructions to the task at hand so that they can *effectively* regulate their conduct.

Delay of Gratification

One of the more fruitful approaches for studying the development of self-control has been the **delay of gratification** paradigm that we discussed briefly in Box 3-1. Recall that children in a typical "delay" study are offered a choice between a small incentive available immediately and a larger one for which they must wait. What these studies reveal is that (1) preschool children find it exceedingly difficult to be patient when the incentives they must resist are in plain sight, although (2) they do become better and better at delaying gratification over the grade-school years, eventually showing a strong preference to wait for delayed incentives by age 10 to 12 (Mischel, 1986). Why does this aspect of self-control improve so dramatically with age? Let's consider two possibilities.

Knowledge of delay strategies.   In an early delay-of-gratification study, Walter Mischel and Ebbe Ebbesen (1970) found that 3- to 5-year-olds simply cannot keep their minds off tempting objects for long. The children in this study were told that, if they waited 15 minutes, they would receive a very attractive snack; but, if they couldn't wait that long, they could signal the experimenter by ringing a bell and would receive a less desirable snack. When both kinds of snacks were visible during the delay period, preschoolers waited an average of only a minute or two before losing their patience, signaling the experimenter, and receiving the less desirable treat. Indeed, only a handful of children were able to wait the entire 15-minute delay period to earn the more valuable incentive. How did they do it? By covering their eyes, singing songs, inventing games, or otherwise *distracting* themselves from the temptations they faced.

However, it should be emphasized that the vast majority of preschoolers do *not* know that distraction can help them to resist immediate temptations. They can be *taught* by adults to use distractive strategies (Mischel & Patterson, 1976) — even very complex ones that require them to mentally transform tempting objects (for example, marshmallows) into less tempting stimuli (for example, white, puffy clouds) — to help them maintain their resolve (Mischel & Baker, 1975). But they do not generate these distractive strategies on their own (Toner & Smith, 1977). In fact, if it is suggested to them that they might become more patient by choosing a self-instructional strategy, preschoolers are much more inclined to focus attention on the *desirable qualities* of

the incentives they are trying to resist (Toner, 1981) — a very *ineffective* means of coping with the frustrations of a delay.

By age 6–8 most children now realize that creating physical distractions (for example, by covering their eyes or the tempting objects) can help them to be more patient. And by age 11–12 they know that *abstract ideation* (that is, cognitive distractions such as the marshmallows-are-clouds transformation or even such untrue self-instructions as "I hate marshmallows") can reduce their frustrations and make waiting easier (Mischel & Mischel, 1983). Why does awareness of abstract ideation take so long to develop? Probably because it rests on hypothetical transformations of present realities — a formal-operational ability. Younger children can use abstract ideation if adults supply these distractors for them, but they will not generate them on their own.

So one reason why self-control improves over the grade-school years is that children learn more about *effective* means of regulating their thinking and conduct.

Self-control as a valued attribute.   Another reason why older children and adolescents are better able to delay gratification, to comply with rules, or to otherwise control their impulses is that they are internalizing norms that stress the value of self-regulation and self-control. Evidence for this process can be seen in the self-descriptions of pre-adolescents and adolescents. When asked what they like about themselves, adolescents will often mention conduct that reflects their self-discipline (for example, being persistent at pursuing their goals or being slow to lose their tempers), and teenagers are often quite concerned about breakdowns in self-control (for example, blowing up at someone over nothing or failing to complete their homework) (Rosenberg, 1979). So by early adolescence a capacity for self-control is viewed as a highly desirable and almost obligatory attribute — one that teenagers hope to incorporate into their own self-concepts.

Could we, then, foster children's self-control by working on their self-concepts — that is, by trying to convince them that they can be patient, persistent, honest, and even tempered whenever they have shown some evidence of displaying these attributes? Might children who are labeled as "honest" or "patient" incorporate these attributions into their self-concepts and try to live up to this new self-image? Indeed they may, for we learned in Box 3-1 that 5½- to 9-year-olds who had been labeled as "patient" by an adult became much more successful at delaying immediate gratification than their age-mates who had been labeled in a task-irrelevant way (Toner, Moore, & Emmons, 1980).

So, in addition to suggesting effective self-instructional strategies for regulating conduct, it appears that adults can promote self-control by bolstering children's images of themselves as patient, honest, or otherwise self-disciplined individuals (see also Casey & Burton, 1982).

Early self-control as a predictor of later life outcomes. Developmentalists who study self-control cannot help but notice that some children are much more self-disciplined than others. Moreover, it is commonly assumed that self-discipline and self-control are adaptive attributes that may forecast many successes in the years ahead. Do children who display early evidence of self-control experience more favorable life outcomes?

Indeed they may. Walter Mischel and his associates have recently conducted ten-year follow-up studies of subjects who had participated as pre-schoolers in Mischel's early delay-of-gratification experiments. In the follow-ups, parents of Mischel's subjects completed questionnaires in which they described the competencies and shortcomings of their adolescent sons and daughters. These descriptions were highly informative. Apparently, self-control is a remarkably stable attribute, for adolescents who had been unable to delay gratification for long during the preschool years were the ones whom parents were now most likely to characterize as impatient and unable to wait for satisfactions (Shoda, Mischel, & Peake, 1990). Moreover, adolescents who had been better at delaying gratification ten years earlier were generally described in more favorable terms (that is, more academically competent, more socially skilled, more confident and self-reliant, and better able to cope with stress) than their counterparts who had shown less self-control as preschoolers (Mischel, Shoda, & Peake, 1988; Shoda et al., 1990). And, consistent with the par-

ents' reports of their teenagers' academic competencies, adolescents who had displayed the most self-control as preschoolers were the ones who made the highest scores on the Scholastic Aptitude Test (SAT) (Shoda et al., 1990).

Now we begin to see why virtually all contemporary developmentalists consider the establishment of self-regulatory skills and the emergence of self-control to be such important developmental hurdles. Not only is self-control a reasonably stable characteristic (see also Block & Block, 1980), but it is reliably associated with the very attributes (cognitive competencies, social skills, self-confidence, self-reliance) that forecast high self-esteem in adolescence (Harter, 1990a) and occupational success and general life satisfaction throughout adulthood (Hunter & Hunter, 1984; Vaillant, 1983). So one's capacity for self-control does appear to be a crucial component of this entity we call the "self" — a conclusion we will reach over and over again as we discuss such topics as achievement, aggression, altruism, moral development, and peer relations.

Summary

In recent years there has been a revival of interest in the psychology of the self. *Self* is a term that researchers use to refer to a person's impressions of the combination of attributes that makes him or her a unique individual. The self seems to have two distinct components: the *I* (or subjective self-as-knower) and the *Me* (or the self-as-an-observable-object that one can think about).

Although there is some disagreement among contemporary theorists, the prevailing point of view is that infants cannot distinguish between the self and nonself (objects, other people) until 4–6 months of age. The "I" (or self-as-knower) develops first. But by 18–24 months of age the "Me" (or self-as-object) has clearly emerged, as children form stable self-images (as indicated by their ability to recognize themselves in mirrors and photographs) and begin to categorize themselves along socially significant dimensions such as age, gender, and (later) race or ethnicity.

Although preschoolers show some awareness of a private, inner self and know how they typically behave in many contexts, their self-descriptions are very concrete, focusing on their physical features, their possessions, and the activities they can perform. By about age 8, children begin to describe themselves in terms of their inner psychological attributes and begin to think of this inner self as a better reflection of their character than the external facade they present to others. Adolescents have an even more integrated and abstract conception of the self—one that includes not only their dispositional qualities (traits, beliefs, attitudes, values) but also a knowledge of how these characteristics might combine or interact with one another and with situational influences to affect their behavior.

Self-esteem, the evaluative component of self, begins to crystalize at about age 8, as children begin to evaluate their academic, social, behavioral, and physical competencies and to construct a sense of general self-worth. Although children differ somewhat in the competencies they consider most important, they frequently base their overall self-worth on their perceived academic and social competencies. Children are most likely to develop high self-esteem if (1) their parents are warm and democratic in enforcing rules and (2) they fare well (in comparison with peers) in the competencies they consider most important. Although some adolescents do experience a decline in self-esteem, most teenagers cope rather well with the biological and social changes of adolescence, showing no decrease or even a modest increase over time in their perceived self-worth.

One of the more challenging tasks of adolescence is that of forming a stable *identity* (or identities) with which to embrace the responsibilities of young adulthood. From the diffusion and foreclosure statuses, many college-age youths progress to the moratorium status (where they experience an *identity crisis*) and ultimately to identity achievement. Identity formation is an uneven process that often continues into adulthood and is fostered by such social experiences as interactions with warm, supportive parents who encourage individuality. Minority youths may be slower to achieve personal identities, owing, in part, to the conflicts they experience between their subcultures and the majority culture. But the vast majority of adolescents do eventually forge an identity, which sets the stage for the establishment of intimate relationships later in life.

Children's capacity for *self-control* is a major achievement—one that represents a shift from external, or environmental, control to internal *self-regulation* of conduct. Although 2-year-olds are voluntarily complying with others' directives, their conduct is still largely externally controlled by the consequences they anticipate for *compliance* (or noncompliance). But, by the middle of the third year, children are displaying an increasing capacity to regulate and control their own thinking and behavior.

Apparently, language plays a crucial role in the child's transition from an externally controlled organism to an agent of self-control. Although 2- to 4-year-olds are not very proficient at instructing themselves to inhibit *ongoing* behaviors, they can use *private speech* to plan their play and problem-solving activities; by age 5 they can effectively resist many temptations through the use of internalized, self-directed speech.

Delay of gratification is an important aspect of self-control—one that improves dramatically with age as children become more knowledgeable about effective delay strategies and internalize norms that stress the value of self-regulation and self-control. Indeed, self-control does become an important component of adolescents' self-concepts. And preschoolers who have already developed a relatively strong capacity for delaying gratification tend to become self-disciplined adolescents whom parents describe as displaying attributes that contribute to high self-esteem and to favorable outcomes later in life.

References

ABOUD, F. E. (1988). *Children and prejudice*. New York: Basil Blackwell.

ABRAHAM, K. G. (1986). Ego-identity differences among Anglo-American and Mexican-American adolescents. *Journal of Adolescence, 9,* 151–166.

ADAMS, G. R., ABRAHAM, K. G., & MARKSTROM, C. A. (1987). The relations among identity development, self-consciousness, and self-focusing during middle and late adolescence. *Developmental Psychology, 23*, 292–297.

AMERICAN ACADEMY OF PEDIATRICS. (1988). Suicide and suicide attempts in adolescents and young adults. *Pediatrics, 81*, 322–324.

ANNIS, R. C., & CORENBLUM, B. (1987). Effect of test language and experimenter's race on Canadian Indian children's racial and self-identity. *Journal of Social Psychology, 126*, 761–773.

ARCHER, S. L. (1982). The lower age boundaries of identity development. *Child Development, 53*, 1551–1556.

BANDURA, A. (1986). *Social foundations of thought and action: A social cognitive theory*. Englewood Cliffs, NJ: Prentice-Hall.

BEHREND, D. A., ROSENGREN, K., & PERLMUTTER, M. (1989). A new look at children's private speech: The effects of age, task difficulty, and parent presence. *International Journal of Behavioral Development, 12*, 305–320.

BERK, L. E. (1986). Relationship of elementary school children's private speech to behavioral accompaniment to task, attention, and task performance. *Developmental Psychology, 22*, 671–680.

BERK, L. E., & GARVIN, R. A. (1984). Development of private speech among low-income Appalachian children. *Developmental Psychology, 20*, 271–286.

BERMAN, A. L., & JOBES, D. A. (1991). *Adolescent suicide: Assessment and intervention*. Washington, DC: American Psychological Association.

BERTENTHAL, B. I., & FISCHER, K. W. (1978). Development of self-recognition in the infant. *Developmental Psychology, 14*, 44–50.

BEUF, A. H. (1977). *Red children in white America*. University Park: Pennsylvania State University Press.

BIVENS, J. A., & BERK, L. E. (1990). A longitudinal study of the development of elementary school children's private speech. *Merrill-Palmer Quarterly, 36*, 443–463.

BLOCK, J. H., & BLOCK, J. (1980). The role of ego-control and ego-resiliency in the organization of behavior. In W. A. Collins (Ed.), *Minnesota symposium on child psychology* (Vol. 13). Hillsdale, NJ: Erlbaum.

BLOUNT, R. (1986, May 4). "I'm about five years ahead of my age." *Atlanta Journal and Constitution*, pp. C17–C20.

BOWLBY, J. (1988). *A secure base: Parent-child attachment and healthy human development*. New York: Basic Books.

BRETHERTON, I., FRITZ, J., ZAHN-WAXLER, C., & RIDGEWAY, D. (1986). Learning to talk about emotions: A functionalist perspective. *Child Development, 57*, 529–548.

BROOKS-GUNN, J., & LEWIS, M. (1981). Infant social perception: Responses to pictures of parents and strangers. *Developmental Psychology, 17*, 647–649.

BULLOCK, M., & LUTKENHAUS, P. (1988). The development of volitional behavior in the toddler years. *Child Development, 59*, 664–674.

BULLOCK, M., & LUTKENHAUS, P. (1990). Who am I? Self-understanding in toddlers. *Merrill-Palmer Quarterly, 36*, 217–238.

BUTLER, R. (1989). Mastery versus ability appraisal: A developmental study of children's observations of peers' work. *Child Development, 60*, 1350–1361.

BUTLER, R. (1990). The effects of mastery and competitive conditions on self-assessment at different ages. *Child Development, 61*, 201–210.

BYNNER, J., O'MALLEY, P., & BACHMAN, J. (1981). Self-esteem and delinquency revisited. *Journal of Youth and Adolescence, 10*, 407–441.

CASEY, W. M., & BURTON, R. V. (1982). Training children to be consistently honest through verbal self-instructions. *Child Development, 53*, 911–919.

CAUCE, A. M. (1987). School and peer competence in early adolescence: A test of domain-specific self-perceived competence. *Developmental Psychology, 23*, 287–291.

CHANDLER, M. J., FRITZ, A. S., & HALA, S. (1989). Small-scale deceit: Deception as an early marker in 2-, 3-, and 4-year-olds' early theories of mind. *Child Development, 60*, 1263–1277.

COLE, D. A. (1991). Change in self-perceived competence as a function of peer and teacher evaluation. *Developmental Psychology, 27*, 682–688.

COOLEY, C. H. (1902). *Human nature and the social order*. New York: Scribner's.

COOPERSMITH, S. (1967). *The antecedents of self-esteem*. New York: W. H. Freeman.

CROCKENBERG, S., & LITMAN, C. (1990). Autonomy as competence in 2-year-olds: Maternal correlates of child defiance, compliance, and self-assertion. *Developmental Psychology, 26*, 961–971.

CROSS, W. E. (1985). Black identity: Rediscovering the distinction between personal identity and reference group orientation. In M. B. Spencer, G. K. Brookins, & W. R. Allen (Eds.), *Beginnings: The social and affective development of black children*. Hillsdale, NJ: Erlbaum.

DAMON, W., & HART, D. (1982). The development of self-understanding from infancy through adolescence. *Child Development, 53*, 841–864.

DeVOS, G., & ROMANUCCI-ROSS, L. (1982). *Ethnic identity*. Chicago: University of Chicago Press.

DUBOW, E. F., KAUSCH, D. F., BLUM, M. C., REED, J., & BUSH, E. (1989). Correlates of suicidal ideation and attempts in a sample of junior high and high school students. *Journal of Clinical Child Psychology, 18*, 158–166.

DUVALL, S., & WICKLUND, R. A. (1972). *A theory of objective self-awareness*. Orlando, FL: Academic Press.

DWECK, C. S., & ELLIOTT, E. S. (1983). Achievement motivation. In P. H. Mussen (Ed.), *Handbook of child psychology*. Vol. 4: *Socialization, personality, and social development*. New York: Wiley.

DYK, P. A., & ADAMS, G. R. (1988). The association between identity development and intimacy during adolescence: A theoretical treatise. *Journal of Adolescent Research, 2*, 223–235.

EDER, R. A. (1989). The emergent personologist: The structure and content of 3½-, 5½-, and 7½-year-olds' concepts of themselves and other persons. *Child Development, 60*, 1218–1228.

EDER, R. A. (1990). Uncovering young children's psychological selves: Individual and developmental differences. *Child Development, 61,* 849–863.

EDWARDS, C. P. (1984). The age group labels and categories of preschool children. *Child Development, 55,* 440–452.

EDWARDS, C. P., & LEWIS, M. (1979). Young children's concepts of social relations: Social functions and social objects. In M. Lewis & L. Rosenblum (Eds.), *The child and its family: The genesis of behavior* (Vol. 2). New York: Plenum.

ERIKSON, E. H. (1950). In M. J. E. Senn (Ed.), *Symposium on the healthy personality.* New York: Josiah Macy, Jr., Foundation.

ERIKSON, E. H. (1963). *Childhood and society* (2nd ed.). New York: Norton.

FISCHER, K. W. (1980). A theory of cognitive development: The control and construction of hierarchies of skills. *Psychological Review, 87,* 477–531.

FITCH, S. A., & ADAMS, G. R. (1983). Ego identity and intimacy status: Replication and extention. *Developmental Psychology, 19,* 839–845.

FRAIBERG, S., & ADELSON, E. (1976). Self-representation in young blind children. In Z. Jastrzembska (Ed.), *The effects of blindness and other impairments on early development.* New York: American Foundation for the Blind.

FRAUENGLASS, M. H., & DIAZ, R. M. (1985). Self-regulatory functions of children's private speech: A critical analysis of recent challenges to Vygotsky's theory. *Developmental Psychology, 21,* 357–364.

FREUD, S. (1960). *A general introduction to psychoanalysis.* New York: Washington Square Press. (Original work published 1935.)

FREY, K. S., & RUBLE, D. N. (1985). What children say when the teacher is not around: Conflicting goals in social comparison and performance assessment in the classroom. *Journal of Personality and Social Psychology, 48,* 550–562.

GALLUP, G. G., JR. (1979). Self-recognition in chimpanzees and man: A developmental and comparative perspective. In M. Lewis & L. A. Rosenblum (Eds.), *Genesis of behavior.* Vol. 2: *The child and its family.* New York: Plenum.

GROTEVANT, H. D., & COOPER, C. R. (1986). Individuation in family relations: A perspective on individual differences in the development of identity and role-taking skills in adolescence. *Human Development, 29,* 82–100.

HALA, S., CHANDLER, M., & FRITZ, A. S. (1991). Fledgling theories of mind: Deception as a marker of three-year-olds' understanding of false belief. *Child Development, 62,* 83–97.

HARTER, S. (1982). The perceived competence scale for children. *Child Development, 53,* 87–97.

HARTER, S. (1983). Developmental perspectives on the self-system. In P. H. Mussen (Ed.), *Handbook of child psychology.* Vol. 4: *Socialization, personality and social development.* New York: Wiley.

HARTER, S. (1986). Cognitive-developmental processes in the integration of concepts about emotions and the self. *Social Cognition, 4,* 119–151.

HARTER, S. (1988). Developmental processes in the construction of the self. In T. D. Yawkey & J. E. Johnson (Eds.), *Integrative processes and socialization: Early to middle childhood.* Hillsdale, NJ: Erlbaum.

HARTER, S. (1990a). Issues in the assessment of the self-concept of children and adolescents. In A. M. LaGreca (Ed.), *Through the eyes of the child: Obtaining self-reports from children and adolescents.* Boston: Allyn & Bacon.

HARTER, S. (1990b). Processes underlying adolescent self-concept formation. In R. Montemayer, G. R. Adams, & T. P. Gullotta (Eds.), *From childhood to adolescence: A transitional period?* Newbury Park, CA: Sage.

HARTER, S., & MONSOUR, A. (1992). Developmental analysis of conflict caused by opposing attributes in the adolescent self-portrait. *Developmental Psychology, 28,* 251–260.

HARTER, S., & PIKE, R. (1984). The pictorial scale of perceived competence and social acceptance for young children. *Child Development, 55,* 1969–1982.

HILL, S. D., & TOMLIN, C. (1981). Self-recognition in retarded children. *Child Development, 53,* 1320–1329.

HOFFNER, C., & BADZINSKI, D. M. (1989). Children's integration of facial and situational cues to emotion. *Child Development, 60,* 411–422.

HUNTER, J. E., & HUNTER, R. F. (1984). Validity and utility of alternative predictors of job performance. *Psychological Bulletin, 96,* 72–98.

ISBERG, R. S., HAUSER, S. T., JACOBSON, A. M., POWERS, S. I., NOAM, G., WEISS-PERRY, B., & FOLLANSBEE, D. (1989). Parental contexts of adolescent self-esteem: A developmental perspective. *Journal of Youth and Adolescence, 18,* 1–23.

JAMES, W. (1890). *Principles of psychology* (Vol. 1). New York: Henry Holt.

JOHNSON, C. N., & WELLMAN, H. M. (1982). Children's developing conceptions of the mind and brain. *Child Development, 53,* 222–234.

KALER, S. R., & KOPP, C. B. (1990). Compliance and comprehension in very young toddlers. *Child Development, 61,* 1997–2003.

KAUFMAN, J., & CICCHETTI, D. (1989). Effects of maltreatment on school-age children's socioemotional development: Assessments in a day-camp setting. *Developmental Psychology, 25,* 516–524.

KELLER, A., FORD, L. H., JR., & MEACHUM, J. A. (1978). Dimensions of self-concept in preschool children. *Developmental Psychology, 14,* 483–489.

KOCHANSKA, G. (1992). Children's interpersonal influence with mothers and peers. *Developmental Psychology, 28,* 491–499.

KOHLBERG, L. (1969). Stage and sequence: The cognitive-developmental approach to socialization. In D. A. Goslin (Ed.), *Handbook of socialization theory and research.* Skokie, IL: Rand McNally.

KOHLBERG, L., YAEGER, J., & HJERTHOLM, E. (1968). Private speech: Four studies and a review of theories. *Child Development, 39,* 691–736.

KOPP, C. B. (1987). The growth of self-regulation: Caregivers and children. In N. Eisenberg (Ed.), *Contemporary topics in developmental psychology.* New York: Wiley.

KROGER, J. (1988). A longitudinal study of ego identity status interview domains. *Journal of Adolescence, 11,* 49–64.

KUCZYNSKI, L., & KOCHANSKA, G. (1990). Development of children's noncompliance strategies from toddlerhood to age 5. *Developmental Psychology, 26,* 398–408.

LAMBORN, S. D., MOUNTS, N. S., STEINBERG, L., & DORNBUSCH, S. M. (1991). Patterns of competence and adjustment among adolescents from authoritative, authoritarian, indulgent, and neglectful families. *Child Development, 62,* 1049–1065.

LARSON, R., & LAMPMAN-PETRAITIS, C. (1989). Daily emotional states as reported by children and adolescents. *Child Development, 60,* 1250–1260.

LEWIS, C., & OSBORNE, A. (1990). Three-year-olds' problems with false belief: Conceptual deficit or linguistic artifact? *Child Development, 61,* 1514–1519.

LEWIS, M., ALESSANDRI, S. M., & SULLIVAN, M. W. (1990). Violation of expectancy, loss of control, and anger expressions in young infants. *Developmental Psychology, 26,* 745–751.

LEWIS, M., & BROOKS-GUNN, J. (1979). *Social cognition and the acquisition of self.* New York: Plenum.

LEWIS, M., BROOKS-GUNN, J., & JASKIR, J. (1985). Individual differences in visual self-recognition as a function of mother-infant attachment relationship. *Developmental Psychology, 21,* 1181–1187.

LEWIS, M., STANGER, S., & SULLIVAN, M. W. (1989). Deception in 3-year-olds. *Developmental Psychology, 25,* 439–443.

LIVESLEY, W. J., & BROMLEY, D. B. (1973). *Person perception in childhood and adolescence.* London: Wiley.

LURIA, A. R. (1961). *The role of speech in the regulation of normal and abnormal behavior.* New York: Liveright.

MACCOBY, E. E. (1980). *Social development: Psychological growth and the parent-child relationship.* San Diego: Harcourt Brace Jovanovich.

MAHLER, M. S., PINE, F., & BERGMAN, A. (1975). *The psychological birth of the human infant.* New York: Basic Books.

MALATESTA, C. Z., CULVER, C., TESMAN, J. R., & SHEPARD, B. (1989). The development of emotion expression during the first two years of life. *Monographs of the Society for Research in Child Development, 54* (Nos. 1–2, Serial No. 219).

MARCIA, J. E. (1966). Development and validation of ego identity status. *Journal of Personality and Social Psychology, 3,* 551–558.

MARCIA, J. E. (1980). Identity in adolescence. In J. Adelson (Ed.), *Handbook of adolescent psychology.* New York: Wiley.

MARKSTROM, C. A. (1987). *A comparison of psychosocial maturity between four ethnic groups during middle adolescence.* Paper presented at the biennial meeting of the Society for Research in Child Development, Baltimore.

MARSH, H. W. (1989). Age and sex effects in multiple dimensions of self-concept: Preadolescence to early adulthood. *Journal of Educational Psychology, 81,* 417–430.

MEAD, G. H. (1934). *Mind, self, and society.* Chicago: University of Chicago Press.

MEILMAN, P. W. (1979). Cross-sectional age changes in ego identity status during adolescence. *Developmental Psychology, 15,* 230–231.

MENDELSON, B. D., & WHITE, D. R. (1985). Development of self-body-esteem in overweight youngsters. *Developmental Psychology, 21,* 90–96.

MILLER, P. H., & ALOISE, P. A. (1989). Young children's understanding of the psychological causes of behavior: A review. *Child Development, 60,* 257–285.

MISCHEL, H. N., & MISCHEL, W. (1983). The development of children's knowledge of self-control strategies. *Child Development, 53,* 603–619.

MISCHEL, W. (1986). *Introduction to personality* (4th ed.). New York: Holt, Rinehart & Winston.

MISCHEL, W., & BAKER, N. (1975). Cognitive appraisals and transformations in delay behavior. *Journal of Personality and Social Psychology, 31,* 254–261.

MISCHEL, W., & EBBESEN, E. B. (1970). Attention in delay of gratification. *Journal of Personality and Social Psychology, 16,* 329–337.

MISCHEL, W., & PATTERSON, C. J. (1976). Substantive and structural elements of effective plans for self-control. *Journal of Personality and Social Psychology, 34,* 942–950.

MISCHEL, W., SHODA, Y., & PEAKE, P. K. (1988). The nature of adolescent competencies predicted by preschool delay of gratification. *Journal of Personality and Social Psychology, 54,* 687–696.

MOHR, D. M. (1978). Development of attributes of personal identity. *Developmental Psychology, 14,* 427–428.

MONTEMAYOR, R., & EISEN, M. (1977). The development of self-conceptions from childhood to adolescence. *Developmental Psychology, 13,* 314–319.

MUNRO, G., & ADAMS, G. R. (1977). Ego-identity formation in college students and working youth. *Developmental Psychology, 13,* 523–524.

MUSSER, L. M., & BROWNE, B. A. (1991). Self-monitoring in middle childhood: Personality and social correlates. *Developmental Psychology, 27,* 994–999.

NATIONAL CENTER FOR HEALTH STATISTICS (1988). *Vital statistics of the United States, 1986.* Vol. 2: *Mortality, Part A* (DHHS Publication No. PHS 88-1122). Washington, DC: U.S. Government Printing Office.

NOTTELMANN, E. D. (1987). Competence and self-esteem during transition from childhood to adolescence. *Developmental Psychology, 23,* 441–450.

OGBU, J. (1988). Black education: A cultural-ecological perspective. In H. P. McAdoo (Ed.), *Black families.* Newbury Park, CA: Sage.

O'MALLEY, P. M., & BACHMAN, J. G. (1983). Self-esteem: Change and stability between ages 13 and 23. *Developmental Psychology, 19,* 257–268.

PETERSEN, A. C. (1988). Adolescent development. *Annual Review of Psychology, 39,* 583–607.

PIPP, S., EASTERBROOKS, M. A., & HARMON, R. J. (1992). The relation between attachment and knowledge of self and mother in one- to three-year-old infants. *Child Development, 63,* 738–750.

POWELL, G. J. (1985). Self-concepts among Afro-American students in racially isolated minority schools: Some regional differences. *Journal of the American Academy of Child Psychiatry, 24,* 142–149.

PRIEL, B., & deSCHONEN, S. (1986). Self-regulation: A study of a population without mirrors. *Journal of Experimental Child Psychology, 41,* 237–250.

ROBINSON, E. J., & MITCHELL, P. (1992). Children's interpretation of messages from a speaker with a false belief. *Child Development, 63,* 639–652.

ROSENBERG, M. (1979). *Conceiving the self.* New York: Basic Books.

ROVEE-COLLIER, C. (1987). Learning and memory in infancy. In J. D. Osofsky (Ed.), *Handbook of infant development* (2nd ed.). New York: Wiley.

RUBENSTEIN, J. L., HEEREN, T., HOUSMAN, D., RUBIN, C., & STECHLER, G. (1989). Suicidal behavior in normal adolescents: Risks and protective factors. *American Journal of Orthopsychiatry, 59,* 59–71.

SALTZ, E., CAMPBELL, S., & SKOTKO, D. (1983). Verbal control of behavior: The effects of shouting. *Developmental Psychology, 19,* 461–464.

SAMUELS, C. (1986). Bases for the infant's development of self-awareness. *Human Development, 29,* 36–48.

SAVIN-WILLIAMS, R. C., & DEMO, D. H. (1984). Developmental change and stability in adolescent self-concept. *Developmental Psychology, 20,* 1100–1110.

SCHEIER, M. F., & CARVER, C. S. (1981). Private and public aspects of self. In L. Wheeler (Ed.), *Review of personality and social psychology* (Vol. 2). Newbury Park, CA: Sage.

SCHNEIDER-ROSEN, K., & CICCHETTI, D. (1984). The relationship between affect and cognition in maltreated infants: Quality of attachment and the development of visual self-recognition. *Child Development, 55,* 648–658.

SCHNEIDER-ROSEN, K., & WENZ-GROSS, M. (1990). Patterns of compliance from eighteen to thirty months of age. *Child Development, 61,* 104–112.

SELMAN, R. L. (1980). *The growth of interpersonal understanding.* Orlando, FL: Academic Press.

SHODA, Y., MISCHEL, W., & PEAKE, P. K. (1990). Predicting adolescent cognitive and self-regulatory competencies from preschool delay of gratification: Identifying diagnostic conditions. *Developmental Psychology, 26,* 978–986.

SIMMONS, R. G., BLYTH, D. A., VAN CLEAVE, E. F., & BUSH, D. M. (1979). Entry into early adolescence: The impact of school structure, puberty, and early dating on self-esteem. *American Sociological Review, 44,* 948–967.

SIMMONS, R. G., BURGESON, R., CARLTON-FORD, S., & BLYTH, D. A. (1987). The impact of cumulative change in early adolescence. *Child Development, 58,* 1220–1234.

SMITH, K., & CRAWFORD, S. (1986). Suicidal behavior among "normal" high school students. *Suicide and Life-Threatening Behavior, 16,* 313–325.

SODIAN, B., TAYLOR, C., HARRIS, P. L., & PERNER, J. (1991). Early deception and the child's theory of mind: False trails and genuine markers. *Child Development, 62,* 468–483.

SPENCER, M. B. (1982). Personal and group identity of black children: An alternative synthesis. *Genetic Psychology Monographs, 103,* 59–84.

SPENCER, M. B. (1988). Self-concept development. In D. T. Slaughter (Ed.), *Black children in poverty: Developmental perspectives.* San Francisco: Jossey-Bass.

SPENCER, M. B., & MARKSTROM-ADAMS, C. (1990). Identity processes among racial and ethnic minority children in America. *Child Development, 61,* 290–310.

SPIKER, D., & RICKS, M. (1984). Visual self-recognition in autistic children: Developmental relationships. *Child Development, 55,* 214–225.

SROUFE, L. A. (1990). An organizational perspective on the self. In D. Cicchetti & M. Beeghly (Eds.), *The self in transition: Infancy to childhood.* Chicago: University of Chicago Press.

STERN, D. N. (1985). *The interpersonal world of the infant.* New York: Basic Books.

STIPEK, D., GRALINSKI, H., & KOPP, C. (1990). Self-concept development in the toddler years. *Developmental Psychology, 26,* 972–977.

STIPEK, D., & Mac IVER, D. (1989). Developmental change in children's assessment of intellectual competence. *Child Development, 60,* 521–538.

THOMPSON, S. K. (1975). Gender labels and early sex-role development. *Child Development, 46,* 339–347.

TONER, I. J. (1981). Role involvement and delay maintenance behavior in preschool children. *Journal of Genetic Psychology, 138,* 245–251.

TONER, I. J., MOORE, L. P., & EMMONS, B. A. (1980). The effect of being labeled on subsequent self-control in children. *Child Development, 51,* 618–621.

TONER, I. J., & SMITH, R. A. (1977). Age and overt verbalization in delay maintenance behavior in children. *Journal of Experimental Child Psychology, 24,* 123–128.

VAILLANT, G. E. (1983). Childhood environment and maturity of defense mechanisms. In D. Magnusson & V. L. Allen (Eds.), *Human development: An interactional perspective.* New York: Academic Press.

VAUGHN, B. E., KOPP, C. B., & KRAKOW, J. B. (1984). The emergence and consolidation of self-control from eighteen to thirty months of age: Normative trends and individual differences. *Child Development, 55,* 990–1004.

VYGOTSKY, L. S. (1962). *Thought and language.* Cambridge, MA: MIT Press. (Original work published 1934.)

WATERMAN, A. S. (1982). Identity development from adolescence to adulthood: An extension of theory and a review of research. *Developmental Psychology, 18,* 341–358.

WATERMAN, A. S. (1988). Identity status theory and Erikson's theory: Commonalities and differences. *Developmental Review, 8,* 185–208.

WELLS, L. E. (1989). Self-enhancement through delinquency: A conditional test of self-derogation theory. *Journal of Research in Crime and Delinquency, 26,* 226–252.

WHITBOURNE, S. K., & TESCH, S. A. (1985). A comparison of identity and intimacy statuses in college students and alumni. *Developmental Psychology, 21,* 1039–1044.

WIGFIELD, A., ECCLES, J. S., Mac IVER, D., REUMAN, D. A., & MIDGLEY, C. (1991). Transitions during early adolescence: Changes in children's domain-specific self-perceptions and general self-esteem across the transition to junior high school. *Developmental Psychology, 27*, 552–565.

WILLIAMS, J. E., BENNETT, S. M., & BEST, D. L. (1975). Awareness and expression of sex stereotypes in young children. *Developmental Psychology, 11*, 635–642.

WINTRE, M. G., POLIVY, J., & MURRAY, M. A. (1990). Self-predictions of emotional response patterns: Age, sex, and situational determinants. *Child Development, 61*, 1124–1133.

WOLFF, P. H. (1969). The natural history of crying and other vocalizations in early infancy. In B. M. Foss (Ed.), *Determinants of infant behavior* (Vol. 4). London: Methuen.

ZUPAN, B. A., HAMMEN, C., & JAENICKE, C. (1987). The effects of current mood and prior depressive history on self-schematic processing in children. *Journal of Experimental Child Psychology, 43*, 149–158.

8 | Achievement

A basic aim of socialization is to urge children to pursue important goals and to take pride in their accomplishments. During my elementary and high school days, my parents and I had several heart-to-heart talks (of the kind you may remember) about the value of writing essays and memorizing the countless passages that were required of me in English and history classes. Both my parents took the position that I should strive to do my best, whatever the assignment, because successful completion of these scholastic activities would promote the self-confidence I would need to become a success in life. My parents' outlook was very typical of that of adults in many Western societies, where children are often encouraged to be independent and competitive and to do well in whatever activities they may undertake—in short, to become "achievers." Although the meaning of "achievement" varies somewhat from society to society, one survey of 30 cultures revealed that people all over the world value such personal attributes as self-reliance, responsibility, and a willingness to work hard to attain important objectives (Fyans et al., 1983).

Must these valued attributes be taught? Social-learning theorists think so, although others disagree. Psychoanalytic theorist Robert White (1959) proposes that children are intrinsically motivated to "master" the environment. He calls this striving for mastery **effectance motivation**—a desire to have an effect on or to cope successfully with the environment and the people within it. We see this effectance, competence, or mastery motive in action as we watch infants struggle to turn knobs, open cabinets, and operate toys—and then notice their pleasure when they succeed. White argued that it is quite natural for human beings to seek out challenges just for the joy of mastering them. Of course, his position is very similar to that of Piaget, who believed that children are intrinsically motivated to *adapt* to the environment by assimilating new experiences and then accommodating to these experiences.

Throughout this text we have stressed that human infants are curious, active explorers who are constantly striving to understand or to exert some control over the world around them. But, even though a basic propensity for competence or mastery may be innate, it is obvious that some children

try harder than others to master their school assignments, their music lessons, or the positions they play on the neighborhood softball team.

If infants are truly mastery oriented and experience great joy in the effects they produce, then why do school-age children vary so dramatically in their achievement strivings? Is there a "motive to achieve" that children must acquire? How do children's self-images and their expectations about succeeding or failing affect their aspirations and accomplishments? And what kinds of home and scholastic settings are likely to promote (or hinder) achievement behavior? These are the major issues that we will consider in the pages that follow.

Definitions of Independence and Achievement

When developmentalists talk about an "independent" person, they mean someone who is able to master challenges and accomplish goals *without assistance*. The concept of achievement extends far beyond a sense of independence. Children who are high achievers not only are self-reliant; they also are likely to appraise the *quality* of their performance against some standard of merit or excellence.

Notice, then, that "achievement" presumes some learning on the individual's part. The child must acquire some idea of what constitutes acceptable or unacceptable performance in any given domain, or context, and learn to use these standards to *evaluate* her accomplishments. But, even though there is widespread agreement that one's propensity for achievement is largely an acquired attribute, different theorists look at this construct in very different ways.

The motivational view of achievement. David McClelland and his associates (1953) speak of the child's **need for achievement (n Ach)**, which they define as a "learned motive to compete and to strive for success whenever one's behavior can be evaluated against a standard of excellence" (p. 78). In other words, high "need-achievers" have learned to take *pride* in their ability to meet or exceed high standards, and it is this sense of *self*-fulfillment that motivates them to work hard, to be successful, and to try to outperform others when faced with new challenges.

McClelland measured achievement motivation by asking subjects to examine a set of four pictures and then write a story about each as part of a test of "creative imagination." These four pictures show people working or studying, although each illustration is sufficiently ambiguous to suggest any number of themes (see Photo 8-1). The subject's need for achievement (*n* Ach) is determined by counting the achievement-related statements that he or she includes in the four stories (the assumption being that subjects are projecting themselves and their motives into their themes). For example, a high need-achiever might respond to Photo 8-1 by saying that these men have been working for months on a new scientific breakthrough that will revolutionize the field of medicine, whereas a low need-achiever might say that the workers are glad the day is over so that they can go home and relax.

A behavioral view of achievement.   In contrast to McClelland's viewpoint, Vaughn Crandall and his associates depict achievement as a behavioral, rather than a motivational, construct. According to Crandall, Katkovsky, and Preston (1960), "Achievement is any *behavior* directed toward the *attainment of approval or the avoidance of disapproval* for competence in performance in situations where standards of excellence are operable" (p. 789; italics added). Crandall and his associates argue that there is no single, overriding motive to achieve that applies to all achievement tasks. Instead, they propose that children will show different strivings in different skill areas (for example, art, schoolwork, sports) depending on the extent to which they value doing well in each area and on their expectations that they can succeed and be recognized for their accomplishments.

Notice that McClelland and Crandall clearly differ on the issue of what reinforces achievement behavior. McClelland and his associates have argued that the sense of *personal pride* stemming from one's high accomplishments is reinforcing (and will sustain achievement behavior in the future) because it satisfies an *intrinsic* need for competence or achieve-

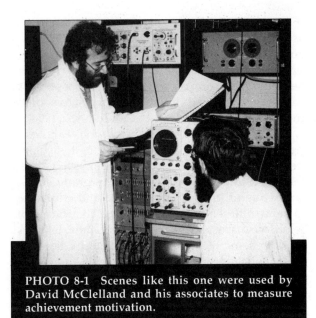

PHOTO 8-1   Scenes like this one were used by David McClelland and his associates to measure achievement motivation.

ment. However, Crandall and his associates counterargue that one need not talk about internal needs that must be satisfied in order to explain why people strive to meet exacting standards. Instead, they propose that achievement behaviors are simply a class of instrumental responses designed to win the *approval* (or to avoid the disapproval) of significant others, such as parents, teachers, and peers.

Which of these viewpoints is correct? Perhaps both of them are. Susan Harter (1981) finds that some children do view achievement tasks as a means of satisfying personal needs for competence or mastery (an **intrinsic orientation** very similar to McClelland's view of *n* Ach), whereas others strive to do well in order to earn external incentives such as grades, prizes, or social approval (an **extrinsic orientation** that other theorists have called "social achievement"). Harter measures children's orientations to achievement with a 30-item questionnaire that asks whether the reasons they perform various activities are intrinsic justifications (I like challenging tasks; I like to solve problems myself) or extrinsic ones (I do things to get good grades, to win the teacher's approval, and so on). And her research reveals that children who are intrinsically oriented are more likely than those who are extrinsically oriented to prefer challenging problems over simpler ones and to view themselves as highly competent at schoolwork. Even when they must seek help to accomplish a task, intrinsically oriented children prefer indirect assistance (hints) that will allow *them* the personal satisfaction of deriving a solution, whereas extrinsically oriented children would just as soon be given the solution (Nelson-LeGall & Jones, 1990).

So, by the early elementary-school years, children already differ in their orientations to achievement. As we will soon see, many theories have been proposed to explain how and why grade-school children (and, indeed, adolescents and adults) respond so differently to the challenges they face. But, before we discuss these theoretical claims, let's first consider some of the milestones that toddlers and preschool children reach as they begin to evaluate their accomplishments.

Early Reactions to One's Accomplishments: From Efficacy to Self-Evaluation

We've noted that even very young infants can take pleasure in mastering a new toy or in producing other interesting outcomes. But when do they first acquire performance standards and begin to evaluate their outcomes as "successes" or "failures"? At what age do they understand the implications of winning or losing at a competitive activity with an agemate? These are important questions in that definitions of achievement typically portray high achievers as those who reliably *evaluate* their accomplishments against standards of excellence and will try to *outperform* others when faced with new challenges.

Recently, Deborah Stipek and her associates (Stipek, Recchia, & McClintic, 1992) reported a program of research that traced the development of 1- to 5-year-olds' reactions to achievement-related outcomes. In the first study, 1- to 5-year-olds played with age-appropriate toys, each of which presented a clear achievement objective (for example, hammering pegs into a pegboard; upsetting plastic pins with a plastic bowling ball), and their reactions to their accomplishments were observed. In study 2, 2- to 5-year-olds worked on puzzles and a cup-

stacking task that were structured so that subjects either could master them (success condition) or could not master them (failure condition), and their responses to their successes and failures were recorded. In study 3, 2- to 5-year-olds competed with a peer at a block-stacking task, and their reactions to winning or losing were noted. Considered together, the findings of these studies led Stipek and her associates to suggest that there are three stages in the development of self-evaluation.

Stage 1—Joy in mastery.[1]   Before age 22 months, infants are visibly pleased when they master a challenge. However, they do not call others' attention to their accomplishments or otherwise seek recognition. Moreover, infants this young are not bothered by mastery failures; instead, they simply shift goals and attempt to master other toys. So mastery outcomes provide young infants with immediate feelings of joy or efficacy of the type White (1959) and others have described; but, before age 22–24 months, infants are not evaluating their outcomes in relation to performance standards that would brand them as "successes" or "failures."

Stage 2—Accomplishments are evaluated.   By age 2 (or shortly before), children become interested in gaining recognition for their accomplishments. After mastering a toy, 2-year-olds often called their mothers' attention to their achievements. When achieving a clear success on tasks performed for an experimenter, 2- to 5-year-olds often smiled, held their heads and chins up high, and would make such statements as "I did it" as they called the experimenter's attention to their accomplishments. By contrast, children who failed would often turn away from the experimenter's gaze, and children older than 3½ were inclined to frown or pout over their lack of success. Thus it seems as if 2-year-olds are already appraising their outcomes as successes or failures and have already learned that approval can be expected for successes and that disapproval may accompany failures. Nevertheless, preschoolers in these studies derived considerable pleasure from their successes, regardless of whether they received any praise. So, even though 2- to 5-year-olds will

[1]The names of these stages are my labels rather than those of Stipek et al. (1992), who chose to leave them nameless.

seek recognition for their accomplishments, they remain *intrinsically* motivated to master challenges. According to Stipek et al. (1992), social approval and disapproval may help children to learn which outcomes are valued in any given context (and perhaps confirm children's personal evaluations of their behavior), but they are not necessary to make a 2- to 5-year-old feel excited by matching a valued standard or disappointed by failing to do so.

Stage 3—Winning is bliss. When do children begin to derive pleasure from winning a competition with an agemate? Stipek's third experiment suggested that, before 33 months of age, competitors were neither happy about winning nor sad about losing. Indeed, successfully completing (mastering) their individual tasks was what was most important to these 24–32-month-olds. By contrast, 33- to 41-month-olds expressed much more positive affect upon mastering a task if they finished first (and won a competition) than if they finished second (and lost). And, by age 42–60 months, losers tended to slow down or stop working when a winner had been declared; apparently they understood the competitive nature of the game and saw little reason for them to rush to finish once an opponent had "won." Stipek et al. (1992) suggest that these older Stage-3 children have internalized a set of performance standards and can experience true *pride* (rather than mere pleasure) in achieving and true *shame* (rather than mere disappointment) when failing to match a standard. Nevertheless, shameful responses were infrequent among preschool children who lost at a *competitive* task. So it appears that, before age 5, winning is divine but losing is not typically interpreted as a clear failure.

The Stipek et al. (1992) monograph looks at *normative* trends in young children's reactions to achievement outcomes—an area that has been largely neglected by developmentalists interested in achievement behavior (but see Heckhausen, 1984; Kagan, 1981). Indeed, the dominant focus of the achievement literature has been to try to explain the *individual differences* that older children and adolescents display in their propensities for achievement. We will now turn to the major theories of achievement to see why individuals might adopt different achievement orientations and how this choice

of an orientation might influence their future accomplishments.

Theories of Achievement Motivation and Achievement Behavior

The theories that have contributed most to our understanding of achievement motivation and achievement behavior are the McClelland/Atkinson need achievement models and more recent attributional (or social information-processing) approaches. In this section we will compare and contrast these influential points of view.

Need Achievement Theory

The first major theory of achievement was the "need achievement" approach, a motivational model that stemmed from the pioneering efforts of David Mc-Clelland and his associates at Wesleyan University and that was later revised by John Atkinson of the University of Michigan.

McCLELLAND'S THEORY OF ACHIEVEMENT MOTIVATION

In 1938 Henry Murray published *Explorations in Personality*, a text that had a profound influence on students of human behavior. Murray outlined a personality theory that included a taxonomy of human needs. He discussed 28 basic human needs—for example, the need for sex, the need for affiliation, the need for nurturance—including the need for achievement (*n* Ach), which he defined as "the desire or tendency to do things as rapidly and/or as well as possible" (p. 164).

David McClelland and his associates at Wesleyan University read Murray's work and became interested in the development of achievement motivation. McClelland et al. (1953) viewed *n* Ach as a learned motive that, like all other complex social motives, is acquired on the basis of the rewards and punishments that accompany certain kinds of behavior. If children are frequently reinforced for independence, competitiveness, and success, and if they meet with disapproval when they fail, their achievement motivation should be rather strong. But a child can hardly be expected to develop a strong need for achievement if he or she is not often encouraged to be independent, competitive, and highly competent in day-to-day activities and endeavors. In sum, the strength of an individual's achievement motive was thought to depend on the quality of his or her "achievement" training. McClelland et al. believed that the quality of achievement training received by children varied as a function of their culture, their social class, and the attitudes of their parents about the value of independence and achievement.

The first task faced by the Wesleyan group was to develop a method of measuring achievement motivation. What was needed was an instrument that measured the strength of one's desire to compete and to excel in situations in which standards of excellence are operable.

McClelland and his associates settled on the story-writing technique described earlier because they believed that a person's true underlying motives may be reflected in his fantasy life—that is, dreams, wishes, idle thoughts, and daydreams. They soon discovered that people varied a great deal in the amount of achievement imagery they displayed when writing stories about ambiguous work or study scenes. The next step, then, was to validate this measure by showing that people who scored high in the need for achievement would actually turn out to be high achievers, whereas those who scored low would display more modest accomplishments.

The relationship between achievement motivation and achievement behavior.

Is achievement motivation related in some meaningful way to achievement behavior? Indeed it is. Several studies conducted during the 1950s revealed that college students who score high in n Ach tend to have higher grade-point averages than those who score low (Bendig, 1958; McClelland et al., 1953; Weiss, Wertheimer, & Groesbeck, 1959). Moreover, Minor and Neel (1958) found that high need-achievers aspire to higher-status occupations than low need-achievers. So it seems that people who express a strong desire to achieve on the McClelland fantasy measure of n Ach

often do achieve at higher levels than those who test low in achievement motivation.

The achieving society.

What would happen if large numbers of high need-achievers were present in a culture at a given time? Would that culture take great strides forward, showing clear signs of technological or economic growth? McClelland asked these questions after reading the work of German sociologist Max Weber. In his book *The Protestant Ethic and the Spirit of Capitalism* (1904/1930), Weber noted that the Protestant countries of Europe were more productive and economically advanced than their Roman Catholic counterparts. He attributed this difference to the "Protestant ethic," a doctrine that encourages self-reliance, delay of gratification, and an evaluation of work as good in itself. In sum, Weber argued that the Protestant religious ideology was conducive to the development of a spirit of capitalism and increased economic productivity.

McClelland reanalyzed these arguments in terms of his own theory of achievement motivation. The central theme of his analysis can be summarized as follows:

Protestant ideology ⟶ Independence and achievement training by socialization agents ⟶ High need-achievers ⟶ Economic growth

There are data consistent with McClelland's model. First, McClelland, Rindlisbacher, and de Charms (1955) found that Protestant parents expect their children to show evidence of independence at an earlier age than Catholic parents do. This finding is consistent with the model's first link, the link between the Protestant ideology and child-rearing techniques. McClelland et al. also report that the Protestants among a group of German boys attained significantly higher n Ach scores than the Catholics. This result, in conjunction with the first, is consistent with the model's second link. Finally, McClelland (1955) found that in 1950—more than four decades after Weber's observations—Protestant countries (such as Australia, Canada, Great Britain, Sweden, and the United States) were still more economically advanced than Catholic countries (such as Austria, France, Ireland, Italy, and Spain). Although a number of factors other than societal differences in n Ach could have contributed to this last finding, McClelland nevertheless proposed a more general hypothesis that *the economic growth and development of a society should be predictable from the average level of achievement motivation of its populace.*

A direct test of this hypothesis appears in McClelland's (1961) book *The Achieving Society*, in which McClelland assessed the mean n Ach of each of 23 countries in a most interesting fashion. He simply obtained readers used in the primary grades in each country and scored the stories in these books for achievement imagery in the same way he typically scored stories that subjects might produce themselves. Children's readers were selected for study because they represent the popular culture of the country and, as such, are probably a reasonably good indication of the amount of achievement training that grade-school children are receiving at any given time. Readers from the 1920s and from the year 1950 were sampled. McClelland's goal was to see whether he could predict the subsequent economic growth of a country from the amount of achievement imagery present in its readers during the 1920s.

Economic growth was indexed by increases in the amount of electricity a country consumed between 1929 and 1950. Why did McClelland use this particular measure? For two reasons. First, use of electricity is highly correlated with most other measures of economic growth. Second and more important, the electricity-consumption index does not automatically handicap countries lacking natural resources such as coal or oil, for electricity can be produced in many ways. As he predicted he would, McClelland found a significant positive correlation ($r = +.53$) between the number of achievement themes in a country's readers during the 1920s and the country's increase in electrical consumption for the period 1929 to 1950. Although this relationship is consistent with his hypothesis, it does not necessarily mean that the n Ach of a society affects its subsequent economic growth. One rival hypothesis is that economic growth already underway during the 1920s was responsible for both a country's preoccupation with achievement during the 1920s and its later economic growth. But, if prior economic growth had been the causal agent, then the country's economic growth between 1929 and 1950 should be highly correlated with the number of achievement themes in its readers in 1950. *No such relationship was observed.* Thus, McClelland's cross-cultural data suggest that achievement motivation precedes economic growth and that a nation's mean n Ach is a barometer of its future economic accomplishments.[2]

Problems with McClelland's approach.   Although McClelland's work implied that achievement motivation is a reliable predictor of achievement behavior at both the individual and the group (or cultural) level, other investigators were having difficulty replicating his findings. Virginia Crandall (1967), for example, found that children high in n Ach outperformed their low-need-achieving agemates in fewer than half the studies she reviewed. Moreover, John Atkinson (1964) noticed that people who actually do accomplish a lot (high achievers) often differed from people who accomplish much less (low achievers) in their emotional reactions to achievement contexts: high achievers welcomed new challenges, whereas low achievers seemed to dread them. Why is it that achievement motivation often fails to forecast achievement behavior? Could there be other, competing motives that make achievement contexts so threatening to some people that their performance is impeded? Atkinson thought so, as we will see in his revision of McClelland's theory.

ATKINSON'S REVISION OF NEED ACHIEVEMENT THEORY

In outlining his theory of achievement motivation, Atkinson (1964) proposed that:

> in addition to a general disposition to achieve success [called the **motive to achieve success (M_s)**, or the achievement motive], there is also a general disposition to avoid failure, called **motive to avoid failure (M_{af})**. Where the motive to achieve might be characterized as a capacity for reacting with pride in accomplishment, the motive to avoid failure can be conceived as a capacity for reacting with shame and embarrassment when the outcome of performance

[2]This conclusion was strengthened by the results of a second study in which the n Ach scores for readers used in 39 countries in the year 1950 predicted the economic growth of those countries between 1952 and 1958 (McClelland, 1961).

is failure. When this disposition is aroused in a person, as it is aroused whenever it is clear . . . that his performance will be evaluated and failure is a distinct possibility, the result is anxiety and a tendency to withdraw from the situation [p. 244].

According to Atkinson, a person's tendency to approach or avoid achievement activities depends on the relative strength of these *two* competing motives. A person who willingly accepts new challenges and accomplishes a lot was presumed to have a motive to attain success that is considerably stronger than her motive to avoid failure (that is, $M_s > M_{af}$). By contrast, the low achiever who shies away from challenges and accomplishes little was thought to have a motive to avoid failure that is stronger than his motive to attain success (that is, $M_{af} > M_s$). So, in Atkinson's theory, the relationship between one's achievement motivation (M_s) and achievement behavior is clearly influenced by the strength of the motive to avoid failure (M_{af}).

Is it worth accomplishing? The value of a particular goal.   Atkinson also believed that the *value* one places on the success he might attain is an important determinant of achievement behavior. Virginia Crandall (1967) agreed. She noted that there are many, many areas in which children might achieve, including schoolwork, sports, hobbies, domestic skills, and friendship making, to name a few. Presumably, a child's willingness to set high standards and to work to attain them may differ from area to area depending, in part, on the **achievement value** of accomplishing these objectives or winning recognition for one's efforts. And it does seem obvious that we are more likely to strive for valuable or important goals than for those we consider trivial or unimportant. In fact, Atkinson (1964) went so far as to argue that global measures of achievement motivation were likely to predict actual accomplishments only for tasks that people consider valuable or important.

This hypothesis was later tested in an interesting study by Joel Raynor (1970). Students from an introductory psychology class took both the McClelland fantasy measure of *n* Ach (used to define M_s) and the *Test Anxiety Questionnaire*, an objective paper-and-pencil test that measures one's anxiety about being evaluated (used to define M_{af}). These stu-

dents also made judgments about how relevant they thought their introductory psychology course would be to their future careers. Raynor predicted that students who are high in achievement motivation (that is, those for whom $M_s > M_{af}$) would be more persistent in their attempts to do well in introductory psychology if they considered the course relevant to their future (high value) rather than irrelevant (low value). By contrast, students who are especially high in the motive to avoid failure (that is, those for whom $M_{af} > M_s$) might not do any better in psychology if the course was perceived as career relevant rather than irrelevant; in fact, the anxiety they may feel about the prospect of doing poorly in a valuable, career-relevant course might even interfere with learning and cause them to do worse.

Table 8-1 presents the results. As predicted, students for whom $M_s > M_{af}$ (those in the top row) obtained significantly *higher* grades if they considered introductory psychology relevant to their future careers. Apparently, achievement motivation is more likely to forecast noteworthy accomplishments when the goals one might attain are considered valuable or important. Notice also that subjects for whom $M_{af} > M_s$ actually obtained *lower* grades if their psychology course was considered career relevant. So a high fear of failure can actually inhibit progress toward valuable goals.

We see, then, that one's performance in achievement contexts depends on far more than his or her level of *n* Ach. To predict how a person is likely to fare when faced with a challenge, it also helps to know something about (1) the person's fear of failure (M_{af}) and (2) the perceived value of success—a *cognitive* variable that differs across individuals and achievement domains and is a crucial determinant of achievement behavior.

Can I achieve? The role of expectancies in achievement behavior.   Finally, Atkinson (1964) proposed that a second *cognitive* variable—our expectations of succeeding or failing should we try to achieve an objective—is a critical determinant of achievement behavior. He claimed that people are more likely to work hard when they feel that they have a reasonable prospect of succeeding than when they see little chance of attaining a goal. How important are these **achievement expectancies**? Very important,

TABLE 8-1 *Mean grade-point averages in introductory psychology as a function of achievement-related motives and the relevance of the course to future careers*

	Relevance of Course to One's Future	
Achievement Profiles	Low	High
$M_s > M_{af}$	2.93	3.37
$M_{af} > M_s$	3.00	2.59

NOTE: Mean grade-point averages are computed on a 4.00 scale where A = 4, B = 3, C = 2, D = 1, F = 0.
SOURCE: From J. O. Raynor, "Relationships between Achievement-Related Motives, Future Orientation, and Academic Performance." *Journal of Personality and Social Psychology*, 1970, 15, 28–33. Copyright © 1970 by the American Psychological Association. Reprinted by permission.

and we can illustrate this point with the following example. Were we to review the literature, we would find that IQ is a moderate-to-strong correlate of academic achievement, with brighter children typically outperforming their average-IQ or low-IQ classmates (Shaffer, 1993). Yet it is not uncommon for children with high IQs and low academic expectancies to earn *poorer* grades than their classmates with lower IQs but higher expectancies (Battle, 1966; Crandall, 1967; Phillips, 1984). In other words, expectations of success and failure are a powerful determinant of achievement behavior; children who expect to achieve usually do, whereas those who expect to fail may spend little time and effort pursuing goals they believe to be "out of reach" (Boggiano, Main, & Katz, 1988; Harter, 1988).

Summing up.   In sum, Atkinson's need achievement theory is a significant revision and extension of McClelland's earlier theory—a model that held that individual differences in achievement behavior are primarily attributable to the levels of achievement motivation (*n* Ach) that people display. Atkinson's theory is properly classified as a motivational model in that one's willingness to work hard to obtain various objectives is said to depend on the relative strength of two achievement-related motives: the motive to attain success (M_s) and the motive to avoid failure (M_{af}). But Atkinson also claims that two cognitive variables—*expectancies* of success (or failure) and the *value* of various objectives—are every bit as important as the motivational variables in

determining our achievement strivings and our actual accomplishments.

Recently, attribution (or social information-processing) theorists have focused more extensively on cognitive determinants of achievement in general and on the origins of achievement expectancies in particular. Let's now turn to the attributional perspective to see what it can tell us about children's propensities for achievement.

Attributional Theories of Achievement

Earlier in this chapter and throughout the text, we have noted that infants and toddlers are likely to view themselves as efficacious and to master many challenges when they have had ample opportunities to *control* their environments—that is, to regulate the behavior of responsive companions and to satisfy other objectives, such as successfully operating age-appropriate toys. Just how important is this sense of personal control to children's achievement expectancies and to the value they are likely to attach to their successes and failures? Let's see what attribution theorists have to say.

WEINER'S ATTRIBUTION THEORY

Bernard Weiner (1974, 1986) has proposed an attributional theory of achievement that claims that a person's achievement behavior depends very critically on how he interprets prior successes and failures and on whether he thinks he can *control* these outcomes. Weiner believes that human beings are active information processors who will sift through the data available to them and formulate explanations, or **causal attributions**, for their achievement outcomes. What kinds of attributions will they make? Although they might not always use these precise labels, Weiner argues that people are likely to attribute their successes or failures to any of four causes: (1) their *ability* (or lack thereof), (2) the amount of *effort* expended, (3) the *difficulty* (or easiness) of the task, or (4) the influence of *luck* (either good or bad).

Notice that two of these causes, ability and effort, are *internal* causes, or qualities of the individual, whereas the other two, task difficulty and luck, are *external* or environmental factors. This grouping of causes along an "internal/external" dimension follows from Virginia Crandall's earlier research on a dimension of personality called **locus of control** (Crandall, 1967). Individuals with an *internal locus of control* assume that they are personally responsible for what happens to them. If they received an A grade on an essay, they would probably attribute the mark to their superior writing ability or to their own hard work (internal causes). Individuals with an *external locus of control* believe that their outcomes depend more on luck, fate, or the actions of others than on their own abilities or efforts. They might say that on A grade was due to luck (the teacher happened to like this one), indiscriminate grading, or some other *external* cause. Crandall proposed that an internal locus of control is conducive to achievement: children must necessarily believe that *they* can produce positive outcomes if they are to strive for success and become high achievers. Children with an external locus of control would not be expected to strive for success or to become high achievers, because they assume that their efforts do not necessarily determine their outcomes.

Children's locus of control is usually measured by administering the *Intellectual Achievement Responsibility Questionnaire*, a 34-item scale that taps one's perceptions of responsibility for pleasant and unpleasant outcomes. Each item describes an achievement-related experience and asks the child to select either an internal or an external cause for that experience (see Figure 8-1 for sample items).

PHOTO 8-2   If youngsters believe they are personally responsible for their successes, they are more likely to become high achievers.

The more "internal" responses the child selects, the higher his or her internality score. Children who choose few internal responses are classified as externalizers.

In their review of more than 100 studies, Maureen Findley and Harris Cooper (1983) found that internalizers do earn higher grades and will typically outperform externalizers on standardized tests of academic achievement. In fact, one rather extensive study of minority students in the United States revealed that children's beliefs in internal control were a better predictor of their academic achievements than were their *n* Ach scores, their parents' child-rearing practices, or the type of classroom and teaching styles to which these students had been exposed (Coleman et al., 1966). So Crandall was right in assuming that a willingness to take personal responsibility for one's successes is conducive to achievement behavior.

How, then, does Weiner's theory differ from Crandall's earlier ideas about locus of control? The answer is straightforward: Weiner claims that the four possible causes for achievement outcomes also differ along a *stability* dimension. Ability and task difficulty are relatively stable or unchangeable. If you have high verbal ability today, you'll have roughly the same high ability tomorrow; and if a

---

1. *If a teacher passes you to the next grade, it would probably be*
   _____ a. because she liked you or
   *_____ b. because of the work that you did

2. *When you do well on a test at school, it is more likely to be*
   *_____ a. because you studied for it
   _____ b. because the test was especially easy

3. *When you read a story and can't remember much of it, it is usually*
   _____ a. because the story wasn't well written or
   *_____ b. because you weren't interested in the story

*Denotes the "internal" response for each sample item.

FIGURE 8-1   Sample items from the Intellectual Achievement Responsibility Questionnaire. (From V. C. Crandall, *Intellectual Achievement Responsibility Questionnaire*. Wright State University School of Medicine, Yellow Springs, Ohio.)

TABLE 8-2   *Weiner's classification of the causes of achievement outcomes (and examples of how you might explain a terrible test grade)*

	Locus of Causality	
	Internal Cause	*External Cause*
Stable Cause	*Ability* "I'm hopeless in math."	*Task difficulty* "That test was incredibly hard and much too long."
Unstable Cause	*Effort* "I should have studied more instead of going out to the concert."	*Luck* "What luck! Every question seemed to be about the days of class I missed."

particular kind of verbal problem is especially difficult, similar problems are also likely to be difficult. By contrast, the amount of effort one expends on a task or the workings of luck are variable, or unstable, from situation to situation. So Weiner classifies the four possible causes for successes and failures along *both* a locus of causality and a stability dimension, as shown in Table 8-2.

Contributions of "stability" and "locus of control" attributions to future achievement behavior.   Why is it important to consider both *locus* of causality and *stability* to classify causal attributions? Simply because each of these judgments has different consequences. According to Weiner, it is the stability dimension that determines achievement *expectancies*: outcomes attributed to stable causes lead to stronger expectancies than those attributed to unstable causes. To illustrate: a *success* that you attribute to your high ability leads you to confidently predict similar successes in the future. Had you attributed your success to an unstable cause that can vary from situation to situation (such as effort or luck), you should not be quite so confident of future successes. Conversely, *failures* attributed to stable causes we can do little about (such as low ability or task difficulty) also lead to strong expectancies—this time to negative expectancies that lead us to anticipate similar failures in the future. By contrast, attributing a failure to an unstable cause (such as not trying very hard) allows for the possibility of improvement and, hence, a less negative expectancy.

If the perceived stability of an achievement-related outcome determines achievement expectan-

cies, what role does locus of causality (or control) play? According to Weiner, judgments about the internality or externality of an outcome determine its *value* to the perceiver. Presumably, successes are most valuable when attributed to *internal* causes such as hard work or high ability; few of us would feel especially proud if we succeeded because of external causes such as blind luck or a ridiculously easy task. Yet, *failures* attributed to internal causes (especially to low ability) can be damaging to our self-esteem and may make us less inclined to strive for future success. Clearly, it seems fruitless to work hard to reverse a poor grade if we think we have little ability in the subject matter; in fact, the course may suddenly seem less valuable or important, and we might be inclined to drop it. But, if we can attribute our poor mark to an *external* cause (such as bad luck or an ambiguous exam), the failure should not make us feel especially critical of ourselves or undermine our feelings about the value of the course.

Notice that Weiner's attribution model resembles Atkinson's theory in stressing the importance of two cognitive variables: achievement expectancies and achievement value. But Weiner's approach assigns a primary role to the cognitive variables. Presumably, the perceived locus of causality for achievement outcomes affects our *valuation* of these successes and failures, whereas our attributions about the stability of these outcomes affect our *achievement expectancies*. Together, these two judgments (expectancy and value) determine our willingness (motivation) to undertake similar achievement-related activities in the future (see Figure 8-2 for a schematic overview of Weiner's theory).

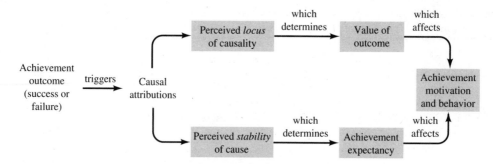

FIGURE 8-2   An overview of Weiner's attribution theory of achievement.

Now, if Weiner's theory is correct, high achievers should generally attribute their successes to stable, internal causes (high ability) and their failures to unstable factors (such as insufficient effort) that they can do something about. By contrast, low achievers might attribute successes to unstable causes (luck or high effort) while ascribing their failures to stable, internal causes (such as low ability) that could undermine their achievement motivation. Do high and low achievers display these different patterns of attributions?

Adults generally do (Weiner, 1982, 1986). Moreover, adults often draw some sophisticated conclusions about the relationships among Weiner's four causal factors, such as assuming that ability and effort are inversely related. For example, if a person succeeds at a challenging task while expending little effort, we assume that she has high ability—much higher ability than a second person who achieves the same success but has to work very hard to do so. Are children capable of distinguishing among the four causal components of Weiner's model? Do they make the same kinds of causal attributions about successes and failures that adults do?

Age differences in children's achievement attributions. Apparently, children do not draw the same kinds of causal inferences about achievement outcomes that adults do. Recall Stipek's finding (Stipek et al., 1992) that older preschool children feel successful and efficacious *whenever* they master a task. Although 4- and 5-year-olds do feel better about winning a competition than about losing, they do not perceive a loss as a "failure" in the same way

that failing to complete a task would be viewed. Other research with young grade-schoolers consistently indicates that, before age 7 or so, children are unrealistic optimists who think they have the ability to succeed on almost any novel task (Dweck & Elliott, 1983; Stipek & Mac Iver, 1989).[3] This rosy optimism is based in part on wishful thinking; the more young children want to succeed, the more they believe they will succeed, even on tasks they have repeatedly failed at in the past (Stipek, Roberts, & Sanborn, 1984). Kindergarten and primary-grade teachers may contribute to this outlook by setting mastery goals (rather than encouraging competition) and by praising children more for their efforts than for the quality of their work, thus leading them to believe that they can accomplish much and "be smart" by working hard (Rosenholtz & Simpson, 1984; Stipek & Mac Iver, 1989). Indeed, young children do seem to have an **incremental view of ability**: they believe that ability is changeable, not stable, and that they can get smarter or become more capable through increased effort and lots of practice (Dweck & Leggett, 1988; Stipek & Mac Iver, 1989).

When do children begin to distinguish ability from effort? When do they adopt an **entity view of ability**—a perspective that ability is a fixed or stable

[3]One exception to this general rule may occur if children are strongly criticized for their mistakes. After pointed criticism, about 10% of the 5- to 6-year-olds in one study quit trying to master the kinds of tasks on which they had received criticism and reported feeling bad about themselves (Heyman, Dweck, & Cain, 1992). But, in the absence of criticism, these youngsters almost invariably felt that they had high ability to perform the experimental tasks, even after they had failed.

TABLE 8-3 *Numbers of children at each grade falling into each of the four levels of reasoning about ability and effort*

	Level of Reasoning			
Grade	1 *Effort or Outcome Is Ability*	2 *Effort Causes Outcomes*	3 *Incomplete Differentiation*	4 *Ability Is Capacity*
2nd (7-year-olds)	10	44	6	0
5th (10-year-olds)	4	22	12	22
8th (13-year-olds)	3	5	9	43

SOURCE: J. G. Nicholls & A. T. Miller, "Reasoning about the Ability of Self and Others: A Developmental Study." *Child Development*, 1984, 55, 1990–1999. Copyright © 1984 by the Society for Research in Child Development.

trait that is not influenced much by effort or practice? John Nicholls and Arden Miller (1984; see also Nicholls, 1989) have reviewed the literature and concluded that children's thinking about ability and effort may progress through as many as four levels, or stages, over the course of middle childhood:

Level 1: Effort or outcome is ability. At this first level, children focus mainly on effort and occasionally on outcomes when making ability judgments. People who try harder are seen as smarter even if they get a lower score. If the child should focus on outcomes, then people who score higher are said to have worked harder (even if they have not) and thus are perceived as smarter.

Level 2: Effort is the cause of outcomes. Now children think that the amount of effort one expends is the primary determinant of success and failure. Equal effort will lead to equal outcomes. And, if two persons achieve the same goal after working different amounts of time, the child will assume that the person who worked longer made mistakes or that the one who spent less time at the task must have tried harder while she was working.

Level 3: Effort and ability are partially differentiated. Effort is still the primary, but no longer the only, cause of achievement outcomes. If two persons experience equal outcomes after unequal efforts, the child may say that one is brighter than the other. However, some confounding of effort

and ability is still apparent, because these same two persons would be expected to achieve exactly the same outcomes if they applied equal effort.

Level 4: Ability is capacity. Ability and effort are now clearly differentiated. The child now realizes that, if two persons have equal attainments, the one who worked harder has *less* ability than the person who breezed through the task.

In their own study of children's thinking about ability and effort, Nicholls and Miller (1984) asked second-, fifth-, and eighth-graders to compare the ability of either themselves or a peer with that of another person who had achieved *exactly the same score* after expending either *more* or *less* effort on a set of experimental tasks. When asked which person was smarter, 7-year-old second-graders reliably chose the person who had expended more effort, whereas the 13-year-old eighth-graders picked the lazier child who had expended little effort. All four levels of reasoning about ability and effort were observed in this study, and, as we see in Table 8-3, there was evidence of a clear age progression: second-graders tended to be at levels 1 and 2, whereas many eighth-graders recognized the inverse relation between ability and effort, thereby falling into level 4.

Nicholls and Miller (1985) have also shown that there are four similar levels of reasoning about the concepts of luck and skill. Five-year-olds believe that children who try harder will perform better on both "luck" tasks (where outcomes are determined by chance) and "skill" tasks (where outcomes really do depend on effort). By contrast, most 12- to 13-year-olds know that only luck influences outcomes in games of chance, whereas effort will affect one's likelihood of success on tasks requiring skill.

Notice that many children are treating ability, effort, luck, and task difficulty as separate and distinct by age 12 to 13—about the time that they are approaching formal operations and might be more capable of the kinds of rapid mental reversals that should enable them to see how these four causes can vary along *two* abstract dimensions (locus of control and stability) at the *same time*. However, social influences are also important in shaping children's causal attributions about achievement outcomes. Consider that, as children progress through grade school, effort ceases to be the major criterion for evaluating performance as teachers place more and more emphasis on *ability* appraisals. Indeed, older children are rarely praised for merely completing assignments. Instead, they receive grades that reflect the *quality* of their work rather than the quantity of effort they've expended. Moreover, these performance evaluations become more frequent in the higher grades and are supplemented by such competitive activities as spelling bees and science fairs, which also place a premium on the quality rather than the quantity of one's efforts. Finally, older grade-school children are often placed into "ability groups" based on the teacher's appraisal of their competencies (Rosenholtz & Simpson, 1984; Stipek & Mac Iver, 1989). So all these practices, combined with older children's increased use of social comparison to appraise their own outcomes (Aboud, 1985; Butler, 1990), may be as important as cognitive development in explaining why preadolescents are clearly distinguishing ability from effort and are beginning to make the kinds of causal attributions that Weiner's theory anticipates (Lord, Umezaki, & Darley, 1990; Stipek & Mac Iver, 1989).

Do these age trends imply that Weiner's theory is not relevant for children younger than 12 or 13? No, they do not. Even though younger children may not always think about Weiner's four causes for achieve-ment-related outcomes in precisely the same ways that many adults do, we will see in the next section that 8–12-year-olds develop general attributional patterns or styles that (1) are clearly based on information about the locus of control and perceived stability of their achievement outcomes and (2) can have a profound effect on their future achievement behavior. Indeed, one of the more fascinating aspects of the work we are about to review is the notion that a strong separation of effort and ability and the adoption of an *entity view* of ability are not always adaptive and can even undermine a child's propensity for achievement. Nowhere is this any more apparent than in Carol Dweck's research on learned helplessness, to which we now turn.

DWECK'S LEARNED-HELPLESSNESS THEORY

Carol Dweck and her associates have carefully analyzed the *patterns* of attributions that children display when explaining their achievement outcomes and the effects of these attributional styles on later achievement behavior. In Dweck's experiments, grade-school children are asked to perform a series of tasks, on which their "successes" and "failures" are arranged by the researcher. Of interest are the kinds of attributions that children offer to account for these outcomes and their willingness to persist at similar achievement tasks in the future.

Dweck and her colleagues (see Dweck & Elliott, 1983; Dweck & Leggett, 1988) find that there are reliable individual differences in the ways children react to achievement outcomes—particularly to *failure* experiences. Some children appear to be **mastery oriented**: they attribute their successes to their high ability but tend to externalize the blame for their failures ("That test was ambiguous and unfair") or to attribute them to unstable causes that they can easily overcome ("I'll do better if I try harder"). These students are called "mastery oriented" because they persist in the face of failure, believing that their increased effort will allow them to succeed. Although they see their ability as a reasonably stable attribute that doesn't fluctuate radically from day to day (which allows them to feel confident about repeating their successes), they do acknowledge that competencies are malleable (an *incremental* viewpoint) and can be improved by trying hard after a failure (Dweck & Leggett, 1988). So mastery-oriented youngsters are highly motivated to "master" important challenges, regardless of whether they have previously succeeded or failed at similar tasks.

By contrast, other children often attribute their successes to the unstable factors of hard work or luck; they do not experience the pride and self-esteem that come from viewing themselves as highly competent. Yet they often attribute their failures to a stable and internal factor—namely, their *lack of ability*—which causes them to form low expectations of future successes and to give up. It appeared to Dweck as if these youngsters were displaying a **learned helplessness orientation**: if failures are attributed to a *stable* cause—lack of ability—that the child thinks he can do little about (an *entity view* of competence), he becomes frustrated and sees little reason to try to improve. So he stops trying and acts helpless.

It is important to note that children who display this learned-helplessness syndrome are *not* just the least competent members of a typical classroom. In fact, Dweck (1978) reports that the previous academic attainments of helpless subjects often equal or exceed those of their mastery-oriented classmates! In a similar vein, Deborah Phillips (1984) has studied the achievement orientations of a large number of *high-ability* fifth-graders, about 20% of whom had academic self-concepts that seriously underestimated their abilities. The high-ability students who held inaccurate self-perceptions displayed several aspects of the learned-helplessness syndrome: compared with children who had accurate perceptions of their own abilities, members of this self-denigrating group (1) set less demanding achievement standards for themselves and held lower expectancies for success; (2) were portrayed by their teachers as showing poor persistence in academic activities; and (3) tended to attribute their successes to unstable causes, such as effort, rather than to stable ones, such as high ability. So it appears that almost anyone, even highly competent children who have often succeeded at achievement

tasks, could eventually learn to stop trying and act helpless in the face of failure.

How does learned helplessness develop? According to Dweck (1978), parents and teachers may unwittingly foster the development of a helpless orientation if they praise the child for *working hard* when she succeeds but *question her ability* when she fails. Apparently, even 5- to 6-year-olds can begin to develop a helpless orientation if their failures are criticized in ways that cause them to doubt their competencies (Heyman et al., 1992). By contrast, if parents and teachers praise the child's *abilities* when she succeeds but emphasize her *lack of effort* when she fails, the child may conclude that she is certainly smart enough and would do even better if she tried harder—the viewpoint adopted by mastery-oriented youngsters. Dweck and her associates (1978) observed fifth-grade teachers as they gave their students evaluative feedback and found that teachers did indeed use different patterns with different students. Some students received the evaluative pattern thought to contribute to a mastery orientation, whereas others (mainly girls) received the pattern thought to contribute to learned helplessness. But do these evaluative patterns really have much effect on children's achievement orientations?

Dweck et al. (1978) tried to answer this question in an interesting experiment. Fifth-graders worked on a series of 20 word puzzles (anagrams), of which half were easy and half were insoluble. The experimenter's evaluation of the child's performance on failure trials was then manipulated. Children assigned to the *mastery pattern* condition heard the experimenter respond to their failure by criticizing their efforts and implying that they needed to work harder. Children assigned to the *helpless pattern* condition heard the experimenter focus on the incorrectness of their solutions, as if to imply that they had little ability at this kind of task. After attempting the word puzzles and working on an unrelated task at which they were told that they were not doing very well, the children were asked to respond anonymously to the following attribution question: "If the man told you that you did not do very well . . . why do you think that was? (a) I did not try hard enough [effort], (b) the man was too fussy [agent], (c) I am not very good at it [ability]."

The answers children gave to this question were quite consistent with Dweck's hypothesis about the importance of evaluative feedback. As we can see in Table 8-4, 75% of the children who had earlier received the helpless pattern of evaluation while working the word puzzles later attributed their failure on the second task to their own lack of ability. By contrast, 75% of the children who had earlier received the mastery pattern of evaluation attributed their failure to a lack of effort or externalized the blame by saying that the evaluator was too fussy. These strikingly different attributional styles are all the more remarkable when we note that they took less than one hour to establish in this experiment. So it seems reasonable to conclude that similar patterns of evaluative feedback from parents or teachers, given consistently over a period of months or years, might well contribute to the development of the contrasting "helpless" and "mastery" orientations so often observed among grade school (and older) students.

On helping the helpless to achieve.   Obviously, a child's giving up in the face of a challenge is not the kind of achievement orientation that adults would hope to encourage — especially in light of recent evidence that, once established, learned helplessness tends to persist over time and will eventually undermine the child's academic performance (Fincham, Hokoda, & Sanders, 1989). What can be done to help these "helpless" children to persist at tasks they have failed? According to Dweck, the most effective therapy might be a form of **attribution retraining**, in which helpless children are persuaded to attribute their failures to unstable causes — namely, insufficient effort — that they can do something about, rather than continuing to view them as stemming from their lack of ability, which is not so easily modifiable.

Dweck (1975) tested her hypothesis by exposing children who had become helpless after failing a series of tough math problems to either of two "therapies." Over a period of 25 therapy sessions, half the children received a *success-only* therapy in which

TABLE 8-4   *Percentage of children in each evaluation condition attributing failure feedback to a lack of ability, a lack of effort, or an overly fussy evaluator*

	Type of Attribution		
Evaluative Pattern	*Lack of Ability*	*Lack of Effort*	*Fussy Evaluator*
Helpless pattern	75	25	0
Mastery pattern	25	65	10

SOURCE: C. S. Dweck, W. Davidson, S. Nelson, & B. Enna, "Sex Differences in Learned Helplessness: II. The Contingencies of Evaluative Feedback in the Classroom; III. An Experimental Analysis." *Developmental Psychology*, 1978, 14, 268–276. Copyright © 1978 by the American Psychological Association.

they worked problems they could solve and received tokens for their successes. The other half received *attribution retraining* — they experienced nearly as many successes over the 25 sessions as did the children in the other group but were also told after each of several prearranged failures that they had not worked fast enough and *should have tried harder*. Thus an explicit attempt was made to convince these youngsters that failures can reflect a lack of effort rather than a lack of ability. Did this therapy work? Yes, indeed! At the end of the experiment, helpless children in the attribution-retraining condition now performed much better on the tough math problems they had initially failed; and, when they did fail one, they usually attributed their outcome to a lack of effort and tried all the harder. By contrast, children in the success-only condition showed no such improvements, giving up once again after failing the original problems. So merely showing helpless children that they are capable of succeeding is not enough! To alleviate learned helplessness, one must teach children to respond more constructively to their *failures* by viewing them as something they can overcome if they try harder.

On a practical note, Licht and Dweck (1984) have proposed that certain academic subjects (such as math and science) may be particularly difficult for helpless children. The problem with these particular subjects is that, at the beginning of new units, they often contain unfamiliar and seemingly confusing terms and concepts—precisely the kinds of material that may pique the curiosity of mastery-oriented youngsters while convincing helpless ones that these subjects are much too complex for them to understand. To test this hypothesis, Licht and Dweck presented groups of helpless and mastery-oriented fifth-graders with two versions of new academic material, provided time for the children to master this material, and then tested them to see what they had learned. One version of the material was written in clearly understandable language in which all new concepts were carefully defined; the second version presented the same material in a somewhat confusing (but grammatically correct) style that would require persistent effort from the child to achieve the same level of understanding. The results of this experiment, which appear in Figure 8-3, were quite consistent with Licht and Dweck's hypothesis. Notice that a sizable majority of both the helpless and the mastery-oriented children did well on the exam if they had read the clear version of the new material. By contrast, only about one-third of the helpless children (compared with 72% of their mastery-oriented classmates) mastered the material presented in the complex version. It appeared that many helpless youngsters simply gave up and stopped trying to learn if they had faced early difficulties in understanding the subject matter.

One implication of these results is that teachers could assist their more "helpless" pupils to assimilate difficult new concepts by restructuring lesson plans to show how new material builds on information that students already know. For example, one might introduce the concept of multiplication by going slowly and showing the child how this operation is really an extension of addition, rather than simply presenting the multiplication tables and requiring children to memorize them. The beauty of this "cumulative" approach is that it links new concepts to familiar ones and, thus, should be less likely to make the helpless child dwell on perceived inadequacies or on the prospect of failing. And, if Licht and Dweck's findings are any guide, it would seem that this cumulative, incremental approach to instruction will benefit the more helpless members

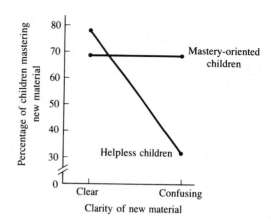

FIGURE 8-3 Percentages of children who mastered new academic material as a function of the clarity of that material and the children's achievement orientations. (From B. G. Licht & C. S. Dweck, "Determinants of Academic Achievement: The Interaction of Children's Achievement Orientations with Skill Area." *Developmental Psychology*, 1984, 20, 628–636. Copyright © 1984 by the American Psychological Association. Reprinted by permission.)

of a class without undermining the performance of their mastery-oriented classmates.

Are attribution retraining and restructuring of lesson plans really the best ways to combat learned helplessness? Can we do better than this? Perhaps we can if we begin to think in terms of *preventing* learned helplessness rather than treating it after the fact. One such preventive strategy that educators might wish to consider is described in Box 8-1.

Reflections on Competence and Achievement

Having now reviewed four major achievement theories, it should be obvious that children's propensities for achievement involve far more than an innate mastery motive or a global need for achievement. Clearly, McClelland and his associates made an important contribution by showing that people reliably differ in their *motivation* to achieve and by suggesting how this motive might be nurtured, although their notion that achievement motivation was a global attribute that predicted one's reactions to all achievement tasks now seems badly overstated. Atkinson's revision of need achievement theory pointed to the existence of a competing "motive to avoid failure" that can make people shy away from challenging tasks to avoid the embarrassment of failing. Of course, Atkinson's model also broke important new ground by emphasizing that achievement-related cognitions — namely, one's *expectancies* of succeeding and the incentive *value* of success — are important determinants of achievement behavior. Weiner's later attribution theory, which grew out of Crandall's earlier work on achievement expectancies and locus of control, has illustrated how our explanations, or *causal attributions*, for achievement outcomes contribute to our achievement expectancies and to the perceived value of our success and failure experiences. Finally, Dweck's learned-helplessness theory takes us back to the starting point by demonstrating how well-ingrained attributional styles affect children's *motivation* to persist at challenging tasks that they have initially failed to master. So, as we concluded when reviewing the various theories of attachment in Chapter 5, it makes no sense to brand any single achievement theory as "correct" and to ignore the others. Each of these theories has helped us to understand why children differ so dramatically when responding to the challenges they face.

Social Influences on Achievement

Now that we have reviewed the major achievement theories, it is time to ask some very practical questions about the development of children's pro-

---

BOX 8-1 | On Restructuring Achievement Goals to Minimize (or Prevent) Learned Helplessness

Theory. Recently, Elaine Elliott and Carol Dweck (1988) argued that children pursue either of two goals in achievement situations: (1) **performance goals**, in which they seek to display their competencies (or avoid looking incompetent), and (2) **learning goals**, in which they seek to *increase* their abilities or master new tasks. According to Elliott and Dweck, mastery-oriented students favor learning goals: when seeking to master a challenge or to improve their competencies, these youngsters treat initial failures as evidence that their learning strategies are inadequate; consequently, they adopt new strategies and keep working. By contrast, helpless children seem to be pursuing performance goals: they give up after failing because their failure has *immediately* undermined their objective, which was to display their competencies. Would children who are prone to helplessness be more persistent at achievement tasks if they adopted a "learning goal" to *improve* their abilities — a goal that is not immediately undermined by an early mistake or two?

Research. To test the plausibility of their goal-based model of helplessness, Elliott and Dweck had fifth-graders perform a novel task, led them to believe they had either high or low ability at this kind of activity, and then told them they would soon be performing similar tasks, some of which would be rather difficult (thus leading the children to anticipate errors). Half the children worked under a *performance goal*, having been told that their performances were going to be compared with those of other children and evaluated by an expert. The remaining children were induced to adopt a *learning goal* through instructions suggesting that, although they would make many mistakes, working at the tasks would "sharpen the mind" and help them at school. As anticipated, children made many errors on the new tasks they performed. And also as anticipated, the only children who displayed telltale signs of help-

pensities for achievement. For example, is a child's achievement orientation at all influenced by the culture or subculture in which he is raised? Anthropologists and sociologists think so, as we will see in the following section. Developmentalists have been concerned with another important issue: are some home environments or patterns of child rearing more conducive to achievement than others? Social-learning theorists have focused on particular social and situational determinants of achievement. How, for example, do peers and other social models influence children's achievement behavior? When should adults try to encourage achievement by providing material rewards, and under what circumstances might such a strategy backfire? And how can we explain the finding that girls and young women reliably underestimate their propensities for achievement, whereas boys and young men tend to overestimate theirs? These are some of the issues we

will consider as we review many of the social and situational contributors to children's achievement orientations.

Cultural and Subcultural Influences on Achievement

There is ample evidence from the anthropological literature that a child's cultural heritage does affect his or her achievement orientation. In one of the larger and more extensive studies, Barry, Child, and Bacon (1959) hypothesized that societies dependent on an agricultural or pastoral economy (those that accumulate food) would stress obedience, responsibility, and cooperation when raising their children. Groups that do not accumulate food (hunting and fishing societies) were expected to train their children to be independent, assertive, and venturesome. In other words, both types of society were

---

B O X **8-1** | *continued*

lessness (that is, deteriorating performance, low ability attributions) were those who thought they had low ability *and* were pursuing a *performance* goal. By contrast, even "low ability" students persisted after initial failures and showed remarkably little distress if they were pursuing a learning goal in which the focus was on *improving* their competencies rather than displaying them.

Applications. As presently structured, most classrooms stress performance goals and foster the development of an *entity view* of ability—a notion that ability is stable and largely unchangeable. Students undertake the same assignments, their performances are compared, and they receive recognition (praise, gold stars, grades, and the like) that places undue attention on their relative abilities—information that seems to undermine many students' intrinsic interest in the subject matter (Butler, 1989, 1990) and may seriously depress the perceived competencies and self-esteem of slower

learners, who compare so unfavorably with their peers (Butler, 1992; Ruble & Flett, 1988). Might we prevent these undesirable consequences by restructuring classroom goals—by emphasizing *individual mastery* of particular learning objectives (learning goals) rather than continuing to place children in direct competition (as teachers often do by saying "Let's see who can finish first," ". . . come up with the best answer," and so on) and making comparative appraisals of their progress? Many contemporary researchers think so (see Butler, 1989, 1990; Stipek & Mac Iver, 1989). And, if Elliott and Dweck's results are any guide, it would seem that a stronger emphasis on individual mastery would be particularly beneficial to the slower learners, who should begin to view their initial mistakes as evidence that they must change strategies to *improve* their competencies (an *incremental view* of ability) rather than treating these errors as proof that they have little ability and simply cannot learn.

expected to stress the kinds of values that are necessary to maintain their way of life. Barry et al. used existing anthropological data to review the economic characteristics and child-rearing techniques of 104 mostly underdeveloped, *preliterate societies* from all over the world. As predicted, they found that agricultural and pastoral societies placed strong pressures on their children to be responsible, cooperative, and obedient, whereas hunting and fishing societies stressed assertiveness, self-reliance, and the pursuit of individual goals.

Berry (1967) extended these findings by comparing members of high- and low-food-accumulative cultures on a measure of independence and conformity. Arctic Eskimo, a people who are forced by their geography to hunt and fish for a living, served as the low-food-accumulative group. The Temne of Sierra Leone, a group whose livelihood depends on the successful planting, harvesting, and rationing of a single crop (rice), were selected as the high-food-accumulative group. Individuals from these two societies were asked to make comparisons among lines that differed in length. For each comparison, the subject was shown a standard line and eight test lines. The subject's task was to select the test line that was the same length as the standard. Before each judgment, the experimenter presented fictitious group norms by telling the subject "Most Temne (Eskimo) people say this line [an incorrect choice] is equal in length to the standard." The incorrect line that was five lines away from the correct one served as the contrived group norm for each trial (see Figure 8-4). The distance of the subject's choice away from the correct line and in the direction of the contrived norm served as a measure of conformity for that trial. A total conformity score was determined by simply adding across trials the number of lines a subject's choice was away from the correct lines.

As expected, Berry found that the Temne largely conformed to the contrived group norms, whereas the Eskimo disregarded normative information and displayed their independence by selecting the correct lines (or lines very close to the correct ones). One Temne illustrated the cultural roots of his conformity by stating "When Temne people choose a

The top line on the stimulus card is the standard. On each trial, the subject is informed that one of the other lines (designated here by the asterisk) was most often perceived to be the same length as the standard by members of a reference group. The correct choice for this card is the second line from the bottom.

FIGURE 8-4 A common method of measuring conformity to group norms. (Adapted from J. W. Berry, "Independence and Conformity in Subsistence-Level Societies." *Journal of Personality and Social Psychology*, 1967, 7, 415–418.)

thing, we must all agree with the decision—that is what we call cooperation" (Berry, 1967, p. 417). Eskimo subjects spoke infrequently while making their judgments, although they sometimes flashed confident smiles as they rejected the group norm in favor of a line much nearer to the correct one.

We see, then, that people from different societies think of achievement in very different ways. To a person from a food-accumulative society, achievement implies that one must suppress individualism and work for the greater good of the group. By contrast, people from other societies are much more likely to stress individual accomplishments and *personal merit* as indications that one has achieved.

Of course, the stress on independence versus cooperation is only one of many cultural values that affect children's achievement orientation. As another example, we can cite a clear cultural difference in the connections that people make between effort and achievement: compared to American mothers, Chinese and Japanese mothers believe that scholastic achievement is far more dependent on the amount of effort a child expends than on his or her innate ability (Stevenson & Lee, 1990). In other words, Oriental parents adopt more of an *incremental* perspective on ability than American parents do—a perspective that seems to carry over to their children and may prevent those youngsters from acting helpless when they experience difficulties with their lessons. We will explore these intriguing cultural differences in more detail when we consider the topic of schooling and scholastic influences in Chapter 14.

Finally, the members of any given culture will vary considerably in their levels of achievement motivation, their expectations of achieving should they try, and their actual achievement behavior. Large multiethnic countries such as the United States and Canada are particularly interesting in this regard, for such a society is more accurately characterized as a collection of subcultures that show certain similarities but differ in many respects. Are there clear subcultural differences in achievement?

ETHNIC VARIATIONS IN ACHIEVEMENT

In a recent review of the literature, Diana Slaughter-Defoe and her associates (1990) noted that there are clear ethnic variations in achievement—at least in the area of academic achievement (which has been most heavily studied). Although tremendous individual differences exist within any ethnic group, African-American, Native-American, and Hispanic children show lower achievement in school than their Anglo classmates, whereas Asian Americans (at least Japanese and Chinese Americans) perform slightly better, on average, than their Anglo classmates (Slaughter-Defoe et al., 1990; Tharp, 1989). What factors might account for these ethnic variations?

One early hypothesis was that ethnic differences in scholastic achievement reflect group differences in intelligence. Indeed, students from underachieving ethnic minority groups do perform at somewhat lower levels on IQ tests than Anglo-American or Asian-American students (Minton & Schneider, 1980). But a word of interpretative caution is in order here, for IQ tests are merely assessments of current intellectual performance and may seriously underestimate the test taker's intellectual *competencies* (Shaffer, 1993). Moreover, even when their cognitive abilities upon entering school match those of Anglo-American students, children from underachieving ethnic minorities are often lagging behind in scholastic achievement by the end of the first grade (see,

for example, Alexander & Entwisle, 1988). So it seems that factors other than intellectual differences must figure prominently in explaining ethnic variations in achievement.

Another explanation for ethnic variations in achievement is that a greater percentage of students from underachieving ethnic minority groups are from lower socioeconomic backgrounds—a factor that is known to be associated with poorer academic performance (see below). In other words, the argument is that ethnic variations in scholastic achievement really represent social-class effects. Consistent with this viewpoint, Charlotte Patterson and her associates (Patterson, Kupersmidt, & Vaden, 1990) recently found that variation in family income (an indicator of socioeconomic status) is a better predictor of the academic competencies of African-American and white schoolchildren than is race per se. Still, even after controlling for social class, African-American students did not perform as well academically as their white classmates. Why is this?

Certainly *not* because their parents devalue the importance of schooling or academic achievement. Indeed, one recent study (Stevenson, Chen, & Uttal, 1990) found that African-American and Hispanic mothers actually expressed *more* concern about their children's education and were *more likely* to see the value of homework, competency testing, and a longer school day than were mothers of Anglo-American children (see also Alexander & Entwisle, 1988). Today many developmentalists believe that ethnic variations in achievement may be attributable not so much to differences in parental attitudes about the value of education as to (1) subtle subcultural differences in parenting practices and (2) differences across ethnic groups in peer endorsement of academics.

Subcultural variations in parenting. Elsie Moore (1986) compared African-American children adopted into white middle-class homes with African-American adoptees in middle-class African-American homes. Both these groups of African-American adoptees displayed above-average cognitive performances when tested at age 7 to 10. But, even though the two groups were from the same social class, children in the white homes were outperforming those from the African-American homes. Why should this be?

Moore tried to find out by carefully observing the children as they took an IQ test and by noting how their mothers interacted with them as the children tried to master a difficult cognitive challenge. What she found is what she believes to be subcultural differences in parenting and in test taking, even within the same social class. For example, children who had been placed into the white homes seemed to enjoy the IQ-testing session more than their counterparts from the African-American homes did: they were more eager to answer questions, they persisted longer at the tasks, and they seemed much more self-confident. By contrast, children from African-American homes often seemed to want to escape the testing situation, and they sometimes shook their heads, as if to say that they didn't know an answer, even before the question was completed. These styles of test taking were linked to the parenting practices mothers used while supervising their children's problem-solving activities. Compared with the African-American mothers, white mothers provided a great deal of *positive* encouragement. They joked to relieve tension, often cheered when their children showed some progress, and seemed to convey the attitude that mastering challenges can be fun. By contrast, African-American mothers were more inclined to try to urge their children onward by showing mild signs of *displeasure* at a child's *lack of progress* (perhaps conveying to the child that tackling challenges involves a risk of disapproval), and their evaluations of their children's performance were somewhat more negative than those of white mothers. Perhaps this is why their children were less comfortable during the IQ-testing session than were children of white mothers.

In sum, Moore's (1986) findings suggest that, even when children from different ethnic backgrounds all grow up in advantaged homes, there may still be subtle differences in parenting styles that contribute to ethnic variations in scholastic achievement (see also Alexander & Entwisle, 1988; Slaughter-Defoe et al., 1990; and Stevenson et al., 1990, for further discussion of this point).

Peer-group influences.   Finally, Lawrence Steinberg and his associates (Steinberg, Dornbusch, & Brown, 1992) have identified what they believe to be a *potent* contributor to ethnic differences in academic achievement: the value that peers place on achieving academic success. Steinberg et al. found that parenting practices and familial values about education simply do not predict the academic performance of African-American and Hispanic adolescents in the same way they do for Anglo-American youths. Why? Because the African-American and Hispanic peer cultures provide little support to youngsters who strive to achieve and may often discourage such activity. Indeed, Steinberg et al. noted that high-achieving African-American students often choose to limit their contact with other African-American youths and to affiliate primarily with students from other ethnic groups (most notably Anglo- and Asian-American peers, who are more inclined to endorse the pursuit of academic excellence). So, even when parents strongly encourage their children to achieve (as most minority parents do) and rely on parenting practices (to be reviewed below) known to promote a positive orientation toward achievement, their efforts may be moderated by a peer culture that devalues scholastic pursuits (Steinberg et al., 1992).

SOCIAL-CLASS DIFFERENCES IN ACHIEVEMENT

In addition to their membership in particular racial or ethnic groups, children also differ in their social-class standing or **socioeconomic status (SES)** — that is, their positions within a society that is stratified according to status and power. In Western societies the most common measures of a family's social class — family income, prestige of parents' occupations, and parents' educational levels — are based on the family's current or prior accomplishments. So in these cultures social class is clearly an achievement-related construct, and it is perhaps not surprising to find that children from middle- and upper-class backgrounds score higher in *n* Ach and are more likely to do well in school than children from the lower socioeconomic strata (see Hess, 1970; Patterson et al., 1990).

As was the case with ethnic variations in achievement, social-class differences in achievement were first attributed to group differences in intelligence. Middle- and upper-class children do tend to score somewhat higher on IQ tests than lower- and working-class youngsters do (Minton & Schneider, 1980), thus implying that children from the higher socioeconomic strata may have an "intellectual advantage" that contributes to their greater achievements. Nevertheless, most contemporary theorists believe that class-linked variations in parenting are probably more important than intelligence in explaining social-class differences in academic achievement. Indeed, it has been argued (and shown) that economic hardship creates psychological distress — a strong dissatisfaction with life's conditions that makes lower-income adults edgy and irritable and reduces their capacity to be sensitive, supportive, and highly involved in their children's learning activities, either as direct participants or as monitors of the child's (or adolescent's) educational progress (Conger et al., 1992; McLoyd, 1990).

Influences from outside the family may also contribute to social-class differences in academic achievement. For example, teachers often respond in stereotyped ways to children from lower socioeconomic backgrounds, subtly (or not so subtly) communicating that they do not expect them to accomplish as much as their middle-class agemates. And, as we will see in Chapter 14, even young grade-school children are aware of these teacher expectancies and may begin to perform in class so as to confirm them. So the very people who are charged with educating our youth may contribute to social-class differences in scholastic achievement.

Although they would not quibble with the conclusions we have drawn, there are some theorists who believe that socioeconomic status is not even the most important contributor to class-linked variations in achievement. One such theorist is Jonathan Turner, whose interesting ideas are presented in Box 8-2.

In sum, a person's propensity for achievement may indeed be influenced by the teachings and values of his culture and subculture. Yet there are dramatic individual differences in achievement

within any cultural or subcultural group — differences that are heavily influenced by variations in children's home and family lives.

Home and Family Influences on Achievement

As early as 6 months of age, infants already differ in their willingness to explore the environment and their attempts to control objects, situations, and the actions of other people (Yarrow et al., 1984). Moreover, these early differences in mastery behavior are better predictors of children's intellectual performance at age 2½ than are the children's own first-year scores on infant intelligence tests (Messer et al., 1986). Which infants are most "mastery oriented" early in life? Leon Yarrow and his associates (1984) find that those who score highest in mastery motivation are the ones whose parents frequently provide *sensory stimulation* designed to amuse them and arouse their curiosity — experiences such as tickling, bouncing, games of pat-a-cake, and so on.

Important as these observations may be, instilling a strong will to achieve requires much more than tickling a child or bouncing her on one's knee. Other especially potent influences on mastery motivation and achievement are the quality of the child's attachments, the character of the home environment, and the child-rearing practices that parents use — practices that can either foster or inhibit a child's achievement motivation.

QUALITY OF ATTACHMENT

There is now ample evidence that secure attachments to parents promote mastery behaviors. Infants who are securely attached to their mothers at age 12–18 months are more likely than those who are insecurely attached to venture away from the mother to explore strange environments (Cassidy, 1986), to persist until they master new challenges (Frankel & Bates, 1990; Matas, Arend, & Sroufe, 1978), and to display a strong sense of curiosity, self-reliance, and eagerness to solve problems some four years later in kindergarten (Arend, Gove, & Sroufe, 1979). It is not that securely attached children are any more intellectually competent; instead, they seem to be more *eager* than insecurely attached children to *apply* their competencies to the new problems they encounter (Belsky, Garduque, & Hrncir, 1984). Apparently, young children need the "secure base" provided by a loving, responsive parent in order to feel comfortable about taking risks and *seeking* challenges.

THE HOME ENVIRONMENT

A young child's tendency to explore, to acquire new skills, and to solve problems will also depend on the character of the home environment and the challenges it provides. Bettye Caldwell and Robert Bradley have developed an instrument called the **HOME inventory** (Home Observation for Measurement of the Environment), which allows a researcher to visit an infant or preschool child at home

and measure just how challenging that home environment is (Caldwell & Bradley, 1984). The HOME inventory consists of 45 statements, each of which is scored *yes* (the statement is true of this home) or *no* (the statement is not true of this home). In order to gather the information to complete the inventory, the researcher will (1) ask the child's mother to describe her daily routine and child-rearing practices, (2) carefully observe the mother as she interacts with her child, and (3) note the kinds of play materials that the parent makes available for the child. The 45 bits of information collected are then grouped into the six categories, or subscales, in Table 8-5. The home then receives a score on each subscale. The higher the scores across all six subscales, the more challenging the home environment.

Does the quality of the home environment predict children's achievement behavior? To find out,

---

B O X **8-2** | *An Alternative Interpretation of Social-Class Differences in Achievement*

Jonathan Turner (1970) has suggested that a child's socioeconomic status may be less important as a determinant of his or her achievement orientation than the role played by the head of the household in attaining that status. Turner reasoned that fathers in entrepreneurial occupations—those who run their own businesses or have supervisory responsibility—are more likely than fathers in nonentrepreneurial occupations to stress independence and achievement when raising their sons. If his reasoning is correct, one could hypothesize that, regardless of their socioeconomic status, boys from entrepreneurial households would exhibit a higher level of achievement motivation than boys whose fathers worked at nonentrepreneurial occupations.

Turner tested his hypothesis by first administering the McClelland test of achievement motivation to 639 seventh- and eighth-grade boys. Each boy also provided information about his father's work, and Turner classified these occupations as *entrepreneurial* or *non-*

entrepreneurial and as *white collar* (nonmanual office or organizational work that is usually considered a middle-class occupation) or *blue collar* (manual labor such as farming or carpentry that is usually considered a working-class occupation). The results of Turner's study were consistent with his hypothesis. As we can see in the table, sons of both white-collar and blue-collar entrepreneurs displayed a higher level of achievement motivation than sons of nonentrepreneurs. Clearly, the role assumed by fathers in their work (entrepreneurial versus nonentrepreneurial) was a better predictor of their sons' achievement motivation than the socioeconomic status of the fathers' occupations. Turner also found that 50% of the white-collar workers in his sample qualified as entrepreneurs, compared with only 16% of the blue-collar workers. This finding suggests that class differences in achievement may occur because a higher percentage of middle-class children are raised in entrepreneurial households, where independence and achievement are likely to be stressed.

William van Doorninck and his associates (1981) visited the homes of 50 12-month-old infants from lower-class backgrounds and used the HOME inventory to classify these settings as stimulating (high HOME scores) or unstimulating (low HOME scores). Five to nine years later the research team followed up on these children by looking at their standardized achievement-test scores and the grades they had earned at school. As we see in Table 8-6, the quality of the home environment at 12 months of age predicted children's academic achievement several years later. Two out of three children from stimulating homes were now performing quite well at school, whereas 70% of those from unstimulating homes were doing very poorly (see also Bradley, Caldwell, & Rock, 1988). Although White and Piaget may well be correct in claiming that the seeds of mastery motivation are innate, it seems that the joy of discovery and problem solving is unlikely to blossom in a barren home environment where the child has few problems to solve and limited opportunities for learning.

Which aspects of the early home environment contribute most to children's propensities for achievement? Robert Bradley and Bettye Caldwell (1984b) find that the HOME subscales measuring the "variety of stimulation" the child receives and the "age-appropriateness of play materials" are strong predictors of children's later scholastic achievement — as strong or stronger than the HOME subscale measuring "parental involvement." Why should the variety and age-appropriateness of the child's stimulation be so important? Perhaps because young children who have many *age-appropriate* toys and experiences will acquire a strong sense of mastery as their attempts to control these objects and events regularly prove successful. By contrast, toys and activities that are too complex for the child may foster

---

B O X **8-2** | *continued*

Turner's study would seem to indicate that children from *any* social class can be high in achievement motivation if the family environment encourages achievement-related activities. Unfortunately, Turner collected no data on the child-rearing practices of the parents in his sample, and so we cannot be sure that parents in entrepreneurial households really do stress independence and achievement more than parents in nonentrepreneurial households. And, even if entrepreneurs were found to be more encouraging of achievement, we would still want to know which of their child-rearing practices are most effective in this regard. There is now a rather extensive literature on parental contributions to children's achievement. These findings are discussed in the pages that follow.

Average achievement-motivation scores of sons as a function of the socioeconomic and entrepreneurial status of their fathers

| | Entrepreneurial Status of Father | |
Social Status of Father	Entrepreneurs	Nonentrepreneurs
White collar (middle class)	9.7 ($N = 136$)	4.7 ($N = 138$)
Blue collar (working class)	8.8 ($N = 57$)	3.6 ($N = 308$)

SOURCE: Adapted from J. H. Turner, "Entrepreneurial Environments and the Emergence of Achievement Motivation in Adolescent Males." *Sociometry*, 1970, *33*, 147–165. Copyright © 1970 by the American Sociological Association. Reprinted by permission.

TABLE 8-5   *Subscales and sample items from the HOME inventory*

Subscale 1: Emotional and Verbal Responsivity of Parent (11 items)

Sample items: Parent responds verbally to child's vocalizations or verbalizations.
Parent's speech is distinct, clear, and audible.
Parent caresses or kisses child at least once.

Subscale 2: Avoidance of Restriction and Punishment (8 items)

Sample items: Parent neither slaps nor spanks child during visit.
Parent does not scold or criticize child during visit.
Parent does not interfere with or restrict child more than three times during visit.

Subscale 3: Organization of Physical and Temporal Environment (6 items)

Sample items: Child gets out of house at least four times a week.
Child's play environment is safe.

Subscale 4: Provision of Appropriate Play Materials (9 items)

Sample items: Child has a push or pull toy.
Parent provides learning facilitators appropriate to age — mobile, table and chairs, highchair, playpen, and so on.
Parent provides toys for child to play with during visit.

Subscale 5: Parental Involvement with Child (6 items)

Sample items: Parent talks to child while doing household work.
Parent structures child's play periods.

Subscale 6: Opportunities for Variety in Daily Stimulation (5 items)

Sample items: Father provides some care daily.
Child has three or more books of his or her own.

SOURCE: Adapted from *Manual for the Home Observation for Measurement of the Environment*, by B. M. Caldwell & R. H. Bradley, 1984. Little Rock: University of Arkansas Press. Adapted by permission of the author.

---

a sense of ineffectiveness and eventually a reluctance to try to master new challenges. Of course, Bradley and Caldwell's findings in no way minimize the importance of having warm and responsive parents; instead, they simply imply that the amount and variety of age-appropriate stimulation that the child receives at home have an effect on achievement above and beyond that predicted by factors related to parental involvement, such as the quality of the child's attachments.

Of course, the demands that parents make of their child and the ways they respond to her accomplishments can also influence the child's will to achieve. Let's now consider some of the child-rearing practices that seem to encourage (or discourage) the development of healthy attitudes about achievement.

CHILD REARING AND ACHIEVEMENT

What kinds of child-rearing practices foster achievement motivation? In their book *The Achievement Motive*, McClelland et al. (1953) proposed that parents who stress **independence training** — doing things on one's own — and who warmly reinforce such self-reliant behavior will contribute in a positive way to the growth of achievement motivation. And research bears this out (Grolnick & Ryan, 1989; Winterbottom, 1958).

However, Bernard Rosen and Ray D'Andrade (1959) were quick to suggest that direct **achievement training** (encouraging children to do things well) is at least as important to the development of achievement motivation as is independence training. To evaluate their hypothesis, Rosen and D'Andrade

TABLE 8-6 *Relation between quality of home environment at 12 months of age and children's grade-school academic achievement five to nine years later*

Quality of Home Environment at Age 12 Months	Academic Achievement	
	Average or High (top 70%)	Low (bottom 30%)
Stimulating	20 children	10 children
Unstimulating	6 children	14 children

SOURCE: Adapted from W. J. van Doorninck, B. M. Caldwell, C. Wright, & W. K. Frankenberg, "The Relationship between Twelve-Month Home Stimulation and School Achievement." *Child Development*, 1981, *52*, 1080–1083. Copyright © 1981 by the Society for Research in Child Development.

visited the homes of boys who had tested either high or low in achievement motivation and asked these 9- to 11-year-olds to work at difficult and potentially frustrating tasks—for example, building a tower out of irregularly shaped blocks while blindfolded and using only one hand. To assess the kind of independence and achievement training the boys were receiving at home, the investigators asked parents to watch their son work and give any encouragement or suggestions that they cared to. The results were clear. Both mothers and fathers of high need-achievers *set lofty standards* for their boys to accomplish and were noticeably concerned about the quality of their sons' performance. They gave many *helpful hints* and were *quick to praise* their sons for meeting one of their performance standards. By contrast, parents of low need-achievers (particularly fathers) stressed neither independence nor achievement training. They often told their sons how to perform the tasks and became rather irritated whenever the boys experienced any difficulty. Finally, the high need-achievers tended to outperform the low need-achievers, and they seemed to enjoy the tasks more as well. So it appears that independence, achievement motivation, and achievement behavior are more likely to develop when parents encourage children to do things on their own *and to do them well.*

Finally, the patterns of praise (or punishment) that accompany the child's achievement outcomes are also important. Children who seek challenges

and display high levels of achievement motivation have parents who *reward their successes and are not overly critical of an occasional failure* (but see Box 8-3 for a caution parents might heed regarding the use of material rewards). By contrast, children who shy away from challenges and are low in achievement motivation have parents who are slow to acknowledge their successes (or who do so in a "matter-of-fact" way) and are inclined to *punish* failures (Baumrind, 1973; Teeven & McGhee, 1972).

We see, then, that parents of children who develop healthy achievement orientations tend to possess three characteristics: (1) they are warm, accepting, and quick to praise the child's accomplishments; (2) they provide guidance and control by setting standards for the child to live up to and then monitoring her progress to ensure that she does; and (3) they permit the child some independence or autonomy, allowing her a say in deciding how best to master challenges and meet their expectations. Diana Baumrind calls this warm, firm, but democratic parenting an **authoritative parenting** style—a style that she and others have found to foster positive attitudes about achievement and considerable

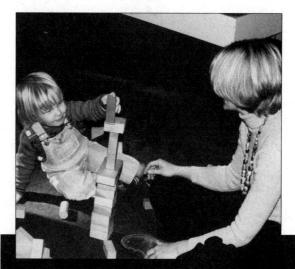

PHOTO 8-3 Parents who encourage achievement and who respond warmly to successes are likely to raise mastery-oriented children who enjoy challenges.

academic success among grade-school children and adolescents, both in Western societies (Baumrind, 1973; Dornbusch et al., 1987; Lamborn et al., 1991; Steinberg, Elmen, & Mounts, 1989) and in the Orient (see Lin & Fu, 1990). Apparently, each of the three components of authoritative parenting makes an independent contribution to children's achievement (Steinberg et al., 1989), and we can see the importance of all three components if we compare children of authoritative parents with those who are raised differently. **Authoritarian parents** are often warm and accepting, and they set firm standards — but they *permit little independence or autonomy*. Their children display average to below-average academic achievement and tend to be hesitant or unenthused about seeking new challenges.[4] **Permissive parents**, on the other hand, allow considerable autonomy — but it is a misguided autonomy in that they *set few standards* and *rarely monitor their children's progress or praise their accomplishments*. So it should come as no surprise that permissive parents often raise children and adolescents who display very little achievement motivation and dismal academic performance (Dornbusch et al., 1987; Maccoby & Martin, 1983).

[4]Asian Americans, who often experience authoritarian parenting, are an exception to this rule, typically displaying average or above-average scholastic performance. Apparently, Asian-American youths do well in school, despite the nonauthoritative parenting they receive, because their Asian-American peers strongly endorse and encourage the pursuit of academic excellence (Steinberg et al., 1992).

BOX 8-3 | *On Turning Fun into Drudgery with Unnecessary Incentives*

Children often take part in achievement-related activities, such as reading storybooks or working numerical puzzles, for the sheer fun of it. Activities that are valued for their own sake and do not require external prompts or rewards for children to perform are said to be *intrinsically* motivated.

Yet schoolwork and other forms of "achievement" behavior are not intrinsically motivating for some young children. Parents and teachers often try to promote an interest in these activities (or at least persuade children to work at them) by offering inducements such as money, praise, and gold stars for achievement at home and in the classroom. Rewards such as these, which are not inherent in the activities they reinforce, are called *extrinsic* reinforcers.

Learning theorists have clearly demonstrated that the offer and presentation of extrinsic reinforcement can promote new learning and motivate young children to undertake and complete activities that are *not* intrinsically satisfying to them (Loveland & Olley, 1979; McLoyd, 1979). For example, a teacher who offers her "nonreaders" a gold star for every ten minutes that they spend reading may well increase the reading activities of these children, who would not ordinarily read on their own. But would this incentive further motivate the class "bookworms" who read avidly because reading is *intrinsically* satisfying?

Although most parents would say yes (Boggiano et al., 1987), attribution theorists strongly disagree. Mark Lepper (1983) contends that children who perform *intrinsically satisfying* activities as a means of obtaining extrinsic reinforcers will come to like these activities *less*! The rationale for this prediction is straightforward: intrinsic interest in an activity may be *discounted* as a cause of one's behavior and even undermined if the child decides he or she is now performing the activity to earn a tangible reward.

An experiment by Lepper, Greene, and Nisbett (1973) provides clear support for the attribution hypothesis. Children aged 3 to 5 who showed considerable intrinsic interest in drawing with colored felt pens were promised a special certificate if they would draw a picture for a visiting adult (expected-reward condition). Other preschool children who were equally interested in drawing with felt pens engaged in the same drawing activities and either received an unexpected certificate for their work (unexpected-reward condition) or did not receive a certificate (no-reward condition). Then, 7 to 14 days later, the children were observed during free-play periods to determine whether

CONFIGURAL INFLUENCES: BIRTH ORDER, FAMILY SIZE, AND CHILDREN'S ACHIEVEMENT BEHAVIOR

Might the size of one's family or the order of one's birth among siblings influence propensity for achievement? Apparently so, at least to some extent. Looking first at birth order, first-born children seem to accomplish more than later-borns do. First-borns are overrepresented among populations of eminent people and college students (Bradley, 1968; Schachter, 1963), and they score higher than later-borns on tests of English and mathematics achievement (Eysenck & Cookson, 1969; Paulhus & Shaffer, 1981), verbal achievement (Breland, 1974), and verbal reasoning (Kellaghan & MacNamara, 1972). In addition, first-borns are somewhat higher in *n* Ach and hold higher educational aspirations than later-borns (Glass, Neulinger, & Brim, 1974; Sampson & Hancock, 1967).

Critics have argued that the lesser attainments of later-borns really reflect social-class differences in family size: since low-SES families have more children, a greater percentage of later-borns would come from low-SES backgrounds, where achievement outcomes are not as good (Schooler, 1972). However, other investigators continued to find birth-order differences in achievement *even when the influences of family size and social class were controlled.* One interesting aspect of this latter research is that family size also has an effect: the more children in

---

BOX 8-3 | *continued*

they still wanted to draw with the felt pens. Lepper et al. found that children who had contracted to draw a picture for an extrinsic reinforcer now spent less of their free time drawing with the pens (8.6%) than children who had received no reward (16.7%) or those who had received the reward as a surprise (18.1%). Note that the reward itself did not undermine intrinsic motivation, for children in the unexpected-reward condition continued to show as much intrinsic interest in drawing as those who were not rewarded. It was only when children had previously drawn *in order to obtain a reward* that intrinsic reinforcement undermined intrinsic interest.

Undermining one's interest in intrinsically satisfying activities is not the only undesirable effect that introduction of external incentives may have. Children who are offered such incentives for undertaking activities they already enjoy may subsequently lower their achievement aspirations, choosing to perform easy rather than difficult problems so as not to miss out on the rewards (Condry & Chambers, 1982). And, unfortunately, this sudden tendency to forgo significant challenges is most apparent among those children who initially displayed the strongest intrinsic interest in the rewarded activities (Pearlman, 1984).

Do these observations mean that parents and teachers should never reward children's noteworthy accomplishments at activities that the children enjoy? No, they do not! Extrinsic rewards can sustain and even increase intrinsic interest in an activity, provided that the reinforcer is given only for *successful* task performance, not merely for working at the task (Pallak et al., 1982). Why? Because rewards given for successes serve an important *informational* function: they allow children to attribute the positive outcomes of their behavior to their *competence* in that activity (a stable, internal cause) rather than to the availability of the reward (an unstable, external cause). Consequently, children are likely to perform the rewarded acts in the future because rewards given for noteworthy successes have increased their perceptions of self-efficacy (Bandura, 1989).

In sum, the implications of this line of research are reasonably clear. Extrinsic reinforcers can be used both at home and in the classroom to strengthen or sustain those activities that children will *not* ordinarily perform on their own. However, parents, teachers, and other social agents must guard against creating unnecessary reward systems that can turn enjoyable tasks that children are motivated to master into pursuits that they may come to view as reward-seeking drudgery.

the family, the lower the child's attainments (see Breland, 1974; Kellaghan & MacNamara, 1972).

Two explanations for these birth-order and family-size effects have appeared in the literature: (1) the **parental socialization hypothesis**, which holds that first-borns (and children from small families) receive more direct achievement training at home than later-borns (and children from large families) do, and (2) the **mental mediation (or confluence) hypothesis**, which suggests that birth order and family size are variables that influence the child's intellectual development, thereby affecting his or her *capacity* to achieve.

Evidence for parental socialization effects. One finding consistent with the parental socialization hypothesis is that parents hold higher achievement expectancies for first-borns than for later-borns (Baskett, 1985). But do these expectancies influence the amount of stimulation and achievement training that parents provide? Apparently so. Using the HOME inventory, Bradley and Caldwell (1984a) found that the early home environments of first-borns are more challenging and stimulating than those of later-borns. And consider what Mary Rothbart (1971) found when she asked mothers to supervise the performance of their 5-year-olds on a series of achievement tasks. Half the children were first-borns and half were later-borns; to control for family size, all were from two-child families. Rothbart discovered that mothers spent an equal amount of time interacting with first-born and later-born children. However, the quality of the interaction differed: mothers gave more complex technical explanations to the first-borns, put more pressure on first-borns to achieve, and were more concerned about the quality of their performance—which perhaps explains why first-borns outperformed later-borns on all but one of the experimental tasks. So it seems that first-borns are more likely to be challenged as infants and to receive more direct achievement training during the preschool years than are later-borns.

The mental mediation (or confluence) hypothesis. The mental mediation (confluence) hypothesis was proposed by Robert Zajonc (1975; Zajonc, Markus,

& Markus, 1979) to explain the remarkable findings of Belmont and Marolla (1973). Analyzing records from nearly 400,000 Dutch soldiers, Belmont and Marolla found that, after controlling for social class, family size had a significant effect on IQ: as we see in Figure 8-5, the brightest soldiers tended to come *from smaller families*. When the researchers then looked at the effects of birth order within any given family size, there was a clear birth-order effect: *first-borns outperformed second-borns, who outperformed third-borns*, and so on down the line. These findings are not unique to Dutch soldiers, having now been replicated in samples of males and females from several countries (Zajonc et al., 1979).

Zajonc offers a very simple explanation for these birth-order and family-size effects, one that rests on an important assumption: a child's intellectual development depends on *the average intellectual level of all family members*—that is, the intellectual climate of the household. Clearly, first-borns should have an advantage because they are initially exposed *only* to adults, whose intellectual levels are relatively high. By contrast, a second child experiences a less stimulating intellectual environment because she is exposed to a cognitively immature older sibling as well as to her parents. A third child is further disadvantaged by the presence of *two* relatively immature older siblings. Zajonc (1975) concludes:

> With each additional child, the family's intellectual environment depreciates. . . . Children who grow up surrounded by people with higher intellectual levels [first-borns and children from small families] have a better chance to achieve their maximum intellectual powers than children . . . from large families who spend more time in a world of child-sized minds, . . . develop more slowly and therefore attain lower IQs [p. 39].

Although Zajonc's confluence model is appealing for its simplicity, its predictions do not always ring true. On the positive side, it appears that the intellectual climate of the household (as indexed by the HOME inventory) does depreciate as family size increases (Bradley & Caldwell, 1984a). Yet Zajonc's model would predict that children growing up in homes with *three* mature adults (say, two parents and a grandparent) should score higher on IQ tests than those exposed only to their two parents; but

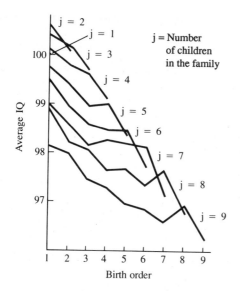

FIGURE 8-5 Average scores on a nonverbal measure of intelligence as a function of the examinee's birth order and the size of his family. Note that subjects from smaller families score higher on this test than subjects from large families. We also see that, within a given family size, children born early tend to obtain higher IQs than those born late. (Adapted from L. Belmont & F. A. Marolla, "Birth Order, Family Size, and Intelligence." *Science*, 1973, *182*, 1096–1101.)

they don't (Brackbill & Nichols, 1982). Moreover, children who live with only one parent (rather than two) do not always show the poorer intellectual performances or the lesser scholastic attainments that confluence theory predicts (Entwisle & Alexander, 1990; Patterson et al., 1990). Finally, it is important to note that birth-order and family-size effects (on intelligence, at least) tend to be quite small and are most likely to be observed when large numbers of families are compared. Thus the trends that emerge for the population as a whole may or may not apply to the members of any *particular* family. Clearly, not all first-borns are brighter than average; nor do all later-borns score lower in IQ (or achieve less) than their older brothers or sisters.

Summing up. After reviewing the literature, it seems reasonable to conclude that the greater attainments of first-borns and children from small families stem, in part, from the fact that these youngsters often receive more direct achievement training than later-borns or children from large families. And although first-borns and children from smaller families do tend to score higher in IQ than later-borns and children from large families, it remains for future research to determine whether these small variations in intellectual performance help to explain birth-order and family-size differences in *achievement*.

Modeling Influences on Children's Achievement

We have seen that all but the most permissive of parents set standards of achievement for their children and expect them to live up to these standards. But a child might also acquire achievement standards by observing the behavior of social models and adopting the criteria that these people use to evaluate their own accomplishments. In fact, several studies indicate that children are quick to adopt a model's achievement standards in situations in which they have no preexisting standards of their own (Bandura, 1977).

It so happens that children are exposed to many models and may often observe discrepant or contradictory standards of achievement. Consider a case in which parents impose a very stringent standard on their child while adopting a very lenient standard for themselves. Such a discrepancy makes one wonder how a child would then behave when not under the watchful eyes of parents. Will the child do as they say or, rather, do as they do? An experiment by McMains and Liebert (1968) suggests an answer.

McMains and Liebert had fourth-graders play a bowling game with an adult model. Although the game appeared to be a game of skill, it was actually "rigged" to produce a fixed pattern of scores. In the training phase of the experiment, the model always imposed a stringent achievement standard on the child: the child had to obtain a score of 20 before receiving a reward. Half the children were assigned to a *consistent-training condition* in which the model used the same stringent standard to evaluate his own performance. The remaining children were assigned to a *discrepant-training condition* in which the model used a more lenient achievement standard (a score of 15) than the one he had imposed on the child. At the end of the training phase, each child was left alone to play the bowling game and to reinforce his or her own performance. Children who reinforced themselves only when they attained a score of 20 were said to have adopted the stringent standard that the model had imposed during the training phase.

The children's average self-leniency scores—that is, the average number of times they rewarded themselves for scores lower than the stringent standard—appear in Table 8-7. Note that children were very likely to do *exactly what the model had done*. When the model used a stringent standard that was *consistent* with the one he had imposed on the child, that standard was adopted by the child; children in the consistent-training condition did not often reward their substandard performances. But, when the model was lenient in evaluating his own behavior, children often abandoned the stringent standard that they had been taught and adopted the lenient standard that the model had actually used. So the achievement standards a child adopts are strongly influenced by the *behavior* of others. Parents who set stringent standards for their children are well advised to reinforce these performance criteria by imposing the same (or even stricter) standards on themselves.

When do children start to evaluate their accomplishments by comparing them with the performance of others? Apparently this kind of **social comparison** begins rather early. Harriet Mosatche and Penelope Bragonier (1981) observed 3- to 4-year-olds at play and noted that the vast majority of them compared themselves with a peer at least once during the 15-minute period when each child was observed (for example, "My spaceship is higher than yours"; "I can run faster than you"). And, by the time children reach the first grade, they become especially interested in using social comparison to evaluate their performance if the other person is in some way *similar* to themselves (France-Kaatrude & Smith, 1985). Yet it is important to note that 6- to 7-year-olds use comparative information mainly to evaluate the *merits* (or lack thereof) of their performance, not to infer their own or others' *abilities* (Aboud, 1985; Butler, 1990; Ruble et al., 1980). Use of comparative performances to infer ability (a dispositional attribute) does not often occur until age 8 or 9, precisely the time that children begin to pay partic-

TABLE 8-7 *Average self-leniency scores as a function of the consistency of the model's and the child's achievement criteria during the training phase of the experiment*

| | Average Self-Leniency Score (5.00 = maximum score possible) | |
Conditions	Boys	Girls
Consistent training (model used stringent standard)	1.83	.25
Discrepant training (model used lenient standard)	4.91	4.04

NOTE: The model always imposed a stringent standard on the child.
SOURCE: M. J. McMains & R. M. Liebert, "The Influence of Discrepancies between Successively Modeled Self-Reward Criteria on the Adoption of a Self-Imposed Standard." *Journal of Personality and Social Psychology*, 1968, 8, 166–171. Copyright © 1968 by the American Psychological Association.

ularly close attention to underlying regularities in behavior and to think of these patterns as reflecting stable traits (Rholes & Ruble, 1984). So it seems that the process of social comparison allows younger children to decide whether they have mastered an activity (and, hence, whether their achievement *outcomes* are good or bad), whereas older children are more inclined to compare themselves with others to decide whether their *ability*, or capacity for achievement, is high, average, or low.

Now we come to an "achievement" question that will serve as a bridge topic to our next chapter (on sex differences and sex-role development): are there sex differences in achievement?

Sex Differences in Achievement

How often have you heard the opinions "That's a man's job," "Women are just not suited for this kind of work (activity) (study)," "A woman's place is in the home"? In the vast majority of the world's societies, men are expected to pursue a career of some sort, whereas women, if not actively discouraged from harboring these aspirations, are at least trained for the tasks of child care and homemaking. Indeed, many who have read the Judeo-Christian scriptures have come away with the impression that such sex-linked divisions of labor are "God's will." No less a religious authority than Pope Pius XII once stated: "A woman's function, a woman's way, a woman's natural bent is motherhood. Every woman is called to be a mother."

Do I repeat these sexist proverbs to enrage my female students and colleagues? Of course not! I do so simply to remind you of the well-ingrained cultural teachings that foster the impression that women ought to serve men, who are, after all, the "achieving" sex. Over the past two decades a plethora of research has revealed that (1) women are no less intelligent or otherwise less capable of achievement than men are (see Maccoby & Jacklin, 1974, for an early review of this literature) and (2) in many Western societies, women have achieved noteworthy successes at virtually all occupations heretofore labeled "masculine" (Tarvis & Wade, 1984). Yet all too often these arguments fall on deaf ears. Even many women (including college students) believe that they are less capable than men and that the successes they do achieve are attributable to factors other than their own abilities (see Chapter 9 for a discussion of these findings).

Let's now set common impressions aside and see what social developmentalists have to say about sex differences in achievement.

Sex differences in achievement expectancies. Although there are tremendous individual differences among members of each sex, girls generally earn higher grades than boys during elementary school, with boys eventually closing the gap and outperforming girls in certain subjects (for example, mathematics) during high school and college (or even sooner if standardized mathematics achievement scores are the performance criteria; cf. Alexander & Entwisle, 1988). But, despite their early accomplishments, grade-school girls consistently *underestimate* their academic competencies (particularly in mathematics), whereas boys consistently overestimate theirs (Crandall, 1969; Lummis & Stevenson, 1990). In fact, kindergarten and first-grade girls already think they are not as good as boys at concept-formation tasks and arithmetic, even though they are earning higher grades in arithmetic and have outperformed their male classmates on tests of concept learning (Entwisle & Baker, 1983; Ruble, Parsons, & Ross, 1976). And it is disturbing to note that

the *brightest* females are the ones who underestimate their competencies the most; high-achieving girls occasionally even display lower expectancies of future success than their average- or low-achieving female classmates (Dweck & Elliott, 1983; Stipek & Hoffman, 1980). How can we account for these puzzling outcomes?

Home influences. Many theorists believe that sex differences in achievement expectancies originate at home. And there is ample evidence for this point of view. Consider that mothers of kindergarten children in the United States, Japan, and Taiwan already believe that boys have greater math aptitude than girls do, even though their children have yet to receive any formal instruction in math (Lummis & Stevenson, 1990). Similarly, Jacquelynne Parsons (Parsons, Adler, & Kaczala, 1982) found that parents of 5th- through 11th-graders expect sons to achieve more than daughters in mathematics, and they believe that math classes are easier, more important, and somewhat more enjoyable for boys than for girls. Do these parental attitudes affect children's own impressions of their math aptitude and their prospects for future success in math? Yes, indeed! Even though the males and females in Parsons' sample *did not differ* in their previous performance in math, the children's beliefs about their own mathematical *abilities* were more in line with their parents' beliefs about their math aptitude and potential than with their own past experiences in math. So it seems that parents' sex-stereotyped beliefs about their children's academic potential may be an important determinant of the sex differences we find in children's academic self-concepts (see also Jacobs & Eccles, 1992). "By attributing their daughters' performances to hard work and their sons' to high ability, parents may be teaching their sons and daughters to draw different inferences regarding their abilities from equivalent achievement experiences" (Parsons, Adler, & Kaczala, 1982, p. 320).

Scholastic influences. Teachers may also contribute to sex differences in achievement expectancies by responding differently to the accomplishments of male and female students. In their observational study of evaluative feedback in the classroom, Dweck et al. (1978) found that teachers' responses to boys' successes and failures were of the kind that promote a mastery orientation; that is, teachers praised the intellectual aspects of the boys' work when a boy succeeded while focusing more on nonintellectual factors (sloppiness of work; lack of effort) to account for his failures. Girls received a different evaluative pattern: teachers often stressed the nonintellectual aspects of a girl's work (neatness; high effort) when she succeeded while focusing on her intellectual shortcomings when she failed. So instructors may unwittingly provide their female students with patterns of verbal evaluation that leave girls little choice but to attribute failures to their own lack of ability. Of course, this is precisely the belief that should lead female students to underestimate the likelihood of future academic success and could even result in learned helplessness.

Why are the brightest female students often the ones who underestimate their future academic accomplishments the most? A study by Jacquelynne Parsons and her associates (Parsons, Kaczala, & Meece, 1982) provides one clue. Parsons et al. looked at teachers' use of praise in five classrooms where male and female students clearly differed in their achievement expectancies. The results were indeed interesting. Teachers were more likely to praise the work of girls they expected to do *poorly* than that of girls they expected to do well. But just the opposite was true of boys, who received more praise if the teacher expected them to do well rather than poorly. Notice that the pattern of praise received by female students in these classrooms does *not* reflect the teachers' true expectations about their future academic accomplishments. Perhaps you can see how a star female student who is rarely praised for her achievements might eventually conclude that she must lack ability or that academic success is not very important for girls, particularly when the star male students and her less competent female classmates receive far more praise from the teacher than she does.

Finally, teachers may contribute to sex differences in children's *patterns* of achievement by virtue of their sex-stereotyped beliefs about the relative abilities of boys and girls in particular subjects. Sixth-grade math teachers, for example, believe that (1) boys have more mathematical ability than girls do but that (2) girls try harder than boys at math (Jussim & Eccles, 1992). And, although teachers often reward girls for the greater effort they perceive them as expending (by assigning them math grades equivalent to or even higher than those assigned to boys; cf. Jussim & Eccles, 1992), their message that girls must try harder to succeed in math may nonetheless convince many girls that their talents might be best directed toward other, nonquantitative achievement domains—an influence that may help to explain why males have continued to dominate such professions as computer science, engineering, and physics, which require extensive training in math.

What can we conclude about sex differences in achievement?   As we have noted previously, women have often been discouraged (and sometimes even prevented) from practicing traditionally masculine occupations. And, given that many contemporary females underestimate their scholastic capabilities and may even conclude that academic success is somehow less important for them than it is for males, it should come as no surprise to learn that women continue to be seriously underrepresented in the so-called achieving roles of most societies (that is, politics and the professions). Indeed, these are precisely the statistics that people often cite when arguing that males achieve more than females or that males are the "achieving" sex.

Yet I would feel incredibly uncomfortable in leaving you with such an impression, particularly in view of the fact that you probably know several women (one of whom may be teaching this course) who have exceeded the educational and occupational attainments of most men. Perhaps the most accurate statement we can make about sex differences in achievement is that men and women have historically differed in their *areas* of achievement rather than in their needs or capacities for achieving. Even as we approach the 21st century, young boys and girls are still being steered toward different social and vocational roles in society (Ruble, 1988), and most high school students continue to aspire toward occupations that are dominated by members of their own sex (Hannah & Kahn, 1989; Reid & Stephens, 1985). This finding may not surprise you, particularly after we examine the sex-typing process in Chapter 9 and see just how powerful the forces are that push males and females in different directions. Nevertheless, there are signs that the times are changing. When America's college class of 1985 began college, in the fall of 1980, 27% of the women said they intended to pursue careers in business, engineering, law, or medicine—a fourfold increase since 1966 (American Council on Education, 1981). And by fall 1990 over 46% of the first-year law class at my home institution was female, as was 44% of the enrollment in the school of business (*University of Georgia Fact Book*, 1991). So there is some reason to suspect that many of the negative stereotypes about the ability of women to succeed in so-called masculine pursuits will eventually crumble as females achieve, in ever-increasing numbers, in politics, professional occupations, skilled trades, and virtually all other walks of life. To oppose such a trend is to waste a most valuable resource: the abilities and efforts of more than half the world's population.

Summary

A major aim of socialization is to encourage children to become self-reliant and to take pride in their accomplishments. An *independent* child is one who is able to accomplish many objectives without the assistance of others. The concept of *achievement* extends beyond a sense of independence: the achieving child not only relies on his or her own efforts to attain many goals but also evaluates personal accomplishments against certain standards of excellence. Historically, achievement has been conceptualized in two very different ways. The motivational viewpoint depicts achievement as a *learned motive* (called the *need for achievement*) to compete and to strive for success. However, behavioral theorists depict achievement as a class of *instrumental behaviors* directed toward attaining social approval (or toward avoiding disapproval) in situations in which standards of excellence are operable.

Between ages 1½ and 5, children are learning to evaluate their accomplishments. Before age 2 they take pleasure in mastering challenges but are not appraising the quality of achievement outcomes in relation to performance standards. Use of acquired standards to evaluate accomplishments emerges at about age 2—the age at which children begin to seek recognition when they succeed and to turn away and avoid a potential evaluator when they fail. By age 3½, children understand the purpose of competition and are noticeably happier when they win such a contest than when they lose. Nevertheless, even 5-year-olds are not yet treating competitive losses as "failures."

Four major theories that seek to explain individual differences in achievement are McClelland's need achievement theory, Atkinson's revision and extension of McClelland's approach, Weiner's attribution theory, and Dweck's learned-helplessness theory. McClelland was the first to demonstrate that people differ in their *motivation* to achieve (n Ach), although his notion that n Ach was a global attribute that predicted one's reactions to all achievement tasks now seems badly overstated. Atkinson's revision of McClelland's theory pointed to the existence of a competing "motive to avoid failure" (M_{af}), which can make people shy away from achievement tasks in order to avoid the embarrassment of failing. Moreover, Atkinson broke new ground by demonstrating that achievement-related cognitions, such as one's *expectancies* of success and failure and the *incentive value* of succeeding, are important determinants of achievement behavior. Weiner's later attribution theory grew out of Crandall's earlier work on locus of control and focused much more intently on how specific beliefs about the *causes* of one's successes and failures contribute to achievement expectancies and the incentive value of various achievement outcomes. Finally, Dweck's learned-helplessness model shows that the *patterns* of attributions that children display when explaining their achievement outcomes will affect their willingness to persist at challenging tasks that they have initially failed to master. Although these four achievement theories differ in many respects, each viewpoint has made important contributions to our understanding of children's achievement orientations.

There is considerable variation among different cultural and subcultural groups in the character of achievement-related goals and activities. Cross-cultural data suggest that the economy of a society influences how its members look at achievement. Societies that depend on an agricultural or pastoral economy train their children to be cooperative and conforming. As a result, these children view achievement as the ability to suppress individualism for the greater good of the group. By contrast, societies that depend on hunting or food gathering train their children to be independent and venturesome and stress *individual* accomplishments as indications of achievement. Ethnic and social-class differences in academic achievement are quite apparent and are multiply determined. Subtle (and not so subtle) differences in parenting styles undoubtedly contribute to these differences, as do the rather modest academic expectancies that many teachers hold for children from disadvantaged backgrounds.

There are many ways in which the home and family context might influence a child's propensity for achievement. Infants who are securely attached to responsive caregivers and whose home environments offer many age-appropriate problems and challenges are likely to become curious nursery-school children who will later do well at school. Parents may either promote or inhibit their child's interest in achievement-related activities by virtue of their child-rearing practices. Early independence and achievement training facilitates the development of achievement motivation if the parent rewards the child's accomplishments and is not overly critical of failure. Indeed, parents who combine all these practices into one parenting style (*authoritative* parenting) tend to raise children who seek challenges and achieve considerable academic success, whereas *authoritarian* parents, who are restrictive and domineering, and *permissive* parents, who set few achievement standards and are lax about monitoring behavior, tend to raise children who accomplish less and are relatively uninterested in achievement.

First-borns and children from small families are likely to display higher levels of academic achievement than later-borns and children from large families. One explanation for these findings that has received some support is the *parental socialization hypothesis*: first-borns and children from smaller families receive more direct achievement training from their parents than later-borns and children from large families. In addition, the *mental mediation hypothesis* suggests that birth order and family size are variables that affect the child's intellectual development, which in turn influences his or her capacity for achievement. Although first-borns and children from smaller families do tend to score higher on IQ tests, it is not yet clear that these minor variations in intellectual performance contribute in any meaningful way to birth-order and family-size differences in achievement.

Children learn many lessons about achievement by observing the behaviors and outcomes of their social acquaintances. They quickly adopt the achievement standards of social models in situations in which they have no standards of their own. Moreover, they compare their accomplishments to those of peers, first to determine whether their work is good or bad (mastery comparisons) and later to assess their ability at the activity in question (ability comparisons).

Although girls often outperform boys in elementary school, they tend to underestimate their academic capabilities and future accomplishments, whereas boys tend to overestimate their own abilities and likelihoods of future success. Parents contribute to these sex differences in achievement expectancies by expecting more of their sons than of their daughters and by attributing sons' achievements to high ability and daughters' achievements to hard work. Teachers may also encourage these latter attributions by reacting differently to the academic accomplishments of males and females. Given that girls often underestimate their scholastic abilities and may even conclude that academic success is less important for them than for boys, it should not be surprising to find that females are underrepresented in the professions and other so-called achieving roles of most societies. However, females are no less capable of achievement than males, and their ever-increasing contributions to virtually all the heretofore "masculine" professions are rapidly exploding the myth that males are the achieving sex.

References

ABOUD, F. E. (1985). Children's application of attribution principles to social comparisons. *Child Development, 56,* 682–688.

ALEXANDER, K. L., & ENTWISLE, D. R. (1988). Achievement in the first two years of school: Patterns and processes. *Monographs of the Society for Research in Child Development, 53* (2, Serial No. 218).

AMERICAN COUNCIL ON EDUCATION (1981, February). More college women pursue traditionally male careers. *Higher Education and National Affairs,* p. 4.

AREND, A., GOVE, F. L., & SROUFE, L. A. (1979). Continuity of individual adaptation from infancy to kindergarten: A predictive study of ego-resiliency and curiosity in preschoolers. *Child Development, 50,* 950–959.

ATKINSON, J. W. (1964). *An introduction to motivation.* Princeton, NJ: Van Nostrand.

BANDURA, A. (1977). *Social learning theory.* Englewood Cliffs, NJ: Prentice-Hall.

BANDURA, A. (1989). Social cognitive theory. In R. Vasta (Ed.), *Annals of child development* (Vol. 6). Greenwich, CT: JAI Press.

BARRY, H., CHILD, I. L., & BACON, M. K. (1959). The relation of child training to subsistence economy. *American Anthropologist, 67,* 51–63.

BASKETT, L. M. (1985). Sibling status effects: Adult expectations. *Developmental Psychology, 21,* 441–445.

BATTLE, E. S. (1966). Motivational determinants of academic competence. *Journal of Personality and Social Psychology, 4,* 634–642.

BAUMRIND, D. (1973). The development of instrumental competence through socialization. In A. Pick (Ed.), *Minnesota symposium on child psychology* (Vol. 7). Minneapolis: University of Minnesota Press.

BELMONT, L., & MAROLLA, F. A. (1973). Birth order, family size and intelligence. *Science, 182,* 1096–1101.

BELSKY, J., GARDUQUE, L., & HRNCIR, E. (1984). Assessing performance, competence, and executive capacity in infant play: Relations to home environment and security of attachment. *Developmental Psychology, 20,* 406–417.

BENDIG, A. W. (1958). Predictive and postdictive validity of need achievement measures. *Journal of Educational Research, 52,* 119–120.

BERRY, J. W. (1967). Independence and conformity in subsistence-level societies. *Journal of Personality and Social Psychology, 7,* 415–418.

BOGGIANO, A. K., BARRETT, M., WEIHER, A. W., McCLELLAND, G. H., & LUSK, C. M. (1987). Use of the maximal-operant principle to motivate children's intrinsic interest. *Journal of Personality and Social Psychology, 53,* 866–879.

BOGGIANO, A. K., MAIN, D. S., & KATZ, P. A. (1988). Children's preference for challenge: The role of perceived competence and control. *Journal of Personality and Social Psychology, 54,* 134–141.

BRACKBILL, Y., & NICHOLS, P. L. (1982). A test of the confluence model of intellectual development. *Developmental Psychology, 18,* 192–198.

BRADLEY, R. H. (1968). Birth order and school-related behavior: A heuristic review. *Psychological Bulletin, 70,* 45–51.

BRADLEY, R. H., & CALDWELL, B. M. (1984a). The HOME inventory and family demographics. *Developmental Psychology, 20,* 315–320.

BRADLEY, R. H., & CALDWELL, B. M. (1984b). The relation of infants' home environments to achievement test performance in the first grade: A follow-up study. *Child Development, 55,* 803–809.

BRADLEY, R. H., CALDWELL, B. M., & ROCK, S. L. (1988). Home environment and school performance: A 10-year follow-up and examination of three models of environmental action. *Child Development, 59,* 852–867.

BRELAND, H. M. (1974). Birth order, family configuration, and verbal achievement. *Child Development, 45,* 1011–1019.

BUTLER, R. (1989). Mastery versus ability appraisal: A developmental study of children's observations of peers' work. *Child Development, 60,* 1350–1361.

BUTLER, R. (1990). The effects of mastery and competitive conditions on self-assessment at different ages. *Child Development, 61,* 201–210.

BUTLER, R. (1992). What young people want to know and when: Effects of mastery and ability goals on different kinds of social comparison. *Journal of Personality and Social Psychology, 62,* 934–943.

CALDWELL, B. M., & BRADLEY, R. H. (1984). *Manual for the Home Observation for Measurement of the Environment.* Little Rock: University of Arkansas Press.

CASSIDY, J. (1986). The ability to negotiate the environment: An aspect of infant competence as related to quality of attachment. *Child Development, 57,* 331–337.

COLEMAN, J. S., CAMPBELL, E. Q., HOBSON, C. J., McPARTLAND, J., MOOD, A. M., WEINFELD, F. D., & YORK, R. L. (1966). *Equality of educational opportunity.* Report from U.S. Office of Education. Washington, DC: U.S. Government Printing Office.

CONDRY, J., & CHAMBERS, J. (1982). Intrinsic motivation and the process of learning. In D. Grune & M. R. Lepper (Eds.), *The hidden costs of rewards.* Hillsdale, NJ: Erlbaum.

CONGER, R. D., CONGER, K. J., ELDER, G. H., JR., LORENZ, F.O., SIMONS, R. L., & EVANS, E. G. (1992). A family process model of economic hardship and adjustment of early adolescent boys. *Child Development, 63,* 526–541.

CRANDALL, V. C. (1967). Achievement behavior in young children. In *The young child: Reviews of research.* Washington, DC: National Association for the Education of Young Children.

CRANDALL, V. C. (1969). Sex differences in expectancy of intellectual and academic reinforcement. In C. P. Smith (Ed.), *Achievement-related motives in children.* New York: Russell Sage Foundation.

CRANDALL, V. J., KATKOVSKY, W., & PRESTON, A. A. (1960). A conceptual formulation of some research on children's achievement development. *Child Development, 31,* 787–797.

DORNBUSCH, S., RITTER, P., LIEDERMAN, P., ROBERTS, D., & FRALEIGH, M. (1987). The relation of parenting style to adolescent school performance. *Child Development, 58,* 1244–1257.

DWECK, C. S. (1975). The role of expectations and attributions in the alleviation of learned helplessness. *Journal of Personality and Social Psychology, 31,* 674–685.

DWECK, C. S. (1978). Achievement. In M. E. Lamb (Ed.), *Social and personality development.* New York: Holt, Rinehart & Winston.

DWECK, C. S., DAVIDSON, W., NELSON, S., & ENNA, B. (1978). Sex differences in learned helplessness: II. The contingencies of evaluative feedback in the classroom; III. An experimental analysis. *Developmental Psychology, 14,* 268–276.

DWECK, C. S., & ELLIOTT, E. S. (1983). Achievement motivation. In E. M. Hetherington (Ed.), *Handbook of child psychology* (Vol. 4). New York: Wiley.

DWECK, C. S., & LEGGETT, E. L. (1988). A social-cognitive approach to motivation and personality. *Psychological Review, 95,* 256–273.

ELLIOTT, E. S., & DWECK, C. S. (1988). Goals: An approach to motivation and achievement. *Journal of Personality and Social Psychology, 54,* 5–12.

ENTWISLE, D. R., & ALEXANDER, K. L. (1990). Beginning school math competence: Minority and majority considerations. *Child Development, 61,* 454–471.

ENTWISLE, D. R., & BAKER, D. P. (1983). Gender and young children's expectations for performance in arithmetic. *Developmental Psychology, 19,* 200–209.

EYSENCK, H. J., & COOKSON, D. (1969). Personality in primary school children: 3. Family background. *British Journal of Educational Psychology, 40,* 117–131.

FINCHAM, F. D., HOKODA, A., & SANDERS, R., JR. (1989). Learned helplessness, test anxiety, and academic achievement: A longitudinal analysis. *Child Development, 60,* 138–145.

FINDLEY, M. J., & COOPER, H. M. (1983). Locus of control and academic achievement: A literature review. *Journal of Personality and Social Psychology, 44,* 419–427.

FRANCE-KAATRUDE, A., & SMITH, W. P. (1985). Social comparison, task motivation, and the development of self-evaluative standards in children. *Developmental Psychology, 21,* 1080–1089.

FRANKEL, K. A., & BATES, J. E. (1990). Mother-toddler problem-solving: Antecedents in attachment, home behavior, and temperament. *Child Development, 61,* 810–819.

FYANS, L. J., JR., SALILI, F., MAEHR, M. L., & DESAI, K. A. (1983). A cross-cultural exploration into the meaning of achievement. *Journal of Personality and Social Psychology, 44,* 1000–1013.

GLASS, D. C., NEULINGER, J., & BRIM, O. G. (1974). Birth order, verbal intelligence, and educational aspiration. *Child Development, 45,* 807–811.

GROLNICK, W. S., & RYAN, R. M. (1989). Parents' styles associated with children's self-regulation and competence in school. *Journal of Educational Psychology, 81,* 143–154.

HANNAH, J. S., & KAHN, S. E. (1989). The relationship of socioeconomic status and gender to the occupational choices of grade 12 students. *Journal of Vocational Behavior, 24,* 161–178.

HARTER, S. (1981). A new self-report scale of intrinsic versus extrinsic orientation in the classroom: Motivational and informational components. *Developmental Psychology, 17,* 300–312.

HARTER, S. (1988). Developmental processes in the construction of the self. In T. D. Yawkey & J. E. Johnson (Eds.), *Integrative processes in socialization: Early to middle childhood.* Hillsdale, NJ: Erlbaum.

HECKHAUSEN, H. (1984). Emergent achievement behavior: Some early developments. In J. Nicholls (Ed.), *Advances in motivation and achievement.* Vol. 3: *The development of achievement motivation.* Greenwich, CT: JAI Press.

HESS, R. D. (1970). Social class and ethnic influences upon socialization. In P. H. Mussen (Ed.), *Carmichael's manual of child psychology* (Vol. 2). New York: Wiley.

HEYMAN, G. D., DWECK, C. S., & CAIN, K. M. (1992). Young children's vulnerability to self-blame and helplessness: Relationship to beliefs about goodness. *Child Development, 63,* 401–415.

JACOBS, J. E., & ECCLES, J. S. (1992). The impact of mothers' gender-role stereotypic beliefs on mothers' and children's ability perceptions. *Journal of Personality and Social Psychology, 63,* 932–944.

JUSSIM, L., & ECCLES, J. S. (1992). Teacher expectations II: Construction and reflection of student achievement. *Journal of Personality and Social Psychology, 63,* 947–961.

KAGAN, J. (1981). *The second year: The emergence of self-awareness.* Cambridge, MA: Harvard University Press.

KELLAGHAN, T., & MacNAMARA, J. (1972). Family correlates of verbal reasoning ability. *Developmental Psychology, 7,* 49–53.

LAMBORN, S. D., MOUNTS, N. S., STEINBERG, L., & DORNBUSCH, S. M. (1991). Patterns of competence and adjustment among adolescents from authoritative, authoritarian, indulgent, and neglectful families. *Child Development, 62,* 1049–1065.

LEPPER, M. R. (1983). Social cognition processes, attributions of motivation, and the internalization of social values. In E. T. Higgins, D. N. Ruble, & W. W. Hartup (Eds.), *Social cognition and social behavior: Developmental perspectives.* Cambridge, England: Cambridge University Press.

LEPPER, M. R., GREENE, D., & NISBETT, R. E. (1973). Undermining children's intrinsic interest with extrinsic reward: A test of the overjustification hypothesis. *Journal of Personality and Social Psychology, 28,* 129–137.

LICHT, B. G., & DWECK, C. S. (1984). Determinants of academic achievement: The interaction of children's achievement orientations with skill area. *Developmental Psychology, 20,* 628–636.

LIN, C. C., & FU, V. R. (1990). A comparison of child-rearing practices among Chinese, immigrant Chinese, and Caucasian-American parents. *Child Development, 61,* 429–433.

LORD, C. G., UMEZAKI, K., & DARLEY, J. M. (1990). Developmental differences in decoding the meanings of appraisal actions of teachers. *Child Development, 61*, 191–200.

LOVELAND, K. K., & OLLEY, J. G. (1979). The effects of external reward on interest and quality of task performance in children of high or low intrinsic motivation. *Child Development, 50*, 1207–1210.

LUMMIS, M., & STEVENSON, H. W. (1990). Gender differences in beliefs and achievement: A cross-cultural study. *Developmental Psychology, 26*, 254–263.

MACCOBY, E. E., & JACKLIN, C. N. (1974). *The psychology of sex differences*. Stanford, CA: Stanford University Press.

MACCOBY, E. E., & MARTIN, J. A. (1983). Socialization in the context of the family: Parent-child interaction. In E. M. Hetherington (Ed.), *Handbook of child psychology*. Vol. 4: *Socialization, personality, and social development*. New York: Wiley.

MATAS, L., AREND, R. A., & SROUFE, L. A. (1978). Continuity of adaptation in the second year: The relationship between quality of attachment and later competence. *Child Development, 49*, 547–556.

McCLELLAND, D. C. (1955). *Studies in motivation*. New York: Appleton-Century-Crofts.

McCLELLAND, D. C. (1961). *The achieving society*. New York: Free Press.

McCLELLAND, D. C., ATKINSON, J. W., CLARK, R. A., & LOWELL, E. L. (1953). *The achievement motive*. New York: Appleton-Century-Crofts.

McCLELLAND, D. C., RINDLISBACHER, A., & de CHARMS, R. C. (1955). Religious and other sources of parental attitudes toward independence training. In D. C. McClelland (Ed.), *Studies in motivation*. New York: Appleton-Century-Crofts.

McLOYD, V. C. (1979). The effects of extrinsic rewards of differential value on high and low intrinsic interest. *Child Development, 50*, 1010–1019.

McLOYD, V. C. (1990). The impact of economic hardships on Black families and children: Psychological distress, parenting, and socioemotional development. *Child Development, 61*, 311–346.

McMAINS, M. J., & LIEBERT, R. M. (1968). The influence of discrepancies between successively modeled self-reward criteria on the adoption of a self-imposed standard. *Journal of Personality and Social Psychology, 8*, 166–171.

MESSER, D. J., McCARTHY, M. E., McQUISTON, S., MacTURK, R. H., YARROW, L. W., & VIETZE, P. M. (1986). Relation between mastery behavior in infancy and competence in early childhood. *Developmental Psychology, 22*, 366–372.

MINOR, C. A., & NEEL, R. G. (1958). The relationship between achievement motive and occupational preference. *Journal of Counseling Psychology, 5*, 39–43.

MINTON, H. L., & SCHNEIDER, F. W. (1980). *Differential psychology*. Pacific Grove, CA: Brooks/Cole.

MOORE, E. G. J. (1986). Family socialization and the IQ test performance of traditionally and transracially adopted black children. *Developmental Psychology, 22*, 317–326.

MOSATCHE, H. S., & BRAGONIER, P. (1981). An observational study of social comparison in preschoolers. *Child Development, 52*, 376–378.

MURRAY, H. (1938). *Explorations in personality*. New York: Oxford University Press.

NELSON-LeGALL, S., & JONES, E. (1990). Cognitive-motivational influences on the task-related help-seeking behavior of Black children. *Child Development, 61*, 581–589.

NICHOLLS, J. G. (1989). *The competitive ethos and democratic education*. Cambridge, MA: Harvard University Press.

NICHOLLS, J. G., & MILLER, A. T. (1984). Reasoning about the ability of self and others: A developmental study. *Child Development, 55*, 1990–1999.

NICHOLLS, J. G., & MILLER, A. T. (1985). Differentiation of the concepts of luck and skill. *Developmental Psychology, 21*, 76–82.

PALLAK, S. R., COSTOMIRIS, S., SROKA, S., & PITTMAN, T. S. (1982). School experience, reward characteristics, and intrinsic motivation. *Child Development, 53*, 1382–1391.

PARSONS, J. E., ADLER, T. F., & KACZALA, C. M. (1982). Socialization of achievement attitudes and beliefs: Parental influences. *Child Development, 53*, 310–321.

PARSONS, J. E., KACZALA, C. M., & MEECE, J. L. (1982). Socialization of achievement attitudes and beliefs: Classroom influences. *Child Development, 53*, 322–339.

PARSONS, J. E., RUBLE, D. N., HODGES, K. L., & SMALL, A. W. (1976). Cognitive-developmental factors in emerging sex differences in achievement-related expectancies. *Journal of Social Issues, 32*, 47–61.

PATTERSON, C. J., KUPERSMIDT, J. B., & VADEN, N. A. (1990). Income level, gender, ethnicity, and household composition as predictors of children's school-based competence. *Child Development, 61*, 485–494.

PAULHUS, D., & SHAFFER, D. R. (1981). Sex differences in the impact of number of younger and number of older siblings on scholastic aptitude. *Social Psychology Quarterly, 44*, 363–368.

PEARLMAN, C. (1984). The effects of level of effectance motivation, IQ, and a penalty/reward contingency on the choice of problem difficulty. *Child Development, 55*, 537–542.

PHILLIPS, D. (1984). The illusion of incompetence among academically competent children. *Child Development, 55*, 2000–2016.

RAYNOR, J. O. (1970). Relationships between achievement-related motives, future orientation, and academic performance. *Journal of Personality and Social Psychology, 15*, 28–33.

REID, P. T., & STEPHENS, D. S. (1985). The roots of future occupations in childhood: A review of the literature on girls and careers. *Youth and Society, 16*, 267–288.

RHOLES, W. S., & RUBLE, D. N. (1984). Children's understanding of dispositional characteristics of others. *Child Development, 55*, 550–560.

ROSEN, B. C., & D'ANDRADE, R. (1959). The psychological origins of achievement motivation. *Sociometry, 22*, 185–218.

ROSENHOLTZ, S. J., & SIMPSON, C. (1984). The formation of ability conceptions: Developmental trend or social construction? *Review of Educational Research, 54*, 31–63.

ROTHBART, M. K. (1971). Birth order and mother-child interaction in an achievement situation. *Journal of Personality and Social Psychology, 17*, 113–120.

RUBLE, D. N. (1988). Sex-role development. In M. H. Bornstein & M. E. Lamb (Eds.), *Developmental psychology: An advanced textbook* (2nd ed.). Hillsdale, NJ: Erlbaum.

RUBLE, D. N., BOGGIANO, A. K., FELDMAN, N. S., & LOEBL, J. H. (1980). Developmental analysis of the role of social comparison in self-evaluation. *Developmental Psychology, 16*, 105–115.

RUBLE, D. N., & FLETT, G. L. (1988). Conflicting goals in self-evaluative information seeking: Developmental and ability level analyses. *Child Development, 59*, 97–106.

RUBLE, D. N., PARSONS, J. E., & ROSS., J. (1976). *Self-evaluative responses in an achievement setting.* Unpublished manuscript, Princeton University.

SAMPSON, E. E., & HANCOCK, F. T. (1967). An examination of the relationship between ordinal position, personality, and conformity: An extension, replication, and partial verification. *Journal of Personality and Social Psychology, 5*, 398–407.

SCHACHTER, S. (1963). Birth order, eminence, and higher education. *American Sociological Review, 28*, 757–767.

SCHOOLER, C. (1972). Birth order effects: Not here, not now! *Psychological Bulletin, 78*, 161–175.

SHAFFER, D. R. (1993). *Developmental psychology: Childhood and adolescence* (3rd ed.). Pacific Grove, CA: Brooks/Cole.

SLAUGHTER-DEFOE, D. T., NAKAGAWA, K., TAKANISHI, R., & JOHNSON, D. L. (1990). Toward cultural/ecological perspectives on schooling and achievement in African- and Asian-American children. *Child Development, 61*, 363–383.

STEINBERG, L., DORNBUSCH, S. M., & BROWN, B. B. (1992). Ethnic differences in adolescent achievement: An ecological perspective. *American Psychologist, 47*, 723–729.

STEINBERG, L., ELMEN, J. D., & MOUNTS, N. S. (1989). Authoritative parenting, psychosocial maturity, and academic success among adolescents. *Child Development, 60*, 1424–1436.

STEVENSON, H. W., CHEN, C., & UTTAL, D. H. (1990). Beliefs and achievement: A study of Black, White, and Hispanic children. *Child Development, 61*, 508–523.

STEVENSON, H. W., & LEE, S. Y. (1990). Contexts of achievement: A study of American, Chinese, and Japanese children. *Monographs of the Society for Research in Child Development, 55* (1–2, Serial No. 221).

STIPEK, D. J., & HOFFMAN, J. M. (1980). Children's achievement related expectancies as a function of academic performance histories and sex. *Journal of Educational Psychology, 72*, 861–865.

STIPEK, D. J., & Mac IVER, D. (1989). Developmental change in children's assessment of intellectual competence. *Child Development, 60*, 521–538.

STIPEK, D. J., RECCHIA, S., & McCLINTIC, S. (1992). Self-evaluation in young children. *Monographs of the Society for Research in Child Development, 57* (1, Serial No. 226).

STIPEK, D. J., ROBERTS, T. A., & SANBORN, M. E. (1984). Preschool-age children's performance expectations for themselves and another child as a function of the incentive value of success and the salience of past performance. *Child Development, 55*, 1983–1989.

TARVIS, C., & WADE, C. (1984). *The longest war: Sex differences in perspective* (2nd ed.). San Diego: Harcourt Brace Jovanovich.

TEEVEN, R. C., & McGHEE, P. E. (1972). Childhood development of fear of failure motivation. *Journal of Personality and Social Psychology, 21*, 345–348.

THARP, R. G. (1989). Psychocultural variables and constants: Effects on teaching and learning in schools. *American Psychologist, 44*, 349–359.

TURNER, J. H. (1970). Entrepreneurial environments and the emergence of achievement motivation in adolescent males. *Sociometry, 33*, 147–165.

UNIVERSITY OF GEORGIA FACT BOOK (1991). Athens: University of Georgia Press.

van DOORNINCK, W. J., CALDWELL, B. M., WRIGHT, C., & FRANKENBERG, W. K. (1981). The relationship between twelve-month home stimulation and school achievement. *Child Development, 52*, 1080–1083.

WEBER, M. (1930). *The Protestant ethic and the spirit of capitalism* (T. Parsons, Trans.). New York: Scribner's. (Original work published 1904.)

WEINER, B. (1974). *Achievement and attribution theory.* Morristown, NJ: General Learning Press.

WEINER, B. (1982). An attribution theory of motivation and emotion. In H. Krohne & L. Laux (Eds.), *Achievement, stress, and anxiety.* Washington, DC: Hemisphere.

WEINER, B. (1986). *An attributional theory of motivation and emotion.* New York: Springer-Verlag.

WEISS, P. M., WERTHEIMER, M., & GROESBECK, B. (1959). Achievement motivation, academic aptitude, and college grades. *Educational and Psychological Measurement, 19*, 663–666.

WHITE, R. W. (1959). Motivation reconsidered: The concept of competence. *Psychological Review, 66*, 297–333.

WINTERBOTTOM, M. (1958). The relation of need for achievement to learning experiences in independence and mastery. In J. Atkinson (Ed.), *Motives in fantasy, action, and society.* Princeton, NJ: Van Nostrand.

YARROW, L. J., MacTURK, R. H., VIETZE, P. M., McCARTHY, M. E., KLEIN, R. P., & McQUISTON, S. (1984). Developmental course of parental stimulation and its relationship to mastery motivation during infancy. *Developmental Psychology, 20*, 492–503.

ZAJONC, R. B. (1975, August). Birth order and intelligence: Dumber by the dozen. *Psychology Today*, pp. 39–43.

ZAJONC, R. B., MARKUS, H., & MARKUS, G. B. (1979). The birth order puzzle. *Journal of Personality and Social Psychology, 37*, 1325–1341.

9 Sex Differences and Sex-Role Development

How important is a child's gender to his or her eventual development? The answer seems to be "very important!" Often the first bit of information that parents receive about their child is his or her sex, and the question "Is it a boy or a girl?" is the very first one that most friends and relatives ask when proud new parents telephone to announce the birth of their baby (Intons-Peterson & Reddel, 1984). Indeed, the ramifications of this gender labeling are normally swift in coming and rather direct. In the hospital nursery or delivery room, parents often call an infant son things like "big guy" or "tiger," and they are likely to comment on the vigor of his cries, kicks, or grasps. By contrast, female infants are more likely to be labeled "sugar" or "sweetie" and to be described as soft, cuddly, and adorable (Maccoby, 1980; MacFarlane, 1977). A newborn infant is usually blessed with a name that reflects his or her gender, and in many Western societies children are immediately adorned in either blue or pink. Mavis Hetherington and Ross Parke (1975, pp. 354-355) describe the predicament of a developmental psychologist who "did not want observers to know whether they were watching boys or girls":

> Even in the first few days of life some infant girls were brought to the laboratory with pink bows tied to wisps of their hair or taped to their little bald heads. . . . When another attempt at concealment of sex was made by asking mothers to dress their infants in overalls, girls appeared in pink and boys in blue overalls, and, "Would you believe overalls with ruffles?"

This gender indoctrination continues during the first year as parents provide their children with "sex-appropriate" clothing, toys, and hairstyles (Pomerleau et al., 1990). Moreover, they often play differently with and expect different reactions from their young sons and daughters (Caldera, Huston, & O'Brien, 1989; MacDonald & Parke, 1986). So it is clear that a child's companions view gender as an important attribute—one that often determines how they will respond to him or her.

Why do people react differently to males and females—especially *infant* males and females? One explanation centers on the biological differences between the sexes. Recall that fathers determine the

PHOTO 9-1   Sex-role socialization begins very early as parents provide their infants with "gender-appropriate" clothing, toys, and hairstyles.

gender of their offspring. A zygote that receives an X chromosome from each parent is a genetic (XX) female that will develop into a baby girl, whereas a zygote that receives a Y chromosome from the father is a genetic (XY) male that will normally assume the appearance of a baby boy. Could it be that this basic genetic difference between the sexes is ultimately responsible for *sex differences in behavior*—differences that might explain why parents often do not treat their sons and daughters alike? We will explore this interesting idea in some detail in a later section of the chapter.

However, there is more to sex differences than biological heritage. Virtually all societies expect males and females to behave differently and to assume different roles. In order to conform to these expectations, the child must understand that he is a boy or that she is a girl and must incorporate this information into his or her self-concept. In this chapter we will concentrate on the interesting and controversial topic of **sex typing**—the process by which children acquire not only a gender identity but also the motives, values, and behaviors considered appropriate in their culture for members of their biological sex.[1]

We begin the chapter by summarizing what people generally believe to be true about sex differences in cognition, personality, and social behavior. As it turns out, some of these stereotypes appear to be reasonably accurate, although many others are best described as fictions or fables that have no basis in fact. We will then look at developmental trends in sex typing and see that youngsters are often well aware of sex-role stereotypes and are displaying sex-typed patterns of behavior long before they are old enough to go to kindergarten. And how do children learn so much about the sexes and sex roles at such an early age? We will address this issue by reviewing several influential theories of sex typing—theories that indicate how biological forces, social experiences, and cognitive development might combine or interact to influence the sex-typing process. And, after examining a new perspective on sex typing, which asserts that traditional sex roles have outlived their usefulness in today's modern society, we will conclude by briefly considering yet another aspect of development that is central to our concept of self as male or female: the growth of human sexuality.

Categorizing Males and Females: Sex-Role Standards

Most of us have learned a great deal about males and females by the time we enter college. In

---

[1]Some writers have used the term *sex* when talking about biological differences between males and females and the term *gender* when discussing masculine and feminine traits and behavioral preferences that are heavily influenced by social forces. This usage is *not* adopted here, on the assumption that differences between males and females on any (and all) psychological attribute(s) could conceivably result from an interaction between biological predispositions and social influences. Thus I use the terms *sex* and *gender* interchangeably and will reserve the term *sexual* for behavior that is directly linked to mating and genital activities.

fact, if you and your classmates were asked to jot down ten psychological dimensions on which men and women are thought to differ, it is likely that every member of the class could easily generate such a list. Here's a head start: Which gender is most likely to display emotions? to be tidy? to be competitive? to use harsh language?

A **sex-role standard** is a value, a motive, or a class of behavior that is considered more appropriate for members of one sex than the other. Taken together, a society's sex-role standards describe how males and females are expected to behave and, thus, reflect the stereotypes by which we categorize and respond to members of each sex.

The female's role as childbearer is largely responsible for the sex-role standards that have prevailed in many societies, including our own. Girls have typically been encouraged to assume an **expressive role** that involves being kind, nurturant, cooperative, and sensitive to the needs of others (Parsons, 1955). These psychological traits, it was assumed, will prepare girls to play the wife and mother roles—to keep the family functioning and to raise children successfully. By contrast, boys have been encouraged to adopt an **instrumental role**, for as a traditional husband and father a male would face the tasks of providing for the family and protecting it from harm. Thus young boys are expected to become dominant, assertive, independent, and competitive. Similar norms and role prescriptions are found in many—though certainly not all—societies (Whiting & Edwards, 1988). In one rather ambitious project, Herbert Barry, Margaret Bacon, and Irving Child (1957) analyzed the sex-typing practices of 110 nonindustrialized societies, looking for sex differences in the socialization of five attributes: nurturance, obedience, responsibility, achievement, and self-reliance. The results are summarized in Table 9-1. Note that achievement and self-reliance were more often expected of young boys, whereas young girls were encouraged to become nurturant, responsible, and obedient.

Children in modern industrialized societies also face strong sex-typing pressures, though not always to the same extent and in the same ways that children in nonindustrialized societies do. (For example, parents in Western societies place roughly equal

TABLE 9-1   *Sex differences in the socialization
of five attributes*

| | Percentage of Societies in Which Socialization Pressures Were Greater for: | |
Attribute	Boys	Girls
Nurturance	0	82
Obedience	3	35
Responsibility	11	61
Achievement	87	3
Self-reliance	85	0

NOTE: The percentages for each attribute do not add to 100, because some of the societies did not place differential pressures on boys and girls with respect to that particular attribute. For example, 18% of the societies for which pertinent data were available did not differentiate between the sexes in the socialization of nurturance.
SOURCE: Adapted from H. Barry III, M. K. Bacon, & I. L. Child, "A Cross-Cultural Survey of Some Sex Differences in Socialization." *Journal of Abnormal and Social Psychology*, 1957, 55, 327–332. Copyright © 1957 by the American Psychological Association.

PHOTO 9-2   In most societies around the world, girls are encouraged to be warm and nurturant.

emphasis on achievement for sons and for daughters; Lytton & Romney, 1991). Moreover, the findings in Table 9-1 do not imply that female self-reliance is frowned on or that disobedience by young males is acceptable. In fact, all five attributes that Barry et al. studied were encouraged of *both* boys and girls, but with different emphases depending on the sex of the child (Zern, 1984). So it appears that the first goal of socialization is to encourage children to acquire those traits that will enable them to become well-behaved, contributing members of society. A second goal (but one that adults view as important nevertheless) is to "sex-type" the child by stressing the importance of relationship-oriented (or expressive) attributes for females and individualistic (or instrumental) ones for males.

When cultural norms demand that females play an expressive role and males play an instrumental role, we may be inclined to assume that females actually display expressive traits and that males possess instrumental qualities. Indeed, surveys conducted during the early 1970s revealed precisely this pattern: when asked to pick out the traits that characterize "typical" men and women, both college students and mental health professionals in the

United States selected expressive traits for females and instrumental traits for males (Broverman et al., 1972). If you are thinking that these stereotypes have disappeared as attention to women's rights has increased and as more women have assumed an instrumental role by entering the labor force, you are wrong! Although some change has occurred, primarily in the direction of viewing high-status, traditionally masculine professions as more appropriate for women (Shaffer et al., 1986), adolescents and young adults still endorse many traditional standards of masculinity and femininity (see Table 9-2) and still tend to prefer individuals who conform to these prescriptions (Lewin & Tragos, 1987; Ruble, 1983; White et al., 1989). Might these stereotypes have any basis in fact? Let's see if they do.

Some Facts and Fictions about Sex Differences

The old French maxim "Vive la difference" reflects a fact that we all know to be true: males and females are anatomically different. Adult males are typically taller, heavier, and more muscular than

TABLE 9-2 *Attributes regarded as clearly masculine and clearly feminine by college students of the 1980s*

Masculine Attributes	Feminine Attributes
Active	Aware of others' feelings
Adventurous	Considerate
Aggressive	Creative
Ambitious	Cries easily
Competitive	Devotes self to others
Dominant	Emotional
Independent	Enjoys art and music
Leadership qualities	Excitable in a crisis
Likes math and science	Expresses tender feelings
Makes decisions easily	Feelings hurt
Mechanical aptitude	Gentle
Not easily influenced	Home oriented
Outspoken	Kind
Persistent	Likes children
Self-confident	Neat
Skilled in business	Needs approval
Stands up under pressure	Tactful
Takes a stand	Understanding

SOURCE: Adapted from T. L. Ruble, "Sex Stereotypes: Issues of Change in the 1970s." *Sex Roles*, 1983, *9*, 397–402. Copyright © 1983 by Plenum Publishing Company. Adapted by permission.

adult females, although females may be hardier in the sense that they live longer and are less susceptible to many diseases. But, despite these obvious physical variations, the evidence for sex differences in psychological functioning is not as clear as most of us might think.

Actual Psychological Differences between the Sexes

In their now-classic review of more than 1500 studies comparing males and females, Eleanor Maccoby and Carol Jacklin (1974) concluded that a few traditional sex-role stereotypes are accurate and that many qualify as "cultural myths" that have no basis in fact. Indeed, Maccoby and Jacklin claimed that only four common gender stereotypes are consistently supported by research:

1. Females have greater *verbal abilities* than males. Girls develop verbal skills at an earlier age than boys and display a small but consistent verbal advantage on tests of reading comprehension, vocabulary, and speech fluency throughout the early

grade-school years. Although sex differences in verbal ability are still detectable in adolescence, they are so small that recent reviewers of the literature have branded them as negligible (Feingold, 1988; Hyde & Linn, 1988).

2. Males outperform females on some tests of **visual/spatial abilities** — that is, the ability to draw inferences about or to otherwise mentally manipulate pictorial information (see Figure 9-1 for two kinds of visual/spatial tasks on which sex differences are found). The male advantage in spatial abilities is not large (Linn & Hyde, 1989), although it is detectable by middle childhood and persists across the life span (Johnson & Meade, 1987; Linn & Petersen, 1985).

3. Beginning in adolescence, boys show a small but consistent advantage over girls on tests of *arithmetic reasoning* (Feingold, 1988; Hyde, Fennema, & Lamon, 1990). Interestingly, boys and girls have equal knowledge of math concepts, and girls outperform boys in computational skills. It is only in performance of complex word problems that males outperform females, and this difference is most apparent at the higher end of the

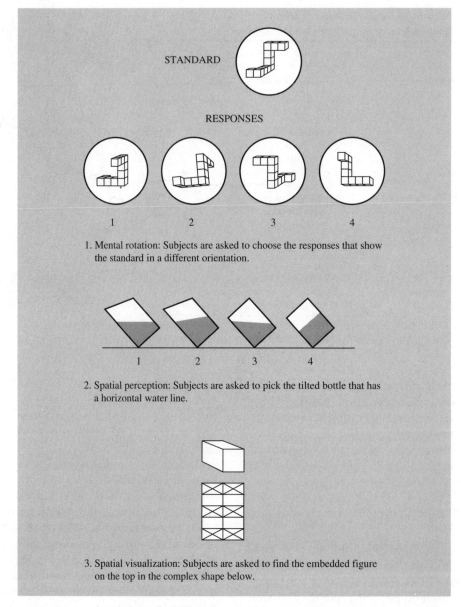

STANDARD

RESPONSES

1   2   3   4

1. Mental rotation: Subjects are asked to choose the responses that show
   the standard in a different orientation.

1   2   3   4

2. Spatial perception: Subjects are asked to pick the tilted bottle that has
   a horizontal water line.

3. Spatial visualization: Subjects are asked to find the embedded figure
   on the top in the complex shape below.

FIGURE 9-1   Types of spatial tasks on which the performance of males and females
has been compared. (From M. C. Linn & A. C. Petersen, 1985, "Emergence and Characteristics of Sex Differences in Spatial Ability: A Meta-Analysis." *Child Development, 56,* 1479–1498. ©
1985 by the Society for Research in Child Development, Inc. Reprinted by permission.)

distribution, where more males than females are
exceptionally talented in math (Hyde et al., 1990).

4. Finally, males are more physically and verbally *aggressive* than females, starting as early as
age 2 (see also Eagly & Steffen, 1986; Hyde, 1984).

Other researchers were quick to criticize Maccoby
and Jacklin's early review, claiming that the procedures they used to gather and tabulate their results led them to underestimate the number of true
sex differences that actually exist (see, for example,

Block, 1976; Huston, 1983). Indeed, new research and new literature reviews point to several additional sex-role stereotypes that seem to be accurate:

5. *Activity level.* Starting in infancy, boys are more physically active than girls (Eaton & Enns, 1986; Eaton & Yu, 1989). Indeed, the heightened activity that boys display may help to explain why they are more likely than girls to initiate and to be receptive to bouts of nonaggressive rough-and-tumble play (DiPietro, 1981; Humphreys & Smith, 1987).

6. *Fear, timidity, and risk taking.* Girls consistently *report* being more fearful or timid in uncertain situations than boys do. Girls are also more cautious in such situations, taking far fewer risks than their male agemates (Christophersen, 1989; Ginsburg & Miller, 1982).

7. *Developmental vulnerability.* From conception, boys are more physically vulnerable than girls to prenatal and perinatal stress and to the effects of disease. Boys are also more likely than girls to display a large number of developmental disorders, including reading disabilities, speech defects, hyperactivity, emotional disorders, and mental retardation (Henker & Whalen, 1989; Jacklin, 1989).

8. *Emotional sensitivity/expressivity.* From about age 4–5 on, girls and women appear to be more interested in and more responsive to infants than boys and men are (Berman & Goodman, 1984; Blakemore, 1981; Reid, Tate, & Berman, 1989), and they rate themselves higher in nurturance and empathy as well (although they often appear no more empathic than boys and men in naturalistic settings; see, for example, Fabes, Eisenberg, & Miller, 1990). Girls and women characterize their emotions as deeper or more intense than boys and men do (Diener, Sandvik, & Larson, 1985). By age 11 or 12, girls feel more comfortable than boys about openly displaying their emotions (Fuchs & Thelen, 1988).

9. *Compliance.* Throughout childhood, girls seem to be more compliant than boys to the demands of parents, teachers, and other authority figures (Cowan & Avants, 1988; Maccoby, 1988). But "pushovers" they are not, for girls are no more (and possibly less) compliant than boys to

PHOTO 9-3   Rough-and-tumble play is more common among boys than among girls.

the demands and directives of agemates (Maccoby, 1988). However, the sexes do differ in the methods used to persuade others or to induce compliance, with girls being more inclined than boys to rely on polite suggestions, cooperation, and verbal negotiations rather than forceful, demanding, and individualistic strategies (Borja-Alvarez, Zarbatany, & Pepper, 1991; Charlesworth & Dzur, 1987; Cowan & Avants, 1988).

In reviewing the evidence for "real" sex differences, we should keep in mind that the data reflect *group averages* that may or may not characterize the behavior of any particular individual. For example, gender accounts for about 5% of the variation children display in aggressive behavior (Hyde, 1984), so the remaining 95% is due to differences between people other than their sex. Moreover, the sex differences in verbal, spatial, and mathematical abilities that Maccoby and Jacklin identified are also small—and even smaller today than they were 20 years ago (Feingold, 1988; Hyde et al., 1990). Finally, gender variations that emerge in one social context may not be evident elsewhere. For example, the sex differences in cognitive abilities found in North American cultures are not found among kibbutz-reared children in Israel, which suggests that they

TABLE 9-3 *Some unfounded beliefs about sex differences*

Belief	Facts
1. Girls are more "social" than boys.	Research indicates that the two sexes are equally interested in social stimuli, equally responsive to social reinforcement, and equally proficient at learning through imitation of social models. At certain ages, boys actually spend more time than girls with playmates.
2. Girls are more "suggestible" than boys.	Most studies of children's conformity find no sex differences. However, some researchers have found that boys are more likely than girls to accept peer-group values that conflict with their own.
3. Girls have lower self-esteem than boys.	The sexes are highly similar in their overall self-satisfaction and self-confidence throughout childhood and adolescence. However, men and women differ in the areas in which they have their greatest self-confidence; girls rate themselves higher in social competence, whereas boys see themselves as more dominant or potent. Thus, males and females apply questionable sex-role stereotypes to themselves.
4. Girls are better at simple repetitive tasks, whereas boys excel at tasks that require higher-level cognitive processing.	The evidence does not support these assertions. Neither sex is superior at role learning, probability learning, or concept formation.
5. Boys are more "analytic" than girls.	Overall, boys and girls do not differ on tests of analytic cognitive style or logical reasoning, although boys do show a slight advantage if the task requires visual/spatial abilities.
6. Girls lack achievement motivation.	No such differences exist in global measures of achievement motivation. However, boys perceive themselves as more competent in the stereotypically "masculine" domains of math, athletics, and mechanical skills, whereas girls have higher expectancies in such stereotypically feminine domains as reading, art, and music. Perhaps the myth of lesser achievement motivation for females has persisted because males and females have generally directed their achievement strivings toward different goals.

SOURCES: Adapted from E. E. Maccoby & C. N. Jacklin, *The Psychology of Sex Differences.* Copyright © 1974 by Stanford University Press. Reprinted by permission of the Board of Trustees for the Leland Stanford Junior University. Also adapted from A. H. Stein, "The Effects of Sex-Role Standards of Achievement and Sex-Role Preference on Three Determinants of Achievement Motivation." *Developmental Psychology,* 1971, 4, 219–231.

are not biologically inevitable and that social/contextual factors must play an important role in the development of males and females (Safir, 1986).

What, then, should we conclude from this research? Although contemporary scholars may quibble at times about which psychological differences between the sexes are real, most developmentalists can agree on this: *males and females are far more psychologically similar than they are different,* and even the most well-documented differences seem to be modest. So it is impossible to accurately predict the aggressiveness, mathematical skill, activity level, or emotional expressivity of any individual simply by knowing his or her gender. Only when group averages are computed do the sex differences emerge.

Cultural Myths

Another conclusion that most developmentalists now endorse is Maccoby and Jacklin's (1974) proposition that most popular sex-role stereotypes are "cultural myths" that have no basis in fact. Among the most widely accepted of these "myths" are those in Table 9-3.

Why do these inaccuracies persist? Maccoby and Jacklin (1974) propose that:

a . . . likely explanation for the perpetuation of "myths" is the fact that stereotypes are such powerful things. An ancient truth is worth restating here: if a generalization about a group of people is believed, whenever a member of the group behaves in a way that is not consistent with the observer's expectations, the instance is likely to pass unnoticed, and the observer's generalized belief is protected from disconfirmation. We believe that this well-documented [selective attention] process occurs continually in relation to the expected and perceived behavior of males and females, and results in the perpetuation of myths that would other-

wise die out under the impact of negative evidence [p. 355].

In other words, sex-role stereotypes are well-ingrained cognitive schemes that we use to interpret and often to distort the behavior of males and females (Martin & Halverson, 1981; see also Box 9-1). People even use these schemes to classify the behavior of infants. In one study (Condry & Condry,

---

B O X **9-1** | *Do Sex Stereotypes Color Children's Interpretations of Counterstereotypic Information?*

Maccoby and Jacklin (1974) proposed that, once people learn sex stereotypes, they are more likely to attend to and remember events that are consistent with these beliefs than events that would disconfirm them. Carol Martin and Charles Halverson (1981) agree. Martin and Halverson argue that gender stereotypes are well-ingrained schemata or naive theories that people use to organize and represent experience. Once established, these gender schemata should have at least two important effects on a child's (or an adult's) cognitive processes: (1) an *organizational* effect on memory, such that information consistent with the schemata will be easier to remember than counterstereotypic events, and (2) a *distortion* effect, such that counterstereotypic information will tend to be remembered as much more consistent with one's gender schemata than the information really is. For example, it should be easier for people to remember that they saw a girl at the stove cooking (sex-consistent information) than a boy partaking in the same activity (sex-inconsistent information). And, if people were to witness the latter event, they might distort what they had seen to make it more consistent with their stereotypes—perhaps by remembering the actor as a girl rather than a boy or by reconstruing the boy's activities as *fixing* the stove rather than cooking.

Martin and Halverson (1983) tested their hypotheses in an interesting study with 5- to 6-year-olds. During a first session, each child was shown 16 pictures, of which half depicted a child performing *gender-consistent* activities (for example, a boy playing with a truck) and half showed children displaying *gender-*

inconsistent behaviors (for example, a girl chopping wood). One week later, children's memory for what they had seen was assessed.

The results of this experiment were indeed interesting. Children easily recalled the sex of the actor for scenes in which gender-consistent activities had been performed. But, when the actor's behavior was gender-*inconsistent*, these youngsters often distorted the scene by saying that the actor's sex was consistent with the activity they recalled (for example, they were likely to say that it had been a boy rather than a girl who had chopped wood). As predicted, children's *confidence* about the sex of the actors was greater for gender-consistent scenes than for gender-inconsistent ones, suggesting that counterstereotypic information is harder to remember. But it is noteworthy that, when children actually distorted a gender-inconsistent scene, they were just as confident about the sex of the actor (which they recalled *incorrectly*) as they were for the gender-consistent scenes in which they correctly recalled the actor's sex. So it seems that children are likely to distort counterstereotypic information to be more consistent with their stereotypes and that these memory distortions are as "real" to them as stereotypical information that has not been distorted (see Cann & Newbern, 1984, for a similar set of findings with 6- to 8-year-olds).

Why, then, do inaccurate sex stereotypes persist? Because we find disconfirming evidence harder to recall and, in fact, will often distort that information in ways that will confirm our initial (and inaccurate) beliefs.

1976), college students watched a videotape of a 9-month-old child who was introduced as either a girl ("Dana") or a boy ("David"). As the students observed the child at play, they were asked to interpret his/her reactions to toys such as a teddy bear or a jack-in-the-box. The resulting impressions of the infant's behavior clearly depended on his or her presumed sex. For example, a strong reaction to the jack-in-the-box was labeled "anger" when the child was presumed to be a male and "fear" when the child had been introduced as a female (see also Stern & Karraker, 1989).

As it turns out, the persistence of unfounded or inaccurate sex-role stereotypes has important consequences for both males and females. We'll now look at some of the more negative implications of these cultural myths.

Evaluating the Accomplishments of Males and Females

In 1968 Phillip Goldberg asked female college students to judge the merits of several professional articles that were attributed either to a male author ("John McKay") or to a female author ("Joan McKay"). Although these manuscripts were identical in every other respect, subjects perceived the articles written by a male to be of higher quality than those by a female.

This tendency to undervalue the accomplishments of females is apparent even when males and females are asked to explain their *own* successes. Females who succeed at *unfamiliar* achievement tasks are much more likely than males to attribute their favorable outcomes to luck, whereas males are more inclined to ascribe their successes to high ability (Dweck & Elliott, 1983). And, in one study in which males and females were asked to explain achievements that are not easily ascribed to luck (for example, the accomplishments of a successful male or female physician), subjects of each sex tended to attribute the male's success to high ability and the female's to her untiring efforts to succeed (Feldman-Summers & Kiesler, 1974). In other words, people believe that females must try harder to accomplish the same feats as males.

When do children first begin to think that males are more competent than females? Earlier, perhaps, than you might imagine. Susan Haugh and her colleagues (Haugh, Hoffman, & Cowan, 1980) asked 3- and 5-year-olds to watch two infants on film, one of whom was presumed to be a male. When told to point to the baby who was "smart," these preschool children typically chose whichever infant had been labeled the boy. (Indeed, one review of the literature indicates that children draw even stronger stereotyped distinctions between babies arbitrarily labeled "boys" and "girls" than adults do; Stern & Karraker, 1989). By the time they enter first grade, children already perceive boys to be more competent at unfamiliar tasks and more worthy of leadership roles than girls are (Pollis & Doyle, 1972). And kindergarten and first-grade girls already believe that they are not as good as boys at concept-formation tasks and arithmetic, even though they are earning as high or even higher grades in arithmetic and have outperformed their male classmates on tests of concept learning (Entwisle & Baker, 1983).

In Chapter 8 we noted how parents (and later teachers) may contribute to these sexist attitudes by (1) communicating different expectancies to boys than to girls (for example, viewing boys as more competent at math; Lummis & Stevenson, 1990) or (2) responding differently to boys' and girls' achievement outcomes (for example, praising boys' abilities and girls' hard work when they achieve a noteworthy success but emphasizing boys' lack of effort and girls' lack of ability when they fail; Dweck et al., 1978). Yet there is some evidence that the pervasive tendency to underestimate women's competencies or to degrade their accomplishments is beginning to wane. About 20 years ago, during the mid-1970s, young adults perceived such high-status professions as medicine, architecture, and college teaching as less valuable or prestigious once they had been led to believe that the proportion of women practitioners in these fields was on the rise (Touhey, 1974). Thus, when women were likely to make significant contributions to a high-status vocation, subjects would reassess the value or prestige of the profession rather than acknowledge the competencies of women! But, when my associates and I replicated this research in 1985, these sexist assessments were no longer apparent (Shaffer et al., 1986). In fact, young adults of the mid-1980s actually considered at least one high-status profession (college professor) to be *higher* in desirability and prestige if they had been led to believe that the proportion of women practitioners would be increasing. So, even though stereotypes are powerful things that often distort the ways we process social information (see Box 9-1), the myth that "males are more competent" should eventually crumble as females lend their talents, in ever-increasing numbers, to all noteworthy domains and occupations heretofore viewed as "masculine" pursuits.

Now let's explore the sex-typing process to see why it is that males and females might come to view themselves so differently and choose to assume complementary roles.

Developmental Trends in Sex Typing

Sex-typing research has traditionally focused on three separate but interrelated topics: (1) the development of **gender identity**, or the knowledge that one is either a boy or a girl and that gender is an unchanging attribute; (2) the development of **sex-role stereotypes**, or ideas about what males and females are supposed to be like; and (3) the development of **sex-typed behavior**—that is, the child's tendency to favor same-sex activities over those normally associated with the other sex. Let's look first at the child's understanding of gender and its implications.

Development of the Gender Concept

The first step in the development of a gender identity is to discriminate males from females and to treat them as categorically distinct. This happens sooner than many of us might imagine. By 6 months of age, infants are already detecting the similarities among different women's voices (that is, forming a "female voice" category) and are using differences

in vocal pitch to discriminate female speech from that of males (Miller, 1983). Categorical perception of male and female faces occurs slightly later; Mary Leinbach and Beverly Fagot (1993; in press) find that about 50% of 9-month-olds and 75% of 12-month-olds can reliably discriminate photographs of male and female adults and are perceiving them as different kinds of people. And it seems that these early gender categories consist mainly of "long-haired" (female) and "short-haired" (male) individuals, for 12-month-old infants cannot reliably discriminate the sexes when the women have short hair (see also Intons-Peterson, 1988). Let's note, however, that the year-old infant's ability to *perceive* males and females as members of different categories does not imply that the child has any conscious awareness of this distinction (Leinbach & Fagot, 1993; in press).

Between ages 2 and 3, children are able to tell us what they know about gender as they acquire such gender labels as "mommy" and "daddy" and "boy" and "girl." Interestingly, 2- to 3-year-olds can apply the correct labels to photographs of adult males and females several months before they can correctly identify photos of children as boys or girls, probably because adults are more salient or important to these youngsters than other children are (Leinbach & Fagot, 1993; in press). By age 2½ to 3 almost all children can label *themselves* as boys or girls (Thompson, 1975), although it will be some time before they recognize that gender is a permanent attribute. Indeed, many 3- to 5-year-olds think that boys could become mommies or girls daddies if they really wanted to or that a person who changes clothing and hairstyles can become a member of the other sex (Fagot, 1985b; Marcus & Overton, 1978; Slaby & Frey, 1975). Children normally begin to understand that sex is an unchanging attribute between the ages of 5 and 7, so that most youngsters have a "stable" identity as a male or a female by the time they enter grade school.

Development of Sex-Role Stereotypes

Remarkable as it may seem, toddlers begin to acquire sex-role stereotypes at about the same time that they begin to label themselves as boys or girls (see Huston, 1983; Weinraub et al., 1984). Deanna Kuhn and her associates (Kuhn, Nash, & Brucken, 1978) showed a male doll ("Michael") and a female doll ("Lisa") to 2½–3½-year-olds and then asked each child which of the two dolls would engage in sex-stereotyped activities such as cooking, sewing, playing with dolls (trucks, trains), talking a lot, giving kisses, fighting, or climbing trees. Almost all the 2½-year-olds had some knowledge of sex-role stereotypes. For example, boys and girls agreed that girls talk a lot, never hit, often need help, like to play with dolls, and like to help their mothers with chores such as cooking and cleaning. By contrast, these young children felt that boys like to play with cars, like to help their fathers, like to build things, and are likely to make statements such as "I can hit you." The 2- to 3-year-olds who know the most about gender stereotypes are those who can correctly label photographs of other children as boys and girls (Fagot, Leinbach, & O'Boyle, 1992). So, understanding of gender labels seems to accelerate the process of sex-role stereotyping.

Over the next several years, children learn more and more about the activities and behaviors of males and females and will eventually begin (by about age 8) to draw sharp distinctions between the sexes on *psychological* dimensions. In one well-known cross-cultural study, for example, Deborah Best and her colleagues (1977) found that 8-year-olds and (especially) 11-year-olds in England, Ireland, and the United States generally agree that women are weak, emotional, soft hearted, sophisticated, and affectionate, whereas men are ambitious, assertive, aggressive, dominating, and cruel.

How seriously do children take the sex-role standards they are rapidly learning? Do they believe that they must conform to these stereotypes? Three- to 6-year-olds do; they reason like little chauvinists, treating sex-role prescriptions as blanket rules that are not to be violated (Martin, 1989). Consider the reactions of one 6-year-old when commenting on a boy named George who likes to play with dolls:

> He should only play with things that boys play with, the things that he is playing with now is girls' stuff. . . . (*Can George play with Barbie dolls if he wants to?*) No sir! . . . (*What should George do?*) He should

stop playing with girls' dolls and start playing with G.I. Joe. (*Why can a boy play with G.I. Joe and not a Barbie doll?*) Because if a boy is playing with a Barbie doll, then he's just going to get people teasing him . . . and if he tries to play more, to get girls to like him, then the girls won't like him either [Damon, 1977, p. 255; italics added].

By age 7 to 9, however, children are becoming much more flexible in their thinking about sex-role stereotypes and much less chauvinistic (Damon, 1977; Martin, 1989). Notice how 9-year-old James reacts to George's doll play, making a clear distinction between moral rules that people are obliged to obey and sex-role standards that are customary but *nonobligatory*:

> (*What do you think [George's] parents should do?*) They should . . . get him trucks and stuff, and see if he will play with those. (*What if . . . he kept on playing with dolls? Do you think they would punish him?*) No. (*How come?*) It's not really doing anything bad. (*Why isn't it bad?*) Because . . . if he was breaking a window, and he kept on doing that, they could punish him, because you're not supposed to break windows. But if you want to you can play with dolls. (*What's the difference?*) Well, breaking windows you're not supposed to do. And if you play with dolls, you can, but boys usually don't [Damon, 1977, p. 263; italics added].

Interestingly, many 12- to 15-year-olds once again become very intolerant of certain cross-sex behaviors (such as a male wearing nail polish or a female sporting a crew cut), even though they remain flexible about the hobbies or occupations that males and females might pursue (see Carter & McCloskey, 1983–1984; Sigelman, Carr, & Begley, 1986; Stoddart & Turiel, 1985). How can we account for this second round of gender chauvinism?

One possibility is that youngsters may tend to exaggerate sex-role stereotypes in order to "get them cognitively clear" during those developmental epochs when gender and gender-related issues are particularly important to them (Maccoby, 1980). The preschool and early grade-school years (ages 3–6 or 7) are one such period, for this is when children are firmly classifying themselves as boys or girls and will want to understand *exactly* how boys and girls are supposed to behave so that they can live up to their self-images. And, given the many gender-linked physical and physiological changes that occur at puberty, a young adolescent's sudden intolerance of personal mannerisms that imply a deviant, cross-sex identification may simply reflect a second attempt to clarify sex-role standards in his or her own mind as a prelude to establishing a mature *personal/social* (or sexual) identity. One implication of this point of view is that college students and other young adults should again become more flexible in their thinking about gender stereotypes once they have resolved their identity crises and have come to feel more comfortable with their masculine or feminine self-concepts. Indeed, young adults are much less rigidly stereotyped in their thinking about sex roles than high school students are (Urberg, 1979).

Development of Sex-Typed Behavior

The most common method of assessing the "sex appropriateness" of children's behavior is to observe whom and what they like to play with. Sex differences in toy preferences develop very early—even before the child has established a clear gender identity or can correctly label various toys as "boy things" or "girl things" (Blakemore, LaRue, & Olejnik, 1979; Fagot, Leinbach, & Hagan, 1986; Weinraub et al., 1984). Boys aged 14 to 22 months usually prefer trucks and cars to other objects, whereas girls of this age would rather play with dolls and soft toys (Smith & Daglish, 1977). In fact, 18- to 24-month-old toddlers will often refuse to play with cross-sex toys, even when there are no other objects available for them to play with (Caldera et al., 1989).

Children's preferences for same-sex playmates also develop very early. In nursery school, 2-year-old girls already prefer to play with other girls (La Freniere, Strayer, & Gauthier, 1984); by age 3, boys are reliably selecting boys rather than girls as companions. At age 4½, children are spending three times as much time playing with same-sex as with cross-sex partners, and by age 6½ the ratio of same-sex to opposite-sex playtime has increased to 11 to 1

(Maccoby, 1988). Moreover, the same pattern of increasing gender segregation has now been observed in 12 different cultures from widely scattered parts of the world (Whiting & Edwards, 1988).

Might these same-sex affiliative preferences reflect a basic incompatibility in the play behaviors of young boys and girls? To find out, Jacklin and Maccoby (1978) dressed pairs of 33-month-old toddlers in gender-neutral clothing (T-shirts and pants) and placed them together in a laboratory playroom that contained several interesting toys. Some of these dyads were same-sex pairs (two boys or two girls), and others were mixed-sex pairs (a boy and a girl). As the children played, an adult observer recorded how often they engaged in solitary activities and in socially directed play. As we see in Figure 9-2, social play varied as a function of the sex of one's playmate: boys directed more social responses to boys than to girls, whereas girls were more sociable with girls than with boys. Interactions between playmates in the same-sex dyads were lively and positive in character. By contrast, girls tended to withdraw from boys in the mixed-sex dyads. Maccoby

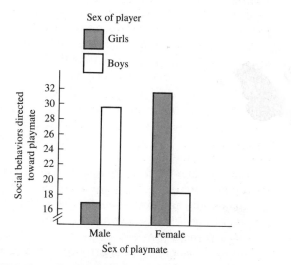

FIGURE 9-2 By age 33 months, toddlers already prefer playmates of their own sex: boys are much more sociable with boys than with girls, whereas girls are more outgoing with girls than with boys. (Adapted from C. N. Jacklin & E. E. Maccoby, "Social Behavior at 33 Months in Same-Sex and Mixed-Sex Dyads." *Child Development*, 1978, *49*, 557–569. Copyright © 1978 by the Society for Research in Child Development.)

(1988, 1990) believes that these findings do reflect basic incompatibilities in boys' and girls' play styles, with boys being too boisterous and domineering to suit the taste of many girls, who prefer less rough-housing and would rather rely on polite negotiations than on demands or shows of force when settling disputes with their playmates.

Sex differences in sex-typed behavior.   Many cultures, including our own, assign greater status to the male sex role (Rosenblatt & Cunningham, 1976), and boys face stronger pressures than girls to adhere to sex-appropriate codes of conduct. Consider that fathers of baby girls are generally willing to offer a truck to their 12-month-old daughters, but fathers of baby boys are likely to withhold dolls from their sons (Snow, Jacklin, & Maccoby, 1983). Moreover, parents of 2- to 9-year-olds (particularly fathers) express more concern about their child's cross-sex play activities if the child is male (Langlois & Downs, 1980; Tauber, 1979b), and they perceive a wider range of behaviors as appropriate for girls than for boys (Fagot, 1978). We seem to live in a male-oriented society where "tomboys" are at least tolerated while "sissies" are ridiculed and rejected (Martin, 1990). In other words, the male role is more clearly defined than the female role, and boys, who face stronger sex-typing pressures than girls, will soon learn what is or is not expected of them as they are criticized for deviating from approved sex-role standards. Walter Emmerich (1959) has suggested that the major task for young girls is to learn how not to be babies, whereas young boys must learn how not to be girls.

Indeed, males are quicker than females to adopt sex-typed preferences and patterns of behavior. Judith Blakemore and her associates (1979) found that 2-year-old boys clearly favor sex-appropriate toys, although some 2-year-old girls may not. And, by age 3 to 4, boys are much more likely than girls to say that they *dislike* opposite-sex toys (Bussey & Bandura, 1992; Eisenberg, Murray, & Hite, 1982).

Between the ages of 4 and 10, both boys and girls are becoming more aware of what is expected of them and conforming to these cultural prescriptions (Huston, 1983). Yet girls are more likely than boys

TABLE 9-4   *Percentages of boys and girls who requested popular "masculine" and "feminine" items from Santa Claus*

	Percentage of Boys Requesting	*Percentage of Girls Requesting*
Masculine items		
Vehicles	43.5	8.2
Sports equipment	25.1	15.1
Spatial/temporal toys (construction sets, clocks, and so on)	24.5	15.6
Race cars	23.4	5.1
Real vehicles (tricycles, bikes, motorbikes)	15.3	9.7
Feminine items		
Dolls (adult female)	.6	27.4
Dolls (babies)	.6	23.4
Domestic accessories	1.7	21.7
Doll houses	1.9	16.1
Stuffed animals	5.0	5.4

SOURCE: Adapted from J. G. Richardson & C. H. Simpson, "Children, Gender, and Social Structure: An Analysis of the Content of Letters to Santa Claus." *Child Development*, 1982, *53*, 429–436. Copyright © 1982 by the Society for Research in Child Development. Adapted by permission.

to retain an interest in cross-sex toys, games, and activities. Consider what John Richardson and Carl Simpson (1982) found when recording the toy preferences of 750 children aged 5 to 9 years as expressed in their letters to Santa Claus. Although most requests were clearly sex typed, we see in Table 9-4 that more girls than boys were asking for "opposite-sex" items. With respect to their actual sex-role preferences, young girls often wish they were boys, but it is unusual for a boy to wish he were a girl (Goldman & Goldman, 1982).

There are probably several reasons why girls are drawn to male activities and the masculine role during middle childhood. For one thing, they are becoming increasingly aware that masculine behavior is more highly valued, and perhaps it is only natural that girls would want to be what is "best" (or at least something other than a second-class citizen) (Frey & Ruble, 1992). And, as we have noted, girls are much *freer* than boys to engage in cross-sex pursuits. Fi-

"Please don't bring me anything that requires my acting out traditional female roles!"

BERRY'S WORLD reprinted by permission. © 1973 NEA, Inc.

nally, it is conceivable that fast-moving games and "action" toys are simply more interesting than the playthings and pastimes (dolls, doll houses, dish sets, cleaning and caretaking utensils) often imposed on girls to encourage their adoption of a nurturant, expressive orientation. Consider the reaction of Gina, a 5-year-old who literally squealed with delight when she received an "action garage" (complete with lube racks, gas pumps, cars, tools, and spare parts) from Santa one Christmas. At the unveiling of this treasure, Gina and her three female cousins (aged 3, 5, and 7) immediately ignored their dolls, doll houses, and unopened gifts to cluster around and play with this unusual and intriguing toy.

In spite of their earlier interest in masculine activities, most girls come to prefer (or at least to comply with) many of the prescriptions for the feminine role by early adolescence. Why? Probably for biological, cognitive, and social reasons. Once they reach puberty (biological growth) and their bodies assume a more womanly appearance, girls often face strong *social* pressures to become more ladylike (Brown, 1957; Kagan & Moss, 1962). Moreover, these young adolescents are also attaining formal operations (cognitive growth), which may help to explain why they become (1) so self-conscious about their changing body images (Von Wright, 1989), (2) so concerned about other people's evaluations of them (Elkind, 1981; remember the *imaginary audience* phenomenon), and, hence, (3) more inclined to adhere to the *social* prescriptions of the female sex role.

How stable is sex typing? Are highly sex-typed children likely to become highly sex-typed adults? At least one longitudinal study of middle-class children suggests that sex typing is reasonably stable over time (Kagan & Moss, 1962): both boys and girls who showed the clearest patterns of sex-typed behavior during middle childhood were likely to display more traditionally sex-typed characteristics as adults than were other men and women whose childhood behaviors had been less firmly sex typed.

Yet it is important to note that an adult's sex-role behavior is hardly set in stone. The birth of a baby, for example, often heralds a change in sex roles: fathers become more concerned about their breadwinner (instrumental) function, whereas mothers become more nurturant and "expressive" (Cowan & Cowan, 1987). And, as adults reach middle age (and beyond), sex roles continue to evolve: males now become more compassionate and expressive (Hyde, Krajnik, & Skuldt-Niederberger, 1991) and females more instrumental and autonomous (Feldman, Biringen, & Nash, 1981; Livson, 1983). So we see that sex typing is really a continuous process and that an adult's enactment of traditional sex-role behaviors may depend more on the utility of these responses at any given point in time than on any overriding personal desire to be "masculine" or "feminine."

Subcultural influences on sex typing. Although it is widely believed that parents from the upper socioeconomic strata are more egalitarian in their child-rearing practices and raise children who are less firmly sex typed, the evidence is not wholly consistent with this assertion (Katz, 1987). Older children and adolescents from middle-class homes do tend to display less stereotyped sex-role attitudes and behaviors than their counterparts from the lower socioeconomic strata (Canter & Ageton, 1984; Emmerich & Shepard, 1982). However, preschoolers from middle-class backgrounds are often found to be no less (and, indeed, sometimes *more*) stereotyped in their sex-role behaviors than disadvantaged children are (Bardwell, Cochran, & Walker, 1986; Nadelman, 1974). Moreover, African-American children in the United States express less stereotyped attitudes toward women than white, middle-class children do (Bardwell et al., 1986).

Researchers have attributed these ethnic and social-class variations in sex typing to differences in family life. For example, children whose mothers are employed outside the home are consistently found to hold less stereotyped views of men and women than do children whose mothers are not employed (Hoffman, 1984, 1989)—and a greater percentage of African-American and disadvantaged children have mothers who are employed. Moreover, African-American children and those from lower socioeconomic backgrounds are more likely than middle-class youngsters to be living in a *single-parent home*—another factor that is associated with less gender stereotyping by children (MacKinnon, Stoneman, & Brody, 1984). So the less stereotyped portrayal of the sexes that has been observed among young African-American children and those from lower socioeconomic backgrounds may simply reflect the fact that their mothers are more likely than middle-class mothers to be assuming both instrumental (male) and expressive (female) functions in their role as parents.

Finally, 6-year-olds raised in "countercultural" or "avant-garde" homes (in which parents strive to promote egalitarian sex-role attitudes) are indeed less sex stereotyped than children from traditional families in their *beliefs* about which activities and occupations are appropriate for males and females (Weisner & Wilson-Mitchell, 1990). Nevertheless, these "countercultural" children are quite aware of traditional gender stereotypes and are just as "sex typed" in their toy and activity preferences as children from traditional families.

In sum, sex-role development proceeds at a remarkable pace. By the time they enter school, youngsters from all social backgrounds have formed a stable gender identity, have acquired many, many stereotypes about males and females, and have developed interests and activity preferences that often forecast how "masculine" or "feminine" they will be as young adults. Now the most intriguing question: how does all this happen so fast?

Theories of Sex Typing and Sex-Role Development

Several theories have been proposed to account for sex differences and the development of sex roles. Some theories emphasize biological differences between males and females as primary contributors to gender differentiation; others stress that *social* influences are more crucial than biology for determining both sex differences in behavior and the outcomes of the sex-typing process. In this section we will first examine the most influential of the biological theories and then evaluate the more exclusively "social" perspectives offered by psychoanalytic theory, social-learning theory, cognitive-developmental theory, and gender schema theory.

Money and Ehrhardt's Biosocial Theory

Many scholars once believed that virtually all sex differences were largely (if not entirely) attributable to biological variations between males and females. What biological differences might be so important? For one, males have a Y chromosome and, hence, some genes that all females lack. For another, the sexes clearly differ in hormonal balance, with males having higher concentrations of androgen and testosterone and lower levels of estrogen than females do. But do these biological *correlates* of gender and gender differences actually cause sex differences in behavior? Do they predispose boys and girls to prefer and to adopt different sex roles?

Today, even biologically oriented theorists take a softer stance, arguing that biological and social influences *interact* to determine a person's behaviors and role preferences. Nowhere is this interactive emphasis any more apparent than in the *biosocial theory* proposed by John Money and Anke Ehrhardt (1972). Although biosocial theory concentrates on biological forces that may channel and constrain the development of boys and girls, it also acknowledges that early biological developments will affect other people's *reactions* to the child and that these social forces play a major part in steering the child toward a particular sex role. Let's take a closer look at this influential theory.

AN OVERVIEW OF GENDER DIFFERENTIATION AND SEX-ROLE DEVELOPMENT

Money and Ehrhardt (1972) propose that there are a number of critical episodes or events that will affect a person's eventual preference for the masculine or the feminine sex role. The first critical event occurs at conception as the child inherits either an X or a Y chromosome from the father. Over the next six weeks the developing embryo has only an undifferentiated gonad, and the sex chromosomes determine whether this structure becomes the male testes or the female ovaries. If a Y chromosome is present, the embryo develops testes; otherwise, ovaries will form.

These newly formed gonads then determine the outcome of episode 2. The testes of a male embryo secrete two hormones: **testosterone**, which stimulates the development of a male internal reproductive system, and **mullerian inhibiting substance (MIS)**, which inhibits the development of female organs. In the absence of these hormones, the embryo develops the internal reproductive system of a female.

At a third critical point, three to four months after conception, secretion of testosterone by the testes normally leads to the growth of a penis and scrotum. If testosterone is absent (as in normal females) or if the male fetus has inherited a rare recessive disorder called **testicular feminization syndrome (TFS)**, which makes the boy insensitive to male sex

hormones, female external genitalia (labia and clitoris) will form. At this juncture, testosterone will also alter the development of the brain and nervous system. For example, it signals the male brain to stop secreting hormones in a cyclical pattern, so that males do not experience menstrual cycles at puberty.

Once a biological male or female is born, social factors immediately come into play. Parents and other people label and begin to react to the child based on the appearance of his or her genitals. If a child's genitals are abnormal, so that he or she is labeled as a member of the other sex, this incorrect label and the corresponding reactions of other people will greatly affect his or her future development. For example, if a biological male were consistently labeled and treated as a girl (as a boy with TFS and female external genitalia might be), he would, by about age 2½ to 3, acquire the gender identity (though not the biological characteristics) of a girl (Money, 1985). Normally, babies are correctly labeled and will acquire a gender identity that matches their biological sex.

Later, at puberty, changes in hormonal functioning underlie the growth of the reproductive system, the appearance of secondary sex characteristics, and the development of sexual urges. These events, in combination with one's earlier self-concept as a male or a female, provide the basis for an adult gender identity and sex-role preference (see Figure 9-3).

EVIDENCE FOR BIOLOGICAL INFLUENCES ON GENDER DIFFERENTIATION AND SEX ROLES

How much influence *do* biological factors have on the behavior of males and females? To answer this question, we must consider what investigators have learned about genetic and hormonal influences.

Genetic influences. Corinne Hutt (1972) believes that genetic differences between the sexes may help to explain why boys are more vulnerable to problems such as reading disabilities, speech defects, various emotional disorders, and certain forms of mental retardation. Since genetic (XY) males have but one X chromosome, they are necessarily more

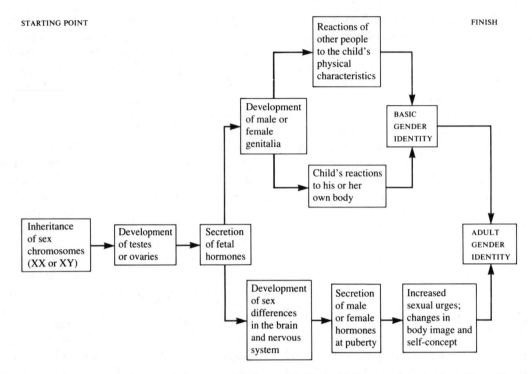

STARTING POINT   FINISH

FIGURE 9-3   Critical events in Money and Ehrhardt's biosocial theory of sex typing. (From *Man and Woman, Boy and Girl,* by John Money & Anke Ehrhardt. Copyright © 1972 by Johns Hopkins University Press. Reprinted by permission.)

susceptible to any **X-linked recessive disorder** for which their mother is a carrier (genetic [XX] females would have to inherit a recessive gene from each parent to show the same disorder). And, since males have more genetic information (by virtue of having some genes that appear only on the Y chromosome that females lack), they may show a wider variety of attributes, including some negative ones. Psychological theories of sex typing cannot easily explain why males often appear to be the "weaker sex," susceptible to many developmental disorders. Hutt's theory is an interesting explanation for this puzzling sex difference—one that should be investigated further.

Although it was once thought that gender variations in visual/spatial abilities and verbal skills might be directly attributable to genetic differences between the sexes, two reviews of the literature provide little support for this notion (Huston, 1983; Linn & Petersen, 1985). **Timing of puberty**—a *bio-*

logical variable regulated in part by one's genes— has a very slight effect on visual/spatial performance: both boys and girls who mature *late* tend to outperform early maturers of their own sex on at least some tests of visual/spatial ability (see Newcombe & Dubas, 1987). However, there are two other important influences on the visual/spatial performance of both males and females: (1) the person's previous involvement in spatial activities and (2) the extent to which the person has acquired masculine personality traits—that is, a masculine self-concept (Signorella & Jamison, 1986; Signorella, Jamison, & Krupa, 1989). These two variables are not closely related to timing of puberty and may, in fact, be *socially* mediated. Which factor is more important to the development of spatial skills? Nora Newcombe and Judith Dubas (1992) believe that having a masculine self-concept is the more critical factor. Indeed, they found that the strength of girls' masculine self-concepts at age 11 predicted both their involvement in spatial activities and their performance on visual/spatial tests five years later at age 16. Interestingly, neither timing of puberty nor involvement in spatial activities *at age 11* could reliably forecast girls' visual/spatial abilities at age 16. Finally, girls who had strong *feminine* self-concepts at age 11 performed more poorly on visual/spatial tests five years later than those who had viewed themselves as less feminine. So it seems that having a strong masculine self-concept promotes interest in spatial activities and the growth of spatial skills, whereas a strong feminine self-concept may inhibit these attributes.

How closely are our masculine and feminine self-concepts related to the genes we have inherited? Results from behavior genetics studies of adolescent twins suggest that genotype accounts for about 50% of the variability in people's masculine self-concepts but only 0–20% of the variability in their feminine self-concepts (Mitchell, Baker, & Jacklin, 1989; Plomin, 1990). So, even though genes determine our biological sex and have some influence on the outcome of sex typing, it appears that a major reason we differ in the psychological traits of masculinity and femininity is that we grow up in different environments.

Hormonal influences. Some sex differences are at least partly attributable to the uneven distribution of sex hormones in males and females. The clearest evidence comes from animal studies revealing that changes in a developing organism's hormonal balance are likely to have both anatomical and behavioral effects. For example, one team of investigators injected pregnant rhesus monkeys with the male hormone testosterone and noted that the female offspring showed malelike external genitalia and a pattern of social behaviors normally more characteristic of males (Young, Goy, & Phoenix, 1964). These masculinized females often threatened other monkeys, engaged in rough-and-tumble play, and would try to "mount" a partner, as males do at the beginning of a sexual encounter. Frank Beach (1965) reports that female rat pups that received testosterone injections in the first three days of life frequently displayed masculine sexual responses such as "mount-ing" in adulthood. The reverse was true for males. That is, castrated pups, who could not produce testosterone, exhibited feminine sexual characteristics such as receptive posturing as adults. Subsequent research has generally confirmed these observations; prenatal exposure to male sex hormones is reliably associated with heightened activity levels, greater aggression, and inadequate maternal behavior in a number of animal species (Moore, 1985).

Human beings may be subject to the same kind of hormonal influences. Indeed, we've already noted that males who display the testicular feminization syndrome (TFS) are insensitive to the effects of testosterone and will develop the external genitalia of a female. John Money and his associates call our attention to the reverse effect in females: a condition known as **adrenogenital syndrome (AGS)** (Ehrhardt & Baker, 1974; Money & Ehrhardt, 1972). Occasionally a female fetus will be exposed to much-higher-than-normal levels of androgen, owing either to a glandular malfunction of her own or to her mother's use of *progestins* — drugs that were once prescribed to prevent miscarriages before it became known that the body converts them to androgen. This overexposure to male sex hormones had the effect of masculinizing female fetuses so that, despite their XX chromosomal endowment and their female internal organs, they were born with external genitalia that resembled those of a boy (for example, a large clitoris that looked like a penis and fused labia that resembled a scrotum).

Money and Ehrhardt (1972; Ehrhardt & Baker, 1974) have studied several of these **androgenized females** whose external organs were surgically altered and who were then raised as girls. Compared with their sisters and other female agemates, many more of the androgenized girls were tomboys who preferred to dress in slacks and shorts, showed almost no interest in jewelry and cosmetics, and clearly favored vigorous athletic activities (and male playmates) over traditionally feminine pastimes. Moreover, their attitudes toward sexuality and achievement were similar to those of males. They expressed some interest in marriage and motherhood but thought in terms of a late marriage with few children — after they had established themselves in a career. During adolescence, most of these girls chose males as romantic partners; however, a higher-than-normal percentage (37%) described themselves as homosexual or bisexual in orientation (Money, 1985). Although it could be argued that other family members had reacted to the girls' abnormal genitalia early in life, treating those girls more like boys, interviews with the girls' parents suggested that they had not (Ehrhardt & Baker, 1974). So we must seriously consider the possibilities that (1) many differences between males and females may be hormonally mediated and (2) prenatal exposure to male sex hormones can influence the attitudes, interests, and activities of human females.[2]

Evidence for the "social" component of biosocial theory.   Although biological forces may steer males and females toward different patterns of behavior, Money and Ehrhardt (1972) believe that social influences are also important—so important, in fact, that they can modify or even *reverse* biological predispositions. Indeed, some of the evidence for this seemingly radical claim comes from Money's own work with androgenized females.

Recall that Money's androgenized females were born with the internal reproductive organs of a normal female even though their external genitalia resembled a penis and scrotum. These children are sometimes labeled boys at birth and raised as such until their abnormalities are detected. Money (1965) reports that the discovery and correction of this condition (by surgery and gender reassignment) present few if any adjustment problems for the child — provided that the sex change occurs *before age 18 months*. After age 3, gender assignment is exceedingly difficult because these genetic females have experienced prolonged masculine sex typing and have already labeled themselves as boys. These data

led Money to conclude that there is a "critical period" between 18 months and 3 years of age for the establishment of gender identity. As illustrated in Box 9-2, it may be more accurate to call the first three years a *sensitive* period, for other investigators have claimed that it is possible to assume a new identity later in adolescence. Nevertheless, Money's findings indicate that early social labeling and sex-role socialization can play a very prominent role in determining a child's gender identity and sex-role preferences.

Margaret Mead's (1935) observations of three New Guinea tribes led to the same conclusion. Mead noted that both males and females of the Arapesh tribe were taught to be cooperative, nonaggressive, and sensitive to the needs of others. This behavioral profile would be considered "expressive" or "feminine" in Western cultures. By contrast, both men and women of the Mundugumor tribe were expected to be hostile, aggressive, and emotionally unresponsive in their interpersonal relationships — a masculine pattern of behavior by Western standards. Finally, the Tchambuli displayed a pattern of sex-role development opposite to that of Western societies: males were passive, emotionally dependent, and socially sensitive, whereas females were dominant, independent, and assertive. In sum, members of these three tribes developed in accordance with the sex roles prescribed by their culture — even when these roles may have been quite inconsistent with sex-linked biological predispositions. Clearly, social forces contribute heavily to sex typing.

In sum, Money and Ehrhardt's biosocial theory stresses the importance of early biological developments that (1) affect how other people label the child at birth and (2) possibly have their own direct effects on the child's behavior and eventual sex-role preferences. Yet the theory also holds that biological and social factors *interact*, for the child's physical appearance largely determines the way he or she is raised, which in turn will strongly influence his or her sex-role development. What biosocial theory does *not* do is specify the precise social processes through which children acquire gender identities and sex-typed patterns of behavior. Other theorists have focused more intently on socialization itself, trying to

---

[2]Yet it is not entirely clear that these girls' preferences for masculine activities are a result of their early exposure to androgen. Many of these androgenized females received cortisone therapy to control their androgen levels and to prevent further masculinization of their bodies, and one side effect of cortisone is to dramatically increase a person's activity level. Thus a plausible alternative interpretation is that the high-intensity "masculine" behaviors of androgenized females are really due more to the cortisone they received than to any prenatal exposure to male sex hormones (Huston, 1983).

9-2 | *Is Biology Destiny?*

When biological sex and social labeling conflict, which wins out? Consider the case of a male identical twin whose penis was damaged beyond repair during circumcision (Money & Tucker, 1975). After seeking medical advice and considering the alternatives, the parents agreed to a surgical procedure that made their 21-month-old son a girl anatomically. After the operation the family began to actively sex-type this boy-turned-girl by changing her hairstyle, dressing her in frilly clothing, giving her feminine toys to play with, and teaching her such feminine behaviors as sitting to urinate. By age 5 the girl twin was quite different from her *genetically identical* brother: she most definitely knew she was a girl, had developed distinct preferences for feminine toys, activities, and apparel, and was far neater and daintier than her brother. Here, then, was a case in which assigned sex and sex-role socialization seemed to overcome biological predispositions. Or did they?

Milton Diamond (1982) describes what had happened by age 13, when the British Broadcasting Corporation (BBC) followed up on this twin, attempting to produce a program about her life. According to her psychiatrists, she was a very maladjusted young lady who was unhappy and uncomfortable in her female role and who very much wanted to become a mechanic. And, despite taking estrogen to prevent further masculinization of her body, she looked somewhat masculine and was rejected by peers, who had been known to call her "cavewoman." Perhaps, then, we should reassess the position that sex-role socialization is all that matters. Apparently biology matters too.

A second source of evidence that biology is important comes from a study of 18 biological males in the Dominican Republic who had a genetic condition (TFS) that made them insensitive prenatally to male sex hormones and caused them to be born with ambiguous genitals (Imperato-McGinley et al., 1979). These children were labeled as girls and raised as such throughout childhood. But, without female hormone therapy at puberty, their male sex hormones caused them to sprout beards and to assume a muscular, masculine appearance. Can a person now adjust to becoming a young man after spending an entire childhood as a girl?

Amazingly, 16 of these 18 individuals seemed quite capable of accepting their late conversion from female to male and adopting masculine lifestyles, including the establishment of heterosexual relationships! One retained a female identity and sex role, and the remaining individual switched to a male gender identity but still dressed as a female. Clearly this research casts some doubt on the notion that socialization during the first three years is "critical" to later sex-role development. In fact, it seems to suggest that hormonal influences are more important than social influences (Imperato-McGinley et al., 1979).

However, Imperato-McGinley's conclusions have been challenged (Ehrhardt, 1985). Little information was provided about how these individuals had been raised, and it is quite possible that Dominican parents, knowing that this genetic disorder was common in their society, treated these girls-turned-boys differently from other "girls" when they were young. Moreover, the girls-turned-boys had genitals that were not completely normal in appearance, and the practice of river bathing in Dominican culture almost certainly means that these youngsters compared themselves to normal girls (and boys) and may have recognized early on that they were "different." So these children may not have received an exclusively feminine upbringing and may actually have been gender-ambivalent—not heavily invested in the female role and ready to go in whichever direction their hormones took them at puberty.

Considering all the evidence, then, is social experience during the first three years (Money's critical period) really so powerful that it overrides biological influences? What studies of people with genital and other hormonal abnormalities (including Money and Ehrhardt's clinical samples) seem to suggest is this: the first three years are a *sensitive* period rather than a critical period for sex-role development, and both biology and society influence a child's gender identity and sex-role preferences. Stated another way, neither biology nor social labeling is "destiny."

identify the kinds of experiences that will convince children that they are boys who should adopt a masculine orientation or girls who should favor feminine pursuits. The first of these "social" theories was Sigmund Freud's psychoanalytic approach.

Freud's Psychoanalytic Theory

Freud's explanation of psychosexual development acknowledges the contributions of both social and biological factors. Recall from our discussion of psychoanalytic theory in Chapter 2 that sexuality (the sex instinct) was said to be innate. Freud also believed that everyone is constitutionally bisexual, having inherited, in varying proportions, the biological attributes of both sexes. What, then, is responsible for the child's adoption of a gender identity that is consistent with his or her (predominant) biological sex?

Freud's answer was that sex typing occurs through the process of **identification**. Recall that identification is the child's tendency to emulate another person, usually the parent of the same sex. Freud argued that a 3- to 6-year-old boy in the **phallic stage** of development will internalize masculine attitudes and behaviors when he is forced to identify with his father (the aggressor) as a means of renouncing his incestuous desires for his mother, reducing his **castration anxiety**, and thus resolving the **Oedipus complex**. However, Freud believed that sex typing is more difficult for a young girl, who already feels castrated and will experience no overriding fear that would compel her to identify with her mother and resolve her **Electra complex**. Why, then, would a girl ever develop a preference for the feminine role? Freud's (1924/1961a, 1924/1961b) view was that girls eventually recognize the impossibility of ever possessing the father as a sex object. As a result, they should gradually begin to identify with the mother and to incorporate the mother's feminine characteristics either (1) to be "in the mother's shoes" and thereby derive *vicarious* pleasure from the mother's relationship with the father, or (2) to prepare themselves for the womanly role they will play in a heterosexual relationship with a man (other than the father) later in life.

PHOTO 9-4   According to psychoanalytic theory, children become appropriately "masculine" or "feminine" by identifying with the same-sex parent.

Some of the evidence we have reviewed is generally consistent with Freudian theory. Children are rapidly acquiring sex-role stereotypes and developing sex-typed behaviors at roughly the same age that Freud says they will (3 to 6). Moreover, boys whose fathers are absent from the home (because of divorce, military service, or death) during the oedipal period frequently have no male role model to emulate and, indeed, are often found to be less masculine in their sex-role behaviors than boys from homes where the father is present (Hetherington, 1966; Stevenson & Black, 1988). Finally, the notion that fathers play an important role in the sex typing of their daughters has now been confirmed (Huston, 1983; Lamb, 1981).

Yet on other counts psychoanalytic theory has not fared well at all. Many preschool children are so ignorant about differences between male and female genitalia that it is hard to see how most boys could fear castration or how most girls could feel castrated and envy males for having a penis (Bem, 1989; Katcher, 1955). Moreover, Freud assumed that a boy's identification with his father is based on fear, but most researchers find that boys identify more strongly with fathers who are warm and nurturant than with overly punitive and threatening ones (Hetherington & Frankie, 1967; Mussen & Rutherford, 1963). Finally, studies of parent/child resemblances reveal that school-age children and adolescents are not all that similar psychologically to either parent (Maccoby & Jacklin, 1974), and one investigator (Tolar, 1968) found that college males actually resembled their mothers more than their fathers! Clearly, these findings are damaging to the Freudian notion that children acquire important personality traits by identifying with the same-sex parent.

In sum, Freud's explanation of sex typing has not received much empirical support, even though children do begin to develop sex-role preferences at about the time that he specified. Let's now consider the social-learning interpretation of sex typing to see whether this approach looks any more promising.

Social-Learning Theory

Prominent social-learning theorists (Bandura, 1989; Mischel, 1970) have argued that children acquire their gender identities, sex-role preferences, and sex-typed behaviors in two ways: through direct tuition and observational learning. *Direct tuition* (or differential reinforcement) refers to the tendency of parents, teachers, and other social agents to "teach" boys and girls how they should behave by encouraging and reinforcing sex-appropriate behaviors and by punishing those actions considered more appropriate for members of the other sex. In addition, every child is thought to acquire a large number of sex-typed attitudes and behaviors by observing the activities of a variety of same-sex models, including peers, teachers, older siblings, and media personalities, as well as the mother or the father. Walter Mischel (1970) has noted that children do not necessarily identify with (that is, hope to emulate) all the models who contribute to their sex-role development. Indeed, imitative responses that psycho-

analysts call "identification" are just as easily described as examples of *observational learning*.

DIRECT TUITION OF SEX ROLES

Do parents "teach" sex roles by actively encouraging sex-typed patterns of behavior? Yes, indeed (Lytton & Romney, 1991), and the shaping of sex-typed behavior begins rather early. As part of a longitudinal study of sex-role development, Beverly Fagot and Mary Leinbach (1989) found that parents are already encouraging sex-appropriate play and responding negatively to cross-sex behaviors during the second year, *before* the child acquires a basic gender identity or displays a clear preference for male or female activities (see also Fagot & Hagan, 1991). By age 20–24 months, daughters are consistently reinforced for such behaviors as dancing, dressing up (as women), following parents around, asking for help, and playing with dolls, and they are likely to be discouraged from manipulating objects, running, jumping, and climbing. By contrast, sons of this age are often punished for "feminine" behaviors (such as playing with dolls or seeking help) and are actively encouraged to play with masculine items such as blocks, trucks, and push-and-pull toys that require large-muscle activity (Fagot, 1978). Are children influenced by the "gender curriculum" their parents provide? Indeed they are! In fact, parents who show the clearest patterns of differential reinforcement have children who are relatively quick to (1) label themselves as boys or girls, (2) develop firm, sex-typed toy and activity preferences, and (3) acquire an understanding of gender stereotypes (Fagot & Leinbach, 1989; Fagot et al., 1992).

A perhaps even more basic strategy that parents use to encourage sex-typed interests is to select gender-consistent toys for their infants and toddlers (Eisenberg et al., 1985). A glance at the bedrooms of young boys and girls is revealing in itself: boys' rooms are likely to contain outer-space toys, construction sets, sporting equipment, and vehicles, whereas girls' rooms will typically contain dolls, domestic toys, floral furnishings, and ruffles (MacKinnon, Brody, & Stoneman, 1982; Pomerleau et al., 1990). Given this early "channeling" of sex-typed interests, parents may find that additional pressures (such as differential reinforcement) are often unnecessary — unless, of course, the child's play patterns and interests seem "inappropriate" to them (Eisenberg et al., 1985).

How strongly do parents react to cross-sex play? To find out, Judith Langlois and Chris Downs (1980) compared the reactions of mothers, fathers, and peers to 3–5-year-olds who were asked (by the experimenter) to play with either same-sex or cross-sex toys. Fathers showed the clearest pattern by rewarding their children for playing with the same-sex items while actively suppressing cross-sex play. Mothers showed a similar pattern with their daughters but permitted their sons to play with either masculine or feminine toys. Finally, peers were quite critical of children who played with cross-sex toys, often ridiculing the offender or disrupting this "inappropriate" play. Apparently, peer pressure for "sex-appropriate" play begins very early: even before establishing a basic gender identity, 21- to 25-month-old boys would belittle or disrupt each other for playing with feminine toys or with a girl, and girls of this same age were critical of other girls who chose to play with boys (Fagot, 1985a).

So it seems that the child's earliest preferences for sex-typed toys and activities may result from the tendency of parents (particularly fathers) to actively encourage sex-appropriate behavior and to discourage acts that they consider sex-inappropriate. As the child grows older, other people, such as teachers, scout leaders, and (especially) peers, will become increasingly important as sources of reinforcement for sex-typed attitudes and behaviors.

OBSERVATIONAL LEARNING

According to Albert Bandura (1989), children acquire many of their sex-typed attributes by observing and imitating same-sex models. Bandura believes that there are two reasons a child might pay particular attention to models of his or her own sex. First, young children may often be reinforced for imitating same-sex siblings or parents. Indeed, you have probably heard a proud parent make comments like "That's my little man; you're just like Daddy!" or "You're as pretty as your mommy when you dress up like that!" As the child acquires a basic gender identity at age 2½ to 3, a second factor should come into play. Same-sex models are now more worthy of attention because children perceive them as *similar* to themselves.

Yet there is some question about just how much social models contribute to sex typing during the preschool years. Although some investigators find that preschool children do pay closer attention to same-sex models (Bussey & Bandura, 1984), others report that the model's sex is of little consequence until relatively late — about 6 to 7 years of age (Ruble, Balaban, & Cooper, 1981; Slaby & Frey, 1975). In fact, John Masters and his associates (1979) found that preschool children are much more concerned about the sex appropriateness of the *behavior* they are observing than about the sex of the model who displays it. For example, 4- to 5-year-old boys will play with objects labeled "boys' toys" even after they have seen a girl playing with them. However, these youngsters are reluctant to play with objects labeled "girls' toys" that boy models have played with earlier. So children's toy choices are affected more by the *labels* attached to the toys than by the sex of the person who served as a model. But, once children recognize that gender is an unchanging aspect of their personalities (at age 6 to 7), they do begin to attend more selectively to same-sex models and are now likely to avoid toys and activities that other-sex models seem to enjoy (Ruble et al., 1981).

Sibling influences on sex typing.   What role do siblings play in sex typing? The answer seems to depend on the number of siblings in the family and their distribution by gender. It might seem that both boys and girls from small families would be more traditionally sex typed if they had a *same-sex* sibling to encourage or model gender-consistent behavior. Indeed, this seems to be the case (Brim, 1958; Sutton-Smith & Rosenberg, 1970). When siblings in two-child families are opposite sex, play behavior is more often determined by the sex of the older child. In fact, boys with an older sister may play "house" just as often as girls with an older sister, whereas boys with an older brother hardly ever partake in such feminine pastimes (Stoneman, Brody, & MacKinnon, 1986).

If one *same-sex* sib promotes traditional sex typing, do many same-sex sibs make a child even more traditional? Interestingly, the answer is no. In fact, Margaret Tauber (1979a) reports that school-age girls who have older sisters and boys from all-boy families are the children who are most likely to enjoy *cross-sex* games and activities. Moreover, Harold Grotevant (1978) found that adolescent girls who have sisters develop a less "feminine" pattern of interests than girls who have brothers. These findings make some sense if children are concerned about establishing a personal niche within the family. A child with other-sex sibs could easily achieve such an individual identity by behaving in a traditionally "masculine" or "feminine" manner. However, a child who is surrounded by same-sex sibs may gravitate toward cross-sex activities as a means of differentiating the self from brothers (or sisters) and avoiding categorization as "one of the boys" (or ". . . girls").

Although we are only beginning to understand how the structure of the family affects children's sex typing, this much is clear: the child's sex-role socialization within the home depends more on the total family environment than on the influence of the same-sex parent.

Media influences.   For the most part, males and females are portrayed in a highly stereotyped fashion in children's storybooks and on TV. Males are usually featured as the central characters who work at professions, make important decisions, respond to emergencies, and assume positions of leadership, whereas females are often depicted as relatively passive and emotional creatures who manage a home or work at "feminine" occupations such as waitressing or nursing (Liebert & Sprafkin, 1988). Not surprisingly, 5- to 11-year-olds who are exposed to these stereotyped portrayals by watching more than 25 hours of TV per week are more likely to prefer gender-appropriate toys and to hold highly stereotyped views of men and women than their classmates who watch little television (McGhee & Frueh, 1980). But, as more women play detectives and more men raise families on television, children's perceptions of male and female roles are likely to change. Indeed, children who regularly watch *The Cosby Show* and other relatively nonsexist programs do hold less stereotyped views of the sexes (Rosenwasser, Lingenfelter, & Harrington, 1989).

In sum, there is a lot of evidence that differential reinforcement and (later) observational learning contribute to sex-role development. However, social-learning theorists have often portrayed children as *passive pawns* in the process: parents, peers, and TV characters show them what to do and reinforce them for doing it. Yet this perspective ignores the child's *own* contribution to sex-role socialization. Consider, for example, that children do not always receive gender-stereotyped Christmas presents *because* their sexist parents force these objects upon them. Instead, many parents who would rather buy gender-neutral or educational toys end up "giving in" to sons who beg for machine guns or daughters who want tea sets (Robinson & Morris, 1986).

Kohlberg's Cognitive-Developmental Theory

Lawrence Kohlberg (1966) has proposed a cognitive theory of sex typing that is quite different from the other theories we have considered and helps to explain why boys and girls might adopt traditional sex roles even when their parents may not want them to. Kohlberg's major themes are these:

1. Sex-role development depends on cognitive development, particularly on children's understanding of gender and its implications for the self.
2. Children *actively socialize themselves*; they are not merely passive pawns of social influence.

According to social-learning theory, children first learn to do "boy" or "girl" things because their parents encourage these activities; later they come to selectively imitate same-sex models, thereby acquiring a stable gender identity. By contrast, Kohlberg suggests that children *first* establish a stable gender identity and then *actively* seek out same-sex models and other information to learn how to act like a boy or a girl. To Kohlberg it's not "I behave like a boy; therefore I must be one" (social-learning position). It's more like "Hey, I'm a boy; therefore I'd better do everything I can to find out how to behave like one" (cognitive self-socialization position).

Kohlberg believes that children pass through the following three stages as they acquire a mature understanding of what it means to be a male or a female:

1. **Basic gender identity**. By age 3, children have labeled themselves as boys or girls.
2. **Gender stability**. Somewhat later, gender is perceived as *stable over time*. The child knows that boys become men and girls grow up to be women.
3. **Gender consistency**. The gender concept is complete when the child realizes that one's sex is also *stable across situations*. Six- to 7-year-olds who have reached this stage are no longer fooled by appearances. They know, for example, that one's sex cannot be altered by cross-dressing or taking up cross-sex activities.

When do children become motivated to socialize themselves—that is, to seek out same-sex models and learn how to act like males and females? According to Kohlberg, self-socialization begins only after children reach *gender consistency*. So, for Kohlberg, a mature understanding of gender (1) instigates true sex typing and (2) is the *cause* rather than the consequence of attending to same-sex models.

Support for Kohlberg's viewpoint.   The results of several studies are consistent with various aspects of Kohlberg's theory. For example, studies of 3- to 7-year-olds indicate that children's understanding of gender develops gradually and is clearly related to other aspects of their cognitive development, such as the conservation of mass and liquids (Marcus & Overton, 1978). Ron Slaby and Karin Frey (1975) have also noted that the gender concept develops *sequentially*, progressing through the three stages Kohlberg describes (indeed, this same sequence has now been observed in children in many cultures; see Munroe, Shimmin, & Munroe, 1984). And there was a second interesting finding in Slaby and Frey's experiment: children who were at the highest stage (gender consistency) were more likely to attend to same-sex models in a movie than were children whose gender concepts were less well developed (see also Ruble et al., 1981). Finally, boys who have reached gender consistency are more inclined than boys who haven't to (1) spend more time with *unattractive* toys that boy models endorse and (2) spend less time with very attractive toys that girl models favor; this finding implies that boys with a mature gender identity feel that they had better "play it safe" and learn all about the "gender-correct" toy before pursuing other options (Frey & Ruble, 1992).[3]

Limitations of Kohlberg's theory.   Of course, the major problem with Kohlberg's cognitive approach is that sex typing is already well underway before the child acquires a mature gender identity. As we have noted, 2-year-old boys prefer masculine toys before they are even aware that these playthings are more appropriate for boys than for girls. Moreover, 3-year-olds of each sex have learned many sex-role stereotypes and already prefer same-sex activities and playmates long before they begin to attend more selectively to same-sex models. It seems that

[3]Gender-consistent girls did not show the same pattern, often choosing to direct their attention to an *attractive* toy that girl models spurned (and boy models favored) and to largely ignore an unattractive toy that girl models endorsed. According to Frey and Ruble (1992), this finding may reflect (1) girls' knowledge that masculine activities are more prestigious than feminine pursuits and (2) the greater freedom that girls are granted to pursue cross-sex interests and activities.

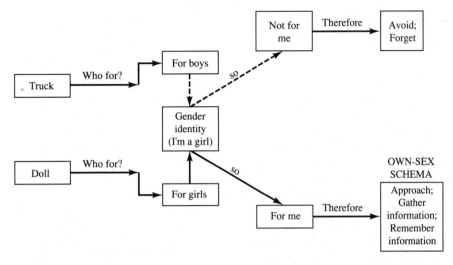

FIGURE 9-4 A model of how gender-relevant information is classified as appropriate or inappropriate for the self and how such classifications stimulate the growth of knowledge about one's own sex role. (Adapted from "The Roles of Cognition in Sex-Roles and Sex-Typing," by C. L. Martin and C. F. Halverson, Jr. In D. B. Carter (Ed.), *Current Conceptions of Sex Roles and Sex-Typing: Theory and Research*. Copyright © 1987 by Praeger Publishing, an imprint of Greenwood Publishing Group, Inc., Westport, CT. Reprinted by permission.)

only a rudimentary understanding of gender is necessary before children will learn about sex-role stereotypes and display sex-appropriate toy preferences and that measures of gender consistency do *not* predict how "sex typed" children are (Bussey & Bandura, 1992; Carter & Levy, 1988; Levy & Carter, 1989). Finally, let's not forget the work of John Money (1965), who found that gender reassignment is exceedingly difficult once children have reached the age of 3 (or Kohlberg's basic gender-identity stage) and have *tentatively* categorized themselves as males or females. So Kohlberg badly overstates the case in arguing that a mature understanding of gender is necessary for sex typing and sex-role development.

Gender Schema Theory

Carol Martin and Charles Halverson (1981, 1987) have proposed a somewhat different cognitive theory of sex typing (actually, an information-processing theory), one that appears quite promising (see Bem, 1983, for a similar viewpoint). Like Kohlberg, Martin and Halverson believe that children are intrinsically

motivated to acquire interests, values, and behaviors that are consistent with their cognitive judgments about the self. But, unlike Kohlberg, they argue that this "self-socialization" begins as soon as the child acquires a *basic gender identity*, at age 2½ or 3, and thus is well underway by age 6 or 7, when the child achieves gender consistency.

According to Martin and Halverson's "gender schema" theory, establishment of a basic gender identity motivates a child to learn about the sexes and to incorporate this information into *gender schemas* — that is, organized sets of beliefs and expectations about males and females that will influence the kinds of information he or she attends to, elaborates, and remembers. First, children acquire a simple **"in-group/out-group schema,"** which allows them to classify some objects, behaviors, and roles as "for males" and others as "for females" (for example, trucks are for boys; dolls are for girls; girls can cry but boys should not). This is the kind of information that investigators normally tap when studying children's knowledge of sex-role stereotypes. In addition, children are said to acquire an **own-sex schema**, which consists of detailed plans of action that one will need to perform various gender-consistent behaviors and enact one's sex role. So a girl who has a basic gender identity might first learn that sewing is "for girls" and building model airplanes is "for boys." Then, because she is a girl and wants to act consistently with her own self-concept, she will gather a great deal of information about sewing to add to her own-sex schema, while largely ignoring information about building model airplanes (see also Figure 9-4).

Once formed, gender schemas "structure" experience by providing an organization for processing social information. The idea here is that people are likely to encode and remember information consistent with their gender schemas and to either forget schema-inconsistent information or transform it so that it becomes consistent with their stereotypes. Support for this idea was presented in Box 9-1; recall that children who heard stories in which actors performed cross-sex behaviors (for example, a girl chopping wood) tended to recall the action but to alter the scene to conform to their gender stereotypes (saying that a boy had been chopping). Surely these strong tendencies to forget or to distort counterstereotypic information help to explain why unfounded beliefs about males and females are so slow to die.

Also consistent with this schematic-processing theory, children do seem to be especially interested in learning about objects and activities that fit their own-sex schemas. In one study, 4- to 9-year-olds were given boxes of gender-neutral objects (for example, hole punches, burglar alarms, and pizza cutters) and were told that the objects were either "boy" items or "girl" items (Bradbard et al., 1986). Boys explored "boy" items more than girls did, whereas girls explored more than boys when the objects were described as things girls enjoy. One week later, children easily recalled whether these objects were "boy" or "girl" items; they had apparently sorted the objects according to their in-group/out-group schemas. Yet boys recalled much more in-depth information about "boy" items than did girls, whereas girls recalled more than boys about these very same objects if they had been labeled "girl" items. If children's information-gathering efforts are consistently guided by their own-sex schemas in

this way, we can easily see how boys and girls might acquire very different stores of knowledge and develop different interests and competencies as they mature.

In sum, Martin and Halverson's gender schema theory is an interesting "new look" at the sex-typing process. Not only does this model describe how sex-role stereotypes might originate and persist over time, but it also indicates how these emerging "gender schemas" might contribute to the development of strong sex-role preferences and sex-typed behaviors long before the child realizes that gender is an unchanging attribute.

An Attempt at Integration

It is likely that some combination of the biosocial, social-learning, and cognitive approaches provides the most accurate explanation of sex differences and sex-role development (Huston, 1983; Ruble, 1988). The biosocial theory of Money and Ehrhardt has contributed in an important way by describing the major biological developments that lead people to label the child as a boy or a girl and to treat him or her accordingly. Yet biosocial theory is not very clear about how (or which) social forces contribute to sex differences and sex-role development.

The cognitive theories of sex typing emphasize the importance of cognitive milestones, information-processing biases, and, indeed, the child's own *desire* to behave like a boy or a girl—developments that occur sometime after age 3. However, an integrative theorist would surely point out that these cognitive approaches largely ignore the important events of the first three years, when a boy, for example, develops a preference for masculine toys and activities because parents, siblings, and even his young peers frequently remind him that he is a boy, reinforce him for doing "boy things," and discourage those of his behaviors that they consider feminine. In other words, it appears that the social-learning theorists have accurately described early sex typing: very young children display gender-consistent behaviors *because other people encourage these activities*.

As a result of this early socialization (and the growth of some basic categorization skills), children

TABLE 9-5 *An overview of the sex-typing process from the perspective of an integrative theorist*

Developmental Period	Events and Outcomes
Prenatal period	The fetus develops the morphological characteristics of a male or a female, which others will react to once the child is born.
Birth to 3 years	Parents and other companions label the child as a boy or a girl, frequently remind the child of his or her gender, and begin to encourage gender-consistent behavior while discouraging cross-sex activities. As a result of these social experiences and the development of very basic classification skills, the young child acquires some sex-typed behavioral preferences and the knowledge that he or she is a boy or a girl (basic gender identity).
3 to 6 years	Once children acquire a basic gender identity, they begin to seek information about sex differences, form gender schemas, and become intrinsically motivated to perform those acts that are viewed as "appropriate" for their own sex. When acquiring gender schemas, children attend to both male and female models. Once their "own-sex" schemas are well established, these youngsters are likely to imitate behaviors considered appropriate for their sex, regardless of the gender of the model who displays them.
6 to 7 and beyond	Children finally acquire a sense of gender consistency—a firm, future-oriented image of themselves as boys who must necessarily become men or girls who will obviously become women. At this point they begin to rely less exclusively on gender schemas and more on the behavior of same-sex models to acquire those mannerisms and attributes that are consistent with their firm categorization of self as a male or female.

acquire a basic gender identity. This is an important development, for Money's research suggests that, as soon as children first label themselves as boys or girls, this self-concept is difficult to change (even though children do not yet recognize that gender itself is invariant). At this point, children begin to (1) actively seek information about sex differences, (2) organize this information into in-group/out-group gender schemas, and (3) learn more about those behaviors they consider appropriate for members of their *own* sex. Although social-learning processes, such as differential reinforcement, may still be implicated in the development of sex-typed behavior, the child is now *intrinsically motivated* to perform those acts that match his or her own-sex gender schema and to avoid activities that are more appropriate for the other sex. This is why 4- to 5-year-old boys, for example, will play with objects labeled "boy" toys even if they have seen a girl playing with and enjoying them. Their gender schemas tell them that "boy" toys are sex appropriate, and they are inclined to approach these objects. The model's sex is of lesser importance, for these youngsters do not yet realize that her gender is invariant; besides, they may simply distort what they have seen to match their gender schemas (for example,

recalling that it was a boy rather than a girl who had enjoyed these "boy" items). And, when they finally understand, at age 6 or 7, that their sex will never change, children begin to focus less exclusively on gender schemas and to pay more attention to same-sex models to decide which activities are most appropriate for members of their sex. So, from age 3 on, children are *self-socializers* who try very hard to acquire the masculine or feminine attributes that they view as consistent with their male or female self-images. This is why parents who hope to discourage their children from adopting traditional gender roles are often amazed that their sons and daughters seem to become little "sexists" all on their own (see Table 9-5 for a brief overview of the integrative viewpoint).

One more point: all theories of sex-role development would agree that what children actually learn about being a male or a female will depend greatly on what their society offers them in the way of a "gender curriculum." In other words, we must view sex-role development through an *ecological* lens and appreciate that there is nothing inevitable about the patterns of male and female development that we see in our society today. (Indeed, recall the gender-role reversals that Mead observed among the

Tchambuli tribe of New Guinea). In another era, in another culture, the sex-typing process can produce very different kinds of boys and girls.

Should we in Western cultures be trying to raise different kinds of boys and girls? As we will see in our next section, some theorists would answer this question with a resounding yes!

Psychological Androgyny: A Prescription for the Future?

Throughout this chapter we have used the term *sex appropriate* to describe the mannerisms and behaviors that societies consider more suitable for members of one sex than the other. Today many developmentalists believe that these rigidly defined sex-role standards are actually harmful, because they constrain the behavior of both males and females. Indeed, Sandra Bem (1978) has stated that her major purpose in studying sex roles is "to help free the human personality from the restrictive prison of sex-role stereotyping and to develop a conception of mental health that is free from culturally imposed definitions of masculinity and femininity."

Psychologists have traditionally assumed that masculinity and femininity are at opposite ends of a single dimension: masculinity supposedly implies the absence of femininity, and vice versa. Bem challenges this assumption by arguing that a person can be **androgynous**—that is, both masculine and feminine, instrumental and expressive, assertive and nonassertive, competitive and noncompetitive, depending on the utility or situational appropriateness of these attributes. The underlying assumption of Bem's theory is that masculinity and femininity are *two separate dimensions*. A person who has many masculine and few feminine characteristics is defined as a *masculine sex-typed individual*. One who has many feminine and few masculine characteristics is said to be *feminine sex typed*. The androgynous person is one who has a large number of both masculine and feminine attributes, whereas people characterized as *undifferentiated* display few masculine or feminine characteristics (see Figure 9-5).

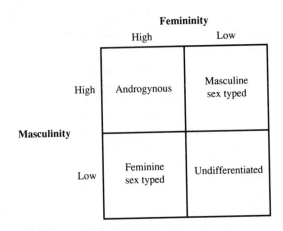

FIGURE 9-5   Categories of sex-role orientation based on viewing masculinity and femininity as separate dimensions of personality.

Do Androgynous People Really Exist?

Bem (1974) and other investigators (Spence & Helmreich, 1978) have developed inventories containing both masculinity and femininity scales that ask people how they perceive themselves. In one large sample of college students (Spence & Helmreich, 1978), roughly 33% of the test takers were "masculine" men or "feminine" women, about 30% were androgynous, and the remaining individuals were either undifferentiated or "sex reversed" (masculine sex-typed females or feminine sex-typed males). Judith Hall and Amy Halberstadt (1980) have developed a similar sex-role inventory for grade-school children and found that 27–32% of their 8- to 11-year-olds could be classified as androgynous (see also Boldizar, 1991). So androgynous individuals do exist, and in sizable numbers.

Are There Advantages to Being Androgynous?

Bem (1975, 1978) has argued that androgynous people are "better off" than sex-typed people because they are not constrained by rigid sex-role concepts and are freer to respond effectively to a wider variety of situations. In her own research, Bem has shown that androgynous men and women are indeed more flexible in their behavior. For example, androgynous people, like masculine sex-typed people, easily display the "masculine" instrumental trait of independence by resisting social pressure to judge very unamusing cartoons as funny just because peers do. Yet they are just as likely as feminine sex-typed individuals to display the "feminine" expressive quality of nurturance by interacting warmly and sensitively with a baby (see also Shaffer, Pegalis, & Cornell, 1991, for further evidence that androgynous people are especially adaptable individuals).

If androgynous people truly are "better off," as Bem has argued, then we might expect them to be popular and to score higher on measures on self-esteem than traditional males and females do. Indeed, recent research indicates that androgynous children and adolescents do enjoy higher self-esteem and are perceived by peers as more likable and better adjusted than classmates who are traditionally sex typed (Boldizar, 1991; Major, Carnevale, & Deaux, 1981; Massad, 1981). Moreover, androgynous females are more likely than sex-typed females to attribute their achievements to ability (rather than effort or luck), to attribute their failures to factors other than lack of ability, and to show little if any decrement in performance (helplessness) after initially failing at an achievement task (Huston, 1983). Clearly, these data imply that androgyny is a desirable attribute.

However, other research challenges Bem's presumption that psychological androgyny is a thoroughly desirable attribute. First, it appears that it is the possession of "masculine" traits rather than androgyny per se that is most strongly associated with good adjustment and high self-esteem (Orlofsky & O'Heron, 1987; Whitley, 1983). Both masculine sex-typed and androgynous individuals have higher self-esteem than feminine sex-typed and undifferentiated persons do—regardless of whether they are men or women. Second, although androgynous adults tend to raise children who also blend masculine and feminine attributes (Orlofsky, 1979), at least one study suggests that 9-year-old children of traditionally sex-typed parents are somewhat more competent and socially responsible than children of androgynous parents, possibly because their parents are firmer and more demanding than androgynous parents are (Baumrind, 1982). Of course, this latter finding doesn't necessarily mean that tradi-

tional adults make better parents. In fact, the benefits of having androgynous parents (or of being androgynous oneself) may be minimal until adolescence, when teenagers (1) become more interested in heterosexual relationships, in which "feminine" sensitivity and nurturance are adaptive attributes, and (2) begin to plan and prepare for a career—activities for which independence, assertiveness, and other "masculine" attributes might be advantageous (Perry & Bussey, 1984). But, even so, any benefits of being androgynous may subside over time, for elderly androgynous people are no more satisfied with life than their traditionally sex-typed peers (Windle, 1986).

In sum, it may be premature to conclude that one is better off in *all* respects to be androgynous than to be either masculine or feminine in orientation. Still, the very fact that androgynous people exist reminds us again that males and females are far more similar psychologically than they are different. Moreover, androgynous females are perceived as no less feminine, and androgynous males no less masculine, simply because they have developed characteristics traditionally associated with the other sex (Major, Carnevale, & Deaux, 1981). Nor do androgynous people show any signs of maladjustment merely because they do not closely conform to traditional sex roles; in fact, they tend to be adaptive, well-adjusted individuals who are liked and respected by their peers (O'Heron & Orlofsky, 1990). Thus we can safely conclude that it is unlikely to be damaging (and may indeed be adaptive) for women to become a little more "masculine" and for men to become a little more like women (see Box 9-3 for a discussion of how we might promote such change—should we choose to).

Development of Sexuality and Sexual Behavior

As children acquire knowledge about males and females and about the roles that society expects males and females to assume, they also become increasingly aware of their own **sexuality**—an aspect of development that will have a major effect on their concepts of self as men or women. In this final section of the chapter we will briefly consider the growth of human sexuality and discuss some changes in adolescent sexual attitudes (and behavior) over the past 60 years.

Origins of "Sexual" Activities

When do children first display signs of sexuality? Might we humans really be "sexual" beings from birth, as Freud assumed? Although this claim might seem a bit outrageous, consider that both male

---

9-3 | *On Modifying Sex-Role Attitudes and Behavior*

Today many people believe that the world would be a better place if sexism were eliminated and if boys and girls were no longer steered toward confining "masculine" or "feminine" roles. In a nonsexist culture, women would no longer suffer from a lack of assertiveness and confidence in the world of work, and men would be freer to display their sensitive, nurturant sides, which many now suppress in the interest of appearing "masculine." How might we reduce sexism and encourage children to be more flexible about the interests and attributes they might display?

Sandra Bem (1983, 1989) believes that parents must take an active role by (1) teaching their young children about genital anatomy as part of a larger lesson that one's sex is unimportant outside the domain of reproduction, and (2) delaying children's exposure to gender stereotypes by encouraging cross-sex as well as same-sex play and by dividing household chores more equitably (with fathers sometimes cooking and cleaning and mothers gardening or making repairs). If preschoolers come to think of gender as a purely biological attribute and often see themselves and their parents pursuing cross-sex interests and activities, they should be less inclined to construct the rigid gender stereotypes that might otherwise evolve in a highly sexist early environment. Indeed, research suggesting that androgynous parents tend to raise androgynous children is consistent with Bem's prescriptions for change (Orlofsky, 1979), as are findings that daughters of employed mothers perceive fewer psychological differences between the sexes and are more likely to be androgynous themselves, compared to daughters of mothers who are not employed (Hansson, Chernovetz, & Jones, 1977; Hoffman, 1989).

How might we reach children from more traditional

backgrounds, who have already received thousands of sex-stereotyped messages from family members, television, and their peers? Apparently, interventions that simply show children the benefits of cross-sex cooperation or that praise them for playing with other-sex toys and play partners have no lasting effect: children soon retreat to same-sex play and continue to prefer same-sex peers after the interventions are over (see Lockheed, 1986; Maccoby, 1988). One particularly ambitious program (Guttentag & Bray, 1976) exposed kinder-

By encouraging and engaging in counter-stereotypic activities, parents may deter their children from developing rigid gender stereotypes.

babies (Kinsey, Pomeroy, & Martin, 1948) and female babies (Bakwin, 1973) have been observed to (1) fondle their genitals; (2) display the grunting, flushing, and sweating that accompany intense sexual arousal; and (3) have what appear to be orgasms before becoming pale and more tranquil. In fact, parents in some cultures are well aware of the pleasure babies receive from sexual gratification and will occasionally use genital stimulation as a means of soothing a fussy or distressed infant (Ford & Beach, 1951).

Of course, infants are "sexual" beings only in the sense that their nervous systems allow sexual

---

B O X **9-3** | *continued*

garten, fifth-grade, and ninth-grade students to age-appropriate readings and activities designed to teach them about the capabilities of women and about the problems created by stereotyping and sexism. This program worked quite well with the younger children—particularly the girls, who often became outraged by what they learned about sexism. However, it actually had a boomerang effect among ninth-grade boys, who seemed to resist the new ideas they were being taught and actually expressed more stereotyped views after the training than before. And, although ninth-grade girls took many of the lessons to heart, they still tended to cling to the idea that women should run the family and men should be the primary breadwinners.

This study and others (see Katz & Walsh, 1991, for a review) suggest that efforts to change sex-role attitudes are more effective with younger children than with older ones and possibly with girls than with boys. It makes some sense that it is easier to alter children's thinking before their stereotypes have become fully crystallized; and, given the cognitive distortions of reality that such stereotypes promote, we may be most effective at changing attitudes by attacking these stereotypes directly. Indeed, Rebecca Bigler and Lynn Liben (1990) recently tried this approach with 6- to 11-year-olds. Through a series of problem-solving discussions, children were taught that (1) the most important considerations in deciding who could perform well at traditionally masculine and feminine occupations (such as construction worker and beautician) are the person's interests and willingness to learn and (2) the person's gender is irrelevant. Compared to control children who received no such training, program participants showed a clear decline in occupational stereotyp-

ing. Moreover, the reduction in stereotyping brought on by the training program was greatest for the *older* (9- to 11-year-old) children, particularly those older participants who had entered the study with the *strongest* stereotypes. Finally, a later information-processing test provided further evidence for the weakening of children's stereotypes: program participants were much more likely than nonparticipants to remember counter-stereotypic information in stories (for example, recalling that the "garbage man" in a story was actually a woman).

Finally, there is some evidence that programs designed to modify children's sex-stereotyped attitudes and behaviors may be more effective when the adult in charge is a male (Katz & Walsh, 1991). Why? Possibly because adult males make stronger distinctions between "gender-appropriate" and "gender-inappropriate" behaviors than adult females do; thus they may be particularly noteworthy as *agents of change*. In other words, children may feel that cross-sex activities and aspirations are quite legitimate indeed if it is a man who encourages (or fails to discourage) these pursuits.

So, new gender-role attitudes can be taught, although it remains to be seen whether such change will persist and generalize to new situations should these attitudes not be reinforced at home or in the culture at large. Our society is slowly changing, however, and some people believe that these changes have already had an impact on children (Etaugh, Levine, & Mennella, 1984). Judith Lorber (1986) sees much hope in her 13-year-old's response to her inquiry about whether a pregnant acquaintance of theirs had delivered a boy or girl: "Why do you want to know?" this child of a new era asked (p. 567).

reflexes and responses. However, it will not be very long before they begin to learn what human sexuality is about and how the members of their society react to sexual behavior.

Sexual Behavior during Childhood

According to Freud, preschoolers in the phallic stage of psychosexual development are very interested in the functioning of their genitals and will seek bodily pleasure through masturbation. However, Freud assumed that the traumas associated with the resolution of their Oedipus or Electra complexes would force school-age children to (1) repress their sexuality and (2) rechannel their energies into schoolwork and nonerotic social activities during the long **latency period** of middle childhood. It turns out that Freud was partly right and partly wrong.

Freud was right about the sexual curiosity and sexual activities of preschool children. However, he was quite incorrect in assuming that sexuality declines during the grade-school years. In fact, masturbation and other forms of sexual experimentation (including cross-sex exploits such as "playing doctor") actually *increase* with age (Rosen & Hall, 1984). In one large survey of 4- to 14-year-olds, more than half the boys and about one-third of the girls reported having masturbated and having engaged in some form of erotic play with same-sex peers (for example, manipulating each other's genitals); and about one-third of the respondents of each sex admitted that they had fondled the genitals of a cross-sex playmate (Elias & Gebhard, 1969). Perhaps Freud was misled by the fact that preschoolers, often unaware of society's rules of etiquette, are more likely to get caught at their sex play than older children are. As Rosen and Hall (1984) put it, older children are very discreet, playing "by adult sexual rules, behaving around adults in the sexless manner that leads observers to believe that they are sexually inactive" (p. 287).

Freud probably would not have been misled about the sexuality of grade-school children had his patients come from *permissive* or *supportive* societies, where children are free to express their sexuality and are even encouraged to prepare for their roles as

PHOTO 9-5   Preschool children are naturally curious about the human body.

mature sexual beings (Currier, 1981; Ford & Beach, 1951). On the island of Ponape, for example, 4- and 5-year-olds receive a thorough "sex education" from adults and are encouraged to experiment with one another. Among the Chewa of Africa, parents believe that practice makes perfect; so, with the blessings of their parents, older boys and girls build huts and play at being husbands and wives in trial marriages.

Of course, Freud might have concluded that humans are largely sexless *throughout childhood* had he worked with people from *restrictive* societies, in which all overt expressions of sexuality are actively suppressed. In New Guinea, for example, Kwoma boys are simply not allowed to touch themselves, and a boy caught having an erection is likely to have his penis beaten with a stick!

Where do Western societies fall on this permissive/restrictive continuum? Most could be classified as *semirestrictive*: there are informal rules prohibiting childhood masturbation and sex play, although these rules are frequently violated and adults rarely punish children unless the violations are flagrant. Nevertheless, anthropologists such as Margaret Mead (1928) have argued that even semirestrictive societies introduce unnecessary conflicts and make the transition to adulthood much harder than it need be by perpetuating horrible myths about normal sexual activities (such as saying that masturbation causes warts or blindness) while denying children opportunities to prepare for sexual relationships later in life.

Adolescent Sexuality

Sexuality assumes far greater importance once children experience puberty and become sexually mature: now adolescents must incorporate concepts of themselves as sexual beings into their male or female self-identities. They must also figure out how to properly express their sexuality. These tasks have never been easy, but they may now be more difficult than ever given the "new morality" that has emerged over the past several decades in Western societies. What are the sexual values of today's teenagers? What is "normal" sexual behavior during adolescence? Why do some adolescents (see Box 9-4) display homosexual rather than heterosexual orientations? Let's see what recent research can tell us.

Teenage sexual morality. Have today's teenagers adopted a new morality that is dramatically different from the standards that their parents and grandparents held? In one sense they have, for adolescents have become increasingly liberal in their thinking about sex throughout this century—and especially during the 1960s and 1970s. Sexual attitudes may now be reverting ever so slightly in a conservative direction, largely as a result of the AIDS problem (Carroll, 1988). But, even before the specter of AIDS, it was clear that few teenagers had completely abandoned the "old" (or traditional) morality.

In his review of the literature on teenage sexuality, Philip Dreyer (1982) noted three major changes in teenagers' sexual attitudes—changes that describe what the "new morality" means to them.

First, most adolescents now believe that *sex with affection* is acceptable. Thus, today's youth are rejecting the maxim that premarital intercourse is always immoral, but they still believe that casual or exploitative sex is wrong (even though they may

themselves have had such experiences). Still, only a surprisingly small percentage of sexually active adolescents in one national survey (6% of the males and 11% of the females) mentioned love as the reason they first had intercourse; instead, nearly 75% of the girls and 80% of the boys attributed their loss of virginity to strong social pressures to initiate sexual relations. They also cited curiosity and sexual desire as important reasons for becoming sexually active (Harris & Associates, 1986).

A second major change in teenage attitudes about sex involves the decline of the *double standard*—the idea that many sexual practices viewed as appropriate for males (premarital sex, promiscuity) are less appropriate for females. The double standard hasn't disappeared, for fathers often seem to condone (or at least not strongly discourage) the sexual exploits of their sons (Brooks-Gunn & Furstenberg, 1989); also, college students of recent times still believed that a woman who has many sexual partners is more immoral than an equally promiscuous man (Robinson et al., 1991). But Western societies have been moving for some time toward a single standard of sexual behavior for both males and females.

Finally, a third change in adolescents' sexual attitudes might be described as *increased confusion about sexual norms*. As Dreyer (1982) notes, the "sex with affection" idea is very ambiguous: must one truly be in love, or is mere liking enough to justify sexual intercourse? It is now up to the individual(s) to decide. Yet these decisions are tough, because adolescents receive mixed messages from many sources. On the one hand, they are often told by parents, the clergy, and advice columnists to value virginity and to avoid such consequences as pregnancy and sexually transmitted diseases. On the other hand, adolescents are strongly encouraged to be popular and attractive, and the more than 9000 glamorous sexual innuendos and behaviors that they see annually on television (most of which occur between *unmarried* couples) may convince them that sexual activity is one means to these ends (American Academy of Pediatrics, 1986). Apparently the behavior of older siblings adds to the confusion, for younger brothers and sisters of a sexually active sib tend to be even more sexually involved at a given age than the older

| *On Sexual Orientation and the Origins of Homosexuality*

One crucial component of sexuality is a person's **erotic orientation**: the gender to which he or she is sexually attracted. Of course, one's erotic orientation strongly influences his or her **sexual orientation**, or the gender to which he or she directs sexual overtures. Although we are accustomed to thinking about two sexual types—homosexuals and heterosexuals—sexual orientation really exists on a continuum, with heterosexuality at one end, homosexuality at the other, and various degrees of bisexuality in between (Ellis, Burke, & Ames, 1987). Nevertheless, the vast majority of adolescents and adults can be classified as primarily homosexual or primarily heterosexual in orientation. Although some uncertainty exists, owing to the reluctance of many homosexuals to make their orientations public, it is estimated that between 4% and 10% of the U.S. population is homosexual (Bell, Weinberg, & Hammersmith, 1981).

How do adolescents become homosexual or heterosexual in orientation? In addressing this issue, John Money (1988) emphasizes that sexual orientation is *not* a choice we make but, rather, something that happens to us. In other words, we do not *prefer* to be gay or straight; we simply turn out that way. How, then, do homosexual individuals become homosexual?

Over the years a large number of environmental hypotheses have been explored, and most have been discredited. For example, the psychoanalytic proposition that homosexuality stems from having a domineering mother and/or a weak father has received little support (Bell et al., 1981), and the long-standing *seduction hypothesis* (that homosexuals have been seduced into the lifestyle by an older same-sex companion) has also been disconfirmed. Indeed, many children and adolescents (perhaps 20–40%) have homosexual experiences, usually with an *agemate*, and the vast majority of these individuals turn out to be *heterosexual* (Masters, Johnson, & Kolodny, 1988; Money, 1988). Even the once-popular notion that fathers who reject their sons will make them effeminate and push them toward homosexuality has failed to gain much support (Bell et al., 1981; Green, 1987). So, to date, no clear environmental pathways to homosexuality have been identified, and parents of gay offspring should not feel that they have done anything to make their children homosexual (Bell et al., 1981; Griffin, Wirth, & Wirth, 1986).

Does this mean that sexual orientations are biologically determined? Not necessarily, even though biological variables may indeed be involved (Ellis & Ames, 1987). For example, we've seen that androgenized females (that is, women with AGS) are more likely than other women to be homosexual or bisexual, an observation implying that hormonal influences during the prenatal period may well influence sexual orientation (Money, 1985). Yet a clear majority of androgenized females turn out to be heterosexual. There are also several studies suggesting that mothers of homosexual men had often experienced more extreme forms of stress during pregnancy than did mothers of heterosexual men—findings bolstered by animal research showing that pregnant rats subjected to extreme stress tend to produce feminized male offspring (see Ellis et al., 1988). But these findings in no way imply that most male offspring of highly stressed mothers will turn out to be homosexual. The concordance of homosexuality is greater among pairs of identical twins than among pairs of fraternal twins, thus implying that there are genetic influences on sexual orientation (Ellis & Ames, 1987). However, not all identical twins share the same sexual orientation. Finally, differences in the structure of certain areas of the brain have been identified in homosexual and heterosexual men (Associated Press, 1992), although it is not known exactly what percentage of men who display the "homosexual" structure actually turn out to be homosexuals.

So the biological influences that have been identified may be just that—*influences*, rather than determinants of homosexuality. And, even if genetic predispositions and prenatal hormones should prove to be powerful contributors to homosexuality, this does not mean that one's experiences are unimportant. John Money (1988) favors an interactive model—one specifying that some individuals who are thus predisposed biologically are more likely to become homosexuals at puberty if their juvenile (childhood) sex play has regularly involved same-sex (rather than other-sex) companions. However, Money's theory is yet to be tested, and the origins of homosexuality remain somewhat mysterious.

TABLE 9-6 *Historical changes in the percentages of high school and college students reporting premarital sexual intercourse*

	High School		College	
Period	Boys	Girls	Boys	Girls
1925–1965	25	10	55	25
1966–1973	35	35	85	65
1974–1979	56	44	74	74
1986	61	53		

SOURCES: P. H. Dreyer, "Sexuality during Adolescence." In B. B. Wolman (Ed.), *Handbook of Developmental Psychology*. New York: Wiley, 1982; L. Harris & Associates, *American Teens Speak: Sex, Myths, TV, and Birth Control. The Planned Parenthood Poll*. New York: Planned Parenthood Federation of America, 1986.

siblings were (Rodgers & Rowe, 1988). One young adolescent, lamenting the strong social pressures she faced to become sexually active, jokingly offered this definition of a virgin: "an awfully ugly third-grader" (Gullotta, Adams, & Alexander, 1986, p. 109). In years gone by, the norms of appropriate behavior were much simpler: sex was fine if you were married (or perhaps engaged), but it should be avoided otherwise. This is not to say that our parents or grandparents always resisted the temptations they faced; but they probably had a lot less difficulty than today's adolescents in deciding whether what they were doing was acceptable or unacceptable.

Sexual behavior.   Not only have sexual attitudes changed, but so have patterns of adolescent sexual behavior. Modern adolescents masturbate more (or at least report doing so more) than those of past eras (Dreyer, 1982), although many still feel guilty or uneasy about it (Coles & Stokes, 1985). And, although only a small minority of today's 15-year-olds have experienced sexual intercourse, we see in Table 9-6 that premarital intercourse has become more common in recent years and that more than half of all adolescents have had intercourse at least once before they leave high school. The table also shows that the sexual behavior of females has changed more than that of males (see also Wielandt & Boldsen, 1989). So the decline of the double standard is clearly not just a matter of changes in attitudes. Indeed, today's 18- to 19-year-old women are about as likely as their male agemates to have had sexual intercourse (Forrest & Singh, 1990).

In sum, both the sexual attitudes and the sexual behaviors of adolescents have changed dramatically in this century—so much so that sexual involvement is now part of the typical adolescent's experience and a part of his or her search for an adult identity and emotional fulfillment (Dreyer, 1982). Unfortunately, many sexually active adolescent couples fail to practice birth control (or do so only sporadically), partly because they are often incredibly misinformed about reproductive issues; for example, only about one teenager in three can identify the phase of the menstrual cycle in which risk of pregnancy is highest (Brooks-Gunn & Furstenberg, 1989; Morrison, 1985). For the 10% of all teenage girls who will give birth before age 18, the consequences can be serious ones: an interrupted education, low income, and a difficult start for both the new mother and her child. And, compared to children of older mothers, children born to teenagers show small but consistent cognitive decrements in the preschool and early grade-school years and markedly lower academic achievement thereafter (Furstenberg, Brooks-Gunn, & Chase-Lansdale, 1989). Meanwhile, the AIDS epidemic continues; although adolescents have become more cautious in their sexual attitudes in response to this threat, they have shown few signs of adopting safer sexual *practices* (Carroll, 1988). Is it any wonder, then, that many educators are now calling for stronger programs of sex education and counseling in our schools? If teenage sexuality is here to stay, then there is little hope of preventing its unwanted consequences unless both boys and girls begin to behave in more sexually responsible ways.

PHOTO 9-6 Sexual involvement has become an integral component of the adolescent's search for an adult identity and emotional fulfillment.

Summary

Differences between males and females can be detected in the physical, psychological, and social realms. Some sex differences are biological in origin, whereas others arise from socialization pressures. Interests, activities, and attributes that are considered more appropriate for members of one sex than the other are called sex-role standards (or sex-role stereotypes). Sex typing is the process by which children acquire a gender identity and assimilate the motives, values, and behaviors considered appropriate in their culture for members of their biological sex.

Some sex-role stereotypes are more accurate than others. Males tend to be more active and aggressive than females and to outperform them on tests of spatial abilities and arithmetic reasoning; females are more emotionally expressive and compliant than males, and they tend to outperform males on tests of verbal abilities. But on the whole these sex differences are quite small, and males and females are psychologically more similar than different. Among the stereotypes that have *no* basis in fact are the notions that females are more sociable, suggestible, and illogical and less analytical and achievement oriented than males. The persistence of these "cultural myths" is particularly damaging to women. For example, members of both sexes tend to devalue women's accomplishments by attributing them to luck or hard work rather than to competence. This tendency to degrade the achievements of females is well established by middle childhood.

Sex typing begins very early. By age 2½ most children know whether they are boys or girls, they tend to favor sex-typed toys and activities, and they are already aware of several sex-role stereotypes. By the time they enter school (or shortly thereafter), they know that gender is an unchanging aspect of their personalities, and they have learned many of the sex-role standards of their society. Boys face stronger sex-typing pressures than girls do; consequently, males are quicker to develop a preference for sex-appropriate patterns of behavior.

Several theories have been proposed to account for sex differences and sex-role development. Money and Ehrhardt's biosocial theory emphasizes the biological developments that occur before a child is born — developments that parents and other social agents will react to when deciding how to socialize the child. Other theorists have focused more intently on the socialization process itself. Psychoanalytic theorists suggest that sex typing is one result of the child's identification with the same-sex parent. Social-learning theorists offer two mechanisms to explain how children acquire sex-typed attitudes and behaviors: (1) direct tuition (reinforcement for sex-appropriate behaviors and punishment for sex-inappropriate ones) and (2) observational learning. Cognitive-developmental theorists point out that the course of sex-role development will depend, in part, on the child's cognitive development. And proponents of gender schema theory have shown how children's active construction of sex-role stereotypes (gender schemata) colors their interpretations of social events and contributes to the development of sex-typed interests, attitudes, and patterns of behavior.

The psychological attributes "masculinity" and "femininity" have traditionally been considered to be at opposite ends of a single continuum. However, one "new look" at sex roles proposes that masculinity and femininity are two separate dimensions and that the *androgynous* person is someone who possesses a fair number of masculine *and* feminine characteristics. Recent research shows that androgynous people do exist, are relatively popular and well adjusted, and may be adaptable to a wider variety of environmental demands than people who are traditionally sex typed.

As Freud had thought, infants are sexual beings from the start; they react physiologically to genital stimulation even though they have no awareness that their responses are "sexual" ones. Moreover, Freud's portrayal of preschool children as "sexually curious beings" was also correct, although he was very wrong in assuming that school-age children repress their sexual urges; in fact, sexual activity actually increases rather than declines during Freud's so-called latency period. Sexual matters become very important to adolescents, who, having reached sexual maturity, must incorporate their sexuality into their changing self-concepts. During this century, sexual attitudes have become much more permissive. The belief that premarital sex is immoral has given way to the view that sex with affection is acceptable; the double standard has weakened; and conflicting norms have increased confusion about what constitutes acceptable sexual conduct. Sexual behavior has increased as well, as more adolescents are engaging in various forms of sexual activity at earlier ages than in the past.

References

AMERICAN ACADEMY OF PEDIATRICS (1986). Sexuality, contraception, and the media. *Pediatrics, 71*, 535–536.

ASSOCIATED PRESS (1992, August 1). New clue to sexual orientation? *Atlanta Journal*, p. B4.

BAKWIN, H. (1973). Erotic feelings in infants and young children. *American Journal of Diseases of Children, 126*, 52–54.

BANDURA, A. (1989). Social cognitive theory. In R. Vasta (Ed.), *Annals of child development* (Vol. 6). Greenwich, CT: JAI Press.

BARDWELL, J. R., COCHRAN, S. W., & WALKER, S. (1986). Relation of parental education, race, and gender to sex-role stereotyping in five-year-old kindergartners. *Sex Roles, 15*, 275–281.

BARRY, H. III, BACON, M. K., & CHILD, I. L. (1957). A cross-cultural survey of some sex differences in socialization. *Journal of Abnormal and Social Psychology, 55*, 327–332.

BAUMRIND, D. (1982). Are androgynous individuals more effective persons and parents? *Child Development, 53*, 44–75.

BEACH, F. A. (1965). *Sex and behavior*. New York: Wiley.

BELL, A. P., WEINBERG, M. S., & HAMMERSMITH, S. K. (1981). *Sexual preference: Its development in men and women*. Bloomington: Indiana University Press.

BEM, S. L. (1974). The measurement of psychological androgyny. *Journal of Consulting and Clinical Psychology, 42*, 155–162.

BEM, S. L. (1975). Sex-role adaptability: One consequence of psychological androgyny. *Journal of Personality and Social Psychology, 31*, 634–643.

BEM, S. L. (1978). Beyond androgyny: Some presumptuous prescriptions for a liberated sexual identity. In J. A. Sherman & F. L. Denmark (Eds.), *The psychology of women: Future directions in research*. New York: Psychological Dimensions.

BEM, S. L. (1983). Gender schema theory and its implications for child development: Raising gender aschematic children in a gender-schematic society. *Signs: Journal of Women in Culture and Society, 8*, 598–616.

BEM, S. L. (1989). Genital knowledge and gender constancy in preschool children. *Child Development, 60*, 649–662.

BERMAN, P. W., & GOODMAN, V. (1984). Age and sex differences in children's responses to babies: Effects of adults' caretaking requests and instructions. *Child Development, 55*, 1071–1077.

BEST, D. L., WILLIAMS, J. E., CLOUD, J. M., DAVIS, S. W., ROBERTSON, L. S., EDWARDS, J. R., GILES, H., & FOWLKES, J. (1977). Development of sex-trait stereotypes among young children in the United States, England, and Ireland. *Child Development, 48*, 1375–1384.

BIGLER, R. S., & LIBEN, L. S. (1990). The role of attitudes and interventions in gender-schematic processing. *Child Development, 61*, 1440–1452.

BLAKEMORE, J. E. O. (1981). Age and sex differences in interaction with a human infant. *Child Development, 52*, 386–388.

BLAKEMORE, J. E. O., LaRUE, A. A., & OLEJNIK, A. B. (1979). Sex-appropriate toy preference and the ability to conceptualize toys as sex-role related. *Developmental Psychology, 15*, 339–340.

BLOCK, J. H. (1976). Issues, problems, and pitfalls in assessing sex differences: A critical review of *The psychology of sex differences. Merrill-Palmer Quarterly, 27*, 283–308.

BOLDIZAR, J. P. (1991). Assessing sex-typing and androgyny in children: The children's sex-role inventory. *Developmental Psychology, 27*, 505–515.

BORJA-ALVAREZ, T., ZARBATANY, L., & PEPPER, S. (1991). Contributions of male and female guests and hosts to peer group entry. *Child Development, 62,* 1079–1090.

BRADBARD, M. R., MARTIN, C. L., ENDSLEY, R. C., & HALVERSON, C. F. (1986). Influence of sex stereotypes on children's exploration and memory: A competence versus performance distinction. *Developmental Psychology, 22,* 481–486.

BRIM, O. G. (1958). Family structure and sex-role learning by children: A further analysis of Helen Koch's data. *Sociometry, 21,* 1–16.

BROOKS-GUNN, J., & FURSTENBERG, F. F., JR. (1989). Adolescent sexual behavior. *American Psychologist, 44,* 249–257.

BROVERMAN, I. K., VOGEL, S. R., CLARKSON, F. E., & ROSENKRANTZ, P. S. (1972). Sex-role stereotypes: A current appraisal. *Journal of Social Issues, 28,* 59–78.

BROWN, D. G. (1957). Masculinity-femininity development in children. *Journal of Consulting Psychology, 21,* 197–202.

BUSSEY, K., & BANDURA, A. (1984). Influence of gender constancy and social power on sex-linked modeling. *Journal of Personality and Social Psychology, 47,* 1292–1302.

BUSSEY, K., & BANDURA, A. (1992). Self-regulatory mechanisms governing gender development. *Child Development, 63,* 1236–1250.

CALDERA, Y. M., HUSTON, A. C., & O'BRIEN, M. (1989). Social interactions and play patterns of parents and toddlers with feminine, masculine, and neutral toys. *Child Development, 60,* 70–76.

CANN, A., & NEWBERN, S. R. (1984). Sex stereotype effects in children's picture recognition. *Child Development, 55,* 1085–1090.

CANTER, R. J., & AGETON, S. S. (1984). The epidemiology of adolescent sex-role attitudes. *Sex Roles, 11,* 657–676.

CARROLL, L. (1988). Concern with AIDS and the sexual behavior of college students. *Journal of Marriage and the Family, 50,* 405–411.

CARTER, D. B., & LEVY, G. D. (1988). Cognitive aspects of early sex-role development: The influence of gender schemas on preschoolers' memories and preferences for sex-typed toys and activities. *Child Development, 59,* 782–792.

CARTER, D. B., & McCLOSKEY, L. A. (1983–1984). Peers and the maintenance of sex-typed behavior: The development of children's conceptions of cross-gender behavior in their peers. *Social Cognition, 2,* 294–314.

CHARLESWORTH, W. R., & DZUR, C. (1987). Gender comparisons of preschoolers' behavior and resource utilization in group problem solving. *Child Development, 58,* 191–200.

CHRISTOPHERSEN, E. R. (1989). Injury control. *American Psychologist, 44,* 237–241.

COLES, R., & STOKES, G. (1985). *Sex and the American teenager.* New York: Harper & Row.

CONDRY, J., & CONDRY, S. (1976). Sex differences: A study in the eye of the beholder. *Child Development, 47,* 812–819.

COWAN, C. P., & COWAN, P. A. (1987). A preventive intervention for couples becoming parents. In C. F. Z. Boukydis (Ed.), *Research on support for parents and infants in the postnatal period.* New York: Ablex.

COWAN, G., & AVANTS, S. K. (1988). Children's influence strategies: Structure, sex differences, and bilateral mother-child influences. *Child Development, 59,* 1303–1313.

CURRIER, R. L. (1981). Juvenile sexuality in global perspective. In L. L. Constantine & F. M. Martinson (Eds.), *Children and sex: New findings, new perspectives.* Boston: Little, Brown.

DAMON, W. (1977). *The social world of the child.* San Francisco: Jossey-Bass.

DIAMOND, M. (1982). Sexual identity, monozygotic twins reared in discordant sex-roles and a BBC follow up. *Archives of Sexual Behavior, 11,* 181–186.

DIENER, E., SANDVIK, E., & LARSON, R. J. (1985). Age and sex effects for emotional intensity. *Developmental Psychology, 21,* 542–546.

DiPIETRO, J. A. (1981). Rough and tumble play: A function of gender. *Developmental Psychology, 17,* 50–58.

DREYER, P. H. (1982). Sexuality during adolescence. In B. B. Wolman (Ed.), *Handbook of developmental psychology.* New York: Wiley.

DWECK, C. S., DAVIDSON, W., NELSON, S., & ENNA, B. (1978). Sex differences in learned helplessness: II. The contingencies of evaluative feedback in the classroom; III. An experimental analysis. *Developmental Psychology, 14,* 268–276.

DWECK, C. S., & ELLIOTT, E. S. (1983). Achievement motivation. In P. H. Mussen (Ed.), *Handbook of child psychology.* Vol. 4: *Socialization, personality, and social development.* New York: Wiley.

EAGLY, A. H., & STEFFEN, V. J. (1986). Gender and aggressive behavior: A meta-analytic review of the social psychological literature. *Psychological Bulletin, 100,* 283–308.

EATON, W. O., & ENNS, L. R. (1986). Sex differences in human motor activity level. *Psychological Bulletin, 100,* 19–28.

EATON, W. O., & YU, A. P. (1989). Are sex differences in child motor activity level a function of sex differences in maturational status? *Child Development, 60,* 1005–1011.

EHRHARDT, A. A. (1985). The psychobiology of gender. In A. S. Rossi (Ed.), *Gender and the life course.* New York: Aldine.

EHRHARDT, A. A., & BAKER, S. W. (1974). Fetal androgens, human central nervous system differentiation, and behavioral sex differences. In R. C. Friedman, R. M. Rickard, & R. L. Van de Wiele (Eds.), *Sex differences in behavior.* New York: Wiley.

EISENBERG, N., MURRAY, E., & HITE, T. (1982). Children's reasoning regarding sex-typed toy choices. *Child Development, 53,* 81–86.

EISENBERG, N., WOLCHIK, S. A., HERNANDEZ, R., & PASTERNACK, J. F. (1985). Parental socialization of young children's play: A short-term longitudinal study. *Child Development, 56,* 1506–1513.

ELIAS, J., & GEBHARD, P. (1969). Sexuality and sexual learning in childhood. *Phi Delta Kappan, 50,* 401–405.

ELKIND, D. (1981). *Children and adolescents: Interpretive essays on Jean Piaget* (3rd ed.). New York: Oxford University Press.

ELLIS, L., & AMES, M. A. (1987). Neurohormonal functioning and sexual orientation: A theory of homosexuality-heterosexuality. *Psychological Bulletin, 101,* 233–258.

ELLIS, L., AMES, M. A., PECKHAM, W., & BURKE, D. M. (1988). Sexual orientation in human offspring may be altered by severe emotional distress during pregnancy. *Journal of Sex Research, 25,* 152–157.

ELLIS, L., BURKE, D. M., & AMES, M. A. (1987). Sexual orientation measures as a continuous variable. *Archives of Sexual Behavior, 16,* 523–529.

EMMERICH, W. (1959). Parental identification in young children. *Genetic Psychology Monographs, 60,* 257–308.

EMMERICH, W., & SHEPARD, K. (1982). Development of sex-differentiated preferences during late childhood and adolescence. *Developmental Psychology, 18,* 406–417.

ENTWISLE, D. R., & BAKER, D. P. (1983). Gender and young children's expectations for performance in arithmetic. *Developmental Psychology, 19,* 200–209.

ETAUGH, C., LEVINE, D., & MENNELLA, A. (1984). Development of sex biases in children: 40 years later. *Sex Roles, 10,* 911–922.

FABES, R. A., EISENBERG, N., & MILLER, P. A. (1990). Maternal correlates of children's vicarious emotional responsiveness. *Developmental Psychology, 26,* 639–648.

FAGOT, B. I. (1978). The influence of sex of child on parental reactions to toddler children. *Child Development, 49,* 459–465.

FAGOT, B. I. (1985a). Beyond the reinforcement principle: Another step toward understanding sex-role development. *Developmental Psychology, 21,* 1097–1104.

FAGOT, B.I. (1985b). Changes in thinking about early sex-role development. *Developmental Review, 5,* 83–98.

FAGOT, B. I., & HAGAN, R. (1991). Observations of parental reactions to sex-stereotyped behaviors: Age and sex effects. *Child Development, 62,* 617–628.

FAGOT, B. I., & LEINBACH, M. D. (1989). The young child's gender schema: Environmental input, internal organization. *Child Development, 60,* 663–672.

FAGOT, B. I., LEINBACH, M. D., & HAGAN, R. (1986). Gender labeling and the adoption of sex-typed behaviors. *Developmental Psychology, 22,* 440–443.

FAGOT, B. I., LEINBACH, M. D., & O'BOYLE, C. (1992). Gender labeling, gender stereotyping, and parenting behaviors. *Developmental Psychology, 28,* 225–230.

FEINGOLD, A. (1988). Cognitive gender differences are disappearing. *American Psychologist, 43,* 95–103.

FELDMAN, S. S., BIRINGEN, Z. C., & NASH, S. C. (1981). Fluctuations of sex-typed self-attributions as a function of stage of family life cycle. *Developmental Psychology, 17,* 24–35.

FELDMAN-SUMMERS, S., & KIESLER, S. B. (1974). Those who are number two try harder: The effect of sex on attribution of causality. *Journal of Personality and Social Psychology, 30,* 846–855.

FORD, C. S., & BEACH, F. A. (1951). *Patterns of sexual behavior.* New York: Harper & Row.

FORREST, J. D., & SINGH, S. (1990). The sexual and reproductive behavior of American women, 1982–1988. *Family Planning Perspectives, 22,* 206–215.

FREUD, S. (1961a). Some physical consequences of the anatomical distinction between the sexes. In J. Strachey (Ed.), *The standard edition of the complete psychological works of Sigmund Freud* (Vol. 19). London: Hogarth Press. (Originally published 1924.)

FREUD, S. (1961b). The dissolution of the Oedipus complex. In J. Strachey (Ed.), *The standard edition of the complete psychological works of Sigmund Freud* (Vol. 19). London: Hogarth Press. (Originally published 1924.)

FREY, K. S., & RUBLE, D. N. (1992). Gender constancy and the "cost" of sex-typed behavior: A test of the conflict hypothesis. *Developmental Psychology, 28,* 714–721.

FUCHS, D., & THELEN, M. H. (1988). Children's expected interpersonal consequences of communicating their affective state and reported likelihood of expression. *Child Development, 59,* 1314–1322.

FURSTENBERG, F. F., JR., BROOKS-GUNN, J., & CHASE-LANSDALE, L. (1989). Teenaged pregnancy and childbearing. *American Psychologist, 44,* 313–320.

GINSBURG, H. J., & MILLER, S. M. (1982). Sex differences in children's risk-taking behavior. *Child Development, 53,* 426–428.

GOLDBERG, P. (1968). Are women prejudiced against women? *Trans/Action, 5,* 28–30.

GOLDMAN, R., & GOLDMAN, J. (1982). *Children's sexual thinking: A comparative study of children aged 5 to 15 years in Australia, North America, Britain, and Sweden.* London: Routledge & Kegan Paul.

GREEN, D. (1987). *The "sissy boy syndrome" and the development of homosexuality.* New Haven, CT: Yale University Press.

GRIFFIN, C. W., WIRTH, M. J., & WIRTH, A. G. (1986). *Beyond acceptance: Parents of lesbians and gays talk about their experiences.* Englewood Cliffs, NJ: Prentice-Hall.

GROTEVANT, H. D. (1978). Sibling constellations and sex-typing of interests in adolescence. *Child Development, 49,* 540–542.

GULLOTTA, T. P., ADAMS, G. R., & ALEXANDER, S. J. (1986). *Today's marriages and families: A wellness approach.* Pacific Grove, CA: Brooks/Cole.

GUTTENTAG, M., & BRAY, H. (1976). *Undoing sex stereotypes: Research and resources for educators.* New York: McGraw-Hill.

HALL, J. A., & HALBERSTADT, A. G. (1980). Masculinity and femininity in children: Development of the Children's Personal Attributes Questionnaire. *Developmental Psychology, 16,* 270–280.

HANSSON, R. O., CHERNOVETZ, M. E., & JONES, W. H. (1977). Maternal employment and androgyny. *Psychology of Women Quarterly, 2,* 76–78.

HARRIS, L., & ASSOCIATES (1986). *American teens speak: Sex, myths, TV, and birth control. The Planned Parenthood poll.* New York: Planned Parenthood Federation of America.

HAUGH, S. S., HOFFMAN, C. D., & COWAN, G. (1980). The eye of the very young beholder: Sex-typing of infants by young children. *Child Development, 51,* 598–600.

HENKER, B., & WHALEN, C. K. (1989). Hyperactivity and attention deficits. *American Psychologist, 44*, 216–223.

HETHERINGTON, E. M. (1966). Effects of paternal absence on sex-typed behaviors in Negro and white preadolescent males. *Journal of Personality and Social Psychology, 4*, 87–91.

HETHERINGTON, E. M., & FRANKIE, G. (1967). Effect of parental dominance, warmth, and conflict on imitation in children. *Journal of Personality and Social Psychology, 6*, 119–125.

HETHERINGTON, E. M., & PARKE, R. D. (1975). *Child psychology: A contemporary viewpoint.* New York: McGraw-Hill.

HOFFMAN, L. W. (1984). Work, family, and the socialization of the child. In R. D. Parke (Ed.), *Review of child development research.* Vol. 7: *The family.* Chicago: University of Chicago Press.

HOFFMAN, L. W. (1989). Effects of maternal employment in the two-parent family. *American Psychologist, 44*, 283–292.

HUMPHREYS, A. P., & SMITH, P. K. (1987). Rough and tumble, friendship, and dominance in school children: Evidence for continuity and change with age. *Child Development, 58*, 201–212.

HUSTON, A. C. (1983). Sex-typing. In P. H. Mussen (Ed.), *Handbook of child psychology.* Vol. 4: *Socialization, personality, and social development.* New York: Wiley.

HUTT, C. (1972). *Males and females.* Baltimore: Penguin Books.

HYDE, J. S. (1984). How large are sex differences in aggression? A developmental meta-analysis. *Developmental Psychology, 20*, 722–736.

HYDE, J. S., FENNEMA, E., & LAMON, S. J. (1990). Gender differences in mathematics performance: A meta-analysis. *Psychological Bulletin, 107*, 139–155.

HYDE, J. S., KRAJNIK, M., & SKULDT-NIEDERBERGER, K. (1991). Androgyny across the life span: A replication and longitudinal follow-up. *Developmental Psychology, 27*, 516–519.

HYDE, J. S., & LINN, M. C. (1988). Gender differences in verbal ability: A meta-analysis. *Psychological Bulletin, 104*, 53–69.

IMPERATO-McGINLEY, J., PETERSON, R. E., GAUTIER, T., & STURLA, E. (1979). Androgyns and the evolution of male gender identity among male pseudohermaphrodites with 5α-reductase deficiency. *New England Journal of Medicine, 300*, 1233–1237.

INTONS-PETERSON, M. J. (1988). *Children's concept of gender.* Norwood, NJ: Ablex.

INTONS-PETERSON, M. J., & REDDEL, M. (1984). What do people ask about a neonate? *Developmental Psychology, 20*, 358–359.

JACKLIN, C. N. (1989). Male and female: Issues of gender. *American Psychologist, 44*, 127–133.

JACKLIN, C. N., & MACCOBY, E. E. (1978). Social behavior at 33 months in same-sex and mixed-sex dyads. *Child Development, 49*, 557–569.

JOHNSON, E. S., & MEADE, A. C. (1987). Developmental patterns of spatial ability: An early sex difference. *Child Development, 58*, 725–740.

KAGAN, J., & MOSS, H. A. (1962). *Birth to maturity.* New York: Wiley.

KATCHER, A. (1955). The discrimination of sex differences by young children. *Journal of Genetic Psychology, 87*, 131–143.

KATZ, P. A. (1987). Variations in family constellation: Effects of gender schemata. In L. S. Liben & M. L. Signorella (Eds.), *New directions for child development.* Vol. 38: *Children's gender schemata.* San Francisco: Jossey-Bass.

KATZ, P. A., & WALSH, P. V. (1991). Modification of children's gender-stereotyped behavior. *Child Development, 62*, 338–351.

KINSEY, A. C., POMEROY, W. B., & MARTIN, C. E. (1948). *Sexual behavior in the human male.* Philadelphia: Saunders.

KOHLBERG, L. (1966). A cognitive-developmental analysis of children's sex-role concepts and attitudes. In E. E. Maccoby (Ed.), *The development of sex differences.* Stanford, CA: Stanford University Press.

KUHN, D., NASH, S. C., & BRUCKEN, L. (1978). Sex-role concepts of two- and three-year-olds. *Child Development, 49*, 445–451.

La FRENIERE, P., STRAYER, F. F., & GAUTHIER, R. (1984). The emergence of same-sex affiliative preferences among preschool peers: A developmental ethological perspective. *Child Development, 55*, 1958–1965.

LAMB, M. E. (1981). *The role of the father in child development.* New York: Wiley.

LANGLOIS, J. H., & DOWNS, A. C. (1980). Mothers, fathers, and peers as socialization agents of sex-typed play behaviors in young children. *Child Development, 51*, 1237–1247.

LEINBACH, M. D., & FAGOT, B. I. (1993; in press). Gender-role development in young children: From discrimination to labeling. *Developmental Review.*

LEVY, G. D., & CARTER, D. B. (1989). Gender schema, gender constancy, and gender-role knowledge: The roles of cognitive factors in preschoolers' gender-role stereotype attributions. *Developmental Psychology, 25*, 444–449.

LEWIN, M., & TRAGOS, L. M. (1987). Has the feminist movement influenced adolescent sex role attitudes? A reassessment after a quarter century. *Sex Roles, 16*, 125–135.

LIEBERT, R. M., & SPRAFKIN, J. (1988). *The early window: Effects of television on children and youth* (3rd ed.). New York: Pergamon Press.

LINN, M. C., & HYDE, J. S. (1989). Gender, mathematics, and science. *Educational Researcher, 18*, 17–27.

LINN, M. C., & PETERSEN, A. C. (1985). Emergence and characterization of sex differences in spatial ability: A meta-analysis. *Child Development, 56*, 1479–1498.

LIVSON, F. B. (1983). Gender identity: A life-span view of sex-role development. In R. B. Weg (Ed.), *Sexuality in the later years: Roles and behavior.* Orlando, FL: Academic Press.

LOCKHEED, M. E. (1986). Reshaping the social order: The case of gender segregation. *Sex Roles, 14*, 617–628.

LORBER, J. (1986). Dismantling Noah's ark. *Sex Roles, 14*, 567–580.

LUMMIS, M., & STEVENSON, H. W. (1990). Gender differences in beliefs and achievement: A cross-cultural study. *Developmental Psychology, 26*, 254–263.

LYTTON, H., & ROMNEY, D. M. (1991). Parents' differential socialization of boys and girls: A meta-analysis. *Psychological Bulletin, 109,* 267–296.

MACCOBY, E.E. (1980). *Social development.* San Diego: Harcourt Brace Jovanovich.

MACCOBY, E. E. (1988). Gender as a social category. *Developmental Psychology, 24,* 755–765.

MACCOBY, E. E. (1990). Gender and relationships: A developmental account. *American Psychologist, 45,* 513–520.

MACCOBY, E. E., & JACKLIN, C. N. (1974). *The psychology of sex differences.* Stanford, CA: Stanford University Press.

MacDONALD, K., & PARKE, R. D. (1986). Parent-child physical play: The effects of sex and age of children and parents. *Sex Roles, 15,* 367–378.

MacFARLANE, A. (1977). *The psychology of childbirth.* Cambridge, MA: Harvard University Press.

MacKINNON, C. E., BRODY, G. H., & STONEMAN, Z. (1982). The effects of divorce and maternal employment on the home environments of preschool children. *Child Development, 53,* 1392–1399.

MacKINNON, C. E., STONEMAN, Z., & BRODY, G. H. (1984). The impact of maternal employment and family form on children's sex-role stereotypes and mothers' traditional attitudes. *Journal of Divorce, 8,* 51–60.

MAJOR, B., CARNEVALE, P. J. D., & DEAUX, K. (1981). A different perspective on androgyny: Evaluations of masculine and feminine personality characteristics. *Journal of Personality and Social Psychology, 41,* 988–1001.

MARCUS, D. E., & OVERTON, W. F. (1978). The development of cognitive gender constancy and sex-role preferences. *Child Development, 49,* 434–444.

MARTIN, C. L. (1989). Children's use of gender-related information in making social judgments. *Developmental Psychology, 25,* 80–88.

MARTIN, C. L. (1990). Attitudes and expectations about children with nontraditional and traditional gender roles. *Sex Roles, 22,* 151–165.

MARTIN, C. L., & HALVERSON, C. F., JR. (1981). A schematic processing model of sex typing and stereotyping in children. *Child Development, 52,* 1119–1134.

MARTIN, C. L., & HALVERSON, C. F., JR. (1983). The effects of sex-typing schemas on young children's memory. *Child Development, 54,* 563–574.

MARTIN, C. L., & HALVERSON, C. F., JR. (1987). The roles of cognition in sex-roles and sex-typing. In D. B. Carter (Ed.), *Current conceptions of sex roles and sex-typing: Theory and research.* New York: Praeger.

MASTERS, J. C., FORD, M. E., AREND, R., GROTEVANT, H. D., & CLARK, L. V. (1979). Modeling and labeling as integrated determinants of children's sex-typed imitative behavior. *Child Development, 50,* 364–371.

MASTERS, W. H., JOHNSON, V. E., & KOLODNY, R. C. (1988). *Masters and Johnson on sex and human loving.* Glenview, IL: Scott Foresman.

McGHEE, P. E., & FRUEH, T. (1980). Television viewing and the learning of sex-role stereotypes. *Sex Roles, 6,* 179–188.

MEAD, M. (1928). *Coming of age in Samoa.* New York: William Morrow.

MEAD, M. (1935). *Sex and temperament in three primitive societies.* New York: William Morrow.

MILLER, C. L. (1983). Developmental changes in male/female voice classification by infants. *Infant Behavior and Development, 6,* 313–330.

MISCHEL, W. (1970). Sex-typing and socialization. In P. H. Mussen (Ed.), *Carmichael's manual of child psychology* (Vol. 2). New York: Wiley.

MITCHELL, J. E., BAKER, L. A., & JACKLIN, C. N. (1989). Masculinity and femininity in twin children: Genetic and environmental factors. *Child Development, 60,* 1475–1485.

MONEY, J. (1965). Psychosexual differentiation. In J. Money (Ed.), *Sex research: New developments.* New York: Holt, Rinehart & Winston.

MONEY, J. (1985). Pediatric sexology and hermaphroditism. *Journal of Sex and Marital Therapy, 11,* 139–156.

MONEY, J. (1988). *Gay, straight, and in-between: The sexology of erotic orientation.* New York: Oxford University Press.

MONEY, J., & EHRHARDT, A. (1972). *Man and woman, boy and girl.* Baltimore: Johns Hopkins University Press.

MONEY, J., & TUCKER, P. (1975). *Sexual signatures: On being a man or a woman.* Boston: Little, Brown.

MOORE, C. L. (1985). Another psychobiological view of sexual differentiation. *Developmental Review, 5,* 18–55.

MORRISON, D. M. (1985). Adolescent contraceptive behavior: A review. *Psychological Bulletin, 98,* 538–568.

MUNROE, R. H., SHIMMIN, H. S., & MUNROE, R. L. (1984). Gender understanding and sex-role preferences in four cultures. *Developmental Psychology, 20,* 673–682.

MUSSEN, P. H., & RUTHERFORD, E. (1963). Parent-child relations and parental personality in relation to young children's sex-role preferences. *Child Development, 34,* 589–607.

NADELMAN, L. (1974). Sex identity in American children: Memory, knowledge, and preference tests. *Developmental Psychology, 10,* 413–417.

NEWCOMBE, N., & DUBAS, J. S. (1987). Individual differences in cognitive ability: Are they related to timing of puberty? In R. M. Lerner & T. T. Foch (Eds.), *Biological-psychosocial interactions in early adolescence: A life-span perspective.* Hillsdale, NJ: Erlbaum.

NEWCOMBE, N., & DUBAS, J. S. (1992). A longitudinal study of predictors of spatial ability in adolescent females. *Child Development, 63,* 37–46.

O'HERON, C. A., & ORLOFSKY, J. L. (1990). Stereotypic and nonstereotypic sex role trait and behavior orientations, gender identity, and psychological adjustment. *Journal of Personality and Social Psychology, 58,* 134–143.

ORLOFSKY, J. L. (1979). Parental antecedents of sex-role orientation in college men and women. *Sex Roles, 5,* 495–512.

ORLOFSKY, J. L., & O'HERON, C. A. (1987). Stereotypic and nonstereotypic sex role trait and behavior organizations: Implications for personal adjustment. *Journal of Personality and Social Psychology, 52,* 1034–1042.

PARSONS, T. (1955). Family structure and the socialization of the child. In T. Parsons & R. F. Bales (Eds.), *Family socialization and interaction processes*. New York: Free Press.

PERRY, D. G., & BUSSEY, K. (1984). *Social development*. Englewood Cliffs, NJ: Prentice-Hall.

PLOMIN, R. (1990). *Nature and nurture: An introduction to human behavioral genetics*. Pacific Grove, CA: Brooks/Cole.

POLLIS, N. P., & DOYLE, D. C. (1972). Sex role, status, and perceived competence among first-graders. *Perceptual and Motor Skills, 34*, 235–238.

POMERLEAU, A., BOLDUC, D., MALCUIT, G., & COSSETTE, L. (1990). Pink or blue: Environmental gender stereotypes in the first two years of life. *Sex Roles, 22*, 359–367.

REID, P. T., TATE, C. S., & BERMAN, P. W. (1989). Preschool children's self-presentations in situations with infants: Effects of sex and race. *Child Development, 60*, 710–714.

RICHARDSON, J. G., & SIMPSON, C. H. (1982). Children, gender, and social structure: An analysis of the contents of letters to Santa Claus. *Child Development, 53*, 429–436.

ROBINSON, C. C., & MORRIS, J. T. (1986). The gender-stereotyped nature of Christmas toys received by 36-, 48-, and 60-month-old children: A comparison between nonrequested vs. requested toys. *Sex Roles, 15*, 21–32.

ROBINSON, I., ZISS, K., GANZA, B., KATZ, S., & ROBINSON, E. (1991). Twenty years of sexual revolution, 1965–1985: An update. *Journal of Marriage and the Family, 53*, 216–220.

RODGERS, J. L., & ROWE, D. C. (1988). Influence of siblings on adolescent sexual behavior. *Developmental Psychology, 24*, 722–728.

ROSEN, R., & HALL, E. (1984). *Sexuality*. New York: Random House.

ROSENBLATT, P. C., & CUNNINGHAM, M. R. (1976). Sex differences in cross-cultural perspective. In B. Lloyd & J. Archer (Eds.), *Exploring sex differences*. London: Academic Press.

ROSENWASSER, S. M., LINGENFELTER, M., & HARRINGTON, A. F. (1989). Nontraditional gender role portrayals on television and children's gender role perceptions. *Journal of Applied Developmental Psychology, 10*, 97–105.

RUBLE, D. N. (1988). Sex-role development. In M. H. Bornstein & M. E. Lamb (Eds.), *Developmental psychology: An advanced textbook*. Hillsdale, NJ: Erlbaum.

RUBLE, D. N., BALABAN, T., & COOPER, J. (1981). Gender constancy and the effects of sex-typed televised toy commercials. *Child Development, 52*, 667–673.

RUBLE, T. L. (1983). Sex stereotypes: Issues of change in the 1970s. *Sex Roles, 9*, 397–402.

SAFIR, M. P. (1986). The effects of nature or of nurture on sex differences in intellectual functioning. *Sex Roles, 14*, 581–590.

SHAFFER, D. R., GRESHAM, A., CLARY, E. G., & THIELMAN, T. J. (1986). Sex-ratios as a basis for occupational evaluations: A contemporary view. *Social Behavior and Personality, 14*, 77–83.

SHAFFER, D. R., PEGALIS, L. J., & CORNELL, D. P. (1991). Interactive effects of social context and sex-role identity on self-disclosure during the acquaintance process. *Sex Roles, 24*, 1–19.

SIGELMAN, C. K., CARR, M. B., & BEGLEY, N. L. (1986). Developmental changes in the influence of sex-role stereotypes on person perception. *Child Study Journal, 16*, 191–205.

SIGNORELLA, M. L., & JAMISON, W. (1986). Masculinity, femininity, androgyny, and cognitive performance: A meta-analysis. *Psychological Bulletin, 16*, 207–228.

SIGNORELLA, M. L., JAMISON, W., & KRUPA, M. H. (1989). Predicting spatial performance from gender stereotyping in activity preferences and in self-concept. *Developmental Psychology, 25*, 89–95.

SLABY, R. G., & FREY, K. S. (1975). Development of gender constancy and selective attention to same-sex models. *Child Development, 46*, 849–856.

SMITH, P. K., & DAGLISH, L. (1977). Sex differences in parent and infant behavior in the home. *Child Development, 48*, 1250–1254.

SNOW, M. E., JACKLIN, C. N., & MACCOBY, E. E. (1983). Sex-of-child differences in father-child interaction at one year of age. *Child Development, 54*, 227–232.

SPENCE, J. T., & HELMREICH, R. L. (1978). *Masculinity and femininity: Their psychological dimensions, correlates, and antecedents*. Austin: University of Texas Press.

STEIN, A. H. (1971). The effects of sex-role standards of achievement and sex-role preference on three determinants of achievement motivation. *Developmental Psychology, 4*, 219–231.

STERN, M., & KARRAKER, K. (1989). Sex stereotyping of infants: A review of gender labeling studies. *Sex Roles, 20*, 501–522.

STEVENSON, M. R., & BLACK, K. N. (1988). Paternal absence and sex-role development: A meta-analysis. *Child Development, 59*, 793–814.

STODDART, T., & TURIEL, E. (1985). Children's concepts of cross-gender activities. *Child Development, 56*, 1241–1252.

STONEMAN, Z., BRODY, G. H., & MacKINNON, C. E. (1986). Same-sex and cross-sex siblings: Activity choices, roles, behavior, and gender stereotypes. *Sex Roles, 15*, 495–511.

SUTTON-SMITH, B., & ROSENBERG, B. G. (1970). *The sibling*. New York: Holt, Rinehart & Winston.

TAUBER, M. A. (1979a). Parental socialization techniques and sex differences in children's play. *Child Development, 50*, 225–234.

TAUBER, M. A. (1979b). Sex differences in parent-child interaction styles during a free-play session. *Child Development, 50*, 981–988.

THOMPSON, S. K. (1975). Gender labels and early sex-role development. *Child Development, 46*, 339–347.

TOLAR, C. J. (1968). An investigation of parent-offspring relationships. *Dissertation Abstracts, 28*(8-B), 3465.

TOUHEY, J. C. (1974). Effects of additional women professionals on ratings of occupational prestige and desirability. *Journal of Personality and Social Psychology, 29*, 86–89.

URBERG, K. A. (1979). Sex-role conceptualization in adolescents and adults. *Developmental Psychology, 15*, 90–92.

VON WRIGHT, M. R. (1989). Body image satisfaction in adolescent boys and girls: A longitudinal study. *Journal of Youth and Adolescence, 18*, 71–83.

WEINRAUB, M., CLEMENS, L. P., SOCKLOFF, A., ETHRIDGE, T., GRACELY, E., & MYERS, B. (1984). The development of sex-role stereotypes in the third year: Relationships to gender labeling, gender identity, sex-typed toy preferences, and family characteristics. *Child Development, 55*, 1493–1503.

WEISNER, T. S., & WILSON-MITCHELL, J. E. (1990). Nonconventional family lifestyles and sex typing in six-year-olds. *Child Development, 61*, 1915–1933.

WHITE, M. J., KRUCZEK, T. A., BROWN, M. T., & WHITE, G. B. (1989). Occupational sex stereotypes among college students. *Journal of Vocational Behavior, 34*, 289–298.

WHITING, B. B., & EDWARDS, C. P. (1988). *Children of different worlds: The formation of social behavior*. Cambridge, MA: Harvard University Press.

WHITLEY, B. E., JR. (1983). Sex-role orientation and self-esteem: A critical meta-analytic review. *Journal of Personality and Social Psychology, 44*, 765–778.

WIELANDT, H., & BOLDSEN, J. (1989). Age at first intercourse. *Journal of Biosocial Science, 21*, 169–177.

WINDLE, M. (1986). Sex-role orientation, cognitive flexibility, and life satisfaction among older adults. *Psychology of Women Quarterly, 10*, 263–273.

YOUNG, W. C., GOY, R. W., & PHOENIX, C. H. (1964). Hormones and sexual behavior. *Science, 143*, 212–218.

ZERN, D. S. (1984). Relationships among selected child-rearing variables in a cross-cultural sample of 110 societies. *Developmental Psychology, 20*, 683–690.

10 *Aggression and Antisocial Conduct*

On a clear afternoon in early May 1970 I found myself lying on the ground, coughing from tear gas and hoping that I would survive the ordeal of the moment. The scene: Kent State University. Just seconds before, a column of Ohio National Guardsmen had turned and fired on a group of bystanders, killing four and wounding several others. Surprisingly, the mood of many people around me was not one of terror but one of retribution. Within minutes there was talk of locating weapons and extracting revenge from the guardsmen. The potential for an even stronger confrontation was apparent, and it is fortunate, I think, that school administrators decided to close the university before additional blood could be spilled.

Human aggression and other forms of antisocial conduct are pervasive phenomena. We need not look beyond the evening news to observe instances of brutality; rapes, kidnappings, shoot-outs, and murders are everyday items for Dan Rather and his colleagues in the network and local news bureaus. Elliot Aronson (1976) has described a book that surely qualifies as the shortest capsule history of the world, a 10- to 15-page chronological listing of the most important events in human history. Perhaps you can guess how it reads. That's right: one war after another, with a few other happenings, such as the birth of Christ, sandwiched in between. If an extraterrestrial being somehow obtained a copy and deciphered it, he or she would be forced to conclude that we are extremely hostile, antisocial creatures who should probably be avoided.

What makes humans aggressive? Most vertebrates do not try to kill members of their own species, as we sometimes do. Is aggression a part of human nature or, rather, something that children must learn? Is there any hope for peaceful coexistence among people with conflicting interests? If so, how can aggression and other forms of antisocial behavior be modified or controlled? These are but a few of the issues that we will consider in the pages that follow.

What Is Aggression?

Most of us have an implicit definition of aggression. Rape is an act that almost everyone would consider violent and aggressive. But the vigorous and passionate lovemaking of consenting partners is generally considered nonaggressive behavior. Whenever I introduce the topic of aggression in my classes, I ask students to define the term in their own words. As I write these definitions on the board, classmates invariably begin to argue about the meaning of aggression and the kinds of behavior that should be considered aggressive. These debates are hardly surprising in view of the fact that social scientists have argued the very same issues for 40 to 50 years. At this point it may be useful to look at some of the most common definitions of aggression.

Aggression as an Instinct

Could aggression be an instinct—a basic component of human nature? Freud thought so, describing the **Thanatos** (or death instinct) as the factor responsible for the generation of aggressive energy in all human beings. Freud held a "hydraulic" view of aggression: hostile, aggressive energy would build up to a critical level and then be discharged through some form of violent, destructive behavior.

Psychoanalytic theorists are not the only ones who have adopted this viewpoint. The famous ethologist Konrad Lorenz (1966) described aggression as a fighting instinct triggered by certain "eliciting" cues in the environment. In his book *African Genesis*, Robert Ardrey (1967) has gone so far as to imply that the human being "is a predator whose natural instinct is to kill with a weapon" (p. 322). Although there are several important differences between psychoanalytic and ethological perspectives on aggression, both schools of thought maintain that aggressive, antisocial conduct results from an innate propensity for violence.

Behavioral Definitions of Aggression

Most behavioral (learning) theorists have rejected an instinctual explanation for violent and destructive acts, choosing instead to think of human aggression and antisocial conduct as a particular category of goal-driven behaviors. Among the more frequently cited **"behavioral" definitions of aggression** is that of Arnold Buss (1961), who characterized an aggressive act as "a response that delivers noxious stimuli to another organism" (p. 3).

Notice that Buss's definition emphasizes the *consequences of an action* rather than the intentions of the actor. According to Buss, any act that delivers pain or discomfort to another creature has to be considered aggressive. Yet how many of us consider our dentists aggressive when they drill our teeth, producing some pain in the process? Is a klutzy dance partner being aggressive when he or she steps on our toes? And is a sniper who misses his target any less aggressive just because no physical harm has been done?

Although you are certainly free to disagree, most people would consider the sniper's behavior aggressive but the dentist's and the dance partner's actions as careless or accidental. In making this pattern of attributions, people are relying on an **intentional definition of aggression**, which implies that an aggressive act is *any form of behavior designed to harm or injure another living being who is motivated to avoid such treatment* (Baron & Byrne, 1991). Note that this intentional definition would classify as aggressive all acts in which harm is intended but not done (for example, a violent kick that misses its target) while excluding accidental injuries or activities (such as rough-and-tumble play) in which participants are enjoying themselves with no harmful intent.

Aggressive acts are often divided into two categories: **hostile aggression** and **instrumental aggression**. If an actor's major goal is to harm or injure a victim (either physically, verbally, or by destroying his work or property), his or her actions qualify as hostile aggression. By contrast, instrumental aggression describes those situations in which one person harms another as a means to a nonaggressive end (for example, knocking a playmate down to obtain his candy). Clearly, the same overt act could be classified as either hostile or instrumental aggression, depending on the circumstances. If a young boy clobbered his sister and teased her for crying, we might consider this hostile aggression. But these same actions might be labeled instrumental aggression (or a mixture of hostile and instrumental aggression) had the boy also grabbed a toy that his sister was using.

Although we will see that the distinction between hostile and instrumental aggression has proved useful to those who study young children, it is often very difficult to tell whether the antisocial conduct of older children, adolescents, or adults is hostile or instrumental in character. Bandura (1973), for example, describes a teenage gang that routinely assaulted innocent victims on the street. But the gang members did not necessarily attack others "for kicks" (hostile motives); they were required to rough up at least ten individuals in order to become full-fledged members of the group (an instrumental goal). So even behaviors that appear to be clear instances of hostile aggression may actually be controlled by hidden reinforcement contingencies.

In sum, the distinction between hostile and instrumental aggression is not so sharp as many would have us believe. Even if we consider these forms conceptually distinct, we must still note that both are common and both have important consequences for victims and aggressors. Bandura (1973) reflects the sentiment of many in calling for a comprehensive theory of aggression and antisocial conduct — one that embraces both hostile and instrumental aggression.

Aggression as a Social Judgment

Although we have talked as if there were a class of intentional behaviors that almost everyone would label "aggressive," such a viewpoint is simply incorrect. Bandura and others (for example, Parke & Slaby, 1983) argue convincingly that "aggression" is really a social label that we apply to various acts, guided by our judgments about the meaning of those acts to us. Presumably, our interpretation of an act as aggressive or nonaggressive will depend on a variety of social, personal, and situational factors, such as our own beliefs about aggression (which may vary as a function of our gender, culture, social class, and prior experiences), the context in which the response occurs, the intensity of the response, and the identities and reactions of the people involved, to name but a few. Accordingly, a high-intensity response such as a hard right hand to someone's jaw is more likely to be labeled aggressive than a milder version of the same action, which we might interpret as a playful prompt or even as a sign of affection (Costabile et al., 1991). Shooting a deer may be seen as much more violent and aggressive by a pacifist vegetarian than by a carnivorous card-carrying member of the National Rifle Association. Scuffles between children are more likely to be labeled aggressive if someone is hurt in the process (Costabile et al., 1991). And, as we see in Box 10-1, the identities of the people involved in a behavioral sequence can play a major role in determining our impressions of their aggressive intent.

In sum, aggression is to no small extent a *social judgment* that we make about the seemingly injurious or destructive behaviors we observe or experience. Clearly, we can continue to think of aggression as behavior that is *intended* to frustrate, harm, injure, or deprive someone, as long as we recognize that the basis for inferring whether an actor has a harmful intent can vary dramatically across perceivers, perpetrators, victims, contexts, and situations, thereby ensuring that people will often disagree about what has happened and whether it qualifies as aggression.

Theories of Aggression

By now you may have guessed that each of the preceding definitions of aggression is based on a theory of some sort. In the pages that follow, we will consider several theories that have been offered as explanations of human aggression.

Instinct Theories of Aggression

Freud's psychoanalytic theory.   Freud believed that we are all born with a death instinct (Thanatos) that seeks the cessation of life and underlies all acts of violence and destruction. His view was that energy derived from food is continually being converted to aggressive energy and that these aggressive urges must be discharged periodically to prevent them from building up to dangerous levels. According to Freud, aggressive energy can be discharged in a socially acceptable fashion through vigorous work or play, or through less desirable activities such as insulting others, fighting, or destroying property. An interesting Freudian notion is that aggressive urges

are occasionally directed inward, resulting in some form of self-punishment, self-mutilation, or perhaps even suicide.

Most contemporary psychoanalytic theorists continue to think of aggression as an instinctual drive but reject Freud's notion that we harbor a self-directed death instinct. Presumably, an instinctual tendency to aggress occurs whenever we are frustrated in our attempts at need satisfaction or face some other threat that hinders the functioning of the ego (Feshbach, 1970). Viewed in this way, aggressive drives are *adaptive*: they help the individual to satisfy basic needs and thus serve to promote life rather than self-destruction.

Lorenz's ethological theory of aggression.   A second instinct theory of aggression stems from the work of ethologist Konrad Lorenz (1966), who argues that humans and animals have a basic fighting (aggressive) instinct that is directed against members of the same species. Like psychoanalytic theorists, Lorenz views aggression as a hydraulic system that generates its own energy. But he believes that aggressive urges continue to build until relieved by an appropriate *releasing stimulus*.

What kinds of stimuli are likely to trigger aggressive behavior? What functions might these displays of aggression serve? According to Lorenz, all instincts, including aggression, serve a basic evolutionary purpose: *to ensure the survival of the individual and the species*. Thus, fights that occur when one animal enters another's territory are said to be adaptive; they disperse individuals over a wider area, thereby preventing large numbers of animals from congregating in the same locale, exhausting all sources of food, and starving. An animal may also fight off an intruder in order to protect its young, thereby allowing them to live, to mature, and eventually to reproduce. Finally, fighting among the males of a species determines which males will mate with available females. Since the stronger males usually win these battles, intraspecies aggression helps to ensure that the hardiest members of the lot will be the ones to reproduce.

From an ethological perspective, aggression helps most species survive because they have evolved various ''instinctual inhibitions'' that prevent them

10-1 | *Adult Reactions to Roughhousing:*
Boys Will Be Boys, but Girls Are Aggressors

Imagine that you are walking down the street on a snowy winter afternoon and you happen to notice a child hitting, jumping on, and throwing snowballs at an agemate. How might you interpret this event? Would your judgment be affected by the identities of the actor and the recipient? What would you think if the children were both boys? Both girls? A boy and a girl?

John Condry and David Ross (1985) conducted an interesting experiment to determine how adults might interpret the rough-and-tumble activities of children they thought to be boys or girls. Subjects first watched a videotape in which two children, whose genders were concealed by snowsuits, played together in the snow. The play soon became quite rough as one child (the target) hit, jumped on, and hurled snowballs at the other (the recipient). Before watching the video, subjects were told that these children were both boys, both girls, a boy target and girl recipient, or a girl target and boy recipient. After the video was over, subjects were asked to rate the behavior of the target child along two dimensions: (1) the amount of aggression the tar-

get displayed toward the recipient and (2) the extent to which the target's behavior was merely active, playful, and affectionate.

The results were indeed interesting. As we see in scanning the figure, the rough-and-tumble behavior of the target child was much less likely to be interpreted as aggressive, and tended to be seen instead as a display of affection, when both the target child and the recipient were said to be boys. So, if we see two children "roughhousing" and think that the two are boys, we say "Boys will be boys" and may fail to intervene. By contrast, boys' roughhousing with girls was definitely interpreted as aggressive behavior. And notice that the high-intensity antics of the girl targets were also seen as highly aggressive, regardless of whether the recipient of those actions was a boy or a girl! In summarizing these data, Condry and Ross say that "It may not be fair, and it certainly is not equal, but from the results of this study, it looks as if boys and girls really are judged differently in terms of what constitutes aggression" (p. 230).

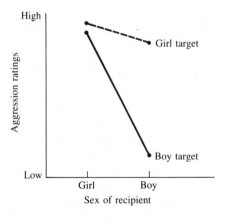 

Average ratings of the aggressiveness and the affection of the target child's behavior as a function of the gender of the target and the recipient. (Adapted from J. C. Condry & D. F. Ross, "Sex and Aggression: The Influence of Gender Label on the Perception of Aggression in Children." *Child Development*, 1985, *56*, 225–233. Copyright © 1985 by the Society for Research in Child Development. Reprinted by permission.)

from killing members of their own kind. For example, many species of fish engage in "threat" displays or ritualized aggressive ceremonies in which one of the participants will "win" without seriously injuring an adversary. Birds of the same species could easily kill one another (or peck one another's eyes out) but rarely do so. Wolves normally refrain from killing each other when the loser of a battle "signals" its defeat by offering its unprotected throat to the teeth of the victor.

According to Lorenz, human beings kill members of their own species because their aggressive instinct is poorly controlled. Because *Homo sapiens* in prehistoric times lacked the innate equipment to kill (such as claws or fangs), there was little need for the evolution of instinctual inhibitions against maiming or killing other human beings. But humans did evolve intellectually, developed weapons of destruction, and, lacking innate inhibitions, showed little reluctance to use this lethal weaponry to defeat human adversaries. Lorenz points out that this lack of aggressive inhibitions, coupled with the recent development of doomsday weapons, presents a crucial challenge to humanity: we must now work very hard to channel our aggressive urges into socially acceptable pursuits or face the very real possibility of becoming an endangered species.

A critique of instinct theories.   It is often argued that instinct theories of aggression are of limited explanatory value. For example, the notion that all aggression stems from inborn, instinctual forces cannot easily explain why some societies are more aggressive than others. Cultures such as the Arapesh of New Guinea, the Lepchas of the Himalayas, and the Pygmies of the Congo all use weapons to procure food but rarely show any kind of intraspecies aggression. When invaded by outsiders, these peace-loving people retreat to inaccessible regions rather than stand and fight (Gorer, 1968). Although these observations do not rule out the possibility of biological influences on aggression, they present a strong challenge to any theory that humans are *instinctively* aggressive.

To date, there is no neurophysiological evidence that the body generates or accumulates aggressive energy (Scott, 1966, 1972). John Scott believes that the instigation of aggression derives from external rather than internal forces. The mere fact that animals fight doesn't mean they are expending pent-up aggressive energy. To assume so is like assuming that "most people find the odor of roses pleasant [because] there is spontaneous internal stimulation to go out and smell the flowers" (Scott, 1966, p. 696).

Now recall one of the central arguments of instinct theory: human aggression is so widespread because it stems from recurring internal forces for which we have no inborn or instinctual inhibitions. Critics scoff at this assertion. It is true that human beings do not bare their throats or rely on other such signals of aggressive appeasement in exactly the same way that animals do. However, Bandura (1973) points out that these primitive gestures are unnecessary for humans, who have evolved a much more intricate system — namely, language — for controlling aggression.

Indeed, ethologists who study *humans* are nowhere near as pessimistic about the prospect of controlling human aggression as Lorenz and Freud were. Ethological studies of children's play groups (Sluckin & Smith, 1977; Strayer, 1980) reveal that even 3- to 5-year-olds form reasonably stable dominance hierarchies (determined on the basis of who dominates whom in conflict situations) and know which of their playmates are likely to dominate or submit to them during a conflict. Strayer (1980) proposes that the function of these dominance hierarchies is to *minimize* aggression, just as similar hierarchies minimize fighting and promote social adaptation among apes and other species. And apparently he is right. In play groups characterized by such dominance hierarchies, children who are attacked rarely counterattack or enlist the aid of teachers and peers. Instead, they generally submit to their more dominant classmates. One recent observational study of conflicts among 5-year-olds found that most disputes were resolved quickly as the "loser" simply stepped back and moved away from his or her adversary. And, in a substantial percentage of these disputes, the nondominant child terminated conflict by making some sort of conciliatory gesture to the dominant one, such as offering to be his friend, offering to share a toy, or even touching the former adversary in a friendly manner

(Sackin & Thelen, 1984). So not only can children successfully end most disputes before they escalate into violent, aggressive exchanges, but they are remarkably proficient at doing so at an early age.

Even if human beings were instinctively aggressive, it is likely that an individual's aggressive inclinations would soon be affected by social experiences. If we look at the animal literature, we find that cats will normally kill rats, a behavior that many people have called instinctive. In one ingenious experiment, Kuo (1930) raised kittens either by themselves, with rat-killing mothers, or with rats as companions. Of the kittens raised with rat-killing mothers, 85% became regular rat killers. But only 45% of the isolated kittens ever killed a rat, and few of those reared with rats (17%) became rat killers. When Kuo later exposed the pacifistic kittens to adult rat-killing models, 82% of the isolated pacifists became vigorous rat killers. However, only 7% of the pacifists that had been reared with rats followed the model's example and attacked rats. Kuo's study nicely illustrates the importance of environmental influences as determinants of aggressive behavior. It appears that aggressive responses that are often labeled instinctive can be substantially modified or even eliminated through social learning. Proponents of instinct theory could reply that all human beings have aggressive instincts and that any differences in their degree of aggressiveness are due to learning. But, as Middlebrook (1974) points out:

> such a response . . . only emphasizes the limited understanding of aggression that the instinct explanation offers. Human aggressive behaviors—whatever their basic origins—have been so modified by learning that it may not be helpful to spend much time on the extent to which their origins are instinctive [p. 265].

Learning Theories of Aggression

THE FRUSTRATION/AGGRESSION HYPOTHESIS

Perhaps the best-known explanation of human aggression was proposed by a group of psychologists and anthropologists at Yale University (Dollard et al., 1939). Their theory, which came to be known as the **frustration/aggression hypothesis**, stated that frustration (the thwarting of goal-directed behavior) always produces some kind of aggression. A related claim was that aggression is always caused by frustration.

Were the Yale theorists proposing an innate link between frustration and aggression? Apparently not, for, in an early review of the literature, Neal Miller (1941) wrote that "no assumptions are made as to whether the frustration-aggression relationship is of innate or of learned origin" (p. 340). However, Robert Sears, another member of this neo-Hullian group, eventually concluded that the connection between frustration and aggression is learned. What seems to be innate, according to Sears (1958) and Feshbach (1964), is a relationship between frustration and *anger*.[1] Angry children tend to throw tantrums and flail their limbs in an agitated manner, often striking other people, animals, or inanimate objects in the process. This observation led Feshbach (1964) to conclude that, during the first two years of life, "frustration produces an instigation to hit rather than to hurt" (p. 262). So how do children come to react aggressively when frustrated? Sears believes that a child learns to attack frustrators when he or she discovers that these attacks alleviate frustration. But the attacks have another important consequence: they produce signs of pain and suffering from the frustrator. If the child associates the frustrator's pain with the positive consequences arising from the removal of frustration, pain cues will assume the characteristics of secondary reinforcers, and the child will have acquired a motive to hurt others (a hostile-aggressive drive).

It soon became apparent that there were real problems with the frustration/aggression hypothesis. Although frustration can lead to aggression, it does not invariably do so (Davitz, 1952). And must we assert that all acts of aggression are instigated by some form of frustration? Leonard Berkowitz didn't think so.

---

[1]Today we know that the relationship between frustration and anger is not inborn. Recall from Chapter 5 that anger first appears over the first several months of life and is not a reliable response to frustration until about 4 months of age (Lewis, Alessandri, & Sullivan, 1990).

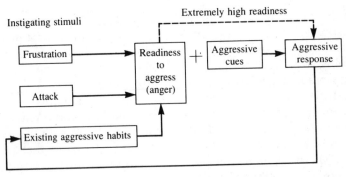

FIGURE 10-1 Berkowitz's revised frustration/aggression hypothesis. (Adapted from L. Berkowitz, "Some Determinants of Impulsive Aggression: Role of Mediated Association with Reinforcement for Aggression." *Psychological Review*, 1974, *81*, 165–176. Copyright © 1974 by the American Psychological Association. Adapted by permission.)

BERKOWITZ'S REVISION OF THE FRUSTRATION/AGGRESSION HYPOTHESIS

Like Robert Sears, Berkowitz believes that frustration creates only a "readiness for aggressive acts," which we may think of as anger. However, he adds that a variety of other causes, such as *attack* by another person and previously acquired *aggressive habits*, may also heighten a person's readiness to aggress. Finally, Berkowitz argues that an angered person who is "ready to aggress" will not necessarily commit an aggressive response:

> Aggressive responses will not occur, even given [a readiness to aggress], unless there are suitable cues, stimuli associated with the present or previous anger instigators. . . . These cues *evoke aggressive responses* from [a person who] is "primed" to make them. The strength of the aggressive response made to the [eliciting] cue is . . . a function of (1) the aggressive cue value of this stimulus—the strength of the association between the eliciting stimulus and the past or present determinants of aggression—and (2) the degree of aggression readiness [1965, p. 308; italics added].

So Berkowitz's theory makes a rather bold assertion—namely, that aggressive cues must be present before an aggressive act will occur. However, Berkowitz eventually modified his position somewhat to allow for the possibility that an extremely angry person may behave aggressively even when

aggressive cues are not present (Berkowitz, 1974). A schematic representation of Berkowitz's theory appears in Figure 10-1.

Notice that Berkowitz's theory anticipates individual differences in aggression: when exposed to aggressive cues, children with well-ingrained aggressive habits should be more inclined to behave aggressively than those whose aggressive habits are not well established. But by far the most provocative of Berkowitz's ideas is the **"aggressive cues" hypothesis**, which implies that exposure to any object or event previously associated with aggression will serve a cuing function and increase the likelihood of aggressive exchanges among young children. Would toys such as guns, tanks, rubber soldiers, and other symbolic implements of destruction have such an effect?

Apparently so. In one study, Seymour Feshbach (1956) exposed 5- to 8-year-olds to structured play sessions that revolved around *aggressive* themes (such as pirates and soldiers) or *neutral* themes (such as circuses, farm activities, and storekeeping). Then, during periods of free play, an adult observer noted aggressive interactions among these children and labeled each as either *thematic* aggression—action that was appropriate in the context of earlier play, such as challenging an enemy pirate—or *inappropriate* aggression—verbal taunts or physical blows that were clearly outside the context of the previous play session. Not surprisingly, thematic

PHOTO 10-1   Although these young boys seem to be enjoying themselves, toys that encourage the enactment of aggressive themes do increase the likelihood of hostile interactions in children's play groups.

aggression was highest for the children who had played with aggressive toys. However, those children were also involved in a greater number of inappropriate aggressive exchanges than were classmates who had played with neutral toys. (See Turner & Goldsmith, 1976, for a similar pattern of results with preschool children.) So it appears that toys that encourage enactment of aggressive themes do increase the likelihood of hostile interactions in children's play groups.

In sum, Berkowitz's revised frustration/aggression hypothesis views aggressive behavior as stemming from a combination of internal forces (anger) and external stimuli (aggressive cues). Although this theory may help to explain how aggressive responses are evoked from a person who is angry at the moment, it has little to say about the development of aggressive habits or about how various stimuli become "aggressive cues." Moreover, other theorists have criticized Berkowitz's model on the grounds that many aggressive acts are committed not out of a sense of anger or outrage but merely as means to nonaggressive ends. And, as we will see, the impact of aggressive cues on children's be-

havior seems to depend more on children's *interpretations* of those stimuli and events (cognitive factors) than on the mere presence of the cues themselves.

BANDURA'S SOCIAL-LEARNING THEORY

Bandura's (1973, 1989) social-learning theory of aggression is noteworthy in several respects. It is the first model to stress cognitive influences on aggression. It treats aggression as a class of social behaviors that are acquired through the same processes as any other type of social behavior. And, whereas most theorists concentrate on factors that instigate aggression, Bandura proceeds a step further by explaining how aggressive behaviors are acquired and maintained.

According to Bandura, aggressive responses are acquired in either of two ways. The first and most important method is *observational learning* — a cognitive process by which children attend to and retain in memory the aggressive responses they see others commit. The now-classic Bandura (1965) experiment that we discussed in Chapter 3 clearly illustrates his point. Recall that children who witnessed an adult model beating up on a Bobo doll clearly learned the aggressive responses they had observed and were likely to direct similar acts toward Bobo — as long as they had not seen the model punished for aggression.

Children may also acquire aggressive responses (or aggressive habits) through *direct experience*. A child who is reinforced for aggressive behavior will be more likely to resort to aggression in the future. In fact, a study by Ivar Lovaas (1961) shows that reinforcement of one type of aggression can make children more inclined to perform other, seemingly unrelated, acts of aggression. Participants in Lovaas's study first played with dolls and were rewarded with trinkets for making either *aggressive, derogatory* statements (for example, "bad doll"; "dirty doll"; "This doll should be spanked") or *nonaggressive* statements as they played. At the end of this initial "training" session, each child was told that he or she could play with a crude pinball apparatus or with "striking dolls," an aggressive toy built so that pressing a lever would cause one doll to hit another with a stick. The number of times the child caused one doll to strike the other during a four-minute testing period served as a measure of the child's *nonverbal* aggression.

Lovaas found that he could easily increase the frequency of verbal aggression by simply reinforcing the hostile utterances of children in the aggressive-training group. Of greater interest was the finding that children who had been reinforced for verbal aggression were more likely than those in the nonaggressive-training group to choose to play with the "striking dolls" toy. The implication is clear: *children who are reinforced for one kind of aggression become more willing to display other (perhaps unrelated) forms of aggression in the future.*

Of course, participants in Lovaas's experiment were aggressing against inanimate objects (dolls). Could these results be replicated in a setting where the child has the opportunity to aggress against another child? Yes, indeed. In one experiment, Slaby and Crowley (1977) asked nursery-school teachers to reinforce children's verbal aggression by paying close attention to hostile utterances and then repeating these utterances in a friendly tone of voice. This treatment continued for one week, and the behavior of each child was carefully recorded. The results were clear: reinforcement of verbal aggression not only increased the incidence of verbally aggressive statements but also increased the likelihood that a child's verbally aggressive utterance would be followed by a physically aggressive response!

How is aggression maintained?   According to Bandura (1973), aggressive behaviors are often maintained (and may become habitual) if they are instrumental in procuring benefits for the aggressor or otherwise satisfying his or her objectives. In other words, highly aggressive children have presumably learned that the use of force is an efficient and effective means to other ends.

Indeed, aggressive children do have more positive *expectancies* about the outcomes of aggression; compared to nonaggressive peers, they are (1) more confident that aggression will yield tangible rewards (such as control of a disputed toy), (2) more certain that aggression will be easy for them and successful at terminating others' noxious behavior,

and (3) more inclined to believe that aggression will enhance their self-esteem and will not cause their victims any permanent harm (Perry, Perry, & Rasmussen, 1986; Quiggle et al., 1992; Slaby & Guerra, 1988). In addition, aggressive children are more likely than nonaggressive children to *value* the outcomes of aggression; that is, they attach much significance to their ability to dominate and control their victims, and they are not particularly concerned about the suffering they may cause or the possibility of being rejected by their peers (Boldizar, Perry, & Perry, 1989; Coie et al., 1991). Moreover, highly aggressive children tend to cluster together in cliques that encourage and *reinforce* aggressive solutions to conflict (Cairns et al., 1988), and they may become so accustomed to dominating others (or attempting to dominate others) that it becomes habitual and especially satisfying. In the language of Bandura's theory, these aggressive individuals "have . . . adopted a self-reinforcement system in which aggressive actions are a source of personal pride" (1973, p. 208). A passage from Toch (1969) nicely illustrates how violence can be self-reinforcing:

> And he said "F--- you man." And the dude got up and we were both on him, man. And we beat him to a pulp. . . . Once we got going we just wasted the dude . . . sent him on down to the hospital. And after that I felt like a king, man. It felt like you know, "I'm the man. You're not going to mess with me." . . . I felt like everybody looking up to me [pp. 91–92).

In sum, Bandura claims that aggressive habits often persist because they are (1) instrumental to the satisfaction of nonaggressive goals, (2) useful as means of terminating others' noxious behaviors, (3) socially sanctioned by aggressive peers, and (4) even intrinsically rewarding for the aggressor.

Internal arousal and aggressive behavior.   Most theories of aggression assume that people are "driven" to aggress by internal forces such as instincts, acquired motives, frustrations, or anger. Bandura takes issue with all these theories by arguing that internal states such as frustration and anger may facilitate aggression but *are not necessary for its occurrence.*

According to Bandura, the role of internal arousal in human aggression is simply to increase the probability that a person will commit an aggressive response in situations in which aggressive cues are present. Moreover, Bandura claims that *any* form of arousal can energize aggressive behavior, as long as the cues available in the situation cause the individual to *interpret* that arousal as frustration or anger. Several experiments conducted with adults support this line of reasoning: compared with subjects who are not aroused, people who have experienced arousal stemming from sources completely unrelated to aggression (for example, exercise, noise, rock music, and even erotica) are likely to reinterpret this arousal as anger and to display heightened aggression when exposed to insults or other provocations (Bryant & Zillmann, 1979; Rule, Ferguson, & Nesdale, 1980).

Controlling aggression. Bandura is optimistic about the possibility of reducing and controlling human aggression. He views aggressive habits as learned responses that can be modified if we work diligently at eliminating the conditions that maintain them. He proposes that people can be taught to respond nonaggressively to "negative" emotional states such as anger and frustration. Of course, he realizes that the changes will not come easily and will require a concentrated effort on the part of parents, teachers, and other agents of socialization, particularly when working with highly aggressive adolescents who have learned to rely on violence and other antisocial acts as means of maintaining or enhancing self-esteem. His advice, then, is to control aggression early, before it becomes a well-ingrained aspect of one's personality (see also Patterson, DeBaryshe, & Ramsey, 1989). Social information-processing theorists would agree that early treatment of hostile, aggressive inclinations is necessary if we hope to eliminate them. However, they believe that the most important characteristic that sets aggressive children apart from nonaggressive peers is not their valuation of aggression but, rather, a **hostile attributional bias**. This bias, established early in childhood, causes aggressive youngsters (1) to overattribute hostile intentions to their peers and thus (2) to view these companions as belligerent adversaries who deserve to be dealt with in a forceful manner. Let's take a closer look.

A Social Information-Processing Theory of Aggression

Imagine that you are an 8-year-old carrying a heavy load when a classmate seated on a bench extends his leg into your path, tripping you and causing you to drop your cargo. As you fall to the sidewalk, you really have very little information about why this incident may have occurred, although you are already aroused. So how would you respond?

Social information-processing theorists believe that a person's reactions to frustration, anger, or an apparent provocation depend not so much on the social cues present in a situation as on the ways in which the person processes and interprets this information. Perhaps the best-known social-cognitive theory of aggression is that of Kenneth Dodge and his associates (Dodge, 1980, 1986; Dodge & Frame, 1982). Dodge assumes that children enter each social situation with a data base of past experiences (that is, a *memory store*) and a *goal* of some sort (for example, making friends, staying out of trouble, having fun, or even simply passing by without stopping to interact). Suddenly an event occurs that requires explanation (such as tripping over someone's leg). Dodge proposes that the child's response to this situation and the social cues it provides will depend on the outcomes of five cognitive "steps" or processes, which are illustrated in Figure 10-2.

The first step is a *decoding* process in which the child gathers information about the event from the environment. When tripped by a classmate, for example, the victim searches for cues. Is there an expression of concern on the classmate's face? Does the classmate look away? Is he laughing? According to Dodge, the child's proficiency at gathering relevant information will affect his responses to such events.

Next comes the *interpretation* phase. Having gathered and focused on situational cues, the child will integrate them with information about similar events from the past, consider the goals that he was

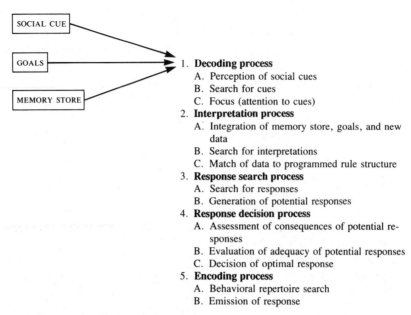

1. **Decoding process**
   A. Perception of social cues
   B. Search for cues
   C. Focus (attention to cues)
2. **Interpretation process**
   A. Integration of memory store, goals, and new data
   B. Search for interpretations
   C. Match of data to programmed rule structure
3. **Response search process**
   A. Search for responses
   B. Generation of potential responses
4. **Response decision process**
   A. Assessment of consequences of potential responses
   B. Evaluation of adequacy of potential responses
   C. Decision of optimal response
5. **Encoding process**
   A. Behavioral repertoire search
   B. Emission of response

FIGURE 10-2   A social information-processing model of aggression. (From a paper presented by K. A. Dodge at the biennial meeting of the Society for Research in Child Development, Boston, 1981.)

pursuing in this situation, and try to decide whether the act in question was accidental or intentional. Presumably, the information he has gathered, as well as his past interpretations of similar events, will influence his perception of the present event.

Once the child has interpreted the situation, the next step is a *response search* process in which he considers alternative courses of action that he might pursue. Then comes the *response decision* phase: he weighs the advantages and disadvantages of various response options and selects the one that is viewed as "best" for this situation. Last comes the *encoding* phase, in which the child enacts his chosen response. However, Dodge points out that children may lack the ability to enact various response options. That is, a child who decides to avoid further hostilities by merely admonishing the aggressor may not have the verbal skills to do so in a non-threatening way and may end up in a fight.

Social information-processing theory clearly anticipates individual differences in aggression, because children vary in both their past experiences (or memory stores) and their information-processing skills. Indeed, Dodge (1980, 1986) believes that

highly aggressive youngsters who have a history of bickering and fighting are likely to carry in memory a powerful expectancy that "other people are often hostile to me." Thus, whenever aggressive children are harmed, they may be predisposed to search for social cues that would confirm this expectancy. Should they then experience truly *ambiguous* harm-doing (such as being tripped without clear evidence of harmful intent), aggressive children should be more likely than nonaggressive children to attribute hostile intent to the harmdoer, thus predisposing them to behave aggressively. The aggressive child's hostile reaction may then trigger counteraggression from his victim, which, as we see in Figure 10-3, should reinforce the aggressive child's impression that other people are hostile, thus starting the vicious cycle all over again.

Tests of Dodge's theory. Do aggressive children really interpret ambiguous information about harmdoing as implying a hostile intent? To find out, Dodge (1980) had highly aggressive and nonaggressive boys from the second, fourth, and sixth grades each work on a jigsaw puzzle in one room while a

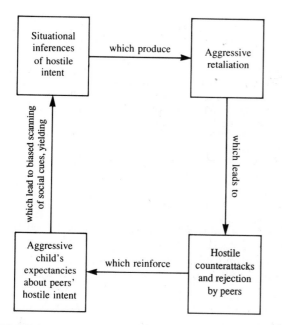

FIGURE 10-3 A social-cognitive model of the aggressive child's social information-processing biases and their behavioral consequences.

peer worked on a similar puzzle in a second room. During a break when the boys had switched rooms to check on each other's progress, the subject heard a voice on the intercom. The voice (ostensibly that of the peer who was examining the subject's puzzle) expressed either a *hostile* intent ("Gee, he's got a lot done—I'll mess it up"), a *benign* intent ("I'll help him—Oh, no, I didn't mean to drop it"), or an *ambiguous* intent ("Gee, he's got a lot done") just before a loud crash (presumably the subject's puzzle being scattered). How did the subjects respond? Dodge found that both aggressive and nonaggressive boys reacted much more aggressively (as measured by dissembling of the harmdoer's puzzle or by verbal hostility) to a hostile intent than to a benign intent. Thus, aggressive boys did not distort social cues when the harmdoer's intentions were obvious. But, when the peer's intent was ambiguous, cue distortion was apparent: aggressive boys often retaliated as if the peer had acted with a hostile intent, whereas nonaggressive boys typically did nothing or said something positive, as if the peer's intentions were honorable ones. Later research reveals

that highly aggressive girls distort cues about ambiguous harmdoing in roughly the same way that aggressive boys do (Dodge, Murphy, & Buchsbaum, 1984; Guerra & Slaby, 1990). And, when aggressive children are led to believe that conflict with a peer may be imminent, cue distortion increases; in fact, aggressive children may now even interpret *accidental* harmdoing as reflecting a hostile intent (Dodge & Somberg, 1987).

Are aggressive children's expectancies valid? It turns out that aggressive youngsters may have some very good reasons for attributing hostile intentions to their peers. Not only do aggressive children provoke a large number of conflicts, but they are also more likely than nonaggressive children to be disliked (Dodge et al., 1990) and to become targets of aggression. In fact, *nonaggressive* children who are harmed under ambiguous circumstances are much more likely to retaliate *if the harmdoer has a reputation as an aggressive child* (Dodge & Frame, 1982; Sancilio, Plumert, & Hartup, 1989). So, by virtue of their hostile inclinations, highly aggressive children ensure that they will often be attacked by their peers.

A preliminary evaluation. Taken together, the studies we have reviewed provide impressive support for a social-cognitive theory of aggression. As predicted by the model, children's behavioral responses to provocations depend more on their own *perceptions* of the harmdoer's intent than on the actual intentions of the harmdoer. Stated another way, the social cues present in a situation are not what determines whether a child will commit an aggressive response. What matters is how these cues are processed and interpreted.

The social information-processing approach is of very recent origin, and, as is often true of new theories, it leaves many questions unanswered. For example, the model aptly describes variations in the information-processing skills of children already known to be aggressive or nonaggressive, but it does not address the issues of how these children came to be aggressive or nonaggressive or why they have different information-processing biases in the first place. Fortunately, social developmentalists are

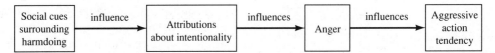

FIGURE 10-4 A mediational model of the relationship among attributions of intentionality, anger, and aggressive behavior. The model predicts that our inferences about a harmdoer's intentionality are the major influence on how angry we become about harmdoing and that our anger (rather than our attributions about intent) most directly influences our behavioral reactions to harmdoing. (Adapted from S. Graham, C. Hudley, & E. Williams, "Attributional and Emotional Determinants of Aggression among African-American and Latino Young Adolescents." *Developmental Psychology*, 1992, *28*, 731–740. Copyright © 1992 by the American Psychological Association. Adapted by permission.)

learning more about the origins of the hostile attributional bias; as we'll see later in the chapter, this tendency to overattribute hostile intentions to others can be acquired very early and often originates at home.

You may also have noticed that Dodge's theory largely ignores the topic of how various *emotional reactions* (for example, anger) might color children's interpretations of social cues or influence their behavioral reactions to harmdoing. This oversight is currently being addressed, both by Dodge (in press) and by other researchers. Sandra Graham and her associates (1992), for example, believe that the attributions we make about a harmdoer's intent influence how angry we become and that it is the *amount of anger we experience* (rather than our attributions about intent) that best predicts how we will respond to the harmdoer (see Figure 10-4 for an overview of this model). Indeed, Graham's study of aggressive and nonaggressive adolescents revealed that (1) perceptions of others' intent do predict how angry subjects become about harmdoing and (2) subjects' anger was a better predictor of their preferred *behavioral* responses to harmdoing than were their attributions of intent. Nevertheless, the data also revealed that anger may have colored the attributions of *highly aggressive* adolescents, making them more likely to believe that ambiguous harmdoing was intentional. So, even though Graham's data do not answer all the questions we may have about the links among cognitive processing biases, anger, and aggression, they reinforce Parke and Slaby's (1983) earlier assessment of social information-processing theory, which held: "The extent to which cognitive

models of aggression [are able to] incorporate other dimensions such as affect [or emotional arousal] will determine their ultimate usefulness; it is unlikely that simple cognitive models alone will suffice" (p. 573).

Developmental Trends in Aggression

Although children have served as subjects in many studies of aggression, relatively few of these studies have addressed developmental issues. In this section we will examine what is known about the origins and changing character of children's aggressive behavior.

Early Conflict and the Origins of Aggression

There is some debate about when children begin to behave in ways that satisfy our intentional definition of aggression. Although young infants can become very angry and may occasionally strike people, it is difficult to think of these actions as having an aggressive intent. Piaget (1952) describes an incident in which he frustrated 7-month-old Laurent by placing his hand in front of an interesting object that Laurent was trying to reach. The boy then smacked Piaget's hand as if to knock it out of the way. Although this looks very much like an example of instrumental aggression, it is unlikely that Laurent intended to frighten or harm his father. Instead, he seems to have been treating his father's hand as a simple obstruction that had to be removed. Indeed, some investigators claim that even 12- to 15-month-olds rarely look at each other as they struggle over a toy; their attention is usually directed toward the toy itself, and their goal seems to be to gain possession of the object rather than to harm or intimidate their adversary (Bronson, 1975; Shantz, 1987).

However, not everyone agrees that tussles among infants are always "nonsocial" events with few if any aggressive overtones. Marlene Caplan and her associates (1991) find that even 1-year-olds can be quite forceful with each other when one child controls a toy that the other desires. It seemed to Caplan and her associates that a child's possession of a toy makes that object a more valuable commodity in the eyes of other infants (a clear social influence): even when duplicate toys were readily available, 12-month-olds would occasionally ignore these objects and try to overpower a peer in order to control the other child's plaything. Clearly the intimidators in these tussles were treating other children as adversaries rather than as inanimate obstacles—implying that the seeds of instrumental aggression may already have been sown by the end of the first year.

Are 2-year-olds any more forceful with playmates than 1-year-olds are? Apparently not. Two-year-olds have just as many conflicts over toys as 1-year-olds do. But 2-year-olds are more likely than 1-year-olds to resolve these disputes by negotiating with an adversary and sharing resources than by fighting with each other. In fact, sharing and other prosocial methods of conflict resolution actually become more common when toys are in short supply (Caplan et al., 1991). So, early conflicts among peers need not be training grounds for aggression. Indeed, Dale Hay (1984) has argued that these squabbles can be quite adaptive, serving as a context in which infants and toddlers can learn how to negotiate and thereby achieve their aims without having to resort to shows of force.

Age-Related Changes in the Nature of Aggression

It is very difficult to determine whether children become any more or less aggressive or antisocial over time, because the aggressive and antisocial acts that 2-year-olds display are not directly comparable to those of an 8-year-old or an adolescent. As a result, researchers have studied age-related changes in both the *form* of aggressive behavior and the situations that elicit aggressive or antisocial contact.

Aggression during the preschool period. Much of what we know about the aggressive behavior of preschool children comes from a handful of studies. One is a project conducted by Florence Goodenough (1931), who asked mothers of 2- to 5-year-olds to keep diaries recording each angry outburst displayed by their children, its apparent causes, and its consequences. A second, longitudinal study conducted by Mark Cummings and his associates (1989) recorded the squabbles that occurred among pairs of children at play, once when the children were 2 years old and again at age 5. Finally, Willard Hartup (1974) conducted an observational study in which he analyzed the causes and consequences of aggressive acts that occurred over a five-week period in groups of 4- to 5-year-olds and 6- to 7-year-olds. Taken together, these studies indicate the following:

1. Unfocused temper tantrums diminish during the preschool period and are uncommon after age 4.
2. The tendency to retaliate in response to attack or frustration increases dramatically for children over age 3.
3. *The primary instigators of aggression vary with the age of the child.* At age 2–3, children are most often aggressive after parents have thwarted or angered them by exerting authority; older children are much more likely to aggress after conflicts with siblings or peers.
4. The *form* of aggression also changes over time. Children aged 2 or 3 are likely to hit or kick an adversary. Most of the squabbles among youngsters of this age concern toys and other possessions, so that their aggression is usually *instrumental* in character. Older nursery-schoolers (and young grade-school children) show less and less physical aggression, choosing instead to tease, taunt, tattle, and call their victims uncomplimentary names. Although

PHOTO 10-2 The squabbles of young children usually center around toys, candy, or other treasured resources and qualify as acts of instrumental aggression.

older children continue to fight over objects, their aggressive outbursts are increasingly *hostile* in character—designed primarily to harm another person.

5. Apparently the frequency of aggressive interactions declines with age, for pairs of 5-year-olds squabble less often (and have conflicts of shorter duration) than was true of these same children observed three years earlier, as 2-year-olds.

Why are aggressive exchanges less common among 5-year-olds than among 2-, 3-, and 4-year-olds? One possibility is that parents and nursery-school teachers are actively preparing older preschoolers for a structured kindergarten environment by refusing to tolerate antisocial conduct and encouraging such alternative prosocial responses as cooperation and sharing (Emmerich, 1966). Of course, older children may also have learned from their own experiences that negotiation can be a relatively painless and efficient method of achieving objectives without undermining their relationships with playmates (Fabes & Eisenberg, 1992; Shantz, 1987).

Aggression during the early grade-school years. During the first few years of elementary school, physical aggression and other forms of antisocial conduct (for example, disobedience) continue to decline as children become increasingly proficient at settling disputes more amicably (Loeber, 1982). Yet, grade-school children will often respond aggressively to direct provocations (Sancilio et al., 1989), and this reactive or **retaliatory aggression,** *which is intended to harm the provocator,* can escalate into rather intense knock-down, drag-out battles (Coie et al., 1991). Clearly, these observations reinforce Hartup's (1974) conclusion that hostile aggression increases with age (even as instrumental aggression and disorderly conduct are declining). Why? Hartup's explanation is that older children are becoming more proficient role takers and, thus, are better able to infer the motives and intentions of other people. So, if a companion behaves in a deliberately harmful way, a grade-school child is more likely than a preschooler to detect the aggressive intent and to retaliate against the harmdoer.

Research on children's perceptions of harmdoing is generally consistent with Hartup's point of view. Although 3- to 5-year-olds may appropriately infer an actor's aggressive intentions if the relevant cues are clear and made very obvious to them, they are nowhere near as proficient at interpreting such information as older children and adolescents are (Nelson-LeGall, 1985). In one study (Dodge et al., 1984), kindergartners, second-graders, and fourth-graders were asked to judge the intentions of a child who had destroyed a peer's tower of blocks accidentally or while portraying either a hostile, a benign, or a prosocial intent. The results were clear: kindergartners correctly discriminated the actor's true intentions less than half the time (42%). Second-graders were more accurate (57% correct) but not nearly so skilled at detecting intentional cues as the fourth-graders (72% correct).

Yet it is important to note that 7- to 12-year-olds, who can easily discriminate accidental from deliberate harmdoing (see Dodge, 1980), may react aggressively to almost any provocation, even one that they know was unintentional (Sancilio et al., 1989; Shantz & Voydanoff, 1973). Why? Because grade-

PHOTO 10-3   As children mature, an increasing percentage of their aggressive acts qualify as examples of hostile aggression.

school children (particularly boys) are reluctant to condemn aggressive *retaliation*, often viewing it as an understandable (though not completely moral) response to provocation (Ferguson & Rule, 1988). So another reason why hostile aggression increases with age is that peers informally sanction the practice of *fighting back*; they view it as a normal reaction to harmdoing (Sancilio et al., 1989).

Finally, displays of hostile aggression are not an equal-opportunity enterprise: researchers who have charted aggressive exchanges among grade-school children find that a small minority of the youngsters are involved in a large majority of the conflicts (Perry, Kusel, & Perry, 1988). Who is most highly involved? In many groups the participants are a handful of highly aggressive children and the 10–15% of their classmates who are regularly abused by these bullies (Olweus, 1984; Perry et al., 1988).

We have already described some of the characteristics of highly aggressive children: they value ag-

gression; they expect aggression to be a successful means of achieving their aims; and they display the *hostile attributional bias* that makes them inclined to overattribute hostile intent to their peers. Indeed, John Coie and his associates (1991) find that highly aggressive grade-school boys who misinterpret others' nonhostile intents actually view themselves as being completely justified, morally and otherwise, when they assault their adversaries. And whom are they most likely to torment? In Box 10-2 we will see what researchers have learned about that small minority of youngsters who are habitually abused by their peers.

Aggression and antisocial conduct among pre-adolescents and adolescents.   In his review of age changes in antisocial and delinquent conduct, Rolf Loeber (1982) concluded that the incidence of fighting and hostile aggression peaks early in adolescence (that is, age 13–15) and declines thereafter. And, in their six-year longitudinal study of aggression from ages 10 to 16, Robert Cairns and his associates (1989) found similar declines in hostile physical attacks from early through mid-adolescence. How, then, might we explain the fact that arrests for assault and other violent crimes increase dramatically between ages 10 and 19, even though the absolute number of physically aggressive incidents is declining over the same period (Cairns & Cairns, 1986)? These seemingly inconsistent findings may simply reflect the fact that adolescents are bigger and stronger and have more access to weapons than preadolescents do; thus they are more likely to inflict serious injuries when they do decide to retaliate against harmdoers (Cairns et al., 1989).

One final point: although aggression may generally decline with age, adolescents are not necessarily becoming any better behaved. Not only does *social ostracism* — that is, malicious gossip and exclusion — increase dramatically among girls as they enter adolescence (Cairns et al., 1989), but so too does the incidence of theft, truancy, substance abuse, sexual misconduct, and other delinquent acts (Loeber, 1982; Newcomb & Bentler, 1989; *Uniform Crime Reports*, 1989). So it seems that adolescents who are becoming less overtly aggressive may simply turn to more *covert* forms of antisocial conduct to express their anger and hostility.

Is aggression a stable attribute?   We have seen that the kinds of aggression and antisocial conduct that children display will change over time. But what about aggressive (or antisocial) dispositions? Do aggressive preschoolers remain highly aggressive throughout the grade-school years? Do highly combative grade-school children become aggressive, antisocial adolescents and young adults?

Apparently, aggression is a reasonably stable attribute. Not only are aggressive toddlers likely to become aggressive 5-year-olds (Cummings et al., 1989), but the amount of physical and verbal aggression that a child displays at ages 6 to 12 is a fairly good predictor of his or her tendency to insult, argue, threaten, and fight with peers later in adolescence (Cairns et al., 1989; Kagan & Moss, 1962; Lerner et al., 1988).

On the basis of one longitudinal study of fewer than 100 individuals (Kagan & Moss, 1962), it has

---

BOX 10-2 | *Victims of Peer Aggression*

Each of us has probably known at least one victimized child—a youngster who repeatedly serves as a target for other children's hostile acts. Who are these children? Why are they singled out for abuse?

Dan Olweus's (1978, 1984) studies of 13- to 16-year-old Swedish "toughs" and their "whipping boys" provide some clues. Based on ratings made by their teachers, about 10% of Olweus's subjects could be described as habitual bullies who regularly subjected another 10% of the sample (their whipping boys) to physical and verbal harassment. Comparing the personality profiles of bullies, victims, and other well-adjusted male classmates, Olweus found that whipping boys showed a number of distinctive characteristics. They were (1) highly anxious, (2) low in self-esteem, (3) socially isolated, (4) physically weak, and (5) afraid to be assertive or to defend themselves. Most of these chronic patsies were "passive victims" in that they rarely fought back and appeared to have done nothing to invite the hostilities they received. But about one victimized adolescent in five could be described as a "provocative victim"—one who was restless, hot tempered, inclined to irritate or tease others, and likely to at least attempt to fight back (unsuccessfully) when attacked by a peer.

Recently, David Perry and his associates (1988; Perry, Williard, & Perry, 1990) have studied patterns of aggression and victimization in U.S. elementary schools, finding that, even among third-graders, about one child in ten was severely and repeatedly abused by highly aggressive classmates. Perry, like Olweus, found that there are two kinds of victims—passive and provocative—and he discovered that both groups are disliked and rejected by their peers. Interestingly, girls are victimized almost as often as boys, although female victims are more likely to be verbally harassed than physically assaulted. Finally, being a victim is apparently a stable attribute, for children who were highly victimized at the beginning of the study were still viewed as extreme victims three months later by their teachers and peers (indeed, Olweus found that his 13-year-old whipping boys were likely to retain that status when observed at age 16).

How are victimized children perceived by their classmates? Why might they be chosen as victims? Perry et al. (1990) addressed these issues by asking fourth- through seventh-graders to contemplate acts of aggression against victimized and nonvictimized peers and to estimate the consequences of these actions. They found that classmates of chronic victims hold very *positive expectancies* about attacking a victimized peer—that is, they felt that victimized children would reinforce them by surrendering tangible resources and by showing signs of distress (or defeat). Moreover, peers seemed to *value* tangible rewards more when taken from a victimized than from a nonvictimized

long been assumed that the stability of aggression from childhood to adulthood is greater for males than for females. However, later research has questioned this assertion. Rowell Huesmann and his associates (1984) tracked one sample of 600 subjects for 22 years and found, *for both males and females*, that childhood measures of aggression at age 8 were solid predictors of adult aggression and antisocial conduct at age 30 (as indexed by criminal behavior, spousal abuse, and self-reported physical aggression; see also Olweus, 1987, for a similar set of findings). Moreover, Avshalom Caspi and his associates (1987) found that *both boys and girls* who had been moody, aggressive, and ill tempered at age 10 tended to be ill-tempered young adults whose relations with their spouses and children were generally unpleasant and conflictual. So it seems that there is some continuity to the aggressive dispositions of female subjects after all.

Of course, these findings reflect group trends and in no way imply that a highly aggressive individual can't become relatively nonaggressive over

---

BOX 10-2 | *continued*

child, and they were relatively unconcerned about the prospect of harming (or being harmed by) these targets of abuse. So both aggressive and nonaggressive peers expect good things to follow from their attacks on chronic victims, and they even *exaggerate* the importance of obtaining these outcomes! Given the high probability of defeating a victimized child and the value attached to dominating these "whipping boys" (and girls), it is easy to see why the field of potential victims narrows considerably (to about 10% of a typical grade-school class) over the course of middle childhood.

Clearly, there is much that we don't know about the causes and consequences of prolonged victimization. Why, for example, are "passive" victims so disliked that their tormentors relish the prospect of dominating them and are relatively unconcerned about the suffering these children may experience? Are these young whipping boys (and girls) at risk of becoming depressed, untrusting adolescents and young adults who are likely to experience serious adjustment problems later in life? And how might we help victimized children to become less inviting targets for their peers? Obviously these are important questions—ones that developmentalists will be trying to answer in the years ahead.

A large percentage of aggressive episodes in children's peer groups involve chronic victims and the highly aggressive youngsters who regularly torment them.

time, or vice versa. However, we should not be surprised to find that aggression is a reasonably stable attribute for many individuals. Shortly we will see that some home settings can serve as early "training grounds" for the development of aggressive habits. And, when children who have learned to react aggressively to conflicts at home later face similar problems at school, they may try their forceful tactics on classmates, thereby inviting counterattacks, which lead the child to assume that peers are hostile toward her. Before long the child finds herself in a vicious cycle (portrayed earlier in Figure 10-3)—a pattern that seems likely to perpetuate her aggressive inclinations.

Are there also biological predispositions toward aggression that could help to explain its stability? Philippe Rushton and his associates (1986) think so. In their study, 296 pairs of identical twins and 277 pairs of fraternal twins completed a self-report measure of hostility and aggression. Even though these twins were adults, most of whom had presumably lived apart from their co-twins for many years, identical-twin pairs were much more alike in self-reported aggression ($r = .40$) than pairs of fraternal twins ($r = .04$). Clearly some caution is warranted in interpreting these results, for the data are simply verbal reports that may or may not accurately reflect the twins' actual aggressive behaviors. Nevertheless, these findings imply that our aggressive inclinations may well be influenced to some extent by the genes we have inherited.

How might one's genotype contribute to aggression and, specifically, to the stability of aggression over time? Perhaps in many ways. For example, active and temperamentally difficult youngsters may regularly *elicit* negative reactions from other people, which in turn may engender hostility and aggression. And recall the concept of active *genotype/environment interactions* (discussed in Chapter 2)—the idea that individuals create or select environmental niches that best suit their genotypes. Perhaps children who are genetically predisposed to be aggressive and who have begun to develop some aggressive habits will choose to associate with people like themselves (that is, aggressive peers). If so, they will have created an environment for them-

selves that could easily perpetuate their aggressive tendencies (Rushton et al., 1986).

Sex Differences in Aggression

Although aggression is a reasonably stable attribute for members of each sex, we noted in Chapter 9 that males are more aggressive than females. Data from more than 100 studies conducted in countries all over the world reveal that boys and men are not only more physically aggressive than girls and women but more verbally aggressive as well (Hyde, 1984; Maccoby & Jacklin, 1974, 1980; Tieger, 1980; Whiting & Edwards, 1988). The probability of becoming a target of aggression also depends on one's sex: conflicts of all kinds are more common in boy/boy than in boy/girl or girl/girl dyads (Barrett, 1979); and, even though boys can be quite verbally abusive toward girls, it seems that they are less likely to physically assault a harmdoer if that person is a female (Barrett, 1979; Cairns et al., 1989). Perhaps boys do take to heart the cultural maxim that it is inappropriate to clobber girls, although their reluctance to do so may also stem from a fear of offending their parents (Perry, Perry, & Weiss, 1989).

Why do males and females differ in aggression? Let's consider three complementary points of view.

The biological viewpoint. According to Maccoby and Jacklin (1974, 1980), there are at least four reasons to suspect that biological factors contribute heavily to sex differences in aggression. First, males are more aggressive than females in almost every society that has been studied. Second, sex differences in aggression appear so early (about age 2 to 2½) that it is difficult to attribute them solely to social learning or to parental child-rearing practices. Third, males tend to be the more aggressive gender among our closest phylogenetic relatives—species such as baboons and chimpanzees. Finally, there is evidence to suggest a link, in both animals and humans, between male hormones (such as testosterone) and aggressive behavior. Let's take a closer look at these hormonal influences.

It has been suggested that males are more aggressive than females because of their higher levels of androgen and testosterone—activating male sex hormones that are thought to promote heightened activity, a readiness to anger, and, hence, a predisposition to behave aggressively (Jacklin, 1989; Maccoby & Jacklin, 1980). The evidence seems quite convincing when experiments are conducted with animals. In Chapter 9 we noted that female rhesus monkeys exposed prenatally to the male hormone testosterone later display patterns of social behavior more characteristic of males: they often threaten other monkeys, initiate rough-and-tumble play, and try to mount a partner, as males do at the beginning of a sexual encounter (Young, Goy, & Phoenix, 1964). By contrast, genetically male rat pups that are castrated and cannot produce testosterone tend to be passive and to display feminine sexual behavior (Beach, 1965).

What about humans? Interestingly, the connection between prenatal androgen exposure and aggression in females is not very compelling. In studies of children with *adrenogenital syndrome (AGS)*, researchers (Ehrhardt & Baker, 1974; Money & Ehrhardt, 1972) have found that, even though androgenized females were extremely active and qualified as "tomboys," they were no more aggressive than their nonandrogenized sisters or other female agemates. However, production of sex hormones increases dramatically at puberty, and there is some evidence for a relationship between hormones and aggression among adolescents. Dan Olweus and his associates (1980), for example, found that 16-year-old boys who label themselves as physically and verbally aggressive do have higher *testosterone* levels than boys who view themselves as nonaggressive. Elizabeth Susman and her colleagues (1987; Inoff-Germain et al., 1988) found a similar link between *androgen* levels and aggressive, domineering behaviors in samples of 9–14-year-old boys *and* girls. Since adolescent males have much greater concentrations of male sex hormones than adolescent females do, these data imply that the sex differences in aggres-

sion that adolescents display could be hormonally mediated.

However, extreme caution is required in interpreting these correlational findings, because a person's hormonal level may depend on his or her experiences. To illustrate: Irwin Bernstein and his associates (Rose, Bernstein, & Gordon, 1975) found that the testosterone levels of male rhesus monkeys rose after they had won a fight but fell after they had been defeated. So it appears that higher concentrations of male sex hormones might be either a cause or an effect of aggressive behavior, and it is difficult to establish conclusively that these hormones either *cause* one to act aggressively or explain sex differences in aggression (Maccoby & Jacklin, 1980).

The social viewpoint.   Not only are proponents of a social viewpoint critical of the hormonal evidence for sex differences in aggression, but they would also point out that very young boys are not always more aggressive than girls. In fact, Marlene Caplan and her associates (1991) found that forceful, aggressive resolutions of disputes over toys were actually more numerous among 1-year-olds when the play groups were dominated *by girls*! Even at age 2, groups dominated by boys were more likely than those dominated by girls to negotiate and share when toys were scarce. It is not until age 2½ to 3 that sex differences in aggression are reliable—and this is clearly enough time for social influences to have steered boys and girls in different directions (see Fagot & Leinbach, 1989; Fagot, Leinbach, & O'Boyle, 1992).

Of course, there are many social influences that might conspire to make boys more aggressive than girls. For example, parents play more roughly with boys than with girls; they react more negatively to the aggressive antics of daughters than to those of sons (Mills & Rubin, 1990; Parke & Slaby, 1983); and they are more likely to side with their sons than with their daughters in disputes with peers (Ross et al., 1990). The ray guns, tanks, missile launchers, and other symbolic implements of destruction that parents buy their sons encourage the enactment of aggressive themes—and actually promote aggressive behavior (see Feshbach, 1956; Turner & Goldsmith,

1976)—whereas the dolls, doll houses, and dish sets that girls receive promote their adoption of a nurturant, expressive (nonaggressive) orientation. Although most parents do not encourage their sons to be physically aggressive (except perhaps to defend themselves), they may indirectly promote such behavior by adopting a "boys will be boys" attitude and downplaying the significance of scuffles among males (recall the results of Box 10-1). These lessons are hardly lost on children. By the time they enter grade school, both boys and girls have categorized aggression as a male attribute in their gender schemas, and their ability to recall information about previous aggressive episodes is much better if the perpetrators were boys rather than girls (Bukowski, 1990). By age 9 to 12, boys expect less parental and peer disapproval for aggression than girls do; they also think that aggression will provide them with more tangible rewards, and they value these outcomes more than girls do (Boldizar et al., 1989; Perry et al., 1989). There are many more observations that could be cited here (see Parke & Slaby, 1983), but the point should be obvious: sex differences in aggression depend to no small extent on the sex-typing process and on sex differences in social learning.

The interactive viewpoint.   Finally, proponents of an interactive viewpoint contend that sex-linked constitutional factors (biology) interact with social-environmental influences to promote sex differences in aggression. Consider some of the constitutional differences between infant males and females. Female infants tend to mature faster, to talk sooner, and to be more sensitive to pain than male infants, whereas males tend to be larger and more muscular, to sleep less, to cry more, and to be somewhat more active, more irritable, and harder to comfort than female infants (Bell, Weller, & Waldrip, 1971; Hutt, 1972; Maccoby, 1980; Moss, 1967). Clearly these (and other) sex-linked constitutional differences could have *direct* effects on a child's behavior; but a more likely possibility is that they have *indirect*, or interactive, effects by influencing the behavior of the child's companions (Tieger, 1980). For example, parents may find that they can play more vigorously with an active, muscular son who may

be somewhat less sensitive to pain than with a docile, less muscular daughter who seems to enjoy these activities less. Or perhaps they are likely to become more impatient with irritable and demanding sons who are difficult to quiet or to comfort. In the first case, parents would be encouraging boys to partake in the kinds of fast-paced, vigorous activities from which aggressive outbursts often emerge. In the second case, parents' greater impatience or irritability with sons than with daughters could push males in the direction of becoming quicker to anger and somewhat more hostile or resentful toward other people. So it is unlikely that sex differences in aggression (or in any other form of social behavior) are automatic or "biologically programmed." Instead, it seems that a child's biological predispositions are likely to affect the *behavior* of caregivers and other close companions, which in turn will elicit certain reactions from the child and influence the activities and interests that the child is likely to display. The implication of this interactive model is that biological factors and social influences are complexly intertwined and that both nature and nurture are important contributors to sex differences in aggression.

Cultural and Familial Influences on Aggression and Delinquency

We have seen that one's genotype and other biological correlates of gender can affect one's propensity for aggressive, antisocial conduct. However, Albert Bandura, Seymour Feshbach, and many other aggression theorists believe that a person's *absolute* level of aggression—that is, how aggressive and antisocial an individual is likely to become—will depend very critically on the social environment in which he or she is raised. We will now consider two important sets of social influences that help to explain why some children and adolescents are more aggressive than others: (1) the norms and values endorsed by their societies and subcultures and (2) the family settings in which they are raised.

Cultural and Subcultural Influences

Cross-cultural studies consistently indicate that some societies and subcultures are more violent and aggressive than others. Indeed, we have already cited the Arapesh of New Guinea and the Pygmies of central Africa as examples of passive, nonaggressive social orders. In marked contrast to these groups is the Ik tribe of Uganda, whose members live in small bands and will steal from, deceive, and even kill one another to ensure their own survival (Turnbull, 1972). Another aggressive society is the Mundugumor of New Guinea, who teach their children to be independent, combative, and emotionally unresponsive to the needs of others (Mead, 1935). These are values that serve the Mundugumor well, for during some periods of their history they were cannibals who routinely killed human beings as prey and considered almost anyone other than close kinfolk fair game. The United States is also an "aggressive" society. On a percentage basis, the incidence of rape, homicide, and assault is higher in the United States than in any other stable democracy (see Figure 10-5), and the United States ranks a close second to Spain (and far above third-place Canada) in the incidence of armed robbery (Wolff, Rutten, & Bayer, 1992).

Studies conducted in the United States and in England also point to social-class differences in aggression: children and adolescents from the lower socioeconomic strata (particularly males from larger urban areas) exhibit more aggressive behavior and higher levels of delinquency than their agemates from the middle class (see Atwater, 1992, and Feshbach, 1970, for reviews). African-American males, in particular, are overrepresented among school-aged children labeled as aggressive and among juveniles arrested for delinquency—so much so that researchers who study childhood aggression often include large numbers of black males in their samples (Graham et al., 1992). However, there is some question about whether African-American youths are really more violent and antisocially inclined than low-SES males from other ethnic backgrounds. Indeed, some studies have shown that low-SES white adolescents commit violent crimes at the same rate as low-SES African Americans but that African-

American males are more likely than their white counterparts to be arrested and charged for their offenses (Cavan & Ferdinand, 1981; Farrington, 1987). So the overrepresentation of minority youths among juvenile arrests and incarcerations may be partly attributable to racism on the part of police and the court system.

Interestingly, social-class differences in delinquency are greatest for violent crimes: low-SES adolescents commit more than three times as many sexual assaults, aggravated assaults, and robberies as middle-class youths do (Elliott & Ageton, 1980). One contributor to this finding seems to be social-class differences in parenting. Parents from the lower socioeconomic strata often display less warmth and more hostility to their children (particularly to sons) than middle-class parents do, and they tend to rely more on physical punishment to discipline aggressive behavior—thus modeling aggression even as they are trying to suppress it (Patterson et al., 1989; Sears, Maccoby, & Levin, 1957). Low-SES parents are also inclined to actively encourage their children to respond aggressively when provoked by peers (Miller & Sperry, 1987)—a practice that may foster the development of a hostile attributional bias. Finally, economic frustrations faced by members of the lower socioeconomic strata can promote antisocial conduct. In one study it was found that crimes of larceny (minor theft) increased dramatically among poorer members of society soon after the introduction of television to their communities (Hennigan et al., 1982). The authors' explanation of this finding was that the poor felt a sense of frustration or "relative deprivation" after viewing mostly affluent people on television; consequently they turned to larceny to obtain some of the good things in life that they were lacking. And it now appears that these same feelings of "relative deprivation" are contributing to the rise of more violent crimes (muggings, armed robberies) as well (Wolff et al., 1992).

In sum, a person's tendencies toward aggression and antisocial conduct will depend, in part, on the extent to which the culture (or subculture) encourages and condones such behavior. Yet not all people in pacifistic societies are kind, cooperative, and helpful, and the vast majority of people raised

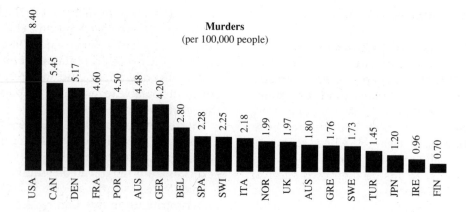

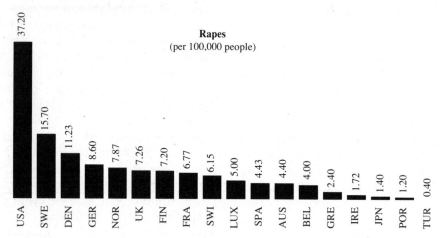

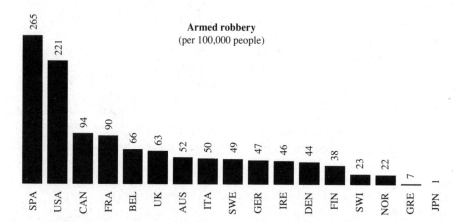

FIGURE 10-5 Frequencies of three major violent crimes in modern industrialized societies. (Adapted from M. Wolff, P. Rutten, & A. F. Bayer III, *Where We Stand: Can America Make It in the Race for Health, Wealth, and Happiness?* Copyright © 1992 by Bantam Books. Reprinted by permission.)

in "aggressive" societies or subcultures are not especially prone to violence. One reason why there are dramatic differences in aggression within any social order is that children are raised in very different families. In our next section we will see how the home setting can sometimes serve as a breeding ground for hostile, antisocial conduct.

Familial Influences

How might one's family and the family setting contribute to violent and aggressive behavior? In the pages that follow, we will consider two interrelated avenues of influence: (1) the effects of particular child-rearing practices and (2) the more global impact of the family environment on children's aggressive inclinations.

PARENTAL CHILD-REARING PRACTICES AND CHILDREN'S AGGRESSIVE BEHAVIOR

When investigators began to study the development of aggression, they operated under the assumption that parents' attitudes and child-rearing strategies play a major role in shaping children's aggressive inclinations. Clearly there is some truth to this assumption. Some of the most reliable findings in the child-rearing literature show that *cold* and *rejecting* parents who apply **power-assertive** discipline (particularly physical punishment) in an *erratic* fashion and often *permit* their child to express aggressive impulses are likely to raise hostile, aggressive children (Dishion, 1990; Olweus, 1980; Parke & Slaby, 1983). Surely these findings make good sense. Cold and rejecting parents are frustrating their children's emotional needs and modeling a lack of concern for others by virtue of their aloofness. By ignoring many of the child's aggressive outbursts, the permissive parent is legitimizing combative activities and failing to provide many opportunities for the child to control his or her aggressive urges. And, when aggression escalates to the point that the parent spanks the child, the adult is serving as a model for the very behavior that he or she is trying to suppress. So it is hardly surprising to find that parents who rely on physical coercion to discipline aggression have children who are highly aggressive out-

PHOTO 10-4 Children who are hit when they displease others are likely to hit others who displease them.

side the home (Patterson et al., 1989; Sears et al., 1957; Weiss et al., 1992). A child who learns that he will be hit, kicked, or shoved when he displeases his parents will probably direct the same kind of responses toward playmates who displease him (Hart, Ladd, & Burleson, 1990).

Can the child be influencing the parent? Although parental attitudes and child-rearing practices certainly contribute to children's aggression and antisocial conduct, the stream of influence may also flow in the opposite direction, from child to parent. In Dan Olweus's (1980) child-rearing study, the best predictors of aggression among young adolescent males were (1) the mothers' permissiveness toward, or willingness to tolerate, the boys' aggressive behavior earlier in childhood and (2) the mothers' cold and rejecting attitudes toward their sons. However, the next best predictor was not a child-rearing variable at all but, rather, a measure of the boys' own temperamental impulsivity (highly active, impulsive boys tended to be the most aggressive). According to Olweus, a boy with an active and impetuous temperament may simply "exhaust his mother, resulting in her becoming more permissive of aggression in the boy" (p. 658). And should the impetuous child really anger his mother, so that she can no longer ignore his conduct, she may express her negative feelings openly or resort to physical punishment as a control tactic, thereby increasing the likelihood that her son will behave in a surly and belligerent manner. Although contemporary theorists disagree about just how much temperament contributes to aggressive, antisocial conduct (see, for example, Dodge, 1990; Lytton, 1990), it seems that children (by virtue of their temperaments) have a hand in creating the very child-rearing environments that will influence their propensities for aggression (Vuchinich, Bank, & Patterson, 1992).

Parents as managers.   Another way that parents may influence their children's aggression and antisocial conduct is through their management and monitoring of the child's whereabouts, activities, and choice of friends. Gerald Patterson and his associates (Capaldi & Patterson, 1991; Patterson et al., 1989; Patterson & Stouthamer-Loeber, 1984) consistently find that *lack* of parental monitoring is associated with such aggressive or delinquent adolescent behaviors as fighting with peers, sassing teachers, destroying property, and generally breaking rules outside the home. According to Patterson and Stouthamer-Loeber (1984), "Parents of delinquents are indifferent trackers of their sons' whereabouts, the kinds of companions they keep, and the type of activities in which they engage. Perhaps this [lack of monitoring] constitutes an operational definition for what is meant by 'the unattached parent'" (p. 1305).

However, not all parents who fail to monitor their children can be described as uncaring or unconcerned. Sanford Dornbusch and his associates (Dornbusch et al., 1985) found that a parent's ability to influence children depends in part on the composition of the family. Specifically, Dornbusch et al. found that the heads of *mother-only* households have a particularly difficult time managing the activities of adolescent sons and daughters without the support of a spouse or some other adult in the home (see also Steinberg, 1987). And, given the association between lack of parental monitoring and deviant adolescent behavior in their own (and other) studies, Dornbusch et al. concluded that "the

raising of adolescents is not a task that can easily be borne by a mother alone" (p. 340).

In sum, it appears that parental awareness of and control over a child's activities may be just as important in determining an adolescent's aggressive inclinations as the particular child-rearing practices that parents have used. Moreover, Dornbusch's finding that the structure of the family affects parental control suggests another interesting conclusion: to understand how aggression develops within the home setting, one must think of the family as a *social system* in which interactions among *all* family members (or the lack thereof) will affect the child's developmental outcomes. We will see just how true this conclusion is in the next section.

THE HOME AS A BREEDING GROUND FOR AGGRESSION

Parental conflict and children's aggression.   Developmentalists have long suspected that the emotional climate of the home can and often does influence children's adjustment. For example, children from strife-ridden homes in which parents often fight tend to display emotional difficulties and a variety of conduct disorders, including aggression (Holden & Ritchie, 1991; Porter & O'Leary, 1980). Proceeding from this kind of correlational data, Mark Cummings and his associates (Cummings, Iannotti, & Zahn-Waxler, 1985) designed an interesting experiment to determine whether exposure to adult conflict would upset children and *cause* them to become more aggressively inclined. Two-year-olds seated together in a play area watched both angry and highly affectionate interactions between two adults in an adjacent room. The children's emotional reactions to these exchanges were recorded, as were their tendencies to fight or otherwise aggress against one another.

The results were clear. Angry exchanges between adults had a much stronger effect on the children than affectionate ones. These angry interactions not only upset the toddlers but also increased their willingness to fight with one another as well (particularly for boys). Often these altercations were rather intense, and they seemed to be more closely related to the children's emotional distress than to any tendency to imitate the angry adults. Moreover, negative reactions to angry adult exchanges were even greater one month later, when the children were exposed to a second such episode. So the results of this tightly controlled experiment provide good reason for believing that regular exposure to parental strife at home can place children on edge emotionally and thereby increase their likelihood of having hostile, aggressive interactions with siblings or peers.

And how might argumentative parents respond to the bickering and fighting they induce in their children (or to any other misconduct, for that matter)? Let's see what developmentalists have learned by conceptualizing families as complex social systems.

Families as social systems. Gerald Patterson (1982, 1986; Patterson et al., 1989) has observed patterns of interaction among children and their parents in families that have at least one highly aggressive child. The aggressive children in Patterson's sample seemed "out of control" — they fought a lot at home and at school and were generally unruly and defiant. These families were then compared with other families of the same size and socioeconomic status that had no problem children.

Patterson found that his problem children were growing up in very atypical family environments. Unlike in most homes, where people frequently express approval and affection, the highly aggressive problem child usually lives in a setting in which family members are constantly struggling with one another: they are reluctant to initiate conversations, and, when they do talk, they tend to needle, threaten, or otherwise irritate other family members rather than conversing positively. Patterson called these settings **coercive home environments** because a high percentage of interactions centered on one family member's attempts to force another to stop irritating him or her. He also noted that **negative reinforcement** was important in maintaining these coercive interactions: when one family member is making life unpleasant for another, the second will learn to whine, yell, scream, tease, or hit because these actions often force the antagonist to stop (and thus are reinforced). Consider the following sequence of events, which may be fairly typical in a coercive home environment:

1. A girl teases her older brother, who makes her stop teasing by yelling at her (yelling is negatively reinforced).
2. A few minutes later the girl calls her brother a nasty name. The boy then chases and hits her.
3. The girl stops calling him names (which negatively reinforces hitting). She then whimpers and hits him back, and he withdraws (negatively reinforcing her hits). The boy then approaches and hits his sister again, and the conflict escalates.
4. At this point the mother intervenes. However, her children are too emotionally disrupted to listen to reason, so she finds herself applying punitive and coercive tactics to make them stop fighting.
5. The fighting stops (thus reinforcing the mother for using punitive methods). However, the children now begin to whine, cry, or yell at the mother. These countercoercive techniques are then reinforced if the mother backs off and accepts peace at any price. Unfortunately, backing off is only a temporary solution. The next time the children antagonize each other and become involved in an unbearable conflict, the mother is likely to use even more coercion to get them to stop. The children once again apply their own methods of countercoercion to induce her to "lay off," and the family atmosphere becomes increasingly unpleasant for everyone.

Patterson finds that mothers of problem children rarely use social reinforcement or social approval as means of behavior control, choosing instead to largely ignore prosocial conduct, to interpret neutral events as antisocial, and to rely almost exclusively on coercive tactics to deal with perceived misconduct. Indeed, the overwhelmingly negative treatment these problem children receive at home (including parents' tendency to label ambiguous events as antisocial) might easily explain why they generally mistrust other people and display the *hostile attributional bias* so commonly observed among highly aggressive children (Dishion, 1990; see also Weiss et al., 1992). And, ironically, children who live in these highly coercive family settings eventually become resistant to punishment: not only have these youngsters learned to fight coercion with countercoercion, but they often defy the parent and may *repeat the very act she is trying to suppress.* Why? Because this is one of the few ways the child can be successful at commanding the attention of an adult who rarely offers praise or shows any signs of affection. No wonder Patterson calls these children "out of control"! By contrast, children from noncoercive families are likely to receive much more positive attention from siblings and parents, so that they don't have to irritate other family members to be noticed (Patterson, 1982, 1986).

So we see that the flow of influence in the family setting is *multidirectional*; coercive parent/parent, parent/child, and child/child interactions will affect the behavior of all family members and may contribute to the development of a hostile family environment—a true breeding ground for aggression. Unfortunately, these problem families may never break out of this destructive pattern of attacking and counterattacking one another unless they receive help. In Box 10-3 we look at one particularly effective ap-

---

B O X | **10-3** | *Helping Children (and Parents) Who Are "Out of Control"*

How does one treat a problem child who is hostile, defiant, and "out of control"? Rather than focusing on the problem child, Gerald Patterson's (1981, 1982) approach is to work with the entire family. Patterson begins by carefully observing the family's interactions and determining just how family members are reinforcing one another's coercive activities. The next step is to describe the nature of the problem to parents and to teach them a new approach to managing their children's behavior. Some of the principles, skills, and procedures that Patterson stresses are the following:

1. Don't give in to the child's coercive behavior.
2. Don't escalate your own coercion when the child becomes coercive.
3. Control the child's coercion with the time-out procedure—a method of punishment in which the child is sent to her room (or some other location) until she calms down and stops using coercive tactics.
4. Identify those of the child's behaviors that are most irritating, and then establish a point system in which the child can earn credits (rewards, privileges) for acceptable conduct or lose them for unacceptable behavior. Parents with older problem children are taught how to formulate "behavioral contracts" that specify how the child is expected to behave at home and at school, as well as how deviations from this behavioral code will be punished. Whenever possible, children should have a say in negotiating these contracts.

5. Be on the lookout for occasions when you can respond to the child's prosocial conduct with warmth and affection. Although this is often difficult for parents who are accustomed to snapping at their children and accentuating the negative, Patterson believes that parental affection and approval will reinforce good conduct and eventually elicit displays of affection from the child—a clear sign that the family is on the road to recovery.

A clear majority of problem families respond quite favorably to these methods. Not only do problem children become less coercive, defiant, and aggressive, but the mother's depression fades as she gradually begins to feel better about herself, her child, and her ability to resolve family crises (Patterson, 1981). Some problem families show an immediate improvement. Others respond more gradually to the treatment and may require periodic "booster shots"—that is, follow-up treatments in which the clinician visits the family, determines why progress has slowed (or broken down), and then retrains the parents or suggests new procedures to correct the problems that are not being resolved. Clearly, this therapy works because it recognizes that "out of control" behavior stems from a *family system* in which both parents and children are influencing each other and contributing to the development of a hostile family environment. Therapies that focus exclusively on the problem child are not enough!

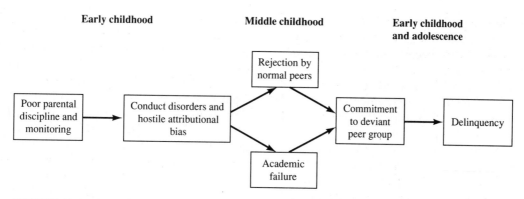

FIGURE 10-6   A model of the development of chronic antisocial behavior. (Adapted from G. R. Patterson, B. D. DeBaryshe, & E. Ramsey, "A Developmental Perspective on Antisocial Behavior." *American Psychologist*, 1989, *44*, 329–335. Copyright © 1989 by the American Psychological Association. Adapted by permission.)

proach to this problem—a method that necessarily focuses on the family as a social system rather than simply on the aggressive child who has been referred for treatment.

Coercive home environments as contributors to chronic delinquency.   How serious are the risks faced by "out of control" children who grow up in a disordered home environment? Patterson and his associates (1989) have addressed this issue by reviewing the literature on problem children and drawing some strong conclusions. As noted above, coercive parenting contributes to the development of children's defiant, aggressive behaviors and hostile attributional biases, which in turn can cause these youngsters to be rejected by peers and to founder academically. These poor outcomes may then cause parents to feel less invested in their children and less inclined to closely monitor their activities (Patterson et al., 1989; Vuchinich et al., 1992).

Moreover, the rejection that problem children experience from peers, coupled with their likely placement in classes or study groups with other academically deficient children, often means that they will have lots of exposure to other relatively defiant, aggressive, and socially unskilled youngsters like themselves. Indeed, Thomas Dishion and his associates (1991) recently found that aggressive preadolescent boys who had been rejected by peers earlier in childhood were now associating mainly with

other hostile, antisocial classmates and were much more likely than nonrejected boys to be involved in antisocial conduct. In other words, aggressive preadolescents were banding together to form deviant cliques (see Cairns et al., 1988, for evidence that aggressive girls also form such alliances)—groups that tend to devalue academics, encourage aggression, and promote such dysfunctional adolescent activities as sexual misconduct, substance abuse, dropping out of school, and a variety of other kinds of delinquent or criminal behaviors (Cairns, Cairns, & Neckerman, 1989; Newcomb & Bentler, 1989; Patterson et al., 1989). So, to return to the question raised above, Patterson et al. (1989) think that living in a coercive home environment poses serious risks indeed, for such an experience is often a crucial first step along the road to chronic antisocial or delinquent behavior (see Figure 10-6 for an overview of Patterson's model).

Although more boys than girls complete the developmental progression described in Figure 10-6 and become chronic delinquents, the delinquency "gender gap" is narrowing (*Uniform Crime Reports,* 1989). Male delinquents still dominate the violent crime statistics; but females are about as likely as males to be involved in larcenies, sexual misconduct, and substance abuse, and they are more likely than males to be arrested for such status offenses as running away from home and engaging in prostitution (*Uniform Crime Reports,* 1989). Although it does seem to take a more disordered home environment to push girls along the path to delinquency (Thornburg, 1986), females can become just as chronically antisocial as males can.

Family interventions of the kind described in Box 10-3 can be quite effective at modifying the antisocial tendencies of preadolescent (and younger) children; however, once antisocial patterns continue into adolescence, so many factors conspire to maintain them that interventions are usually unsuccessful (Kazdin, 1987; Patterson et al., 1989). Note the implication here: to cope with the problem of chronic delinquency, we must think in terms of *preventive* interventions—ideally, programs that would (1) teach parents more effective child-management techniques, (2) foster children's social skills to prevent them from being rejected by their peers, and (3) provide any academic remediation that may be necessary to keep children on track at school and to lessen the likelihood that they will fall in with deviant peer groups and/or become high school dropouts. Of course, any intervention that makes aggressive, antisocial conduct a less viable or attractive option for young children would be a step in the right direction. In the final section of the chapter, we will consider some of the many procedures developmentalists have touted as effective methods for reducing children's aggression.

Methods of Controlling Aggression and Antisocial Conduct

What methods other than family therapy might help parents and teachers to control the aggressive antics of young children so that antisocial approaches to conflict do not become habitual? Over the years, a variety of solutions have been offered, including procedures to eliminate the payoffs for aggression, modeling and coaching strategies, creating nonaggressive play environments, and training children to empathize with victims of harmdoing. But few solutions have been so highly touted as the recommendation that we offer children harmless ways to express their anger or frustrations. Let's consider this "popular" alternative first.

Catharsis: A Dubious Strategy

Sigmund Freud believed that hostile, aggressive urges build over time, and he urged people to find *harmless* ways to release them every now and then (that is, to experience *catharsis*) before they reach dangerous levels and trigger a truly violent outburst. The implications of this **catharsis hypothesis** are clear: if we encourage young children to vent their anger or frustrations on inanimate objects such as Bobo dolls, they should drain away their aggressive energies and become less inclined to harm other people.

Popular as this **cathartic technique** has been, it does *not* work and *may even backfire*. In one study (Walters & Brown, 1963), children who had been encouraged to slap, punch, and kick an inflatable Bobo doll were found to be much more aggressive in their later interactions with peers than were classmates who had not had an opportunity to beat on the doll. Other investigators have noted that children who are first angered by a peer and then given an opportunity to aggress against an inanimate object become no less aggressive toward the peer who had angered them in the first place (Mallick & McCandless, 1966). So, cathartic techniques do not reduce children's aggressive urges. In fact, they may teach youngsters that hitting and kicking are acceptable methods of expressing their anger or frustrations.

Eliminating the Payoffs for Aggression

It is possible to reduce aggression by eliminating the rewards that sustain aggressive acts. However, this approach is not as simple as it sounds, for any number of objects and events may reinforce an act of aggression.

Suppose that 5-year-old Mike wrests an attractive toy away from his 3-year-old sister, Gail, causing her to cry. If Mike's aggression were motivated by the prospect of obtaining the toy, his mother could simply return the toy to Gail and thus deny him his reward. Mike's tendency to attack should then wane, for this aggressive strategy has not "paid off" (Bandura, 1973).

Unfortunately, this solution wouldn't always work, for it is possible that Gail's submissive behavior is the "reward" that sustains Mike's aggression

(Patterson, Littman, & Bricker, 1967). And suppose that Mike is an insecure child who has attacked his sister *in order to attract his mother's attention*; under these circumstances the mother would be reinforcing Mike's aggression if she attended to it at all. But we cannot recommend that the mother ignore Mike's aggressive outburst, for Siegal and Kohn (1959) have shown that young children may interpret an adult's nonintervention as tacit approval for their aggressive deeds. So what is the mother to do?

The incompatible-response technique. One proven method that she might use is the **incompatible-response technique**—a strategy of ignoring all but the most serious of Mike's aggressive antics (thereby denying him an "attentional" reward) while reinforcing acts (such as cooperation and sharing) that are incompatible with aggression. In the classic study of this technique, Paul Brown and Rogers Elliot (1965) instructed nursery-school teachers to turn their backs on all but the most severely aggressive exchanges among their pupils. At the same time, teachers were asked to reward all instances of prosocial behavior, such as sharing toys or playing together cooperatively. Within two weeks this treatment had significantly reduced the incidence of both physical and verbal aggression among the children, and the program was ended. A follow-up treatment given several weeks later brought about further reductions in aggressive behavior. In a second study, Ron Slaby (Slaby & Crowley, 1977) found that merely encouraging children to say nice things about one another produced an increase in prosocial behavior and a corresponding decrease in aggression. Clearly the reinforcement of responses that are incompatible with aggression can inhibit hostile behavior. The beauty of this nonpunitive approach is that it does not reinforce children who seek attention through their hostile acts, it does not make children angry or resentful, and it does not expose them to a punitive or aggressive model. Thus many of the negative side effects associated with punishment can be avoided.

The "time-out" procedure. Of course, the incompatible-response technique will be somewhat less than effective if the child's "reward" for aggression is dominating other children and/or obtaining control of their possessions. And obviously parents cannot turn their backs on incidents in which children are likely to do *serious* harm to one another. So how might they inhibit serious hostilities without "reinforcing" them with their attention? One effective approach is the **time-out technique** (that is, time out from the opportunity to receive positive reinforcement) that Patterson favors—a technique in which the adult "punishes" by disrupting or otherwise preventing the aggressive antics the child finds reinforcing (for example, by sending the aggressor to his room until he is ready to behave appropriately). Although this technique may generate some resentment, the punitive agent is not physically abusing the child, is not serving as an aggressive model, and is not likely to unwittingly reinforce the child who misbehaves as a means of attracting attention. The time-out procedure is most effective at controlling children's hostilities when the adult in charge also reinforces cooperative or helpful acts that are incompatible with aggression (Parke & Slaby, 1983).

Modeling and Coaching Strategies

Responses incompatible with aggression may also be instilled by modeling or by coaching strategies. When children see a model choose a nonaggressive solution to a conflict or are explicitly coached in the use of nonaggressive methods of problem solving, they become more likely to enact similar solutions to their own problems (Chittenden, 1942; Zahavi & Asher, 1978). Indeed, coaching of effective methods of conflict resolution is particularly useful with chronically aggressive children, who often resort to aggressive tactics because they overattribute hostile intentions to others and are not very skilled at generating amiable solutions on their own (Rabiner, Lenhart, & Lochman, 1990; Shure, 1989). In one recent study (Guerra & Slaby, 1990), a group of violent adolescent offenders were coached in such skills as (1) looking for nonhostile cues that might be associated with harmdoing, (2) controlling their impulses (or anger), and (3) generating nonaggressive solutions to conflict. Not only did these violent offenders show dramatic improvements in their social problem-solving skills, but they also became less inclined to endorse beliefs supporting aggression and less aggressive in their interactions with authority figures and other inmates.

Yet it is important to note that any reduction in hostilities that results from these social-cognitive training programs could be short lived if the principles subjects have learned are quickly undermined in a coercive home environment (Pettit, Dodge, & Brown, 1988) or in the company of chronically aggressive friends who value and endorse aggression (Cairns et al., 1988). Indeed, two years after their release, the "trained" offenders in Guerra and Slaby's (1990) study were only slightly less likely to have stayed clean and not violated their parole (34% had violated parole) than other offenders who had not been trained (46% were parole violators). Although these long-term outcomes are in the right direction, Guerra and Slaby concluded that "To the extent that an offender's postrelease environment may lack the social support for maintaining the new pattern of [social-cognitive skills], the offender may be expected eventually to revert to his or her old pattern of [violent, antisocial conduct]" (p. 276).

Creating "Nonaggressive" Environments

Yet another method that adults may use to reduce children's aggression is to create play areas that minimize the likelihood of interpersonal conflict. For example, providing ample space for vigorous play helps to eliminate the kinds of accidental body contacts (such as tripping and shoving) that often provoke aggressive incidents (Hartup, 1974). Paul Gump (1975) points out that shortages in play materials also contribute to conflicts and hostilities. However, additional children can easily be assimilated into a play area without any increase in aggression if the number of slides, swings, and other toys is sufficient to prevent playmates from having to compete for scarce resources (Smith & Connolly, 1980).

Finally, we have seen that toys that suggest aggressive themes (guns, tanks, and so on) are likely to provoke hostile, aggressive incidents (Feshbach, 1956; Turner & Goldsmith, 1976). If our goal is to reduce the incidence of aggression, we may be better off in the long run to advise parents and teachers against making aggressive toys available to young children.

Empathy as a Deterrent to Aggression

A number of years ago a very dear friend of mine confessed to having recurring nightmares about the year he had spent as a combat infantryman in Vietnam. The event that triggered his discomfort would seem quite horrifying to most of us. He had once shot a man (a North Vietnamese) at close range and then watched this person suffer the agony of a slow, painful death. So distressed was my friend by this experience that he refused to bear arms any longer. He was granted a medical discharge from the service, but the nightmares remained.

Here is an example where pain cues emitted by a victim inhibited further aggression on the part of the perpetrator. This is not unusual: grade-school children, adolescents, and adults will normally back off and stop attacking a victim who shows signs of pain or suffering (Perry & Bussey, 1977). However, many *preschool* children and *highly aggressive* grade-school boys may continue to attack a suffering victim (Perry & Perry, 1974) and express little concern about the harm they have done (Boldizar, et al., 1989). One possible explanation for this seemingly sadistic behavior is that young preschoolers and other highly aggressive individuals may not *empathize* with their victims. In other words, they may not feel bad or suffer themselves when they have harmed another person.

Does **empathy** inhibit aggression? Apparently so. Grade-school children who score high in empathy are rated low in aggression by their teachers, whereas classmates who test very low in empathy tend to be more aggressive (Bryant, 1982; Feshbach, 1978). Moreover, Michael Chandler (1973) found that highly aggressive 11–13-year-old delinquents who participated in a ten-week program designed to make them more aware of other people's feelings subsequently became less hostile and aggressive, compared with a second group of delinquents who had not participated in the program. (See also Feshbach & Feshbach, 1982, for similar results in an empathy-training program with 9- to 11-year-olds.)

In the home setting, adults can foster the development of empathy by modeling empathic concern (Barnett, 1987; Zahn-Waxler, Radke-Yarrow, & King, 1979) and by using disciplinary techniques that (1) point out the harmful consequences of the child's aggressive actions and (2) encourage the child to put himself in the victim's place and imagine how the victim feels (Brody & Shaffer, 1982; Hoffman, 1988). In our next chapter we will see that parents who rely mainly on these rational, nonpunitive disciplinary techniques tend to raise sympathetic children who seem genuinely concerned about the welfare of others.

Summary

Human aggression is a pervasive phenomenon—so pervasive as to lead many theorists to believe that aggression is a part of human nature. Sigmund Freud proposed that we are driven by a destructive instinct, the Thanatos, which he considered responsible for the generation of hostile, aggressive impulses. Ethologists describe aggression as a fighting instinct triggered by certain eliciting cues in the environment. Although there are several important differences between psychoanalytic and ethological theories of aggression, both schools of thought contend that human beings are instinctively aggressive.

This view was challenged by learning theorists, who initially argued that aggression is the result of frustration and that frustrating events invariably lead to aggression. This *frustration/aggression hypothesis* was soon amended when it became apparent that frustration could lead to outcomes other than aggression.

Leonard Berkowitz has formulated a revised frustration/aggression hypothesis that emphasizes the interaction between an aggressor's internal emotional state and the environment. Berkowitz contends that frustration and a variety of other factors (such as an attack or one's aggressive habits) produce a *readiness to aggress* (anger). But aggressive responses will not occur unless *aggressive cues* are present in the environment—cues that have been associated with aggression in the past and that elicit aggressive responses from people who are "ready to aggress."

Bandura's social-learning theory treats aggression as a specific type of social behavior that is acquired by direct tuition or observational learning. Aggression is defined as *any behavior directed toward the goal of harming or injuring another organism*. Once acquired, aggressive habits are said to be maintained because they are (1) instrumental to the satisfaction of nonaggressive goals, (2) useful for terminating others' noxious behaviors, (3) socially sanctioned by other aggressive peers, and (4) intrinsically rewarding for the perpetrator. Most theories of aggression assume that people are "driven" to aggress by some sort of internal motivation such as frustration or anger. Bandura takes issue with all these theories by arguing that internal states may facilitate aggression but are not necessary for its occurrence.

Dodge's social information-processing theory is an interesting new approach that emphasizes cognitive contributions to aggression. Presumably, a person's reactions to frustration, anger, or an apparent provocation depend not so much on the social cues actually present in the situation as on how the person *processes* and *interprets* this information. Support for the model comes from studies showing that highly aggressive youngsters distort ambiguous information about harmdoing, viewing it as implying an aggressive intent. Thus, compared with nonaggressive agemates, aggressive children are more likely to retaliate when harmed under ambiguous circumstances.

Instrumental aggression emerges by the end of the first year, as infants begin to quarrel with siblings and peers over toys and other possessions. During the preschool period, children become less likely to throw temper tantrums or to hit others and more likely to resort to verbally aggressive tactics such as name calling or ridiculing. Grade-school children continue to fight over objects, but an increasing number of their aggressive exchanges are person-directed hostile outbursts. Although the incidence of aggression declines with age, adolescents are not necessarily any "better behaved," often turning instead to more covert forms of antisocial conduct to express their anger or frustrations. Aggression is a reasonably stable attribute for both boys and girls; that is, aggressive preschoolers are likely to become aggressive grade-school children, and an aggressive 8-year-old is likely to be relatively high in aggression and antisocial conduct as an adolescent or young adult.

Although aggression is equally stable for members of each sex, males are more physically and verbally aggressive than females and are more likely than females to become targets of aggression. These well-established sex differences in aggression reflect the interactive influence of biological and social forces.

A person's tendencies toward violence and aggression depend, in part, on the culture, subculture, and family setting in which he or she is raised. Cold and rejecting parents who rely on physical punishment and often permit aggression are likely to raise highly aggressive children. However, the "socialization" of aggression is a two-way street, for characteristics of the child (such as temperament or reactions to discipline) can affect parental attitudes and child-rearing practices. Strife-ridden homes appear to be breeding grounds for aggression. Highly aggressive youngsters who are "out of control" often live in *coercive home environments* where family members are constantly struggling with one another. To help these highly combative children, it is often necessary to treat the entire family. Long-term exposure to a coercive home environment seems to be a major contributor to poor life outcomes, as these highly aggressive, defiant children eventually alienate their teachers and normal peers and begin to form deviant peer cliques that encourage antisocial behavior and a variety of delinquent activities. And, once highly aggressive individuals reach adolescence, family therapy and other treatments are generally unsuccessful at modifying their antisocial conduct.

For these reasons, most developmentalists now believe that delinquency must be *prevented* rather than remediated. In addition to family therapy, a number of other strategies for reducing young children's antisocial conduct have been attempted. Proceeding in accordance with the *catharsis hypothesis* — the belief that children become less aggressive after letting off steam against an inanimate object — is an *ineffective* control tactic that may instigate aggression. Some proven methods of controlling children's aggression are (1) using the *incompatible-*

response technique, (2) using the *time-out* procedure to punish aggression, (3) modeling and coaching nonaggressive solutions to conflict, (4) creating play environments that minimize the likelihood of conflict, and (5) encouraging children to recognize the harmful effects of their aggressive acts and to *empathize* with victims of aggression.

References

ARDREY, R. (1967). *African genesis*. New York: Dell.

ARONSON, E. (1976). *The social animal*. New York: W. H. Freeman.

ATWATER, E. (1992). *Adolescence* (2nd ed.). Englewood Cliffs, NJ: Prentice-Hall.

BANDURA, A. (1965). Influence of models' reinforcement contingencies on the acquisition of imitative responses. *Journal of Personality and Social Psychology, 1*, 589–595.

BANDURA, A. (1973). *Aggression: A social learning analysis*. Englewood Cliffs, NJ: Prentice-Hall.

BANDURA, A. (1989). Social cognitive theory. In R. Vasta (Ed.), *Annals of child development* (Vol. 6). Greenwich, CT: JAI Press.

BARNETT, M. A. (1987). Empathy and related responses in children. In N. Eisenberg & J. Strayer (Eds.), *Empathy and its development*. Cambridge, England: Cambridge University Press.

BARON, R. A., & BYRNE, D. (1991). *Social psychology: Understanding human interaction* (6th ed.). Newton, MA: Allyn & Bacon.

BARRETT, D. W. (1979). A naturalistic study of sex differences in children's aggression. *Merrill-Palmer Quarterly, 25*, 193–203.

BEACH, F. A. (1965). *Sex and behavior*. New York: Wiley.

BELL, R. Q., WELLER, G. M., & WALDRIP, M. F. (1971). Newborn and preschooler: Organization of behavior and relations between periods. *Monographs of the Society for Research in Child Development, 36*(1–2, Serial No. 142).

BERKOWITZ, L. (1965). The concept of aggressive drive: Some additional considerations. In L. Berkowitz (Ed.), *Advances in experimental social psychology* (Vol. 2). Orlando, FL: Academic Press.

BERKOWITZ, L. (1974). Some determinants of impulsive aggression: Role of mediated association with reinforcement for aggression. *Psychological Review, 81*, 165–176.

BOLDIZAR, J. P., PERRY, D. G., & PERRY, L. C. (1989). Outcome values and aggression. *Child Development, 60*, 571–579.

BRODY, G. H., & SHAFFER, D. R. (1982). Contributions of parents and peers to children's moral socialization. *Developmental Review, 2*, 31–75.

BRONSON, W. C. (1975). Developments in behavior with age mates during the second year of life. In M. Lewis & L. A.

Rosenblum (Eds.), *The origins of behavior: Friendship and peer relations.* New York: Wiley.

BROWN, P., & ELLIOT, R. (1965). Control of aggression in a nursery school class. *Journal of Experimental Child Psychology, 2,* 103–107.

BRYANT, B. K. (1982). An index of empathy for children and adolescents. *Child Development, 53,* 413–425.

BRYANT, J., & ZILLMANN, D. (1979). Effect of intensifications of annoyance through unrelated residual excitation on substantially delayed hostile behavior. *Journal of Experimental Social Psychology, 15,* 470–480.

BUKOWSKI, W. J. (1990). Age differences in children's memory of information about aggressive, socially withdrawn, and prosociable boys and girls. *Child Development, 61,* 1326–1334.

BUSS, A. H. (1961). *The psychology of aggression.* New York: Wiley.

CAIRNS, R. B., & CAIRNS, B. D. (1986). The developmental-interactional view of social behavior: Four issues of adolescent aggression. In D. Olweus, J. Block, & M. Radke-Yarrow (Eds.), *Development of antisocial and prosocial behavior: Research, theories, and issues.* New York: Academic Press.

CAIRNS, R. B., CAIRNS, B. D., & NECKERMAN, H. J. (1989). Early school dropout: Configurations and determinants. *Child Development, 60,* 1437–1452.

CAIRNS, R. B., CAIRNS, B. D., NECKERMAN, H. J., FERGUSON, L. L., & GARIEPY, J. (1989). Growth and aggression: 1. Childhood to early adolescence. *Developmental Psychology, 25,* 320–330.

CAIRNS, R. B., CAIRNS, B. D., NECKERMAN, H. J., GEST, S. D., & GARIEPY, J. (1988). Social networks and aggressive behavior: Peer support or peer rejection. *Developmental Psychology, 24,* 815–823.

CAPALDI, D. M., & PATTERSON, G. R. (1991). Relation of parental transitions to boys' adjustment problems: I. A linear hypothesis. II. Mothers at risk for transition and unskilled parenting. *Developmental Psychology, 27,* 489–504.

CAPLAN, M., VESPO, J., PEDERSEN, J., & HAY, D. F. (1991). Conflict and its resolution in small groups of one- and two-year-olds. *Child Development, 62,* 1513–1524.

CASPI, A., ELDER, G. H., JR., & BEM, D. J. (1987). Moving against the world: Life-course patterns of explosive children. *Developmental Psychology, 23,* 308–313.

CAVAN, R., & FERDINAND, T. (1981). *Juvenile delinquency* (4th ed.). Philadelphia: Lippincott.

CHANDLER, M. J. (1973). Egocentrism and antisocial behavior: The assessment and training of social perspective taking skills. *Developmental Psychology, 9,* 326–332.

CHITTENDEN, G. E. (1942). An experimental study in measuring and modifying assertive behavior in young children. *Monographs of the Society for Research in Child Development, 7* (Serial No. 31).

COIE, J. D., DODGE, K. A., TERRY, R., & WRIGHT, V. (1991). The role of aggression in peer relations: An analysis of aggression episodes in boys' play groups. *Child Development, 62,* 812–826.

CONDRY, J. C., & ROSS, D. F. (1985). Sex and aggression: The influence of gender label on the perception of aggression in children. *Child Development, 56,* 225–233.

COSTABILE, A., SMITH, P. K., MATHESON, L., ASTON, J., HUNTER, T., & BOULTON, M. (1991). Cross-national comparison of how children distinguish serious and playful fighting. *Developmental Psychology, 27,* 881–887.

CUMMINGS, E. M., IANNOTTI, R. J., & ZAHN-WAXLER, C. (1985). Influence of conflict between adults on the emotions and aggression of young children. *Developmental Psychology, 21,* 495–507.

CUMMINGS, E. M., IANNOTTI, R. J., & ZAHN-WAXLER, C. (1989). Aggression between peers in early childhood: Individual continuity and developmental change. *Child Development, 60,* 887–895.

DAVITZ, J. (1952). The effects of previous training on postfrustration behavior. *Journal of Abnormal and Social Psychology, 47,* 309–315.

DISHION, T. J. (1990). The family ecology of boys' peer relations in middle childhood. *Child Development, 61,* 874–892.

DISHION, T. J., PATTERSON, G. R., STOOLMILLER, M., & SKINNER, M. L. (1991). Family, school, and behavioral antecedents to early adolescent involvement with antisocial peers. *Developmental Psychology, 27,* 172–180.

DODGE, K. A. (1980). Social cognition and children's aggressive behavior. *Child Development, 51,* 162–170.

DODGE, K. A. (1986). A social information processing model of social competence in children. In M. Perlmutter (Ed.), *Minnesota symposia on child psychology* (Vol. 18). Hillsdale, NJ: Erlbaum.

DODGE, K. A. (1990). Nature versus nurture in childhood conduct disorder: It is time to ask a different question. *Developmental Psychology, 26,* 698–701.

DODGE, K. A. (in press). Emotion and social information-processing. In J. Garber & K. A. Dodge (Eds.), *The development of emotion regulation and deregulation.* New York: Cambridge University Press.

DODGE, K. A., COIE, J. D., PETTIT, G. S., & PRICE, J. M. (1990). Peer status and aggression in boys' groups: Developmental and contextual analyses. *Child Development, 61,* 1289–1309.

DODGE, K. A., & FRAME, C. L. (1982). Social cognitive biases and deficits in aggressive boys. *Child Development, 53,* 620–635.

DODGE, K. A., MURPHY, R. R., & BUCHSBAUM, K. (1984). The assessment of intention-cue detection skills in children: Implications for developmental psychopathology. *Child Development, 55,* 163–173.

DODGE, K. A., & SOMBERG, D. R. (1987). Hostile attributional biases among aggressive boys are exacerbated under conditions of threats to the self. *Child Development, 58,* 213–224.

DOLLARD, J., DOOB, L. W., MILLER, N. E., MOWRER, O. H., & SEARS, R. P. (1939). *Frustration and aggression.* New Haven, CT: Yale University Press.

DORNBUSCH, S. M., CARLSMITH, J. M., BUSHWALL, S. J., RITTER, P. L., LEIDERMAN, H., HASTORF, A. H., & GROSS, R. T. (1985). Single parents, extended households, and the control of adolescents. *Child Development, 56*, 326–341.

EHRHARDT, A. A., & BAKER, S. W. (1974). Fetal androgens, human central nervous system differentiation, and behavioral sex differences. In R. C. Friedman, R. M. Richard, & R. L. Van de Wiele (Eds.), *Sex differences in behavior.* New York: Wiley.

ELLIOTT, D. S., & AGETON, S. S. (1980). Reconciling race and class differences in self-reported and official estimates of delinquency. *American Sociological Review, 45*, 95–110.

EMMERICH, W. (1966). Continuity and stability in early social development: II. Teacher's ratings. *Child Development, 37*, 17–27.

FABES, R. A., & EISENBERG, N. (1992). Young children's coping with interpersonal anger. *Child Development, 63*, 116–128.

FAGOT, B. I., & LEINBACH, M. D. (1989). The young child's gender schema: Environmental input, internal organization. *Child Development, 60*, 663–672.

FAGOT, B. I., LEINBACH, M. D., & O'BOYLE, C. (1992). Gender labeling, gender stereotyping, and parenting behaviors. *Developmental Psychology, 28*, 225–230.

FARRINGTON, D. P. (1987). Epidemiology. In H. C. Quay (Ed.), *Handbook of juvenile delinquency.* New York: Wiley.

FERGUSON, T. J., & RULE, B. G. (1988). Children's evaluations of retaliatory aggression. *Child Development, 59*, 961–968.

FESHBACH, N. (1978). Studies of the development of children's empathy. In B. Maher (Ed.), *Progress in experimental personality research.* Orlando, FL: Academic Press.

FESHBACH, N., & FESHBACH, S. (1982). Empathy training and the regulation of aggression: Potentialities and limitations. *Academic Psychology Bulletin, 4*, 399–413.

FESHBACH, S. (1956). The catharsis hypothesis and some consequences of interaction with aggressive and neutral play objects. *Journal of Personality, 24*, 449–461.

FESHBACH, S. (1964). The function of aggression and the regulation of aggressive drive. *Psychological Review, 71*, 257–272.

FESHBACH, S. (1970). Aggression. In P. H. Mussen (Ed.), *Carmichael's manual of child psychology* (Vol. 2). New York: Wiley.

GOODENOUGH, F. L. (1931). *Anger in young children.* Minneapolis: University of Minnesota Press.

GORER, G. (1968). Man has no "killer" instinct. In M. F. A. Montague (Ed.), *Man and aggression.* New York: Oxford University Press.

GRAHAM, S., HUDLEY, C., & WILLIAMS, E. (1992). Attributional and emotional determinants of aggression among African-American and Latino young adolescents. *Developmental Psychology, 28*, 731–740.

GUERRA, N. G., & SLABY, R. G. (1990). Cognitive mediators of aggression in adolescent offenders: 2. Intervention. *Developmental Psychology, 26*, 269–277.

GUMP, P. V. (1975). Ecological psychology and children. In E. M. Hetherington (Ed.), *Review of child development research* (Vol. 5). Chicago: University of Chicago Press.

HART, C. H., LADD, G. W., & BURLESON, B. R. (1990). Children's expectations of the outcomes of social strategies: Relations with socioeconomic status and maternal disciplinary styles. *Child Development, 61*, 127–137.

HARTUP, W. W. (1974). Aggression in childhood: Developmental perspectives. *American Psychologist, 29*, 336–341.

HAY, D. F. (1984). Conflict in early childhood. In G. J. Whitehurst (Ed.), *Annals of child development* (Vol. 1). Greenwich, CT: JAI Press.

HENNIGAN, K. M., Del ROSARIO, M. L., HEATH, L., COOK, T. D., WHARTON, J. D., & CALDER, B. J. (1982). Impact of the introduction of television on crime in the United States: Empirical findings and theoretical implications. *Journal of Personality and Social Psychology, 42*, 461–477.

HOFFMAN, M. L. (1988). Moral development. In M. H. Bornstein & M. E. Lamb (Eds.), *Developmental psychology: An advanced textbook* (2nd ed.). Hillsdale, NJ: Erlbaum.

HOLDEN, G. W., & RITCHIE, R. L. (1991). Linking extreme marital discord, child rearing, and child behavior problems: Evidence from battered women. *Child Development, 62*, 311–327.

HUESMANN, L. R., ERON, L. D., LEFKOWITZ, M. M., & WALDER, L. O. (1984). Stability of aggression over time and generations. *Developmental Psychology, 20*, 1120–1134.

HUTT, C. (1972). *Males and females.* Baltimore: Penguin Books.

HYDE, J. S. (1984). How large are gender differences in aggression? A developmental meta-analysis. *Developmental Psychology, 20*, 722–736.

INOFF-GERMAIN, G., ARNOLD, G. S., NOTTLEMAN, E. D., SUSMAN, E. J., CUTLER, G. B., JR., & CHROUSOS, G. P. (1988). Relations between hormone levels and aggressive behavior of young adolescents in family interactions. *Developmental Psychology, 24*, 129–139.

JACKLIN, C. N. (1989). Male and female: Issues of gender. *American Psychologist, 44*, 127–133.

KAGAN, J., & MOSS, H. A. (1962). *Birth to maturity.* New York: Wiley.

KAZDIN, A. E. (1987). *Conduct disorders in childhood and adolescence.* Newbury Park, CA: Sage.

KUO, Z. Y. (1930). The genesis of the cat's response to the rat. *Journal of Comparative and Physiological Psychology, 11*, 1–35.

LERNER, J. V., HERTZOG, C., HOOKER, K. A., HASSIBI, K. A., & THOMAS, A. (1988). A longitudinal study of negative emotional states and adjustment from early childhood through adolescence. *Child Development, 59*, 356–366.

LEWIS, M., ALESSANDRI, S. M., & SULLIVAN, M. W. (1990). Violation of expectancy, loss of control, and anger expressions in young children. *Developmental Psychology, 26*, 745–751.

LOEBER, R. (1982). The stability of antisocial behavior: A review. *Child Development, 53*, 1431–1446.

LORENZ, K. (1966). *On aggression.* San Diego: Harcourt Brace Jovanovich.

LOVAAS, O. I. (1961). Interaction between verbal and nonverbal behavior. *Child Development, 32*, 329–336.

LYTTON, H. (1990). Child and parent effects in boys' conduct disorder: A reinterpretation. *Developmental Psychology, 26,* 683–697.

MACCOBY, E. E. (1980). *Social development: Psychological growth and the parent-child relationship.* San Diego: Harcourt Brace Jovanovich.

MACCOBY, E. E., & JACKLIN, C. N. (1974). *The psychology of sex differences.* Stanford, CA: Stanford University Press.

MACCOBY, E. E., & JACKLIN, C. N. (1980). Sex differences in aggression: A rejoinder and reprise. *Child Development, 51,* 964–980.

MALLICK, S. K., & McCANDLESS, B. R. (1966). A study of the catharsis of aggression. *Journal of Personality and Social Psychology, 4,* 591–596.

MEAD, M. (1935). *Sex and temperament in three primitive societies.* New York: William Morrow.

MIDDLEBROOK, P. N. (1974). *Social psychology and modern life.* New York: Knopf.

MILLER, N. E. (1941). The frustration-aggression hypothesis. *Psychological Review, 48,* 337–342.

MILLER, P., & SPERRY, L. (1987). The socialization of anger and aggression. *Merrill-Palmer Quarterly, 33,* 1–31.

MILLS, R. S. L., & RUBIN, K. H. (1990). Parental beliefs about problematic social behaviors in early childhood. *Child Development, 61,* 138–151.

MONEY, J., & EHRHARDT, A. (1972). *Man and woman, boy and girl.* Baltimore: Johns Hopkins University Press.

MOSS, H. A. (1967). Sex, age, and state as determinants of mother-infant interaction. *Merrill-Palmer Quarterly, 13,* 19–36.

NELSON-LeGALL, S. A. (1985). Motive-outcome matching and outcome foreseeability: Effects on attribution of intentionality and moral judgments. *Developmental Psychology, 21,* 332–337.

NEWCOMB, M. D., & BENTLER, P. M. (1989). Substance use and abuse among children and teenagers. *American Psychologist, 44,* 242–248.

OLWEUS, D. (1978). *Aggression in the schools: Bullies and whipping boys.* Washington, DC: Hemisphere.

OLWEUS, D. (1980). Familial and temperamental determinants of aggressive behavior in adolescent boys: A causal analysis. *Developmental Psychology, 16,* 644–660.

OLWEUS, D. (1984). Aggressors and their victims: Bullying at school. In H. Frude & H. Gault (Eds.), *Disruptive behaviors in schools.* New York: Wiley.

OLWEUS, D. (1987, Fall). Schoolyard bullying: Grounds for intervention. *School Safety,* pp. 4–11.

OLWEUS, D., MATTSSON, A., SCHALLING, D., & LOW, H. (1980). Testosterone, aggression, physical and personality dimensions in normal adolescent males. *Psychosomatic Medicine, 42,* 253–269.

PARKE, R. D., & SLABY, R. G. (1983). The development of aggression. In P. H. Mussen (Ed.), *Handbook of child psychology.* Vol. 4: *Socialization, personality, and social development.* New York: Wiley.

PATTERSON, G. R. (1981). Mothers: The unacknowledged victims. *Monographs of the Society for Research in Child Development, 45*(5, Serial No. 186).

PATTERSON, G. R. (1982). *Coercive family processes.* Eugene, OR: Castilia Press.

PATTERSON, G. R. (1986). The contribution of siblings to training for fighting: A microsocial analysis. In D. Olweus, J. Block, & M. Radke-Yarrow (Eds.), *Development of antisocial and prosocial behavior.* Orlando, FL: Academic Press.

PATTERSON, G. R., DeBARYSHE, B. D., & RAMSEY, E. (1989). A developmental perspective on antisocial behavior. *American Psychologist, 44,* 329–335.

PATTERSON, G. R., LITTMAN, R. A., & BRICKER, W. (1967). Assertive behavior in children: A step toward a theory of aggression. *Monographs of the Society for Research in Child Development, 32*(5, Serial No. 113).

PATTERSON, G. R., & STOUTHAMER-LOEBER, M. (1984). The correlation of family management practices and delinquency. *Child Development, 55,* 1299–1307.

PERRY, D. G., & BUSSEY, K. (1977). Self-reinforcement in high- and low-aggressive boys following acts of aggression. *Child Development, 48,* 653–657.

PERRY, D. G., KUSEL, S. J., & PERRY, L. C. (1988). Victims of peer aggression. *Developmental Psychology, 24,* 807–814.

PERRY, D. G., & PERRY, L. C. (1974). Denial of suffering in the victim as a stimulus to violence in aggressive boys. *Child Development, 45,* 55–62.

PERRY, D. G., PERRY, L. C., & RASMUSSEN, P. (1986). Cognitive social learning mediators of aggression. *Child Development, 57,* 700–711.

PERRY, D. G., PERRY, L. C., & WEISS, R. J. (1989). Sex differences in the consequences that children anticipate for aggression. *Developmental Psychology, 25,* 312–319.

PERRY, D. G., WILLIARD, J. C., & PERRY, L. C. (1990). Peers' perceptions of the consequences that victimized children provide aggressors. *Child Development, 61,* 1310–1325.

PETTIT, G. S., DODGE, K. A., & BROWN, M. M. (1988). Early family experience, social problem-solving patterns, and children's social competence. *Child Development, 59,* 107–120.

PIAGET, J. (1952). *The origins of intelligence in children.* New York: International Universities Press.

PORTER, B., & O'LEARY, K. D. (1980). Marital discord and childhood behavior problems. *Journal of Abnormal Child Psychology, 8,* 287–295.

QUIGGLE, N. L., GARBER, J., PANAK, W. F., & DODGE, K. A. (1992). Social information processing in aggressive and depressed children. *Child Development, 63,* 1305–1320.

RABINER, D. L., LENHART, L., & LOCHMAN, J. E. (1990). Automatic versus reflective social problem solving in relation to children's sociometric status. *Developmental Psychology, 26,* 1010–1016.

ROSE, R. M., BERNSTEIN, I. S., & GORDON, T. P. (1975). Consequences of social conflict on plasma testosterone levels in rhesus monkeys. *Psychosomatic Medicine, 37,* 50–61.

ROSS, H., TESLA, C., KENYON, B., & LOLLIS, S. (1990). Maternal intervention in toddler peer conflict: The socialization of principles of justice. *Developmental Psychology, 26,* 994–1003.

RULE, B. G., FERGUSON, T. J., & NESDALE, A. R. (1980). Emotional arousal, anger, and aggression: The misattribution principle. In P. Pliner, K. Blankstein, & T. Spiegel (Eds.), *Advances in communication and affect.* Hillsdale, NJ: Erlbaum.

RUSHTON, J. P., FULKER, D. W., NEALE, M. C., NIAS, D. K. B., & EYSENCK, H. J. (1986). Altruism and aggression: The heritability of individual differences. *Journal of Personality and Social Psychology, 50,* 1192–1198.

SACKIN, S., & THELEN, E. (1984). An ethological study of peaceful associative outcomes to conflict in preschool children. *Child Development, 55,* 1098–1102.

SANCILIO, M. F. M., PLUMERT, J. M., & HARTUP, W. W. (1989). Friendship and aggressiveness as determinants of conflict outcomes in middle childhood. *Developmental Psychology, 25,* 812–819.

SCOTT, J. P. (1966). Agonistic behavior in mice and rats: A review. *American Zoologist, 6,* 683–701.

SCOTT, J. P. (1972). Hostility and aggression. In B. Wolman (Ed.), *Handbook of genetic psychology.* Englewood Cliffs, NJ: Prentice-Hall.

SEARS, R. R. (1958). Personality development in the family. In J. M. Seidman (Ed.), *The child.* New York: Holt, Rinehart & Winston.

SEARS, R. R., MACCOBY, E. E., & LEVIN, H. (1957). *Patterns of child rearing.* New York: Harper & Row.

SHANTZ, C. U. (1987). Conflicts between children. *Child Development, 58,* 283–305.

SHANTZ, D. W., & VOYDANOFF, D. A. (1973). Situational effects on retaliatory aggression at three age levels. *Child Development, 44,* 149–153.

SHURE, M. B. (1989). Interpersonal competence training. In W. Damon (Ed.), *Child development today and tomorrow.* San Francisco: Jossey-Bass.

SIEGAL, A. E., & KOHN, L. G. (1959). Permissiveness, permission, and aggression: The effect of adult presence or absence on aggression in children's play. *Child Development, 30,* 131–141.

SLABY, R. G., & CROWLEY, C. G. (1977). Modification of cooperation and aggression through teacher attention to children's speech. *Journal of Experimental Child Psychology, 23,* 442–458.

SLABY, R. G., & GUERRA, N. G. (1988). Cognitive mediators of aggression in adolescent offenders: 1. Assessment. *Developmental Psychology, 24,* 580–588.

SLUCKIN, A. M., & SMITH, P. K. (1977). Two approaches to the concept of dominance in preschool children. *Child Development, 48,* 917–923.

SMITH, P. K., & CONNOLLY, K. J. (1980). *The ecology of preschool behavior.* New York: Cambridge University Press.

STEINBERG, L. (1987). Single parents, stepparents, and the susceptibility of adolescents to antisocial peer pressure. *Child Development, 58,* 269–275.

STRAYER, F. F. (1980). Social ecology of the preschool peer group. In W. A. Collins (Ed.), *Minnesota Symposia on Child Psychology.* Vol. 13: *Development of cognition, affect, and social relations.* Hillsdale, NJ: Erlbaum.

SUSMAN, E. J., INOFF-GERMAIN, G., NOTTELMAN, E. D., LORIAUX, D. L., CUTLER, G. G., JR., & CHROUSOS, G. P. (1987). Hormones, emotional dispositions, and aggressive attributes in young adolescents. *Child Development, 58,* 1114–1134.

THORNBURG, H. D. (1986). Adolescent delinquency and families. In G. K. Leigh & G. W. Peterson (Eds.), *Adolescents in families.* Cincinnati: South-Western.

TIEGER, T. (1980). On the biological bases of sex differences in aggression. *Child Development, 51,* 943–963.

TOCH, H. (1969). *Violent men.* Hawthorne, NY: Aldine.

TURNBULL, C. M. (1972). *The mountain people.* New York: Simon & Schuster.

TURNER, C. W., & GOLDSMITH, D. (1976). Effects of toy guns and airplanes on children's antisocial free play behavior. *Journal of Experimental Child Psychology, 21,* 303–315.

UNIFORM CRIME REPORTS FOR THE UNITED STATES, 1989. Federal Bureau of Investigation. Washington, DC: U.S. Government Printing Office.

VUCHINICH, S., BANK. L., & PATTERSON, G. R. (1992). Parenting, peers, and the stability of antisocial behavior in preadolescent boys. *Developmental Psychology, 28,* 510–521.

WALLERSTEIN, J. S., & KELLY, J. B. (1980). *Surviving the breakup: How children and parents cope with divorce.* New York: Basic Books.

WALTERS, R. H., & BROWN, M. (1963). Studies of reinforcement of aggression: Transfer of responses to an interpersonal situation. *Child Development, 34,* 562–571.

WEISS, B., DODGE, K. A., BATES, J. E., & PETTIT, G. S. (1992). Some consequences of early harsh discipline: Child aggression and a maladaptive social information processing style. *Child Development, 63,* 1321–1335.

WHITING, B. B., & EDWARDS, C. P. (1988). *Children of different worlds: The formation of social behavior.* Cambridge, MA: Harvard University Press.

WOLFF, M., RUTTEN, P., & BAYER, A. F. III (1992). *Where we stand: Can America make it in the race for health, wealth, and happiness?* New York: Bantam Books.

YOUNG, W. C., GOY, R. W., & PHOENIX, C. H. (1964). Hormones and sexual behavior. *Science, 143,* 212–218.

ZAHAVI, S., & ASHER, S. R. (1978). The effect of verbal instructions on preschool children's aggressive behavior. *Journal of School Psychology, 16,* 146–153.

ZAHN-WAXLER, C., RADKE-YARROW, M., & KING, R. A. (1979). Child rearing and children's prosocial initiations toward victims of distress. *Child Development, 50,* 319–330.

11 Development of Altruism and Prosocial Behavior

At some point during the prehistoric era, humans became social animals. Groups of men, women, and children began to form collectives, or tribal units, which provided increased protection against common enemies and allowed individuals to share the many labors necessary for their survival. One rule of order that undoubtedly characterized these early cooperative social groupings was some version of what we now know as the **norm of social responsibility** (see Berkowitz & Daniels, 1963), which prescribes that *one should help others who need help*. This ideal is endorsed by most people in most cultures (Krebs, 1970), and its widespread acceptance has led many social philosophers to conclude that a concern for one's fellow human beings is a basic value of our species.

However, several psychoanalytic and social-learning theorists have not given prosocial behavior (behavior that benefits others) a prominent place in their overall view of personality development. They have traditionally stressed our self-serving side, depicting us as creatures who strive to attain power or self-advancement. Consequently, one individual is thought to help another only when he or she expects some personal gain or reward for doing so.

Surely this view of human nature is oversimplified. All of us can probably recall an occasion when one person has made a great personal sacrifice to help another without expecting anything in return. For example, what self-serving principle motivates the soldier who hurls himself on a live grenade in order to save his buddies? What personal gain could possibly have motivated the behavior of the many Germans who *risked their lives* to save Jewish citizens during World War II? Many of these "rescuers" did not even know the names of the people they saved, much less receive rewards from them (Rosenhan, 1972a). In short, people often help others, even if this helping involves some cost to themselves and promises very little in the way of personal gain or reward.

In this chapter we will explore the issue of how children acquire the capacity to give of themselves in order to benefit others. Our first task is to determine what psychologists mean by the terms *prosocial behavior* and *altruism*. We will then discuss several theoretical explanations for these interesting and often self-sacrificial forms of social behavior. Next we will chart the development of prosocial behavior from infancy to adolescence, noting who is most likely to benefit whom, and when. Finally, we will review the effects of many variables that are thought to foster prosocial inclinations and then conclude by discussing some strategies that adults might use to promote children's concern about the welfare of others.

What Are Altruism and Prosocial Behavior?

Prosocial behavior is *any action that benefits other people*, such as sharing with someone less fortunate than oneself, comforting or rescuing a distressed person, cooperating with someone or helping him or her to achieve an objective, or even simply making others feel good by complimenting them on their appearance or accomplishments. Now, before proceeding further, briefly scan the nine situations presented in Figure 11-1. Most of us would probably agree that these acts are examples of prosocial behavior. But would you consider each of them to be *altruistic*?

Were I to ask this question of 30 students, there would be disagreement on whether several of the acts in Figure 11-1 qualify as **altruism**. Moreover, psychologists interested in prosocial behavior would debate the very same points, and for reasons that should become quite apparent as we discuss the two most common definitions of altruism.

A Motivational/Intentional Definition of Altruism

Those who favor a **motivational/intentional definition of altruism** focus on the motives, or intentions, that underlie prosocial acts. According to this perspective, an act of kindness can be labeled "altruistic" if the actor's *primary* motive, or intent, is to provide positive consequences for another person. In

| | Altruistic? | | |
Situation	Yes	Undecided	No
1. John S., a millionaire, makes a $50,000 contribution to AIDS research.	___	___	___
2. Sam P., a talented professional football player, agrees to donate his time to tape a commercial for the United Way.	___	___	___
3. Susie Q., an 8-year-old, freely chooses to spend Halloween night trick-or-treating for the March of Dimes.	___	___	___
4. Noriko H. comforts a crying child who is lost in a large department store.	___	___	___
5. Odell W. intervenes to help a woman who is being mugged, and he is stabbed to death.	___	___	___
6. Tammy P. gives part of her 25¢ allowance to a friend who has no money.	___	___	___
7. John B. gives a pint of blood to a blood bank and receives $10 for his donation.	___	___	___
8. Juan K. repays Jim L. for a previous favor by offering to help Jim paint his garage.	___	___	___
9. Jack R., a used-car salesman, gives a quarter to the child of a customer when the child cries that she is thirsty for a soft drink.	___	___	___

You may want to compare your responses with those of your friends or other members of your class. Looking at the pattern of your own responses, do you favor a motivational or a behavioral definition of altruism?

FIGURE 11-1   When is a prosocial act altruistic?

other words, the true altruist acts more out of a concern for others than for the positive outcomes he or she may obtain as a result of helping, sharing with, or comforting them. Proponents of the motivational definition would classify a prosocial act as non-altruistic if the actor hopes to reap significant personal gains from his or her benevolence or is simply repaying the recipient for a favor.

Although a majority of my students endorse a motivational definition of altruism, the more skepti-

cal minority seriously doubt that any form of helping is motivated solely out of a concern for others, without regard for the self. The minority may have a point, for it is often difficult to determine exactly what motivates a helping act. Consider situation 1 of Figure 11-1. John S. could be considered altruistic if we conclude that his donation was prompted by a desire to help find a cure for AIDS. But we would probably label his act nonaltruistic if we learned that John suffers from AIDS or if we decided that his donation was intended as a tax write-off. Even Odell W. in situation 5 could conceivably be seeking the adulation of the female victim or "doing the right thing" in order to maintain his own self-respect or to ensure that he makes it to heaven. If so, his behavior does not qualify as altruism under a motivational definition. Consider one more example: suppose you found a wallet containing a large sum of money, returned it to its owner, and subsequently declined a monetary offering with the statement "Your thanks is my reward." Is this "thank you" a sufficient reward to render your behavior nonaltruistic? The problems involved in inferring a helper's true intentions have led many psychologists to conclude that altruism is best defined behaviorally.

A Behavioral Definition of Altruism

According to the **behavioral definition of altruism**, an altruistic act is one that benefits another person, *regardless of the actor's motives*. In other words, altruism and prosocial behavior are viewed as roughly synonymous concepts, so that any and all of the acts described in Figure 11-1 could be labeled "altruistic."

What kinds of behaviors do children view as altruistic? How do their views differ from those of adults? Lizette Peterson and Donna Gelfand (1984) addressed these issues by asking college students and first-, fourth-, and sixth-graders to rate the altruistic motivation of different children who had helped adults (1) out of empathy, (2) to obtain a tangible reward, (3) to win praise, (4) to repay a favor, or (5) to avoid criticism. Even the first-graders knew that an actor who helped in order to avoid criticism was not displaying an altruistic motive. However, they felt that all the other actors were about equally altruistic, regardless of their reasons for helping. Surprisingly, perhaps, fourth- and sixth-graders showed roughly the same pattern of results—thus indicating that even 9–12-year-olds often fail to discriminate the motives underlying prosocial acts and seem to favor a behavioral definition of altruism. By contrast, the adults in this study favored the motivational definition, for they attributed greater altruism to helpers who had empathized with the recipient than to those who were simply repaying a favor or

who had something to gain (praise or a tangible reward) from their assistance.

Yet, even though adults generally favor a motivational definition of altruism, neither they nor most developmentalists make sharp distinctions between altruism and prosocial behavior when referring (or responding) to the benevolence of young children. One reason they don't is that people (even second-graders) generally perceive themselves as having less obligation to do something nice for others (the positive side of morality) than to inhibit harmdoing and antisocial conduct (the negative side of morality) (Grusec, 1991; Kahn, 1992). In other words, benevolent acts, although socially sanctioned, often have a *discretionary* quality about them and, thus, are often *not* mandatory. So, in the interest of promoting such nonobligatory behaviors, parents and other socialization agents are likely to view a variety of benevolent acts as "good" and worthy of praise (even if not wholly altruistic).

Nevertheless, there are developmentalists who argue that the motivational bases of children's early acts of kindness have important implications for predicting future conduct. David Rosenhan (1972b), for example, has proposed a distinction between **autonomous altruism** (those prosocial acts motivated by a concern for others) and **normative altruism** (those acts of kindness committed in expectation of receiving personal benefits or avoiding criticism for failing to act). Later in the chapter we will see that this distinction may indeed be useful, for these two kinds of prosocial conduct may evolve along separate developmental paths.

Theories of Altruism and Prosocial Development

Several theorists have debated the issue of whether altruism is innate or learned. *Ethologists* and *sociobiologists* believe that altruism is a preadapted, genetically programmed attribute—a basic component of human nature—that helps to ensure the survival of the species. By contrast, *psychoanalytic* and *social-learning theorists* argue that a child's prosocial inclinations derive not from his or her genes or evolutionary history but, rather, from experiences with social agents (altruism is acquired). *Cognitive-developmental theorists* can certainly agree with this latter point of view; however, they would add that both the form and the frequency of a child's prosocial conduct will depend, in part, on his or her cognitive skills and level of intellectual development.

It will become apparent from our review that each of these theories has a particular focus that is not shared by the others, and, as a result, no one of them provides a complete explanation of human altruism. Yet these models have stimulated a plethora of research from which we have gained important insights about the origins and development of children's altruistic concern.

Biological Theories:
Are We "Programmed" for Prosocial Conduct?

In 1965 Donald Campbell argued that altruism is, in part, instinctive—a basic component of human nature. His argument hinged on the assumption that individuals, be they animal or human, are more likely to receive protection from natural enemies and to satisfy their basic needs if they live together in cooperative social units. If this assumption is correct, then cooperative, altruistic individuals would be most likely to survive and to pass along "altruistic genes" to their offspring. Thus, over thousands of years, evolutionary processes would favor the development of innate prosocial motives.[1] Campbell aptly notes that "the tremendous survival value of being social makes innate social motives as likely on *a priori* grounds as self-centered ones" (1965, p. 301).

Sociobiologists have extended Campbell's theory, arguing that altruism is particularly adaptive when our benevolence promotes the survival of *our*

own genes* (Cunningham, 1986; Rushton, 1989). Accordingly, we should be more inclined to comfort, share with, or help close relatives who share our genes (a process known as *kin selection*) than other people to whom we are unrelated. Cunningham (1986) has tested this **"kin selection" hypothesis** in a study with adults. Subjects were given a long list of prosocial behaviors and were asked which of these acts they would be willing to perform for a number of recipients, ranging from close relatives to complete strangers. The results were clear: subjects' willingness to act in the interest of others was directly related to the degree of kinship between them and the prospective recipients. Close relatives were more likely to be helped than distant relatives, who in turn would receive more assistance than nonrelatives. Though consistent with the kin-selection hypothesis, these data are obviously amenable to alternative interpretations. For example, one might argue that we have developed attachments to our relatives (particularly to close relatives) and that these emotional outgrowths of our social lives are what really account for our heightened benevolence toward close kin.

If there is a genetic basis for altruism, then what exactly do we inherit that makes us prosocially inclined? Martin Hoffman (1981, 1988) proposes that a capacity for *empathy*—the tendency to become aroused by another person's distress—may be the biological mediator of altruistic concern. Indeed, we noted in Box 2-2 that newborn infants may be displaying a primitive empathic reaction when they become distressed at the sound of another infant's cries. And we also learned (in Chapter 2) that empathy is a heritable attribute, for identical twins are much more alike in empathic concern than fraternal twins (Matthews et al., 1981). Later in this chapter we will see that there is a meaningful relationship between a person's empathic sensitivities and his or her prosocial behavior. However, this does not necessarily imply that altruism is biologically programmed, for, as Hoffman (1981) has argued, an inborn capacity for empathy is subject to environmental influence and may be fostered or dramatically inhibited by the social environments in which children are raised. With that comment in mind, let's

---

[1]One such motive might be *reciprocal altruism*—the idea that people are genetically programmed to help others because one day these recipients of aid will reciprocate by aiding the original benefactor and/or his genetic relatives, thus serving to ensure their survival (Trivers, 1971, 1983).

turn to other theories that stress environmental contributions to children's prosocial development.

Psychoanalytic Theory:
Let Your Conscience Be Your Guide

Recall from our discussion of psychoanalytic theory
(Chapter 2) that its originator, Sigmund Freud,
described the young, unsocialized child as a self-
serving creature constantly driven by id-based, hedonistic impulses. This characterization of human
nature might seem to suggest that the concept of
altruism offers a severe challenge to a psychoanalytic account of personality development: how is it
possible for a selfish, egoistic child to acquire a
sense of altruistic concern that will occasionally dictate that he or she make self-sacrificing responses to
benefit others?

The challenge is not so formidable as it first appears. According to proponents of psychoanalytic
theory, altruistic norms and principles—for example, the social responsibility norm and the Golden
Rule—are but a few of the many prescriptions and
values that may be internalized during the period of
childhood in which the superego develops. We will
examine the process of superego development in
some detail when we discuss moral development
(Chapter 12), but for the moment it should be noted
that a necessary condition for the development of
altruism is exposure to altruistic values within the
context of a warm, nurturant parent/child relationship. Once altruistic principles are internalized and
become part of the ego-ideal, the child strives to
help others in need in order to avoid punishment
from the conscience (guilt, shame, self-degradation)
for failing to render such assistance.

Social-Learning Theory: What's in It for Me?

Altruism presents an interesting paradox for social-
learning theory (Rosenhan, 1972a). A central premise of the social-learning approach is that people
repeat behaviors that are reinforced and avoid repeating responses that prove costly or punishing.
Yet many prosocial acts seem to defy this view of
human nature: altruists often choose to take dangerous risks, forgo personal rewards, and donate
their own valuable resources (thereby incurring a
loss) in order to benefit others. The challenge for
social-learning theorists is to explain how these self-
sacrificial tendencies are acquired and maintained.

Responses to the challenge have been many and
varied. On a conceptual level, several reinforcement
theorists have taken the position that all prosocial
acts, even those that prove extremely costly to the
benefactor, are prompted by some form of subtle reward or self-gain. For example, we could argue that
the German citizens who risked their lives to rescue
Jews from Nazi tormentors did so in order to increase their self-esteem, to win a favorable evaluation from future generations, or to reap the benefits
afforded to morally righteous people in the afterlife.
The major problem with this explanation is its circu-
larity: it is assumed that, since helping behavior occurred, its consequences must have been reinforcing (Sigelman, 1984).

Although tangible rewards do not always follow
altruistic responses, altruism may still be a function
of social learning and reinforcement. Let's consider
three ways in which children might learn that altruism "pays off."

Conditioning of empathic responses.
Our capacity
for empathy may help to explain why we might
help, comfort, or share with others in situations in
which there are no obvious tangible rewards to sustain helping behavior. In Chapter 10 we defined empathy as the ability to recognize and experience the
emotions of others. If an empathizer were to observe a happy or joyful person, she too might experience a pleasant, positive feeling and might be
motivated to prolong the person's happiness as a
means of sustaining her own good mood. Similarly,
an empathizer might experience pain and suffering
if exposed to a person who expresses these negative
emotions. Assisting a suffering victim not only
would relieve the victim's distress but also might reinforce the benefactor by relieving her vicarious distress. In sum, prosocial responses may often appear
to be self-sacrificing when, in fact, they *reinforce* the
helper by making her feel good or by relieving empathic discomfort.

How and when do children begin to associate
their own empathic reactions with the performance

of altruistic responses? According to Eleanor Maccoby (1980), the empathic mediation of altruism may develop through classical conditioning and begin very early in life:

> With empathic distress the process would work in the following way: A twelve-month-old has cried on hundreds of different occasions and the sound of crying has repeatedly been associated with the child's own distress. And so by a process of [classical conditioning], the sound of crying—anyone's crying—can now evoke feelings of distress . . . and even tears. If the young listener thinks of a way to make the other person stop crying, he or she will feel better. From the standpoint of simple self-interest, then, we should expect children to learn to perform such "altruistic" actions [p. 347].

Direct tuition of altruism.   Neo-Hullian and operant-learning theorists argue that we may often behave altruistically without expecting immediate payoffs because previous rewards for similar acts of kindness have made such behavior intrinsically reinforcing. The process might work this way: Parents, teachers, Sunday-school instructors, and other socializing agents often preach the virtues of prosocial conduct and reward children who behave accordingly. Over a period of time (and reinforcements), some of the positive affect stemming from these rewards becomes associated with the prosocial acts that are rewarded, so that altruistic gestures eventually become conditioned, or secondary, reinforcers that, when enacted, make the child feel good. And, because individuals in most cultures receive periodic praise, recognition, or other forms of extrinsic reinforcement for their benevolence, prosocial acts may retain their "satisfying" qualities and become extremely resistant to extinction.

Observational learning of altruism.   Although conceding that altruistic habits might be acquired through classical-conditioning processes or direct tuition, Albert Bandura (1989) believes that the most pervasive influence on children's altruism is the behavior of other people—the social models to which they are exposed. And he may be right, for it is now apparent that children who witness the charitable acts of an altruistic model often become more altru-

istic themselves (see Radke-Yarrow, Zahn-Waxler, & Chapman, 1983, for a review). In one study, Rosenhan and White (1967) had fourth- and fifth-graders take turns playing a bowling game with an adult model. Each "winning" score of 20 attained by either the child or the adult earned the player two five-cent gift certificates that were redeemable at a local candy store. Children exposed to a *charitable* model saw the adult place one of his two gift certificates into a container labeled "Trenton Orphans' Fund" after each of his winning trials. In a *control* condition, the model did not donate any of his gift certificates to the orphans. At the conclusion of this "training" phase, the model pretended to have work to do elsewhere. The child was then left alone to play the bowling game. Before departing, the model told the child to return to the classroom after completing 20 plays. The outcomes for these 20 trials were rigged so that each child had four winning scores and thus four opportunities to donate gift certificates to needy children.

The results were clear. Of the children who had been exposed to a charitable model, 63% contributed to the orphans' fund during the training trials when the model was present. Perhaps these donations represent nothing more than normative altruism, for they may have been made in an attempt to win the approval of a charitable adult. Would these children behave in a similar fashion *when the model left the room*? Presumably, donations made in the model's absence are motivated by a concern for others (autonomous altruism) rather than by a desire to win the model's approval. Rosenhan and White found that 47.5% of the children who had witnessed the charitable model donated some of their gift certificates when the model was absent. However, not one of the children in the control group made a donation to the orphans' fund *at any time during the procedure*. So it appears that observation of a charitable model can promote both normative and autonomous altruism in grade-school children.

We have noted on many occasions that observers are especially willing to imitate a social model if the model's behavior is reinforced. Thus it might seem that the influence of altruistic modeling presents a challenge for social-learning theory. Why should

PHOTOS 11-1   Children learn many prosocial lessons by observing the behavior of altruistic models.

children follow the lead of prosocial models when these charitable individuals incur personal costs and receive little or no tangible benefits for their exemplary behavior?

The answer may lie in the ways children process the relevant social information and interpret what they have seen. For example, Kohlberg (1969) argues that the model's behavior merely informs the child of what older, more competent people consider an "appropriate" or mature response under the circumstances. Presumably, the child then follows the model's example as part of his attempt to emulate the behavior of competent others; that is, imitating competent people is intrinsically reinforcing. A second possibility is that the model's prosocial acts simply remind children of the norm of social responsibility, which they may have already internalized. Finally, children may learn that altruism is *self-reinforcing* if altruistic models reinforce themselves by expressing happiness or some other form of positive affect when they help others. Indeed, Midlarsky and Bryan (1972) discovered that models who express positive affect while helping—for example, "Giving to the poor makes me feel *good*"— elicit more prosocial behavior from fourth- and fifth-grade children than equally charitable models who express positive affect that is unrelated to their acts of kindness (such as "This game is fun").

In sum, learning theorists have offered several plausible explanations for children's willingness to perform prosocial acts that promise few if any tangible rewards and may even be costly to themselves. In a later section of the chapter we will follow up on these ideas by taking a closer look at the contributions of reinforcement, empathy, and social-modeling influences to children's prosocial development.

Cognitive Theories of Altruism: Is Maturity the Medium?

Both cognitive-developmental theorists and social information-processing theorists assume that prosocial responses such as cooperating, sharing, giving reassurance and comfort, and volunteering to help others should become increasingly apparent over the course of childhood (Chapman et al., 1987; Eisenberg, Lennon, & Roth, 1983; Kohlberg, 1969). The basis for this prediction is straightforward: as children develop intellectually, they will acquire important cognitive skills that will affect both their reasoning about prosocial issues and their motivation to act in the interests of others.

Cognitive theorists have proposed that there are four broad phases of prosocial development. The first phase, in which some sharing and demonstrations of sympathy are observed, occurs in the second year of life and is thought to be tied to the infant's ability to recognize himself and to differentiate the self from other people (Hoffman, 1988; Zahn-Waxler et al., 1992). As we will see in our next section, this is the period when infants begin to react more reliably to others' distress, often becoming distressed themselves (that is, empathizing) and occasionally trying to cheer a distressed companion. The second broad phase of development roughly coincides with Piaget's preoperational period (ages 3–6). Presumably, young preschool children are still relatively egocentric, and their thinking about prosocial issues (as well as their actual behavior) is often self-serving, or hedonistic: acts that benefit others are considered worth performing if those acts will also benefit the self. During middle childhood and preadolescence (or Piaget's concrete-operational stage), children are becoming less egocentric, are acquiring important role-taking skills, and should now begin to focus on the legitimate needs of others as a justification for prosocial behavior. This is the period when children begin to think that any act of kindness that most people would condone is probably "good" and should be performed. It is also the stage at which empathic or sympathetic responses should become an important mediator of altruism. Finally, adolescents who have reached formal operations have begun to understand and appreciate the implications of abstract prosocial norms—universal principles (such as the norm of social responsibility or the Golden Rule) that (1) encourage them to direct their acts of kindness to a wider range of prospective recipients and (2) trigger strong attributions of personal responsibility for prosocial conduct and feelings of guilt or self-condemnation should they callously ignore their obligations (Chapman et al., 1987; Eisenberg et al., 1983).

Most cognitively oriented researchers have not attempted to delineate the stages of prosocial development that children pass through, choosing instead to explore the relationship between the growth of particular cognitive skills (for example, role taking) and children's prosocial behavior. Yet, in recent years, Nancy Eisenberg and her associates have begun to chart age-related changes in children's reasoning about prosocial issues, and her results are indeed interesting. We will review both these lines of inquiry in a later section of the chapter.

A Final Comment

Although research on the nature of children's moral transgressions and the development of moral inhibitions has a long and storied history (which we will discuss in Chapter 12), only within the past 25 years have social developmentalists taken a strong interest in altruism and the growth of prosocial behavior.[2] And, even though ethologists, sociobiologists, and behavior geneticists have called our attention to possible biological bases of prosocial conduct and have proposed a number of intriguing ideas that are definitely worth pursuing, most of the existing work on prosocial development stems from either the social-learning or the cognitive approach. These two theories are often viewed as more conflicting or contradictory than they really are. In truth, they emphasize *different* aspects of development:

> The social-learning approach emphasizes the role of antecedent and consequent environmental events (e.g., the presence or absence of a model or reinforcement), [whereas] the cognitive-developmental approach emphasizes the role of cognitive structures as measured, for example, by role-taking tasks and moral judgment stories [Rushton, 1976, p. 909].

I will simply add that predictions derived from both theories have received empirical confirmation, sometimes in the same experiment! For example, Rushton (1975) found that children exposed to charitable models were later more charitable themselves than were agemates exposed to selfish models—a finding consistent with social-learning theory. However, closer inspection of the data revealed that

---

[2]One reason for this earlier lack of interest in altruism was the widespread belief (mostly among academics influenced by operant-learning theory) that true altruism—a willingness to make self-sacrifices without expectations of benefiting oneself—never occurs. Indeed, one of my student colleagues in graduate school (during the late '60s) was not allowed to pursue his chosen thesis topic (the child-rearing antecedents of *self-sacrifice*) because no faculty member at our university would supervise research addressing what the faculty labeled a "nonexistent phenomenon."

children who had tested relatively high (that is, mature) in their levels of moral reasoning were much more charitable overall and were more likely to criticize the stinginess of a selfish model than those who had tested lower (or less mature) in their moral reasoning—findings that are clearly anticipated by cognitive-developmental theory. So, in light of these results and other empirical evidence that we will examine, it seems wise to consider the social-learning and the cognitive-developmental perspectives as complementary, rather than contradictory, statements about the origins and development of altruism.

Developmental Trends in Prosocial Behavior

A genuine concern about the welfare of other people and a willingness to act on that concern are attributes that most adults hope their children will acquire. In fact, many parents are already encouraging altruistic acts such as sharing, cooperating, and helping while their children are still in diapers! Until recently, experts in child development would have claimed that these well-intentioned adults were wasting their time, for infants and toddlers were thought to be too egocentric to consider the needs of anyone other than themselves. But the experts were wrong!

Origins of Prosocial Behavior

Long before children receive any formal moral or religious training, they may display behavior that resembles the prosocial behavior of older people. At 12 months of age, infants are often "sharing" interesting experiences by pointing, and they will occasionally offer toys to their companions (Hay et al., 1991; Leung & Rheingold, 1981). By age 18 months, some children are already jumping in and trying to help with household chores such as sweeping, dusting, or setting the table (Rheingold, 1982). And the prosocial conduct of very young children even has a certain "rationality" about it. For example, 2-year-olds are more likely to offer toys to a peer

when playthings are scarce than when plentiful (Hay et al., 1991). Moreover, a type of *reciprocity* appears by the end of the third year. In one study (Levitt et al., 1985), 29- to 36-month-old toddlers who had previously received a toy from a peer when they had had none of their own typically returned the favor (given a little maternal prompting) when they later found themselves with several toys to play with and the peer without any. Yet, if that peer had earlier refused to share, the toddlers almost invariably hoarded the toys when it was their turn to control them.

Are toddlers capable of expressing sympathy and behaving compassionately toward their companions? Yes, indeed, and these displays of prosocial concern are not all that uncommon (see Radke-Yarrow et al., 1983; Zahn-Waxler et al., 1992). Consider the reaction of 21-month-old John to his distressed playmate Jerry:

> Today Jerry was kind of cranky; he just started . . . bawling and he wouldn't stop. John kept coming over and handing Jerry toys, trying to cheer him up. . . . He'd say things like "Here Jerry," and I said to John "Jerry's sad; he doesn't feel good; he had a shot today." John would look at me with his eyebrows wrinkled together like he really understood that Jerry was crying because he was unhappy. . . . He went over and rubbed Jerry's arm and said "Nice Jerry," and continued to give him toys [Zahn-Waxler, Radke-Yarrow, & King, 1979, pp. 321-322].

Clearly, John was concerned about his little playmate and did what he could to make him feel better.

Although some toddlers will often try to comfort distressed companions, others rarely do. These individual differences are due, in part, to cognitive development, for 23–25-month-olds who have achieved self-recognition (as assessed by the rouge test and other similar measures) are more likely than those who haven't to display some sympathy for and to try to comfort a victim of distress (Zahn-Waxler et al., 1992). By contrast, younger infants often became personally distressed (rather than concerned) by others' distress and were less inclined to show compassion—sometimes even behaving aggressively.

Individual differences in early compassion may also depend on parental socialization practices. Carolyn Zahn-Waxler and her associates (1979) asked mothers to keep records of (1) the reactions of their 1½- to 2½-year-olds to the distress of other children and (2) their own reactions when their child had been the cause of that distress. The results of this study were indeed interesting. Mothers of less compassionate toddlers tended to discipline acts of harmdoing with such coercive tactics as *physical restraint* ("I just moved him away from the baby"), *physical punishment* ("I swatted her a good one"), or *unexplained prohibitions* ("I said 'Stop that'"). By contrast, mothers of highly compassionate toddlers frequently disciplined harmdoing with **affective explanations**, which helped the child to see the relationship between his or her own acts and the distress they had caused (for example, "You made Doug cry; it's not nice to bite"; "You must never poke anyone's eyes!"). According to Eleanor Maccoby (1980), these affective explanations may be a form of *empathy training*—that is, the mother's scolding distresses the child and simultaneously draws attention to the discomfort of another person. Once children begin to associate their own distress with that of their victims, the foundation for compassionate behavior has been laid. All that the child now needs to learn is that he can eliminate his own conditioned discomfort by relieving the distress of others.

Age Differences in Altruism

Although many 2- to 3-year-olds will show some sympathy and compassion toward distressed companions, they are not particularly eager to make truly self-sacrificial responses, such as sharing a treasured cookie with a peer. Sharing and other benevolent acts are more likely to occur if adults instruct a toddler to consider others' needs (Levitt et al., 1985) or if a peer should actively elicit sharing through a request or a threat of some kind, such as "I won't be your friend if you won't gimme some" (Birch & Billman, 1986). But, on the whole, acts of *spontaneous* self-sacrifice in the interest of others are relatively infrequent among toddlers and young preschool children. Can this be because toddlers are largely oblivious to others' needs and to the good they might do by sharing or helping their compan-

PHOTO 11-2   Young children are not very altruistic and often must be coaxed to share.

ions? Probably not, for at least one observational study in a nursery-school setting found that 2½–3½-year-olds often took pleasure in performing acts of kindness for others during *pretend play*; by contrast, 4–6-year-olds performed more *real* helping acts and rarely "play-acted" the role of an altruist (Bar-Tal, Raviv, & Goldberg, 1982).

Sharing, helping, and other forms of prosocial behavior become much more common from the early elementary-school years through preadolescence (Underwood & Moore, 1982; Whiting & Edwards, 1988). The relationship between age and sharing is illustrated nicely in an early study of 291 Turkish children (Ugurel-Semin, 1952). Each child was asked to divide an odd number of nuts between himself and another known child of the same age. Children were classified as *altruistic* if they either gave more nuts than they kept or shared equally by refusing to assign the odd item and as *selfish* if they kept more than they gave. Sharing clearly increased with age. Only 33% of the 4–6-year-old children chose an altruistic division of resources, compared with 69% of the 6–7-year-olds, 81% of the 7–9-year-olds, and 96% of the 9–12-year-olds. Handlon and Gross (1959) performed a conceptual replication of Ugurel-Semin's study with American preschool, kindergarten, and fourth-, fifth-, and sixth-grade

TABLE 11-1   *Altruistic behavior of boys from four age groups*

Altruistic Response	Age Group			
	5–6	7–8	9–10	13–14
Average number of candy bars shared	1.36 (60%)	1.84 (92%)	2.88 (100%)	4.24 (100%)
Percentage of children who picked up pencils	48%	76%	100%	96%
Percentage of children who volunteered to work for needy children	96%	92%	100%	96%

NOTE: Figures in parentheses indicate percentage of children sharing at least one candy bar.
SOURCE: Adapted from F. P. Green & F. W. Schneider, "Age Differences in the Behavior of Boys on Three Measures of Altruism." *Child Development*, 1974, *45*, 248–251. Copyright © 1974 by the Society for Research in Child Development. Reprinted by permission.

children. This study also revealed that children of preschool and kindergarten age are selfish in their allocation of resources to a peer and that generosity increases with age.

Green and Schneider (1974) sought to determine whether aspects of altruism other than sharing also increase with age. Boys from four age groups—5–6, 7–8, 9–10, and 13–14—were given opportunities to (1) share candy with classmates who would not otherwise receive any, (2) help an experimenter who had "accidentally" dropped some pencils on the floor, and (3) volunteer to work on a project that would benefit poor children. The age trends for these three types of altruism appear in Table 11-1. The sharing data are consistent with the previous literature: generosity increases over the course of middle childhood. Further, this developmental increase in altruistic concern apparently generalizes to at least one other measure of helping—picking up pencils for the experimenter. There were no age differences on the volunteering-to-work index; over 90% of the boys in each age group were willing to sacrifice some of their playtime to help needy children. This lack of age differences may be due to an inability of younger children to anticipate or understand the costs that they would incur (giving up free time) as a result of their helpfulness.

Contributing factors.   Why might older children be more generous or helpful than younger ones? One possibility is that they are better *social information*

processors and, thus, more likely than younger children to detect subtle cues that indicate the need for benevolent action. A study by Ruth Pearl (1985) supports this interpretation. In Pearl's study, 4-year-olds and 9-year-olds watched a series of brief vignettes in which the central character needed some kind of assistance (in one vignette, for example, a boy was struggling to open a cookie jar). The social cues reflecting the actor's distress ranged from very subtle (the boy gave up and looked sadly at the cookie jar) to very explicit (the boy gave up, saying "Rats! The top is stuck," and looked sadly at the cookie jar). After viewing the vignettes, children were questioned to determine whether they knew the central characters were distressed, and they were also asked to suggest a solution for each vignette. Pearl found that 4-year-olds were just as likely as 9-year-olds to notice the actors' distress and to suggest helpful solutions when the distress cues were very explicit. Yet, when these cues were subtle, younger children were much less likely than older ones to perceive an actor's need for help or to suggest a helpful response.

In addition to their greater ability to recognize others' needs for compassionate or helpful behavior, older children may also feel more *responsible* for helping others and more *competent* to render assistance. Lizette Peterson (1983) tested these hypotheses in an experiment with 4-, 7-, and 12-year-olds. Children were first trained at certain tasks (for example, opening a tricky lock) to establish their competence at these activities. Then the experimenter left the room, telling subjects to "watch over things" while she was gone (*responsibility focus* condition) or to simply wait until she returned (*control* condition). Shortly thereafter a second adult entered the room and soon found herself needing assistance with tasks (1) at which the children were competent (for example, opening the lock) or (2) at which the children had not been trained (for example, tying a string around a package). The results were clear. Younger children were as likely as older children to help with the tasks at which they felt competent, particularly if responsibility for "watching over things" had been assigned to them. But, on tasks at which children had not explicitly been made to feel competent, age differences were quite apparent: 12-year-olds were more helpful than 7-year-olds, who were more helpful than 4-year-olds. In sum, the latter findings do seem to imply that age-related increases in altruism may often reflect older children's greater feelings of responsibility for helping and, in particular, their impressions that they are sufficiently competent to help.

And some exceptions to the rule. Although older children are more likely to help or to share with others, it would be inappropriate to conclude that all forms of prosocial behavior increase with age or that older children are always more generous or helpful than younger children. For example, Marian Radke-Yarrow and her associates (1983) reviewed much of the available literature and found *no* consistent age trends for two kinds of prosocial conduct: demonstrations of compassionate behavior and willingness to cooperate with peers. In fact, several studies in this review found that American children actually become less cooperative and more competitive between the ages of 4 and 12.

A series of experiments by Ervin Staub (1970, 1974) shows just how complex the relation between age and altruism can become. In one experiment (Staub, 1970), children from kindergarten through sixth grade were seated in one room when they heard a crash in the next room followed by a series of sobs and moans. Would these child bystanders help the victim by entering the room or informing the experimenter of the victim's distress? Much to

his surprise, Staub found a curvilinear relation between age and helping: helpfulness increased from kindergarten through second grade (age 5 to 7) and then decreased from second through sixth grades (see Midlarsky & Hannah, 1985, for a similar pattern of results). When questioned about their inaction, the younger children often say they lack the necessary competence to assist the injured victim (Midlarsky & Hannah, 1985), or they feel that they are not supposed to step in and help when adults are somewhere nearby (Caplan & Hay, 1989). However, the oldest children explained their inaction by saying that they feared *disapproval* from either the experimenter (for leaving their work) or the injured victim. Typical responses were "I thought I should stay here" or "If I went in there, I might get yelled at."

Were those concerns genuine? That is, will older children, who are often more altruistic than younger ones, actually allow vague, unstated "rules" of appropriate conduct to restrain their helpfulness? Staub (1974) tried to answer this question in the following experiment. Seventh-grade girls were taken to a room and asked to complete a questionnaire. Before leaving the child alone in the room, the experimenter either said nothing (*no information* condition), gave the child permission to play with some games in the next room (*permission* condition), or said that the girl in the next room was not to be bothered (*prohibition* condition). Ninety seconds later, subjects heard a crash followed by sounds of distress from the girl in the adjoining room. If seventh-grade children are greatly concerned about the possibility of violating *unstated* rules or prohibitions, then girls in the no-information condition should have been *less* helpful than girls who had permission to enter the next room and no more helpful than girls who were told that the person in the next room was not to be bothered. Staub's results confirmed these predictions; over 90% of the subjects who had permission to leave the room took some action to assist the victim, compared with 36% of the no-information subjects and 45% of the subjects in the prohibition group. Staub (1974) concluded:

> The inhibitory effect of no information on children's helping behavior suggests that . . . socializing

agents . . . may overemphasize the teaching of prohibitions against "improper" behavior without sufficient emphasis on norms which prescribe prosocial behavior. . . . *The data suggest that behavior that
manifests concern about others' welfare is relatively fragile, and easily yields to counterinfluences* [p. 315, italics
added].

Of course, these data dovetail nicely with the observations cited earlier that prosocial acts are viewed as
having a discretionary quality about them and,
thus, are much less obligatory than the need to refrain from antisocial conduct (Kahn, 1992).

Fortunately, older high school students and
adults eventually become less concerned about violating unstated rules or prohibitions that conflict
with the obvious needs of an injured victim (Midlarsky & Hannah, 1985; Staub, 1979). Nevertheless,
even adolescents and adults may be very reluctant
to help an injured party (or anyone else who could
use some assistance) if they suspect that their benevolence will make the recipient feel embarrassed
or incompetent (Midlarsky & Hannah, 1985).

Is Altruism a Consistent and Stable Attribute?

Although it appears that many kinds of prosocial
behavior become more common as children mature,
we might wonder just how consistent individuals
are from situation to situation. Will a child who
shares cookies with a playmate also share his bicycle
with a visiting cousin? Will another youngster who
refuses to cooperate or to play by the rules of a game
later decline to comfort or share with one of her
playmates should the opportunity present itself?

Several studies have found that there is a fair degree of consistency in children's prosocial inclinations from situation to situation. Not only are children who help or share in one situation more likely
than their nonaltruistic agemates to help or share in
similar situations (Rushton, 1980), but there is some
consistency across different kinds of prosocial behavior as well. For example, sympathetic 4-year-
olds are more likely than their less sympathetic agemates to share with or help their peers (Grusec &
Lytton, 1988), and children who have often cared for
younger siblings tend to be more generous, helpful,

and compassionate than those who have had few
caregiving responsibilities (Radke-Yarrow et al.,
1983; Whiting & Edwards, 1988). Yet the correlations
that emerge across different prosocial indexes are
often rather modest (Green & Schneider, 1974). So
it seems reasonable to conclude that there is a moderate degree of consistency at best in children's
willingness to display different kinds of prosocial
behavior.

Is altruism a *temporally stable* attribute? Is a socially concerned 2-year-old likely to become a compassionate 6-year-old, adolescent, or adult? Does
early sharing predict later generosity? Although few
longitudinal studies of children's altruism have
been conducted, the limited information we do have
suggests that children's modes of altruistic expression are reasonably stable over time. For example,
Radke-Yarrow and Zahn-Waxler (1983) found considerable variation among 2-year-olds in their responses to distressed companions. Some children
were very emotional and tried to comfort whoever
was distressed. Others adopted a more combative
style of prosocial behavior (for example, "I'll hit the
person who made you cry"), whereas a third group
of toddlers tried to shut out others' distress signals
by turning or running away from them. When these
children were retested at age 7, about two-thirds of
them exhibited the *same general style* of response to
distressed companions (that is, emotional, combative, or avoidant) that they had shown as 2-year-
olds. Nevertheless, the fact that one-third of the
sample now reacted in a *different* way to others' distress indicates that early patterns of altruistic expression can be modified. So, for some children, development means change rather than consistency or
stability.

Who Benefits Whom: Some Personal and Situational Influences on Prosocial Conduct

Not only do children differ in their willingness
to behave kindly or helpfully toward others, but it
seems that not all people who could use some com-

forting or assistance are equally effective at eliciting altruistic responses from potential benefactors. In this section we will consider several characteristics of benefactors and recipients that affect prosocial behavior.

Are There Sex Differences in Altruism?

Although people commonly assume that girls are (or will become) more compassionate, generous, and helpful than boys (see Shigetomi, Hartmann, & Gelfand, 1981; Zarbatany et al., 1985), two major reviews of the literature strongly dispute this notion (Radke-Yarrow et al., 1983; Rushton, 1980). Girls often do emit stronger *facial* expressions of sympathy or concern than boys do (Eisenberg et al., 1988; Fabes, Eisenberg, & Miller, 1990; Zahn-Waxler et al., 1992). But the vast majority of studies find that girls and women do not differ from boys and men either in the amount of sympathy they *say* they experience or in their willingness to comfort, help, or share resources with people in need. In fact, boys are occasionally more helpful than girls on some measures, such as active rescue behaviors.

Does the sex of the person who needs help or comforting affect children's prosocial inclinations? Apparently so, at least for young children. Rosalind Charlesworth and Willard Hartup (1967) observed the interactions of nursery-school children over a five-week period and found that these youngsters generally directed their acts of kindness to playmates of the same sex. However, the sex of a prospective recipient becomes a less important consideration during the grade-school years. In one study (Ladd, Lange, & Stremmel, 1983), kindergartners and first-, third-, and fourth-graders were given an opportunity to help other children complete some schoolwork. Some of these potential recipients clearly needed more help than others. Ladd et al. found that kindergartners and first-graders often disregarded recipients' apparent needs, choosing instead to help children of their own sex. However, this same-sex bias was much less apparent among third- and fourth-graders, who typically based their helping decisions on a recipient's need for help rather than his or her gender.

Dependency: Does This Person Need (and Deserve) My Help?

One morning as I was about to enter my office building, I paused to allow the person in front of me to open the door. A few seconds passed before I noticed that he was carrying an armload of laboratory equipment that prevented him from turning the doorknob. I then stepped forward and opened the door for him. His burden had made me feel that he was somewhat dependent on me for assistance.

Children also are inclined to help those persons who seem to depend on them for assistance. In fact, we have just seen that third- and fourth-graders are more likely to assist someone who needs a lot of help than someone who needs very little (Ladd et al., 1983). Moreover, Elizabeth Midlarsky and Mary Hannah (1985) found that children between the ages of 6 and 16 are quicker to help a toddler who has been hurt than an agemate who has suffered the same injury, particularly when the injury appears to be severe. One interpretation of these findings is that children viewed toddlers as more dependent on them for assistance. Indeed, Midlarsky and Hannah's subjects indicated that they were much less concerned about lacking the competence to help or about embarrassing the victim if the injured party was a toddler who seemed to require their assistance.

However, there clearly are limits to these dependency effects. Adults often base their helping decisions on the attributions they make about the *cause* of the victim's need and are more likely to help if the person's misfortune seems to stem from factors beyond his control, such as illness or bad luck (Baron & Byrne, 1991). Children make similar attributions about the causes of others' misfortunes and are much less likely to feel sympathy or be altruistic toward a person whose need stems from laziness, greed, or some other controllable factor (Barnett & Mcminimy, 1988; Eisenberg, 1990).

Getting By with a Little Help from My Friends

To whom do you turn when you require aid or comfort? If you are like most people, you probably seek the attention of a very close companion—perhaps your spouse, a relative, or your best friend. Indeed, relationships between friends or relatives seem to imply a sense of mutual dependency and an obligation to help each other.

Are children more likely to comfort, assist, or share valuable resources with friends than with acquaintances or strangers? The answer is yes, and this tendency to favor friends appears rather early. Even nursery-school children (3- to 6-year-olds) are more likely to share favorite snacks or to make sacrifices for another child if the recipient is a friend rather than a mere acquaintance (Birch & Billman, 1986; see also Box 11-1). Children are particularly generous or helpful toward a friend if they think that the friendship is threatened and view their acts of kindness as ways of solidifying or restoring the relationship (Staub & Noerenberg, 1981). However, if grade-school children think that their relationship with a friend is *secure*, they are sometimes more generous with a stranger than with a *good* friend. Thus,

when Wright (1942) asked 8-year-old boys to divide two toys that differed in attractiveness between a good friend and a stranger, many of them gave the attractive toy to the stranger. Those who favored the stranger often remarked that their generosity would help to eliminate the inequality between the friend, who knew he was liked, and the stranger. They also believed that they might win a new friend with their generosity and that the "deprived" friend would understand their actions.

Would children be more generous with friends than with strangers in *competitive* situations in which the sharing of resources (such as a crayon) is necessary for both children to complete an assignment and/or win a prize? The evidence bearing on this issue is somewhat mixed. Diane Jones (1985) found that kindergartners, second-graders, and fourth-graders were more generous with friends than with acquaintances under these competitive circumstances. Even when they refused to share,

---

B
O
X

11-1 | *Me Sacrifice for Someone Else? Well . . . That Depends*

Frederick Kanfer and his associates (Kanfer, Stifter, & Morris, 1981) designed an interesting experiment to see whether 3½–6-year-olds would delay immediate gratification in order to produce a desirable outcome for somebody else. Each of Kanfer's young subjects first learned how to perform a dull chip-sorting task and earned five prize tokens that could be used later to purchase a toy. The child was then given a choice between playing with an array of attractive toys (small immediate incentive) and continuing to sort chips in order to earn more prize tokens with which to buy additional toys (larger delayed incentive). Some of the children were led to believe that they would be using their later "earnings" to buy *themselves* attractive toys. Others were told that their future earnings would be used to buy toys for (1) *another little boy or girl* (anonymous-other condition), (2) a *"classmate"* whom the experimenter would select as the recipient, or (3) a *"friend"* whom the child liked very much. Finally, children in the *control* condition were simply told that they

could either play with the toys or sort chips if they wanted to but that no more prize tokens would be given for chip sorting. If the child began to sort chips (the delay choice), the experimenter left the room and observed the child's activities from an adjacent area for a maximum of 15 minutes. After 15 minutes had elapsed (or the child had quit working and started to play with the toys), the experimenter returned and praised the child for his or her work. The subject was then allowed to exchange the tokens earned at the beginning of the session for a toy.

The results of the experiment appear in the table. In evaluating these data, let's first note that not one child in the control condition chose to continue the chip-sorting task when his efforts would earn him no more tokens. Even preschool children won't work for nothing. And will they work for themselves? Yes, indeed, for 75% of those who could earn tokens to buy themselves additional toys chose to work rather than play, and most of these youngsters worked for the en-

children were more likely to explain to friends why they had done so, whereas the queries of acquaintances often elicited nothing more than a terse "no!" Grade-school boys will occasionally compete more with friends and cooperate more with strangers in "competitive" contexts, apparently trying to prevent the distasteful experience of being upstaged by a friend; however, this tendency is relatively short lived, as young adolescent males are much more inclined to compete with strangers and to stress equality in their interactions with friends (Berndt, Hawkins, & Hoyle, 1986).

Feeling Good and Feeling Blue: Effects of Moods on Altruism

Remarkable as it may seem, our willingness to help a person in need is often influenced by temporary fluctuations in mood. Suppose you had just succeeded beyond your wildest expectations on an im-

portant exam, earning the highest grade in the class. Would you be any more willing under these circumstances to help or comfort someone than if you had scored only about average on the test or had actually failed it?

EFFECTS OF GOOD MOODS

It seems that good moods do clearly enhance the altruistic inclinations of both children and adults. Subjects who are feeling good after succeeding at a game or a test are typically more charitable and helpful than those whose performance was only average or below average (see Isen, 1970; Shaffer, 1986). And this "feel good/do good" effect is by no means limited to people who are experiencing the warm glow of success. For example, Isen and Levin (1972) reported that subjects who had found a dime in a telephone booth (good-mood condition) were more likely than those who had not found a dime

---

B O X **11-1** | *continued*

tire 15 minutes. Now for the question that stimulated this research: will preschool children set aside personal pleasures in order to do something nice for somebody else? As we see in the table, the answer depends on whom they would be working for. The majority of these 3½–6-year-olds refused to do anything

to benefit an anonymous child or a "classmate" whose identity was left unspecified. However, 55% of the children were willing to defer immediate gratification and perform the dull chip-sorting task when the person who would benefit from their sacrifice was a friend.

Number of children who worked at the dull chip-sorting task for all, part, or none of the 15-minute delay interval

	Control (no tokens earned)	Self as Recipient	Anonymous Other as Recipient	Classmate as Recipient	Friend as Recipient
No work	20 (100%)	5 (25%)	19 (95%)	15 (75%)	9 (45%)
Part-time work	0 (0%)	2 (10%)	1 (5%)	2 (10%)	1 (5%)
Maximum work	0 (0%)	13 (65%)	0 (0%)	3 (15%)	10 (50%)

SOURCE: Adapted from F. H. Kanfer, E. Stifter, & S. J. Morris, "Self-Control and Altruism: Delay of Gratification for Another." *Child Development,* 1981, *52,* 674–682. Copyright © 1981 by the Society for Research in Child Development. Adapted by permission.

(neutral-mood condition) to help a stranger who had dropped some papers. Even good weather can brighten our spirits and make us more prosocially inclined, for people leave waitresses larger tips and are more likely to volunteer as participants in research projects on bright and sunny days than on dull and dreary ones (Cunningham, 1979).

Why do positive moods promote altruism? Recent research by Michael Cunningham and his associates (Cunningham, 1988; Cunningham et al., 1990) provides some strong clues. Cunningham finds that people experiencing positive moods are much more optimistic and self-confident and much less preoccupied about personal concerns than people experiencing neutral or negative moods. Moreover, good-mood subjects are more likely to engage in a variety of social activities (such as dancing or chatting with a new acquaintance) than subjects who are feeling "down" or depressed. Thus, positive moods may promote altruism because they (1) direct our attention outward toward other people, rather than inward on personal concerns, and (2) make us feel more confident or optimistic that we can successfully alleviate the distress of a person in need.

EFFECTS OF BAD MOODS

Do negative moods, then, make one *less* altruistically inclined? To answer this question, Moore, Underwood, and Rosenhan (1973) asked 7- and 8-year-olds to recall events from their lives that had made them feel very happy (good-mood condition) or very sad (bad-mood condition). Children assigned to the control condition did not reminisce about prior experiences and were assumed to be in a neutral mood. After the mood manipulation, subjects were given an opportunity to donate some of the 25 pennies they had received for participating in the experiment to other children who would not have an opportunity to participate and earn pennies. Children were told that they could share their money if they wanted to but that they did not have to. The experimenter then left the room, thus providing each child an opportunity to make an anonymous donation to his or her less fortunate peers.

The results, summarized in Figure 11-2, reveal that subjects who had recalled happy events donated significantly more money to the children's

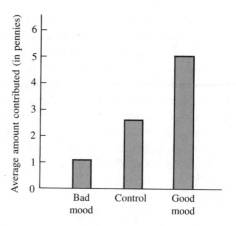

FIGURE 11-2 Average donations by children in the good-mood, bad-mood, and control conditions. (Adapted from B. S. Moore, B. Underwood, & D. L. Rosenhan, "Affect and Altruism." *Developmental Psychology*, 1973, *8*, 99–104. Copyright © 1973 by the American Psychological Association. Reprinted by permission.)

fund than control subjects did. And subjects who had recalled unhappy events contributed significantly *less* than control subjects. Moore et al. (1973) concluded that "brief, even fleeting, affective experiences appear to have significant implications for behavior toward others. The transient experience of [mood-induced] positive affect makes children more generous to others, while the equally ephemeral experience of negative affect appears to make them more niggardly" (p. 102).

However, later research shows that negative moods do not always suppress altruism. Using a procedure similar to that of Moore et al. (1973), Robert Cialdini and Douglas Kenrick (1976) found that bad moods inhibited sharing among 6- to 8-year-olds but actually *enhanced* the generosity of older children and adolescents. Moreover, there is now a good deal of evidence to indicate that adults who are feeling "down" or depressed are often *more* prosocially inclined than those experiencing neutral moods (see Shaffer, 1986, for a review). How might we explain these inconsistent outcomes?

The "negative state relief" hypothesis.   One possibility is that the effects of negative moods on altruism change with age. Indeed, Cialdini and Kenrick (1976) proposed that altruism eventually becomes *self-reinforcing* for an older child, who will have had many opportunities to associate prosocial responses with positive outcomes (such as praise and tangible reinforcement) and to learn that "helping makes *me* feel good." Thus an older child who is feeling blue may be motivated to help others in order to make *himself* feel better and thereby overcome his negative mood (the **"negative state relief" hypothesis**). Younger children who are feeling "down" would not be so prosocially inclined because they do not yet realize that altruism is self-reinforcing and can be used to brighten their own spirits.

The "focus of attention" hypothesis. In contrast to Cialdini and Kenrick's developmental model, Mark Barnett and his associates (Barnett, King, & Howard, 1979) have proposed that a cognitive variable — *focus of attention* — determines whether a negative mood will enhance or inhibit altruism. After carefully reviewing the literature, Barnett et al. concluded that, in studies showing that bad moods increase altruism, subjects were generally thinking about the misfortunes of others. By contrast, in studies showing that bad moods inhibit altruism, subjects were generally reflecting on their *own* misfortunes (for example, thinking about a sad personal experience or a personal failure). Thus the implication is that people whose bad moods stem from an outward focus on the problems or misfortunes of other people are likely to be altruistically inclined, whereas an inward focus on one's own problems should heighten self-concern at the expense of concern for others.

Barnett et al. (1979) tested this **"focus of attention" hypothesis** by telling 7- to 12-year-old children to discuss a very sad incident that had happened to themselves or to another child. Children assigned to the control group provided information either about themselves or about another child that was essentially devoid of emotional content (data about the child's age, address, and so on). Soon thereafter, subjects were given an opportunity to anonymously donate some of the valuable prize chips they had received for their participation to a group of unfortunate children who would have no opportunity to earn prize chips. The results were clear: children who had been saddened by focusing outward on the misfortunes of another child shared significantly *more* prize tokens than their counterparts in

the control group, whereas saddened children who focused on their own misfortunes were much *less* generous than those in the control group (see also Thompson, Cowan, & Rosenhan, 1980, for a similar set of findings with adult subjects). Because these "focusing" effects were apparent among even the youngest (7- to 8-year-old) subjects in Barnett's sample, it would appear to be one's attentional focus, rather than one's age or socialization history, that determines the effect of negative moods on altruism.

Summing up. Although Barnett's study seems to discredit some of the developmental implications of the negative state relief hypothesis, that theory may still be partly correct. People who are feeling sad and are focusing *inward* on their own concerns are often more altruistic than those experiencing neutral moods if (1) the needs of a prospective recipient are made obvious to them and (2) the type of prosocial response that is called for is not unpleasant or costly and thus offers some promise of improving their negative mood (see Shaffer, 1986, for a review of this literature). In other words, the prosocial behavior of these saddened and self-focused individuals has distinct *hedonistic* overtones: I'll help if it will make *me* feel better, but I'll decline if the act will do nothing to brighten my spirits. By contrast, people who are experiencing *positive* moods are much more concerned about the benefits accruing to the recipient than about the consequences of their actions for themselves. In fact, happy people may even undertake very unpleasant or costly prosocial acts in the interests of others, whereas saddened and self-focused people routinely decline to help if the costs of their benevolence outweigh the benefits they can expect to receive (Cunningham et al., 1990; Shaffer & Graziano, 1983).

Cognitive and Affective Contributors to Altruism

Earlier we noted that generosity and other types of helping behavior become more frequent during middle childhood (ages 6 to 12). In addition, middle childhood is a period when children are be-coming less egocentric, are developing more profi-ciency at role taking (that is, imagining themselves in the place of others), and are displaying some in-teresting changes in their moral reasoning. Propo-nents of cognitive theories of altruism believe that increases in prosocial behavior during middle child-hood are closely linked to the development of role-taking abilities, prosocial moral reasoning, and em-pathy, as well as to a better understanding of the responsibilities implied should we view ourselves as helpful, compassionate, or otherwise altruistic individuals. Let's see if there is any support for these ideas.

Role Taking and Altruism

It makes some sense to assume that proficient role takers might be more altruistic than poor role takers if their role-taking skills help them to recognize and appreciate the factors that contribute to another per-son's distress or misfortune. Indeed, we discussed a study in Chapter 4 that is consistent with this point of view. Recall that, when second-graders taught kindergartners how to make caterpillars from con-struction paper, both good and poor role takers were quite helpful if the younger children explicitly asked for help. But, if the younger children's needs were subtle or their requests were indirect, good role takers recognized them and offered assistance, whereas poor role takers simply smiled at their young charges and resumed their own activities (Hudson, Forman, & Brion-Meisels, 1982).

So do role-taking, or perspective-taking, skills consistently predict children's altruistic inclina-tions? Measures of physical perspective taking (that is, imagining what another person can see or sense) don't; however, measures of children's **social per-spective taking** (identifying what another is think-ing or intending or what goals he is pursuing) and **affective perspective taking** (identifying what an-other person is feeling) are reliable predictors of prosocial conduct (Underwood & Moore, 1982), par-ticularly when the kind of role taking assessed is similar to the kind children must display to infer the feelings or needs of an actual recipient (Carlo et al., 1991). Specifically, children who are proficient at so-cial and affective role taking do tend to be more prosocially inclined than poor role takers; and the relationship between role-taking skills and altruism becomes stronger with age (Underwood & Moore, 1982).

Unfortunately, the data we have reviewed are correlational patterns and do not necessarily imply that proficiency at role taking *causes* children to be-have more altruistically. Yet, if role taking truly me-diates altruism, we might predict that children who receive training to further their role-taking skills should become more altruistic. Indeed, evidence for such a causal link is quite clear in studies showing that children and adolescents who are coached to be better social and affective role takers do subse-quently become more charitable, more cooperative, and more concerned about the needs of others when compared with agemates who receive no training (Chalmers & Townsend, 1990; Iannotti, 1978). However, role taking is only one of several cognitive attributes that play a part in the develop-ment of altruistic behavior. Three other contributors are children's level of **prosocial moral reasoning**, their empathic reactions to the distress of other peo-ple, and their emerging self-concepts as altruistic individuals.

Prosocial Moral Reasoning and Altruistic Behavior

Recently, researchers have begun to chart the devel-opment of children's reasoning about prosocial is-sues and its relationship to altruistic behavior. For example, Nancy Eisenberg and her colleagues have presented children with stories in which the central character has to decide whether or not to help or comfort someone when the prosocial act would be personally costly to the helpgiver. The following story illustrates the kinds of dilemmas children were asked to think about (Eisenberg-Berg & Hand, 1979):

> One day a girl named Mary was going to a friend's birthday party. On her way she saw a girl who had fallen down and hurt her leg. The girl asked Mary to go to her house and get her parents so that [they] could come and take her to a doctor. But if Mary did . . . , she would be late to the party

TABLE 11-2   *Levels of prosocial moral reasoning*

Level	Brief Description	Age Range
1. Hedonistic (self-centered)	Concern is for oneself; helpgiving is most likely when it will in some way benefit the self	Preschool and young elementary-school children
2. Needs-oriented	Will base helping decisions on the needs of others; not much evidence of sympathy or guilt for not helping at this level	Elementary-school children and a few preschoolers
3. Approval-oriented	Concern is for performing altruistic acts that other people see as good or praiseworthy; being good or socially appropriate is important	Elementary-school and some high school students
4. Empathic or transitional	Judgments now include evidence of sympathetic responding, evidence of guilt for failing to respond, and evidence of feeling good for having done the right thing; vague references are made to abstract principles, duties, and values	High school students and some older elementary-school children
5. Strongly internalized	Justifications for helping are based on strongly internalized values, norms, convictions, and responsibilities; to violate one's internalized principles will now undermine self-respect	A small minority of high school students and virtually no elementary-school children

SOURCE: Adapted from N. Eisenberg, R. Lennon, & K. Roth, "Prosocial Development: A Longitudinal Study." *Developmental Psychology*, 1983, *19*, 846–855. Copyright © 1983 by the American Psychological Association. Reprinted by permission.

and miss the ice cream, cake, and all the games. What should Mary do?

As illustrated in Table 11-2, reasoning about these prosocial moral dilemmas may progress through as many as five levels between early childhood and adolescence. Notice that preschoolers' responses are frequently *hedonistic*: these youngsters often say that Mary should go to the party so as not to miss out on the goodies. But, as children mature, they tend to become increasingly responsive to the needs and wishes of others—so much so that some high school students feel that they could no longer respect themselves were they to ignore the appeal of a person in need in order to pursue their own interests (Eisenberg et al., 1983; Eisenberg, Miller, et al., 1991).

Eisenberg does *not* view these levels of prosocial moral reasoning as integrated and hierarchical "stages" that unfold in an invariant sequence. Indeed, both cross-sectional and longitudinal research reveals that older children may reason at different levels when resolving different prosocial dilemmas, using empathic concern, for example, to justify helping an injured victim while relying on needs-oriented or even hedonistic reasoning to justify a decision not to share. Nevertheless, Eisenberg's longitudinal studies indicate that lower levels of prosocial moral reasoning become increasingly less common and higher levels more common between kindergarten age and mid-adolescence (Eisenberg et al., 1987; Eisenberg, Miller, et al., 1991).

Does the child's predominant level of prosocial moral reasoning predict his or her altruistic inclinations? To some extent it does. Eisenberg-Berg and Hand (1979) found that preschoolers who had begun to consider the needs of others when responding to prosocial moral dilemmas later displayed more *spontaneous* sharing with peers than did their nursery-school classmates whose prosocial reasoning was more hedonistic. And, in a later study of older subjects, Eisenberg (1983) found that mature moral reasoners among her high school sample might even help someone they *disliked* if that person really needed their assistance, whereas immature moral reasoners were likely to ignore the needs of a person they did not like (see also Eisenberg, Miller, et al., 1991).

Why are mature moral reasoners so sensitive to the needs of others—even disliked others? Although we don't yet know the answer to this question, Eisenberg and her associates (1987; Eisenberg, Miller, et al., 1991) report that the ability to empathize easily with others aids children in reaching the higher stages of prosocial moral reasoning. So it is possible that mature moral reasoners experience particularly strong empathic responses to the distress of other people and that these emotional reactions trigger some form of altruistic behavior. In the following section we will consider what researchers have learned about the relationship between empathy and altruism.

Empathy: An Important Affective Mediator of Altruism

Empathy refers to a person's ability to experience the emotions of other people. According to Martin Hoffman (1981, 1988), empathy is a universal human response, has a neurological basis, and can be either fostered or suppressed by environmental influences. Hoffman believes that empathic arousal will eventually become an important mediator of altruism. Why else, Hoffman asks, would we set aside our own selfish motives to help other people or to avoid harming them unless we had the capacity to share their emotions?

Although infants and toddlers do seem to recognize and will often react to the distress of their companions (Zahn-Waxler et al., 1979; see also Box 2-4), their responses are not always helpful ones. Indeed, some young children experience *personal* distress upon witnessing the distress or misfortunes of others (this may be the predominant response early in life) and may turn away from a person in need, or even

attack him or her, in order to relieve their *own* discomfort. Yet other children (even some young ones) are more inclined to interpret their empathic arousal as concern for distressed others, and it is this **sympathetic empathic arousal**, rather than **self-oriented empathic distress**, that should eventually come to mediate altruism (Batson, 1987; Eisenberg et al., 1992; Hoffman, 1988).

As we noted in Chapter 10 and earlier in this chapter when discussing the origins of compassion in toddlers, parents can help to promote sympathetic empathic arousal by (1) modeling sympathetic concern and (2) relying on affectively oriented forms of discipline that help young children to understand the harmful effects of any distress they may have caused others (Barnett, 1987; Eisenberg, Fabes, et al., 1991; Zahn-Waxler et al., 1979, 1992). Mothers who *explicitly verbalize* their own sympathetic reactions to others are also contributing to the development of sympathy, particularly for boys, who seem to be somewhat less sensitive than girls to mothers' sympathetic facial displays (Eisenberg et al., 1992).

So what is the relationship between empathy and altruism? The answer depends, in part, on how empathy is measured and how old the research participants are. In studies that assess empathy by having children report their own feelings about the misfortunes of story characters, researchers have found little association between empathy and altruism. However, teacher ratings of children's empathic sensitivities and children's own facial expressions of emotion in response to others' misfortunes are better predictors of prosocial behavior (Chapman et al., 1987; Eisenberg et al., 1990). With respect to the age variable, it seems that evidence for a link between empathy and altruism is weak at best for preschool and young grade-school children but stronger for preadolescents, adolescents, and adults (Underwood & Moore, 1982).

One possible explanation for these age trends is that it simply takes some time for children to become more reliable at suppressing personal distress to others' misfortunes so that they can respond more sympathetically. And it is likely that cognitive development plays an important role in this process, for younger children may lack the role-taking

PHOTO 11-3 As children mature and develop better role-taking skills, they are more likely to sympathize with distressed companions and to provide them with comfort or assistance.

skills to fully understand and appreciate (1) *why* others are distressed and, hence, (2) *why* they are experiencing empathic arousal. For example, when kindergartners see a series of slides showing a boy becoming depressed after his dog runs away, they usually attribute his sadness to an external cause (the dog's disappearance) rather than to a more "personal" or internal one, such as the boy's longing for his pet (Hughes, Tingle, & Sawin, 1981). And, although kindergartners report that they feel sad after seeing the slides, they usually provide egocentric explanations for their empathic arousal—ones that seem to reflect *personal distress* (for example, "I might lose my dog"). However, 7–9-year-olds are beginning to associate their own empathic emotions with those of the story character as they put themselves in his place and infer the psychological basis for his sadness (for example, "I'm sad because he's sad . . . because, if he really liked the dog, then . . ."). So empathy may become an impor-

tant mediator of altruism once children become more proficient at inferring others' points of view (role taking) and understanding the causes of their own empathic emotions—causes that can help them to feel sympathy for distressed or needy companions (see also Eisenberg et al., 1988).

Another demonstration of the interrelationship among role taking, empathy, and altruism comes from an interesting experiment by Mark Barnett and associates (1982). Sixth-graders rated high or low in empathy by their teachers were first asked to reminisce about something very sad. Half the children were asked to think about a sad event that had happened to someone else (other-focused, role-taking condition), whereas the other half were asked to think about a sad event that had happened to themselves (self-focused condition). A few minutes later these youngsters were given an opportunity to make "color and activity" booklets to cheer up sick children who were hospitalized. The results were clear. As we see in the left-hand portion of Figure 11-3, a child's capacity for empathy, by itself, does not predict her willingness to do something nice for sick peers if she has been thinking about a personal misfortune. The only time that the highly empathic 12-year-olds were more helpful than their less empathic classmates was when they had been thinking

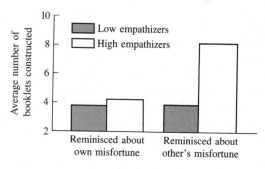

FIGURE 11-3 Average number of "color and activity" booklets constructed by high- and low-empathic 12-year-olds who had reminisced about a sad event that had happened to themselves or to another person. (Adapted from M. A. Barnett, J. A. Howard, E. M. Melton, & G. A. Dino, "Effect of Inducing Sadness about Self or Other on Helping Behavior in High- and Low-Empathetic Children." *Child Development*, 1982, 53, 920–923. Copyright © 1982 by the Society for Research in Child Development. Reprinted by permission.)

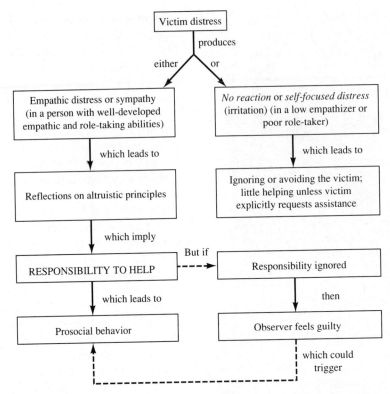

FIGURE 11-4   How empathy promotes altruism: A "felt responsibility" interpretation.

about another person's misfortune—a form of role taking that apparently triggered strong sympathetic responses from high empathizers, which then increased their motivation to aid and comfort a group of unfortunate children.

Now an important question: *how* exactly does empathic arousal mediate altruism? One possibility is that a child's empathic distress causes him to reflect on altruistic lessons he has learned—lessons such as the Golden Rule, the *norm of social responsibility* (that is, help others who need help), or even the knowledge that other people approve of helping behavior. As a result of this reflection, the child is likely to assume some personal *responsibility* for aiding a victim in distress (see Figure 11-4) and would now feel guilty for callously ignoring that obligation (Chapman et al., 1987). Notice that this **"felt responsibility" hypothesis** is reflected in Eisenberg's

higher stages of prosocial moral reasoning (see Table 11-2) and may help to explain why the link between empathy and altruism becomes stronger with age. Since older children are likely to have learned (and internalized) more altruistic principles than younger children, they should have much more to reflect on as they experience empathic distress. Consequently, they are more likely than younger children to feel responsible for helping a distressed person and to follow through by rendering the necessary assistance.

Viewing Oneself as Altruistic: A Social-Cognitive Contributor

A person's willingness to sacrifice in order to benefit others may also hinge very critically on how altruistic she believes herself to be. Research with adults consistently indicates that people with strong altruistic self-concepts really are more prosocially inclined than those who do not view themselves as particularly compassionate, charitable, or helpful (see Baron & Byrne, 1991; Shaffer & Smith, 1987). Might the same be true of children? Could we promote altruism by persuading youngsters to think of themselves as generous or helpful individuals?

Joan Grusec and Erica Redler (1980) sought to answer these questions by first urging 5- and 8-year-olds to (1) donate marbles to poor children, (2) share colored pencils with classmates who didn't have any, and (3) help an experimenter with a dull and repetitive task. Once children had donated, shared, or begun to work on the repetitive task, they either were told that they were "nice" or "helpful" persons for the good that they had done (self-concept training condition) or were told nothing (control condition). One to two weeks later the children were asked by another adult to donate drawings and craft materials to help cheer up sick children at a local hospital.

Grusec and Redler found that self-concept training had a much greater effect on the 8-year-olds than the 5-year-olds. The 8-year-olds who were told that they were "nice" or "helpful" were more likely than those in the control condition to make drawings for and to share their possessions with sick children. Why was the self-concept training so effective with 8-year-olds but not with 5-year-olds? The research we reviewed in Chapter 7 provides a strong clue. Recall that 8-year-olds are just beginning to describe the self in psychological terms and to see these "traits" as stable aspects of their character. Thus, when told that they were "nice" or "helpful," Grusec and Redler's 8-year-olds apparently incorporated these traitlike attributions into their self-concepts and were trying to live up to this new, more altruistic self-image by generously volunteering assistance when help was needed.

So, encouraging youngsters to think of themselves as altruistic is one way to promote acts of kindness—at least among children old enough to understand and appreciate the implications of traitlike attributions. Might we ever be effective at persuading younger children to view themselves as "helpers" or "comforters" and to make internal attributions for their acts of kindness? Probably so, but only if our self-concept training focuses directly on the helper's desirable intentions and is stated in *explicit behavioral terms*—precisely the kind of information that younger children use to describe the self (for example, "I hear that you are a nice boy who wants to share his toys [cookies, marbles] with other boys and girls"). Although the success of this kind of "behavioral" self-concept training has yet to be demonstrated for altruistic behavior, Fiona Ritchie and Ignatius Toner (1984) find that children only 3 years old will become more *patient* (by forgoing immediate rewards to wait for a larger, delayed incentive) if the experimenter has labeled them as a boy or girl who "can wait for nice things when you can't get them right away." So there is reason to believe that a form of self-concept training that is carefully tailored to the younger child's social information-processing capabilities might prove to be an effective means of altering self-perceptions and inducing prosocial behavior.

In our next section we consider a number of other social and cultural factors that have a bearing on how altruistic children are likely to become.

Cultural and Social Influences on Altruism

According to prominent social-learning theorists (for example, Bandura, 1989), our altruistic inclinations are heavily influenced by the company we keep. We will now consider how such social influences as our culture and our family help determine why some of us are more altruistic than others.

Cultural Influences

Cultures clearly differ in their endorsement or encouragement of altruism. In one interesting cross-cultural study, Beatrice and John Whiting (1975) observed the altruistic behavior of 3- to 10-year-olds in six cultures—Kenya, Mexico, the Philippines, Okinawa, India, and the United States. As we see in

TABLE 11-3   *Prosocial behavior in six cultures:*
Percentages of children in each culture who
scored above the median altruism score for
the cross-cultural sample as a whole

Type of Society	Percentage Scoring High in Altruism
Nonindustrialized	
Kenya	100
Mexico	73
Philippines	63
Industrialized	
Okinawa	29
India	25
United States	8

SOURCE: Reprinted by permission of the publishers from
Children of Six Cultures: A Psycho-Cultural Analysis, by B. B.
Whiting & J. W. M. Whiting. Cambridge, MA: Harvard
University Press. Copyright © 1975 by the President and
Fellows of Harvard College.

Table 11-3, the cultures in which children were most altruistic were the less industrialized societies where people tend to live in large families with everyone contributing to the family welfare. The Whitings concluded that children who are assigned important responsibilities, such as producing and processing food or caring for infant brothers and sisters, are likely to develop a cooperative, altruistic orientation at an early age.

Another possible explanation for the very low altruism scores among children from industrialized nations is that many Western societies place a tremendous emphasis on competition and stress individual rather than group goals. By contrast, Native American and Mexican children (and, indeed, children from many nonindustrialized societies) are taught to suppress individualism, to cooperate with others, and to avoid interpersonal conflicts. The impact of these cultural teachings is apparent in a number of contexts. For example, Anne Marie Tietjen (1986) finds that children from a cooperative society in New Guinea typically become less other-oriented and more self-centered in their thinking about prosocial issues once they have spent three years attending Westernized schools. And, when children are asked to play games in which partners must cooperate to earn scores high enough to win a prize, Mexican children, who are taught to cooperate, clearly outperform their more competitive Mexican-American and Anglo-American agemates (Kagan & Masden, 1971, 1972). In fact, many 7- to 9-year-old American children are so competitive at these games that they will attempt to lower their partner's outcomes even though they receive no direct benefits for doing so. Apparently this competitive orientation can be acquired very early and may interfere with prosocial activities such as sharing. In one study of American nursery-school children, highly competitive 4-year-olds were already less inclined than other preschoolers to share candy with their two best friends (Rutherford & Mussen, 1968).

Although cultures may differ in the emphasis they place on altruism, most people in most societies endorse the *norm of social responsibility* — the rule of thumb prescribing that one should help others who need help. Let's now consider some of the ways adults might persuade young children to adopt this important value and to become more concerned about the welfare of other people.

Reinforcing Altruism

Might we promote altruism by offering children tangible rewards for their generous or helpful acts? Probably not. Although the practice of giving children toys or bubble gum for acts of kindness does increase the frequency of such behavior in the short run (Fischer, 1963), rewarded children are actually *less likely* than other "nonrewarded" peers to make sacrifices for others once the rewards stop (Fabes et al., 1989). What seems to be happening is that children who are "bribed" with tangible incentives for prosocial conduct attribute their acts of kindness to the rewards rather than to the recipient's needs or to their own inclinations to be kind to others. Consequently, tangible rewards can undermine children's altruistic motivation in much the same way that rewards can undermine interest in intrinsically satisfying activities (see Box 8-3). Apparently, parents understand that a strong concern for others is not easily established through bribery, for mothers of 4- to 7-year-olds report that they rarely use tangible rewards to promote prosocial behavior (Grusec, 1991); and the mothers who are most likely to do so have children who are the least prosocially inclined (Fabes et al., 1989).

On the other hand, *verbal reinforcement* can promote altruistic behavior if it is administered by a warm and charitable person whom children respect and admire (Mills & Grusec, 1989; Yarrow, Scott, & Waxler, 1973). Perhaps verbal approval is effective under these circumstances because children hope to live up to standards set by a liked and respected person, and praise that accompanies their kindly acts suggests that they are accomplishing that objective. But, as we see in Box 11-2, the use of praise to promote altruism can function in much the same way that tangible reinforcers do if the person providing the praise is not altruistically inclined.

Another way in which adults might subtly reinforce altruism is to structure play activities so that children are likely to discover the benefits of cooperating and helping one another. Indeed, Terry Orlick (1981) finds that preschool children who have been trained to play cooperative games in which they must join forces to achieve various goals are later more cooperative in other contexts (for example, with peers on the playground) than agemates who have spent an equal amount of time playing very similar but individualistic games that do not require cooperation. Orlick also finds that youngsters in his "cooperative activities" training usually become more generous about sharing treats and possessions—even when the peers who would benefit from their acts of kindness are unknown to them. By contrast, children who participated in traditional (individualistic) activities often became stingier with their possessions as the training wore on. So it seems that a program designed to teach children to cooperate not only accomplishes that objective but may also promote completely different forms of altruism, such as sharing.

Modeling Influences: Practicing and Preaching Altruism

Social-learning theorists have assumed that adults who encourage altruism and who practice what they preach will affect children in two ways. By practicing altruism, the adult model may induce the child to perform similar acts of kindness. In addition, regular exposure to the model's **altruistic exhortations** provides the child with opportunities to internalize principles (such as the norm of social responsibility) that should contribute to the development of an altruistic orientation.

Laboratory experiments consistently indicate that young children who observe charitable or helpful models become more charitable or helpful themselves. But do these modeling effects so often seen in laboratory studies stand the test of time and/or generalize to contexts outside the laboratory? Apparently they can. Elizabeth Midlarsky and James Bryan (1972) found that a model who donated valuable tokens to a charity increased children's willingness to donate a *different* commodity (candy) to the same charity, even though the candy donations were solicited ten days later in a different setting by a person the children had never seen before (see Yarrow et al., 1973, for a similar set of findings with preschool children). Other investigators have noted that children who observe charitable models are more generous than those who observe selfish models, even when they are tested *two to four months later* (Rice & Grusec, 1975; Rushton, 1980). Taken together, these findings suggest that encounters with altruistic models may indeed foster the development of prosocial habits and altruistic values.

The importance of "practicing what we preach."   Although most parents encourage their children to be kind, generous, and helpful to others, they don't always practice what they preach. How do children respond to these inconsistencies? James Bryan and his associates (Bryan & Schwartz, 1971; Bryan & Walbek, 1970) addressed this issue by exposing grade-school children to models who *behaved* either charitably or selfishly while *preaching* either charity ("It's good to donate to poor children") or greed ("Why should I give my money to other people?"). When children were later given an opportunity to donate some of their own valuable resources to charity, the size of their donations was influenced by the model's behavior but *not* his exhortations. In other words, children who saw a model refuse to donate while preaching charity (or greed) showed a low level of altruism themselves, whereas those who observed a charitable model who exhorted greed (or charity) gave sizable amounts to charity. These findings appear to have an important implication for child rearing: parents would be well advised to back up their verbal exhortations with altruistic deeds if they hope to instill a strong sense of altruistic concern in their children.

Are altruistic exhortations ever effective? Although a model's actions may speak louder than his or her words, it would be inappropriate to conclude that words are wasted on children. Midlarsky and Bryan (1972) suspected that the charitable exhortations used in previous studies were weak—doing little more than reminding children of the norm of social responsibility. By contrast, parents often provide their children with meaningful cognitive rationales for sharing with, comforting, or helping others. Perhaps stronger exhortations that justify acts of kindness on the basis of their positive impact on recipients would prove more successful at eliciting prosocial responses from children.

Midlarsky and Bryan tested this hypothesis by exposing children to an adult model who took ten turns at a game, winning five times and losing five times. On winning trials, the model behaved either *charitably*, by donating some of his winnings to a needy-children's fund, or *selfishly*, by keeping all of his winnings for himself. On losing trials, the model

---

B O X 11-2 | *When Praise Fails: The Aversive Approval Effect*

Can you think of an occasion when the verbal reinforcement of prosocial responses will *inhibit* altruism? Paradoxical as this may seem, Elizabeth Midlarsky, James Bryan, and Philip Brickman (1973) were able to imagine one such occasion. They hypothesized that a child would become reluctant to share valuable resources with others if his or her charitable acts were reinforced by a *selfish* person. If we can assume that children disapprove of selfishness and dislike selfish people, then approval from a selfish person may lead the child to expect disapproval from other important people, who share a dislike for the selfish person. In other words, approval from a disliked source may prove "aversive" and actually inhibit, rather than strengthen, the behavior it was intended to reinforce (in this case, sharing behavior).

Midlarsky et al. conducted an interesting experiment to test this hypothesis. Twelve-year-old girls were exposed to an adult model who demonstrated how to play a pinball game. Some of the subjects saw the model behave in a *charitable* manner by donating a sizable portion of her winnings to a fund for needy children. Other children saw the model act *selfishly* by refusing to share any of her winnings with needy children. Each child then played the game several times and won 20 tokens that could be redeemed for valuable prizes. In the *social approval* condition, the adult model smiled and gave verbal praise (for example, "That's really sweet of you") whenever the subject donated part of her winnings to needy children. Subjects assigned to a *no approval* condition were not praised for their charitable acts.

The results of this experiment are shown in the figure. As we might expect, charitable models elicited larger donations than selfish models. But the effects of social approval depended on its source. Approval from a charitable model enhanced altruism, whereas approval from a selfish model appeared to *inhibit* it. A later experiment replicated this **"aversive approval" effect** among groups of 8- to 9-year-old children.

Why does approval from a selfish person inhibit altruism? The answer is not immediately obvious. When children rated the attractiveness of the adult models, the selfish model was rated *no less* attractive or well liked than the charitable model. This finding suggests that children who received social approval from a selfish model *did not* fear disapproval from others for accepting praise from an "unattractive" person. Perhaps

either preached *charity* and emphasized the positive impact of charitable acts on recipients ("I know that I don't have to give, but it would make some children very happy") or preached *greed* and stressed the undesirable aspects of charity ("I could really use some spending money this week; it makes some children feel bad to get charity"). Each child then played the game, won five times, and thus had five opportunities to donate money to needy children.

Table 11-4 summarizes the results. As expected, children who observed a charitable model donated a larger percentage of their winnings (35.8%) than children who observed a selfish model (14%). Furthermore, the model's verbal exhortations had a

TABLE 11-4 *Average percentage of winnings donated by children exposed to charitable or selfish models who preached charity or greed*

Model's Behavior	Model's Verbal Preaching		Row Averages
	Charity	Greed	
Charitable	44.0	27.5	35.8
Selfish	17.5	10.5	14.0
Column Averages	30.8	19.0	

SOURCE: Adapted from E. Midlarsky & J. H. Bryan, "Affect Expressions and Children's Imitative Altruism." *Journal of Experimental Research in Personality*, 1972, 6, 195–203. Copyright © 1972 by Academic Press, Inc. Adapted by permission.

11-2 | *continued*

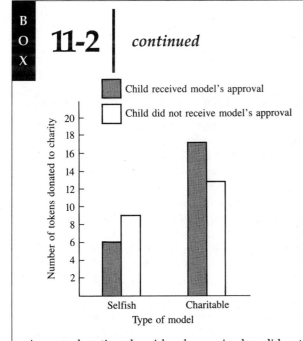

Average donations by girls who received or did not receive social approval for donating from charitable or selfish models. (Adapted from E. Midlarsky, J. H. Bryan, & P. Brickman, "Aversive Approval: Interactive Effects of Modeling and Reinforcement on Altruistic Behavior." *Child Development*, 1973, 44, 321–328. Copyright © 1973 by the Society for Research in Child Development. Reprinted by permission.)

the approving responses of a selfish model made the inconsistency between the model's actions and her verbal behavior obvious to the child. This inconsistency may then have prompted the child to think about the inequity of the situation and wonder "Why should I give when the model has not?"

The results Midlarsky et al. obtained have straightforward implications for parents and other socializing agents:

> This research indicates that an adult's inconsistency [between his actions and the behavior he reinforces] may cause him to lose the ability to exert positive influence in the domain of moral behavior . . . or to lose the ability to exercise one of the two most important means of [socializing a child], social reinforcement. . . . The parent who models selfishness may be better advised to do nothing than to attempt to reinforce altruism, if teaching altruism is his aim [1973, pp. 326–328].

significant effect: models who exhorted charity elicited larger donations from the children (30.8%) than models who exhorted greed (19%). So charitable exhortations can increase children's generosity if they are strongly stated and are justified in terms of the needs of prospective recipients. However, the relatively large donations prompted by the charitable model who preached charity serve as a reminder that our altruistic exhortations are most effective when we practice what we preach.

Now let's turn to the child-rearing literature to see if the variables that promote altruism in the laboratory have similar effects on children in the natural environment.

Who Raises Altruistic Children?

Implications from studies of prosocial activists. Might we learn more about the encouragement of altruism by studying prosocial activists and trying to determine why they are so altruistically inclined? David Rosenhan (1970) thought so. Rosenhan's strategy was to conduct extensive interviews with people who had participated in the civil rights movement in the southern United States during the early to mid-1960s. His interviews suggested that these "freedom riders" could be divided into two groups: (1) *fully committed* activists who had given up their homes, jobs, and educations to participate extensively in the civil rights movement and (2) *partially committed* activists who had limited their involvement to one or two freedom rides without altering the course of their lives in a significant way.

The two groups held similar attitudes about racial equality and civil rights. But there were two striking differences between fully and partially committed activists, both involving events that had taken place in childhood. First, the fully committed subjects had parents who themselves had been prosocial activists for other causes in an earlier era. For example, one member of the fully committed group noted that his mother "felt close to Jesus and . . . [had] devoted her entire life to Christian education." By contrast, the partially committed activists had parents who had often preached but rarely practiced altruism.

The second difference between the two groups centered on their emotional relationships with their parents. Fully committed activists had generally maintained a warm, cordial relationship with at least one parent, whereas the partially committed activists described their parental relations as hostile during childhood and rather cool at the time they were interviewed.

It seemed to Rosenhan (1972b) that the behavior of the fully committed activists qualified as *autonomous altruism*, for these people had ignored their present or future careers to advance the cause of others. The antecedents of their deep sense of altruistic commitment appeared to be a *warm, nurturant relationship with parents who were good altruistic models*.[3] These findings are reminiscent of the laboratory evidence we have reviewed, which indicates that altruistic models who are warm and nurturant are especially likely to elicit prosocial responses from children.

Partially committed activists did not incur many personal costs and were only minimally committed to the cause. Rosenhan suspected that their participation was prompted by group *esprit* or social conformity and thus qualified as *normative altruism*. Recall that these individuals had experienced rather cool relations with parents who often failed to practice what they preached. The literature we have reviewed does indeed suggest that a cool relationship with a relatively nonaltruistic (or hypocritical) model is not conducive to the development of a strong sense of altruistic concern.

Unfortunately, one disadvantage of interview data such as Rosenhan's is that they could be inaccurate. For example, were the parents of the fully committed participants really that altruistic? Or, rather, were these altruistic activists simply being charitable in their memories of their parents? One way to assess the merits of Rosenhan's ideas about the antecedents of altruism would be to identify groups of

[3]London (1970) reached a similar conclusion in his study of prosocial activists: Christians who had risked their lives to save Jews from the Nazis during World War II reported that they had had close ties with moralistic parents who always acted in accordance with their ethical principles, regardless of the personal costs for doing so.

PHOTO 11-4   Children who are committed to performing prosocial acts often have parents who have encouraged altruism and who have practiced what they preach.

toward the victim (Zahn-Waxler et al., 1979). Research with older children paints a similar picture: parents who continue to rely on rational, nonpunitive disciplinary techniques in which they regularly display sympathy and concern for others tend to raise children who are sympathetic and self-sacrificing, whereas frequent use of forceful and punitive discipline appears to inhibit altruism and lead to the development of self-centered values (Brody & Shaffer, 1982; Eisenberg et al., 1992; Fabes et al., 1990).

If we think about it, there are several reasons why rational, affectively oriented discipline that is heavy on reasoning might inspire children to become more altruistic. First, it encourages the child to assume another person's perspective (role taking) and to experience that person's distress (empathy training). It also teaches the child to perform helpful or comforting acts that may make both the self and the other person feel better. And, last but not least, these reparative responses provide opportunities for parents to persuade their older (grade-school) children that they can be "nice," "helpful," or "sympathetic" people, thus promoting a *positive self-image* that children may try to live up to by performing other acts of kindness in the future.

people who had had the same kinds of childhood experiences as Rosenhan's fully committed and partially committed activists and then see whether the former group is *subsequently* more altruistic than the latter group. The research described in Box 11-3 relied on this type of *prospective* methodology, and, as we will see, its results provide striking support for Rosenhan's earlier conclusions.

Parental discipline.   Parental reactions to a child's harmdoing also play an important role in the development of altruism. For example, we've noted that mothers of less compassionate infants and toddlers react to harmdoing in punitive or forceful ways, whereas mothers of compassionate toddlers rely more heavily on nonpunitive, affective explanations in which they persuade their child to accept personal responsibility for her harmdoing and urge her to direct some sort of comforting or helpful response

Aggression and Altruism Revisited — And a Look Ahead

Now that we've examined the development of both aggression and altruism, it might seem that these two dispositional qualities are at opposite ends of a "social responsibility" dimension, with (1) aggressive individuals generally displaying self-centeredness and a lack of concern for others and (2) relatively altruistic souls being more likely to consider others' needs and to make personal sacrifices, if necessary, to ensure that those needs are met. Yet such a depiction may mislead us into believing that (1) highly aggressive individuals have few if any prosocial qualities and (2) altruists are more other-oriented and less self-serving than they may actually be. Personally, I like to think of aggression and altruism as two separate aspects of character that are often negatively correlated (with aggressive individuals being low in prosocial concern and altruistic individuals being low in aggression/antisocial conduct) *but need not be*. The proposal, then, is that people can vary, from high to low, in both aggression and altruism, so that it is possible (theoretically, at least) to identify children and adolescents who display high, intermediate, or low levels of both aggression/antisocial conduct and prosocial concern.

Indeed, there is some support in the literature for conceptualizing aggression and altruism as separable aspects of character, rather than as opposite ends of a single personality dimension. In their recent study of peer popularity among middle-school students (that is, 12–14-year-olds), Jennifer Parkhurst and Steven Asher (1992) constructed independent measures of children's prosocial and antisocial conduct and found that different combinations of these two attributes were associated with different peer statuses. Many of the children who were actively *rejected* by peers were indeed high in aggression/antisocial conduct and low in prosocial inclinations, whereas *popular* students tended to be low in aggression and high in prosocial conduct. And yet there were many relatively aggressive students who were *not* rejected—apparently because they also displayed *at least average levels of prosocial conduct*. Moreover, other children who were low in aggression were rejected nonetheless—apparently because they were easy to dominate and showed *little* prosocial behavior toward peers. Finally, middle-school students who displayed intermediate, or average, levels of both prosocial and antisocial conduct were often *neglected* (rather than actively rejected) by their classmates. So, by treating aggres-

---

**B
O
X**

11-3 | *Do Childhood Experiences Predict Adult Altruism?*

Gil Clary and Jude Miller (1986) have conducted an important replication of Rosenhan's study that differs from the civil rights project in one very crucial way. These investigators first obtained reports of subjects' childhood experiences with parents. They then observed these subjects over a period of time to determine whether the kinds of experiences subjects reported having had with their parents would *predict* the subjects' future altruistic behaviors.

The participants in this study were adult volunteers at a crisis counseling agency in Minneapolis, Minnesota. During the period when the volunteers were trained, each of them completed an extensive questionnaire about his or her childhood experiences. On the basis of their responses (and Rosenhan's earlier classification scheme), subjects were classified as "autonomous altruists" (that is, those who reported having had warm relations with altruistic parents who practiced what they preached) or "normative altruists" (those reporting cooler relations with parents who had

rarely modeled altruism). As the volunteers were being trained, the cohesiveness, or *esprit de corps*, of their training group was also measured and was classified as high or low. All trained volunteers were expected to fulfill a six-month commitment to the crisis counseling agency—a commitment requiring them to work one four-hour shift each week. The dependent variable in this study was a measure of *sustained* altruism—that is, whether the volunteer actually completed his or her six-month commitment to the agency.

The results of this study were quite interesting. The table reveals that a majority of subjects classified as normative altruists completed their obligations to the agency *if their training group happened to be a cohesive one*; however, 70% of the normative altruists *failed* to fulfill their commitments if their groups were less cohesive. So, consistent with Rosenhan's earlier results, the pleasantness of the social context, or *group esprit*, was critical in determining the sustained altruism of subjects classified as normative altruists. By contrast, a

sion and altruism as separable aspects of character (rather than as opposite poles of a single dimension), Parkhurst and Asher (1992) were able to provide a much richer description of the behavioral correlates of various peer statuses than that which had emerged from earlier research.[4]

If aggression and altruism are separable aspects of personality, how, then, can we explain why many aggressive children are not especially concerned about others, or why many concerned children are not very aggressive? My own speculation about this issue is that the development of both aggressive and altruistic inclinations depends very heavily on the growth of *self-regulatory processes* and *self-control*—a topic we discussed earlier in Chapters 3 and 7. Children who are generally proficient at regulating their

conduct and controlling their emotions may simply be better than their more impulsive agemates at appraising social situations. That is, they are better at finding cues that would signal a harmdoer's nonhostile intent or would elicit a sympathetic response to a victim's distress—cues that would then help them to inhibit aggression and/or to behave more kindly toward others. Indeed, Kathryn Wentzel (1991) finds that 11- to 12-year-olds who actively attempt to *regulate* their social conduct (by striving to be kindly, helpful, and compliant with teachers and peers) are viewed by other students as much more prosocially inclined and much less aggressive, or antisocial, than agemates who have set few such self-regulatory objectives.

Here, then, is yet another clue that self-regulation and self-control are critically important aspects of social and personality development. Just how important are they? We address this issue in our next

---

[4]The determinants of one's peer status and popularity will be discussed at length in Chapter 15.

<table>
<tr><td>**B O X**</td><td>**11-3**</td><td>*continued*</td></tr>
</table>

clear majority of volunteers who had been classified by their childhood experiences as autonomous altruists followed through to complete their commitments to the agency, *regardless of the level of cohesiveness of their training groups*. Apparently, social benefits stemming from the volunteer experience itself were less important to these individuals than the services they might provide to clients who needed crisis counseling. In other words, the motivation for their helpfulness did seem to come from within and to reflect a sense of *autonomous* altruism.

So here, then, is important converging evidence for Rosenhan's proposition that different childhood experiences can promote different kinds of altruism. Parents who are not particularly nurturant or altruistic are likely to raise children whose prosocial inclinations are situationally determined and will depend to a large extent on the benefits they can expect to receive. By contrast, nurturant parents who frequently encourage and display altruism are more likely to raise children whose

prosocial acts are internally motivated and reflect a genuine concern for the welfare of other people.

Percentages of subjects completing their obligation to a crisis counseling agency as a function of their prior childhood experiences and the cohesiveness of their training groups

	Group Cohesiveness	
Childhood Experiences	Low	High
Normative (cool relations with nonaltruistic parents)	30	60
Autonomous (warm relations with altruistic parents)	57	62

SOURCE: Adapted from E. G. Clary & J. Miller, "Socialization and Situational Influences on Sustained Altruism." *Child Development*, 1986, *57*, 1358–1369. Copyright © 1986 by the Society for Research in Child Development. Adapted by permission.

chapter, where we will see that, regardless of their often contrasting theoretical positions, students of moral development view the ability to monitor and control one's own conduct as the *essential foundation* for the growth of moral maturity.

Summary

Most people in most cultures endorse the *norm of social responsibility*, which prescribes that one should help others who need help. The widespread acceptance of this principle has sparked a controversy about human nature. One school of thought contends that all prosocial behavior — behavior that benefits others — is motivated by expectations of self-gain or self-reinforcement; other theorists argue that such behavior often stems from a genuine concern for the welfare of others.

Altruism, a form of prosocial behavior, is usually defined in one of two ways. Proponents of a *motivational* definition contend that an act is altruistic if it benefits others and if the helper is acting more out of a concern for others than for the positive outcomes he or she might obtain. Advocates of a *behavioral* definition note that it is often difficult to infer a helper's true intentions. As a result, they define altruism as an act that provides assistance to others, regardless of the helper's motives.

Several theoretical explanations of altruism have been proposed. Evolutionary theorists argue that altruism is a preadapted, genetically programmed motive that evolved because it promotes the survival of the individual (or the individual's genes) and the species. By contrast, proponents of psychoanalytic, social-learning, and cognitive-developmental theories believe that children must *acquire* a sense of altruistic concern. Psychoanalytic theorists assume that altruistic values are internalized and become a part of one's superego. Social-learning theorists believe that altruistic habits are acquired and maintained because children learn that prosocial behavior is rewarding. Cognitive-developmental theorists argue that the growth of altruistic concern depends on fundamental cognitive changes that occur during childhood; these changes include (1) the toddler's ability to recognize the self and to differentiate self from others, (2) the gradual decline in egocentrism that occurs over the preschool period, (3) the development of role-taking skills, and (4) the growth of empathic sensitivity and prosocial moral reasoning.

Although infants and toddlers will occasionally offer toys to playmates, try to help their parents with household chores, and attempt to soothe distressed companions, examples of altruism become increasingly common over the first 10–12 years of life — due, in part, to age-related increases in children's feelings of competency to help and responsibility to do so. By middle childhood there is a moderate degree of consistency in children's prosocial inclinations: those who help or share in one situation are likely to behave in a helpful or kindly manner in related situations; moreover, children's manner of responding to others' distress is often stable over time.

Contrary to popular belief, females are not more altruistic than males, although there is some evidence that young children are more inclined to assist or comfort members of their own sex. By middle childhood the sex of a prospective recipient is less important in determining children's willingness to help than is the recipient's apparent need for help. Generally speaking, children are more likely to comfort, assist, or share valuable resources with friends than with acquaintances or strangers. And a child's prosocial behavior may be influenced by his or her mood. Children are more prosocially inclined if they are experiencing positive emotions, whereas the effects of negative moods are quite complex. If one's negative affect stems from personal misfortunes, it is likely to inhibit altruism. However, blue moods stemming from a consideration of someone else's misfortunes may increase altruism, in both children and adults.

A child's role-taking abilities and level of *prosocial moral reasoning* will affect his or her altruistic behavior. Children with good *social* and *affective* role-taking skills are often more prosocially inclined than poor role takers, and the link between role taking and altruism becomes stronger with age. Mature moral reasoners are more generous and helpful than immature moral reasoners. In fact, mature moral reasoners may often help someone they dislike, whereas immature moral reasoners are much more inclined to ignore the needs of a distressed other.

Although young children may often empathize with a person in need, their behavioral responses to the person's distress are not always helpful ones. Children whose empathic distress is sympathetic (rather than self-oriented) are more prosocially inclined. Yet the evidence for a link between empathy and altruism is weak for young children and becomes stronger with age. Empathy is a more reliable mediator of altruism once children acquire the role-taking skills that will enable them to understand that the distress or misfortune of others is the cause of their own empathic emotions. And, given this understanding, empathy may trigger altruism by causing children to reflect on the prosocial norms they have learned, which in turn induce them to assume personal responsibility for aiding people in distress. Parents, teachers, and other socialization agents may also promote altruism by persuading young children to think of themselves as "kindly" or "helpful" persons—a self-image that youngsters may try to perpetuate by being more kindly or helpful in the future.

A person's altruistic inclinations are clearly influenced by the cultural and family settings in which he or she is raised. Prosocial behavior is more common among children when their society emphasizes cooperation over competition and when children must assume important family responsibilities at an early age. Tangible reinforcement for prosocial conduct may undermine altruistic motivation, but *social reinforcement* can be quite effective at promoting altruism—as long as the praise is administered by someone children like and respect. Children exposed to altruistic models often become more altruistic themselves, particularly if they know and respect the model and have previously established a warm and friendly relationship with this benevolent companion. Although a model's actions speak louder than his or her words, it is inappropriate to conclude that words are wasted on children. Verbal exhortations will promote altruism if they are strongly stated and provide the child with a meaningful cognitive rationale for sharing with, comforting, or helping others.

Who raises altruistic children? The conclusions we can draw dovetail nicely with laboratory work on the development of altruism. Prosocial activists tend to have warm relationships with parents who have exhorted and praised altruism and have practiced what they preached. Moreover, parents who rely on rational, affective-oriented modes of discipline that are heavy on reasoning tend to promote the role-taking skills and the sympathetic emotional responses to distress that are associated with a concern for others and self-sacrificial behaviors. Forceful and punitive forms of discipline appear to inhibit altruism and lead to the development of self-centered values.

References

BANDURA, A. (1989). Social cognitive theory. In R. Vasta (Ed.), *Annals of child development* (Vol. 6). Greenwich, CT: JAI Press.

BARNETT, M. A. (1987). Empathy and related responses in children. In N. Eisenberg & J. Strayer (Eds.), *Empathy and its development*. New York: Cambridge University Press.

BARNETT, M. A., HOWARD, J. A., MELTON, E. M., & DINO, G. A. (1982). Effect of inducing sadness about self or other on helping behavior in high- and low-empathic children. *Child Development, 53,* 920–923.

BARNETT, M. A., KING, L. M., & HOWARD, J. A. (1979). Inducing affect about self or other: Effects on generosity in children. *Developmental Psychology, 15,* 164–167.

BARNETT, M. A., & McMINIMY, V. (1988). Influence of the reason for other's affect on preschoolers' empathy response. *Journal of Genetic Psychology, 149,* 153–162.

BARON, R. A., & BYRNE, D. (1991). *Social psychology: Understanding human interaction* (6th ed.). Newton, MA: Allyn & Bacon.

BAR-TAL, D., RAVIV, A., & GOLDBERG, M. (1982). Helping behavior among preschool children: An observational study. *Child Development, 53,* 396–402.

BATSON, C. D. (1987). Prosocial motivation: Is it ever truly altruistic? In L. Berkowitz (Ed.), *Advances in experimental social psychology* (Vol. 20). New York: Academic Press.

BERKOWITZ, L., & DANIELS, L. (1963). Responsibility and dependence. *Journal of Abnormal and Social Psychology, 66,* 429–436.

BERNDT, T. J., HAWKINS, J. A., & HOYLE, S. G. (1986). Changes in friendship during a school year: Effects on children's and adolescents' impressions of friendship and sharing with friends. *Child Development, 57,* 1204–1297.

BIRCH, L. L., & BILLMAN, J. (1986). Preschool children's food sharing with friends and acquaintances. *Child Development, 57,* 387–395.

BRODY, G. H., & SHAFFER, D. R. (1982). Contributions of parents and peers to children's moral socialization. *Developmental Review, 2,* 31–75.

BRYAN, J. H., & SCHWARTZ, T. H. (1971). The effects of filmed material upon children's behavior. *Psychological Bulletin, 75,* 50–59.

BRYAN, J. H., & WALBEK, N. (1970). Preaching and practicing self-sacrifice: Children's actions and reactions. *Child Development, 41,* 329–353.

CAMPBELL, D. T. (1965). Ethnocentric and other altruistic motives. In D. Levine (Ed.), *Nebraska Symposium on Motivation* (Vol. 13). Lincoln: University of Nebraska Press.

CAPLAN, M. Z., & HAY, D. F. (1989). Preschoolers' responses to peers' distress and beliefs about bystander intervention. *Journal of Child Psychology and Psychiatry, 30,* 231–242.

CARLO, G., KNIGHT, G. P., EISENBERG, N., & ROTENBERG, K. J. (1991). Cognitive processes and prosocial behaviors among children: The role of affective attributions and reconciliations. *Developmental Psychology, 27,* 456–461.

CHALMERS, J. B., & TOWNSEND, M. A. R. (1990). The effects of training in social perspective taking on socially maladjusted girls. *Child Development, 61,* 178–190.

CHAPMAN, M., ZAHN-WAXLER, C., COOPERMAN, G., & IANNOTTI, R. J. (1987). Empathy and responsibility in the motivation of children's helping. *Developmental Psychology, 23,* 140–145.

CHARLESWORTH, R., & HARTUP, W. W. (1967). Positive social reinforcement in the nursery school peer group. *Child Development, 38,* 993–1002.

CIALDINI, R. B., & KENRICK, D. T. (1976). Altruism as hedonism: A social development perspective on the relationship of negative mood state and helping. *Journal of Personality and Social Psychology, 34,* 907–914.

CLARY, E. G., & MILLER, J. (1986). Socialization and situational influences on sustained altruism. *Child Development, 57,* 1358–1369.

CUNNINGHAM, M. R. (1979). Weather, mood, and helping behavior: Quasi-experiments with the sunshine Samaritan. *Journal of Personality and Social Psychology, 37,* 1947–1956.

CUNNINGHAM, M. R. (1986). Levites and brother's keepers: A sociobiological perspective on prosocial behavior. *Humboldt Journal of Social Relations, 13,* 35–67.

CUNNINGHAM, M. R. (1988). What do you do when you're happy or blue? Mood, expectancies, and behavioral interest. *Motivation and Emotion, 12,* 309–331.

CUNNINGHAM, M. R., SHAFFER, D. R., BARBEE, A. P., WOLFF, P. L., & KELLEY, D. J. (1990). Separate processes in the relation of elation and depression to helping: Social versus personal concerns. *Journal of Experimental Social Psychology, 26,* 13–33.

EISENBERG, N. (1983). Children's differentiations among potential recipients of aid. *Child Development, 54,* 594–602.

EISENBERG, N. (1990). Prosocial development in early and mid-adolescence. In R. Montemayor, G. R. Adams, & T. P. Gullotta (Eds.), *From childhood to adolescence: A transitional period?* Newbury Park, CA: Sage.

EISENBERG, N., FABES, R. A., CARLO, G., TROYER, D., SPEER, A. L., KARBON, M., & SWITZER, G. (1992). The relations of maternal practices and characteristics to children's vicarious emotional responsiveness. *Child Development, 63,* 583–602.

EISENBERG, N., FABES, R. A., MILLER, P. A., SHELL, R., SHEA, C., & MAY-PLUMLEE, T. (1990). Preschoolers' vicarious emotional responding and their situational and dispositional prosocial behavior. *Merrill-Palmer Quarterly, 36,* 507–529.

EISENBERG, N., FABES, R. A., SCHALLER, M., CARLO, G., & MILLER, P. A. (1991). The relations of parental characteristics and practices in children's vicarious emotional responding. *Child Development, 62,* 1393–1408.

EISENBERG, N., LENNON, R., & ROTH, K. (1983). Prosocial development: A longitudinal study. *Developmental Psychology, 19,* 846–855.

EISENBERG, N., MILLER, P. A., SHELL, R., McNALLEY, S., & SHEA, C. (1991). Prosocial development in adolescence: A longitudinal study. *Developmental Psychology, 27,* 849–857.

EISENBERG, N., SCHALLER, M., FABES, R. A., BUSTAMANTE, D., MATHY, R. M., SHELL, R., & RHODES, K. (1988). Differentiation of personal distress and sympathy in children and adolescents. *Developmental Psychology, 24,* 766–775.

EISENBERG, N., SHELL, R., PASTERNACK, J., LENNON, R., BELLER, R., & MATHY, R. M. (1987). Prosocial development in middle childhood: A longitudinal study. *Developmental Psychology, 23,* 712–718.

EISENBERG-BERG, N., & HAND, M. (1979). The relationship of preschoolers' reasoning about prosocial moral conflicts to prosocial behavior. *Child Development, 50,* 356–363.

FABES, R. A., EISENBERG, N., & MILLER, P. A. (1990). Maternal correlates of children's vicarious emotional responsiveness. *Developmental Psychology, 26,* 639–648.

FABES, R. A., FULTZ, J., EISENBERG, N., MAY-PLUMLEE, T., & CHRISTOPHER, F. S. (1989). Effects of rewards on children's prosocial motivation: A socialization study. *Developmental Psychology, 25,* 509–515.

FISCHER, W. F. (1963). Sharing in pre-school children as a function of the amount and type of reinforcement. *Genetic Psychology Monographs, 68,* 215–245.

GREEN, F. P., & SCHNEIDER, F. W. (1974). Age differences in the behavior of boys on three measures of altruism. *Child Development, 45,* 248–251.

GRUSEC, J. E. (1991). Socializing concern for others in the home. *Developmental Psychology, 27,* 338–342.

GRUSEC, J. E., & LYTTON, H. (1988). *Social development: History, theory, and research.* New York: Springer-Verlag.

GRUSEC, J. E., & REDLER, E. (1980). Attribution, reinforcement, and altruism: A developmental analysis. *Developmental Psychology, 16*, 525–534.

HANDLON, B. J., & GROSS, P. (1959). The development of sharing behavior. *Journal of Abnormal and Social Psychology, 59*, 425–428.

HAY, D. F., CAPLAN, M., CASTLE, J., & STIMSON, C. A. (1991). Does sharing become increasingly "rational" in the second year of life? *Developmental Psychology, 27*, 987–993.

HOFFMAN, M. L. (1981). Is altruism part of human nature? *Journal of Personality and Social Psychology, 40*, 121–137.

HOFFMAN, M. L. (1988). Moral development. In M. H. Bornstein & M. E. Lamb (Eds.), *Developmental Psychology: An advanced textbook*. Hillsdale, NJ: Erlbaum.

HUDSON, L. M., FORMAN, E. R., & BRION-MEISELS, S. (1982). Role-taking as a predictor of prosocial behavior in cross-age tutors. *Child Development, 53*, 1320–1329.

HUGHES, R., JR., TINGLE, B. A., & SAWIN, D. B. (1981). Development of empathic understanding in children. *Child Development, 52*, 122–128.

IANNOTTI, R. J. (1978). Effect of role-taking experiences on role-taking, empathy, altruism, and aggression. *Developmental Psychology, 14*, 119–124.

ISEN, A. M. (1970). Success, failure, attention, and reaction to others: The warm glow of success. *Journal of Personality and Social Psychology, 15*, 294–301.

ISEN, A. M., & LEVIN, P. F. (1972). Effects of feeling good on helping: Cookies and kindness. *Journal of Personality and Social Psychology, 21*, 384–388.

JONES, D. C. (1985). Persuasive appeals and responses to appeals among friends and acquaintances. *Child Development, 56*, 757–763.

KAGAN, S., & MASDEN, M. C. (1971). Cooperation and competition of Mexican, Mexican-American, and Anglo-American children of two ages and four instructional sets. *Developmental Psychology, 5*, 32–39.

KAGAN, S., & MASDEN, M. C. (1972). Rivalry in Anglo-American and Mexican children of two ages. *Journal of Personality and Social Psychology, 24*, 214–220.

KAHN, P. H., JR. (1992). Children's obligatory and discretionary moral judgments. *Child Development, 63*, 416–430.

KANFER, F. H., STIFTER, E., & MORRIS, S. J. (1981). Self-control and altruism: Delay of gratification for another. *Child Development, 47*, 51–61.

KOHLBERG, L. (1969). Stage and sequence: The cognitive-developmental approach to socialization. In D. A. Goslin (Ed.), *Handbook of socialization theory and research*. Skokie, IL: Rand McNally.

KREBS, D. L. (1970). Altruism — An examination of the concept and a review of the literature. *Psychological Bulletin, 73*, 258–302.

LADD, G. W., LANGE, G., & STREMMEL, A. (1983). Personal and situational influences on children's helping behavior: Factors that mediate compliant helping. *Child Development, 54*, 488–501.

LEUNG, E. H. L., & RHEINGOLD, H. L. (1981). Development of pointing as a social gesture. *Developmental Psychology, 17*, 215–220.

LEVITT, M. J., WEBER, R. A., CLARK, M. C., & McDONNELL, P. (1985). Reciprocity of exchange in toddler sharing behavior. *Developmental Psychology, 21*, 122–123.

LONDON, P. (1970). The rescuers: Motivational hypotheses about Christians who saved Jews from the Nazis. In J. Macaulay & L. Berkowitz (Eds.), *Altruism and helping behavior*. Orlando, FL: Academic Press.

MACCOBY, E. E. (1980). *Social development*. San Diego: Harcourt Brace Jovanovich.

MATTHEWS, K. A., BATSON, C. D., HORN, J., & ROSENMAN, R. H. (1981). "Principles in his nature which interest him in the fortune of others. . . .": The heritability of empathic concern. *Journal of Personality, 49*, 237–247.

MIDLARSKY, E., & BRYAN, J. H. (1972). Affect expressions and children's imitative altruism. *Journal of Experimental Research in Personality, 6*, 195–203.

MIDLARSKY, E., BRYAN, J. H., & BRICKMAN, P. (1973). Aversive approval: Interactive effects of modeling and reinforcement on altruistic behavior. *Child Development, 44*, 321–328.

MIDLARSKY, E., & HANNAH, M. E. (1985). Competence, reticence, and helping by children and adolescents. *Developmental Psychology, 21*, 534–541.

MILLS, R. S. L., & GRUSEC, J. E. (1989). Cognitive, affective, and behavioral consequences of praising altruism. *Merrill-Palmer Quarterly, 35*, 299–326.

MOORE, B. S., UNDERWOOD, B., & ROSENHAN, D. L. (1973). Affect and altruism. *Developmental Psychology, 8*, 99–104.

ORLICK, T. D. (1981). Positive socialization via cooperative games. *Developmental Psychology, 17*, 426–429.

PARKHURST, J. T., & ASHER, S. R. (1992). Peer rejection in middle school: Subgroup differences in behavior, loneliness, and interpersonal concerns. *Developmental Psychology, 28*, 231–241.

PEARL, R. (1985). Children's understanding of others' need for help: Effects of problem explicitness and type. *Child Development, 56*, 735–745.

PETERSON, L. (1983). Influence of children's age, task competence, and responsibility focus on children's altruism. *Developmental Psychology, 19*, 141–148.

PETERSON, L., & GELFAND, D. M. (1984). Causal attributions of helping as a function of age and incentives. *Child Development, 55*, 504–511.

RADKE-YARROW, M., & ZAHN-WAXLER, C. (1983). Roots, motives, and patterns in children's prosocial behavior. In J. Reykowski, T. Karylowski, D. Bar-Tal, & E. Staub (Eds.), *Origins and maintenance of prosocial behaviors*. New York: Plenum.

RADKE-YARROW, M., ZAHN-WAXLER, C., & CHAPMAN, M. (1983). Children's prosocial dispositions and behavior. In E. M. Hetherington (Ed.), *Handbook of child psychology*. Vol.

4: *Socialization, personality, and social development*. New York: Wiley.

RHEINGOLD, H. L. (1982). Little children's participation in the work of adults, a nascent prosocial behavior. *Child Development, 53*, 114–125.

RICE, M. E., & GRUSEC, J. E. (1975). Saying and doing: Effects on observer performance. *Journal of Personality and Social Psychology, 32*, 584–593.

RITCHIE, F. K., & TONER, I. J. (1984). Direct labeling, tester expectancy, and delay maintenance behavior in Scottish preschool children. *International Journal of Behavioral Development, 7*, 333–341.

ROSENHAN, D. L. (1970). The natural socialization of altruistic autonomy. In J. Macaulay & L. Berkowitz (Eds.), *Altruism and helping behavior*. Orlando, FL: Academic Press.

ROSENHAN, D. L. (1972a). Learning theory and prosocial behavior. *Journal of Social Issues, 28*, 151–163.

ROSENHAN, D. L. (1972b). Prosocial behavior of children. In W. W. Hartup (Ed.), *The young child* (Vol. 2). Washington, DC: National Association for the Education of Young Children.

ROSENHAN, D. L., & WHITE, G. M. (1967). Observation and rehearsal as determinants of prosocial behavior. *Journal of Personality and Social Psychology, 5*, 424–431.

RUSHTON, J. P. (1975). Generosity in children: Immediate and long term effects of modeling, preaching, and moral judgment. *Journal of Personality and Social Psychology, 31*, 459–466.

RUSHTON, J. P. (1976). Socialization and the altruistic behavior of children. *Psychological Bulletin, 83*, 898–913.

RUSHTON, J. P. (1980). *Altruism, socialization, and society*. Englewood Cliffs, NJ: Prentice-Hall.

RUSHTON, J. P. (1989). Genetic similarity, human altruism, and group selection. *Behavioral and Brain Sciences, 12*, 503–559.

RUTHERFORD, E., & MUSSEN, P. H. (1968). Generosity in nursery school boys. *Child Development, 39*, 755–765.

SHAFFER, D. R. (1986). Is mood-induced altruism a form of hedonism? *Humboldt Journal of Social Relations, 13*, 195–216.

SHAFFER, D. R., & GRAZIANO, W. G. (1983). Effects of positive and negative moods on helping tasks having pleasant or unpleasant consequences. *Motivation and Emotion, 7*, 269–278.

SHAFFER, D. R., & SMITH, J. D. (1987). Self-consciousness, self-reported altruism, and helping behavior. *Social Behavior and Personality, 15*, 215–220.

SHIGETOMI, C. C., HARTMANN, D. P., & GELFAND, D. M. (1981). Sex differences in children's altruistic behavior and reputations for helpfulness. *Developmental Psychology, 17*, 434–437.

SIGELMAN, C. K. (1984). Prosocial behavior. In K. Deaux & L. S. Wrightsman, *Social psychology in the '80s* (4th ed.). Pacific Grove, CA: Brooks/Cole.

STAUB, E. A. (1970). A child in distress: The influence of age and number of witnesses on children's attempts to help. *Journal of Personality and Social Psychology, 14*, 130–140.

STAUB, E. A. (1974). Helping a distressed person: Social, personality, and stimulus determinants. In L. Berkowitz (Ed.), *Advances in experimental social psychology* (Vol. 7). Orlando, FL: Academic Press.

STAUB, E. A. (1979). *Positive social behavior and morality* (Vol. 2). Orlando, FL: Academic Press.

STAUB, E. A., & NOERENBERG, H. (1981). Property rights, deservingness, reciprocity, friendship: The transactional character of children's sharing behavior. *Journal of Personality and Social Psychology, 40*, 271–289.

THOMPSON, W. C., COWAN, C. L., & ROSENHAN, D. L. (1980). Focus of attention mediates the impact of negative mood on altruism. *Journal of Personality and Social Psychology, 38*, 291–300.

TIETJEN, A. M. (1986). Prosocial reasoning among children and adults in a Papua New Guinea society. *Developmental Psychology, 22*, 861–868.

TRIVERS, R. L. (1971). The evolution of reciprocal altruism. *Quarterly Review of Biology, 46*, 35–57.

TRIVERS, R. L. (1983). The evolution of cooperation. In D. L. Bridgeman (Ed.), *The nature of prosocial development*. New York: Academic Press.

UGUREL-SEMIN, R. (1952). Moral behavior and moral judgment of children. *Journal of Abnormal and Social Psychology, 47*, 463–474.

UNDERWOOD, B., & MOORE, B. (1982). Perspective-taking and altruism. *Psychological Bulletin, 91*, 143–173.

WENTZEL, K. R. (1991). Relations between social competence and academic achievement in early adolescence. *Child Development, 61*, 1066–1078.

WHITING, B. B., & EDWARDS, C. P. (1988). *Children of different worlds: The formation of social behavior*. Cambridge, MA: Harvard University Press.

WHITING, B. B., & WHITING, J. W. M. (1975). *Children of six cultures*. Cambridge, MA: Harvard University Press.

WRIGHT, B. A. (1942). Altruism in children and perceived conduct of others. *Journal of Abnormal and Social Psychology, 37*, 218–233.

YARROW, M. R., SCOTT, P. M., & WAXLER, C. Z. (1973). Learning concern for others. *Developmental Psychology, 8*, 240–260.

ZAHN-WAXLER, C., RADKE-YARROW, M., & KING, R. A. (1979). Childrearing and children's prosocial initiations towards victims of distress. *Child Development, 50*, 319–330.

ZAHN-WAXLER, C., RADKE-YARROW, M., WAGNER, E., & CHAPMAN, M. (1992). Development of concern for others. *Developmental Psychology, 28*, 126–136.

ZARBATANY, L., HARTMANN, D. P., GELFAND, D. M., & VINCIGUERRA, P. (1985). Gender differences in altruistic reputation: Are they artifactual? *Developmental Psychology, 21*, 97–101.

12 | *Moral Development*

Suppose a large sample of new parents were asked "What is the most important aspect of a child's social development?" Surely this question could elicit any number of responses. However, it's a good bet that many parents would hope above all else that their children would acquire a strong sense of morality—right and wrong—to guide their everyday exchanges with other people.

The **moral development** of each successive generation is of obvious significance to society. One of the reasons why people can live together in peace is that they have evolved codes of ethics that sanction certain practices and prohibit others. Although moral standards may vary from culture to culture, every society has devised rules that its citizens must obey in order to remain members in good standing (Garbarino & Bronfenbrenner, 1976). Thus the moral education of each succeeding generation serves two important functions: (1) to maintain the social order and (2) to enable the individual to function appropriately within his or her culture (or subculture).

Sigmund Freud once argued that moral education is the largest hurdle that parents face when raising a child, and many of his contemporaries agreed. In one of the first social psychology texts, William McDougall (1908) said:

> The fundamental problem of social psychology is the moralization of the individual into the society into which he was born as an amoral and egoistic infant. There are successive stages, each of which must be traversed by every individual before he can attain the next higher: (1) the stage in which . . . [innate] impulses are modified by the influence of rewards and punishments, (2) the stage in which conduct is controlled . . . by social praise or blame, and (3) the highest stage in which conduct is regulated by an ideal that enables a man to act in a way that seems to him right regardless of the praise or blame of his immediate social environment [p. 6].

If we look carefully at McDougall's proposed sequence of moral stages, we again encounter a familiar theme: the notion that young children must learn to *regulate* and to *control* their impulses in order to comply with socially defined rules of order. Although material and social incentives may be necessary early in life to gain such compliance, the third stage in McDougall's theory suggests that children

do not go through life submitting to society's moral dictates because they expect rewards for complying or fear punishments for transgressing. Rather, they eventually internalize the moral principles that they have learned and will behave in accordance with these ideals even when authority figures are not present to enforce them. As we will see, almost all contemporary theorists consider **internalization**—the shift from externally controlled actions to conduct that is governed by internal standards and principles—to be a crucial step in the development of morality.

What Is Morality (and Moral Maturity)?

We all have some idea of what **morality** is, although the ways we define the term may depend, in part, on our backgrounds and general outlooks on life. A theologian, for example, might mention the relationship between human beings and their Creator. A philosopher's definition of morality may depend on the assumptions that he or she makes about human nature. Psychologists are generally concerned with the feelings, thoughts, and actions of people who are facing moral dilemmas. And, when young adults are asked "What does morality mean to you?" they generally agree that it implies a *set of principles* that help a person *(1) to distinguish right from wrong, (2) to act on this distinction, and (3) to experience pride in virtuous conduct and guilt (or shame) over acts that violate their standards* (Quinn, Houts, & Graesser, 1993; Shaffer, 1993).

How Developmentalists Look at Morality

Interestingly, developmental theorizing and research have centered on the same three moral components that laypersons most often mention in their consensual definition of morality:

1. An *affective*, or emotional, component, which consists of the feelings that surround "right" or

PHOTO 12-1 Resisting temptation is a difficult feat for young children, particularly when there is no one around to help them to exercise willpower.

"wrong" actions and that often motivate moral thoughts and deeds.

2. A *cognitive* component, which centers on the way we conceptualize right and wrong and make decisions about how to behave.
3. A *behavioral component*, which reflects how we actually behave when we experience the temptation to violate moral rules.

As it turns out, each of the three major theories of moral development has focused on a different component of morality. Psychoanalytic theorists emphasize the affective component, or powerful **moral affects**. They believe that children are motivated to act in accordance with their ethical principles in order to experience positive affects such as pride and to avoid negative moral emotions such as guilt and shame. Cognitive-developmental theorists have concentrated on the cognitive aspects of morality, or **moral reasoning**, and have found that the ways children think about right and wrong may change

rather dramatically as they mature. Finally, the research of social-learning and social information-processing theorists has helped us to understand how children learn to resist temptation and to practice **moral behavior**, inhibiting actions (such as lying, stealing, and cheating) that violate moral norms.

Defining and Assessing Moral Maturity

Like McDougall, most contemporary researchers believe that moral development proceeds toward the internalization of a set of ethical principles or norms against which the appropriateness of various feelings, thoughts, and actions is evaluated. Thus, "moral maturity" implies an ability and a willingness to abide by one's chosen (internalized) ethical standards, even when authority figures are not around to approve of praiseworthy conduct or to punish transgressions.

By contrast, those whose conduct is controlled by the expectation of rewards for acceptable behaviors and/or fear of punishment for prohibited acts are said to have an **external moral orientation**. These persons have not selected and internalized a set of ethical principles to guide their conduct; thus they could be considered "morally immature."

Over the years, researchers have devised several methods of assessing moral maturity. The most common measure of moral affect is some index of the amount of guilt, shame, or self-criticism that children associate with the commission of prohibited acts. Typically, subjects are presented with an incomplete story in which a child of the same age and sex has committed a transgression that is unlikely to be detected. The subject is asked to complete the story by telling what the protagonist thinks or feels and what will happen as a result of these feelings. Of course, the assumption is that children will project onto the story character the reactions that they themselves experience after a transgression. If a child says that the protagonist feels little emotion or feels anxious and runs away to avoid punishment, his answer is interpreted as a sign of an external moral orientation (and moral immaturity). A more mature, or "internal," response would be one in which the child expresses remorse, guilt, shame, or some other self-critical reaction.

The cognitive component of morality, or moral reasoning, is typically measured by (1) questioning subjects about the meaning of rules and having them make judgments about the naughtiness of different rule violations or (2) asking them to think about moral dilemmas that require a choice between obeying a rule, law, or authority figure and endorsing an action that conflicts with this rule while serving a human need. The purpose of these procedures (which will be described in much greater detail later in the chapter) is to determine how children think about moral issues and to what extent their moral reasoning centers on external sanctions for harmdoing.

Traditionally, moral conduct has been assessed in either of two ways: (1) by tempting the child to cheat or to violate other prohibitions when there is no one around to detect this transgression or (2) by measuring (through projective stories or parental interviews) the child's tendency to confess to or accept responsibility for deviant behavior when the possibility of its detection is remote. Of course, the child's willingness to share, comfort, or help others is also a behavioral indicator of morality — the positive side of morality (prosocial concern, discussed in Chapter 11).

Although different theories emphasize different aspects of morality and moral development, in real life these moral components may well be interrelated — at least to some extent. For example, a child's confession of wrongdoing (moral conduct) may be driven by her intense feelings of guilt (moral affect). Another child's willingness to violate a prohibition in the absence of external surveillance (moral conduct) may stem from a belief (moral reasoning) that violations that go undetected and unpunished are really not all that harmful.

In this chapter we will be discussing the development of all three aspects of moral character. We will begin by examining each of the major theories of moral development and the research it has generated. After we have seen how each theory approaches the topic of moral growth and development, we will take a closer look at the relationships among moral affect, moral reasoning, and moral behavior. This information should help us to decide whether a person really has a unified "moral character" that is stable over time and across situations. Finally, we will consider how various child-rearing practices may affect a child's moral development and, in so doing, will attempt to integrate much of the information that we have reviewed.

Psychoanalytic Explanations of Moral Development

According to Freud (1935/1960), the personality consists of three basic components: the id, the ego, and the superego. Recall from Chapter 2 that the id is impulsive and hedonistic; its purpose is to gratify the instincts. The function of the ego is to restrain the id until realistic means for satisfying needs can be worked out. The superego is the final component of the personality to develop; its role is to determine whether id impulses and the means of impulse satisfaction produced by the ego are acceptable or unacceptable (moral or immoral).

Freud believed that infants and toddlers are basically amoral and hedonistic because they are dominated by their ids. Before the superego has formed, parents must reward behaviors that they consider acceptable and punish those that they consider unacceptable if they hope to restrain the child's hedonistic impulses. Once the superego develops, it will monitor the child's thoughts and actions and become an *internal* censor. Indeed, Freud argued that a well-developed superego is a harsh master that will punish the ego for moral transgressions by producing guilt, shame, and a loss of self-esteem. Presumably, the morally mature child will then resist temptation to violate moral norms in order to avoid these dreaded forms of negative moral affect.

Freud's Theory of Oedipal Morality

According to Freud, the superego develops during the phallic stage (age 3–6), when children were said to experience a hostile rivalry with the same-sex parent stemming from their incestuous desire for the other-sex parent (that is, an Oedipus complex for males and an Electra complex for females). Freud proposed that hostilities arising from the Oedipus complex would build until a boy came to fear his father (castration anxiety) and was forced to identify with him in order to reduce this fear. By identifying with the father, the boy would internalize many of his father's attributes, including the father's moral standards. Similarly, a girl was said to resolve her Electra complex by identifying with her mother and internalizing her mother's moral standards. Yet, Freud argued that girls are never quite as afraid of their mothers as boys are of their fathers, because, in the worst of all imaginable circumstances, their mothers could never castrate them. Thus, girls experience no intense fear that would absolutely compel them to identify with their mothers; for this reason, Freud assumed that girls develop weaker superegos than boys do!

We might applaud Freud for pointing out that moral emotions such as pride, shame, and guilt are potentially important determinants of ethical conduct and that the internalization of moral principles is a crucial step along the road to moral maturity. Yet the specifics of his theory are largely unsupported. For example, threatening and punitive parents do not raise children who are morally mature. Quite the contrary; parents who rely on punitive forms of discipline tend to have children who often misbehave and who rarely express feelings of guilt, remorse, shame, or self-criticism (Brody & Shaffer, 1982; Hoffman, 1988; Kochanska, 1991). Furthermore, there is simply no evidence that males develop stronger superegos than females. In fact, investigators who have left children alone in the face of a temptation usually find no sex differences in moral behavior, or they find differences favoring females (Hoffman, 1975b). Finally, Freud's proposed age trends for moral development miss the mark in many respects. Older infants and toddlers, for example, are nowhere near as impulsive and hedonistic as Freud made them out to be. Not only do 2–3-year-olds seem to appreciate the implications of many rules that they are supposed to follow (Kagan, 1987), but they often try to correct (without adult intervention) the mishaps they think they have caused (Cole, Barrett, & Zahn-Waxler, 1992); in ad-

dition, they are already displaying complex emotions that look very much like *pride* when they live up to a standard and *shame* when they fail to do so (Lewis, Alessandri, & Sullivan, 1992; Stipek, Recchia, & McClintic, 1992). All of this occurs before these young children would even have experienced much of an Oedipus or Electra complex, much less having resolved it or established a mature superego. Moreover, 6–7-year-olds, who have presumably resolved their oedipal conflicts, are nowhere near as morally mature as Freud made them out to be. Indeed, not until age 10 do children even seem to distinguish the two negative moral emotions (guilt and shame) that Freud thought so important (Ferguson, Stegge, & Damhuis, 1991),[1] and we will soon see that at least one aspect of moral development — moral reasoning — continues to evolve well into young adulthood. So, even though Freud's broader themes about the significance of moral emotions may indeed have some merit, it is perhaps time to lay his theory of **Oedipal morality** to rest.

Neo-Freudian Explanations of Moral Development

Many psychoanalytic theorists (such as Erikson, 1963; Hartmann, 1960) have largely rejected Freud's theory of oedipal morality, arguing that children internalize the moral principles of *both* parents. According to the neo-Freudians, moral development can be traced to *social* (rather than sexual) conflicts that begin during the second year, when the child starts to submit to parental authority (literally, to the parents' superegos) in order to avoid losing their love. The preschool period is viewed as a trying time for children. Presumably, 2- to 5-year-olds very much resent parental attempts to restrict and control their behavior. They would love to find a way of getting back at (or getting even with) their dominating

---

[1]Lest you wonder, guilt implies that we have failed to live up to interpersonal obligations and motivates us to *approach* others — that is, to make reparations to those we have failed. Shame, which may stem from moral transgressions, personal failures, or social blunders, often undermines our feeling of self-esteem and motivates us to *withdraw* from social contact, at least temporarily, while we rethink our abilities and attributes and decide how we would ideally like to be or to behave (Higgins, 1987).

and controlling parents, but they realize that, if they retaliate, they could lose Mom's and Dad's love. To resolve this social dilemma, children repress their hostilities and seek parental affection by internalizing the parents' moral standards. This identification with one's parents is a kind of insurance for *both boys and girls*, who believe "If I become like Mom and Dad, they'll have to love me."

Unlike Freud, the neo-Freudians believe that both the *ego* and the superego play important roles in moral development. The superego dictates to the ego the kinds of behavior that are morally acceptable and unacceptable. But, unless the ego is strong enough to inhibit the id's undesirable impulses, the child will be unable to resist the id, regardless of the strength of the superego. So the neo-Freudians assume that morality is a product of both the internalized rules of the superego and the restraining forces of the ego that enable the child to obey these rules.

Two predictions flow directly from this neo-Freudian theory of moral development:

1. Parents who rely heavily on *love-oriented* disciplinary techniques (withholding affection; refusing to speak to the child) that generate anxiety over a loss of love should raise children who develop stronger superegos than would youngsters whose parents rely on threats and other physically coercive disciplinary strategies.

2. Since the ego plays a major role in moral development, children with strong egos (as measured by such self-regulatory activities as toddlers' complying with rather than defying maternal commands, or children's deferring immediate gratification in the service of long-term goals) should be more morally mature than those with weaker egos.

As we will see later in the chapter, there is little evidence that parents' use of love-oriented disciplinary techniques promotes moral maturity (Brody & Shaffer, 1982); rather, the practice of making young children feel unworthy of affection may cause them (1) to blame themselves for causing the disciplinarian's distress, (2) to feel guilty about upsetting him or her, and (3) eventually to avoid the disciplinarian and to become depressed, rather than

to develop a strong sense of morality and altruistic concern (Zahn-Waxler et al., 1990). However, there are data consistent with the **"ego strength" hypothesis**. For example, compliant toddlers are more likely than noncompliant ones to show clear signs of an internal moral orientation (that is, strong empathic reactions to others' distress; feelings of guilt and insistence on making reparations for transgressions; intolerance of violations such as cheating) six years later, during middle childhood (Kochanska, 1991). In addition, young children who have shown a strong capacity for deferring immediate gratification are (1) better able than their more impulsive agemates to resist the temptation to cheat at experimental games (Mischel, 1974) and (2) rated by adults as more "socially responsible" ten years later, in adolescence (Mischel, Shoda, & Peake, 1988; Shoda, Mischel, & Peake, 1990).

Although the "ego strength" research is consistent with neo-Freudian theory, it is also easily interpreted within the framework of other theories, most notably the cognitive approach. Since the ego is the rational component of the personality—the seat of all higher intellectual functions—the neo-Freudians are arguing that moral development depends, in part, on intellectual development. The cognitive developmentalists definitely agree.

Cognitive-Developmental Theory: The Child as a Moral Philosopher

Cognitive developmentalists study morality by charting the development of *moral reasoning*—the thinking children display when deciding whether various acts are right or wrong. The most basic assumption of the cognitive approach is that moral development depends very heavily on cognitive development. Moral reasoning is said to progress through an **invariant sequence** of "stages," each of which is a consistent way of thinking about moral issues that is different from the stage preceding and following it. Presumably each moral stage evolves from and replaces its immediate predecessor, so that there can be no skipping of stages. If these assumptions sound familiar, they should, for they are the same ones that Piaget made about his stages of intellectual development.

In this section we will consider two cognitive-developmental theories of morality: Jean Piaget's model and Lawrence Kohlberg's revision and extension of Piaget's approach.

Piaget's Theory of Moral Development

According to Piaget (1932/1965), moral maturity implies both a respect for rules and a sense of social justice — that is, a concern that all people be treated fairly and equitably under the socially defined rules of order. Piaget studied the development of respect for rules by rolling up his sleeves and playing marbles with a large number of Swiss children. As he played with children of different ages, Piaget would ask them questions about the rules of the game — questions such as "Where do these rules come from?" "Must everyone obey a rule?" "Can these rules be changed?" Once he had identified developmental stages in the understanding and use of rules, he proceeded to study children's conceptions of social justice by presenting them with moral dilemmas in the form of stories. Here is one example:

> *Story A.* A little boy who is called John is in his room. He is called to dinner. He goes into the dining room. But behind the door there was a chair, and on the chair there was a tray with 15 cups on it. John couldn't have known that there was all this behind the door. He goes in, the door knocks against the tray, bang go the 15 cups, and they all get broken.
>
> *Story B.* Once there was a little boy whose name was Henry. One day when his mother was out, he tried to reach some jam out of the cupboard. He climbed onto a chair and stretched out his arm. But the jam was too high up, and he couldn't reach it. . . . While he was trying to get it, he knocked over a cup. The cup fell down and broke [Piaget, 1932/1965, p. 122].

Having heard the stories, subjects were asked "Are these children equally guilty?" and "If not, which child is naughtier? Why?" Subjects were also asked how the naughtier child should be punished. Through the use of these research techniques, Piaget formulated a theory of moral development that includes a premoral period and two moral stages.

THE PREMORAL PERIOD

According to Piaget, preschool children show little concern for or awareness of rules. In a game of marbles, these **premoral** children do not play systematically with the intent of winning. Instead, they seem to make up their own rules, and they think the point of the game is to take turns and have fun. Toward the end of the premoral period (ages 4 to 5), children become more aware of rules by watching older children and imitating their rule-bound behavior. But the premoral child does not yet understand that rules represent a cooperative agreement about how a game should be played.

THE STAGE OF MORAL REALISM, OR HETERONOMOUS MORALITY

Between the ages of 5 and 10 the child develops a strong respect for rules and a belief that they must be obeyed at all times. Children at this **heteronomous** stage assume that rules are laid down by authority figures such as God, the police, or their parents, and they think these regulations are sacred and unalterable.[2] Try exceeding the speed limit with a 6-year-old at your side and you may see what Piaget was talking about. Even if you are rushing to the hospital in a medical emergency, the young child may note that you are breaking a "rule of the road" and consider your behavior unacceptable conduct that deserves to be punished. In sum, heteronomous children think of rules as *moral absolutes*. They see a "right" side and a "wrong" side to any moral issue, and right always means following the rules.

Heteronomous children are also likely to judge the naughtiness of an act by its objective consequences rather than the actor's intent. For example, Piaget found that many 5–9-year-olds judged John, who broke 15 cups while performing a well-intentioned act, to be naughtier than Henry, who broke one cup while stealing jam. Perhaps this focus on objective harm done stems from the fact that young children are often punished if and when their behavior produces harmful consequences. For

---

[2]Indeed, the term *heteronomous* means subject to externally imposed laws or under the authority of another.

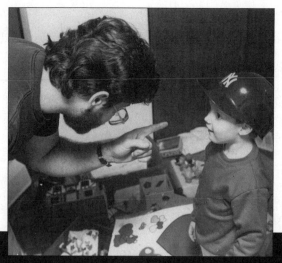

PHOTO 12-2   According to Piaget, young children judge the naughtiness of an act by its objective consequences rather than the actor's intent.

example, a girl who bumps into a table without doing any harm is less likely to be reprimanded for her clumsiness than a second youngster who nudges the table and knocks over a number of plants in the process.

Heteronomous children favor **expiatory punishment**—punishment for its own sake, with no concern for its relation to the nature of the forbidden act. For example, a 6-year-old might favor spanking a boy who had broken a window rather than making the boy pay for the window from his allowance. Moreover, the heteronomous child believes in **immanent justice**—the idea that violations of social rules will invariably be punished in one way or another (see, for example, Dennis's warning to Joey in the cartoon). So, if a 6-year-old boy were to fall and skin his knee while stealing cookies, he might conclude that this injury was the punishment he deserved for his transgression. Life for the heteronomous child is fair and just.

THE STAGE OF MORAL RELATIVISM, OR AUTONOMOUS MORALITY

By age 10 or 11 most children have reached Piaget's second moral stage—the stage of moral relativism,

or **autonomous morality**. Older, autonomous children now realize that social rules are arbitrary agreements that can be challenged and even changed with the consent of the people they govern. They are also likely to feel that rules can be violated in the service of human needs. Thus a driver who speeds during a medical emergency may no longer be considered a wrongdoer, even though she is breaking the law. Judgments of right and wrong now depend more on the actor's intent to deceive or to violate social rules than on the objective consequences of the act itself. For example, 10-year-olds reliably say that Henry, who broke one cup while stealing some jam (bad intent), is naughtier than John, who broke 15 cups while coming to dinner (good or neutral intent).

When deciding how to punish transgressions, the morally autonomous child usually favors **reciprocal punishments**—that is, treatments that tailor punitive consequences to the "crime" so that the rule breaker will understand the implications of a transgression and perhaps be less likely to repeat it. So an autonomous child may decide that the boy who deliberately breaks a window should pay for it out of his allowance (and learn that windows cost money) rather than simply submit to a spanking. Finally, autonomous youngsters no longer believe in immanent justice, because they have learned from experience that violations of social rules often go undetected and unpunished.

MOVING FROM HETERONOMOUS TO AUTONOMOUS MORALITY

Piaget believes that two cognitive deficits contribute to the young child's rigid and absolutistic moral reasoning. The first is *egocentrism*—a difficulty in recognizing perspectives other than one's own. The second is *realism*—the tendency to confuse subjective experience (one's own thoughts) with external reality. Perhaps you can see how these cognitive shortcomings might lead to a sense of moral realism. When parents or other authority figures enforce a rule, the young child assumes that this dictate must be sacred and unalterable, particularly since it comes from a powerful person who can make the rule stick (realism). And, since the child at this age

"HEY, CAREFUL, JOEY! GOD SEES EVERYTHING WE DO, THEN HE GOES AN' TELLS SANTA CLAUS!"

Dennis the Menace® used by permission of Hank Ketcham and © by North American Syndicate.

without any assistance from adults, if they are to play together cooperatively or accomplish other group goals. While settling disputes, each child will assume the roles of "governor" and "governed" and see that rules are merely social contracts that derive their power from the mutual consent of the group members rather than from an external authority figure. So Piaget believes that equal-status contacts with peers lead to a more flexible morality because they (1) lessen the child's unilateral respect for adult authority, (2) increase his or her self-respect and respect for peers, and (3) illustrate that rules are arbitrary agreements that can be changed with the consent of the people they govern.

And what role do parents play? According to Piaget, parents may actually slow the progress of moral development by reinforcing the child's unilateral respect for authority figures. If, for example, a parent enforces a demand with a threat or a statement such as "Do it because *I* told you to," the young child will likely conclude that rules are "absolutes" that derive their "teeth" from the parent's power to enforce them. Although Piaget believes that the peer group plays the greater role in the development of autonomous morality, he suggests that parents could help by relinquishing some of their power and establishing a more egalitarian relationship with their children.

assumes that other people see things as she does (egocentrism), she will conclude that various rules must be "absolutes" that apply to everyone.

According to Piaget, both cognitive maturation and social experience play a role in the transition from heteronomous to autonomous morality. The cognitive advances that are necessary for this shift are a general decline in egocentrism and the development of role-taking skills that will enable the child to view moral issues from several perspectives. The kind of social experience that Piaget considers important is *equal-status* contact with peers. Beginning at about age 6, the child spends four to six hours a day at school surrounded by other children of approximately the same age. Conflicts will often arise because members of the group will not always agree on how they should play games or solve problems. Since everyone has roughly equal status, children will soon learn that they must compromise, often

Tests of Piaget's Theory

Many researchers have used Piaget's methods in an attempt to replicate his findings, and much of the evidence they have collected is consistent with his theory. In Western cultures there is a clear relationship between children's ages and stages of moral reasoning: younger children are more likely than older children to display such aspects of heteronomous morality as a strong belief in immanent justice and a tendency to weigh the consequences of an act much more heavily than the actor's intentions when making moral judgments (Hoffman, 1970; Jose, 1990; Lickona, 1976). Apparently the child's level of moral reasoning does depend, in part, on his or her level of cognitive development. For example, IQ and moral maturity are positively correlated

(Lickona, 1976), and children who score high on tests of role taking tend to make more advanced moral judgments than agemates whose role-taking skills are less well developed (Ambron & Irwin, 1975; Selman, 1971). Finally, there is even some support for Piaget's "peer participation" hypothesis: popular children who often take part in social activities and who assume positions of leadership in the peer group tend to make mature moral judgments (Keasey, 1971). Moreover, 5- to 7-year-olds who have had a hand in formulating the rules of a new game (peer participation) are later more flexible about changing these rules than their agemates who simply learned the same rules from an adult (Merchant & Rebelsky, 1972).

Yet, in spite of this supportive evidence, there are reasons to believe that Piaget has badly underestimated the moral sophistication of preschool and young grade-school children. Let's take a closer look.

DO YOUNGER CHILDREN
IGNORE ACTORS' INTENTIONS?

Recent research indicates that younger children may often consider an actor's intentions when evaluating his behavior. Two problems with Piaget's moral-decision stories are that they (1) confounded intentions and consequences by always asking whether a person who caused little harm with a bad intent was naughtier than one who caused a larger amount of damage while serving good intentions, and (2) made information about the consequences of an act *much clearer* (or easier to detect) than information about the actor's intentions. Since younger children give more weight to concrete evidence (for example, cups breaking) that they can see or easily imagine than to abstract information (that is, an actor's motive) that they must infer from the story, it is hardly surprising that they would consider the person who did the more damage to be the naughtier of the two (Surber, 1982).

Sharon Nelson (1980) corrected these methodological flaws in an interesting experiment with 3-year-olds. Each child listened to a story in which a character threw a ball to a playmate. The actor's intent was described as *good* (his friend had nothing to

FIGURE 12-1 Example of drawings used by Nelson to convey an actor's intentions to preschool children. (Adapted from S. A. Nelson, "Factors Influencing Young Children's Use of Motives and Outcomes as Moral Criteria." *Child Development*, 1980, *51*, 823–829. Copyright © 1980 by the Society for Research in Child Development. Reprinted by permission.)

play with) or *bad* (the actor was mad at his friend), and the consequences of his act were either *positive* (the friend caught the ball and was happy to play with it) or *negative* (the ball hit the friend in the head and made him cry). To ensure that these young subjects would understand the actor's intentions, they were shown drawings such as that in Figure 12-1, which happens to depict a negative intent.

How did these 3-year-olds judge the actor's behavior? As we see in Figure 12-2, they did judge acts that had positive consequences more favorably than those producing negative outcomes. Yet the more interesting finding was that the well-intentioned child who had wanted to play was evaluated much more favorably than the child who intended to hurt his friend, *regardless of the consequences of his actions*. In a later study using a very similar methodology (Nelson-Le Gall, 1985), 3- to 4-year-olds judged negative consequences that the actor could have *foreseen* to be more intentional and naughtier than the same consequences produced by an actor who could not have foreseen them. By age 4, children rate a harmful consequence much more negatively if the actor lies about it (deceitful intent) than if nothing is said (Bussey, 1992). And, by age 5 to 7, children believe that harmful acts stemming from carelessness or negligence are more blameworthy than those that are purely accidental (Shultz, Wright, & Schleifer, 1986; Yuill & Perner, 1988). Taken together, these findings are clearly inconsistent with Piaget's view of younger children as "moral realists" who focus exclusively on objective harm done when assigning

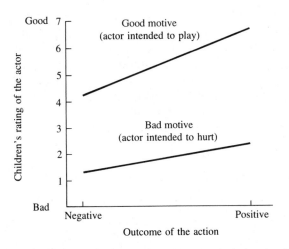

FIGURE 12-2   Average ratings of an actor's behavior for actors who produced positive or negative outcomes while serving either good or bad intentions. (Adapted from S. A. Nelson, "Factors Influencing Young Children's Use of Motives and Outcomes as Moral Criteria." *Child Development*, 1980, *51*, 823–829. Copyright © 1980 by the Society for Research in Child Development. Reprinted by permission.)

moral responsibility. Apparently, preschool children can and often do consider intentions when making moral judgments if this information is clear to them. But Piaget was right in one respect: younger children do assign more weight to consequences and less weight to intentions than older children do, even though both younger and older children consider both sources of information when evaluating others' conduct (Olthof, Ferguson, & Luiten, 1989; Surber, 1982).

DO YOUNGER CHILDREN RESPECT
ALL RULES (AND ADULT AUTHORITY)?

According to Piaget, young children think of rules as sacred and obligatory prescriptions that are laid down by respected authority figures and are not to be questioned or changed. However, Elliot Turiel (1983) notes that toddlers and preschool children actually encounter two kinds of rules: (1) **moral rules**, which focus on the rights and privileges of individuals, and (2) **social-conventional rules**, which are determined by consensus and tell us what is appropriate in a particular social setting. Moral rules include rules against hitting, lying, stealing, or

otherwise violating other people's rights. Social-conventional rules are more like rules of social etiquette and include rules of games as well as school rules that forbid snacking in class or using the restroom without permission. Do children treat these two kinds of rules as equivalent?

Apparently not. Judith Smetana (1981, 1985, 1989) finds that even 2½–3-year-olds make important distinctions between moral and social-conventional rules—distinctions that are also seen in Oriental cultures such as Korea, where respect for adult authority is much more heavily emphasized than in Western societies (Song, Smetana, & Kim, 1987). Basically, young children view moral transgressions such as hitting, stealing, and refusing to share as much more serious and more deserving of punishment than social-conventional violations such as snacking in class or not saying "please" when requesting a toy. And, when asked whether a violation would be OK if there were no rule against it, children said that moral transgressions are always wrong but social-conventional violations are OK in the absence of any explicit rule. Although preschoolers may not always feel guilty about violating a moral rule (see Nunner-Winkler & Sodian, 1988), they do indeed understand the need for and importance of these prescriptions by age 2½ to 3—much sooner than Piaget had assumed they would.

Do 6- to 10-year-old "heteronomous" children show the special reverence for adults and adult authority that Piaget attributed to them? Once again the answer is apparently not! Six- to 11-year-olds typically acknowledge that their parents are justified in making and enforcing rules about moral issues such as stealing; but they feel that a parent is unjustified and is behaving inappropriately when he or she imposes rules that seriously restrict their choice of friends or leisure activities—areas that they perceive as under their own *personal* jurisdiction (Tisak & Tisak, 1990). Moreover, Marta Laupa (1991; Laupa & Turiel, 1986) finds that 7- to 11-year-olds are more likely to obey (and to view as legitimate) the commands of a *peer* authority (for example, a playground monitor) than those of an adult nonauthority (for example, a woman who lives across the street from the playground). And, although it is true that 6- to 11-year-olds are likely to comply with many different kinds of legitimate adult authorities, including librarians in a library and lifeguards at a public pool, they tend to explain such obedience in terms of their *own beliefs* about the benefits of complying (for example, "If kids don't listen, they will get hurt")—an *internal* justification that seems rather *non*heteronomous indeed (Braine et al., 1991). In sum, 6- to 11-year-olds have quite

clear opinions about what constitutes legitimate authority, and these ideas are hardly based on an unwavering respect for the sanctity or wisdom of adults, as Piaget had assumed.

Finally, the research presented in Box 12-1 suggests that Piaget badly overstated the case when he implied that parents typically *impede* the growth of their children's moral reasoning.

B O X **12-1** | *Parental Influence on Children's Moral Reasoning*

Might we alter children's moral reasoning by exposing them to adult models (such as parents) whose moral judgments are more sophisticated than their own? Piaget says no. He expects a young child's moral judgments to be very difficult to modify because (1) they are based on the child's underlying thought structures (which depend on the child's level of cognitive development), and (2) young premoral children and those at the heteronomous stage are simply too intellectually immature to understand and appreciate a parent's autonomous moral reasoning.

Contrary to Piaget's claims, several investigators have found that children's moral reasoning is subject to modeling influences, and even 3-year-olds, who should be at Piaget's premoral level, can be trained to reason at Piaget's *autonomous* level (see, for example, Schleifer & Douglas, 1973). Yet cognitive theorists doubt that subjects in these experiments really changed their moral orientations; instead, they argue that social models merely teach children "conforming" responses that are likely to be displayed in the short run to win the model's approval but are unlikely to persist over time.

If children's moral judgments are not readily amenable to social influence, as the cognitive theorists have proposed, then the moral reasoning of 6- to 7-year-old "heteronomous" youngsters should bear little resemblance to that of their parents. But, if moral judgments are truly subject to social influence, as social-learning theorists (for example, Bandura, 1977, 1991) have argued, then there ought to be at least some correspondence between the moral reasoning of young children and that of their parents. Several years ago, Manual

Leon (1984) conducted an interesting experiment to compare the moral decisions of 6- to 7-year-old boys with those of their mothers. The boys were tested first while their mothers were off in an adjacent room. Each boy listened to nine stories in which boys like himself had done no damage, a little damage, or lots of damage (consequences information) by accident, out of displaced anger, or with malice (intentions information). After listening to each story, the boy indicated the amount of punishment (from none to severe) that the actor deserved. When the boy had finished, he was dismissed and his mother was summoned to listen to the same stories and to recommend punishments for the same actors her son had evaluated.

Leon found that different mothers used different "rules" in assigning punishments to the story characters. The three types of reasoning that mothers used were as follows:

1. *Intent + damage linear rule*. These mothers ($N = 18$) combined intentions and consequences information when making punishment decisions. Thus the most severe punishment was assigned to actors who did a lot of damage with malicious intent, whereas the least punishment was assigned when the actor did no damage in an accident.
2. *Accident-configural rule*. These mothers ($N = 10$) also combined intentions and consequences information if the story character had acted out of displaced anger or with a malicious intent. However, they always assigned mild punishment, regardless of the damage done, when the act in question was accidental.

Developmentalists are indebted to Piaget for suggesting that children's moral reasoning develops in stages that are closely tied to cognitive growth. His early theory stimulated an enormous amount of research and several new insights—including the findings above, which indicate that children younger than 10 are considerably more sophisticated in their moral reasoning than Piaget made them out to be. But is moral reasoning fully developed by age 10 to 11, as Piaget had assumed? Lawrence Kohlberg certainly didn't think so.

Kohlberg's Theory of Moral Development

Kohlberg (1963, 1984) has refined and extended Piaget's theory of moral development by asking 10-,

---

B O X | **12-1** | *continued*

3. *Damage-only rule.* These mothers ($N = 4$) ignored the actors' intentions and assigned punishment solely on the basis of the amount of damage the actors had caused.

From a Piagetian perspective, the damage-only rule is pure heteronomous moral reasoning, whereas the linear rule and especially the configural rule (accidents are viewed as totally unintentional and hence not blameworthy) are more characteristic of autonomous moral reasoning.

How did the boys' moral judgments compare with those of their mothers? Remarkable as it may seem, the rules used by the majority of these 6- to 7-year-olds to assign punishments to the story characters were *virtually identical* to those of their own mothers. Recall that the boys had been tested first and, thus, were not merely "imitating" their mothers' judgments. The implication, then, is that the moral reasoning of young children is much more amenable to social influence than Piaget had thought. Moreover, the finding that 6- to 7-year-olds use a relatively mature configural rule if their mothers do suggests that parents may often *foster* (rather than inhibit) the growth of children's moral reasoning.

How exactly might parents influence their child's reasoning? Lawrence Walker and John Taylor (1991a) recently addressed this issue by (1) asking each child and his (her) parents to discuss a real-life moral dilemma that the child had experienced and then (2) following up on the child two years later to see if there were any aspects of the earlier "family" discussions that predicted how much moral growth the child had shown. The findings were interesting indeed. First, most parents adjusted their moral reasoning to the child's competencies; that is, they reasoned at a level slightly above the child's and significantly lower than that they normally displayed when resolving moral issues by themselves. Second, different discussion styles were associated with different patterns of moral growth over the next two years. Children who showed the most growth had parents who encouraged the child to clearly state his or her own position and who often paraphrased this logic, in a warm and supportive way, as they presented higher-order moral reasoning. By contrast, children who showed little moral growth had parents who tended to *challenge* the child's moral judgments and to present higher-order reasoning in a lecture-like format as lessons to be learned.

What are the implications of these findings? Perhaps we can argue that Piaget was partly right and partly wrong in his views on parents as agents of moral socialization. He was right in assuming that parents do not foster moral growth if they adopt a heavy-handed or authoritarian approach and attempt to impose new modes of thinking on their children. But apparently he was wrong in assuming that parents typically impede moral development. Leon's study shows that children often make moral judgments that are more mature than Piaget expects, as long as their parents do. And Walker and Taylor (1991a) show how this is possible: by tailoring their reasoning to the child's competencies and presenting new moral perspectives in a supportive (rather than challenging) way, parents can *promote* their children's moral development!

13-, and 16-year-old boys to resolve a series of "moral dilemmas."[3] Each dilemma challenged the respondent by requiring him to choose between (1) obeying a rule, law, or authority figure and (2) taking some action that conflicts with these rules and commands while serving a human need. The following story is the best known of Kohlberg's moral dilemmas:

> In Europe, a woman was near death from a special kind of cancer. There was one drug that doctors thought might save her. It was a form of radium that a druggist in the same town had recently discovered. The drug was expensive to make, but the druggist was charging $2000, or 10 times the cost of the drug, for a small (possible life-saving) dose. Heinz, the sick woman's husband, borrowed all the money he could, about $1000, or half of what he needed. He told the druggist that his wife was dying and asked him to sell the drug cheaper or to let him pay later. The druggist replied "No, I discovered the drug, and I'm going to make money from it." Heinz then became desperate and broke into the store to steal the drug for his wife. Should Heinz have done that?

Kohlberg was actually less interested in the subject's decision (that is, what Heinz should have done) than in the underlying rationale, or "thought structures," that the subject used to justify his decision. So, if a subject says "Heinz should steal the drug to save his wife's life," it is necessary to determine why her life is so important. Is it because she cooks and irons for Heinz? Because it's a husband's duty to save his wife? Or because the preservation of life is among the highest of human values? To determine the "structure" of a subject's moral reasoning, Kohlberg asked probing questions: Does Heinz have an obligation to steal the drug? If Heinz doesn't love his wife, should he steal it for her? Should Heinz steal the drug for a stranger? Is it important for people to do everything they can to save another life? Is it against the law to steal? Does that make it morally wrong? Of course, the purpose of the probes is to clarify how individual participants reason about obedience and authority on the one hand and about human needs, rights, and privileges on the other.

Through his use of these elaborate *clinical interviews*, Kohlberg's first discovery was that moral development is far from complete when the child reaches age 10 to 11, or Piaget's autonomous stage. Indeed, moral reasoning seemed to evolve and become progressively more complex throughout adolescence and into young adulthood. Careful analyses of his subjects' responses to several dilemmas led Kohlberg to conclude that moral growth progresses through an *invariant sequence* of three moral levels, each of which is composed of two distinct moral stages. According to Kohlberg, the order of these moral levels and stages is invariant because each depends on the development of certain cognitive abilities that evolve in an invariant sequence. Like Piaget, Kohlberg assumes that each succeeding stage evolves from and replaces its predecessor; once the individual has attained a higher stage of moral reasoning, he or she should never regress to earlier stages.

Before we look at Kohlberg's sequence of stages, it is important to emphasize that each stage represents a particular perspective, or *method of thinking* about moral dilemmas, rather than particular type of moral decision. As we will see, decisions are not very informative in themselves, because subjects at each moral stage might well endorse either of the alternative courses of action when resolving one of these ethical dilemmas.[4]

The basic themes and defining characteristics of Kohlberg's three moral levels and six stages are as follows:

LEVEL 1: PRECONVENTIONAL MORALITY

At the level of **preconventional morality**, rules are truly external to the self rather than internalized.

---

[3]Lawrence Kohlberg was born in 1927 and died in 1987. As a youth he put his own moral principles into action by helping to transport Jewish refugees from Europe to Israel after World War II. He devised his theory of moral development as a doctoral student at the University of Chicago and then spent most of his career at Harvard University, studying moral development and promoting moral education.

[4]There is, however, a strong tendency for subjects at Kohlberg's highest moral level to favor serving human needs over complying with rules or laws that conflict with such needs.

The child conforms to rules imposed by authority figures to avoid punishment or obtain personal rewards. Morality is self-serving: what is right is what one can get away with or what is personally satisfying.

Stage 1: Punishment-and-obedience orientation. The goodness or badness of an act depends on its consequences. The child will obey authorities to avoid punishment but may not consider an act wrong if it will not be detected and punished. The greater the harm done or the more severe the punishment, the more "bad" the act is. The following two responses reflect a punishment-and-obedience orientation to the Heinz dilemma:

> *Protheft*: It isn't really bad to take the drug—he did ask to pay for it first. He wouldn't do any other damage or take anything else, and the drug he'd take is only worth $200, not $2000.
> *Antitheft*: Heinz doesn't have permission to take the drug. He can't just go and break through a window. He'd be a bad criminal doing all that damage—and stealing anything so expensive would be a big crime.

Stage 2: Naive hedonism. A person at this second stage of moral development conforms to rules in order to gain rewards or satisfy personal objectives. There is some concern for the perspective of others, but other-oriented behaviors are ultimately motivated by the hope of benefit in return. "You scratch my back and I'll scratch yours" is the guiding philosophy. Here are two samples of this hedonistic, self-serving morality (see also Calvin's moral philosophy in the cartoon):

> *Protheft*: Heinz isn't really doing any harm to the druggist, and he can always pay him back. If he doesn't want to lose his wife, he should take the drug.
> *Antitheft*: Hey, the druggist isn't wrong, he just wants to make a profit like everybody else. That's what you're in business for, to make money.

LEVEL 2: CONVENTIONAL MORALITY

At the level of **conventional morality**, the individual now strives to obey rules and social norms in order to win others' approval or to maintain social order. Social praise and the avoidance of blame have now replaced tangible rewards and punishments as motivators of ethical conduct. The perspectives of other people are clearly recognized and given careful consideration.

Stage 3: "Good boy" or "good girl" orientation. Moral behavior is that which pleases, helps, or is approved of by others. Actions are evaluated on the basis of the actor's intent. "He means well" is a common expression of moral approval at this stage. As we see in the following responses, the primary objective of a Stage-3 respondent is to be thought of as a "good" person.

Protheft: Stealing is bad, but Heinz is only doing something that is natural for a good husband to do. You can't blame him for doing something out of love for his wife. You'd blame him if he didn't save her.

Antitheft: If Heinz's wife dies, he can't be blamed. You can't say he is heartless for failing to commit a crime. The druggist is the selfish and heartless one. Heinz tried to do everything he really could.

Stage 4: Social-order-maintaining morality. At this stage the individual considers the perspectives of the generalized other — that is, the will of society as reflected in law. Now what is right is what conforms to the rules of *legitimate* authority. The motive for conforming is not a fear of punishment but a belief that rules and laws maintain a social order that is worth preserving. As we see in the following responses, laws always transcend special interests for the Stage-4 respondent:

Protheft: The druggist is leading the wrong kind of life if he just lets somebody die; so it's Heinz's duty to save [his wife]. But Heinz just can't go around breaking laws — he must pay the druggist back and take his punishment for stealing.

Antitheft: It's natural for Heinz to want to save his wife, but it's still always wrong to steal. You have to follow the rules regardless of your feelings or the special circumstances.

*LEVEL 3: POSTCONVENTIONAL
(OR PRINCIPLED) MORALITY*

At the level of **postconventional morality**, a person now defines right and wrong in terms of broad principles of justice that could conflict with written laws or with the dictates of authority figures. Morally right and legally proper are not always one and the same.

Stage 5: Morality of contract, individual rights, and democratically accepted law. At this "social contract" stage the individual is now aware that the purpose of just laws is to express the will of the majority and further human values. Laws that accomplish these ends and are impartially applied are viewed as social contracts that one has an obligation to follow, but imposed laws that compromise hu-

man rights or dignity are considered unjust and worthy of challenge. (By contrast, the person at Stage 4 will not ordinarily challenge the sanctity of an established law and may be suspicious of those who do.) Notice how distinctions between what is legal and what is moral begin to appear in the following Stage-5 responses to Heinz's dilemma:

Protheft: Before you say stealing is morally wrong, you've got to consider this whole situation. Of course, the laws are quite clear about breaking into a store. And . . . Heinz would know that there were no *legal* grounds for his actions. Yet it would be reasonable for anybody, in that kind of situation, to steal the drug.

Antitheft: I can see the good that would come from illegally taking the drug. But the ends don't justify the means. The law represents a consensus of how people have agreed to live together, and Heinz has an obligation to respect these agreements. You can't say Heinz would be completely wrong to steal the drug, but even these circumstances don't make it right.

Stage 6: Morality of individual principles of conscience. At this "highest" moral stage the individual defines right and wrong on the basis of the self-chosen ethical principles of his or her own conscience. These principles are not concrete rules such as the Ten Commandments. They are abstract moral guidelines or principles of universal justice (and respect for individual rights) that *transcend* any law or social contract that may conflict with them. Kohlberg (1981) described Stage-6 thinking as a kind of "moral musical chairs" in which the person facing a moral dilemma is able to take the perspective of each and every other person who could potentially be affected by a decision and arrive at a solution that would be regarded as "just" by all. Here are two Stage-6 responses to the Heinz dilemma:

Protheft: When one must choose between disobeying a law and saving a human life, the higher principle of preserving life makes it morally *right* to steal the drug.

Antitheft: With many cases of cancer and the scarcity of the drug, there may not be enough to go around to everybody who needs it. The correct course of action can only be the one that is "right" by all people concerned. Heinz ought to act not on emotion or the law, but according to what he thinks an ideally just person would do in this case.

Stage 6 is Kohlberg's vision of ideal moral reasoning. But, because it is so very rare and virtually no one functions consistently at this level, Kohlberg came to view it as a hypothetical construct—that is, the stage to which people would progress were they to develop beyond Stage 5. In fact, the later versions of Kohlberg's manual for scoring moral judgments no longer attempt to measure Stage-6 reasoning (Colby & Kohlberg, 1987).

Tests of Kohlberg's Theory

Although Kohlberg sees his stages as an invariant and universal sequence of moral growth that is closely tied to cognitive development, he also claims that cognitive growth, by itself, is not sufficient to guarantee moral development. To ever move beyond the preconventional level of moral reasoning, children must be exposed to persons or situations that introduce *cognitive disequilibria*—that is, conflicts between existing moral concepts and new ideas that will force them to reevaluate their viewpoints. So, like Piaget, Kohlberg believes that both cognitive development and relevant social experiences underlie the growth of moral reasoning.

How much support is there for these ideas? Let's review the evidence, starting with data bearing on Kohlberg's invariant-sequence hypothesis.

ARE KOHLBERG'S STAGES AN INVARIANT SEQUENCE?

If Kohlberg's stages represent a true developmental sequence, we should find a strong positive correlation between age and maturity of moral reasoning. Kohlberg reports such a relationship in his original work with 10- to 16-year-olds, and similar findings have emerged from studies in Mexico, the Bahamas, Taiwan, Indonesia, Turkey, Honduras, India, Nigeria, and Kenya (see Colby & Kohlberg, 1987; Lei & Cheng, 1989; Snarey, 1985). In all these cultures, adolescents and young adults typically reason about moral issues at higher levels than preadolescents and younger children do. So it seems that Kohl-

berg's levels and stages of moral reasoning are "universal" structures that are age related—just as we would expect them to be if they formed a development sequence. But do these studies establish that Kohlberg's stages form a fixed, or *invariant*, sequence?

No, they do not! The problem is that subjects at each age level were *different* people, and we cannot be certain that a 25-year-old at Stage 5 has progressed through the various moral levels and stages in the order specified by Kohlberg's theory. How can we evaluate the invariant-sequence hypothesis? By examining two important sources of evidence: (1) experimental attempts to modify children's moral judgments and (2) longitudinal studies of the moral development of individual children.

The experimental evidence. If Kohlberg's stages represent an invariant sequence, then children might be influenced by models who reason about moral issues at one stage higher than their own. Reasoning that is less advanced should be rejected as too simplistic, and moral judgments that are two stages higher should be too difficult for subjects to comprehend.

Most of the available evidence is consistent with these hypotheses. When exposed to moral reasoning that is one stage above ($+1$) or one stage below (-1) their own, children generally favor and are more influenced by the more sophisticated set of arguments (Rest, 1983). Moreover, relatively few children understand or appreciate moral reasoning that is two stages higher ($+2$) than their own (see Turiel, 1966; Walker, 1982).

Who in the real world is most likely to reason at levels just beyond the child's own, thereby introducing the cognitive disequilibria that foster moral growth? Although adults may fit the bill, peers are really the more likely candidates. In Box 12-2 we will focus on peers as agents of moral socialization and see that the lessons they have taught us provide additional support for Kohlberg's invariant-sequence hypothesis.

The longitudinal evidence. Clearly the most compelling evidence for Kohlberg's invariant-sequence hypothesis would be a demonstration that individual children progress through the moral stages in precisely the order that Kohlberg says they should. Ann Colby and her associates (1983) have reported the results of a 20-year longitudinal study of 58 American males who were 10, 13, or 16 years old at the beginning of the project. These boys responded to Kohlberg's moral dilemmas when the study began and again in five follow-up sessions administered at three- to four-year intervals. As shown in Figure 12-3, moral reasoning developed very gradually, with use of preconventional reasoning (stages 1 and 2) declining sharply in adolescence—the same period in which conventional reasoning (stages 3 and 4) is on the rise. Conventional reasoning remained the dominant form of moral expression in young adulthood, with very few subjects ever moving beyond it to postconventional morality (Stage 5). But, even so, Colby et al. found that subjects proceeded through the stages they did attain in precisely the order Kohlberg predicted and that no subject ever skipped a stage. Similar results have been reported in a 9-year longitudinal study of adolescents in Israel and a 12-year longitudinal project conducted in Turkey (Colby & Kohlberg, 1987). So Kohlberg's moral stages do seem to represent an invariant sequence.

BOX 12-2 | Peers as Agents of Moral Socialization

One sure way to encounter differences in moral perspectives is to discuss the burning issues of the day with your peers. Like Piaget, Kohlberg (1985) felt that interactions among social equals probably contribute much more to moral development than *one-sided* discussions in which children and adolescents are expected to defer to the adult authority figures. Is there any evidence for this idea?

Indeed there is! Children do seem to think more deeply about both their own and their parents' moral ideas in discussions with peers than in talks with their mothers (Kruger & Tomasello, 1986). Moreover, children and adolescents who discuss moral issues in groups show clear advances in their levels of moral reasoning (particularly those youngsters who scored lower than their peers before the discussions). How much change is possible? The many studies reviewed by Andre Schlaefli and his associates (Schlaefli, Rest, & Thoma, 1985) suggest that average changes representing the equivalent of about four to five years of natural development can be achieved in intensive discussion programs lasting from 3 to 12 weeks. Finally, it is important to note that the advances in moral reasoning shown by the "changers" in these discussions are not merely a modeling effect. Berkowitz and Gibbs (1983) report that change is unlikely to occur unless the discussions are characterized by **transactive interactions**— that is, exchanges in which each discussant performs mental operations on the reasoning of his or her partner (for example, "Your reasoning misses an important distinction"; "Here's an elaboration of your position"; "We can combine our positions into a common view").

This latter finding is crucial, for it reinforces Kohlberg's contention that social experiences promote moral growth by introducing cognitive challenges to one's current reasoning—challenges to which the *less mature* individual will adapt by assimilating and accommodating to the other person's logic. Why do the more mature discussants not move in the direction of their less mature partners? Because the challenges introduced by their less mature counterparts are based on reasoning that they have already rejected. Indeed, their lack of change in the face of such logic provides additional support for Kohlberg's invariant-sequence hypothesis.

Now an important issue: Recall from Box 12-1 that parents who *directly challenge* a child's moral judgments, through the kinds of transactive interactions that Berkowitz and Gibbs (1983) describe, do not seem to foster moral growth. But peers who use this same discussion style do promote advances in moral reasoning. How can we account for this inconsistency?

THE RELATIONSHIP OF KOHLBERG'S STAGES TO COGNITIVE DEVELOPMENT

According to Kohlberg (1963), the young, preconventional child reasons about moral issues from an egocentric point of view. At Stage 1 the child thinks that certain acts are bad because they are punished. At Stage 2 the child shows a limited awareness of the needs, thoughts, and intentions of others but still judges self-serving acts as "right" or appropriate. However, conventional reasoning clearly requires some role-taking abilities. A person at Stage 3, for example, must necessarily recognize others'

points of view before she will evaluate intentions that would win their approval as "good" or morally acceptable. Furthermore, postconventional, or "principled," morality would seem to require much more than a decline in egocentrism and a capacity for mutual role taking: the person who bases moral judgments on abstract principles must be able to reason abstractly and to take all possible perspectives on a moral issue, rather than simply adhering to the rule of law or to concrete moral norms. So Kohlberg believes that the highest level of intellect, *formal operations*, is necessary for principled moral reasoning (Stage 5).

B O X **12-2** | *continued*

Walker and Taylor (1991a) believe that there is a rather simple explanation. They argue that cognitive conflict introduced in a challenging way by a parent (who then offers his or her own point of view) is likely to be perceived as hostile criticism and thus to arouse defensiveness in a child or adolescent. By contrast, the same kind of criticism is less likely to be perceived as threatening when voiced by a social equal; in fact, children may be especially inclined to listen carefully and to assimilate and accommodate to a peer's position because they are so highly motivated to establish and maintain good relations with peers. Although more research is needed to confirm this explanation, it seems that parents and peers do promote moral growth in very different ways.

So, if you are a person who likes to discuss contemporary social issues in bull sessions with peers, and if you are not too "bullheaded" to carefully consider or comment constructively on what they have to say, you are probably contributing in a positive way to your own and your peers' moral growth (Kohlberg, 1985). Indeed, the simple experience of hashing out everyday decisions jointly with one's spouse can also contribute to moral development (Walker, 1986). Peers *are* important agents of moral socialization!

Discussing important ethical issues with peers often promotes the growth of moral reasoning.

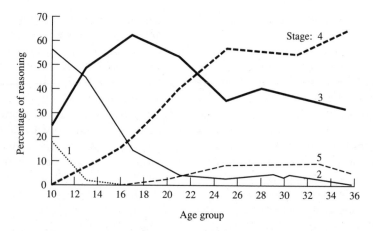

FIGURE 12-3 Use of Kohlberg's moral stages at ages 10 through 36 by male participants studied longitudinally over a 20-year period. (Adapted from "A Longitudinal Study of Moral Judgment," by A. Colby, L. Kohlberg, J. Gibbs, and M. Lieberman, 1983, *Monographs of the Society for Research in Child Development, 48* (Nos. 1–2, Serial No. 200). Copyright © 1983 by the Society for Research in Child Development. Adapted by permission.)

Much of the available research is remarkably consistent with Kohlberg's hypotheses (Krebs & Gillmore, 1982; Moir, 1974; Walker, 1980). For example, Lawrence Walker's (1980) study of 10- to 13-year-olds found that all subjects who had reached Kohlberg's third stage of moral reasoning ("good boy/good girl" morality) were proficient at mutual role taking. However, not all the proficient role takers had reached Stage 3 in their moral reasoning. So Walker's results imply that mutual role-taking skills are *necessary but not sufficient* for the development of conventional morality.

Carol Tomlinson-Keasey and Charles Keasey (1974) administered Kohlberg's moral dilemmas and tests of cognitive development to sixth-grade girls (age 11–12) and to college women. An interesting pattern emerged. All the subjects who reasoned at the postconventional level (Stage 5) on the dilemmas showed at least some formal-operational thinking on the cognitive tests. But not all the formal operators reasoned at the postconventional level on the dilemmas test. This same pattern also resulted in a later study by Deanna Kuhn and her associates (1977). So it seems that formal operations are *necessary but not sufficient* for the development of postconventional morality.

In sum, Kohlberg's moral stages are clearly related to one's level of cognitive development. Proficiency at mutual perspective taking may be necessary for the onset of conventional morality, and formal operations appear to be necessary for postconventional, or "principled," morality. Yet it is important to emphasize, as Kohlberg himself has, that intellectual growth does not guarantee moral development, for a person who has reached the highest stages of intellect (or role taking) may continue to reason at the preconventional level about moral issues. The implication, then, is that both *intellectual growth* and *relevant social experiences* (exposure to persons or situations that force a reevaluation of one's current moral concepts) are necessary before children can progress from preconventional morality to Kohlberg's higher stages.

EVIDENCE FOR KOHLBERG'S "SOCIAL EXPERIENCE" HYPOTHESIS

Does the literature support the proposition that social experience contributes to moral growth? Indeed it does, and we've already discussed two important examples: in Boxes 12-1 and 12-2 we saw that both parents and peers can promote the growth of children's moral reasoning.

Advanced education also contributes to moral growth. People who receive a university education reason at higher levels than those who do not (Boldizar, Wilson, & Deemer, 1989), and the differences in moral reasoning between college students and their nonstudent peers become greater with each successive year of school that the college students complete (Rest & Thoma, 1985). Being a leader among one's peers is another experience that seems to promote the growth of moral reasoning. Even in preliterate societies, tribal leaders who must often resolve interpersonal conflicts tend to reason at somewhat higher levels than their followers (Harkness, Edwards, & Super, 1981; Tietjen & Walker, 1985).

Finally, still another relevant social experience is living in a complex, diverse, democratic society. Cross-cultural studies indicate that postconventional moral reasoning emerges primarily in Western democracies, and it is not at all unusual to find that people from rural villages in underdeveloped countries show absolutely no signs of postconventional morality (Boyes & Walker, 1988; Harkness et al., 1981; Snarey, 1985). It seems that people governed at the village or tribal level need be concerned only with the customs and conventions of their immediate social group. They have little if any experience with the kinds of social and political compromise among diverse ethnic, racial, religious, and political factions that characterize large democracies and seem to contribute to Stage-5 reasoning — the social contract orientation. Note, however, that their conventional (mostly Stage-3) reasoning, with its emphasis on cooperation, loyalty to the immediate social group, and adherence to principles of goodness (such as those that underlie the Golden Rule), is perfectly adaptive and hence mature within their own social systems (Harkness et al., 1981).

SOME LINGERING QUESTIONS
ABOUT KOHLBERG'S APPROACH

Does moral reasoning predict moral behavior?
One common criticism of Kohlberg's theory is that it is based on subjects' responses to hypothetical and somewhat artificial dilemmas that they haven't faced themselves. Would children reason in the same way about the moral dilemmas they actually encounter? Would an individual who said that Heinz should steal the drug actually do so if he were in Heinz's shoes? Can we ever predict a person's moral behavior from a knowledge of his or her stage of moral reasoning?

Many researchers have found that the moral judgments of young children do *not* predict their actual behavior in situations in which they are induced to cheat or violate other moral norms (Nelson, Grinder, & Biaggio, 1969; Santrock, 1975; Toner & Potts, 1981). However, studies of older grade-school children, adolescents, and young adults often find at least some consistency between moral reasoning and moral conduct. Individuals at higher stages of moral reasoning are more likely than those at lower stages to behave altruistically and conscientiously (Linn, 1989), to favor free speech, and to oppose capital punishment (de Vries & Walker, 1986; Rest, 1986); also, they are less likely to cheat or partake in delinquent or criminal activity (Blasi, 1980). For example, Kohlberg (1975) found that only 15% of those students who reasoned at the postconventional level actually cheated on a test when given an opportunity, compared with 55% of the "conventional" students and 70% of those at the preconventional level.

Just as Kohlberg expected, however, the relationship between moral reasoning and moral behavior is far from perfect.[5] For example, even though many

[5]An examination of the persuasion literature from social psychology (see Tesser & Shaffer, 1990, for a review) implies that the consistency between moral reasoning and moral behavior may be much higher than many of the developmental studies might indicate. Persuasion researchers have found that, if you want to predict a *specific* behavior (for example, newspaper recycling) from a subject's attitudes, you will achieve better success if you measure a *specific* attitude (attitudes about recycling) rather than a more global one (for example, attitudes about the environment). Yet, developmentalists typically use *global* measures of moral maturity (the person's level of reasoning across several kinds of moral dilemmas) to try to predict *specific* behaviors (one's willingness to cheat on a test). Thus, existing studies probably underestimate the consistency between moral reasoning and moral behavior. If you want to predict who is likely to lie, you should ask subjects to resolve an ethical dilemma about lying (specific moral judgment) rather than use their *global* responses to measures such as Kohlberg's moral judgment interview.

juvenile delinquents reason at the preconventional level, a fair number of them are conventional moral reasoners who break the law anyway (Blasi, 1980). So there must be personal qualities other than one's level of moral reasoning, and many situational factors as well, that influence a person's moral conduct in daily life (Kurtines, 1986; Thoma, Rest, & Davison, 1991).

Is there any consistency to moral reasoning?   Recall that Kohlberg viewed his stages as "structured wholes"—that is, reasonably stable and consistent ways of conceptualizing moral issues. And one interesting aspect of Kohlberg's research is that subjects are fairly consistent in the type (or stage) of reasoning they use to resolve the different moral dilemmas that make up Kohlberg's moral judgment interview. Does this coherence confirm Kohlberg's **"structured wholes" hypothesis**? Or, alternatively, does it simply reflect the fact that all of Kohlberg's dilemmas are abstract and hypothetical? Would subjects be as consistent when reacting to more common moral issues—ones that they have experienced?

Lawrence Walker and his associates (1987) sought to answer these questions by asking each of 240 6–65-year-olds to resolve three of Kohlberg's hypothetical dilemmas and a fourth, *real-life* dilemma that the subject had faced and had considered very important. The results were interesting: 62% of the participants reasoned at the same stage when resolving real-life and hypothetical dilemmas, whereas 20% reasoned at a higher stage on the hypothetical dilemmas than on the real one, and 18% reasoned at a higher stage on the real dilemma than on the hypothetical ones. Yet, even when subjects operated at different levels on the hypothetical and the real-life dilemmas, they still ended up reasoning at adjacent stages on the two types of issues (for example, Stage 3 on the real-life dilemma and a mix of Stage-3 and Stage-4 reasoning on the hypothetical ones). So it seems that there is an underlying consistency to moral reasoning after all—a coherence that is not attributable merely to the abstract and hypothetical nature of Kohlberg's moral dilemmas.

Even the minor inconsistencies that subjects display point to the overall coherence of moral development. In Figure 12-4, for example, we see three individuals whose predominant (or modal) stage of moral reasoning is Stage 2. Individual 1 displays a *negative bias*—that is, more of his reasoning that is *not* at Stage 2 is at the lower stage (Stage 1) than at the higher stage (Stage 3). Person 2 shows *consolidation*—the vast majority of her judgments are at the modal stage, with very few judgments at either the lower or the higher stage. Finally, individual 3 displays a *positive bias* in that more of his "nonmodal" reasoning is at the higher than the lower stage. If the direction of moral reasoning is forward (toward higher stages over time), as Kohlberg's theory predicts, then people displaying a positive bias should be more inclined than those displaying a negative bias to move to the next highest modal stage in the near future. And that is precisely the pattern that Lawrence Walker and John Taylor (1991b) observed in their recent two-year longitudinal study: seven times as many "positive-bias" subjects moved to the next higher stage over the two-year period as did "negative-bias" subjects. So, rather than undermining Kohlberg's "structured wholes" hypothesis, the minor inconsistencies in moral reasoning that subjects display actually allow us to predict who among a group of participants is most likely (or least likely) to move anytime soon to the next higher stage.

Is Kohlberg's theory biased against women?   No criticism of Kohlberg has stirred more heat than the charge that his theory is biased against women. Carol Gilligan (1977, 1982; Gilligan & Attanucci, 1988) has been disturbed by the fact that Kohlberg's stages were based on interviews with males and that, in some studies, women seemed to be the moral inferior of men, typically reasoning at Stage 3, whereas men usually reasoned at Stage 4. Her response was that (1) females develop a different moral orientation than males do—one that is not adequately represented in Kohlberg's theory—and (2) these different moral orientations are a product of sex typing. According to Gilligan, the independence and assertiveness training that boys receive encourages them to consider moral dilemmas as inevitable conflicts of interest between *individuals*—conflicts that laws and other social conventions are designed to resolve. She calls this orientation the *morality of justice*—a perspective that approximates

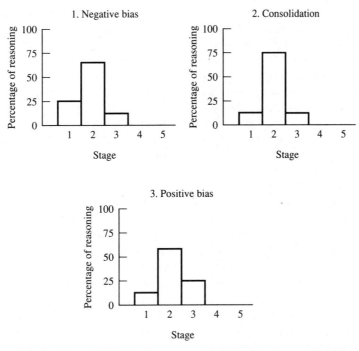

FIGURE 12-4 Three patterns of moral judgments observed among Stage-2 moral reasoners. (Adapted from L. J. Walker & J. H. Taylor, "Stage Transitions in Moral Reasoning: A Longitudinal Study of Developmental Processes." *Developmental Psychology*, 1991, 27, 330–337. Copyright © 1991 by the American Psychological Association. Adapted by permission.)

Stage 4 in Kohlberg's scheme. By contrast, girls are taught to be nurturant, empathic, and concerned about others—in short, to define their sense of "goodness" in terms of their interpersonal *relationships*. So, for females, morality implies a sense of caring or compassionate concern for human welfare—a **morality of care** that sounds like Stage 3 in Kohlberg's scheme. Gilligan also insists that the morality of care that females adopt can become quite abstract or "principled," even though Kohlberg's scheme might place it at Stage 3 because of its focus on interpersonal obligations.

Gilligan then derived stages in the development of a morality of care by analyzing interviews with 29 women facing the difficult dilemma of deciding whether to have an abortion. In the first stage, *self-interest* guides decisions; women said they would do what was best for them. At a second, or *self-sacrificing*, stage, a woman is willing to sacrifice her personal interests to the welfare of others. Finally, Gilligan detected a third, "postconventional" stage—one in which the abstract principle of *nonviolence* causes a woman to try to avoid hurting anyone. This mature morality of care is reflected in the thinking of one 25-year-old: "I would not be doing myself or the child a favor by having this child. . . . I don't need to pay off my imaginary debts to the world through this child, and I don't think that it is right to bring a child into the world and use it for that purpose" (Gilligan, 1977, p. 505).

Has research supported Gilligan's claims that there are sex differences in moral reasoning, moral orientations, and moral development? Not very convincingly, it hasn't. At this point there is little support for the claim that Kohlberg's theory is biased against females, for most studies indicate that women reason just as complexly as men do when their answers are scored by Kohlberg's criteria

(Thoma, 1986; Walker, 1984, 1989). Nor is there much evidence that females travel a different moral path and come to emphasize a morality of care more than males do. In fact, there is evidence to the contrary: when reasoning about real-life moral dilemmas that they have faced, *both* males and females raise issues of compassion and interpersonal responsibility about *as often as* or *more often than* issues of law, justice, and individual rights (Ford & Lowery, 1986; Walker et al., 1987; see also Kahn, 1992; Smetana, Killen, & Turiel, 1991).

Although Gilligan's ideas about sex differences in moral reasoning have not been supported, her work is valuable nonetheless. The most important lessons she has taught us are (1) that there is much more to morality than a concern with laws, rules, rights, and justice and (2) that reasoning based on compassionate concerns and interpersonal responsibility can be just as "principled" (and hence mature) as the "justice" orientation that Kohlberg has emphasized. What Gilligan has given us, then, is a broader view of the meaning of morality. Perhaps it is now appropriate to describe a moral person, whether male or female, as "one whose moral choices reflect reasoned . . . judgments that ensure justice will be accorded to each person while maintaining a passionate concern for the well-being and care of each individual" (Brabeck, 1983, p. 289).

Summing up. Kohlberg's theory is an important statement about the moral development of children, adolescents, and young adults. He has identified a sequence of moral stages that is related to cognitive growth and appears to be universal across cultures.[6] Each of Kohlberg's stages does seem to be a relatively coherent mode of thinking that is likely to determine how an individual will reason about both hypothetical and real-life moral issues. So is this influential theory the final word on moral development?

No indeed! Despite its many strengths, there are those who argue that Kohlberg's theory is woefully incomplete. Consider, for example, that, although reasoning corresponding to each of Kohlberg's stages (the first four stages, at least) is found in all cultures, people in non-Western societies sometimes think about moral issues in ways that Kohlberg didn't anticipate. When resolving the Heinz dilemma, for example, people from India and New Guinea sometimes take a collectivist orientation and say that only through changing society's values can an ideal solution to Heinz's problem be reached (Snarey, 1985; Vasudev & Hummel, 1987). Clearly, this latter reasoning seems highly abstract and even "postconventional"; in fact, Snarey (1985) argues that the failure to find "principled" (Stage-5) moral reasoning in many non-Western societies may simply reflect Kohlberg's failure to recognize all possible forms of postconventional morality.

By focusing solely on legalistic conflicts or dilemmas that laws are designed to resolve, Kohlberg completely ignores other "nonlegalistic" forms of justice that govern the social interactions of very young children. For example, the concept of **distributive justice** — deciding what is a "fair" allocation of limited resources (toys, candies, etc.) among a group of deserving recipients — is not adequately represented in Kohlberg's theory. And, as we will see in Box 12-3, the growth of this positive, distributive-justice reasoning progresses rapidly during middle childhood — so much so that many 8- to 10-year-olds, who are hopelessly mired in Kohlberg's Stage 1, have some reasonably sophisticated ideas about how to distribute resources in a fair and just way.

Finally, other theorists have argued that Kohlberg's singular focus on moral cognition overlooks much of what we need to know about moral growth and development. Norma Haan and her colleagues (1985), for example, point out that moral dilemmas in everyday life tend to arouse strong *emotions* (moral affects) that Kohlberg largely ignores, even though they may have a powerful influence on our moral conduct (see also Hart & Chmiel, 1992). According to Haan, what we should ultimately be interested in when we study morality is (1) how people actually behave when confronted with a moral dilemma and (2) what factors cause them to behave as they do — moral reasoning being only one such cause. In our next section we will examine a third

---

[6]Perhaps it is more accurate to say that the first four stages of Kohlberg's sequence are "universal," for, as we have noted, postconventional reasoning simply does not exist in some societies and only a small minority of adults in any society ever reach the postconventional level.

12-3

How Shall We Divide These Cookies?
Children's Understanding of Distributive Justice

In everyday life, children must often decide how to dispense limited resources (cookies, group earnings, etc.) among a number of deserving parties. What do they think is a fair distribution of rewards? How do their allocations change over time?

William Damon (1977, 1980) addressed these issues by asking 4- to 12-year-olds to provide their views on hypothetical distributive-justice dilemmas. In one dilemma, four children had made bracelets for an adult, who then gave them ten candy bars as a reward. The story provided information that might pertain to children's allocation decisions: for example, one child had made the most and the prettiest bracelets; another child was bigger than the others; a third was younger and unable to work as quickly. The subject's task was to resolve the dilemma by deciding on a fair and just allocation of the ten candy bars among the four participants.

Damon found a stagelike progression in children's reasoning about distributive justice. Four-year-olds are often dominated by *self-interest*: irrespective of what they have contributed, they believe they should get more rewards than other collaborators simply because they want more. Some 4- and 5-year-olds cite objective characteristics (such as size or popularity) as a justification for granting more rewards to a particular child, but they are not yet tying allocations to work performed. By age 5 to 6, children recognize that all collaborators have a legitimate claim to the rewards, and they favor resolving these claims with an *equality rule*—dividing rewards equally among participants, whatever their respective inputs (Damon & Colby, 1987; Damon & Killen, 1982). By age 6 to 7, children begin to show some awareness of deservingness based on work performed; now it is considered fair to give more reward to those who do more work, although these *equity allocations* are not always in exactly the correct proportions (Hook, 1983). Finally, children 8 and older recognize conflicting claims to distributive justice—equality, merit, and need—and will consider these claims (as well as what might be good for promoting group solidarity) when making their allocations. For example, when a child must divide rewards between himself and an agemate who has performed less work, he may use an *equity* rule if he expects little future interaction with

that party but an *equality* rule (thus promoting friendship or group solidarity) if future contact with that child is anticipated (Graziano, 1987).

As children grow older, their thinking about distributive justice becomes increasingly sensitive to social and contextual information. In one recent study (Sigelman & Waitzman, 1991), 5-, 9-, and 13-year-olds were asked to make allocations to three collaborators: an older child, a child who was very poor, and a third child who was a better worker (more productive) than the other two. The allocations were made under three different contexts: one that required a division of money made from the sale of artwork (performance-based context), one that involved allocating a total of nine votes to select a new game to buy (equality context), and one that required the division of a monetary gift that the benefactor hoped would be distributed on the basis of children's needs (charity context). Five-year-olds were totally insensitive to the contextual information, simply preferring an equal distribution of resources among the three children in all three contexts. By contrast, the 9- and the 13-year-olds were quite sensitive to the social context, using an *equity* rule to divide earnings, an *equality* rule to apportion votes, and a *need-based* rule to assign more of a charitable gift to the poor child than to his or her companions.

The development of distributive-justice reasoning obviously depends to some extent on such cognitive advances as children's understanding of proportions (which underlies equity-based allocations). However, the contextual variations in older American children's allocations point to the impact of *cultural lessons* as well—lessons that workers should be rewarded in proportion to their inputs, that all citizens deserve to have an equal say (vote) in group decisions, and that welfare resources should be directed to the needy (Sigelman & Waitzman, 1991). Notice that these complex, internalized concepts of fairness evolve very early (by age 9). Moreover, fear of punishment, deference to authority, and other legalistic themes do not even appear in children's distributive-justice rationales. So, by focusing solely on legalistic conceptions of morality, Kohlberg has clearly underestimated the sophistication of young children's moral judgments.

theory—the social-learning approach—which attempts to specify some of the important cognitive, social, and emotional influences on a child's moral conduct and eventual moral development.

Morality as a Product of Social Learning (and Social Information Processing)

Unlike psychoanalytic theorists, who assume that the development of the superego implies a consistent moral orientation, social-learning theorists propose a **doctrine of specificity**. The implications of these opposing views can be seen in the following example. Suppose we expose a young girl to two tests of moral conduct. In the first test the child is told not to play with some attractive toys and is then left alone with them. The second test is one in which the child is left to play a game that is "rigged" in such a way that she must cheat in order to win a valuable prize. Each situation requires the child to resist the temptation to do something she is not supposed to do in order for her behavior to be labeled morally responsible. If morality is a stable and **unitary** attribute, as psychoanalysts contend, our subject should either resist temptation on both tests or transgress on both. But, if morality is specific to the situation, the child might well behave inconsistently by resisting temptation on one test and transgressing on the other.

How Consistent Are Moral Conduct and Moral Character?

Perhaps the most extensive study of children's moral conduct is one of the oldest—the Character Education Inquiry reported by Hugh Hartshorne and Mark May (1928–1930). The purpose of this five-year project was to investigate the moral "character" of 10,000 children aged 8–16 by tempting them to lie, cheat, or steal in a variety of situations. The most noteworthy finding of this massive investigation was that children tended *not* to be consistent in their moral behavior; a child's willingness to cheat in one situation did not predict his willingness to lie, cheat, or steal in other situations. Of particular interest was the finding that children who cheated in a

particular setting were just as likely as those who did not to state that cheating is wrong! Hartshorne and May concluded that "honesty" is largely specific to the situation rather than stable.

This "doctrine of specificity" has been questioned by other researchers. Roger Burton (1963, 1976) reanalyzed Hartshorne and May's data using newer and more sophisticated statistical techniques. His analyses provide some support for behavioral consistency. For example, a child's willingness to cheat or not cheat in one context (for example, on tests in class) is reasonably consistent, although the same child may behave very differently in highly unrelated contexts (for example, at competitive games on the playground; see also Nelson, Grinder, & Mutterer, 1969). Phil Rushton (1980) drew a similar conclusion after finding that children who help (or share) in one situation are more likely than their nonaltruistic agemates to help (or share) in other *similar* situations. So it seems that moral behaviors *of a particular kind* (for example, cheating on exams; helping needy others) are not nearly so situationally specific as Hartshorne and May had thought. Furthermore, it appears that both the consistency of moral behaviors and the correlations among measures of moral affect, moral reasoning, and moral conduct become progressively stronger between the grade-school years and young adulthood (Blasi, 1980).

In sum, the doctrine of specificity is clearly an overstatement, for all three aspects of morality become more consistent and more highly interrelated over time. However, this is not to imply that morality ever becomes a wholly stable and unitary attribute, for one's willingness to lie, cheat, or violate other moral norms may always depend to some extent on contextual factors, such as the importance of the goal one might achieve by transgressing or the amount of encouragement provided by peers for deviant conduct (Burton, 1976). In other words, the moral character of even the most mature of adults is unlikely to be perfectly consistent across all situations.

Learning to Resist Temptation

From society's standpoint the most important index of morality is the extent to which an individual is

PHOTO 12-3 Sometimes it is difficult to tell whether children are working together, helping each other, or using each other's work. Although there is some consistency to children's moral behavior, a child's conduct in any particular situation is likely to be influenced by factors such as the importance of the goal that might be achieved by breaking a moral rule and the probability of being caught should he or she commit a transgression.

able to resist pressures to violate moral norms, *even when the possibility of detection and punishment is remote* (Hoffman, 1970). A person who resists temptation in the absence of external surveillance not only has learned a moral rule but also is *internally motivated* to abide by that rule. How do children acquire moral standards, and what motivates them to obey these learned codes of conduct? Social-learning theorists have attempted to answer these questions by studying the effects of reinforcement, punishment, and social modeling on children's moral behavior.

REINFORCEMENT AS A DETERMINANT OF MORAL CONDUCT

We have seen on several occasions that the frequency of many behaviors can be increased if these acts are reinforced. Moral behaviors are certainly no exception. For example, David Perry and Ross Parke (1975) found that children were more likely to obey a prohibition against touching attractive toys if they had been reinforced for playing with other, less at-

tractive items. So the practice of rewarding alternative behaviors that are *incompatible* with prohibited acts can be an effective method of instilling moral controls. In addition, punishment administered by a warm, loving (socially reinforcing) parent is more successful at producing resistance to temptation than the same punishment given by a cold, rejecting parent (Sears, Maccoby, & Levin, 1957). Thus the effectiveness of punishment as a means of establishing moral prohibitions will depend, in part, on the disciplinarian's past history as a reinforcing agent.

THE ROLE OF PUNISHMENT IN ESTABLISHING MORAL PROHIBITIONS

Although reinforcing acceptable behaviors is an effective way to promote desirable conduct, adults will often fail to recognize that a child has *resisted* a temptation and is deserving of praise. By contrast, people are quick to inform a child of his or her misdeeds by *punishing* moral transgressions. Is punishment an effective way to foster the development of **inhibitory controls**? As we will see, the answer depends very critically on the child's *interpretation* of these aversive experiences.

Early research. Ross Parke (1972, 1977) has used the **"forbidden toy" paradigm** to study the effects of punishment on children's resistance to temptation. During the first phase of a typical experiment, subjects are punished (by hearing a noxious buzzer) whenever they touch an attractive toy; however, nothing happens when they play with unattractive toys. Once the child has learned the prohibition, the experimenter leaves and the child is surreptitiously observed to determine whether he or she plays with the forbidden toys.

Parke soon discovered that not all punishments were equally effective at promoting the development of moral controls. As illustrated in Table 12-1, *stronger* (rather than milder) punishments, administered *immediately* (rather than later) and *consistently* by a *warm* (rather than an aloof) disciplinarian proved most effective at inhibiting the child's undesirable conduct after the adult had left the room. Yet, Parke's most important discovery was that all forms of punishment become more effective when accompanied by a cognitive rationale that provides

TABLE 12-1   Characteristics of punishment and the punitive context that influence a child's resistance to temptation

Timing of punishment	Punishment administered as children initiate deviant acts is more effective than punishment given after the acts have been performed. Early punishment makes children apprehensive as they prepare to commit a transgression, so that they are less likely to follow through. By contrast, late punishment makes children apprehensive *after* the act is completed, so that they may perform the act again and only then feel anxious.
Intensity of punishment	High-intensity punishment (a loud buzzer or a forceful *no!*) is more effective at inhibiting undesirable conduct than milder forms of the same punitive consequences. However, a caution is in order. Although the high-intensity punishments used in this research were certainly discomforting, they were probably a lot less aversive than a forceful spanking or a week's restriction to one's room. If high-intensity punishments are perceived as "cruel and unusual," children may become hostile toward the punitive agent and/or concerned only with not getting caught—hence they may be willing to commit the prohibited acts, perhaps "out of spite," when the disciplinarian is not around to oversee their activities.
Consistency of punishment	To be effective, punishment must be administered *consistently*. As most prohibited acts are themselves satisfying to the child, he or she will experience positive outcomes on those occasions when transgressions are not punished. In other words, inconsistent punishment may result in the *partial reinforcement* of unacceptable behavior, which strengthens these responses and makes them extremely resistant to extinction—even after the disciplinarian begins to punish them on a regular basis.
Relationship to the punitive agent	Punishment is more effective in establishing moral prohibitions when administered by someone who has previously established a warm and friendly (rewarding) relationship with the child. Children who are punished by a warm, caring person may perceive the reprimand as a loss of affection and may inhibit the punished act as a means of regaining approval. However, children who are punished by a cold, rejecting adult should not be highly motivated to inhibit forbidden acts, because they have no expectation of reestablishing a warm relationship with this cool or aloof disciplinarian.

the transgressor with reasons for inhibiting a forbidden act. In fact, rationales alone were more effective than mild punishments at persuading children not to touch attractive toys. However, let's not conclude that parents should abandon punishment in favor of rationales, for a combination of *mild punishment and a rationale* is much more effective than either of these treatments by itself.

Explaining the effects of cognitive rationales: Hoffman's social information-processing analysis of punitive suppression. It was once thought that punishment suppressed undesirable behaviors by conditioning fear or anxiety to the punished act. Thus, whenever a child thought about committing a transgression, he would feel highly anxious and would inhibit the prohibited act in order to reduce this conditioned anxiety (Aronfreed, 1976).

Martin Hoffman (1984, 1988) points out that this older, conditioning viewpoint doesn't easily explain why rationales *increase* the effectiveness of punishment, especially mild or delayed punishments that produce little anxiety or moral restraint by themselves. According to Hoffman's *attributional (or social information-processing) theory*, rationales enhance the effectiveness of punishment because they provide children with information specifying why the punished act is wrong and why *they* should feel guilty or shameful if they repeat it. So, when these youngsters think about committing the forbidden act in the future, they should experience a general uneasiness (stemming from previous disciplinary encounters), should be inclined to make an *internal* attribution for this arousal (for example, "I'd feel guilty if I were to deviate," "I'd violate my positive self-image"), and should now be more likely to inhibit

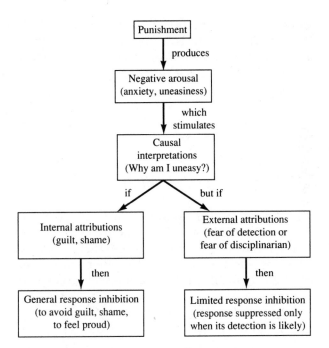

FIGURE 12-5 The social information-processing model of the suppressive effects of punishment.

the forbidden act and to feel rather good about their "mature and responsible" conduct (see Figure 12-5). By contrast, children who receive no rationales or who have been exposed to reasoning that focuses their attention on the negative consequences they can expect for future transgressions (for example, "You'll be spanked again if you do it") will experience just as much uneasiness when they think about committing the forbidden act. However, these youngsters should tend to make *external* attributions for their emotional arousal (for example, "I'm worried about getting caught and punished") — attributions that might make them comply with moral norms in the presence of authority figures but that should do little to inhibit deviant conduct if there is no one around to detect a transgression.

We see, then, that fear of detection and punishment is not enough to persuade children to resist temptations in the absence of external surveillance. In order to establish truly internalized, *self*-controls, adults must structure disciplinary encounters to include an appropriate rationale — a rationale that informs the child why the prohibited act is wrong and why *she* should feel guilty or shameful were she to

repeat it (Hoffman, 1988). Stated another way, true *self*-restraint is largely under *cognitive* control; the ability to resist temptation depends on what's in children's heads rather than on the amount of fear or uneasiness in their guts.

Although rational forms of punishment can be quite successful at inhibiting children's undesirable conduct, we should not necessarily assume that punitive tactics are the most effective way to establish moral controls. The major problem with punishment is that it often has undesirable side effects that limit its usefulness (for example, making children angry or resentful; modeling coercive, antisocial modes of problem solving; or even reinforcing a child who deviates to attract attention). In Box 12-4 we will consider two alternative techniques adults can use to promote children's resistance to temptation while avoiding many of these side effects.

EFFECTS OF SOCIAL MODELS ON CHILDREN'S MORAL BEHAVIOR

Social-learning theorists have generally assumed that modeling influences play an important role in the child's moral development. And they are undoubtedly correct, for, as we have seen, young children often imitate the compassionate and helpful acts of altruistic models. But helpful acts are *active* responses that will capture a child's attention. Will children learn *inhibitory* controls from models who exhibit socially desirable behavior in a "passive" way by failing to commit forbidden acts?

Indeed they will, as long as they recognize that the "passive" model is actually resisting the temptation to violate a moral norm (Toner, Parke, & Yussen, 1978). Joan Grusec and her associates (1979) find that a temptation-resisting model can be particularly effective at inspiring children to behave in kind if he clearly verbalizes that he is following a rule and states a rationale for not committing the deviant act. Moreover, rule-following models whose rationales match the child's customary level of moral reasoning are more influential than models whose rationales are beyond that level (Toner & Potts, 1981).

Of course, a model who violates a moral norm may *disinhibit* observers by giving them reason to think that they too can break the rule, particularly if the model is not punished for his deviant acts (Rosenkoetter, 1973). Thus, social models play two roles in a child's moral development, sometimes leading him or her to resist temptation and sometimes serving as ''bad influences'' who encourage inappropriate conduct.

Finally, an experiment by Nace Toner and his associates (Toner, Moore, & Ashley, 1978) produced a very interesting outcome: 6- to 8-year-olds who were persuaded to serve as models of moral restraint for other children became more likely than agemates who had not served as exemplary models to obey rules during later tests of resistance to temptation. It was almost as if serving as a model had produced a change in children's *self-concepts*, so that they now defined themselves as ''people who follow rules.'' The implications for child rearing are obvious: perhaps parents could succeed in establishing inhibitory controls in their older children by appealing to their maturity and persuading them to serve as models of self-restraint for their younger brothers and sisters.

Who Raises Morally Mature Children?

About 25 years ago, Martin Hoffman (1970) reviewed the child-rearing literature to determine whether the disciplinary techniques that *parents* use have any effect on the moral development of their children. Three major approaches were compared:

BOX 12-4 | *Nonpunitive Methods of Promoting Moral Restraint*

In recent years, social-learning and social information-processing theorists have searched for nonpunitive methods of persuading children to comply with rules and to display self-restraint. Two such strategies that appear especially promising are (1) the self-instructional approach and (2) moral self-concept training.

Self-instructional strategies. If a child's willingness to resist temptation is truly under cognitive control, as social-learning and social information-processing theorists have argued, then it should be possible to teach young children how to *instruct themselves* to follow rules and to resist temptations. To test this hypothesis, Walter Mischel and Charlotte Patterson (1976) asked preschool children to work on a very dull task in the presence of a talking ''clown box'' that tried to persuade them to break their promise to work. Children who had been taught to say to themselves ''I'm not going to look at Mr. Clown Box . . . when Mr. Clown Box says to look at him'' were better able than those who had received no self-instructional strategy to resist this tempting distraction and keep on working.

So we see that even very simple plans or ''blueprints for action'' that children have available for use in the face of temptation will enhance their ability to live up to their promises and follow rules.

Instilling a ''moral'' self-concept. The idea that moral self-restraint is under cognitive control implies that we should be able to promote compliance with moral rules by convincing children that they are ''good'' or ''honest'' people who are inhibiting the temptation to lie, cheat, or steal because they want to (an internal attribution). Indeed, children who incorporate attributions of ''goodness,'' ''honesty,'' or ''strength of character'' into their self-concepts may strive to live up to these positive self-images and could become highly self-critical or remorseful should they violate a rule.

Apparently this kind of moral self-concept training does indeed work. William Casey and Roger Burton (1982) found that 7–10-year-olds became much more honest while playing games if being ''honest'' was stressed and the players had learned to remind themselves to follow the rules. Yet, when honesty was not stressed, the players were likely to cheat—even when they had been told to periodically remind themselves

1. **Love withdrawal:** withholding attention, affection, or approval after a child misbehaves — or, in other words, creating anxiety over a loss of love.
2. **Power-assertion:** using superior power to control the child's behavior (includes techniques such as forceful comments, physical restraint, spankings, and withdrawal of privileges — techniques that may generate fear, anger, or resentment).
3. **Induction:** explaining why a behavior is wrong and should be changed by emphasizing how it affects other people; often suggests how the child might undo any harm done.

Although only a limited number of child-rearing studies had been conducted by 1970, their results suggested that (1) neither love withdrawal nor power assertion was particularly effective at promoting moral maturity, but that (2) induction seemed to foster the development of all three aspects of morality — moral emotions, moral reasoning, and moral behavior (Hoffman, 1970). Table 12-2 summarizes the relationships among the three patterns of parental discipline and various measures of children's moral maturity that emerged from a later review of the literature that included many more studies (Brody & Shaffer, 1982). Clearly these data confirm Hoffman's conclusions: parents who rely on inductive discipline tend to have children who are morally mature, whereas frequent use of power assertion is more often associated with moral immaturity than with moral maturity. The few cases in which induction was *not* associated with moral

---

B O X **12-4** | *continued*

to comply with the rules. Moreover, David Perry and his associates (1980) found that 9–10-year-olds who had been told that they were especially good at carrying out instructions and following rules (moral self-concept training) behaved very differently after succumbing to a nearly irresistible temptation (leaving a boring task to watch an exciting TV show) than did peers who had not been told they were especially good. Specifically, children who had heard positive attributions about themselves were more inclined than control subjects to *punish their own transgressions* by giving back many of the valuable prize tokens they had been paid for working at the boring task.

So it seems that labeling children as "good" or "honest" not only increases the likelihood that they will resist temptations but also contributes to children's feelings of guilt or remorse should they behave inappropriately and violate their positive self-images. Indeed, Perry et al. (1980) suggest that the expectation of feeling guilty or remorseful over deviant conduct may be what motivates children with positive self-concepts to resist temptations in the first place.

Summing up. Clearly, children can become effective allies in their own moral socialization if they are often encouraged to be "good" or "honest" persons and have learned how to instruct or remind themselves of the rules they must follow to behave appropriately and to maintain a "good" or "honest" self-image. Unlike punishment, which is easily applied after a transgression, the nonpunitive strategies that we have reviewed will require a substantial amount of planning on the part of the adult. But, despite the effort that one must expend, the potential advantages of these alternatives to punishment are many. For example, a parent who is obviously concerned about helping the child to *prevent future transgressions* is likely to be perceived as caring and loving — an impression that should increase the child's motivation to comply with parental requests. Moreover, self-concept training and the use of self-instruction should help to convince the child that "I'm resisting this temptation because I want to" and thus lead to the development of truly *internalized* controls, rather than response inhibitions based on a fear of detection and punishment. And, last but not least, these nonpunitive techniques produce few if any of the undesirable side effects that often accompany punishment.

TABLE 12-2   *Relationships between parents' use of three disciplinary strategies and children's moral development*

Direction of Relationship between Parent's Use of a Disciplinary Strategy and Children's Moral Maturity	Type of Discipline		
	Power-Assertion	Love Withdrawal	Induction
+ (positive correlation)	7	8	38
− (negative correlation)	32	11	6

NOTE: Table entries represent the number of occasions on which a particular disciplinary technique was found to be associated (either positively or negatively) with a measure of children's moral affect, reasoning, or behavior.
SOURCE: Adapted from G. H. Brody & D. R. Shaffer, "Contributions of Parents and Peers to Children's Moral Socialization." *Developmental Review*, 1982, 2, 31–75. Copyright © 1982 by Academic Press, Inc.

maturity all involved children under age 4. However, other recent research indicates that induction can be highly effective with 2- to 5-year-olds, reliably promoting sympathy and compassion for others as well as a willingness to comply with parental requests; by contrast, use of such high-intensity power-assertive tactics as becoming angry and physically restraining or spanking the child is already associated with (and seems to promote) noncompliance, defiance, and a lack of concern for others (Crockenberg & Litman, 1990; Hart et al., 1992; Kochanska, 1991; Kuczynski & Kochanska, 1990; Zahn-Waxler, Radke-Yarrow, & King, 1979).

Why is inductive discipline effective?   Hoffman believes that there are several reasons why the use of inductive tactics is such an effective disciplinary strategy. First, the inductive disciplinarian provides *cognitive standards* (or rationales) that children can use to evaluate their conduct. And, when the inductive discipline is other-oriented, parents are furnishing their child with the kinds of experiences that should foster the development of *empathy* and *role-taking skills* — two cognitive abilities that contribute to the growth of mature moral reasoning. Second, use of inductive discipline allows parents to talk about *moral emotions* (such as guilt and shame), which are not easily discussed with a child who is made emotionally insecure by love-oriented discipline or angry by power-assertive techniques. Indeed, this inward focus on the child's moral emotions should foster *internal attributions* for one's uneasiness when tempted to deviate (for example, "I'm feeling ashamed for considering this action")

or for one's decision to abide by rules (for example, "I'm resisting this temptation because I want to") — precisely the kinds of attributions that contribute to truly *internalized* moral controls. By contrast, power-assertion and love withdrawal are more likely to focus the child's attention on the aversive consequences of having been caught at a transgression (for example, a loss of affection; a sore butt), which in turn may lead to *external attributions* for one's uneasiness about prohibited acts (that is, fear of the disciplinarian) and a willingness to perform them when the probability of detection is remote. Finally, parents who rely heavily on inductive discipline are likely to explain to the child (1) what he or she *should have done* when tempted to violate a prohibition and (2) what he or she *can now do* to make up for a transgression. So it appears that induction is an effective method of moral socialization because it clearly illustrates the affective, cognitive, and behavioral aspects of morality and may help the child to integrate them.

Does induction promote moral maturity? Or, rather, do morally mature children elicit more inductive forms of discipline from their parents? Since the child-rearing studies are correlational in nature, either of these possibilities could explain Hoffman's findings. Yet, Hoffman (1975a) contends that parents exert far more constraints on their children's behavior than children exert on parents. In other words, he believes that parental use of inductive discipline promotes moral maturity rather than the other way around. And there is some *experimental* support for Hoffman's claim in that induction is much more effective than other forms of discipline

"IF YOU'RE TRYIN' TO GET SOMETHING INTO MY HEAD, YOU'RE WORKIN' ON THE WRONG END!"

Dennis the Menace® used by permission of Hank Ketcham and © by North American Syndicate.

at persuading children to keep their promises and to comply with rules imposed by unfamiliar adults (Kuczynski, 1983). Moreover, parents' preexisting attitudes about child rearing or implicit theories of discipline play a major part in determining how they react to children's undesirable conduct (Dix, Ruble, & Zambarano, 1989). For example, mothers who believe that they can do little to control problem behaviors are the ones who react most negatively and coercively to such antics, regardless of whether they are overseeing their own or someone else's child (Bugental, Blue, & Cruzcosa, 1989; Bugental, Blue, & Lewis, 1990).

Yet, children clearly have a hand in determining how they are treated by their overseers. Youngsters who have a history of conduct disorders, for example, are more likely than normal children to elicit coercive, punitive forms of discipline when they misbehave—both from their mothers and from other adults who have been asked to monitor their activities (see Anderson, Lytton, & Romney, 1986; Lytton, 1990). A child's reactions to previous disciplinary encounters are also important. Ross Parke (1977) finds that children who had ignored a disciplinarian or who had pleaded for mercy were dealt with much more forcefully during the next disciplinary encounter than those who had reacted to the earlier discipline by offering to undo the harm they had done. So, moral socialization in the home is a two-way street: although inductive discipline may indeed promote the development of moral controls, children with a history of good conduct who respond more favorably to disciplinary encounters are the ones who are likely to be treated in a rational, nonpunitive manner by their parents.

Finally, it is important to note that few if any parents are totally inductive, love oriented, or power-assertive in their approach to discipline; most make at least some use of all three disciplinary techniques. Although parents classified as "inductive" rely heavily on inductive methods, they will occasionally take punitive measures whenever punishment is necessary to command the child's attention or to discipline repeated transgressions. So the style of parenting that Hoffman refers to as induction may be very similar to the "rationale + mild punishment" treatment that is so effective in the laboratory.

A child's-eye view of discipline.   What do children think about various disciplinary strategies? Do they feel (as many developmentalists do) that physical punishment and love withdrawal are ineffective methods of promoting moral restraint? Would they favor inductive techniques? Or is it conceivable that children would prefer that their parents adopt a more permissive attitude and not be so quick to discipline transgressions?

Michael Siegal and Jan Cowen (1984) addressed these issues by asking 100 children and adolescents between the ages of 4 and 18 to listen to stories describing different kinds of misdeeds and to evaluate strategies that mothers had used to discipline these antics. Five kinds of transgressions were described: (1) simply disobeying a directive (the child refused to clean his room), (2) causing physical harm to others (the child punched a playmate), (3) causing physical harm to oneself (ignoring an order not to touch a hot stove), (4) causing psychological harm to others (making fun of a physically disabled person), and (5) causing physical damage (breaking a lamp while roughhousing). The four disciplinary techniques on which mothers were said to have relied were *induction* (reasoning with the culprit by pointing out the harmful consequences of his or her actions), *physical punishment* (striking the child), *love withdrawal* (saying they wanted nothing more to do with the culprit), and *permissive nonintervention* (ignoring the incident and assuming that the child would learn important lessons on his or her own). Each participant heard 20 stories that resulted from pairing each of the four maternal disciplinary strategies with each of the five transgressions. After listening to or reading each story, the subject indicated whether the mother's approach to the problem was "very wrong," "wrong," "half right and half wrong," "right," or "very right."

Although the perceived appropriateness of each disciplinary technique varied somewhat across transgressions, the most interesting findings overall were that (1) induction was the most preferred disciplinary strategy for subjects of all ages (even preschoolers), and (2) physical punishment was the next most favorably evaluated technique. So all participants seemed to favor a rational disciplinarian who relies heavily on reasoning that is occasionally backed by power-assertion. By contrast, love withdrawal and permissiveness were favorably evaluated by no age group. In fact, the younger children in the sample (that is, the 4- to 9-year-olds) favored *any* form of discipline, even love withdrawal, over a permissive attitude on the mother's part (which they viewed as "wrong" or "very wrong"). Apparently, young children see the need for adults to step in and restrain their inappropriate conduct, for they were quite bothered by the stories in which youngsters were generally free to do their own thing, largely unencumbered by adult constraints.

We see, then, that the disciplinary style that children favor (induction backed by occasional use of power-assertion) is the one most closely associated with measures of moral maturity in the child-rearing studies and with resistance to temptation in the laboratory. Perhaps another reason why induc-

tive discipline promotes moral maturity is simply that children view this approach as the "right" way to deal with transgressions, and they may be highly motivated to accept influence from a disciplinarian whose "world view" matches their own. By contrast, children who favor induction but are usually disciplined in other ways may see little justification for internalizing the values and exhortations of a disciplinarian whose very methods of inducing compliance seem unwise, unjust, and hardly worthy of respect.

Summary

Many theorists consider morality and the growth of moral controls to be critical aspects of social and personality development. Morality has been defined in many ways, although almost everyone agrees that it implies *a set of principles or ideals that help the individual to distinguish right from wrong, to act on this distinction, and to experience pride in virtuous conduct and guilt (or shame) over conduct that violates one's standards.* Thus, morality has three basic components: *moral affect, moral reasoning,* and *moral behavior.*

Psychoanalytic theorists emphasize the affective, or "emotional," aspects of morality. According to Freud, the character of the parent/child relationship largely determines the child's willingness to internalize the moral standards of the same-sex parent. This internalization is said to occur during the phallic stage and results in the development of the superego. Once formed, the superego functions as an internal censor that will reward the child for virtuous conduct and punish moral transgressions by making the child feel anxious, guilty, or ashamed. Although Freud's broader themes about the importance of moral emotions have some merit, the particulars of his theory of oedipal morality have not received much empirical support.

Neo-Freudians have proposed a theory of moral development that differs from Freud's version in two important respects. First, the superego is said to result from social (rather than sexual) conflicts that cause the child to internalize the moral standards of *both* parents in order to avoid losing their love and affection. Second, both the ego and the superego are said to play important roles in determining the child's moral conduct and character. The neo-Freudian hypothesis that moral development depends, in part, on the strength of one's ego has been confirmed, although the evidence cited to support this claim is easily explained by other theories.

Cognitive-developmental theorists have emphasized the cognitive component of morality by studying the development of moral reasoning. Jean Piaget was the pioneer. He formulated a two-stage model of moral development based on changes that occur in children's conceptions of rules and their sense of social justice. Although Piaget did identify some important processes and basic trends in the development of moral reasoning, recent research suggests that his two-stage theory badly underestimated the moral sophistication of preschool and young grade-school children while overestimating the moral maturity of adolescents.

Lawrence Kohlberg's revision and extension of Piaget's theory views moral reasoning as progressing through an invariant sequence of three levels, each composed of two distinct stages. According to Kohlberg, the order of progression through the levels and stages is invariant because each of these modes of thinking depends, in part, on the development of cognitive abilities that evolve in a fixed sequence. Yet, Kohlberg also claimed that no moral growth occurs in the absence of social experiences that would cause a person to reevaluate her existing moral concepts.

Research indicates that Kohlberg's stages do form an invariant sequence and that both cognitive development and such relevant social experiences as higher education and peer interaction contribute to the growth of moral reasoning. Moreover, each of Kohlberg's stages is a reasonably consistent mode of thinking that is likely to guide an individual's reasoning about both hypothetical and real-world dilemmas. And research has consistently failed to support the claim that Kohlberg's theory is biased against women. However, Kohlberg's singular focus on the *legalistic* moral judgments of *Westernized* sub-

jects caused him to overlook (1) types of postconventional reasoning that appear in other cultures and (2) the positive, nonlegalistic forms of *distributive justice* that govern the interactions of grade-school children.

Social-learning theorists emphasize the behavioral component of morality, and their research has helped us to understand how children resist temptation and inhibit acts that violate moral norms. Although the consistency of children's moral conduct from situation to situation is only moderate at best, measures of moral affect, moral reasoning, and moral behavior become more consistent and more highly interrelated over time. However, morality never becomes a wholly stable and unitary attribute, even among the most mature of adults.

Among the processes that are important in establishing inhibitory controls are (1) reinforcing the child for following rules and (2) punishing transgressions. The most effective punitive tactics are those that include a cognitive rationale explaining why the punished act is wrong and why the child should want to inhibit such conduct. Nonpunitive techniques such as teaching the child how to instruct herself to avoid temptations or convincing the child that she is a "good" or "honest" person are also quite effective at promoting moral self-restraint. Indeed, any technique that induces children to make *internal attributions* for their uneasiness in the face of temptation or for their compliance with rules is likely to contribute to their moral development. Children may also acquire inhibitory controls by observing models who show moral restraint or by serving as rule-following models for other children.

Martin Hoffman has looked at the relationship between parental disciplinary practices and children's moral development. His findings indicate that warm and loving parents who rely mainly on *inductive discipline* tend to raise children who are morally mature. Induction is an effective method of moral socialization because it often illustrates and may help the child to integrate the affective, cognitive, and behavioral aspects of morality. And, because children generally prefer induction to other disciplinary techniques, viewing it as the wise choice for handling most transgressions, they may be highly motivated to accept influence from an "inductive" adult whose methods they can respect.

References

AMBRON, S. R., & IRWIN, D. M. (1975). Role-taking and moral judgment in five- and seven-year-olds. *Developmental Psychology, 11,* 102.

ANDERSON, K. E., LYTTON, H., & ROMNEY, D. M. (1986). Mothers' interactions with normal and conduct-disordered boys: Who affects whom? *Developmental Psychology, 22,* 604–609.

ARONFREED, J. (1976). Moral development from the standpoint of a general psychological theory. In T. Lickona (Ed.), *Moral development and behavior.* New York: Holt, Rinehart & Winston.

BANDURA, A. (1977). *Social learning theory.* Englewood Cliffs, NJ: Prentice-Hall.

BANDURA, A. (1991). Social cognitive theory of moral thought and action. In W. M. Kurtines & J. L. Gewirtz (Eds.), *Handbook of moral behavior and development* (Vol. 1). Hillsdale, NJ: Erlbaum.

BERKOWITZ, M. W., & GIBBS, J. C. (1983). Measuring the developmental features of moral discussion. *Merrill-Palmer Quarterly, 29,* 399–410.

BLASI, A. (1980). Bridging moral cognition and moral action: A critical review of the literature. *Psychological Bulletin, 88,* 1–45.

BOLDIZAR, J. P., WILSON, K. L., & DEEMER, D. K. (1989). Gender, life experience, and moral judgment development: A process-oriented approach. *Journal of Personality and Social Psychology, 57,* 229–238.

BOYES, M. C., & WALKER, L. J. (1988). Implications of cultural diversity for the universality claims of Kohlberg's theory of moral reasoning. *Human Development, 31,* 44–59.

BRABECK, M. (1983). Moral judgment: Theory and research on differences between males and females. *Developmental Review, 3,* 274–291.

BRAINE, L. G., POMERANTZ, E., LORBER, D., & KRANTZ, D. H. (1991). Conflicts with authority: Children's feelings, actions, and justifications. *Developmental Psychology, 27,* 829–840.

BRODY, G. H., & SHAFFER, D. R. (1982). Contributions of parents and peers to children's moral socialization. *Developmental Review, 2,* 31–75.

BUGENTAL, D. B., BLUE, J., & CRUZCOSA, M. (1989). Perceived control over caregiving outcomes: Implications for child abuse. *Developmental Psychology, 25,* 532–539.

BUGENTAL, D. B., BLUE, J., & LEWIS, J. (1990). Caregiver beliefs and dysphoric affect directed to difficult children. *Developmental Psychology, 26,* 631–638.

BURTON, R. V. (1963). The generality of honesty reconsidered. *Psychological Review, 70,* 481–499.

BURTON, R. V. (1976). Honesty and dishonesty. In T. Lickona (Ed.), *Moral development and behavior.* New York: Holt, Rinehart & Winston.

BUSSEY, K. (1992). Lying and truthfulness: Children's definitions, standards, and evaluative reactions. *Child Development, 63,* 129–137.

CASEY, W. M., & BURTON, R. V. (1982). Training children to be consistently honest through verbal self-instructions. *Child Development, 53,* 911–919.

COLBY, A., & KOHLBERG, L. (1987). *The measurement of moral judgment. Vol. 1: Theoretical foundations and research validation.* Cambridge, England: Cambridge University Press.

COLBY, A., KOHLBERG, L., GIBBS, J., & LIEBERMAN, M. (1983). A longitudinal study of moral judgment. *Monographs of the Society for Research in Child Development, 48* (Nos. 1–2, Serial No. 200).

COLE, P. M., BARRETT, K. C., & ZAHN-WAXLER, C. (1992). Emotion displays in two-year-olds during mishaps. *Child Development, 63,* 314–324.

CROCKENBERG, S., & LITMAN, C. (1990). Autonomy as competence in 2-year-olds: Maternal correlates of child defiance, compliance, and self-assertion. *Developmental Psychology, 26,* 961–971.

DAMON, W. (1977). *The social world of the child.* San Francisco: Jossey-Bass.

DAMON, W. (1980). Patterns of change in children's social reasoning: A two-year longitudinal study. *Child Development, 51,* 1010–1017.

DAMON, W., & COLBY, A. (1987). Social influence and moral change. In W. M. Kurtines & J. L. Gewirtz (Eds.), *Moral development through social interaction.* New York: Wiley.

DAMON, W., & KILLEN, M. (1982). Peer interaction and the process of change in children's moral reasoning. *Merrill-Palmer Quarterly, 28,* 347–367.

de VRIES, B., & WALKER, L. J. (1986). Moral reasoning and attitudes toward capital punishment. *Developmental Psychology, 22,* 509–513.

DIX, T., RUBLE, D. N., & ZAMBARANO, R. J. (1989). Mothers' implicit theories of discipline: Child effects, parent effects, and the attribution process. *Child Development, 60,* 1373–1391.

ERIKSON, E. H. (1963). *Childhood and society.* New York: Norton.

FERGUSON, T. J., STEGGE, H., & DAMHUIS, I. (1991). Children's understanding of guilt and shame. *Child Development, 62,* 827–839.

FORD, M. R., & LOWERY, C. R. (1986). Gender differences in moral reasoning: A comparison of the use of justice and care orientations. *Journal of Personality and Social Psychology, 50,* 777–783.

FREUD, S. (1960). *A general introduction to psychoanalysis.* New York: Washington Square Press. (Original work published 1935.)

GARBARINO, J., & BRONFENBRENNER, U. (1976). The socialization of moral judgment and behavior in cross-cultural perspective. In T. Lickona (Ed.), *Moral development and behavior.* New York: Holt, Rinehart & Winston.

GILLIGAN, C. (1977). In a different voice: Women's conceptions of self and morality. *Harvard Educational Review, 47,* 481–517.

GILLIGAN, C. (1982). *In a different voice: Psychological theory and women's development.* Cambridge, MA: Harvard University Press.

GILLIGAN, C., & ATTANUCCI, J. (1988). Two moral orientations: Gender differences and similarities. *Merrill-Palmer Quarterly, 34,* 223–237.

GRAZIANO, W. G. (1987). Lost in thought at the choice point: Cognition, context, and equity. In J. C. Masters & W. P. Smith (Eds.), *Social comparison, social justice, and relative deprivation.* Hillsdale, NJ: Erlbaum.

GRUSEC, J. E., KUCZYNSKI, L., RUSHTON, J. P., & SIMUTIS, Z. (1979). Learning resistance to temptation through observation. *Developmental Psychology, 15,* 233–240.

HAAN, N., AERTS, E., & COOPER, B. A. B. (1985). *On moral grounds: The search for practical morality.* New York: New York University Press.

HARKNESS, S., EDWARDS, C. P., & SUPER, C. M. (1981). Social roles and moral reasoning: A case study in a rural African community. *Developmental Psychology, 17,* 595–603.

HART, C. H., DeWOLF, D. M., WOZNIAK, P., & BURTS, D. C. (1992). Maternal and paternal disciplinary styles: Relations with preschooler's playground behavioral orientations and peer status. *Child Development, 63,* 879–892.

HART, D., & CHMIEL, S. (1992). Influence of defense mechanisms on moral judgment development: A longitudinal study. *Developmental Psychology, 28,* 722–730.

HARTMANN, H. (1960). *Psychoanalysis and moral values.* New York: International Universities Press.

HARTSHORNE, H., & MAY, M. S. (1928–1930). *Studies in the nature of character.* Vol. 1: *Studies in deceit.* Vol. 2: *Studies in self-control.* Vol. 3: *Studies in the organization of character.* New York: Macmillan.

HIGGINS, E. T. (1987). Self-discrepancy: A theory relating self and affect. *Psychological Review, 94,* 319–340.

HOFFMAN, M. L. (1970). Moral development. In P. H. Mussen (Ed.), *Carmichael's manual of child psychology* (Vol. 2). New York: Wiley.

HOFFMAN, M. L. (1975a). Moral internalization, parental power, and the nature of parent-child interaction. *Developmental Psychology, 11,* 228–239.

HOFFMAN, M. L. (1975b). Sex differences in moral internalization and values. *Journal of Personality and Social Psychology, 32,* 720–729.

HOFFMAN, M. L. (1984). Empathy, its limitations, and its role in a comprehensive moral theory. In W. M. Kurtines & J. L. Gewirtz (Eds.), *Morality, moral behavior, and moral development.* New York: Wiley.

HOFFMAN, M. L. (1988). Moral development. In M. H. Bornstein & M. E. Lamb (Eds.), *Developmental psychology: An advanced textbook* (2nd ed.). Hillsdale, NJ: Erlbaum.

HOOK, J. (1983). The development of children's equity judgments. In R. L. Leahy (Ed.), *The child's construction of social equality.* New York: Academic Press.

JOSE, P. E. (1990). Just world reasoning in children's immanent justice judgments. *Child Development, 61,* 1024–1033.

KAGAN, J. (1987). Introduction. In J. Kagan & S. Lamb (Eds.), *The emergence of morality in young children.* Chicago: University of Chicago Press.

KAHN, P. H., JR. (1992). Children's obligatory and discretionary moral judgments. *Child Development, 63,* 416–430.

KEASEY, C. B. (1971). Social participation as a factor in the moral development of preadolescents. *Developmental Psychology, 5,* 216–220.

KOCHANSKA, G. (1991). Socialization and temperament in the development of guilt and conscience. *Child Development, 62,* 1379–1392.

KOHLBERG, L. (1963). The development of children's orientations toward a moral order: I. Sequence in the development of moral thought. *Vita Humana, 6,* 11–33.

KOHLBERG, L. (1975, June). The cognitive-developmental approach to moral education. *Phi Delta Kappan,* pp. 670–677.

KOHLBERG, L. (1981). *Essays on moral development.* Vol. 1 *The philosophy of moral development.* San Francisco: Harper & Row.

KOHLBERG, L. (1984). *Essays on moral development.* Vol. 2: *The psychology of moral development.* San Francisco: Harper & Row.

KOHLBERG, L. (1985). The just community approach to moral education in theory and practice. In M. W. Berkowitz & F. Oser (Eds.), *Moral education: Theory and application.* Hillsdale, NJ: Erlbaum.

KREBS, D., & GILLMORE, J. (1982). The relationship among the first stages of cognitive development, role-taking abilities, and moral development. *Child Development, 53,* 877–886.

KRUGER, A. C., & TOMASELLO, M. (1986). Transactive discussions with peers and adults. *Developmental Psychology, 22,* 681–685.

KUCZYNSKI, L. (1983). Reasoning, prohibitions, and motivations for compliance. *Developmental Psychology, 19,* 126–134.

KUCZYNSKI, L., & KOCHANSKA, G. (1990). Development of children's noncompliance strategies from toddlerhood to age 5. *Developmental Psychology, 26,* 398–408.

KUHN, D., KOHLBERG, L., LANGER, J., & HAAN, N. (1977). The development of formal operations in logical and moral judgment. *Genetic Psychology Monographs, 95,* 97–188.

KURTINES, W. M. (1986). Moral behavior as rule governed behavior: Person and situation effects on moral decision making. *Journal of Personality and Social Psychology, 50,* 784–791.

LAUPA, M. (1991). Children's reasoning about three authority attributes: Adult status, knowledge, and social position. *Developmental Psychology, 27,* 321–329.

LAUPA, M., & TURIEL, E. (1986). Children's conceptions of adult and peer authority. *Child Development, 57,* 405–412.

LEI, T., & CHENG, S. (1989). A little but special light on the universality of moral judgment development. In L. Kohlberg, D. Candee, & A. Colby (Eds.), *Rethinking moral development.* Cambridge, MA: Harvard University Press.

LEON, M. (1984). Rules mothers and sons use to integrate intent and damage information in their moral judgments. *Child Development, 55*, 2106–2113.

LEWIS, M., ALESSANDRI, S. M., & SULLIVAN, M. W. (1992). Differences in shame and pride as a function of children's gender and task difficulty. *Child Development, 63*, 630–638.

LICKONA, T. (1976). Research on Piaget's theory of moral development. In T. Lickona (Ed.), *Moral development and behavior*. New York: Holt, Rinehart & Winston.

LINN, R. (1989). Hypothetical and actual moral reasoning of Israeli selective conscientious objectors during the war in Lebanon (1982–1985). *Journal of Applied Developmental Psychology, 10*, 19–36.

LYTTON, H. (1990). Child and parent effects in boys' conduct disorder: A reinterpretation. *Developmental Psychology, 26*, 683–697.

McDOUGALL, W. (1908). *An introduction to social psychology*. London: Methuen.

MERCHANT, R. L., & REBELSKY, F. (1972). Effects of participation in rule formation on the moral judgment of children. *Genetic Psychology Monographs, 85*, 287–304.

MISCHEL, W. (1974). Processes in the delay of gratification. In L. Berkowitz (Ed.), *Advances in experimental social psychology* (Vol. 7). Orlando, FL: Academic Press.

MISCHEL, W., & PATTERSON, C. J. (1976). Substantive and structural elements of effective plans for self-control. *Journal of Personality and Social Psychology, 34*, 942–950.

MISCHEL, W., SHODA, Y., & PEAKE, P. K. (1988). The nature of adolescent competencies predicted by preschool delay of gratification. *Journal of Personality and Social Psychology, 54*, 687–696.

MOIR, J. (1974). Egocentrism and the emergence of conventional morality in preadolescent girls. *Child Development, 45*, 299–304.

NELSON, E. A., GRINDER, R. E., & BIAGGIO, A. M. B. (1969). Relationships between behavioral, cognitive-developmental and self-report measures of morality and personality. *Multivariate Behavioral Research, 4*, 483–500.

NELSON, E. A., GRINDER, R. E., & MUTTERER, M. L. (1969). Sources of variance in behavioral measures of honesty in temptation situations: Methodological analyses. *Developmental Psychology, 1*, 265–279.

NELSON, S. A. (1980). Factors influencing young children's use of motives and outcomes as moral criteria. *Child Development, 51*, 823–829.

NELSON-LeGALL, S. A. (1985). Motive-outcome matching and outcome foreseeability: Effects on attribution of intentionality and moral judgments. *Developmental Psychology, 21*, 332–337.

NUNNER-WINKLER, G., & SODIAN, S. (1988). Children's understanding of moral emotions. *Child Development, 59*, 1323–1338.

OLTHOF, T., FERGUSON, T. J., & LUITEN, A. (1989). Personal responsibility and antecedents of anger and blame reactions in children. *Child Development, 60*, 1326–1336.

PARKE, R. D. (1972). Some effects of punishment on children's behavior. In W. W. Hartup (Ed.), *The young child* (Vol. 2).

Washington, DC: National Association for the Education of Young Children.

PARKE, R. D. (1977). Some effects of punishment on children's behavior—Revisited. In E. M. Hetherington & R. D. Parke (Eds.), *Contemporary readings in child psychology*. New York: McGraw-Hill.

PERRY, D. G., & PARKE, R. D. (1975). Punishment and alternative response training as determinants of response inhibition to children. *Genetic Psychology Monographs, 91*, 257–279.

PERRY, D. G., PERRY, L. C., BUSSEY, K., ENGLISH, D., & ARNOLD, G. (1980). Processes of attribution and children's self-punishment following misbehavior. *Child Development, 51*, 545–551.

PIAGET, J. (1965). *The moral judgment of the child*. New York: Free Press. (Original work published 1932.)

QUINN, R. A., HOUTS, A. C., & GRAESSER, A. C. (1993). Naturalistic conceptions of morality: A question-answering approach. *Journal of Personality*.

REST, J. R. (1983). Morality. In P. H. Mussen (Ed.), *Handbook of child psychology*. Vol. 3: *Cognitive development*. New York: Wiley.

REST, J. R. (1986). *Moral development: Advances in research and theory*. New York: Praeger.

REST, J. R., & THOMA, S. J. (1985). Relation of moral judgment development to formal education. *Developmental Psychology, 21*, 709–714.

ROSENKOETTER, L. I. (1973). Resistance to temptation: Inhibitory and disinhibitory effects of models. *Developmental Psychology, 8*, 80–84.

RUSHTON, J. P. (1980). *Altruism, socialization, and society*. Englewood Cliffs, NJ: Prentice-Hall.

SANTROCK, J. W. (1975). Moral structure: The interrelations of moral behavior, moral judgment, and moral affect. *Journal of Genetic Psychology, 127*, 201–213.

SCHLAEFLI, A., REST, J. R., & THOMA, S. J. (1985). Does moral education improve moral judgment? A meta-analysis of intervention studies using the Defining Issues Test. *Review of Educational Research, 55*, 319–352.

SCHLEIFER, M., & DOUGLAS, V. I. (1973). Effects of training on the moral judgment of young children. *Journal of Personality and Social Psychology, 28*, 62–68.

SEARS, R. R., MACCOBY, E. E., & LEVIN, H. (1957). *Patterns of child rearing*. New York: Harper & Row.

SELMAN, R. L. (1971). The relation of role-taking to the development of moral judgment in children. *Child Development, 42*, 79–91.

SHAFFER, D. R. (1993). Do naturalistic conceptions of morality provide any [novel] answers? *Journal of Personality*.

SHODA, Y., MISCHEL, W., & PEAKE, P. K. (1990). Predicting adolescent cognitive and self-regulatory competencies from preschool delay of gratification: Identifying diagnostic conditions. *Developmental Psychology, 26*, 978–986.

SHULTZ, T. R., WRIGHT, K., & SCHLEIFER, M. (1986). Assignment of moral responsibility and punishment. *Child Development, 57*, 177–184.

SIEGAL, M., & COWEN, J. (1984). Appraisals of intervention: The mother's versus the culprit's behavior as determinants of children's evaluations of discipline techniques. *Child Development*, 55, 1760–1766.

SIGELMAN, C. K., & WAITZMAN, K. A. (1991). The development of distributive justice orientations: Contextual influences on children's resource allocations. *Child Development*, 62, 1367–1378.

SMETANA, J. G. (1981). Preschool children's conceptions of moral and social rules. *Child Development*, 52, 1333–1336.

SMETANA, J. G. (1985). Preschool children's conceptions of transgressions: Effects of varying moral and conventional domain-related attributes. *Developmental Psychology*, 21, 18–29.

SMETANA, J. G. (1989). Toddlers' social interactions in the context of moral and conventional transgressions in the home. *Developmental Psychology*, 25, 499–508.

SMETANA, J. G., KILLEN, M., & TURIEL, E. (1991). Children's reasoning about interpersonal and moral conflicts. *Child Development*, 62, 629–644.

SNAREY, J. R. (1985). Cross-cultural universality of social-moral development: A critical review of Kohlbergian research. *Psychological Bulletin*, 97, 202–232.

SONG, M., SMETANA, J. G., & KIM, S. Y. (1987). Korean children's conceptions of moral and conventional transgressions. *Development Psychology*, 23, 577–582.

STIPEK, D., RECCHIA, S. & McCLINTIC, S. (1992). Self-evaluation in young children. *Monographs of the Society for Research in Child Development*, 57 (1, Serial No. 226).

SURBER, C. F. (1982). Separable effects of motives, consequences, and presentation order on children's moral judgments. *Developmental Psychology*, 18, 257–266.

TESSER, A., & SHAFFER, D. R. (1990). Attitudes and attitude change. *Annual Review of Psychology*, 41, 479–523.

THOMA, S. J. (1986). Estimating gender differences in the comprehension and preference of moral issues. *Developmental Review*, 6, 165–180.

THOMA, S. J., REST, J. R., & DAVISON, M. L. (1991). Describing and testing a moderator of the moral judgment and action relationship. *Journal of Personality and Social Psychology*, 61, 659–669.

TIETJEN, A. M., & WALKER, L. J. (1985). Moral reasoning and leadership among men in a Papua New Guinea society. *Developmental Psychology*, 21, 982–992.

TISAK, M. S., & TISAK, J. (1990). Children's conceptions of parental authority, friendship, and sibling relations. *Merrill-Palmer Quarterly*, 36, 347–368.

TOMLINSON-KEASEY, C., & KEASEY, C. B. (1974). The mediating role of cognitive development in moral judgment. *Child Development*, 45, 291–298.

TONER, I. J., MOORE, L. P., & ASHLEY, P. K. (1978). The effect of serving as a model of self-control on subsequent resistance to deviation to children. *Journal of Experimental Child Psychology*, 26, 85–91.

TONER, I. J., PARKE, R. D., & YUSSEN, S. R. (1978). The effect of observation of model behavior on the establishment and stability of resistance to deviation in children. *Journal of Genetic Psychology*, 132, 283–290.

TONER, I. J., & POTTS, R. (1981). Effect of modeled rationales on moral behavior, moral choice, and level of moral judgment in children. *Journal of Psychology*, 107, 153–162.

TURIEL, E. (1966). An experimental test of the sequentiality of developmental stages in the child's moral judgments. *Journal of Personality and Social Psychology*, 3, 611–618.

TURIEL, E. (1983). *The development of social knowledge: Morality and convention*. Cambridge, England: Cambridge University Press.

VASUDEV, J., & HUMMEL, R. C. (1987). Moral stage sequence and principled reasoning in an Indian sample. *Human Development*, 30, 105–118.

WALKER, L. J. (1980). Cognitive and perspective-taking prerequisites for moral development. *Child Development*, 51, 131–139.

WALKER, L. J. (1982). The sequentiality of Kohlberg's stages of moral development. *Child Development*, 53, 1330–1336.

WALKER, L. J. (1984). Sex differences in the development of moral reasoning: A critical review. *Child Development*, 55, 677–691.

WALKER, L. J. (1986). Experimental and cognitive sources of moral development in adulthood. *Human Development*, 29, 113–124.

WALKER, L. J. (1989). A longitudinal study of moral development. *Child Development*, 60, 157–166.

WALKER, L. J., de VRIES, B., & TREVETHAN, S. D. (1987). Moral stages and moral orientations in real-life and hypothetical dilemmas. *Child Development*, 58, 842–858.

WALKER, L. J., & TAYLOR, J. H. (1991a). Family interactions and the development of moral reasoning. *Child Development*, 62, 264–283.

WALKER, L. J., & TAYLOR, J. H. (1991b). Stage transitions in moral reasoning: A longitudinal study of developmental processes. *Developmental Psychology*, 27, 330–337.

YUILL, N., & PERNER, J. (1988). Intentionality and knowledge in children's judgments of actor's responsibility and recipient's emotional reaction. *Developmental Psychology*, 24, 358–365.

ZAHN-WAXLER, C., KOCHANSKA, G., KRUPNICK, J., & McKNEW, D. (1990). Patterns of guilt in children of depressed and well mothers. *Developmental Psychology*, 26, 51–59.

ZAHN-WAXLER, C., RADKE-YARROW, M., & KING, R. A. (1979). Child rearing and children's prosocial initiations toward victims of distress. *Child Development*, 50, 319–330.

13 *The Family*

Have humans always been social animals? Although no one can answer this question with absolute certainty, the archeological record provides some strong clues. Apparently our closest evolutionary ancestors (dating back before the Neanderthals) were already living in small bands, or tribal units, which provided increased protection against common enemies and allowed individuals to share the many labors necessary for their survival (Weaver, 1985). Of course, there are no written records of social life among these early collectives. But it is clear that, at some point during the prehistoric era, early human societies (and perhaps even the protohuman aggregations) evolved codes of conduct that defined the roles of various tribal members and sanctioned certain behaviors while prohibiting others. Once a workable social order was established, it then became necessary to "socialize" each succeeding generation.

Socialization is the process by which children acquire the beliefs, values, and behaviors deemed significant and appropriate by the older members of their society. The socialization of each generation serves society in at least three ways. First, it is a means of regulating children's behavior and controlling their undesirable or antisocial impulses. Second, the socialization process helps to promote the personal growth of the individual. As children interact with and become like other members of their culture, they acquire the knowledge, skills, motives, and aspirations that should enable them to adapt to their environment and function effectively within their communities. Finally, socialization perpetuates the social order. Socialized children become socialized adults who will impart what they have learned to their own children.

All societies have developed various mechanisms, or institutions, for socializing their young. Examples of these socializing institutions are the family, the church, the educational system, children's groups (for example, Boy and Girl Scouts), and the mass media.

Central among the many social agencies that impinge on the child is that institution we call the family. More than 99% of children in the United States are raised in a family of one kind or another (U.S. Bureau of the Census, 1989), and most children in most societies grow up in a home setting with at least one biological parent or other relative. Often children have little exposure to people outside the family for several years, until they are placed in day care or nursery school or until they begin formal schooling. So the family has a clear head start on other institutions when it comes to socializing a child. And, since the events of the early years are very important to the child's social, emotional, and intellectual development, it is perhaps appropriate to think of the family as society's most important instrument of socialization.

Our focus in this chapter is on the family as a social system—an institution that both influences and is influenced by its young. What is a family, and what functions do families serve? How does the birth of a child affect other family members? Do the existing (or changing) relationships among other members of the family have any effect on the care and training that a young child receives? Are some patterns of child rearing better than others? Do parents decide how they will raise their children—or might children influence parental decisions? Does the family's socioeconomic status affect parenting and parent/child interactions? Do siblings play an important part in the socialization process? How do children react to divorce, maternal employment, or a return to the two-parent family when a single parent remarries? And why do some parents mistreat their offspring? These are the issues we will consider as we look at the important roles that families play in the cognitive, social, and emotional development of their children.

Functions of the Family

Families serve society in many ways. They produce and consume goods and services, thereby playing a role in the economy. Traditionally, the family has served as an outlet for the sexual urges of its adult members and as the means of replenishing the population. And, historically, families have cared for their elderly, although this function is now less common in Western societies with the advent of such institutions as Social Security, socialized medical care, and nursing homes. But perhaps the most widely recognized functions of the family—those that are served in all societies—are the caregiving, nurturing, and training that parents and other family members provide for young children.

Three goals of parenting.   After studying the child-rearing practices of many diverse cultures, Robert LeVine (1974, p. 238) concluded that families in all societies have three basic goals for their children:

1. The **survival goal**—to promote the physical survival and health of the child, ensuring that he or she will live long enough to have children too.
2. The **economic goal**—to foster the skills and behavioral capacities that the child will need for economic self-maintenance as an adult.
3. The **self-actualization goal**—to foster behavioral capabilities for maximizing other cultural values (for example, morality, religion, achievement, wealth, prestige, and a sense of personal satisfaction).

According to LeVine, these universal goals of parenting form a hierarchy. Parents and other caregivers are initially concerned about maximizing the child's chances of survival, and all higher-order goals are placed on the back burner until it is clear that the youngster is healthy and likely to survive. When physical health and security can be taken for granted, then parents begin to encourage those characteristics that are necessary for economic self-sufficiency. Only after survival and the attributes necessary for economic productivity have been established do parents begin to encourage the child to seek status, prestige, and self-fulfillment.

LeVine's ideas stem from observations of child-rearing practices in societies where infants often die before their second birthday. Regardless of whether one is observing African Bushmen, South American Indians, or Indonesian tribes, parents in societies where infant mortality is high tend to maintain close contact with their infants 24 hours a day, often carrying them on their hips or their backs in some sort of sling or cradleboard. LeVine suggests that these practices increase the infants' chances of survival by reducing the likelihood of their becoming ill or dehydrated, crawling into a river or a campfire, or am-

PHOTO 13-1   In many cultures, parents increase their babies' chances of survival by keeping them close at all times.

bling off to be captured by a predator. Sleeping with parents at night is also a common practice in these societies (Whiting & Edwards, 1988)—one that may promote survival by sensitizing parents to infants' breathing-control errors which, if not corrected, could otherwise result in *sudden infant death syndrome* (McKenna, 1986; Morelli et al., 1992).[1] Although infants are kept close at all times, their parents rarely chat with or smile at them and may seem almost uninterested in their future psychological development. Could this pattern of psychologically

[1]Sudden infant death syndrome (SIDS; also known as "crib death") refers to the silent death of a seemingly healthy baby who, without apparent cause, simply stops breathing (usually at night while sleeping). In the United States this mysterious affliction accounts for nearly 13% of all infant deaths—more than any other single factor (Colon & Colon, 1989).

aloof yet competent physical caregiving be a defensive maneuver that prevents parents from becoming overly attached to an infant who might well die? Perhaps so, for many cultures in which infant mortality is high still institutionalize practices like not speaking to neonates as if they were human beings or not naming them until late in the first year, when it is more probable that they will survive (Brazelton, 1979).

The next task that parents face is to promote those characteristics and competencies that will enable children to care for themselves and their own future families. Anthropologist John Ogbu (1981) points out that the economy of a culture (that is, the way in which people support themselves, or subsist) will determine how families socialize their young. To illustrate his point, he cites a well-known cross-cultural study by Herbert Barry and his associates (1959), who hypothesized that societies that depend on an agricultural or pastoral economy (those that accumulate food) would stress obedience, cooperation, and responsibility when raising their children. By contrast, groups that do not accumulate food (hunting, trapping, and fishing societies) were expected to train their children to be independent, assertive, and venturesome. In other words, both types of society were expected to emphasize the values, competencies, and attributes necessary to maintain their way of life. Barry et al. used existing anthropological records to review the economic characteristics and child-rearing techniques of 104 **preliterate societies** all over the world. As predicted, they found that agricultural and pastoral societies did place strong pressures on their children to be cooperative and obedient, whereas hunting and fishing societies stressed assertiveness, self-reliance, and individual achievement.

Even in industrial societies such as the United States, a family's social position or socioeconomic status affects child-rearing practices. For example, parents from the lower socioeconomic strata, who typically work for a boss and must defer to his or her authority, tend to stress obedience, neatness, cleanliness, and respect for power—attributes that should enable their children to function effectively within a blue-collar economy. By contrast, middle-class parents, particularly those who work for them-

selves or who are professionals, are more likely to stress ambition, curiosity, creativity, and independence when raising their children (Kohn, 1979). The latter finding would hardly surprise LeVine, who would argue that middle-class parents who have the resources to promote their child's eventual economic security are freer to encourage initiative, achievement, and personal self-fulfillment (the third set of parenting goals) at a very early age.

Understanding the Family and Its Contributions to Human Development

Our brief overview of LeVine's three parenting goals may make it sound as if parents consciously decide how they will raise their young and that their child-rearing practices determine how their children will behave and develop. Indeed, early family researchers focused almost entirely on the mother/child relationship, operating under the assumption that mothers (and, to a lesser extent, fathers) were the ones who molded children's conduct and character. However, modern family theorists have rejected this simple, unidirectional model of family socialization in favor of a more comprehensive "systems" approach—one that is similar to Urie Bonfenbrenner's (1986, 1989) *ecological theory*, which we discussed in Chapter 2. The "systems" approach recognizes that parents influence their children. But it also stresses that (1) children influence the behavior and child-rearing strategies of their parents, and (2) families are complex social systems—that is, networks of reciprocal relationships and alliances that are constantly evolving and are greatly affected by the larger social contexts in which they are embedded. Let's now consider some of the implications of this systems perspective.

The Family as a System

What does it mean to say that a **family** is a **social system**? To Jay Belsky (1981), it means that the family, much like the human body, is a *holistic structure* consisting of interrelated parts, each of which affects and is affected by every other part and each of which contributes to the functioning of the whole.

As an illustration, let's consider the simplest of **nuclear families**, consisting of a mother, a father, and a first-born child. According to Belsky (1981), even this man/woman/infant "system" is a complex entity. An infant interacting with his or her mother is already involved in a process of **reciprocal influence**, as is evident when we notice that the infant's smile is likely to be greeted by the mother's smile or that a mother's concerned expression often makes her infant wary. And what happens when Dad arrives? The mother/infant dyad is suddenly transformed into a *"family system* [comprising] a husband-wife as well as mother-infant and father-infant relationships" (Belsky, 1981, p. 17).

One implication of viewing the family as a system is that interactions between any two family members should change in the presence of a third family member. As it turns out, the mere presence of the second parent does affect the way the first parent interacts with his or her child. For example, fathers talk less and display less affection toward their infants and toddlers when the mother is present (Hwang, 1986), and mothers are less likely to initiate play activities or to hold their youngsters when the father is around (Belsky, 1981), particularly if the child is a male (Liddell, Henzi, & Drew, 1987). In early adolescence, mother/son interactions are less conflict ridden in the presence of the father, whereas the entry of the mother into father/son interactions often erodes the quality of that contact by causing the father to withdraw and become less involved in the boy's activities (Gjerde, 1986). Finally, the quality of the marriage (that is, the husband/wife relationship) can affect parent/child interactions, which in turn can have a reciprocal effect on the quality of the marriage (Cox et al., 1989, 1992; Minuchin, 1985). In short, every individual and every relationship within the family affects every other individual and relationship through pathways of reciprocal influence (see Figure 13-1). Now we see why it was rather naive to think that we could understand how families influence children by concentrating on the mother/child relationship.

Now think about how complex the family system becomes with the birth of a second child and the

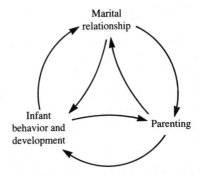

FIGURE 13-1 A model of the family as a social system. As implied in the diagram, a family is bigger than the sum of its parts. Parents affect infants, who affect each parent and the marital relationship. Of course, the marital relationship may affect the parenting the infant receives, the infant's behavior, and so on. Clearly, families are complex social systems. As an exercise, you may wish to rediagram the patterns of influence within a family after adding a sibling or two. (From J. Belsky, "Early Human Experience: A Family Perspective." *Developmental Psychology*, 1981, 17, 3–23. Copyright © 1981 by the American Psychological Association. Reprinted by permission.)

addition of sibling/sibling and sibling/parent relationships. Or consider the complexity of an **extended family** household, a nearly universal practice in some cultures, in which parents and their children live with other kin—grandparents or aunts, uncles, nieces, and nephews. It turns out that living in extended families is a fairly common arrangement for African Americans—and an adaptive one in that large numbers of economically disadvantaged black mothers must work, are often supporting their offspring without the father, and can surely use the assistance they receive from the grandparents, siblings, uncles, aunts, and cousins who may live with them and serve as surrogate parents for young children (Pearson et al., 1990; Wilson, 1989). Until recently, family researchers have largely ignored extended families or have looked upon them as unhealthy contexts for child rearing. That view is changing, thanks in part to research showing that support from members of extended families (particularly grandmothers) can help disadvantaged single mothers to cope with the stresses they face, to become more sensitive caregivers, and to establish more secure emotional relationships with their infants and toddlers (Crockenberg, 1987; Wilson, 1989). Indeed, disadvantaged African-American children in extended families do better at school and are better adjusted psychologically than their disadvantaged agemates from nuclear families (Wilson, 1986). And, in cultures such as the Sudan, where social life is governed by ideals of communal interdependence and intergenerational harmony, children routinely display better patterns of psychological adjustment if raised in extended-family households than in Westernized, two-parent nuclear families (Al Awad & Sonuga-Barke, 1992). Thus it seems that the healthiest family context for child development will depend very heavily on both the needs of individual families and the values that families (within particular cultural and subcultural contexts) are trying to promote.

Families are developing entities. Not only are families complex systems, but they are dynamic ones as well. Consider that every family member is a *developing* individual and that relationships between husband and wife, parent and child, and sibling and sibling will also change in ways that can influence the growth of each family member. Many such changes are planned, as when parents allow toddlers to do more things on their own as a means of encouraging autonomy and individual initiative. Yet a host of unplanned or unforeseen changes (such as the death of a sibling or the souring of the husband/wife relationship) can greatly affect family interactions and the development of its children. So the family itself is like a developing organism—one that not only promotes change but is changed by the development of its members.

Families are embedded entities. Finally, we should constantly remind ourselves of the lesson we learned when discussing the significance of extended families: all families are embedded within larger cultural or subcultural contexts, and the ecological niche a family occupies (for example, the family's religion, its socioeconomic status, and the values that prevail within a culture, a subculture, a community, or even a neighborhood) can affect fam-

ily interactions and the development of a family's children (Bronfenbrenner, 1986, 1989). According to Jay Belsky (1981), future advances in the study of family socialization will stem from broadly conceived, *interdisciplinary* efforts in which developmentalists, family sociologists, and community psychologists pool their expertise to gain a better understanding of the ways in which families (within particular social contexts) influence and are influenced by their young. Focusing narrowly on parent/child interactions is not enough!

A Changing Family System in a Changing World

Not only is the family a social system that changes over time, but it exists and develops in a world that is constantly changing. During the latter half of the 20th century, several dramatic social changes have altered the makeup of the typical family as well as the nature of the family experience. Here are some of the most noteworthy changes:

1. *Increased numbers of single adults.* More adults are living as singles today than in the past. In 1991 only 61% of American adults were married, down from 72% in 1971 (Teegardin, 1992). Marriage isn't "out," however, as about 90% of today's young adults will eventually marry (Norton & Moorman, 1987).

2. *Active postponement of marriage.* Many young singles are postponing marriage to pursue educational and career goals. Although the average age of first marriage actually decreased during the first half of this century, it has risen again to about 24 for women and 26 for men (Teegardin, 1992), despite the high rates of teenage pregnancy (Furstenberg, Brooks-Gunn, & Chase-Lansdale, 1989).

3. *Decreased childbearing.* Today's adults are not only waiting longer after they marry to have children, but they are having fewer of them. During the Baby Boom era after World War II, American women of childbearing age were having an average of slightly more than three children, a figure that dropped to 2.1 children by 1988 (U.S. Bureau of the Census, 1990). Moreover, increasing numbers of young women are now choosing to remain childless.

4. *Increased female participation in the labor force.* Today most young women, including a majority of those with children, are employed outside the home (Hoffman, 1989). Fewer and fewer children have a mother whose full-time job is homemaking.

5. *Increases in divorce.* Divorce rates have increased over the past 30 years, to the point that 40%–50% of newly married couples will eventually divorce (Glick & Lin, 1987). Each year an additional one *million* American children are affected by their parents' divorce (Teegardin, 1992). Yet it seems that the Baby Boom generation is the group most prone to divorce, and post-Boomers, like earlier generations, may have a somewhat lower divorce rate (Norton & Moorman, 1987).

6. *Increased numbers of single-parent families.* Partly because of a large number of out-of-wedlock births, but mostly because of rising divorce rates, it was projected that 40%–50% of all children born in the 1970s and 1980s would spend an average of about five years in a **single-parent family** (Glick & Lin, 1987). At present about 20%–25% of American children live in such a family, nine times out of ten with their mothers.

7. *Increased remarriage.* Because more married couples are divorcing, more adults (about 72% of divorced mothers and 80% of divorced fathers) are remarrying, forming **reconstituted families** that involve at least one child, his or her biological parent, and a stepparent and that often blend multiple children from two families into a new family system (Glick, 1989). About 25% of American children will spend some time in a stepparent family (Hetherington, 1989).

What these changes tell us is that modern families are much more diverse than ever. Our stereotyped image of the model family — the *Leave It to Beaver* nuclear aggregation with a breadwinning father, a housewife mother, and at least two children — is just that: a stereotype. By one estimate, this "ideal" family represented 70% of American households in 1960 but only 12% in 1990 (Teegardin, 1992). Although the family is by no means dying, we must broaden our image of it to include the many dual-career, single-parent, and reconstituted families that exist today and are influencing the development of the *majority* of our children. Bear that in

PHOTO 13-2 Families are more diverse than ever before. Fewer than one in five American families fit the stereotyped "ideal" nuclear aggregation of a breadwinning father, a homemaker mother, and two (or more) children.

mind as we begin our excursion into family life at the beginning — with the impending arrival of an infant.

Interchanges between Parents and Their Infants

A child begins to influence the behavior of other family members long before he or she is born. Adults who have hoped to conceive and who eagerly anticipate their baby's arrival will often plan for the blessed event by selecting names for the infant, buying or making baby clothes, decorating a nursery, moving to larger quarters, changing or leaving jobs, and preparing older children in the family for the changes that are soon to come (Grossman et al., 1980). Of course, the impact of an unborn child may be far less pleasant for an unwed mother or a couple who do not want their baby, who cannot afford a child, or who receive very little encouragement and support from friends, relatives, and other members of the community.

How is the birth of a child likely to influence the mother, the father, and the marital relationship? Do the changes that parents experience affect their reactions to the baby? Are some parents more capable than others of coping with a difficult infant? Is there any truth to the claim that shaky marriages can be strengthened by having a child? In addressing these issues, we will see why researchers have come to think of families as complex entities that they are only now beginning to understand. However, this much is certain: the arrival of an infant transforms the marital dyad into a rather intricate social system that can influence the behavior and emotional well-being of all family members.

The Transition to Parenthood

The birth of a baby is a highly significant event that alters the behavior of both mothers and fathers and may affect the quality of their marital relationship (Fleming et al., 1990; Levy-Shiff, Goldshmidt, & Har-Even, 1991). As we noted in Chapter 9, the onset of parenthood often produces changes in sex-role behaviors. Even among egalitarian couples who have previously shared household tasks, new mothers typically become more "expressive," partake in more traditionally feminine activities, and feel more "feminine," whereas new fathers are likely to focus more intently on their role as a provider (Cowan & Cowan, 1987). If both parents previously worked, it is nearly always the mother who stays home to look after the baby. However, new fathers do often report feeling more "feminine" after the birth of a baby, owing perhaps to the increased nurturance and affection they display while interacting with their infants (Feldman & Aschenbrenner, 1983).

How does the birth of a child affect the marital relationship? Many family sociologists believe that the advent of parenthood is a "crisis" of sorts for a marriage. Couples must now cope with greater financial responsibilities, a possible loss of income, changes in sleeping habits, and less time to themselves—events that may be perceived as aversive and could well disrupt the bond between husbands and wives. Indeed, Jay Belsky and his associates (Belsky, Lang, & Rovine, 1985) find that marital sat-

isfaction usually does drop after the birth of a baby and that this decline in marital bliss is generally steeper for women than for men, probably because the burden of child-care responsibilities typically falls more heavily on the mother. But, as shown in Figure 13-2, a new mother's increased negativity toward the father is usually short-lived and does little to discourage her growing sense of affection for the baby.

Nevertheless, there are dramatic individual differences in adjustment to new parenthood: some couples do experience a significant, *lasting* reduction in intimacy and spousal affection after the birth of a first child, whereas others report that becoming a new parent is only mildly stressful. Which couples cope best with this important life transition? Jay Belsky (1981) finds that the impact of a new baby on the marital relationship tends to be less severe or disruptive when parents are older, conceive after the marriage ceremony, and have been married for longer periods before conceiving. Moreover, parents' own family histories have an effect. If both husband and wife were treated in a warm and accepting manner by their own parents, their marriage is unlikely to suffer as they make the transition to parenthood. But, if either the husband or wife was raised in an aloof or rejecting manner, the couple will likely experience some marital discord after their child is born (Belsky & Isabella, 1985).

Of course, the infant's behavior can also influence a couple's adjustment to parenthood. Parents of temperamentally difficult infants who cry a lot, have feeding problems, and are often "on the move" report more disruption of normal activities and greater dissatisfaction in their marital relationships than parents of "quiet" or "easy" babies (Levitt, Weber, & Clark, 1986; Wilkie & Ames, 1986; Wright, Henggeler, & Craig, 1986). Moreover, many parents of infants who require special care (for example, babies with Down's syndrome or with illnesses that demand constant monitoring) have problems with their spouses and often say that rearing a "special" child has made their marriage worse (Bristol, Gallagher, & Schopler, 1988; Gath, 1985). But, for every couple who experience marital disharmony as a result of caring for a special child, there is at least one other couple who believe that their ab-

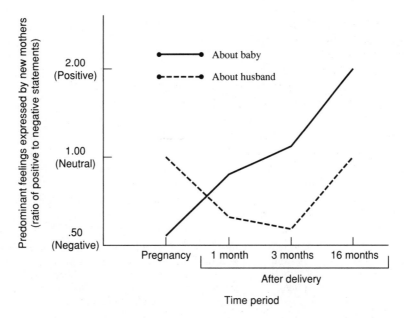

FIGURE 13-2 Changes over time in the feelings expressed by new mothers about their husbands and their babies. (Adapted from A. S. Fleming, D. N. Ruble, G. L. Flett, & V. Van Wagner, "Adjustment in First-Time Mothers: Changes in Mood and Mood Content during the Early Postpartum Months." *Developmental Psychology*, 1990, 26, 137–143. Copyright © 1990 by the American Psychological Association. Adapted by permission.)

normal infant has had no effect on their marriage or has even brought them closer together (Floyd & Zmich, 1991; Gath, 1985). So it seems that the arrival of a baby who requires special attention may disrupt the balance of a vulnerable marriage without shaking the foundation of one already on firm ground.

Effects of Parents on Their Infants

In Chapter 6 we reviewed a large body of research that sought to determine how parents affect the social, emotional, and intellectual development of their infants and toddlers. Recall that this work was remarkably consistent in its implications: warm and sensitive mothers who often talk to their infants and try to stimulate their curiosity are contributing in a positive way to the establishment of secure emotional attachments (Ainsworth, 1979) as well as to the child's curiosity and willingness to explore (Belsky, Garduque, & Hrncir, 1984; Cassidy, 1986), sociability (Waters, Wippman, & Sroufe, 1979), and

intellectual growth (Bradley et al., 1989; Bradley, Caldwell, & Elardo, 1979). Indeed, Jay Belsky (1981) argues that maternal warmth/sensitivity "is *the* most influential dimension of mothering in infancy: it not only fosters healthy psychological functioning during this developmental epoch, but it also lays the foundation on which future experience will build" (p. 8).

Does the mother's age make a difference? Popular wisdom suggests that women should have their children between ages 18 and 35 — and this practice makes good medical sense.[2] But are younger or older mothers any less sensitive and responsive to their infants than women who give birth during the "optimal" childbearing years?

[2]Indeed, mothers younger than 17 and those older than 35 face far greater risks of bearing a stillborn fetus or a baby who will fail to survive than do mothers in their twenties and early thirties. For a discussion of the probable causes of these age trends, see Shaffer (1993).

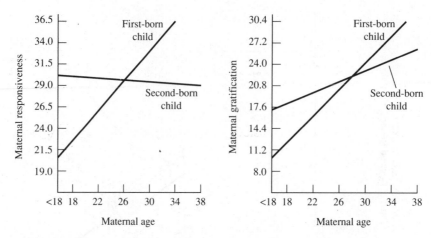

FIGURE 13-3   Relationship of mothers' age to their responsiveness to and satisfaction with first-born and second-born infants. (Adapted from A. S. Ragozin, R. B. Basham, K. A. Crnic, M. T. Greenberg, & N. M. Robinson, "Effects of Maternal Age on Parenting Role." *Developmental Psychology*, 1982, *18*, 627–634. Copyright © 1982 by the American Psychological Association. Adapted by permission.)

Although there are many exceptions to the rule, teenage mothers tend to express much less favorable attitudes about child rearing than mothers in their twenties. Indeed, Susan Crockenberg (1987) finds that adolescent mothers who were rejected by their own parents and who lack the support of a spouse or other close companions are likely to be harsh and insensitive caregivers. And, even when adolescent mothers do have a close companion to provide social support, their parenting still tends to be less sensitive and responsive than that of older women. Part of the problem is that these young mothers, who are not very knowledgeable about babies, usually seek advice and support from other unknowledgeable sources—namely, their own adolescent peers (Garcia Coll, Hoffman, & Oh, 1987). Very young mothers also provide less stimulating home environments for their infants and toddlers than older mothers do, which perhaps explains why children born to teenagers are likely to show some deficits in intellectual functioning during the preschool and grade-school years and very poor academic performances by the time they reach adolescence (Furstenberg et al., 1989).

Are older mothers who delay childbearing until they are well established in their careers any less sensitive and responsive to their infants than mothers who are in their twenties? Apparently not. Arlene Ragozin and her associates (1982) observed the behavior of mothers aged 16 to 38 as they interacted with their 4-month-old infants. As shown in Figure 13-3, older mothers were quite responsive to their babies (particularly first-borns), and they claimed to derive more satisfaction from interacting with either a first-born or a second-born infant than younger mothers did. Clearly, these data argue against the popular belief that women in their twenties are the ones who are best suited psychologically for the responsibilities of motherhood.

Fathers' influence on infants.   Now that developmentalists have embraced the idea that the family is truly a social system, they have discovered that fathers are part of the family too. But are fathers as competent as mothers to care for an infant? Do they really contribute that much to the development of infants and toddlers?

Although gender stereotypes might have us believe otherwise, most fathers are quite competent as caregivers. For example, they are no less capable than mothers of responding sensitively to infants at feeding time and ensuring that milk is consumed

(Parke & Sawin, 1976). Similarly, fathers are quite capable of soothing and comforting distressed infants, and they eventually become objects of affection who serve as "secure bases" for their infants' explorations (Lamb, 1981). But, just because fathers are capable of sensitive parenting does not necessarily mean that they will play the same roles in their infants' lives as mothers do (Parke & Tinsley, 1987). Fathers and mothers differ in both the quality and the quantity of the parenting they provide.

Consider first the matter of *quantity*. Mothers simply attend more to infants than fathers do, even when fathers are home from work (Parke & Tinsley, 1987). Several years ago, Freda Rebelsky and Cheryl Hanks (1971) attached microphones to ten infants and recorded how often their fathers spoke to them between the ages of 2 weeks and 3 months. On an average day the fathers in this study addressed their infants only 2.7 times for a total of approximately 40 seconds. Although it seems that today's fathers are spending more time than this with their very young infants and will become increasingly involved with them over the first year (Easterbrooks & Goldberg, 1984; Ricks, 1985), even today, with more mothers than ever working outside the home, it is still the mother who performs the majority of the family's domestic activities *and* who attends most closely to an infant's needs (Ninio & Rinott, 1988). So mothers devote considerably more effort to parenting than fathers do.

Now consider the issue of *quality*. Just how do mothers and fathers differ in their typical interactions with young children? Mothers spend a large proportion of their time providing care: offering food, wiping noses, changing diapers, and so on. By contrast, fathers spend a greater proportion of their time involved in *play* (Parke & Tinsley, 1987). And the play styles of fathers differ from those of mothers. Fathers play unusual and unpredictable games that tend to be a bit rowdy, whereas mothers are more inclined to hold, soothe, talk to, and play quietly with their infants (Lamb, 1981).

By assuming the role of "special playmate," the father is in a unique position to influence the activities and preferences of his children — particularly sons, for fathers tend to spend more time with sons than with daughters (Barnett & Baruch, 1987; Cox

PHOTO 13-3   Fathers play a central role in the lives of their children, serving as teachers, playmates, caregivers, and confidants, as well as an important source of emotional security.

et al., 1989). Evidence for such influence was presented in Chapter 9, where we noted that fathers are more likely than mothers to encourage their infants (particularly boys) to play with sex-typed toys and to avoid playful activities considered more appropriate for the other sex (Snow, Jacklin, & Maccoby, 1983).

Yet it is important to add that fathers are more than activity directors or substitute caregivers. For example, in Chapter 6 we learned that a secure attachment to the father can help to offset the social deficiencies and emotional disturbances that could otherwise result when an infant is insecurely attached to the mother. And, compared to less involved fathers, those who are highly involved in child care and who have positive attitudes about parenting tend to foster secure attachments and to view their infants as more *competent* (Cox et al., 1992; Ninio & Rinott, 1988) — findings that may help to explain why children of both sexes benefit intellectually and will achieve more in school when they have enjoyed a nurturant relationship with a highly involved father (Belsky, 1981; Lamb, 1981).

In sum, fathers richly deserve the increased attention and respect they have been getting from developmentalists lately. Not only are they capable of sensitive and responsive caregiving, but they can contribute in many positive ways to their children's development when they take an active part in child rearing and *apply* their competencies.

Indirect effects.   The notion that families are social systems implies that parents may have **indirect effects** on their children by virtue of their influence on the behavior of their spouses. Consider how a father might indirectly influence the mother/infant relationship. If husband and wife are experiencing marital tension, the father's negativity toward the mother may disrupt the mother's caregiving routines and interfere with her ability to enjoy her infant (Belsky, 1981). Indeed, Frank Pedersen and his associates (1977) found that both mothers and fathers were likely to be unresponsive or even negative toward their 5-month-old infants in families characterized by marital strife (see also Cox et al., 1989). So it would seem that unhappily married couples are ill advised to have children as a means of solidifying a shaky marriage. Not only is this practice unlikely to strengthen the marital bond, but it is almost guaranteed to lead to poor parent/child relations.

Of course, the indirect effects of either parent may often be positive ones. For example, fathers tend to be much more involved with their infants when mothers believe that the father should play an important role in the child's life (Palkowitz, 1984) and when the two parents talk frequently about the baby (Belsky, Gilstrap, & Rovine, 1984; Lamb & Elster, 1985). In these studies it appeared that mothers were exerting an indirect influence on father/infant interactions by encouraging fathers to become more knowledgeable and concerned about the development of their children. Apparently the influence of parents on each other is often reciprocal, for mothers who have a close, supportive relationship with their husbands tend to be more patient with their infants and more sensitive to their needs than mothers who receive little or no support

from their spouses and feel that they are raising their children on their own (see, for example, Cox et al., 1989; Howes & Markman, 1989). In fact, intimate support from the husband seems to be more important to a mother's life satisfaction than any other kind of social support that she might receive—particularly if her infant is temperamentally difficult (Levitt et al., 1986). We see, then, that happily married couples seem to function as sources of *mutual* support and encouragement, so that many child-rearing problems are easier to overcome (Crnic et al., 1983; Goldberg & Easterbrooks, 1984). Indeed, parents of babies who are at risk for later emotional problems (as indicated by the baby's poor performance on the Brazelton Neonatal Behavioral Assessment Scale) will typically establish "synchronous" and satisfying relationships with their infants *unless they are unhappily married* (Belsky, 1981).

From these data on parent/infant interactions we see that even the simplest of families is a true social system that is bigger than the sum of its parts. Not only does each family member influence the behavior of every other, but the relationship that any two family members have can affect the interactions and relationships among all other members of the family. Clearly, socialization within the family is not just a two-way street—it is more accurately described as the busy intersection of many avenues of influence.

Parental Socialization during Childhood and Adolescence

During the second and third years, parents continue to be caregivers and playmates, but they also become more concerned with teaching children how to behave (or how not to behave) in a variety of situations. According to Erik Erikson (1963), this is the period when socialization begins in earnest. Parents must now manage the child's budding autonomy in the hope of instilling a sense of social propriety and self-control, while taking care not to undermine the child's curiosity, initiative, and feelings of personal competence.

Two Major Dimensions of Child Rearing

Erikson believed that two aspects of parenting are especially important during the preschool and grade-school years: *parental warmth* and *parental control*.

Parental warmth (or **warmth/hostility**) refers to the amount of responsiveness and affection that a parent displays. Parents classified as warm and responsive often smile at, praise, and encourage their children, even though they can be quite critical when a child misbehaves. By contrast, "hostile" (aloof/unresponsive) parents are often quick to criticize, belittle, punish, or ignore a child; they rarely act in ways that would let the child know that he is valued or loved.

Parental control refers to the amount of regulation or supervision parents undertake with their children. Controlling parents limit their children's freedom of expression by imposing many demands and actively monitoring their children's behavior to ensure that these rules and regulations are followed. Uncontrolling parents are much less restrictive; they make fewer demands and allow children considerable freedom to pursue their interests, express their opinions and emotions, and make decisions about their own activities. A common assumption is that parents become less restrictive as their children mature, although the available longitudinal data suggest that, if anything, middle-class parents actually become somewhat *more* controlling from the early elementary school years through mid-adolescence (McNally, Eisenberg, & Harris, 1991; Roberts, Block, & Block, 1984).

These two dimensions of child rearing are reasonably independent, so that we find parents who are warm and controlling, warm and uncontrolling, aloof and controlling, and aloof and uncontrolling (see Figure 13-4). How are these aspects of parenting related to a child's social, emotional, and intellectual development? Let's look first at the correlates of parental warmth.

PARENTAL WARMTH/HOSTILITY

How important is it that a child be (or feel) accepted by his or her parents? You should already know the

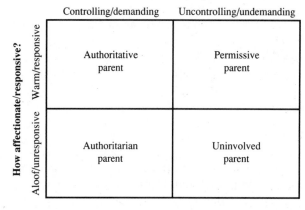

FIGURE 13-4 Two major dimensions of parenting. When we cross the two dimensions, we come up with four parenting styles: warm/controlling (or "authoritative"), warm/uncontrolling (or "permissive"), aloof/controlling (or "authoritarian"), and aloof/uncontrolling (or "uninvolved"). Which parenting style do you think would be associated with the most favorable outcomes? The least favorable outcomes? (Data from E. E. Maccoby & J. A. Martin, "Socialization in the Context of the Family: Parent-Child Interaction." In E. M. Hetherington (Ed.; P. H. Mussen, General Ed.), *Handbook of Child Psychology.* Vol. 4: *Socialization, Personality, and Social Development* (4th ed.). Copyright © 1983 by John Wiley & Sons.)

answer to this question, for throughout the text we have discussed many studies indicating that parental warmth and affection are powerful contributors to healthy cognitive, social, and emotional outcomes. By way of review, here are some of the attributes that characterize the children of warm and responsive parents:

1. They are securely attached at an early age. Of course, secure attachments are an important contributor to the growth of curiosity, exploratory competence, problem-solving skills, and positive social relations with both adults and peers (see Chapters 5 and 6).
2. They tend to be competent students during the grade-school years — students who make steady scholastic progress and score average or above on IQ tests (Estrada et al., 1987; see Chapter 8).
3. They are relatively altruistic, especially when their parents preach altruistic values and practice what they preach (see Chapter 11).

4. They are generally obedient, noncoercive youngsters who get along reasonably well with parents and peers (see Chapter 10).

5. They tend to be high in self-esteem and role-taking skills; when they are disciplined, they usually feel that their parents' actions are justified (Brody & Shaffer, 1982; see Chapter 7).

6. They are satisfied with their gender identities and are likely to be firmly sex typed or androgynous (see Chapter 9).

7. They will often refer to internalized norms rather than fear of punishment as a reason for complying with moral rules (Brody & Shaffer, 1982; see Chapter 12).

Now compare this behavioral profile with that of a group of "unwanted" Czechoslovakian children whose mothers had tried repeatedly to gain permission to abort them (Matejcek, Dytrych, & Schuller, 1979). Compared with "wanted" children from similar family backgrounds, the unwanted children had less stable family ties; were described as anxious, emotionally frustrated, and irritable; had more physical health problems; made poorer grades in school (even though they were comparable in IQ to the "wanted" children); were less popular with peers; and were more likely to require psychiatric attention for serious behavior disorders. Children simply do not thrive when they are rejected; nor are they likely to become happy, well-adjusted adults (MacDonald, 1992; see also Box 13-1).

In sum, warmth and affection are clearly important components of effective parenting. As Eleanor Maccoby (1980) points out:

> Parental warmth binds children to their parents in a positive way—it makes children responsive and more willing to accept guidance. If the parent-child relationship is close and affectionate, parents can exercise what control is needed without having to apply heavy disciplinary pressure. It is as if parents' responsiveness, affection, and obvious commitment to their children's welfare have earned them the right to make decisions and exercise control [p. 394].

Kevin MacDonald (1992) agrees with Maccoby, speculating that parental affection may be a flexible evolutionary adaptation that allows adults to influ-

PHOTO 13-4   Warmth and affection are crucial components of effective parenting.

ence children's behaviors in a variety of ways that evolution could never have foreseen.

Now what about parental control? Is it better for parents to be highly controlling? Or, rather, should they impose few restrictions and grant their children considerable autonomy? To answer these questions, we need to be more specific about the degrees of restrictiveness that parents use and to look carefully at patterns of parental affection *and* control.

PATTERNS OF PARENTING

Perhaps the best-known research on parenting styles is Diana Baumrind's (1967, 1971) studies of preschool children and their parents. Each child in Baumrind's sample was observed on several occasions in nursery school and at home. These data were used to rate the child on such behavioral dimensions as sociability, self-reliance, achievement, moodiness, and self-control. Parents were also interviewed and observed while interacting with their children at home. When Baumrind analyzed the parental data, she found that individual parents generally used one of three parenting styles, which can be summarized as follows:

1. **Authoritarian parenting**—a very restrictive pattern of parenting in which adults impose many

rules, expect strict obedience, will rarely if ever explain to the child why it is necessary to comply with all these regulations, and will often rely on punitive, forceful tactics (that is, power-assertion or love withdrawal) to gain compliance. Authoritarian parents are not sensitive to a child's conflicting viewpoints, expecting instead for the child to accept their word as law and to respect their authority.

2. **Authoritative parenting**—a more flexible style of parenting in which adults allow their children considerable freedom but are careful to provide rationales for the restrictions they impose and to ensure that the children follow these guidelines.

B O X | **13-1** | *Parental Rejection as a Contributor to Adult Depression*

Several years ago, Thomas Crook, Allen Raskin, and John Eliot (1981) proposed that adults who are clinically depressed and view themselves as inferior or worthless are often the product of a home environment in which they were clearly rejected by one or both parents. To evaluate their hypothesis, Crook et al. asked 714 adults who were hospitalized for depression to describe their childhood relationships with their mothers and fathers by indicating whether each of 192 statements characterized the behavior of either or both parents (for example, "Did your mother [father] worry about you when you were away? Threaten not to love you if you misbehaved? Often make you feel guilty? Set firm standards? Consistently enforce her [his] rules? Often ridicule you?"). As a comparison group, 387 nondepressed adults answered the same questions. Since an adult's self-reports of childhood experiences may be distorted and unreliable, the investigators also interviewed siblings, relatives, and long-time friends of the subjects as a check on the accuracy of their reflections. Data collected from these "independent sources" were then used to rate each subject's mother and father on the warmth/hostility and the autonomy/control (permissiveness/restrictiveness) dimensions.

The results of this study were straightforward. Subjects hospitalized for depression rated *both their mothers and their fathers* as less "accepting" and more "hostile," "detached," and "rejecting" than nondepressed adults in the comparison sample. Although the parents of depressed patients were not rated as any more "restrictive" or "controlling" than parents of nondepressed adults, they were perceived as exercising control in a more derisive way, often choosing to ridicule, belittle, or withdraw affection from their children. So even the guidance and discipline that depressed adults received during childhood were administered in a hostile, rejecting manner.

Data collected from the "independent sources" were quite consistent with the subjects' own reports. Both the mothers and fathers of the depressed patients were described as less affectionate and less involved with their children than the parents of nondepressed adults.

More recently, Monroe Lefkowitz and Edward Tesiny (1984) have conducted a *prospective* study to determine whether parental rejection measured *during childhood* would predict a person's depressive tendencies in adolescence. Mothers and fathers of 8-year-old girls completed a child-rearing questionnaire containing items designed to assess their satisfaction with their child and her behavior (extremely low scores were taken as indications of parental rejection). Ten years later these girls (who were now 18-year-old adolescents) completed the Depression scale of the Minnesota Multiphasic Personality Inventory, a well-known diagnostic test. As expected, girls whose mothers and fathers were rejecting during childhood scored significantly higher on the Depression scale as adolescents than did their counterparts whose parents were not so rejecting.

In sum, it appears that a primary contributor to adult depression is a family setting in which one or both parents treat the child as if he or she were unworthy of their love and affection. Perhaps it is fair to say that parents who blatantly reject their children are committing an extremely powerful form of child abuse—one that could leave emotional scars that will last a lifetime.

Authoritative parents are responsive to their children's needs and points of view and will often seek their children's input in family decisions. However, they expect the child to comply with the restrictions they view as necessary and will use both power, if necessary, and reason (that is, inductive discipline) to ensure that she does.

3. **Permissive parenting**—a warm but lax pattern of parenting in which adults make relatively few demands, permit their children to freely express their feelings and impulses, do not closely monitor their children's activities, and rarely exert firm control over their behavior.

On the basis of her observations in the nursery-school setting, Baumrind identified three groups of preschool children: *energetic-friendly*, *conflicted-irritable*, and *impulsive-aggressive*. As shown in Table 13-1, each of these patterns of child behavior was closely related to a particular parenting style. Authoritative parents generally had energetic-friendly youngsters who were cheerful, socially responsive, self-reliant, achievement oriented, and cooperative with adults and peers. By contrast, children of authoritarian parents tended to fall into the conflicted-irritable category: they were moody and seemingly unhappy much of the time, easily annoyed, relatively aimless, and not very pleasant to be around. Finally, permissive parents often had children classified as impulsive-aggressive. These youngsters (particularly the boys) tended to be bossy and self-centered, rebellious, aggressive, rather aimless, and quite low in independence and achievement.

What do Baumrind's findings imply about parental control? For one thing, it appears that restrictive parenting is preferable to a laissez-faire approach, for young children of permissive parents are often aimless and defiant little terrors—in a word, spoiled brats. Moreover, the ways in which parents introduce and enforce restrictions are also important. Note that both authoritative and authoritarian parents set many standards for their children and are quite controlling. But there is a clear difference in the way control is exercised. The authoritarian parent dominates the child, allowing little if any freedom of expression, whereas the authoritative parent is careful to permit the child enough autonomy

TABLE 13-1 *Patterns of parental control and corresponding patterns of children's behavior*

Parental Classification	Children's Behavioral Profile
Authoritative parenting	*Energetic-friendly* Self-reliant Self-controlled Cheerful and friendly Copes well with stress Cooperative with adults Curious Purposive Achievement oriented
Authoritarian parenting	*Conflicted-irritable* Fearful, apprehensive Moody, unhappy Easily annoyed Passively hostile Vulnerable to stress Aimless Sulky, unfriendly
Permissive parenting	*Impulsive-aggressive* Rebellious Low in self-reliance and self-control Impulsive Aggressive Domineering Aimless Low in achievement

SOURCE: From D. Baumrind, "Child Care Practices Anteceding Three Patterns of Preschool Behavior." *Genetic Psychology Monographs*, 1967, 75, 43–88. Copyright © 1967 by Academic Press, Inc. Reprinted by permission of the author.

so that he or she can develop initiative, self-reliance, and a sense of pride in personal accomplishments. Baumrind's results indicate that maintaining a firm sense of control over a child can be a very beneficial child-rearing practice. It is only when the controlling parent severely restricts the child's autonomy and uses arbitrary or irrational methods of control that the child is likely to be surly or sulky in social situations and lacking in initiative and achievement.

Although Baumrind's findings clearly favor authoritative parenting, one might legitimately wonder whether children of authoritarian or permissive parents might eventually "outgrow" the emotional

TABLE 13-2   *Relationship between patterns of parental control during the preschool period and children's cognitive and social competencies during the grade-school years*

Pattern of Parenting during Preschool Period	Children's Competencies at Age 8–9	
	Girls	*Boys*
Authoritative	Very high cognitive and social competencies	High cognitive and social competencies
Authoritarian	Average cognitive and social competencies	Average social competencies; low cognitive competencies
Permissive	Low cognitive and social competencies	Low social competencies; very low cognitive competencies

SOURCE: From D. Baumrind, *Socialization Determinants of Personal Agency*. Paper presented at the biennial meeting of the Society for Research in Child Development, New Orleans, March 1977. Excerpted by permission.

conflicts and behavioral disturbances they displayed as preschoolers. Seeking to answer this question, Baumrind (1977) observed her subjects (and their parents) once again when the children were 8 to 9 years old. As we see in Table 13-2, children of authoritative parents were still relatively high in both *cognitive competencies* (that is, showed originality in thinking, had high achievement motivation, liked intellectual challenges) and *social skills* (for example, were sociable and outgoing, participated actively and showed leadership in group activities), whereas children of authoritarian parents were generally average to below average in cognitive and social skills and children of permissive parents were relatively unskilled in both areas. And dovetailing nicely with Baumrind's research, other investigators have recently found that children of authoritative parents are much more autonomous and self-reliant later as *adolescents* and enjoy greater academic success than their counterparts raised by authoritarian or permissive parents (Dornbusch et al., 1987; Lamborn et al., 1991; Steinberg, Elmen, & Mounts, 1989).

The uninvolved parent.   One limitation of Baumrind's research is that almost all the parents in her sample were reasonably warm and accepting; even her authoritarian parents, who could be described as more self-centered and unresponsive than child-centered and responsive, did not clearly reject their children. It turns out that the least successful parenting style is what might be termed **uninvolved parenting**—an extremely lax, uncontrolling approach displayed by parents who have either *rejected* their children or are so overwhelmed with their own stresses and problems that they haven't much time or energy to devote to child rearing (Becker, 1964; Maccoby & Martin, 1983). Not only are children of these neglectful parents deficient both socially and academically, but they tend to become very hostile and rebellious adolescents who are prone to such antisocial or delinquent acts as alcohol and drug abuse, sexual misconduct, truancy, and a variety of criminal offenses (see Lamborn et al., 1991; Patterson, DeBaryshe, & Ramsey, 1989; Pulkkinen, 1982). In effect, these youngsters have "unattached" parents who seem to be saying "I don't care about you or about what you do"—a message that undoubtedly breeds resentment and willingness to strike back at these aloof, uncaring adversaries or at other symbols of authority.

Summing up.   It appears, then, that authoritative parenting—warmth combined with *moderate* parental control—is the parenting style most closely associated with positive developmental outcomes. Children apparently need love *and* limits—a set of rules that help them to structure and to evaluate their conduct. Without such guidance, they may not learn self-control and may become quite selfish, unruly, and lacking in clear achievement goals. But, if they receive too much guidance and are hemmed in by restrictions, they may have few opportunities to become self-reliant and may lack confidence in their own decision-making abilities (Grolnick & Ryan, 1989; Steinberg et al., 1989).

Does authoritative parenting really foster positive traits in children? Or is it that easygoing, manageable children cause parents to be authoritative? Baumrind (1983, 1991) insists that authoritative parenting causes children to be well behaved rather than the other way around. And at least one study of disciplinary conflict among mothers and their 2-year-olds does imply that a mother's approach to parenting has a much greater impact on the child's behavior than the child has on the mother (Crockenberg & Litman, 1990). Specifically, authoritative mothers who dealt firmly but rationally with noncompliance had toddlers who became more compliant; by contrast, authoritarian mothers who used arbitrary, power-assertive control strategies had children who became more *defiant*. Yet it is also true that extremely difficult, stubborn, and aggressive children tend to elicit more coercive forms of discipline and may eventually wear their parents out, causing them to become lax, less affectionate, and possibly even hostile and uninvolved (Anderson, Lytton, & Romney, 1986; Lytton, 1990). So, as we concluded when considering the impact of discipline on moral development in Chapter 12, socialization within the family is a matter of *reciprocal* influence: parents certainly influence their children, but children can also influence the parenting they receive.

Social-Class Differences in Parenting

Social class, or socioeconomic status (SES), refers to one's position within a society that is stratified according to status or power. Unlike in many countries such as India, where social standing is fixed at birth by the status of one's parents, we in the United States are fond of saying that anyone can rise above his or her origins if that person will work hard enough to succeed. Indeed, this proverb is the cornerstone of the American dream.

However, sociologists tell us that the "American dream" is a belief that is most likely to be endorsed by members of the middle and upper classes—those elements of society that have the economic resources to maintain or improve on their lofty economic status (Hess, 1970). As we will see, many people from the lower and working classes face very

different kinds of problems, pursue different goals, and often adopt different values. In short, they live in a different world than middle-class people do, and these ecological considerations may well affect the approaches they take when raising their children.

PATTERNS OF CHILD REARING IN HIGH-SES AND LOW-SES FAMILIES

Eleanor Maccoby (1980) has reviewed the child-rearing literature and concluded that **high-SES** (middle- and upper-class) parents differ from **low-SES** (lower- and working-class) parents in at least four respects:

1. Low-SES parents tend to stress obedience and respect for authority, neatness, cleanliness, and staying out of trouble. Higher-SES parents are more likely to stress happiness, curiosity, independence, creativity, and ambition.
2. Lower-SES parents are more restrictive and authoritarian, often setting arbitrary standards and enforcing them with power-assertive forms of discipline. Higher-SES parents tend to be either permissive or authoritative, and they are more likely to use inductive forms of discipline.
3. Higher-SES parents talk more with their children, reason with them more, and may use somewhat more complex language than lower-SES parents.
4. Higher-SES parents tend to show more warmth and affection toward their children.

According to Maccoby, these relationships seem to be true in many cultures and across racial and ethnic groups within the United States. However, there is some evidence that differences between high-SES and low-SES parenting are much more pronounced for boys than for girls. For example, John Zussman (1978) found that lower-class parents were more likely than middle-class parents to use power-assertion with their sons, whereas parents from both social classes used very low levels of power-assertion with their daughters (see also Simons et al., 1991).

Of course, we should keep in mind that these class-linked differences in parenting represent *group averages* rather than absolute contrasts; some

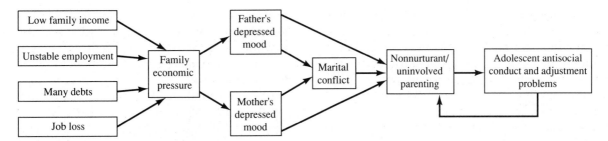

FIGURE 13-5 A model of the relationship among family economic stress, patterns of parenting, and adolescent adjustment. (Adapted from R. D. Conger, K. J. Conger, G. H. Elder, Jr., F. O. Lorenz, R. L. Simons, & L. B. Whitbeck, "A Family Process Model of Economic Hardship and Adjustment of Early Adolescent Boys." *Child Development*, 1992, *63*, 526–541. Copyright © 1992 by The Society for Research in Child Development. Adapted by permission.)

middle-class parents are highly restrictive, power-assertive, and aloof in their approach to child rearing, whereas many lower- and working-class parents function more like their counterparts in the middle class (Kelley, Power, & Wimbush, 1992; Laosa, 1981). But, on average, it appears that lower- and working-class parents are somewhat more critical, more punitive, and more intolerant of disobedience than parents from the middle and upper socioeconomic strata.

EXPLAINING SOCIAL-CLASS DIFFERENCES IN CHILD REARING

Undoubtedly, many factors contribute to social-class differences in child rearing, and economic considerations may head the list. Consider that a low income may mean that living quarters are crowded, that family members must sometimes make do without adequate food, clothing, or medical care, and that parents are constantly tense and anxious about living under these marginal conditions. Eleanor Maccoby (1980) suggests that low-income living is probably much more *stressful* for parents and that stress affects the ways in which parental functions are carried out. Vonnie McLoyd (1989, 1990) agrees. His recent reviews of the literature suggest that economic hardship creates its own psychological distress—a most pervasive discomfort that makes lower-income adults more edgy and irritable and more vulnerable to all negative life events (including the daily hassles associated with child rearing), thereby diminishing their capacity to be warm,

supportive parents. Indeed, in their study of lower- and working-class families, Rand Conger and his associates (1984) found a rather strong correlation between the number of environmental (and primarily economic) stresses that a parent experiences (for example, having less education, having low income, being a single parent, relying on welfare payments) and the treatment that children receive from their mothers. Specifically, the greater the number of environmental stressors the family was experiencing, the less supportive mothers were when interacting with their children, the more likely they were to make derogatory statements about their youngsters or to threaten, slap, push, or grab them, and the more authoritarian they became when expressing their views on child rearing.

In a second study, focusing on families with young adolescents, Conger and his associates (1992) found impressive support for a link among economic distress, nonnurturant/uninvolved parenting, and poor adolescent outcomes. As shown in Figure 13-5, greater economic distress predicted parental depression and marital conflict, which in turn were associated with nonnurturant/uninvolved parenting. And in this study (as in those we reviewed earlier), nonnurturant, uninvolved parenting was reliably associated with such adolescent adjustment problems as poor scholastic performance and peer relations, depression, hostility, and aggression. Of course, the patterns of antisocial conduct that a family's adolescent displays can further exasperate parents and cause them to remain relatively nonnurturant and/or uninvolved with him or her (Vuchinich, Bank, & Patterson, 1992). So it seems that Maccoby and McLoyd were correct in asserting that economic stresses and hardships contribute to the relatively coercive and/or aloof styles of parenting often observed in lower- and working-class families.

In addition, John Ogbu (1981) has argued that the way a family earns its livelihood may affect the strategies parents use to raise their children. Consider, for example, that the majority of lower- and working-class breadwinners are blue-collar workers who must please a supervisor and defer to his or her authority. So lower-SES parents may emphasize respect, obedience, neatness, and staying out of trouble because these are precisely the attributes they view as critical for success in the blue-collar economy. By contrast, high-SES parents may reason or negotiate more with their children while emphasizing individual initiative and achievement because these are the skills, attributes, and abilities that high-SES parents find necessary in their own roles as businesspersons, white-collar workers, or professionals.

Finally, it is possible that children themselves may contribute to social-class differences in child rearing. Low-SES mothers, who often are younger and receive less adequate prenatal care, are more likely than middle-class mothers to deliver prematurely or to experience other complications of childbirth (Kessner, 1973). As a result, low-SES families are more likely to have irritable, unresponsive, or otherwise difficult babies who may be harder to care for and love.

When we look at the data, it may seem that high-SES parenting is somehow "better" or more competent. After all, the responsive, authoritative parenting often observed in middle-class families is reliably associated with positive developmental outcomes in all the demographic (that is, racial and ethnic) groups studied to date in the United States (Lamborn et al., 1991; Steinberg et al., 1991). Yet there is another side to this issue—one that researchers in Western societies sometimes fail to consider. Perhaps middle-class parenting is "better" for children who are expected to become productive members of a middle-class subculture. However, a middle-class pattern of parenting that stresses individual initiative, intellectual curiosity, and competitiveness may actually represent "incompetent" parenting among the Temne of Sierra Leone, a society in which everyone must pull together and suppress individualism if the community is to successfully plant, harvest, and ration the meager crops on which its livelihood absolutely depends (Berry, 1967). And, since many children from Western societies will choose a career within the blue-collar economy, it is unreasonable to conclude that a pattern of child rearing that prepares them for this undertaking is in some way deficient or "incompetent."

The closest thing to a general law of parenting is that warm, sensitive caregiving seems to be associated with positive developmental outcomes in virtually all the cultures and subcultures that social scientists have studied. But people are being somewhat **ethnocentric** when they suggest that a particular style of child rearing (for example, authoritative parenting) that produces favorable outcomes in one context (middle-class Western societies) is the optimal pattern for children in all other cultures and subcultures. Louis Laosa (1981, p. 159) makes this same point, noting that "indigenous patterns of child care throughout the world represent largely successful adaptations to conditions of life that have long differed from one people to another. Women are 'good mothers' by the only relevant standards, those of their own culture."

The Quest for Autonomy: Renegotiating the Parent/Child Relationship during Adolescence

One of the most important developmental tasks that adolescents face is to achieve a mature and healthy sense of **autonomy**. This complex attribute has two major components: (1) *emotional autonomy*, or an ability to serve as one's own source of emotional strength rather than childishly depending on parents to provide comfort, reassurance, and emotional security, and (2) *behavioral autonomy*, or an ability to make one's own decisions, to govern one's own affairs, and to take care of oneself (Steinberg, 1985). If adolescents are to "make it" as adults, they can't be rushing home for loving hugs after every little setback. Nor can they continue to rely on parents to get them to work on time or to remind them of their duties and obligations. Indeed, parents want their adolescents to become autonomous, and adolescents actively seek the freedom to become autonomous.

So what happens within the family system when teenagers mature and begin to act more autonomously? Sparks fly! As boys reach the period of greatest pubertal growth, they become more assertive, more argumentative, and more inclined to interrupt parental words of wisdom to voice their own opinions (Steinberg, 1981). Similarly, conflicts between girls and their mothers also heighten once girls reach puberty (Brooks-Gunn & Zahaykevich, 1989; Holmbeck & Hill, 1991). Conflicts occur mostly over mundane details of family life, such as the adolescent's physical appearance, her choice of friends, or her neglect of schoolwork and household chores. And much of the friction stems from the different perspectives that parents and adolescents adopt: parents view conflicts through a *social-conventional* lens, feeling that they have a duty to regulate the child's conduct, whereas the adolescent, locked in his quest for autonomy, views his nagging parents as infringing on *personal* rights and choices (Smetana, 1989).

As a result of these power struggles, adolescents (particularly boys) gain influence in family decision making, usually at the expense of their mothers (Steinberg, 1981). And, as teenagers continue to assert themselves and parents grant them more and more influence, the parent/child relationship gradually evolves from a parent-dominated enterprise to one in which parents and adolescents are on a more equal footing (Feldman & Gehring, 1988; Furman & Burhmester, 1992; Steinberg, 1981; Youniss & Smollar, 1985). Do these experiences undermine the closeness of the parent/child emotional bond?

Ideally, they do not. Although researchers once believed that achieving autonomy meant separating from parents—cutting the cords—they are beginning to realize that maintaining a close attachment to one's family may be just as important to an adolescent's psychological adjustment as the ability to fend for oneself (Grotevant & Cooper, 1986;

PHOTO 13-5   As adolescents begin their quest for autonomy, conflicts with parents become more commonplace.

Youniss & Smollar, 1985). There really is no need for teenagers to become emotionally detached from parents in order to achieve autonomy (Ryan & Lynch, 1989). In fact, high self-esteem and psychosocial maturity are more characteristic of adolescents who emphasize the positive side of autonomy—the quest for self-governance—than of those who believe that their primary mission is to break away from their parents (Moore, 1987).

From their interviews with teenagers, James Youniss and Jacqueline Smollar (1985) have learned how parents might successfully nurture autonomy in their adolescents. It seems that parents of well-adjusted teenagers gradually loosened the reins as their school-aged children reached adolescence; but by no means did they cease to set rules or stop monitoring their children's behavior. They gave adolescents more freedom to venture away from home with friends, but they still watched closely to see that their youngsters were keeping up in school and were not developing any serious behavior problems. By viewing their children as more mature, parents not only gave them more freedom but demanded more of them in the way of self-governance as well. And, although adolescents reported that they stopped treating their parents as all-knowing authority figures and began to ask them to justify their rules and restrictions, they continued to respect parental opinions (particularly well-reasoned ones) and very much wanted their parents' approval.

So it seems that adolescents are most likely to achieve a healthy sense of autonomy if their parents keep their rules and restrictions to a reasonable minimum, explain them, and continue to be warm and supportive (Hill, 1987). Does this parenting style sound familiar? It should, for this winning combination of parental warmth and a pattern of control that is neither too lax nor overly restrictive is an *authoritative* approach—the same style that appears to foster

---

BOX 13-2   *Does Part-Time Employment Foster a Healthy Sense of Autonomy (and Positive Developmental Outcomes)?*

Most adolescents in the United States and Canada work at least part time during their high school days, and it seems reasonable to assume that these early work experiences could have any number of effects on their development. On the positive side, the money teenagers earn might foster a sense of self-sufficiency and economic autonomy from parents, which in turn could contribute to higher self-esteem. In addition, working youths just might be (1) quicker than nonworking peers to establish a positive work orientation (that is, pride in a job well done) and (2) more knowledgeable about the world of work, consumer issues, and financial management. Yet there are some potential disadvantages to part-time employment as well. Some developmentalists have wondered whether hours spent at work will detract from scholastic activities and undermine teenagers' academic performance. Others have feared that teens who work long hours will be less closely monitored by parents, thus having both the freedom and the economic means (from their earnings) to partake heavily in such antisocial activities as drug and alcohol abuse. So what have researchers learned about the effects of adolescent employment? Is work a positive or a negative force in the lives of most teens?

Lawrence Steinberg and his associates (Greenberger & Steinberg, 1986; Steinberg, 1984; Steinberg & Dornbusch, 1991) have addressed these issues by comparing working and nonworking youths on a variety of outcome measures (for example, autonomy from parents, self-esteem, attitudes about work, investment and performance in school, psychological adjustment, and involvement in delinquent activities), seeking to determine if there are meaningful associations between the number of hours adolescents work and their standing on these developmental indexes. Overall, Steinberg and his colleagues report far more bad news than good about teenagers who work—particularly about those who work more than 15–20 hours per week during the school year. Although working youths did know more than their nonworking peers about consumer issues and financial management, there was no consistent evidence that increasing involvement in the world of work fosters the development of a healthy orientation toward work; in fact, working adolescents often develop some rather cynical attitudes about work and become more tolerant of such unethical practices as overreporting work hours (to boost their pay).

Even more discouraging were the findings that adolescents who worked more than 20 hours a week were less involved in school, made lower grades, and were *lower* in self-esteem than agemates who worked 10 or fewer hours a week. Although these findings held for all racial groups, the negative impact of long working hours on scholastic achievement was greatest for Caucasian and Asian-American students—the two groups that ordinarily do best at school.

And there is more. Adolescents who worked more than 20 hours a week were granted much more autonomy over day-to-day decisions than were agemates who worked 10 hours a week or less. Yet this greater autonomy seemed to be directed toward "cutting the cords" to parents—the less adaptive form of independence—for teenagers who worked long hours were much less invested in family activities and were mon-

healthy developmental outcomes in childhood. It is mainly when parents react negatively to a teenager's push for autonomy and become overly strict or overly permissive that adolescents are likely to rebel and to get into trouble (Balswick & Macrides, 1975; Patterson et al., 1989). Of course, we must remind ourselves that socialization within the family is a matter of reciprocal influence, and it is much easier for a parent to respond authoritatively to a responsible, level-headed adolescent than to one who is rude, hostile, and unruly.

In sum, the parent/adolescent relationship might be viewed as more of a partnership — the quality of which depends on what both parents and children

---

BOX 13-2 | continued

itored less closely by older family members. And, as shown in the figure, the psychological and behavioral correlates of all this freedom were downright gloomy: teenagers working more than 20 hours per week reported higher levels of anxiety, depression, and somatic symptoms (for example, headaches, stomach aches, and colds) and more frequent involvement in alcohol and drug use and other delinquent activities than did agemates working 10 or fewer hours a week (Steinberg & Dornbusch, 1991).

In sum, the personal, social, and educational *costs* of working long hours appear to be formidable indeed for most American adolescents, and even employment on a more limited scale seems to offer few benefits (beyond providing teens with more spending money).

Why is working not a more positive contributor to adolescent development? One major reason may be that teenagers typically work at relatively menial and repetitive "fast food" or manual-labor jobs that offer so few opportunities for self-direction or decision making (Steinberg, 1984). Given the hard economic times that many Western economies have experienced in recent years, it may be unrealistic to expect teenagers not to work when so many of their parents find it increasingly difficult to provide for all their needs. Nevertheless, Steinberg's research implies that parents, educators, and policymakers would be serving our youth well by carefully monitoring (and limiting as necessary) the number of hours that adolescents work during the school year.

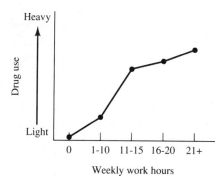
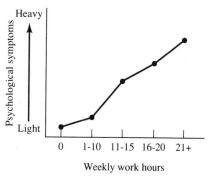

Relations between the number of hours worked per week and adolescents' drug use and reported psychological symptoms. (Adapted from L. Steinberg & S. M. Dornbusch, "Negative Correlates of Part-Time Employment during Adolescence: Replication and Elaboration." *Developmental Psychology*, 1991, 27, 304–313. Copyright © 1991 by the American Psychological Association. Adapted by permission.)

do when renegotiating their ties. Although power struggles are an inevitable consequence of the adolescent's quest for autonomy, most parents and their teenagers are able to resolve their differences and maintain positive feelings for one another as they rework their relationship so that it becomes more equal (Furman & Buhrmester, 1992). As a result, most adolescents achieve autonomy and become more self-reliant while also developing a more "friendlike" attachment to their parents.

The Influence of Siblings and Sibling Relationships

Although families are getting smaller, the majority of American children still grow up with at least one sibling, and there is certainly no shortage of speculation about the roles that brothers and sisters play in a child's life. For example, many parents are distressed by the fighting and bickering that their children display, and they often fear that such rivalrous conduct will undermine the growth of children's prosocial concerns and their ability to get along with others. At the same time, the popular wisdom is that only children are likely to be lonely, overindulged "brats" who would profit both socially and emotionally from having siblings to teach them that they are not nearly so "special" as they think they are (Falbo, 1984).

Although rivalries among siblings are certainly commonplace, we will see that siblings can play some very positive roles in a child's life, often serving as caregivers, teachers, playmates, and confidants. Yet we will also see that only children may not be nearly so disadvantaged by their lack of sibling relationships as people have commonly assumed.

And Baby Makes Four: Changes in the Family System with the Birth of a Second Child

Judy Dunn and Carol Kendrick (1982) have studied how children adapt to a new baby, and the account they provide is not an entirely cheerful one. After the baby arrives, mothers typically devote less warm and playful attention to their first-borns, who are likely to respond to this perceived "neglect" by becoming difficult and demanding, crying a lot, clinging to their mothers, and sometimes even hitting or pinching their tiny brother or sister (see also Stewart et al., 1987). So most first-borns are not entirely thrilled to have an attention-grabbing new baby in the home. They resent losing the mother's attention, may harbor animosities toward the baby for stealing it, and will do whatever they can to make their feelings known and recapture the mother's love.

Thus, **sibling rivalry**—a spirit of competition, jealousy, or resentment between siblings—often begins as soon as a younger brother or sister arrives. How can it be minimized? Fathers can play an important role by increasing the time they devote to first-borns as mothers are decreasing theirs (Stewart et al., 1987). Mothers can also help by talking to older children about the infant's feelings and competencies and by appealing to the older child's maturity, encouraging him or her to assist in caring for the baby (Dunn & Kendrick, 1982; Howe & Ross, 1990). Setting aside a little "quality time" to let the older child know she is still loved and considered important is also a useful strategy for mothers to pursue. Yet some caution is required here, for Dunn and Kendrick (1982) found that older girls whose parents showered them with attention in the weeks after a baby was born were the ones who played *least* with and were *most negative* toward their baby brother or sister 14 months later. The older children who were most positive toward younger siblings (both 14 months later and at age 6) were those whose mothers had not permitted them to brood or respond negatively toward the baby (Dunn, 1984). We see, then, that parents may have to walk a thin line between two traps: becoming so attentive toward the new baby that they deprive the older child of attention or undermine his security, and becoming so indulgent of the first-born that he resents any competition from the younger sib. Indeed, researchers are consistently finding that sibling relationships are friendlier and less conflictual when both mothers and fathers respond warmly and sensitively to *all* their children and do not consistently favor one child over the others (Brody, Stoneman, & Burke, 1987; Brody et al., 1992; Stocker, Dunn, & Plomin, 1989; Teti & Ablard, 1989).

Sibling Relationships over the Course of Childhood

Fortunately, most older siblings adjust fairly quickly to having a new brother or sister, becoming much less anxious and less inclined to display the problem behaviors that they showed early on. But, even in the best of sibling relationships, conflict is normal. Actual confrontations often become more frequent and intense once the younger child reaches 18 to 24 months of age and is better at "holding his own" by hitting or teasing the older sib or by directing a parent's attention to an older sib's misconduct (Dunn & Munn, 1985).

Although rivalrous conduct among siblings occurs throughout the preschool and grade-school years, researchers who have observed siblings at home find that their interactions are more often positive and supportive than oppositional and conflictual (Abramovitch et al., 1986; Baskett & Johnson, 1982). There are some reliable differences in the behavior of older and younger siblings, with older siblings generally being the more domineering and aggressive parties and younger siblings the more compliant (Abramovitch et al., 1986; Berndt & Bulleit, 1985). Yet, older sibs also initiate more helpful, playful, and other prosocial behaviors—a finding that may reflect the pressure parents place on them to demonstrate their maturity by looking after a younger brother or sister.

In some ways, sibling relationships are truly paradoxical, because they are often both *close* and *conflictual*. Wyndol Furman and Duane Buhrmester (1985a, 1985b), for example, found that grade-school siblings who were similar in age reported more warmth and closeness than other sibling pairs—but, at the same time, more friction and conflict. Moreover, children viewed their sibling relations as more conflict ridden and less satisfying than their relations with either parent, their grandparents, or their friends. Yet, when children were asked to rate the *importance* of different social relationships and the *reliability* of their various social alliances, siblings were viewed as more important and more reliable than friends!

As is true of parent/child relationships, sibling relationships become much more egalitarian during the adolescent years. Siblings now quarrel less fre-

PHOTO 13-6   Coercive and rivalrous conduct between siblings is a normal aspect of family life.

quently, and their relationships become otherwise less intense—probably because teenagers are spending less time with brothers and sisters, who are, after all, part of the family from whom they want to develop some autonomy (Buhrmester & Furman, 1990; Furman & Buhrmester, 1992). But, even though they are immersing themselves in close friendships and romantic entanglements, older adolescents once again come to perceive their siblings as important and intimate associates—people to whom they can turn for support and companionship, despite the fact that relations with them have often been rather stormy (Buhrmester & Furman, 1990; Furman & Buhrmester, 1992).

Perhaps these seemingly paradoxical data make perfectly good sense if we carefully reexamine the findings on the nature of sibling/sibling interactions. Yes, rivalries and conflicts between siblings are a very normal part of family life. Yet the observational record consistently shows that brothers and sisters often do nice things for one another and that these acts of kindness and affection are typically much more common than hateful or rivalrous conduct.

Positive Aspects of Sibling Interaction

What positive roles might siblings play in one another's lives? One important contribution that older siblings make is to provide *caretaking* services for younger brothers and sisters. Indeed, one survey of child-rearing practices in 186 societies found that older children were the *principal* caregivers for infants and toddlers in 57% of the groups studied (Weisner & Gallimore, 1977). Even in industrialized societies such as the United States, older siblings (particularly girls) are often asked to look after their younger brothers and sisters (McHale & Gamble, 1989). Of course, their role as caregivers provides older children opportunities to influence their younger siblings in many ways, by serving as their teachers, playmates, and advocates, as well as important sources of emotional security.

Siblings as attachment objects.

Do infants become attached to older brothers and sisters, viewing them as providers of security? To find out, Robert Stewart (1983) exposed 10–20-month-old infants to a variation of Ainsworth's strange-situations test. Each infant was left with a 4-year-old sibling in a strange room that a strange adult soon entered. The infants typically showed signs of distress as their mothers departed, and they were wary in the company of the stranger. Stewart noted that these distressed infants would often approach their older brother or sister, particularly when the stranger appeared. And most of the 4-year-olds offered some sort of comforting or caregiving to their baby brothers and sisters.

Other investigators have replicated these findings and shown that the older children who are most inclined to comfort an infant sibling are those who themselves are securely attached to their mothers (Teti & Ablard, 1989) and who have developed the role-taking skills to understand the basis for the infant's distress (Stewart & Marvin, 1984). So it appears that older siblings can become important sources of emotional support who help younger sibs to cope with uncertain situations when their parents are not around. Moreover, infants are likely to venture much farther away to explore a strange environment if a sensitive and attentive older sibling is nearby to serve as a "secure base" for exploration (Samuels, 1980; Stewart & Marvin, 1984).

Finally, Patricia East and Karen Rook (1992) report that a secure tie to a favorite sibling can help to offset certain adjustment problems (for example, insecurity, social anxiety) that children often display if they are ignored or neglected by their peers. So siblings can be meaningful companions indeed!

Siblings as social models.

In addition to providing a sense of security and promoting the younger child's exploratory competencies, older siblings serve as models for their younger brothers and sisters. As early as 12 to 20 months of age, infants are already becoming very attentive to their older sibs, often choosing to imitate their actions or to take over toys that the older children have abandoned (Abramovitch, Corter, & Pepler, 1980; Samuels, 1977). Younger siblings tend to look up to their older brothers and sisters throughout childhood and very much value the things they learn by observing and interacting with them (Buhrmester & Furman, 1990). By contrast, older siblings typically select parents (or other adults) as social models and will pay little attention to the behavior of younger sibs, unless they happen to be squabbling or playing with them (Baskett, 1984; Samuels, 1977).

Siblings as teachers.

Do older siblings take it upon themselves to oversee a younger sib's activities and to promote his or her competencies? Yes, indeed. In one study (Brody, Stoneman, & MacKinnon, 1982), 8- to 10-year-olds played a popular board game with (1) a younger (4½- to 7-year-old) sibling, (2) an 8- to 10-year-old peer, and (3) a younger sib and a peer. As the children played, observers noted how often each child assumed the following roles: *teacher*, *learner*, *manager* (child requests or commands an action), *managee* (child is the target of management), and *equal-status playmate*. Older siblings dominated the sibling/sibling interactions by assuming the teacher and manager roles much more often than younger sibs did. Yet, when playing with a peer, these 8- to 10-year-olds usually assumed the role of equal-status playmate and rarely tried to dominate their friends. And, when all three children played together, it was the older sibling rather than the peer who assumed responsibility for "managing" the younger child. So older siblings are likely to make an active attempt to instruct their younger brothers and sisters, particularly when playing alone with them. Although the teaching that older sibs performed in this study may seem rather trivial, other research indicates that younger siblings who experience little difficulty in learning to read are likely to have older brothers and sisters who played "school" with them and who taught them important lessons such as the ABCs (Norman-Jackson, 1982).

If we reexamine the ground we have covered, it may seem as if younger siblings are reaping all the benefits. Yet studies of peer tutoring, in which older children teach academic lessons to younger pupils, consistently find that the tutors show significant gains in academic achievement—bigger gains than those posted by agemates who have not had an opportunity to tutor a younger child (Feldman, Devin-Sheehan, & Allen, 1976). Closer to home, it seems that, the greater the number of younger siblings (up to three) that college women have had an opportunity to tutor, the higher these women score on the SAT, or Scholastic Aptitude Test (Paulhus & Shaffer, 1981). So it appears that the teacher/learner roles that siblings often assume at play are beneficial to *both* parties: older siblings learn by tutoring their younger brothers and sisters, while their young tutees also appear to profit from the instruction they receive.

Sibling effects on social competence. How do experiences with siblings affect a child's social relationships outside the family? Here is one area where developmentalists know relatively little. There is some evidence that later-born children tend to be somewhat *more popular*, on average, than first-borns are (see, for example, Miller & Maruyama, 1976). Why? One reason may be that some older siblings who reliably use their greater power to dominate a younger brother or sister will employ these same coercive tactics with peers (Berndt & Bulleit, 1985)—a move that is not likely to enhance their popularity or status in the peer group. Yet another reason why later-borns may eventually become more popular than first-borns is that they have learned to defer to and to negotiate with their older and more powerful siblings, thereby acquiring cooperative and concilia-

tory interpersonal skills that should serve them well when interacting with peers (Miller & Maruyama, 1976).

However, it is important to add that these **ordinal position** effects on peer popularity are small in magnitude and that there are many, many exceptions to the rule. Some first-borns are immensely popular, whereas some later-borns lack social skills and are actually *rejected* by their peers. What these qualifications tell us, then, is that much more research is needed before we will fully understand how children's experiences with siblings affect their social standing outside the family.

Characteristics of Only Children

Are only children who grow up without siblings the spoiled, selfish, overindulged brats that people often presume them to be? Hardly! After reviewing the pertinent literature, Toni Falbo and Denise Polit (1986) found that only children (1) are more obedient and slightly more intellectually competent, on average, than children with siblings, and (2) are likely to establish very good relations with peers. Since only children enjoy an exclusive relationship with their parents, they may receive more quality time from parents and more direct achievement training than children with siblings do, which perhaps explains their tendency to be relatively friendly, well behaved, and instrumentally competent (Baskett, 1985; Rothbart, 1971). Moreover, these singletons have no younger sibs that they can bully and, like later-borns, may soon learn that they must negotiate and be accommodating if they hope to play successfully with *peer* playmates, most of whom are probably at least as powerful as they are. So, important as siblings may be to children who have them, it is quite possible for a child to develop normally and even to flourish without brothers and sisters. Indeed, the generally positive social outcomes that only children display suggest that many singletons are able to gain through their peer alliances whatever they may miss by not having siblings at home.[3]

---

[3]Peer influences on child and adolescent development are examined in detail in Chapter 15.

The Impact of Divorce

Earlier in the chapter we learned that 40–50% of today's marriages will end in divorce and that about 40–50% of American children born in the 1970s and 1980s will spend some time in a single-parent home—usually one headed by the mother. And it is important to emphasize that divorce is *not* a singular life event; instead, it represents a series of stressful experiences for the entire family that begins with marital conflict before the actual separation and includes a multitude of life changes afterward. As Mavis Hetherington and Kathleen Camara (1984) see it, families must often cope with "the diminution of family resources, changes in residence, assumption of new roles and responsibilities, establishment of new patterns of [family] interaction, reorganization of routines . . . , and [possibly] the introduction of new relationships [that is, stepparent/child and stepsibling relationships] into the existing family" (p. 398).

Only recently have investigators begun to conduct longitudinal studies to determine how family members cope with divorce and whether this dissolution of the nuclear family will have any long-term effects on children's social, emotional, and intellectual development. Let's see what they have learned.

Immediate Effects: Crisis and Reorganization

Most families going through a divorce experience a *crisis period* of a year or more in which the lives of all family members are seriously disrupted (Hetherington, 1981, 1989; Hetherington, Cox, & Cox, 1982; Wallerstein & Kelly, 1980b). Typically, both spouses experience emotional as well as practical difficulties. The wife, who obtains custody of any children in about 90% of divorcing families, is likely to be angry, depressed, lonely, or otherwise distressed, although often relieved as well. The husband is also likely to be distressed, particularly if he feels shut off from his children. Having just become single adults, both parents often feel isolated from former married friends and other bases of social support on which they had relied as marrieds. And women with children usually face the added problems of adjusting to a seriously reduced income, moving to a lower-income neighborhood, and trying to work and raise young children single-handedly.

As you might suspect, psychologically distressed adults do not make the best parents. Hetherington and her associates (1982) find that custodial mothers, overwhelmed by responsibilities and by their own emotional reactions to divorce, often become edgy, impatient, and insensitive to their children's needs, and they typically adopt more punitive and coercive methods of child rearing. Indeed, divorced mothers often appear (to their children, at least) to have been transformed into more hostile, less caring parents (Fauber et al., 1990). Meanwhile, noncustodial fathers are likely to change in a different way, becoming somewhat overpermissive and indulgent during visits with their children.

We trust that you can imagine how these changes in parenting are likely to be received by the children of divorce. They themselves are often angry, fearful, and depressed about recent events and may be feeling guilty as well, especially if they are preschoolers, who are likely to think that they are somehow responsible for their parents' separation (Hetherington, 1981). What frequently happens is that these distressed youngsters react vigorously to their mother's seemingly aloof, impatient, and coercive parenting by becoming whiny, argumentative, disobedient, and downright disrespectful. Parent/child relationships during this crisis phase are best described as a vicious circle in which the child's emotional distress and problem behaviors and the adult's ineffective parenting styles feed on each other and make everyone's life unpleasant (Baldwin & Skinner, 1989).

The low point in mother/child relations comes about a year after the divorce. One divorced mother described her family's ordeal as a "struggle for survival," and another characterized experiences with her children as like "getting bitten to death by ducks" (Hetherington et al., 1982, p. 258). Not surprisingly, the stresses associated with a divorce and a breakdown in effective parenting often lead not only to problem behaviors at home but also to a disruption of children's peer relations and to academic difficulties and conduct disorders at school (Allison & Furstenberg, 1989; Doherty & Needle, 1991; Fauber et al., 1990).

Although older, preadolescent and adolescent children are better able to understand the reasons for their parents' divorce, they are nonetheless upset by the breakup of their nuclear families and show an increase in problem behaviors and disruptions in their relationships with other family members (Bray, 1988; Hetherington, Clingempeel, & Associates, 1992). Often preadolescents and adolescents will react to the turmoil at home by disengaging from the family and becoming involved in extrafamilial alliances with peers or with the family of a close friend (Hetherington, 1989; Wallerstein & Kelly, 1980a, 1980b). And custodial mothers are not as effective as two parents are at monitoring adolescent activities, with the result being that adolescents in single-parent homes are granted (or assume) greater autonomy and experience fewer conflicts about autonomy issues than agemates from intact nuclear families (Anderson, Hetherington, & Clingempeel, 1989; Smetana et al., 1991). However, this greater freedom may come at some cost, for investigators consistently find that antisocial and delinquent behaviors are much more common among adolescents from divorced homes than among those from intact families (see Capaldi & Patterson, 1991; Dornbusch et al., 1985; Hetherington et al., 1992).

The question of sex differences. Although the finding is by no means universal (see, for example, Allison & Furstenberg, 1989; Hetherington et al., 1992), many investigators report that the impact of marital strife and divorce is more powerful and enduring for boys than for girls. Even before the divorce occurs, boys are already showing more behavioral disruptions than girls (Block, Block, & Gjerde, 1986, 1988). And at least two longitudinal studies found that girls had largely recovered from their social and emotional disturbances two years after a divorce, whereas boys, who improved dramatically over this same period, were nevertheless continuing to show signs of emotional stress and problems in their relationships with parents, siblings, teachers, and peers (Hetherington et al., 1982; Wallerstein & Kelly, 1980b; see also Emery, 1988).

Why might marital turmoil and dissolution strike harder at boys? The most popular explanation is that boys may feel closer to fathers than girls do (recall that fathers often spend more time with sons than with daughters), so that they experience more frustration and a deeper sense of loss when the father is no longer readily available to them (Lamb, 1981). However, it could also be that boys look so poorly adjusted because investigators have focused more on overt behavior problems that are easy to detect than on other, more subtle outcome measures, such as covert psychological distress (Zaslow, 1989). Indeed, at least two recent studies suggest that, even prior to a divorce (and for up to five years afterward), girls experience more *covert distress* than boys do (Allison & Furstenberg, 1989; Doherty & Needle, 1991). Moreover, a disproportionate number of girls from divorced families show precocious sexual activity at adolescence and a persistent lack of self-confidence in their relationships with boys and men (Hetherington, Stanley-Hagan, & Anderson, 1989; Wallerstein & Corbin, 1989). So divorce seems to affect boys and girls in different ways.

Yet another reason why boys may look bad is that most researchers have limited their studies to the most common custodial arrangement: mother-headed households. Interestingly, those few boys whose fathers assume custody fare much better than boys who live with their mothers; in fact, children and adolescents of *both* sexes seem to be better adjusted and less likely to drop out of high school when they live with their same-sex parent (Camara & Resnick, 1988; Zaslow, 1989; Zimiles & Lee, 1991).[4]

So a divorce can strike very hard at children of either sex. Clearly, we would be overstating the case (not to mention being insensitive to girls) were we to conclude that this disruptive life experience is anything but a major struggle for the majority of boys *and* girls.

---

[4]However, at least one recent study (Buchanan, Maccoby, & Dornbusch, as cited by Hetherington, Clingempeel, & Associates, 1992) reports that both sons and daughters in father-custody homes may be more prone to delinquent conduct than those who live with their mother.

On staying together for the good of the children.
The conventional wisdom used to be that unhappily married couples should remain together for the good of the children. Yet, researchers are consistently finding that children in stable, single-parent (or stepparent) homes are usually better adjusted than those who remain in conflict-ridden two-parent families (Hetherington, 1989; Long & Forehand, 1987). In fact, many of the behavior problems that children display after a divorce are actually evident well *before* the divorce and may be related to long-standing family conflict rather than to the divorce itself (Block et al., 1986, 1988; Demo & Acock, 1988). Hetherington (1981) believes that an eventual escape from conflict may be the most positive outcome of divorce for many children. Judith Wallerstein and Joan Kelly (1980a) definitely agree, adding that "today's conventional wisdom holds . . . that an unhappy couple might well *divorce* for the good of the children; that an unhappy marriage for the adults is also unhappy for the children; and that a divorce that promotes the happiness of the adults will benefit the children as well" (p. 67).

Long-Term Reactions to Divorce

Although many of the emotional and behavioral disturbances that accompany a divorce will diminish considerably over the next two years, the whole experience is not forgotten. Compared to children in harmonious, two-parent families, children of divorce are still showing more evidence of psychological distress and academic difficulties four to six years later, particularly if they were very young at the time of their parents' divorce (Allison & Furstenberg, 1989; Hetherington, 1989; Hetherington et al., 1992; Kurdek, Blisk, & Siesky, 1981). Interestingly, children who show the most positive changes over time in their attitudes about the divorce often report that having friends whose parents were divorced had helped them cope with their earlier feelings of bitterness and resentment (Kurdek et al., 1981).

Judith Wallerstein's (1987; Wallerstein & Blakeslee, 1989) studies of children ten years after their parents' divorce are generally consistent with the earlier follow-ups, with one interesting difference:

PHOTO 13-7   Youngsters who live in conflict-ridden nuclear families often suffer physically and emotionally. In the long run, children of divorce are usually better adjusted than those whose unhappily married parents stay together "for the sake of the children."

those who were grade-school children or adolescents when their parents divorced were the ones most heavily burdened by painful memories ten years later, even though they had suffered less than preschoolers had at the time of the divorce. Yet another interesting long-term reaction is that children from divorced families are more likely than those from intact families to fear that their own marriages will be unhappy (Franklin, Janoff-Bulman, & Roberts, 1990; Wallerstein & Blakeslee, 1989). It is not that children of divorce fear intimacy or think that they will be unable to find happiness in love relationships; rather, they differ from other respondents only in their optimism about the success of their *marriages* (Franklin et al., 1990).

In sum, divorce tends to be a most unsettling and troubling life event — one that few children feel very positive about, even after ten years have elapsed. But, despite their sentiments, it seems that a conflict-ridden nuclear family is often more detrimental to the child's development than the absence of a divorced parent. Moreover, not all divorced families experience all the difficulties we've described; in fact, some divorced adults and their children manage this transition quite well and may even thrive afterward (Hetherington, 1989). Who are these survivors? Box 13-3 provides some clues by exploring the factors that seem to promote a positive adjustment to divorce.

Children in Reconstituted Families

Within three to five years after a divorce, about 75% of single-parent families will experience yet another major change when the parent remarries and the children acquire a stepparent—and perhaps new siblings as well (Hetherington, 1989). Remarriage often improves the financial and other life circumstances of custodial parents, and most remarried adults report that they are satisfied with their second marriages. Yet these reconstituted families introduce new challenges for children, who must now adjust not only to the parenting of an unfamiliar adult but also to the behavior of stepsiblings (if any) and to the possibility of receiving less attention from both their custodial and noncustodial parents (Hetherington, 1989). Moreover, second marriages are somewhat more likely to end in divorce than first marriages are (Glick & Lin, 1987). Imagine, then, the stresses experienced by those adults and children who find themselves in a recurring cycle of marriage, marital conflict, divorce, single parenthood, and remarriage (see Brody, Neubaum, & Forehand, 1988)!

How do children fare when their custodial parents remarry? We can begin by saying that there is often an initial period of conflict and disruption as new family roles and relationships are ironing themselves out (Hetherington, 1989). After this initial transition phase, an interesting sex difference emerges: boys often seem to benefit more than girls from gaining a *stepfather*, enjoying higher self-esteem, being less anxious and angered about their new living arrangements, and eventually overcoming most of the adjustment problems they displayed before their mothers remarried (Baumrind, 1989; Clingempeel, Ievoli, & Brand, 1984; Hetherington, 1989; Santrock et al., 1982; Zaslow, 1989). Why do girls not fare as well? Certainly *not* because fathers are treating stepdaughters any worse than step-

sons; in fact, Hetherington and her associates (1989; Vuchinich et al., 1991) find that just the opposite is true during the early stages of remarried life. Yet, no matter how hard stepfathers tried, their stepdaughters rejected them! Apparently girls view stepfathers as major threats to their relationships with their mothers, and they are likely to resent their mothers for remarrying and becoming less attentive to their needs (Hetherington, 1989; Santrock et al., 1982).

Much less is known about children's reactions to *stepmothers*, because stepmother families are still relatively uncommon (recall that fathers receive custody of their children in only about 10% of all custody hearings). There are some data to indicate that introduction of a stepmother into the family system is somewhat more disruptive initially than introduction of a stepfather, perhaps because stepmothers play more active roles as behavior monitors and disciplinarians than stepfathers do (Clingempeel et al., 1984; Furstenberg, 1988; Santrock & Sitterle, 1987). And it appears that the transition from a father-headed single-parent home to a two-parent *stepmother* family is once again more disruptive and difficult for girls than for boys, particularly if the biological mother maintains frequent contact with her children (Brand, Clingempeel, & Bowen-Woodward, 1988; Clingempeel & Segal, 1986). The problem seems to be that girls in single-parent homes are often so closely allied with their mothers that they are bothered by either a stepfather competing for their mother's attention or a stepmother attempting to play a substitute-mother role. But the emotional disruption and resentment that daughters may initially experience in stepmother families are often short-lived, for "over time, the relative childrearing roles of biological mother and stepmother [are] effectively negotiated, and girls may [actually] benefit from a support system augmented by a second mother figure" (Clingempeel & Segal, 1986, p. 482).

In sum, stable second marriages often work out well for two groups: custodial parents and their sons. Custodial parents gain the satisfaction of companionship and some assistance in child rearing, and boys usually fare better in reconstituted families than in single-parent homes headed by their mothers. Yet, girls are not so clearly advantaged by gaining a stepparent, and it remains for future research to determine whether their long-range outcomes are any better (or worse) in reconstituted families than in single-parent homes.

A final note: preadolescent and young adolescent children of both sexes find it much more difficult to adjust to life in a reconstituted family than younger children do (Hetherington, 1989). In fact, Mavis Hetherington and her associates (1992) found that, even after spending more than two years in a stepparent home, most adolescent males and females were less well adjusted than agemates from intact homes and had shown little improvement over the 26-month course of the study. Of course, not all these adolescents were functioning poorly (cf. Maccoby, 1992), and authoritative parenting (by both

---

B O X   **13-3** | *Smoothing the Rocky Road to Recovery after Divorce*

Some adults and children cope quite well with a divorce, whereas others suffer many negative and long-lasting effects. Although an individual's temperament and social problem-solving skills will influence how well he or she adjusts (Hetherington, 1989), several other factors can make the individual's task much easier.

Adequate Financial Support
Families fare much better after a divorce if their finances are not seriously undermined (Hetherington, 1989; Menaghan & Lieberman, 1986). Unfortunately, many mother-headed families experience a precipitous drop in income, which may necessitate a move to a lower-income neighborhood and a mother's return to work at precisely the time her children need stability and increased attention. Moreover, a lack of money for trips, treats, and other amenities to which children may be accustomed can be a significant contributor to family quarrels and bickering. Recent efforts to ensure that more noncustodial parents pay their fair share of child support should help the cause.

Adequate Parenting from the Custodial Parent
The custodial parent obviously plays a crucial role in the family's adjustment to divorce. If she or he can respond in a warm, consistent, and authoritative manner, children are much less likely to experience serious problems (Hetherington et al., 1992; Kline et al., 1989). Of course, it is difficult to be an effective parent when one is depressed and under stress. Yet both the custodial parent and the children can benefit immensely from receiving outside social support—not the least important of which is that provided by the *noncustodial* parent.

Social/Emotional Support
from the Noncustodial Parent
If divorced parents continue to squabble and are hostile to each other, both are likely to be upset, the custodial parent's parenting is likely to suffer, and children will feel torn in their loyalties and may display any number of behavior problems (Buchanan, Maccoby, & Dornbusch, 1991; Fauber et al., 1990; Kline et al., 1989). Children may also suffer if they lose contact with their noncustodial parent, and, unfortunately, about one-third of those children who live with their mothers lose all contact with their fathers (Seltzer & Bianchi, 1988). By contrast, regular contact with a father who *supports* the mother in her parenting role helps children (particularly sons) to make a positive adjustment to life in a single-parent home (Camara & Resnick, 1988; Hetherington et al., 1989). Ideally, then, children should be permitted to maintain affectionate ties with *both* parents and should be shielded from any continuing conflict between parents.

Is *joint physical custody* the answer? Obviously, children will have regular contact with both parents when they live part of the time in each parent's home. Yet this "contact advantage" may be offset by new kinds of instability (that is, changes in residence and sometimes in schools and peer groups) that often leave children distressed and confused (MacKinnon & Wallerstein,

the custodial parent and the stepparent) was associated with better adjustment outcomes than were authoritarian or uninvolved parenting. Nevertheless, there is clear evidence, both from this study and from several others, that the incidence of deviant or delinquent behavior is higher among adolescents in stepparent homes than among agemates living with both biological parents (see also Capaldi & Patterson, 1991; Dornbusch et al., 1985; Steinberg, 1987).

How might we explain these findings? One possibility is that adolescents, who are becoming increasingly autonomous, simply view any rules imposed by a stepparent as more intrusive or unwarranted than those coming from a natural parent. Another possibility that has received some support (see Hetherington, 1989; Hetherington et al., 1992) is that many stepparents are hesitant to impose restrictions on adolescents or to carefully monitor

---

B O X | **13-3** | *continued*

1986). Unfortunately, there is not much research that speaks to the advantages and disadvantages of joint physical custody. But what research there is suggests that children in this increasingly popular living arrangement show no fewer disturbances and no better social and emotional adjustment than sole-custody children do (Kline et al., 1989; Luepnitz, 1986). Not surprisingly, joint custody works best when the two custodial parents have a harmonious relationship. When the parents' relationship is hostile and conflictual, however, children in dual residences often feel "caught in the middle"—a perception that is associated with high levels of stress and very poor adjustment outcomes (Buchanan et al., 1991).

Additional Social Support
There are a number of other social supports that make a divorce easier to bear. For example, divorcing adults are less depressed and are more sensitive as caregivers if they have close confidants to whom they can turn (Hetherington, 1989; Menaghan & Lieberman, 1986). Moreover, children benefit from peer support programs in which they and other children of divorce are encouraged to share their feelings, correct their misconceptions, and learn positive coping skills (Pedro-Carroll & Cowen, 1985; Stolberg & Garrison, 1985). Adolescents in single-parent homes also appear to be less likely to engage in delinquent activities if a second adult (a grandmother, for example) lives in the home and bears some responsibility for child rearing and conduct monitoring (Dornbusch et al., 1985). In sum,

friends, peers, school personnel, and other sources of social support outside the nuclear family can do much to help families adjust to divorce.

Minimizing Additional Stressors
Generally, families respond most positively to divorce if additional disruptions are kept to a minimum—for example, if parents do not have to go through messy divorce trials and custody hearings, seek new jobs or residences, cope with the loss of their children, and so on (Buehler et al., 1986). One way to accomplish some of these aims is through *divorce mediation*—meetings prior to the divorce in which a trained professional tries to help divorcing parents reach amicable agreements on disputed issues such as child custody and property settlements. Divorce mediation does increase the likelihood of out-of-court settlements and often promotes better feelings between divorcing adults (Emery & Wyer, 1987); thus it may well have a beneficial effect on children's adjustment to the family break-up (although this latter effect remains to be confirmed by research).

Here, then, we have some effective first steps in the path toward a positive postdivorce adjustment. We also have yet another excellent example of the family as a social system embedded in larger social systems. Mother, father, and children will all influence one another's adjustment to divorce, and the family's experience will also depend on the supports available within the neighborhood, the schools, the community, and the family members' own social networks.

their activities, preferring to leave these tasks to the biological parent, who has difficulty accomplishing them on her or his own. Clearly, the issue of deviant conduct among adolescents in reconstituted families is a topic that begs for additional research. Yet it is important to emphasize that most adolescents who live with a stepparent are perfectly normal teenagers who are unlikely to display any psychopathological tendencies (Maccoby, 1992).

Maternal Employment—Revisited

In Chapter 6 we learned that a clear majority of American mothers now work outside the home and that this arrangement need not undermine the emotional security of their children. Infants and toddlers are likely to become or to remain securely attached to their working mothers if they have good day care and receive responsive caregiving when their parents are home from work.

Looking beyond primary attachments, research with older children suggests that maternal employment, by itself, is unlikely to impede a child's social and emotional development. Indeed, children of working mothers (particularly daughters) tend to be more independent and to hold higher educational and occupational aspirations and less stereotyped views of men and women than children whose mothers are not employed (Hoffman, 1989). And studies of toddlers (Schachter, 1981), grade-school children (Gold & Andres, 1978b), and adolescents (Gold & Andres, 1978a) consistently indicate that children of employed mothers are as confident in social settings as children whose mothers remain at home and are somewhat more sociable with peers. Moreover, at least one recent study of a national sample of *low-income* families links maternal employment to children's cognitive *competence*: second-graders whose mothers had worked a great deal outperformed those whose mothers had worked less (if at all) in mathematics, reading, and language achievement (Vandell & Ramanan, 1992). Although there have been reports that young children of working mothers are somewhat more aggressive

and less obedient than children cared for at home by mothers who are not employed (Clarke-Stewart, 1989; Hoffman, 1989), these "negative returns" are not always found and are generally limited to children receiving low-quality day care that includes a lack of close supervision (Howes, 1990; Vandell, Henderson, & Wilson, 1988).

Why might children of employed mothers so often experience favorable (rather than unfavorable) developmental outcomes? One reason may be that employed mothers are more likely than unemployed mothers to grant their children independence and autonomy when they are ready for it—which may be why many children of employed women look so socially mature (Hoffman, 1989). And, when mothers are satisfied with their working role, receive adequate social support, and are highly committed to being a parent, they perceive their children in relatively favorable ways, rely less on power-assertion to control their behavior, and are inclined to take an authoritative approach to child rearing—precisely the parenting style that is so often associated with favorable cognitive, social, and emotional outcomes (Crockenberg & Litman, 1991; Greenberger & Goldberg, 1989; Lerner & Galambos, 1985). Of course, outcomes may not be as good for children whose working mothers are dissatisfied with their jobs, who are not so highly committed to being a parent, or who receive little social support in their parenting role. Under these circumstances, working mothers are often aloof, impatient, and restrictive caregivers, which in turn makes children more argumentative and difficult (Hock, DeMeis, & McBride, 1988; Lerner & Galambos, 1985, 1988).

Against this backdrop of generally favorable outcomes associated with maternal employment is a recurring finding that has caused some concern: *middle-class boys* (but not girls) of working mothers tend to score lower in intelligence and academic achievement than boys whose mothers are not employed (Bronfenbrenner, 1986; Gold & Andres, 1978a), particularly when their mothers work more than 40 hours a week (Gottfried, Gottfried, & Bathurst, 1988). Yet even these results must be qualified, for Ann Crouter and her associates (1990) find that maternal employment is associated with lower academic achievement only when a boy's working parents fail to carefully monitor his activities. Indeed, boys in dual-earner families are just as competent academically as boys (and girls) of non-employed mothers when parents keep close tabs on their daily experiences and ensure that they devote sufficient attention to schoolwork (Crouter et al., 1990; see also Moorehouse, 1991).

The importance of parental monitoring raises another employment-related issue: after-school supervision of children whose mothers work. In the United States at least 2 to 4 million grade-school youngsters between the ages of 6 and 13 qualify as **self-care (or latchkey) children** — youngsters who care for themselves after school with little or no adult supervision (Zigler & Finn Stevenson, 1993). Are these children at risk of poor developmental outcomes such as feeling lonely, neglected, and low in self-esteem? Are they deficient academically? Is there a danger that, in the absence of adult supervision, self-care children will be prone to delinquent or antisocial conduct?

Unfortunately, we have little solid information about the effects of self-care on a child's development, and what research exists is often contradictory. Some studies report no differences between supervised and self-care children in self-esteem, self-confidence, peer popularity, academic achievement, and conduct at school (Galambos & Maggs, 1991; Steinberg, 1986; Vandell & Corasantini, 1988), whereas other research suggests that self-care children display more anxiety, more problems at school, and higher levels of drug and alcohol abuse than supervised youngsters do (Cole & Rodman, 1987; Richardson et al., 1989; Rodman & Cole, 1987).

How might we explain these inconsistent outcomes? Lawrence Steinberg (1986) suggests that the effects of self-care may depend very heavily on the way self-care children spend their time and on whether parents are supervising them *in absentia*. Steinberg's own studies of 10–16-year-olds revealed that self-care children who were allowed to "hang out" after school were likely to describe themselves as willing to engage in delinquent or antisocial conduct with peers. By contrast, self-care children who came home after school and whose parents *monitored them from a distance* (by phoning them or by assigning chores to be completed) were no more susceptible to deviant peer influences than children supervised at home by a parent. Moreover, Stein-

berg found that authoritative parenting greatly increased latchkey children's resistance to undesirable peer influences, even when these children are not closely monitored in the afternoon and when peer pressure for deviant conduct is reasonably strong (see also Galambos & Maggs, 1991).

So it appears that there are steps that working parents can take to minimize some of the potential risks of leaving schoolchildren to care for themselves — namely, requiring them to go home after school, supervising them *in absentia* to ensure that they do, and parenting them in an authoritative manner. Indeed, authoritative parenting may be the most important factor of all, for the social responsibility and *self*-control that are fostered by this warm but demanding parental style were often sufficient to buffer children against deviant peer pressure, even when they were not monitored from afar by an adult. Nevertheless, we should not take these results as a ringing endorsement of self-care arrangements, for there are a multitude of potential risks that Steinberg's results do not address — risks that can be identified only by future research.[5] In the meantime we might encourage politicians and community leaders to provide affordable after-school-care alternatives, thereby preventing children of working mothers from having to face the risks of being alone in the afternoon and early evening.

When Parenting Breaks Down: The Problem of Child Abuse

Family relationships can be our greatest source of nurturance and support, but they can also be a powerful source of anguish. Nowhere is this more obvious than in cases of **child abuse**. Every day, thousands of infants, children, and adolescents are burned, bruised, beaten, starved, suffocated,

---

[5]As examples of these "other risks," researchers have found repeatedly that as many as one out of six residential fires involved an unattended child (Baker & Waller, 1989), and self-care children appear to be more vulnerable to sexual abuse and to harm at the hands of burglars as well (Zigler & Finn Stevenson, 1993).

sexually molested, or otherwise mistreated by their caregivers. Other children may not be targets of these physical forms of abuse but are victims of such *psychological abuse* as being rejected, ridiculed, or even terrorized by their parents (Hart & Brassard, 1987). Still others are *neglected* and deprived of the basic care and stimulation that they need to develop normally. Although instances of severe battering are the most visible forms of child abuse and are certainly horrible, many investigators now believe that strong and recurrent psychological abuse and neglect may prove to be even more harmful to children in the long run (Emery, 1989; Hart & Brassard, 1987).

Child abuse is a very serious problem. In 1987 over 1.9 *million* reports of child maltreatment of all sorts were filed in the United States (American Humane Association, 1989), and, in one survey of two-parent families, Murray Straus and Richard Gelles (1986) found that almost 11% of the children had been kicked, bitten, punched, beaten up, hit with an object, or threatened with a knife or a gun by their parents in the past year.[6] Moreover, a random survey of women living in one major U.S. city revealed that 2.5% had been coerced into oral, anal, or genital intercourse by their father, stepfather, or brother before age 18 (Russell, 1983, as cited by Emery, 1989). It is not a pretty picture, is it? And, since many cases of child abuse and neglect are never detected or reported, these figures may represent only the tip of the iceberg.

Clearly, there are many factors that contribute to a problem as widespread as child abuse. To date, researchers have attempted to understand this complex phenomenon by seeking answers for three basic questions: (1) Who are the abusers? (2) Whom are they likely to abuse? (3) Under what circumstances is abuse most likely to occur?

Who Are the Abusers?

Anyone examining a badly beaten child might immediately suspect that the abuser must be psycho-

logically deranged. But, strange as it may seem, only about one child abuser in ten appears to have a severe mental illness (Kempe & Kempe, 1978). Although the incidence of child abuse is higher in low-SES than in high-SES families, the fact is that people who abuse their children come from all races, ethnic groups, and social classes, and many of them appear to be rather typical, loving parents—except for their tendency to become extremely irritated with their children and to do things they will later regret (Trickett et al., 1991; U.S. Department of Health and Human Services, 1988).

Yet there are differences between parents who abuse their children and those who do not. For example, a fairly high proportion of child abusers were abused, neglected, or unloved by their own parents (Belsky, 1980; Egeland, Jacobvitz, & Sroufe, 1988). Moreover, abusive and nonabusive mothers clearly differ in their reactions to young children. Byron Egeland (1979; Egeland, Sroufe, & Erickson, 1983) found that, when infants cry to communicate needs such as hunger, nonabusive mothers treated these cries as signs of discomfort (correct interpretation), whereas abusive mothers often inferred that the baby was somehow criticizing or rejecting them! Indeed, many abusive parents reach a point where even a baby's smiles are unpleasantly arousing, and they are much less inclined than nonabusive parents to interact with a smiling baby (Frodi & Lamb, 1980). Finally, abusive parents clearly favor authoritarian control and power-assertive forms of discipline over authoritative and inductive techniques (which they view as much less effective). Although abusive parents do not report using physical punishment any more often than nonabusive parents do, they do admit to relying heavily on the most severely punitive tactics—actions such as yanking children's hair, hitting them in the face, or striking them with objects (Trickett & Susman, 1988). And, as we noted earlier in the chapter, use of these arbitrary, high-intensity tactics often elicits *defiance* from young children rather than the compliance their parents had hoped for (Crockenberg & Litman, 1990).

In sum, abusive parents seem to find caregiving more stressful, more ego threatening, and far less enjoyable than nonabusive parents do (Bugental, Blue, & Cruzcosa, 1989; Trickett & Susman, 1988).

---

[6]When Straus and Gelles omitted the act of hitting a child with an object (a practice that many parents believe to be an appropriate form of discipline), the percentage of children who had been severely abused dropped to about 2%.

Still, there are many *nonabusive* parents who display all these characteristics, and it has been very difficult to specify *in advance* exactly who will become a child abuser (Trickett et al., 1991).

Who Is Abused?

Interestingly, abusive parents often single out only one child in the family as a target, which implies that some children may bring out the worst in their parents (Gil, 1970). No one is suggesting that children are to *blame* for this abuse, but some children do appear to be more at risk than others. For example, infants who are emotionally unresponsive, hyperactive, irritable, or ill are far more likely to be abused than quiet, healthy, and responsive babies who are easy to care for (Egeland & Sroufe, 1981; Sherrod et al., 1984). Similarly, defiant children may elicit stronger and stronger forms of physical punishment from their caregivers until the line between spanking and abuse is crossed (Parke & Lewis, 1981). Yet it is important to emphasize that many "difficult" children are never abused, whereas many cheerful and seemingly easygoing children will be mistreated. Just as caregiver characteristics cannot fully predict or explain why abuse occurs, neither can characteristics of children, although the combination of a high-risk parent and a high-risk child spells trouble (see Bugental et al., 1989).

But even a match of high-risk children and caregivers does not invariably result in child abuse. In fact, recent research indicates that high-risk parents who were rejected, mistreated, or otherwise emotionally deprived as children are likely to become angry, punitive, or abusive parents *only* if they are currently experiencing other kinds of social or environmental stress (Crockenberg, 1987; Egeland et al., 1988). Let's now consider some of the social and contextual factors that can contribute to child abuse.

Social-Situational Triggers: The Ecology of Child Abuse

Child abuse is most likely to occur in families under stress. Consider, for example, that battered children often come from large families in which overburdened caregivers have many small children to attend to (Light, 1973). The probability of abuse under these stressful circumstances is further compounded if the mother is relatively young, is poorly educated, and receives little child-rearing assistance from the father, from a friend or relative, or from some other member of her social network (Crockenberg, 1987; Egeland et al., 1983, 1988). Other significant life changes (such as the death of a family member, the loss of a job, or a move to a new home) can disrupt social and emotional relationships within a family and thereby contribute to neglectful or abusive parenting (Bronfenbrenner, 1986; McLoyd, 1989). Finally, children are much more likely to be abused or neglected if their parents abuse alcohol or drugs, are experiencing legal problems, or are unhappily married (Belsky, 1980; Egeland et al., 1988; Emery, 1989).

Of course, families are embedded in a broader social context (for example, a neighborhood, a community, and a culture) that may well affect a child's chances of being abused. Some areas can be labeled **"high risk" neighborhoods** because they have much higher rates of child abuse than other neighborhoods that are demographically and socioeconomically alike. What are these high-risk areas like? According to James Garbarino and Deborah Sherman (1980), they tend to be deteriorating neighborhoods—physically unattractive and socially impoverished settings in which families not only are struggling financially but also are isolated from formal and informal support systems (for example, friends, relatives, the church, services such as scouting or recreation centers, and a sense of "community"). Although the quality of a neighborhood will depend, in part, on the people who live there, let's also note that the actions of government and industry can have an effect. For example, a decision to rezone a low-risk area or to locate a highway there can lead to a destruction of play areas, declining property values, a loss of pride in the neighborhood, and the eventual isolation of families from friends, community services (which may no longer exist), and other bases of social support. James Garbarino (1982) is one of many theorists who believe that large numbers of American children are likely to be mistreated because of political or economic decisions that have undermined the health and stability of low-risk, family-oriented neighborhoods.

Other researchers have argued that child abuse is rampant in the United States because people in this society (1) have a permissive attitude about violence and (2) generally sanction the use of physical punishment as a means of controlling children's behavior. Indeed, there may be some truth to these assertions, for cross-cultural studies reveal that children are rarely abused in societies that discourage the use of physical punishment (see Belsky, 1980; Hart & Brassard, 1987).

In sum, child abuse is a very complex phenomenon that has many causes and contributing factors. Clearly we have come a long way from those early theories that focused almost exclusively on the abusive parent (and his or her personality) as the primary contributor to abuse.

Long-Term Consequences of Abuse and Neglect

Child abuse and neglect often have rather grave long-term consequences. Recall that abusive mothers tend to misinterpret the causes of their infants' distress and are often unpleasantly aroused by even positive social signals such as a baby's smile. Indeed, some of these same characteristics can already be observed in abused infants and toddlers. In one study of day-care children, Mary Main and Carol George (1985) observed the reactions of abused and nonabused 1- to 3-year-olds to the fussing and crying of peers. As shown in Figure 13-6, nonabused toddlers typically reacted to a peer's distress by attending carefully to the other child and/or by displaying concern. By contrast, not one abused toddler showed any concern in response to the distress of an agemate. Instead, the abused toddlers were likely to emit disturbing patterns of behavior, often becoming angry at this fussing and then *physically attacking* the crying child. Even after spending significant amounts of time with nonabusive day-care providers, abused preschoolers are still more likely than their nonabused classmates to respond inappropriately and aggressively to a distressed peer (Klimes-Dougan & Kistner, 1990). So it seems that abused children are likely to be abusive companions who have apparently learned from their own experiences at home that distress signals are particularly irritating to others and will often elicit angry re-

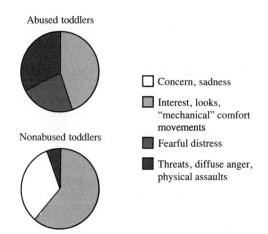

FIGURE 13-6   Responses to the distress of peers observed in abused and nonabused toddlers in the day-care setting. (The figures show the mean proportion of responses falling in each category for the nine abused and nine nonabused toddlers.) (Adapted from M. Main & C. George, "Responses of Abused and Disadvantaged Toddlers to Distress in Agemates: A Study in the Day-Care Setting." *Developmental Psychology*, 1985, *21*, 407–412. Copyright © 1985 by the American Psychological Association. Reprinted by permission.)

sponses rather than displays of sympathy and compassion.[7] And, given this early learning history, we should hardly be surprised to find that abused preschoolers and grade-school children tend to be highly aggressive youngsters who are not very successful in their interactions with playmates and are often rejected by their peers (Downey & Walker, 1989; Haskett & Kistner, 1991; Trickett et al., 1991).

Abused and neglected youngsters also tend to be fearful, anxious, depressed, and low in self-esteem (Emery, 1989; Trickett et al., 1991). Adults who were *sexually abused* in childhood show all of these characteristics and also are likely to feel ashamed, stigmatized, and distrustful of other people (Brassard & McNeill, 1987; Haugaard & Reppucci, 1988). Not surprisingly, they are often maladjusted themselves and are prone to such antisocial or self-destructive acts as running away from home, becoming sexually promiscuous, attempting or committing suicide,

---

[7]Interestingly, children of battered women display roughly the same behavioral characteristics as abused children do (Holden & Ritchie, 1991), which suggests that both witnessing violence and experiencing violence may teach similar lessons about other people and the character of social interactions.

and abusing drugs (Artenstein, 1990; Haugaard & Reppucci, 1988).

The good news is that many abused or neglected youngsters are remarkably resilient, especially if they are able to establish a warm, secure, and supportive relationship with a nonabusive parent, a grandparent, or some other member of the family (Egeland et al., 1988; Egeland & Sroufe, 1981). And, even though abused children are at risk of becoming abusive parents, the majority of these maltreated individuals do *not* abuse their own children (Kaufman & Zigler, 1987; Widom, 1989). Abused parents who succeed at breaking this cycle of abuse are more likely than those who do not to (1) have received emotional support from a nonabusive adult during childhood, (2) have participated in therapy at some point in their lives, and (3) have a nonabusive, satisfying relationship with their spouse (Egeland et al., 1988).

Despite our better understanding of the causes of child abuse and our observations that its often severe consequences can be lessened or even overcome, we are still a long way from solving the problem. Rather than conclude on that depressing note, let's consider some of the methods that have been used to assist the abused child and his or her abusers.

How Do We Solve the Problem?

A number of strategies have been devised in an attempt to prevent or control the problem of child abuse. Let's look first at preventive measures.

PREVENTING ABUSE

To prevent child maltreatment before it begins, we must be able to identify high-risk families—a task that is greatly aided by the kinds of studies we have reviewed. For example, extremely irritable or unresponsive babies who are at risk of alienating their caregivers can be identified through neonatal assessment programs, and their parents can be taught methods to make these infants respond more favorably to their caregiving. Indeed, we have already seen that Brazelton testing and training programs (Box 5-1) are effective methods of preventing the "miscommunications" between infants and caregivers that can contribute to child abuse.

Other efforts to prevent abuse have been targeted directly at high-risk parents. Steven Schinke and his associates (1986), for example, worked with one high-risk group of mothers—single teenagers who were under a great deal of stress. The goal was to teach a wide range of stress-management skills: relaxation techniques, problem-solving strategies, communication skills that would enable mothers to request help and to refuse unreasonable demands, and even techniques for building stronger social support networks. Three months later, mothers who had received the training outperformed those in a control group on several measures. They had improved their problem-solving skills, had established stronger support networks, now enjoyed higher self-esteem, and were more confident about their parenting skills. It seems likely that high-risk parents who have learned effective techniques for coping with stress will be better able to deal with the sometimes-overwhelming challenges they face without resorting to violence. These parents can also benefit from programs to teach them effective child-management skills (Wolfe et al., 1988).

The demonstrated success of these and other similar interventions has led child-welfare agencies in several states to develop family support and education programs designed to prevent child abuse (Zigler & Finn Stevenson, 1993). For example, the **Ounce of Prevention program**, a collaborative effort of the Illinois Department of Children and Family Services and the Pittway Corporation, attempts to head off child abuse by offering parent-education classes that teach effective child-management techniques and by providing such support services (through churches, medical clinics, and schools) as child-care programs, medical assistance, and job training. Other similar family support systems, which are regularly evaluated to ensure that they are meeting families' needs, are now available in Arkansas, Iowa, Oregon, and Vermont (Zigler & Finn Stevenson, 1993).

CONTROLLING ABUSE

How do we deal with parents who are already abusive? It is clear that a few visits from a social worker are unlikely to solve the problem (Oates, 1986). Kempe and Kempe (1978) report that a fair percentage of abusive parents will stop physically maltreating their children if they can be persuaded to use certain services, such as 24-hour "hotlines" or crisis nurseries, that will enable them to discuss their hostile feelings with a volunteer or to get away from their children for a few hours when they are about to lose control. However, these are only stopgap measures that will probably not work for long unless the abuser also takes advantage of other services—such as **Parents Anonymous** or family therapy—that are designed to help the caregiver understand his or her problem while providing the emotional support that an abusive parent so often lacks.[8]

Other approaches to the problem include media campaigns in newspapers and magazines and on television that are designed to educate the public about child abuse, to publicize formal support systems (for example, Parents Anonymous or crisis nurseries) available to abusive parents, and to teach effective, nonpunitive child-management techniques that could minimize family conflict and decrease the likelihood of abuse (Rosenberg & Reppucci, 1985).

In recent years, another control tactic has become more common—one that involves arresting and prosecuting parents for acts of violence that would be considered criminal assault if they occurred between strangers (Emery, 1989). Yet, child abuse is often difficult to prove (beyond the reasonable doubt required for criminal conviction), and American courts are quite hesitant to take children from abusive parents, even when there is reason to suspect a child has been repeatedly abused. One reason for this reluctant attitude is that, historically, children have been treated as their parents' possessions (Hart & Brassard, 1987). Another is that abused children and their parents are often attached to each other, so that neither the abusive adult nor the battered child wishes to be separated. However, it is

4 out of 5 convicts were abused children.

In the United States, an average of 80% of our prisoners were abused children. That is why we are working so hard to help these children today, before

they develop into a threat to others tomorrow.

With your support, we can have a full staff of trained people available 24 hours a day. Abused

children desperately need us. Please let us be there to help. Write for our free brochure, or send in your tax-deductible donation today.

San Francisco Child Abuse Council, Inc.
4093 24th Street, San Francisco, CA 94114

PHOTO 13-8 **Many programs attempt to prevent and control the problem of child abuse.**

essential that we carefully weigh the child's rights against the rights and wishes of parents, for some abusive adults (perhaps as many as 2000 per year in the United States) will go as far as to kill their children, regardless of the counseling they receive (American Humane Association, 1989; Hart, 1991).

Although some people may disagree, developmentalists the world over have argued that no caregiver has the right to abuse a child (Hart, 1991). And, in cases of severe abuse or neglect, developmentalists generally agree that our first priority must be to provide for the health and safety of mistreated children—even if that means terminating the abusers' legal rights of parenthood and placing their children in foster care or adoptive homes. The challenge we now face is to become much more successful at preventing and controlling child abuse so that the difficult decision of whether to separate children from their parents will need to be made less frequently than it is at present.

[8]Fortunately, these services are often free. Chapters of Parents Anonymous are now located in many cities and towns in the United States (for the location of a nearby chapter, consult a telephone directory or write to Parents Anonymous, 6733 South Sepulveda Blvd., Suite 270, Los Angeles, CA 90045). In addition, many cities and counties provide free family therapy to abusive parents. Often the therapists are lay volunteers who have been trained to serve in this capacity.

Reflections on the Family

If you do not yet fully appreciate the awesome significance of the family for children and adolescents, reflect for a moment on how very badly things can go when the family does not fulfill its important functions. Start with a neglected infant who not only may fail to thrive physically (see Chapter 5) but does not experience anything faintly resembling warm, sensitive, and responsive parenting. How is this child to form the secure attachments that serve as foundations for later social and intellectual competencies? Or think about the child whose parents are downright hostile—either providing no guidance at all or hemming the child in with rules and punishing his every misstep. How is this child to learn how to care about other people, to become appropriately autonomous, and to fit into society?

You get the picture; it is easy to illustrate the grave importance of families by accentuating the negative. Fortunately, most of us have fared much better than this, even though we do not always acknowledge just how significant our families may have been in underwriting our developmental successes. So think about what you have learned in this chapter the next time you gather with the closest members of your own family. Chances are you will understand why adults who are asked to reflect on what is really important in their lives almost invariably speak of their families (Whitbourne, 1986). Although we change and our families change as we get older, it seems that we never cease to affect, or to be affected by, those folks we call "family."

Summary

The family is the primary agent of socialization—the setting in which children begin to acquire the beliefs, attitudes, values, and behaviors considered appropriate in their society. Basic goals of parenting in all societies include (1) ensuring the child's survival, (2) preparing the child for economic self-sufficiency, and (3) encouraging the child to maximize other cultural values such as morality, religion, and achievement.

Whether nuclear or extended in form, families are best viewed as changing social systems embedded in larger social systems that are also changing. Social trends affecting family life today include greater numbers of single adults, later marriages, a decline in childbearing, more female participation in the work force, and more divorces, single-parent families, and remarriages.

The birth of a child is a highly significant event that alters the behavior of both parents and may change the character of their marital relationship. The transition to parenthood tends to be less severe or disruptive when parents are older and have been married for some time before the child is conceived. Warm, responsive parenting during infancy contributes to the establishment of secure parent/child attachments and promotes the child's exploratory competence and intellectual growth. Although fathers interact less with their very young infants than mothers do, they soon become more involved with their children and begin to play an important role in the child's life. The quality of the marital relationship is very important. Unhappily married couples often establish shaky emotional relations with their children, whereas parents who are happily married provide the mutual support and encouragement that usually enable them to establish good relations with their infants—even those who require special care or are temperamentally difficult.

Parents differ along two broad dimensions—warmth/hostility and permissiveness/restrictiveness (or control)—that, when considered together, yield four styles of parenting. Generally speaking, warm and restrictive (that is, authoritative) parents who appeal to reason in order to enforce their demands are likely to raise highly competent, well-adjusted children. Outcomes of other parenting styles are not as favorable; indeed, children of hostile and permissive (that is, uninvolved) parents are often deficient in all aspects of psychological functioning.

Parents from different cultures and social classes have different values, concerns, and outlooks on life, which influence their child-rearing strategies. Lower- and working-class parents, who tend to be more punitive and authoritarian than their middle-class counterparts, stress obedience, respect, neatness, cleanliness, and avoidance of trouble — precisely the attributes their children will need to succeed in a blue-collar economy. By contrast, middle-class parents are more likely to stress independence, creativity, ambition, and self-control — the attributes that their children will need to succeed in business or a profession. Thus, parents from all socioeconomic strata (and from different cultures) emphasize the characteristics that contribute to *success as they know it*, and it is inappropriate to conclude that one particular style of parenting is somehow "better" or more competent than all others.

Parent/child relationships are renegotiated as adolescents seek to become more autonomous. Although family conflict escalates during this period, adolescents are likely to become appropriately autonomous if their parents willingly grant them more freedom, explain the rules and restrictions that they do impose, and continue to be loving and supportive guides.

Although sibling rivalries are a normal aspect of family life that may begin as soon as a younger sibling arrives, there is a positive side to having siblings. Siblings are typically viewed as intimate associates who can be counted on for support. Older sibs frequently serve as attachment objects, models, and teachers for their younger siblings, and they often profit themselves from the instruction and guidance they provide. Yet, sibling relationships are not essential for normal development, and only children are just as socially, emotionally, and intellectually competent (or slightly more so), on average, as children with siblings are.

Divorce represents a drastic change in family life that is stressful and unsettling for children and their parents. Children's initial reactions often include anger, fear, depression, and guilt — feelings that may last more than a year. The emotional upheaval that follows a divorce may influence the parent/child relationship. Children often become cranky, disobedient, or otherwise difficult, while the custodial parent may suddenly become more punitive and controlling. The stresses resulting from a divorce and this new coercive lifestyle often affect the child's peer relations and schoolwork. But, in the long run, children of divorce are usually better adjusted than those who remain in conflict-ridden two-parent families. Girls adjust better than boys to life in a single-parent, mother-headed home, whereas, after a period of initial disruption in which new roles are ironed out, boys seem to fare better than girls in reconstituted families. Among the factors that help children to make positive adjustments to divorce are adequate financial and emotional support from the noncustodial parent, additional social support (from friends, relatives, and the community) for custodial parents and their children, and a minimum of additional stressors surrounding the divorce itself.

As long as mothers are satisfied in their working role and are committed to being a parent, their employment does not seem to disrupt children's social and emotional development. In fact, children of working mothers are often found to be more independent and more sociable and to have less stereotyped views of men and women than children whose mothers are not employed. Although middle-class boys of working mothers do score somewhat lower in intelligence and academic achievement than boys whose mothers are not employed, it seems that these deficits are limited to boys whose working parents fail to carefully monitor their daily activities. Parental monitoring could be a problem with latchkey children — those who care for themselves after school. But, despite great public concern, the limited evidence available indicates that self-care youngsters show few if any developmental deficiencies if they are required to come right home after school and are monitored from a distance by their parents.

There are many contributors to the very serious problem of child abuse. Abusers come from all social strata and walks of life, although many of them were themselves abused as children. Defiant children and those who are hyperactive, irritable, emotionally unresponsive, or ill are more vulnerable to abuse than happy, healthy children who are easy to care for. Child abuse is more likely in families under social, financial, or environmental stress. Programs designed to assist abused children and their abusive parents have achieved some success. However, we are still a long way from solving the problem.

References

ABRAMOVITCH, R., CORTER, C., & PEPLER, D. J. (1980). Observations of mixed-sex sibling dyads. *Child Development, 51,* 1268–1271.

ABRAMOVITCH, R., CORTER, C., PEPLER, D. J., & STANHOPE, L. (1986). Sibling and peer interaction: A final follow-up and a comparison. *Child Development, 57,* 217–229.

AINSWORTH, M. D. S. (1979). Attachment as related to mother-infant interaction. In J. S. Rosenblatt, R. A. Hinde, C. Beer, & M. Busnel (Eds.), *Advances in the study of behavior* (Vol. 9). New York: Academic Press.

AL AWAD, A. M. H., & SONUGA-BARKE, E. J. S. (1992). Childhood problems in a Sudanese city: A comparison of extended and nuclear families. *Child Development, 63,* 906–914.

ALLISON, P. D., & FURSTENBERG, F. F., JR. (1989). How marital dissolution affects children: Variations by age and sex. *Developmental Psychology, 25,* 540–549.

AMERICAN HUMANE ASSOCIATION (1989). *Highlights of official aggregate child neglect and abuse reporting, 1987.* Denver: Author.

ANDERSON, E. R., HETHERINGTON, E. M., & CLINGEMPEEL, W. G. (1989). Transformations in family relations at puberty: Effects of family conflict. *Journal of Early Adolescence, 9,* 310–314.

ANDERSON, K. E., LYTTON, H., & ROMNEY, D. M. (1986). Mothers' interactions with normal and conduct-disordered boys: Who affects whom? *Developmental Psychology, 22,* 604–609.

ARTENSTEIN, J. (1990). *Runaways in their own words: Kids talking about living on the street.* New York: Tor Books.

BAKER, S., & WALLER, A. (1989). *Childhood injury: State-by-state mortality facts.* Washington, DC: National Maternal and Child Health Clearinghouse.

BALDWIN, D. V., & SKINNER, M. L. (1989). Structural model for antisocial behavior: Generalization to single-mother families. *Developmental Psychology, 25,* 45–50.

BALSWICK, J. O., & MACRIDES, C. (1975). Parental stimulus for adolescent rebellion. *Adolescence, 10,* 253–266.

BARNETT, R. C., & BARUCH, G. K. (1987). Determinants of father's participation in family work. *Journal of Marriage and the Family, 49,* 29–40.

BARRY, H., CHILD, I. L., & BACON, M. K. (1959). The relation of child training to subsistence economy. *American Anthropologist, 61,* 51–63.

BASKETT, L. M. (1984). Ordinal position differences in children's family interactions. *Developmental Psychology, 20,* 1026–1031.

BASKETT, L. M. (1985). Sibling status effects: Adult expectations. *Developmental Psychology, 21,* 441–445.

BASKETT, L. M., & JOHNSON, S. M. (1982). The young child's interaction with parents versus siblings: A behavioral analysis. *Child Development, 53,* 643–650.

BAUMRIND, D. (1967). Child care practices anteceding three patterns of preschool behavior. *Genetic Psychology Monographs, 75,* 43–88.

BAUMRIND, D. (1971). Current patterns of parental authority. *Developmental Psychology Monographs, 4*(1, Part 2).

BAUMRIND, D. (1977, March). *Socialization determinants of personal agency.* Paper presented at the biennial meeting of the Society for Research in Child Development, New Orleans.

BAUMRIND, D. (1983). Rejoinder to Lewis's reinterpretation of parental firm control effects: Are authoritative families really harmonious? *Psychological Bulletin, 94,* 132–142.

BAUMRIND, D. (1989, April). *Sex-differentiated socialization effects in childhood and adolescence in divorced and intact families.* Paper presented at the meeting of the Society for Research in Child Development, Kansas City, MO.

BAUMRIND, D. (1991). Effective parenting during the early adolescent transition. In P. A. Cowan & E. M. Hetherington (Eds.), *Family transitions.* Hillsdale, NJ: Erlbaum.

BECKER, W. C. (1964). Consequences of different kinds of parental discipline. In M. L. Hoffman & L. W. Hoffman (Eds.), *Review of child development research* (Vol. 1). New York: Russell Sage Foundation.

BELSKY, J. (1980). Child maltreatment: An ecological integration. *American Psychologist, 35,* 320–335.

BELSKY, J. (1981). Early human experience: A family perspective. *Developmental Psychology, 17,* 3–23.

BELSKY, J., GARDUQUE, L., & HRNCIR, E. (1984). Assessing performance, competence, and executive capacity in infant play: Relations to home environment and security of attachment. *Developmental Psychology, 20,* 406–417.

BELSKY, J., GILSTRAP, B., & ROVINE, M. (1984). The Pennsylvania infant and family development project: I. Stability and change in mother-infant and father-infant interaction in a family setting at one, three, and nine months. *Child Development, 55,* 692–705.

BELSKY, J., & ISABELLA, R. A. (1985). Marital and parent-child relationships in family of origin and marital change following the birth of a baby: A retrospective analysis. *Child Development, 56,* 342–349.

BELSKY, J., LANG, M. E., & ROVINE, M. (1985). Stability and change in marriage across the transition to parenthood: A second study. *Journal of Marriage and the Family, 47,* 855–865.

BERNDT, T. J., & BULLEIT, T. N. (1985). Effects of sibling relationships on preschoolers' behavior at home and at school. *Developmental Psychology, 21,* 761–767.

BERRY, J. W. (1967). Independence and conformity in subsistence-level societies. *Journal of Personality and Social Psychology, 7,* 415–418.

BLOCK, J. H., BLOCK, J., & GJERDE, P. F. (1986). The personality of children prior to divorce: A prospective study. *Child Development, 57,* 827–840.

BLOCK, J. H., BLOCK, J., & GJERDE, P. F. (1988). Parental functioning and the home environment of families of divorce: Prospective and current analyses. *Journal of the American Academy of Child and Adolescent Psychiatry, 27,* 207–213.

BRADLEY, R. H., CALDWELL, B. M., & ELARDO, R. (1979). Home environment and cognitive development in the first 2 years: A cross-lagged panel analysis. *Developmental Psychology, 15,* 246–250.

BRADLEY, R. H., CALDWELL, B. M., ROCK, S. L., RAMEY, C. T., BARNARD, K. E., GRAY, C., HAMMOND, M. A., MITCHELL, S., GOTTFRIED, A. W., SIEGEL, L., & JOHNSON, D. L. (1989). Home environment and cognitive development in the first 3 years of life: A collaborative study involving six sites and three ethnic groups in North America. *Developmental Psychology, 25,* 217–235.

BRAND, E., CLINGEMPEEL, W. G., & BOWEN-WOODWARD, K. (1988). Family relationships and children's psychological adjustment in stepmother and stepfather families: Findings and conclusions from the Philadelphia Stepfamily Research Project. In E. M. Hetherington & J. D. Arasteh (Eds.), *Impact of divorce, single-parenting, and stepparenting on children.* Hillsdale, NJ: Erlbaum.

BRASSARD, M. R., & McNEILL, L. E. (1987). Child sexual abuse. In M. R. Brassard, R. Germain, & S. Hart (Eds.), *Psychological maltreatment of children and youth.* New York: Pergamon Press.

BRAY, J. H. (1988). Children's development during early remarriage. In E. M. Hetherington & J. D. Arasteh (Eds.), *Impact of divorce, single-parenting, and stepparenting on children.* Hillsdale, NJ: Erlbaum.

BRAZELTON, T. B. (1979). Behavioral competence of the newborn infant. *Seminars in Perinatology, 3,* 35–44.

BRISTOL, M. M., GALLAGHER, J. J., & SCHOPLER, E. (1988). Mothers and fathers of young developmentally disabled and nondisabled boys: Adaptation and spousal support. *Developmental Psychology, 24,* 441–445.

BRODY, G. H., NEUBAUM, E., & FOREHAND, R. (1988). Serial marriage: A heuristic analysis of an emerging family form. *Psychological Bulletin, 103,* 211–222.

BRODY, G. H., & SHAFFER, D. R. (1982). Contributions of parents and peers to children's moral socialization. *Developmental Review, 2,* 31–75.

BRODY, G. H., STONEMAN, Z., & BURKE, M. (1987). Child temperaments, maternal differential behavior, and sibling relationships. *Developmental Psychology, 23,* 354–362.

BRODY, G. H., STONEMAN, Z., & MacKINNON, C. E. (1982). Role asymmetries in interactions among school-aged children, their younger siblings, and their friends. *Child Development, 53,* 1364–1370.

BRODY, G. H., STONEMAN, Z., McCOY, J. K., & FOREHAND, R. (1992). Contemporaneous and longitudinal associations of sibling conflict with family relationship assessments and family discussions about sibling problems. *Child Development, 63,* 391–400.

BRONFENBRENNER, U. (1986). Ecology of the family as a context for human development: Research perspectives. *Developmental Psychology, 22,* 723–742.

BRONFENBRENNER, U. (1989). Ecological systems theory. In R. Vasta (Ed.), *Annals of child development.* Vol. 6: *Theories of child development: Revised formulations and current issues.* Greenwich, CT: JAI Press.

BROOKS-GUNN, J., & ZAHAYKEVICH, M. (1989). Parent-daughter relationships in early adolescence: A developmental perspective. In K. Kreppner & R. M. Lerner (Eds.), *Family systems and life-span development.* Hillsdale, NJ: Erlbaum.

BUCHANAN, C. M., MACCOBY, E. E., & DORNBUSCH, S. M. (1991). Caught between parents: Adolescents' experiences in divorced homes. *Child Development, 62,* 1008–1029.

BUEHLER, C. A., HOGAN, M. J., ROBINSON, B. E., & LEVY, R. J. (1986). The parental divorce transition: Divorce-related stressors and well-being. *Journal of Divorce, 9,* 61–81.

BUGENTAL, D. B., BLUE, J., & CRUZCOSA, M. (1989). Perceived control over caregiving outcomes: Implications for child abuse. *Developmental Psychology, 25,* 532–539.

BUHRMESTER, D., & FURMAN, W. (1990). Perceptions of sibling relationships during middle childhood and adolescence. *Child Development, 61,* 1387–1398.

CAMARA, K. A., & RESNICK, G. (1988). Interparental conflict and cooperation: Factors moderating children's postdivorce adjustment. In E. M. Hetherington & J. D. Arasteh (Eds.), *Impact of divorce, single-parenting, and stepparenting on children.* Hillsdale, NJ: Erlbaum.

CAPALDI, D. M., & PATTERSON, G. R. (1991). Relation of parental transitions to boys' adjustment problems: I. A linear hypothesis. II. Mothers at risk for transition and unskilled parenting. *Developmental Psychology, 27,* 489–504.

CASSIDY, J. (1986). The ability to negotiate the environment: An aspect of infant competence as related to quality of attachment. *Child Development, 57,* 331–337.

CLARKE-STEWART, K. A. (1989). Infant day care: Maligned or malignant? *American Psychologist, 44,* 266–273.

CLINGEMPEEL, W. G., IEVOLI, R., & BRAND, E. (1984). Structural complexity and the quality of stepparent-stepchild relationships. *Family Processes, 23,* 547–560.

CLINGEMPEEL, W. G., & SEGAL, S. (1986). Stepparent-stepchild relationships and the psychological adjustment of children in stepmother and stepfather families. *Child Development, 57,* 474–484.

COLE, C., & RODMAN, H. (1987). When school-age children care for themselves: Issues for family life educators and parents. *Family Relations, 26,* 92–96.

COLON, P. A., & COLON, A. R. (1989). The health of America's children. In F. J. Macchiarola & A. Gartner (Eds.), *Caring for America's children.* New York: Academy of Political Science.

CONGER, R. D., CONGER, K. J., ELDER, G. H., JR., LORENZ, F. O., SIMONS, R. L., & WHITBECK, L. B. (1992). A family process model of economic hardship and adjustment of early adolescent boys. *Child Development, 63,* 526–541.

CONGER, R. D., McCARTY, J. A., YANG, R. K., LAHEY, B. B., & KROPP, J. (1984). Perception of child, child-rearing values, and emotional distress as mediating links between environmental stressors and observed maternal behavior. *Child Development, 55,* 2234–2247.

COWAN, C. P., & COWAN, P. A. (1987). A preventive intervention for couples becoming parents. In C. F. Z. Boukydis (Ed.), *Research on support for parents and infants in the postnatal period.* New York: Ablex.

COX, M. J., OWEN, M. T., HENDERSON, V. K., & MARGAND, N. A. (1992). Prediction of infant-father and infant-mother attachment. *Developmental Psychology, 28,* 474–483.

COX, M. J., OWEN, M. T., LEWIS, J. M., & HENDERSON, V. K. (1989). Marriage, adult adjustment, and early parenting. *Child Development, 60,* 1015–1024.

CRNIC, K. A., GREENBERG, M. T., RAGOZIN, A. S., ROBINSON, N. M., & BASHAM, R. B. (1983). Effects of stress and social support on mothers and premature and full-term infants. *Child Development, 54,* 209–217.

CROCKENBERG, S. (1987). Predictors and correlates of anger toward and punitive control of toddlers by adolescent mothers. *Child Development, 58,* 964–975.

CROCKENBERG, S., & LITMAN, C. (1990). Autonomy as competence in 2-year-olds: Maternal correlates of child defiance, compliance, and self-assertion. *Developmental Psychology, 26,* 961–971.

CROCKENBERG, S., & LITMAN, C. (1991). Effects of maternal employment on maternal and two-year-old child behavior. *Child Development, 62,* 930–953.

CROOK, T., RASKIN, A., & ELIOT, J. (1981). Parent-child relationships and adult depression. *Child Development, 52,* 950–957.

CROUTER, A. C., MacDERMID, S. M., McHALE, S. M., & PERRY-JENKINS, M. (1990). Parental monitoring and perceptions of children's school performance and conduct in dual- and single-career families. *Developmental Psychology, 26,* 649–657.

DEMO, D. H., & ACOCK, A. C. (1988). The impact of divorce on children. *Journal of Marriage and the Family, 50,* 619–648.

DOHERTY, W. J., & NEEDLE, R. H. (1991). Psychological adjustment and substance abuse among adolescents before and after a parental divorce. *Child Development, 62,* 328–337.

DORNBUSCH, S. M., CARLSMITH, J. M., BUSHWALL, S. J., RITTER, P. L., LEIDERMAN, P. H., HASTORF, A. H., & GROSS, R. T. (1985). Single parents, extended households, and the control of adolescents. *Child Development, 56,* 326–341.

DORNBUSCH, S. M., RITTER, P. L., LEIDERMAN, P. H., ROBERTS, D. F., & FRALEIGH, M. J. (1987). The relation of parenting style to adolescent school performance. *Child Development, 58,* 1244–1257.

DOWNEY, G., & WALKER, E. (1989). Social cognition and adjustment in children at risk for psychopathology. *Developmental Psychology, 25,* 835–845.

DUNN, J. (1984). Sibling studies and the developmental impact of critical incidents. In P. B. Baltes & O. G. Brim, Jr. (Eds.), *Life-span development and behavior* (Vol. 6). Orlando, FL: Academic Press.

DUNN, J., & KENDRICK, C. (1982). *Siblings: Love, envy, and understanding.* Cambridge, MA: Harvard University Press.

DUNN, J., & MUNN, P. (1985). Becoming a family member: Family conflict and the development of social understanding in the second year. *Child Development, 56,* 480–492.

EAST, P. L., & ROOK, K. S. (1992). Compensatory patterns of support among children's peer relationships: A test using school friends, nonschool friends, and siblings. *Developmental Psychology, 28,* 163–172.

EASTERBROOKS, M. A., & GOLDBERG, W. A. (1984). Toddler development in the family: Impact of father involvement and parenting characteristics. *Child Development, 55,* 740–752.

EGELAND, B. (1979). Preliminary results of a prospective study of the antecedents of child abuse. *International Journal of Child Abuse and Neglect, 3,* 269–278.

EGELAND, B., JACOBVITZ, D., & SROUFE, L. A. (1988). Breaking the cycle of abuse. *Child Development, 59,* 1080–1088.

EGELAND, B., & SROUFE, L. A. (1981). Attachment and early maltreatment. *Child Development, 52,* 44–52.

EGELAND, B., SROUFE, L. A., & ERICKSON, M. (1983). The developmental consequences of different patterns of maltreatment. *International Journal of Child Abuse and Neglect, 7,* 459–469.

EMERY, R. E. (1988). *Marriage, divorce, and children's adjustment.* Beverly Hills, CA: Sage.

EMERY, R. E. (1989). Family violence. *American Psychologist, 44,* 321–328.

EMERY, R. E., & WYER, M. M. (1987). Divorce mediation. *American Psychologist, 42,* 472–480.

ERIKSON, E. H. (1963). *Childhood and society* (2nd ed.). New York: Norton.

ESTRADA, P., ARSENIO, W. F., HESS, R. D., & HOLLOWAY, S. D. (1987). Affective quality of the mother-child relationship: Longitudinal consequences for children's school-relevant cognitive functioning. *Developmental Psychology, 23,* 210–215.

FALBO, T. (1984). Only children: A review. In T. Falbo (Ed.), *The single-child family.* New York: Guilford Press.

FALBO, T., & POLIT, D. F. (1986). Quantitative review of the only child literature: Research evidence and theory development. *Psychological Bulletin, 100,* 176–189.

FAUBER, R., FOREHAND, R., THOMAS, A. M., & WIERSON, M. (1990). A mediational model of the impact of marital conflict on adolescent adjustment in intact and divorced families: The role of disrupted parenting. *Child Development, 61,* 1112–1123.

FELDMAN, R. S., DEVIN-SHEEHAN, L., & ALLEN, V. L. (1976). Children tutoring children: A critical review of research. In V. L. Allen (Ed.), *Children as teachers: Theory and research on tutoring.* New York: Academic Press.

FELDMAN, S. S., & ASCHENBRENNER, B. (1983). Impact of parenthood on various aspects of masculinity and femininity: A short-term longitudinal study. *Developmental Psychology, 19*, 278–289.

FELDMAN, S. S., & GEHRING, T. M. (1988). Changing perceptions of family cohesion and power across adolescence. *Child Development, 59*, 1034–1045.

FLEMING, A. S., RUBLE, D. N., FLETT, G. L., & VAN WAGNER, V. (1990). Adjustment in first-time mothers: Changes in mood and mood content during the early postpartum months. *Developmental Psychology, 26*, 137–143.

FLOYD, F. J., & ZMICH, D. E. (1991). Marriage and the parenting partnership: Perceptions and interactions of parents with mentally retarded and typically developing children. *Child Development, 62*, 1434–1448.

FRANKLIN, K. M., JANOFF-BULMAN, R., & ROBERTS, J. E. (1990). Long-term impact of parental divorce on optimism and trust: Changes in general assumptions or narrow beliefs? *Journal of Personality and Social Psychology, 59*, 743–755.

FRODI, A. M., & LAMB, M. E. (1980). Child abusers' responses to infant smiles and cries. *Child Development, 51*, 238–241.

FURMAN, W., & BUHRMESTER, D. (1985a). Children's perceptions of the personal relationships in their social networks. *Developmental Psychology, 21*, 1016–1024.

FURMAN, W., & BUHRMESTER, D. (1985b). Children's perceptions of the qualities of sibling relationships. *Child Development, 56*, 448–461.

FURMAN, W., & BUHRMESTER, D. (1992). Age and sex differences in perceptions of networks of personal relationships. *Child Development, 63*, 103–115.

FURSTENBERG, F. F., JR. (1988). Child care after divorce and remarriage. In E. M. Hetherington & J. D. Arasteh (Eds.), *Impact of divorce, single-parenting, and stepparenting on children.* Hillsdale, NJ: Erlbaum..

FURSTENBERG, F. F., JR., BROOKS-GUNN, J., & CHASE-LANSDALE, L. (1989). Teenaged pregnancy and childbearing. *American Psychologist, 44*, 313–320.

GALAMBOS, N. L., & MAGGS, J. L. (1991). Out-of-school care of young adolescents and self-reported behavior. *Developmental Psychology, 27*, 644–655.

GARBARINO, J. (1982). The human ecology of school crime. In B. Emrich (Ed.), *Theoretical perspective on school crime.* Davis, CA: National Council on Crime and Delinquency.

GARBARINO, J., & SHERMAN, D. (1980). High-risk neighborhoods and high-risk families: The human ecology of child maltreatment. *Child Development, 51*, 188–198.

GARCIA COLL, C. T., HOFFMAN, J., & OH, W. (1987). The social ecology and early parenting of Caucasian adolescent mothers. *Child Development, 58*, 955–963.

GATH, A. (1985). Down's syndrome in the first nine years. In A. R. Nicol (Ed.), *Longitudinal studies in child psychology and psychiatry.* New York: Wiley.

GIL, D. G. (1970). *Violence against children.* Cambridge, MA: Harvard University Press.

GJERDE, P. F. (1986). The interpersonal structure of family interaction settings: Parent-adolescent relations in dyads and triads. *Developmental Psychology, 22*, 297–304.

GLICK, P. C. (1989). Remarried families, stepfamilies, and stepchildren: A brief demographic profile. *Family Relations, 38*, 24–47.

GLICK, P. C., & LIN, S. (1987). Remarriage after divorce: Recent changes and demographic variations. *Sociological Perspectives, 30*, 162–179.

GOLD, D., & ANDRES, D. (1978a). Developmental comparisons between adolescent children with employed and nonemployed mothers. *Merrill-Palmer Quarterly, 24*, 243–254.

GOLD, D., & ANDRES, D. (1978b). Developmental comparisons between 10-year-old children with employed and nonemployed mothers. *Child Development, 49*, 75–84.

GOLDBERG, W. A., & EASTERBROOKS, M. A. (1984). Role of marital quality in toddler development. *Developmental Psychology, 20*, 504–514.

GOTTFRIED, A. E., GOTTFRIED, A. W., & BATHURST, K. (1988). Maternal employment, family environment and children's development: Infancy through the school years. In A. E. Gottfried & A. W. Gottfried (Eds.), *Maternal employment and children's development: Longitudinal research.* New York: Plenum.

GREENBERGER, E., & GOLDBERG, W. A. (1989). Work, parenting, and the socialization of children. *Developmental Psychology, 25*, 22–35.

GREENBERGER, E., & STEINBERG, L. (1986). *When teenagers work: The psychological and social costs of adolescent employment.* New York: Basic Books.

GROLNICK, W. S., & RYAN, R. M. (1989). Parent styles associated with self-regulation and competence in school. *Journal of Educational Psychology, 81*, 143–154.

GROSSMAN, F. K., EICHLER, L. S., WINICKOFF, S. A., & ASSOCIATES (1980). *Pregnancy, birth, and parenthood: Adaptations of mothers, fathers, and infants.* San Francisco: Jossey-Bass.

GROTEVANT, H. D., & COOPER, C. R. (1986). Individuation in family relations: A perspective on individual differences in the development of identity and role-taking skills in adolescence. *Human Development, 29*, 82–100.

HART, S. N. (1991). From property to person status: Historical perspective on children's rights. *American Psychologist, 46*, 53–59.

HART, S. N., & BRASSARD, M. R. (1987). A major threat to children's mental health: Psychological maltreatment. *American Psychologist, 42*, 160–165.

HASKETT, M. E., & KISTNER, J. A. (1991). Social interactions and peer perceptions of young physically abused children. *Child Development, 62*, 979–990.

HAUGAARD, J. J., & REPPUCCI, N. D. (1988). *The sexual abuse of children.* San Francisco: Jossey-Bass.

HESS, R. D. (1970). Social class and ethnic influences upon socialization. In P. H. Mussen (Ed.), *Carmichael's manual of child psychology* (Vol. 2). New York: Wiley.

HETHERINGTON, E. M. (1981). Children and divorce. In R. W. Henderson (Ed.), *Parent-child interaction: Theory, research, and prospects*. New York: Academic Press.

HETHERINGTON, E. M. (1989). Coping with family transitions: Winners, losers, and survivors. *Child Development, 60,* 1–14.

HETHERINGTON, E. M., & CAMARA, K. A. (1984). Families in transition: The processes of dissolution and reconstitution. In R. D. Parke (Ed.), *Review of child development research.* Vol. 7: *The family.* Chicago: University of Chicago Press.

HETHERINGTON, E. M., CLINGEMPEEL, W. G., & ASSOCIATES (1992). Coping with marital transitions. *Monographs of the Society for Research in Child Development, 57*(Nos. 2–3, Serial No. 227).

HETHERINGTON, E. M., COX, M., & COX, R. (1982). Effects of divorce on parents and children. In M. E. Lamb (Ed.), *Nontraditional families.* Hillsdale, NJ: Erlbaum.

HETHERINGTON, E. M., STANLEY-HAGAN, M., & ANDERSON, E. R. (1989). Marital transitions: A child's perspective. *American Psychologist, 44,* 303–312.

HILL, J. P. (1987). Research on adolescents and their families: Past and prospect. In C. E. Irwin, Jr. (Ed.), *Adolescent social behavior and health.* San Francisco: Jossey-Bass.

HOCK, E., DeMEIS, D., & McBRIDE, S. (1988). Maternal separation: Its role in the balance of employment and motherhood in mothers of infants. In A. E. Gottfried & A. W. Gottfried (Eds.), *Maternal employment and children's development: Longitudinal research.* New York: Plenum.

HOFFMAN, L. W. (1989). Effects of maternal employment in the two-parent family. *American Psychologist, 44,* 283–292.

HOLDEN, G. W., & RITCHIE, K. L. (1991). Linking extreme marital discord, child rearing, and child behavior problems: Evidence from battered women. *Child Development, 62,* 311–327.

HOLMBECK, G. N., & HILL, J. P. (1991). Conflictive engagement, positive affect, and menarche in families with seventh-grade girls. *Child Development, 62,* 1030–1048.

HOWE, N., & ROSS, H. S. (1990). Socialization, perspective-taking, and the sibling relationship. *Developmental Psychology, 26,* 160–165.

HOWES, C. (1990). Can the age of entry into child care and the quality of child care predict adjustment in kindergarten? *Developmental Psychology, 26,* 292–303.

HOWES, P., & MARKMAN, H. J. (1989). Marital quality and child functioning: A longitudinal investigation. *Child Development, 60,* 1044–1051.

HWANG, C. P. (1986). Behavior of Swedish primary and secondary caretaking fathers in relation to mother's presence. *Developmental Psychology, 22,* 749–751.

KAUFMAN, J., & ZIGLER, E. (1987). Do abused children become abusive parents? *American Journal of Orthopsychiatry, 57,* 186–192.

KELLEY, M. L., POWER, T. G., & WIMBUSH, D. D. (1992). Determinants of disciplinary practices in low-income Black mothers. *Child Development, 63,* 573–582.

KEMPE, R. S., & KEMPE, C. H. (1978). *Child abuse.* Cambridge, MA: Harvard University Press.

KESSNER, D. M. (1973). *Infant death: An analysis by maternal risk and health care.* Washington, DC: National Academy of Sciences.

KLIMES-DOUGAN, B., & KISTNER, J. (1990). Physically abused preschoolers' responses to peers' distress. *Developmental Psychology, 26,* 599–602.

KLINE, M., TSCHANN, J. M., JOHNSTON, J. R., & WALLERSTEIN, J. S. (1989). Children's adjustment to joint and sole physical custody families. *Developmental Psychology, 25,* 430–438.

KOHN, M. L. (1979). The effects of social class on parental values and practices. In D. Reiss & H. A. Hoffman (Eds.), *The American family: Dying or developing?* New York: Plenum.

KURDEK, L. A., BLISK, D., & SIESKY, A. E., JR. (1981). Correlates of children's long-term adjustment to their parents' divorce. *Developmental Psychology, 17,* 565–579.

LAMB, M. E. (1981). *The role of the father in child development.* New York: Wiley.

LAMB, M. E., & ELSTER, A. B. (1985). Adolescent mother-infant-father relationships. *Developmental Psychology, 21,* 768–773.

LAMBORN, S. D., MOUNTS, N. S., STEINBERG, L., & DORNBUSCH, S. M. (1991). Patterns of competence and adjustment among adolescents from authoritative, authoritarian, indulgent, and neglectful families. *Child Development, 62,* 1049–1065.

LAOSA, L. M. (1981). Maternal behavior: Sociocultural diversity in modes of family interaction. In R. W. Henderson (Ed.), *Parent-child interaction: Theory, research, and prospects.* Orlando, FL: Academic Press.

LEFKOWITZ, M. M., & TESINY, E. P. (1984). Rejection and depression: Prospective and contemporaneous analyses. *Developmental Psychology, 20,* 776–785.

LERNER, J. V., & GALAMBOS, N. L. (1985). Maternal role satisfaction, mother-child interaction, and child temperament: A process model. *Developmental Psychology, 21,* 1157–1164.

LERNER, J. V., & GALAMBOS, N. L. (1988). The influence of maternal employment across life: The New York Longitudinal Study. In A. E. Gottfried & A. W Gottfried (Eds.), *Maternal employment and children's development: Longitudinal research.* New York: Plenum.

LeVINE, R. A. (1974). Parental goals: A cross-cultural view. *Teachers College Record, 76,* 226–239.

LEVITT, M. J., WEBER, R. A., & CLARK, M. C. (1986). Social network relationships as sources of maternal support and well-being. *Developmental Psychology, 22,* 310–316.

LEVY-SHIFF, R., GOLDSHMIDT, I., & HAR-EVEN, D. (1991). Transition to parenthood in adoptive families. *Developmental Psychology, 27,* 131–140.

LIDDELL, C., HENZI, S. P., & DREW, M. (1987). Mothers, fathers, and children in an urban park playground: A comparison of dyads and triads. *Developmental Psychology, 23,* 262–266.

LIGHT, R. J. (1973). Abused and neglected children in America: A study of alternative policies. *Harvard Educational Review, 43,* 556–598.

LONG, N., & FOREHAND, R. (1987). The effects of parental divorce and marital conflict on children: An overview. *Journal of Developmental and Behavioral Pediatrics, 8,* 292–296.

LUEPNITZ, D. A. (1986). A comparison of maternal, paternal, and joint custody: Understanding the varieties of post-divorce family life. *Journal of Divorce, 9,* 1–12.

LYTTON, H. (1990). Child and parent effects in boys' conduct disorder: A reinterpretation. *Developmental Psychology, 26,* 683–697.

MACCOBY, E. E. (1980). *Social development.* San Diego: Harcourt Brace Jovanovich.

MACCOBY, E. E. (1992). Family structure and children's adjustment: Is quality of parenting the major mediator? In E. M. Hetherington, W. G. Clingempeel, & Associates, Coping with marital transitions. *Monographs of the Society for Research in Child Development, 57*(Nos. 2–3, Serial No. 227).

MACCOBY, E. E., & MARTIN, J. A. (1983). Socialization in the context of the family: Parent-child interaction. In E. M. Hetherington (Ed.; P. H. Mussen, General Ed.), *Handbook of child psychology*: Vol. 4: *Socialization, personality, and social development* (4th ed.). New York: Wiley.

MacDONALD, K. (1992). Warmth as a developmental construct: An evolutionary analysis. *Child Development, 63,* 753–773.

MacKINNON, R., & WALLERSTEIN, J. S. (1986). Joint custody and the preschool child. *Behavioral Sciences and the Law, 4,* 169–183.

MAIN, M., & GEORGE, C. (1985). Responses of abused and disadvantaged toddlers to distress in agemates: A study in the day-care setting. *Developmental Psychology, 21,* 407–412.

MATEJCEK, Z., DYTRYCH, Z., & SCHULLER, V. (1979). The Prague study of children born from unwanted pregnancies. *International Journal of Mental Health, 7,* 63–74.

McHALE, S. M., & GAMBLE, W. C. (1989). Sibling relationships of children with disabled and nondisabled brothers and sisters. *Developmental Psychology, 25,* 421–429.

McKENNA, J. (1986). An anthropological perspective on the Sudden Infant Death Syndrome (SIDS): The role of parental breathing cues and speech breathing adaptations. *Medical Anthropology, 10,* 90–92.

McLOYD, V. C. (1989). Socialization and development in a changing economy: The effects of paternal job and income loss on children. *American Psychologist, 44,* 293–302.

McLOYD, V. C. (1990). The impact of economic hardship on Black families and children: Psychological distress, parenting, and socioemotional development. *Child Development, 61,* 311–346.

McNALLY, S., EISENBERG, N., & HARRIS, J. D. (1991). Consistency and change in maternal child-rearing practices and values: A longitudinal study. *Child Development, 62,* 190–198.

MENAGHAN, E. G., & LIEBERMAN, M. A. (1986). Changes in depression following divorce: A panel study. *Journal of Marriage and the Family, 48,* 319–328.

MILLER, N., & MARUYAMA, G. (1976). Ordinal position and peer popularity. *Journal of Personality and Social Psychology, 33,* 123–131.

MINUCHIN, P. (1985). Families and individual development: Provocations from the field of family therapy. *Child Development, 56,* 289–302.

MOORE, D. (1987). Parent-adolescent separation: The construction of adulthood by late adolescents. *Developmental Psychology, 23,* 298–307.

MOOREHOUSE, M. J. (1991). Linking maternal employment patterns to mother-child activities and children's school competence. *Developmental Psychology, 27,* 295–303.

MORELLI, G. A., ROGOFF, B., OPPENHEIM, D., & GOLDSMITH, D. (1992). Cultural variation in infants' sleeping arrangements: Questions of independence. *Developmental Psychology, 28,* 604–613.

NINIO, A., & RINOTT, N. (1988). Fathers' involvement in the care of their infants and their attributions of cognitive competence to infants. *Child Development, 59,* 652–663.

NORMAN-JACKSON, J. (1982). Family interactions, language development, and primary reading achievement of Black children in families of low income. *Child Development, 53,* 349–358.

NORTON, A. J., & MOORMAN, J. E. (1987). Current trends in marriage and divorce among American women. *Journal of Marriage and the Family, 49,* 3–14.

OATES, K. (1986). *Child abuse and neglect: What happens eventually.* New York: Brunner/Mazel.

OGBU, J. U. (1981). Origins of human competence: A cultural-ethological perspective. *Child Development, 52,* 413–429.

PALKOWITZ, R. (1984). Parental attitudes and fathers' interactions with their 5-month-old infants. *Developmental Psychology, 20,* 1054–1060.

PARKE, R. D., & LEWIS, N. G. (1981). The family in context: A multilevel interactional analysis of child abuse. In R. W. Henderson (Ed.), *Parent-child interaction: Theory, research, and prospects.* New York: Academic Press.

PARKE, R. D., & SAWIN, D. B. (1976). The father's role in infancy. In J. Osofsky (Ed.), *Handbook of infant development* (2nd ed.). New York: Wiley.

PARKE, R. D., & TINSLEY, B. J. (1987). Family interaction in infancy: A reevaluation. *Family Coordinator, 25,* 365–371.

PATTERSON, G. R., DeBARYSHE, B. D., & RAMSEY, E. (1989). A developmental perspective on antisocial behavior. *American Psychologist, 44,* 329–335.

PAULHUS, D., & SHAFFER, D. R. (1981). Sex differences in the impact of number of older and number of younger siblings on scholastic aptitude. *Social Psychology Quarterly, 44,* 363–368.

PEARSON, J. L., HUNTER, A. G., ENSMINGER, M. E., & KELLAM, S. G. (1990). Black grandmothers in multigenerational households: Diversity in family structure and parenting involvement in the Woodlawn community. *Child Development, 61,* 434–442.

PEDERSEN, F., ANDERSON, B., & CAIN, R. (1977, March). *An approach to understanding linkages between parent-infant and spouse relationships*. Paper presented at the biennial meeting of the Society for Research in Child Development, New Orleans.

PEDRO-CARROLL, J. L., & COWEN, E. L. (1985). The children of divorce intervention program: An investigation of the efficacy of a school-based prevention program. *Journal of Consulting and Clinical Psychology*, 53, 603–611.

PULKKINEN, L. (1982). Self-control and continuity from childhood to adolescence. In P. B. Baltes & O. G. Brim, Jr. (Eds.), *Life-span development and behavior* (Vol. 4). Orlando, FL: Academic Press.

RAGOZIN, A. S., BASHAM, R. B., CRNIC, K. A., GREENBERG, M. T., & ROBINSON, N. M. (1982). Effects of maternal age on parenting role. *Developmental Psychology*, 18, 627–634.

REBELSKY, F., & HANKS, C. (1971). Fathers' verbal interaction with infants in the first three months of life. *Child Development*, 42, 63–68.

RICHARDSON, J. L., DWYER, K., McGUIGAN, K., HANSEN, W. B., DENT, C., JOHNSON, C., SUSSMAN, S. Y., BRANNON, B., & FLAY, B. (1989). Substance use among eighth-grade students who take care of themselves after school. *Pediatrics*, 84, 556–560.

RICKS, S. S. (1985). Father-infant interactions: A review of empirical research. *Family Relations*, 34, 505–511.

ROBERTS, G. C., BLOCK, J. H., & BLOCK, J. (1984). Continuity and change in parents' child-rearing practices. *Child Development*, 55, 586–597.

RODMAN, H., & COLE, C. (1987). Latchkey children: A review of policy and resources. *Family Relations*, 36, 101–105.

ROSENBERG, M. S., & REPPUCCI, N. D. (1985). Primary prevention of child abuse. *Journal of Consulting and Clinical Psychology*, 53, 576–585.

ROTHBART, M. K. (1971). Birth order and mother-child interaction in an achievement situation. *Journal of Personality and Social Psychology*, 17, 113–120.

RYAN, R. M., & LYNCH, J. H. (1989). Emotional autonomy versus detachment: Revisiting the vicissitudes of adolescence and young adulthood. *Child Development*, 60, 340–356.

SAMUELS, H. R. (1977, March). *The sibling in the infant's social environment*. Paper presented at the biennial meeting of the Society for Research in Child Development, New Orleans.

SAMUELS, H. R. (1980). The effect of older siblings on infant locomotor exploration of a new environment. *Child Development*, 51, 607–609.

SANTROCK, J. W., & SITTERLE, K. A. (1987). Parent-child relationships in stepmother families. In K. Pasley & M. Ihinger-Tallman (Eds.), *Remarriage and stepparenting: Current research and theory*. New York: Guilford Press.

SANTROCK, J. W., WARSHAK, R. A., LINDBERGH, C., & MEADOWS, L. (1982). Children's and parents' observed social behavior in stepfather families. *Child Development*, 53, 472–480.

SCHACHTER, F. F. (1981). Toddlers with employed mothers. *Child Development*, 52, 958–964.

SCHINKE, S. P., SCHILLING, R. F. II, BARTH, R. P., GILCHRIST, L. D., & MAXWELL, J. S. (1986). Stress-management intervention to prevent family violence. *Journal of Family Violence*, 1, 13–26.

SELTZER, J. A., & BIANCHI, S. M. (1988). Children's contact with absent parents. *Journal of Marriage and the Family*, 50, 663–677.

SHAFFER, D. R. (1993). *Developmental psychology: Childhood and adolescence* (3rd ed.). Pacific Grove, CA: Brooks/Cole.

SHERROD, K. B., O'CONNOR, S., VIETZE, P. M., & ALTEMEIER, W. A. III (1984). Child health and maltreatment. *Child Development*, 55, 1174–1183.

SIMONS, R. L., WHITEBECK, L. B., CONGER, R. D., & CHYI-IN, W. (1991). Intergenerational transmission of harsh parenting. *Developmental Psychology*, 27, 159–171.

SMETANA, J. G. (1989). Adolescents' and parents' reasoning about actual family conflict. *Child Development*, 60, 1052–1067.

SMETANA, J. G., YAU, J., RESTREPO, A., & BRAEGES, J. L. (1991). Adolescent-parent conflict in married and divorced families. *Developmental Psychology*, 27, 1000–1010.

SNOW, M. E., JACKLIN, C. N., & MACCOBY, E. E. (1983). Sex-of-child differences in father-child interaction at one year of age. *Child Development*, 54, 227–232.

STEINBERG, L. (1981). Transformations in family relations at puberty. *Developmental Psychology*, 17, 833–840.

STEINBERG, L. (1984). The varieties and effects of work during adolescence. In M. E. Lamb, A. L. Brown, & B. Rogoff (Eds.), *Advances in developmental psychology* (Vol. 3). Hillsdale, NJ: Erlbaum.

STEINBERG, L. (1985). *Adolescence*. New York: Knopf.

STEINBERG, L. (1986). Latchkey children and susceptibility to peer pressure: An ecological analysis. *Developmental Psychology*, 22, 433–439.

STEINBERG, L. (1987). Single parents, stepparents, and the susceptibility of adolescents to antisocial peer pressure. *Child Development*, 58, 269–275.

STEINBERG, L., & DORNBUSCH, S. M. (1991). Negative correlates of part-time employment during adolescence: Replication and elaboration. *Developmental Psychology*, 27, 304–313.

STEINBERG, L., ELMEN, J. D., & MOUNTS, N. S. (1989). Authoritative parenting, psychosocial maturity, and academic success among adolescents. *Child Development*, 60, 1424–1436.

STEINBERG, L., MOUNTS, N. S., LAMBORN, S., & DORNBUSCH, S. M. (1991). Authoritative parenting and adolescent adjustment across various ecological niches. *Journal of Research on Adolescence*, 1, 19–36.

STEWART, R. B. (1983). Sibling attachment relationships: Child-infant interactions in the strange situation. *Developmental Psychology*, 19, 192–199.

STEWART, R. B., & MARVIN, R. S. (1984). Sibling relations: The role of conceptual perspective-taking in the ontogeny of sibling caregiving. *Child Development*, 55, 1322–1332.

STEWART, R. B., MOBLEY, L. A., VAN TUYL, S. S., & SALVADOR, M. A. (1987). The firstborn's adjustment to the birth of a sibling: A longitudinal assessment. *Child Development, 58*, 341–355.

STOCKER, C., DUNN, J., & PLOMIN, R. (1989). Sibling relationships: Links with child temperament, maternal behavior, and family structure. *Child Development, 60*, 715–727.

STOLBERG, A. L., & GARRISON, K. M. (1985). Evaluating a primary prevention program for children of divorce. *American Journal of Community Psychology, 13*, 111–124.

STRAUS, M. A., & GELLES, R. J. (1986). Societal change and change in family violence from 1975 to 1985 as revealed by two national surveys. *Journal of Marriage and the Family, 48*, 465–478.

TEEGARDIN, C. (1992, July 17). Delayed marriages, divorce transformed families during '80s. *Atlanta Journal*, A1, A7.

TETI, D. M., & ABLARD, K. E. (1989). Security of attachment and infant-sibling relationships: A laboratory study. *Child Development, 60*, 1519–1528.

TRICKETT, P. K., ABER, J. L., CARLSON, V., & CICCHETTI, D. (1991). Relationship of socioeconomic status to the etiology and developmental sequelae of physical child abuse. *Developmental Psychology, 27*, 148–158.

TRICKETT, P. K., & SUSMAN, E. J. (1988). Parental perceptions of child-rearing practices in physically abusive and nonabusive families. *Developmental Psychology, 24*, 270–276.

U.S. BUREAU OF THE CENSUS (1989). *Statistical abstract of the United States, 1989* (109th Ed.). Washington, DC: U.S. Government Printing Office.

U.S. BUREAU OF THE CENSUS (1990). *Current population reports, Series P-20*. Washington, DC: U.S. Government Printing Office.

U.S. DEPARTMENT OF HEALTH AND HUMAN SERVICES (1988). *Study of the national incidence and prevalence of child abuse and neglect.* Washington, DC: U.S. Government Printing Office.

VANDELL, D. L., & CORASANTINI, M. A. (1988). The relation between third graders' after-school care and social, academic, and emotional functioning. *Child Development, 59*, 868–875.

VANDELL, D. L., HENDERSON, V. K., & WILSON, K. S. (1988). A follow-up of children in excellent, moderate, and poor quality day care. *Child Development, 59*, 1286–1292.

VANDELL, D. L., & RAMANAN, J. (1992). Effects of early and recent maternal employment on children from low-income families. *Child Development, 63*, 938–949.

VUCHINICH, S., BANK, L., & PATTERSON, G. R. (1992). Parenting, peers, and the stability of antisocial behavior in preadolescent boys. *Developmental Psychology, 28*, 510–521.

VUCHINICH, S., HETHERINGTON, E. M., VUCHINICH, R. A., & CLINGEMPEEL, W. G. (1991). Parent-child interaction and gender differences in early adolescents' adaptation to stepfamilies. *Developmental Psychology, 27*, 618–626.

WALLERSTEIN, J. S. (1987). Children of divorce: Report of a ten-year follow-up of early latency children. *American Journal of Orthopsychiatry, 57*, 119–211.

WALLERSTEIN, J. S., & BLAKESLEE, S. (1989). *Second chances: Men, women, and children a decade after divorce.* New York: Ticknor & Fields.

WALLERSTEIN, J. S., & CORBIN, S. B. (1989). Daughters of divorce: Report from a ten-year follow-up. *American Journal of Orthopsychiatry, 59*, 593–604.

WALLERSTEIN, J. S., & KELLY, J. B. (1980a, January). California's children of divorce. *Psychology Today*, pp. 67–76.

WALLERSTEIN, J. S., & KELLY, J. B. (1980b). *Surviving the breakup: How children and parents cope with divorce.* New York: Basic Books.

WATERS, E., WIPPMAN, J., & SROUFE, L. A. (1979). Attachment, positive affect, and competence in the peer group: Two studies in construct validation. *Child Development, 50*, 821–829.

WEAVER, K. F. (1985). Stones, bones, and early man: The search for our ancestors. *National Geographic, 168*, 561–623.

WEISNER, T. S., & GALLIMORE, R. (1977). My brother's keeper: Child and sibling caretaking. *Current Anthropology, 18*, 169–190.

WHITBOURNE, S. K. (1986). *The me I know: A study of adult identity.* New York: Springer-Verlag.

WHITING, B., & EDWARDS, C. P. (1988). *Children in different worlds.* Cambridge, MA: Harvard University Press.

WIDOM, C. S. (1989). Does violence beget violence? A critical examination of the literature. *Psychological Bulletin, 106*, 3–28.

WILKIE, C. F., & AMES, E. W. (1986). The relationship of infant crying to parental stress in the transition to parenthood. *Journal of Marriage and the Family, 48*, 545–550.

WILSON, M. N. (1986). The black extended family: An analytical consideration. *Developmental Psychology, 22*, 246–258.

WILSON, M. N. (1989). Child development in the context of the Black extended family. *American Psychologist, 44*, 380–385.

WOLFE, D. A., EDWARDS, B., MANION, I., & KOVEROLA, C. (1988). Early intervention for parents at risk of child abuse and neglect: A preliminary investigation. *Journal of Consulting and Clinical Psychology, 56*, 40–47.

WRIGHT, P. J., HENGGELER, S. W., & CRAIG, L. (1986). Problems in paradise? A longitudinal examination of the transition to parenthood. *Journal of Applied Developmental Psychology, 7*, 277–291.

YOUNISS, J., & SMOLLAR, J. (1985). *Adolescent relations with mothers, fathers, and friends.* Chicago: University of Chicago Press.

ZASLOW, M. J. (1989). Sex differences in children's response to parental divorce: 2. Samples of variables, ages, and sources. *American Journal of Orthopsychiatry, 59*, 118–141.

ZIGLER, E. F., & FINN STEVENSON, M. F. (1993). *Children in a changing world: Development and social issues.* Pacific Grove, CA: Brooks/Cole.

ZIMILES, H., & LEE, V. E. (1991). Adolescent family structure and educational progress. *Developmental Psychology, 27*, 314–320.

ZUSSMAN, J. U. (1978). Relationship of demographic factors to parental disciplinary techniques. *Developmental Psychology, 14*, 685–686.

14 | *Extrafamilial Influences I: Television and Schooling*

In Chapter 13 we focused on the family as an agent of socialization, looking at the ways parents and siblings affect developing children. Although families have an enormous impact on their young throughout childhood and adolescence, it is only a matter of time before other societal institutions begin to exert their influence as well. For example, infants and toddlers are often exposed to alternative caregivers and a host of new playmates when their working parents place them in some kind of day care. Even those toddlers who remain at home will soon begin to learn about the outside world once they develop an interest in television. Between the ages of 2 and 5, many American children spend several hours of every weekday away from home, attending nursery school. And by the age of 6 to 7 virtually all children in Western societies are going to elementary school, a setting that requires them to interact with other little people who are similar to themselves and to adjust to the rules and regulations of a brave new world — one that may be very dissimilar to the home environment from which they came.

So, as they mature, children are becoming increasingly familiar with the outside world and will spend much less time under the watchful eyes of their parents. How do these experiences affect their lives? Our final two chapters explore this issue as we consider the impact of three **extrafamilial influences** on socialization: television and schools (in this chapter) and children's peer groups (Chapter 15).

The Early Window: Effects of Television on Children and Youth[1]

It seems almost incomprehensible that only 50 years ago the average person in the United States could not have answered the question "What is a television?" When first introduced in the late 1940s,

---

[1]The title of this section is taken from a book of the same name (Liebert & Sprafkin, 1988). I highly recommend this volume to students who are seeking a reasonably comprehensive and readable overview of the effects of television on developing children.

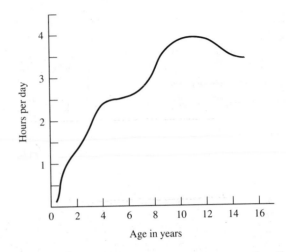

FIGURE 14-1 Average number of hours per day that American children and adolescents spent watching television in 1987. (From Robert M. Liebert & Joyce Sprafkin, *The Early Window: Effects of Television on Children and Youth*, Third Edition. Copyright © 1988. Reprinted by permission of Allyn & Bacon.)

television was an expensive luxury for the wealthy — one that made the children of well-to-do parents immensely popular with their peers. Now virtually all American homes have one or more televisions, and children between the ages of 3 and 11 watch an average of two to four hours of TV a day (Huston et al., 1990; Liebert & Sprafkin, 1988). As we see in Figure 14-1, time spent watching television gradually increases until about age 12 and then declines somewhat during adolescence. And a survey of television use in Australia, Canada, and several European countries reported virtually the same developmental trends in children's viewing habits (Murray, 1980). To place these findings in perspective, we need only note that, by age 18, a child born today will have spent more time watching television than performing any other single activity except sleeping (Liebert & Sprafkin, 1988).

Clearly, this heavy exposure to the electronic media has the potential to influence children in many ways. Does television undermine the quality of family life, as some critics have maintained? Are children who watch a lot of TV likely to be socially withdrawn and less interested in schoolwork? How do children react to televised violence and to the social stereotyping of women and minorities that often appears in commercial programming? Might television be used to reduce social prejudices and to teach prosocial lessons such as cooperation and sharing? Does educational programming promote cognitive growth? In the pages that follow, we will discuss each of these issues as we consider what is known about the effects of television on children's cognitive, social, and emotional development.   *nb*

Television and Children's Lifestyles

Has television changed children's lifestyles and the character of family life? In some ways it has. One early survey found that a majority of families altered their sleeping patterns and mealtimes once they had purchased a television (Johnson, 1967). The presence of a TV at home also had the effect of decreasing the amount of time that parents spent with their youngsters in non-TV-related leisure activities such as games and family outings, and most parents at least occasionally used television as an "electronic babysitter." Although family members may spend many hours in close proximity as they watch television together, many critics believe that this form of family interaction is not very meaningful for the younger set—particularly if they are often told to sit still or keep their mouths shut until the commercials come on. Urie Bronfenbrenner (1970) has argued:

> The primary danger of . . . television . . . lies not so much in the behavior it produces—although there is danger there—as in the behavior that it prevents: the talks, games, the family festivities and arguments through which much of the child's learning takes place and through which his character is formed. Turning on the television can turn off the process that transforms children into people.

But, despite these concerns, there is very little evidence that television has undermined the quality of children's family life. In fact, the reverse may occasionally be true, for children of highly punitive, insensitive parents tend to be very heavy TV viewers, perhaps using television as a means of insulating themselves from unpleasantness at home (Tangney, 1988).

Does exposure to television deaden young minds or transform children into social isolates who become less interested in making friends or less competent as playmates? A study of Canadian children who were observed before and after the introduction of television to their remote community gives us some cause for concern (Corteen & Williams, 1986; Harrison & Williams, 1986). Prior to the coming of television, grade-school children in "Notel" tested higher in both reading skills and creativity than did agemates in other comparable Canadian towns served by television. But, two to four years after television broadcasts became available in their village, these youngsters' creativity and reading proficiency scores had declined to the levels shown by children in the other towns. Moreover, the coming of television was associated with a dramatic rise in children's aggression during free-play periods and with a sharp decline in adolescents' participation in community activities.

Although these findings are sobering, they are by no means universal. Apparently, involvement with television is not all that harmful to peer relations, for popular children who partake in many sports and extracurricular activities tend to watch about as much TV as their less popular peers (Lyle & Hoffman, 1972). Moreover, a study of Native Americans in Alaska found that the introduction of television to their remote villages had little if any effect on children's cognitive competencies (Lonner et al., 1985). Finally, one recent review of the literature found *little or no support* for the common presumption that the more TV children watch, the poorer their academic performance (Anderson & Collins, 1988). In fact, the data imply that students in the primary grades may actually learn a great deal of useful information from watching television—particularly educational programming. So in moderate doses, at least, television does not seem to stunt intellectual growth or impair academic achievement, although youngsters who watch *far* more television than their peers (particularly cartoons and situation comedies) may fall behind in their reading skills (Beentjes & VanderVoort, 1988).

In sum, the overall effects of exposure to television do not appear to be so uniformly negative as some critics have charged. But aren't we missing something if we focus only on children's access to television or on the amount of programming they watch? Shouldn't we be asking *what* they are watching? Viewing a steady diet of murder and carnage may have very different effects than watching educational programs such as *Sesame Street*. And indeed it does!

Effects of Televised Violence

As early as 1954, complaints raised by parents, teachers, and students of human development prompted Senator Estes Kefauver, then Chairman of the Senate Subcommittee on Juvenile Delinquency, to question the need for violence in television programming. As it turns out, American television is incredibly violent. Eighty percent of all prime-time television programs contain at least one incident of physical violence, and it is estimated that the average child of 16 will have already witnessed more than 13,000 killings on television (Gerbner et al., 1986; Liebert & Schwartzberg, 1977). This remarkable statistic often shocks college students, particularly those who have young children of their own. Yet they would probably not be surprised by these figures were they to sit down and watch Saturday-morning television. George Gerbner and his associates (1986) report that the most violent programs on commercial television are those designed for children—especially Saturday-morning cartoon shows, which contain more than 20 violent incidents per hour. And, despite many popular claims to the contrary, violence rates on commercial television have remained remarkably stable since the late 1960s (Liebert & Sprafkin, 1988).

THEORETICAL PERSPECTIVES ON MEDIA VIOLENCE

Does heavy exposure to media violence encourage spectators to behave aggressively or to partake in other kinds of antisocial conduct? Proponents of the catharsis hypothesis say no. In fact, Seymour Feshbach (1970) argued that people may often experience catharsis (that is, a draining away of aggressive energy) by merely thinking aggressive thoughts (fantasy aggression). If this is the case, exposure

to televised violence should *reduce* aggressive impulses by providing fantasy material that viewers can use for cathartic purposes.

By contrast, *social-learning theorists* such as Albert Bandura (1973) offer several reasons why media violence might *enhance* the aggressive or antisocial inclinations of children who watch it. First, there is physiological evidence that children become *emotionally aroused* when they see others fight (Cline, Croft, & Courrier, 1973; Osborn & Endsley, 1971)—arousal that might be reinterpreted as anger and thereby energize aggressive behavior if children should soon experience a situation that seems to suggest an aggressive response. Second, actors who portray violence on television serve as *aggressive models* who teach children a variety of violent acts that they may not know about or would not otherwise have considered performing. Robert Liebert and Joyce Sprafkin (1988) provide several dramatic illustrations of how children have acquired and performed unusual aggressive responses after watching similar actions on television. Here is one example:

> In Los Angeles, a housemaid caught a seven-year-old boy in the act of sprinkling ground glass into the family's lamb stew. There was no malice behind the act. It was purely experimental, having been inspired by curiosity to learn whether it would really work as well as it did on television [p. 9].

Finally, televised violence may reduce children's *inhibitions* about aggression if people in the story approve (or do not disapprove) of the actor's aggressive behavior. I am reminded of the "Thanks!" that townspeople typically shouted to the Lone Ranger as he rode into the sunset after shooting the villain of that particular episode or conspiring with Tonto to beat him to a pulp. If an actor's aggressive behavior is "legitimized" by social approval, observers may expect less risk of punishment or loss of self-respect should they engage in similar behavior.

In sum, Bandura's position on the effects of TV violence is diametrically opposed to that of Feshbach and other proponents of the catharsis hypothesis. Attempts to resolve this theoretical controversy involve three types of research: (1) *correlational surveys* that assess the relationship between television viewing habits and aggressive behavior, (2) *laboratory investigations* in which subjects are exposed to aggressive films and then faced with a situation in which they may choose to behave aggressively, and (3) *field experiments* in which the content of television programming is manipulated over a period of time in a real-world setting in order to measure the effects of the manipulation on viewers' aggressive inclinations. We will briefly consider examples of each type of research as we evaluate the relative merits of the catharsis and the social-learning hypotheses.

1) RESULTS OF CORRELATIONAL SURVEYS

The vast majority of correlational surveys conducted to date have found that children and adolescents who watch a lot of televised violence tend to be more aggressive than their classmates who watch little violence. Indeed, this positive relationship between the amount of violence one observes on TV and aggressive behavior in naturalistic settings has been documented over and over with preschool, grade-school, high school, and adult subjects in the United States and with grade-school boys and girls in Australia, Canada, Finland, Great Britain, and Poland (Liebert & Sprafkin, 1988; Parke & Slaby, 1983). But does early-childhood exposure to televised violence predict how aggressive or how antisocial one may be as an adolescent or young adult?

Indeed it may! In their now-classic *longitudinal* survey, Leonard Eron and his associates (1972) found that the best predictor of aggression among adolescent males was the boys' preference for violent TV programming as expressed 11 years earlier, when they were in the third grade. In other words, boys who favored violent programming at age 8 tended to be highly aggressive at age 19. Subsequent longitudinal studies of different populations indicate that (1) an earlier preference for televised violence predicts later aggression for both girls *and* boys and (2) children who are more aggressive are likely to watch more violence on television (Eron, 1982; Huesmann, Lagerspitz, & Eron, 1984). The latter finding is important because it suggests that the link between televised violence and children's aggression is *bidirectional*: viewing TV violence may

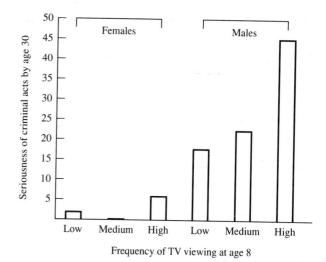

FIGURE 14-2 Although males commit more criminal acts than females, heavy childhood exposure to TV violence is associated with higher levels of criminal activity for both males and females. (Adapted from "Psychological Processes Promoting the Relation between Exposure to Media Violence and Aggressive Behavior by the Viewer," by L. R. Huesmann, 1986. *Journal of Social Issues, 42*, 125–139. Copyright © 1986 by Journal of Social Issues. Adapted by permission.)

instigate aggressive behavior, which stimulates interest in violent programming, which promotes further aggression, and so on down the line (Huesmann et al., 1984). Although longitudinal surveys are correlational research and do *not* demonstrate causality, their results are at least consistent with the argument that early exposure to a heavy diet of televised violence can lead to the development of hostile, antisocial habits that persist over time. Indeed, when Rowell Huesmann (1986) followed up on participants from Eron's original longitudinal survey when they were 30 years old, he found that their earlier preferences for violent television at age 8 predicted not only their aggressiveness as adults but also their involvement in serious criminal activities (see Figure 14-2).

2) RESULTS OF LABORATORY EXPERIMENTS

One method of assessing whether televised violence really does instigate (or reduce) aggression is to expose children to violent programming and then give them an opportunity to commit aggressive responses. By 1972, 18 such laboratory experiments had been conducted, and 16 of them found that children became *more* aggressive after watching violent sequences on television (Liebert & Baron, 1972).[2]

Despite the consistency of these laboratory findings, this method has its shortcomings. For example, it has been argued that a laboratory session in which subjects give their undivided attention to a televised sequence is very dissimilar to the viewing that occurs at home—a setting where parents may berate aggressors and where much of one's "viewing time" is spent talking to others, reading, playing with toys or pets, going to the refrigerator, and so on. Perhaps these exhortations and interruptions lessen the impact of televised violence in a naturalistic setting. We might also note that children at home rarely have a tailor-made opportunity to aggress immediately after watching violent programs. Is it possible that the instigating effects of TV violence are extremely short-lived and thus are a problem only in a laboratory setting where subjects are "encouraged" to be aggressive by the requirements of the task they face soon after observing violent programming? Liebert, Neale, and Davidson (1973) acknowledge these possibilities, noting that "we know from laboratory studies what type of relationship can exist between television violence and aggression, but cannot be wholly certain that this relationship *does* exist in the complex world of free-ranging behavior" (p. 69).

RESULTS OF FIELD EXPERIMENTS

The field experiment is probably the best method of assessing the impact of televised violence on children's behavior, because it combines the naturalistic approach of a correlational survey with the more rigorous control of an experiment. In other words, well-conducted field experiments can determine whether real-life exposure to violent television increases the incidence of aggressive behavior in real-life settings.

[2] A well-controlled and rather dramatic example of this research (Liebert & Baron, 1972) was used in Chapter 1 to illustrate the strengths of laboratory experimentation.

An experiment with young children. In a study by Lynette Friedrich and Aletha Stein (1973), previously discussed in Chapter 2, nursery-school children were first observed to establish a baseline level of aggression for each child and were then exposed to daily episodes of either violent TV shows (for example, *Batman* and *Superman*) or nonviolent programming (for example, *Mr. Rogers' Neighborhood*). Following these month-long television diets, the children were observed daily for two additional weeks to measure the effects of the programming. The results were clear: children who had watched violent programming were subsequently more aggressive in their interactions with nursery-school classmates than were those who had watched nonviolent programming. Although the impact of violent programming was significant only for those youngsters who were above average in aggression on the initial baseline measure, these "initially aggressive" children were by no means extreme or deviant. They simply represented the more aggressive members of a normal nursery-school peer group. Stein and Friedrich remind us that "these effects occurred in [a naturalistic context] that was removed both in time and in environmental setting from the viewing experience. They occurred with a small amount of exposure . . . and they endured during the postviewing period" (1972, p. 247).

An experiment with adolescents. The effects of violent and nonviolent movies on the interpersonal behavior of adolescent males were assessed in a field experiment by Leyens, Parke, Camino, and Berkowitz (1975). The subjects were Belgian delinquents who lived together in cottages at a minimum-security institution for secondary-school boys. Baseline observations suggested that the institution's four cottages could be divided into subgroups consisting of two cottages populated by relatively aggressive inmates and two cottages populated by less aggressive peers. For a period of one week, *aggressive* films (such as *Iwo Jima, Bonnie and Clyde,* and *The Dirty Dozen*) were shown to one of the two cottages in each subgroup, and *neutral* films (such as *Lily, Daddy's Fiancée,* and *La Belle Américaine*) were shown to the other. Instances of physical and verbal aggression among the residents of each cottage were recorded twice daily (at lunchtime and in the evenings after the movie) during the movie week and once daily (at lunchtime) during a posttreatment week.

Perhaps the most striking result of this research was the significant increase in *physical* aggression that occurred in the evenings among residents of *both* cottages assigned to the aggressive-film condition (see Figure 14-3). Since the violent movies contained a large number of physically aggressive incidents, it appears that they evoked similar responses from the boys who watched them. By contrast, boys who watched neutral films showed few signs of physical aggression after the movies. In fact, highly aggressive boys who saw *neutral* films showed a significant *decrease* in physical aggression compared with the baseline period (see Figure 14-3).

There was also evidence of a generalization of aggressive responses over time. That is, highly aggressive boys who watched violent movies became more *verbally* assaultive during the movie week and retained this heightened level of verbal aggressiveness throughout the posttreatment period. Neutral films had the opposite effect: highly aggressive boys who saw neutral films became less verbally aggressive during the movie week and remained low in verbal aggression during the posttreatment week. In sum, the experiment by Leyens et al. shows that (1) violent programming can instigate aggressive responses in naturalistic settings, especially among groups of viewers who are already high in interpersonal aggression, and (2) lighthearted, comical movies may actually reduce the incidence of aggression among a highly aggressive group of spectators. Similar field experiments conducted with adolescents in the United States have reported similar results (Parke et al., 1977).

Although some field experiments have failed to find that violent programming increases children's aggression (see Freedman, 1984), most of the literature is consistent with the research we have reviewed. Indeed, investigators who have conducted large-scale reviews of both the experimental and the survey literatures have concluded that the aggression-instigating effects of TV violence are (1) ob-

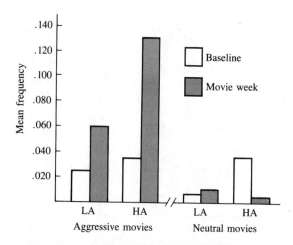

FIGURE 14-3 Mean physical aggression scores in the evening for highly aggressive (HA) and less aggressive (LA) boys under baseline conditions and after watching aggressive or neutral movies. (Adapted from J. P. Leyens, R. D. Parke, L. Camino, & L. Berkowitz, "Effects of Movie Violence on Aggression in a Field Setting as a Function of Group Dominance and Cohesion." *Journal of Personality and Social Psychology*, 1975, 32, 346–360. Copyright © 1975 by the American Psychological Association. Reprinted by permission.)

served among *both* boys and girls, (2) strongest when the violence appears justified, and (3) sufficiently powerful to cultivate aggressive habits and antisocial behavior among heavy viewers (Hearold, 1986; Rosenthal, 1986). Of course, we should heed the cautions expressed by these researchers, who have stressed that televised violence is only one of many contributors to children's hostile, antisocial conduct—but a potent contributor nonetheless (Liebert & Sprafkin, 1988). Finally, there is virtually no support for the notion that exposure to media violence leads to a reduction of viewers' aggressive impulses through catharsis.

Why might televised violence instigate aggression? One possibility is that successful violence perpetrated by story protagonists (that is, the "good guys") not only exposes children to aggressive models but may also persuade them that aggression is socially condoned (Liebert & Sprafkin, 1988). Moreover, a steady diet of violent programming may lead the viewer to believe that the outside world is a violent place inhabited by people who typically rely on aggressive solutions to their interpersonal problems.

PHOTO 14-1   Heavy exposure to media violence may blunt children's emotional reactions to real-life aggression and convince them that the world is a violent place populated mainly by hostile and aggressive people.

Indeed, Leonard Eron and his associates (1983) found that 7- to 9-year-old boys and girls who were judged highly aggressive by their peers not only preferred violent television programs—they also believed that violent shows were an accurate portrayal of everyday life.

TELEVISED VIOLENCE AS A DESENSITIZING AGENT

In addition to promoting aggressive behavior, a steady diet of televised violence may *desensitize* children to violence—that is, make them less emotionally upset by violent acts and more willing to tolerate them in real life. Ronald Drabman and Margaret Thomas (1974) tested this **desensitization hypothesis** with 8- to 10-year-olds. Half the children watched a violent Hopalong Cassidy film that contained several gun battles and fistfights. The remaining children were assigned to a control condition and did not see a film. Each child was then asked to watch a television monitor in order to ensure that two kindergartners who were playing in another room didn't get into any trouble while the experimenter was away at the principal's office. The experimenter took great care to explain to the child that he or she was to come to the principal's office for help should *anything* go wrong. Each child then observed the same sequence, in which the two kindergartners (who were actually on videotape) got into an intense battle. The tape ended with a loud crash that occurred shortly after the video portion had gone dead.

The results of this study were straightforward: children who had watched the violent film reacted much more slowly to what they believed to be a real-world altercation than their classmates who had not seen a film. Drabman and Thomas concluded that an exposure to media violence may blunt viewers' emotional reactions to later aggressive episodes and perhaps even make them feel that aggressive acts are a part of everyday life and do not necessarily warrant a response.

In a second experiment, Thomas and her colleagues (1977) exposed 8- to 10-year-olds to either a *violent* film from the then-popular police series *S.W.A.T.* or a *nonviolent* but exciting film of a championship volleyball match. The viewers were hooked up to a physiograph that recorded their emotional reactions to the films (which were equally arousing). After the film was over, the experimenter switched channels and asked the child to monitor the activities of two younger children who were playing in an adjacent room. At this point the experimenter departed, leaving the child hooked up to the physiograph. The child then observed the same videotaped altercation that was used in Drabman and Thomas's experiment, and his or her emotional reactions to these events were recorded.

Once again, the results were clear: children who had watched the violent programming were subsequently *less aroused* by the "real-life" altercation than their classmates who had seen the nonviolent film. Here, then, is an explanation for children's tolerance of aggression in the first experiment: if exposure to media violence really lessens a viewer's emotional reactivity to later aggressive acts, then this emotionally desensitized person is unlikely to experience strong empathic distress for the victims of aggression. Consequently, he or she may be less inclined to do anything to help them.

ON REDUCING THE HARMFUL EFFECTS OF TV VIOLENCE

How might we reduce the potentially negative effects that media violence can have on children? Perhaps the most obvious strategy might be to carefully monitor what children are watching and to try to interest them in programs that contain little or no violence. Indeed, many parents are concerned about their children's exposure to violent programming and do attempt to regulate it, often achieving some degree of success (St. Peters et al., 1991). Anyone who would like a list of programs that experts consider too violent for children can obtain one by writing to **Action for Children's Television (ACT)**, 46 Austin Street, Boston, MA 02160.

Another step that concerned adults might take is to complain to the networks, to local network affiliates, and to sponsors of violent programs about the highly violent and aggressive programming directed at young children. Indeed, write-in campaigns organized by groups such as ACT and the National Association for Better Broadcasting have been successful at persuading some advertisers to avoid sponsoring extremely violent television shows, and it is likely that these protests would be even more effective if more concerned citizens became involved (Huston, Watkins, & Kunkel, 1989).

In the meantime, parents can help their children to critically evaluate media violence by watching with them and commenting on the inappropriate conduct they observe. One reason why young children are so responsive to aggressive modeling influences is that they don't always interpret the violence they see in the same way adults do, often missing subtleties such as an aggressor's motives and intentions or the unpleasant consequences that perpetrators suffer as a result of their aggressive acts (Collins, Sobol, & Westby, 1981; see Box 14-1). When adults highlight this information while strongly disapproving of a perpetrator's conduct, children gain a much better understanding of media violence and are less affected by what they have seen — particularly if the adult commentator also suggests how these perpetrators might have approached their problems in a more constructive way (Collins, 1983; Liebert & Sprafkin, 1988). Moreover, Leonard Eron

and Rowell Huesmann (1984) have developed a training program designed to teach heavy consumers of TV violence how to discriminate fantasy aggression from real-life events. The results are encouraging: two years later, children exposed to the training sessions were rated much less aggressive by their peers than were other heavy consumers of TV violence who had not received the training.

So adults can play an important role in reducing children's aggression by helping youngsters to interpret the meaning and implications of the violence they see. Unfortunately, this may be an underutilized strategy, for, as Michele St. Peters and her associates (1991) have noted, coviewing at home most often occurs *not* during action/adventure shows or other highly violent fare but during the evening news, sporting events, or prime-time dramas — programming that is not particularly captivating for young children.

Some Other Potentially Undesirable Effects of Television

Besides its potential for instigating aggressive behavior and cultivating hostile, antisocial attitudes, there are several other undesirable lessons that TV might teach young viewers. Let's briefly consider two such influences that seem to annoy or even anger many adults.

TELEVISION AS A SOURCE OF SOCIAL STEREOTYPES

Commercial television programming often represents a young child's first exposure to many societal groups and institutions. For example, toddlers and preschool children may have little or no contact with police officers, lawyers, teachers, people from different racial and ethnic groups, or the elderly, and their impressions of individuals who fall into these categories are likely to be heavily influenced by what they see on television.

Unfortunately, much of what children see on commercial television involves highly stereotyped portrayals of other people. In Chapter 9 we noted that sex-role stereotyping is common on television

Part of pt 1

14-1 | *Punishing Aggression on TV:*
Does It Inhibit Children's Aggressive Behavior?

It is often assumed that children will be reluctant to imitate the actions of aggressive models if they see the aggressors punished for their behavior. Indeed, Bandura, Ross, and Ross (1963) report that children who had seen an aggressive model punished for his actions were subsequently less aggressive than those who had seen the aggressive model rewarded. Yet, children who had seen the model punished were *no less aggressive* than a third group of children who had not been exposed to an aggressive model. The latter finding is important, for it implies that we would be at least as successful at restraining children's aggression were we to regulate what they watch and try to minimize their exposure to violent media models.

An interesting experiment by Andrew Collins (1973) supports this contention. Third-, sixth-, and tenth-graders were given an aggression "test" and then, 18 days later, watched a TV program in which a criminal attacked federal agents and was punished for his actions (he was mortally wounded in a gunfight). The program was edited to yield two versions. In the *separation* version, four-minute commercials were inserted between the inciting incidents in the drama and the aggression and again between the aggression and its punishment. The *no-separation* version presented the entire aggressive scenario uninterrupted by commercials. About a third of the children from each grade level watched each version of the aggressive film. The remaining third saw a *nonaggressive travelogue*. After watching their film, the children took the aggression test a second time.

Children in all three experimental conditions showed an increase in aggression from the pretest to the posttest. However, there were two additional findings that are particularly noteworthy. First, as we see in the figure, third-graders in the no-separation condition, who saw the model punished immediately, were not appreciably less aggressive on the posttest than their agemates who had watched a nonaggressive travelogue. So even immediate punishment of a model's inappropriate aggression did not make young viewers any less aggressively inclined. Second—and of major importance to our discussion—*third-graders* became *much more* aggressive on the posttest if the filmed aggression and its negative consequences were separated

by a commercial than if they occurred in sequence, uninterrupted by another event. Apparently, third-graders did not associate the aggression with its punishment when these two events were separated in time.

On television and in the real world, aggressors are seldom punished immediately after committing aggressive acts; usually hours, days, or weeks—or, on TV, numerous commercials—intervene before an aggressor gets his or her due. Collins's study suggests that exposing young children to aggressive models who are punished later—even a short time later—is *not* an effective means of reducing aggression. *Quite the contrary*: such an exposure appears to instigate aggression and may even foster the development of aggressive habits that are difficult to overcome.

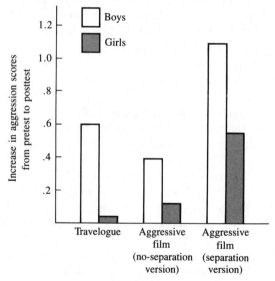

Average increase in the aggression scores of third-graders exposed to different versions of an aggressive film or to a nonaggressive travelogue. (Adapted from W. A. Collins, "Effect of Temporal Separation between Motivation, Aggression, and Consequences: A Developmental Study." *Developmental Psychology*, 1973, *8*, 215–221. Copyright © 1973 by the American Psychological Association. Reprinted by permission.)

and that grade-school children who watch a lot of commercial TV are likely to hold more traditional views of men and women than their classmates who watch little television. Indeed, once television was introduced to the isolated Canadian village of "Notel," both boys and girls showed a sharp increase in sex-role stereotyping (Kimball, 1986). And it seems that the youngsters most affected by sex-role stereotypes on television are girls of above-average intelligence from middle-class homes — precisely the group that is otherwise least likely to hold traditionally sexist attitudes (Morgan, 1982).

Stereotyping of minorities.   Until the mid- to late 1970s, ethnic minorities other than blacks were practically ignored on television. African Americans who did appear on TV were usually cast into comical or subservient roles. The one black show that appeared in the early days of television — *Amos and Andy* — presented such an unfavorable image of African Americans that the National Association for the Advancement of Colored People (NAACP) demanded that CBS take it off the air. African Americans now appear on television in a much wider range of occupations, and their numbers approximate their proportions in the population. However, Hispanics and other ethnic minorities remain underrepresented. And, when nonblack minorities do appear, they are usually portrayed in an unfavorable light, often cast as villains or victims (Liebert & Sprafkin, 1988).

Surprisingly, Liebert and Sprafkin's (1988) recent review found only one study (Graves, 1975) that has examined the effects of media stereotyping on children's racial attitudes. Black and white children watched a series of cartoons in which black people were portrayed either positively (as competent, trustworthy, and hard working) or negatively (as inept, lazy, and powerless). On a later test of racial attitudes, both black and white children became more favorable toward blacks if they had seen the positive portrayals. But, when the depictions of blacks were negative, an interesting racial difference emerged: black children once again became more favorable in their racial attitudes, but whites became much *less* favorable. So the way blacks are portrayed on television may have a striking effect on the racial attitudes of white viewers, whereas the mere presence of black TV characters may be sufficient to produce more favorable attitudes toward blacks among a young black audience.

Countering stereotypes on television.   In recent years, attempts have been made to design programs for the younger set that counter inaccurate racial, sexual, and ethnic stereotypes while fostering goodwill among children from different social backgrounds. In 1969 *Sesame Street* led the way with positive portrayals of blacks and Hispanics. And one early study (Gorn, Goldberg, & Kanungo, 1976) found that white preschool children soon became more willing to include nonwhites in their play activities after watching episodes of *Sesame Street* that depicted minority youngsters as cheerful companions. Among the other shows that have been effective at fostering international awareness and reducing children's ethnic stereotypes are *Big Blue Marble*, a program designed to teach children about people in other countries, and *Vegetable Soup*, a show that portrays many ethnic groups in a favorable light (Liebert & Sprafkin, 1988). Moreover, such recent commercial offerings as *The Cosby Show* and *A Different World*, which depict minorities as family oriented and socially influential professionals, also encourage children and adults to change their views of minorities and may persuade more minority youngsters to pursue higher education (Wilson & Gutierrez, 1985).

Programs designed to counteract gender stereotypes by showing girls and women excelling at traditionally masculine pastimes are also enjoying at least some limited success (Johnston & Ettema, 1982; Rosenwasser, Lingenfelter, & Harrington, 1989). However, the effectiveness of these programs would undoubtedly be enhanced were they combined with the kinds of cognitive training efforts (described in Box 9-3) that directly undermine the erroneous *beliefs* on which gender stereotypes rest (Bigler & Liben, 1990).

In sum, television can either reinforce or reduce inaccurate and potentially harmful social stereotypes — depending, of course, on the type of programming to which people are exposed. Unfortunately, the stereotyped depictions of gender, race, and ethnicity that often appear on commercial TV are far more numerous than nonstereotyped trayals, which are still largely limited to selected programs on public (educational) television.

CHILDREN'S REACTIONS TO COMMERCIAL MESSAGES

In the United States the average child is exposed to nearly 20,000 television commercials each year—many of which extol the virtues of toys, fast foods, and sugary treats that adults may not wish to purchase. Nevertheless, young children continue to ask for products that they have seen advertised on television, and conflicts often ensue when parents refuse to honor their requests (Atkin, 1978). Young children may be so darn insistent because they rarely understand the manipulative (selling) intent of ads, often treating them more like public service announcements that are meant to be helpful and informative to viewers (Liebert & Sprafkin, 1988). By age 9–11 most children realize that ads are designed to persuade and sell, and by 13–14 they will have acquired a healthy skepticism about product claims and advertising in general (Linn, de Benedictis, & Delucchi, 1982; Robertson & Rossiter, 1974). Nevertheless, even adolescents are often persuaded by the ads they see, particularly if the product endorser is a celebrity or if the appeals are deceptive and misleading (Huston et al., 1989).

In addition to creating friction among family members, commercials could have indirect effects on children's sociability and peer relations. In one study (Goldberg & Gorn, 1977, cited in Liebert & Sprafkin, 1988), 4- and 5-year-olds saw a program that had either no commercials or two commercials for an attractive toy. Later, children were asked whether they would rather play with this toy or with friends in a sandbox. Compared to children who had seen no commercials, those who had were about twice as likely to choose the toy and to shun their friends. And, when asked whether they would rather play with a "nice boy" without the toy or a "not-so-nice boy" with the toy, 70% of the commercial viewers chose the not-so-nice boy who possessed the advertised item, compared with only 30% of those in the no-commercial group. Is it any wonder, then, that parents are often concerned about the impact of commercials on their children? Not only do children's ads often push products that are unsafe or of poor nutritional value, but they may

also contribute to conflictual family interactions and poor peer relations. Indeed, Action for Children's Television considers commercials aimed at children to be an even greater problem than televised violence! And policymakers are beginning to respond to the outcries, as evidenced by a recent law limiting the number of commercials on children's programs and requiring broadcasters to offer more educational programming or risk losing their licenses (Zigler & Finn Stevenson, 1993).

Television as an Educational Instrument

Thus far we've cast a wary eye at television, talking mostly about its capacity to do harm. Yet there is reason to believe that this "early window" could become a most effective way of teaching a number of valuable lessons if only its content were altered to convey such information. Let's examine some of the evidence to support this claim.

EDUCATIONAL TELEVISION AND CHILDREN'S PROSOCIAL BEHAVIOR

Emotional

A number of programs broadcast on the Public Broadcasting System (PBS) are designed to supplement the everyday learning experiences of preschool children. For example, *Sesame Street* was created to entertain preschoolers while fostering their intellectual and social development. A typical episode combines fast action and humorous incidents with a carefully designed educational curriculum designed to teach (among other things) letters of the alphabet, numbers, counting, vocabulary, and many social and emotional lessons. Another program, *Mister Rogers' Neighborhood*, is designed to promote the child's social and emotional development. To accomplish these objectives, Mister Rogers talks directly to his audience about things that may interest or puzzle children (for example, crises such as the death of a pet); he reassures them about common fears such as riding in airplanes; he encourages viewers to learn from and to cooperate with children of different races and social backgrounds; and he helps children to see themselves in a favorable light by repeatedly emphasizing "There is only one person in the whole wide world like you, and I like you just the way you are."

Both these programs have a positive influence on the social behavior of young viewers. When preschool children watch either program over a long period, they often become more affectionate, considerate, cooperative, and helpful toward their nursery-school classmates (Friedrich & Stein, 1975; Hearold, 1986; Paulson, 1974). However, it is important to emphasize that merely parking young children in front of the tube to watch *Sesame Street*, *Mister Rogers*, or other programs with prosocial themes is not an effective training strategy, for this programming has few if any *lasting* benefits unless adults monitor the programs and encourage children to rehearse and enact the prosocial lessons they have learned (Friedrich & Stein, 1975; Friedrich-Cofer et al., 1979). Furthermore, children exposed to prosocial programming may well become more compassionate, helpful, or cooperative without becoming any less aggressive (Friedrich-Cofer et al., 1979). Why? Possibly because youngsters who watch prosocial programming will typically become more outgoing and thus will have more opportunities to argue with their peers. Nevertheless, it seems that the positive effects of prosocial programming greatly outweigh the negatives and that prosocial television actually promotes prosocial conduct to a greater extent than violent television promotes aggression (Hearold, 1986)! Hearold believes that these findings have important and far-reaching policy implications:

> Many organizations and groups have chosen to work for the removal of . . . violence in television programs. It is a defensive position: eliminate the negative. Alternatively, I would recommend accentuating the positive: apply money and effort to creating new entertainment programs with prosocial themes. . . . Although fewer studies exist on prosocial effects, the effect size[3] [of prosocial programming] is so much larger [than that of violent programming], holds up better under more stringent experimental conditions, and is consistently higher for boys and girls, that the potential for prosocial effects overrides the smaller but persistent negative effects of antisocial programs (1986, p. 116).

[3]An "effect size" is a statistical term that indicates the strength of a relationship between variables (for example, between exposure to prosocial television programming and subsequent prosocial behavior) when results of many different studies are combined.

PROMOTING GOOD NUTRITION ON TELEVISION

Most food advertisements on children's television are for high-calorie or high-sodium foods and snacks that contain few beneficial nutrients (Stoneman & Brody, 1981). Since a diet containing too much of these foods has been established as a risk factor in a number of diseases (for example, high blood pressure) and dental problems, researchers have hoped to counter the influence of such advertising by producing pronutritional messages and commercials for nutritious snacks. Do these attempts to promote healthful eating practices affect children's dietary habits?

The evidence is mixed. Polly Peterson and her colleagues (1984) exposed 6-year-olds to pronutritional messages from shows such as *Mulligan Stew* (a PBS series) and *Captain Kangaroo* and found that children (1) *learned* the pronutritional information and (2) showed an increased *verbal preference* for nutritious foods. But, when given a choice between nutritious and nonnutritious snacks, these youngsters were no more likely to select nutritious foods than they had been before viewing the programs. However, Joan Galst (1980) found that 3- to 6-year-olds who had watched pronutritional programming did tend to choose nutritious rather than nonnutritious snacks if they had heard an adult comment on ads for nonnutritious foods by stressing these products' poor nutritional value and threats to one's dental health. So there is reason to believe that *regular* exposure to pronutritional television programming could be effective in teaching pronutritional concepts and perhaps even in altering children's dietary habits. Yet the success of such programming may depend very critically on having an adult present for at least some of the broadcasts to help children interpret what they have seen and to translate these lessons into action.

TELEVISION AS A CONTRIBUTOR TO COGNITIVE DEVELOPMENT

In 1968 the U.S. government and a number of private foundations provided funds to create **Children's Television Workshop (CTW)**, an organization committed to producing TV programs that would hold children's interest and facilitate their

PHOTO 14-2   Children learn many valuable lessons from educational TV programs such as *Sesame Street*.

intellectual development. CTW's first production, *Sesame Street*, was unveiled in 1969 and quickly became the world's most popular children's series — one that is seen an average of three times a week by about half of America's preschool children and is broadcast to nearly 50 other countries around the world (Liebert & Sprafkin, 1988). Targeted at 3- to 5-year-olds, *Sesame Street* attempts to foster important cognitive skills such as recognizing and discriminating numbers and letters, counting, ordering and classifying objects, and solving simple problems. It was hoped that children from disadvantaged backgrounds would be much better prepared for school after viewing this programming on a regular basis. Has the show accomplished its objectives?

Evaluating **Sesame Street.**   During the first season that *Sesame Street* was broadcast, its impact was assessed by the Educational Testing Service. About 950 3- to 5-year-olds from five areas of the United States participated in the study. At the beginning of the project, children took a pretest that measured their cognitive skills and determined what they knew about letters, numbers, and geometric forms.

At the end of the season they took this test again to see what they had learned.

When the data were analyzed, it was clear that *Sesame Street* was achieving its objectives. As shown in Figure 14-4, children who watched *Sesame Street* the most (groups Q_3 and Q_4, who watched four or more times a week) were the ones who showed the biggest improvements in their total test scores (panel A), their scores on the alphabet test (panel B), and their ability to write their names (panel C). The 3-year-olds posted bigger gains than the 5-year-olds, probably because the younger children knew less to begin with. The results of a second, similar study that included only urban disadvantaged preschoolers paralleled those of the original study (Bogatz & Ball, 1972), and others have found that regular exposure to *Sesame Street* is associated with impressive gains in preschoolers' vocabularies and prereading skills as well (Rice et al., 1990). Finally, disadvantaged children who had been heavy viewers of *Sesame Street* were later rated by their first-grade teachers as better prepared for school and more interested in school activities than classmates who had rarely watched the program (Bogatz & Ball, 1972).

The Electric Company.   In 1970 CTW consulted with reading specialists to create *The Electric Company*, a TV series designed to teach reading skills to young elementary-school children. The programming was heavily animated, and, to interest children in the content, well-known personalities such as Bill Cosby often appeared. The curriculum attempted to teach children the correspondence between letters (or letter combinations) and sounds — knowledge that should help them to decode words. Reading for meaning and grammar were also taught (Liebert & Sprafkin, 1988).

The success of *The Electric Company* was evaluated by administering a battery of reading tests to first- through fourth-grade children. Although home viewing had little or no effect on children's reading skills, those who watched *The Electric Company* at school attained significantly higher scores on the reading battery than nonviewers (Ball & Bogatz, 1973; Corder-Bolz, 1980). In other words, *The Electric Company* was achieving many of its objectives when

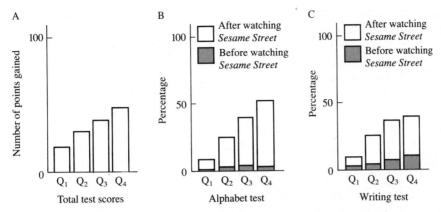

Q_1 = Rarely watch; Q_2 = Watch 2-3 times a week; Q_3 = Watch 4-5 times a week; Q_4 = Watch more than 5 times a week

FIGURE 14-4   Relationship between amount of viewing of *Sesame Street* and children's abilities: A, improvement in total test scores for children grouped into different quartiles according to amount of viewing; B, percentage of children who recited the alphabet correctly, grouped according to quartiles of amount of viewing; C, percentage of children who wrote their first names correctly, grouped according to quartiles of amount of viewing. (From Robert M. Liebert & Joyce Sprafkin, *The Early Window: Effects of Television on Children and Youth*, Third Edition. Copyright © 1988. Reprinted by permission of Allyn & Bacon.)

children watched the program with an adult—in this case the teacher—who could help them to apply what they had learned.[4]

Other educational programs.   In recent years, CTW and other noncommercial producers have created children's programs to teach subjects such as math (*Square One*), logical reasoning (*Think About*), science (*3-2-1 Contact*), and social studies (*Big Blue Marble*). Although these offerings have been quite popular in the areas where they are broadcast, it remains to be seen how well they are achieving their objectives.

Criticisms of educational programming.   One recurring criticism of educational television is that it is essentially a one-way medium in which the pupil is a passive recipient of information rather than an active constructor of knowledge. Critics fear that heavy TV viewing (be it educational TV or otherwise) will blunt children's curiosity, and they be-

lieve that a child's viewing time would be more profitably spent in active, imaginative activities under the guidance of an adult (Singer & Singer, 1983). Indeed, we've seen that programs such as *The Electric Company* (as well as pronutritional messages and programs stressing prosocial behavior) are unlikely to achieve their objectives unless children watch *with an adult* who encourages them to apply what they have learned. Perhaps John Wright and Aletha Huston (1983) are correct in arguing that television's potential as a teaching device will be greatly enhanced once it becomes *computer integrated* and interactive, thereby allowing the viewer to be more actively involved in the learning process (see Box 14-2 for some early returns on the impact of computers on developing children).

Although *Sesame Street* was primarily targeted at disadvantaged preschoolers in an attempt to narrow the intellectual gap between these youngsters and their advantaged peers, early research suggested that children from advantaged backgrounds were the ones who were more likely to watch the program. Thus it was feared that *Sesame Street* might actually end up *widening* the intellectual and academic

---

[4]In 1985 *The Electric Company* went off the air. However, episodes are still available to schools on videocassette for classroom use.

gaps between advantaged and disadvantaged youth (Cook et al., 1975). Yet this particular concern now appears unfounded. Later research suggests that children from disadvantaged backgrounds are not only watching *Sesame Street* about as often as their advantaged peers (Pinon, Huston, & Wright, 1989)

but are learning just as much from it (Rice et al., 1990). Moreover, children benefit from viewing this series even when they watch it alone (Rice et al., 1990). So *Sesame Street* appears to be a potentially valuable resource for *all* preschool children—and a true educational bargain that costs less than a penny

---

B O X　**14-2** | *The Computer: A Second "Early Window"*
That May Influence Children

Like television, the computer is a modern technological device that has the potential to influence children's learning and lifestyles. But in what ways? If we take our cues from Hollywood, we might be led to believe that young computer "hackers" will grow up to be *brainy* but socially inept introverts, like those curiously lovable misfits from the movie *Revenge of the Nerds*. Indeed, many educators believe that the microcomputer is an effective supplement to classroom instruction—a tool that helps children to learn more and to have more fun doing so. And parents, many of whom may be "computer illiterates," are nevertheless rushing out to buy home computers, prompted, in part, by TV ads suggesting that they may be undermining their child's chances of success if they don't. Do computers really help children to learn, to think, or to create? Is there a danger that young "hackers" will become so enamored of computer technology and so reclusive or socially unskilled that they risk being ostracized by their peers?

Only recently have researchers begun to explore the impact of computers on children's lives, and the early returns are interesting. For example, James Kulik and his associates (Kulik, Kulik, & Bangert-Drowns, 1985) find that children do learn more and seem to enjoy school more when they receive at least some *computer-assisted instruction (CAI)*. Some CAI is simply drill, although computer-drill programs can diagnose learning problems (from the kinds of errors made), individualize questions for the student, and provide instantaneous feedback (much as a human tutor might). Other, more elaborate forms of CAI are guided tutorials that pose challenging problems and permit children to assimilate new academic materials in the

context of highly motivating and thought-provoking games. After considering several recent reviews of the literature, Mark Lepper and Jean-Luc Gurtner (1989) came to agree with Kulik that CAI promotes academic achievement and more positive attitudes about learning—particularly for disadvantaged students and other low achievers. Moreover, the benefits of CAI are strongest when programs are made up of highly involving "tutorials" rather than simple "drills."

Douglas Clements (1986) believes that teaching students to *program* a computer has advantages beyond those associated with the performance of computer-assisted academic exercises. In his own research, Clements gave first- and third-graders 22 weeks of training in *Logo*, a computer language that allows children to take drawings they've made and translate them into input statements so that they eventually succeed at reproducing their drawings on the computer monitor. Of what benefit is this kind of problem-solving activity? Although Clements's "Logo" children performed no better on achievement tests than agemates who participated in the more usual kinds of computer-assisted academic exercises, Logo users scored higher on tests of Piagetian concrete-operational abilities, metacognition (knowledge about thinking and thought processes), and creativity. These data are intriguing, for they suggest that computers are useful not only for teaching children academic lessons but for helping them to *think* in new ways as well (see also Lehrer & Randle, 1987).

Aside from its instructional function, the computer is also a *tool* that can further children's basic writing and communication skills (Lepper & Gurtner, 1989). For example, word-processing programs eliminate the

a day per viewer (Palmer, 1984). The formidable task lies ahead—that being to convince more parents that episodes of *Sesame Street* (and other educational programs) are indeed rewarding and valuable experiences, ones that they and their children should not be missing.

Should Television Be Used to Socialize Children?

Although television is often criticized as an instigator of violence or an "idiot box" that undermines the intellectual curiosity of our young, we have seen

---

drudgery of handwriting and increase the likelihood that students will edit, revise, and polish their work. Programs that check spelling or grammar may help children to improve those skills. And it seems that computer-prompted metacognitive strategies can help students to organize their thoughts into more coherent essays (Saloman & Globerson, 1988, as cited by Lepper & Gurtner, 1989).

But what about the social consequences? Are young computer users likely to become reclusive misfits who are shunned by their peers? Daniel Kee (1986) says no. Kee's observations led him to believe that children often use the computer to attract playmates, almost as if it were any other desirable toy. And research in the classroom indicates that children who are learning Logo engage in *more* collaborative activities with classmates than students who are working on traditional assignments (Hawkins et al., 1982; Weinstein, 1991). In sum, computers seem to promote rather than inhibit social interaction. (Of course, it is possible that some withdrawn children with poor social skills could become even more reclusive should they find that their nonevaluative computer is more "user friendly" than most peers.)

Obviously there is much more that we need to learn about the effects of computers on developing children. For example, there is some concern that economically disadvantaged students, who rarely have access to home computers, may fall even further behind in academic achievement (Lepper & Gurtner, 1989). And, since boys are much more likely than girls to take an active interest in computers and to sign up for computer camps, it is possible that the computer revolution may widen the gender gap that already exists in math

and science achievement (Lepper, 1985). Judging from what we know about the effects of television, it is a good bet that computers will prove to influence children in both positive and negative ways. Outcomes may be less than desirable if a child's primary use of the machine is to hole up by himself in the bedroom, zapping mutant aliens from space. But the news may be rather positive indeed for children who use computers to learn, to think in new ways, and to collaborate with siblings and peers.

Learning by computer is an effective complement to classroom instruction and an experience that can teach young children to collaborate.

that the medium can have many positive effects on children's social, emotional, and intellectual development. Should we now work at harnessing television's potential—at using this "early window" as a means of socializing our children? Many developmentalists think so, although not everyone agrees, as we see in the following newspaper account of a conference on behavioral control through the media. To set the stage: the conference participants were reacting to the work of Dr. Robert M. Liebert, a psychologist who had produced some 30-second TV spots to teach children cooperative solutions to conflict. Here is part of the account that appeared in the *New York Times*:

> The outburst that followed Liebert's presentation flashed around the conference table. Did he believe that he had a right to . . . impose values on children? Should children . . . be taught cooperation? Did ghetto kids perhaps need to be taught to slug it out in order to survive in this society? Was it not . . . immoral to create a TV ad . . . to influence kids' behavior? Liebert was accused of . . . manipulation and even brainwashing. One would have thought he had proposed setting up Hitler Youth Camps on Sesame Street.
> However, I understand why the hackles had gone up around the . . . table. I am one of those people who [are] terrified of manipulation. A Skinnerian world filled with conditioned people scares the daylights out of me—even if those people do hate war and . . . love their fellow man. [Behavior control through technology may come] . . . at the cost of our freedom [Rivers, 1974, quoted in Liebert & Sprafkin, 1988, pp. 243-244].

The concern of those conference participants is perhaps understandable, for television is often used as a means of political indoctrination in many countries. And is the use of television for socialization not a subtle form of brainwashing? Perhaps it is. However, one could argue that television in this country is already serving as a potent agent of socialization and that much of what children see in the media helps to create attitudes and to instigate actions that the majority of us may not condone. Perhaps the question we should be asking is "Can we somehow alter television to make it a more effective agent of socialization—one that teaches attitudes, values, and behaviors that more accurately reflect the mores of a free society?" Surely we can, although it remains to be seen whether we will.

The School as a Socialization Agent

Of all the formal institutions that children encounter in their lives away from home, few have as much of an opportunity to influence their behavior as the schools they attend. Starting at age 5 or 6, the typical child in the United States spends about five hours of each weekday at school. And children are staying there longer than ever before. In 1870 there were only 200 public high schools in the United States, and only half of all American children were attending during the three to five months that school was in session. Today the school term is about nine months long (180 school days); more than 75% of American youth are still attending high school at age 17; and nearly 50% of U.S. high school graduates enroll in some form of higher education (U.S. Bureau of the Census, 1989).

If asked to characterize the mission of the schools, we are likely to think of them as the place where children acquire basic knowledge and academic proficiencies: reading, writing, arithmetic, computer skills, and, later, foreign languages, social studies, higher math, and science. But schools have an **informal curriculum** as well. Children are expected to obey rules, to cooperate with their classmates, to respect authority, to learn about their society's way of life, and to become upstanding citizens. Today we see the schools providing information and moral guidance in an attempt to combat almost every social problem affecting children, including racism, teenage sex, and substance abuse (Comer, 1991; Linney & Seidman, 1989). And much of the influence that peers may have on developing children occurs in the context of school-related activities and may depend very critically on the type of school a child attends and the quality of a child's school experiences. So it is quite proper to think of the school as a socialization agent—one that is likely to affect children's social and emotional development as well as imparting knowledge and helping to prepare students for a job and economic self-sufficiency.

In this section we will focus on the ways in which schools influence children. First we will consider whether formal classroom experiences are likely to promote children's intellectual development. Then we will see that schools clearly differ in "effectiveness"—that is, the ability to accomplish both curricular goals and noncurricular objectives that contribute to what educators often call "good citizenship." After reviewing the characteristics of effective and less effective schools, we will examine some of the ways teachers might influence the social behavior and academic progress of their pupils. Finally, we will discuss a few of the obstacles that handicapped students and disadvantaged youths may encounter at school as we consider whether our educational system is currently meeting the needs of our children.

Does Schooling Promote Cognitive Development?

If you have completed the first two years of college, you may already know far more biology, chemistry, and physics than many of the brightest college professors of only 100 years ago. Clearly, students acquire a vast amount of knowledge about their world from the schooling they receive. But, when developmentalists ask "Do schools promote cognitive growth?" they want to know whether formal education hastens intellectual development or encourages modes of thinking and methods of problem solving that are less likely to develop in the absence of schooling.

To address these issues, investigators have typically studied the intellectual growth of children from developing countries where schooling is not compulsory or not yet available throughout the society. Studies of this type generally find that children who attend school are quicker to reach certain Piagetian milestones (for example, conservation) and will perform better on tests of memory and **metacognitive knowledge** than agemates from similar backgrounds who do not go to school (see Rogoff,

1990; Sharp, Cole, & Lave, 1979). And it seems that, the more schooling children complete, the better their cognitive performance. Consider what Frederick Morrison (1991) found when comparing the cognitive performance of children who had just made the age cutoff for entering first grade with that of those who had just missed the cutoff and had spent the year in kindergarten. When tested at the end of the school year, the first-graders outperformed the nearly *identically aged* kindergartners in memory, language, and reading skills. In a similar study of fourth-, fifth-, and sixth-graders in Israel (Cahan & Cohen, 1989), children at any given grade performed at higher levels on a variety of intellectual and achievement tests than their chronological *agemates* in the next lower grade—another clear indication that intellectual performance is influenced, in part, by the *amount* of schooling one has had (see also Ceci, 1991).

So schooling does seem to promote cognitive growth, both by transmitting general knowledge and by teaching children a variety of rules, principles, strategies, and problem-solving skills (including an ability to concentrate and an appreciation for abstraction) that they can apply to many different kinds of information (Ceci, 1991). Yet there are limits to these schooling effects (see Box 14-3), and it is important to note that differences between schooled and unschooled subjects are likely to be small on any cognitive test (for example, recognition memory) or testing situation with which both groups of test takers feel equally comfortable and performance does not depend on the use of strategies acquired at school (Rogoff & Morelli, 1989; Sharp et al., 1979).

Determinants of Effective and Ineffective Schooling

One of the first questions that parents often ask when searching for a new residence is "What are the schools like here?" or "Where should we live so that our children will get the best education?" These concerns reflect the common belief that some schools are "better" or "more effective" than others. But are they?

Should Preschoolers Attend School?

In recent years, children in the United States have begun their schooling earlier and earlier. Not only is kindergarten compulsory in most states, but there is talk of requiring school for 4-year-olds (Zigler, 1987). And already many preschoolers spend 6–8-hour days in day-care settings or nursery schools that have a strong academic emphasis and attempt to ready them for the classroom. Indeed, some wealthy parents will do almost anything to get their youngsters into the "right" settings, including enrolling their toddlers in courses that prepare them for admission interviews with exclusive nursery schools (Geist, 1985)!

Is attending preschool beneficial? As we noted in Chapters 6 and 13, children in structured day-care or preschool programs often develop social skills at an earlier age than those who remain at home, particularly if their activities are closely monitored by their preschool or day-care supervisors. However, most children who attend preschool programs are no more nor less intellectually competent than those who remain at home. The notable exceptions are economically disadvantaged youngsters who attend compensatory-education programs specially designed to prepare them for school; these youngsters do display more cognitive growth and achieve more success in school than similarly disadvantaged children who either stay at home or attend other kinds of nursery schools (Burchinal, Lee, & Ramey, 1989; Lee et al., 1990).

In sum, the data indicate that attending a well-monitored preschool program may provide social benefits to most children and intellectual benefits to those from economically disadvantaged homes. But, even so, developmentalists such as Edward Zigler (1987) and David Elkind (1981), author of *The Hurried Child*, believe that the push for early education may be going too far. They fear that young children today are not given enough time simply to be children—to play and socialize as they choose. Elkind even worries that children may lose their self-initiative and burn out on learning when their lives are orchestrated by parents who incessantly push them to achieve. And one recent study of 4-year-olds in academically oriented versus nonacademically oriented preschool programs seems to corroborate Elkind's concerns (Hyson, Hirsch-Pasek, & Rescorla, 1989). Children in the academically oriented preschools were found to score higher on tests of academic skills (for example, knowledge of letters, numbers, and shapes) than their counterparts in the nonacademic program. But this initial advantage in academic skills was no longer apparent one year later, when children from both groups had completed kindergarten. Moreover, children who had attended the academically oriented preschools were judged to be *less* creative than agemates from nonacademic preschools; and by the end of kindergarten they already showed *more* signs of **test anxiety** and held *more negative attitudes toward school* than their counterparts from nonacademic preschools. Hyson and her associates concluded:

> For many middle- and upper-middle-class children, a strong emphasis on formal academic learning in the preschool years appears unnecessary. In our study, academic skills were acquired by virtually all children by the end of kindergarten regardless of family or preschool emphasis, and broader intellectual abilities [such as IQ] were not enhanced by structured academic programs. In summary, our results indicated that effort spent on formal, teacher-directed *academic* learning in preschool may not be the best use of children's time at this point in their development [p. 15; italics added].

A final point: no one is suggesting that nursery-school experiences per se are harmful. In fact, most experts believe that *nonacademic* nursery schools, which encourage free play and such group activities as storytelling and show-and-tell, are beneficial because they foster the development of social and communication skills and an appreciation for rules and routines—attributes that will help youngsters to make the transition from individual learning at home to group learning in a formal grade-school classroom (Zigler & Finn Stevenson, 1993).

Michael Rutter (1983) certainly thinks so. According to Rutter, **effective schools** are those that promote academic achievement, social skills, polite and attentive behavior, positive attitudes toward learning, low absenteeism, continuation of education beyond the age at which attendance is mandatory, and acquisition of skills that will enable students to find and hold a job. Rutter argues that some schools are more successful than others at accomplishing these objectives, regardless of the students' racial, ethnic, or socioeconomic backgrounds. Let's examine the evidence for this claim.

In one study, Rutter and his associates (1979) conducted extensive interviews and observations in 12 high schools serving lower- to lower-middle-class populations in London, England. As the children entered these schools, they were given a battery of achievement tests to measure their prior academic accomplishments. At the end of the secondary-school experience, the pupils took another major exam to assess their academic progress. Other information, such as attendance records and teacher ratings of classroom behavior, was also available. When the data were analyzed, Rutter et al. found that the 12 schools clearly differed in "effectiveness": students from the "better" schools exhibited fewer problem behaviors, attended school more regularly, and made more academic progress than students from the less effective schools. We get some idea of the importance of these "schooling effects" from Figure 14-5. The "bands" on the graph refer to the pupils' academic accomplishments *at the time they entered* high school (band 3, low achievers; band 1, high achievers). In all three bands, students attending the "more effective" schools outperformed those in the "less effective" schools in the final assessment of academic achievement. Even more revealing is the finding that the initially poor students (band 3) who attended the "better" schools ended up scoring just as high on this final index of academic progress as the initially good (band 1) students who attended the least effective schools. Similar findings were obtained in other large studies of elementary and high schools in the United States. Even after controlling for important variables such as the racial composition and socio-

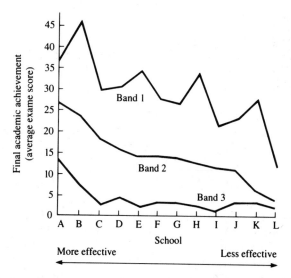

FIGURE 14-5 Average level of academic achievement in secondary school as a function of initial achievement at the time of entry (bands 1–3) and the school that pupils were attending (schools A–L). Note that pupils in all three bands performed at higher levels on this final academic assessment if they attended the more effective schools. Moreover, students in band 2 performed like band-1 students in the more effective schools but like band-3 students in the least effective schools. (Reprinted by permission of the publishers from *Fifteen Thousand Hours: Secondary Schools and Their Effects on Children*, by Michael Rutter, Barbara Maughan, Peter Mortimore, Janet Ouston, & A. Smith. Cambridge, MA: Harvard University Press. Copyright © 1979 by Michael Rutter, Barbara Maughan, Peter Mortimore, and Janet Ouston.)

economic backgrounds of the student bodies and the type of communities served, some schools were found to be much more "effective" than others (Brookover et al., 1979; Hill, Foster, & Gendler, 1990).

So the school that children attend can make a difference. And you may be surprised by some of the factors that do and do not have a bearing on how "effective" a school is.

SOME MISCONCEPTIONS ABOUT EFFECTIVE SCHOOLING

There are several variables that really contribute very little to a school's effectiveness, even though many people have stressed their importance. Let's briefly review some of the common misconceptions about effective schooling.

Monetary support.   Surprising as it may seem, a school's level of support has little to do with the quality of education it provides. The amount of money spent per pupil, the number of books in the school library, teachers' salaries, and teachers' academic credentials play only a minor role in determining student outcomes (Rutter, 1983). To be sure, some minimal level of support must exist for a school to accomplish its objectives, and there are recent, distressing indications that fewer and fewer school districts in the United States are properly adjusting for inflation and for technological innovations to preserve these minimums (Seabrook, 1991). But, as long as adequate support is maintained, merely adding more dollars to the school's budget will not substantially improve the quality of education students receive (Rutter, 1983).

School and class size.   Another variable that contributes minimally, at best, to a school's effectiveness is average class size: in typical elementary- and secondary-school classes ranging from 20 to 40 students, class size has little or no effect on academic achievement. Consequently, it seems that across-the-board decreases in class size—say, from 36 to 24 students—are unlikely to improve student outcomes in any major way (Rutter, 1983). Yet there are some exceptions to this very general rule. Michael Rutter and others (Cooper, 1989; Educational Research Service, 1978) find that smaller classes of 15–20 pupils are beneficial in the primary grades and for students who have special educational needs, as is often true of handicapped children or those from economically disadvantaged backgrounds. So, if a school district were to have the money to hire additional instructors, the wisest course might be to devote these "personnel resources" to remedial instruction or to the primary grades—precisely the settings in which smaller classes seem to promote academic achievement.

There is some evidence that the size of one's school affects student participation in structured extracurricular activities—settings in which aspects of the "informal curriculum" (such as cooperation, fair play, and healthy attitudes toward competition) are likely to be stressed. Roger Barker and Paul Gump (1964) surveyed the activities of high school students in schools ranging in size from 100 pupils to more than 2000. Although the larger schools offered more extracurricular activities to their students, it was the pupils in the smaller schools who were (1) more heavily involved, (2) more likely to hold positions of responsibility or leadership, and (3) more satisfied with their after-school experiences (see also Garbarino, 1980). Moreover, there were few "isolates" in small schools, where almost everyone was encouraged to join in one or more activities. By contrast, students in larger schools received less encouragement to participate; they could easily get lost in the crowd and often felt isolated or even alienated from their peers—feelings that may help to explain why the incidence of truancy, delinquency, substance abuse, and dropping out of school is higher in large schools than in smaller ones (Dusek, 1991; Linney & Seidman, 1989). So, to the extent that a sense of belonging and the lessons stemming from extracurricular activities are important aspects of schooling, there may be some clear advantages to attending smaller schools.

Ability tracking.   The merits of **ability tracking**—a procedure in which students are grouped by IQ or academic achievement and then taught in classes made up of students of comparable "ability"—have been debated for years. Some theorists believe that students learn more when surrounded by peers of equal ability. Others argue that ability tracking will undermine the self-esteem of lower-ability students and contribute to their poor academic achievement and high dropout rate.

In his review of the literature, Rutter (1983) found that neither ability tracking nor mixed-ability teaching has decisive advantages: both procedures are common in highly effective and less effective schools. A closer inspection of the data suggested that mixed-ability instruction may be advantageous with younger children and that ability tracking makes more sense in secondary schools, where it is difficult to teach advanced subjects to students who vary considerably in their background knowledge. However, ability tracking is occasionally found to have negative effects on the self-esteem and academic achievement of low-ability students. After reviewing the tracking systems of effective and ineffective schools, Rutter (1983) concluded that *effective* ability tracking achieves the following:

1. Categorizes students on the basis of their *tested abilities* in *particular subjects* rather than using an across-the-board assignment based on teachers' ratings or IQ scores.
2. Ensures that students in *all* ability groups have some exposure to the more experienced, popular, or "effective" teachers rather than simply assigning the best teachers to the high-ability groups.
3. Integrates the bottom-track students into the nonacademic aspects of schooling, such as sports and extracurricular activities. By taking part in such activities and occasionally being picked for positions of responsibility, bottom-track students are less likely to be stigmatized in a negative way or to suffer a loss of self-esteem.

Classroom structure. Chances are that you were educated in **traditional classrooms** where the seats were arranged in neat rows facing the teacher, who lectured and gave demonstrations at a desk or chalkboard. In a traditional classroom the curriculum is highly structured. Normally, everybody will be studying the same subject at a given moment, and students are expected to interact with the teacher rather than with one another. One interesting aspect of this classroom arrangement is that teachers end up interacting with some students more than others. As we see in Figure 14-6, children who sit in front or at the center of the class are more likely to catch the teacher's eye and participate in classroom discussions than their classmates who sit outside this "zone of activity" (Adams & Biddle, 1970).

Over the past 25 years, however, many North American classrooms have become less formal or structured. "Open education" is a philosophy

Teacher

FIGURE 14-6 In a traditional classroom, the students in the shaded area are more likely to capture teachers' attention and to participate in classroom activities than their classmates who sit outside this "zone of activity."

based on the premise that children are curious explorers who will achieve more by becoming *actively involved* in the learning process than by simply listening to a teacher recite facts, figures, and principles. In an **open classroom**, all the children are rarely doing the same thing at once. A more typical scenario is for students to distribute themselves around the room, working individually or in small groups at reading stories, playing word games, solving math puzzles, creating art, or working on the class's science project. And, rather than being centers of attention or central authority figures, teachers in open classrooms help children to decide what they will learn about and will circulate around the room, guiding and instructing students in response to their individual needs (Minuchin & Shapiro, 1983).

Is the open classroom more effective than the highly structured traditional setting? Proponents of open education certainly think so, although their claim is difficult to evaluate because students attending open nursery and elementary schools often come from different (usually more affluent) backgrounds than those who receive traditional instruction. It does seem that students generally prefer an "open" atmosphere and are more cooperative and create fewer disciplinary problems than students in traditional classrooms (Minuchin & Shapiro, 1983).

PHOTO 14-3   Children at work in an open classroom.

Moreover, the open classroom may be effective at helping elementary-school children to develop novel ideas and concepts (Rutter, 1983). Yet many investigators find no differences in the academic performance (or the conduct) of students in open and traditional classrooms, and others have concluded that students actually learn more in a *traditional* classroom whenever the subject matter requires teachers to illustrate very difficult concepts or transmit a lot of factual information (Good, 1979). So open education is hardly the panacea that its proponents claimed it to be. After reviewing the literature, Rutter (1983, p. 21) concluded that "debates on whether 'open classrooms' are better than traditional [ones] . . . or whether formal methods are preferable to 'informal' methods . . . are misplaced. Neither system has overall superiority, but both include elements of good practice."

FACTORS THAT DO CONTRIBUTE TO EFFECTIVE SCHOOLING

Composition of the student body.   To some extent, the "effectiveness" of a school is a function of what it has to work with. On average, academic achievement is lowest in schools with a preponderance of economically disadvantaged students (Brookover et al., 1979; Rutter et al., 1979), and it appears that *any* child is likely to make more academic progress if taught in a school with a higher concentration of intellectually capable peers. However, this does *not* mean that a school is only as good as the students it serves, for many schools that draw heavily from disadvantaged minority populations are highly effective at motivating students and preparing them for jobs or higher education (Rutter, 1983). The implication, then, is that there must be something about the "atmosphere" or "learning environment" that allows some schools to accomplish their objectives, regardless of the clientele they serve. Let's explore this idea further.

The scholastic atmosphere of successful schools. Recent reviews of the literature (see Linney & Seidman, 1989; Rutter, 1983) point to several values and practices that characterize "effective" schools. For example:

1. *Academic emphasis.* Effective schools have a clear focus on academic goals. Children are regularly assigned homework, which is checked, corrected, and discussed with them. Effective secondary schools require all students to complete a basic, or "core," curriculum rather than allowing pupils a great deal of latitude in setting learning objectives (Hill et al., 1990). Teachers in effective schools expect a lot from their students and devote a high proportion of their time to active teaching and to monitoring of activities so that their expectations can be met.

2. *Classroom management.* In effective schools, teachers spend little time setting up equipment, handing out papers, and dealing with disciplinary problems. Lessons begin and end on time. Pupils are told exactly what is expected of them and receive clear and unambiguous feedback about their academic performance. The classroom atmosphere is comfortable; all students are actively encouraged to work to the best of their abilities, and ample praise is given to acknowledge good work.

3. *Discipline.* In effective schools, the staff is firm in enforcing rules and does so on the spot rather than sending offenders off to the principal's

office. Rarely do instructors resort to physical sanctions (slapping or spanking) that contribute to truancy, defiance, and a tense classroom atmosphere.

4. *Strong leadership.* Effective schools have active, energetic administrators who are successful at persuading their faculties to work as a team at planning and implementing curricular goals and monitoring student progress.

In sum, the effective school environment is a *comfortable* but *businesslike* setting in which academic successes are expected and students are *motivated* to learn. After reviewing the literature, Rutter (1983) concluded that the task of motivating students was of critical importance, for "in the long run, good pupil outcomes were [nearly always] dependent on pupils *wanting* to participate in the educational process" (p. 23).

And whose job is it to motivate students? Traditionally we have assigned this responsibility to the classroom instructor.

The Teacher's Influence

Once they reach school age, many children spend nearly as much time around their teachers as they do around their parents. Indeed, teachers are often the first adults outside the immediate family to play a major role in a child's life, and the functions that teachers serve will change rather dramatically as children progress through the educational system (Minuchin & Shapiro, 1983). Nursery-school and kindergarten classes are in some ways similar to home life: teachers serve as companions or substitute caregivers who provide reassurance if needed while striving to help their pupils achieve the objectives of the preschool curriculum. Elementary-school classrooms are more structured: teachers are focusing mainly on curricular goals, and grade-school children are now more inclined to perceive their instructors as evaluators and authority figures than as pals. During the adolescent years, teachers continue to serve as evaluators and authority figures. But, since high school and college students change classes hourly and have many different teachers, it is less likely that any particular instruc-

tor will exert as much influence as was true during the grade-school years. Instead, high school students tend to think of school as a complex social organization. Their orientation is now more diffuse, centering on the school as a whole—on peer groups, extracurricular activities, sports, and, yes, even curricular matters—rather than on a particular classroom or classroom instructor.

Much of the research on teacher influences has focused on two very broad topics: (1) influences stemming from the teacher's evaluation of students and (2) the effects of teaching styles and instructional techniques on pupil outcomes.

TEACHERS AS APPRAISERS AND EVALUATORS

Teacher expectancy effects. Teachers form distinct impressions of their students' scholastic potential, and these expectancies can affect children's academic progress. In their landmark study of teacher expectancy effects, Robert Rosenthal and Lenore Jacobson (1968) gave first- through sixth-graders an IQ test and then led their teachers to believe that this test predicted which students would show sudden bursts of intellectual growth during the academic year. Each teacher was given the names of five students who might very well prove to be "rapid bloomers." In fact, the so-called rapid bloomers had been randomly selected from the class rosters. The only way they differed from other children was that their teachers expected more of them. Yet, when students were retested eight months later, Rosenthal and Jacobson found that, among the first- and second-graders, *the so-called rapid bloomers showed significantly greater gains in IQ and reading achievement than other students in the class.* In other words, children who were expected to do well did, in fact, do better than other students of comparable ability. It seemed that these students were becoming the objects of their teachers' *self-fulfilling prophecies*, in what Rosenthal and Jacobson called the **Pygmalion effect**.

Although some investigators have failed to replicate Rosenthal and Jacobson's results (Cooper, 1979), many others have reported similar findings, showing that (1) students expected by teachers to do well are likely to live up to these positive expectancies, whereas (2) those expected to perform poorly often do earn lower grades and score lower on standardized tests than classmates of comparable ability for whom the teacher has no negative expectancies (see Harris & Rosenthal, 1986; Weinstein et al., 1987). And there is really nothing mystical about the Pygmalion effect: it occurs because teachers treat high-expectancy students very differently from those expected to founder (Brophy, 1983; Harris & Rosenthal, 1986). Basically, teachers expose high-expectancy students to more challenging materials, demand better performances from them, and are more likely to praise these youngsters for answering questions correctly (perhaps leading them to infer that they have *high ability*). And, when high-expectancy students do not answer correctly, they often hear the question rephrased so that they can get it right (thus implying that failures can be overcome by *persisting* and *trying harder*). By contrast, low-expectancy students are not often challenged and are more likely to be criticized when they answer questions incorrectly—a practice that may convince them that they have *little ability* and that undermines their motivation to achieve (Brophy, 1983; Dweck & Elliott, 1983). Even first-graders are aware of their teachers' expectations, and between first and fifth grades, they increasingly expect of themselves the kind of performance that their teachers expect of them (Weinstein et al., 1987).

One final point—and an important one: unlike the teachers in Rosenthal and Jacobson's experiment, who had an "expectancy" handed to them, the positive or negative expectancies that most teachers form are firmly rooted in reality, *based largely on students' current or previous academic accomplishments* (Brophy, 1983). Students expected to do poorly have generally performed poorly in lower grades (or on achievement tests), whereas those expected to do well have typically accomplished a lot. So teacher expectancies and the patterns of teacher/student interactions associated with them may not *create* self-fulfilling prophecies as much as they simply serve to *maintain* the excellent, average, or poor performances that students have already displayed (Jussim & Eccles, 1993). Nevertheless,

teachers should be made aware of the impact that their expectancies (and associated classroom behaviors) may have on their pupils. Indeed, the clever instructor might even use this knowledge to "get the most out of" nearly every child in the class by (1) setting educational objectives that the child can realistically achieve, (2) communicating these *positive* expectancies to the child, and then (3) praising the *ability* the child has shown whenever he or she reaches one of these academic milestones.

Impact of testing procedures.   You may recall from Chapter 8 that children often lose interest and shy away from challenging tasks if they fare very poorly by comparison to their classmates. And this undermining of motivation is especially apparent when teachers encourage competition in the classroom (thus calling attention to students' relative abilities) rather than emphasizing individual mastery of learning objectives (Butler, 1989, 1990; see also Box 8-1). Indeed, highly competitive assessments of performance can be very stressful for many *capable* students as well.

Consider that teachers often hear students say "I know the material but froze during the test" or "I worried so much about finishing that I made stupid mistakes." Are these kinds of statements merely rationalizations for poor marks? Probably not. A sizable minority of any group of students will become highly anxious during tests, and this **test anxiety** can interfere with their academic performance, *particularly if the test is timed*. In one study (Hill & Eaton, 1977), highly anxious and less anxious grade-schoolers took an arithmetic test under one of two conditions. Some of the children had all the time they needed to complete the test, whereas the remaining youngsters had a time limit imposed on them—one ensuring that they would fail to finish. The results were clear. On the timed test, highly anxious children made three times as many errors and spent twice as much time per problem as their low-anxious classmates. But, if time pressures were removed, the highly anxious students worked just as quickly and performed just as well on the test as their less anxious peers. We see, then, that the way teachers structure their evaluative procedures can have a major impact on the academic performance of students high in test anxiety. Although any test has the potential to elicit some concern about being evaluated, it appears that teachers who favor and use highly stressful evaluative techniques may inadvertently underrate the scholastic abilities and perhaps undermine the achievement motivation of their more anxious pupils.

Teachers' evaluations of children's conduct. Finally, it seems that the ways in which teachers respond to a child's appropriate and inappropriate classroom behaviors can influence the child's popularity with peers. In one recent experiment (White & Kistner, 1992), kindergartners, first-, and second-graders observed a videotape of a classroom scene in which a target child responded appropriately in class (for example, by paying close attention) much of the time but was disruptive (for example, by giggling or by flying a paper airplane) at other times. The teacher's responses to this child were varied in different versions of the videotape. Some children saw teachers accentuate the positive by praising the target child's appropriate behaviors. Others saw the teacher focus on the child's inappropriate conduct either by offering *corrective* feedback (for example ". . . stop making airplanes and get back to work") or by *derogating* the offender (saying, for example, "I've had just about enough, Billy"). Children in a fourth condition saw the teacher praise the target child's appropriate conduct *and* offer corrective feedback for inappropriate conduct. Finally, children in a *control* condition heard the teacher make neutral statements to the entire class without responding either positively or negatively to the target child's conduct. After viewing one of the above videotapes, subjects judged the target child's likability and were asked to indicate whether the target child was likely to display such positive behaviors as helping others and such negative behaviors as pushing and shoving other kids.

The results were interesting. Compared to the target child in the control condition, the target child who was praised for appropriate conduct was judged to be somewhat more likable and was viewed as more likely to display positive charac-

teristics such as helping others. By contrast, the effects of teacher reactions to inappropriate conduct were more complex. If the teacher responded by providing corrective feedback or by combining corrective feedback with praise for appropriate conduct, there was little effect on subjects' evaluation of the target child. But, when the target child received *derogatory* feedback, he was judged as significantly less likable (see Figure 14-7) and much more inclined to display negative behaviors such as hitting and shoving than was the target child in the control condition. So it seems that teachers may either promote a child's status in the eyes of peers (by praising appropriate conduct) or undermine it (by *derogating* inappropriate behavior). And a teacher's influence on a child's popularity is potentially important, for (as we will see in Chapter 15) children who are rejected by peers early in the grade-school years often retain their "rejectee" status and are at risk for experiencing a variety of adjustment problems later in life. Although teachers may find it impossible not to react to the behavior of a habitually disruptive pupil, they may be doing both themselves and the disruptive child a favor by correcting rather than derogating inappropriate conduct and by looking for opportunities to praise such children for their appropriate behaviors.[5]

TEACHING STYLES AND INSTRUCTIONAL TECHNIQUES

Earlier we saw that teachers in "effective" schools will typically set clear-cut standards for their students to achieve, emphasize successes more than failures, firmly enforce rules without derogating an offender or becoming overly punitive, and use praise rather than threats to encourage each child to work to the best of his or her ability. Perhaps you have noticed that these managerial characteristics are in some ways similar to the pattern of control

---

[5]Indeed, derogatory feedback may even *reinforce* inappropriate conduct if the child is disrupting the class as a means of seeking attention. By contrast, corrective feedback (perhaps backed by "time out," if necessary, at the principal's office) provides less attention to a disruptive child and, coupled with the use of praise for appropriate on-task behaviors, is an example of the *incompatible-response technique* that has often proved effective at modifying children's aggressive inclinations (see Chapter 10).

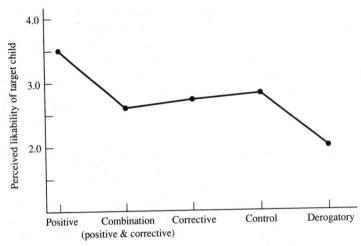

FIGURE 14-7   Average likability ratings for a disruptive child as a function of the type of verbal feedback the teacher provides. (Adapted from K. J. White & J. Kistner, "The Influence of Teacher Feedback on Young Children's Peer Preferences and Perceptions." *Developmental Psychology*, 1992, *28*, 933–940. Copyright © 1992 by the American Psychological Association.)

that Diana Baumrind calls authoritative parenting. Indeed, Baumrind (1972) believes that the three major patterns of control that characterize parent/child interactions are also found in the classroom. Teachers who use an **authoritarian** style tend to dominate their pupils, relying on power-assertive methods to enforce their demands. The **authoritative** teacher is also controlling but will rely on reason to explain his or her demands, encourage verbal give-and-take, and value autonomy and creative expression as long as the child is willing to live within the rules that the teacher has established. Finally, the **laissez-faire** (or permissive) instructor makes few demands of students and provides little or no active guidance. Baumrind believes that teachers who use an authoritative style will promote children's intellectual curiosity, their academic achievement, and their social and emotional development.

A classic study by Kurt Lewin and his associates (Lewin, Lippitt, & White, 1939) is certainly relevant. Eleven-year-old boys who met after school to participate in hobby activities, such as making papier-mâché theater masks, were supervised by adults who functioned as (1) *authoritarian* leaders (by rigidly assigning jobs and work partners and by dictating policies without providing rationales for these edicts), (2) authoritative, or *democratic*, leaders (by guiding the boys as they chose their own jobs and work partners and participated in policy making), or (3) *laissez-faire* leaders (by providing little or no guidance and remaining noncommittal for the most part). How did the boys react to these supervisory styles? Authoritarian leadership produced tension, restlessness, hostile outbursts, and a general dissatisfaction with the group experience. Productivity (as indexed by the number of theater masks constructed) was high under authoritarian leadership while the leader was present. But, when the leader left the room, work patterns disintegrated. Democratic leadership was more effective; the boys were friendly toward one another and happier with the leader. Although productivity was not as high under democratic supervision, the boys continued working in the leader's absence and the work they completed was of higher quality than that produced under authoritarian or laissez-faire leaders. Finally, the laissez-faire approach resulted in an apathetic group atmosphere and very low productivity. All but 1 of the 20 boys in this experiment clearly favored democratic supervision.

These findings also hold in the classroom, where students prefer a democratic atmosphere (Rosenthal, Underwood, & Martin, 1969; U.S. Department of Education, 1986) and often achieve more under a flexible, nondictatorial instructional style as well (Minuchin & Shapiro, 1983). Yet a word of caution is in order, for the instructional techniques that a teacher uses will not affect all children in the same way. For example, Brophy (1979) notes that teachers get the most out of *high-ability* students by moving at a quick pace and demanding high standards of performance. By contrast, *low-ability* and disadvantaged children respond much more favorably to slow-paced instruction from a teacher who is warm and encouraging rather than intrusive and demanding (see also U.S. Department of Education, 1986).

In sum, authoritative instruction does seem to promote academic achievement. Yet there are many ways in which authoritative instructors might attempt to motivate their pupils, and the techniques that work best will depend, in part, on the type of student they are trying to reach.

Do Our Schools Meet the Needs of Our Children?

From the beginning, the U.S. public school system was intended to be an instrument of social change. The push for compulsory education in the United States arose not so much from a desire to produce an educated work force (most people were then employed as farmers or as unskilled laborers and required little education) as from the need to "Americanize" an immigrant population—to teach them the values and principles on which the country was founded so as to assimilate them into the mainstream of American society (Rudolph, 1965). In recent years, policy decisions such as those regarding school desegregation and equal education for handicapped youngsters have brought new groups of students into the mainstream of American education. And, as we noted in introducing the topic of schooling, our educational system has become a potential intervention site for combatting almost every kind of social problem affecting children.

Today our public schools are often criticized for failing to accomplish their missions (Linney & Seidman, 1989). Some critics contend that educators are not doing enough to meet the needs of disadvantaged students or those who are in some way handicapped. Others believe that any major concessions made to these groups or any time devoted to such nonacademic social problems as sex education or drug education will detract from the school's instructional mission and place us at risk of failing to properly prepare our youth for the increasingly technical workaday world of a modern industrial society. So how well *are* our schools doing? Let's begin to address this issue by considering the progress of disadvantaged youngsters in our public schools.

THE SCHOOL AS A MIDDLE-CLASS INSTITUTION: EFFECTS ON DISADVANTAGED YOUTH

Public schools in the United States are middle-class institutions largely staffed by middle-class instructors who preach middle-class values. Some theorists have argued that this particular emphasis places children from lower-class or minority subcultures at an immediate disadvantage. After all, these youngsters must adjust to an environment that may seem altogether foreign and somewhat foreboding to them—a problem with which white middle-class students do not have to contend.

Many lower-income and minority students do have problems at school. They are more likely than middle-class youngsters to make poor marks, to be disciplined by the staff, to be "held back" in one or more grades, and to drop out before completing high school (Dusek, 1991). Why is this? Let's consider three possibilities.

Parental involvement. Twenty years ago it was fashionable to claim that the poor academic performance of disadvantaged students stemmed largely from the very modest academic expectancies their parents held for them (Hess, 1970). Although this conclusion may have been valid then, the times have clearly changed. Today, parents of disadvantaged and minority youth (1) value education as much as or more than other parents do, (2) spend as much or more time helping their children with

PHOTO 14-4   Children are more likely to do well in school if their parents value education and are interested and involved in school activities.

homework, and (3) are just as inclined as other parents to expect their children to do well at school (Hare & Castanell, 1985; Stevenson, Chen, & Uttal, 1990). However, parents from the lower socioeconomic strata are often less knowledgeable about the school system and less involved in many school activities, and this lack of participation may partially counteract their exhortations that school is important. But when lower-income or minority parents *are* highly involved in school activities, their children do well in school (Brookover et al., 1979; Slaughter-Defoe et al., 1990). So active parental involvement can make a big difference.

"Relevance" of educational materials.

The textbooks that children read are clearly centered on the lives and experiences of middle-class people, and it has been argued that lower-income and minority youth may simply be less inspired by these educational materials, which are often irrelevant to their own experiences. Indeed, there may be some truth to this assertion. English-speaking minority students often score far below their white, middle-class

agemates in reading proficiency — an academic area in which textbooks adequately represent the white, middle-class culture but are much less pertinent to the daily lives of young blacks and Hispanics (Kagan & Zahn, 1975; Stevenson, Chen, & Uttal, 1990). However, these same minority students show a much smaller achievement gap in mathematics, presumably because math texts contain less culturally irrelevant information. The implication is clear: perhaps we should be using more "culturally relevant" educational materials in school systems heavily populated by underachieving ethnic minorities.

Teachers' reactions to low-income and minority students.

In his book *Dark Ghetto*, Kenneth Clark (1965) argues that the classroom represents a "clash of cultures" in which teachers who have adopted middle-class values fail to appreciate the difficulties that minority students face in trying to adjust to the quiet, orderly "middle-class" atmosphere of the classroom. According to Clark, teachers in schools serving lower-income minority populations make nearly three times as many negative comments to their students as their colleagues in middle-income schools. And teachers often have lower expectancies for children from low-income families (Minuchin & Shapiro, 1983). Even before they have any academic information about their students, many instructors are already placing them into "ability groups" on the basis of their grooming, the quality of their clothing, and their use or misuse of standard English (Rist, 1970). Moreover, the language customs of children from minority subcultures often differ from those employed in school. For example, black children are asked fewer questions at home than white children are, and the questions they are asked are typically open-ended prompts that call for them to recount their knowledge or experiences through long, elaborate verbal responses (Brice-Heath, 1982, 1989). Consequently, these youngsters are often hesitant to answer what, for them, are "unusual" knowledge-training questions (requiring brief, factually correct answers) at school and may thus be branded by teachers as unknowledgeable or uncooperative. In one study (Gottlieb, 1966), teachers were asked to select from a checklist those attributes that best described their lower-income and minority pupils. Middle-class respondents consistently checked adjectives such as *lazy, fun loving,* and *rebellious.* Clearly, these instructors did not expect much of their disadvantaged students—an attitude that undoubtedly contributes to social-class and ethnic differences in achievement.

Ironically, lower-income and minority students are often convinced that they are doing well in elementary school, even when performing far below grade level (Fulkerson, Furr, & Brown, 1983; Stevenson, Chen, & Uttal, 1990). But, by the time they reach high school, many disadvantaged students are foundering academically and seem to have lost all motivation to achieve; and, to the dismay of their parents, they are at much greater risk of dropping out of school than are white children from middle-class backgrounds (American Council on Education, as cited by Associated Press, 1991).

Why is this? One reason may be that the greater demands of the junior and senior high school curricula may transform the classroom from the place of success that it appeared to be during elementary school to one of potential failure (Stevenson, Lee, et al., 1990). And, if students with substandard skills have been routinely promoted through the elementary grades, their academic deficiencies are likely to place them in the lower tracks of a high school's ability-tracking system. Now they are likely to receive even fewer challenges and less stimulation from secondary-school teachers, who don't expect them to accomplish very much (Reed, 1988). In addition, the relevant peer cultures for disadvantaged youth often endorse negative attitudes toward school and academic achievement (Slaughter-Defoe et al., 1990; Steinberg, Dornbusch, & Brown, 1992). So all these influences, coupled with a growing awareness of social prejudice and the limitations it places on vocational opportunities (see Ogbu, 1988), may cause many disadvantaged students to abandon earlier beliefs about the importance of academic achievement and to seek incentives outside the classroom.

How might we prevent disadvantaged preadolescents from becoming "turned off" by school? One suggestion favored by many educational reformers is to find ways to encourage parents and teachers to work more closely together to achieve educational objectives. As we have noted, disadvantaged youth are much less likely to fail at school when their parents are active partners in the educational process. Another model of educational reform (Banks & Banks, 1989) stresses that virtually all instruction should be made as "multicultural" (and hence "involving" for minority students) as possible without lowering curricular standards. As one example, all students might find social studies more interesting were they asked by teachers to consider the westward movement of whites in North America from the perspectives of both American pioneers and Native Americans.

Clearly there is a critical need to motivate and to better educate our disadvantaged students, for the societal costs of failing to do so are staggering. The Carnegie Council on Adolescent Development (1989) estimates that, over their lifetime, each year's class of dropouts, who are often unemployed or stuck in low-paying, dead-end jobs, will cost the United States some $260 billion in lost earnings and tax revenues. And, by the year 2000, people from economically disadvantaged backgrounds will make up more than one-third of America's school-children and future work force. As Diana Slaughter-Defoe and her associates (1990) point out, "unless the educational prospects of [these] students can be reversed, the potential for future social unrest is enormous" (p. 377).

EFFECTS OF SCHOOL DESEGREGATION ON MINORITY YOUTH

In its landmark decision in the 1954 case of *Brown* v. *Board of Education,* the U.S. Supreme Court ruled that racially segregated schools were "inherently unequal" and ordered that they be desegregated. It was hoped that, by integrating America's classrooms, black students would achieve more academically than they had in all-black schools and would show distinct improvements in self-esteem. It was also hoped that increased interracial contact would promote more favorable racial attitudes (that is, less prejudice) among both black and white students. Were these hopes realized?

Not as clearly as the Supreme Court had hoped. Focusing first on racial attitudes, one major review of the literature found that black students' prejudice toward white students decreased in 50% of the studies reviewed, whereas white prejudice toward blacks decreased in only 13% of the studies (Stephan, 1978). Even in communities where school desegregation proceeded without serious incidents, it was not at all uncommon for both black and white students in integrated schools to be *more* negative toward the other group than were students in segregated schools (Green & Gerard, 1974; Stephan, 1977). Moreover, the *self-esteem* of black students in integrated schools was no higher (and often lower) than that of black children in segregated schools (Stephan, 1978). The most encouraging news was that minority students tended to achieve a little more in integrated classrooms, especially if they began to attend an integrated school early in their academic careers (St. John, 1975).

One reason why school desegregation has not been more successful at improving race relations is that members of various racial and ethnic groups tend to stick together, without interacting much with their classmates from other groups. In fact, Neal Finkelstein and Ron Haskins (1983) found that kindergartners who were just entering an integrated school already preferred same-race peers and that these racial cleavages became even stronger over the course of the school year. Other investigators have noted that children's preferences for same-race friends become progressively stronger across grades in integrated schools (Hartup, 1983) and that few of the students who have a close other-race school friend report much contact with him or her away from school (DuBois & Hirsch, 1990). However, other-race friendships are more common in ethnically diverse schools consisting of white, black, Hispanic, and Asian-American students who are of *similar socioeconomic status* (Howes & Wu, 1990). Moreover, race relations often improve when students from different backgrounds are persuaded to cooperate as *social equals* while pursuing important academic goals, extracurricular objectives, or even "victories" as members of multiethnic sports teams (Hallinan & Teixeira, 1987; Minuchin & Shapiro, 1983). Clearly these latter findings support Finkelstein and Haskins's (1983) view that "school desegregation will not, by itself, . . . lead to a destruction of the color barriers that have plagued our

society. . . . If such barriers are to be reduced, schools will need to design, implement, and monitor programs aimed at facilitating [equal-status] social contacts between blacks and whites" (p. 508).

EDUCATING THE HANDICAPPED— IS MAINSTREAMING THE ANSWER?

In 1975 the U. S. Congress passed Public Law 94-142, the *Education for All Handicapped Children Act*. This law requires schools to provide an education equivalent to that received by normal children to all handicapped youngsters, 80% of whom are mentally retarded, speech impaired, or learning disabled. The intent of the law was to help handicapped people acquire the skills they would need to participate in a society largely populated by nonhandicapped individuals, while helping nonhandicapped people to better understand the handicapped. How might schools provide a comparable education to handicapped youngsters? Most school districts have opted for **mainstreaming**—the practice of integrating handicapped children into regular classrooms for all or large parts of the day, as opposed to segregating them in special schools or classrooms.

Has mainstreaming achieved its objectives? Not very well, it hasn't. Although handicapped students who attend regular classes are occasionally found to perform a little better academically than their handicapped agemates in special-education classes (Madden & Slavin, 1983; Zigler & Muenchow, 1979), they rarely show an increase in self-esteem. In fact, their perceived self-worth often declines because normal children tend to ridicule them and are reluctant to choose them as friends or playmates (see Guralnick & Groom, 1988; Taylor, Asher, & Williams, 1987). What can be done to make mainstreaming a more positive and fruitful experience?

Robert Slavin (1986) and his colleagues have had some success using **cooperative learning methods**, in which students of different races and ability levels are assigned to "math teams" and are reinforced for performing well *as a team*. Each team member is given problems to solve that are appropriate for his or her own ability level, but all children on a team are encouraged to monitor the activities of their teammates and to offer assistance when necessary. As encouragement for this teamwork, groups that complete the most "math units" are rewarded in some way—for example, by earning special certificates designating the winning groups as "Superteams." Here, then, is a procedure ensuring that children of different races and ability levels will interact in a context in which the efforts of even the least capable team members are important to the group's success.

Slavin finds that elementary-school students in these cooperative learning groups come to like math better and will learn more about it than they do when they receive traditional math instruction. Moreover, team members gain self-esteem from their successes, and minority-group and handicapped youngsters are more fully accepted by their peers (see also Johnson, Johnson, & Maruyama, 1983). So it seems that both racial integration and mainstreaming could have more positive academic and social consequences if educators were to deliberately design learning experiences that encourage students from different backgrounds and ability levels to pull together, work hard, and pool their individual efforts to achieve common goals (Weinstein, 1991).

HOW SUCCESSFUL ARE OUR SCHOOLS?
A CROSS-CULTURAL COMPARISON

How successful are our schools at imparting academic skills to their pupils? Large surveys of the reading, writing, and mathematical achievement of 9- to 17-year-old American students reveal that most of them do learn to read during the elementary-school years and have acquired such mathematical proficiencies as basic computational skills and graph-reading abilities by the time they finish high school (Dossey et al., 1988; National Education Goals Panel, 1992; U.S. Department of Education, 1990; White, 1991). However, American youths do not write very well; in fact, more than one-third of all 17-year-olds could not produce a coherent paragraph. Are these findings cause for alarm?

Many educators think so (see National Education Goals Panel, 1992), especially in view of the results of several cross-national surveys of children's academic achievement—studies indicating that the average scores obtained by American schoolchildren in mathematics, science, and verbal skills are consis-

tently lower (and sometimes much lower) than those made by students in many other industrialized nations (McKnight et al., 1987; National Education Goals Panel, 1992; Stevenson, Lee, & Stigler, 1986). Harold Stevenson and his associates (Stevenson & Lee, 1990; Stevenson et al., 1986; Stevenson, Lee, et al., 1990; Uttal, Lummis, & Stevenson, 1988) have been monitoring the academic progress of elementary-school children in Japan, Taiwan, the United States, and the People's Republic of China. Their findings indicate that (1) Chinese and Japanese students are outperforming American students in math from the time they enter school and (2) these differences become progressively larger from grades 1 to 5. In fact, the average math score obtained by the highest-scoring fifth-grade American classroom was below that obtained by *all* the Japanese classrooms and by *all but one* of the Chinese classrooms. Cross-national differences in reading are not so large; nevertheless, Taiwanese students score significantly higher in reading achievement than Americans, who perform at about the same levels in reading as Japanese and mainland Chinese students do (Chen & Stevenson, 1989).

In sum, the cross-national surveys clearly brand Americans as academic underachievers, especially in math and science. But why? Certainly not because they are any "dumber" than other students, for American children entering school perform just as well on IQ tests as their Asian counterparts do (Stevenson et al., 1985). Instead, the achievement gap between Asian and American students seems to center around cultural differences in educational attitudes, educational practices, and the involvement of both parents and students in the learning process. For example:

1. *Classroom instruction.* Academic success is more strongly emphasized in Asian cultures, where teachers (and parents) are more inclined than their U.S. counterparts to believe that any child can master the curricula if they try hard enough (Stevenson et al., 1986). Consequently, Asian students spend more hours per day and more days per year going to school. The Asian classroom is a businesslike, no-nonsense enterprise in which students spend about 95% of their time on such "on-task" activities as listening

PHOTO 14-5   Children in Asian classrooms are required to stay in their seats working on assignments or, as shown here, paying close attention to their teachers.

carefully to the teacher or completing assignments; by contrast, American students spend approximately 20% of their class time "off-task," as they daydream, visit with classmates, or wander around the room (Stigler, Lee, & Stevenson, 1987). Asian teachers devote two to three times as many hours a week to math instruction as American teachers do (see Figure 14-8), and they appear to be better prepared and more enthused about teaching mathematics as well (Stigler et al., 1987; Stevenson, Lee, et al., 1990).

2. *Parental involvement*. Asian parents are strongly committed to ensuring their children's academic success. They hold higher achievement expectancies for their children than American parents do, and, even though their children are excelling by American standards, Asian parents are much less likely than American parents to be satisfied with their child's current academic performance (Stevenson, Lee, et al., 1990). Asian parents think that homework is more important and they spend more time helping their children with homework than American parents do (Stevenson, Lee, et al., 1990). Asian parents also work very closely with teachers, who (1) make periodic visits to students'

homes to discuss student progress and (2) regularly send written messages home to outline school assignments and to suggest how parents might encourage or otherwise assist their child (Stevenson & Lee, 1990). By contrast, communications between U.S. parents and teachers are often limited to brief annual parent/teacher conferences.

3. *Student involvement*. Not only do Asian students spend more days of the year in class and more class time on academic assignments than American children do, but they are assigned and complete more homework as well (see Figure 14-8). Although Japanese children do not spend as much time on homework as Chinese youngsters, about half of all Japanese schoolchildren attend after-school classes (*juku*), working there on assignments that substitute for homework (Chen & Stevenson, 1989).

What steps might U.S. educators take to bridge the achievement gap between American students and pupils elsewhere? James Stigler suggests that

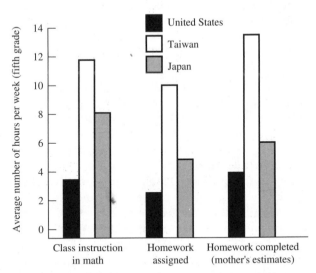

FIGURE 14-8   Average number of hours per week of class instruction in mathematics and of homework (of all kinds) that teachers assign and that mothers report their children completing. (Adapted from "Homework: A Cross-Cultural Examination," by C. Chen and H. W. Stevenson, *Child Development, 60*, 551–561; and "Contexts of Achievement: A Study of American, Chinese, and Japanese Children," *Monographs of the Society for Research in Child Development, 55* (1–2, Serial No. 221).

they increase the percentage of instructional effort devoted to math and science and decrease the amount of class time that both teachers and students spend on irrelevant nonacademic activities (Stigler et al., 1987). Better training (and pay) for math and science teachers would also help, as would the establishment of more formal pathways of communication between teachers and parents, who generally want to be involved in their children's education (Stevenson, Lee, et al., 1990) and may well do so if they receive regular updates on their child's progress and are told how they can help. One encouraging sign is that many states, cities, and local school districts have begun to respond to the cross-national surveys by strengthening curricula and standards for teacher certification, by raising the requirements for grade-to-grade promotions in elementary school and for high school graduation, and even by implementing alternative academic calendars that shorten summer vacation, thereby increasing student retention of previously learned material and giving teachers in the next grade a better chance of achieving their instructional objectives. Obviously these educational reformers believe that improving the academic achievement and vocational skills of America's youth is an attainable objective — and they recognize it as a crucial one if Americans are to maintain a leadership role in the ever-changing technological world in which they live (National Education Goals Panel, 1992; White, 1991).

Summary

This chapter has focused on two extrafamilial agents of socialization: television and the schools.

Once television became widely available, children soon began to watch it — so much so, in fact, that children today spend more time watching television than in any other waking activity. But, despite this heavy exposure, it seems that TV viewing, in moderate doses, is unlikely to impair children's cognitive development, academic achievement, or peer relations. Commercial television programming is often violent, however, and there is ample evidence that a heavy diet of televised violence can instigate aggressive behavior, cultivate the development of aggressive, antisocial habits, and make children and adolescents more tolerant of aggression. Television is also an important source of information about people in the outside world. But, unfortunately, the information that children receive is often inaccurate and misleading — frequently consisting of stereotyped portrayals of men, women, and various racial and ethnic groups. Children are also influenced by television commercials, often developing preferences for unhealthy foods or unsafe toys and becoming angry or resentful if a parent refuses to buy a product that they have requested.

Yet the effects of television are not all bad. Children are likely to learn prosocial lessons and to put them into practice after watching acts of kindness on television. Parents can help by watching shows such as *Mister Rogers' Neighborhood* with their children and then encouraging them to verbalize or role-play the prosocial lessons they have observed. Educational programs such as *Sesame Street* and *The Electric Company* have been quite successful at fostering basic cognitive skills, particularly when children watch with an adult who discusses the material with them and helps them to apply what they have learned.

By age 6, children are spending several hours of each weekday at school. Schools seem to have two missions: to impart academic knowledge and to teach children how to become "good citizens." Schooling also appears to promote cognitive development, both by transmitting general knowledge and by teaching children a variety of rules, principles, and problem-solving strategies that they can apply to many different kinds of information.

Some schools are more "effective" than others at producing positive outcomes such as low absenteeism, an enthusiastic attitude about learning, academic achievement, occupational skills, and socially desirable patterns of behavior. What makes a school effective is not its physical characteristics, classroom structure, class size, or amount of money spent per pupil but, rather, its *human resources*. Effective schools are comfortable but businesslike settings in which pupils are motivated to learn. Administrators and teachers work together to create such an atmosphere by formulating clear educational goals and providing the active guidance and feedback students need to meet these objectives.

Traditionally, the task of motivating students has been assigned to classroom instructors. Teacher expectancies may create a self-fulfilling prophecy: students usually do well when teachers expect them to succeed, whereas they often fall short of their potential when teachers expect them to do poorly. Teachers who emphasize competition in the classroom and who favor stressful evaluative procedures are likely to undermine the academic performance of their slower students and those high in test anxiety. And teachers' reactions to a child's appropriate and inappropriate classroom behaviors can even influence a child's popularity with peers. In particular, elementary-school teachers who tend to derogate inappropriate conduct (rather than correcting it) may undermine the offender's status in the peer group, whereas praise given for appropriate behavior seems to promote peer acceptance.

Teaching styles can also affect pupil outcomes. Generally speaking, it appears that an authoritative style is more likely than either authoritarian or permissive instruction to motivate students to do their best. Yet even the authoritative teacher may have to use different instructional techniques with different children in order to "get the most out of" each pupil.

The middle-class bias of most schools may hinder the academic progress of disadvantaged children or those from minority subcultures. Textbooks and other materials tend to portray middle-class values and experiences that may seem irrelevant and uninteresting to these students. Parents of disadvantaged students are often less involved in school activities, and teachers tend to hold negative academic expectancies for lower-income and minority students. All these factors seem to contribute to the academic difficulties often experienced by disadvantaged youth. At best, legally mandated school desegregation and mainstreaming have led to modest improvements in the academic performance of racial minorities and handicapped students; but these policies have done little to reduce racial prejudice or to enhance the self-esteem of either hand-

icapped pupils or minority youth. Fortunately, newly developed cooperative learning programs hold some promise of making "integration" a more fruitful experience for these students.

Cross-national surveys of academic achievement clearly brand American students as "underachievers," especially in math and science. American children are not any less intelligent than children from other countries. Instead, the achievement gap that exists between American schoolchildren and those in other industrialized societies centers around cultural differences in educational attitudes, educational practices, and the involvement of both parents and students in the learning process. Steps are now being taken at local, state, and national levels to try to bridge this achievement gap.

References

ADAMS, R. S., & BIDDLE, B. J. (1970). *Realities of teaching.* New York: Holt, Rinehart & Winston.

ANDERSON, D. R., & COLLINS, P. A. (1988). *The impact on children's education: Television's influence on cognitive development.* Washington, DC: U.S. Department of Education.

ASSOCIATED PRESS (1991, January 21). Hispanics on rise, but not in schools. *Atlanta Journal,* p. A14.

ATKIN, C. (1978). Observation of parent-child interaction in supermarket decision-making. *Journal of Marketing, 42,* 41–45.

BALL, S., & BOGATZ, C. (1973). *Reading with television: An evaluation of The Electric Company.* Princeton, NJ: Educational Testing Service.

BANDURA, A. (1973). *Aggression: A social learning analysis.* Englewood Cliffs, NJ: Prentice-Hall.

BANDURA, A., ROSS, D., & ROSS, S. A. (1963). Vicarious reinforcement and imitative learning. *Journal of Abnormal and Social Psychology, 67,* 601–607.

BANKS, J. A., & BANKS, C. A. (1989). *Multicultural education: Issues and perspectives.* Boston: Allyn & Bacon.

BARKER, R. G., & GUMP, P. V. (1964). *Big school, small school.* Stanford, CA: Stanford University Press.

BAUMRIND, D. (1972). From each according to her ability. *School Review, 80,* 161–197.

BEENTJES, J. W., & VANDERVOORT, T. H. (1988). Television's impact on children's reading skills. *Reading Research Quarterly, 23,* 389–413.

BIGLER, R. S., & LIBEN, L. S. (1990). The role of attitudes and interventions in gender-schematic processing. *Child Development, 61,* 1440–1452.

BOGATZ, G. A., & BALL, S. (1972). *The second year of Sesame Street: A continuing evaluation.* Princeton, NJ: Educational Testing Service.

BRICE-HEATH, S. (1982). Questioning at home and at school: A comparative study. In G. Spindler (Ed.), *Doing the ethnography of schooling: Educational anthropology in action*. New York: Holt, Rinehart & Winston.

BRICE-HEATH, S. (1989). Oral and literate traditions among black Americans living in poverty. *American Psychologist, 44*, 367–373.

BRONFENBRENNER, U. (1970). *Who cares for America's children?* Invited address presented at the Conference of the National Association for the Education of Young Children, Washington, DC.

BROOKOVER, W., BEADY, C., FLOOD, P., SCHWEITZER, J., & WISENBAKER, J. (1979). *School social systems and student achievement: Schools can make a difference*. New York: Praeger.

BROPHY, J. E. (1979). Teacher behavior and its effects. *Journal of Educational Psychology, 71*, 733–750.

BROPHY, J. E. (1983). Research on the self-fulfilling prophecy and teacher expectations. *Journal of Educational Psychology, 75*, 631–661.

BURCHINAL, M., LEE, M., & RAMEY, C. (1989). Type of daycare and preschool intellectual development in disadvantaged children. *Child Development, 60*, 128–137.

BUTLER, R. (1989). Mastery versus ability appraisal: A developmental study of children's observations of peers' work. *Child Development, 60*, 1350–1361.

BUTLER, R. (1990). The effects of mastery and competitive conditions on self-assessment at different ages. *Child Development, 61*, 201–210.

CAHAN, S., & COHEN, N. (1989). Age versus schooling effects on intelligence development. *Child Development, 60*, 1239–1249.

CARNEGIE COUNCIL ON ADOLESCENT DEVELOPMENT (1989). *Turning points: Preparing American youth for the 21st century*. New York: Carnegie Corp.

CECI, S. J. (1991). How much does schooling influence general intelligence and its cognitive components? *Developmental Psychology, 27*, 703–722.

CHEN, C., & STEVENSON, H. W. (1989). Homework: A cross-cultural examination. *Child Development, 60*, 551–561.

CLARK, K. B. (1965). *Dark ghetto*. New York: Harper & Row.

CLEMENTS, D. (1986). Effects of Logo and CAI environments on cognition and creativity. *Journal of Educational Psychology, 78*, 309–318.

CLINE, V. E., CROFT, R. G., & COURRIER, S. (1973). Desensitization of children to television violence. *Journal of Personality and Social Psychology, 27*, 360–365.

COLLINS, W. A. (1973). Effect of temporal separation between motivation, aggression, and consequences: A developmental study. *Developmental Psychology, 8*, 215–221.

COLLINS, W. A. (1983). Interpretation and inference in children's television viewing. In J. R. Bryant & D. R. Anderson (Eds.), *Children's understanding of television: Research on attention and comprehension*. New York: Academic Press.

COLLINS, W. A., SOBOL, B. L., & WESTBY, S. (1981). Effects of adult commentary on children's comprehension and inferences about a televised aggressive portrayal. *Child Development, 52*, 158–163.

COMER, J. (1991). The black child in school. In M. Lewis (Ed.), *Child and adolescent psychiatry: A comprehensive textbook*. Baltimore: Williams & Wilkins.

COOK, T. D., APPLETON, H., CONNER, R. F., SHAFFER, A., TABKIN, G., & WEBER, J. S. (1975). *Sesame Street revisited*. New York: Russell Sage Foundation.

COOPER, H. M. (1979). Pygmalion grows up: A model for teacher expectation, communication, and performance influence. *Review of Educational Research, 49*, 389–410.

COOPER, H. M. (1989). Does reducing student-to-instructor ratios affect achievement? *Educational Psychologist, 24*, 79–98.

CORDER-BOLZ, C. R. (1980). Mediation: The role of significant others. *Journal of Communication, 30*, 106–118.

CORTEEN, R. S., & WILLIAMS, T. (1986). Television and reading skills. In T. Williams (Ed.), *The impact of television: A natural experiment in three communities*. Orlando, FL: Academic Press.

DOSSEY, J. A., MULLIS, I. V. S., LINDQUIST, M. M., & CHAMBERS, D. L. (1988). *The Mathematics Report Card: Are we measuring up?* Princeton, NJ: Educational Testing Service.

DRABMAN, R. S., & THOMAS, M. H. (1974). Does media violence increase children's toleration of real-life aggression? *Developmental Psychology, 10*, 418–421.

DuBOIS, D. L., & HIRSCH, B. J. (1990). School and neighborhood friendship patterns of Blacks and Whites in early adolescence. *Child Development, 61*, 524–536.

DUSEK, J. B. (1991). *Adolescent development and behavior* (2nd ed.). Englewood Cliffs, NJ: Prentice-Hall.

DWECK, C. S., & ELLIOTT, E. S. (1983). Achievement motivation. In E. M. Hetherington (Ed.), *Handbook of child psychology*. Vol. 4: *Socialization, personality, and social development*. New York: Wiley.

EDUCATIONAL RESEARCH SERVICE (1978). *Class size: A summary of research*. Arlington, VA: Author.

ELKIND, D. (1981). *The hurried child: Growing up too fast too soon*. Reading, MA: Addison-Wesley.

ERON, L. D. (1982). Parent-child interaction, television violence, and aggression of children. *American Psychologist, 37*, 197–211.

ERON, L. D., & HUESMANN, L. R. (1984). The control of aggressive behavior by changes in attitudes, values, and the conditions of learning. In R. J. Blanchard & C. Blanchard (Eds.), *Advances in the study of aggression* (Vol. 2). Orlando, FL: Academic Press.

ERON, L. D., HUESMANN, L. R., BRICE, P., FISCHER, P., & MERMELSTEIN, R. (1983). Age trends in the development of aggression, sex-typing, and related television habits. *Developmental Psychology, 19*, 71–77.

ERON, L. D., HUESMANN, L. R., LEFKOWITZ, M. M., & WALDER, L. O. (1972). Does television violence cause aggression? *American Psychologist, 27*, 253–263.

FESHBACH, S. (1970). Aggression. In P. H. Mussen (Ed.), *Carmichael's manual of child psychology* (Vol. 2). New York: Wiley.

FINKELSTEIN, N. W., & HASKINS, R. (1983). Kindergarten children prefer same-color peers. *Child Development, 54,* 502–508.

FREEDMAN, J. L. (1984). Effect of television violence on aggressiveness. *Psychological Bulletin, 96,* 227–246.

FRIEDRICH, L. K., & STEIN, A. H. (1973). Aggressive and prosocial television programs and the natural behavior of preschool children. *Monographs of the Society for Research in Child Development, 38* (Serial No. 151).

FRIEDRICH, L. K., & STEIN, A. H. (1975). Prosocial television and young children: The effects of verbal labeling and role-playing on learning and behavior. *Child Development, 46,* 27–38.

FRIEDRICH-COFER, L. K., HUSTON-STEIN, A., KIPNIS, D. M., SUSMAN, E. J., & CLEWETT, A. S. (1979). Environmental enhancement of prosocial television content: Effects on interpersonal behavior. *Developmental Psychology, 15,* 637–646.

FULKERSON, K. F., FURR, S., & BROWN, D. (1983). Expectations and achievement among third-, sixth-, and ninth-grade black and white males and females. *Developmental Psychology, 19,* 231–236.

GALST, J. P. (1980). Television food commercials and pronutritional public service announcements as determinants of young children's snack choices. *Child Development, 51,* 935–938.

GARBARINO, J. (1980). Some thoughts on school size and its effects on adolescent development. *Journal of Youth and Adolescence, 9,* 19–31.

GEIST, W. E. (1985, November 3). New Yorkers trying to stop nursery school madness. *Lexington Herald-Leader,* p. A14.

GERBNER, G., GROSS, L., SIGNORIELLI, N., & MORGAN, M. (1986). *Television's mean world: Violence Profile No. 14–15.* University of Pennsylvania, Annenberg School of Communications, Philadelphia.

GOOD, T. L. (1979). Teacher effectiveness in the elementary school: What do we know about it now? *Journal of Teacher Education, 30,* 52–64.

GORN, G. J., GOLDBERG, M. E., & KANUNGO, R. N. (1976). The role of educational television in changing the intergroup attitudes of children. *Child Development, 47,* 277–280.

GOTTLIEB, D. (1966). Teaching and students: The views of Negro and white teachers. *Sociology of Education, 37,* 344–353.

GRAVES, S. B. (1975, April). *How to encourage positive racial attitudes.* Paper presented at the biennial meeting of the Society for Research in Child Development, Denver.

GREEN, J. A., & GERARD, H. B. (1974). School desegregation and ethnic attitudes. In H. Franklin & J. Sherwood (Eds.), *Integrating the organization.* New York: Free Press.

GURALNICK, M. J., & GROOM, J. M. (1988). Friendships of preschool children in mainstreamed playgroups. *Developmental Psychology, 24,* 595–604.

HALLINAN, M. T., & TEIXEIRA, R. A. (1987). Opportunities and constraints: Black-white differences in the formation of interracial friendships. *Child Development, 58,* 1358–1371.

HARE, B. R., & CASTANELL, L. A., JR. (1985). No place to run, no place to hide: Comparative status and future prospects for black boys. In M. B. Spencer, G. K. Brookins, & W. R. Allen (Eds.), *Beginnings: The social and affective development of black children.* Hillsdale, NJ: Erlbaum.

HARRIS, M. J., & ROSENTHAL, R. (1986). Four factors in the mediation of teacher expectancy effects. In R. S. Feldman (Ed.), *The social psychology of education: Current research and theory.* Cambridge, England: Cambridge University Press.

HARRISON, L. F., & WILLIAMS, T. (1986). Television and cognitive development. In T. Williams (Ed.), *The impact of television: A natural experiment in three communities.* Orlando, FL: Academic Press.

HARTUP, W. W. (1983). Peer relations. In E. M. Hetherington (Ed.), *Handbook of social psychology.* Vol. 4: *Socialization, personality, and social development.* New York: Wiley.

HAWKINS, J., SHEINGOLD, K., GEARHART, M., & BERGER, C. (1982). Microcomputers in schools: Impact on the social life of elementary classrooms. *Journal of Applied Developmental Psychology, 3,* 361–373.

HEAROLD, S. (1986). A synthesis of 1043 effects of television on social behavior. In G. Comstock (Ed.), *Public communications and behavior: Volume I.* New York: Academic Press.

HESS, R. D. (1970). Social class and ethnic influences upon socialization. In P. H. Mussen (Ed.), *Carmichael's manual of child psychology* (Vol. 2). New York: Wiley.

HILL, K. T., & EATON, W. O. (1977). The interaction of test anxiety and success-failure experiences in determining children's arithmetic performances. *Developmental Psychology, 13,* 205–211.

HILL, P. T., FOSTER, G. E., & GENDLER, T. (1990). *High schools with character: Alternatives to bureaucracy.* Santa Monica, CA: Rand Corp.

HOWES, C., & WU, F. (1990). Peer interactions and friendships in an ethnically diverse school setting. *Child Development, 61,* 537–541.

HUESMANN, L. R. (1986). Psychological processes promoting the relation between exposure to media violence and aggressive behavior by the viewer. *Journal of Social Issues, 42,* 125–139.

HUESMANN, L. R., LAGERSPITZ, K., & ERON, L. D. (1984). Intervening variables in the TV violence-aggression relation: Evidence from two countries. *Developmental Psychology, 20,* 746–775.

HUSTON, A. C., WATKINS, B. A., & KUNKEL, D. (1989). Public policy and children's television. *American Psychologist, 44,* 424–433.

HUSTON, A. C., WRIGHT, J. C., RICE, M. L., KERKMAN, D., & ST. PETERS, M. (1990). Development of television viewing patterns in early childhood: A longitudinal investigation. *Developmental Psychology, 26,* 409–420.

HYSON, M. C., HIRSCH-PASEK, K., & RESCORLA, L. (1989). *Academic environments in early childhood: Challenge or pressure?* Summary report to the Spencer Foundation.

JOHNSON, D. W., JOHNSON, R. T., & MARUYAMA, G. (1983). Interdependence and interpersonal attraction among heterogeneous and homogeneous individuals: A theoretical formulation and a meta-analysis of the research. *Review of Educational Research, 53,* 5–54.

JOHNSON, N. (1967). *How to talk back to your television.* Boston: Little, Brown.

JOHNSTON, J., & ETTEMA, J. S. (1982). *Positive images.* Newbury Park, CA: Sage.

JUSSIM, L., & ECCLES, J. S. (1993). Teacher expectations II: Construction and reflection of student achievement. *Journal of Personality and Social Psychology, 63,* 947–961.

KAGAN, S., & ZAHN, G. L. (1975). Field dependence and the school achievement gap between Anglo-American and Mexican-American children. *Journal of Educational Psychology, 67,* 643–650.

KEE, D. W. (1986). Computer play. In A. W. Gottfried & C. C. Brown (Eds.), *Play interactions: The contribution of play materials and parental involvement to children's development.* Lexington, MA: Lexington Books.

KIMBALL, M. M. (1986). Television and sex-role attitudes. In T. Williams (Ed.), *The impact of television: A natural experiment in three communities.* Orlando, FL: Academic Press.

KULIK, J. A., KULIK, C. C., & BANGERT-DROWNS, R. I. (1985). Effectiveness of computer-based education in elementary schools. *Computers in Human Behavior, 1,* 59–74.

LEE, V. E., BROOKS-GUNN, J., SCHNUR, E., & LIAW, F. (1990). Are Head Start efforts sustained? A longitudinal follow-up comparison of disadvantaged children attending Head Start, no preschool, and other preschool programs. *Child Development, 61,* 495–507.

LEHRER, R., & RANDLE, L. (1987). Problem-solving, metacognition, and composition: The effects of interactive software for first grade children. *Journal of Educational Computing Research, 3,* 409–427.

LEPPER, M. R. (1985). Microcomputers in education: Motivation and social issues. *American Psychologist, 40,* 1–18.

LEPPER, M. R., & GURTNER, J. (1989). Children and computers: Approaching the twenty-first century. *American Psychologist, 44,* 170–178.

LEWIN, K., LIPPITT, R., & WHITE, R. K. (1939). Patterns of aggressive behavior in experimentally created "social climates." *Journal of Social Psychology, 10,* 271–299.

LEYENS, J. P., PARKE, R. D., CAMINO, L., & BERKOWITZ, L. (1975). Effects of movie violence on aggression in a field setting as a function of group dominance and cohesion. *Journal of Personality and Social Psychology, 32,* 346–360.

LIEBERT, R. M., & BARON, R. A. (1972). Some immediate effects of televised violence on children's behavior. *Developmental Psychology, 6,* 469–475.

LIEBERT, R. M., NEALE, J. M., & DAVIDSON, E. S. (1973). *The early window: Effects of television on children and youth.* New York: Pergamon Press.

LIEBERT, R. M., & SCHWARTZBERG, N. S. (1977). Effects of mass media. In M. R. Rosenzweig & L. W. Porter (Eds.), *Annual review of psychology* (Vol. 28). Palo Alto, CA: Annual Reviews.

LIEBERT, R. M., & SPRAFKIN, J. N. (1988). *The early window: Effects of television on children and youth* (3rd ed.). New York: Pergamon Press.

LINN, M. C., de BENEDICTIS, T., & DELUCCHI, K. (1982). Adolescent reasoning about advertisements: Preliminary investigations. *Child Development, 53,* 1599–1613.

LINNEY, J. A., & SEIDMAN, E. (1989). The future of schooling. *American Psychologist, 44,* 336–340.

LONNER, W. J., THORNDIKE, R. M., FORBES, N. E., & ASHWORTH, C. (1985). The influence of television on measured cognitive abilities: A study with native Alaskan children. *Journal of Cross-Cultural Psychology, 16,* 355–380.

LYLE, J., & HOFFMAN, H. R. (1972). Children's use of television and other media. In E. H. Rubenstein, G. A. Comstock, & J. P. Murray (Eds.), *Television in day-to-day life: Patterns of use.* Washington, DC: U.S. Government Printing Office.

MADDEN, N. A., & SLAVIN, R. E. (1983). Mainstreaming students with mild handicaps: Academic and social outcomes. *Review of Educational Research, 53,* 519–569.

McKNIGHT, C. C., CROSSWHITE, F. J., DOSSEY, J. A., KIFER, E., SWAFFORD, J. O., TRAVERS, K. J., & COONEY, T. J. (1987). *The underachieving curriculum: Assessing U.S. school mathematics from an international perspective.* Champaign, IL: Stipes.

MINUCHIN, P. P., & SHAPIRO, E. K. (1983). The school as a context for social development. In E. M. Hetherington (Ed.), *Handbook of child psychology. Vol. 4: Socialization, personality, and social development.* New York: Wiley.

MORGAN, M. (1982). Television and adolescents' sex-role stereotypes: A longitudinal study. *Journal of Personality and Social Psychology, 43,* 947–955.

MORRISON, F. J. (1991, April). *Making the cut: Early schooling and cognitive growth.* Paper presented at the meeting of the Society for Research in Child Development, Seattle.

MURRAY, J. P. (1980). *Television and youth: 25 years of research and controversy.* Boys Town, NE: Boys Town Center for the Study of Youth Development.

NATIONAL EDUCATION GOALS PANEL (1992). *The National Education Goals Report, 1992.* Washington, DC: U.S. Department of Education.

OGBU, J. (1988). Black education: A cultural-ecological perspective. In H. P. McAdoo (Ed.), *Black families.* Newbury Park, CA: Sage.

OSBORN, D. K., & ENDSLEY, R. C. (1971). Emotional reactions of young children to TV violence. *Child Development, 42,* 321–331.

PALMER, E. L. (1984). Providing quality television for America's children. In J. P. Murray & G. Salomon (Eds.), *The future of children's television.* Boys Town, NE: Boys Town Center for the Study of Youth and Development.

PARKE, R. D., BERKOWITZ, L., LEYENS, J., WEST, S., & SEBASTIAN, R. J. (1977). Some effects of violent and nonviolent movies on the behavior of juvenile delinquents. In L. Berkowitz (Ed.), *Advances in experimental social psychology* (Vol. 10). Orlando, FL: Academic Press.

PARKE, R. D., & SLABY, R. G. (1983). The development of aggression. In E. M. Hetherington (Ed.), *Handbook of child psychology. Vol. 4: Socialization, personality, and social development.* New York: Wiley.

PAULSON, F. L. (1974). Teaching cooperation on television: An evaluation of *Sesame Street*'s social goals and programs. *AV Communication Review, 22,* 229–246.

PETERSON, P. E., JEFFREY, D. B., BRIDGEWATER, C. A., & DAWSON, B. (1984). How pronutritional television programming affects children's dietary habits. *Developmental Psychology, 20,* 55–63.

PINON, M., HUSTON, A. C., & WRIGHT, J. C. (1989). Family ecology and child characteristics that predict young children's educational television viewing. *Child Development, 60,* 846–856.

REED, R. J. (1988). Education and achievement of young black males. In J. T. Gibbs (Ed.), *Young, black, and male in America: An endangered species.* Dover, MA: Auburn House.

RICE, M. L., HUSTON, A. C., TRUGLIO, R., & WRIGHT, J. (1990). Words from "Sesame Street": Learning vocabulary while viewing. *Developmental Psychology, 26,* 421–428.

RIST, R. C. (1970). Student social class and teacher expectations: The self-fulfilling prophecy in ghetto education. *Harvard Educational Review, 40,* 411–451.

ROBERTSON, T. S., & ROSSITER, J. R. (1974). Children and commercial persuasion: An attribution theory analysis. *Journal of Consumer Research, 1,* 13–20.

ROGOFF, B. (1990). *Apprenticeship in thinking: Cognitive development in social context.* New York: Oxford University Press.

ROGOFF, B., & MORELLI, G. (1989). Perspectives on children's development from cultural psychology. *American Psychologist, 44,* 343–348.

ROSENTHAL, R. (1986). Media violence, antisocial behavior, and the social consequences of small effects. *Journal of Social Issues, 42,* 141–154.

ROSENTHAL, R., & JACOBSON, L. (1968). *Pygmalion in the classroom.* New York: Holt, Rinehart & Winston.

ROSENTHAL, T., UNDERWOOD, B., & MARTIN, M. (1969). Assessing classroom incentive practices. *Journal of Educational Psychology, 60,* 370–376.

ROSENWASSER, S. M., LINGENFELTER, M., & HARRINGTON, A. F. (1989). Nontraditional gender role portrayals and children's gender role perceptions. *Journal of Applied Developmental Psychology, 10,* 97–105.

RUDOLPH, F. (1965). *Essays on early education in the republic.* Cambridge, MA: Harvard University Press.

RUTTER, M. (1983). School effects on pupil progress: Research findings and policy implications. *Child Development, 54,* 1–29.

RUTTER, M., MAUGHAN, B., MORTIMORE, P., OUSTON, J., & SMITH, A. (1979). *Fifteen thousand hours: Secondary schools and their effects on children.* Cambridge, MA: Harvard University Press.

SEABROOK, C. (1991, January 9). Real spending for education declines in 1980s. *Atlanta Journal,* p. 21A.

SHARP, D., COLE, M., & LAVE, C. (1979). Education and cognitive development: The evidence from experimental research. *Monographs of the Society for Research in Child Development, 44* (1–2, Serial No. 178).

SINGER, J. L., & SINGER, D. G. (1983). Implications of childhood television viewing for cognition, imagination, and emotion. In J. Bryant & D. R. Anderson (Eds.), *Children's understanding of television.* New York: Academic Press.

SLAUGHTER-DEFOE, D. T., NAKAGAWA, K., TAKANISHI, R., & JOHNSON, D. J. (1990). Toward cultural/ecological perspectives on schooling and achievement in African- and Asian-American children. *Child Development, 61,* 363–383.

SLAVIN, R. E. (1986). Cooperative learning: Engineering social psychology in the classroom. In R. S. Feldman (Ed.), *The social psychology of education: Current research and theory.* Cambridge, England: Cambridge University Press.

STEIN, A. H., & FRIEDRICH, L. K. (1972). Television content and young children's behavior. In J. P. Murray, E. A. Rubinstein, & G. A. Comstock (Eds.), *Television and social behavior.* Vol. 2: *Television and social learning.* Washington, DC: U.S. Government Printing Office.

STEINBERG, L., DORNBUSCH, S. M., & BROWN, B. B. (1992). Ethnic differences in adolescent achievement. *American Psychologist, 47,* 723–729.

STEPHAN, W. G. (1977). Cognitive differentiation and intergroup perception. *Sociometry, 40,* 50–58.

STEPHAN, W. G. (1978). School desegregation: An evaluation of the predictions made in *Brown v. Board of Education. Psychological Bulletin, 85,* 217–238.

STEVENSON, H. W., CHEN, C., & UTTAL, D. H. (1990). Beliefs and achievement: A study of Black, White, and Hispanic children. *Child Development, 61,* 508–523.

STEVENSON, H. W., & LEE, S. Y. (1990). Contexts of achievement: A study of American, Chinese, and Japanese children. *Monographs of the Society for Research in Child Development, 55* (1-2, Serial No. 221).

STEVENSON, H. W., LEE, S. Y., CHEN, C., LUMMIS, M., STIGLER, J. W., FAN, L., & FANG, G. (1990). Mathematics achievement of children in China and the United States. *Child Development, 61,* 1053–1056.

STEVENSON, H. W., LEE, S. Y., & STIGLER, J. W. (1986). Mathematics achievement of Chinese, Japanese, and American children. *Science, 231,* 693–699.

STEVENSON, H. W., STIGLER, J. W., LEE, S. Y., LUCKER, G. W., LITAMURA, S., & HSU, C. (1985). Cognitive performance and academic achievement of Japanese, Chinese, and American children. *Child Development, 56,* 718–734.

STIGLER, J. W., LEE, S. Y., & STEVENSON, H. W. (1987). Mathematics classrooms in Japan, Taiwan, and the United States. *Child Development, 58,* 1272–1285.

ST. JOHN, N. H. (1975). *School desegregation: Outcomes for children.* New York: Wiley.

STONEMAN, Z., & BRODY, G. H. (1981). Peers as mediators of television food advertisements aimed at children. *Developmental Psychology, 17,* 853–858.

ST. PETERS, M., FITCH, M., HUSTON, A. C., WRIGHT, J. C., & EAKINS, D. J. (1991). Television and families: What do young children watch with their parents? *Child Development, 62,* 1409–1423.

TANGNEY, J. P. (1988). Aspects of the family and children's television viewing content preferences. *Child Development, 59,* 1070–1079.

TAYLOR, A. R., ASHER, S. R., & WILLIAMS, G. A. (1987). The social adaptation of mainstreamed mildly retarded children. *Child Development, 58,* 1321–1334.

THOMAS, M. H., HORTON, R. W., LIPPINCOTT, E. C., & DRABMAN, R. S. (1977). Desensitization to portrayals of real-life aggression as a function of exposure to television violence. *Journal of Personality and Social Psychology, 35,* 450–458.

U.S. BUREAU OF THE CENSUS (1989). *Statistical abstract of the United States, 1989* (10th ed.). Washington, DC: U.S. Government Printing Office.

U.S. DEPARTMENT OF EDUCATION (1986). *What works—Research about teaching and learning.* Washington, DC: U.S. Government Printing Office.

U.S. DEPARTMENT OF EDUCATION (1990). *National assessment of educational progress.* Washington, DC: U.S. Government Printing Office.

UTTAL, D. H., LUMMIS, M., & STEVENSON, H. W. (1988). Low and high mathematics achievement in Japanese, Chinese, and American elementary-school children. *Developmental Psychology, 24,* 335–342.

WEINSTEIN, C. S. (1991). The classroom as a social context for learning. *Annual Review of Psychology, 42,* 493–525.

WEINSTEIN, R. S., MARSHALL, H. H., SHARP, L., & BOTKIN, M. (1987). Pygmalion and the student: Age and classroom differences in children's awareness of teacher expectations. *Child Development, 58,* 1079–1093.

WHITE, B. (1991, September 30). U.S. education behind goals, report reveals. *Atlanta Journal,* pp. A1, A16.

WHITE, K. J., & KISTNER, J. (1992). The influence of teacher feedback on young children's peer preferences and perceptions. *Developmental Psychology, 28,* 933–940.

WILSON, C. C., & GUTIERREZ, F. (1985). *Minorities and the media: Diversity and the end of mass communication.* Newbury Park, CA: Sage.

WRIGHT, J. C., & HUSTON, A. C. (1983). A matter of form: Potentials of television for young viewers. *American Psychologist, 38,* 835–843.

ZIGLER, E. (1987). Formal schooling for four-year-olds? No. *American Psychologist, 42,* 254–260.

ZIGLER, E., & FINN STEVENSON, M. F. (1993). *Children in a changing world: Development and social issues.* Pacific Grove, CA: Brooks/Cole.

ZIGLER, E., & MUENCHOW, S. (1979). Mainstreaming: The proof is in the implementation. *American Psychologist, 34,* 993–996.

15 | *Extrafamilial Influences II: Peers as Socialization Agents*

Throughout this text we have concentrated on adults as the major source of influence on developing children. In their various roles as parents, teachers, coaches, scoutmasters, and religious leaders, adults clearly represent the power, authority, and expertise of a society. But grownups are by no means the sole influence on the social development of children — even very young children. In this final chapter we will concentrate on yet another important agency of socialization: other children and the society of one's peers.

Although youngsters spend an enormous amount of time and energy socializing with one another, only within the past 25 years have developmentalists given much thought to how contacts with peers might influence developing children. Perhaps owing to early research on the behavior of adolescent gangs (see Hartup, 1983), peers have often been characterized as potentially subversive agents who may erode the influence of adults and lead the child into a life of delinquency and antisocial conduct. Popular novels and films such as *Lord of the Flies* and *A Clockwork Orange* reinforce this point of view.

However, this perspective on peer relations is distorted and unnecessarily negative. Although peers occasionally are "bad influences," they clearly have the potential to affect their playmates in positive ways. Try to imagine what your life would be like if other children had not been available as you were growing up. Would you have acquired the social skills to mix comfortably with others, to cooperate, to engage in socially acceptable forms of competition, or to make appropriate social (or sexual) responses to love objects other than your parents? No one can say for sure, but the following letter written by a farmer from the Midwestern United States provides a strong clue that interactions with other children may be an important aspect of the socialization process.[1]

---

[1]This letter appears with the permission of its author and its recipient, Dr. Shirley G. Moore.

Dear Dr. Moore:

I read the report in the Oct. 30 issue of _____ about your study of only children. I am an only child, now 57 years old, and I want to tell you some things about my life. Not only was I an only child, but I grew up in the country where there were no nearby children to play with. . . . [And] from the first year of school, I was teased and made fun of. . . . I dreaded to get on the school bus and go to school because the other children on the bus called me "Mommy's baby." In about the second grade I heard the boys use a vulgar word. I asked what it meant and they made fun of me. So I learned a lesson — don't ask questions. This can lead to a lot of confusion to hear talk one doesn't understand and not be able to learn what it means.

I never went out with a girl while I was in school — in fact I hardly talked to them. In our school the boys and girls did not play together. Boys were sent to one part of the playground and girls to another. So I didn't learn anything about girls. When we got into high school and boys and girls started dating, I could only listen to their stories about their experiences.

I could tell you a lot more, but the important thing is I have never married or had any children. I have not been very successful in an occupation or vocation. I believe my troubles are not all due to being an only child . . . but I do believe you are right in recommending playmates for . . . school agers and not have them strictly supervised by adults. . . . Parents of only children should make special efforts to provide playmates for them.

Sincerely yours,

If we assume that peers are important agents of socialization, there are a number of questions that remain to be answered. For example, who qualifies as a peer? How do peers influence one another? What is it about peer influence that is unique? What are the consequences (if any) of poor peer relations? Is it important to have special peer alliances, or friendships? Do peers eventually become a more potent source of influence than parents or other adults? These are some of the issues that have been raised as developmentalists turn in ever-increasing numbers to the study of peer influence.

Who Is a Peer, and What Functions Do Peers Serve?

Webster's New Collegiate Dictionary defines a **peer** as "one that is of equal standing with another." Developmentalists also think of peers as *"social equals"* or as individuals *who, for the moment at least, are operating at similar levels of behavioral complexity* (Lewis & Rosenblum, 1975). Notice that this "activity-based" definition treats the quality of "being a peer" as a transient thing, tied directly to a particular activity or interaction. So older or younger associates (or even pets) may become peers if these "companions" share with the child capabilities and goals that in some way facilitate their interaction. Although the vast majority of peer-oriented research has concentrated on the influence of agemates, we will see that this activity-based definition of a peer has opened exciting new avenues of inquiry by leading investigators to consider the significance of **mixed-age peer interactions** for a child's social development.

The Adaptive Significance of Peer Interaction

Contemporary research on peer influence has been heavily influenced by theorists from the *ethological* tradition, who have sought to determine the *adaptive significance* of child/child interactions. You may recall from Chapters 10 and 11 that conflicts among peers when resources (toys) are scarce can help youngsters learn how to resolve their differences amicably through prosocial modes of conflict resolution, such as sharing (Caplan et al., 1991). We also noted that even blatantly hostile exchanges among 3–5-year-olds may prove adaptive by helping to create *dominance hierarchies* that establish the relative power and status of individual group members and thereby *minimize* the likelihood of future aggression within the peer group (Sackin & Thelen, 1984; Strayer, 1980). Based on such observations, ethologists propose that peer interaction may be a special form of social behavior that has been "selected" over the centuries to promote the development of adaptive patterns of social conduct in each successive generation. Let's now consider some of the specific functions that child/child interactions might serve.

SAME-AGE (OR EQUAL-STATUS) INTERACTIONS

We get some idea why contacts among agemates may be important by contrasting them to exchanges that occur at home. A child's interactions with parents and older siblings are rarely equal-status contacts; typically, young children are placed in a subordinate position by an older member of the family who is instructing them, issuing orders, or otherwise overseeing their activities. By contrast, agemates are much less critical and directive, and children are freer to try out new roles, ideas, and behaviors when interacting with someone of similar status. And, in so doing, they are likely to learn important lessons about themselves and others — lessons such as "She quits when I don't take turns," "He hits me when I push him," or "Nobody likes a cheater." Many theorists believe that peer contacts are important precisely because they are *equal-status* contacts; that is, they teach children to understand and appreciate the perspectives of people *just like themselves* and thereby contribute to the development of social competencies that may be difficult to acquire in the nonegalitarian atmosphere of the home.

MIXED-AGE INTERACTIONS

According to Hartup (1983), interaction among children of *different* ages is also a critically important context for social and personality development. Although cross-age interactions tend to be somewhat *asymmetrical*, with one child (typically the elder) possessing more power or status than the other, it is precisely these asymmetries that may help children to acquire certain social competencies. For example, the presence of younger peers may foster the development of sympathy and compassion, caregiving and prosocial inclinations, assertiveness, and leadership skills in older children (see, for example, French et al., 1986). At the same time, younger children may benefit from mixed-age interactions by learning how to seek assistance and how to defer gracefully to the wishes and directives of older, more powerful peers. Moreover, younger children are potentially in a position to acquire many socially and intellectually adaptive patterns of behavior by instruction (tutoring) from elder playmates or by observation and imitation of the competent behaviors of these "older and wiser" companions.

In their survey of children's social contacts in several cultures, Whiting and Edwards (1988) found that mixed-age interactions do differ in important ways from those among agemates. Nurturant and prosocial behaviors occurred more frequently in mixed-age groups, whereas casually sociable acts (such as conversation and cooperative play) as well as antisocial ones (such as aggression) were more likely to occur among agemates. Older children usually take charge of mixed-age interactions and will adjust their behavior to the competencies of their younger companions (see also Brody, Graziano, & Musser, 1983; Graziano et al., 1976). Even 2-year-olds show such powers of leadership and accommodation, for they are more inclined to take the initiative and to display simpler and more repetitive play routines when paired with an 18-month-old toddler than with an agemate (Brownell, 1990).

By the time children enter grade school, they know that same-age and mixed-age interactions serve different purposes, and their preferences for associating with older, younger, or same-age peers clearly depend on the goals they are pursuing (French, 1984). Six- to 9-year-olds, for example, prefer agemates to younger or older children if their objective is to pick a friend. However, older children are preferred over agemates if the child feels the need for sympathy or guidance, whereas younger children are the ones subjects choose if the situation calls for them to display compassion or to teach another child what they already know.

Perhaps you have noticed that mixed-age peer interactions are presumed to benefit older and younger children in many of the same ways that sibling

PHOTO 15-1   Both older and younger children benefit from mixed-age interactions.

interactions benefit older and younger siblings (see Chapter 13). But there is a crucial difference between sibling and peer contacts, for one's status as either a younger or an older sibling is *fixed* by order of birth, whereas one's peer status is *flexible*, depending on whom he or she is associating with. Thus, mixed-age *peer* interactions may provide children with experience they might otherwise miss in their sibling interactions and, in fact, may be the primary context in which (1) a habitually domineering elder sibling learns to be more accommodating (when interacting with older peers), (2) an oppressed younger sib learns to lead and to show compassion (when dealing with even younger children), and (3) an only child (who has no sibs) acquires both sets of social competencies. Viewed in this way, mixed-age peer interactions may be important experiences indeed.

Frequency of Peer Contacts

As you might expect, the amount of contact that children have with their peers increases with age. Sharri Ellis and her colleagues (1981) observed the daily activities of 436 children aged 2 to 12 to determine how often they interacted with adults, age-

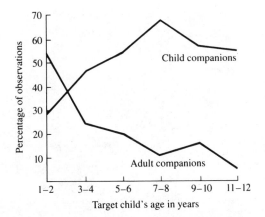

FIGURE 15-1 Developmental changes in children's companionship with adults and other children. (Adapted from S. Ellis, B. Rogoff, & C. C. Cromer, "Age Segregation in Children's Social Interactions." *Developmental Psychology*, 1981, 17, 399–407. Copyright © 1981 by the American Psychological Association. Adapted by permission.)

mates, and other children who differed in age by more than a year. As we see in Figure 15-1, children's exposure to other children increases steadily from infancy through middle childhood, while their contacts with adults show a corresponding decrease.

Same-age versus mixed-age interactions. Since children in Western cultures attend age-graded schools, it seems reasonable to conclude that they would play most often with agemates. However, Ellis et al. (1981) found that they do not! As we see in Figure 15-2, youngsters of all ages spend much less time with agemates than with children who differ in age by more than a year (see also Barker & Wright, 1955).

Same-sex versus mixed-sex interactions. In Chapter 9 we noted that preschool children already prefer playmates of their own sex. In their observational study, Ellis et al. found that even 1- to 2-year-olds were playing more often with same-sex companions and that this like-sex bias became increasingly apparent with age. The fact that *infants* are already playing more often with children of their own sex probably reflects their parents' idea that boys should be playing with boys and girls with girls.

And, as children acquire gender stereotypes and sex-typed interests, it is hardly surprising that they would begin to choose same-sex playmates who enjoy the same kind of activities that they do.

What may be most surprising about the naturalistic studies of peer interaction is the sheer amount of contact that children have with one another before they go to school. Even 5–6-year-olds are spending as much leisure time (or more) in the company of children as around adults (Barker & Wright, 1955; Ellis et al., 1981). And what is the "peer group" like? It consists primarily of same-sex children of *different* ages. Now we see why developmentalists define peers as people who interact at similar levels of behavioral complexity, for only a small percentage of a youngster's "child associates" are actually agemates.

Peers as Promoters of Social Competence

To this point we have speculated that peer interactions may promote the development of many social

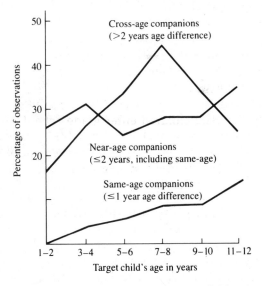

FIGURE 15-2 Developmental changes in children's companionship with children of different ages. (Adapted from S. Ellis, B. Rogoff, & C. C. Cromer, "Age Segregation in Children's Social Interactions." *Developmental Psychology*, 1981, 17, 399–407. Copyright © 1981 by the American Psychological Association. Adapted by permission.)

and personal competencies that are not easily acquired within the decidedly nonegalitarian parent/child relationship. Is there truly any basis for such a claim? And, if so, just how important are these peer influences? Developmentalists became very interested in these questions once they learned of Harry Harlow's research with rhesus monkeys.

Harlow's work with monkeys.   Will youngsters who have little or no contact with peers turn out to be abnormal or maladjusted? To find out, Harlow and his associates (Alexander & Harlow, 1965; Suomi & Harlow, 1978) raised groups of rhesus monkeys with their mothers and denied them the opportunity to play with peers. These **"mother only" monkeys** failed to develop normal patterns of social behavior. When finally exposed to agemates, the peer-deprived youngsters preferred to avoid them. On those occasions when they did approach a peer, these social misfits tended to be highly (and inappropriately) aggressive, and their antisocial tendencies often persisted into adulthood.

Is peer contact the key to normal social development? Not entirely. In later experiments, Harlow and his colleagues separated rhesus monkeys from their mothers and raised them with continuous exposure to their peers. These **"peer only" monkeys** were observed to cling tenaciously to one another and to form strong mutual attachments. Yet their social development was somewhat atypical in that they became highly agitated over minor stresses or frustrations (see also Higley et al., 1992); as adults they were unusually aggressive toward monkeys from outside their peer groups.

And a human parallel.   In 1951 Anna Freud and Sophie Dann reported a startling human parallel to Harlow's peer-only monkeys. During the summer of 1945, six 3-year-olds were found living by themselves in a Nazi concentration camp. By the time these children were 12 months old, their parents had been put to death. Although they received minimal caregiving from a series of inmates who were periodically executed, these children had, in effect, reared themselves.

When rescued at war's end, the six orphans were flown to a special treatment center in England,

PHOTO 15-2   Monkeys raised only with peers form strong mutual attachments and will often attack other monkeys from outside their peer group.

where attempts were made to "rehabilitate" them. How did these "peer only" children respond to this treatment? They began by breaking nearly all their toys and damaging their furniture. Moreover, they often reacted with cold indifference or open hostility toward the staff at the center. And, like Harlow's monkeys, these children:

> had no other wish than to be together and became upset when they were separated . . . even for short moments. No child would remain upstairs while the others were downstairs. . . . If anything of the kind happened, the single child would constantly ask for the other children, while the group would fret for the missing child. . . .
>
> There was no occasion to urge the children to "take turns"; they did it spontaneously. They were extremely considerate of each other's feelings. . . . At mealtimes handing food to the neighbor was of greater importance than eating oneself [Freud & Dann, 1951, pp. 131–133].

Although these orphans were closely attached to one another and very suspicious of outsiders, they were certainly not psychotic. In fact, they eventually established positive relationships with their adult caregivers and acquired a new language during the first year at the center. The story even has a happy ending, for, 35 years later, these orphans were leading effective, productive lives as middle-aged adults. According to Hartup (1983), "No more graphic account exists in the literature to demonstrate resilience in social development and to display that peer interaction can contribute importantly to the socialization of the individual child" (p. 158).

Taken together, Harlow's monkey research and Freud and Dann's observations of their war orphans suggest that parents and peers each contribute something different and perhaps unique to a child's (or a monkey's) social development. Regular contacts with sensitive, responsive parents not only permit infants to acquire some basic interactive skills but also provide a sense of *security* that enables them to venture forth to explore the environment and to discover that other people can be interesting companions (Hartup, 1989; Higley et al., 1992). By contrast, contacts with peers may allow children to elaborate their basic interactive routines and to develop competent and adaptive patterns of social behavior with associates who are more or less similar to themselves. Indeed, Harlow's peer-only monkeys lacked the security of a mother/infant relationship, which perhaps explains why they clutched at one another, were reluctant to explore, and were terrified by (and aggressive toward) outsiders. But *within their own peer groups* they developed competent interactive routines and displayed normal patterns of social and sexual behavior (Suomi & Harlow, 1978).

Just how important is it for human beings to establish and maintain *harmonious* relations with their peers? Apparently it is very important. One recent review of more than 30 studies revealed that youngsters who had been rejected by their peers during grade school were much more likely than those who had enjoyed good peer relations to drop out of school, to become involved in delinquent or criminal activities, and to display serious psychological difficulties later in adolescence and young adulthood (Parker & Asher, 1987; see also Kupersmidt & Coie, 1990; Morison & Masten, 1991). So mere contact with peer associates is not enough to ensure normal developmental outcomes; getting along with peers is important too.

In sum, peers do seem to be significant agents of socialization, and the task of becoming *appropriately* sociable with peers is a most important developmental hurdle. In our next section we will focus on the growth of peer sociability and on some of the factors that influence how appropriately (or inappropriately) sociable a child turns out to be.

The Development of Peer Sociability

Sociability is a term that describes the child's willingness to engage others in social interaction and to seek their attention or approval. In Chapter 5 we noted that even young infants are sociable creatures: months before they form their first attachments, they are already smiling, cooing, or otherwise trying to attract the attention of their companions. By 6 weeks of age many infants already prefer human company to other nonsocial forms of stimulation, and they are likely to protest whenever any *adult* puts them down or walks off and leaves them alone (Schaffer & Emerson, 1964). But would they be so positively disposed to a peer—that is, an infant or a toddler companion?

Peer Sociability during the First Two Years

Clearly, young infants' sociable gestures are much more elaborate when they are interacting with socially skilled partners, such as their parents, than with less responsive companions, such as another infant or a toddler sibling (Vandell & Wilson, 1987). Nevertheless, even another baby may elicit a sociable response from a young infant. Touching among infants first occurs at 3–4 months of age (Vincze, 1971), and by the middle of the first year infants will occasionally smile at their tiny companions, vocalize, offer toys, and gesture to one another (Hay, Nash, & Pedersen, 1983; Vandell, Wilson, & Buchanan, 1980). These sociable activities become much more common during the second half of the first year, as do other more complex activities, such as pointing out toys to a peer and even imitating a peer's simple actions with a toy (Eckerman & Stein, 1982).

Despite these observations, investigators have often wondered just how "sociable" infant/infant interactions really are. Consider that year-old infants in the same room may direct a response toward each other less than once per minute, and sustained social interactions are even less common (Eckerman & Stein, 1982; Hartup, 1983). Indeed, 1-year-olds would much rather play with toys or with socially skilled partners (such as their mothers) than with socially immature playmates like themselves.

During the first half of the second year, infants are paying more attention to the activities of other infants and will sometimes try to regulate a peer's behavior, as we see in the following example:

> Larry sits on the floor and Bernie turns and looks toward him. Bernie waves his hand and says "da," still looking at Larry. He repeats the vocalization three more times before Larry laughs. Bernie vocalizes again and Larry laughs again. This same sequence is repeated twelve more times before Bernie . . . walks off [Mueller & Lucas, 1975, p. 241].

Are these brief "action/reaction" episodes examples of true social discourse? Perhaps, but it is also possible that infants at this stage are so egocentric that they regard peers as particularly interesting and responsive "toys" over which they have some control (Brownell, 1986).

By 18 months of age, however, almost all infants are beginning to display *coordinated interactions* with agemates that are clearly social in character. They now take great delight in *imitating* each other and will often gaze and smile at their partners as they turn their imitative sequences into social games (Eckerman, Davis, & Didow, 1989; Eckerman & Stein, 1990; Howes & Matheson, 1992). By age 24 months, toddlers are assuming *complementary* roles, such as chaser and chasee in games of tag, and they will occasionally coordinate their actions (that is, cooperate) to achieve a shared goal, as illustrated by one child's operating a handle, thereby enabling the second to retrieve attractive toys from a container (Brownell & Carriger, 1990).

PHOTO 15-3   With age, infants' interactions with one another become increasingly skilled and reciprocal.

Notice, then, that children are beginning to respond more purposively and contingently to the actions of peers by 18–24 months of age—about the time or soon after they can recognize themselves in a mirror and can discriminate photographs of themselves from those of other infants (see Chapter 7). This may be no accident. Celia Brownell and Michael Carriger (1990) propose that infants must first realize that both they and their companions are autonomous causal agents who can make things happen before they are likely to play complementary games or try to coordinate their actions to accomplish a goal. Indeed, Brownell and Carriger found that toddlers who cooperated successfully to achieve a goal did score higher on a test of self/other differentiation than their less cooperative agemates, thus suggesting that infants' interactive skills may depend very heavily on their social-cognitive development.

Peer Sociability during the Preschool Period

Between the ages of 2 and 5, children not only become more outgoing but also direct their social gestures to a wider audience. Observational studies suggest that 2- to 3-year-olds are more likely than older children to remain near an adult and to seek physical affection, whereas the sociable behaviors of 4- to 5-year-olds normally consist of playful bids for attention or approval that are directed at *peers* rather than adults (Harper & Huie, 1985; Hartup, 1983).

Just as children are becoming more peer oriented during the preschool years, the character of their peer interactions is changing as well. Between ages 2 and 5, preschoolers become less inclined to stand around and watch a playmate or to take part in simple initiative games; instead, they engage in increasingly sophisticated, reciprocal exchanges, many of which will require players not only to assume complementary roles but also to agree on how these roles are to be played if their play activities are to continue successfully.

In a classic study of preschoolers at play, Mildren Parten (1932) observed 2- to 4½-year-old nursery-school children during free-play periods, hoping to identify a meaningful developmental progression in the *social complexity* of peer interactions. Her observations suggested that the play activities of pre-school children could be placed into four categories, arranged from least to most social:

1. *Solitary play* — children play alone, typically with toys, and largely ignore what other youngsters are doing.
2. *Parallel play* — children play side by side with similar toys or materials but interact very little and do not try to influence the behavior of other players.
3. *Associative play* — children now interact by sharing toys, swapping materials, and following each other's lead, but they do not assume distinct roles or cooperate to complete a shared goal.
4. *Cooperative play* — most complex form of play, in which children join forces to achieve a common goal. They can divide the labor necessary to create joint products (that is, collaborate); they can assume reciprocal roles such as mommie and baby in pretend play; and (according to Parten) they can follow the rules of simple games.

PHOTO 15-4   Solitary play.

Parten found that play becomes increasingly social over the preschool years. As shown in Figure 15-3, solitary and parallel play declined with age, whereas associative and cooperative play (the most social forms of play activity) became more common. She concluded that her data reflect a three-step developmental sequence in which solitary play emerges first and is least mature, followed by parallel play, which eventually gives way to the more mature forms of associative and cooperative play.

Other researchers have challenged Parten's conclusions, noting that solitary play is actually quite common throughout the preschool period and need not be considered immature (Hartup, 1983). If solitary play is *functional* in character, involving such cognitively simplistic and repetitive actions as rolling a ball back and forth or running around a room, then it might be properly labeled "immature." However, most of the solitary play of the preschool period is more cognitively complex and *constructive* in nature, as children work alone to build towers of blocks, draw pictures, or complete puzzles. And preschoolers who spend much of their playtime in such constructive solitary pursuits are often bright

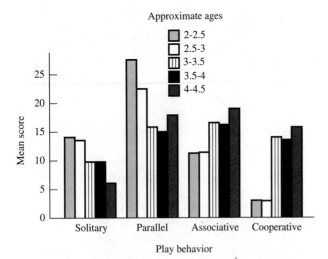

FIGURE 15-3 Frequency of activities engaged in by preschool children of different ages. With age, solitary and parallel play occur less frequently, whereas associative and cooperative play occur more frequently. (Adapted from M. Parten, "Social Participation among Preschool Children." *Journal of Abnormal and Social Psychology*, 1932, 27, 243–269. Copyright © 1932 by the American Psychological Association.)

youngsters who have few if any difficulties interacting with peers.

Notice, then, that the "maturity" of preschool play activities may depend as much (or more) on their cognitive complexity as on their social or nonsocial character. Carolee Howes and Catherine Matheson (1992) have recently proposed a new developmental sequencing of young children's play based on the *cognitive complexity* of children's *social* activities. Their six categories of play (from least to most complex) are as follows:

1. *Parallel play* — two children perform similar activities without acknowledging each other.
2. *Parallel aware play* — children engage in parallel play with eye contact.
3. *Simple social play* — children engage in similar activities while talking, smiling, sharing toys, or otherwise interacting.
4. *Complementary and reciprocal play* — children demonstrate action-based role reversals in social games such as run-and-chase or peek-a-boo.

5. *Cooperative social pretend play* — children play complementary *nonliteral*, or "pretend," roles (for example, mommie and baby) but without any planning or communicating about the meaning of the roles or the form that the play will take.
6. *Complex social pretend play* — children actively *plan* their pretend play. They name and explicitly assign roles, propose a play script, and may stop playing to modify the script if necessary.

To determine whether these six forms of play develop sequentially, Howes and Matheson (1992) conducted a longitudinal study in which the play activities of a group of 1- to 2-year-olds were repeatedly observed (at six-month intervals) over the next three years. The observers also rated each child's social competencies with peers at each observation period. Howes and Matheson found that the categories of play described above did develop sequentially. Consistent with findings we discussed earlier, most infants were displaying simple social play soon after their first birthday and complementary and reciprocal play by age 19–24 months. By age 2½ to 3, most children had progressed to cooperative social pretend play, and nearly half had displayed complex social pretend play by age 3½ to 4. Moreover, there was a clear relationship between the complexity of a child's play and the child's social competence with peers: children who engaged in more complex play at any given age were rated as more outgoing and prosocially inclined and as less aggressive and withdrawn at the next observation period six months later. So it seems that the complexity of a child's play (particularly pretend play) is a reliable predictor of his or her future social competencies and popularity with peers (see also Connolly & Doyle, 1984; Doyle et al., 1992; Rubin, Fein, & Vandenberg, 1983).

Peer Interactions in Middle Childhood and Adolescence

Peer interactions become increasingly sophisticated throughout the grade-school years. Not only do cooperative forms of complex social pretend play become more commonplace, but, by age 7–10, children have become enthusiastic participants in games (such as jacks, hopscotch, and marbles) that are governed by formal sets of rules (Hartup, 1983; Piaget, 1965).

Another very noticeable way in which peer interactions change during middle childhood is that contacts among grade-school children more often occur in true **peer groups**. When psychologists talk about peer groups, they are referring not merely to a collection of playmates but, rather, to a confederation that (1) interacts on a regular basis, (2) defines a sense of belonging, (3) shares implicit or explicit *norms* that specify how members are supposed to behave, and (4) develops a structure or hierarchical organization that enables the members to work together toward the accomplishment of shared goals. Older nursery-school children do share common interests, assume different roles while playing together, and conform to loosely defined norms or rules of conduct. But the membership of these pre-school "play groups" may fluctuate from day to day, and the guidelines to which the children conform are often laid down by adults. The group activities of elementary-school children, however, are very different. Members now share norms that *they* have had a hand in creating, and they begin to assume stable roles or "statuses" within the peer society. Moreover, elementary-school children clearly identify with their groups; to be a "Brownie," a "Blue Knight," or "one of Smitty's gang" is often a source of great personal pride. So it seems that middle childhood (ages 6–10) is the period when children are assuming membership in what we can call true peer groups.

Under what conditions will a collection of individuals coalesce, forming a true group? Obviously, one prerequisite is that the members of an aggregation be in a setting that permits and in some way encourages them to interact regularly. But interaction alone does not necessarily imply the formation of a group. Groups are composed of people who are drawn together by common goals or motives.

The importance of proximity and shared goals to the formation and functioning of children's groups has been demonstrated by Muzafer Sherif and his associates (1961) in an elaborate field experiment known as the "Robber's Cave" study. There were three distinct phases to this classic piece of research, and, as we see in Box 15-1, the results of each phase have taught us important lessons about children's experiences in peer groups.

Children become increasingly peer oriented over the course of middle childhood. This happens so much so that, by early adolescence, youngsters are spending more time with their peers—particularly with close friends and with friendship networks known as **cliques**—than with parents, siblings, or any other agent of socialization (Berndt, 1989; Medrich et al., 1982). Peer cliques often develop very distinct and colorful norms that specify how group members are expected to dress, to talk, to think, and to act; and teenagers (as well as college students in fraternities and sororities and adult members of many clubs and organizations) face very real pressures to adhere to the dictates of their peer groups and will risk social ostracism should they fail to do so. Developmentalists have long been concerned about the potential of adolescent cliques to subvert the positive influence of parents and teachers while promoting antisocial conduct. Although such negative peer influences are certainly not unknown, we will see later in the chapter that experiences within the adolescent peer culture are much more likely to promote healthy and adaptive patterns of behavior than unhealthy or maladaptive outcomes.

Personal and Social Influences on Sociability and Peer Relations

Were you to carefully observe children of any age, you would soon discover that some of them are drawn to peers and seem to thrive on social interaction, whereas others appear rather unsociable or even withdrawn. How might we account for these individual differences in peer sociability?

THE GENETIC HYPOTHESIS: IS SOCIABILITY A HERITABLE ATTRIBUTE?

There is now ample evidence to suggest that genotype influences one's responsiveness to other people (Goldsmith, 1983). Over the first year, identical twins are much more similar than fraternal twins in their frequency of social smiling and their fear of

15-1

Robber's Cave: An Experimental Analysis of Group Formation and Intergroup Conflict

More than 30 years ago, Muzafer Sherif and his colleagues (Sherif, 1956; Sherif et al., 1961) designed an ingenious field experiment to study the formation and functioning of children's peer groups. The three phases of this experiment and the lessons learned from each are described below.

Phase 1: Group Formation

The 22 subjects who participated in the "Robber's Cave" experiment were 11-year-old boys at a summer camp in Oklahoma. Initially the campers were divided into two sets and housed in different areas of a large, woodsy preserve. Neither aggregation was aware of the other's presence.

The boys in each aggregation lived closely together and participated in many enjoyable activities, such as hiking, crafts, organized games, and the building of "hideouts." To encourage the formation of group structures, camp counselors arranged for the boys to work at tasks requiring them to assume different roles and to coordinate their efforts in order to accomplish shared goals. For example, one evening the boys came to dinner, only to discover that the staff had not prepared the meal. However, the ingredients (for example, raw meat, Kool-Aid, watermelon) were available. Under these circumstances, the hungry boys soon divided the labor: some cooked, others sliced watermelon or mixed drinks, and others either served food or cleaned up. This and other such cooperative activities soon led to the development of cohesive groups. Leaders emerged, individual members assumed different statuses, and each group developed rules or norms to govern its daily activities. The groups even assumed names, becoming the "Eagles" and the "Rattlers."

Let's now summarize this first phase. When previously unacquainted children were thrust together and encouraged to work cooperatively at necessary and/or attractive tasks, they formed cohesive groups, assumed different roles, and developed norms to regulate their interactions and accomplish group goals. But interesting questions remained. For example, what would happen to "group *esprit*" should the Eagles and Rattlers come in conflict with each other?

Phase 2: Intergroup Conflict

Next the investigators chose to study intergroup rivalry and its effects on the structure of a peer group. They first arranged for the Eagles and Rattlers to "accidentally" discover each other and then talked the groups into a series of competitions—baseball games, tugs-of-war, and the like. Prizes were to be awarded to the winners (for example, money, trophies, pocket knives), and the boys practiced intently for the coming events.

Once the competitions began, the investigators were careful to observe the boys' reactions to success and failure. The immediate effect of failure was internal friction, mutual accusation, and blame—in short, decreased group cohesion and a shake-up in the group structure. So, when the Rattlers emerged victorious from the first baseball game, Mason (the Eagles' best athlete) threatened to "beat up" certain Eagles if they "didn't try harder" in the future. Craig, the Eagle leader, was eventually deposed for failing to give his all at athletic competition.

As the competitions progressed and boys in each group assumed new statuses, both the Eagles and the Rattlers became more cohesive than ever before. New norms emerged, and increased solidarity within each group was apparent from the hostilities these rival factions displayed toward each other. At first these exchanges were limited to verbal taunts such as "You're not Eagles—you're pigeons." But, after losing a series of contests, the Eagles vented their frustrations by securing the Rattlers' flag and burning it. The Rattlers then lost two consecutive contests, endured the verbal scoffs of the Eagles, and suffered internal disharmony. They finally decided that the Eagles had used unfair tactics in the most recent tug-of-war, and they reacted by staging a raid on the Eagles' cabin, stealing comic books and a pair of jeans belonging to the Eagle leader. The jeans were painted orange and displayed as a flag by the Rattlers. Armed with rocks, the Eagles started on a retaliatory raid, but the counselors stopped them before any serious injuries could result.

So the second phase of the experiment revealed that intergroup conflict may bring about changes in the in-

BOX 15-1 | *continued*

ternal structures of rival groups, particularly within the group that is placed in a subordinate position by losing. As conflict continues, members of opposing groups develop strong "we versus they" attitudes that help to reestablish a sense of ingroup solidarity and to maintain the group's animosity toward its rivals.

Phase 3: Reducing Intergroup Hostility

Sherif and his associates had created a monster. By the end of phase 2 the Eagles and Rattlers had reached a point at which their contacts with each other invariably resulted in name calling, threats, and fisticuffs. The third phase of the experiment was designed to reduce these hostilities.

It soon became apparent that intergroup conflicts were easier to create than to reduce. One of the first strategies was to bring the boys together in a pleasant, noncompetitive setting—for example, at the movies. This plan failed miserably: the boys used these occasions to call each other names and squabble, and, if anything, the hostilities became even more intense. Several other ploys were tried and found ineffective. For example, both groups attended religious services emphasizing cooperation and brotherly love, but the boys reverted to their rivalrous conduct immediately after the services were over. "Summit" meetings between the two group leaders were not attempted, for it was felt that any concessions made by the leaders would be interpreted by followers as traitorous behavior.

Finally, Sherif et al. devised a strategy that they thought would work. If the two groups were to face common problems that could not be solved by either group working alone, they would be forced to "pull together," which should decrease intergroup hostilities. The counselors then cleverly engineered a series of these problems, or **"superordinate goals."** On one occasion the Eagles and the Rattlers pooled their money to rent an interesting film when it appeared that neither group had the resources to rent it on its own. On another occasion, when everyone was hungry and the camp truck would not start, the boys combined their efforts to get the truck going so that they would have supplies for dinner that night. As a result of these

and other cooperative exchanges, the two groups became much less antagonistic toward each other. In fact, friendships developed across group lines, and the Eagles, who had won a monetary prize in the previous athletic competition, ended up using the money to treat their former rivals. Sherif has summarized these results in the following way:

> What our limited experiments have shown is that the possibilities for achieving harmony are greatly enhanced when groups are brought together to work toward common ends. Then favorable information about a disliked group is seen in a new light, and leaders are in a position to take bolder steps toward cooperation. In short, hostility gives way when groups pull together to achieve overriding goals that are real and compelling to all concerned [Sherif, 1956, p. 58].

Notice, then, that the same factors that promote *within-group* cohesion—namely, working toward a common goal—can also help to reduce *between-group* hostilities. Surely the results of phase 3 are applicable far beyond the camp setting in which they were obtained. Although feelings have waxed and waned over the years, Americans and Russians have been much more positive in their impressions of each other whenever their governments were actively pressing for the attainment of a shared goal—halting the arms race. And perhaps the only way to reduce well-ingrained animosities between rivalrous, inner-city adolescent gangs or between such ethnic groups as Arabs and Israelis, English and French Canadians, and South African blacks and whites is for leaders of these rival factions to identify common problems that must be solved and that neither group is likely to resolve without the other's cooperation. The challenge, of course, is to identify superordinate goals that are attractive and will be received enthusiastically by members of different groups. But, in any case, the search for a common ground will surely prove far less costly in terms of both economic and human resources than a continuation and possible escalation of intense intergroup conflicts.

strangers (Freedman, 1974), and these differences in sociability are still apparent when pairs of identical and fraternal twins are retested at 18 and 24 months of age (Matheny, 1983). In fact, Sandra Scarr's (1968) study of 6–10-year-old twin pairs suggests that genetic influences on sociability are often detectable well into middle childhood. Even when identical twins have been *mistakenly reared* as fraternals, they are still (1) as similar as identical twins who have been raised as identicals on aspects of sociability such as friendliness and shyness and (2) much more similar on these same measures than are pairs of true fraternal twins.

Although sociability appears to be a heritable attribute, environmental factors play a major role in its expression. For example, Denise Daniels and Robert Plomin (1985) recently found a significant correlation between the shyness of adopted toddlers and the sociability of their *biological* mothers: shy toddlers tended to have mothers who were low in sociability, whereas nonshy toddlers had mothers who were more outgoing. This finding argues for a genetic influence on sociability, since biological mothers and their adopted-away toddlers have genes in common. Yet Daniels and Plomin also found a significant correlation between the shyness of adopted toddlers and the sociability of their *adoptive* mothers, and the magnitude of this relationship was nominally greater than that between the toddlers and their biological mothers! Since adoptive mothers and their adopted children have no genes in common, environmental factors must have been responsible for their resemblance on these sociability measures.

What environmental experiences are likely to influence a child's responsiveness to peers? Let's consider the direct and the indirect roles that *parents* play in fostering (or inhibiting) peer interactions.

DIRECT PARENTAL EFFECTS ON PEER INTERACTION

There are several ways in which parents directly influence the amount of contact their children have with peers. Their choice of a residence is one such influence. If parents choose to live in a neighborhood where there are parks, playgrounds, and many young children, their sons and daughters will have ample opportunities to interact with peers. By contrast, a decision to reside in a neighborhood with big yards, widely spaced houses, and few playgrounds or available playmates could seriously restrict children's access to peers (Medrich et al., 1982).

The amount of contact children have with peers will also depend on whether parents act as "booking agents" for peer interaction—whether they arrange visits by playmates, enroll their children in nursery school, or encourage their participation in organized children's activities such as little league or scouting. Of course, parents who arrange home visits by peer playmates are also in a position to influence their child by monitoring his or her peer interactions to ensure that play proceeds smoothly and amiably, without major conflicts. This brings us to an interesting issue.

How closely should parents monitor children's play?   Is it a good idea for parents to closely monitor or to intrude upon playful interactions between young children? Gary Ladd and Beckie Golter (1988) conducted a study in an attempt to answer this question. Parents of preschool children were interviewed in the evenings and asked whether their children had had any interactions with peers at home that day. When parents reported a peer interaction, they were then asked if and how they had monitored the interaction. Not surprisingly, the vast majority of parents felt it necessary to monitor the activities of young preschool children. Some parents reported that they had closely watched over the children or had even participated in their play activities (direct monitoring), whereas others said that they checked occasionally on the children without often intruding or becoming involved as a playmate (indirect monitoring). Which form of monitoring is associated with successful and harmonious peer interactions? Ladd and Golter's findings clearly favor indirect parental monitoring. As shown in Figure 15-4, preschoolers whose parents indirectly monitored their peer interactions (1) were better liked and less often disliked by their nursery-school classmates and (2) were rated as less hostile and ag-

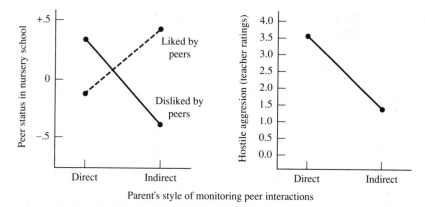

FIGURE 15-4 Nursery-school children enjoy a more favorable status with peers and are rated as less aggressive by their teachers when parents have indirectly monitored their interactions with playmates. (Adapted from G. W. Ladd & B. S. Golter, "Parents' Management of Preschoolers' Peer Relations: Is It Related to Children's Social Competence?" *Developmental Psychology*, 1988, 24, 109–117. Copyright © 1988 by the American Psychological Association.)

gressive by nursery-school teachers than their counterparts whose parents closely scrutinized and often intruded on their play activities (see also Putallaz, 1987).

Do these findings imply that parents would be well advised to butt out entirely and allow their children to resolve whatever difficulties they may have with playmates on their own? No indeed! Recall from our discussion in Chapter 10 that parents who consistently fail to monitor their children's (or adolescents') whereabouts, activities, or associates tend to raise surly and aggressive youngsters who are often rejected by peers (Dishion, 1990). Moreover, we noted in Chapter 13 that, although preschool children in day-care settings are occasionally found to be more aggressive and disobedient than children reared at home, these "negative returns" are largely limited to children receiving low-quality day care in which their interactions with peers are often *not* monitored by their day-care providers (Howes, 1990; Vandell, Henderson, & Wilson, 1988). So it seems that parental encouragement and indirect monitoring of peer interactions — monitoring just sufficient to prevent major conflicts while allowing children the autonomy to choose their own play activities and to resolve minor squabbles on their

own — is the practice most closely associated with the development of positive interactional skills with other children (see also Ladd & Hart, 1992).

Effects of nursery school on children's peer interactions.   Another way that parents might directly influence their children's peer relations is to enroll them in nursery school. In Chapter 14 we noted that a major objective of many nursery schools is to prepare preschoolers for a formal scholastic environment by introducing them to a "social" curriculum that fosters the growth of communicative and interactive skills and an appreciation for rules of social etiquette. Does nursery school have any noticeable effect on children's sociability with peers? Does the amount of nursery-school experience that children have make a difference?

John Shea (1981) addressed these issues by observing 3- and 4-year-olds as they entered nursery school and attended classes two, three, or five days a week. As children mingled on the playground, their behavior was videotaped, and individual acts were classified on five dimensions: aggression, rough-and-tumble play, distance from the nearest child, distance from the teacher, and frequency of peer interaction. Over a ten-week observation period, children gradually ventured farther from the teacher as they became much more playful and outgoing with one another and much less forceful and aggressive. Moreover, these changes were most noticeable for the children who attended school five days a week and least apparent (but detectable nevertheless) for those who attended twice a week. Shea concluded that nursery-school attendance has a very positive effect on young children's reactions to other children.

Why is nursery school beneficial? Surely the guidance offered by nursery-school teachers is a key ingredient to the success of a nursery-school curriculum. However, it also appears that peer interactions contribute directly to the growth of children's social skills. Consider that children who attend nursery school on a regular basis become quite familiar with their classmates and that familiarity (among children at least) breeds liking and sociability rather than contempt. As children get to know their classmates better, their interactions become less awkward and tentative and much bolder and more synchronous. Indeed, play among preschoolers is much more complex among familiar than among unfamiliar playmates (Doyle, Connolly, & Rivest, 1980; Harper & Huie, 1985), and collaborative problem solving proceeds much more smoothly among familiar than among unfamiliar playmates as well (Brody et al., 1983). Experience with nursery-school peers can also help children make a positive adjustment to formal classroom settings, for Gary Ladd (1990) found that children who enter kindergarten along with peers they had known in nursery school seem to like school better and show fewer adjustment problems than those who have had little nursery-school experience or who enter kindergarten without familiar companions. So it seems that parents can indeed foster their children's social competence with peers by enrolling them in nursery school.

INDIRECT PARENTAL EFFECTS ON PEER SOCIABILITY

In addition to their role as initiators and monitors of peer interactions, parents may indirectly influence their children's reactions to peers by virtue of their behavior as caregivers, playmates, authority figures, and disciplinarians.

Parents as caregivers.   In Chapter 6 we learned that different patterns of caregiving during the first year are reliably associated with the development of different kinds of attachments. Although attachment behaviors and peer sociability represent different social systems, attachment theorists (Ainsworth, 1979; Sroufe, 1983) argue that the quality of a child's primary attachments will influence his or her reactions to other people later in life. Specifically, they believe that children who are insecurely attached to one or more unresponsive caregivers may be rather anxious and inhibited in the presence of unfamiliar companions and much less sociable than children who are securely attached.

Most of the available evidence is consistent with this notion. Recall from our discussion in Chapter 6 that infants who were securely attached to their mothers at 12–18 months of age are more likely than those who were insecurely attached to act sociably around other infants and toddlers and to be friendly, outgoing, and popular with their peers some three to four years later in nursery school and kindergarten. Moreover, we learned that (1) boys who are still securely attached to their mothers at age 6 are less aggressive and are more popular with their first-grade peers than boys whose current attachments are insecure (Cohn, 1990), and (2) adults who recall their early attachments as secure are less lonely and are likely to receive more social support from companions than those who portray their childhood attachments as insecure (Kobak & Sceery, 1988). Apparently two secure attachments are better than one, for toddlers who are secure with both parents are more socially responsive and less conflicted about contacts with strangers than are those who are insecure with one parent or both (Main & Weston, 1981). Finally, infant twins who are insecure with their mothers are less friendly and outgoing, even with their co-twins, than other twin pairs in which both twins were securely attached (Vandell, Owen, et al., 1988). Perhaps Ainsworth (1979) is right in arguing that securely attached children are sociable children because they have learned to trust their responsive caregivers and they assume that other people will also welcome their bids for attention.

Parents as playmates. The finding that securely attached youngsters are generally outgoing and even popular with other children suggests that sensitive, responsive caregiving contributes to the development of sociability. Kevin MacDonald and Ross Parke (1984) believe that the character of *playful* interactions between parents and their children is especially significant in this regard, for parents' conduct while serving as "playmates" will undoubtedly influence the ways in which the child reacts to other playmates, such as siblings and peers. Clearly this idea has some merit. Nine-month-old infants whose mothers provide many opportunities for playful turn taking are already more responsive to peer playmates than are agemates who have experienced less turn taking with their mothers (Vandell & Wilson, 1987). And, in his studies of playful interactions between 3–5-year-olds and their parents, MacDonald (1987; MacDonald & Parke, 1984) finds that, if parents are *directive, controlling* playmates (that is, always issuing commands and rarely allowing the child to regulate their play), their children tend to have poor social skills and nonharmonious peer interactions (see also Russell & Finnie, 1990; Youngblade & Belsky, 1992). Perhaps a controlling parent who is always barking orders will inhibit sociability by simply taking all the fun out of play activities. Or, alternatively, these parents may be teaching their children to be bossy and dictatorial themselves—a style that is likely to elicit negative reactions from playmates and convince the child that contacts with peers are not all that pleasant (Ladd & Golter, 1988; Russell & Finnie, 1990).

Patterns of child rearing and peer sociability. Perhaps you have gleaned from our discussion thus far that parents of appropriately sociable preschool children tend to be warm, sensitive companions and playmates who (1) monitor their children's interactions to ensure that they comply with rules of social etiquette but who also (2) allow children considerable autonomy in structuring play episodes (both

with themselves and with peers), as long as they follow the rules of social discourse that have been presented as guidelines. Clearly this pattern of warmth, sensitivity, and moderate control sounds very much like the *authoritative* pattern of child rearing that we have commented favorably upon throughout the text. Indeed, investigators are consistently finding that warm, authoritative parents who rely on reason (induction) rather than forceful coercive methods (power-assertion) to control their children's conduct are likely to raise well-adjusted sons and daughters who (1) display many prosocial and few disruptive or antisocial behaviors toward peers and (2) are likely to be accepted by or even popular with their playmates (Baumrind, 1971; Dekovic & Janssens, 1992; Hart et al., 1992; Youngblade & Belsky, 1992). By contrast, highly authoritarian (and uninvolved) parents who rely heavily on power-assertion as a control tactic tend to raise youngsters who (1) display the hostile attributional bias we discussed in Chapter 10, (2) are often disruptive and aggressive when interacting with other children, and (3) are likely to be *disliked* by their peers (Dekovic & Janssens, 1992; Hart et al., 1992; Weiss et al., 1992).

So it does seem as if the path to positive (or negative) peer interactions often begins at home. As Putallaz and Heflin have noted:

> Parental involvement, warmth, and moderate control appear to be important in terms of children's social competence. Within the social context of the family, children appear to learn certain interactional skills and behaviors that then transfer to their interactions with peers [1990, p. 204].

Peer Acceptance and Status in the Peer Group

Perhaps no other aspect of children's social lives has received more attention than peer acceptance. When we speak of peer acceptance, we are referring to two attributes: a child's **popularity**, or likability, and his or her **status**—a reflection of the child's perceived worth as a contributor to the attainment of group goals (Hartup, 1983). Although these two attributes tend to be positively correlated—popular children enjoy high status, and vice versa—the correlations are often rather modest. Thus it is possible for a child to be a leader (high status) even though she is not well liked or to be very popular but have only average status in the peer group.

Some determinants of peer acceptance are specific to a particular group or setting. For example, toughness, hostile attitudes toward outgroups, and an ability to handle a motorcycle may make you a valued Hell's Angel, but it is doubtful that these qualities would enhance your standing among the members of your monthly investment club. Clearly, different groups value different attributes, and those who are accepted possess the characteristics that are valued by their peer groups. Nevertheless, there are a number of factors that seem to affect a person's social standing in many kinds of groups, regardless of the age, sex, or sociocultural backgrounds of the members. These are the qualities on which we will focus as we review the determinants of one's popularity in children's peer groups.

Measuring Children's Popularity with Peers

Developmentalists generally rely on **sociometric techniques** to assess a child's status in the peer group or his popularity with peers. These techniques require children to state their preferences for other group members with respect to some specific criterion. If you wanted to measure popularity, for example, you might use the *rating-scale technique* and ask each child to rate every other child in the group on a 5-point likability scale (ranging from "really like to play with" to "really don't like to play with"). Other investigators favor a *paired-comparison* approach in which the child is presented with the names of two group members at a time and asked to pick the one whom he or she likes better. Because all pairs of group members are eventually presented, this technique yields an overall measure of popularity for each child in the group. However, the approach that many investigators favor (and that seems to provide the sharpest distinctions among

different categories of peer acceptance; see Terry & Coie, 1991) is the **nominations technique**: each child is asked to name a specific number of peers (often three) whom he or she *really likes* (or would prefer as playmates) and the same number of peers whom he or she *least likes* (or would not want as play partners). Even 3- to 5-year-olds can respond appropriately to sociometric surveys, for they already know who among their nursery-school classmates are perceived as likable or dislikable (Denham et al., 1990; Howes, 1988). And, lest you wonder, the sociometric classifications that children receive from these measures (1) are positively correlated with teacher ratings of peer popularity and (2) accurately predict the character of children's peer interactions as well (Green et al., 1980; Howes, 1988; Hymel, 1983). So it seems that sociometric surveys provide *valid* assessments of children's social standing in their peer groups.

How is a child's social standing determined? With the often-used nominations technique, the number of positive and negative nominations that each child receives determines his or her standing along two sociometric dimensions. First, the number of negative nominations (as a disliked peer) is subtracted from the number of positive nominations (as a liked peer) to locate the child on a *social preference* dimension. Children who receive more positive than negative nominations have positive social-preference scores, whereas those receiving more negative than positive nominations fall toward the negative end of this dimension. Then the child's *total number* of positive and negative nominations are added to locate him or her on a *social impact* dimension. Children high in social impact thus receive many nominations and are quite noticeable to their peers, whereas those who receive few nominations (and are low in social impact) do not stand out and may seem almost invisible in the peer group.

Categories of peer acceptance. Having located a child on the social-preference and the social-impact dimensions, it is usually possible to assign him or her to one of five sociometric categories. As shown in Figure 15-5, children classified as **popular** are

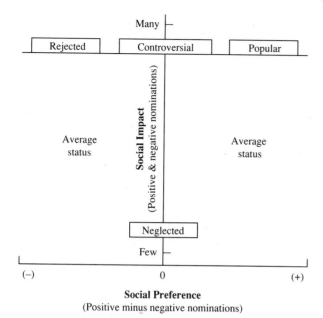

Many ┤

| Rejected | Controversial | Popular |

Social Impact
(Positive & negative nominations)

Average
status

Average
status

| Neglected |

Few ┤

(−)   0   (+)

Social Preference
(Positive minus negative nominations)

FIGURE 15-5 Five sociometric classifications (statuses) that children might attain based on the number and patterning of nominations each receives as a "liked" or a "disliked" peer. (Adapted from T. J. Berndt, *Child Development*, p. 501. Copyright © 1992 by Holt, Rinehart & Winston, Inc. Ft. Worth, TX.)

high in both social preference and social impact, having received many positive nominations and few negative ones from their peers. By contrast, **rejected children** are high in social impact but low in social preference; they are disliked by many children and liked by few. Children classified as **neglected** receive very few positive or negative nominations; they are *low* in social impact and intermediate (neither high nor low) on the social-preference dimension. Children labeled **controversial** receive many positive *and* many negative nominations. Like neglected children, they score intermediate on the social-preference dimension; they differ from neglectees, however, in that they are *high* in social impact. Together, these four types of children make up about two-thirds of the pupils in a typical elementary-school classroom. The remaining one-third are of **average** sociometric status, having received moderate numbers of positive and negative nominations (Coie, Dodge, & Coppotelli, 1982).

A couple of notes about these sociometric classifications are in order. First, controversial children have not been studied extensively, because they make up only about 5% of the students in a typical elementary-school classroom and they often do not remain controversial for long. In fact, one study found that nearly 60% of children initially classified as controversial had achieved another status in the peer group over intervals as brief as one month (Newcomb & Bukowski, 1984). Second, it seems that rejected children fall in roughly equal numbers into two distinct subcategories: those who are highly and inappropriately aggressive (*aggressive rejectees*) and those who are anxious, low in self-esteem, and inclined to withdraw from peer contacts (*nonaggressive rejectees*; see Boivin & Begin, 1989; French, 1988). And one recent study of *nonaggressive* rejectees suggests that this subgroup can be further subdivided into (1) shy-rejected children and (2) another category of generally noncombative youngsters who are outgoing but uncooperative and are poor social problem solvers (Cillessen et al., 1992).

Notice that both neglected children and rejected children are not well received by their peers. Yet it is not nearly so bad to be ignored by other children as to be rejected by them. Neglectees do not feel as lonely as rejectees do (Asher & Wheeler, 1985; Cassidy & Asher, 1992), and they are much more likely than rejected children to eventually attain an average sociometric status (or even to become popular) should they enter a new class at school or a new play group (Coie & Dodge, 1983). In addition, it is the rejected child, particularly the *aggressive* rejectee, who runs the greater risk of displaying deviant, antisocial behavior and other serious adjustment problems later in life (Asher & Coie, 1990; Kupersmidt & Coie, 1990; Morison & Masten, 1991; Roff, 1974).

Why do neglected children seem to fare better in the long run than their rejected classmates? And why are not all rejectees equally at risk of displaying long-term adjustment problems? Answers to these questions should become more apparent as we examine the research presented in Box 15-2 and look more carefully at other causes and correlates of children's sociometric classifications in the pages that follow.

Why Are Children Accepted, Neglected, or Rejected by Peers?

At several points throughout the text we have discussed factors that seem to contribute to children's popularity or social status. By way of review:

1. *Parenting styles.* As noted earlier in the chapter, warm, sensitive, and authoritative caregivers who rely on reasoning rather than power to guide and control children's conduct tend to raise youngsters who are securely attached and who are liked by both adults and peers. By contrast, highly au-thoritarian and/or emotionally unresponsive parents who rely heavily on power-assertion as a control tactic often have uncooperative, aggressive, or disruptive youngsters who are actively disliked by peers.

2. *Ordinal position effects.* Later-born children who must learn to negotiate with older and more powerful siblings tend to be more popular than first-borns (see Chapter 13).

3. *Cognitive skills.* Both cognitive and social-cognitive skills predict children's peer acceptance. Among groups of third- through eighth-graders,

---

B O X

15-2 | Why Rejectees Often Remain Rejected

In an interesting five-year longitudinal study, John Coie and Kenneth Dodge (1983) found that not all so-ciometric classifications are equally stable over time. The most popular children in the sample tended to lose some of their very favorable status, although they typically remained "accepted" members of the peer group. And, although some neglected youngsters remained neglected, many showed meaningful *gains* in social acceptance. The sociometric classification that proved to be most highly stable was rejectee: once rejected, a very sizable minority of youngsters remained rejected over the long run. As we will see in the text, rejected children typically display patterns of behavior that alienate their peers, and the persistence of these annoying antics does help to explain why rejectees might remain rejected. Yet there is now reason to suspect that, even if rejectees begin to respond more positively and constructively to their peers, they may find it exceedingly difficult to climb out of the hole they have dug for themselves and become accepted members of the peer group. But why?

Shelly Hymel (1986; Hymel et al., 1990) has proposed that, once children achieve a particular sociometric status, this social standing, or reputation, will color other children's impressions of their subsequent behavior. Specifically, Hymel contends that positive acts are likely to be attributed to stable internal causes (that is, the child's good character) if displayed by a *liked* peer but to less stable causes (for example, ulterior motives) if displayed by a child who is *disliked*. Conversely, a negative act is likely to be attributed to unstable causes if displayed by a child who is *liked* (for example, he was just kidding around) but to stable ones if the child is *disliked* (for example, she's mean and nasty). If these information-processing biases exist, it is easy to see why rejected children might remain rejected: their positive acts may be interpreted as having few if any implications for their future behavior and will probably be discounted as unimportant, whereas their negative acts are likely to be perceived as indicative of future conduct and, thus, as a basis for continued rejection of these individuals. But do such interpretive biases exist?

To find out, Hymel (1986) had second-, fifth-, and tenth-graders think about situations in which either a liked or a disliked peer had done something positive or negative that had personally affected him or her. Here are some examples of these scenarios:

1. The liked (disliked) peer invites (does not invite) you to a birthday party.
2. The liked (disliked) peer helps you pick up papers you dropped (laughs at you for being so clumsy).

the most popular children are those who have well-developed role-taking skills (Kurdek & Krile, 1982; Pellegrini, 1985), and children who have established intimate friendships score higher on tests of role taking than classmates without close friends (McGuire & Weisz, 1982). There is also a positive relationship between intelligence and peer acceptance: brighter children tend to be the more popular members of many peer groups (Hartup, 1983). Even during the preschool period, popular children score higher than their less popular peers on such indicators of cognitive maturity as mental

age (Quay & Jarrett, 1984) and complexity of pretend play (Connolly & Doyle, 1984). Finally, peers are often attracted to students who do well in school and who have good academic self-concepts (Green et al., 1980; Hartup, 1983), whereas children who fail miserably at school are often rejected by their classmates (Dishion et al., 1991). Indeed, one research team provided extensive academic skills training to low-achieving, socially rejected fourth-graders and found that this treatment improved not only the children's reading and math achievement but their social standing as

---

B O X | **15-2** | *continued*

Subjects were then asked to explain why the peer in each scenario had behaved as he or she did.

The results were clear. At all three age levels, subjects attributed *positive* behaviors of the liked peer to relatively stable, personal causes (for example, "he invited me because he likes me") but felt that the same behavior displayed by a disliked peer was less stable and often attributable to situational factors (for example, "her mother made her invite me"). By contrast, *negative* behaviors of liked peers were often attributed to unstable, situational causes (for example, "he didn't invite me because he ran out of invitations"), whereas the same behaviors displayed by a disliked peer were viewed as reflecting personal motives or dispositions (for example, "she's mean; she wanted to make me feel bad"). Thus, liked peers are given the benefit of the doubt should they respond negatively to their playmates — a finding that helps to explain why accepted children tend to remain accepted. Conversely, disliked children are assigned personal responsibility for their negative antics without gaining appropriate credit for any acts of kindness or compassion that might help them to overcome their bad reputations and low social status.

Let's note, however, that the majority of rejected children in Coie and Dodge's longitudinal study did eventually succeed at improving their status and be-

coming accepted by their peers. Which children are most likely to retain their bad reputations and remain rejected? Apparently it is those youngsters who fall into the *aggressive* rejectee category (Cillessen et al., 1992). And research reviewed in Chapter 10 provides some very strong clues as to why this may be. Recall that highly aggressive youngsters who are disliked by most peers often choose to associate with other highly aggressive youngsters like themselves (Cairns et al., 1988), eventually forming deviant peer cliques that (1) shun (and are shunned by) more typical peer aggregations and (2) often promote such dysfunctional adolescent activities as sexual misconduct, substance abuse, dropping out of school, and a variety of other kinds of delinquent or criminal behaviors (Cairns, Cairns, & Neckerman, 1989; Dishion et al., 1991; Newcomb & Bentler, 1989; Patterson, DeBaryshe, & Ramsey, 1989). So, by virtue of the peers to whom they are drawn and the values this peer group endorses, it is easy to see why *aggressive* rejectees might retain their "rejected" status over time and why they are more likely than nonaggressive rejectees to display antisocial behavior or serious psychological disturbances later in life.

well. One year after the training had ended, these former rejectees were now "accepted" and enjoyed average status in the peer group (Coie & Krehbiel, 1984).

There are at least three additional characteristics that seem to affect children's standing among their peers: their names, their physical attributes, and their patterns of interpersonal behavior.

Names.   What's in a name? Apparently quite a lot, in the eyes (or ears) of grade-school children. John McDavid and Herbert Harari (1966) asked four groups of 10- to 12-year-olds to rate the attractiveness of a large number of first names. At a later date the subjects were asked to indicate the three most popular and the three least popular children in their classes. McDavid and Harari found that children with attractive names (for example, Steven, John, Susan, or Kim) were rated as more popular by their peers than children with unusual and less attractive names (for example, Herman or Chastity). And in a later study Harari and McDavid (1973) found that teachers tend to have more positive achievement expectancies for children with attractive names.

These outcomes, like all correlational findings, must be interpreted with caution. Perhaps having a strange name does handicap children by making them the object of scorn or ridicule. However, we must also consider the possibility that parents who give their children unusual names may also encourage unusual behaviors that contribute to the problems that the Myrtles and the Mortimers may have with their peers.

Physical characteristics.   Despite the maxim that "beauty is only skin deep," many of us seem to think otherwise. Even 6-month-old infants can easily discriminate attractive from unattractive faces (Langlois et al., 1991), and 12-month-old infants already prefer to interact with attractive rather than unattractive strangers (Langlois, Roggman, & Rieser-Danner, 1990). By the preschool period, attractive youngsters are often described in more favorable ways (that is, friendlier, smarter) than their less attractive classmates by both teachers and peers

(Adams & Crane, 1980; Langlois, 1986), and attractive children are generally more popular than unattractive children from elementary school onward (Langlois, 1986). Indeed, this link between facial attractiveness and peer acceptance even begins to make some sense when we consider how attractive and unattractive children interact with their playmates. Although attractive and unattractive 3-year-olds do not yet differ a great deal in the character of their social behaviors, by age 5 unattractive youngsters are more likely than attractive ones to be active and boisterous during play sessions and to respond aggressively toward peers (Langlois & Downs, 1979). So, unattractive children do seem to develop patterns of social interaction that could alienate other children.

Why might this happen? Some theorists have argued that parents, teachers, and other children may contribute to a self-fulfilling prophecy by subtly (or not so subtly) communicating to attractive youngsters that they are smart and are expected to do well in school, behave pleasantly, and be likable. Information of this sort undoubtedly has an effect on children: attractive youngsters may become progressively more confident, friendly, and outgoing, whereas unattractive children who receive less favorable feedback may suffer a loss of self-esteem and become more resentful, defiant, and aggressive. This is precisely how a "beautiful is good" stereotype could become a reality (Langlois & Downs, 1979).

Body build (or physique) is another physical attribute that can affect a child's self-concept and popularity with peers. In one study (Staffieri, 1967), 6–10-year-olds were shown full-length silhouettes of *ectomorphic* (thin, linear), *endomorphic* (soft, rounded, chubby), and *mesomorphic* (athletic, muscular) physiques (see Figure 15-6). After stating which body type they preferred, the children were given a list of adjectives and asked to select those that applied to each body type. Finally, each child listed the names of five classmates who were good friends and three classmates whom he or she didn't like very well.

The results were clear. Not only did children prefer the mesomorphic silhouette, but they attributed

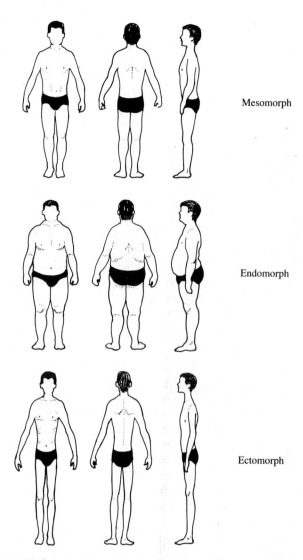

Mesomorph

Endomorph

Ectomorph

FIGURE 15-6   The three body types used in Staffieri's experiment.

positive adjectives—for example, *brave, strong, neat,* and *helpful*—to this figure while assigning much less favorable adjectives to the ectomorphic and endomorphic figures. Among the children themselves, there was a definite relationship between body build and popularity: the mesomorphs in the class turned out to be the most popular children, whereas endomorphic classmates were least popular (see also Sigelman, Miller, & Whitworth, 1986).

Other research with adolescents and adults paints a similar picture: mesomorphs are generally popular individuals who often rise to positions of leadership, whereas ectomorphs and particularly endomorphs tend to be much less popular with their peers (Clausen, 1975; Lerner, 1969).

Finally, there are tremendous individual differences in the age at which children reach puberty, and the timing of this maturational milestone can have important social consequences, at least for males.[2] Longitudinal research conducted at the University of California suggests that early-maturing males tend to be poised and confident in social settings and to be overrepresented among pupils who have won athletic honors or student elections. Early maturers were also rated as more attractive, more masculine, less "childish," and less inclined to actively seek others' attention than their later-maturing classmates (Jones & Bayley, 1950). Other investigators have found that late maturers tend to feel somewhat socially inadequate and inferior and that they often express a need for sympathy and understanding (Duke et al., 1982; Livson & Peskin, 1980). The down side to early maturation is that boys who reach puberty early are sometimes found to have less self-control (Susman et al., 1985) and to be somewhat more inclined to drink and use drugs than their later-maturing agemates (Duncan et al., 1985). But, on the whole, the advantages of early maturation for males appear to outweigh the disadvantages, and there is even some evidence that these benefits are long lasting: when retested during their thirties, the early maturers from Jones and Bayley's (1950) sample were still more sociable, self-confident, and popular with peers than members of the late-maturing group (Jones, 1965).

[2]Although early-maturing girls are sometimes found to be *less* popular than those who reach puberty at the same time as or later than their female classmates (Aro & Taipale, 1987; Duncan et al., 1985), this "timing of puberty" effect is not large and does not last very long. Why does it appear at all? Possibly because early-maturing girls experience more conflicts with parents, who themselves are feeling the strain of having to closely regulate the behavior of a young but sexually mature daughter (Savin-Williams & Small, 1986). This conflictual relationship with parents may thus contribute to a surly, defiant attitude that could color the girl's interactions with peers in ways that temporarily decrease her social standing in the peer group.

Why is the early-maturing male in such an advantageous position? One reason may be that his greater size and strength make him a more capable athlete, which in turn is likely to bring social recognition from adults and peers (Simmons & Blyth, 1987). The early maturer's adultlike appearance may also prompt others to overestimate his competencies and to grant him privileges and responsibilities normally reserved for older individuals. Indeed, parents do hold higher educational and achievement aspirations for early-maturing than for late-maturing sons (Duke et al., 1982), and they have fewer conflicts with early maturers about such issues as acceptable curfews and the boy's choice of friends (Savin-Williams & Small, 1986). Perhaps you can see how this generally positive, harmonious atmosphere might promote the poise or self-confidence that enables many early maturers to become popular and to assume positions of leadership within the peer group. By contrast, if parents, teachers, and peers continue to treat a "boyish-looking" late maturer as if he were somehow less competent or less worthy of privileges or responsibility, it is easy to imagine how he could become unsure of himself and feel somewhat inferior.

Behavioral characteristics.   Although attractive names, attractive physical features, and cognitive/scholastic/athletic prowess are all meaningfully related to peer acceptance, even the brightest and most attractive children may be very unpopular if peers consider their conduct inappropriate or antisocial (Dodge, 1983; Langlois & Styczynski, 1979). Indeed, popular, rejected, and neglected children typically respond to peers in very different ways, displaying distinctive behavioral profiles that help to establish and to maintain their social standings in the peer group.

What behavioral characteristics seem to be most important in influencing a child's standing with peers? Several studies of preschool, grade-school, and middle-school (young adolescent) children report pretty much the same findings. *Popular* children are observed to be relatively calm, outgoing, friendly, and supportive companions who can successfully initiate and maintain interactions and can resolve disputes amicably (see Coie, Dodge, &

Kupersmidt, 1990; Denham et al., 1990; Ladd, Price, & Hart, 1988, 1990). Stated another way, these "sociometric stars" are warm, cooperative, and compassionate souls who display many prosocial behaviors and are seldom disruptive or aggressive (Hart et al., 1992; Parkhurst & Asher, 1992).

Neglected children, by contrast, often appear shy or withdrawn. They are not very talkative; they make fewer attempts than children of average status to enter play groups; and they seldom call attention to themselves (Coie et al., 1990; Coie & Kupersmidt, 1983). Nevertheless, these youngsters are no less socially skilled than children of average status; nor are they any more lonely or more distressed about the character of their social relationships (Asher & Wheeler, 1985; Cassidy & Asher, 1992; Parkhurst & Asher, 1992). Their withdrawn behavior appears to stem more from their own social anxieties and their beliefs that they are not socially skilled than from any active ostracism or exclusion by their peer groups (Cassidy & Asher, 1992; Younger & Daniels, 1992).

Finally, *rejected* children display many characteristics that are likely to annoy or anger their peers. Clearly, the most consistent predictor of peer rejection is aggression—particularly aggression that is unprovoked and is intended to dominate and control other children and their resources (Coie et al., 1991; Dodge et al., 1990). Additionally, rejected children are often disruptive braggarts who tend to be uncooperative and critical of peer-group activities and who display poor social problem-solving skills and low levels of prosocial behavior (Coie et al., 1990; Parkhurst & Asher, 1992).

Now let's consider a thorny interpretive issue: Do the behavioral profiles that children display really *cause* them to become popular, rejected, or neglected by peers? Do popular children, for example, become popular because they are friendly, cooperative, and nonaggressive? Or is it that children become friendlier, more cooperative, and less aggressive after achieving their popularity? One way to test these competing hypotheses is to place children in play groups with *unfamiliar* peers and then see whether the behaviors they display will predict their eventual status in the peer group. Several studies of this type have been conducted (Coie &

Kupersmidt, 1983; Dodge, 1983; Dodge et al., 1990; Ladd et al., 1988), and the results are reasonably consistent: the patterns of behavior that children display do predict the status they will achieve with their peers. Children who are ultimately accepted by unfamiliar peers are effective at initiating social interactions and at responding positively to others' bids for attention. When they want to join a group activity, for example, these socially skilled, *soon-to-be-accepted* children will first watch and attempt to understand what is going on and then comment pleasantly and constructively about the proceedings as they blend smoothly into the group. By contrast, children who are ultimately *rejected* are pushy and self-serving; they will often criticize or disrupt group activities and may even threaten reprisals if they are not allowed to join in. Children who end up being *neglected* by their peers tend to hover around the edges of a group, initiating few interactions and shying away from other children's bids for attention. Interestingly, some children who are neglected by familiar playmates will suddenly become quite sociable with *unfamiliar* peers (Coie & Kupersmidt, 1983), whereas other extremely withdrawn neglectees are likely to retain this status or even to become nonaggressive *rejectees* (French, 1988; Rubin, LeMare, & Lollis, 1990).

Who among withdrawn children are most likely to be rejected in the long run? Although the evidence is not extensive, it appears that the withdrawn children whom peers ultimately reject are those who are not especially cooperative and who are hypersensitive to teasing, often interpreting such verbal banter as evidence that peers dislike them (Cillessen et al., 1992; Parkhurst & Asher, 1992). It seems that their heightened sensitivity to criticism and teasing prompts these youngsters to *actively isolate* themselves from peers, who eventually conclude that they are thin-skinned, hypercritical playmates who can't take a joke and are generally dislikable (Parkhurst & Asher, 1992; Younger & Daniels, 1992).

Earlier we noted that it is aggressive rejectees rather than nonaggressive rejectees who face the greater risk of adjustment problems later in life. Yet Ken Rubin and his associates (1990) have recently hypothesized that these socially withdrawn, nonag-

gressive rejectees may eventually show signs of clinical depression or other internalizing disorders later in life. Moreover, Parkhurst and Asher (1992) find that nonaggressive rejectees are perceived by peers as "easy to push around," and they speculate that these youngsters may become especially inviting targets for bullies (recall from Box 10-2 that chronically victimized children are typically passive youngsters who are clearly rejected by their peers). So there may well be meaningful risks associated with the "nonaggressive rejectee" status after all.

On Improving the Social Skills of Unpopular Children

The finding that peer acceptance is a strong predictor of current and future psychological well-being has prompted many investigators to devise interventions, or "therapies," aimed at improving the social skills (and sociometric statuses) of unpopular children. Among the more common of these approaches are the following.

Reinforcing socially appropriate behaviors. In an early review of interventions based on social-learning principles, Melinda Combs and Diana Slaby (1977) concluded that adults can shape socially skilled behaviors such as cooperation and sharing by reinforcing these actions and ignoring examples of "inappropriate" behavior such as aggression, disruptive conduct, and solitary play. But, to be effective, contingent reinforcement of socially skilled behaviors must be administered on a regular basis to the *entire peer group*—a procedure that not only reinforces the socially skillful acts of the target children but also allows them to see others reinforced for this kind of behavior. There are several ways for adults to structure play environments so that it becomes possible to reinforce groups of children for their appropriate social conduct. For example, they might persuade youngsters to work at tasks or strive for goals that require cooperation among all present (see Box 15-1). Even simple strategies such as giving children "social" toys to play with (cards, checkers, and the like) should provide ample opportunities for adults to reinforce examples of appropriate social behavior.

Modeling social skills.   Early in the development of his social-learning theory, Bandura (Bandura & Menlove, 1968) discovered that modeling techniques were effective at persuading children to approach objects (dogs) that they had previously feared and avoided. Would a similar form of therapy help shy or otherwise withdrawn youngsters to become less apprehensive about approaching and interacting with peers?

Apparently it can. In one study (Cooke & Apolloni, 1976), live models demonstrated certain social skills—for example, smiling at others, sharing, initiating positive physical contacts, and giving verbal compliments—to withdrawn grade-school children. This procedure proved effective at increasing each type of behavior that the model had enacted. The training also had two desirable side effects. First, the withdrawn children began to show increases in other positive social behaviors that had not been modeled. Second, the frequency of positive social responses among *untrained* children also increased, apparently in direct response to the friendly gestures made by their classmates who had received the social-skills training. So modeling strategies can produce marked changes in a child's social skills—changes that benefit both the child and the peers with whom he or she interacts. And it seems that the modeling approach works best when the model is similar to the child, when he initially acts shy and withdrawn, and when his socially skillful actions are accompanied by some form of commentary that directs the observer's attention to the purposes and benefits of behaving appropriately toward others (Asher, Renshaw, & Hymel, 1982).

Cognitive approaches to social-skills training.   The fact that modeling strategies work better when accompanied by verbal rationales and explanations implies that interventions that induce the child to think about or to imagine the consequences of various social overtures are likely to be effective. Why? Because the child's active cognitive involvement in the social-skills training may increase her understanding and appreciation of the principles that are taught, thereby persuading her to internalize and then rely on these lessons when interacting with peers.

Coaching is a cognitive social-learning technique in which the therapist displays one or more social skills, carefully explains the rationales for using them, allows children to practice such behavior, and then suggests how the children might improve on their performances. Sherri Oden and Steven Asher (1977) coached third- and fourth-grade social isolates on four important skills: how to participate in play activities, how to take turns and share, how to communicate effectively, and how to give attention and help to peers. Not only did the children who were coached become more outgoing and positive, but follow-up measures a year later revealed that these former isolates had achieved even further gains in social status (see also Bierman, 1986; Ladd, 1981). Coaching strategies have been employed successfully with preschool as well as grade-school children (Mize & Ladd, 1990), and apparently the benefits of this approach are even greater when it is combined with other forms of social-skills training, such as encouraging children to work together toward the attainment of cooperative goals (Bierman & Furman, 1984).

Other cognitive interventions, firmly grounded in cognitive-developmental theory, include attempts to improve children's *role-taking* skills and *social problem-solving abilities* (Chandler, 1973; Rabiner, Lenhart, & Lochman, 1990; Yeates & Selman, 1989). These techniques can be especially effective with aggressive rejectees who often display a *hostile attributional bias* (a tendency to overattribute hostile intentions to their companions) that has been acquired at home from coercive parents who mistrust other people and endorse aggression (Keane, Brown, & Crenshaw, 1990; Pettit, Dodge, & Brown, 1988). In order to help these aggressive rejectees, the training must not only emphasize that aggression is inappropriate but also help them to generate nonaggressive solutions to conflict. One approach that looks promising is the **social problem-solving training** that Myrna Shure and George Spivack (1978; Shure, 1989) devised to help preschoolers generate and then evaluate amicable solutions to interpersonal problems. Over a ten-week period, children role-

PHOTO 15-5 Coaching can be effective at improving the social skills of withdrawn children.

played conflict scenarios with puppets and were encouraged to discuss the impact of their solutions on the feelings of all parties involved in a conflict. Shure and Spivack found that fewer aggressive solutions were offered the longer the children had participated in the program. Moreover, the children's classroom adjustment (as rated by teachers) improved as they became better able to think through the social consequences of their own actions.

Qualifications about social-skills training. How does one decide when to institute social-skills training? Who should be trained and by what method? In addressing these issues, let's first recall that, despite their withdrawn demeanor, most *neglected* children are not all that socially unskilled or unhappy about the quality of their social relationships. If a neglectee shows signs of becoming especially wary of peer contacts or of being hypersensitive to teasing or criticism (signals that he could eventually be rejected), then an approach that produces immediate results (such as contingent reinforcement, modeling, or coaching) might be used to draw him out of his shell and illustrate that peer contacts can

be satisfying. But many (perhaps most) neglectees require no intervention at all.

Second, aggressive rejectees who receive social-skills training often gain status in the eyes of other youngsters with whom they are trained without becoming any more popular with their regular classmates (Bierman, Miller, & Stabb, 1987). Why does their standing with classmates not improve? Perhaps because their negative reputations make classmates hesitant to give them the benefit of the doubt when they begin to behave more positively (see Box 15-2). To increase the effectiveness of interventions with rejected children, it may be crucial to enlist many of their peers and perhaps even their classroom teachers as participants in the training. If teachers and peers are involved, they are more likely to notice changes in the rejected child's behavior and should be more inclined to change their opinions of him or her (Bierman & Furman, 1984; White & Kistner, 1992).

Finally, the long-term success of any intervention is likely to be compromised if the social skills and problem-solving strategies that aggressive children have learned are undermined by coercive, mistrusting parents who endorse aggressive solutions to conflict or by highly aggressive friends. For these reasons, Gregory Pettit and his associates (1988) favor *preventive* therapies—family-based interventions in which parents who are likely to value and encourage aggression are identified early and retrained themselves, thus possibly preventing their children from ever becoming highly aggressive or being rejected by their peers. Moreover, the academic skills training that we discussed earlier in the chapter is also a preventive strategy: rejected children who gain in scholastic competence not only become better liked by peers (Coie & Krehbiel, 1984) but also are less likely to select highly aggressive children as friends or to become members of deviant peer cliques (Dishion et al., 1991). Today we are seeing a much stronger emphasis on preventive interventions—programs that are undertaken as soon as a child's problems with peers become apparent. And such an emphasis is clearly warranted, for (as we learned in Chapter 10) social-skills training programs rarely succeed once a child's deviant, antisocial conduct has continued beyond the first few grades at school (Kazdin, 1987; Patterson, DeBaryshe, & Ramsey, 1989).

Children and Their Friends

As young children become more outgoing and are exposed to a wider variety of peers, they typically form close ties to one or more playmates—bonds that we call **friendships**. In this portion of the chapter we will first consider how children define friendships and see what they expect from their "special" companions. We will then compare the social interactions of friends with those of acquaintances and discuss some of the roles that friends may play in a person's social and emotional development.

Children's Conceptions of Friends and Friendships

What qualifies someone as a friend? Recall from our discussion in Chapter 4 that the answer seems to depend on the child's age and level of social-cognitive development (Berndt, 1988; Selman, 1980). Before age 8 the principal basis for friendship is *common activity*: children view friends as associates who live nearby, who enjoy similar play activities, and who like to play with them. Between 8 and 12, children's ever-increasing abilities to assume other people's perspectives enable them to become more proficient at inferring one another's needs, motives, intentions, and desires. Now the bases for friendship are relevant *psychological similarities*—shared interests, traits, and motives—as well as an expectation that friends can be *trusted* to be loyal, kind, cooperative, and sensitive to each other's social and emotional needs (Berndt, 1986; Reid et al., 1989; Rotenberg & Mann, 1986).

Although adolescents continue to think that trustworthiness and shared psychological attributes are characteristics that friends should display, their conceptions of friendship now focus much more in-

PHOTO 15-6   Sometimes nothing is as reassuring as the affection and encouragement of a friend.

tently on *reciprocal emotional commitments*. Friends are viewed as *intimate* associates who truly understand and *accept* each other's strengths and shortcomings and are willing to discuss their innermost thoughts and feelings. Indeed, 16- to 17-year-olds say that, above all, friends are people whom they can count on for guidance, intimate emotional support, and validation of their worth as an individual (Parker & Gottman, 1989; Smollar & Youniss, 1982). So, for older adolescents, close friendship seems to imply a unit relation or a "shared identity" in which "me and you" have become a "we" (Hartup, 1983).

Although young children may have many playmates, few of these companions become close friends. How do friendships develop? One way to find out is to randomly pair unacquainted same-age playmates and then observe their play over a period of weeks for clues as to why some pairs become friends and others do not. John Gottman (1983) tried this approach with pairs of initially unacquainted 3- to 9-year-olds. Each pair of playmates met in the home of one of the children for several play sessions over a period of four weeks. At the end of the study, mothers responded to a questionnaire on which they indicated whether their children had become friends with their new playmates. Moreover, observers had recorded children's behavior during the play sessions, hoping to use these observations as a way of determining how the interactions of children who become friends differ from those of eventual nonfriends.

As expected, Gottman found that some of the playmate pairs became fast friends whereas others did not. He also found several important differences in the play activities of eventual friends and nonfriends. First, even though eventual friends didn't always initially agree on which play activities to pursue, they were much more successful than eventual nonfriends at *resolving conflicts* and establishing a *common-ground activity* — that is, at agreeing on what and how to play. Eventual friends were also more successful at *communicating clearly* with each other and *exchanging information*. And some of the information exchanged was very personal in nature, for eventual friends were more likely than children who did not become friends to engage in **self-disclosure**. So it seemed to Gottman as if children who generally agreed about play activities early on simply "hit it off," thus becoming more inclined to show affection and approval toward their partners and to reveal personal information about themselves — processes that allowed their relationship to gel as a friendship. Do these same processes that help to create friendships also characterize interactions among longer-term friends? Let's see if they do.

Social Interactions among Friends and Acquaintances

As early as age 2 to 3, children are establishing mutual (or reciprocated) friendships and are reacting very differently to friends than to mere acquaintances (Hartup, 1989; Howes, 1988). For example, friends display more advanced forms of social play than acquaintances do — as well as more affection and more approval (Guralnick & Groom, 1988; Hinde et al., 1985). Indeed, friends often do nice

things for each other, and many altruistic behaviors may first appear within these early alliances of the preschool era. Frederick Kanfer and his associates (1981), for example, found that 3- to 6-year-olds were generally willing to give up their own valuable playtime to perform a dull task if their efforts would benefit a friend; yet this same kind of self-sacrifice was almost never made for a mere acquaintance (see Box 11-1 for a more complete description of this research). Moreover, young children express more sympathy in response to the distress of a friend than to that of an acquaintance, and they are more inclined to try to relieve the friend's negative emotional state as well (Costin & Jones, 1992). Finally, 3- to 6-year-olds respond much more constructively to strange settings or to novel routines when they face them with friends than with mere acquaintances — suggesting, perhaps, that the presence of friends reduces a young child's apprehension about uncertain situations (Ladd, 1990; Schwartz, 1972). Notice, then, that *preschool* friendships are already characterized by a sense of mutual caring and emotional support, even though years may pass before children will *say* that these qualities are what define a good friendship.

We've all heard the colloquial expressions that there is a "chemistry" to close friendships and that true friends are "in tune with each other" or are "on the same wavelength." Recent research provides some support for these notions. Tiffany Field and her associates (1992) filmed pairs of sixth-graders as they conversed face to face for ten minutes on topics of their own choosing. They found that interactions between pairs of friends were much more lively and "in synch" than those between mere acquaintances. For example, friends were more attentive and involved in the conversations and appeared to be more relaxed and playful with each other than acquaintances were. Moreover, friends were more likely than acquaintances to be displaying the same behavioral state (for example, playfulness) at the same time. Finally, a measure of participants' saliva cortisol levels (a physiological correlate of stress) taken after the interactions suggested that casual conversations between acquaintances are more stressful than those between friends.

So perhaps it is fair to say that interactions between friends have a favorable "chemistry" about them—a spirit that is evident in group activities as well. For example, when 6- to 8-year-olds work together on such challenging tasks as a tower-building game, groups of friends do not necessarily build bigger towers than groups of acquaintances. However, friends are more talkative, pay more attention to equity rules (for example, "If we take turns, we'll all make more points"), and usually direct their remarks to the group ("Let's do it this way") rather than to each other as individuals ("Put your block over there") (Newcomb, Brady, & Hartup, 1979). This is not to say that friends never lock horns; in fact, they squabble about as often or even more often than acquaintances do (Hartup et al., 1988). But, as we noted in Chapter 4, disagreeing friends are more likely than disagreeing acquaintances to fully explain the basis for their conflicting points of view, thus providing each other with information that might foster the development of role-taking skills (Nelson & Aboud, 1985) as well as an ability to compromise.

How long do children's friendships last? It may surprise you to learn that even preschool friendships can be highly stable. Carollee Howes (1988), for example, found that children who attend the same day-care center for several years often keep the same close friends for more than a year. Research with grade-school children paints a similar picture. Friendship networks (that is, the list of *all* individuals a child might nominate as "friends") are not terribly stable from year to year, although *best* friendships are highly stable, particularly if the pair of friends share similar interests and perceive their relationship as very close (Berndt, Hawkins, & Hoyle, 1986; Berndt & Hoyle, 1985). Interestingly, friendship networks shrink over time, so that an eighth-grader is likely to lose more friends during the course of a school year than she gains (Berndt & Hoyle, 1985). This net loss of friends may simply reflect the young adolescent's growing awareness that the obligations of friendship—which now include the exchange of intimate information and the provision of emotional support—are easier to live up to if one selects a smaller circle of very close friends.

Are There Distinct Advantages to Having Friends?

Do friends play a unique role in shaping a child's development? Do children who have established adequate peer relations but no close friends turn out any differently than those who have one or more of these special companions? Might an unpopular child who has one or more socially skilled friends stand a better chance than other rejectees of improving her social status? Unfortunately, no one has answers to all of these questions, for not many longitudinal studies of the effects of having (or not having) friends have been conducted. Nevertheless, the data that are available permit some speculation about the roles friends play as socializing agents.

Friends as promoters of social competence. Consider first the issue of whether having a socially skilled friend might help an unpopular child improve his or her status with peers. In her study of peer relations among preschoolers, Howes (1988) found that rejected children were much more likely to gain entry into ongoing peer-group activities if they tried to join with a friend or if they had a friend in the play group. Moreover, rejected children who had a close friend were more skilled interactants and displayed more mature forms of social play than other rejectees who had no friends. Howes concluded that having a mutual friend may indeed help an unpopular child to gain access to peers and to acquire more appropriate social skills—two obvious prerequisites for improving one's social status. In her own words, "The implications of [these] findings include expanding intervention programs for at-risk children to include friendship-making opportunities as well as social skill training" (Howes, 1988, p. 51).

Friends as providers of security and social support. The fact that children respond more constructively to novel environments in the presence of friends suggests that friendships provide an emotional safety net—a kind of security that not only makes children a little bolder when faced with new challenges but also may make almost any other form of stress (for example, coping with a divorce or with a rejecting parent) a little easier to bear. Indeed, Gary Ladd (1990; Ladd & Price, 1987) finds that children who enter kindergarten along with their friends seem to like school better and have fewer adjustment problems than those who enter school without many friends. Moreover, we saw in Chapter 13 that children who respond most constructively to their parents' divorce are often those who have the support of friends whose parents are also divorced. We can also gauge the security and support that young children derive from friendships by looking at what happens should they lose a close friend who moves away. Such a loss is often a devastating experience for preschool children — one that can quickly undermine their emotional security and the quality (or maturity) of their interactions with peers (Howes, 1988).

So friends are potentially important sources of security and **social support**, and they become increasingly significant in fulfilling this role as children grow older. Fourth-graders, for example, say that their parents are their primary sources of social support; however, *same-sex* friends are perceived to be (1) as supportive as parents by seventh-graders and (2) the most frequent providers of social support by tenth-grade adolescents (Furman & Buhrmester, 1992).

Friendship as an impetus for amicable conflict resolution. Since friendships are usually characterized as pleasant and mutually rewarding relationships that are worth preserving, children should be highly motivated to resolve any conflicts with these "special companions" (Hartup, 1989). We've noted that disagreements among friends may foster the development of role-taking skills because friends try harder than acquaintances to fully explain the bases for their conflicting points of view. And, given the possibility that one may lose something (or someone) valuable if conflicts remain unresolved, it is likely that squabbles among friends provide an impetus for compromise that is simply not present to the same degree in interactions among acquaintances. Even during the preschool period, disagreeing friends are more likely than disagreeing

acquaintances to step away before their battles become intense, to make concessions by accepting equal outcomes, and to continue to play together after the conflict is over (Hartup et al., 1988). So the experience of amicably resolving conflicts with a friend is undoubtedly an important contributor to the growth of mature social problem-solving skills — one of the strongest predictors of a healthy sociometric status with peers.

Friendships as preparation for romantic attachments and adult love relationships. Although close friendships at all ages are *reciprocal* relationships, we've seen that they are characterized by increasing intimacy and mutuality from middle childhood through adolescence. Could these relatively intense and intimate ties to what are overwhelmingly same-sex companions be necessary for the development of the deep interpersonal sensitivity and commitment so often observed in stable adult love relationships? Harry Stack Sullivan (1953) thought so. Sullivan reported that many of his mentally disturbed patients had failed to form close friendships when they were young, and he concluded that the close bonds that develop between same-sex friends (or "chums") during preadolescence provide the *essential* foundation of caring and compassion that a person needs to establish and maintain intimate love relationships (as well as close friendships) later in life. Although this latter conclusion remains to be confirmed, Sullivan was correct in assuming that adolescents who have succeeded in establishing *intimate* friendships would be better adjusted (more sociable; less hostile, anxious, and depressed; higher in self-esteem) than those whose friendships are not so deep (see Buhrmester, 1990).

So there are good reasons to suspect that close friends contribute importantly (and perhaps uniquely) to social and personality development, and it will be interesting to see whether our speculations pan out in the years ahead as researchers learn more about the long-term implications of having (or not having) friends.

One final point — and an important one: although many children and adolescents have smooth, synchronous, and supportive relationships with close friends, others have friendships that are conflictual, often nonsupportive, and lacking in trust. How might we explain these individual differences in the quality of children's friendships?

Recent research implies that the pathway to stable, high-quality friendships begins at home and is a reflection of the child's relationships with parents. In Chapter 6, for example, we discussed a study by Park and Waters (1989) in which interactions between pairs of 4-year-old "best friends" were much less conflictual and more harmonious when both members of the pair were securely attached to their mothers than when either of the friends was insecurely attached. Lise Youngblade and Jay Belsky (1992) have since replicated this finding in a study of friendships among 5-year-olds. Moreover, they found that the character of children's playful interactions with fathers at age 3 predicted the quality of their friendships at age 5: children whose fathers had been sensitive, supportive, and nonintrusive playmates tended to interact in a synchronous manner with their close friends and to have harmonious relationships with them, whereas children whose fathers had been more intrusive and controlling tended to have more asynchronous and conflictual relationships with their friends. Here, then, are data suggesting that some of the same family variables (for example, attachment quality, the character of parent/child interactions) that affect a child's general sociability with peers will also influence the character or quality of her friendships. Of course, these findings are also consistent with a major proposition of attachment theory that we discussed at length in Chapter 6—namely, that the quality of early parent/child attachments can have very important implications for the kind of close relationships that people are likely to have (with friends, romantic partners, spouses, and their own children) later in life.

How Do Peers Exert Their Influence?

To this point we have seen that it is important for children to establish good peer relations because they will acquire many competent and adaptive patterns of social behavior through their interactions with peers. How exactly do peers exert their influence? In many of the same ways that parents do—by reinforcing, modeling, discussing, and even pressuring one another to comply with the values and behaviors they condone.

Peer Reinforcement, Modeling Influences, and Social Comparison Processes

It is easy to see that parents, teachers, and other powerful authority figures are in a position to reward or punish the behavior of children. Yet we might legitimately wonder whether a peer, who shares a similar status with the child, can become an effective agent of reinforcement. Wonder no longer—the evidence is clear: peers are rather potent sources of reinforcement.

Consider what Michael Lamb and his associates (1980) found while observing the reactions of 3- to 5-year-olds to their playmates' sex-appropriate or sex-inappropriate (cross-sex) activities. Children generally reinforced their companions for sex-appropriate play and were quick to criticize or disrupt a playmate's cross-sex activities. But were these playmates influenced by the treatment they received? Indeed they were. Children who were reinforced for sex-appropriate play tended to keep playing, whereas those who were punished for sex-inappropriate play usually terminated this activity in less than a minute (Lamb, Easterbrooks, & Holden, 1980).

Many of the reinforcers that children provide one another are quite subtle or unintentional. For example, a child who "caves in" to a bully not only has reinforced the bully's aggressive tactics without meaning to, but also has set herself up to be victimized again. Yet, when a potential victim "punishes" a tormentor by fighting back, she may persuade him to seek other victims and may even learn that fighting "pays off," thus becoming more aggressive herself (Patterson, Littman, & Bricker, 1967).

So peers *are* important sources of social reinforcement. Although we have sampled only two studies from a voluminous literature, the evidence clearly indicates that children's social behaviors are often strengthened, maintained, or virtually eliminated by the favorable or unfavorable reactions they elicit from peers.

Modeling influences.   Peers influence one another by serving not only as reinforcing and punishing agents but also as social models. For example, we've noted that children who are afraid of dogs will often overcome their phobic reactions after witnessing other children playing with these once-terrifying creatures (Bandura & Menlove, 1968). Among the other attributes and activities that are easily acquired by observing peer models are socially responsive behaviors (Cooke & Apolloni, 1976), achievement behaviors (Sagotsky & Lepper, 1982), moral judgments (Dorr & Fey, 1974), an ability to delay gratification (Stumphauzer, 1972), and sex-typed attitudes and behaviors (Ruble, Balaban, & Cooper, 1981), to name a few. You may recall that several of these findings were discussed at length in earlier chapters.

Another function that peer models serve is to inform the child how he or she is supposed to behave in different situations. For example, a new child at school may not know whether it is acceptable to visit the water fountain during a study period without first asking the teacher, but she will quickly conclude that this behavior is allowed if she sees her classmates doing it.

Peers as objects for social comparison.   Finally, children often reach conclusions about their competencies and other personality attributes by comparing their behaviors and accomplishments against those displayed by peers. If a 10-year-old consistently outperforms all her classmates on math tests, she is likely to conclude that she is "smart" or at least "good in math." A 6-year-old who loses every foot race that he has with peers will soon come to think of himself as a slow runner. Because peers are similar in age (and are presumed to be reasonably similar in many other respects), the peer group is the most logical choice for these kinds of *social comparisons* (see Festinger, 1954; France-Kaatrude & Smith, 1985). It matters little to our "smart" 10-year-old that she knows less math than her teenage sis-

ter. And our "snail-like" 6-year-old is not at all comforted by the fact that he can run faster than his 4-year-old brother. In matters of social comparison and self-definition, peers simply have no peer.

Peers as Critics and Agents of Persuasion

Another way peers influence each other is by discussing and debating issues on which they disagree. Typically, both parties to these discussions (which can become rather heated) are invested in their own points of view and are trying to persuade their partner to adopt (or at least move toward) the position they are advocating. Indeed, we learned in Chapter 12 that older children and young adolescents can be persuaded to change their perspectives on moral issues should a peer challenge their existing viewpoints (that is, induce cognitive disequilibrium) and present a more sophisticated set of arguments for them to assimilate and adopt as their own. Moreover, peers may be the *most effective* agents of persuasion-via-cognitive-conflict, for you may recall from our earlier discussion (see Boxes 12-1 and 12-2) that cognitive challenges from *authority figures* (parents) are often perceived by children as heavy-handed criticism and are generally less successful than other methods at inducing youngsters to change their viewpoints. By contrast, a peer is an equal-status associate whose *well-reasoned* challenges (1) are less likely to be perceived as derisive and (2) should carry some weight in that most children and adolescents are very interested in establishing or maintaining good peer relations (Walker & Taylor, 1991).

The Normative Function of Peer Groups

As we noted earlier, an increasing percentage of peer interactions from middle childhood onward occur in true *peer groups* — confederations that influence group members by setting implicit or explicit norms specifying how members are supposed to look, think, and act. You may recall from your own childhood or adolescence that pressures to conform to group norms can be intense and that those who ignore the dictates of peers risk all sorts of sanctions, ranging from simply being labeled a "nerd" to facing outright rejection. For many youngsters it is quite a feat to be accepted as "one of the gang" while maintaining respectability in the eyes of parents, teachers, and other important adults.

People often assume that children become increasingly responsive to peer pressure as they grow older and that adolescence is the period when the peer group is most influential. Clearly there is an element of truth to these ideas. In his study of **peer conformity**, Thomas Berndt (1979) asked 3rd-through 12th-graders to indicate the likelihood that they would bend to peer pressure when peers were advocating various prosocial or antisocial acts. He found that conformity to peer pressure for prosocial behaviors did not change much with age. Instead, the most striking developmental change was a sharp increase in conformity to peers' advocating *antisocial* behavior. This receptivity to peer-sponsored misconduct peaked in the 9th grade (or about age 15; see Figure 15-7) and then declined throughout the high school years (see also Brown, Clasen, & Eicher, 1986; Steinberg & Silverberg, 1986). So parents may have some grounds for worrying that their 12- to 15-year-olds could wind up in trouble by going along with the crowd. Peer pressure of all kinds is especially strong at this age, and being accepted by peers is particularly important (Gavin & Furman, 1989).

Why do older adolescents become increasingly less susceptible to peer pressure for deviant conduct? Perhaps this trend reflects the progress they are making in their quest for autonomy; that is, older adolescents are better able to make their own decisions and are now much less dependent on the opinions of *either* parents or peers. According to Lawrence Steinberg and Susan Silverberg (1986), strong conformity to peer pressure early in adolescence may even be a necessary step in the development of autonomy: young adolescents who are struggling to become less dependent on their parents may need the security that peer acceptance provides before they can develop the confidence to take their own stands and stick by them. And they are unlikely to gain such acceptance if they conform too closely to adult rules and values without taking a chance and going along with peers every now and then (Allen, Weissberg, & Hawkins, 1989). Al-

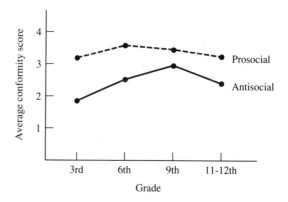

FIGURE 15-7   Average scores by grade for conformity to peer pressure for prosocial and antisocial behaviors. (Adapted from T. J. Berndt, "Developmental Changes in Conformity to Peers and Parents." *Developmental Psychology*, 1979, *15*, 608–616. Copyright © 1979 by the American Psychological Association. Adapted by permission.)

though the parent whose teenager is nabbed with his friends for cherry-bombing mailboxes or deflating tires may not be totally comforted by this thought, it does seem that a period of heavy peer influence may pave the way for later independence.

Peer versus Adult Influence: The Question of Cross-Pressures

In years gone by, adolescence was often characterized as a stormy period when all youths experience **cross-pressures** — severe conflicts between the practices advocated by parents and those favored by peers. How accurate is this "life portrait" of the teen years? It may have some merit for some adolescents, especially those "rejected" youths who form deviant peer groups and endorse behaviors that are likely to alienate parents, teachers, and normal peers (Cairns et al., 1988; Dishion et al., 1991; Patterson et al., 1989). But there are several reasons to believe that the "cross-pressures problem" is not a problem for most adolescents.

Even though mid-adolescence is a time of high susceptibility to negative peer pressure, most parents need not worry about having protracted wars with their teenagers or about losing their ability to influence them (Hartup, 1983). It seems that adolescents who have established warm relations with parents who are neither too controlling nor too lax will rarely experience strong cross-pressures (Bixenstine, DeCorte, & Bixenstine, 1976; Brook, Whiteman, & Gordon, 1983; Smetana, 1988). They have often internalized many of their parents' most basic values and have little need to rebel or to desperately seek acceptance from peers when they are so warmly received at home. Fortunately, most adolescents do enjoy reasonably cordial relations with their parents and very much want their parents' approval (Grotevant & Cooper, 1986; Larson & Richards, 1991; Youniss & Smollar, 1985). And, even when teenagers are at odds with a parent over status issues, privileges, or academic matters, these disagreements do not necessarily make them any more susceptible to peer influence. In fact, Raymond Montemayor (1982) finds that adolescents who argue a lot with their mothers often react to these conflicts by spending more time alone or with their fathers rather than becoming more involved with peers (see also Larson & Richards, 1991).

In addition, parent/peer conflicts are often kept to a minimum because parents and peers tend to exert their influence in different domains. Hans Sebald (1986), for example, has asked adolescents whether they would seek the advice of their parents or the advice of their peers on a number of different issues. *Peers* were likely to be more influential than parents on such issues as what styles to wear and which clubs, social events, hobbies, and other recreational activities to choose. By contrast, adolescents claimed that they would depend more on their *parents* when the issue involved scholastic or occupational goals or other future-oriented decisions (see also Brittain, 1963; Wilks, 1986). So it seems that peers are the primary reference group for questions of the form "Who am I?" whereas the advice of parents and other significant adults will carry more weight when teenagers grapple with the question "Who am I to be?"

A final reason why the cross-pressures "problem" is not that disruptive for most adolescents is that peer-group values are rarely as deviant as people commonly assume. Even at mid-adolescence, when negative peer pressures are greatest, teenagers report that their friends and associates are more likely to *discourage* antisocial behavior than to

PHOTO 15-7 Although teenagers are often characterized as wild and rebellious, typically their norms and values are a reflection of adult society.

condone it (Brown et al., 1986). And on many issues for which parental and peer norms might seem to be in conflict, the adolescent's behavior is actually a product of *both* parental and peer influences. Consider the following example: Denise Kandel (1973) studied a group of adolescents whose best friends either did or did not smoke marijuana and whose parents either did or did not use psychoactive drugs. Among those teenagers whose parents used drugs but whose friends did not, only 17% were marijuana users. When parents did not use drugs but best friends did, 56% of the adolescents used marijuana. From these findings we can conclude that the peer group is more influential than parents over marijuana use. However, the highest rate of marijuana smoking (67%) occurred among teen-agers whose parents and peers *both* used psychoactive drugs, and a similar pattern emerges when we look at parental and peer influences on use of alcohol, tobacco, and other illicit drugs (Chassin et al., 1986; Newcomb & Bentler, 1989).

In sum, adolescent socialization is not a continual battle between parents and peers; instead, these two important sources of influence *combine* to affect one's development. Most adolescents have cordial relationships with their parents, have accepted many of their parents' values, and are reluctant to stray too far from these guidelines and undermine their parents' approval. And most parents know how important it is for their children and adolescents to establish close relationships with social equals. They seem to appreciate what the lonely farmer whose letter opened this chapter has learned the hard way: many of the social competencies that will serve people well are the fruits of their alliances with close friends and peers.

Summary

Peer contacts represent a second world for children—a world of equal-status interactions that is very different from the nonegalitarian environment of the home. Contacts with peers increase dramatically with age, and, during the preschool or early elementary-school years, children are already spending at least as much of their leisure time with peers as with adults. The "peer group" consists mainly of *same-sex* playmates of *different* ages. Indeed, developmentalists define peers as "those who interact at similar levels of behavioral complexity," because only a small percentage of the child's associates are actually agemates.

Research with monkeys and young children indicates that peer contacts are important for the development of competent and adaptive patterns of social behavior. Children who fail to establish and maintain adequate relations with their peers will run the risk of experiencing any number of serious adjustment problems later in life.

Sociable gestures between peers begin by the middle of the first year. By age 18–24 months, infants' sociable interactions are becoming much more complex and coordinated as they reliably imitate each other, assume complementary roles in simple social games, and occasionally coordinate their actions to achieve shared goals. Play becomes increasingly social and more cognitively complex throughout the preschool years as children develop and refine the skills necessary to plan and monitor their enactment of *nonliteral* complementary roles during social pretend play. The maturity of a preschool child's play activities is a reasonably good predictor of his or her present and future social competencies and popularity with peers. During middle childhood an increasing percentage of peer interactions occur in true *peer groups*—confederations that associate regularly, define a sense of group membership, and formulate norms that specify how group members are supposed to behave. By early adolescence, youngsters are spending even more time with peers—particularly with their closest friends and with social networks known as *cliques*.

Several factors contribute to individual differences in peer sociability, and among the more important influences are the child's genotype, the security of the child's attachments, and the child-rearing practices that parents employ. Parents can directly influence their children's interactions with peers by virtue of the neighborhood in which they choose to live, their function as booking agents for peer contacts, and their monitoring of the children's behavior with playmates. The character of parent/child interactions indirectly influences children's peer sociability and social competencies. Warm, sensitive, and authoritative parents tend to raise appropriately sociable youngsters who establish good relations with their peers, whereas authoritarian or uninvolved parents—particularly those who rely on power-assertion as a control tactic—tend to raise disruptive, aggressive youngsters whom peers may dislike.

Children clearly differ in popularity—the extent to which other youngsters view them as likable (or dislikable) companions. Using *sociometric techniques*, developmentalists find that there are five categories of peer acceptance: (1) *popular children* (liked by many and disliked by few), (2) *rejected children* (disliked by many and liked by few), (3) *controversial children* (liked by many and disliked by many), (4) *neglected children* (seldom nominated by others as likable or dislikable), and (5) *average-status children* (those who are liked or disliked by a moderate number of peers). Neither neglected children nor rejected children are well received by peers; however, it is the rejected child who is typically the lonelier of the two and at greater risk of displaying serious adjustment problems later in life.

Although a child's ordinal position among siblings, physical attractiveness, and cognitive prowess may contribute meaningfully to his popularity with peers, the strongest predictor of peer acceptance is his pattern of social conduct. Popular children are generally warm, cooperative, and compassionate companions who display many prosocial behaviors and are rarely disruptive or aggressive. Neglected children often have adequate social skills, but they may underestimate their social competencies or experience social anxieties that cause them to appear shy and to hover at the edge of peer-group activities, rarely calling attention to themselves. Rejected children display many unpleasant and annoying behaviors and few prosocial ones. Many rejectees are highly disruptive, uncooperative, and aggressive, whereas other "nonaggressive" rejectees are hypersensitive to criticism and have actively isolated themselves from peers. Several techniques have been devised to improve the peer acceptance of rejected children. These social-skills training programs work better (1) with younger than with older children, and (2) when the target children's classmates also participate in the intervention.

Children typically form close ties, or friendships, with one or more members of their play group. Younger children view a friend as a harmonious playmate, whereas older children and adolescents come to think of friends as close companions who share similar interests and values and are willing to provide them with intimate social and emotional support. Interactions among friends are warmer, more cooperative, more compassionate, and more synchronous (though not necessarily less conflictual) than those among acquaintances. Although

the unique roles that friends might play in one's social development have not been firmly established, there are indications that solid friendships (1) provide a sense of security and social support that helps children and adolescents to respond more constructively to stresses and challenges, (2) promote the development of role-taking skills and an ability to compromise, and (3) foster the growth of caring and compassionate feelings, which are the foundations of intimate love relationships later in life.

Peers influence a child in many of the same ways that parents do — by modeling, reinforcing, discussing, and pressuring associates to conform to the behaviors and values they condone. Conformity pressures peak at mid-adolescence, when teenagers are most susceptible to peer-sponsored misconduct. Yet, adolescents who have established warm relations with their parents have generally internalized many of the parents' values and will continue to seek parental advice about scholastic matters and future-oriented decisions. Moreover, peer-group values are often very similar to those of parents, and peers are more likely to discourage than to condone antisocial conduct. So adolescent socialization is not a continual battle between parents and peers; instead, these two important influences *combine* to affect one's development.

References

ADAMS, G. R., & CRANE, P. (1980). An assessment of parents' and teachers' expectations of preschool children's social preference for attractive or unattractive children and adults. *Child Development, 51,* 224–231.

AINSWORTH, M. D. S. (1979). Attachment as related to mother-infant interaction. In J. G. Rosenblatt, R. A. Hinde, C. Beer, & M. Busnel (Eds.), *Advances in the study of behavior* (Vol. 9). Orlando, FL: Academic Press.

ALEXANDER, B. K., & HARLOW, H. F. (1965). Social behavior in juvenile rhesus monkeys subjected to different rearing conditions during the first 6 months of life. *Zoologische Jarbucher Physiologie, 60,* 167–174.

ALLEN, J. P., WEISSBERG, R. P., & HAWKINS, J. A. (1989). The relation between values and social competence in early adolescence. *Developmental Psychology, 25,* 458–464.

ARO, H., & TAIPALE, V. (1987). The impact of timing of puberty on psychosomatic symptoms among fourteen- to sixteen-year-old Finnish girls. *Child Development, 58,* 261–268.

ASHER, S. R., & COIE, J. D. (1990). *Peer rejection in childhood.* New York: Cambridge University Press.

ASHER, S. R., RENSHAW, P. D., & HYMEL, S. (1982). Peer relations and the development of social skills. In S. G. Moore (Ed.), *The young child: Reviews of research* (Vol. 3). Washington, DC: National Association for the Education of Young Children.

ASHER, S. R., & WHEELER, V. A. (1985). Children's loneliness: A comparison of rejected and neglected peer status. *Journal of Consulting and Clinical Psychology, 53,* 500–505.

BANDURA, A., & MENLOVE, F. L. (1968). Factors determining vicarious extinction of avoidance behavior through symbolic modeling. *Journal of Personality and Social Psychology, 8,* 99–108.

BARKER, R. G., & WRIGHT, H. F. (1955). *Midwest and its children.* New York: Harper & Row.

BAUMRIND, D. (1971). Current patterns of parental authority. *Developmental Psychology Monographs, 4*(1, 2).

BERNDT, T. J. (1979). Developmental changes in conformity to peers and parents. *Developmental Psychology, 15,* 608–616.

BERNDT, T. J. (1986). Children's comments about their friendships. In M. Perlmutter (Ed.), *Minnesota symposia on child psychology.* Vol. 18: *Cognitive perspectives on children's social and behavioral development.* Hillsdale, NJ: Erlbaum.

BERNDT, T. J. (1988). The nature and significance of children's friendships. In R. Vasta (Ed.), *Annals of child development* (Vol. 5). London: JAI Press.

BERNDT, T. J. (1989). Friendships in childhood and adolescence. In W. Damon (Ed.), *Child development today and tomorrow.* San Francisco: Jossey-Bass.

BERNDT, T. J., HAWKINS, J. A., & HOYLE, S. G. (1986). Changes in friendship during a school year: Effects on children's and adolescents' impressions of friendship and sharing with friends. *Child Development, 57,* 1284–1297.

BERNDT, T. J., & HOYLE, S. G. (1985). Stability and change in childhood and adolescent friendships. *Developmental Psychology, 21,* 1007–1015.

BIERMAN, K. L. (1986). Process of change during social skills training with preadolescents and its relation to treatment outcome. *Child Development, 57,* 230–240.

BIERMAN, K. L., & FURMAN, W. (1984). The effects of social skills training and peer involvement on the social adjustment of preadolescents. *Child Development, 55,* 157–162.

BIERMAN, K. L., MILLER, C. L., & STABB, S. C. (1987). Improving the social behavior and peer acceptance of rejected boys: Effects of social skill training with instructions and prohibitions. *Journal of Consulting and Clinical Psychology, 55,* 194–200.

BIXENSTINE, V. C., DeCORTE, M. S., & BIXENSTINE, B. A. (1976). Conformity to peer-sponsored misconduct at four grade levels. *Developmental Psychology, 12,* 226–236.

BOIVIN, M., & BEGIN, G. (1989). Peer status and self-perception among elementary school children: The case of rejected children. *Child Development, 60,* 591–596.

BRITTAIN, C. V. (1963). Adolescent choices and parent-peer cross pressures. *American Sociological Review, 28,* 358–391.

BRODY, G. H., GRAZIANO, W. G., & MUSSER, L. M. (1983). Familiarity and children's behavior in same-age and mixed-age peer groups. *Developmental Psychology, 19,* 568–576.

BROOK, J. S., WHITEMAN, M., & GORDON, A. S. (1983). Stages of drug use in adolescence: Personality, peer, and family correlates. *Developmental Psychology, 19,* 269–277.

BROWN, B. B., CLASEN, D. R., & EICHER, S. A. (1986). Perceptions of peer pressure, peer conformity dispositions, and self-reported behavior among adolescents. *Developmental Psychology, 22,* 521–530.

BROWNELL, C. A. (1986). Convergent developments: Cognitive-developmental correlates of growth in infant/toddler peer skills. *Child Development, 57,* 275–286.

BROWNELL, C. A. (1990). Peer social skills in toddlers: Competencies and constraints illustrated by same-age and mixed-age interaction. *Child Development, 61,* 838–848.

BROWNELL, C. A., & CARRIGER, M. S. (1990). Changes in cooperation and self/other differentiation during the second year. *Child Development, 61,* 1164–1174.

BUHRMESTER, D. (1990). Intimacy of friendship, interpersonal competence, and adjustment during preadolescence and adolescence. *Child Development, 61,* 1101–1111.

CAIRNS, R. B., CAIRNS, B. D., & NECKERMAN, H. J. (1989). Early school dropout: Configurations and determinants. *Child Development, 60,* 1437–1452.

CAIRNS, R. B., CAIRNS, B. D., NECKERMAN, H. J., GEST, S. D., & GARIEPY, J. (1988). Social networks and aggressive behavior: Peer support or peer rejection? *Developmental Psychology, 24,* 815–823.

CAPLAN, M., VESPO, J., PEDERSEN, J., & HAY, D. F. (1991). Conflict and its resolution in small groups of one- and two-year-olds. *Child Development, 62,* 1513–1524.

CASSIDY, J., & ASHER, S. R. (1992). Loneliness and peer relations in young children. *Child Development, 63,* 350–365.

CHANDLER, M. J. (1973). Egocentrism and antisocial behavior: The assessment and training of social perspective taking skills. *Developmental Psychology, 9,* 326–332.

CHASSIN, L., PRESSON, C. C., SHERMAN, S. J., MONTELLO, D., & McGREW, J. (1986). Changes in peer and parent influence during adolescence: Longitudinal versus cross-sectional perspectives on smoking initiation. *Developmental Psychology, 22,* 327–334.

CILLESSEN, A. H. N., van IJZENDOORN, H. W., van LIESHOUT, C. F. M., & HARTUP, W. W. (1992). Heterogeneity among peer-rejected boys: Subtypes and stabilities. *Child Development, 63,* 893–905.

CLAUSEN, J. A. (1975). The social meaning of differential physical maturation. In D. Drugastin & G. H. Elder (Eds.), *Adolescence in the life cycle.* New York: Halsted Press.

COHN, D. A. (1990). Child-mother attachment of 6-year-olds and social competence at school. *Child Development, 61,* 152–162.

COIE, J. D., & DODGE, K. A. (1983). Continuities and changes in children's social status: A five-year longitudinal study. *Merrill-Palmer Quarterly, 19,* 261–282.

COIE, J. D., DODGE, K. A., & COPPOTELLI, H. (1982). Dimensions and types of social status: A cross-age perspective. *Developmental Psychology, 18,* 557–570.

COIE, J. D., DODGE, K. A., & KUPERSMIDT, J. B. (1990). Peer group behavior and social status. In S. R. Asher & J. D. Coie (Eds.), *Peer rejection in childhood.* New York: Cambridge University Press.

COIE, J. D., DODGE, K. A., TERRY, R., & WRIGHT, V. (1991). The role of aggression in peer relations: An analysis of aggression episodes in boys' play groups. *Child Development, 62,* 812–826.

COIE, J. D., & KREHBIEL, G. (1984). Effects of academic tutoring on the social status of low-achieving, socially rejected children. *Child Development, 55,* 1465–1478.

COIE, J. D., & KUPERSMIDT, J. B. (1983). A behavioral analysis of emerging social status in boys' groups. *Child Development, 54,* 1400–1416.

COMBS, M. L., & SLABY, D. A. (1977). Social skills training with children. In B. B. Lahey & A. E. Kazdin (Eds.), *Advances in clinical child psychology.* New York: Plenum.

CONNOLLY, J. A., & DOYLE, A. (1984). Relation of social fantasy play to social competence in preschoolers. *Developmental Psychology, 20,* 797–806.

COOKE, T., & APOLLONI, T. (1976). Developing positive social-emotional behaviors: A study of training and generalization effects. *Journal of Applied Behavior Analysis, 9,* 65–78.

COSTIN, S. E., & JONES, D. C. (1992). Friendship as a facilitator of emotional responsiveness and prosocial interventions among young children. *Developmental Psychology, 28,* 941–947.

DANIELS, D., & PLOMIN, R. (1985). Origins of individual differences in infant shyness. *Developmental Psychology, 21,* 118–121.

DEKOVIC, M., & JANSSENS, J. M. A. M. (1992). Parents' child-rearing style and children's sociometric status. *Developmental Psychology, 28,* 925–932.

DENHAM, S. A., McKINLEY, M., COUCHOUD, E. A., & HOLT, R. (1990). Emotional and behavioral predictors of preschool peer ratings. *Child Development, 61,* 1145–1152.

DISHION, T. J. (1990). The family ecology of boys' peer relations in middle childhood. *Child Development, 61,* 874–892.

DISHION, T. J., PATTERSON, G. R., STOOLMILLER, M., & SKINNER, M. L. (1991). Family, school, and behavioral antecedents to early adolescent involvement with antisocial peers. *Developmental Psychology, 27,* 172–180.

DODGE, K. A. (1983). Behavioral antecedents of peer social status. *Child Development, 54,* 1386–1399.

DODGE, K. A., COIE, J. D., PETTIT, G. S., & PRICE, J. M. (1990). Peer status and aggression in boys' groups: Developmental and contextual analyses. *Child Development, 61,* 1289–1309.

DORR, D., & FEY, S. (1974). Relative power of symbolic adult and peer models in the modification of children's moral choice behavior. *Journal of Personality and Social Psychology, 29,* 335–341.

DOYLE, A. B., CONNOLLY, J., & RIVEST, L. (1980). The effects of playmate familiarity on the social interaction of very young children. *Child Development, 51,* 217–223.

DOYLE, A. B., DOEHRING, P., TESSIER, O., de LORIMIER, S., & SHAPIRO, S. (1992). Transitions in children's play: A sequential analysis of states preceding and following social pretence. *Developmental Psychology, 28,* 137–144.

DUKE, P. M., CARLSMITH, J. M., JENNINGS, D., MARTIN, J. A., DORNBUSCH, S. M., GROSS, R. T., & SIEGEL-GORELICK, B. (1982). Educational correlates of early and late sexual maturation in adolescence. *Journal of Pediatrics, 100,* 633–637.

DUNCAN, P., RITTER, P. L., DORNBUSCH, S. M., GROSS, R. T., & CARLSMITH, J. M. (1985). The effects of pubertal timing on body image, school behavior, and deviance. *Journal of Youth and Adolescence, 14,* 227–235.

ECKERMAN, C. O., DAVIS, C. C., & DIDOW, S. M. (1989). Toddlers' emerging ways of achieving social coordinations with a peer. *Child Development, 60,* 440–443.

ECKERMAN, C. O., & STEIN, M. R. (1982). The toddler's emerging interactive skills. In K. H. Rubin & H. S. Ross (Eds.), *Peer relationships and social skills in childhood.* New York: Springer-Verlag.

ECKERMAN, C. O., & STEIN, M. R. (1990). How imitation begets imitation and toddlers' generation of games. *Developmental Psychology, 26,* 370–378.

ELLIS, S., ROGOFF, B., & CROMER, C. C. (1981). Age segregation in children's social interactions. *Developmental Psychology, 17,* 399–407.

FESTINGER, L. (1954). A theory of social comparison processes. *Human Relations, 7,* 117–140.

FIELD, T., GREENWALD, P., MORROW, C., HEALY, B., FOSTER, T., GUTHERTZ, M., & FROST, P. (1992). Behavior state matching during interactions of preadolescent friends versus acquaintances. *Developmental Psychology, 28,* 242–250.

FRANCE-KAATRUDE, A., & SMITH, W. P. (1985). Social comparison, task motivation, and the development of self-evaluative standards in children. *Developmental Psychology, 21,* 1080–1089.

FREEDMAN, D. G. (1974). *Human infancy: An evolutionary perspective.* Hillsdale, NJ: Erlbaum.

FRENCH, D. C. (1984). Children's knowledge of the social functions of younger, older, and same-age peers. *Child Development, 55,* 1429–1433.

FRENCH, D. C. (1988). Heterogeneity of peer-rejected boys: Aggressive and nonaggressive subtypes. *Child Development, 59,* 976–985.

FRENCH, D. C., WASS, G. A., STRIGHT, A. L., & BAKER, J. A. (1986). Leadership asymmetrics in mixed-age children's groups. *Child Development, 57,* 1277–1283.

FREUD, A., & DANN, S. (1951). An experiment in group upbringing. In R. Eisler, A. Freud, H. Hartmann, & E. Kris (Eds.), *The psychoanalytic study of the child* (Vol. 6). New York: International Universities Press.

FURMAN, W., & BUHRMESTER, D. (1992). Age and sex differences in perceptions of networks of personal relationships. *Child Development, 63,* 103–115.

GAVIN, L. A., & FURMAN, W. (1989). Age differences in adolescents' perceptions of their peer groups. *Developmental Psychology, 25,* 827–834.

GOLDSMITH, H. H. (1983). Genetic influences on personality from infancy to adulthood. *Child Development, 54,* 331–355.

GOTTMAN, J. M. (1983). How children become friends. *Monographs of the Society for Research in Child Development, 48* (3, Serial No. 201).

GRAZIANO, W. G., FRENCH, D., BROWNELL, C. A., & HARTUP, W. W. (1976). Peer interaction in same- and mixed-age triads in relation to chronological age and incentive condition. *Child Development, 47,* 707–714.

GREEN, K. D., FOREHAND, R., BECK, S. J., & VOSK, B. (1980). An assessment of the relationship among measures of children's social competence and children's academic achievement. *Child Development, 51,* 1149–1156.

GROTEVANT, H. D., & COOPER, C. R. (1986). Individuation in family relations: A perspective on individual differences in the development of identity and role-taking skills in adolescence. *Human Development, 29,* 82–100.

GURALNICK, M. J., & GROOM, J. M. (1988). Friendships of preschool children in mainstreamed playgroups. *Developmental Psychology, 24,* 595–604.

HARARI, H., & McDAVID, J. W. (1973). Teachers' expectations and name stereotypes. *Journal of Educational Psychology, 65,* 222–225.

HARPER, L. V., & HUIE, K. S. (1985). The effects of prior group experience, age, and familiarity on the quality and organization of preschoolers' social relationships. *Child Development, 56,* 704–717.

HART, C. H., De WOLF, D. M., WOZNIAK, P., & BURTS, D. C. (1992). Maternal and paternal disciplinary styles: Relations with preschoolers' playground behavioral orientations and peer status. *Child Development, 63,* 879–892.

HARTUP, W. W. (1983). Peer relations. In E. M. Hetherington (Ed.), *Handbook of child psychology.* Vol. 4: *Socialization, personality, and social development.* New York: Wiley.

HARTUP, W. W. (1989). Social relationships and their developmental significance. *American Psychologist, 44,* 120–126.

HARTUP, W. W., LAURSEN, B., STEWART, M. I., & EASTENSON, A. (1988). Conflict and friendship relations of young children. *Child Development, 59,* 1590–1600.

HAY, D. F., NASH, A., & PEDERSEN, J. (1983). Interaction between six-month-old peers. *Child Development, 54,* 557–562.

HIGLEY, J. D., HOPKINS, W. D., THOMPSON, W. W., BYRNE, E. A., HIRSH, R. M., & SUOMI, S. J. (1992). Peers as primary attachment sources in yearling rhesus monkeys. *Developmental Psychology, 28,* 1163–1171.

HINDE, R. A., TITMUS, G., EASTON, D., & TAMPLIN, A. (1985). Incidence of "friendship" and behavior toward strong associates versus nonassociates in preschoolers. *Child Development, 56,* 234–245.

HOWES, C. (1988). Peer interaction of young children. *Monographs of the Society for Research in Child Development, 53* (1, Serial No. 217).

HOWES, C. (1990). Can the age of entry into child care and the quality of child care predict adjustment in kindergarten? *Developmental Psychology, 26,* 292–303.

HOWES, C., & MATHESON, C. C. (1992). Sequences in the development of competent play with peers: Social and social pretend play. *Developmental Psychology, 28,* 961–974.

HYMEL, S. (1983). Preschool children's peer relations: Issues in sociometric assessment. *Merrill-Palmer Quarterly, 19,* 237–260.

HYMEL, S. (1986). Interpretations of peer behavior: Affective bias in childhood and adolescence. *Child Development, 57,* 431–445.

HYMEL, S., RUBIN, K. H., ROWDEN, L., & LeMARE, L. (1990). Children's peer relationships: Longitudinal prediction of internalizing and externalizing problems from middle to late childhood. *Child Development, 61,* 2004–2021.

JONES, M. C. (1965). Psychological correlates of somatic development. *Child Development, 36,* 899–911.

JONES, M. C., & BAYLEY, N. (1950). Physical maturing among boys as related to behavior. *Journal of Educational Psychology, 41,* 129–148.

KANDEL, D. (1973). Adolescent marijuana use: Role of parents and peers. *Science, 181,* 1067–1070.

KANFER, F. H., STIFTER, E., & MORRIS, S. J. (1981). Self-control and altruism: Delay of gratification for another. *Child Development, 52,* 674–682.

KAZDIN, A. E. (1987). *Conduct disorders in childhood and adolescence.* Newbury Park, CA: Sage.

KEANE, S. P., BROWN, K. P., & CRENSHAW, T. M. (1990). Children's intention-cue detection as a function of maternal social behavior: Pathways to social rejection. *Developmental Psychology, 26,* 1004–1009.

KOBAK, R. R., & SCEERY, A. (1988). Attachment in late adolescence: Working models, affect regulation and representation of self and others. *Child Development, 59,* 135–146.

KUPERSMIDT, J. B., & COIE, J. D. (1990). Preadolescent peer status, aggression, and school adjustment as predictors of externalizing problems in adolescence. *Child Development, 61,* 1350–1362.

KURDEK, L. A., & KRILE, D. (1982). A developmental analysis of the relation between peer acceptance and both interpersonal understanding and perceived social self-competence. *Child Development, 53,* 1485–1491.

LADD, G. W. (1981). Effectiveness of a social learning method for enhancing children's social interaction and peer acceptance. *Child Development, 52,* 171–178.

LADD, G. W. (1990). Having friends, keeping friends, making friends, and being liked by peers in the classroom: Predictors of children's early school adjustment. *Child Development, 61,* 1081–1100.

LADD, G. W., & GOLTER, B. S. (1988). Parents' management of preschoolers' peer relations: Is it related to children's social competence? *Developmental Psychology, 24,* 109–117.

LADD, G. W., & HART, C. H. (1992). Creating informal play opportunities: Are parents' and preschoolers' initiations related to children's competence with peers? *Developmental Psychology, 28,* 1179–1187.

LADD, G. W., & PRICE, J. M. (1987). Predicting children's social and school adjustment following the transition from preschool to kindergarten. *Child Development, 58,* 1168–1189.

LADD, G. W., PRICE, J. M., & HART, C. H. (1988). Predicting preschoolers' play status from their playground behaviors. *Child Development, 59,* 986–992.

LADD, G. W., PRICE, J. M., & HART, C. H. (1990). Preschoolers' peer networks and behavioral orientations: Relationship to school and school adjustment. In S. R. Asher & J. D. Coie (Eds.), *Peer rejection in childhood.* New York: Cambridge University Press.

LAMB, M. E., EASTERBROOKS, M. A., & HOLDEN, G. W. (1980). Reinforcement and punishment among preschoolers: Characteristics, effects, and correlates. *Child Development, 51,* 1230–1236.

LANGLOIS, J. H. (1986). From the eye of the beholder to behavioral reality: Development of social behaviors and social relations as a function of physical attractiveness. In C. P. Herman, M. P. Zanna, & E. T. Higgins (Eds.), *Physical appearance, stigma, & social behavior: The Ontario Symposium* (Vol. 3). Hillsdale, NJ: Erlbaum.

LANGLOIS, J. H., & DOWNS, A. C. (1979). Peer relations as a function of physical attractiveness: The eye of the beholder or behavioral reality? *Child Development, 50,* 409–418.

LANGLOIS, J. H., RITTER, J. M., ROGGMAN, L. A., & VAUGHN, L. S. (1991). Facial diversity and infant preferences for attractive faces. *Developmental Psychology, 27,* 79–84.

LANGLOIS, J. H., ROGGMAN, L. A., & RIESER-DANNER, L. A. (1990). Infants' differential social responses to attractive and unattractive faces. *Developmental Psychology, 26,* 153–159.

LANGLOIS, J. H., & STYCZYNSKI, L. (1979). The effects of physical attractiveness on the behavioral attributions and peer preferences of acquainted children. *International Journal of Behavioral Development, 2,* 325–341.

LARSON, R., & RICHARDS, M. H. (1991). Daily companionship in late childhood and early adolescence: Changing developmental contexts. *Child Development, 62,* 284–300.

LERNER, R. M. (1969). The development of stereotyped expectancies of body build relations. *Child Development, 40,* 137–141.

LEWIS, M., & ROSENBLUM, M. A. (1975). *Friendship and peer relations.* New York: Wiley.

LIVSON, N., & PESKIN, H. (1980). Perspectives on adolescence from longitudinal research. In J. Adelson (Ed.), *Handbook of adolescent psychology.* New York: Wiley.

MacDONALD, K. (1987). Parent-child physical play with rejected, neglected, and popular boys. *Developmental Psychology, 23,* 705–711.

MacDONALD, K., & PARKE, R. D. (1984). Bridging the gap: Parent-child play interaction and peer interactive competence. *Child Development, 55,* 1265–1277.

MAIN, M., & WESTON, D. R. (1981). The quality of the toddler's relationship to mother and father: Related to conflict and the readiness to establish new relationships. *Child Development, 52,* 932–940.

MATHENY, A. P. (1983). A longitudinal twin study of the stability of components from Bayley's Infant Behavior Record. *Child Development, 54,* 356–360.

McDAVID, J. W., & HARARI, H. (1966). Stereotyping of names and popularity in grade school children. *Child Development, 37,* 453–459.

McGUIRE, K. D., & WEISZ, J. R. (1982). Social cognition and behavioral correlates of preadolescent chumship. *Child Development, 53,* 1478–1484.

MEDRICH, E. A., ROSEN, J., RUBIN, V., & BUCKLEY, S. (1982). *The serious business of growing up.* Berkeley: University of California Press.

MIZE, J., & LADD, G. W. (1990). A cognitive-social learning approach to social skill training with low-status preschool children. *Developmental Psychology, 26,* 388–397.

MONTEMAYOR, R. (1982). The relationship between parent-adolescent conflict and the amount of time adolescents spend alone with parents and peers. *Child Development, 53,* 1512–1519.

MORISON, P., & MASTEN, A. S. (1991). Peer reputation in middle childhood as a predictor of adaptation in adolescence: A seven-year follow-up. *Child Development, 62,* 991–1007.

MUELLER, E., & LUCAS, T. (1975). A developmental analysis of peer interactions among toddlers. In M. Lewis & L. Rosenblum (Eds.), *Friendship and peer relations.* New York: Wiley.

NELSON, J., & ABOUD, F. E. (1985). The resolution of social conflict among friends. *Child Development, 56,* 1009–1017.

NEWCOMB, A. F., BRADY, J. E., & HARTUP, W. W. (1979). Friendship and incentive condition as determinants of children's task-oriented social behavior. *Child Development, 50,* 878–881.

NEWCOMB, A. F., & BUKOWSKI, W. M. (1984). A longitudinal study of the utility of social preference and social impact sociometric classification schemes. *Child Development, 55,* 1434–1447.

NEWCOMB, M. D., & BENTLER, P. M. (1989). Substance use and abuse among children and teenagers. *American Psychologist, 44,* 242–248.

ODEN, S., & ASHER, S. R. (1977). Coaching children in social skills for friendship making. *Child Development, 48,* 495–506.

PARK, K. A., & WATERS, E. (1989). Security of attachment and preschool friendships. *Child Development, 60,* 1076–1081.

PARKER, J. G., & ASHER, S. R. (1987). Peer relations and later adjustment: Are low-accepted children "at risk"? *Psychological Bulletin, 102,* 357–389.

PARKER, J. G., & GOTTMAN, J. M. (1989). Social and emotional development in a relational context: Friendship interactions from early childhood to adolescence. In T. J. Berndt & G. Ladd (Eds.), *Peer relations in child development.* New York: Wiley.

PARKHURST, J. T., & ASHER, S. R. (1992). Peer rejection in middle school: Subgroup differences in behavior, loneliness, and interpersonal concerns. *Developmental Psychology, 28,* 231–241.

PARTEN, M. (1932). Social participation among preschool children. *Journal of Abnormal and Social Psychology, 27,* 243–269.

PATTERSON, G. R., DeBARYSHE, B. D., & RAMSEY, E. (1989). A developmental perspective on antisocial behavior. *American Psychologist, 44,* 329–335.

PATTERSON, G. R., LITTMAN, R. A., & BRICKER, W. (1967). Assertive behavior in children: A step toward a theory of aggression. *Monographs of the Society for Research in Child Development, 32* (5, Serial No. 113).

PELLEGRINI, D. S. (1985). Social cognition and competence in middle childhood. *Child Development, 56,* 253–264.

PETTIT, G. S., DODGE, K. A., & BROWN, M. M. (1988). Early family experience, social problem solving patterns, and children's social competence. *Child Development, 59,* 107–120.

PIAGET, J. (1965). *The moral judgment of the child.* New York: Free Press.

PUTALLAZ, M. (1987). Maternal behavior and children's sociometric status. *Child Development, 58,* 324–340.

PUTALLAZ, M., & HEFLIN, A. H. (1990). Parent-child interaction. In S. R. Asher & J. D. Coie (Eds.), *Peer rejection in childhood.* New York: Cambridge University Press.

QUAY, L. C., & JARRETT, O. S. (1984). Predictors of social acceptance in preschool children. *Developmental Psychology, 20,* 793–796.

RABINER, D. L., LENHART, L., & LOCHMAN, J. E. (1990). Automatic versus reflective social problem solving in relation to children's sociometric status. *Developmental Psychology, 26,* 1010–1016.

REID, M., LANDESMAN, S., TREDER, R., & JACCARD, J. (1989). "My family and friends": Six- to twelve-year-old children's perceptions of social support. *Child Development, 60,* 896–910.

ROFF, M. F. (1974). Childhood antecedents of adult neurosis, severe bad conduct, and psychological health. In D. F. Ricks, A. Thomas, & M. Roff (Eds.), *Life history research in psychopathology* (Vol. 3). Minneapolis: University of Minnesota Press.

ROTENBERG, K. J., & MANN, L. (1986). The development of the norm of the reciprocity of self-disclosure and its function in children's attraction to peers. *Child Development, 57,* 1349–1357.

RUBIN, K. H., FEIN, G., & VANDENBERG, B. (1983). Play. In E. M. Hetherington (Ed.), *Handbook of child psychology.* Vol. 4: *Socialization, personality, and social development.* New York: Wiley.

RUBIN, K. H., LeMARE, L., & LOLLIS, S. (1990). Social withdrawal in childhood: Developmental pathways to peer rejection. In S. R. Asher & J. D. Coie (Eds.), *Peer rejection in childhood.* New York: Cambridge University Press.

RUBLE, D. N., BALABAN, T., & COOPER, J. (1981). Gender constancy and the effects of sex-typed televised toy commercials. *Child Development, 52,* 667–673.

RUSSELL, A., & FINNIE, V. (1990). Preschool children's social status and maternal instructions to assist group entry. *Developmental Psychology, 26,* 600–611.

SACKIN, S., & THELEN, E. (1984). An ethological study of peaceful associative outcomes to conflict in preschool children. *Child Development, 55,* 1098–1102.

SAGOTSKY, G., & LEPPER, M. R. (1982). Generalization of changes in children's preferences for easy or difficult goals induced through peer modeling. *Child Development, 53,* 372–375.

SAVIN-WILLIAMS, R. C., & SMALL, S. A. (1986). The timing of puberty and its relationship to adolescent and parent perceptions of family interactions. *Developmental Psychology, 22,* 342–347.

SCARR, S. (1968). Environmental bias in twin studies. *Eugenics Quarterly, 15,* 34–40.

SCHAFFER, H. R., & EMERSON, P. E. (1964). The development of social attachments in infancy. *Monographs of the Society for Research in Child Development, 29*(3, Serial No. 94).

SCHWARTZ, J. C. (1972). Effects of peer familiarity on the behavior of preschoolers in a novel situation. *Journal of Personality and Social Psychology, 24,* 276–284.

SEBALD, H. (1986). Adolescents' shifting orientation toward parents and peers: A curvilinear trend over recent decades. *Journal of Marriage and the Family, 48,* 5–13.

SELMAN, R. L. (1980). *The growth of interpersonal understanding.* Orlando, FL: Academic Press.

SHEA, J. D. C. (1981). Changes in interpersonal distances and categories of play behavior in the early weeks of preschool. *Developmental Psychology, 17,* 417–425.

SHERIF, M. (1956). Experiments in group conflict. *Scientific American, 195,* 54–58.

SHERIF, M., HARVEY, O. J., WHITE, B. J., HOOD, W. R., & SHERIF, C. W. (1961). *Intergroup conflict and cooperation: The Robber's Cave experiment.* Norman: University of Oklahoma Press.

SHURE, M. B. (1989). Interpersonal competence training. In W. Damon (Ed.), *Child development today and tomorrow.* San Francisco: Jossey-Bass.

SHURE, M. B., & SPIVACK, G. (1978). *Problem-solving techniques in childrearing.* San Francisco: Jossey-Bass.

SIGELMAN, C. K., MILLER, T. E., & WHITWORTH, L. A. (1986). The early development of stigmatizing reactions to physical differences. *Journal of Applied Developmental Psychology, 7,* 17–32.

SIMMONS, R. G., & BLYTH, D. A. (1987). *Moving into adolescence: The impact of pubertal change in school context.* New York: A. de Gruyter.

SMETANA, J. G. (1988). Adolescents' and parents' conceptions of parental authority. *Child Development, 59,* 321–335.

SMOLLAR, J., & YOUNISS, J. (1982). Social development through friendship. In K. H. Rubin & H. S. Ross (Eds.), *Peer relations and social skills in childhood.* New York: Springer-Verlag.

SROUFE, L. A. (1983). Infant-caregiver attachment and patterns of adaptation in preschool: The roots of maladaptation. In L. Perlmutter (Ed.), *Minnesota Symposia on Child Development* (Vol. 16). Hillsdale, NJ: Erlbaum.

STAFFIERI, J. R. (1967). A study of social stereotype of body image in children. *Journal of Personality and Social Psychology, 7*, 101–104.

STEINBERG, L., & SILVERBERG, S. B. (1986). The vicissitudes of autonomy in early adolescence. *Child Development, 57*, 841–851.

STRAYER, F. F. (1980). Social ecology of the preschool peer group. In W. A. Collins (Ed.), *Minnesota Symposia on Child Psychology*. Vol. 13: *Development of cognition, affect, and social relations*. Hillsdale, NJ: Erlbaum.

STUMPHAUZER, J. S. (1972). Increased delay of gratification in young inmates through imitation of high-delay peer models. *Journal of Personality and Social Psychology, 21*, 10–17.

SULLIVAN, H. S. (1953). *The interpersonal theory of psychiatry*. New York: Norton.

SUOMI, S. J., & HARLOW, H. F. (1978). Early experience and social development in rhesus monkeys. In M. E. Lamb (Ed.), *Social and personality development*. New York: Holt, Rinehart & Winston.

SUSMAN, E. J., NOTTELMAN, E. D., INHOFF-GERMAIN, G. E., DORN, L. D., CUTLER, G. B., LORIAUX, D. L., & CHROUSOS, G. P. (1985). The relation of development and socio-emotional behavior in young adolescents. *Journal of Youth and Adolescence, 14*, 245–264.

TERRY, R., & COIE, J. D. (1991). A comparison of methods for defining sociometric status among children. *Developmental Psychology, 27*, 867–880.

VANDELL, D. L., HENDERSON, V. K., & WILSON, K. S. (1988). A follow-up of children in excellent, moderate, and poor quality day care. *Child Development, 59*, 1286–1292.

VANDELL, D. L., OWEN, M. T., WILSON, K. S., & HENDERSON, V. K. (1988). Social development in infant twins: Peer and mother-child relationships. *Child Development, 59*, 168–177.

VANDELL, D. L., & WILSON, K. S. (1987). Infants' interactions with mother, sibling, and peer: Contrasts and relations between interaction systems. *Child Development, 58*, 176–186.

VANDELL, D. L., WILSON, K. S., & BUCHANAN, N. R. (1980). Peer interaction in the first year of life: An examination of its structure, content, and sensitivity to toys. *Child Development, 51*, 481–488.

VINCZE, M. (1971). The social contacts of infants and young children reared together. *Early Child Development and Care, 1*, 99–109.

WALKER, L. J., & TAYLOR, J. H. (1991). Family interactions and the development of moral reasoning. *Child Development, 62*, 264–283.

WEISS, B., DODGE, K. A., BATES, J. E., & PETTIT, G. S. (1992). Some consequences of early harsh discipline: Child aggression and a maladaptive social information processing style. *Child Development, 63*, 1321–1335.

WHITE, K. J., & KISTNER, J. (1992). The influence of teacher feedback on young children's peer preferences and perceptions. *Developmental Psychology, 28*, 933–940.

WHITING, B. B., & EDWARDS, C. P. (1988). *Children of different worlds: The formation of social behavior*. Cambridge, MA: Harvard University Press.

WILKS, J. (1986). The relative importance of parents and friends in adolescent decision making. *Journal of Youth and Adolescence, 15*, 323–334.

YEATES, K. O., & SELMAN, R. L. (1989). Social competence in the schools: Toward an integrative developmental model for intervention. *Developmental Review, 9*, 64–100.

YOUNGBLADE, L. M., & BELSKY, J. (1992). Parent-child antecedents of 5-year-olds' close friendships: A longitudinal analysis. *Developmental Psychology, 28*, 700–713.

YOUNGER, A. J., & DANIELS, T. M. (1992). Children's reasons for nominating their peers as withdrawn: Passive withdrawal versus active isolation. *Developmental Psychology, 28*, 955–960.

YOUNISS, J., & SMOLLAR, J. (1985). *Adolescent relations with mothers, fathers, and friends*. Chicago: University of Chicago Press.

Glossary

ability tracking: the practice of placing students in categories on the basis of IQ or academic achievement and then educating them in classes with pupils of comparable academic or intellectual ability.

accommodation: Piaget's term for the process by which children modify their existing schemes in order to incorporate or adapt to new experiences.

achievement expectancies: cognitive expectations of succeeding or failing at a particular achievement-related activity.

achievement training: encouraging children to do things well — that is, to meet or exceed high standards as they strive to accomplish various objectives.

achievement value: perceived value of attaining a particular goal should one strive to achieve it.

Action for Children's Television (ACT): a group of concerned citizens who monitor television programming and try to reduce its harmful impact on children.

active genotype/environment interactions: the notion that our genotypes affect the types of environments that we prefer and will seek out.

activity/passivity issue: a debate among developmental theorists about whether children are active contributors to their own development or, rather, passive recipients of environmental influence.

adaptation: inborn tendency to adjust to the demands of the environment.

adoption design: a study in which adoptees are compared to their biological relatives and their adoptive relatives to estimate the heritability of an attribute or attributes.

adrenogenital syndrome (AGS): a congenital disorder caused by prenatal exposure to androgens. Females

who experience AGS are born with external genitalia that resemble those of a male.

affective explanations: a rational form of discipline in which the disciplinarian helps the young child to appreciate the distress he has caused a victim by virtue of his harmdoing.

affective perspective taking: the ability to accurately infer the feelings or emotions that others are experiencing.

aggression: *behavioral definition:* any action that delivers noxious stimuli to another organism. *Intentional definition:* any form of behavior intended to harm or injure another living being who is motivated to avoid such treatment.

"aggressive cues" hypothesis: Berkowitz's notion that the presence of stimuli previously associated with aggression can evoke aggressive responses from an angry individual.

altruism: a concern for the welfare of others that is expressed through such prosocial acts as sharing, cooperating, and helping. *Behavioral definition:* behavior that benefits another person, regardless of the actor's motives. *Motivational/intentional definition:* beneficial acts for which the actor's primary motive or intent was to address the needs of others. (*See also* **autonomous altruism**.)

altruistic exhortations: verbal encouragements to help, comfort, share, or cooperate with others.

anal stage: Freud's second stage of psychosexual development (from 1 to 3 years of age), in which anal activities such as defecation become the primary methods of gratifying the sex instinct.

androgenized females: girls who display the adrenogenital syndrome — that is, malelike external genitalia at birth and (later) a preference for malelike interests, behaviors, and playmates.

androgyny: a sex-role orientation in which the individual has incorporated a large number of both masculine and feminine attributes into his or her personality.

asocial stage: the first six weeks of life, in which infants respond in an equally favorable manner to interesting social and nonsocial stimuli.

assimilation: Piaget's term for the process by which children try to adapt to new experiences by incorporating them into existing schemes.

attachment: a close emotional relationship between two persons, characterized by mutual affection and a desire to maintain proximity.

attachment object: a close companion to whom one is attached.

Attachment Q-Set: a set of 90 written statements that caregivers or observers sort into categories labeled descriptive or nondescriptive of a child's attachment behaviors; used as an alternative to the "strange situations" to assess the security of children's attachments.

attribution retraining: therapeutic intervention in which helpless children are persuaded to attribute failures to their lack of effort rather than to a lack of ability.

attribution (or social information-processing) theory: social-cognitive theory stating that the explanations we construct for social experiences largely determine how we perceive and react to those experiences.

authoritarian instruction: a restrictive style of instruction in which the teacher makes absolute demands and uses threats or force (if necessary) to ensure that students comply.

authoritarian parenting: a restrictive pattern of parenting in which adults set many rules for their children, expect strict obedience, and rely on power rather than reason to elicit compliance.

authoritative instruction: a controlling style of instruction in which the teacher makes many demands but also allows some autonomy and individual expression as long as students are staying within the guidelines that the teacher has set.

authoritative parenting: a flexible style of parenting in which adults allow their children autonomy but are careful to explain the restrictions they impose and will ensure that their children follow these guidelines.

autonomous altruism: prosocial acts motivated by a concern for others with no expectations of being repaid for such favors.

autonomous morality: Piaget's second stage of moral development, in which children realize that rules are

arbitrary agreements that can be challenged and even changed with the consent of the people they govern.

autonomy: the capacity to make decisions independently, to serve as one's own source of emotional strength, and to otherwise manage one's life tasks without depending on others for assistance; an important developmental task of adolescence.

autonomy versus shame and doubt: the second of Erikson's psychosocial stages, in which toddlers either assert their wills and attend to their own basic needs or else become passive, dependent, and lacking in self-confidence.

average-status children: children who receive a moderate number of nominations as a liked and/or a disliked individual from members of their peer group.

"aversive approval" effect: the finding that social reinforcement of altruistic acts will *inhibit* altruism if administered by a selfish or otherwise nonaltruistic individual.

avoidant attachment: an insecure infant/caregiver bond, characterized by little separation protest and a tendency of the child to avoid or ignore the caregiver.

baby biography: a detailed record of an infant's growth and development over a period of time.

basic gender identity: the stage of gender identity in which the child first labels the self as a boy or a girl.

basic trust versus mistrust: the first of Erikson's eight psychosocial stages, in which infants must learn to trust their closest companions or else run the risk of mistrusting other people later in life.

behavioral comparisons phase: the tendency to form impressions of others by comparing and contrasting their overt behaviors.

behavioral definition of aggression: *see* **aggression** (*behavioral definition*).

behavioral definition of altruism: *see* **altruism** (*behavioral definition*).

behavioral inhibition: a temperamental characteristic reflecting one's tendency to withdraw from unfamiliar people or situations.

behavioral schemes: organized patterns of behavior that are used to represent and respond to objects and experiences.

behavior genetics: the scientific study of how one's hereditary endowment interacts with environmental influences to determine such attributes as intelligence, temperament, and personality.

behaviorism: a school of thinking in psychology holding that conclusions about human development should be based on controlled observations of overt behavior rather than on speculation about unconscious motives or other unobservable phenomena; the philosophical underpinning for social-learning theories.

Brazelton Neonatal Behavioral Assessment Scale (NBAS): An evaluation of a neonate's neurological status and responsiveness to environmental stimuli.

caregiving hypothesis: Ainsworth's notion that the type of attachment an infant develops with a particular caregiver depends primarily on the kind of caregiving she has received from that person.

case study: a research method in which the investigator gathers extensive information about the life of an individual and then tests developmental hypotheses by analyzing the events of the person's life history.

castration anxiety: in Freud's theory, a young boy's fear that his father will castrate him as punishment for his rivalrous conduct.

categorical self: a person's classification of the self along socially significant dimensions such as age and sex.

catharsis hypothesis: the notion that aggressive urges are reduced when people witness or commit real or symbolic acts of aggression.

cathartic technique: a strategy for reducing aggression by encouraging children to vent their anger or frustrations on inanimate objects.

causal attributions: inferences made about the underlying causes of one's own or another person's behavior.

centered thinking (centration): the tendency to focus on only one aspect of a problem when two or more aspects are relevant.

child abuse: term used to describe any extreme maltreatment of children, involving physical battering, sexual molestation, physical or emotional neglect, and psychological insults such as persistent ridicule, rejection, and terrorization.

Children's Television Workshop (CTW): an organization committed to producing TV programs that hold children's interest and facilitate their social and intellectual development.

classical conditioning: a type of learning in which an initially neutral stimulus is repeatedly paired with a meaningful stimulus so that the neutral stimulus comes to elicit the response originally made only to the meaningful stimulus.

clinical method: a type of interview in which a participant's reponse to each successive question (or problem) determines what the investigator will ask next.

clique: a small, tightly knit group of peers who share common interests and viewpoints and who set themselves apart from other peers.

coaching: method of social-skills training in which an adult displays and explains various socially skilled behaviors, allows the child to practice them, and provides feedback aimed at improving the child's performances.

coercive home environment: a home in which family members often annoy one another and use aggressive tactics as a method of coping with these aversive experiences.

cognitive development: age-related changes that occur in mental activities such as attending, perceiving, learning, thinking, and remembering.

cognitive operation: an internal mental activity that one performs on objects of thought.

cohort effect: age-related difference among cohorts that is attributable to cultural/historical differences in cohorts' growing-up experiences rather than to true developmental change.

collaborative (or guided) learning: learning that occurs through participation in an activity under the guidance of a more competent associate.

compensation: the ability to consider more than one aspect of a problem at a time (also called *decentration*).

complex emotions: self-conscious and self-evaluative emotions that emerge in the second year and depend, in part, on cognitive development.

compliance: the act of willingly obeying the requests or commands of others.

concordance rate: the percentage of cases in which a particular attribute is present for both members of a twin pair if it is present for one member.

concrete-operational stage: Piaget's third stage of cognitive development, lasting from about age 7 to age 11, when children are acquiring cognitive operations and thinking more logically about real objects and experiences.

"conditioned anxiety" hypothesis: notion that infants fear separations from caregivers (and strangers who might cause such separations) because prior discomforts have been especially intense when caregivers were not present to relieve them.

conditioned reinforcer: an initially neutral stimulus that acquires reinforcement value by virtue of its repeated association with other reinforcing stimuli.

conditioned response (CR): a learned response to a stimulus that was not originally capable of producing the response.

conditioned stimulus (CS): an initially neutral stimulus that comes to elicit a particular response after being paired with an unconditioned stimulus (UCS) that always elicits the response.

consensus schema: attributional heuristic implying that actions that almost everybody would perform are likely to be externally (or situationally) caused, whereas unique actions reflect internal dispositions.

conservation: the recognition that the properties of an object or substance do not change when its appearance is altered in some superficial way.

consistency schema: attributional heuristic implying that actions that a person consistently performs are likely to be internally caused (reflecting a dispositional characteristic).

constructivist: one who gains knowledge by acting or otherwise operating on objects or events to discover their properties.

continuity/discontinuity issue: a debate among theorists about whether developmental changes are best characterized as gradual, quantitative, and connected over time or, rather, are abrupt, qualitative, and often unconnected to earlier developments.

controversial children: children who receive many nominations by peers as a liked individual and many as a disliked individual.

conventional morality: Kohlberg's term for the third and fourth stages of moral reasoning, in which moral judgments are based on a desire to gain approval (Stage 3) or to uphold laws that maintain social order (Stage 4).

"cooperative activities" training: programs that require children to play cooperative games in which they must pool their efforts or resources to achieve shared objectives; thought to be a subtle way of teaching children to value cooperation, sharing, and other prosocial acts.

cooperative learning methods: an educational practice whereby children of different races or ability levels are assigned to teams; each team member works on problems geared to his or her ability level, and all members are reinforced for "pulling together" and performing well as a team.

coos: vowel-like sounds that young infants repeat over and over during periods of contentment.

correlational design: a type of research design that indicates the strength of associations among variables; although correlated variables are systematically related, these relationships are not necessarily causal.

correlation coefficient: a numerical index, ranging from -1.00 to $+1.00$, of the strength and direction of the relationship between two variables.

critical period: a brief period in the development of an organism when it is particularly sensitive to certain environmental influences; outside this period the same influences will have little if any effect.

cross-cultural comparison: a study that compares the behavior and/or development of people from different cultural or subcultural backgrounds.

cross-generational problem: the fact that long-term changes in the environment may limit conclusions of a longitudinal project to that generation of children who were growing up while the study was in progress.

cross-pressures: conflicts between the practices advocated by parents and those favored by peers.

cross-sectional design: a research design in which subjects from different age groups are studied at the same point in time.

deferred imitation: reproduction of a modeled activity that has been witnessed at some point in the past.

defiance: active resistance to others' requests or demands; noncompliant acts that are accompanied by anger and an intensification of ongoing behavior.

delay of gratification: a form of self-control that involves the capacity to inhibit impulses to seek small rewards available immediately in the interest of obtaining larger, delayed incentives.

dependent variable: the aspect of behavior that is measured in an experiment and assumed to be under the control of the independent variable.

deprivation dwarfism: a retardation in physical growth that is apparently triggered by emotional distress and/or a lack of love and affection.

desensitization hypothesis: the notion that people who watch a lot of media violence will become less aroused by aggression and more tolerant of violent and aggressive acts.

developmental stage: a distinct phase within a larger sequence of development; a period characterized by a particular set of abilities, motives, behaviors, or emotions that occur together and form a coherent pattern.

difficult temperament: temperament in which the child is irregular in his or her daily routines and adapts slowly to new experiences, often responding negatively and intensely.

discounting principle: attributional heuristic whereby we are less likely to attribute a behavior to any particular cause when other plausible explanations are available.

disequilibriums: imbalances or contradictions between one's thought processes and environmental events. By contrast, *equilibrium* refers to a balanced, harmonious relationship between one's cognitive structures and the environment.

disorganized/disoriented attachment: an insecure infant/caregiver bond, characterized by the infant's dazed appearance on reunion or a tendency to first seek and then abruptly avoid the caregiver.

distinctiveness schema: attributional heuristic implying that unusual or distinctive actions are likely to be externally (or situationally) caused rather than attributable to the actor's dispositions.

distributive justice: concepts of what is "fair" or "just" concerning the allocation of resources among the members of a group.

doctrine of specificity: a viewpoint, shared by many social-learning theorists, holding that moral affect, moral reasoning, and moral behavior depend more on the situation one faces than on an internalized set of moral principles.

early-experience hypothesis: the notion that the social and emotional events of infancy are very influential in determining the course of one's future development.

easy temperament: temperament such that the child quickly establishes regular routines in infancy, is generally good natured, and adapts easily to new experiences.

eclectic approach: tendency (common among contemporary developmentalists) to seek explanations by borrowing from many theories and attempting to integrate their contributions into a holistic portrait of development.

ecological perspective: an approach to studying development that focuses on individuals within their natural environments.

ecological systems model: Bronfenbrenner's view emphasizing that the developing person is embedded in a series of environmental systems that interact with one another and with the person to influence development.

ecological validity: state of affairs in which the findings of one's research are an accurate representation of processes that occur in the natural environment.

economic goal: LeVine's second priority of parenting—to promote skills that children will need for economic self-sufficiency.

effectance motivation: an inborn motive to explore, understand, and control one's environment (sometimes called *mastery motivation*).

effective schools: schools that are generally successful at achieving curricular and noncurricular objectives, regardless of the racial, ethnic, or socioeconomic backgrounds of the student population.

ego: psychoanalytic term for the rational component of the personality.

egocentrism: the tendency to view the world from one's own perspective while failing to recognize that others may have different points of view.

"ego strength" hypothesis: the neo-Freudian notion that moral maturity is impossible to attain unless one's ego is strong enough to inhibit the id, thus allowing one to comply with the dictates of the superego.

Electra complex: female version of the Oedipus complex, in which a 4- to 6-year-old girl is said to envy her father for possessing a penis and desires him as a sex object in the hope of sharing the organ that she lacks.

emotional bonding: term used to describe the positive emotional ties that parents may feel toward their newborn infant; some theorists believe bonding occurs through physical contact with the neonate during a sensitive period.

emotional display rules: culturally defined rules specifying which emotions should or should not be expressed under which circumstances.

empathic concern: a measure of the extent to which an individual recognizes the needs of others and is concerned about their welfare.

empathy: the ability to experience the same emotions that someone else is experiencing.

engrossment: paternal analogue of maternal bonding; term used to describe fathers' fascination with their neonates, including their desire to touch, hold, caress, and talk to the newborn baby.

entity view of ability: belief that one's ability is a highly stable trait that is not influenced much by increased effort or practice.

environmental determinism: the notion that children are passive creatures who are molded by their environments.

Eros: Freud's name for instincts (such as respiration, hunger, and sex) that help the individual (and the species) to survive.

erotic orientation: the gender to which an individual is sexually attracted.

ethnocentrism: the tendency to view one's own culture as "best" and to use one's own cultural standards as a basis for evaluating other cultures.

ethology: the study of the bioevolutionary bases of behavior.

evocative genotype/environment interactions: the notion that our heritable attributes will affect others' behavior toward us and thus will influence the social environment in which development takes place.

exosystem: social system that children and adolescents do not directly experience but that may nonetheless influence their development; the third of Bronfenbrenner's layers of context.

experimental control: steps taken by an experimenter to ensure that all extraneous factors that could influence the dependent variable are roughly equivalent in each experimental condition; these precautions must be taken before an experimenter can be reasonably certain that observed changes in the dependent variable were caused by the manipulation of the independent variable.

experimental design: a research design in which the investigator introduces some change in the participant's environment and then measures the effect of that change on the participant's behavior.

expiatory punishment: punitive consequences that bear no relation to the nature of the forbidden act.

expressive role: a social prescription, usually directed toward females, that one should be cooperative, kind, nurturant, and sensitive to the needs of others.

extended family: a group of blood relatives from more than one nuclear family (for example, grandparents, aunts, uncles, nieces, and nephews) who live together, forming a household.

external moral orientation: moral compliance that is induced by anticipation of rewards or praise for following rules and punishment or blame for transgressions; thought to be an immature moral orientation.

extrafamilial influences: social agencies other than the family that influence a child's cognitive, social, and emotional development.

extrinsic orientation: a desire to achieve in order to earn external incentives such as grades, prizes, or the approval of others.

"failure to thrive" syndrome: a condition in which seemingly healthy infants fail to grow normally and are much smaller than their agemates.

falsifiability: a criterion for evaluating the scientific merit of theories. A theory is falsifiable when it is capable of generating predictions that could be disconfirmed.

family social system: the complex network of relationships, interactions, and patterns of influence that characterize a family with three or more members.

"felt responsibility" hypothesis: the theory that empathy may promote altruism by causing one to reflect on altruistic norms and, thus, to feel some obligation to help distressed others.

field experiment: an experiment that takes place in a naturalistic setting such as the home, the school, or a playground.

fixation: arrested development at a particular psychosexual stage; often occurs as a means of coping with existing conflicts and preventing movement to the next stage, where stress may be even greater.

"focus of attention" hypothesis: the proposal that negative moods promote altruism if one is focused on others' misfortunes but inhibit altruism if one is focused on personal concerns.

"forbidden toy" paradigm: a method of studying children's resistance to temptation by noting whether youngsters will play with forbidden toys when they believe that this transgression is unlikely to be detected.

foreclosure: identity status characterizing individuals who have prematurely committed themselves to occupations or ideologies without really thinking about these commitments.

foreseeability heuristic: attributional scheme by which voluntary acts with predictable effects are more likely to be viewed as intentional than are other acts having unpredictable outcomes.

formal-operational stage: Piaget's fourth and final stage of cognitive development, from age 11 to 12 and beyond, when the individual begins to think more rationally and systematically about abstract concepts and hypothetical events.

friendship: a strong and often enduring relationship between two individuals, characterized by loyalty, intimacy, and mutual affection.

frustration/aggression hypothesis: early learning theory of aggression, holding that frustration triggers aggression and that all aggressive acts can be traced to frustrations.

gender consistency: the stage of gender identity in which the child recognizes that a person's gender is invariant despite changes in the person's activities or appearance (also known as *gender constancy*).

gender identity: one's awareness of one's gender and its implications.

gender stability: the stage of gender identity in which the child recognizes that gender is stable over time.

genital stage: Freud's final stage of psychosexual development (from puberty onward), in which the underlying aim of the sex instinct is biological reproduction.

genotype: the genetic endowment that an individual inherits.

"goodness of fit" model: Thomas and Chess's notion that development is likely to be optimized when parents' child-rearing practices are adapted to (or are compatible with) the child's temperamental characteristics.

growth hormone: a pituitary hormone that stimulates rapid growth and development of body cells.

habits: well-learned associations between various stimuli and responses; represent the stable aspects of one's personality.

heritability: the amount of variation in a trait that is attributable to hereditary factors.

heritability coefficient: a numerical estimate, ranging from .00 to +1.00, of the amount of variation in an attribute that is due to hereditary factors.

heteronomous morality: Piaget's first stage of moral development, in which children view the rules of authority figures as sacred and unalterable.

heuristic value: a criterion for evaluating the scientific merit of theories. A heuristic theory is one that continues to stimulate new research and new discoveries.

"high risk" neighborhood: a residential area in which the incidence of child abuse is much higher than in other neighborhoods with the same demographic and socioeconomic characteristics.

high-SES: a term that refers to the middle and upper social classes—that is, the economically advantaged members of society.

holistic perspective: a unified view of the developmental process that emphasizes the interrelationships among the physical/biological, mental, social, and emotional aspects of human development.

HOME inventory: a measure of the amount and type of intellectual stimulation provided by a child's home environment.

hostile aggression: aggressive acts in which the actor's major goal is to harm or injure a victim.

hostile attributional bias: tendency to view harm done under ambiguous circumstances as having stemmed from a hostile intent on the part of the harmdoer; characterizes highly aggressive children and adolescents.

hypothesis: a theoretical prediction about some aspect of experience.

hypothetical-deductive reasoning: a style of problem solving in which the possible solutions to a problem are generated and then systematically evaluated to determine the correct answer(s).

I (or private self): those inner, or subjective, aspects of the self that are not readily available for public scrutiny.

id: psychoanalytic term for the inborn component of the personality that is driven by the instincts.

identification: Freud's term for the child's tendency to emulate another person, usually the same-sex parent.

identity: one's mature self-definition; a sense of who one is, where one is going, and how one fits into society.

identity achievement: identity status characterizing individuals who have carefully considered identity issues and have made firm commitments to an occupation and ideologies.

identity crisis: Erikson's term for the uncertainty and discomfort that adolescents experience when they become confused about their present and future roles in life.

identity diffusion: identity status characterizing individuals who are not questioning who they are and have not yet committed themselves to an identity.

imaginal representational system: Bandura's term for the images observers generate to retain a model's behavior.

imaginary audience: a form of adolescent egocentrism that involves confusing your own thoughts with those of a hypothesized audience and concluding that others share your preoccupations.

immanent justice: the notion that unacceptable conduct will invariably be punished and that justice is ever present in the world.

imprinting: an innate or instinctual form of learning in which the young of certain species will follow and become attached to moving objects (usually their mothers).

incompatible-response technique: a nonpunitive method of behavior modification in which adults ignore undesirable conduct while reinforcing acts that are incompatible with these responses.

incremental view of ability: belief that one's ability can be improved through increased effort and practice.

independence training: encouraging children to become self-reliant by accomplishing goals without others' assistance.

independent variable: the aspect of the environment that an experimenter modifies or manipulates in order to measure its impact on behavior.

indirect effects: instances in which the relationship between two individuals in a family is modified by the behavior or attitudes of a third family member.

induction: a nonpunitive form of discipline in which an adult explains why a child's behavior is wrong and should be changed by emphasizing its effects on others.

industry versus inferiority: the psychosocial crisis of the grade-school years, in which children must acquire important social and intellectual skills or else will view themselves as incompetent.

informal curriculum: noncurricular objectives of schooling, such as teaching children to cooperate, to respect authority, to obey rules, and to become good citizens.

"in-group/out-group" schema: one's general knowledge of the mannerisms, roles, activities, and behaviors that characterize males and females.

inhibitory control: an ability to display acceptable conduct by resisting the temptation to commit a forbidden act.

initiative versus guilt: the third of Erikson's psychosocial stages, in which preschool children either develop goals and strive to achieve them or feel guilty when their ambitions are thwarted by others.

innate purity: the idea that infants are born with an intuitive sense of right and wrong that is often misdirected by the demands and restrictions of society.

inner experimentation: the ability to solve simple problems on a mental, or symbolic, level without having to rely on trial-and-error experimentation.

instrumental aggression: aggressive acts in which the actor's major goal is to gain access to objects, territory, or privileges.

instrumental role: a social prescription, usually directed toward males, that one should be dominant, independent, assertive, competitive, and goal oriented.

intentional definition of aggression: *see* **aggression** *(intentional definition)*.

internalization: the process of adopting the attributes or standards of other people — taking these standards as one's own.

internal working models: cognitive representations of self, others, and relationships that infants construct from their interactions with caregivers.

intimacy versus isolation: the sixth of Erikson's psychosocial conflicts, in which young adults must commit themselves to a shared identity with another person (that is, intimacy) or else remain aloof and unconnected to others.

intrinsic orientation: a desire to achieve in order to satisfy one's personal needs for competence or mastery.

introversion/extraversion: the opposite poles of a personality dimension: introverts are shy, anxious around others, and ready to withdraw from social situations; extraverts are highly sociable and enjoy being with others.

intuitive thought: Piaget's term for reasoning that is dominated by appearances (or perceptual characteristics of objects and events) rather than by rational thought processes.

invariant developmental sequence: a series of developments that occur in one particular order because each

development in the sequence is a prerequisite for the next.

kewpie-doll effect: the notion that infantlike facial features are perceived as cute and lovable and will elicit favorable responses from others.

"kin selection" hypothesis: sociobiological notion that altruistic acts directed toward genetic relatives are adaptive because they increase the likelihood that the altruist's genes will survive.

kinship: the extent to which two individuals have genes in common.

laissez-faire instruction: a permissive style of instruction in which the teacher makes few demands of students and provides little or no active guidance.

latency period: Freud's fourth stage of psychosexual development (age 6 to puberty), in which sexual desires are repressed and the child's available libido is channeled into socially acceptable outlets such as schoolwork or vigorous play.

learned helplessness: the failure to learn how to respond appropriately in a situation because of previous exposures to uncontrollable events in the same or similar situations.

learned helplessness orientation: a tendency to give up or to stop trying after failing because failures have been attributed to a lack of ability that one can do little about.

learning: relatively permanent changes in behavior (or behavioral potential) that result from one's experiences or practice.

learning goal: desire to increase one's abilities at achievement-related activities or to master new challenges.

libido: Freud's term for the biological energy of the sex instinct.

locus of control: personality dimension distinguishing people who assume that they are personally responsible for their life outcomes (internal locus) from those who believe that their outcomes depend more on circumstances beyond their control (external locus).

longitudinal design: a research design in which one group of subjects is studied repeatedly over a period of months or years.

looking-glass self: the idea that a child's self-concept is largely determined by the ways other people respond to him or her.

love withdrawal: a form of discipline in which an adult withholds attention, affection, or approval in order to modify or control a child's behavior.

low-SES: a term that refers to the lower and working classes—that is, the economically disadvantaged members of society.

macrosystem: the larger cultural or subcultural context in which development occurs; Bronfenbrenner's fourth layer of context.

mainstreaming: an educational practice in which handicapped children are integrated into regular classrooms.

manic-depression: a psychotic disorder characterized by extreme fluctuations in mood.

mastery orientation: a tendency to persist at challenging tasks because of a belief that one has high ability and/or that earlier failures can be overcome by trying harder.

matching rule: attributional scheme by which young children view actions that match the actor's motives as intentional; actions that produce unwanted consequences are viewed as unintentional.

maternal deprivation hypothesis: the notion that socially deprived infants develop abnormally because they have failed to establish attachments to a primary caregiver.

maturation: developmental changes in the body or behavior that result from the aging process rather than from learning, injury, illness, or some other life experience.

Me (or public self): those aspects of self that others can see or easily infer.

mental mediation (or confluence) hypothesis: that notion that first-borns (and children from small families) achieve more than later-borns (and children from large families) because their home environments are more conducive to the development of their intellectual potential.

mere exposure: the finding that repeated exposure to an object results in greater attraction to that object.

mesosystem: the interconnections among an individual's immediate settings, or microsystems; the second of Bronfenbrenner's layers of context.

metacognitive knowledge: one's knowledge about cognition and about the regulation of cognitive activities.

microsystem: the immediate settings (including role relationships and activities) that the person actually encounters; the innermost of Bronfenbrenner's layers of context.

mixed-age peer interaction: interactions among children who differ in age by a year or more.

moral affect: the emotional component of morality, including feelings such as guilt, shame, and pride in ethical conduct.

moral behavior: the behavioral component of morality; actions that are consistent with one's moral standards in situations in which one is tempted to violate a prohibition.

moral development: the process by which children acquire society's standards of right and wrong.

morality: a set of principles or ideals that help the individual to distinguish right from wrong, to act on this distinction, and to feel pride in virtuous conduct and guilt (or shame) for conduct that violates one's standards.

morality of care: Gilligan's term for what she presumes to be the dominant moral orientation of females—an orientation focusing more on compassionate concerns for human welfare than on socially defined justice as administered through law.

moral reasoning: the cognitive component of morality; the thinking that people display when deciding whether various acts are right or wrong.

moral rules: standards of acceptable and unacceptable conduct that focus on the rights and privileges of individuals.

moratorium: identity status characterizing individuals who are currently experiencing an identity crisis and are actively exploring occupational and ideological positions in which to invest themselves.

"motherless mothers": Harlow's term for rhesus monkey mothers who were reared in isolation and received no mothering as infants.

"mother only" monkeys: monkeys who are raised with their mothers and denied any contact with peers.

motivational/intentional definition of altruism: *see* **altruism** *(motivational/intentional definition).*

motive to achieve success (M_s): Atkinson's term for the disposition describing one's tendency to approach challenging tasks and to take pride in mastering them; analogous to McClelland's need for achievement.

motive to avoid failure (M_{af}): Atkinson's term for the disposition describing one's tendency to shy away from challenging tasks so as to avoid the embarrassment of failing.

mullerian inhibiting substance (MIS): hormone secreted by the testes that inhibits the development of a female reproductive system.

natural (or quasi) experiment: a study in which the investigator measures the impact of some naturally occurring event that is assumed to affect people's lives.

naturalistic observation: a method in which the scientist tests hypotheses by observing people as they engage in everyday activities in their natural habitats (for example, at home, at school, or on the playground).

natural selection: an evolutionary process, proposed by Charles Darwin, stating that individuals with characteristics that promote adaptation to the environment will survive, reproduce, and pass these adaptive characteristics to offspring; those lacking these adaptive characteristics will eventually die out.

nature/nurture controversy: the debate within developmental psychology over the relative importance of biological predispositions (nature) and environmental influences (nurture) as determinants of human development.

need for achievement (*n* Ach):   a learned motive to compete and to strive for success in situations in which one's performance can be evaluated against some standard of excellence.

negative reinforcer: any stimulus whose removal or termination, as the consequence of an act, increases the probability that the act will recur.

"negative state relief" hypothesis: the proposal that people experiencing bad moods are willing to perform prosocial acts in order to make themselves feel better (that is, to relieve their negative states).

neglected children: children who receive few nominations as either a liked or a disliked individual from members of their peer group.

neo-Hullian theory: early social-learning theory that attempted to explain Freudian psychoanalytic phenomena within the framework of Clark Hull's animal learning theory.

neonate: a newborn infant from birth to approximately one month of age.

nominations technique: sociometric measure in which children are asked to nominate a specific number of peers as liked and the same number as disliked. The number and patterning of positive and negative nominations a child receives determine his or her sociometric status.

nonrepresentative sample: a subgroup that differs in important ways from the larger group (or population) to which it belongs.

nonshared environmental influence: an environmental influence that people living together do not share and that makes these individuals different from one another.

normative altruism: prosocial acts that are performed with the expectation of receiving some personal benefit for acting or avoiding criticism for failing to act.

norm of social responsibility: the principle that we should help others who are in some way dependent on us for assistance.

nuclear family: a family unit consisting of a wife/mother, a husband/father, and their dependent children.

object permanence: the realization that objects continue to exist when they are no longer visible or detectable through the other senses.

observational learning: learning that results from observing the behavior of others.

observer bias: a tendency of an observer to over- or underinterpret naturally occurring experiences rather than simply recording the events that take place.

oedipal morality: Freud's theory that moral development occurs during the phallic period (ages 3 to 6), when children internalize the moral standards of the same-sex parent as they resolve their Oedipus or Electra conflicts.

Oedipus complex: Freud's term for the conflict that 3- to 6-year-old boys were said to experience when they develop an incestuous desire for their mothers and a jealous and hostile rivalry with their fathers.

open classroom: a classroom arrangement in which there is a separate area for each educational activity and children distribute themselves around the room, working individually or in small groups.

operant (or instrumental) conditioning: a form of learning in which freely emitted acts (or operants) become either more or less probable, depending on the consequences they produce.

operational schemes: Piaget's term for schemes that utilize cognitive operations, or mental "actions of the head," that enable one to transform objects of thought and to reason logically.

oral stage: Freud's first stage of psychosexual development (from birth to 1 year), in which children gratify the sex instinct by stimulating the mouth, lips, teeth, and gums.

ordinal position: the child's order of birth among siblings (also called *birth order*).

organization: an inborn tendency to combine and integrate available schemes into coherent systems or bodies of knowledge.

original sin: the idea that children are inherently negative creatures who must be taught to rechannel their selfish interests into socially acceptable outlets.

Ounce of Prevention program: community-based attempt to prevent child abuse by educating parents in effective child management techniques and providing such family support services as child-care programs, job training, and medical assistance.

own-sex schema: detailed knowledge or plans of action that enable a person to perform gender-consistent activities and to enact his or her sex role.

parental control: a dimension of parenting that describes how restrictive and demanding parents are.

parental socialization hypothesis: the notion that first-borns (and children from small families) achieve more than later-borns (and children from large families) because they receive more direct achievement training from their parents.

Parents Anonymous: an organization of reformed child abusers (modeled after Alcoholics Anonymous) that functions as a support group and helps parents to understand and overcome their abusive tendencies.

parsimony: a criterion for evaluating the scientific merit of theories; a parsimonious theory is one that uses relatively few explanatory principles to explain a broad set of observations.

passive genotype/environment interactions: the notion that the rearing environments that biological parents provide are influenced by the parents' own genes and, hence, are correlated with the child's own genotype.

peer conformity: the tendency to go along with the wishes of peers or to yield to peer-group pressures.

peer group: a confederation of peers that interacts regularly, defines a sense of membership, and formulates norms that specify how members are supposed to look, think, and act.

"peer only" monkeys: monkeys who are separated from their mothers (and other adults) soon after birth and raised with peers.

peers: two or more persons who are operating at similar levels of behavioral complexity.

performance goal: desire to display one's competencies at achievement-related activities and to avoid appearing incompetent.

performance standards: Bandura's term for personally chosen standards that must be met or exceeded to experience self-reinforcement; performance falling below these standards is unacceptable and may result in self-punishment.

permissive parenting: lax or indulgent style of parenting in which adults make few demands of their children and do not closely monitor their conduct.

personal agency: the understanding that one can be the cause of events.

personal fable: a form of adolescent egocentrism in which the individual thinks that he and his thoughts and feelings are special or unique.

phallic stage: Freud's third stage of psychosexual development (from 3 to 6 years of age), in which children gratify the sex instinct by fondling their genitals and developing an incestuous desire for the parent of the other sex.

phenotype: the ways in which a person's genotype is expressed in observable or measurable characteristics.

pleasure principle: tendency of the id to seek immediate gratification for instinctual needs, even when realistic methods for satisfying these needs are unavailable.

popular children: children who are liked by many members of their peer group and disliked by very few.

popularity: measure of a person's likability (or dislikability) in the eyes of peers.

positive reinforcer: any stimulus whose presentation, as the consequence of an act, increases the probability that the act will recur.

postconventional morality: Kohlberg's term for the fifth and sixth stages of moral reasoning, in which moral judgments are based on social contracts and democratic law (Stage 5) or on universal principles of ethics and justice (Stage 6).

power-assertion: a form of discipline in which an adult relies on his or her superior power (for example, by administering spankings or withholding privileges) to modify or control a child's behavior.

preadapted characteristic: an innate attribute that is a product of evolution and serves some function that increases the chances of survival for the individual and the species.

preconventional morality: Kohlberg's term for the first two stages of moral reasoning, in which moral judgments are based on the tangible punitive consequences (Stage 1) or rewarding consequences (Stage 2) of an act for the actor, rather than on the relationship of that act to society's rules and customs.

preliterate society: a society in which there is little or no formal schooling, so that many children never learn to read and write.

premoral period: in Piaget's theory, the first five to six years of life, when children have little respect for or awareness of socially defined rules.

preoperational stage: Piaget's second stage of cognitive development, lasting from about age 2 to age 7, when children are thinking at a symbolic level but are not yet using cognitive operations.

primary circular reaction: a pleasurable response, centered on the infant's own body, that is discovered by chance and performed over and over.

primary drives: neo-Hullian term for innate (unlearned) motives such as hunger and sex.

primary emotions: the set of emotions present at birth or emerging early in the first year that some theorists believe to be biologically programmed.

private speech: Vygotsky's term for the self-directed speech children use to regulate their activities as they strive to achieve important goals.

prosocial behavior: actions, such as sharing, helping, or comforting, that benefit other people.

prosocial moral reasoning: the thinking that people display when deciding whether to help, share with, or comfort others when these actions could prove costly to themselves.

psychological comparisons phase: tendency to form impressions of others by comparing and contrasting these individuals on abstract psychological dimensions.

psychological constructs phase: tendency to base one's impressions of others on the stable traits these individuals are presumed to have.

punishment: any consequence of an act that suppresses that act and/or decreases the probability that it will recur.

Pygmalion effect: the tendency of teacher expectancies to become self-fulfilling prophecies, causing students to perform better or worse depending on their teacher's estimation of their potential.

questionnaire: a research instrument that asks the persons being studied to respond to a number of written questions.

random assignment: a control technique in which participants are assigned to experimental conditions through an unbiased procedure so that the members of the groups are not systematically different from one another.

reality principle: tendency of the ego to defer immediate gratification in order to find rational and realistic methods for satisfying the instincts.

reciprocal determinism: the notion that the flow of influence between children and their environments is a two-way street: the environment may affect the child, but the child's behavior will also influence the environment.

reciprocal influence: the notion that each person in a social relationship influences and is influenced by the other person(s).

reciprocal punishment: punitive consequences that are tailored to the forbidden act so that a rule breaker will understand the implications of a transgression.

reconstituted families: new families that form after the remarriage of a single parent.

regression: a defense mechanism whereby the ego copes with stress and conflict by producing behaviors more characteristic of an earlier stage of development.

reinforcer: any consequence of an act that increases the probability that the act will recur.

rejected children: children who are disliked by many peers and liked by few.

reliability: the extent to which a measuring instrument yields consistent results, both over time and across observers.

repression: a type of motivated forgetting in which anxiety-provoking thoughts and conflicts are forced out of conscious awareness.

resistant attachment: an insecure infant/caregiver bond, characterized by strong separation protest and a tendency by the child to resist contact initiated by the caregiver, particularly after a separation.

retaliatory aggression: aggressive acts elicited by real or imagined provocations.

reversibility: the ability to reverse, or negate, an action by mentally performing the opposite action.

role taking: the ability to assume another person's perspective and to understand his or her thoughts, feelings, and behaviors.

rouge test: test of infants' self-recognition; if they have achieved self-recognition, infants whose faces are marked with rouge will touch their own faces (rather than that of a mirror image) when placed before a mirror.

scaffolding: method of instruction in which the tutor adjusts the level of assistance provided in relation to the tutee's performance, the goal being to constantly challenge the tutee and (ultimately) to promote her mastery of the activity.

scheme: an organized pattern of thought or action that a child constructs to make sense of some aspect of experience. Piaget sometimes used the term *cognitive structures* as a synonym for *schemes*.

schizophrenia: a serious form of mental illness characterized by disturbances in logical thinking, emotional expression, and interpersonal behavior.

scientific method: an attitude or value about the pursuit of knowledge dictating that investigators must be objective and must allow their data to decide the merits of their theorizing.

secondary circular reaction: a pleasurable response, centered on an object external to the self, that is discovered by chance and performed over and over.

secondary drives: neo-Hullian term for all motives that are not present at birth and are acquired as a result of experience.

secure attachment: an infant/caregiver bond in which the child welcomes contact with a close companion and uses this person as a secure base from which to explore the environment.

secure-base phenomenon: the tendency of infants to venture away from a close companion to explore the environment.

self: the combination of physical and psychological attributes that is unique to each individual.

self-actualization goal: LeVine's third priority of parenting—to promote the child's cognitive and behavioral capacity for maximizing such cultural values as morality, achievement, prestige, and personal satisfaction.

self-assertion: noncompliant acts that are undertaken by children in the interest of doing things for themselves or otherwise establishing autonomy.

self-care (or latchkey) children: children who care for themselves after school or in the evenings while their parents are working.

self-concept: one's perceptions of one's unique attributes or traits.

self-control: the capacity to inhibit responses that are unacceptable or that conflict with a goal.

self-disclosure: the act of revealing private or intimate information about oneself to another person.

self-efficacy: Bandura's concept referring to the person's belief that he or she can successfully master various challenges.

self-esteem: one's evaluation of one's worth as a person based on an assessment of the qualities that make up the self-concept.

self-oriented empathic distress: feelings of *personal* discomfort or distress that may be elicited when we experience the emotions of (that is, empathize with) a distressed other; thought to inhibit altruism.

self-recognition: the ability to recognize a physical representation of oneself (in a mirror or photograph).

self-regulated behavior: Bandura's term for behavior that is controlled by intrinsic reinforcers or intrinsic punishments that we produce ourselves.

self-regulation: internal processes by which we monitor and control our actions, thoughts, or emotions for the purpose of achieving a goal.

sensitive period: a particular period during which an organism is especially sensitive to certain environmental influences; weaker form of the **critical period** concept.

sensitive-period hypothesis: Klaus and Kennell's notion that mothers will develop the strongest possible affection for their babies if they have close physical contact with them within 6–12 hours after giving birth.

sensorimotor stage: Piaget's first stage of cognitive development, from birth to 2 years, when infants are relying on behavioral schemes to adapt to the environment.

separation anxiety: a wary or fretful reaction that infants and toddlers often display when separated from the person(s) to whom they are attached.

sequential design: a research design in which subjects from different age groups are studied repeatedly over a period of months or years.

seriation: a cognitive operation that allows one to order a set of stimuli along a quantifiable dimension such as height or weight.

sex-role standard: a behavior, value, or motive that members of a society consider more typical or appropriate for members of one sex.

sex-role stereotypes: widely held beliefs about the mannerisms and attributes that males and females display.

sex-typed behaviors: behaviors and behavioral preferences more commonly displayed by members of one sex than the other.

sex typing: the process by which a child becomes aware of his or her gender and acquires motives, values, and behaviors considered appropriate for members of that sex.

sexuality: aspect of self referring to the individual's erotic thoughts, actions, and orientation.

sexual orientation: the gender to which an individual directs sexual overtures.

shared environmental influence: an aspect of environment that is experienced (shared) by people living together; can make these people similar to one another or, in interaction with other variables, can contribute to personal dissimilarities.

sibling rivalry: the spirit of competition, jealousy, and resentment that may arise between two (or more) siblings.

single-parent family: a family system consisting of one parent (either the mother or the father) and the parent's dependent child(ren).

slow-to-warm-up temperament: temperament in which the child is inactive and moody and displays mild passive resistance to new routines and experiences.

sociability: one's willingness to interact with others and to seek their attention or approval.

social cognition: the thinking one displays about the self, other people, and interpersonal relationships.

social comparison: the process of defining and evaluating the self by comparing oneself to other people.

social-conventional rules: standards of conduct, determined by social consensus, that indicate what is appropriate within a particular social setting.

socialization: the process by which children acquire the beliefs, values, and behaviors considered desirable or appropriate by the society to which they belong.

social perspective taking: the ability to infer others' thoughts, intentions, motives, and attitudes.

social problem-solving training: method of social-skills training in which an adult helps children (through role playing or role-taking training) to make less hostile attributions about harmdoing and to generate non-aggressive solutions to conflict.

social referencing: the use of others' emotional expressions to infer the meaning of otherwise ambiguous situations.

social stimulation hypothesis: the notion that socially deprived infants develop abnormally because they have had little contact with companions who respond contingently to their social overtures.

social support: tangible and intangible resources provided by other people in times of uncertainty or stress.

sociobiology: a branch of biology that focuses on the evolutionary origins of social motives and behaviors.

socioeconomic status (SES): one's position within a society that is stratified according to status and power.

sociometric techniques: procedures that ask children to identify those peers whom they like or dislike or to rate peers for their desirability as companions; these methods are used to measure children's peer acceptance (or nonacceptance).

stage of indiscriminate attachments: period between 6 weeks and 6–7 months of age in which infants prefer social to nonsocial stimulation and are likely to protest whenever any adult puts them down or leaves them alone.

stage of multiple attachments: term used to describe infants who have formed attachments to two or more close companions.

stage of specific attachments: period between 7 and 9 months of age when infants are attached to one close companion (usually the mother).

status: a measure of a person's perceived worth as a contributor to the attainment of group goals.

stimulus generalization: the fact that one stimulus can be substituted for another and produce the same response that the former stimulus did.

stranger anxiety: a wary or fretful reaction that infants and toddlers often display when approached by an unfamiliar person.

strange-situations test: a series of eight mildly stressful situations to which infants are exposed in order to determine the quality of their attachments to one or more close companions.

structured interview or questionnaire: a technique in which all participants are asked the same questions in precisely the same order so that the responses of different participants can be compared.

structured observation: an observational method in which the investigator cues the behavior of interest and observes participants' responses in a laboratory.

"structured wholes" hypothesis: Kohlberg's claim that each of his stages of moral reasoning is a consistent perspective on morality that will determine how subjects think about most moral issues.

sublimation: a defense mechanism by which the ego finds socially acceptable outlets for the id's undesirable impulses.

superego: psychoanalytic term for the component of the personality that consists of one's internalized moral standards.

superordinate goals: important objectives that cannot be achieved unless rivaling groups or factions set their differences aside and pull together to work as a team.

survival goal: LeVine's first priority of parenting—to promote the physical health and safety (survival) of young children.

symbolic function: the ability to use symbols (for example, images and words) to represent objects and experiences.

symbolic representations: the images and verbal labels that observers generate in order to retain the important aspects of a model's behavior.

symbolic schemes: internal mental symbols (such as images or verbal codes) that one uses to represent aspects of experience.

sympathetic empathic arousal: feelings of sympathy or compassion that may be elicited when we experience the emotions of (that is, empathize with) a distressed other; thought to become an important mediator of altruism.

synchronized routines: generally harmonious interactions between two persons in which each participant adjusts his or her behavior in response to the partner's actions.

tabula rasa: the idea that the mind of an infant is a "blank slate" and that all knowledge, abilities, behaviors, and motives are acquired through experience.

temperament: a person's characteristic modes of response to the environment, including such attributes as activity level, irritability, self-regulation, fearfulness, and sociability.

temperament hypothesis: Kagan's view that the strange-situations test measures individual differences in infants' temperaments rather than the quality of their attachments.

tertiary circular reaction: an exploratory scheme in which infants devise new methods of acting on objects to reproduce interesting results.

test anxiety: a concern about being evaluated that can undermine performance, especially under highly stressful, competitive testing procedures.

testicular feminization syndrome (TFS): a genetic anomaly in which a male fetus is insensitive to the effects of male sex hormones and will develop female-like external genitalia.

testosterone: a type of androgen, secreted by the testes, that stimulates the development of a male internal reproductive system during the prenatal period.

Thanatos: Freud's name for inborn, self-destructive instincts, which were said to characterize all human beings.

theory: a set of concepts and propositions designed to organize, describe, and explain an existing set of observations.

time-out technique: a strategy in which the disciplinary agent "punishes" a child by disrupting or preventing the prohibited activity that the child seems to enjoy.

"timing of puberty" effect: the finding that people who reach puberty late perform better on visual/spatial tasks than those who mature early.

traditional classroom: a classroom arrangement in which all pupils sit facing an instructor, who normally teaches one subject at a time by lecturing or giving demonstrations.

transactive interactions: verbal exchanges in which individuals perform mental operations on the reasoning of their discussion partners.

transitivity: the ability to infer relations among elements in a serial order (for example, if $A > B$ and $B > C$, then $A > C$).

twin design (or twin study): study in which sets of twins differing in zygosity (kinship) are compared to determine the heritability of an attribute, or attributes.

unconditioned response (UCR): the unlearned response elicited by an unconditioned stimulus.

unconditioned stimulus (UCS): a stimulus that elicits a particular response without any prior learning.

unconscious motivation: Freud's term for feelings, experiences, and conflicts that influence a person's thinking and behavior but lie outside the person's awareness.

uninvolved parenting: a pattern of parenting that is both aloof (or even hostile) and overpermissive — almost as if parents don't care about their children or about what they may become.

unitary morality: the notion that moral affect, moral reasoning, and moral behavior are interrelated components of a "moral character" that is consistent across situations.

validity: the extent to which a measuring instrument accurately reflects what the researchers intended to measure.

verbal/nonverbal consistency rule: attributional scheme by which children infer the truth or sincerity of another person's statements. If nonverbal cues are inconsistent in implication with the speaker's verbal message, the speaker is assumed to be lying (or insincere).

verbal representational system: Bandura's term for the verbal labels/codes observers generate to retain a model's behavior.

visual/spatial abilities: the ability to mentally manipulate or otherwise draw inferences about pictorial information.

warmth/hostility: a dimension of parenting that describes the amount of responsiveness and affection that a parent displays toward a child.

X-linked recessive disorder: an attribute determined by a recessive gene that appears only on X chromosomes; since the gene determining these characteristics is recessive (that is, dominated by other genes that might appear at the same location on X chromosomes), such characteristics are more common among males, who have only one X chromosome; also called *sex-linked trait.*

younger-peer therapy: a method of rehabilitating emotionally withdrawn individuals by regularly exposing them to younger but socially responsive companions.

zone of proximal development: Vygotsky's term for the difference between what children can accomplish on their own and what they can accomplish with the guidance of a more competent associate.

Name Index

Subject Index